energy

and the challenge of sustainability

**United Nations
Development Programme**

**United Nations
Department of Economic
and Social Affairs**

World Energy Council

World Energy Assessment

The editorial phase and the production of the World Energy Assessment benefited from contributions from the governments of Austria, Finland, Norway, and Sweden, and the Energy Foundation. The consultative and outreach phases of the report have been made possible through funding from the United Nations Foundation.

United Nations Development Programme
Bureau for Development Policy
One United Nations Plaza
New York, NY 10017

Library of Congress Cataloging-in-Publication Data
World energy assessment : energy and the challenge of sustainability / United Nations Development Programme, United Nations Department of Economic and Social Affairs, World Energy Council ; [edited by José Goldemberg].
   p. cm.
Includes index.
   ISBN 92-1-126126-0
  1. Power resources. 2. Energy Development. I. Goldemberg, José, 1928. II. United Nations Development Programme. III. United Nations Dept. of Economic and Social Affairs. IV. World Energy Council. V. Title.
  TJ163.2 .W657 2000
  333.79–dc21

00-012327

Sales Number: 00.III.B.5

Final editing by Communications Development Incorporated, Washington, D.C.

Design by Julia Ptasznik, Suazion, Staten Island, NY

Printed on recycled, acid-free paper

contents

PART I. ENERGY AND MAJOR GLOBAL ISSUES

Chapter 4. Energy Security 111
Hisham Khatib (Jordan)

PART II. ENERGY RESOURCES AND TECHNOLOGY OPTIONS

Chapter 7. Renewable Energy Technologies 219
Wim C. Turkenburg (Netherlands)

PART III. ARE SUSTAINABLE FUTURES POSSIBLE?

PART 5. FURTHER INFORMATION AND REFERENCE MATERIAL

foreword

Mark Malloch Brown
Administrator
United Nations
Development Programme

Nitin Desai
Under Secretary-General
United Nations
Department of Economic
and Social Affairs

Gerald Doucet
Secretary General
World Energy Council

M ore than 175 governments have committed to Agenda 21, the programme for achieving human-centred sustainable development adopted at the 1992 United Nations Conference on Environment and Development in Rio de Janeiro. Agenda 21 noted energy's importance to sustainable development. The June 1997 Special Session of the UN General Assembly, convened to review progress on Agenda 21, went further. It emphasised that sustainable patterns of energy production, distribution, and use are crucial to continued improvements in the quality of life. It also declared that the ninth session of the United Nations Commission on Sustainable Development (CSD-9), in 2001, should focus on issues related to the atmosphere and energy and to energy and transport.

To inform the discussion and debate, the United Nations Development Programme (UNDP), United Nations Department of Economic and Social Affairs (UNDESA), and World Energy Council (WEC) initiated the World Energy Assessment in late 1998. This report analyses the social, economic, environmental, and security issues linked to energy supply and use, and assesses options for sustainability in each area.

We offer the World Energy Assessment as an input to the CSD-9 process, the "Rio Plus Ten" meeting in 2002, and beyond. We believe that a synthesis of reviewed and validated information on energy production and consumption patterns will be a valuable tool for energy planners at the regional and national levels, and for many other audiences as well.

Our energy future will largely depend on the actions not only of governments, but also regional alliances, the private sector, and civil society. For this reason, this assessment is the centrepiece of an outreach effort by UNDP, UNDESA, and WEC. This outreach includes regional dialogues, exchanges among developing countries and between developing and industrialised countries, and consultations with a wide range of stakeholders, including the private sector, which is not always brought into debates.

The World Energy Assessment represents a collaborative effort involving the three founding organisations, 12 convening lead authors, and the teams of experts they assembled. Drafts of the report were sent out to a wide audience of experts and government representatives for review and consultation. This review included a special Advisory Panel meeting, an electronic posting, and consultations at the local, regional, and global levels, as well as with non-governmental organisations. The Editorial Board considered the content of the chapters at six meetings over the course of 16 months. Whereas the overview reflects the combined judgement and scrutiny of the Editorial Board, each chapter is the responsibility of its convening lead author. ■

preface

José Goldemberg
Chair, World Energy Assessment

Energy is central to achieving the interrelated economic, social, and environmental aims of sustainable human development. But if we are to realise this important goal, the kinds of energy we produce and the ways we use them will have to change. Otherwise, environmental damage will accelerate, inequity will increase, and global economic growth will be jeopardised.

We cannot simply ignore the energy needs of the 2 billion people who have no means of escaping continuing cycles of poverty and deprivation. Nor will the local, regional, and global environmental problems linked to conventional ways of using energy go away on their own. Other challenges confront us as well: the high prices of energy supplies in many countries, the vulnerability to interruptions in supply, and the need for more energy services to support continued development.

The World Energy Assessment affirms that solutions to these urgent problems are possible, and that the future is much more a matter of choice than destiny. By acting now to embrace enlightened policies, we can create energy systems that lead to a more equitable, environmentally sound, and economically viable world.

But changing energy systems is no simple matter. It is a complex and long-term process—one that will require major and concerted efforts by governments, businesses, and members of civil society. Consensus on energy trends and needed changes in energy systems can accelerate this process.

The World Energy Assessment was undertaken, in part, to build consensus on how we can most effectively use energy as a tool for sustainable development. Its analysis shows that we need to do more to promote energy efficiency and renewables, and to encourage advanced technologies that offer alternatives for clean and safe energy supply and use. We also need to help developing countries find ways to avoid retracing the wasteful and destructive stages that have characterised industrialisation in the past.

Considerable work by many individuals went into this publication, and my hope is that it contributes to a more equitable, prosperous, and sustainable world. ∎

ACKNOWLEDGEMENTS

This publication would not have been possible without the strenuous efforts of many people, starting with the members of the Editorial Board and the authors of each chapter, as well as those who represented the establishing institutions. The establishing institutions greatly appreciate their efforts.

The editorial process was skilfully guided by Chair José Goldemberg of Brazil. His extensive experience in energy, policy issues, and international relations has been invaluable, and his unwavering commitment to the success of this project has been an inspiration to everyone involved. We are also deeply grateful to the other members of the Editorial Board for their painstaking work in preparing and reviewing this publication under an extremely tight schedule, for their willingness to challenge one another while maintaining a spirit of cooperation, and for their shared commitment to the idea of energy as a tool for sustainable human development.

Project manager Caitlin Allen was instrumental to the success of this project. Her desk was the nexus of communications for the members of the Editorial Board, who were located all over the world. She also managed the administrative, editorial, and graphic design staff that assisted in the preparation of this book, and planned and implemented the outreach phase.

We appreciate the dedicated work of the entire World Energy Assessment team, including Janet Jensen for editorial assistance throughout the project, Nerissa Cortes for handling myriad administrative details, and Natty Davis for assisting with the outreach phase. We are grateful to Julia Ptasznik for creating the distinctive look of the publication and associated materials, and to Communications Development Incorporated for final editing and proofreading.

The establishing organisations also thank the Advisory Panel, peer reviewers, and participants in the consultative and outreach phases of the book. ■

editorial board

Chair
José Goldemberg, Brazil

Vice-chairs
John W. Baker, United Kingdom
Safiatou Ba-N'Daw, Côte d'Ivoire
Hisham Khatib, Jordan
Anca Popescu, Romania
Francisco L. Viray, Philippines

Convening lead authors
Dennis Anderson, United Kingdom
John P. Holdren, United States
Michael Jefferson, United Kingdom
Eberhard Jochem, Germany
Nebojsa Nakićenović, Austria
Amulya K.N. Reddy, India
Hans-Holger Rogner, Germany
Kirk R. Smith, United States
Wim C. Turkenburg, Netherlands
Robert H. Williams, United States

Establishing institutions
Thomas B. Johansson, UNDP representative
JoAnne DiSano and Kui-nang Mak, UNDESA representatives
Gerald Doucet and Emad El-Sharkawi, WEC representatives

Caitlin Allen, project manager
Janet Jensen, managing editor

establishing institutions

The United Nations Development Programme's (UNDP) mission is to help countries achieve sustainable human development by assisting their efforts to build their capacity to design and carry out development programmes in poverty eradication, employment creation and sustainable livelihoods, empowerment of women, and protection and regeneration of the environment, giving first priority to poverty eradication. UNDP focuses on policy support and institution building in programme countries through its network of 136 country offices.

The United Nations Department of Economic and Social Affairs (UNDESA) facilitates intergovernmental processes and, through its Division for Sustainable Development, services such bodies as the UN Commission on Sustainable Development and the UN Committee on Energy and Natural Resources for Development. UNDESA also undertakes, among other things, statistical and analytical work to monitor the environment and sustainable development, provides policy and technical advisory services, and implements technical cooperation projects at the request of developing countries in the followup to the 1992 Earth Summit.

The World Energy Council (WEC) is a multi-energy, non-governmental, global organisation founded in 1923. In recent years, WEC has built a reputation in the energy field through its studies, technical services, and regional programmes. Its work covers long-term energy scenarios, developing country and transitional economy energy issues, energy financing, energy efficiency and liberalization policies, and environmental concerns. Through its member committees in close to 100 countries, it has encouraged the participation of private industry throughout the editorial and consultative process for this report.

For more information on the activities and publications of the three establishing organisations, please visit the following Websites:
UNDP: http://www.undp.org/seed/eap
UNDESA: http://www.un.org/esa
WEC: http://www.worldenergy.org ■

overview

Energy and the challenge of sustainability

INTRODUCTION The World Energy Assessment provides analytical background and scientific information for decision-makers at all levels. It describes energy's fundamental relationship to sustainable development and analyses how energy can serve as an instrument to reach that goal. This overview synthesises the key findings of the report, which is divided into four parts.

Part 1 (chapters 1–4) begins with an introduction to energy, especially its relationship to economic development. It then considers the linkages between the present energy system and major global challenges, including poverty alleviation, health, environmental protection, energy security, and the improvement of women's lives. The chapters find that although energy is critical to economic growth and human development, affordable commercial energy is beyond the reach of one-third of humanity, and many countries and individuals are vulnerable to disruptions in energy supply. Further, energy production and use have negative impacts at the local, regional, and global levels that threaten human health and the long-term ecological balance.

Part 2 (chapters 5–8) examines the energy resources and technological options available to meet the challenges identified in part 1. It concludes that physical resources are plentiful enough to supply the world's energy needs through the 21st century and beyond, but that their use may be constrained by environmental and other concerns. Options to address these concerns—through greater energy efficiency, renewables, and next-generation technologies—are then analysed. The analysis indicates that the technical and economic potential of energy efficiency measures are under-realised, and that a larger contribution of renewables to world energy consumption is already economically viable. Over the longer term, a variety of new renewable and advanced energy technologies may be able to provide substantial amounts of energy safely, at affordable costs and with near-zero emissions.

Part 3 (chapters 9–10) synthesises and integrates the material presented in the earlier chapters by considering whether sustainable futures—which simultaneously address the issues raised in part 1 using the options identified in part 2—are possible. As a way of answering that question, chapter 9 examines three scenarios to explore how the future might unfold using different policy approaches and technical developments. The analysis shows that a reference scenario based on current trends does not meet several criteria of sustainability. Two other scenarios, particularly one that is ecologically driven, are able to incorporate more characteristics of sustainable development. Chapter 10 examines the challenge of bringing affordable energy to rural areas of developing countries. It presents approaches to widening access to liquid and gaseous fuels for cooking and heating and to electricity for meeting basic needs and stimulating income-generating activities.

Part 4 (chapters 11–12) analyses policy issues and options that could shift current unsustainable practices in the direction of sustainable development (as called for by every major United Nations conference of the 1990s), using energy as an instrument to reach that goal. Creating energy systems that support sustainable development will require policies that take advantage of the market to promote higher energy efficiency, increased use of renewables, and the development and diffusion of cleaner, next-generation energy. Given proper signals, the market could deliver much of what is needed. But because market forces alone are unlikely to meet the energy needs of poor people, or to adequately protect the environment, sustainable development demands frameworks (including consistent policy measures and transparent regulatory regimes) to address these issues. ■

One way of looking at human development is in terms of the choices and opportunities available to individuals. Energy can dramatically widen these choices. Simply harnessing oxen, for example, multiplied the power available to a human being by a factor of 10. The invention of the vertical waterwheel increased productivity by another factor of 6; the steam engine increased it by yet another order of magnitude. The use of motor vehicles greatly reduced journey times and expanded human ability to transport goods to markets.

Today the ready availability of plentiful, affordable energy allows many people to enjoy unprecedented comfort, mobility, and productivity. In industrialised countries people use more than 100 times as much energy, on a per capita basis, as humans did before they learned to exploit the energy potential of fire.[1]

Although energy fuels economic growth, and is therefore a key concern for all countries, access to and use of energy vary widely among them, as well as between the rich and poor within each country. In fact, 2 billion people—one-third of the world's population—rely almost completely on traditional energy sources and so are not able to take advantage of the opportunities made possible by modern forms of energy (World Bank, 1996; WEC-FAO, 1999; UNDP, 1997).[2] Moreover, most current energy generation and use are accompanied by environmental impacts at local, regional, and global levels that threaten human well-being now and well into the future.

In Agenda 21 the United Nations and its member states have strongly endorsed the goal of sustainable development, which implies meeting the needs of the present without compromising the ability of future generations to meet their needs (WCED, 1987, p. 8).[3] The importance of energy as a tool for meeting this goal was acknowledged at every major United Nations conference in the 1990s, starting with the Rio Earth Summit (UN Conference on Environment and Development) in 1992.[4] But current energy systems, as analysed in this report and summarised here, are not addressing the basic needs of all people, and the continuation of business-as-usual practices may compromise the prospects of future generations.

Energy produced and used in ways that support human development over the long term, in all its social, economic, and environmental dimensions, is what is meant in this report by the term *sustainable energy*. In other words, this term does not refer simply to a continuing supply of energy, but to the production and use of energy resources in ways that promote—or at least are compatible with— long-term human well-being and ecological balance.

Many current energy practices do not fit this definition. As noted in Agenda 21, "Much of the world's energy…is currently produced and consumed in ways that could not be sustained if technology were to remain constant and if overall quantities were to increase substantially" (UN, 1992, chapter 9.9).[5] Energy's link to global warming through greenhouse gas emissions (most of which are produced by fossil fuel consumption) was addressed by the United Nations Framework Convention on Climate Change, adopted in 1992. And in 1997 a United Nations General Assembly Special Session identified energy and transport issues as being central to achieving a sustainable future, and set key objectives in these areas.

The energy industry also recognises the need to address energy issues within a broad context. For example, the conclusions and recommendations of the 17th Congress of the World Energy Council discuss the need to provide commercial energy to those without it, and to address energy-linked environmental impacts at all levels (WEC, 1998).[6]

Although there seem to be no physical limits to the world's energy supply for at least the next 50 years, today's energy system is unsustainable because of equity issues as well as environmental, economic, and geopolitical concerns that have implications far into the future. Aspects of the unsustainability of the current system include:

- Modern fuels and electricity are not universally accessible, an inequity that has moral, political, and practical dimensions in a world that is becoming increasingly interconnected.
- The current energy system is not sufficiently reliable or affordable to support widespread economic growth. The productivity of one-third of the world's people is compromised by lack of access to commercial energy, and perhaps another third suffer economic hardship and insecurity due to unreliable energy supplies.
- Negative local, regional, and global environmental impacts of energy production and use threaten the health and well-being of current and future generations.

More specific—and more quantifiable—elements of sustainability are identified below in the section on energy scenarios. Before looking into the future, however, some basic features of energy and its relationship to economic development are described, and the linkages between energy and major global challenges are analysed.

Part 1 analyses the linkages between energy and the economy, social and health issues, environmental protection, and security, and describes aspects of energy use that are incompatible with the goal of sustainable development. It shows that:

- Affordable, modern energy supplies—including gaseous and liquid fuels, electricity, and more efficient end-use technologies—are not accessible by 2 billion people. This constrains their opportunities for economic development and improved living standards. Women and children are disproportionately burdened by a dependence on traditional fuels.
- Wide disparities in access to affordable commercial energy and energy services are inequitable, run counter to the concept of human development, and threaten social stability.
- Unreliable supplies are a hardship and economic burden for a large portion of the world's population. In addition, dependence on imported fuels leaves many countries vulnerable to disruptions in supply.
- Human health is threatened by high levels of pollution resulting from energy use at the household, community, and regional levels.
- The environmental impacts of a host of energy-linked emissions—including suspended fine particles and precursors of acid deposition—contribute to air pollution and ecosystem degradation.
- Emissions of anthropogenic greenhouse gases, mostly from the production and use of energy, are altering the atmosphere in ways that may already be having a discernible influence on the global climate.

Finding ways to expand energy services while simultaneously addressing the environmental impacts associated with energy use represents a critical challenge to humanity. The resources and options available to meet this challenge—energy efficiency, renewables, and advanced energy technologies—are analysed in the next sections.

An introduction to energy

An energy system is made up of an energy supply sector and energy end-use technologies. The object of the energy system is to deliver to consumers the benefits that energy offers. The term *energy services* is used to describe these benefits, which in households include illumination, cooked food, comfortable indoor temperatures, refrigeration, and transportation. Energy services are also required for virtually every commercial and industrial activity. For instance, heating and cooling are needed for many industrial processes, motive power is needed for agriculture, and electricity is needed for telecommunications and electronics.

The energy chain that delivers these services begins with the collection or extraction of primary energy that, in one or several steps, may be converted into energy carriers, such as electricity or diesel oil, that are suitable for end uses. Energy end-use equipment—stoves, light bulbs, vehicles, machinery—converts final energy into useful energy, which provides the desired benefits: the energy services. An example of an energy chain—beginning with coal extraction from a mine (primary energy) and ending with produced steel as an energy service—is shown in figure 1.

Energy services are the result of a combination of various technologies, infrastructure (capital), labour (know-how), materials, and primary energy. Each of these inputs carries a price tag, and they are partly substitutable for one another. From the consumer's perspective, the important issues are the economic value or utility derived from the services. Consumers are often unaware of the upstream activities required to produce energy services.

Per capita consumption of primary energy in the United States was 330 gigajoules in 1995, more than eight times as much as used by an average Sub-Saharan African (who used 40 gigajoules that year when both commercial and traditional energy are included). Many people in the least developed countries use much less. Figure 2 shows commercial and non-commercial energy consumption in various regions.

In most low-income developing countries, a small, affluent minority uses various forms of commercial energy in much the same way as do most people in the industrialised world. But most people in low-income developing countries rely on traditional, non-commercial sources of energy using inefficient technologies such as unventilated stoves or open fires. Traditional energy sources are generally not reflected in energy statistics. Analysis based on per capita consumption of commercially distributed energy resources is common because the data are much easier to collect. The resulting analysis, however, does not accurately reflect the world's energy situation, which is why estimates of non-commercial energy use are included in table 1 and figure 2. Though less well documented, non-commercial energy is very significant globally, and is used far more widely than commercial energy in rural areas of many developing countries, particularly the least developed countries.

The rate of global commercial energy consumption is thousands of times smaller than the energy flows from the sun to the earth. Primary energy consumption is reliant on fossil fuels (oil, natural gas, and coal), which represent nearly 80 percent of the total fuel mix (table 1). Nuclear power contributes slightly more than 6 percent, and hydropower and new renewables each contribute about 2 percent.

World-wide, traditional (often non-commercial) energy accounts for about 10 percent of the total fuel mix. But the distribution is uneven: non-commercial energy accounts for perhaps 2 percent of energy consumption in industrialised countries, but an average of 30 percent in developing ones. In some low-income developing countries, traditional biomass accounts for 90 percent or more of total energy consumption.

If the global growth rate of about 2 percent a year of primary energy use continues, it will mean a doubling of energy consumption by 2035 relative to 1998, and a tripling by 2055. In the past 30 years developing countries' commercial energy use has increased at a rate three and a half times that of OECD countries, the result of life-style changes made possible by rising personal incomes, coupled with higher population growth rates and a shift from traditional to commercial energy. On a per capita basis, however, the increase in total primary energy use has not resulted in any notable way in more equitable access to energy services between industrialised and developing countries. Clearly, more energy will be needed to fuel global economic growth and to deliver opportunities to the billions of people in developing countries who do not have access to adequate energy services.

However, the amount of additional energy required to provide the energy services needed in the future will depend on the efficiencies with which the energy is produced, delivered, and used. Energy efficiency improvements could help reduce financial investments in new energy supply systems, as they have over the past 200 years. The degree of interdependence between economic activity and energy use is neither static nor uniform across regions. Energy intensity (the ratio of energy demand to GDP) often depends on a country's stage of development. In OECD countries, which enjoy abundant energy services, growth in energy demand is less tightly linked to economic productivity than it was in the past (figure 3).

The trend towards a reduction in energy intensity as economic development proceeds can be discerned over a long historical period, as shown in figure 4, which includes the developing country examples of China and India. A detailed, long-term analysis of energy intensity for a number of countries reveals a common pattern of energy use driven by the following factors:

- The shift from non-commercial to commercial forms of energy, industrialisation, and motorisation initially increase the commercial energy-GDP ratio. (In the 1990s this ratio increased in transition in economies, mainly because of slower economic growth.)
- As industrialisation proceeds and incomes rise, saturation effects, as well as an expansion of the service sector (which is less energy intensive), decrease the ratio of commercial energy to GDP after it reaches a peak. This maximum energy intensity has been passed by many countries, but not by low-income developing countries.
- As a result of world-wide technology transfer and diffusion, energy efficiency improvements can be the main limiting factor in the growth of energy demand arising from increasing populations and growing production and incomes.
- The more efficient use of materials in better-quality, well-designed, miniaturised products, the recycling of energy-intensive materials, and the saturation of bulk markets for basic materials in industrialised countries contribute to additional decreases in energy intensity.
- In developing countries, technological leapfrogging to the use of highly efficient appliances, machinery, processes, vehicles, and transportation systems offers considerable potential for energy efficiency improvements.

These drivers are leading to a common pattern of energy use per unit of GDP in industrialised and developing countries.

Energy prices influence consumer choices and behaviour and can affect economic development and growth. High energy prices can lead to increasing import bills, with adverse consequences for business, employment, and social welfare. High energy prices can also stimulate exploration and development of additional resources, create a pull for innovation, and provide incentives for efficiency improvements.

Although some impacts of energy prices are fairly steady, others are more transient. For example, different absolute price levels have had little effect on economic development in OECD European countries or Japan relative to the much lower energy prices in the United States and some developing countries. What affected economic growth in all energy-importing countries were the price hikes of the 1970s. It appears that economies are more sensitive to price changes than to prices per se.

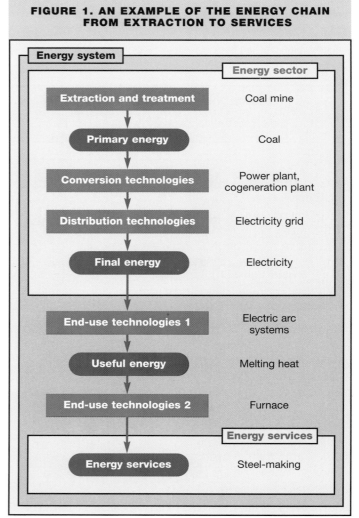

FIGURE 1. AN EXAMPLE OF THE ENERGY CHAIN FROM EXTRACTION TO SERVICES

Source: Adapted from chapter 6.

TABLE 1. WORLD PRIMARY ENERGY CONSUMPTION, 1998

Source	Primary energy (exajoules)	Primary energy (10^9 tonnes of oil equivalent)	Percentage of total	Static reserve-production ratio (years)[a]	Static resource base–production ratio (years)[b]	Dynamic resource base–production ratio (years)[c]
Fossil fuels	**320**	**7.63**	**79.6**			
Oil	142	3.39	35.3	45	~ 200	95
Natural gas	85	2.02	21.1	69	~ 400	230
Coal	93	2.22	23.1	452	~ 1,500	1,000
Renewables	**56**	**1.33**	**13.9**			
Large hydro	9	0.21	2.2	Renewable		
Traditional biomass	38	0.91	9.5	Renewable		
'New' renewables[d]	9	0.21	2.2	Renewable		
Nuclear	**26**	**0.62**	**6.5**			
Nuclear[e]	26	0.62	6.5	50[f]	>> 300[f]	
Total	**402**	**9.58**	**100.0**			

a. Based on constant production and static reserves. b. Includes both conventional and unconventional reserves and resources. c. Data refer to the energy use of a business-as-usual scenario—that is, production is dynamic and a function of demand (see chapter 9). Thus these ratios are subject to change under different scenarios. d. Includes modern biomass, small hydropower, geothermal energy, wind energy, solar energy, and marine energy (see chapter 7). Modern biomass accounts for about 7 exajoules, and 2 exajoules comes from all other renewables. e. Converted from electricity produced to fuels consumed assuming a 33 percent thermal efficiency of power plants. f. Based on once-through uranium fuel cycles excluding thorium and low-concentration uranium from seawater. The uranium resource base is effectively 60 times larger if fast breeder reactors are used. *Source: Chapter 5.*

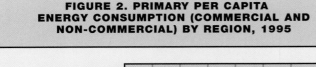

FIGURE 2. PRIMARY PER CAPITA ENERGY CONSUMPTION (COMMERCIAL AND NON-COMMERCIAL) BY REGION, 1995

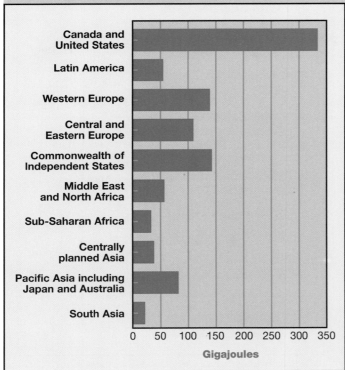

Source: World Bank, 1997; WRI, 1998.

Capital investment is a prerequisite for energy development. Energy system development and structural change are the results of investment in plants, equipment, and energy system infrastructure. Difficulties in attracting capital for energy investment may impede economic development, especially in the least developed countries. Scarce public funds, especially in developing countries, are needed for many projects—ranging from rural development, education, and health care to energy supplies. Because energy supply, more than any other alternative, is often seen as more readily capable of generating early revenues, energy investments are increasingly viewed as a private sector affair. Yet private funds are not flowing into many developing countries for a variety of reasons, especially risks to investors.

Foreign direct investment approached $400 billion in 1997—up from $50 billion in 1984—and represents an increasing share of international investment flows.[7] Foreign direct investment is generally commercially motivated, and investors not only expect to recover the initial capital but also count on competitive returns. These outcomes cannot be guaranteed in developing countries with potentially fragile governments or without free markets. In fact, very little foreign direct investment reaches the least developed countries.

Unlike foreign direct investment, official development assistance has remained flat relative to gross world product. In 1997 it totalled $56 billion, or 0.25 percent of the GDP of OECD countries—which have agreed in principle to a target of 0.7 percent of GDP.[8] Against this backdrop, financing is inadequate for energy projects in developing countries. Until the economic risks to foreign investors can be managed (for example, through clear and stable rules for energy and financial markets, steady revenue generation through bill collection, and profit transfers), most developing countries may have to continue to finance their energy development from domestic savings.

Although energy investment as a share of total investment varies greatly among countries and at different stages of economic development, on balance, 1.0–1.5 percent of GDP is invested in the energy sector. This ratio is expected to remain relatively stable. Based on these rules of thumb, current energy supply sector investment totals $290–430 billion a year. But this does not include investment in end-use energy efficiency.

Energy and social issues

Energy use is closely linked to a range of social issues, including poverty alleviation, population growth, urbanisation, and a lack of opportunities for women. Although these issues affect energy demand, the relationship is two-way: the quality and quantity of energy services, and how they are achieved, have an effect on social issues as well.

Poverty is the overriding social consideration for developing countries. Some 1.3 billion people in the developing world live on less than $1 a day. Income measurement alone, however, does not fully capture the misery and the absence of choice that poverty represents. The energy consumption patterns of poor people—especially their reliance on traditional fuels in rural areas—tend to keep them impoverished.

World-wide, 2 billion people are without access to electricity and an equal number continue to use traditional solid fuels for cooking. As shown in the next section, cooking with poorly vented stoves has significant health impacts. In addition, hundreds of millions of people—mainly women and children—spend several hours a day in the drudgery of gathering firewood and carrying water, often from considerable distances, for household needs. Because of these demands on their time and energy, women and children often miss out on opportunities for education and other productive activities.

Lack of electricity usually means inadequate illumination and few labour-saving appliances, as well as limited telecommunications and possibilities for commercial enterprise. Greater access to electricity and modern fuels and stoves for cooking can enable people to enjoy both short-term and self-reinforcing, long-term advances in their quality of life. Table 2 summarises some of the specific improvements that may result.

Limited income may force households to use traditional fuels and inefficient technologies. Figure 5 shows the average primary energy demand for various fuels as a function of income levels in Brazil. For low-income households, firewood is the dominant fuel. At higher incomes, wood is replaced by commercial fuels and electricity, which offer much greater convenience, energy efficiency, and cleanliness. Because convenient, affordable energy can contribute to a household's productivity and income-generating potential, its availability can become a lever for breaking out of a

World-wide, 2 billion people are without access to electricity and an equal number continue to use traditional solid fuels for cooking.

cycle of poverty.

Although population growth tends to increase energy demand, it is less widely understood that the availability of adequate energy services can lower birth rates. Adequate energy services can shift the relative benefits and costs of fertility towards a lower number of desired births in a family. An acceleration of the demographic transition to low mortality and low fertility (as has occurred in industrialised countries) depends on crucial developmental tasks, including improving the local environment, educating women, and ameliorating the extreme poverty that may make child labour a necessity. All these tasks have links to the availability of low-cost energy services.

The growing concentration of people in urban centres is another key demographic issue linked to energy. Although the general trend towards urbanisation has many components and may be inevitable, providing more options to rural residents through energy interventions could potentially slow migration and reduce pressure on rapidly growing cities. Although the negative externalities associated with energy use in urban areas can be severe, various strategies can mitigate their effects and promote energy conservation. Taking energy into consideration in land-use planning, and in designing physical infra-structure, construction standards, and transportation systems, can reduce some of the growth in energy demand that accompanies rapid urbanisation.

Transportation systems may be especially important in this regard, given the rapid growth in the number of motor vehicles world-wide. Since about 1970 the global fleet has been increasing by 16 million vehicles a year, and more than 1 billion cars will likely be on the road by 2020. Most of these cars will be driven in the cities of the developing world, where they will create more congestion, aggravate urban pollution, and undermine human health—even with optimistic projections about efficiency improvements and alternative fuels.

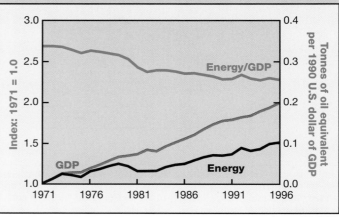

FIGURE 3. GDP AND PRIMARY ENERGY CONSUMPTION IN OECD COUNTRIES, 1971–96

Source: IEA, 1999.

FIGURE 4. PRIMARY ENERGY INTENSITIES IN VARIOUS COUNTRIES, 1850–2000

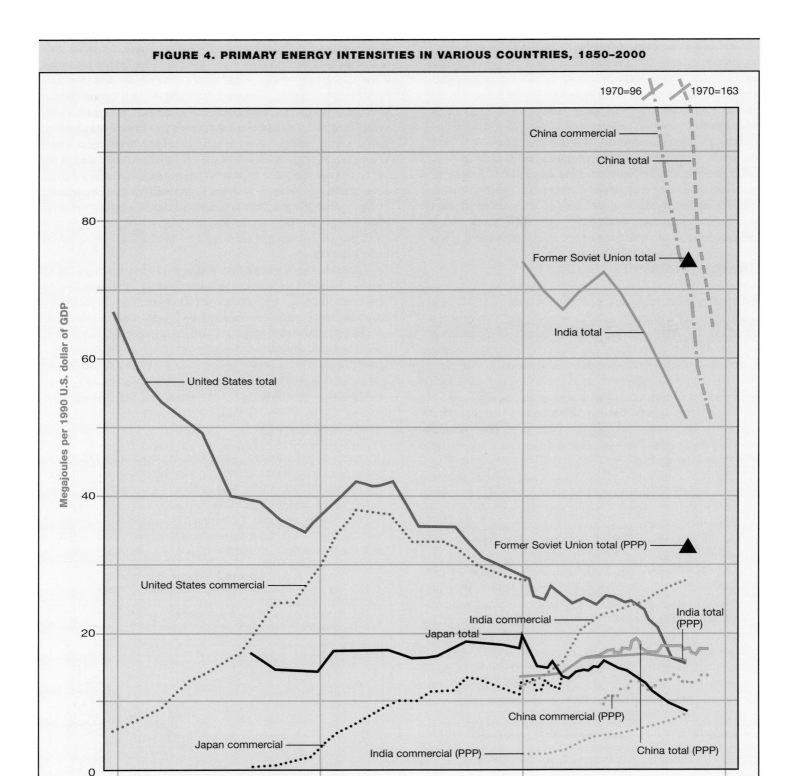

Two energy intensity paths are shown for Japan and the United States, one based on total energy consumption from all sources and the other only on commercial energy. The paths converge where traditional sources have been replaced by commercial energy. Because of distortions from market fluctuations, energy intensity paths for China and India are calculated in two ways: using total and commercial energy divided by GDP measured at market exchange rates (as with Japan and the United States), and divided by GDP measured at purchasing power parities (PPP). Energy intensities for the former Soviet Union, derived using both market exchange rates and PPP, are data points only.   *Source: Nakićenović, Grübler, and McDonald, 1998.*

In developing countries, addressing the energy needs of the poor, who represent a large majority, will require major structural changes. On the other hand, in industrialised countries adequate access to affordable energy is problematic only for a minority, and thus more amenable to social policy solutions. Throughout the world, however, poor households pay a larger fraction of their incomes for energy than do the rich, and so are vulnerable to rapid increases in the price of energy. Increases in the price of oil in the winter of 1999/2000, for example, posed a hardship for many people, even in some industrialised countries.

Eradicating poverty is a long-term goal of development. But long before that goal is achieved, convenient and affordable energy services could dramatically improve living standards and offer more oppor-

tunities to people. Today's inequity is unsustainable. Satisfying the energy needs of the poor with modern technologies has the potential to improve standards of living and health, and to create new jobs and business opportunities. Allowing one-third of the world's population to continue to endure the constraints associated with traditional energy is unacceptable from a humanitarian and moral standpoint. Making commercial energy more widely available makes sense from a political perspective as well. The wave of democratisation sweeping the world is putting political power in the hands of the economically disenfranchised. Societies with grave inequalities and disparities tend to be unstable, and large populations below the poverty line are fertile ground for social upheavals.

Energy, the environment, and health

The environmental impacts of energy use are not new. For centuries, wood burning has contributed to the deforestation of many areas. Even in the early stages of industrialisation, local air, water, and land pollution reached high levels. What is relatively new is an acknowledgement of energy linkages to regional and global environmental problems and of their implications. Although energy's potential for enhancing human well-being is unquestionable, conventional energy[9] production and consumption are closely linked to environmental degradation. This degradation threatens human health and quality of life, and affects ecological balance and biological diversity.

The environment-energy linkage is illustrated in table 3, which shows the share of toxic emissions and other pollutants attributable to the energy supply. The human disruption index is the ratio of the human-generated flow of a given pollutant (such as sulphur dioxide) to the natural, or baseline, flow. Thus, in the case of sulphur, the index is 2.7, which means that human-generated emissions of 84

Social challenge	Energy linkages and interventions
Alleviating poverty in developing countries	• Improve health and increase productivity by providing universal access to adequate energy services—particularly for cooking, lighting, and transport—through affordable, high-quality, safe, and environmentally acceptable energy carriers and end-use devices. • Make commercial energy available to increase income-generating opportunities.
Increasing opportunities for women	• Encourage the use of improved stoves and liquid or gaseous fuels to reduce indoor air pollution and improve women's health. • Support the use of affordable commercial energy to minimise arduous and time-consuming physical labour at home and at work. • Use women's managerial and entrepreneurial skills to develop, run, and profit from decentralised energy systems.
Speeding the demographic transition (to low mortality and low fertility)	• Reduce child mortality by introducing cleaner fuels and cooking devices and providing safe, potable water. • Use energy initiatives to shift the relative benefits and costs of fertility—for example, adequate energy services can reduce the need for children's physical labour for household chores. • Influence attitudes about family size and opportunities for women through communications made accessible through modern energy carriers.
Mitigating the problems associated with rapid urbanisation	• Reduce the 'push' factor in rural-urban migration by improving the energy services in rural areas. • Exploit the advantages of high-density settlements through land planning. • Provide universal access to affordable multi-modal transport services and public transportation. • Take advantage of new technologies to avoid energy-intensive, environmentally unsound development paths.

TABLE 2. ENERGY-RELATED OPTIONS TO ADDRESS SOCIAL ISSUES

Source: Adapted from chapter 2.

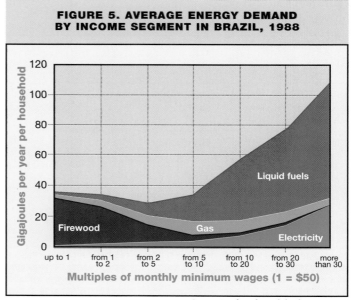

FIGURE 5. AVERAGE ENERGY DEMAND BY INCOME SEGMENT IN BRAZIL, 1988

Source: De Almeida and de Oliveira, 1995.

million tonnes a year are 2.7 times the natural baseline flow of 31 million tonnes a year. The table indicates that, together with other human activities, energy systems significantly affect the global cycling of important chemicals. Although by itself the index does not demonstrate that these emissions translate into negative impacts, their magnitudes provide warning that such impacts could be considerable.

Some impacts, as discussed below, are already significant.

Just in the course of the past 100 years, during which the world's population more than tripled, human environmental insults[10] grew from local perturbations to global disruptions. The human disruptions of the 20th century—driven by more than 20-fold growth in the use of fossil fuels, and augmented by a tripling in the

TABLE 3. ENVIRONMENTAL INSULTS DUE TO HUMAN ACTIVITIES BY SECTOR, MID-1990s

Insult	Natural base-line (tonnes per year)	Human disruption index[a]	Share of human disruption caused by			
			Commercial energy supply	Traditional energy supply	Agriculture	Manufacturing, other
Lead emissions to atmosphere[b]	12,000	18	41% (fossil fuel burning, including additives)	Negligible	Negligible	59% (metal processing, manufacturing, refuse burning)
Oil added to oceans	200,000	10	44% (petroleum harvesting, processing, and transport)	Negligible	Negligible	56% (disposal of oil wastes, including motor oil changes)
Cadmium emissions to atmosphere	1,400	5.4	13% (fossil fuel burning)	5% (traditional fuel burning)	12% (agricultural burning)	70% (metals processing, manufacturing, refuse burning)
Sulphur emissions to atmosphere	31 million (sulphur)	2.7	85% (fossil fuel burning)	0.5% (traditional fuel burning)	1% (agricultural burning)	13% (smelting, refuse burning)
Methane flow to atmosphere	160 million	2.3	18% (fossil fuel harvesting and processing)	5% (traditional fuel burning)	65% (rice paddies, domestic animals, land clearing)	12% (landfills)
Nitrogen fixation (as nitrogen oxide and ammonium)[c]	140 million (nitrogen)	1.5	30% (fossil fuel burning)	2% (traditional fuel burning)	67% (fertiliser, agricultural burning)	1% (refuse burning)
Mercury emissions to atmosphere	2,500	1.4	20% (fossil fuel burning)	1% (traditional fuel burning)	2% (agricultural burning)	77% (metals processing, manufacturing, refuse burning)
Nitrous oxide flows to atmosphere	33 million	0.5	12% (fossil fuel burning)	8% (traditional fuel burning)	80% (fertiliser, land clearing, aquifer disruption)	Negligible
Particulate emissions to atmosphere	3,100 million[d]	0.12	35% (fossil fuel burning)	10% (traditional fuel burning)	40% (agricultural burning)	15% (smelting, non-agricultural land clearing, refuse)
Non-methane hydrocarbon emissions to atmosphere	1,000 million	0.12	35% (fossil fuel processing and burning)	5% (traditional fuel burning)	40% (agricultural burning)	20% (non-agricultural land clearing, refuse burning)
Carbon dioxide flows to atmosphere	150 billion (carbon)	0.05[e]	75% (fossil fuel burning)	3% (net deforestation for fuelwood)	15% (net deforestation for land clearing)	7% (net deforestation for lumber, cement manufacturing)

Note: The magnitude of the insult is only one factor determining the size of the actual environmental impact.
a. The human disruption index is the ratio of human-generated flow to the natural (baseline) flow. b. The automotive portion of human-induced lead emissions in this table is assumed to be 50 percent of global automotive emissions in the early 1990s. c. Calculated from total nitrogen fixation minus that from nitrous oxide. d. Dry mass. e. Although seemingly small, because of the long atmospheric lifetime and other characteristics of carbon dioxide, this slight imbalance in natural flows is causing a 0.4 percent annual increase in the global atmospheric concentration of carbon dioxide. *Source: Chapter 3.*

use of traditional energy forms such as biomass—have amounted to no less than the emergence of civilisation as a global ecological and geochemical force. In other words, the accelerating impact of human life is altering the world at the global level.

At every level (local, regional, global), the environmental consequences of current patterns of energy generation and use make up a significant fraction of human impacts on the environment. At the household level, solid fuel use for cooking and heat has significant health impacts. Poor air quality—at the household, local, and regional levels—is associated with increased sickness and premature death. About 2 million premature deaths a year—disproportionately of women and children—are estimated to occur from exposure to indoor air pollution caused by burning solid fuels in poorly ventilated spaces. Particulate matter (which is both emitted directly and formed in the air as the result of the emissions of gaseous precursors in the form of oxides of sulphur and nitrogen) and hydrocarbons are growing concerns world-wide. They are especially troublesome in many parts of the developing world, where dirtier fuels predominate with little emissions abatement. No safe threshold level for exposure to small particulate matter has been established.

Fossil fuel combustion is problematic on several levels (although natural gas produces significantly fewer harmful emissions than do oil or coal). The main pollutants emitted in the combustion of fossil fuels are sulphur and nitrogen oxides, carbon monoxide, and suspended particulate matter. Ozone is formed in the troposphere from interactions among hydrocarbons, nitrogen oxides, and sunlight. Energy-related emissions from fossil fuel combustion, including in the transport sector, are major contributors to urban air pollution. Precursors of acid deposition from fuel combustion can be precipitated thousands of kilometres from their point of origin—often crossing national boundaries. The resulting acidification is causing significant damage to natural systems, crops, and human-made structures; and can, over time, alter the composition and function of entire ecosystems. In many regions acidification has diminished the productivity of forests, fisheries, and farmlands. Large hydropower projects often raise environmental issues related to flooding, whereas in the case of nuclear power, issues such as waste disposal raise concern.

Fossil fuel combustion produces more carbon dioxide (CO_2) than any other human activity. This is the biggest source of the anthropogenic greenhouse gas emissions that are changing the composition of the atmosphere and could alter the global climate system, including the amount and pattern of rainfall. Achieving a stable atmospheric CO_2 concentration at any level would require that CO_2 emissions eventually be cut by more than half from current levels. Stabilising CO_2 at close to the present concentration would require reducing emissions to half of current levels within the next few decades. Instead, CO_2 emissions continue to increase. Current CO_2

Numerous energy strategies could simultaneously benefit the environment, the economy and human well-being.

emission trends, if not controlled, will lead to more than a doubling of atmospheric concentrations before 2070, relative to pre-industrial levels. Changes have been observed in climate patterns that correspond to scientific projections based on increasing concentrations of greenhouse gases. The balance of evidence, according to the Intergovernmental Panel on Climate Change, suggests that there is already a discernible human influence on global climate.

Because, by definition, sustainable energy systems must support both human and ecosystem health over the long term, goals on tolerable emissions should look well into the future. They should also take into account the public's tendency to demand more health and environmental protection as prosperity increases.

Although the scope of environmental problems related to energy may seem overwhelming, numerous 'win-win' strategies could simultaneously benefit the environment (at several levels), the economy, and human well-being. For example, the replacement of solid fuels for cooking with gaseous or liquid fuels could have significant environmental benefits at the local, community, regional, and global scales, with attendant benefits for health and productivity.

Energy security

Energy security means the availability of energy at all times in various forms, in sufficient quantities, and at affordable prices. These conditions must prevail over the long term if energy is to contribute to sustainable development.

Attention to energy security is critical because of the uneven distribution both of the fossil fuel resources on which most countries currently rely and of capacity to develop other resources. The energy supply could become more vulnerable over the near term due to the growing global reliance on imported oil. For example, the oil dependence (net imports as a share of total demand) of OECD countries is expected to grow from 56 percent in 1996 to 72 percent in 2010.

In addition, although energy security has been adequate for the past 20 years, and has in fact improved, the potential for conflict, sabotage, disruption of trade, and reduction in strategic reserves cannot be dismissed. These potential threats point to the necessity of strengthening global as well as regional and national energy security. Options to enhance energy security include:

■ Avoiding excessive dependence on imports by increasing end-use efficiency and encouraging greater reliance on local resources (particularly those whose development will have other positive externalities such as job creation, capacity building, and pollution reduction), provided these do not involve disproportionate costs or waste scarce resources.

■ Diversifying supply (including both suppliers and energy forms).

■ Fostering greater political stability through international cooperation and long-term agreements among energy-importing countries and between importing and exporting countries. Examples might include wider adoption—and more effective implementation of—the Energy Charter Treaty,[11] as well as increased sharing of infrastructure for transporting natural gas.

■ Encouraging technology transfers (for example, through joint ventures and public-private partnerships) to developing countries so they can develop local resources and improve energy efficiencies.

■ Increasing national and regional strategic reserves of crude oil and oil products through increased investment and advanced exploration technologies.

Although markets play a prominent role in securing energy supply in OECD countries, their role is modest in some developing countries and absent in others. Where markets do not flourish, the security of supply and services depends almost solely on government action and multinational companies, which may not serve the best interests of consumers. In such situations, energy security can be enhanced by encouraging the development of frameworks that allow markets to contribute to the allocation of energy resources.

Because of small fuel requirements, nuclear power contributes to the diversity of supply and to supply security. But public concerns about economic necessity, reactor safety, and radioactive waste transport and disposal—as well as weapons proliferation—have curbed nuclear energy development in many countries. A nuclear accident anywhere in the world or a proliferation incident linked to nuclear power could further reduce support for nuclear power programmes, with long-term loss in the diversity of the energy supply mix. But if generally accepted responses could be found to the above concerns, nuclear energy could contribute significantly to secure electricity generation in many parts of the world.

Individuals and commercial enterprises are also vulnerable to disruptions of energy supply. Although the trend towards the liberalisation of energy markets generally has enhanced energy security by offering more options, supplies, and competition, it has also raised concerns that those who are impoverished will be left out of the process, resulting in continued energy insecurity for some individuals.

PART 2. ENERGY RESOURCES AND TECHNOLOGICAL OPTIONS

Physical resources and technical opportunities are available—or could become available—to meet the challenge of sustainable development. Without policy changes, cost differentials may favour conventional fuels for years to come. Options for using energy in ways that support sustainable development, which requires addressing environmental concerns, include:

■ **More efficient use of energy, especially at the point of end use in buildings, electric appliances, vehicles, and production processes.**

■ **Increased reliance on renewable energy sources.**

■ **Accelerated development and deployment of new energy technologies, particularly next-generation fossil fuel technologies that produce near-zero harmful emissions—but also nuclear technologies, if the problems associated with nuclear energy can be resolved.**

All three options have considerable potential, but realising this potential will require removing obstacles to wider diffusion, developing market signals that reflect environmental costs, and encouraging technological innovation.

Energy resources

Careful analysis of the long-term availability of energy resources, starting with conventional and unconventional oil and gas, indicates that these resources could last another 50–100 years—and possibly much longer—with known exploration and extraction technologies and anticipated technical progress in upstream operations. Coal resources and nuclear materials are so abundant that they could, respectively, last for centuries or millennia. Moreover, although fossil fuel prices may rise slowly over time, the large, cost-driven increases in energy prices projected in the 1970s and 1980s will not take place in the foreseeable future.

As evidenced by rising oil prices in the winter of 1999/2000, however, prices are subject to volatility. This may occur, for example, if cartels set prices independent of production costs. Some fluctuations in prices can also be expected, especially during the transition to a large-scale use of unconventional oil and gas resources, because the timing of investments in upstream production capacities may not correspond with demand. Other cost-pushing factors could arise from the environmentally more challenging extraction of unconventional oil resources.

Renewable resources are more evenly distributed than fossil and nuclear resources, and energy flows from renewable resources are more than three orders of magnitude higher than current global energy use. But the economic potential of renewables is affected by many constraints—including competing land uses, the amount and timing of solar irradiation, environmental concerns, and wind patterns.

Although there are no real limitations on future energy availability from a resource point of view, the existence of resources is of little relevance without consideration of how these can contribute to the supply of (downstream) energy services. Rather, the key concerns are: Can technologies to extract, harvest, and convert these vast energy stocks and flows be developed in time? Will these processes have adverse implications? Will the energy services eventually generated from these resources be affordable? Historical evidence suggests that these concerns may be at least partly offset by technological progress, but that such progress needs to be encouraged—by regulations to improve market performance, temporary subsidies, tax incentives, or other mechanisms—if it is to occur in a timely fashion.

> Over the next 20 years the amount of primary energy required for a given level of energy services could be cost-effectively reduced by 25–35 percent in industrialised countries.

Energy end-use efficiency

The quadrupling of oil prices in the 1970s, the growing awareness of energy-related pollution, and the possibility of climate change have all contributed to a re-evaluation of energy use. The result has been an improvement in the efficiency with which energy is used in industry and power generation as well as in lighting, household appliances, transportation, and heating and cooling of buildings. This more efficient use of energy is a major factor contributing to the improvements in energy intensity that have occurred historically in almost all OECD countries, and more recently in many transition economies, as well as in some in fast-growing developing countries such as Brazil and China.

Today the global energy efficiency of converting primary energy to useful energy is about one-third (see figure 1). In other words, two-thirds of primary energy is dissipated in the conversion processes, mostly as low-temperature heat. Further significant losses occur when the useful energy delivers the energy service. Numerous and varied economic opportunities exist for energy efficiency improvements, particularly in this final conversion step from useful energy to energy services. Taking advantage of these opportunities, which have received relatively little attention, has the largest potential for cost-effective efficiency improvements. It would mean less costly energy services and lower energy-related pollution and emissions.

Over the next 20 years the amount of primary energy required for a given level of energy services could be cost-effectively reduced by 25–35 percent in industrialised countries (the higher figure being achievable by more effective policies). These reductions are mostly in the conversion step of useful energy to energy services in the residential, industrial, transportation, public, and commercial sectors. Reductions of more than 40 percent are cost-effectively achievable in transition economies. And in most developing countries—which tend to have high economic growth and old capital and vehicle stocks—the cost-effective improvement potentials range from 30 to more than 45 percent, relative to energy efficiencies achieved with existing capital stock.[12]

The improvements of about 2 percent a year implied by the above figures could be enhanced by structural changes in industrialised and transition economies, by shifts to less energy-intensive industrial production, and by saturation effects in the residential and transportation sectors. These combined effects, made up by efficiency improvements and structural changes, could lead to decreases in energy intensity of 2.5 percent a year. How much of this potential will be realised depends on the effectiveness of policy frameworks and measures, changes in attitudes and behaviour, and the level of entrepreneurial activity in energy conservation.

The next few decades will likely see new processes, motor systems, materials, vehicles, and buildings designed to reduce useful energy

demand. Because the demand for cars is expected to grow rapidly in the developing world, gaining greater efficiencies in this area will be very important. In addition, rapidly industrialising countries could greatly profit from the introduction of radically new and more efficient technologies in their energy-intensive basic materials processing. Because these countries are still building their physical infrastructure, they have a growing demand for basic materials. This opens a window of opportunity to innovate and improve efficiencies of production, particularly in countries undergoing market reform. The opportunities are larger at the point of new investment, relative to retrofitting.

Over the long term, additional and dramatic gains in efficiency are possible at all stages of energy conversion, particularly from useful energy to energy services. Analysis shows that current technologies are not close to reaching theoretical limits, and that improvements of an order of magnitude for the whole energy system may eventually be achieved.[13]

For a number of reasons the technical and economic potentials of energy efficiency, as well as its positive impact on sustainable development, have traditionally been under-realised. Achieving higher end-use efficiency involves a great variety of technical options and players. Because it is a decentralised, dispersed activity, it is a difficult issue for which to organise support. And because it has little visibility, energy efficiency is not generally a popular cause for politicians, the media, or individuals looking for recognition and acknowledgement. In addition, significant barriers—primarily market imperfections that could be overcome by targeted policy instruments—prevent the realisation of greater end-use efficiencies. These barriers include:

- Lack of adequate information, technical knowledge, and training.
- Uncertainties about the performance of investments in new and energy-efficient technologies.
- Lack of adequate capital or financing possibilities.
- High initial and perceived costs of more efficient technologies.
- High transaction costs (for searching and assessing information and for training).
- Lack of incentives for careful maintenance.
- The differential benefits to the user relative to the investor (for example, when energy bills are paid by the renter rather than the property owner).
- External costs of energy use, not included in energy prices.
- Patterns and habits of consumers, operators, and decision-makers, which may be influenced by many factors, including ideas of social prestige and professional norms.

Realising cost-effective energy efficiency potentials will be beneficial not only for individual energy consumers, but also for the economy as a whole. For example, saved energy costs can be used to produce energy-saving domestic goods and services. And as cost-effective energy improvements are realised, additional profitable opportunities for improvement will continue to open up as a result of research and development, learning curves, and economies of scale. That means that continual cost-effective energy efficiency improvements can be expected.

Energy efficiency policies that use direct or indirect price mechanisms (such as the removal of subsidies and the incorporation of externalities) are effective in lowering consumption trends in price-sensitive sectors and applications. But even without changing the overall price environment, energy efficiency policies should be pursued to address market failures. For example, efficiency standards, appliance and product labelling, voluntary agreements, and professional training or contracting can increase GDP growth by improving environmental and economic performance, using a given quantity of energy. Legal standards; well-informed consumers, planners, and decision-makers; motivated operators; and an adequate payments system for energy are central to the successful implementation of energy efficiency improvements.[14]

Renewable energy technologies

Renewable energy sources (including biomass, solar, wind, geothermal, and hydropower) that use indigenous resources have the potential to provide energy services with zero or almost zero emissions of both air pollutants and greenhouse gases. Currently, renewable energy sources supply 14 percent of the total world energy demand. The supply is dominated by traditional biomass used for cooking and heating, especially in rural areas of developing countries. Large-scale hydropower supplies 20 percent of global electricity. Its scope for expansion is limited in the industrialised world, where it has nearly reached its economic capacity. In the developing world, considerable potential still exists, but large hydropower projects may face financial, environmental, and social constraints.

Altogether, new renewable energy sources contributed 2 percent of the world's energy consumption in 1998, including 7 exajoules from modern biomass and 2 exajoules for all other renewables (geothermal, wind, solar, and marine energy, and small-scale hydropower). Solar photovoltaics and grid-connected wind installed capacities are growing at a rate of 30 percent a year. Even so, it will likely be decades before these new renewables add up to a major fraction of total energy consumption, because they currently represent such a small percentage.

Substantial price reductions in the past few decades have made some renewables competitive with fossil fuels in certain applications in growing markets. Modern, distributed forms of biomass seem particularly promising for their potential to provide rural areas with clean forms of energy based on the use of biomass resources that have traditionally been used in inefficient, polluting ways. Biomass can be economically produced with minimal or even positive environmental impacts through perennial crops. Wind power in coastal and other windy regions is promising as well.

Unlike hydropower and conventional thermal power sources, wind and solar thermal or electric sources are intermittent.

Renewable energy sources have the potential to provide energy services with zero or almost zero emissions of both air pollutants and greenhouse gases.

Nevertheless, they can be important energy sources in rural areas where grid extension is expensive. They can also contribute to grid-connected electricity supplies in appropriate hybrid configurations. Intermittent renewables can reliably provide 10–30 percent of total electricity supplies if operated in conjunction with hydropower- or fuel-based power generation. Emerging storage possibilities and new strategies for operating grids offer promise that the role of intermittent technologies could be considerably larger.

Significant barriers, which could be overcome by appropriate frameworks and policies, stand in the way of the accelerated development of renewable technologies. These barriers include economic risks, regulatory obstacles, limited availability of products, information and technology gaps, and lack of investment. The greatest challenge is financial, even though costs have come down significantly over the past several decades. Table 4 summarises the status of various renewable technologies, and also provides information on trends in cost and capacity.

Many renewable technologies, because they are small in scale and modular, are good candidates for continued cost-cutting as a result of field experience. The cost reductions of manufactured goods, which are typically rapid at first and then taper off as the industry matures, are called experience curves. These curves resulted in industry-wide cost declines of about 20 percent for each cumulative doubling of production for solar photovoltaics, wind generators, and gas turbines—due to learning effects, marginal technological improvements, and economies of scale (figure 6). Similar declines are expected for other small-scale renewables.

A rapid expansion of renewable-based energy systems will require actions to stimulate the market in this direction. This expansion can be achieved by finding ways to drive down the relative cost of renewables in their early stages of development and commercialisation, while still taking advantage of the economic efficiencies of the marketplace. Pricing based on the full costs of conventional energy sources (including phasing out subsidies and internalising externalities) will make renewables more competitive. Because internalising external costs may be controversial for some time, 'green' pricing of electricity and heat (which lets consumers pay more for environmentally benign energy supplies if they choose) may be an immediate option in industrialised countries.

Advanced energy technologies

Fossil energy

Sustainability goals indicate the importance of evolving fossil energy technologies towards the long-term goal of near-zero air pollutant and greenhouse gas emissions without complicated end-of-pipe control technologies. Near-term technologies and strategies should support this long-term goal.

The technological revolution under way in power generation,

where advanced systems are replacing steam turbine technologies, does support this long-term goal. Natural-gas-fired combined cycles offering low costs, high efficiency, and low environmental impacts are being chosen wherever natural gas is readily available—in some countries even displacing large new hydropower projects. Cogeneration is more cost-effective and can play a much larger role in the energy economy—if based on gas turbines and combined cycles rather than on steam turbines.

Reciprocating engines and emerging microturbine and fuel cell technologies are also strong candidates for cogeneration at smaller scales, including commercial and apartment buildings. Coal gasification by partial oxidation with oxygen to produce syngas (mainly carbon monoxide and hydrogen) makes it possible to provide electricity through integrated gasifier combined cycle (IGCC) plants with air pollutant emissions nearly as low as for natural gas combined cycles. Today power from IGCC cogeneration plants is often competitive with power from coal steam-electric plants in either cogeneration or power-only configurations.

Although synthetic liquid fuels made in single-product facilities are not competitive, superclean syngas-derived synthetic fuels (such as synthetic middle distillates and dimethyl ether) produced in polygeneration facilities that make several products simultaneously may soon be. Syngas can be produced from natural gas by steam reforming or other means or from coal by gasification using oxygen, as noted. Expanding markets for clean synthetic fuels are likely to result from toughening air pollution regulations. Synthetic fuels produced through polygeneration will be based on natural gas if it is readily available. Synthetic middle distillates so produced are likely to be competitive where low-cost natural gas is available (as at remote developing country sites); the technology might facilitate exploitation of relatively small remote natural gas fields.

In natural-gas-poor, coal-rich regions, polygeneration based on coal gasification is promising. Such systems might include production of extra syngas for distribution by pipelines to small-scale cogeneration systems in factories and buildings—making possible clean and efficient use of coal at small as well as large scales. Rapidly growing polygeneration activity is already under way in several countries based on the gasification of low-quality

TABLE 4. CURRENT STATUS AND POTENTIAL FUTURE COSTS OF RENEWABLE ENERGY TECHNOLOGIES

Technology	Increase in installed capacity in past five years (percent a year)	Operating capacity, end 1998	Capacity factor (percent)	Energy production, 1998	Turnkey investment costs (U.S. dollars per kilowatt)	Current energy cost	Potential future energy cost
Biomass energy							
Electricity	≈ 3	40 GWe	25–80	160 TWh (e)	900–3000	5–15 ¢/kWh	4–10 ¢/kWh
Heat[a]	≈ 3	> 200 GWth	25–80	> 700 TWh (th)	250–750	1–5 ¢/kWh	1–5 ¢/kWh
Ethanol	≈ 3	18 billion litres		420 PJ		8–25 $/GJ	6–10 $/GJ
Wind electricity	≈ 30	10 GWe	20–30	18 TWh (e)	1100–1700	5–13 ¢/kWh	3–10 ¢/kWh
Solar photovoltaic electricity	≈ 30	500 MWe	8–20	0.5 TWh (e)	5000–10000	25–125 ¢/kWh	5 or 6–25 ¢/kWh
Solar thermal electricity	≈ 5	400 MWe	20 – 35	1 TWh (e)	3000–4000	12–18 ¢/kWh	4–10 ¢/kWh
Low-temperature solar heat	≈ 8	18 GWth (30 million m²)	8–20	14 TWh (th)	500–1700	3–20 ¢/kWh	2 or 3–10 ¢/kWh
Hydroelectricity							
Large	≈ 2	640 GWe	35–60	2510 TWh (e)	1000–3500	2–8 ¢/kWh	2–8 ¢/kWh
Small	≈ 3	23 GWe	20–70	90 TWh (e)	1200–3000	4–10 ¢/kWh	3–10 ¢/kWh
Geothermal energy							
Electricity	≈ 4	8 GWe	45–90	46 TWh (e)	800–3000	2–10 ¢/kWh	1 or 2–8 ¢/kWh
Heat	≈ 6	11 GWth	20–70	40 TWh (th)	200–2000	0.5–5¢/kWh	0.5–5 ¢/kWh
Marine energy							
Tidal	0	300 MWe	20–30	0.6 TWh (e)	1700–2500	8–15 ¢/kWh	8–15 ¢/kWh
Wave	–	exp. phase	20–35	Unclear	1500–3000	8–20 ¢/kWh	Unclear
Current	–	exp. phase	25–35	Unclear	2000–3000	8–15 ¢/kWh	5–7 ¢/kWh
OTEC	–	exp. phase	70–80	Unclear	Unclear	Unclear	Unclear

Note: The cost of grid-supplied electricity in urban areas ranges from 2-3 c/kWh (off-peak) to 15-25c/kWh (peak). See chapter 11.
a. Heat embodied in steam (or hot water in district heating), often produced by combined heat and power systems using forest residues, black liquor, or bagasse.

Source: Chapter 7.

petroleum feedstocks—activity that is helping to pave the way for coal-based systems.

Barriers to widespread deployment of advanced cogeneration and polygeneration systems are mainly institutional. Most systems will produce far more electricity than can be consumed on-site, so achieving favourable economics depends on being able to sell co-product electricity at competitive prices into electric grids. Utility policies have often made doing so difficult, but under the competitive market conditions towards which electric systems are evolving in many regions, cogeneration and polygeneration systems will often fare well.

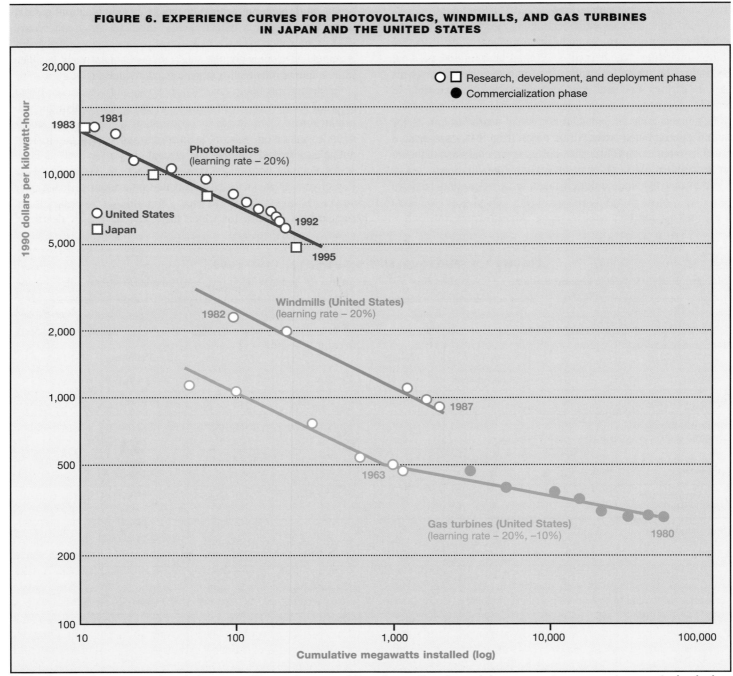

FIGURE 6. EXPERIENCE CURVES FOR PHOTOVOLTAICS, WINDMILLS, AND GAS TURBINES IN JAPAN AND THE UNITED STATES

○ □ Research, development, and deployment phase
● Commercialization phase

○ United States
□ Japan

Photovoltaics (learning rate – 20%)

Windmills (United States) (learning rate – 20%)

Gas turbines (United States) (learning rate – 20%, –10%)

Technology performance and costs improve with experience, and there is a pattern to such improvements common to many technologies. The specific shape depends on the technology, but the persistent characteristic of diminishing costs is termed the 'learning' or 'experience' curve. The curve is likely to fall more sharply as technologies first seek a market niche, then full commercialisation, because lower costs become increasingly important for wider success.

Source: Nakićenović, Grübler, and McDonald, 1998.

Overview

The near-term pursuit of a syngas-based strategy could pave the way for widespread use of hydrogen (H_2) as an energy carrier, because for decades the cheapest way to make H_2 will be from fossil-fuel-derived syngas. The successful development of fuel cells would facilitate the introduction of H_2 for energy. Fuel cells are getting intense attention, especially for transportation, because they offer high efficiency and near-zero air pollutant emissions. Automakers are racing to develop fuel cell cars, with market entry targeted for 2004–10. The fuel cell car will compete for the role of 'car of the future' with the hybrid internal combustion engine/battery powered car already being introduced into the market.

Syngas-based power and H_2 production strategies also facilitate separation and storage of CO_2 from fossil energy systems, making it possible to obtain useful energy with near-zero emissions of green-house gases without large increases in energy costs. Recent research suggests that the global capacity for secure disposal of CO_2 in geological reservoirs might be adequate to dispose of CO_2 from fossil fuel use for hundreds of years, although more research is needed to be sure about this.

Other advanced technologies (ultrasupercritical steam plants, pressurised fluidised-bed combustion, coal IGCC based on partial oxidation in air for power generation, direct coal liquefaction for synthetic fuels production) offer benefits relative to conventional technologies. But unlike syngas-based technologies, such options in the near term would not offer clear paths to the long-term goal of near-zero emissions without significant increases in costs for energy services.

Nuclear energy

World-wide, nuclear energy accounts for 6 percent of energy and 16 percent of electricity. Although nuclear energy dominates electricity generation in some countries, its initial promise has not been widely realised. Most analysts project that nuclear energy's contribution to global energy will not grow—and might decline during the initial decades of the 21st century. Nuclear power is more costly than originally projected, competition from alternative technologies is increasing, and there has been a loss of public confidence because of concerns related to safety, radioactive waste management, and potential nuclear weapons proliferation.

But because nuclear power can provide energy without emitting conventional air pollutants and greenhouse gases, it is worth exploring if advanced technologies could offer simultaneously lower costs, boost public confidence in the safety of nuclear reactors, assure that peaceful nuclear programs are not used for military purposes, and demonstrate effective nuclear waste management practices. Unlike Chernobyl-type reactors, the light water reactors (LWRs) that dominate nuclear power globally have a good safety record—although this record has been achieved at considerable cost to minimise the risk of accidents.

If wise decisions are not made during the next few decades, certain development opportunities might not be achievable.

The potential linkage between peaceful and military uses of nuclear energy was recognised at the dawn of the nuclear age. Efforts to create a non-proliferation regime through the Nuclear Non-Proliferation Treaty and a series of regional treaties, controls on commerce in nuclear materials and goods and services that might be used to further military ambitions, and safeguards applied to nuclear materials in peaceful nuclear applications have been largely successful in separating peaceful and military uses. If there is to be an energy future in which nuclear power eventually contributes much more than at present, stronger institutional measures will be needed to maintain this separation. These measures should be complemented by technological advances aimed at limiting opportunities to acquire nuclear weapons under the guise of peaceful nuclear energy applications and to steal weapons-usable nuclear materials.

Reactor development activity for the near term has involved both evolutionary LWRs and new concepts. Reactor vendors now offer several evolutionary LWRs with improved safety features and standardised designs, for which there can be a high degree of confidence that performance and cost targets will be met. Another evolutionary activity involves modifying LWRs to make them more proliferation resistant through a denatured uranium or thorium fuel cycle. One concept being revisited, the pebble bed modular reactor, offers the potential for a high degree of inherent safety without the need for complicated, capital-intensive safety controls. A pebble bed modular reactor could also be operated on a proliferation resistant denatured uranium- or thorium fuel cycle.

Access to low-cost uranium supplies could constrain nuclear power development based on LWRs. The plutonium breeder reactor, which requires reprocessing spent fuel to recover plutonium for recycling in fresh fuel, was once thought to be a viable option for addressing this challenge. But electricity costs for breeders would probably be higher than for LWRs, at least until late in the 21st century, and preventing proliferation is much more challenging with reprocessing and plutonium recycling than with LWRs operated on once-through fuel cycles.

Other long-term options for addressing the nuclear resource constraint are alternative breeder concepts—including particle-accelerator-driven reactors, uranium from seawater, and thermonuclear fusion. The prospective costs, safety, and proliferation resistance features of such alternative breeder concepts are uncertain, and the concepts would take decades to develop. Recent research suggests it might be feasible, at relatively low cost, to extract uranium from seawater, where its concentration is low but total quantities are vast. If the technology could be deployed at globally significant scales, it might be feasible to avoid making major commitments to nuclear fuel reprocessing and plutonium recycling. Fusion could provide an almost inexhaustible energy supply, but it will probably not be commercially available before 2050.

Radioactive waste by-products of nuclear energy must be isolated so that they can never return to the human environment in concentrations that could cause significant harm. Although the safety of long-term waste disposal has not been proven, the technical community is confident that this objective can be realised—largely because of the small volumes of wastes involved. But in most countries there is no social consensus on the goals and standards for radioactive waste disposal and on strategies (both interim and long-term) for implementing them. The issues involved are only partly technical. The current social stalemate on waste disposal not only clouds prospects for nuclear expansion, it also has made spent fuel reprocessing a de facto interim nuclear waste management strategy in some countries. This has happened even though fuel reprocessing does not offer economic gains and does not solve the waste disposal problem—it merely buys time and is creating large inventories of plutonium that must be disposed of with low proliferation risk.

PART 3. ARE SUSTAINABLE FUTURES POSSIBLE?

Analysis using energy scenarios indicates that it is possible to simultaneously address the sustainable development objectives set forth in part 1 using the resources and technical options presented in part 2. The scenarios exercise and subsequent sections suggest that:

- **Continuing along the current path of energy system development is not compatible with sustainable development objectives.**
- **Realising sustainable futures will require much greater reliance on some combination of higher energy efficiencies, renewable resources, and advanced energy technologies.**
- **A prerequisite for achieving an energy future compatible with sustainable development objectives is finding ways to accelerate progress for new technologies along the energy innovation chain, from research and development to demonstration, deployment, and diffusion.**
- **Providing energy services to rural areas poses particular challenges. But it also offers considerable opportunity for improving the lives of billions of people within a relatively short period. Promising approaches include decentralised solutions, appropriate technologies, innovative credit arrangements, and local involvement in decision-making.**

Energy scenarios

Energy scenarios provide a framework for exploring future energy perspectives, including various combinations of technology options and their implications. Many scenarios in the literature illustrate the degree to which energy system developments will affect the global issues analysed in part 1. Some describe energy futures that are compatible with sustainable development goals. Key developments in sustainable scenarios include increases in energy efficiencies and the adoption of advanced energy supply technologies. Sustainable development scenarios are characterised by low environmental impacts (local, regional, and global) and equitable allocation of resources and wealth.

The three cases of alternative global developments presented in chapter 9 suggest how the future could unfold in terms of economic growth, population trends, and energy use. The challenge is formidable. For example, by 2100, 6–8 billion additional people—significantly more than today's world population—will need access to affordable, reliable, flexible, and convenient energy services.[15] All three cases achieve this through different energy system developments, but with varying degrees of success in terms of sustainability (table 5).

A middle-course, or reference, case (B) includes one scenario and is based on the general direction in which the world is now headed. This scenario assumes the continuation of an intermediate level of economic growth and modest technological improvement, and it leads to adverse environmental impacts, including regional acidification and climate change. Although this middle-course scenario represents a substantial improvement relative to the current situation, it falls short of achieving a transition towards sustainable development. The other two scenarios and their variants lead to higher economic development with vigorous improvement of energy technologies. They both—and especially the ecologically driven case (C)—achieve, to a much higher degree, a transition towards sustainable development (table 6).

For instance, one of the three high-growth case A scenarios (A3) achieves some goals of sustainable development, primarily through rapid economic growth and a shift towards environmentally more benign energy technologies and options. In this scenario, higher levels of affluence result from impressive technological development, including a significant role for clean fossil, renewable, and nuclear energy. Dedicated decarbonisation of the energy system contributes to environmental sustainability. Two other variants of this high-growth case are also considered. Both lead to higher dependence on carbon-intensive fossil fuels, resulting in high energy-related emissions. Consequently, they are unsustainable from an environmental point of view.

A third case (C) includes two scenarios and is ecologically driven, with high growth in developing countries (towards being

TABLE 5. SUMMARY OF THREE ENERGY DEVELOPMENT CASES IN 2050 AND 2100 COMPARED WITH 1990

		Case A High growth	Case B Middle growth	Case C Ecologically driven
Population (billions)	1990	5.3	5.3	5.3
	2050	10.1	10.1	10.1
	2100	11.7	11.7	11.7
Gross world product (trillions of 1990 dollars)	1990	20	20	20
	2050	100	75	75
	2100	300	200	220
Gross world product (annual percentage change)	1990–2050	**High**	**Medium**	**Medium**
	1990–2100	2.7	2.2	2.2
		2.5	2.1	2.2
Primary energy intensity (megajoules per 1990 dollar of gross world product)	1990	19.0	19.0	19.0
	2050	10.4	11.2	8.0
	2100	6.1	7.3	4.0
Primary energy intensity improvement rate (annual percentage change)	1990–2050	**Medium**	**Low**	**High**
	1990–2100	−0.9	-0.8	−1.4
		−1.0	-0.8	−1.4
Primary energy consumption (exajoules)	1990	379	379	379
	2050	1,041	837	601
	2100	1,859	1,464	880
Cumulative primary energy consumption, 1990–2100 (thousands of exajoules)	Coal	8.9 – 30.7	17.5	7.1 – 7.2
	Oil	27.6 – 15.7	15.3	10.9
	Natural gas	18.4 – 28.7	15.8	12.2 – 12.9
	Nuclear energy	6.2 – 11.2	10.5	2.1 – 6.2
	Hydropower	3.7 – 4.2	3.6	3.6 – 4.0
	Biomass	7.4 – 14.3	8.3	9.1 – 10.1
	Solar energy	1.8 – 7.7	1.9	6.3 – 7.4
	Other	3.0 – 4.7	4.3	1.4 – 2.2
	Global total	94.0 – 94.9	77.2	56.9
Energy technology cost reductions (through learning)	Fossil	**High**	**Medium**	**Low**
	Non-fossil	**High**	**Medium**	**High**
Energy technology diffusion rates	Fossil	**High**	**Medium**	**Medium**
	Non-fossil	**High**	**Medium**	**High**
Environmental taxes (excluding carbon dioxide taxes)		**No**	**No**	**Yes**
Sulphur dioxide emissions (millions of tonnes of sulphur)	1990	58.6	58.6	58.6
	2050	44.8 – 64.2	54.9	22.1
	2100	9.3 – 55.4	58.3	7.1
Carbon dioxide emission constraints and taxes		**No**	**No**	**Yes**
Net carbon dioxide emissions (gigatonnes of carbon)	1990	6	6	6
	2050	9 – 15	10	5
	2100	6 – 20	11	2
Cumulative carbon dioxide emissions (gigatonnes of carbon)	1990–2100	910 – 1,450	1,000	540
Carbon dioxide concentrations (parts per million by volume)	1990	358	358	358
	2050	460 – 510	470	430
	2100	530 – 730	590	430
Carbon intensity (grams of carbon per 1990 dollar of gross world product)	1990	280	280	280
	2050	90 – 140	130	70
	2100	20 – 60	60	10
Investments in energy supply sector (trillions of 1990 dollars)	1990–2020	15.7	12.4	9.4
	2020–50	24.7	22.3	14.1
	2050–2100	93.7	82.3	43.3
Number of scenarios		**3**	**1**	**2**

The three cases unfold into six scenarios of energy system alternatives: three case A scenarios (A1, ample oil and gas; A2, return to coal; and A3, non-fossil future), a single case B scenario (middle course), and two case C scenarios (C1, new renewables; and C2, new renewables and new nuclear). Some of the scenario characteristics, such as cumulative energy consumption, cumulative carbon dioxide emissions, and decarbonisation, are shown as ranges for the three case A and two C scenarios.

Source: Nakićenović, Grübler, and McDonald, 1998.

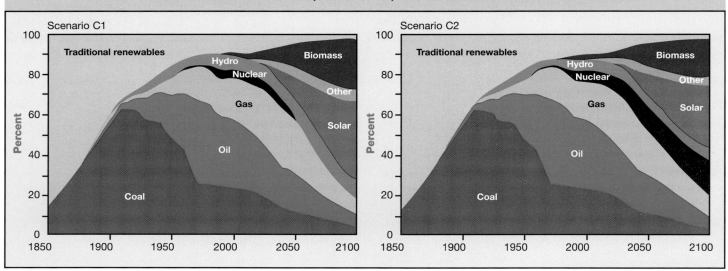

FIGURE 7. PRIMARY ENERGY SHARES, 1850–1990, AND IN SCENARIOS C1 AND C2 TO 2100

Source: Nakićenović, Grübler, and McDonald, 1998.

rich and 'green'). The difference between the two scenarios is that one, C1, assumes a global phase-out of nuclear energy by 2100, whereas the other, C2, does not. Both assume the introduction of carbon and energy taxes directed at promoting renewables and end-use efficiency improvements. The revenues from carbon and energy taxes are assumed to be used to enhance economic growth and promote renewables and end-use efficiency, rather than to reduce other taxes in industrialised regions.

Both case C scenarios assume decentralisation of energy systems and reliance on local solutions. They also require considerably lower supply-side investments than the others. They would, however, require substantial investments in the end-use sector, which is not captured in the scenarios. Ambitious policy measures control local and regional pollutants, and a global regime results in reduced greenhouse gas emissions. Of the three cases considered, case C is the most compatible with the aims of sustainable development, as analysed in part 1 (table 6). In scenario C1 this occurs through a diminishing contribution of coal and oil to the primary energy mix, with a large increase in the share of solar and biomass energy by 2100 (figure 7).

Also shown for illustrative purposes is the primary energy mix for scenario C2, in which nuclear energy could play a large role if the problems associated with it (cost, safety, waste disposal and weapons proliferation) can be adequately resolved.

The considerable differences in expected total energy consumption among the scenarios reflect different approaches to addressing the needs for energy services in the future, and they demonstrate clearly that policy matters (figure 8). Achieving the two scenarios with characteristics of sustainable development will require a substantial increase in private and public research, development, and deployment

efforts to support new energy technologies. Otherwise, most clean fossil and renewable technologies, as well as many energy-efficient end-use technologies, may not reach competitiveness. (The mix of needed efforts may vary depending on the maturity of the specific technology.) Significant technological advances will be required, as will incremental improvements in conventional energy technologies.

In terms of their expected high growth in energy demand, developing countries are well-positioned to take advantage of innovations in energy technologies and policies that support them. In general, scenarios A3, C1, and C2 require significant policy and behavioural changes within the next several decades to achieve more sustainable development paths. Taken together, the outcomes of these changes, which are described in more detail in part 4, represent a clear departure from a business-as-usual approach.

Another crucial prerequisite for achieving sustainability in the scenarios is near-universal access to adequate, affordable energy services and more equitable allocation of resources. Finally, environmental protection—from indoor pollution to climate change—is an essential characteristic of sustainable development in these scenarios. The resolution of these future challenges offers a window of opportunity between now and 2020. The nature of the decisions made during this time will largely determine whether the evolution of the energy system is consistent with current practices (along the lines of the B scenario), or whether it achieves the transition towards more sustainable development paths (along the lines of the A3, C1, and C2 scenarios).

Because of the long lifetimes of power plants, refineries, steel plants, buildings, and other energy-related investments such as transportation infrastructure, there is not sufficient turnover of such facilities to reveal large differences among the alternative scenarios presented here before 2020. But the seeds of the post-2020 world will have been sown by then. Thus choices about the world's future energy systems are relatively wide open now. This window of opportunity is particularly significant where much infrastructure has yet to be installed, offering the possibility of a rapid introduction of new, environmentally sound technologies.

Once the infrastructure is in place, a phase of largely replacement investments begins. Changes can be made in this phase, but they take much longer to affect average system performance. If wise decisions are not made during the next few decades, we will be locked into those choices, and certain development opportunities might not be achievable. Thus the achievement of sustainable development demands a global perspective, a very long time horizon, and the timely introduction of policy measures.

Rural energy in developing countries

Between 1970 and 1990 about 800 million additional people were reached by rural electrification programmes. Some 500 million saw their lives improve substantially through the use of better methods for cooking and other rural energy tasks, particularly in China.

An effective strategy to address the energy needs of the rural populations is to promote the climbing of the 'energy ladder'.

Despite these enormous efforts to improve energy services to rural populations in the past 20–30 years, the unserved population has remained about the same in absolute numbers— 2 billion people.

Although the unavailability of adequate energy services in rural areas is probably the most serious energy problem confronting humanity in the near future, rural energy remains low on the list of priorities of most government and corporate planners. And the increased demands of the more influential (and rapidly growing) urban population will make it more difficult to keep rural development on the agenda.

An effective strategy to address the energy needs of rural populations is to promote the climbing of the 'energy ladder'. This implies moving from simple biomass fuels (dung, crop residues, firewood) to the most convenient, efficient form of energy appropriate to the task at hand—usually liquid or gaseous fuels for cooking and heating and electricity for most other uses. Such climbing involves not only a shift to modern fuels but is often also complemented by the synergistic use of modern, more efficient end-use devices such as cooking stoves.

Climbing the energy ladder does not necessarily mean that all the rungs used in the past should be reclimbed. In the case of cooking,

TABLE 6. CHARACTERISTICS OF SUSTAINABILITY IN THREE ENERGY DEVELOPMENT SCENARIOS IN 2050 AND 2100 COMPARED WITH 1990

Indicator of sustainability	1990	Scenario A3	Scenario B	Scenario C1
Eradicating poverty	Low	Very high	Medium	Very high
Reducing relative income gaps	Low	High	Medium	Very high
Providing universal access to energy	Low	Very high	High	Very high
Increasing affordability of energy	Low	High	Medium	Very high
Reducing adverse health impacts	Medium	Very high	High	Very high
Reducing air pollution	Medium	Very high	High	Very high
Limiting long-lived radionuclides	Medium	Very low	Very low	High
Limiting toxic materials[a]	Medium	High	Low	High
Limiting GHG emissions	Low	High	Low	Very high
Raising indigenous energy use	Medium	High	Low	Very high
Improving supply efficiency	Medium	Very high	High	Very high
Increasing end-use efficiency	Low	High	Medium	Very high
Accelerating technology diffusion	Low	Very high	Medium	Medium

a. For this row only, the qualitative indicators are not based on quantitative features of the scenarios, but were specified by the authors on the basis of additional assumptions.

Source: Chapter 9.

for example, users do not have to go from fuelwood to kerosene to liquefied petroleum gas (LPG) or electricity. What users should do—whenever possible—is leapfrog directly from fuelwood to the most efficient end-use technologies and the least polluting energy forms (including new renewables) available. Because of the emergence of new technologies, it is also possible to introduce new rungs on the energy ladder, and gain even greater efficiencies and environmental acceptability.

The energy-related sustainable development goals for rural areas are to:

- Satisfy basic human needs by providing all households with minimally adequate amounts of electricity for uses such as lighting and fans, in addition to cleaner cooking fuels. Specifically, all households should move away from unprocessed solid fuels (biomass and coal) for cooking and heating to modern energy forms, which may potentially be derived from renewable sources (biomass and solar) or fossil fuels.
- Provide electricity that is sufficiently affordable to support industrial activity in rural areas, which can provide employment and help curb urban migration.

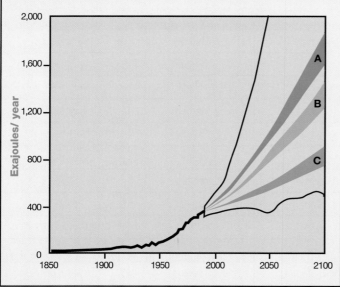

FIGURE 8. GLOBAL PRIMARY ENERGY REQUIREMENTS, 1850–1990, AND IN THREE CASES, 1990–2100

The figure also shows the wide range of future energy requirements for other scenarios in the literature. The vertical line that spans the scenario range in 1990 indicates the uncertainty across the literature of base-year energy requirements.

Source: Nakićenović, Grübler, and McDonald, 1998; Morita and Lee, 1998; Nakićenović, Victor, and Morita, 1998.

The current path of energy development, and the rate of change, are not compatible with key elements of sustainable development.

In many cases the rural poor are willing and able to pay for energy services if appropriate financing options are offered to help them meet high first costs. The economics of providing basic electricity to rural households should be evaluated according to the costs of supplying comparable energy services through less efficient carriers. In most cases home solar photovoltaic systems can provide energy services at a lower cost than the kerosene and batteries they replace and can be an economically viable source of rural household power, even at relatively low levels of service provision.

The availability of affordable and adequate energy services in rural areas could lead to significant improvements in living conditions and to the fulfilment of basic human needs over a relatively short time frame. The amount of energy needed to provide such services in rural areas is relatively small. Modern ways of using biomass more efficiently could go a long way towards achieving this objective. Experience has shown that to find the most viable and appropriate solutions to rural energy, the active participation of the people who will use it is a must.

The challenge is to find ways to make modern energy carriers affordable to satisfy the basic needs of all rural residents—which may, at least initially, require subsidies. The key is to introduce market efficiencies if possible to use the smallest subsidy needed to achieve social objectives. If a subsidy is required, it might be provided as an integral part of a new social contract, whereby energy providers serve rural energy needs while simultaneously, highly competitive conditions are created in the energy sector (a key element of energy reforms). One way to finance the subsidies that might be needed would be to complement the creation of competitive markets with the establishment of a public benefits fund generated by non-bypassable wire and pipe charges on electricity and on gas providers. Such funds have been adopted or are under consideration in several countries as a means of protecting public benefits under competitive market conditions. Other options include carefully designed economic incentives, perhaps using tax regimes.

Specifically, some of these revenues could be used to subsidise the very poorest households until they are able to work themselves out of poverty. This strategy could be made entirely consistent with a shift to greater reliance on market forces to efficiently allocate resources. If, for example, a rural energy concession was the preferred approach for bringing adequate energy services at a set price to a particular rural area, and if the concession was awarded competitively, market forces would be brought into play to find the least costly mix of energy technologies with the least amount of subsidy to satisfy the concessionaire's obligation to provide affordable energy services to all.

Part 4 identifies key strategies and policies for achieving both economic growth and sustainable human development. They include:

■ Setting the right framework conditions—including continued market reforms, consistent regulations, and targeted policies—to encourage competition in energy markets, reduce the cost of energy services to end users, and protect important public benefits.

■ Sending accurate price signals, including phasing out subsidies to conventional energy and internalising externalities.

■ Removing obstacles or providing incentives, as needed, to encourage greater energy efficiency and the development and diffusion to wider markets of new sustainable energy technologies.

The challenge of sustainable energy will require a concerted effort from national governments, the energy community, civil society, the private sector, international organisations, and individuals. Whatever the difficulties of taking appropriate action, they are small relative to what is at stake. Because today's world is in a dynamic and critical period of economic, technological, demographic, and structural transition, and because energy systems take decades to change, the time to act is now.

Energy and economic prosperity

The demand of industrialised and transition economies for energy services is likely to grow, although increasing efficiency in conversion and end uses may result in a levelling off or even a reduction in the demand for primary energy. In developing countries, however, primary energy demand is expected to grow at about 2.5 percent a year as industrialisation and motorisation proceed and living standards improve.

Meeting these projected demands will be essential if developing countries are to achieve economic prosperity. It will require considerable investment—on the order of 2.0–2.5 percent of the GDP of developing countries over the next 20 years. This is close to historical norms and, with good financial and economic policies, should be affordable. In the past, energy investments in developing countries rested heavily—and unnecessarily—on government subsidies, and too little on the financial resources that would be generated by real cost-based pricing, regulatory policies, and efficient management.

In general, there is no reason the energy sector should not be financially self-sufficient in the following sense: appropriate pricing and regulatory policies would raise revenues to cover operating costs and generate returns on investment sufficient to attract large-scale private finance and investment. Indeed, one of the primary aims of market liberalisation and the new forms of regulation introduced in many countries in the 1990s was precisely this: to reduce the need for government subvention and to attract private capital and investment to the energy sector. The other aims were to encourage innovation, cost-effectiveness, and managerial efficiency.

But temporary government subsidies may be needed to help people who are excluded from the market by extreme poverty. Just as poor areas in today's industrialised countries benefited in the past from non-market energy policies, such options should be still available, when justified, in developing countries. Moreover, the poor may need to be shielded from economic hardships caused by trends over which they have no control. In some developing countries, for instance, the oil price increases of the 1970s and early 1980s contributed to large increases in external debt—up to 50 percent in some cases.[16] The effects of that debt—impoverishment of the country and widespread unemployment—were particularly hard on the poor, even though their main source of fuel was and continues to be firewood rather than oil. The debt burden from the 1970s persists in many developing countries.

Although there seem to be no physical limitations on total energy resources, potentially severe problems are likely if appropriate economic, technological, and environmental policies are not developed in a timely manner. Rational energy pricing is part of what is needed, but so is a willingness to prompt markets to find technological solutions to problems before they begin exacting high societal and environmental costs. Finding ways to curb energy-related greenhouse gas emissions and to address other environmental problems, while still expanding energy services, will require enlightened research, development, and demonstration policies. Much therefore will depend on the energy and environmental policies that are introduced, and on their relationship to the forces of globalisation and liberalisation (discussed below).

Thanks to technological advances and better information on impacts, developing countries are in a position to address local and regional environmental problems early in the 21st century, and at an earlier stage of development than industrialised countries did. By addressing these negative externalities of energy generation and use early on, developing countries would find their overall economic well-being and the prospects of their people improved, not diminished. The issue of global climate change, however, may prove more difficult to reconcile with high levels of economic growth.

Overall, however, the analysis in this report suggests that there are no fundamental technological, economic, or resource limits constraining the world from enjoying the benefits of both high levels of energy services and a better environment. This is not to suggest that these benefits are to be expected—only that they are achievable. As the scenarios discussed above demonstrate, sustainable futures depend on ambitious policy measures and support for technological innovation.

In analysing appropriate policies, it is important to keep in mind key features of the political and economic environment in which new energy systems will evolve:

- The broad structure of macroeconomic and development policies—particularly those for education and broad-based growth. Below a certain level of per capita income, subsistence needs other than energy dominate household budgets and priorities. Income growth among groups without access is the most important determinant of whether they will be willing to pay for energy services (and thus provide the demand required for markets to work effectively). This, in turn, depends on policies beyond the control of energy industries.
- The widespread liberalisation of energy markets and the restructuring of the energy sector. These changes are driven by inefficient monopolies, government budget constraints, and expanding technological opportunities—especially in electric power generation. Liberalisation and restructuring can lower costs and generate the finance required for the expansion and extension of supplies (as long as it is profitable to do so). But in restructured energy markets, cross-subsidies will not be available to increase access in areas that are not attractive to investors, unless restructuring is accompanied by policy measures that specifically address such concerns.
- Globalisation and the transformations of the information age. Related to the liberalisation of markets is globalisation—the world-wide expansion of major companies and their acquisition of, or partnership with, local companies. Procurement of materials and services from distant and foreign sources has become common. New technologies are also diffusing at rates faster than ever before, spurred by world-wide access to the Internet and other information technologies. This expansion can expedite the awareness of sustainable energy options and the deployment of new technologies.

Energy policies for sustainable development

The scenarios exercise showed that, although energy can contribute to sustainable development, its performance in this respect will depend on a range of factors. These include attitudes and behaviour, information and technologies, the availability of finance and supporting institutions, and—in particular—policies and policy frameworks that encourage change in the desired direction. The current path of energy development, and the rate of change, are not compatible with key elements of sustainable development. The divergence of alternative futures that becomes apparent in the scenarios after about 20 years reflects the long-term nature of energy systems. It also indicates that if governments, corporations, and international institutions do not introduce appropriate policies and measures now, critical windows of opportunity are likely to close. It will then become even more difficult to change course.

The most critical issues that sustainable energy strategies and the policies derived from them need to address are how to widen access to reliable and affordable modern energy supplies, and how to ease the negative health and environmental impacts of energy use.

Given proper frameworks, pricing signals, and regulatory regimes, markets can efficiently deliver on the economic objectives of sustainable development. But markets alone cannot be expected to meet the needs of the most vulnerable groups and to protect the environment. Where markets fail to protect these and other important public benefits, targeted government policies and consistent regulatory approaches will be needed. The problem is that government interventions are usually less efficient than market approaches. Government intervention may have unintended consequences at odds with its original aims. For that reason, there is a need to try different approaches and learn from the experiences of other countries.

Policies and policy frameworks in support of sustainable development should focus on widening access, encouraging energy efficiency, accelerating new renewable energy diffusion, and expanding the use of advanced clean fossil fuel technologies, while keeping open the nuclear option. These policy areas, as well as related decisions on private-public transportation and city planning, have the greatest relevance to the environmental and safety problems associated with conventional fuels.

The broad strategies for encouraging sustainable energy systems are straightforward. But achieving them will require wide acknowledgement of the challenges we face and stronger commitment to specific policies. The strategies are largely aimed at harnessing market efficiencies to the goal of sustainable development and using additional measures to speed up innovation, overcome obstacles and market imperfections, and protect important public benefits. Among the basic strategies, six stand out.

Making markets work better

Driven by the forces of competition, markets do a better job than administered systems in allocating resources. But the marketplace fails to adequately account for the social and environmental costs of energy provision and use. Policies that reduce market distortions—that level the playing field—would give sustainable energy (renewable sources, energy efficiency measures, new technologies with near-zero emissions) a considerably better market position relative to current uses and practices.

Market distortions can be reduced by phasing out permanent subsidies to conventional energy (estimated at $250–300 billion a year in the mid-1990s) and by including social and environmental costs in prices. Several countries have experimented with energy and environment taxes as a way to address the latter. In many cases incentives will be needed to induce or accelerate changes. One such option is a targeted, time-limited (through a 'sunset clause') subsidy. Where energy markets cannot function effectively because of absolute poverty, additional resources, including official development assistance, are required.

Another aspect of making markets work better is finding ways to overcome obstacles to energy end-use efficiency measures. Even in the absence of subsidies, market barriers—such as lack of technological knowledge, different interests of investors and users, and high transaction costs of individual investors—keep energy efficiency measures from reaching their cost-effective potential. Options to overcome these barriers include voluntary or mandatory standards (effectively applied) for appliances, vehicles, and buildings, labelling schemes to better inform consumers, procurement policies to achieve higher standards and economies of scale, technical training in new energy efficiency technologies and their maintenance, and credit mechanisms to help consumers meet higher first costs.

Complementing energy sector restructuring with regulations that encourage sustainable energy

The ongoing, world-wide restructuring of the energy industry—largely driven by the increasing globalisation of the economy—will lead to more economically efficient energy markets. This restructuring presents a window of opportunity for ensuring that the energy-related public benefits needed for sustainable development are adequately addressed in emerging policies for energy market reform. The process could be enhanced if governments set goals that define the performance characteristics of qualifying sustainable energy technologies (for example, by specifying air pollution emission limits or minimum standards on plants, machinery, and vehicles).

These goals for suppliers can be complemented by mechanisms that favour sustainable energy technologies in energy market choices. Other regulatory approaches supportive of sustainable energy include mandating that a certain percentage of energy comes from renewable sources, requiring that energy grids be open to independent power producers, and ensuring that rural populations are served. Such regulations are based on the recognition that energy market restructuring in itself may not help achieve sustainable development.

Mobilising additional investments in sustainable energy

Energy markets in many countries are rapidly becoming more competitive. For that reason, successful sustainable energy policies, whether involving financing, incentives, taxes, or regulations, must engage the private sector and catalyse private investment on a large scale. But for political or institutional reasons, many of the transition and developing economies that most need investment have problems attracting private enterprise and gaining access to financial markets. Reliable commercial legislation and jurisdiction, as well as incentives, may be needed to encourage private companies to invest in sustainable energy—or to defray the risks associated with such investments.

Official developement assistance may also need to play a greater role in the least developed countries, especially in those where the conditions that attract private sector investment are lacking. Political stability, application of the rule of law, avoidance of arbitrary intervention, and the existence of institutions that facilitate savings and investment are generally important for promoting investment. Supportive financial and credit arrangements (including microcredit arrangements like those now in existence) will be needed to introduce commercial energy to people excluded from markets, especially in rural areas.

Encouraging technological innovation

Currently applied technologies are not adequate and profitable enough to deliver the energy services that will be needed in the 21st century and simultaneously protect human health and environmental stability. Adequate support for a portfolio of promising advanced and new technologies is one way to help ensure that options will be available as the need for them becomes more acute. Energy innovations face barriers all along the energy innovation chain (from research and development, to demonstration projects, to cost buy-down, to widespread diffusion). Some of these barriers reflect market imperfections, some inadequacies in the public sector, and some different views about needs, corporate priorities, relevant time horizons, and reasonable costs.

The public support needed to overcome such barriers will vary from one technology to the next, depending on its maturity and market potential. Obstacles to technology diffusion, for example, may need to be given higher priority than barriers to innovation. Direct government support is more likely to be needed for radically new technologies than for incremental advances, where the private sector usually functions relatively effectively. Options to support technological innovation, while still using competition to keep down costs, include tax incentives, collaborative research and development ventures, government or cooperative procurement policies, 'green' labelling schemes, and market transformation initiatives.

Supporting technological leadership and capacity building in developing countries

Because most of the projected growth in energy demand will occur in the developing world, innovation and leadership in energy technologies could be highly profitable for developing countries in economic, environmental, and human terms. Developing economies need to further develop their resources—human, natural, and technological—so they can create energy systems appropriate to their own circumstances. But they also need assistance with technology transfer, financing, and capacity building.

The declining share of official development assistance relative to required investment capital suggests that much of this investment will need to be led by the private sector or private-public partnerships. International industrial collaboration offers one means by which the private sector could gain markets while fostering the private research institutes, and regional institutes that provide training in technological management offer additional possibilities for furthering technology sharing and capacity building.

Encouraging greater cooperation at the international level

The ongoing process of globalisation means that ideas, finances, and energy flow from one country to another. Productive ways of moving forward might include combining national efforts, for example, in the procurement of renewable energy technologies. Other options include international harmonisation of environmental taxes and emissions trading (particularly among industrialised countries), as

Innovation and leadership in energy technologies could be highly profitable for developing countries in economic, environmental, and human terms.

well as energy efficiency standards for mass-produced products and imports of used machinery and vehicles. The need for concerted action on energy is clear from Agenda 21, which emerged from the 1992 Earth Summit.

The challenge of sustainable energy includes crucial enabling roles for governments, international organisations, multilateral financial institutions, and civil society, including non-governmental organisations and individual consumers. Partnerships will be required, based on more integrated, cooperative approaches and drawing on a range of practical experience. A common denominator across all sectors and regions is setting the right framework conditions and making public institutions work effectively and efficiently with the rest of society and other economic actors to reach beneficial, shared objectives.

Clearly, energy can serve as a powerful tool for sustainable development. Redirecting its power to work towards that overarching goal, however, will require major changes of policy within an enabling overall framework. Poverty, inequity, inefficiency, unreliable service, immediate environmental priorities, a lack of information and basic skills, and an absence of needed institutions and resources—require changes to be made. Unless these changes occur within the next few decades, many of the opportunities now available will be lost, the possibilities for future generations diminished, and the goal of sustainable development unrealised. ■

> Clearly, energy can serve as a powerful tool for sustainable development.

References

De Almeida, E., and A. de Oliveira. 1995. "Brazilian Life Style and Energy Consumption". In *Energy Demand, Life Style Changes and Technology Development*. London: World Energy Council.

IEA (International Energy Agency). 1999. *Energy Balances of OECD Countries*. Paris.

Morita, T., and H.-C. Lee. 1998. "IPCC SRES Database, Version 0.1, Emission Scenario". Database prepared for IPCC Special Report on Emissions Scenarios, http://www.cger.nies.go.jp/ cger-e/db/ipcc.html

Nakićenović, N., A. Grübler, and A. McDonald, eds. 1998. *Global Energy Perspectives*. Cambridge: Cambridge University Press.

Nakićenović, N., N. Victor, and T. Morita. 1998. "Emissions Scenarios Database and Review of Scenarios". *Mitigation and Adaptation Strategies for Global Change 3* (2–4): 95–120.

UN (United Nations). 1992. *Earth Summit Agenda 21: The United Nations Programme of Action from Rio*. New York.

UNDP (United Nations Development Programme). 1997. *Energy after Rio*. New York.

WCED (World Commission on Environment and Development). 1987. *Our Common Future*. Oxford: Oxford University Press.

WEC (World Energy Council). 1998. *Round Up: 17th Congress of the World Energy Council*. London.

———. 2000. *Statement 2000: Energy for Tomorrow's World—Acting Now!* London.

WEC-FAO (World Energy Council and Food and Agriculture Organization of the United Nations). 1999. *The Challenge of Rural Energy Poverty in Developing Countries*. London.

World Bank. 1996. Rural Energy and Development: Improving Energy Supplies for Two Billion People. Washington, D.C.

———. 1997. World Development Indicators 1997. Washington, D.C.

WRI (World Resources Institute). 1998. *A Guide to the Global Environment*. Oxford: Oxford University Press.

Notes

1. In this report the term *industrialised countries* refers primarily to high-income countries that belong to the Organisation for Economic Co-operation and Development (OECD). *Developing countries* generally refers to lower income countries that are members of the G-77 and China. Although many *transition economies* also have a high degree of industrialisation, they are often considered and discussed separately because of their specific development requirements.

2. In this report the terms *traditional energy* and *non-commercial energy* are used to denote locally collected and unprocessed biomass-based fuels, such as crop residues, wood, and animal dung. Although traditional energy sources can be used renewably, in this report the term *new renewables* refers to modern biofuels, wind, solar, small-scale hydropower, marine, and geothermal energy.

3. The Brundtland Report, as the World Commission on Environment and Development report is commonly known, set forth a global agenda for change.

4. Energy's links to sustainable development were most recently acknowledged by the UN General Assembly Special Session on Small Island Developing States in 1999. The major conferences that noted the importance of energy issues were the UN Conference on Population and the UN Conference on Small Island Developing States in 1994, the Copenhagen Social Summit and the Beijing Fourth World Conference on Women in 1995, and the World Food Summit and HABITAT II in 1996. The energy issues emerging from these conferences are summarised in chapters 1 and 2 of UNDP (1997).

5. Agenda 21 is the plan of action for sustainable development adopted at the Rio Earth Summit.

6. Means for achieving these objectives are discussed in more detail in WEC (2000).

7. Unless otherwise noted, all prices are in U.S. dollars.

8. This target was reaffirmed in 1992 (in chapter 33 of Agenda 21).

9. In this report the term *conventional energy* is used to refer to fossil fuel, nuclear energy, and large-scale hydropower.

10. In this report the word *insult* is used to describe a physical stressor produced by the energy system, such as air pollution. The word *impact* is used to describe the resulting outcome, such as respiratory disease or forest degradation.

11. The Energy Charter Treaty, together with a protocol on energy efficiency and related environmental aspects, entered into force in 1998. It has been signed by about 50 countries, including the members of the European Union and the Commonwealth of Independent States, Australia, and Japan.

12. Analysis of efficiency potentials in end-use sectors in the next 20 years appears in chapter 6 of this report and is based on detailed techno-economic studies and examples of best practices.

13. Conventionally, energy efficiency has been defined on the basis of the first law of thermodynamics. The second law of thermodynamics recognises that different forms of energy have different potentials to carry out specific tasks. For example, a gas boiler for space heating may operate at close to 100 percent efficiency (in terms based on the first law of thermodynamics). This seems to suggest that limited additional efficiency improvements are possible. But by extracting heat from the ground or other sources, a gas-driven heat pump could generate considerably more low-temperature heat with the same energy input. The second example illustrates the potential for energy efficiency improvements according to the second law of thermodynamics.

14. An adequate payments system means using meters and payment collection to ensure that all energy services have a price that is paid by all users on a regular basis.

15. Both figures include the 2 billion currently without access to commercial energy. UN population projections were revised downwards in 1998, after the scenarios described here were developed. Although the population assumption used for the scenarios described here (11.7 billion by 2100) is slightly higher than the UN medium scenario (10.4 billion), the two are not inconsistent.

16. The policies of industrialised countries and inflationary pressures from petro-dollars could also have contributed to debt levels.

part I
energy and major global issues

an introduction to energy

CHAPTER 1

Hans-Holger Rogner (Germany)
Anca Popescu (Romania)

L ife is but a continuous process of energy conversion and transformation. The accomplishments of civilisation have largely been achieved through the increasingly efficient and extensive harnessing of various forms of energy to extend human capabilities and ingenuity. Energy is similarly indispensable for continued human development and economic growth. Providing adequate, affordable energy is essential for eradicating poverty, improving human welfare, and raising living standards world-wide. And without economic growth, it will be difficult to address environmental challenges, especially those associated with poverty.

But energy production, conversion, and use always generate undesirable by-products and emissions—at a minimum in the form of dissipated heat. Energy cannot be created or destroyed, but it can be converted from one form to another. The same amount of energy entering a conversion process, say, natural gas in a home furnace, also leaves the device—some 80–90 percent as desirable space heat or warm water, the rest as waste heat, most through the smokestack. Although it is common to discuss energy consumption, energy is actually transformed rather than consumed. What is consumed is the ability of oil, gas, coal, biomass, or wind to produce useful work. Among fossil fuels the chemical composition of the original fuel changes, resulting in by-products of combustion, or emissions.

This chapter provides a brief introduction to energy's importance for human life and economic functioning, and paints a broad picture of the current energy scene. (More extensive data on energy trends appear in the annexes to this report.) Chapters 2, 3, and 4 examine in greater detail the links between energy and important global challenges, including social issues, health and the environment, and energy security. Chapter 11 analyses prospects for achieving widespread and sustainable prosperity and for reconciling high levels of energy services with environmental protection.

What is sustainable energy development?

In its 1987 report, *Our Common Future*, the World Commission on Environment and Development defines sustainable development as development that "meets the needs of the present without compromising the ability of future generations to meet their own needs" (p. 8). The report further describes sustainable development "as a process of change in which the exploitation of resources, the direction of investments, the orientation of technological development, and institutional change are all in harmony and enhance both current and future potentials to meet human needs and aspirations" (p. 46). In its broadest sense, the report notes, "the strategy for sustainable development aims to promote harmony among human beings and between humanity and nature" (p. 65).

The relationship between energy production and use and sustainable development has two important features. One is the importance of adequate energy services for satisfying basic human needs, improving

> The production and use of energy should not endanger the quality of life of current and future generations and should not exceed the carrying capacity of ecosystems.

social welfare, and achieving economic development—in short, energy as a source of prosperity. The other is that the production and use of energy should not endanger the quality of life of current and future generations and should not exceed the carrying capacity of ecosystems.

Throughout the 20th century, the ready availability of commercial energy fuelled global economic development. But much of the developing world continues to rely on non-commercial energy sources, mainly fuelwood, and has limited access to modern energy such as electricity and liquid fuels. Lack of capital and technological capacity hinders the development of adequate supplies, with deleterious effects on economic and social development.

Because they affect affordability and economic competitiveness, energy prices need to be taken into account when analysing options for sustainable energy development. Moreover, energy supplies should be secure and reliable. For that reason, attention should be given to:

- The dependence on energy supplies from politically unstable regions or unevenly distributed locations.
- The possible disruption of energy supplies due to severe accidents.
- The sociocultural environment in which energy systems operate.
- The eventual exhaustion of finite energy resources such as coal, crude oil, natural gas, and uranium, for which alternative options must be developed.

Finally, the development and introduction of sustainable energy technology must occur in a socially acceptable manner, with a broad range of citizens participating in decision-making.

No energy production or conversion technology is without risk or waste. Somewhere along all energy chains—from the extraction of resources to the provision of energy services—pollutants are produced, emitted, or disposed of, often with severe impacts on human health and the environment. The combustion of fossil fuels is responsible for most urban air pollution, regional acidification, and risks of human-induced climate change. The use of nuclear power has created a number of concerns about the safety of nuclear installations, the storage and disposal of high-level radioactive waste, and the proliferation of nuclear weapons. The manufacturing of photovoltaic panels generates toxic waste, and in some developing countries the use of biomass contributes to desertification and biodiversity losses.

As noted, to be considered sustainable, energy systems must not overload the carrying capacity of ecosystems. Nor should the use of finite resources compromise the ability of future generations to meet their energy service requirements. Efficient use of resources, clean conversion processes, and the timely development of inexhaustible supply options—such as renewable forms or nuclear energy based on breeding or fusion—are therefore the principal strategies for sustainable energy development.

Evolution of the energy system

From the perspective of society, energy is not an end in itself. The energy system is designed to meet demands for a variety of services such *as cooking, illumination, comfortable indoor climate, refrigerated storage, transportation, information, and consumer goods. People are interested not in energy, but in energy services.*

> Technology is a critical link between the supply of energy services and access, affordability, and environmental compatibility.

An energy system comprises an energy supply sector and the end-use technology needed to provide energy services (see figure 1 the overview and figure 6.1). The energy supply sector involves complex processes for extracting energy resources (such as coal or oil), for converting these into more desirable and suitable forms of energy (such as electricity or gasoline), and for delivering energy to places where demand exists. The end-use part of the system transforms this energy into energy services (such as illumination or mobility).

Energy services are the result of a combination of technology, infrastructure (capital), labour (know-how), materials, and energy carriers. All these inputs carry a price and, within each category, are partly substitutable for one another. From the perspective of consumers, the important issues are the economic value or utility derived from the services. The energy carrier and the source of that carrier often matter little. Consumers are generally unaware of the upstream activities of the energy system. The energy system is service driven (from the bottom up), whereas energy flows are driven by resource availability and conversion processes (from the top down). Energy flows and driving forces interact intimately (see below). Thus the energy sector should never be analysed in isolation. It is not sufficient to consider only how energy is supplied; the analysis must also include how and for what purposes energy is used.

Modern energy systems rely on manufactured or processed fuels and sophisticated conversion equipment. Traditional energy usually means unprocessed fuels close to their primary form and low-technology conversion devices (or no technology). Low-technology energy conversion usually implies low efficiency and high pollution. Thus technology is a critical link between the supply of energy services and access, affordability, and environmental compatibility. Technology is more than a power plant, an automobile, or a refrigerator. It includes infrastructure such as buildings, settlement patterns, road and transportation systems, and industrial plants and equipment. It also includes social and cultural preferences as well as laws and regulations that reflect the compatibility of technology options with social preferences and capabilities and cultural backgrounds.

The overall efficiency of an energy system depends on individual process efficiencies, the structure of energy supply and conversion, and energy end-use patterns. It is the result of compounding the efficiencies of the entire chain of energy supply, conversion, distribution, and end-use processes. The weakest link in the analysis of the efficiency of various energy chains is the determination of energy services and their quantification, mostly due to a lack of data on end-use devices and actual patterns of their use.

In 1997 the global efficiency of converting primary energy (including non-commercial energy) to final energy, including electricity, was about 70 percent (279 exajoules over 399 exajoules). The efficiency of converting final energy to useful energy is lower, with an estimated global average of 40 percent (Nakićenović and others, 1990; Gilli, Nakićenović, and Kurz, 1995). The resulting average global efficiency of converting primary to useful energy is the product of these two efficiencies, or 28 percent. Because detailed statistics do not exist for most energy services and many rough estimates enter the efficiency calculations, the overall efficiency reported in the literature spans a wide range, from 15 to 30 percent (Olivier and Miall, 1983; Ayres, 1989; Wall, 1990; Nakićenović and others, 1990; Schaeffer and Wirtshafter, 1992; and Wall, Scuibba, and Naso, 1994).

Specific energy services are supplied by various combinations of energy and technology. In this context, technology is often viewed as capital and know-how. To a large extent, energy and technology, capital, and know-how can substitute for one another. Replacing less efficient and dirty technology with more efficient and cleaner technology is the substitution of capital and know-how for energy. Capital investment, however, typically involves energy embedded in materials, manufacturing, and construction, as well as labour and know-how.

The core business of the energy sector has traditionally involved delivering electricity to homes and businesses, natural gas to industries, and gasoline to gas stations. In the past, electricity supply—especially electrification of unserved areas—was a matter of sociopolitical development strategy. As a matter of state importance, energy supply was often directed by a regional utility under essentially monopolistic conditions. More recently, energy sector liberalisation has turned strategic goods into commodities, changing the sector from selling kilowatt-hours or litres of gasoline to selling energy services. With competition among suppliers, energy companies will become increasingly active in providing energy services, which may also include end-use technologies.

Demand for energy services

The structure and size of the energy system are driven by the demand for energy services. Energy services, in turn, are determined by driving forces, including:

- Economic structure, economic activity, income levels and distribution, access to capital, relative prices, and market conditions.
- Demographics such as population, age distribution, labour force participation rate, family sizes, and degree of urbanisation.
- Geography, including climatic conditions and distances between major metropolitan centres.
- Technology base, age of existing infrastructure, level of innovation, access to research and development, technical skills, and technology diffusion.
- Natural resource endowment and access to indigenous energy resources.
- Lifestyles, settlement patterns, mobility, individual and social preferences, and cultural mores.

- Policy factors that influence economic trends, energy, the environment, standards and codes, subsidies, and social welfare.
- Laws, institutions, and regulations.

The structure and level of demand for energy services, together with the performance of end-use technologies, largely determine the magnitude of final energy demand. The amount of final energy per unit of economic output (usually in terms of gross domestic product, or GDP), known as the final energy intensity, is often used to measure the effectiveness of energy use and the consumption patterns of different economies. Economies with a large share of services in GDP and a large share of electricity in the final energy mix usually have lower final energy intensities than do economies based on materials and smokestack-based industries and fuelled by coal and oil. The final energy demand mix, the structure and efficiency of energy supply (resource extraction, conversion, transmission, and distribution), domestic resource availability, supply security, and national energy considerations then determine primary energy use.

Global primary energy use expanded by about 2 percent a year in 1970–98 (table 1.1). This growth rate fell to just under 1 percent a year in 1990–98 as a result of regional differences in socioeconomic development. First, the severe economic collapse of transition economies in Eastern Europe and the former Soviet Union reduced income by 40 percent and primary energy use by 35 percent between 1990 and 1998. Second, the rapid growth experienced by developing countries in the 1980s slowed in the early 1990s and slowed even more during the financial crisis of 1997–98. Third, among OECD regions, energy growth exceeded the long-term global average only in Pacific OECD countries. In North America, despite continued economic expansion and the availability of inexpensive energy services throughout the 1990s, total energy use grew by just 1.4 percent a year (the same as the OECD average). If corrected for weak economic performance in transition economies and the 1997–98 financial crisis, global energy use would have continued to grow by 2 percent a year throughout the 1990s.

Energy use by developing countries has increased three to four times as quickly as that by OECD countries—the result of life-style changes made possible by rising incomes and higher population growth. As a result the share of developing countries in global commercial energy use increased from 13 percent in 1970 to almost 30 percent in 1998. On a per capita basis, however, the increase in primary energy use has not resulted in more equitable access to energy services between developed and developing countries. (Annex C provides energy data and trends related to the discussion in this chapter, disaggregated by country and region.)

In Africa per capita energy use has barely increased since 1970 and remains at less than 10 percent of per capita use in North America (annex table C2). The same is true for Asia despite a near-doubling in per capita energy use since 1970. In essence this means that most Africans and Asians have no access to commercial energy. Latin America saw little improvement, while China and especially the Middle East made above-average progress in providing access to modern energy services. Energy use in non-OECD Europe and the former Soviet Union has been affected by economic restructuring, which in the former Soviet Union led to negative per capita growth in energy use between 1971 and 1997. Per capita energy use stayed nearly constant in North America, while substantial growth occurred in the Pacific OECD.

TABLE 1.1. COMMERCIAL PRIMARY ENERGY USE BY REGION, 1970–98[a]

Region	1970 (exajoules)	1980 (exajoules)	1990 (exajoules)	1998 (exajoules)	1998 as share of world total (percent)	Annual growth rate, 1970–98 (percent)	Annual growth rate, 1970–80 (percent)	Annual growth rate, 1980–90 (percent)	Annual growth rate, 1990–98 (percent)
North America	74.7	85.6	93.4	104.3	29.4	1.2	1.4	0.9	1.4
Latin America	5.7	9.2	11.3	15.1	4.3	3.6	4.9	2.1	3.7
OECD Europe[b]	51.6	61.9	66.5	70.1	19.7	1.1	1.8	0.7	0.7
Non-OECD Europe[c]	3.6	6.1	6.5	4.8	1.3	1.0	5.3	0.5	-3.8
Former Soviet Union	31.8	47.2	58.5	37.5	10.6	0.6	4.0	2.2	-5.4
Middle East	3.0	5.6	10.6	15.4	4.3	6.0	6.4	6.6	4.7
Africa	2.9	5.6	8.9	11.0	3.1	4.8	6.6	4.8	2.7
China	9.8	17.8	28.5	36.0	10.1	4.8	6.2	4.8	3.0
Asia[d]	6.0	10.6	18.8	28.1	7.9	5.7	5.9	5.9	5.2
Pacific OECD[e]	14.1	19.4	26.0	32.8	9.2	3.0	3.2	3.0	2.9
World total	**203.2**	**269.0**	**328.9**	**354.9**	**100.0**	**2.0**	**2.8**	**2.0**	**1.0**
OECD countries	140.4	166.9	185.9	207.2	58.4	1.4	1.7	1.1	1.4
Transition economies	35.4	53.3	65.0	42.3	11.9	0.6	4.2	2.0	-5.2
Developing countries	27.4	48.8	78.0	105.5	29.7	4.9	5.9	4.8	3.8

a. Excluding commercial biomass. b. Includes Czech Republic, Hungary, and Poland. c. Excludes the former Soviet Union. d. Excludes China. e. Australia, Japan, Republic of Korea, and New Zealand.

Source: BP, 1999.

Regional energy use is even more inequitable when viewed in terms of per capita electricity use. The difference between the least developed countries (83 kilowatt-hours per capita) and the OECD average (8,053 kilowatt-hours per capita) is two orders of magnitude (see annex table C.2).

The link between energy use and economic activity is neither static nor uniform across regions. In the past, energy and economic development were closely related. But this relationship does not necessarily hold at higher levels of economic development. During 1960–78 changes in primary energy use and GDP grew at the same rate in OECD countries (figure 1.1). Thereafter, a change in elasticity between energy and economic activity suggests that the often-postulated one-to-one relationship between primary energy use and economic activity can be changed, at least temporarily. Because of its versatility, convenience, cleanliness (at point of use), and productivity-enhancing features, the increase in electricity use has outpaced GDP growth in all regions—often by a large margin. In addition, the efficiency of converting electricity from final energy to energy services is the highest of all fuels.

Energy transformation is the fastest-growing sector in all countries except transition economies, generally followed by transportation. Electricity generation dominates energy transformation, reflecting the continued importance of electricity for economic development. Oil refining, coal transformation (coking), gasworks, centralised heat production, transmission, and distribution losses account for the rest of the energy used by energy transformation.

Energy trade patterns and globalisation

The growing share of traded goods and services in gross world product reflects a continued shift towards integrated global commodity markets. This share approached 43 percent in 1996, up from 25 percent in 1960. The value share of energy in trade peaked in 1979 at almost 14 percent, then fell to 3–5 percent in the 1990s.

Still, the world energy system has become more integrated, as evidenced by the rising share of energy crossing borders before reaching final consumers. Energy trade slipped to 40 percent of primary energy use in 1985 (down from 50 percent in 1970) but rebounded after the collapse in oil prices in 1986. By the end of the 20th century this share was approaching 55 percent.

The fast-growing Asian economies contributed significantly to this increase. Their energy imports tripled between 1985 and 1997, reaching 13 percent of world energy imports. The share of OECD countries in global energy trade dropped 6 percentage points thanks to stepped-up intraregional trade and increased domestic production of oil (accounting for 13 percent of domestic oil production in 1990, up from 6 percent in 1985) and gas (30 percent of domestic gas production in 1985). OECD countries in Europe cut their share of global imports from 25 percent in 1985 to 16 percent in 1997, while North America doubled its share to 8 percent over the same period.

Global energy trade remains dominated by crude oil and oil products. Despite steady growth in coal trade and accelerated penetration of natural gas in the 1990s, the share of crude oil and oil products in trade only fell from 90 percent in 1971 to 77 percent in 1997. While trade in coal, natural gas, and even oil products expanded largely unaffected by world oil market prices, trade in crude oil definitely responds—though with a lag—to market price changes. Thus crude oil remains the world's swing fuel, with Middle Eastern countries as the swing supplier despite the fact that the Middle East has the lowest production costs.

Crude oil and oil products

Developing countries have almost doubled their share of crude oil and oil product imports since 1979. While other major importers such as Western Europe and Japan have reduced or held steady their share of the global oil trade, the U.S. thirst for oil has reached an all-time high, accounting for 25 percent of global oil trade. In 1998 some 46 percent of oil trade originated in the Middle East— up from 38 percent in 1985. The region is on track to regain market shares of well above 50 percent. Its low production costs (on average, less than $5 a barrel) exposes investments in oil production capacity elsewhere to above-average risks. It appears that Organisation of the Petroleum Exporting Countries (OPEC) countries have regained their monopoly power lost in 1986, and can control oil market prices in either direction.

For importing countries, concerns about oil import dependence and supply security appear to have given way to market forces and high expectations that new exploration and development will bring new oil to the market at a rate commensurate with demand. Moreover, in the wake of globalisation and non-polarisation, quasi-open access to OPEC oil has accelerated the shift of oil from a strategic good to a commodity, further lowering supply security concerns.

Still, the world oil market remains fragile. In March 1999 OPEC countries cut production by 85 million tonnes a year, or 2.5 percent of world oil production. This was in addition to an earlier cut of 125 million tonnes. As a result of strong world oil demand, including that from

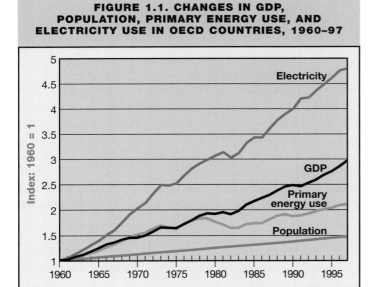

FIGURE 1.1. CHANGES IN GDP, POPULATION, PRIMARY ENERGY USE, AND ELECTRICITY USE IN OECD COUNTRIES, 1960–97

Electricity

GDP

Primary energy use

Population

Index: 1960 = 1

1960 1965 1970 1975 1980 1985 1990 1995

Source: IEA, 1999.

the rebounding Asian economies and the surging U.S. economy, market prices almost tripled within about a year. (World market prices for API Gravity 2 oil were $9.39 a barrel in December 1998 and $27.55 a barrel in March 2000.)

The impact of oil market prices or of high dependence on oil imports (or both) on the economies of several developing countries is shown in figure 1.2. In several countries oil imports absorb a large share of export earnings. The low oil market prices of the mid-1990s benefited these economies relative to 1985 (the year before oil prices collapsed) and 1990 (when prices soared during the Gulf war). The pattern for Haiti differs from those of the other countries in figure 1.2. There the share of export earnings spent on oil imports has more than doubled since 1985. The 1999 hike in oil prices will likely absorb similar shares of export earnings as in 1985 and 1990.

Coal

World coal production runs about 4,500 million tonnes, equivalent to some 2,230 million tonnes of oil equivalent (Mtoe), 210 Mtoe of which corresponds to steam coal trade. In recent years coal exports have grown by 4 percent a year. There is no indication that demand will outstrip supply in the foreseeable future. Production capacity is well developed, and new market entrants (Colombia, Kazakhstan, Russia, Venezuela) are eager to join the trade.

Over the past 20 years a quasi-unified coal market has emerged in which the United States has assumed the role of marginal supplier. Indeed, U.S. capacities are among the world's highest-cost supplies. Everything else being equal, prices tend to gravitate towards the production costs of the marginal producer. Because productivity

Since 1990 electricity rates have declined steadily, especially in countries where electricity market deregulation has been or is about to be introduced.

advances determine the cost of U.S. production, U.S. productivity levels determine the world price of coal.

Natural gas

Unlike oil and coal markets, natural gas has yet to play a significant role in global markets. Some 20 percent of global gas crosses borders before reaching final consumers. About 75 percent of that gas is traded by pipe between essentially neighbouring countries. Hence natural gas trade has developed primarily at the regional level or between adjacent regions. Pipeline transmission is capital-intensive and allows little flexibility in the choice of buyers and sellers. Still, pipeline gas is traded between production and consumption sites more than 4,000 kilometres apart. Three major regional gas trade markets have emerged:

■ The almost fully integrated North American market, characterised by accelerated growth of Canadian exports to the U.S. market (from 26 Mtoe in 1990 to 79 Mtoe in 1998). There have also been minor exchanges between Mexico and the United States.

■ The European market, with the following principal suppliers: the former Soviet Union (with a pipeline producing 108 Mtoe in 1998), Norway (pipeline producing 38 Mtoe), and the Netherlands (pipeline producing 33 Mtoe), and Algeria with minor liquefied natural gas supplies from Libya (pipeline and liquefied natural gas producing 47 Mtoe). Gas trade expanded by 2.7 percent a year in 1990–98.

■ The Asian gas market is dominated by liquefied natural gas (which increased from 47 Mtoe in 1990 to 77 Mtoe in 1998). The main suppliers are Indonesia, Malaysia, Australia, Brunei, the United Arab Emirates, and Qatar. Japan, the Republic of Korea, China, and Taiwan (China) are the main customers.

A gas market has also begun to develop in Latin America, with exports from Bolivia to Argentina and Argentina to Chile.

Energy prices and taxes

Energy prices influence consumer choices and behaviour and can affect economic development and growth. High energy prices can lead to skyrocketing import bills, with adverse consequences for business, employment, and social welfare. Energy exporters benefit from high energy prices. High energy prices also stimulate exploration and development of additional resources, foster innovation, and encourage efficiency improvements.

While some impacts of energy prices are fairly steady, others are more transient. For example, higher absolute prices have had little impact on economic development in Japan and OECD countries in Europe relative to the much lower prices in the United States and some developing countries. The price hikes of the 1970s affected economic growth in all energy-importing countries, however. Thus it appears that economies are more sensitive to price changes than to price levels. But even price changes appear not to cause the turbulence of the past. The recent near-tripling in world oil market prices has, at least in OECD countries, not yet had any impact on economic development.

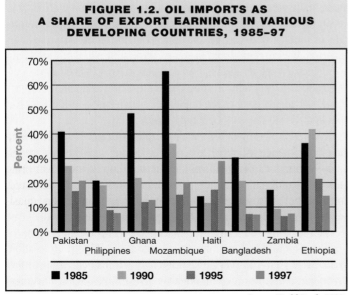

FIGURE 1.2. OIL IMPORTS AS A SHARE OF EXPORT EARNINGS IN VARIOUS DEVELOPING COUNTRIES, 1985–97

(Percent; countries: Pakistan, Philippines, Ghana, Mozambique, Haiti, Bangladesh, Zambia, Ethiopia; series: 1985, 1990, 1995, 1997)

Source: World Bank, 1999.

Energy prices, which include taxes, must be clearly distinguished from costs, average costs from marginal costs, and contract markets from spot markets. Two types of exchange modes—contract markets and spot markets—prevail in most major energy markets. Contracts are long-term trade agreements between exporters and, in the case of oil, refineries. Contracts account for about 80 percent of traded oil. The prices associated with these contracts are usually not disclosed. Contract prices are quasi-fixed for the contract period but include certain adjustment mechanisms that account for major market changes.

The remaining 15–20 percent of international oil is traded in spot markets. Spot sales are more or less instantaneous sales of entire cargoes. Initially, spot market transactions served as a mechanism to clear markets for a small share of production that was not contracted or became available for other reasons—say, seasonal market fluctuations. The spot market has since become the principal mechanism for setting oil prices as well as an essential ingredient for managing risk.

Steam coal prices are less volatile than oil, which is one reason coal remains a popular fuel for electricity generation. In addition, coal can be significantly cheaper than natural gas and oil. While internationally traded energy prices are an important factor in the approximately $450 billion business (at $20 a barrel), the energy bills presented to users are considerably higher than the trade prices because most countries tax energy use. In general, OECD taxes on residential energy use are higher than those on industry. In some developing and transition economies taxes are higher for industry, usually as a cross-subsidy to provide energy services to the poor. Energy taxes and subsidies are an important tool for governments pursuing energy development objectives.

Since 1990 electricity rates have declined steadily, especially in countries where electricity market deregulation has been or is about to be introduced. Market liberalisation has a more profound impact on the electricity rates of industry than of households. Prices for light oil at the national level largely mirror movements in the global market price for oil. Light oil prices are much lower in India and other developing countries than in OECD countries, reflecting government subsidies.

Energy investments

Capital investment is a prerequisite for energy development. Energy system development and structural change are the results of investments in plants and equipment as well as in energy system infrastructure. Difficulties in attracting capital for energy investments may impede economic development, especially in the least developed countries. Although energy investments account for only a small share of the global capital market, the provision of the capital required to finance the growing needs of the energy sector cannot be assumed, especially in developing countries.

Market size and product mobility often favour investments in oil exploration and development over, for example, natural gas or energy efficiency.

General features

The challenges of raising funds for energy investments include the perceived risk to investors and the uncertainty on rates of return. Returns on energy investments do not always compare well to those on other infrastructure investments. During 1974–92 electricity projects supported by the World Bank achieved average rates of return of 11 percent a year—while returns to urban development projects were 23 percent and to transport projects, 21 percent (Hyman, 1994). Also important is the allocation of funds within the energy sector. Rate of return considerations discriminate against small-scale, clean, and innovative energy supplies and against investments in energy efficiency. Market size and product mobility often favour investments in oil exploration and development over, for example, natural gas or energy efficiency.

Investments in energy plants, equipment, and infrastructure must be viewed in the context of economic growth, savings, and the size and degree of liberalisation of capital markets. The current average global savings rate is about 22 percent of GDP—21 percent in developed countries and 24 percent in developing countries. In transition economies recent declines in GDP have been matched by reduced savings, keeping the savings rate at about 20 percent (World Bank, 1999). Although energy investments as a share of total investments vary greatly among countries and between stages of economic development, an average of 1.0–1.5 percent of GDP is invested in energy. This share is expected to remain relatively stable.

Thus current energy investments amount to $290–430 billion a year. But such investments do not include investments in end-use devices and appliances, energy efficiency improvements in buildings, and so on. Including these investments doubles capital requirements.

Energy investments have long lives. Investments in electricity generating plants, refineries, and energy-related infrastructure made in the next 10 years will likely still be in operation in 2050 and beyond. Hence there is a fair amount of inertia with regard to the rate of change that can be introduced in the energy system. For example, the current global average conversion efficiency for coal-fired electricity generation is 34 percent and for gas-fired electricity generation, 37 percent. The best commercially available coal and gas power plants have much higher efficiencies: 43–48 percent for coal and 55–60 percent for natural gas.

Given the longevity of the existing capital stock, it is unlikely that the global average will reach, say, 45 percent for coal-fired electricity by 2050 unless the most efficient plants are adopted universally. But most efficient does not always mean least cost—low-cost domestic coal can be burnt more economically in a medium-efficient plant than in a high-efficient but more capital-intensive alternative.

The efficiency of electricity generation also varies widely among regions. The Middle East introduced coal for electricity generation in the early 1980s and, because most coal is imported, adopted the latest coal combustion technology. As a result the region's average conversion efficiency exceeds that of OECD countries. Another aspect affecting efficiency is the introduction of sulphur and nitrogen oxide abatement equipment, which tends to reduce efficiency (as in Asia and Africa).

Capital flows

The globalisation of economic production has led to an acceleration of capital flows. Indeed, capital markets have been growing faster than GDP for some time, and this trend is unlikely to change. Annual global energy investments account for about 7 percent of international credit financing, which is about $3.6 trillion (Hanke, 1995). With capital markets growing relative to GDP, and assuming relatively stable future energy investment ratios, capital market size does not appear to be a limiting factor for energy sector finance.

Scarce public funds, especially in developing countries, are sought by many needy projects ranging from rural development, education, and health care to energy supply. Because energy supply, more than any other alternative, is often seen as more readily capable of generating revenues early on, energy investments are increasingly viewed as a private sector affair. Yet private funds are not flowing into most developing countries.

Foreign direct investment approached $400 billion in 1997, up from $50 billion in 1984, and accounted for 1.8 percent of OECD GDP (up from 0.6 percent in 1984; figure 1.3). Foreign direct investment in energy projects is estimated at 5–15 percent of the total (Victor, 2000). Foreign direct investment is generally commercially motivated, with the sponsor of investments expecting not only to recover the initial capital but also counting on competitive returns. This cannot always be guaranteed in developing countries with potentially fragile governments or the absence of free markets. Indeed, 25 countries received 89 percent of global foreign direct investment in 1996, and only 10 of these are developing countries—none are among the 47 least developed countries. Brazil, China, and Mexico are the only developing countries to receive more than 2 percent of the world total.

In contrast to foreign direct investment, official development assistance is meant as development aid in the form of grants. Official development assistance increased from $34 billion in 1984 to $69 billion in 1995 but slipped to $56 billion in 1997, or 0.25 percent of OECD GDP—a far cry from the 0.7 percent target agreed to by developed countries (see figure 1.3).

Against these recent developments in international financial and capital flows, prospects for financing energy projects in developing countries generally look bleak. Most foreign investors lack confidence in the ability of developing country energy projects to provide stable (and competitive) returns until the investment has been recovered. Hence, until the economic risk to foreign investors can be eliminated (through deregulated energy and financial markets, steady revenue generation through bill collection, firm policies on profit transfers, and the like), developing countries will have to continue to finance their energy development from domestic savings. ■

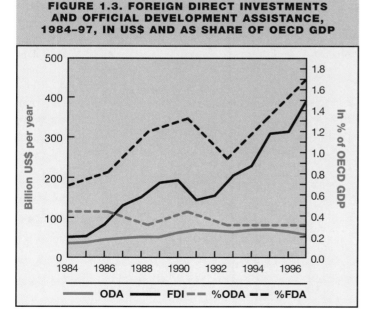

FIGURE 1.3. FOREIGN DIRECT INVESTMENTS AND OFFICIAL DEVELOPMENT ASSISTANCE, 1984–97, IN US$ AND AS SHARE OF OECD GDP

Source: World Bank, 1999.

References

Ayres, R.U. 1989. *Energy Inefficiency in the US Economy: A New Case for Conservation.* RR-89-12. International Institute for Applied Systems Analysis, Laxenburg, Austria.

BP (British Petroleum). 1999. *BP Statistical Review of World Energy.* London.

Gilli, P.-V., N. Nakićenović, and R. Kurz. 1995. "First- and Second-Law Efficiencies of the Global and Regional Energy Systems." Paper presented at the World Energy Council's 16th Congress, 8–13 October, Tokyo.

Hanke, T. 1995. "Die Mäerkte spielen verrüeckt." *Die Zeit* 18: 33.

Hyman, L. S. 1994: "Financing Electricity Expansion." *World Energy Council Journal* (July): 15–20.

IEA (International Energy Agency). 1999. *Energy Balances.* Paris: Organisation for Economic Co-operation and Development.

IMF (International Monetary Fund). 1998. *International Financial Statistics (May).* Washington, D.C.

Nakićenović, N., L. Bodda, A. Gruebler, and P.-V. Gilli. 1990. "Technological Progress, Structural Change and Efficient Energy Use: Trends Worldwide and in Austria." International part of a study supported by the Öesterreichische Elektrizitäetswirtschaft AG and International Institute for Applied Systems Analysis, Laxenburg, Austria.

Olivier, D., and H. Miall. 1983. *Energy Efficient Futures: Opening the Solar Option.* London: Earth Resources Limited.

Schaeffer, R. and R. M. Wirtshafter. 1992. "An Exergy Analysis of the Brazilian Economy: From Energy Product to Final Energy Use." *Energy* 17: 841–61.

Victor, D. 2000. Private communication. Council of Foreign Relations, 9 March, New York, NY.

Wall, G. 1990. "Exergy Conversion in the Japanese Society." *Energy* 15: 435–44.

Wall, G., E. Scuibba, and V. Naso. 1994. "Exergy Use in the Italian Society." *Energy* 19: 1267–74.

WCED (World Commission on Environment and Development). 1987. *Our Common Future.* Oxford: Oxford University Press.

World Bank. 1999. *World Development Indicators 1999 CD-ROM.* Washington, D.C.

energy and social issues

CHAPTER 2

Amulya K.N. Reddy (India)

LEAD AUTHORS: Wendy Annecke (South Africa), Kornelis Blok (Netherlands), David Bloom (United States), Brenda Boardman (United Kingdom), Anton Eberhard (South Africa), Jamuna Ramakrishna (India), Quentin Wodon (Belgium), and Anita Kaniz Mehdi Zaidi (United Kingdom and Pakistan)

ABSTRACT Poverty is the most fundamental reality of developing countries—and the energy consumption patterns of poor people tend to add to their misery and aggravate their poverty. A direct improvement in energy services would allow the poor to enjoy both short-term and long-term advances in living standards. Required are energy strategies based on increasing the use of energy carriers other than biomass, or on using biomass in modern ways. Poverty alleviation and development depend on universal access to energy services that are affordable, reliable, and of good quality.

It has been noted that "poverty has a woman's face". Energy and women are linked in many diverse ways, particularly through the nature of the (predominantly biomass) energy resource base, the characteristics of the household and community economy, the features of energy policy, and the position of women in families and communities. Energy can be a vital entry point for improving the position of women in households and societies.

Many of today's global problems arise from the availability and use of natural resources, which depend on the size of the human population putting pressure on them. But population is more than just an external factor influencing energy consumption. Energy consumption patterns can also influence population growth through their effect on the desired number of births in a family and the relative benefits and costs of fertility.

Energy is linked to urbanisation through its implications for land use, transportation, industry, construction, infrastructure, domestic appliances and products, biomass consumption, and gender. Energy strategies can be designed to improve the urban environment—particularly for transport, industrialisation, mitigation of heat island effects, and construction.

Although energy devices (houses, vehicles, appliances) have become much more efficient in industrialised countries, the number and use of these devices have increased markedly. If appliances and their use (the material basis of lifestyles) are taken as determinants of energy consumption, then strategies can be devised based on reducing the number and use of energy-intensive appliances.

Almost every industrialised country has poor and disadvantaged populations. But the energy aspects of poverty are radically different for industrialised and developing countries. Energy exacerbates poverty in industrialised countries—for example, through the disconnection of energy services or the absence in cold countries of universal affordable warmth.

There are two-way linkages between energy and poverty, women, population growth, urbanisation, and lifestyles. That is, these global issues determine energy consumption, and energy systems influence the issues. Current energy consumption patterns are aggravating these global issues, leading to unsustainability. But energy can also help solve major global problems—particularly those related to poverty, women, population growth, urbanisation, and lifestyles. To realise this potential, energy must be brought to centre stage and given the same importance as the other major global issues. ■

H uman society cannot survive without a continuous use, and hence supply, of energy. The original source of energy for social activities was human energy—the energy of human muscle provided the mechanical power necessary at the dawn of civilisation. Then came the control and use of fire from the combustion of wood, and with this, the ability to exploit chemical transformations brought about by heat energy, and thereby to cook food, heat dwellings, and extract metals (bronze and iron). The energy of flowing water and wind was also harnessed. The energy of draught animals began to play a role in agriculture, transport, and even industry. Finally, in rapid succession, human societies acquired control over coal, steam, oil, electricity, and gas. Thus from one perspective, history is the story of the control over energy sources for the benefit of society.

Modern economies are energy dependent, and their tendency has been to see the provision of sufficient energy as the central problem of the energy sector. Indeed, the magnitude of energy consumed per capita became an indicator of a country's 'modernisation' and progress. Energy concerns have long been driven by one simple preoccupation: increasing the supply of energy. Over the past few decades, however, serious doubts have arisen about the wisdom of pursuing a supply-obsessed approach. Attention is shifting towards a more balanced view that also looks at the demand side of energy. But access to, and the use of, energy continues to be a necessary and vital component of development.

In the supply-driven approach, the appetite for energy often exceeded the capacity of local sources of supply. The energy supplies of some countries had to be brought from halfway round the world. Efforts to establish control over oil wells and oil sea routes have generated persistent tensions and political problems. This situation has also shaped national policies for foreign affairs, economics, science, and technology—and influenced the political map of the world. The security of energy supplies was a major geostrategic issue throughout the 20th century.

At the same time, the magnitude and intensity of energy production and use began to have deleterious impacts on the environment. By the late 1960s the gravity of the environmental problems arising from toxic substances had become clear. Awareness of the environmental issue of acid rain followed. The problems of urban air pollution have been known for a long time. Climate change discussions intensified in the mid-1970s. All these problems are directly related to the quality and quantity of fuel combustion.

Then came the oil shocks of 1973 and 1979, along with price increases that led to economic disruption at international, national, and local levels. The oil shocks thrust the energy problem into the range of awareness of individuals. Some oil-importing developing countries suffered serious balance of payments problems, and in some cases landed in debt traps. The development of indigenous fossil fuel resources and power generation faced the hurdle of capital availability. And more recently, the accumulation of greenhouse gases in the atmosphere resulting from energy consumption has focussed attention on the threat of climate change, with the possibility of far-reaching consequences. In parallel, the lack of control over energy resources has highlighted the importance of national and local self-reliance (as distinct from self-sufficiency).[1]

Thus, quite apart from the critical issues related to the supply of fossil fuels, the political, social, and economic institutions dealing with energy have failed to overcome a new series of grave problems—problems of economics (access to capital), empowerment (self-reliance), equity, and the environment. Many of the human-made threats to the species and the biosphere, indeed to civilisation's future, are energy-related. Awareness of the energy dimensions of these issues has arisen more recently, but the underlying energy bases of the issues are still imperfectly appreciated by decision-makers, perhaps because this understanding has not been disseminated widely.

This chapter is devoted to the main linkages between energy and social issues. It shows that energy strategies have impacts on major issues related to poverty, women, population, urbanisation, and lifestyles. Data on infant mortality, illiteracy, life expectancy, and total fertility as a function of energy use are shown in figure 2.1, which is not meant to suggest that there is a causal relation between the parameters represented.[2]

These linkages imply that energy has to be tackled in such a way that social problems are at least not aggravated—which is what conventional energy strategies tend to do, because they are so preoccupied with energy supplies that they ignore these problems completely or deal with them inadequately. Because of its linkages to social problems, energy can contribute to their solution. Unfortunately, energy and the major problems of today's world are not being dealt with in an integrated way by national and international policy-makers.

Towards a new approach to energy for human uses

Another approach is called for: one that recognises that the satisfaction of social needs by energy is best achieved by treating neither energy supply nor energy consumption as ends in themselves. After all, what human beings want is not oil or coal, or even gasoline or electricity per se, but the services that those energy sources provide. Thus it is important to focus on the demand side of the energy system, the end uses of energy, and the services that energy provides.

In fact, one can identify a rather small set of the most important of these energy services. They include the basic services of cooking, heating, lighting, space conditioning, and safe storage of food. In addition, the provision of clean water and sanitation, which is facilitated by energy, affects public health in cities as well as rural areas. Societies also require services such as transportation, motive power for industry and agriculture, heat for materials processing

> What human beings want is not oil or coal, or even gasoline or electricity per se, but the services that those energy sources provide.

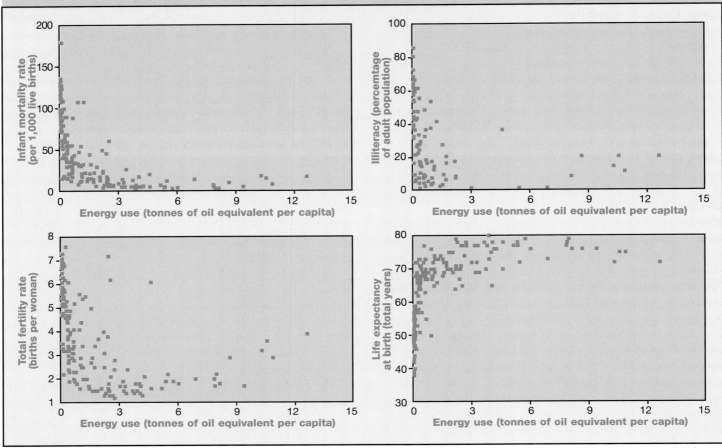

FIGURE 2.1. COMMERCIAL ENERGY USE AND INFANT MORTALITY, ILLITERACY, LIFE EXPECTANCY, AND FERTILITY IN INDUSTRIALISED AND DEVELOPING COUNTRIES

Note: Data on commercial energy use are for 1994; data on social indicators are for 1995.

Source: World Bank, 1997.

(steel, cement, and so on), and energy for commerce, communication, and other economic and social activities.

The demand-side, end-use-oriented energy services approach stresses another difference. The end user cares less about the original sources or fuels used to provide the service than about crucial attributes of the final energy carrier from a social standpoint. Among the most important attributes are energy's accessibility (particularly for the poor, women, and those in remote areas), affordability, adequacy, quality, reliability, safety, and impact (particularly on the immediate environment).

The traditional supply-side approach tends to forecast energy demand on the basis of projections of past and present economic and demographic trends. It tends to ignore the large variety of scenarios that are feasible considering the opportunities and potentials offered by changes in energy demand, improvements in energy efficiency, shifts from traditional energy sources to modern energy carriers, and dissemination of new energy technologies.

To best serve humanity, the energy system should help achieve the goals laid down at the 1992 United Nations Conference on Environment and Development (the so-called Earth Summit) in Rio de Janeiro, and in other UN contexts. These goals include the promotion of economically viable, socially harmonious, environmentally safe, and strategically secure societies. Meeting these goals requires five crucial components: economic efficiency, equity (particularly for the poor, women, ethnic minorities, and those in remote areas), empowerment or self-reliance, environmental soundness, and peace. Together these components can be taken as some of the most essential measures of sustainable development.

The Earth Summit led to greater awareness that development needs to be sustainable if it is to serve humanity's short- and long-term goals. More than 150 governments committed themselves to the protection of the environment through the Rio Declaration and Agenda 21. Government representatives considered that key commitments related to energy would be covered under the United Nations Framework Convention on Climate Change (UNFCCC), which was signed on this occasion. Agenda 21 makes this important statement:

Energy is essential to economic and social development and improved quality of life. Much of the world's energy, however, is currently produced and consumed in ways that could not be sustained if technology were to remain constant and if overall quantities were to increase substantially. The need to control atmospheric emissions and other gases and substances will increasingly need to be based on efficiency in energy production, transmission, distribution and consumption, and on growing reliance on environmentally sound energy systems, particularly new and renewable sources of energy. (UN, 1993b, ch. 9.9)

The Framework Convention on Climate Change, which has been ratified by 164 countries, defines an ecological target—without linking this target to social impacts!— that implies the implementation of energy measures. The Intergovernmental Panel on Climate Change (IPCC) also has presented scientific assessments of data related to climate change and prospects for inputs, adaptation, and mitigation of climate change and their relationship to energy issues.

Since the Earth Summit many other initiatives have been taken at various levels to promote sustainable energy through increased energy efficiency, support for renewable energy sources, and integrated energy resource planning. There are now good examples, significant benchmarks, and success stories all around the world of efforts in these areas. But these efforts are dispersed. Though they provide a good starting point, they cannot meet the tremendous energy challenges facing humanity during the 21st century.

Energy issues tend to get sidelined in many international forums. Such major global issues as poverty, women, population, urbanisation, lifestyles, undernutrition, environment, economics, and security tend to get higher priority than energy. But missing from most discussions of these issues is the important linkage between each of them and global and local energy systems. It is too little appreciated that achieving progress in these other arenas can be greatly assisted by manipulation of energy systems.

Even when this linkage is mentioned, the discussion focuses on how these global issues determine energy consumption patterns. Energy is treated as the dependent variable. Very little attention is directed at understanding whether current energy patterns are aggravating these issues, and almost no attention is given to how alternative energy strategies can contribute to their solution.

Thus a fresh conceptual framework is required. The framework elaborated in this chapter, and depicted in figure 2.2, concerns the linkage between energy, on the one hand, and poverty, women, population, urbanisation, and lifestyles, on the other.[3]

The linkage between energy and food security is also crucial, particularly because it concerns the important social problem of undernutrition that is so widespread and serious, especially in developing countries. Despite this, the energy-undernutrition dimension is not addressed in this chapter, primarily because of space considerations. Moreover, the energy-undernutrition link has been treated adequately in other contexts, particularly in *Energy after Rio: Prospects and Challenges* (UNDP, 1997a), which explains how energy strategies can play a powerful role in increasing the supply of food as well as building an environment in which food is absorbed more effectively.

As humankind enters the new millennium, it is important to highlight energy's critical relationship to major global problems. The timeliness of the challenge derives from three critical elements that are converging to make the world thirstier for energy services: aspirations for a higher living standards, booming economies in large regions, and population growth.

The assessment that follows draws together a number of diverse elements that are relevant to sustainable development, and for which issues of supply and demand of energy are significant. It goes on to show new options for using energy more efficiently, and also how both renewable and fossil sources of energy can be used in cleaner, more efficient ways to help create a more sustainable future. In fact, the global goal for energy can be stated very simply: sustainable development of the world. Energy services therefore are a necessary condition for sustainable development.

Energy and poverty in developing countries

Poverty is the most fundamental reality of developing countries.[4] Poverty refers to an individual's (or family's) lack of access—associated primarily with inadequate income—to basic human needs such as food, shelter, fuel, clothing, safe water, sanitation, health care, and education. Poverty is manifested as the inability to achieve a minimum standard of what is needed for material well-being. Human poverty also entails the denial of opportunities and choices most vital to human development—including a long, healthy, creative life, a decent standard of living, dignity, self-esteem, the respect of others, and the things that people value in life.

Dimensions of poverty

Poverty is usually conceptualised and measured in terms of the proportion of people who do not achieve specified levels of health,

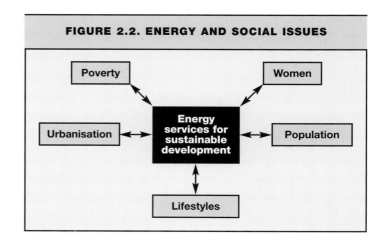

FIGURE 2.2. ENERGY AND SOCIAL ISSUES

education, or body weight. Operationally, however, poverty standards are typically expressed in a single dimension: the monetary resources that would enable an individual to consume either a fixed bundle of basic goods and services (absolute poverty[5]), or a fraction of the bundle of goods and services that a reference group is able to, or actually does, consume (relative poverty).

UNDP's human poverty index goes beyond mere income poverty. It measures deprivation in three essential dimensions of human life: longevity (or vulnerability to death at an early age), knowledge (access to reading and communication), and a decent standard of living in terms of overall economic and social needs (percentage of people without access to safe water and health services and the percentage of underweight children under five).

Whether measured directly with a range of indicators of basic human outcomes, or indirectly with a single monetary dimension, poverty is indisputably among the world's largest, most urgent, and most fundamental problems. Its pervasiveness—as revealed by the extent to which elementary minimum needs are not satisfied—is undeniable. Whether food, shelter, health, education, or employment is considered, living standards of the majority in most developing countries are pathetically low. They represent a full-time struggle for survival—a type of existence largely unknown, and perhaps even unimaginable, in industrialised countries. This struggle is quite apart from associated psychological reactions of deprivation and feelings of hopelessness and social disempowerment, often accompanied by deep feelings of personal need.

In perhaps the most ambitious and careful attempt yet undertaken to measure absolute poverty in developing countries, it has been estimated that, as of 1993, roughly 1.3 billion people in developing countries—30 percent of their total population—consumed less than $1 a day worth of goods and services.[6]

Statistics on the inability of people in developing countries to satisfy basic human needs corroborate the enormous scale of poverty and highlight its breadth and complexity. For example, an estimated 20 percent of people in developing countries do not have access to health services, 30 percent lack access to safe water, and 61 percent lack access to sanitation (UNDP, 1996). And infant and child mortality rates in developing countries are more than 5 times higher than in industrialised countries, the proportion of children below age five who are underweight is 8 times higher, the maternal mortality rate is 14 times higher, and the proportion of births not attended by trained health personnel is 37 times higher.

Significant and widening disparities in human development and poverty are also found within countries between the rich and the poor, between rural and urban areas, between regions, between different ethnic groups, and between women and men. And income and development inequalities are greater within developing countries than within industrialised OECD countries. The richest 10 percent account for nearly half of national income or consumption in Brazil

Because efficient devices tend to have higher first costs, the poor invariably end up with less efficient devices that consume more energy for a given level of service.

and South Africa. In contrast, the richest 10 percent in countries such as Germany, Japan, Norway, Switzerland, and the United States account for about 25 percent of their country's national income and spending. Industrialised countries not only have higher human development and lower poverty indexes; they are also more equitable than developing countries. But there has been overall progress in human development over the past 30 years, as indicated by an examination of measures such as UNDP's Human Development Index (HDI). On average, a child born in a developing country today can expect to live 16 years longer than a child born in 1970. Adult literacy rates since then have increased by nearly half (UNDP, 1998).

Yet these favourable aggregate trends mask slow progress or even setbacks in many countries, especially among the poorest people. For example, life expectancy in Africa is still 20 years lower than in East Asia or Latin America and the Caribbean. And adult literacy rates in South Asia (51 percent) are shockingly lower than in Southeast Asia (90 percent) or in nearly all industrialised countries (UNDP, 1998).

The alleviation, if not eradication, of poverty is among the world's largest, most urgent, and most fundamental challenges—and not merely for humanitarian reasons. Societies with grave inequalities and disparities tend to be unstable. Large populations below the poverty line are explosive material for social upheavals. Thus poverty has politically unsustainable characteristics. It merits urgent consideration and immediate action.

The energy-poverty nexus

Energy services are a crucial input to the primary development challenge of providing adequate food, shelter, clothing, water, sanitation, medical care, schooling, and access to information. Thus energy is one dimension or determinant of poverty and development, but it is vital. Energy supports the provision of basic needs such as cooked food, a comfortable living temperature, lighting, the use of appliances, piped water or sewerage, essential health care (refrigerated vaccines, emergency and intensive care), educational aids, communication (radio, television, electronic mail, the World Wide Web), and transport. Energy also fuels productive activities, including agriculture, commerce, manufacture, industry, and mining. Conversely, lack of access to energy contributes to poverty and deprivation and can contribute to economic decline.

The energy dimension of poverty—energy poverty—may be defined as the absence of sufficient choice in accessing adequate, affordable, reliable, high-quality, safe, and environmentally benign energy services to support economic and human development. The numbers are staggering: 2 billion people are without clean, safe cooking fuels and must depend on traditional biomass sources; 1.7 billion are without electricity. Increased access to such energy services will not, in itself, result in economic or social development. But lack of adequate energy inputs can be a severe constraint on development. Universally accessible energy services that are adequate, affordable, reliable, of good quality, safe, and environmentally benign are therefore a necessary but insufficient condition for development.

The energy ladder and household decisions about fuel choice

Poor people tend to rely on a significantly different set of energy carriers than the rich. The poor use proportionately more wood, dung, and other biomass fuels in traditional ways, and less electricity and liquefied petroleum gas (LPG). To illustrate this point, evidence from Brazil is shown in figure 2.3.

The observation that roughly 2 billion people depend mainly on traditional fuels for cooking is significant in part because indoor air pollution is a major by-product of the traditional use of biomass. This pollution diminishes the quality of life, especially for women and young children.

Households use fuel for a variety of activities, including cooking, water heating, lighting, and space heating. Different energy carriers can be used for each of these activities. For instance, firewood, dung, charcoal, coal, kerosene, electricity, and LPG can be used for cooking; and kerosene and electricity for lighting.

These carriers (for a particular activity) form what is commonly referred to as an 'energy ladder' for that activity. Each rung corresponds to the dominant (but not sole[7]) fuel used by a particular income group, and different income groups use different fuels and occupy different rungs (Hosier and Dowd, 1987; Reddy and Reddy, 1994). Wood, dung, and other biomass fuels represent the lowest rung on the energy ladder for cooking. Charcoal and coal (when available) and kerosene represent higher steps up the ladder to the highest rungs, electricity and LPG.

The ordering of fuels on the energy ladder also tends to correspond to the efficiency of the associated systems (the fraction of energy released from the carrier that is actually used by the end-use device) and their 'cleanliness'. For example, the cook-stove efficiencies of firewood (as traditionally used), kerosene, and gas are roughly 15, 50, and 65 percent, respectively. As one proceeds up the energy ladder, the emission into the air of carbon dioxide, sulphur dioxide, and particulates also tends to decline.

Households seem to make choices among energy carrier options on the basis of both the household's socioeconomic characteristics and attitudes and the attributes of alternative carriers. Income is the main characteristic that appears to influence a household's choice of carrier (Leach, 1992; Reddy and Reddy, 1994).

Relevant attributes of energy carriers include accessibility, convenience, controllability, cleanliness, efficiency, current cost, and expected distribution of future costs. Because different fuels require different appliances—stoves, lamps, and so on—with varying costs and durability, fuel costs have both fixed and variable components.

The importance of this distinction between fixed and variable costs is magnified by three factors: the presence of quasi-fixed costs, such as fixed monthly charges for a natural gas or electricity hookup; the need to make large 'lumpy' purchases of some fuels, such as tanks for storing propane gas; and the need to make sometimes

sizeable security deposits, either to guarantee the payment of monthly bills or the return of equipment such as LPG cylinders or canisters. Despite the fact that they are refundable, security deposits impose a present cost on households, the magnitude of which depends upon the return on those funds in their next best use, or their 'opportunity cost'.

The division of costs into fixed, quasi-fixed, and variable components affects household decisions about fuel choice. The outcome of these decisions depends on the household's preparedness to forgo present consumption for future benefits. The degree to which a household discounts future benefits may be determined in part by its level of wealth and its liquidity. Households may apply high discount rates to fuel consumption decisions, because of the high cost of either diverting resources from other uses or of borrowing funds to cover up-front capital costs. Thus they will tend to prefer fuel carriers that involve lower up-front or first costs. Poor people use much higher discount rates than the rich when making energy carrier decisions (Reddy and Reddy, 1994). Lack of reliable income may force them to think almost solely in terms of the first cost, rather than the life-cycle cost. Because efficient devices tend to have higher first costs, the poor invariably end up with less efficient devices that consume more energy for a given level of service. Fuel costs may be determined either in a market or implicitly in terms of the opportunity cost of time spent gathering the fuel, such as firewood.

Energy strategies for alleviating poverty in developing countries

The poor pay more money, or spend more time for energy services, than those who are better off. This has a powerful implication. The economic hardship endured by poor households is understated

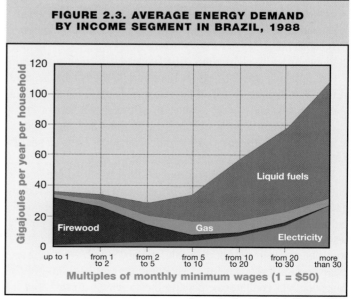

FIGURE 2.3. AVERAGE ENERGY DEMAND BY INCOME SEGMENT IN BRAZIL, 1988

Source: De Almeida and de Oliveira, 1995.

when their income (consumption expenditure) is evaluated in terms of its command over the basket of goods and services purchased by households with average income or consumption expenditures.

Further, in many places, poor households could achieve the same level of energy services at much less daily cost if they could move up the energy ladder to LPG or electricity. Demonstration projects have shown that the price that the poorest household is prepared to pay for electric lighting is near the full cost because the alternative of kerosene lamps involves much higher expenditures.

Substitution of energy carriers or devices that enable greater efficiency would confer sizeable gains in purchasing power on poor urban households. This analysis of the expenditure patterns of households in different income groups suggests that such an increase in effective resources would be devoted almost entirely to better satisfying basic needs for food, shelter, clothing, health, education, and additional fuel. Thus cost-effective improvements in energy efficiency have considerable potential to reduce poverty in all of its key dimensions.

It appears that the energy consumption patterns of poor people tend to add to their misery and aggravate their poverty for the following reasons:

- Because the poor pay more for daily energy needs, they are less likely to accumulate the wealth needed to make the investments that are necessary to make use of cheaper and more efficient fuels and appliances.
- The use of biomass compromises the health of household members, especially when it is burned indoors without either a proper stove to help control the generation of smoke or a chimney to draw the smoke outside. Thus in addition to its relatively high cost, the use of biomass fuel may promote higher medical care expenditures and diminish the poor's ability to work productively (chapter 3).
- Biomass also has deleterious environmental consequences outside the household. These effects are reinforced by the fact that biomass users are less likely to boil the water they drink, for reasons of cost or custom. Insofar as the use of biomass in urban areas promotes deforestation, reliance on biomass may also tend to increase its future cost, further diminishing the living standards of the poor (Leach, 1992; Dasgupta, 1993).

The linkages between energy and poverty have implications for strategies to alleviate poverty. The standard poverty alleviation strategies of macroeconomic growth, human capital investment, and wealth redistribution do not directly address the energy-poverty nexus in developing countries. If patterns of energy use among the poor depress their nutrition, health, and productivity, the poor are likely to absorb the benefits of economic growth only very slowly. Education will continue to increase their earning capacity, but by less when kerosene rather than electricity is the main illuminant,

> Dramatic increases in living standards in developing countries can theoretically be achieved with small inputs of energy.

when lighting is poor, and when access to knowledge though radio and television is limited. The situation is worsened when traditional biomass is the dominant cooking fuel: school attendance flags because of the burden of collecting it and the respiratory illness caused by cooking with it.

In contrast, strategies that, in addition to standard poverty alleviation strategies and rural development, include direct improvement of energy services allow the poor to enjoy both short-term and self-reinforcing long-term advances in their living standards. Such strategies should promote increased use of energy carriers other than biomass, or use of biomass in modern ways.

In fact, this approach suggests that major advances in poverty alleviation can be achieved with relatively small inputs of energy, as evidenced from the so-called 1 kilowatt per capita scenario (Goldemberg and others, 1985). This scenario was based on a 'thought experiment' in which the following question was explored: If all developing countries achieved a level of energy services comparable to that of Western Europe in the 1970s,[8] and if they deployed the most efficient energy technologies and energy carriers available in the 1980s, what would be the per capita energy consumption corresponding to this vastly improved standard of living?

The surprising answer was that, provided that the most energy-efficient technologies and energy carriers available are implemented, a mere 1 kilowatt per capita—that is, a 10 percent increase in today's energy per capita—would be required for the populations of developing countries to enjoy a standard of living as high as that of Western Europe in the 1970s. In other words, dramatic increases in living standards in developing countries can theoretically be achieved with small inputs of energy.[9]

Energy and poverty in industrialised countries

Almost every industrialised country has its poor and disadvantaged, but the energy aspects of their poverty are radically different from those for developing countries. The poor in industrialised countries are not energy poor in an absolute sense. Indeed, the direct use of energy by the poor in the United States for homes and automobiles is 1.65 times the average use in developing countries for all purposes, including the indirect use of energy for industrial and commercial purposes and public transportation. The high energy expenditures of the poor relative to those in developing countries are also not an indicator of affluence. These expenditures are essential to meet basic needs in the industrialised country context. The poor in industrialised countries consume much more energy than their counterparts in developing countries because of the much wider use of energy-intensive technologies.

Despite this apparent energy affluence of the poor in industrialised countries relative to the masses in developing countries, their economic plight cannot be ignored. The poor in industrialised countries spend a larger fraction of their income on energy relative to the average. Energy patterns clearly exacerbate poverty in industrialised countries—just as they do in developing ones. This linkage is not taken into account in conventional energy planning and policy-making. Rather, conventional energy strategies adopt the 'energy trickle-down' approach to social welfare and implicitly assume that if energy supplies are increased, these problems will take care of themselves. In industrialised countries the problem is not that the poor do not have access to enough energy to satisfy their needs, but rather that their circumstances require them to consume too much energy and therefore to spend too large a fraction of their income on it. If they cannot meet this expenditure, their access to energy is disrupted.

An alternative energy strategy is needed that addresses the energy-poverty link in industrialised countries and makes the poor less vulnerable to the high costs of energy. The most promising approach is to make available to the poor more energy-efficient technologies for space heating, household appliances, and transportation services.

A central challenge for many developing countries is the expansion of access to electricity for the poor. In contrast, maintaining access is the critical issue in some medium-income countries and economies in transition, as well as in OECD countries. The uninterrupted availability of access to vital energy services is particularly important to the poor, highlighting the health and other hazards associated with the lack of heating and light. Disconnection can be life-threatening. It is part of the general question of how the poor should be protected during the liberalisation and privatisation that are sweeping electric utilities around the world. There is increasing recognition of the importance of dealing with material hardship (lack of access to energy) rather than just income poverty in both industrialised and developing countries.

Energy and women

Poverty has a woman's face. Of the approximately 1.3 billion people living in poverty, 70% are women. (UNDP, 1997a. p. 12)

Compared to men, women in developing countries spend long hours working in survival activities…[This] time spent…is largely invisible in current methods of reporting energy patterns and statistics. (UNDP, 1997a, p. 15)

In developing countries, biomass accounts for about one-third of all energy and nearly 90% in some of the least-developed countries. About two billion people rely mainly or exclusively on traditional fuels (mostly biomass) for their daily energy needs. (UNDP, 1997a, pp. 36–37)

Human energy conservation must be central to any energy strategy, as it is a major component of energy used at the domestic level. The traditional division of labour allocates most tasks to women in the household. (Viklund, 1989, p. 10)

Energy and women are linked in many diverse ways.[10] These linkages vary spatially, over time, across classes, between urban and rural areas, and between countries. Some of these variations are common to women, men, and children of a given era, class, or country. But certain features of the relationship between energy and women are worth considering.

Factors determining energy-women linkages

Four main factors influence the nature of linkages between energy and women: the nature of the (energy) resource base, the characteristics of the household and community economy, the features of energy policy, and the position of women in families and communities.

Resource base. The survival and lives of most people in the developing world depend on the biomass resource base, rather than on coal, oil, or nuclear energy. Their consumption of energy (other than human energy and animate energy sources) is for survival needs, primarily cooking. For these needs, most people depend on biomass sources such as fuelwood, crop residues, and animal dung.

But this biomass resource base is being degraded.[11] As a result, in the course of a single generation, the time and effort required to meet minimum household energy needs have increased. Because many households rely on biomass fuels that are gathered or received as payment for services rendered, national energy accounts tend to under-represent the importance of biomass fuels as energy sources.

Likewise, labour and human investment (contributed primarily by women) added to this resource base are not fully understood or recognised. In fact, only fairly recently has it become accepted that deforestation in most areas is not caused by household use of fuelwood. Nonetheless, the cost (human effort and financial outlay) involved in securing household energy needs has escalated to such an extent that many households have been forced to shift to less efficient and less clean fuels. The health impacts on women and children of exposure to high concentrations of particulate matter, carbon monoxide, and hundreds of other pollutants emitted when biomass fuels are burned have been investigated and documented in some depth during the past 20 years (see chapter 3).

Household and community economy. Energy choices depend on the extent to which the local economy is based on subsistence agriculture or on raising livestock. A further issue is the degree of monetisation of the economy, and whether wages are paid in cash or in kind—for instance, in grain or, more pertinently, in crop residues. Each of these variables may influence the choices made— whether fuel is gathered or bought, whether improved (more efficient and less polluting) stoves are adopted, and what type of fuel is used.

Like the resource base, the local economy is dynamic, particularly now that macroeconomic factors are bringing about vast changes in microeconomies. These factors will determine the disposable income of households, as well as the opportunity costs of depending on the labour and time of women and children to supply household energy needs.

Energy policy. The linkages between women and energy are also shaped by the prevailing energy policy, especially its degree of sensitivity to the needs and priorities of (rural) women. Particularly in many developing countries, energy policy is designed in such a way that energy resources are not equally available to all. Industrial, commercial, urban, and male users receive priority service and attention in energy policies. At the bottom of the list are agricultural, domestic, rural, and female users. The structure and functioning of the energy sector also cater to those in the favoured categories.

The effect of these biases and predilections is evident in the rural areas of most developing countries. Even well-intentioned initiatives such as rural electrification often begin and end with a 'pole in every village'. Few affordable, viable options have been developed for the domestic sector, where much of women's work occurs.

Position of women in families and communities. One can see evidence in many places of a highly degraded biomass energy resource base. Yet investments to improve kitchens, stoves, and cooking fuels either do not figure in the hierarchy of household expenditures or appear very low on the list. Why?

A partial answer is that the livelihoods of people living in such environments are also under threat. In other words, they have other, even more urgent priorities. But another and crucial part of the answer is related to the position of women in families and communities.

The four factors discussed here—the energy resource base, the local economy, energy policy, and the position of women in families and communities—are closely connected. But the last of these factors is perhaps more fundamental than the others. It is a root cause, the reason it is necessary to study linkages not only between women and energy but also between women and a range of productive assets and social services. Women, by virtue of their position in society (or lack thereof), stand disadvantaged in decision-making processes in family, community, and country, as well as in accessing productive assets. Poor women in developing

countries are doubly disadvantaged, while their sisters in rural areas are triply disenfranchised. Two aspects of this disenfranchisement that have particular bearing on the linkages between women and energy deserve closer attention: the value assigned to women's labour and the value placed on women's time.

■ Valuing women's labour. Across cultures and economic rankings, women's work has been under-valued, sometimes to the extent that it has been rendered invisible. This applies not only to women's reproductive work and household work but also to their immensely active participation in the so-called informal sector of the economy. This under-valuation, in terms of what is included in the UN System of National Accounts (SNA) and what is not, is similar in industrialised and developing countries.[12] In both cases only about one-third of women's work is taken into account. Two-thirds is left out.

Women's contribution to world output is also under-valued, and to a much greater extent (figure 2.4). According to published statistics, world output in 1993 totalled $23 trillion. But this reflects only recorded economic activity—and the unrecorded economic contributions of women are almost 45 percent of this amount (UNDP, 1995).

Furthermore, women are under-paid relative to men for the same tasks. Again, this applies both in industrialised and developing countries. Women also shoulder the burden of household survival activities (cooking, cleaning, collecting fuel and water, and caring for children, plus sometimes raising kitchen gardens), all of which are largely unacknowledged. The result is that across the globe, women work longer hours than men. One of the most tangible linkages between women and energy is that the growing scarcity and cost of cooking fuel have lengthened women's workdays and made them more arduous.

■ Valuing women's time. Rural women in developing countries have been forced to become experts at multitasking.[13] Faced with impossible workloads and only their own time and labour to fall back on, poor rural women have become very efficient at managing time. These skills are not assigned any value in the labour market. Even women often do not consider what they do as 'work'. Though the survival of the family—in literal as well as economic terms—may depend on the skill with which a woman manages her household, she has little or no economic decision-making power, and her time and her work have very low status. Not only are the cash-earning activities of the male members of the household given higher status, but even the leisure time of men may rank higher than the work time of women (Nathan, 1997).

To summarise, many of the world's women (roughly 400 million) rely on energy sources that are not part of the market economy in order to fulfil their survival activities and household responsibilities. They often depend on these sources for their economic activities as well. Women are more vulnerable than men to environmental degradation, because there is often a direct impact on their workload. They are also more likely to be directly affected by increases in fuel prices and by scarcity. Often the only asset that women can turn to

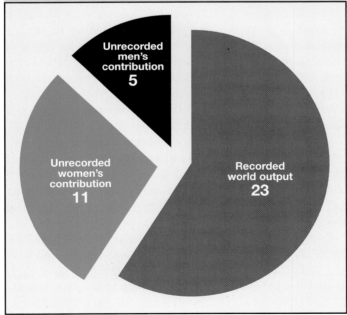

FIGURE 2.4. WOMEN'S SHARE OF WORLD OUTPUT, 1993 (TRILLIONS OF U.S. DOLLARS)

Unrecorded men's contribution 5

Unrecorded women's contribution 11

Recorded world output 23

Source: De Almeida and de Oliveira, 1995.

in times of scarcity or high prices is their own bodies, their own labour. This results not only in longer workdays but also in declining health, nutrition, and a score of other ill effects. Apart from the overwhelming importance of biomass energy, the role of human energy and particularly of women's energy must be recognised (chapter 3).

Specific concerns and priority areas

Health and sanitation. Thus there is a very direct link between energy and women's health. Most of the burdens placed by energy scarcity are borne by women. Even where biomass energy is relatively easily available, women feel the health impacts of having to collect fuelwood. These impacts may range from cuts, falls, bites, and back injuries to sexual harassment (Government of India, 1988). Often these problems are compounded by having to haul water for the household as well.

Exposure to indoor air pollution is another well-documented health risk associated with the use of biomass fuels in traditional stoves that are little more than shielded fires in poorly ventilated kitchens (WHO, 1992). Rural women and children in developing countries are most affected by this pollution. The rural-urban differential in pollutant concentrations and exposures is marked, as are differences between countries at different stages of human development (figure 2.5). The urban-rural differential is reversed in high-HDI countries, where exposures are higher due to the greater amount of time spent indoors and due to building characteristics and materials.

Fuel scarcity has wider implications. Women may be forced to move to foods that can be cooked more quickly or to eat more raw food. Such a shift can have health repercussions for the whole family, especially children (Batliwala, 1982; Ramakrishna, 1992).

An additional critical factor related to health is the lack of sanitation in many rural areas of developing countries, which is directly related to the difficulty of accessing clean water. There is an energy-sanitation link here because energy often has to be used to lift 'clean' sub-soil water or to boil water to reduce the health risk from contamination. The convenience of the water supply—for instance, the distance to the source and the number of sources—correlates with the amount of water used daily per capita. For most rural people in developing countries, the amount of clean water available per capita is well below the minimum required for maintaining sanitation. In addition, the supply of drinking water is highly inadequate. As water drawers and carriers and household managers, women feel the impact of water shortages most keenly. The availability, supply, and quality of water could be greatly improved by increasing the amount of energy available for these functions.

Environmental quality. Energy scarcity often relates directly to environmental quality for households and for communities in general. The implications of this relationship are particularly relevant for women. Deteriorating environmental quality places greater burdens on women's time and labour. In addition, as mentioned above, women's health and productivity may be significantly undermined. This is only partly due to the increased effort required to meet minimum household energy requirements. Energy, after all, is only one of the inputs that women must secure for survival. Water also becomes scarce with increasing environmental degradation. In cases of severe environmental decline, male migration often increases, as in Sub-Saharan Africa. In such circumstances women have to bear the additional responsibility of heading households. A key intervention to arrest or slow environmental degradation in many developing countries would be to increase the energy options for poor rural women. In particular, the potential of renewable energy sources has not been realised.

Economic activities. The linkages between women's economic activities and energy have two aspects. One is the strong correlation between the time women have for economic activities and the time they have for survival activities, including collecting and preparing cooking fuels. The other is securing energy inputs for economic activities. The main point is that women's choices are often very restricted, and they do not have much margin for error for the

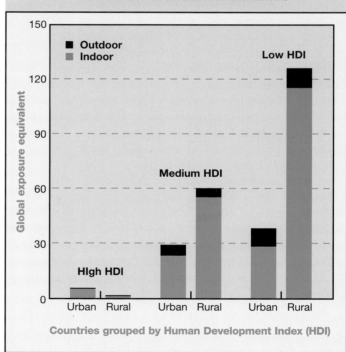

FIGURE 2.5. GLOBAL EXPOSURE EQUIVALENTS FOR PARTICULATES IN 12 MAJOR MICROENVIRONMENTS

The global exposure equivalent is defined as the equivalent (particulate) concentration that the entire world's population would have to breathe continuously to equal the population exposure in each micro-environment.
Note: Data are for various years from the late 1980s to early 1990s.
Source: Based on Smith, 1993.

unforeseen. Given that most women, whether bakers, brewers, or food processors, are small-scale producers whose businesses are frequently biomass-energy intensive, both technology development and improved energy supply could greatly enhance their productivity.

Education. Despite momentous advances in the literacy of women, much remains to be done. As long as the drudgery of survival activities continues to grow, given the division of labour in most households, getting girls into schools will be an uphill battle. Improved access to better-quality, affordable, reliable cooking fuels could make an enormous difference. As it is, girls are the first to be called on to shoulder survival activities that cannot be managed by the adult women of the household. Invariably, girls' education suffers as a result.

Human productivity. The gravest consequence of energy scarcity is probably that human productivity—especially women's productivity—is depressed. When survival of the family becomes the goal, there is no opportunity to develop human potentials and talents. This is a loss not only to the individual, but to society as well.

Energy for improving the position of women

Energy can be a vital entry point or 'lever' for improving the position of women in the household and society. As a bottleneck and burden, the lack of affordable energy has often constrained the options and opportunities available to women. But there are many strategic advantages in using energy as an entry point.

Energy scarcity condemns many women to spend all their days and a good part of their nights meeting basic survival needs. Enhancing their access to affordable, clean energy sources would go a long way towards reducing the drudgery they face, and allow them to use their time and energy for other purposes. This could lead to improved health, education, nutrition, and economic status, not only for women but for their families as well. The greatest benefit would accrue to the next generation; and in particular to girls, who would gain—as their workload at home decreases—better health and nutrition and opportunities to go to school.

Energy is also a key productive asset for strengthening the economic standing of women. In many cases it is also necessary for providing equal access to productive resources (Batliwala and Reddy, 1996). Whether a woman is engaged in food processing or in farming, her economic return largely depends on a dependable supply of energy and on improvements in energy technology products relevant to her trade.

Energy is a good organising issue for women, because energy is a primary concern in their daily lives—especially poor women's. Energy resource scarcity, cost, quality, and reliability are their constant concerns. Whereas alone each woman may be able to do little to improve the situation, together their power could be fairly easily demonstrated. In some countries farmers (mainly men) have organised themselves to demand affordable and reliable energy

> Energy can be
> a vital entry point or 'lever'
> for improving the position of
> women in the household
> and society.

supplies. Women can broaden these movements by adding their agenda.

Finally, energy provides many opportunities for skill building among women. That these skills would be non-traditional ones, and would not restrict women to the kitchen and home (as do those perennial-favourite income-generation schemes tailoring and pickle-making) are added advantages. The exploitation of such opportunities, combined with improved access to credit for women, could result in considerable entrepreneurial activity.

This perspective can also be turned on its head with good effect. Involving women more integrally in the energy sector could be a boon for the sector as well. The energy sector has evolved as a capital-intensive, expert-dominated, centralised sector. But there is a role for decentralised energy in which women can play an important part. In fact, the 'engendering' of the energy sector could be its salvation in the long run, leading to decentralisation, longer-term perspectives, and investment, and a better fit between energy source, energy quality, and end use—in other words, to a greater emphasis on renewable energy sources, in keeping with the underlying philosophy of sustainable development.

Energy and population

Many of today's global problems arise from the availability and use of natural resources, which depend on the size of the human population putting pressure on them. This pressure has been escalating in an alarming manner.

The world's population has increased explosively over the past 100 years. "It took the world population millions of years to reach the first billion, then 123 years to get to the second, 33 years to the third, 14 years to the fourth, 13 years to the fifth billion" (Sen, 1994). Additions to the population have been unprecedented: "Between 1980 and 1990, the number of people on earth grew by about 923 million, an increase nearly the size of the total world population in Malthus' time" (about 1800; Sen, 1994).

This explosive growth has led to talk of a runaway population inexorably bringing humanity to its doom and of a situation of 'standing room only' on this planet. But these predictions have generally assumed the persistence of the very high population growth rates of the 1950s, which corresponded to a doubling every 23 years or so.

Demographic transitions

The recent tremendous increase in world population is associated with what is known as a demographic transition. In such a transition, the population moves from a pre-industrial balance of high mortality and high fertility to a post-industrial balance of low mortality and low fertility.

Demographic transitions have occurred in the past—in Western Europe in the 19th century, and in Southern and Eastern Europe in the first quarter of the 20th century. They are now taking place all over the developing world. In some countries they are just starting. In others they are well under way. And in the remaining countries they are over or almost over.

The demographic transition currently under way in developing countries has been initiated by the rapid fall in mortality in these countries, brought about by improvements in public health and advances in medical technology. For example, an increase in life expectancy from 40 to 50 years was accomplished in developing countries in just 15 years, from 1950–65. In comparison, a similar increase of life expectancy required 70 years (from 1830–1900) in Western Europe and 25 years (from 1900–25) in southern and Eastern Europe.

If a large reduction in mortality were not accompanied by a fall in fertility, the population would increase indefinitely. But what happened in industrialised countries is that fertility also fell, and the low value of mortality was balanced by a new low value of fertility. Thus the growth rate of population is low both before and after the demographic transition during which the population grows rapidly:

The rate of world population growth is certainly declining, and even over the last two decades, its percentage growth rate has fallen from 2.2 percent per year between 1970 and 1980 to 1.7 percent between 1980 and 1992. This rate is expected to go down steadily until the size of the world's population becomes nearly stationary (Sen, 1994).

The crucial question, therefore, is whether the reduction in mortality that took place in developing countries from 1950–65 has been followed by a fall in fertility. The evidence seems clear. Until the mid-1960s there was no sign of a fertility decline, but since then fertility has begun to fall in almost all developing countries, except those in Sub-Saharan Africa. The average total fertility rate in developing countries fell from 5.9 to 4.7, that is, by about 20 percent, from 1965–70.[14]

It is important to note that the response of fertility is not as rapid as the decline in mortality—fertility is not in sync with mortality. The delay in fertility decline leads to a 'bulge' in the time variation of population. This bulge gives rise to the problems associated with population size. Thus it seems that a demographic transition is taking place and that the population of developing countries and of the world is likely to stabilise eventually. But the world is sure to have a growing population for quite some time because of 'population momentum (Sen, 1994).

Population momentum

Population momentum has important geographic, locational, and age dimensions. First, the geographic distribution of population growth is uneven—90 percent of the growth is taking place in developing countries. These additions to population are primarily in populous countries with a low average income. In addition, the population explosion is worse in countries that already have a severe population problem. Second, the locational distribution of population growth is such that the urban share of growth has increased and will continue to go up.

Third, the age distribution of the population is changing in all countries, but the nature of the change varies among them. The population is becoming older in rich countries because life expectancy is increasing while infant mortality is relatively stable. In poor countries the age distribution depends on the phase of the demographic transition. In the initial phase the dependent non-working-age population grows faster because infant mortality is declining much more than the increase in life expectancy. In the middle phase the growth of the working-age population (with the potential of being economically active) is relatively greater.[15] And in the final phase, the elderly population grows faster.[16]

It is important to estimate this future population. An average of the 1992 UN medium estimate and the World Bank estimate of the future population yields 9.79 billion in 2050,[17] 11.15 billion in 2100, and 11.45 billion in 2150. In 1998 the UN Population Division projected 8.9 billion people by 2050, thanks to the fertility rate decreasing around the world (New York Times, 21 October 1998, p. A8). The bulk of the population increase is expected to take place in developing countries, where the population is expected to triple to 9 billion by 2110.

The increase in global population before its expected stabilisation by about 2100 means that per capita resources will continuously decline in the near future. In fact, per capita estimates conceal the differential growth that is likely to take place in industrialised and developing countries, which will exacerbate the already serious disparities between these two worlds.

The energy-population nexus

Population levels influence the magnitude of energy demand in a straightforward way: The larger the population, the more total energy is required, with the magnitude of this total energy depending on per capita energy consumption. This is perhaps the basis of a view that population increases in developing countries represent the most serious threat to the global atmosphere through the phenomenon of global warming (Atiq, Robins, and Roncerel, 1998).

There is an another view, however. The patterns of energy consumption in rich industrialised and poor developing countries, and the rich and poor within developing countries, are such that industrialised countries, and the rich within developing countries, have—because of their energy-intensive consumption patterns—far greater per capita impact on the global atmosphere. Hence the greater rates of population growth of poor developing countries, and the poor within developing countries, are far less relevant to global warming than the lower rates of population growth of industrialised countries, and the rich within developing countries. In fact, 49 percent of the growth in world energy demand from 1890–1990 was due to population growth, with the remaining 51 percent due to increasing energy use per capita.[18] This relationship will hold true for the future if per capita energy consumption does not change significantly.

Thus the conventional view of the energy-population nexus is that population is an external factor influencing energy consumption.

This exogenous impact of population on energy is the well-known (and obvious) aspect of the population-energy connection, although many people seem not to realise the scale of its impact even today.

But there can be another connection, in which energy strategies may lessen the intensity of the population problem. If energy consumption and population growth are a dialectical pair—each transforming the other, and each being an effect when the other is the cause—then the pattern of energy consumption should also have an effect on population growth.

This is the other side of the coin—energy consumption patterns influencing the rate of population growth through their effect on the desired number of births in a family and the relative benefits and costs of fertility. These patterns can retard or accelerate the demographic transition (Goldemberg and others, 1988).

This dimension of the energy-population nexus—not yet elaborated sufficiently—will be sketched through the influence of energy consumption on population growth at two levels: the micro level of villages in developing countries and the macro level of the world. The implication is that energy can play a key role in accelerating the demographic transition, particularly by achieving dramatic reductions in fertility to stabilise global population as quickly as possible and at as low a level as possible.

Rural energy consumption and population implications

To proceed, several features of rural energy consumption in developing countries must be highlighted. Though these features vary with country and agroclimatic conditions, a few numbers typical of south Indian villages are presented to give a flavour of the features involved (ASTRA, 1982):

■ Commercial energy accounts for a very small percentage of the inanimate energy used in villages; the bulk of the energy comes from fuelwood.[19]

■ Animate sources—human beings and draught animals such as bullocks—account for less than 10 percent of the total energy, but the real significance of this contribution is that these animate sources represent the bulk of the energy used in agriculture.

■ Nearly all the energy consumption comes from traditional renewable sources. Thus agriculture is largely based on human beings and bullocks, and domestic cooking (which uses the bulk of the total inanimate energy) is based entirely on fuelwood.[20] But the environmental soundness of this pattern of dependence on renewable resources comes at an exorbitant price. Levels of agricultural productivity are very low, and large amounts of human energy are spent on fuelwood gathering (for example, about 2–6 hours and 4–8 kilometres a day per family to collect about 10 kilograms of fuelwood).

■ Fetching water for domestic consumption also uses a great deal of human energy (an average of 1.5 hours and 1.6 kilometres a day per household) to achieve an extremely low per capita water

Industrialised countries have—because of their energy-intensive consumption patterns—far greater per capita impact on the global atmosphere.

consumption of 1.7 litres a day.

■ Almost half of the human energy is spent on grazing livestock (5–8 hours a day per household), which is a crucial source of supplementary household income in these parts of the country.

■ Children contribute about one-third of the labour for gathering fuelwood, fetching water, and grazing livestock. Their labour contributions are vital to the survival of families. This point is usually ignored by population and education planners.

■ The end uses of human energy in villages show that their inhabitants, particularly women and children, suffer burdens that have been largely eliminated in urban settings by the deployment of inanimate energy. For example, gathering fuelwood and fetching water can be eliminated by changing, respectively, the supply of cooking fuel and water. There are also serious gender and health implications of rural energy consumption patterns (Batliwala, 1982).

To understand the population implications of these features of energy consumption in villages, it is necessary to consider how these features influence the desired number of births in a family and the relative benefits and costs of fertility. A useful starting point is the general preconditions for a decline of fertility, as set forth by the demographer A. J. Coale (1973, 1983):

■ Fertility must be within the calculus of conscious choice. Potential parents must consider it an acceptable mode of thought and form of behaviour to balance advantages and disadvantages before deciding to have another child.

■ Reduced fertility must be advantageous. Perceived social and economic circumstances must make reduced fertility seem an advantage to individual couples.

■ Effective fertility reduction techniques must be available. Procedures that will prevent births must be known, and there must be sufficient communication between spouses and sufficient sustained will, in both, to use them successfully.

The exercise of choice in matters of fertility is a culture-dependent issue, and awareness and availability of fertility-reduction techniques depend on specific technologies and the success with which they are spread. But the desired number of births, and therefore the relative benefits and costs of fertility, depend upon socioeconomic factors such as

■ Infant mortality and the probability of offspring surviving. The lower this probability, the larger the number of children aspired to and the greater the exposure of the mother to the possibility of additional pregnancies.

■ The role of women in arduous, time-consuming household chores. The greater this role, the smaller the scope and emphasis on women's education and the lower the age of marriage.

■ The use of children to perform essential household tasks. The greater the use of children for these tasks, the more they become essential for the survival of the household.

■ Opportunities for children to earn wages. Wage-earning children become desirable as economic assets.

Only a few of these factors enter into perceptions of advantages and disadvantages of fertility and family size. Nevertheless, the reduction of fertility, and therefore the acceleration of the demographic transition, depends on crucial developmental tasks. These tasks include an increase in life expectancy, improvement of the immediate environment (including drinking water, sanitation, and housing), education of women, and diversion of children away from household support tasks and employment to schooling.

Further, almost every one of these socioeconomic preconditions for smaller family size and fertility decline depends on energy-using technologies. Infant mortality has much to do with inadequate, unsafe supplies of domestic water and with an unhealthy indoor environment resulting from polluting fuel-stove cooking systems. The conditions for women's education become favourable if the drudgery of their household chores is reduced with efficient energy sources and devices for cooking and with energy-using technologies to supply water for domestic uses. The deployment of energy for industries that generate employment and income for women can also help delay the marriage age, which is an important determinant of fertility. And if the use of energy results in child labour becoming unnecessary for crucial household tasks (cooking, gathering fuelwood, fetching drinking water, grazing livestock), an important rationale for large families is eliminated.

From this standpoint, it is obvious that prevailing patterns of energy consumption in villages do not emphasise energy inputs for the following tasks:

- Providing safe and sufficient supplies of drinking water.
- Maintaining a clean and healthy environment.
- Reducing the drudgery of household chores traditionally performed by women.
- Relieving children of menial tasks.
- Establishing income-generating industries in rural areas.

Thus current energy consumption patterns exclude the type of energy-using technologies needed to promote the socioeconomic preconditions for fertility decline. In fact, they encourage an increase in the desired number of births in a family and an increase in the relative benefits of fertility (Batliwala and Reddy, 1996).

Traditional biomass-based cooking and demographic indicators

Traditional biomass-based cooking is predominant in most developing countries, particularly in rural areas. The negative health impacts of this are discussed in chapter 3. The low efficiencies of traditional biomass stoves derive from the incomplete combustion of the biomass, resulting in a number of health-damaging pollutants, particularly suspended particulates and carbon monoxide. These pollutants exceed acceptable levels inside poorly ventilated houses, especially those without chimneys. Thus one would expect to find a correlation between the percentage of biomass use in total energy use and a number of demographic indicators, especially those related to women and young children, who are thought to be most vulnerable.

Indeed, such a correlation has been revealed by recent work on a large number of developing countries (Bloom and Zaidi, 1999). Table 2.1 shows that, as the percentage of biomass increases, life expectancy decreases, infant (and child) mortality increases, and the annual population growth rate increases. Such trends do not prove causality but are consistent with the view that traditional biomass use impedes the demographic transition.

Energy-population nexus at the global level

One way of considering the energy-population nexus at the global level is through the 1 kilowatt per capita scenario (Goldemberg and others, 1985) described above. That scenario shows that, if the most energy-efficient technologies and energy carriers available today were implemented, a mere 10 percent increase in the magnitude of energy would be required for the populations of developing countries to enjoy a standard of living as high as that in Western Europe in the 1970s. In other words, under the conditions of this scenario, energy supplies need not become a constraint, and dramatic increases in living standards can be attained in developing

TABLE 2.1 BIOMASS USE AND DEMOGRAPHIC INDICATORS

Indicator	Percentage of biomass in total fuel use				
	0–20	20–40	40–60	60–80	Above 80
Number of countries	70.00	12.00	14.00	10.00	16.00
Female life expectancy (years)	74.70	68.80	62.00	56.10	48.30
Life expectancy (years)	71.50	66.50	59.90	54.50	47.00
Male life expectancy (years)	68.50	64.00	57.80	53.00	45.80
Infant mortality (per 1,000 live births)	22.50	46.60	64.70	82.60	116.80
Under-five mortality (per 1,000 live births)	27.50	59.30	93.00	135.30	173.00
Total fertility rate	2.51	3.26	4.64	5.35	6.33
Crude birth rate	19.20	26.20	35.00	39.10	45.00
Crude death rate	8.60	7.60	10.90	12.80	18.10
Annual population growth rate (percent)	1.00	1.61	2.43	2.74	2.52
Female-male life expectancy gap (years)	6.20	4.50	4.20	3.10	2.60

Sources: UN, 1993a; World Bank, 1998.

countries. It follows that, if energy-efficient technologies and modern energy carriers were implemented to enable the populations of developing countries to realise higher living standards, then these standards would likely result in low growth rates for developing country populations, similar to rates in Western European countries. Insofar as current energy strategies do not sufficiently emphasise energy-efficient technologies and modern energy carriers, they are not addressing directly the population problem.

Energy and urbanisation

A century ago, even visionaries could not imagine a city with more than 1 million inhabitants.[21] Yet by 2010 more than 500 such concentrations will dot the globe, 25 of them with more than 10 million people (so-called megacities). The availability of energy sources in combination with the phenomena of motorisation and industrialisation have substantially altered the manner in which people relate to their environment.

Urban dwellers will soon outnumber those in traditionally rural areas and constitute half the world's population. Of the 1.23 billion urban residents added to the world population since 1970, 84 percent have been in less developed regions. The global population is growing by 2.5 percent a year (3.5 percent a year in less developed regions, and 0.8 percent in more industrialised regions). The annual growth is 61 million people—roughly the equivalent of adding six cities with a population of 10 million to the urban population world-wide. By 2020–25 the global annual urban growth rate will have declined to less than 2 percent, but the urban population will increase by 93 million people a year—more than the current annual increase in the total world population.

The rate of urbanisation and its attendant impacts differ in regions across the globe. Thus strategies to capitalise on the positive factors of urbanisation and to mitigate the negative factors will also differ by region. Latin America is the most urbanised region in the developing world. Nearly three-quarters of Latin Americans live in urban areas. Although Africa is the least urbanised region, it is experiencing the highest urban growth rate, and already a third of its people live in cities. However Asia contains almost half the world's megacities and continues to urbanise rapidly. Given its current annual growth rate, Asia's urban population is expected to double in less than 20 years.

Increasingly, larger portions of the world's people live in the biggest cities. In addition, more live in intermediate-sized cities than ever before. In 1950 there were 83 cities or urban areas with more than 1 million people. Today 280 such urban areas exist. The growth of large cities also affects smaller cities, particularly in less developed regions. Over the next 15 years the number of cities with 5–10 million residents will increase significantly. Further, the number of people in them will more than double, as will the population of cities in the 1–5 million and 0.5–1.0 million ranges. This means that while megacities are the most visible symbols of problems and challenges, smaller cities are no less significant.

Urbanisation reflects more than demographic change. It is both driven by and profoundly influences the context and processes of development. It exerts both direct and indirect advantages in the struggle towards global sustainability and human development. The origins of many global environmental problems related to air and water pollution are located in cities—this is the urbanisation-pollution linkage. Unsustainable consumption and production patterns are also a feature of cities. But it is also in cities that one can find potential solutions, because they have several positive features.

Birth rates are three to four times lower in urban areas than in rural areas, thereby reducing environmental pressures from population growth. Cities provide greater accessibility to education, services, and training. They increase the access of residents to information on environmental issues and facilitate their integration into the policy process according to identified needs and priorities. Because of their concentrated form and efficiencies of scale, cities offer major opportunities to reduce energy demand and minimise pressures on surrounding land and natural resources. Women are also the direct beneficiaries of urbanisation, because their interests and demands are more easily articulated and negotiated in their new, dynamic social environment.

Cities are the engines of economic growth and centres of employment and opportunity for expanding and diversified national economies. Eleven of the twelve urban agglomerations with 10 million or more people are located within one of the 25 largest economies. The economic prosperity of nations will depend on the performance of their cities. With a focus on cities, appropriate energy policy can be targeted more effectively and resources leveraged far more efficiently to affect large numbers of individuals, communities, industries, and services. But a lack of competent and accountable urban governance can lead to the loss of much of the potential contribution of cities to sustainable economic and social development and, at worst, to a completely dysfunctional living environment. Concerned and innovative urban development planning, on the other hand, can enable growing urban populations to contribute towards sustainable human development by empowering individuals to convert their creative assets into global wealth.

Urbanisation and energy linkages

The 1996 United Nations Conference on Sustainable Human Settlements, known as Habitat II, reaffirmed that the vast majority of population growth in developing countries will occur in urban centres. The type and scale of urban development will largely affect future energy consumption. In turn, urbanisation also has a profound effect on the amount and type of energy consumed. Other factors—including economic development, industrialisation, and such social-cultural particularities as consumption patterns—also drive the global increase in energy demand. Although traditional rural societies rely heavily on human and animal energy and on wood for fuel, today's urban societies rely primarily on fossil fuels and electricity.

Per capita energy consumption remains low in the developing world. For many urban Africans and Asians, biomass fuels meet a large portion of energy needs. As these countries urbanise, energy demand increases, and traditional bulky fuels (such as wood and charcoal, which require energy-intensive forms of transportation), food, and other materials consumed in urban areas must be transported across greater distances. Urban manufacturing and industry also require more energy than traditional agriculture. In addition, the provision of infrastructure and services to new urban residents requires energy that is not typically consumed in rural settlements.

Urbanisation imposes enormous demands on the ecosphere, because most urban activities at the industrial, community, and household levels are based on natural capital depletion. Housing construction, transportation, economic activities, and the generation of residential heat and electricity all put stress on the environment and compete for ecological space. Energy use is already high in industrialised countries and is increasing rapidly in developing countries as they industrialise. But energy can be an instrument for sustainable development with an emphasis on more efficient use of energy, and an increased use of renewable energy sources, among other measures.

Urbanisation and energy strategies

Although many countries prepared national plans of action for Habitat II, most did not formulate a national policy on the linkages between urbanisation and energy. Few governments have allocated significant resources to encouraging more effective use of non-renewable energy resources or to increasing the long-term supply of renewable energy resources. In light of current urbanisation trends and the opportunities presented by new energy-efficient technologies and processes, the moment is opportune for this discussion to take place.

Cities have the potential to be far more environmentally benign. The spatial concentration of humans and their activities can minimise pressures on surrounding land and natural resources. Well-designed cities can channel development far away from wetlands and other sensitive areas, and protect natural resources. By integrating land-use and transportation planning, cities can reduce both congestion and pollution.

Cities offer important opportunities for protecting the environment. With proper planning, dense settlement patterns can ease pressures on per capita energy consumption and provide opportunities to increase energy efficiency. For example, recycling becomes more feasible due to the large quantities of materials and the number of industries that can benefit from it. In addition, land use, infrastructure, and services are better used, and the need for extensive transportation networks and residential heating is reduced. Low-density communities tend to have the opposite characteristics.

Transportation. Mobility and access remain among the greatest challenges for cities in the developing world, especially considering the growing proportion of lower-income people. A city that cannot be accessed by all its inhabitants is not sustainable. Because motor vehicle ownership remains relatively low in many of these cities,

The new millennium is ushering in a new urbanised era. For the first time ever, more people will reside in urban settlements than in rural.

there is a window of opportunity to avoid the mistakes made in the industrialised world and design urban transportation systems that facilitate walking, bicycling, and public transportation. Such measures can improve the environmental health of cities and citizens as well as mitigate the threat of global warming.

Cities are centres of employment, residence, and leisure, and of the integration between them. Mobility and access are therefore complementary aspects of the same problem. Mobility implies movement: people going to work, people going to the market, people bringing vegetables to sell in the market. Access implies the ability to take advantage of urban functions: people developing 'backyard industries', people being able to find in their neighbourhoods the services they need, people being able to walk to work. A sensible balance between mobility and accessibility concerns should result in a more energy-efficient transport strategy based on demand management. In this regard, the systemic integration between land use and transport is much more important than an isolated concern with vehicles, fuels, and emissions. These are also important complementary concerns.

To illustrate, given the opportunity to work legally at home (for example, inputting data or transcribing reports from remote places), the informal sector, a thriving and integral sector in developing economies, would be formalised and backyard industries would proliferate, reducing the need for urban residents to commute to places of employment. The integration of sustainable transport and employment-related strategies could reduce stress on the local environment, promote more creative employment options (especially for women), and lead to a general improvement in quality of life.

Patterns of energy consumption also depend on the means and availability of transport. Where extensive road networks, vehicles, and other transport infrastructure exist, there is a high risk of depending on a supply-driven vicious circle. As is well known, conventional traffic planning based on individual modes of transport can lead to potentially difficult situations, as has occurred, for example, in Bangkok (Thailand), Kuala Lumpur (Malaysia), Mexico City, and São Paulo (Brazil). The creation of appropriate land-use legislation for residential and commercial sites and access to public transportation services can mediate the demand for more energy-intensive transport use.

Considerable opportunity exists to design more efficient transportation systems and create more liveable cities. A critical step for industrialised and developing countries is to move towards managing urban travel demand rather than simply increasing the supply by reducing or averting over-reliance on the privately owned car through appropriate pricing, spatial settlement policies, and regulatory measures.

A number of strategies are available to governments to advance a sustainable transport sector (Rabinovitch, 1993; UN, 1996):

- Exploration of surface (rather than above-ground or underground) solutions based on affordable technologies. Buses should be considered before a high-technology rail system.

- Development of an integrated transport strategy that explores the full array of technical and management options and pays due attention to the needs of all population groups, especially those whose mobility is constrained because of disability, age, poverty, or other factors.
- Coordination of land-use and transport planning to encourage spatial settlement patterns that facilitate access to basic needs such as places of employment, schools, health centres, and recreation, thereby reducing the need to travel.
- Encouragement and promotion of public access to electronic information services and technology.
- Promotion, regulation, and enforcement of quiet, use-efficient, low-polluting technologies, including fuel-efficient engine and emission controls, fuel with a low level of polluting emissions, and other alternative forms of energy.
- Provision or promotion of effective, affordable, physically accessible, and environmentally sound public transport and communication systems that give priority to collective means of transport, with adequate carrying capacity and frequency to support basic needs and reduce traffic flows.
- Exploration of partnerships with private-sector providers. Ideally the public sector should provide monitoring and operational standards, and the private sector should invest in capacity and contribute managerial comparative advantages and entrepreneurship.

Construction. Low-energy building materials such as timber, soil, sand, and stone require little energy in their manufacture and processing. The durability of many of these materials can be improved without large energy expenditures. These materials are often used in the construction of housing in developing countries. It is often possible to improve the use of such materials through appropriate construction methods and design techniques that maximise their functionality and natural advantage.

One example is construction using earth, in which the mechanical energy required is ultimately much more efficient than that for ceramic building materials, which require large amounts of heat (usually applied inefficiently). The low costs of locally available renewable energy resources could potentially ensure a continuous supply of energy to meet the demand of domestic, agricultural, and small-scale industrial sectors. These materials also have the advantage of being familiar to local building operators and planners.

Energy to improve the urban environment

The new millennium is ushering in a new urbanised era. For the first time ever, more people will reside in urban settlements than in rural. Perhaps the forces of change—economic, social, technological, and political—render this process inevitable. If so, policy design

The rapid expansion of urbanised areas, especially in developing countries, creates a unique opportunity to implement 'leapfrogging' approaches.

and prescriptions should be targeted differently. Rather than attempting to arrest rural-urban migration, it is important to make rural life less difficult and arduous and more pleasant and attractive. Energy interventions can play a positive role in this task through electrification of homes for lighting, labour-saving appliances, and entertainment, as well as for the supply of safe piped water. Thus an improvement in the quality of rural life can decrease the negative aspects of urbanisation, making it wise to pursue balanced urban and rural development and to ensure synergies between the two. The focus of development efforts should be redirected towards achieving more sustainable urban and rural living environments in light of the inevitability of a mostly urban world.

Rapid urbanisation is associated with a rise in energy demand— which potentially threatens the sustainability of human settlements and the natural environment. The spatial concentration and diversification of human and economic activities hasten the demand for resources and compromise the carrying capacity of final disposal systems and infrastructure. In addition, the rise in disposable income of urban populations is likely to lead to a concomitant desire for more material goods and services.

Yet many of the negative effects of urbanisation can be mitigated through innovative energy policies. In developing countries rapid urbanisation and its attendant demands on material and financial resources have severely compromised the ability of governments to foster sustainable environment. Although the use of fossil fuels in industrial processes, heating, electricity, and motor vehicles tends to expand with economic growth, measures can be taken to promote renewable, clean technologies that lessen the burden of economic activity on human populations and ecosystems. In cities in industrialised countries, control of motor vehicle emissions has led to a dramatic reduction in ground-level ozone and carbon monoxide levels on or near major roads.

Urban areas offer enormous potential for easing the demand for energy-intensive materials and increasing the efficiency of resource use. The agglomeration of social networks fosters an environment that is more accessible to public awareness campaigns, creating a favourable learning environment for changing wasteful patterns of consumption on a large scale. The application of new energy-efficient technology is more easily accelerated in an urban setting because business and industry may be more amenable to experimentation and thus bypass the environmentally deleterious path of excessive technological use that has often been followed in industrialised countries.

Most technologies used in cities in the industrialised world were invented about a century ago. The rapid expansion of urbanised areas, especially in developing countries, creates a unique opportunity to implement 'leapfrogging' approaches. Widespread urbanisation may provide the economies of scale needed to implement innovative affordable technologies.

The urban environment is also conducive to offering education opportunities and creating jobs. This facilitates capacity-building efforts to deal with the operation and maintenance of environmentally friendly energy infrastructure based on renewable sources. Opportunities for reducing the material inputs of production by recycling waste by-products are more feasible in urban areas. For urban services such as transportation, a reduction in cost and in the share of energy-intensive services provides an additional means by which energy strategies can take advantage of the positive aspects of urbanisation. A prime example is the promotion of surface bus modes of transportation rather than expensive solutions such as subways.

Energy and lifestyles

After the oil shocks of the 1970s, one of the issues that often arose in discussions of energy was the sustainability of a world with glaring and grave disparities in per capita energy consumption between industrialised and developing countries. A related issue was the need for convergence in per capita consumption through minimisation, if not removal, of these disparities.

These discussions were set aside because of optimists' belief in the enormous potential of efficiency improvements. These improvements—it was believed—would enable industrialised countries to sustain their energy services (and therefore living standards and lifestyles) with far less energy consumption. At the same time, the improvements would enable developing countries to achieve dramatic improvements in their standards of living with only marginal increases in their inputs of energy. Now, almost 30 years after the oil shocks, the time has come to revisit these fundamental issues by analysing the experiences of industrialised countries.

Energy use in the United States

Consider the United States.[22] Following the oil shocks and for almost 10 years, from 1973–83, the United States reduced its consumption even as its population and economy expanded. "Americans learned to do more with less" (Myerson, 1998). For instance, there was an emphasis on thicker insulation and tighter windows to cut space-heating bills. Compact, fuel-efficient cars became popular. There was investment in more efficient appliances, machines, and engines. As a result per capita residential energy consumption fell by a tenth. It looked as if energy patterns were following the hopes of the optimists.

But during the next 15 years, from 1983–98, the United States lost all the gains in energy conservation it achieved in 1973–83. Declining energy prices offset the conservation gains. In 1983–98 per capita residential energy consumption rose by 10 percent, offsetting its 10 percent reduction from 1973–83 and rising to within 2 percent of its 1973 peak. Americans returned to consuming nearly as much energy as before the oil shocks.

In 1999 Americans were expected to burn more fuel per capita than in 1973. U.S. dependence on oil imports has increased—in 1973 imports were 35 percent of consumption; in 1998, 50 percent. In 1973, 5 percent of oil imports came from the Gulf; in 1998, 10 percent. The reduction in the energy intensity of the U.S. economy has tapered off; from 1972–86 energy per unit of GDP fell 43 percent; but from 1987–97 the fall was only 8 percent. It appears as if, to one-third of Americans, "conservation means doing less, worse or without, i.e., privation, discomfort and curtailment" (Myerson, 1998).

Houses. The number of people in the average U.S. household has shrunk by one-sixth, but the area of the average new home has grown by one-third. In 1973 the average new home was 1,600 square feet for the average family of 3.6 people; by 1998 the average size had increased to 2,100 square feet even though the average family had shrunk to 3.0 people. In addition, many energy-intensive changes have taken place inside the home. For example, the average ceiling height, which was 8 feet in 1973, had risen to 9 feet by 1998. Ceilings are often so high that ceiling fans are required in winter to blow back rising heat.

Appliances. The penetration of energy-intensive appliances has increased. For example, in 1973 fewer than 40 percent of homes had central air conditioning. But in 1998 more than 80 percent had it. Forty percent of homes had two or more television sets in 1970; by 1997, the percentage was 85 percent. And homes with dishwashers increased from 19 percent in 1970 to 57 percent in 1996. There has also been an invasion of new always-on, electricity-sucking 'vampires' such as computers, videocassette recorders, microwave ovens, and telecommunications equipment. The energy consumption of these gadgets is rising 5 percent a year, and they will soon consume more per household than a refrigerator.

Transport. Americans are driving automobiles more than ever, primarily because there are more wage earners per family and more urban sprawl. The number of women working or looking for work increased from 47 percent in 1975 to 72 percent in 1997. Households with three or more cars increased from 4 percent in 1969 to 20 percent in 1998. From 1983–95 average commuting distance increased by one-third, from 9.72 to 11.6 miles. And only 15 percent of commuters use public transit.

Fuel-intensive minivans, sport utility vehicles, and pickup trucks are growing in popularity. As a result the average horsepower of motor vehicles increased from 99 in 1982 to 156 in 1996. It took 14.4 seconds to accelerate from 0–60 miles per hour in 1982, but only 10.7 seconds in 1996.

Gasoline prices are a key factor in these developments. The 1973 per gallon price (adjusted for inflation) was $1.10, but the 1998 price was only $1.00. U.S. gasoline prices are only about a third of those in Europe and Japan. No wonder U.S. per capita consumption is much higher than that in Europe and Japan.

Industry and commerce. U.S. corporations have all but stopped making improvements solely to save energy. Industrial and commercial energy use fell 18 percent from 1973–83 but rose 37 percent from 1983–97.

Environment. Clearly, energy prices and environmental concerns point in opposite directions. At the 1992 Earth Summit, U.S. President George Bush pledged to reduce carbon emissions by 7 percent between 1990 and 2010. But the U.S. Energy Information Administration predicts that emissions will rise 33 percent. If fears of global warming are justified, it looks as if the pattern of U.S. energy consumption during the past 25 years has grave implications for the global environment—even though U.S. national and urban environments are much cleaner.

Energy and income. How have changes in lifestyle influenced the pattern of energy use in industrialised countries?[23] What are the determinants of energy consumption? What are the driving forces of energy consumption patterns?

The general relationship between per capita GDP and per capita energy use has been established in many studies (Nakićenović and John, 1991). The relationship is non-linear—energy use typically grows slower than GDP. For instance, in 1985–95 per capita GDP in OECD countries grew 1.6 percent a year, whereas per capita energy use grew 0.8 percent (IEA, 1997).

It is instructive to look at energy use from the point of view of individual consumers or households. Households use energy directly (for example, electricity, natural gas, and gasoline) as well as indirectly, in the goods and services that they purchase. The sum of direct and indirect use represents the total energy requirements of a household. If it is assumed that, in the ultimate analysis, all products and services of society are produced for the service of households, then an overall picture of the energy requirements of society can be obtained.

The relationship between household income and energy requirements (using input-output analysis) has been known for a long time. In the early 1970s it was found that, if the income of households increases by 1 percent, their use of energy increases by 0.7–0.8 percent—that is, the income elasticity of energy requirements for any year lies between 0.7 and 0.8 (Roberts, 1975). More detailed research in the Netherlands using a combination of process analysis and input-output analysis came to similar findings; for 1990 the income elasticity of energy requirements was 0.63.

The most salient finding is that income is the main determinant of energy consumption. Other household characteristics, such as size, age of oldest member, life-cycle phase, degree of urbanisation, education level, and so on, turn out to be relatively unimportant (Vringer and Blok, 1995; Vringer, Gerlach, and Blok, 1997).

Income elasticity is smaller than unity because the growth of direct energy consumption is less than the growth of income. In contrast the indirect part of energy consumption grows in proportion to income. Thus a shift to less energy-intensive products does not take place as household income grows.

In the case of direct energy use, saturation effects occur. Lower-income households already use a large amount of natural gas (or other energy carriers for space heating). Gasoline consumption saturates at a much higher income level. Electricity consumption did not saturate in the income categories considered.

While some saturation effects occur, lifestyles in industrialised countries still evolve towards higher levels of energy use.

A cross-sectional analysis for 1948–96 yielded similar results. Indirect energy use grew at a rate more or less proportional to income. Direct energy consumption shows a different behaviour; from 1976–96 it grew at less than average income levels (Vringer and Blok, 1995).

Thus the lifestyle issue becomes an income issue. Seen from the perspective of households, income is by far the main driver of energy requirements. There does not seem to be any tendency to adopt less energy-intensive consumption patterns with rising incomes.

Trends towards increased energy use

Increasing income levels tend to lead to a higher use of energy services by citizens of modern society. Some saturation effects occur, but they do not have a dominant effect on energy consumption. The effects of energy-efficiency improvements, especially in space heating and large appliances, may be more important. Nevertheless, lifestyles in industrialised countries still evolve towards higher levels of energy use.

Many of the driving forces described here cannot easily be altered to lead to lower energy use. But energy-efficiency improvement (including design that stimulates energy-efficient use of equipment) had a considerable impact in the early 1980s. Hence increasing the rate of efficiency improvement seems to be the most straightforward approach to limiting the growth of energy consumption.

If it is necessary to go beyond the limits of efficiency improvements, it is not sufficient to identify income as the determinant. After all, one cannot look for income reduction strategies. But income is only a proxy for more fundamental determinants of energy use. Income is translated into consumption, which is the material expression (more appliances, bigger homes, heavier cars, more goods) of lifestyles. If one takes these material expressions as determinants, one can think of strategies directed towards altering the consumption patterns associated with the most energy-intensive categories of energy use without impairing quality of life. But a great deal of thought and action will be required to influence lifestyles in this way. They may require a fundamental change in current pricing and taxing policies—not to mention taking advantage of the Internet revolution to change trends.

Conclusion

This chapter has clarified the two-way linkages between energy, on the one hand, and poverty, women, population, urbanisation, and lifestyles, on the other. The relationship between energy and these major global issues is dialectical—the global issues determine energy consumption, and in turn, energy systems influence the issues. If attention is focussed on the global issues as the cause, then energy becomes the effect. But if the focus is on energy as the cause, then one can see the myriad ways in which energy shapes the global issues.

It has also been shown that current energy consumption patterns are aggravating various global problems, leading to further unsustainability. But energy can also contribute to the solution of problems; in particular, poverty, the situation of women, population growth, unplanned urbanisation, and excessively consumptive lifestyles. To realise energy's enormous potential in these areas, it must be brought to centre stage and given the same importance as other major global concerns.

A goal is an objective to be achieved, a strategy is a broad plan to achieve the goal, and a policy is a specific course of action to implement a strategy. Policies are implemented through policy agents working with policy instruments.

The goal for energy systems is sustainable development. Energy strategies to advance this goal should be derived from the details of the linkages between energy and social issues. In particular strategies should emerge from the manner in which energy can contribute to the solution of social problems.

Thus poverty alleviation in developing countries should involve the energy strategy of universal access to adequate, affordable, reliable, high-quality, safe, and environmentally benign modern energy services, particularly for cooking, lighting, income generation, and transport. Poverty alleviation in industrialised countries requires the energy strategy of universal protection and maintenance of access to affordable energy services, particularly for space heating and lighting.

Improvement in the position of women requires energy strategies that minimise, if not eliminate, arduous physical labour at home and at work, replace traditional biomass-based fuel-stove cooking systems with modern (preferably gaseous) fuels and cooking devices, and use the intrinsic managerial and entrepreneurial capabilities of women in decentralised energy systems.

Control over population growth can benefit from energy strategies that increase life expectancy and reduce infant (and child) mortality in developing countries through modern fuels and cooking devices that render unnecessary the physical labour of children for household chores such as gathering fuelwood, cooking, fetching drinking water, and grazing livestock—and that improve the quality of life of women.

Accentuating the positive aspects of urbanisation and alleviating its negative aspects require energy strategies that exploit the advantages of high-density settlements, provide universal access to affordable multi-modal public transportation, and reduce the 'push' factor in rural-urban migration by improving energy services in rural settlements.

Finally, reducing energy consumption through lifestyle changes requires a strategy—using pricing and taxation—of discouraging the use of energy-intensive devices and encouraging the use of energy-conserving devices.

To be successful, the strategies outlined above must harness both appropriate supply and end-use technologies. The strategies must also be converted into policies wielded by policy agents through policy instruments. Complete hardware plus 'software'—policies, management, financing, training, institutions—solutions are essential for the deployment of energy as an instrument of sustainable development. These challenges will be discussed in the chapters that follow. ■

Notes

1. Self-reliance does not preclude imports and exports but requires that control over destiny be indigenous.

2. Energy use is taken as a proxy for useful energy, which means that the efficiency of energy use has been held constant.

3. The linkages between energy and security, between energy and economics, and between energy and environment are dealt with in later chapters.

4. This section is based on inputs from Anton Eberhard and Wendy Annecke of the Energy Research Development Centre, University of Cape Town, and from David Bloom, Harvard University.

5. Unfortunately, estimates of absolute poverty are quite sensitive to the methods used to make these adjustments. In addition, all such methods focus on the cost of a standardised bundle consumed by an average household, not on the typical bundle consumed by a poor household. Insofar as market baskets consumed by poor households tend to be filled with relatively high proportions of less costly non-tradable goods and services, absolute poverty will be overstated with all methods of estimation.

6. This number has been adjusted for differences in the purchasing power of different national currencies in 1985 using estimates contained in Penn World Table 5.6 (Center for International Comparisons at the University of Pennsylvania, 2000).

7. Because of irregularities in supply, price rises, and so on, households have, in addition to a preferred or dominant fuel, other fuels as back-ups. Thus when LPG, for instance, is in short supply, households may be forced to switch to electricity.

8. The thought experiment was not intended to recommend Western European living standards as the goal for developing countries or to establish activity level targets for these countries to be achieved by some particular date. The appropriate mix and levels of activities for the future in developing countries will have to be different to be consistent with their climate, culture, and development goals. Rather, the purpose of the thought experiment was to show that it is possible not only to meet basic human needs but also to provide improvements in living standards that go far beyond the satisfaction of basic needs, without significant increases in per capita energy use. Thus energy supply availability need not be a fundamental constraint on development.

9. The correspondence between the 1 kilowatt per capita increase (about 30 gigajoules per capita annually) and a vastly improved standard of living is not very different from the threshold of 1 tonne of oil equivalent per capita (about 40 gigajoules per capita annually), above which infant mortality, illiteracy, life expectancy, and fertility all show substantial improvement and saturation (see figure 2.1).

10. This section is based on the paper prepared for this chapter by Jamuna Ramakrishna, Humanist Institute for Cooperation with Developing Countries (HIVOS), Bangalore, India.

11. The initial (early 1970s) belief that this degradation was the result of villagers' dependence on biomass for cooking has given way to a broader understanding that includes factors such as urban demand for biomass, industrial needs, logging, and clearing for agriculture. The fact remains that biomass cover (indicated, for instance, by remote sensing) is decreasing.

12. Under the criteria set forth in the 1993 revision of the SNA, the boundary between productive activities that are market-oriented and those that are not is drawn in such a way that the majority of household work and community voluntary work is excluded from the SNA. Education is also excluded. Although this leads to a gross under-estimation of women's economic contributions, the 1993 revision is actually an improvement over the previous version of the SNA, which excluded production of household goods for own consumption and activities such as carrying water (UNDP, 1995).

13. This section is based on the paper prepared for this chapter by Jamuna Ramakrishna, HIVOS, Bangalore, India.

14. Total fertility is a measure of the average number of children a woman will bear throughout her child-bearing years if at each age she has the average fertility corresponding to that age group.

15. Incidentally, the growth in the percentage of the working-age population capable of being economically active (relative to the total population) has been ascribed a key role in the East Asian economic miracle in conjunction with educational, health, and institutional measures to realise the economic potential of this boom in the labour

force. Thus the middle phase of the demographic transition has important implications for economic growth.

16. The importance of the percentage of working-age population was brought out by Bloom and Williamson (1998).

17. The 'demographic indicators for countries of the world, 1950–2050, medium variant' (UN, 1996) estimates 9.37 billion in 2050.

18. Data are from John Holdren, Harvard University.

19. In one of the villages studied, fuelwood consumption corresponded to about 217 tonnes of firewood per year; that is, about 0.6 tonnes per day for the village, or 0.6 tonnes per year per capita.

20. Unlike in some rural areas of India, dung cakes are not used as cooking fuel in the region studied. In situations where agro-wastes (such as coconut husks) are not abundant, it appears that, if firewood is available within some convenient range (determined by the capacity of head-load transportation), dung cakes are never burnt as fuel. Instead dung is used as manure.

21. This section is based on the paper prepared for this chapter by Jonas Rabinovitch, senior urban development adviser, UNDP, with the assistance of Raquel Wexler.

22. Apart from information provided by the U.S. Energy Information Administration, an excellent article is Myerson (1998).

23. This section is based on the input of Kornelis Blok, Utrecht University.

References

ASTRA (Centre for the Application of Science and Technology to Rural Areas). 1982. "Rural Energy Consumption Patterns: A Field Study." *Biomass* 2 (4): 255–80.

Atiq R.A., N. Robins, and A. Roncerel, eds. 1998. *Exploding the Population Myth: Consumption versus Population—Which Is the Population Bomb?* Dhaka: Dhaka University Press.

Batliwala, S. 1982. "Rural Energy Scarcity and Nutrition: A New Perspective." *Economic and Political Weekly* 17 (9): 329–33.

———. 1984. "Rural Energy Situation: Consequences for Women's Health." *Socialist Health Review* 1 (2): 75.

———. 1987. "Women's Access to Food." *Indian Journal of Social Work* 48 (3): 255–71.

Batliwala, S., and A.K.N. Reddy. 1994. "Energy Consumption and Population." In *Population: The Complex Reality.* London: The Royal Society.

———. 1996. "Energy for Women and Women for Energy (Engendering Energy and Empowering Women)." Paper presented at a meeting of Energia: Women and Energy Network, 4–5 June, University of Twente, Enschede, Netherlands.

Bloom, D.E., and J.G. Williamson. 1998. "Demographic Transitions and Economic Miracles in Emerging Asia." *The World Bank Economic Review* 12 (3): 419–55.

Bloom, D.E., and A. Zaidi. 1999. "Energy-Population Linkages in Developing Countries." Paper presented at World Energy Assessment Lead Authors Meeting, London, March.

Bloom, D.E., P. Craig, and P. Malaney. 2000. *The Quality of Life in Rural Asia.* Hong Kong: Oxford University Press.

Center for International Comparisons at the University of Pennsylvania. 2000. Penn World Table, http://pwt.econ.upenn.edu/

Coale, A.J. 1973. "The Demographic Transition Reconsidered." Paper presented at International Population Conference, Liège, Belgium.

———. 1983. "Recent Trends in Fertility in Less Developed Countries." *Science* 221: 828–32.

Dasgupta, P.S. 1993. *Scientific American*: 26–31.

De Almeida, E., and A. de Oliveira. 1995. "Brazilian Life Style and Energy Consumption." In *Energy Demand, Life Style Changes and Technology Development.* London: World Energy Council.

Goldemberg, J., T.B. Johansson, A.K.N. Reddy, and R.H. Williams. 1985. "Basic Needs and Much More with One Kilowatt per Capita." *Ambio* 14 (4–5): 190–200.

———. 1988. *Energy for a Sustainable World.* New Delhi: Wiley-Eastern.

Government of India. 1988. Shramshakti Report. *Report of the National Commission of Self-Employed Women and Women in the Informal Sector.* New Delhi.

Hosier, R.H., and J. Dowd. 1987. "Household Fuel Choice in Zimbabwe: An Empirical Test of the Energy Ladder Hypothesis." *Resources and Energy* 13 (9): 347–61.

IEA (International Energy Agency). 1997. *Indicators of Energy Use and Energy Efficiency.* Paris.

Leach, G. 1992. "The Energy Transition." *Energy Policy* 20 (2): 116–23.

Myerson, A.R. 1998. "U.S. Splurging on Energy after Falling Off Its Diet." *New York Times,* 22 October: A1.

Nakićenović, N., and A. John. 1991. "CO_2 Reduction and Removal: Measures for the Next Century." *Energy, the International Journal* 16: 1347–77.

Nathan, D. 1997. "Economic Factors in Adoption of Improved Stoves." *Wood Energy News* 12 (1): 16–18.

Rabinovitch, J. 1993. "Urban Public Transport Management in Curitiba, Brazil." *UNEP Industry and Environment* (January–June): 18–20.

Ramakrishna, J. 1992. "Improved Stoves, Time, Fuel: Implications for the Nutrition and Health of Women and Children." *Boiling Point* 27: 4–6.

Reddy, A.K.N., and B.S. Reddy, 1994. "Substitution of Energy Carriers for Cooking in Bangalore." *Energy* 19 (5): 561–71.

Roberts, P.C. 1975. "Energy Analysis in Modelling." In I.M. Blair, B.D. Jones, and A.J. van Horn, eds., *Aspects of Energy Conversion.* Oxford: Pergamon Press.

Sen, A. 1994. "Population: Delusion and Reality." *New York Review of Books* 41 (15): 1–8.

Smith, K.R. 1993. "Fuel Combustion, Air Pollution Exposure, and Health: The Situation in Developing Countries." *Annual Review of Energy and Environment* 18: 529–66.

UN (United Nations). 1993a. *Energy Statistics Yearbook* 1993. New York.

———. 1993b. *Report of the United Nations Conference on Environment and Development (UNCED), Agenda 21.* Document A/Conf. 151/26/Rev. 1., Vol. 1. New York.

———. 1996. *Habitat Agenda and Istanbul Declaration.* New York: United Nations Department of Public Information.

UNDP (United Nations Development Programme). 1995. *Human Development Report 1995.* New Delhi: Oxford University Press.

———. 1996. *Human Development Report 1996.* New Delhi: Oxford University Press.

———. 1997a. *Energy after Rio: Prospects and Challenges.* New York: UNDP, in collaboration with International Energy Initiative, Stockholm Environment Institute, and United Nations Conference on Environment and Development.

———. 1997b. *Human Development Report 1997.* New Delhi: Oxford University Press.

———. 1998. *Human Development Report 1998.* New Delhi: Oxford University Press.

Viklund, E., ed. 1989. *Nordic Seminar on Domestic Energy in Developing Countries: A Seminar Report.* Publication 31. Lund University, Lund Centre for Habitat Studies, Sweden.

Vringer, K., and K. Blok. 1995. "The Direct and Indirect Energy Requirement of Households in the Netherlands." *Energy Policy* 23: 893–910.

Vringer, K., T. Gerlach, and K. Blok. 1997. "The Direct and Indirect Energy Requirement of Netherlands' Households in 1995 [in Dutch]." Utrecht University, Department of Science, Technology and Society, Utrecht, Netherlands.

WHO (World Health Organisation). 1992. *Epidemiological, Social, and Technical Aspects of Indoor Air Pollution from Biomass Fuels: Report of a WHO Consultation,* June 1991. Geneva.

World Bank. 1998. *World Development Indicators 1998.* Washington, D.C.

energy, the environment, and health

CHAPTER 3

John P. Holdren (United States)
Kirk R. Smith (United States)

LEAD AUTHORS: Tord Kjellstrom (New Zealand), David Streets (United States), and Xiaodong Wang (China)

CONTRIBUTING AUTHORS: Susan Fischer (United States), Donna Green (Australia), Emi Nagata (Japan), and Jennifer Slotnick (United States)

MAJOR REVIEWERS: Jyoti Parikh (India) and Yasmin Von Schirnding (South Africa)

ABSTRACT

In this chapter, the principal environmental and health impacts of energy are discussed according to the *scale* at which they occur. About half of the world's *households* use solid fuels (biomass and coal) for cooking and heating in simple devices that produce large amounts of air pollution—pollution that is probably responsible for 4–5 percent of the global burden of disease. The chief ecosystem impacts relate to charcoal production and fuelwood harvesting.

At the *workplace* scale, solid-fuel fuel cycles create significant risks for workers and have the largest impacts on populations among energy systems. In *communities*, fuel use is the main cause of urban air pollution, though there is substantial variation among cities in the relative contributions of vehicles and stationary sources. Diesel-fuelled vehicles, which are more prominent in developing countries, pose a growing challenge for urban health. The chief ecosystem impacts result from large-scale hydropower projects in forests, although surface mining causes significant damage in some areas.

At the *regional* scale, fine particles and ozone are the most widespread health-damaging pollutants from energy use, and can extend hundreds of kilometres from their sources. Similarly, nitrogen and sulphur emissions lead to acid deposition far from their sources. Such deposition is associated with damage to forests, soils, and lakes in various parts of the world. At the *global* scale, energy systems account for two-thirds of human-generated greenhouse gas increases. Thus energy use is the human activity most closely linked to potential climate change. Climate change is feared to have significant direct impacts on human health and on ecosystems.

There are important opportunities for 'no regrets' strategies that achieve benefits at more than one scale. For example, if greenhouse gas controls are targeted to reduce solid fuel use in households and other energy systems with large health impacts (such as vehicle fleets), significant improvements can occur at the local, community, regional, and global scales. ■

Because of their ubiquity and size, energy systems influence nearly every category of environmental insult and impact.

T he harvesting, processing, distribution, and use of fuels and other sources of energy have major environmental implications. Insults include major land-use changes due to fuel cycles such as coal, biomass, and hydropower, which have implications for the natural as well as human environment.[1] Perhaps the most important insult from energy systems is the routine and accidental release of pollutants. Human activities disperse a wide variety of biologically and climatologically active elements and compounds into the atmosphere, surface waters, and soil at rates far beyond the natural flows of these substances. The results of these alterations include a 10-fold increase in the acidity of rain and snow over millions of square kilometres and significant changes in the global composition of the stratosphere (upper atmosphere) and troposphere (lower atmosphere).

The rough proportions of various pollutants released into the environment by human activities are shown in table 3.1. Note the importance of energy supply systems, both industrial and traditional, in the mobilisation of such toxic substances as sulphur oxides and particles as well as in the release of carbon dioxide, the principal greenhouse gas. Also shown is the human disruption index for each substance, which is the ratio of the amount released by human activities to natural releases. This indicates that together with other human activities, energy systems are significantly affecting the cycling of important chemical species at the global scale. Although by themselves these indexes do not demonstrate that these insults are translated into negative impacts, their magnitudes provide warning that such impacts could be considerable.

In the past hundred years most of these phenomena have grown from local perturbations to global disruptions. The environmental transition of the 20th century—driven by more than 20-fold growth in the use of fossil fuels and augmented by a tripling in the use of traditional energy forms such as biomass—has amounted to no less than the emergence of civilisation as a global ecological and geochemical force.

The impacts from energy systems, however, occur from the household to the global scale. Indeed, at every scale the environmental impacts of human energy production and use account for a significant portion of human impacts on the environment.

This chapter examines the insults and impacts of energy systems according to the scale at which the principal dynamics occur— meaning the scale at which it makes the most sense to monitor, evaluate, and control the insults that lead to environmental impacts. In addition, some cross-scale problems are considered to illustrate the need to control insults occurring at one scale because of the impacts they have at other scales. Impacts are divided into two broad categories: those directly affecting human health (environmental health impacts) and those indirectly affecting human welfare through impacts on the natural environment (ecosystem impacts).

Because of their ubiquity and size, energy systems influence nearly

every category of environmental insult and impact. Indeed, large multiple-volume treatises have been devoted to discussing the environmental problem of just part of the energy system in single countries (as with U.S. electric power production in ORNL and RFF, 1992–98). A detailed review of the environmental connections of energy systems world-wide is beyond the scope of this volume. Indeed, simply cataloguing the routes of insults and types of impacts of energy systems world-wide would take substantially more space than is available here, even if accompanied by little comment.

In addition, for three other reasons reproducing catalogues involving simple listings of insults and impacts for each of the many types of energy systems would not serve the interests of readers. First, many detailed studies in recent years have done this job much better than we could here. Thus we will cite a range of such material to enable interested readers to expand their understanding. In addition, there is a substantial amount of such information in other chapters, for example, on the environmental and health impacts of renewable energy systems in chapter 7 and of fossil and nuclear power systems in chapter 8. Chapter 8 also addresses the technological implications of reducing urban pollution according to changes in local willingness to pay for health improvements. Chapter 1 discusses some of the relationships between environment and energy development, and chapter 9 has much discussion of the implications of various future energy scenarios for greenhouse gas emissions.

The second reason relates to our desire to help readers understand the relative importance of the problems. The significance of known environmental impacts from energy systems varies by orders of magnitude, from the measurable but minuscule to the planet-threatening. Just as the other chapters in this volume must focus on just a few of the most important energy system issues for the next half-century, we must do so for environmental impacts.

Finally, we feel that it is as important to give readers a framework for thinking about environmental impacts as it is to document current knowledge about individual problems. Thus we have devoted much of our effort to laying out the problems in a systematic manner using scale as the organising principle. Near the end of the chapter we also discuss two of the most common analytical frameworks for making aggregate comparisons involving a range of environmental impacts from energy systems: economic valuation and comparative risk assessment using fuel-cycle analysis.

Given space limitations and the reasons summarised above, we focus below on the two or three most important environmental insults and impacts at each scale. This approach brings what may seem to be a geographic bias as well—examples at each scale tend to be focused not only on the most important problems but also on the places in the world where the problems are most severe. We recognise that there are innumerable other impacts and places that could be mentioned as well, but we offer this set as candidates for those that ought to have the highest priority in the next few decades.

Indeed, if these environmental problems were brought under control, the world would have moved most of the way towards a sustainable energy future from an environmental standpoint.

This chapter focuses almost entirely on the environmental insults and impacts associated with today's energy systems, in line with this report's goal of exploring the sustainability of current practices. In later chapters, as part of efforts to examine the feasibility of advanced energy conversion technologies, new sources of energy, and enhanced end-use efficiencies, the potential environmental impacts of future energy systems are explored.

TABLE 3.1. ENVIRONMENTAL INSULTS DUE TO HUMAN ACTIVITIES BY SECTOR, MID-1990S

Insult	Natural baseline (tonnes a year)	Human disruption index[a]	Share of human disruption caused by			
			Commercial energy supply	Traditional energy supply	Agriculture	Manufacturing, other
Lead emissions to atmosphere[b]	12,000	18	41% (fossil fuel burning, including additives)	Negligible	Negligible	59% (metal processing, manufacturing, refuse burning)
Oil added to oceans	200,000	10	44% (petroleum harvesting, processing, and transport)	Negligible	Negligible	56% (disposal of oil wastes, including motor oil changes)
Cadmium emissions to atmosphere	1,400	5.4	13% (fossil fuel burning)	5% (traditional fuel burning)	12% (agricultural burning)	70% (metals processing, manufacturing, refuse burning)
Sulphur emissions to atmosphere	31 million (sulphur)	2.7	85% (fossil fuel burning)	0.5% (traditional fuel burning)	1% (agricultural burning)	13% (smelting, refuse burning)
Methane flow to atmosphere	160 million	2.3	18% (fossil fuel harvesting and processing)	5% (traditional fuel burning)	65% (rice paddies, domestic animals, land clearing)	12% (landfills)
Nitrogen fixation (as nitrogen oxide and ammonium)[c]	140 million (nitrogen)	1.5	30% (fossil fuel burning)	2% (traditional fuel burning)	67% (fertiliser, agricultural burning)	1% (refuse burning)
Mercury emissions to atmosphere	2,500	1.4	20% (fossil fuel burning)	1% (traditional fuel burning)	2% (agricultural burning)	77% (metals processing, manufacturing, refuse burning)
Nitrous oxide flows to atmosphere	33 million	0.5	12% (fossil fuel burning)	8% (traditional fuel burning)	80% (fertiliser, land clearing, aquifer disruption)	Negligible
Particulate emissions to atmosphere	3,100 million[d]	0.12	35% (fossil fuel burning)	10% (traditional fuel burning)	40% (agricultural burning)	15% (smelting, non-agricultural land clearing, refuse)
Non-methane hydrocarbon emissions to atmosphere	1,000 million	0.12	35% (fossil fuel processing and burning)	5% (traditional fuel burning)	40% (agricultural burning)	20% (non-agricultural land clearing, refuse burning)
Carbon dioxide flows to atmosphere	150 billion (carbon)	0.05[e]	75% (fossil fuel burning)	3% (net deforestation for fuelwood)	15% (net deforestation for land clearing)	7% (net deforestation for lumber, cement manufacturing)

Note: The magnitude of the insult is only one factor determining the size of the actual environmental impact. a. The human disruption index is the ratio of human-generated flow to the natural (baseline) flow. b. The automotive portion of anthropogenic lead emissions in the mid-1990s is assumed to be 50 percent of global automotive emissions in the early 1990s. c. Calculated from total nitrogen fixation minus that from nitrous oxide. d. Dry mass. e. Although seemingly small, because of the long atmospheric lifetime and other characteristics of carbon dioxide, this slight imbalance in natural flows is causing a 0.4 percent annual increase in the global atmospheric concentration of carbon dioxide.

Source: Updated from Holdren, 1992 using Houghton and others, 1994; IPCC, 1996b; Johnson and Derwent, 1996; Lelieveld and others, 1997; Nriagu, 1989, 1990; Smithsonian Institution, 1996; Smith and Flegal, 1995; and WRI, 1998.

Household scale

The oldest human energy technology, the home cooking fire, persists as the most prevalent fuel-using technology in the world. For much of the world's population, the home cooking fire accounts for most direct energy demand. Household fuel demand accounts for more than half of energy demand in most countries with per capita incomes under $1,000 (see figure 2.1).

The 'energy ladder' is a useful framework for examining trends and impacts of household fuel use (see figure 10.1). The ladder ranks household fuels along a spectrum running from simple biomass fuels (dung, crop residues, wood) through fossil fuels (kerosene and gas) to the most modern form (electricity). The fuel-stove combinations that represent rungs in the ladder tend to become cleaner, more efficient, more storable, and more controllable in moving up the ladder.[2] But capital costs and dependence on centralised fuel cycles also tend to increase in moving up the ladder (OTA, 1992).

Although there are local exceptions, history has generally shown that when alternatives are affordable and available, populations tend to move up the ladder to higher-quality fuel-stove combinations. Although all of humanity had its start a quarter of a million years ago at the top of the energy ladder in those times (wood), only about half has moved up to higher-quality rungs (figure 3.1). The remaining half is either still using wood or has been forced by local wood shortages down the ladder to crop residues, dung, or, in some severe situations, to the poorest-quality fuels such as shrubs and grass.

Throughout history in places where coal is easily available, local wood shortages have led some populations to move to coal for household use. This shift occurred about a thousand years ago in the United Kingdom, for example, although it is relatively uncommon there today (Brimblecome, 1987). In the past 150 years such transitions occurred in Eastern Europe and China, where coal use still persists

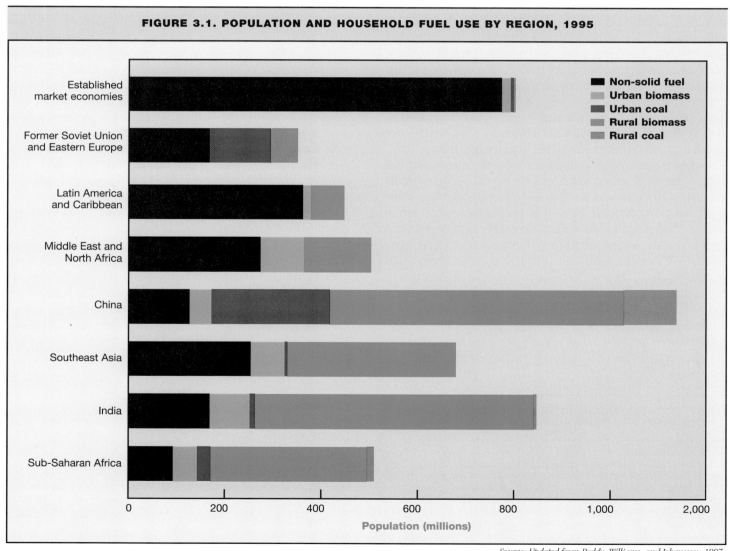

FIGURE 3.1. POPULATION AND HOUSEHOLD FUEL USE BY REGION, 1995

Legend:
- Non-solid fuel
- Urban biomass
- Urban coal
- Rural biomass
- Rural coal

Regions (y-axis):
- Established market economies
- Former Soviet Union and Eastern Europe
- Latin America and Caribbean
- Middle East and North Africa
- China
- Southeast Asia
- India
- Sub-Saharan Africa

Population (millions) (x-axis): 0, 200, 400, 600, 800, 1,000, 2,000

Source: Updated from Reddy, Williams, and Johansson, 1997.

in millions of households (see figure 3.1). In terms of the energy ladder, coal represents an upward movement in terms of efficiency and storability. Because of these characteristics and its higher energy densities, it is possible to ship coal economically over longer distances than wood and to efficiently supply urban markets. In these senses, coal is like other household fossil fuels. Unlike kerosene and gas, however, coal is often a dirtier fuel than wood.

Harvesting

The chief environmental impacts of household fuel cycles relate to harvesting and combustion. In the 1970s books and newspapers called attention to the 'other' energy crisis, referring to the growing and alarming shortage of woodfuel affecting a large fraction of the world population that depended on it. Since deforestation and desertification were often also occurring in such places, it was perhaps a logical conclusion that fuel demand was to blame. It is still common today to read that deforestation is caused by fuel gathering in rural areas of developing countries. Detailed studies in many areas around the world, however, have rarely documented cases in which fuel demand is a significant cause of deforestation. The most important cause by far seems to be expansion of agricultural lands, followed by lumbering and road building. Indeed, the causation is more often the reverse—that is, the shortage of fuelwood is due to deforestation, rather than the other way around.

Part of the misunderstanding stems from the assumption that rural households gather woodfuel from forests. In many areas villagers gather significant amounts of fuelwood from what Gerald Leach has called 'invisible trees'—the trees around fields, next to houses, along roads, and so on that do not show up in most satellite remote sensing surveys or national forest statistics. Thus when estimates of local fuelwood demand appear to exceed growth rates in local forests, it does not necessarily imply that deforestation is taking place. Conversely, if deforestation is known to be occurring, it does not mean that fuel demand is necessarily the reason.

Similarly, desertification in the Sahel and elsewhere in Sub-Saharan Africa has links to fuel demand. But it has been difficult to separate out the influence of all the relevant factors, including climate change, intensification of grazing, land-use shifts, and fuel harvesting. Nevertheless, as with deforestation, there are some poor areas where harvesting of wood and brush plays an important role.

Although the link between fuelwood harvesting and deforestation is far from universal, there are localised cases in which fuelwood demand seems to contribute significantly to forest depletion. Most prominent among these are places, mainly in Sub-Saharan Africa, where commercial charcoal production is practised. In these areas temporary kilns (legal or illegal) in forested areas are used until local wood resources are depleted, then moved or rebuilt elsewhere. Charcoal, being a relatively high-quality and high-density fuel, can be trucked economically across long distances to urban markets. Thus large charcoal-using cities can have 'wood sheds' extending hundreds of kilometres along roadways, though there is evidence that significant regrowth often occurs over long enough periods. In some arid and semiarid areas, harvesting by woodfuel traders to meet urban demand seems to contribute to forest depletion, although, again, regrowth is often occurring. The quality of regrowth in terms of biodiversity and other ecosystem parameters is not well documented, however.

The harvesting of dung and crop residues as fuel does not have much direct environmental impact. But in some areas it may deprive local soils of needed nutrients and other conditioners. Indeed, in most rural areas the use of dung as fuel rather than fertiliser is probably a sign of poverty and lack of fuel alternatives. Crop residues, on the other hand, consist of a wide variety of materials, many of which do not have much value as fertiliser or soil conditioner. Indeed, in some cases disposal becomes a serious problem if these residues are not gathered for fuel. In these cases the usual practice is to burn the residues in place on the fields, with consequent pollution implications (although sometimes with benefits in terms of pest control). Consequently, regardless of development level, air pollution from post-harvest burning of farmland is a significant seasonal source of air pollution in many agricultural areas around the world (see chapter 10). Harvesting and preparation of household biomass fuels also have occupational health impacts on women and children, due, for example, to heavy loads and burns (see the section on workplace scale, below).

> Physical form and contaminant content are the two characteristics of fuels that most affect their pollutant emissions when burned.

BOX 3.1. HEALTH-DAMAGING POLLUTANTS IN SOLID FUEL SMOKE FROM HOUSEHOLD STOVES IN INDIA

Biomass smoke
- Small particles, carbon monoxide, nitrogen dioxide.
- Formaldehyde, acrolein, benzene, 1,3-butadiene, toluene, styrene, and so on.
- Polyaromatic hydrocarbons such as benzo(a)pyrene.

Coal smoke
- All the above plus, depending on coal quality, sulphur oxides and such toxic elements as arsenic, lead, fluorine, and mercury.

Combustion

Physical form and contaminant content are the two characteristics of fuels that most affect their pollutant emissions when burned. It is generally difficult to pre-mix solid fuels sufficiently with air to assure good combustion in simple small-scale devices such as household stoves. Consequently, even though most biomass fuels contain few noxious contaminants, they are usually burned incompletely in household stoves and so produce a wide range of health-damaging pollutants (box 3.1). Wood and other biomass fuels would produce little other than non-toxic products, carbon dioxide, and water when

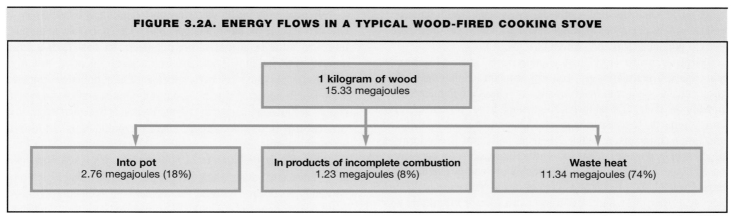

FIGURE 3.2A. ENERGY FLOWS IN A TYPICAL WOOD-FIRED COOKING STOVE

1 kilogram of wood
15.33 megajoules

Into pot
2.76 megajoules (18%)

In products of incomplete combustion
1.23 megajoules (8%)

Waste heat
11.34 megajoules (74%)

Source: Smith and others, 2000 a.

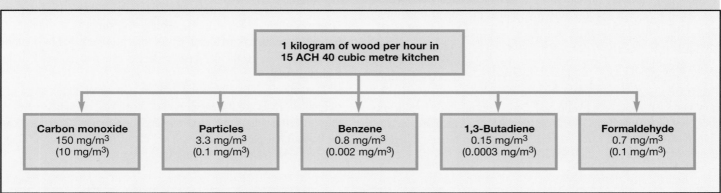

**FIGURE 3.2B. INDOOR CONCENTRATIONS OF HEALTH-DAMAGING POLLUTANTS
FROM A TYPICAL WOOD-FIRED COOKING STOVE**

1 kilogram of wood per hour in
15 ACH 40 cubic metre kitchen

Carbon monoxide
150 mg/m^3
(10 mg/m^3)

Particles
3.3 mg/m^3
(0.1 mg/m^3)

Benzene
0.8 mg/m^3
(0.002 mg/m^3)

1,3-Butadiene
0.15 mg/m^3
(0.0003 mg/m^3)

Formaldehyde
0.7 mg/m^3
(0.1 mg/m^3)

Note: Dozens of other health-damaging pollutants are known to be in woodsmoke. Mg/m^3 stands for milligrams per cubic metre. Numbers in parentheses are typical standards set to protect health. *Source: Smith and others, 2000 a.*

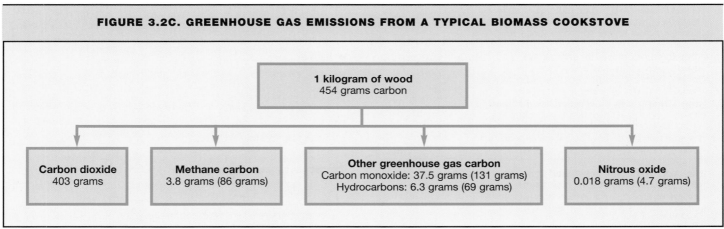

FIGURE 3.2C. GREENHOUSE GAS EMISSIONS FROM A TYPICAL BIOMASS COOKSTOVE

1 kilogram of wood
454 grams carbon

Carbon dioxide
403 grams

Methane carbon
3.8 grams (86 grams)

Other greenhouse gas carbon
Carbon monoxide: 37.5 grams (131 grams)
Hydrocarbons: 6.3 grams (69 grams)

Nitrous oxide
0.018 grams (4.7 grams)

Note: Numbers in parentheses are carbon dioxide equivalents of non-carbon dioxide gases. *Source: Smith and others, 2000 a.*

combusted completely. But in practice sometimes as much as one-fifth of the fuel carbon is diverted to products of incomplete combustion, many of which are important health-damaging pollutants.

Coal, on the other hand, is not only difficult to burn completely because it is solid, but also often contains significant intrinsic contaminants that add to its emissions of health-damaging pollutants. Most prominent among such emissions are sulphur oxides (see box 3.1). But in many areas coal also contains arsenic, fluorine, and other toxic elements that can lead to serious health-damaging pollutants. Tens of millions of people in China, for example, are exposed to such pollutants from household coal use.

Petroleum-based liquid and gaseous fuels, such as kerosene and liquefied petroleum gas, can also contain sulphur and other contaminants, though in much smaller amounts than in many coals. In addition, their physical forms allow much better pre-mixing with air in simple devices, assuring much higher combustion efficiencies and lower emissions of health-damaging pollutants in the form of products of incomplete combustion. Furthermore, stoves for petroleum-based liquid and gaseous fuels are much more energy efficient than those for coal. As a result emissions of health-damaging pollutants per meal from these fuels are at least an order of magnitude less than those from solid fuels (Smith and others, 2000 a).

Not only do solid-fuel stoves produce substantial emissions of health-damaging pollutants per meal, but a large fraction do not have chimneys for removing the emissions from the home. Consequently, indoor concentrations of health-damaging pollutants can reach very high levels. Figure 3.2a shows the energy flows of a typical wood-fired cooking stove, in which a large fraction of the fuel energy is lost because of low combustion efficiency or low transfer of the heat to the pot. Figure 3.2b shows the excessive pollutant levels commonly reached in these circumstances, well beyond World Health Organization guidelines. Even in households with chimneys, however, heavily polluting solid-fuel stoves can produce significant local outdoor pollution. This is particularly true in dense urban slums, where such 'neighbourhood' pollution can be much higher than average urban pollution levels.

To estimate the health damage from pollution, it is necessary to take into account the amount of pollution released. Equally important, however, is the behaviour of the population at risk. Even a large amount of pollution will not have much health impact if little of it reaches people. But a relatively small amount of pollution can have a big health impact if it is released at the times and places where people are present, such that a large fraction is breathed in. Thus it is necessary to look not only at where the pollution is but also at where the people are.

Unfortunately, pollution from household stoves is released right at the times and places where people are present—that is, in every household every day. This is the formula for high pollution exposures: significant amounts of pollution often released in poorly ventilated spaces at just the times when people are present. Moreover, because of their nearly universal responsibility for cooking, women and their youngest children are generally the most exposed.

Thus, although the total amount of health-damaging pollution released from stoves world-wide is not high relative to that from large-scale use of fossil fuels, human exposures to a number of important pollutants are much larger than those created by outdoor pollution. As a result the health effects can be expected to be higher as well.

In many ways the harvesting impacts and air pollution from use of biomass fuels are the result of fuel shortages, particularly where inferior forms (dung and crop residues) are in use. Thus these can be considered part of the health effects of too little energy, along with lower nutrition and chilling (box 3.2).

BOX 3.2. HEALTH EFFECTS OF TOO LITTLE WOODFUEL

Lack of sufficient fuel for heating and cooking has several negative health impacts. First, in many places women and children must walk further and work harder to gather fuel, using more energy and time and placing themselves at increased risk of assault and natural hazards such as leeches and snakes. In addition, nutrition can be negatively affected if families have to walk long distances to gather cooking fuel. When seasonal changes result in longer fuel collection times, families are unable to compensate by reducing the time spent on agricultural activities. Instead the time is subtracted from resting and food preparation.

Inferior fuels, such as twigs and grass, that are used as substitutes in times of shortage require more attention from women during cooking, keeping them from other tasks. These fuels also produce more health-damaging smoke and are inadequate for processing more nutritious foods such as cereals and beans (since they have long cooking times). The figure at right outlines some coping strategies adopted by households to deal with fuel shortages and their health consequences.

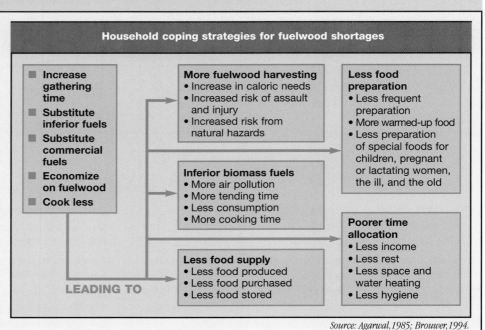

Source: Agarwal, 1985; Brouwer, 1994.

BOX 3.3. NATIONAL BURDEN OF DISEASE FROM HOUSEHOLD SOLID FUEL USE IN INDIA

National surveys, including the 1991 national census, show that nearly 80% of Indian households use biomass as their primary cooking fuel. As a result, a large portion of the Indian population is potentially exposed to indoor and outdoor levels of pollution produced by cooking stoves. Based on risks derived solely from studies of the health effects of individual diseases occurring in biomass-using households in developing countries, many in India itself, it is possible to estimate the total national burden of disease in India from use of these fuels:

Acute respiratory infection. More than a dozen studies around the world have found that household use of solid fuels is associated with acute respiratory infection in young children (although, as with all the diseases discussed here, there are other important risk factors, including malnutrition and crowding). Acute respiratory infection is the leading cause of death of the world's children and the largest category of ill health in the world in terms of disease burden. Almost 9 percent of the global burden of ill health and 12 percent of India's is due to acute respiratory infection. Acute respiratory infection linked to solid fuel use is estimated to cause 290,000–440,000 premature deaths a year in Indian children under 5.

Tuberculosis has been associated with household solid fuel use in a national survey in India involving nearly 90,000 households as well as in smaller studies. Although this relationship is not yet established with complete certainty, it would be highly significant because tuberculosis is on the rise in many developing countries due to HIV infection and the increase in drug-resistant strains. In India 50,000–130,000 cases of tuberculosis in women under 15 are associated with solid fuel use.

Chronic respiratory disease, such as chronic bronchitis, is almost entirely due to smoking in the industrialised world. But studies in Asia and Latin America have found the chronic respiratory disease develops in women after long years of cooking with solid fuels. In India 19,000–34,000 women under 45 suffer from chronic respiratory disease linked to solid fuel use.

Lung cancer, which is also dominated by smoking in industrialised countries, has been found to result from long-term exposure to cooking with coal in more than 20 studies in China. No such effect has been shown for biomass fuels, however. In India 400–800 women under 45 suffer from lung cancer linked to solid fuel use; the number is small because households rarely use coal.

Cardiovascular (heart) disease. Although there are apparently no studies in biomass-using households, studies of urban air pollution suggest that in India 50,000–190,000 women under 30 suffer from pollution-related heart disease.

Adverse pregnancy outcomes. Stillbirth and low birthweight have been associated with solid fuel use by pregnant women in Latin America and India. Low birthweight is a big problem in developing countries because it is a risk factor for a range of health problems. In India, however, there are too few studies to calculate the impacts of solid fuel use on adverse pregnancy outcomes.

Total. Because there is more uncertainty in the estimates for tuberculosis and heart disease, only the low ends of the estimated ranges are used. In India 410,000–570,000 premature deaths a year in women and children, of 5.8 million total, seem to be due to biomass fuel use. Given the age distribution of these deaths and the associated days of illness involved, 5–6 percent of the national burden of disease in women and young children can be attributed to biomass fuel use in households. For comparison, about 10 percent of the Indian national burden of disease is attributed to lack of clean water and sanitation.

Source: Smith, 2000; Smith and others, 2000; Murray and Lopez, 1996.

Estimated health effects

Considering the sizes of the relevant populations and the exposures to health-damaging pollutants, there has been relatively little scientific investigation of the health effects of indoor air pollution in developing countries relative to studies of outdoor air pollution in cities. Nevertheless, enough has been done to enable rough estimates of the total impact of air pollution, at least for women and young children (who suffer the highest exposures).

Four main types of health effects are thought to occur, based on studies in households that use solid fuels and corroborated by studies of active and passive smoking and outdoor air pollution (Smith, 1998):

- Infectious respiratory diseases such as acute respiratory infections and tuberculosis.
- Chronic respiratory diseases such as chronic bronchitis and lung cancer.
- Adverse pregnancy outcomes such as stillbirth and low birthweight in babies born to women exposed during pregnancy.
- Blindness, asthma, and heart disease (less evidence to date).

The best estimates of such effects for developing countries have been done for India (box 3.3). These indicate that household solid fuel use causes about 500,000 premature deaths a year in women and children under 5. This is 5–6 percent of the national burden of ill health, or 6–9 percent of the burden for these two population groups.[3] This is comparable to, though somewhat less than, the estimated national health impacts of poor water and sanitation at the household level—and more than the national burdens of such major health hazards as malaria, tuberculosis, tobacco, AIDS, heart disease, or cancer (Murray and Lopez, 1996).

Given that India contains about one-quarter of the world's solid-fuel cooking stoves, the global impact could be expected to be about four times larger, or about 2 million deaths a year in women and children. This is roughly compatible with World Health Organization estimates of about 2.5 million, estimates that were generated by extrapolating studies from industrialised country cities to developing country conditions (WHO, 1997). The global burden of disease from major risk factors, including indoor air pollution, is shown in figure 3.3.

Greenhouse gases

The same incomplete combustion processes that produce emissions of health-damaging pollutants from household solid-fuel stoves also produce greenhouse gas emissions. (Greenhouse gas emissions and their global impacts are described below, in the section on the global scale.) A large amount of fuel carbon is typically diverted to gaseous products of incomplete combustion, all of which cause greater global warming per carbon atom than would be the case if complete combustion occurred and all the carbon was released as carbon dioxide (see figure 3.2c). The most powerful of these is methane, which over a 20-year period causes more than 20 times the global warming from the same amount of carbon as carbon dioxide (equivalent to a discount rate of about 4 percent).

Greenhouse gas emissions from several of the most important household fuels in developing countries (as measured in India) are shown in figure 3.4. Because of significant emissions of non–carbon

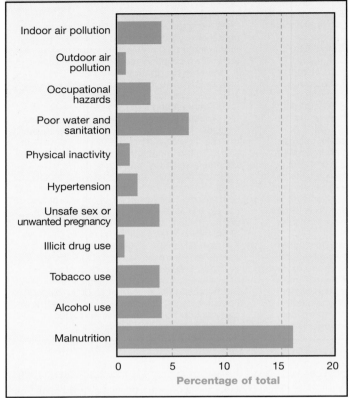

FIGURE 3.3. GLOBAL BURDEN OF DISEASE FROM SELECTED MAJOR RISK FACTORS, 1995

Note: Burden of indoor air pollution extrapolated from data for India.

Source: Smith, 2000; Murray and Lopez, 1996.

dioxide greenhouse gases, solid biomass fuels, even though renewable, can have a larger greenhouse gas commitment per meal than fossil fuels, kerosene, and liquefied petroleum gas. These relationships have several important policy implications:

- Even if renewably harvested, many biomass fuel cycles are not greenhouse gas neutral because of their substantial production of products of incomplete combustion.
- In some situations, therefore, substitution of fossil fuels for renewable biomass might be recommended to reduce greenhouse gas emissions.
- To be greenhouse gas neutral, biomass fuel cycles must be based on renewable harvesting and must have close to 100 percent combustion efficiency (which most do not in their current configurations).
- Improved biomass stoves should be designed to increase overall efficiency and to reduce combustion inefficiency, which is the cause of greenhouse gas and health-damaging pollutants.

Stoves using biogas, which is made in household or village anaerobic digesters from dung (see chapter 10), have by far the least greenhouse gas emissions per meal—only about 10 percent of those for liquefied petroleum gas and a factor of 80 less than the average stove burning dung directly (see figure 3.4). A complete comparison of these fuel-stove combinations would require evaluating greenhouse gas emissions over the entire fuel cycle in each case, for example, including methane leaking from biogas digesters and releases from oil refineries making kerosene. Nevertheless, the extremely low greenhouse gas emissions from biogas stoves illustrate the potentially great advantage for greenhouse gas emissions of processed biomass fuels such as biogas. Such fuels can be both renewably harvested as well as burned as liquids or gases with high combustion efficiency. (The section on cross-scale impacts, below, discusses some of the potential opportunities for reducing impacts at the household and global scales through improvements in household cooking.)

Reducing the human health and global warming impacts of household stoves will require better stoves with higher efficiency, lower emissions, and cleaner fuels. These issues are discussed in chapter 10. Of course, the largest greenhouse gas emissions are from energy systems used in industrialised countries, as discussed in later sections.

Workplace scale

The extraction, transport, use, and waste management of energy sources involve important health hazards related to the work and workplaces involved in these activities. Many of the jobs involved, such as forestry and mining for solid fuels, are particularly dangerous. Many workers are engaged in these jobs, particularly in countries that are rapidly developing their industries and the energy sources that the industries require. In addition, much of the work needed for household energy supply in developing countries is carried out as a household task that does not figure in national statistics as an 'occupational issue'.

This section analyses these health issues based on the type of energy source and give examples of how the effects have been documented in different countries. The fourth edition of the International Labour Organisation's *Encyclopaedia of Occupational Safety and Health* (Stellman, 1998) provides additional detail about energy jobs and their health hazards.

Biomass

As noted, wood, crop residues, dung, and the like are common energy sources for poor households in developing countries. Wood is also still widely used in industrialised countries, in some cases promoted in the interest of reducing greenhouse gas emissions. Wood and agricultural waste are often collected by women and children (Sims, 1994). Such collection is part of daily survival activities, which also include water hauling, food processing, and cooking (see chapters 2 and 10). An analysis in four developing countries found that women spend 9–12 hours a week on these activities, while men spend 5–8 hours (Reddy, Williams, and Johansson, 1997). Women's role in firewood collection is most prominent in Nepal (2.4 hours a day for women and 0.8 hours for men).

Firewood collection may be combined with harvesting of wood for local use in construction and small-scale cottage industry manufacturing. This subsistence work is often seasonal, unpaid, and not recorded in national economic accounts. Globally about 16 million people are involved in forestry (Poschen, 1998), more than

14 million of them in developing countries and 12.8 million in subsistence forestry.

A number of health hazards are associated with the basic conditions of the forest. Forest workers have a high risk of insect bites, stings from poisonous plants, leech infestation, cuts, falls, and drowning. In tropical countries the heat and humidity put great strain on the body, while in temperate countries the effects of cold are a potential hazard. The work is outside, and in sunny countries ultraviolet radiation can be another health hazard, increasing the risk of skin cancer and eye cataracts (WHO, 1994). All forestry work is hard physical labour, with a risk of ergonomic damage such as painful backs and joints as well as fatigue, which increases the risk of injuries. Heavy loads of firewood contribute to ergonomic damage (Poschen, 1998). Women carrying heavy loads of firewood are a common sight in areas with subsistence forestry (Sims, 1994). Falling trees, sharp tools, dangerous machinery, and falls from heights are the main causes of injuries. In addition, the living conditions of forestry workers are often poor, and workers may be spending long periods in simple huts in the forest with limited protection against the weather and poor sanitary facilities.

Urbanisation leads to the development of a commercial market for firewood and larger-scale production of firewood from logs or from smaller waste material left over after logs have been harvested. Energy forestry then becomes more mechanised, exposing workers to additional hazards (Poschen, 1998). Motorised hand tools (such as chain saws) become more common, resulting in high risks of injuries, noise-induced hearing losses, and 'white finger disease' caused by vibration of the hands. In addition, fertilisers and pesticides become part of the production system, with the potential for poisoning those who spray pesticides. As forestry develops further, more logging becomes mechanised, with very large machinery reducing the direct contact between workers and materials. Workers in highly mechanised forestry have only 15 percent of the injury risk of highly skilled forestry workers using chain saws (Poschen, 1998). Still, firewood production remains an operation that requires manual handling of the product at some stage and so tends to remain hazardous.

Another health aspect of wood-based energy is the risk of burning wood that has been treated against insect damage with copper-arsenic compounds or that has been painted with lead paint. Such wood may be harder to sell and so may be used to a greater extent by firewood production workers in stoves and open fires. When burned, poisonous arsenic and lead compounds will be emitted with the smoke. These compounds are health hazards when inhaled.

Coal

Coal is a major global energy source, accounting for 23 percent of total energy consumption. It was the primary energy source from 1900 until 1960, when it was overtaken by oil (WHO, 1997). Coal can be produced through surface (open cast) mining or underground mining. Like mining in general, both operations are inherently dangerous to the health of the workers. About 1 percent of the global workforce is engaged in mining, but these workers account for 8 percent of the 15,000 fatal occupational accidents each year. Armstrong and Menon (1998) offer a detailed review of occupational health and safety issues in coal mining and other mining.

Underground coal miners are exposed to the hazards of excavating and transporting materials underground. These hazards include injuries from falling rocks and falls into mine shafts, as well as injuries from machinery used in the mine. There are no reliable data on injuries of this type from developing countries (Jennings, 1998), but in industrialised countries miners have some of the highest rates of compensation for injuries—and the situation is likely to be worse in developing countries. In addition, much of the excavation involves drilling into silica-based rock, creating high levels of silica dust inside the mine. Pneumoconiosis silicosis is therefore a common health effect in coal miners (Jennings, 1998).

> Pollution from household stoves is released right at the times and places where people are present— that is, in every household every day.

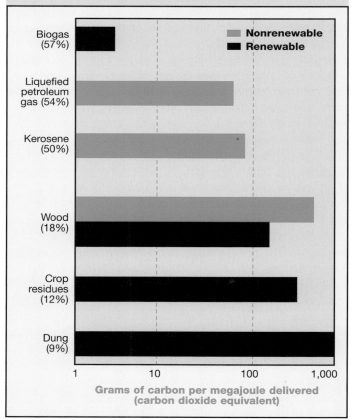

FIGURE 3.4. GREENHOUSE GAS EMISSIONS FROM HOUSEHOLD FUELS

Grams of carbon per megajoule delivered (carbon dioxide equivalent)

Note: Includes warming from all greenhouse gases emitted: carbon dioxide, methane, carbon monoxide, non-methane hydrocarbons, and nitrous oxide. Weighted by stove distribution in India. Numbers in parentheses are average stove energy efficiency. *Source: Smith and others, 2000 b.*

Other health hazards specific to underground coal mining include coal dust, which can cause 'coal worker's pneumoconiosis' or anthracosis, often combined with silicosis. Coal dust is explosive, and explosions in underground coal mines are a constant danger for coal miners. Coal inherently burns, and fires in coal mines are not uncommon. Once such a fire has started, it may be almost impossible to extinguish. Apart from the danger of burns, the production of smoke and toxic fumes create great health risks for the miners.

Even without fires, the coal material produces toxic gases when it is disturbed: carbon monoxide, carbon dioxide, and methane (Weeks, 1998). Carbon monoxide is extremely toxic because it binds to haemoglobin in the blood, blocking oxygen transport and creating chemical suffocation (Bascom and others, 1996). Carbon monoxide is a colourless and odourless gas and so gives no warning before the symptoms of drowsiness, dizziness, headache, and unconsciousness occur. Carbon dioxide, also colourless and odourless, displaces oxygen in underground air and can also cause suffocation. Another health hazard in mining is exhaust from the diesel engines used in underground machinery and transport vehicles. This exhaust contains very fine particles, nitrogen oxides, and carbon monoxide, all of which pose serious health hazards (Bascom and others, 1996). Exposure to fine particles in diesel exhaust increases the risk of lung cancer (Holgate and others, 1999).

Surface coal mining avoids some of the hazards of working underground. Still, it involves the risk of injuries from machinery, falls, and falling rocks. In addition, coal mining is energy-intensive work, and heat, humidity, and other weather factors can affect workers' health. The machinery used is also noisy, and hearing loss is a common among miners. Another health hazard is the often squalid conditions under which many coal workers and their families in developing countries live, creating particular risk for the diseases of poverty. In addition, such workers are likely to receive part of their compensation in the form of coal for use as household fuel, with consequent indoor and neighbourhood pollution.

After extraction, coal needs to be processed and transported to residential areas, power stations, and industries. This creates other types of occupational hazards (Armstrong and Menon, 1998). For instance, coal for residential use is often ground and formed into briquettes. This work involves high levels of coal dust as well as noise hazards. Loading, transportation, and off-loading of large amounts of coal involves ergonomic, noise, and injury hazards.

The large-scale use of coal in power stations and industry creates yet more hazards. One is the conversion of coal to coke in steel production. This process distils a large number of volatile polycyclic aromatic hydrocarbons in coal, the so-called coal tar pitch volatiles (Moffit, 1998). Exposure to these hydrocarbons puts coke oven workers at twice the lung cancer risk of the general population (IARC, 1984). (This process is not entirely associated with energy supply, as an important aim is to provide carbon to reduce iron oxides

Solid biomass fuels, even though renewable, can have a larger greenhouse gas commitment per meal than fossil fuels, kerosene, and liquefied petroleum gas.

to elemental iron.) Additional health hazards are created for workers when the large amounts of ash produced by power stations and industry need to be transported and deposited. Crane (1998) reviews the health hazards faced by power generation workers.

Oil and gas

Oil and gas exploration, drilling, extraction, processing, and transport involve a number of the same hazards as mining: heavy workload, ergonomic hazards, injury risk noise, vibration, and chemical exposures (Kraus, 1998). This work is often carried out in isolated areas with inclement weather conditions. Long-distance commuting may also be involved, causing fatigue, stress, and traffic accident risks.

The ergonomic hazards lead to risks of back pain and joint pain. Injury hazards include burns and explosions. Skin damage from exposure to oil and to chemicals used in drilling creates a need for well-designed protective clothing. In addition, many oil and gas installations have used asbestos to insulate pipes and equipment. Inhalation of asbestos dust in the installation and repair of such equipment creates a risk of lung cancer, asbestosis, and mesothelioma (WHO, 1998a).

A lot of exploration and drilling for oil and gas occur offshore. This involves underwater diving, which is dangerous. In addition, weather-related exposures can be extreme, particularly since the work often requires round-the-clock operations (Kraus, 1998).

Hydropower and other renewables

Major hazards occur when a hydroelectric power station is built, because this usually requires constructing a large dam, excavating underground water channels, and building large structures to house the generator. McManus (1998) lists 28 occupational hazards potentially involved in the construction and operation of hydroelectric power stations. These include asbestos exposure, diesel and welding fumes, work in confined spaces or awkward positions, drowning, electrocution, noise, heat, electromagnetic fields, vibration, weather-related problems, and chemical exposures from paints, oils, and PCBs (polychlorinated biphenyls). As in any industry, however, proper attention to health and safety can keep the risks to acceptable levels.

The manufacture of wind and solar power equipment involves the typical hazards in manufacturing: injuries, noise, chemical exposures, and so on. In addition, the technologies for solar electricity generation involve new chemical compounds, some based on rare metals with poorly known toxic properties (Crane, 1998).

Nuclear danger

Nuclear power generation has its own hazards due to the radiation danger involved in mining, processing, and transporting uranium, as well as the radiation in nuclear power stations. In addition, occupational hazards will develop as countries start to deal with the backlog of radioactive waste. Due to the major potential risk to the general public from a malfunctioning nuclear power station, the safety of stations is always paramount. This has contributed to a low average occupational health risk for workers in the stations (Morison, 1998).

The mining of uranium has been an important occupational health hazard in nuclear power generation, as underground mining for uranium often entails high exposure to radon, a radioactive gas emitted from uranium. Radon exposure leads to an increased risk of lung cancer. In addition, the same occupational hazards in mining noted above occur, although the relatively high energy content of uranium ore means that there are fewer health effects per unit of electricity produced.

Until the Chernobyl accident, relatively few nuclear power station workers had been affected by radiation exposure. In that accident, however, 40 workers lost their lives in the fire or due to acute radiation exposure. The long-term impact on workers exposed during the accident in the form of cancer and other radiation-related effects is not yet known, however. The clean-up after the accident may eventually create substantially more effects. As many as 900,000 army, police, and other workers were called on to take part. Many workers were needed because they were only allowed to work for a short time, until they had reached the maximum allowable radiation dose. In some cases this dose was reached in a few minutes. Studies are now being undertaken to establish the exposure of each clean-up worker and the long-term health impacts (WHO, 1996).

Number of workers and quantitative health effects estimates

It is difficult to estimate the number of workers involved in meeting the energy requirements of communities. As noted, in poor communities much of this work is carried out by family members, particularly women, who are not formally employed. In addition, much of this work is carried out by small industries that are not always recorded in national employment statistics.

As noted, an estimated 16 million people are involved in forestry, most of them in developing countries. In industrialised countries with reliable statistics, the occupational mortality rate for agricultural workers is 5–10 times the average for all workers (Kjellstrom, 1994). Because of the additional risks in forestry, mortality rates for these workers are possibly twice as high again, or 32,000–160,000 at a global level. Not all of this activity is directly related to fuel demand, however.

As noted, miners are a large occupational group in international statistics (UN Demographic Yearbooks). They represent up to 2 percent of the economically active population in certain developing countries. Mining is an extremely dangerous occupation. Recent data show that occupational mortality rates for miners are up to 20 times the average for all occupations (ILO, 1998). The range of mortality rates may be as wide as that for forestry (2–10 per 1,000 workers per year). In most countries the economically active population is 40–60 percent of the population over 15. Thus miners may account for 1 percent of the population over 15, or about 30 million people world-wide. If half of these miners are coal miners, the number of miners killed each year in accidents would be about the same as for forestry workers (30,000–150,000). Another approach to this calculation is through total coal production. If applied to the world's coal production today, about 70 percent of which is in developing countries, the mean death rate in U.S. mines from 1890–1939 of 3.1 deaths per million tons produced would predict 16,000 coal mining deaths a year world-wide (ORNL and RFF, 1994a). This may be low, however, because China alone has about 6,500 coal mining deaths a year according to official statistics, which tend to be incomplete (Horii, 1999). The estimate of 6,500 of 16,000 deaths, on the other hand, is roughly consistent with China's 30 percent share of global production (BP, 1998).

For energy production and distribution as a whole, occupational mortality may sum to 70,000–350,000 a year. These numbers are likely to exclude many cases of occupational disease (such as cancers caused by asbestos or radiation) and deaths among the many workers in informal workplaces. The upper limit of the numbers, however, may also be inflated by the crude estimates of mortality rates and number of workers. Occupational mortality rates in energy jobs in industrialised countries are generally 10–30 times lower than in developing countries (Kjellstrom, 1994; ILO, 1998), indicating that more effective prevention programs could eliminate more than 90 percent of the deaths referred to above. Still, energy-related jobs have inherent health risks that need to be considered when assessing the full impact of energy production and distribution.

Although too often ignored in discussions of environmental health risks, the burden of occupational disease and injury is substantial on a global scale. It is conservatively estimated that with well over 1 million deaths a year, nearly 3 percent of the global burden of ill health is directly attributable to occupational conditions (Leigh and others, 1996). This is substantial, accounting for more than motor vehicles, malaria, or HIV and about equal to tuberculosis or stroke. Although the fraction due directly to supplying energy is unclear, energy systems employ many millions of people world-wide in jobs substantially riskier than average—particularly in jobs producing solid fuels.

Community scale

Energy systems are associated with a vast array of insults and impacts (see table 3.1). Many of these are expressed at the community scale, including problems associated with coal and uranium mining, petroleum and gas extraction, water use and contamination by power plants, thermal pollution, and noise from wind farms. Here we can only focus on the largest of these impacts world-wide.

Urban air pollution is the chief environmental impact of energy systems at the community level. Although there are industrial and other sources of some pollutants, the vast bulk—whether measured by mass or by hazard—is generated by fuel combustion or, as in the case of photochemical smog, is created in the urban atmosphere by precursor chemicals largely released in the course of fuel use. From the 1930s to the 1950s a number of urban air pollution episodes in the industrialised world brought air pollution to the attention of the public. The first major improvements came by banning the burning of refuse and coal within city limits. By the early 1970s the infamous London smogs (and their parallels in other cities), caused by coal combustion, were memories. Two other community-level impacts are also discussed in this section: those due to large hydroelectric dams and to nuclear power.

Fuel-derived air pollution in cities of industrialised countries

During the past 25 years the cities of the industrialised world have generally brought energy-derived urban air pollutants under even greater control. In the United States, for example, emissions per unit of useful energy from power plants and automobiles—the two largest urban energy polluters—have fallen 65 percent and 50 percent in health hazard (weighted by the relative standards for each pollutant).[4] Japan and Western Europe have achieved similar results.

In the power sector these achievements have mostly come about by relying more on nuclear power and natural gas and by requiring smokestack controls for particles and nitrogen and sulphur oxides at coal-fired power plants. In addition, thermal power plants have become more efficient, and more improvements are expected, particularly for those using gas (see chapter 8). For vehicles, the reductions have come from a mix of improvements in engine combustion, increases in fuel efficiency (in North America), and the nearly universal requirement of catalytic converters (devices to help control pollutant emissions). Thus, despite significant increases in power production and vehicle use since 1975, overall emissions of most pollutants are now lower.

As a result of these emission reductions, urban air quality has generally improved throughout the industrialised world. Although fuel combustion produces a number of health-damaging pollutants, as explained above, small particles are probably the best single indicator. Suspended small particles are a mix of primary combustion particles—carbonaceous materials and associated trace elements—and secondary conversion products such as sulphate and nitrate aerosols. In many parts of the world, windblown and urban dust can also be significant contributors to suspended particles.

Small particles are deposited deep in the lungs, where their clearance is slow and their ability to cause damage is enhanced. Small particles also carry adsorbed trace metals and carcinogenic hydrocarbons into the lungs, intensifying the potential for health damage. Assessments of the human health effects of air pollutants increasingly focus on these small particles. Still, there are few measurements of these particles in most cities, although more cities are measuring PM_{10} (particles less than 10 microns), which is considered a better indicator than simple total particulate levels

(National Research Council, 1998).[5]

In the late 1990s the mean annual cocentration of PM_{10} in North American, Western European, and Japanese cities ranged from 30–45 micrograms per cubic metre (figure 3.5). (The U.S. standard is 50 micrograms per cubic metre.) In the 1960s particulate levels were probably two to four times higher. (Small particles were not measured routinely until the mid-1980s, so previous levels have to be inferred from measurements of total particles.)

Still, industrialised countries face a number of energy-related air pollution challenges. Nitrogen dioxide and ozone levels exceed standards in many cities, particularly in sunny cities with large auto fleets such as Los Angeles (California) and Athens (Greece). The recent evidence suggesting that small particles (less than 2.5 micrograms) may be even better indicators of ill health than PM_{10} has led the United States to propose new regulations aimed at $PM_{2.5}$, potentially putting a number of cities out of compliance. European countries are also considering such regulations. Since long-term data are not widely available, it is not clear how much $PM_{2.5}$ levels have decreased in recent decades, partly because such particles are transported over much larger areas than larger particles.

This focus on even smaller particles has brought diesel exhaust particles under more scrutiny. Unlike gasoline, diesel produces a significant amount of emissions of particles that are not only smaller but may have chemical properties that make them more dangerous. This feature raises questions about the future of diesel-fuelled vehicles, even though such vehicles can be slightly more fuel-efficient and cost-effective than gasoline-fuelled vehicles. The tendency for many countries to keep diesel prices low relative to gasoline—as a means of assisting farming, fishing, and other industries—can artificially promote diesel passenger vehicles. (See the section on cross-scale impacts, below, for a discussion of the economic implications of diesel particle health effects.)

Since the 1980s studies have seemed to indicate that there is no threshold for the health effects of particle pollution. In other words, there no longer seems to be an identifiable level that can be termed safe. All that can be said is that the effect is lower at lower levels, but does not seem to disappear even at the lowest (background) concentrations. Indeed, in the late 1990s European and global offices of the World Health Organization revised their particle guidelines to reflect the absence of thresholds (figure 3.6).

Because it is rarely (if ever) practical to set a standard of zero for pollutants with significant natural sources, standard setting is much harder for pollutants with no threshold for significant effects. Policy-makers must determine that the benefits of fuel combustion outweigh the extra mortality produced by the resulting pollution— for example, that the 5 percent increase in mortality 'allowed' by a PM_{10} standard of 50 micrograms per cubic metre above background (see figure 3.6) is acceptable given the societal advantages of fuel use. This is a difficult determination, and much more politically

About 1 percent of the global workforce is engaged in mining, but these workers account for 8 percent of the 15,000 fatal occupational accidents each year.

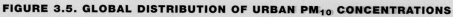

FIGURE 3.5. GLOBAL DISTRIBUTION OF URBAN PM$_{10}$ CONCENTRATIONS

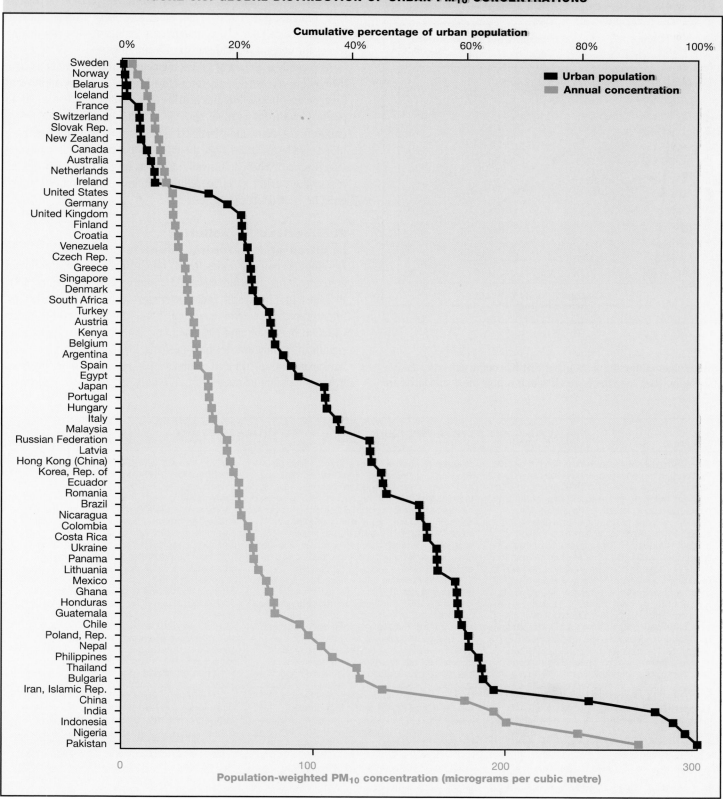

Note: In many cases, PM$_{10}$ levels have been entirely estimated from measurements of total particles.

Source: WRI, 1998; WHO, 1998b.

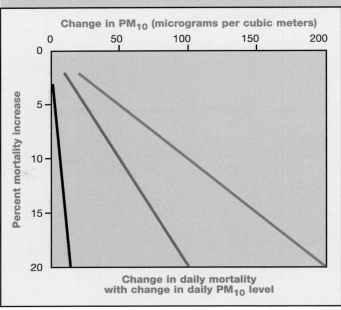

FIGURE 3.6. PROVISIONAL GLOBAL AIR QUALITY GUIDELINES FOR PARTICLES

Change in PM$_{10}$ (micrograms per cubic meters)

Percent mortality increase

Change in daily mortality with change in daily PM$_{10}$ level

Source: WHO, 1999.

difficult than endorsing a standard that has some scientific validity of being below a 'no effects' level, which is how most standards are set. The likely result will be continuous pressure to tighten particle standards, with stronger incentives for lower particle emissions from vehicles, power plants, and other fuel-using sources. Indeed, as discussed in later chapters, emission reductions are the driving forces for new power and transport technologies.

As recently as the early 1990s, the main source of lead emissions throughout the world was tetra-ethyl-lead used as an additive to raise octane in gasoline. But nearly every country now has a plan to remove lead from gasoline (box 3.4). Still, significant numbers of children in many industrialised and developing countries have blood lead levels above those thought to affect cognitive development (intelligence). These levels will decline as lead is removed from the rest of the world's gasoline, although industrial and other sources must be controlled as well.

Fuel-derived air pollution in cities of developing countries

Developing country cities have much higher mean pollutant concentrations than industrialised country cities (see figure 3.5). In cities in China and India, averages seem to be nearly 200 micrograms per cubic metre of PM$_{10}$, though there is much variation by season and city. Such concentrations must be causing significant premature deaths—perhaps 15 percent or more above background levels. Indeed, estimates for premature mortality from urban air pollution range from 170,000–290,000 a year in China

---

BOX 3.4. GETTING THE LEAD OUT: A SLOW SUCCESS STORY

"The current consensus is that no amount of Pb [lead] in the environment can be considered safe" (Schwela and Zali, 1999). Although this was not the first reason to remove lead from gasoline, it soon became the driving force. The introduction of catalytic converters spawned the need for unleaded gasoline to protect the devices. Shortly after, concerns about the health effects of lead emissions led to an increase in sales of unleaded gas and a reduction in the lead content of leaded fuel. Since leaded gasoline has been responsible for about 90 percent of lead emissions, it was the most logical target for reduction (Lovei, 1998).

Many nations have taken action to phase out lead from fuel. Canada, Japan, and the United States have completely phased out leaded gasoline (Lovei, 1998; Schwela and Zali, 1999). Los Angeles (California) saw a 98 percent reduction in the lead exposure of commuters between 1979 and 1989. In Western Europe leaded gasoline has a very low lead content, and unleaded fuel has a large market share in most countries. In addition, a few developing nations have lowered or even banned lead in gasoline (Lovei, 1998).

Over the past 20 years Singapore has taken significant steps to phase out lead in fuel. Between 1980 and 1987 the lead content of leaded gasoline fell to a low 0.15 grams a litre. In 1991 unleaded petrol was introduced and taxes were changed to make it cheaper than leaded fuel. By the end of 1997 unleaded fuel accounted for about 75 percent of gasoline sales. In addition, more stringent exhaust emission standards were implemented for gasoline-fuelled vehicles, promoting an unleaded fuel market. Finally, oil companies agreed to phase out leaded gasoline by July 1998.

Mexico has also taken steps to reduce the lead content of fuel, though it still has far to go. Since 1994 the lead content of leaded fuel has been cut to 0.15 grams a litre. But it appears that the Mexican National Petroleum Co. has recently raised lead levels. No government agency has the authority to ensure fuel quality, making enforcement of low lead levels a challenge. Unleaded gasoline accounts for 46 percent of sales in Mexico City and 84 percent in Monterrey (which is wealthier and closer to the U.S. border). Leaded fuel is still cheaper, however. Mexico is implementing new standards requiring catalytic converters and so unleaded gas.

But large problems remain in many developing countries. The biggest lead problems are in Africa and in petroleum-exporting nations. These countries, including Venezuela and those in the Middle East, are dominated by powerful oil companies and state-owned refineries.

Although in 1994 two-thirds of global gasoline sales were unleaded, additional efforts are needed. Several mechanisms can encourage the reduction of lead in gasoline. The most promising is to set fuel taxes so that unleaded gasoline is cheaper than leaded fuel. Fuel filler inlets should be required in automobiles to allow only the narrower nozzles of unleaded fuel pumps to be used. Requiring catalytic converters in vehicles would further decrease the use of leaded fuel. Emphasising other benefits of using unleaded gasoline, such as lower exhaust emissions of hydrocarbons, also promotes the reduction of lead in gasoline (Schwela and Zali, 1999). Finally, as shown in Brazil, it is possible to substitute 5–10 percent ethanol for lead as an octane booster, thereby promoting renewable fuels.

An enduring urban myth exists that some older cars need lead to operate well. As long as the fuel has the correct octane level, no engine needs lead. Indeed, in many cases the removal of lead will have direct benefits in the form of less engine maintenance. The persistence of this myth slows the introduction of low-lead fuels despite technical evidence to the contrary.

(World Bank, 1997; Florig, 1997) and 90,000–200,000 in India (Murray and Lopez, 1996; Saksena and Dayal, 1997).

The causes of air pollution in developing country cities are much more varied than in industrialised countries. Although automobile ownership rates are much lower, there tend to be many other types of vehicles as well, including two- and three-wheelers using highly polluting two-stoke engines. There also tend to be larger portions of light-duty and heavy-duty vehicles using diesel rather than gasoline. In addition to power plants and large industries with limited pollution controls, developing country cities tend to have large numbers of small boilers, engines, and open fires in the commercial and light-industry sectors, as well as in informal sectors such as street food. These enterprises tend to rely on the most inexpensive and thus dirty fuels in inefficient applications without pollution controls—and so have high emissions per unit of useful energy.

Furthermore, such cities often do not have adequate refuse and garbage collection, leading to street-side trash burning, a highly polluting activity. Even when collected, trash often burns uncontrollably in landfills in or near cities, wasting potential energy and producing clouds of noxious emissions. Another major non-energy source of particle pollution in many cities is dust from construction sites and unmanaged empty land. Finally, unlike in industrialised countries, a large fraction of urban households in developing countries still use solid fuels for cooking and space heating in inefficient stoves with no pollution controls (see figure 3.1). Although individually small, their large number means that these stoves can contribute significantly to urban pollution.

In addition to dealing with trash, dust, and other non-energy issues, the most pressing need for pollution control in developing country cities is to reduce and eventually eliminate small- and medium-scale combustion of dirty fuels. For stationary sources, this means shifting away from solid fuels (coal and biomass) and high-sulphur fuels of any kind. For mobile sources, it means dealing soon with, in order of priority, two-stroke engines, poorly operating diesel engines, and gasoline-fuelled vehicles without catalytic converters. In addition, as is happening in Bangkok (Thailand) and New Delhi (India), there is great advantage in shifting vehicle fleets (taxis, buses, government vehicles) to clean-burning gaseous fuels such as compressed natural gas or liquefied petroleum gas (Mage and Zali, 1992).

Urban pollution control in the longer run

Because the best commercial technology in terms of energy efficiency and emissions has not been deployed completely in industrialised countries and has been used little in developing countries, much improvement is possible in the next 20 years without switching to advanced technologies. In the longer term, however, if air pollution levels are to be brought down to and kept at low levels given the projected increase in population, urbanisation, economic activity, and energy use, it will be necessary to develop and deploy new, even cleaner and more efficient energy-using technologies. A number of advanced power plant technologies potentially offer such performance (see chapter 8).

In addition, some near-commercial vehicle technologies may allow vehicle densities in developing country cities to grow for several decades and still meet air quality goals (box 3.5). Strong pollution controls will be needed to bring these technologies into wide use, however.

In addition to technical changes in vehicles of all types (not just private cars), a range of other improvements will be needed if the world's cities are to accommodate the greater demand for transport that increases in population and income will bring. These include improvements that result in significant and sustained enhancement in the attractiveness of public transport, land-use planning to reduce the need for intraurban trips, and implementation of policy tools such as time-of-day, congestion, and central-zone pricing. In addition, significant switches to public transport might occur through such means as including the cost of vehicle insurance in the price of fuel and taxing employer-provided parking as income (see chapter 11).

Hydroelectric dams[6]

Dams, large and small, have brought tremendous benefits to many regions, including important contributions to development in industrialised countries. It is important not to deny these benefits to developing countries. But such dams need to be designed and constructed with care. Although dams frequently serve many purposes—including flood control, irrigation, navigation, and recreation—major dams (those over 150 metres high, with 25 cubic kilometres of storage, or 1,000 megawatts of electricity) tend to have hydropower as one of the their main objectives. Such dams often have big impacts on the environment. There are more than 300 major dams world-wide, and nearly all have hydropower as a major component of their function. The environmental impact per unit of electricity production, however, can often be smaller for large than for small dams. The type rather than the size can be the most important factor (Gleick, 1992).

With a total capacity of about 640,000 megawatts of electricity, hydropower provides about one-fifth of the world's electricity (Gleick, 1992). In Central and South America hydropower provides about 60 percent of electricity; in Asia this figure is about 15 percent. Itaipu, on the border of Brazil and Paraguay, is the most powerful hydropower dam built to date, with a capacity of 12,600 megawatts of electricity. It cost $20 billion to build. When finished, China's Three Gorges Dam will produce about 18,200 megawatts of electricity and may cost as much as $75 billion (*The Economist*, 1999). Thus hydroelectric dams are the most expensive energy projects in the world.

Dams affect Earth at scales rivalling other major human activities, such as urbanisation and road building.

No major river in the world is without existing or planned hydro-electric dams. Nearly four-fifths of the discharge of the largest rivers in Canada, Europe, the former Soviet Union, and the United States are strongly or moderately affected by flow regulation, diversions, and the fragmentation of river channels by dams (Dynesius and Nilsson, 1994). More than 500,000 square kilometres—the area of Spain—have been inundated by dam reservoirs world-wide, though not all for hydropower (Collier, Webb, and Schmidt, 1996). (Indeed, many hydropower plants have no reservoirs.) Globally, about 200 cubic kilometres of water a year—about 7 percent of the freshwater consumed by human activities—are evaporated from the surface of reservoirs due to their increased exposed surface area (Shiklomanov, 1998). Thus dams affect Earth at scales rivalling other major human activities, such as urbanisation and road building.

Direct human impacts. During the 20th century 30–60 million people were flooded off their lands by dams (Dunn, 1998). The World Bank, using Chinese government figures, estimates that 10.2 million people were displaced by reservoirs in China between 1950 and 1989 (World Bank, 1993). Given that a number of major dams are under construction or planned in developing countries, there will be no slackening in the pace of population displacement. China's Three Gorges Dam, for example, is expected to displace more than 1 million people, and the proposed Pa Mong Dam between Lao PDR and Thailand is expected to displace more than 500,000 (Gleick, 1998).

Large population resettlements can have a number of direct

BOX 3.5. ALTERNATIVE VEHICLES

With growing energy and environmental concerns surrounding today's conventional vehicles, a great deal of research is going into alternative vehicles. Four main types of alternative vehicles have the potential to reduce the environmental and efficiency deficits of conventional vehicles and to become commercially available in the near future.

Electric vehicles are powered by rechargeable batteries and have no internal combustion engines. The battery, which can be made of lead-acid, nickel-metal hydride, and lithium-polymer, can be recharged at home or, in the future, at recharging stations. Electric vehicles have several environmental benefits relative to conventional vehicles, including no tailpipe emissions and lower hydrocarbon, carbon monoxide, and nitrogen oxide emissions (including emissions from the production of electricity). Other advantages include lower maintenance costs and the elimination of the need for complicated tailpipe emission controls.

But electric vehicles also have several disadvantages, such as the environmental concerns of an increase in electricity use, increasing emissions of sulphur oxides, and possible contamination from the disposal and recycling of batteries. There are also disadvantages in terms of convenience and cost, such as lengthy recharging and lack of infrastructure for recharging stations, short driving ranges (though electric vehicles are good for local trips and commuting for two-car households), an inability to maintain high speeds, and high battery costs. Today electric vehicles cost about $30,000, which is too expensive for most markets.

Hybrid electric vehicles combine the battery and electric motor of an electric vehicle with the internal combustion engine and fuel tank of a conventional vehicle, to obtain the benefits from both technologies. The engine, which is much smaller than that in a conventional vehicle, operates at a constant power load and so is

more efficient, and less polluting, and generates only the power required for most operations. Hybrid electric vehicles have several advantages over conventional vehicles and fewer disadvantages than electric vehicles. Hybrid electric vehicles have higher fuel economy and lower emissions than vehicles with internal combustion engines, and better range and more rapid refuelling than electric vehicles. Hybrid electric vehicles also reduce petroleum consumption and increase energy diversity by using alternative engines, which can use a range of fuels. But hybrid electric vehicles are still expensive and not yet fully developed. Programs are in place to develop and improve hybrid electric vehicles, and several automobile manufacturers are or will soon be marketing models.

Compressed natural gas vehicles are powered by an abundant, inexpensive fuel composed largely of methane. Natural gas is a clean-burning fuel with lower carbon dioxide, carbon monoxide, hydrocarbon, and nitrous oxide emissions than gasoline. This is partly due to the lower carbon content per unit of energy in natural gas relative to other fossil fuels. In addition to its environmental benefits, natural gas vehicles are cheaper to maintain, requiring service less frequently than conventional vehicles as well as having a lower cost of refuelling. Converting vehicle fleets such as taxis, three-wheelers, and buses to natural gas is an important interim way to improve air quality in developing country cities. Conversion costs are relatively small, although baggage space is reduced because of the need to add pressurised tanks. It is hard to use compressed natural gas for private vehicles because of the need to create many fuelling stations. Urban vehicle fleets, on the other hand, can operate with relatively few centralised fuelling stations.

Fuel-cell vehicles operate by combining hydrogen and oxygen gases into an electrochemical device, a cell, that converts them

into water and electricity without using combustion. The hydrogen gas can come from a number of sources, including multiple forms of pure hydrogen and a variety of hydrocarbon fuels. Fuel-cell vehicles have many advantages over conventional vehicles. Fuel cells have a much greater engine efficiency and fuel economy, drastically reduce pollution emissions (including greenhouse gas emissions), and can use a wide variety of fuels, promoting energy diversity.

In addition, they are quieter and smoother in operation, have tested at high performance levels, have long driving ranges, and have about the same operating costs as conventional automobiles. Still, there are several drawbacks to fuel-cell vehicles, including the lack of infrastructure to distribute hydrogen or another fuel (unless gasoline is used), difficult storage of pure hydrogen, and possible safety concerns. Major automobile companies are planning to have commercially available fuel-cell vehicles by 2004 and are currently demonstrating prototypes and improving on them. Large cost reductions need to occur, however, and fuel infrastructure issues must be resolved before fuel-cell vehicles are ready for the marketplace.

Of these four alternatives to conventional vehicles, electric vehicles have the fewest barriers to market entry. But they probably have the least consumer appeal in terms of environmental improvements and convenience. Fuel-cell vehicles will probably be found to be the most environmentally friendly, but they are the furthest from commercial development. Hybrid electric vehicles also offer a good option in the near future, with convenience and environmental benefits. All these cars will likely begin to enter the market in the next 5–10 years, and infrastructure will have to be built to accommodate all of them as well as today's automobiles.

Source: American Honda Motor Company, 1999; California Energy Commission, 1998; California Environmental Protection Agency, 1999; Ford Motor Company, 1998, 2000; General Motors Corporation, 1999; Global Toyota, 1999; Gould and Golob, 1997; Hanisch, 1999; Krebs, 1999; Kremer, 2000; Mark, Ohi, and Hudson, 1994; Matsumoto, Inaba, and Yanagisawa, 1997; Mendler, 1997; National Fuel Cell Research Center, 1999; Natural Gas Vehicle Coalition. 2000a, b; Neil, 1999; Steinbugler and Williams, 1998; USDOE, 1995; USEPA, 1994, 1998b.

TABLE 3.2. ECOLOGICAL INSULTS AND IMPACTS OF LARGE DAMS

Insult caused by dam	Impacts seen	Severity of impact	Example of impact
Changes in the chemical properties of release water	Deterioration of downstream ecosystem cased by inability to process the increased dissolved minerals	Depends on the sensitivity of the affected ecosystem (tropical ecosystems are especially sensitive)	Enhanced algae growth in the reservoir consumes the oxygen in the epilimnion and, as it decays, the mass sinks to the already oxygen-deficient hypolimnion, where decay processes reduce the oxygen concentration even further, resulting in acid conditions at lower levels and the dissolution of minerals from the reservoir bed.
Changes in the thermal properties of release water	Thermal pollution often results in species diversity reduction, species extinction, and productivity changes in the reservoir	Diversity, biomass, distribution, and density of fish stocks can be affected, disrupting breeding cycles	Productivity levels in the surface waters of new reservoirs often increase before long-term declines occur (Horne, 1994). China's Three Gorges Dam may be the final critical factor for driving to extinction the Yangtze River dolphin.
Changes in the flow rate and timing of release water	Erosion increases downstream of dam. Settling of sediments in the reservoir causes high sediment loads to be picked up in the area immediately below the dam	Erosion of natural riverbeds can disturb the nurseries and spawning of many aquatic organisms, disturbing their breeding cycles	Changes in the downstream river morphology and ecosystem productivity.
Changes in the sediment load of the river	High trap efficiencies of dams prevent the natural processes of sediments and associated nutrients refreshing downstream soils	Effects often noticed most severely in high-productivity areas downstream from the dam that no longer receive annual fertilisation	Before the Aswan High Dam was constructed, the Nile carried about 124 million tonnes of sediment to the sea each year, depositing nearly 10 million tonnes on the floodplain and the delta. Today 98 percent of the sediment remains behind the dam, resulting in a drop in soil productivity and depth, among other serious changes to Egypt's floodplain agriculture (Pottinger, 1997).
Changes in the dynamics of downstream riverbeds	Increased likelihood of lower water tables, which can create problems in areas near the dam where groundwater is a major source	Reduced access to potable water is a huge problem in many developing countries	Within nine years of the closure opening of the Hoover Dam, 110 million cubic metres of material had been washed away from the first 145 kilometres of riverbed below the dam (McCully, 1996).
Changes in the coastal area morphology	The loss of sediment in the rivers flowing through deltas and into the sea often results in a gradual process of delta and coastal degradation	Financially expensive for many areas where there is a large population living near the coastal zone.	Over the past 80 years dams have reduced by four-fifths the sediment reaching the coasts of southern California. This has reduced the beach cover at the base of cliffs along these shorelines, causing cliffs to collapse (Jenkins and others, 1988).

social and health impacts. The social and cultural stress, loss of income, disruption of traditional support services, and other problems facing displaced populations often lead to lowered health status. Even when efforts are made to resettle people in new areas, it is difficult to locate land of similar productivity because other groups are likely to already occupy the best areas. Some 13,500 people have been swept to their deaths by the 200 or so dams (outside China) that have collapsed or been overtopped in the 20th century. In 1975 in Henan, China, about 230,000 people died from a series of dam bursts (Gleick, 1998).

Disease can spread from vectors that thrive in secondary dam systems, such as irrigation canals and even dam reservoirs. Mosquitoes carrying malaria, for example, have thrived in conditions created by dams. The parasitic disease schistosomiasis has also become more prevalent through the creation of habitats for snails that act as the disease vector. Nearby populations, for example, suffered nearly universal infection after several large African dams were filled, including Aswan (Egypt), Akosombo (Ghana), and Sennar (Sudan) (Nash, 1993).

Ecosystem impacts. An internal survey of World Bank hydroelectric dam projects found that 58 percent were planned and built without any consideration of downstream impacts—even when these impacts could be predicted to cause coastal erosion, pollution, and other problems (Dixon, 1989). The main ecological insults and impacts of large dams (not just those producing hydropower) are summarised in table 3.2.

Dams and greenhouse gases. The work assessing the impacts of dams on greenhouse gas emissions is incomplete, but some estimates have been made. The most immediate changes are in the carbon flow between the flooded vegetation and the atmosphere. The decomposition of plants and soils causes the gradual release of their stored carbon (Rudd and others, 1993).

From a greenhouse gas standpoint, it might be thought that vegetation decaying in a reservoir would be no worse than the same amount of deforestation. Because of the low-oxygen conditions near and in the bottoms of many reservoirs, however, relative to deforestation a larger fraction of the biomass carbon is likely to be released as methane rather than as carbon dioxide. Since methane is a much more powerful greenhouse gas than carbon dioxide, the global warming impacts are greater than the same amount of carbon released as carbon dioxide.

The peak greenhouse gas emissions, however, are unlikely to rival those of a similarly sized fossil power plant, emissions from which would not decrease with age like those from a reservoir. In addition, it is difficult to determine the baseline in tropical forests—that is, how much methane and other non-carbon dioxide greenhouse gases are released in natural conditions. In colder climates reservoirs apparently emit greenhouse gases at much lower rates (Gagnon, 1998).

Nuclear power

There are two main environmental concerns about nuclear power, both mostly with regard to its potential impacts on human health. One involves the highly radioactive products produced by nuclear fission inside power reactors. Such products require careful management at the reactor and during and after disposal. The other concern revolves around the weapons-grade plutonium or uranium that might be clandestinely derived from the nuclear power fuel cycle to make bombs or other weapons of mass destruction by nations or subnational groups (see chapter 8).

The routine (non-accidental) emissions of pollutants from the harvesting, processing, and conversion of nuclear fuels are not negligible. And more than many technologies, they are vulnerable to being enhanced by mismanagement. Still, the impacts of these emissions are generally substantially less than those involved with producing power with current coal technologies, the chief competitor in many areas. Although involving different pollutants, routine emissions from nuclear power systems are probably no more dangerous than those from new natural gas power systems—with the important exception of carbon dioxide, which is not produced by nuclear power. If public concerns about reactor safety, proliferation, and waste disposal can be satisfied, nuclear power may be able to play a significant role in de-carbonising the world energy system in the next 50 years (see chapter 8).

Regional scale

Nested between local-scale issues—such as the health effects of urban pollution—and global-scale issues—such as climate change—are a number of regional-scale problems that affect human health and ecosystems over areas the size of countries and continents. The most important regional-scale issues are acid deposition, tropospheric ozone, and suspended fine particles.

Matched with the regional spatial scale is a temporal scale that requires air pollutants to remain aloft for periods ranging from days to weeks and thereby be transported by prevailing winds and transformed by chemical reactions. Gases and fine particles meet this criterion; larger particles (greater than 1 micron or so in diameter) tend to settle out quickly and are considered contributors to local, rather than regional, impacts. Fine particles may be solid (such as elemental 'black' carbon) or liquid (such as aerosol droplets).

Contributing to regional pollution are a number of precursor species, most of which are generated by the use of fossil fuels and biofuels. Prominent among them are sulphur dioxide (SO_2) and nitrogen oxides (NO_x). Sulphur dioxide is released during the combustion of the sulphur found naturally in fossil fuels, while nitrogen oxides originate either as fuel nitrogen or as atmospheric nitrogen oxidised during combustion. Other species of importance are particulate matter (PM), carbon monoxide (CO), methane (CH_4), and

TABLE 3.3. ANTHROPOGENIC EMISSIONS OF IMPORTANT SPECIES BY REGION, 1990 (MILLIONS OF TONNES)

Region	Sulphur dioxide (as sulphur)		Nitrogen oxides (as nitrogen)		Carbon monoxide		Non-methane volatile organic compounds		Methane	
	Energy-related	Non-energy-related	Energy-related	Non-energy-related	Energy-related	Non-energy-related	Energy-related	Non-energy-related	Energy-related	Non-energy-related
Western Europe	8.8	2.5	3.6	0.4	45	23	10.1	7.6	5.5	18.0
Eastern Europe and former Soviet Union	13.5	3.4	3.5	0.6	47	36	13.9	6.2	37.6	20.3
North America	11.6	0.7	7.6	0.3	82	24	13.2	8.7	23.9	21.5
Asia	17.9	3.0	5.6	1.9	165	132	30.7	24.2	25.7	98.6
Rest of world	8.8	4.1	3.2	4.4	105	316	31.7	31.2	15.5	54.0
Total	60.6	13.6	23.5	7.6	444	531	99.6	77.9	108.2	212.3
		74.2		31.1		975		177.5		320.4

Note: These numbers are slightly different from those in table 3.1 because of different assumptions and methods. Energy-related sources include the combustion, extraction, processing, and distribution of fossil fuels and biofuels. Non-energy-related sources include industrial processes, deforestation, savannah burning, agricultural waste burning, and uncontrolled waste burning.

Source: Olivier and others, 1996.

non-methane volatile organic compounds (NMVOC), released during incomplete combustion and other activities. Ammonia (NH_3) is a significant regional pollutant, but fuel combustion is not its primary source.

When emissions of these primary species are released into the atmosphere, they form a complex, reactive 'soup,' the chemical and physical behaviour of which is determined by such factors as temperature, humidity, and sunlight. The primary species are transported and deposited, influencing the health of humans and of natural ecosystems. But these primary species are also transformed into secondary species—such as sulphate, nitrate, acids, ozone, and miscellaneous organic compounds—that can have effects even more damaging than their precursors and in areas far removed from the primary sources. This can lead to transboundary problems, where a country or region has little control over the emissions that damage its environment.

Emissions and energy

A snapshot of global and regional anthropogenic (human-caused) emissions in 1990 is provided in table 3.3. The emissions are partitioned into those derived from energy-related activities (including combustion, extraction, processing, and distribution of fossil fuels and biofuels) and those derived from non-energy activities (which have a wide variety of sources, including industrial processes, deforestation, savannah burning, agricultural waste burning, and uncontrolled waste burning). Non-anthropogenic sources (volcanoes, soils) are not included.

Energy activities account for 82 percent of anthropogenic emissions of sulphur dioxide and 76 percent for nitrogen oxides. Energy activities play a less dominant role for the three other species—56 percent for non-methane volatile organic compounds, 46 percent for carbon monoxide, and 34 percent for methane. The smaller role of energy in emissions of these three species reflects the important contributions of deforestation, savannah burning, and agricultural waste burning in the generation of products of incomplete combustion, coupled with rice cultivation and enteric fermentation in the case of methane. Nevertheless, table 3.3 demonstrates the critical contribution of energy to emissions of regional-scale pollutants. It also highlights the importance of the developing world in current patterns of regional emissions.

Sulphur dioxide and nitrogen oxides play a role in the formation of acid deposition, because they can be transformed to acids in the atmosphere. The transformation products are fine particles, solid or aerosol, in the form of sulphates and nitrates. In addition, nitrogen oxides are a major precursor to the formation of regional tropospheric ozone. Finally, sulphates and nitrates have the ability to scatter and absorb radiation and so contribute to global and regional climate change, probably with a net cooling effect.

Carbon monoxide is an important regional atmospheric pollutant from several perspectives. It acts as an indirect greenhouse gas with

Energy activities account for 82 percent of anthropogenic emissions of sulphur dioxide and 76 percent for nitrogen oxides.

a potential for global warming (see above, in the section on greenhouse gases) on a 20-year time horizon of about 4.5 due to its influence on the atmospheric lifetime of methane (IPCC, 1990). In addition, carbon monoxide is toxic to humans and is a critical component of many photochemical reactions in the atmosphere. It is a scavenger of hydroxyl radicals and so influences the production of ozone. There are many relatively easy ways to reduce carbon monoxide emissions—catalytic converters for automobiles, improved household stoves, and reuse of carbon monoxide gas in industry.

Non-methane volatile organic compounds consist of a variety of chemical species. In China, for example, the mix of organic compounds is 46 percent paraffins, 32 percent olefins, 21 percent aromatics, and 1 percent aldehydes (Piccot, Watson, and Jones, 1992). These compounds are important in the chemistry of the atmosphere because of their influence on the formation and destruction of ozone and methane. Non-methane volatile organic compounds are a product of the incomplete combustion of fossil fuels, biofuels, and other carbonaceous materials. They are also emitted during the extraction, processing, and handling of gaseous and liquid fossil fuels. And they are released through the evaporation of miscellaneous organic products in industry and households.

Ammonia is a significant component of regional emissions. Being an alkaline substance, it neutralises acids in the atmosphere. But once it is deposited on land, it can be converted to acid through biochemical processes in the soil. Ammonia emissions are largely derived from animal waste, fertiliser application, and fuel combustion. In 1990 energy-related activities accounted for just 5 percent of global ammonia emissions—2.7 of 52.0 teragrams (Olivier and others, 1998). Most ammonia emissions are from Asia and other developing countries, due to the rural nature of these countries, the intensive use of fertiliser for food production, and the heavy use of fossil fuels. In 1990 ammonia emissions in Asia were 22.5 teragrams, compared with 3.5 teragrams in Western Europe and 4.1 teragrams in North America.

Future emissions

Sulphur dioxide. The latest energy projections indicate that global sulphur dioxide emissions will likely stay roughly constant between 1990 and 2020, at about 59 teragrams of sulphur (Nakićenović, Grübler, and McDonald, 1998). This 'middle-course' scenario incorporates modest economic growth, continued reliance on fossil fuels, and the elimination of trade barriers. At the regional level, however, a distinctive pattern emerges for all the important species. Emissions will decline in the industrialised regions of the Northern hemisphere—Europe, the former Soviet Union, North America—and increase sharply the developing regions of the Southern hemisphere and the Far East—Latin America, Africa, Asia (figure 3.7).

In Western Europe strong national environmental policies, changes in national energy policies, and implementation of the

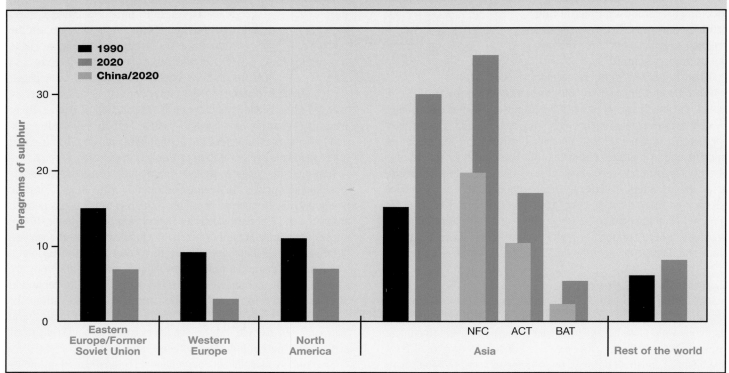

FIGURE 3.7. SULPHUR DIOXIDE EMISSIONS BY REGION, 1990 AND 2020 (PROJECTED)

Source: Nakićenović, Grübler, and McDonald, 1998; Foell and others, 1995.

1985 Helsinki Protocol and 1994 Oslo Protocol (under the 1979 Convention on Long-range Transboundary Air Pollution) have driven down sulphur dioxide emissions. As a result the region could see a 60 percent drop in sulphur dioxide emissions between 1990 and 2020. Similarly, in North America the adoption by the United States of the 1990 amendments to the Clean Air Act has reduced sulphur dioxide emissions. North America's sulphur dioxide emissions in 2020 are expected to be about 35 percent below 1990 levels. In Central and Eastern Europe and the former Soviet Union, a 50 percent reduction is anticipated.

The problem of sulphur dioxide emissions has shifted to the developing world, with emissions in Latin America, Africa, and the Middle East expected to increase by about 30 percent between 1990 and 2020. The main problem region is Asia, where emissions are already high—with 17 teragrams of sulphur emissions in 1990—and could double by 2020. If that happens, Asia will account for 58 percent of global emissions, much of them from China.

Three emission scenarios from the RAINS-ASIA model are also shown in figure 3.7 (Foell and others, 1995; Arndt and others, 1997; Streets and others, 1999). Driven by a similar energy forecast, the model projects that Asia's sulphur dioxide emissions in 2020 will be bounded by an upper value of 40 teragrams of sulphur (under the assumption of no further control policies beyond those in place in 1990—the NFC scenario) and a lower value of 6 teragrams of sulphur (with the assumption of very tight controls, similar to those in Western

Europe). A mid-range estimate is 20 teragrams of sulphur, to be achieved if all large, new facilities are fitted with flue-gas desulphurisation units and other fossil-fuel users switch to low-sulphur fuels.

China continues to be the largest contributor to Asia's sulphur dioxide emissions, emitting about half of the continental total. But the establishment in 1997 of China's Two Control Zone policy for sulphur dioxide emissions has generated optimism that emissions will not grow as fast as once thought. Emissions of 11.9 teragrams of sulphur in 1995 are used as a baseline, and the plan is to limit national emissions to 12.3 teragrams of sulphur in 2000 by capping emissions in certain provinces at their 1995 levels. While implementation and enforcement questions linger, there is a commitment at the highest level in China to holding down sulphur dioxide emissions. The official (but undocumented) estimate for China's emissions in 2020 is 19.5 teragrams of sulphur.

The message from figure 3.7 is one of opportunity. With rapid growth in Asia, many of the coal-fired plants projected to be needed after 2000 have yet to be built. Thus the opportunity exists to fit these plants with emission controls or lower-emission technology at the time of construction. The incremental cost of emission reduction is then the only hurdle to be overcome—though it is a high hurdle ($25 billion a year for the ACT scenario, rising to $65 billion a year for the BAT scenario). Substitution of natural gas for coal is an attractive interim measure, and any possibilities for increasing the efficiency of energy use and moving towards renewable energy would reduce emissions of sulphur, nitrogen, and other species. The ecologically driven scenario (chapter 9), for example, would lower global 2020 emissions from 59 teragrams of sulphur to 34 teragrams.

Nitrogen oxides. The situation for nitrogen oxides emissions is even more challenging, because of the added emissions from transportation. Though nitrogen emissions were not estimated by Nakićenović, Grübler, and McDonald (1998), other analyses suggest a regional pattern similar to that of sulphur dioxide. An earlier study, *Energy for Tomorrow's World* (WEC, 1993), which was more optimistic about economic growth, forecast a 13 percent increase in global emissions of nitrogen oxide between 1990 and 2020 (from 24 teragrams of nitrogen to 27 teragrams) under case B assumptions. The increase in Asia was 70 percent (from 6.8 teragrams of nitrogen to 11.5 teragrams). Use of the RAINS-ASIA model, with its daunting view of the growth of fossil-fuel-based energy systems in Asia, yields an estimated increase of more than 300 percent in this period (van Aardenne and others, 1999).

Carbon monoxide and non-methane volatile organic compounds. Though there are no published projections for emissions of carbon monoxide and non-methane volatile organic compounds, carbon monoxide emissions are unlikely to increase in Asia, because inefficient combustion of biofuels will fall and inefficient vehicles will be replaced. On the other hand, emissions of non-methane volatile organic compounds may grow rapidly as expanding industrial production calls for greatly increased solvent use, increased vehicle use generates more hydrocarbons, and rising living standards increase the demand for domestic and commercial paints and solvents. Together, the expected rise in emissions of nitrogen oxides non-methane volatile organic compounds bodes ill for the formation of regional ozone in the developing world.

Acid deposition

Acid deposition—or acid precipitation in its 'wet' form—is perhaps the most important regional-scale manifestation of energy generation through fuel combustion. Acid deposition occurs when sulphur dioxide and nitrogen oxides are oxidised in the atmosphere to—sulphuric acid (H_2SO_4) and nitric acid (HNO_3), respectively, and dissolved in rainwater. Clean rainwater is naturally acidic, with a pH of about 5.6. In the industrialised regions of Europe, North America, and Asia, rainfall pH values of 4.0-6.0 are common—and values as low as 3.0 have been measured in isolated events.

Acid deposition is a problem because it causes damage to natural and human-made surfaces with which it comes into contact. If soils contain insufficient alkali to neutralise the acid, damage can be caused to vegetation, particularly sensitive tree species and agricultural crops. Lakes can become acidified, leading to the demise of fish populations. Over time the entire natural structure and function of ecosystems can change. Manufactured materials can be attacked: metal surfaces rust, and alkaline materials like concrete, limestone, and marble are eroded (box 3.6).

In Europe forest damage has long been attributed to acid deposition. Despite emission reductions, the health of European forests still seems to be deteriorating (UNECE, 1996). In a 1995 survey of 117,000 trees in 30 countries, more than 25 percent showed signs of significant defoliation, and more than 10 percent showed significant leaf discoloration. Both direct and indirect effects of air pollution, of which acid deposition is but one part, are considered the cause. Surveys of forest soils show that, while sulphur deposition has dropped drastically since the 1970s, nitrogen deposition is still high, impairing soil chemistry and nutrient status. For acidification

---

BOX 3.6. ENVIRONMENTAL IMPACTS OF ACID DEPOSITION

In general, the exposure-response relationships between acid deposition and impacts on ecosystems, materials, visibility, and human health are complex. Some are reasonably well understood, but others involve poorly known relationships involving climate, geography, other chemicals, and time. Much research has been devoted to studies in North America and Western Europe, while relatively little has been done in Asia—where most of the growth in acid-depositing emissions is expected over the next few decades.

Acid deposition has harmful effects on many lakes and rivers, hurting aquatic life. In affected regions such as eastern Canada, lakes have acid levels that are unsafe for fish and other aquatic life. While species of fish vary in their sensitivities to acidification, those with low tolerance decline in population, at times to the point of extinction. This not only affects the species directly harmed, but loss of species diversity damages the ecosystem as a whole due to the interdependence among species (Curren and Nixon, 1992).

Although the impacts of acid rain on terrestrial systems are known with less certainty, several aspects are likely outcomes of acid deposition. Effects on soil include reducing the availability of nutrients and enhancing the solubility of metals. But nitrogen deposition into the soil can enhance its nutrient content, and some soils are fairly resistant to damage. Acid deposition can cause damage to foliage of trees and crops, however (Curren and Nixon, 1992). Forests, especially those at high elevations, are also affected by acid deposition directly through increased susceptibility to natural stresses and indirectly through a loss of nutrients obtained from soil (USEPA, 1999). Considerable uncertainty relates to long-term impacts that may not yet have been observed (NAPAP, 1998).

Several human health problems are linked to acid deposition. For example, many respiratory diseases, including bronchitis and emphysema, are likely caused or aggravated by sulphur particulates and nitrogen oxides. Respiratory problems are particularly noted in

sensitive populations, such as children and asthmatics, as in Hong Kong, China (Hong Kong Municipal Government, 1999). Another potential human health problem comes from increased levels of toxic metals leached from soil, especially aluminium, into drinking water in rural areas (Environment Canada, 1999).

Acid precipitation is also known to have negative non-ecological consequences. It causes the erosion of materials and structures, leading to aesthetic and functional damage as well as increased maintenance costs. This damage to structures includes those that have a great deal of historical significance and are considered highly valuable. Another impact of acid deposition is haze, or a lessening of visibility, largely an aesthetic problem (USEPA, 1999).

The largest documented economic disruptions have been to fishery, forestry, and agricultural industries. The damage occurring to their products is causing a loss of productivity and jobs (Environment Canada, 1999). Furthermore, recreational use of aquatic regions and forests has diminished, causing a loss in revenue (NAPAP, 1998).

of surface waters, there appears to be an overall improvement (with higher pH, for example), probably as a result of reductions in acid deposition (UNECE, 1997). With projected reductions in sulphur and nitrogen emissions through 2020, continued progress is expected towards healthier ecosystems in Europe.

North America has seen significant reductions in the sulphate concentration and pH of precipitation as a result of the 1990 amendments to the Clean Air Act. Reductions in nitrate concentration have not been observed, however, because requirements for lower nitrogen oxide emissions did not go into effect until 1996 (NAPAP, 1998). On the whole, it is too early to tell if there has been significant improvement in the health of ecosystems. There is evidence of recovery in some New England lakes, but the U.S. Environmental Protection Agency has reported that additional reductions in sulphur and nitrogen deposition will be needed to fully restore the health of sensitive Adirondack lakes (USEPA, 1999). High-elevation spruce fir forests in the eastern United States continue to show signs of damage. But, as in Europe, there is reason to hope for improvement.

Asia is the region of greatest concern. Acid deposition is being reported throughout Asia (Wang and Wang, 1995), with many areas receiving levels that exceed the carrying capacity of their soils. Long-range transport is receiving scientific and political attention as countries receive increasing pollution from neighbouring and even distant countries (Huang and others, 1995; Ichikawa and Fujita, 1995; Streets and others, 1999). By far the worst episodes of acid deposition occur in southwestern China (Zhao and Xiong, 1988). Average rainwater pH values of 4.0–5.0 are observed in the Sichuan Basin, and values below 3.0 have been recorded in individual episodes. Atmospheric conditions in Sichuan and Guizhou provinces, with weak winds and frequent temperature inversions, are conducive to high pollutant concentrations. Emissions are also high there because of the widespread burning of high-sulphur coal in small stoves and medium-size industrial boilers.

Southwestern China has seen damage from acid deposition. Sulphur deposition levels are more than 10 grams of sulphur per square metre per year, making the situation comparable to the worst parts of the former Czechoslovakia in the 1960s and 1970s. Zhao and Xiong (1988) report the following effects in the vicinity of Chongqing and the provinces of Sichuan and Guizhou:

■ A 50 percent dieback of pine forests on Nanshan Mountain, about 20 kilometres from Chongqing, attributed to acid deposition and air pollution.

■ A more than 50 percent reduction in biomass production in commercial spruce forests in areas experiencing rain with a pH of less than 4.5.

■ A yellowing of rice in large areas near Chongqing after rainfalls with a pH of less than 4.5.

Seip and others (1995) sampled soil water and stream water in a 7-hectare catchment near Guiyang in Guizhou Province, about 350 kilometres south of Chongqing. Sulphate concentrations were very high, pH values were as low as 4.3, and aluminium concentrations were elevated. Despite these factors, no apparent damage to vegetation

was observed. It appears that neutralisation of acid inputs by deep soils and underlying bedrock may be averting ecosystem damage. Because of the heterogeneity of Chinese soils, however, local acidification and damage may be occurring in sensitive areas that have not been studied. A more recent survey of acidification in China by the Norwegian Institute for Water Research (Lydersen and others, 1997) reported severe effects of acid deposition on soils, water bodies with high loadings showing typical signs of acidification, and observed effects on surface water organisms.

Zhao and Xiong (1988, p. 342) describe some of the severe materials damage observed in Chongqing: "Metal structures are scraped of rust and painted once every 1–3 years. Shells of buses are generally replaced every 1–2 years. Structural components made of stainless steel become rusty after a few years. Some concrete works built in the 1950s have corroded in such a manner that the gravel is exposed. It is estimated that the corrosion depth reaches 0.5 cm in less than 30 years".

In northern China, by contrast, rainwater pH values are typically 6.0–7.0. Although emissions are high in many parts of northern China, meteorological conditions are more conducive to pollutant dispersion, and windblown dust from central Asian deserts tends to neutralise the acidity. The line delineating acid precipitation in China (pH of 5.6) extends just west of Beijing and along the eastern edge of the Greater Khingan mountain range. Since 1982 the area receiving acid deposition may have expanded by 600,000–700,000 square kilometres (Wang and Wang, 1995).

Acidification is responsible for much of the air pollution–related damage in China, though the relative roles of acid rain, dry deposition of sulphur dioxide, nitrates, particulates, ozone, and other factors have not been determined. Areas with lower rain acidity see much less damage than Chongqing and neighbouring cities of southwestern China. Acid rain damage to crops, forests, materials, and human health in China in 1995 is estimated to total more than $13 billion (*China Daily,* 9 March 1998).

In Asia there is also considerable concern about the fate of cultural materials as pollution levels rise. Concerns about the deterioration of the Taj Mahal were raised as far back as 1981 (Lal, Gauri, and Holdren, 1981). Throughout Asia, cultural buildings and monuments made of alkaline-based materials are vulnerable to attack. Glass, paper, textiles, and archives are also subject to accelerated deterioration in the warm, moist, polluted atmospheres of Asia. These problems are greatly under-appreciated and should be given high priority in future research before rich areas of cultural heritage are destroyed.

Finally, although not yet major emitters, Sub-Saharan Africa and Latin American have the potential for significant sulphur emissions as fossil fuel use increases.

Tropospheric ozone

Ozone is an important air pollutant that can cause damage to crops, trees, and human health. It is a major component of the harmful smog that forms in urban areas during periods of high temperature, intense solar radiation, low wind speed, and an absence of precipitation. In the polluted air mass, ozone is produced by a complex set of chemical reactions involving nitrogen oxides and non-methane volatile organic compounds. North America and Europe are developing coordinated strategies to reduce emissions of ozone precursors and thereby reduce some of the health and ecosystem damage attributed to it. Although there is still progress to be made in these regions, it is again in Asia that concern is greatest.

Episodes of high ozone concentrations are now common in the megacities (cities containing more than 10 million people) of southern Asia that have industrial emissions (producing volatile organic compounds), transportation (producing nitrogen oxides), and conducive climates—Bangkok (Thailand), Hong Kong (China), Mumbai (India), and Shanghai (China), to name a few. In addition, the formation and transport of regional ozone have been observed in measurement campaigns such as PEM-West (Akimoto and others, 1996; Jaffe and others, 1996). Ozone concentrations were observed to be regionally enhanced by photochemical activity in continental air masses passing through areas with high nitrogen oxides emissions.

The potential effects of elevated ozone concentrations on human health and crop production in Asia are just beginning to be explored (Chameides and others, 1994). Studies in the West have established that crop yields are depressed by repeated exposures to ozone levels above 50–70 parts per billion; these concentrations are exceeded in fall and winter throughout large areas of southern China. There is concern that damage to winter wheat and other crops in the Yangtze Delta may endanger China's ability to meet increasing food demands. These analyses are still in their infancy, however, and much more work is needed on meteorological analysis, the gathering of monitoring data, field studies on crop responses to elevated concentrations, and regional assessments of economic impact. Until more of this work is done in Asia, a definitive statement cannot be made about the relationship between regional emissions of non-methane volatile organic compounds and nitrogen oxides and impacts on human health and vegetation.

Suspended fine particles

Particulate emissions are relatively well controlled in the industrialised world. Control systems on stationary and mobile sources are effective in limiting the release of primary particles, and secondary fine particles (such as aerosols) are being checked by reductions in emissions of their precursors. In the outdoor environments of many Asian cities, however, concentrations of fine particles are very high, exacerbated by domestic solid-fuel combustion, small-scale industrial activities, and inefficient transportation systems (see above). In many parts of the world the build-up of secondary fine particles over large regional areas during hot, dry spells leads to regional haze, impaired visibility, inhalation health effects, and related ecosystem problems.

Acid deposition is being reported throughout Asia, with many areas receiving levels that exceed the carrying capacity of their soils.

Alkaline dust is also important in Asia because of its ability to neutralise the acidity of precipitation and deposition. In the spring (March, April, May) large dust storms build in the Taklamakan and Gobi deserts and the loess plateau areas of China and Mongolia. These storms are associated with strong cold fronts and prevailing westerly winds. Dust particles are lifted as high as 6 kilometres into the atmosphere and transported over long distances to eastern China, the Republic of Korea, Japan, the Pacific Ocean, and even North America. The dust contains high concentrations of calcium, which neutralises part of the acidity in rainfall. Thus, while sulphate levels in northeast Asian deposition are high and similar to those in North America and Europe, pH values are less acid (typically 5.3–7.0+).

Although large amounts of carbonaceous particles are emitted from the burning of coal, most of the larger particles fall to ground quickly and are not part of the regional emissions picture. Similarly, a large portion of particles is collected, for even in the most polluted regions some form of particulate collection is usually employed. Nevertheless, a certain portion of fine particles from fuel combustion is carried aloft and transported over long distances. These particles are usually less than 1 micron in diameter and consist of carbonaceous solids—so-called black carbon—and organic compounds in aerosol form. These particles can participate in chemical reactions, contribute to reduced visibility, and lead to soiling of surfaces. They scatter and absorb solar radiation and hence play a role in global warming. They also affect cloud albedo (ability to reflect sunlight), because their hydrophilic qualities increase the number of cloud condensation nuclei. On balance, black carbon is thought to contribute a net warming of about 0.5 degrees Celsius (C) globally (Penner, Ghan, and Walton, 1991).

The combustion of biofuels and coal in rural households and diesel fuel in vehicles is a prime contributor to these fine particles. There is an urgent need to better characterise the anthropogenic emissions of primary particles from Asian sources, both by size and chemical and physical characteristics. Diesel vehicles that are poorly designed, operated, and maintained emit large quantities of fine particles in much of the developing world.

Forest fires are a large source of particle emissions in all size ranges. Some of these fires are of natural origin (caused by lightning strikes), while others are caused by human activities such as forest clearing. The fires in Indonesia in the summer of 1997 caused a months-long regional air pollution episode in Indonesia, Malaysia, Singapore, and parts of Thailand and the Philippines. The health of tens of millions of people was affected. Increases in acute respiratory infections, asthma, and conjunctivitis were noted in Kuala Lumpur (Malaysia), Sarawak (Malaysia), and Singapore. Tests on school children in Malaysia noted significant decreases in lung function, the chronic effects of which will not be known for a long time (Brauer and Hisham-Hashim, 1998). Fine particles from such fires can be transported thousands of kilometres if atmospheric conditions are conducive.

Regional climate change

In the early 1990s it was recognised that sulphate aerosols can influence the global climate by scattering and absorbing incoming solar radiation (Charlson and others, 1992) and hence exerting a cooling effect. The role of sulphate aerosols has now been clarified (IPCC, 1996a). Indeed, sulphate aerosols contribute negative radiative forcing (of about –0.4 watts per square metre) that offsets the positive forcing of carbon dioxide and other greenhouse gases. Hence a reduction in sulphur dioxide or nitrogen oxide emissions would be expected to reduce sulphate aerosol concentrations and increase the potential for global warming. The radiative forcing is spatially inhomogeneous, with values as large as –11 watts per square metre over heavily polluted areas such as Central Europe and eastern China.

Lal and others (1995) have suggested that sulphate aerosols can also interfere with local climates. The cooling effect of the aerosol haze reduces the difference between land and sea temperatures and weakens the monsoon. In addition, the cooler land surface reduces evaporation and lowers the amount of water vapour in the atmosphere. The authors estimate that sulphate aerosols in the Asian atmosphere will reduce monsoon rainfall over India and parts of China by the middle of this century. The calculated reduction of 7–14 percent over the fertile north and central Indian plains would be a serious threat to agricultural production. It also appears that large-scale forest fires can reduce rainfall regionally.

Global scale: climate change from greenhouse gases

The two most important human-caused problems associated with environmental processes operating at the global scale are:

- The disruption of climate as the result of energy-related emissions of heat-trapping (greenhouse) gases with long atmospheric residence times.
- The depletion of stratospheric ozone as a result of emissions of chlorofluorocarbons and related compounds from air-conditioning and refrigeration equipment (among other sources).

The character and origins of the first of these are discussed in this section. Stratospheric ozone is not addressed here because it is not primarily an energy issue, although it has connections to energy end-use technologies.[7]

It has been known since the work of Swedish scientist Gustav Arrhenius at the end of the 19th century that certain gases present in Earth's atmosphere in trace quantities exert a thermal blanketing effect that keeps the planet's surface much warmer than it would otherwise be. These are called 'greenhouse gases' because they work in a way analogous to one of the functions of the glass in a greenhouse, letting sunlight in but trapping outgoing heat by absorbing it and re-radiating some of it back to the ground.

The most important greenhouse gas naturally present in Earth's atmosphere is water vapour. Next in importance is carbon dioxide (CO_2), followed by methane (CH_4) and nitrous oxide (N_2O). The concentrations of these gases in the atmosphere before the start of the industrial revolution kept the mean global surface air temperature about 33 degrees Celsius warmer than it would have been in absence of an atmosphere with such natural levels of greenhouse gases. (This natural 'greenhouse effect' is highly beneficial to life on Earth, since without it the average temperature would be far below freezing.[8])

Although water vapour contributes the largest part of the natural greenhouse effect, its concentration in the atmosphere globally—on which the size of the water-vapour contribution to the greenhouse effect depends—is not significantly affected by emissions of water vapour from human activities. The most important anthropogenic greenhouse gas emissions are those of carbon dioxide (CO_2), which arise mainly from combustion of fossil and biomass fuels and from deforestation (see below).[9, 10] An important indirect effect of human activities on the atmospheric concentration of water vapour results from increased evaporation of water from the surface of Earth because of the warming caused by increasing concentrations of anthropogenic greenhouse gases in the atmosphere. The resulting increase in atmospheric water-vapour content further warms Earth's surface—a significant 'positive feedback' in the anthropogenic greenhouse effect.[11]

Concerns developed many decades ago that human-caused increases in the carbon dioxide content of the atmosphere might accentuate the natural greenhouse effect enough to disturb the global climatic patterns to which human habitation, agriculture, forestry, and fisheries had become accustomed. As a result, in 1958 scientists began to take direct measurements of the atmospheric concentration of carbon dioxide at locations far from its main human sources.[12] The continuous record of such measurements, at various remote locations on land and from ships and aircraft, has revealed a steady increase in the global atmospheric inventory of carbon dioxide, reaching 14 percent above the 1958 level by 1995.

Reconstruction of the earlier history of atmospheric carbon dioxide content (by analysis of air bubbles trapped in layered cores taken from polar ice sheets) has established that the increase from pre-industrial times to 1958 was about 13 percent. Thus the ratio of the 1995 concentration to the pre-industrial one is 1.14 x 1.13 = 1.29, representing an increase of 29 percent (figure 3.8). The rise in the atmosphere's inventory of carbon dioxide closely tracks the rise in global fossil-fuel burning over the past 150 years. Moreover, studies based on relatively abundant carbon isotopes confirm the role of fossil-fuel-derived carbon in the observed increase. There is reason to believe that the slower increase in the 100 years before that was due mainly to widespread deforestation for timber, fuelwood, and charcoal.

Not all of the carbon added to the atmosphere by human activities stays there. A substantial part is absorbed by dissolution into the surface layer of the world's oceans (from which oceanic mixing processes gradually transport the dissolved carbon dioxide into the much larger volume of water in the deep oceans). And part is absorbed into forests and soils in areas where the forest 'standing crop' or soil carbon inventory is growing.[13] Estimates for the balance of sources, sinks, and atmospheric accumulation of anthropogenic carbon during the 1980s are summarised in table 3.4. The mean

FIGURE 3.8. ATMOSPHERIC CONCENTRATIONS OF CARBON DIOXIDE, 1850–1995

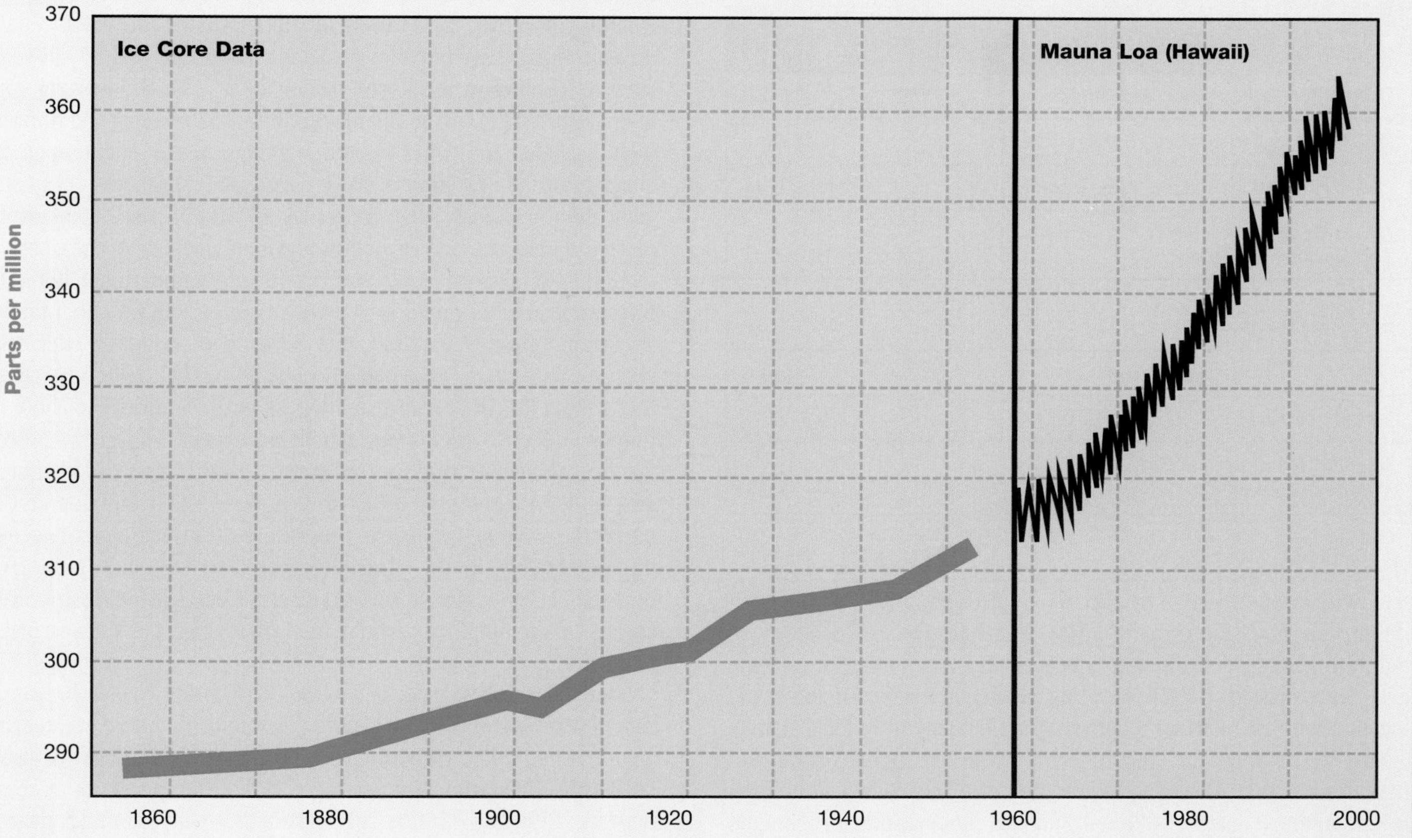

Source: OSTP, 2000.

residence time in the atmosphere of carbon dioxide contributed by human activities, relative to the processes that remove it, is more than 100 years.

Measurements and analyses over the past 20 years have revealed that the atmospheric concentrations of two other naturally occurring greenhouse gases—methane (CH_4) and nitrous oxide (N_2O)—have increased by 145 percent and 14 percent since pre-industrial times. Apparently these increases are at least partly due to direct inputs from human activities as well as to alteration of ecological conditions. The wholly anthropogenic chlorofluorocarbons (CFCs) implicated in the depletion of stratospheric ozone are potent greenhouse gases as well. The warming effect of ozone, itself a greenhouse gas, has been increased in the troposphere (as a result of anthropogenic emissions of hydrocarbons and nitrogen oxides) by more than CFCs have decreased it in the stratosphere.

Changes in the atmospheric concentrations of methane, nitrous oxide, chlorofluorocarbons, and ozone since pre-industrial times are thought to have increased by about 75 percent the warming potential that would be expected from the observed increases in carbon dioxide concentrations alone. Increases over this same period

in the atmospheric concentrations of particulate matter produced by combustion of fossil fuels and biomass have offset part of the warming effect of the greenhouse gas increases.[14] This offset, for which the best estimate is about half of the overall warming effect

TABLE 3.4. SOURCES AND FATES OF ANTHROPOGENIC CARBON EMISSIONS, 1980S

Source	Billions of tonnes of contained carbon
Emissions from fossil fuel combustion and cement production	5.5 ± 0.5
Emissions from tropical deforestation	1.6 ± 1.0
Total anthropogenic emissions	7.1 ± 1.1
Fate	
Storage in the atmosphere	3.3 ± 0.2
Uptake by the oceans	2.0 ± 0.8
Uptake by terrestrial ecosystems	1.8 ± 1.6

Source: IPCC, 1996.

TABLE 3.5. CHANGES IN EARTH'S ENERGY BALANCE, PRE-INDUSTRIAL TIMES–1992

Effect	Global average watts per square metre
Direct effect of increasing carbon dioxide	1.6 ± 0.2
Direct effect of increasing methane	0.5 ± 0.1
Direct effect of increasing halocarbons	0.25 ± 0.04
Direct effect of increasing tropospheric ozone	0.4 ± 0.2
Direct effect of decreasing stratospheric ozone	0.1 ± 0.02
Direct effect of tropospheric aerosols	-0.5 ± 0.3
Indirect effect of tropospheric aerosols	-0.8 ± 0.8
Direct effect of natural changes in solar output (since 1850)	0.3 ± 0.1

Source: IPCC, 1996b.

that would otherwise have occurred through 1995, is likely to diminish as emissions of particulates and their precursors are more tightly regulated.[15] Estimated effects of the various anthropogenic greenhouse gases on Earth's energy balance are shown in table 3.5, together with estimates of other changing influences on this balance.

Are the changes in climate being observed in the forms and magnitudes that theory predicts for the measured increases in greenhouse gases? Although natural fluctuations in climatic variables would tend to mask human-caused disruption in its early stages, a variety of evidence indicates that the 'signal' of anthropogenic change is becoming visible despite the 'noise' of these fluctuations. Specifically:

■ Near-surface air temperatures around the globe have increased by 0.3–0.6 degrees Celsius since the late 19th century.[16] The 11 hottest years since 1860 have all occurred since 1983 (notwithstanding the multiyear cooling effect of particulate matter injected into the stratosphere by a major volcanic eruption in 1991).

■ Directly measured ocean surface-water temperatures have also increased by 0.3–0.6 degrees Celsius on a global average over the past century. In the same period the global sea level, as determined from tidal-range measurements, rose 10–25 centimetres (4–10 inches). Mountain glaciers have generally been in retreat all over the world, and mid- to high-latitude cloudiness and precipitation have generally been increasing.

These observed changes in climatic variables are consistent, in overall magnitudes and in the general pattern of their geographic distribution, with the predictions of basic theory for the effects of the changes in greenhouse gas and particulate matter concentrations known to have occurred over this period.

The observed climatic changes are also similar to the predictions of the most sophisticated computer models of global climate, when these models include the observed build-up of greenhouse gases (corrected for the effect of atmospheric particulate matter).[17] This agreement among theory, observation, and computer modelling extends, moreover, to a variety of subtler trends for which reliable measurements have become available only for the past 15–25 years, such as cooling in the lower stratosphere, reduction of day-night temperature differences, and maximum surface warming in northern high latitudes in winter. Taken together, these phenomena are 'fingerprints' of greenhouse gas–induced climate change—consistent with the hypothesis that increases in those gases explain the observed changes, and inconsistent with alternative hypotheses.

Based on the evidence and arguments summarised here, the Intergovernmental Panel on Climate Change (IPCC) concluded in its Second Assessment that "the balance of evidence suggests a discernible human influence on climate" (IPCC, 1996b, p. 4). In that report the IPCC also extended its earlier analyses of how the human influence on climate would be expected to grow under a business-as-usual trajectory of future greenhouse gas emissions and under higher and lower trajectories. The panel found that, under the range of trajectories considered (and taking into account the uncertainty in the global temperature response to a given increase in greenhouse gas concentrations), the global average surface air temperature would be 1.0–3.5 degrees Celsius higher in 2100 than in 1990.[18]

In all these cases, according to the IPCC (1996b, p. 5), the average rate of warming in the 21st century "would probably be greater than any seen in the last 10,000 years". In the IPCC's 'business-as-usual' emissions scenario, the average global temperature increase between 1990 and 2100 is 2.0 degrees Celsius—about 2.5 degrees Celsius above the temperature a century ago—which would make the world warmer than it has been at any time in the last 125,000 years. In this scenario the sea level would rise 50 centimetres between 1990 and 2100, then "continue to rise at a similar rate in future centuries beyond 2100, even if concentrations of greenhouse gases were stabilized by that time, and would continue to do so even beyond the time of stabilization of global mean temperature" (IPCC, 1996b, p. 5).

The IPCC assessment gives due consideration to the range of possible outcomes and to the size of the uncertainties attached to the group's best estimates. Still, the range of expected ecological and social impacts of climate changes in the next century leaves little room for complacency even at the lower end of the range. And the uncertainties include the possibility of unpleasant surprises that would extend the upper end:

Further unexpected, large and rapid climate system changes (as have occurred in the past) are, by their nature, difficult to predict. This implies that future climate changes may also involve "surprises". In particular these arise from the non-linear nature of the climate system. When rapidly forced, non-linear systems are especially subject to unexpected behavior. Progress can be made by investigating non-linear processes and subcomponents of the climate system. Examples of such non-linear behavior include rapid circulation changes in the North Atlantic and feedbacks associated with terrestrial ecosystem changes (IPCC, 1996b, p. 6).[19]

Since the IPCC's Second Assessment, scientific evidence has continued to accumulate concerning human influences on the global climate system.[20] In particular, the data and analyses show more compellingly than ever that Earth's average surface temperature is increasing and that this increase can largely be attributed to the accumulation of greenhouse gases in the atmosphere caused by human activities. Among the recent findings:

- *1998 appears to have been the warmest year in a millennium,* and the 1990s were the warmest decade in 1,000 years for the Northern hemisphere. Scientists have reconstructed the millennial temperature record in the Northern hemisphere using proxy data for temperatures, such as ice cores, lake sediments, corals, and tree rings (Mann, Bradley, and Hughes, 1999).
- *Greenhouse gases from human activities are the driver of these temperature increases.* While solar variability, volcanic eruptions, and El Niño cycles also contribute to these global temperature patterns, the 20th century record cannot be explained solely by invoking these phenomena (Mann, Bradley, and Hughes, 1998).
- *Regional patterns of temperature change across Earth's surface and vertical patterns of temperature change in the atmosphere provide further evidence of human-induced global warming.* These patterns are consistent with what is expected under anthropogenic climate change—and are inconsistent with hypotheses that suggest that solar variability or the urban-heat island effect can be used to explain the instrumental temperature record (see Wigley, Smith, and Santer, 1998; Wentz and Schabel, 1998; and Peterson and others, 1999).

Consequences of greenhouse gas–induced climate change

There is a natural tendency to suppose that an average global warming of 2.5 degrees Celsius—around the mid-range projection for the year 2100 relative to 1900—would not be such a bad thing. Raising Earth's average surface temperature from 15.0 to 17.5 degrees Celsius (from 59.0 to 63.5 degrees Fahrenheit) does not, at first glance, seem to be especially problematic. Some regions would have longer growing seasons, and some would have shorter seasons of freezing weather. What would be so bad about that?

Such complacency is unwarranted for several reasons. Most important, small changes in the average global surface temperature will cause many changes in other climatic variables—latitudinal temperature differences, frequency of extreme temperatures, atmospheric circulation patterns, precipitation patterns, humidity, soil moisture, ocean currents, and more—that affect human well-being in myriad ways. Climatic conditions are the 'envelope' in which all other environmental conditions and processes exist and operate. Thus climate exerts powerful influences over, for example,

Mountain glaciers have generally been in retreat all over the world.

the productivity of farms, forests, and fisheries, the geography of human disease, and the abundance and distribution of the plants, animals, and microorganisms constituting biodiversity, as well as determining the availability of water, the frequency and intensity of damage from storms and floods, the combination of heat and humidity that determines liveability (and requirements for air conditioning) in warm regions in summer, and the potential property loss from rising sea level.

The average global surface temperature, then, is not a number that by itself reveals the features of climate that matter most—the spatial and temporal patterns of hot and cold, wet and dry, wind and calm, frost and thaw that constitute the climate locally and regionally, where people live. Rather, it is a single, highly aggregated index of the global climatic state that is correlated in complicated ways with those crucial local and regional climatic features. When the average global temperature increases, the regional increases will be greater on land than on the ocean surface, greater inland than near the coasts, and greater at high latitudes than near the equator. In mid-latitude, mid-continent regions—the midwestern United States, for example—the increase in average temperature is expected to be 1.3–2.0 times the average global increase (hence as much as a 5 degree Celsius increase when the global average has gone up by 2.5 degrees; Wigley, 1999 and IPCC, 1996b). At higher latitudes—central Canada, northern Russia—the increase could be three times the global average, or more.

Evaporation and, hence, precipitation are expected to increase about 3 percent for each 1 degree Celsius increase in the average global temperature. (Thus a 2.5 degree Celsius increase in the average global temperature would produce a 7.5 percent increase in precipitation.) In addition, a larger fraction of the precipitation is expected to occur during extreme precipitation events, leading to an increase in flooding.[21] Notwithstanding the increase in precipitation, the increase in evaporation will likely reduce summer soil moisture over large regions, increasing the frequency and severity of droughts in some. At the same time, humid regions will likely become more so. Climate simulations conducted at the Geophysical Fluid Dynamics Laboratory of the U.S. National Oceanographic and Atmospheric Administration show that the average heat index (a discomfort indicator combining temperature and humidity) for the southeastern United States in July will increase from about 30 degrees Celsius (86 degrees Fahrenheit) today to about 35 degrees Celsius (95 degrees Fahrenheit) by the time the average global surface temperature has increased 2.5 degrees Celsius (GFDL, 1997).

As the average temperature and average heat index go up, the frequency of days with extremely high temperature and humidity increases disproportionately. An average warming of 1 degree Celsius might increase the number of days over a particular threshold by 10 percent, while a 2 degree Celsius increase would increase the number of days over that threshold by substantially more than 20 percent (Wigley, 1999; IPCC, 1996b). This result portends not only much higher summer discomfort in a greenhouse gas–warmed climate but also a possibility of substantial increases in death rates from heat stress in areas that are already hot and humid in summer. A decrease in cold-related deaths in winter would partly offset this effect, but for a variety of reasons seems unlikely to offset it entirely (IPCC, 1996a).

An increase in sea level at the mid-range value of 50 centimetres between 1990 and 2100 would be devastating to low-lying islands and seriously damaging to coastal wetlands and many coastal communities. As with temperature, the damage will come not just from the increase in the average but from the increase in extremes. In the case of sea level, this refers to the damage done by storm surges and storm waves starting from a higher baseline (IPCC, 1996a).

As for the frequency and intensity of damaging storms themselves—hurricanes and typhoons in particular—some lines of argument and evidence suggest increases in a greenhouse gas–warmed world, but the origins and dynamics of such storms are complicated. The higher sea surface temperatures and higher atmospheric moisture contents associated with a warmer world tend to produce more powerful storms, all else being equal, but other relevant factors that could be affected by climate change might offset this tendency. There is evidence of an increase in the frequency of Atlantic hurricanes based on a correlation with sea surface temperatures, and there are simulation results indicating higher wind speeds and lower pressures in tropical storms world-wide under global temperature increases in the range expected for the 21st century (see Wigley, 1999 and Knutson, Tuleya, and Kurihara, 1998).

Also subject to considerable uncertainty are the effects of global warming on the large-scale patterns of atmospheric and oceanic circulation that are so crucial in determining regional climates. One thinks particularly of the El Niño/Southern Oscillation phenomenon that affects climates across the central Pacific and the Americas and all the way to Africa, the monsoons that are so critical across Africa and South Asia, and the North Atlantic thermohaline circulation that drives the Gulf Stream and greatly moderates the winter climate in Western and Northern Europe. Although there is every reason to expect that global warming would influence these phenomena, neither historical correlations nor the ocean-atmosphere models used to simulate global climate have proven adequate for predicting with confidence what the exact effects will be.

There are, however, some suggestive preliminary findings. Some modelling results, for example, indicate a substantial weakening of the North Atlantic thermohaline circulation from greenhouse gas–induced warming, setting in well before the pre-industrial carbon dioxide concentration has doubled (Broecker, 1997; GFDL, 1997). Such a weakening would, somewhat paradoxically, make Europe much colder in winter in a world that was warmer overall.

And even bigger changes, such as some that might ensue from ocean-atmosphere-ice interactions, cannot be ruled out. One such scenario involves the complete melting of the Arctic sea ice (with no

In a range of cases considered by the IPCC, the average rate of warming in the 21st century "would probably be greater than any seen in the last 10,000 years."

effect on sea level, since floating ice displaces its weight in water, but with large potential effects on oceanic and atmospheric circulations). Another involves the collapse of the largely land-borne but ocean-anchored West Antarctic Ice Sheet, the slow slide of which into the ocean if the anchor points melted away could raise sea level by 5 metres in 500 years (Oppenheimer, 1998).

If the ways in which global warming will affect regional climates are uncertain, the ecological consequences of those regional changes are even more so. Certainly both the averages and extremes of temperature, humidity, and precipitation are critical in governing the distribution and abundance of terrestrial animals, plants, and microorganisms, just as the averages and extremes of ocean temperatures, salinities, and current patterns are critical to marine life. The organisms in question include, of course, the plants that are the foundation of all terrestrial and oceanic food chains—including all those that support the human population—and they include the pests and pathogens that can destroy crops, fell farm animals, ravage forests, and bring debilitating diseases to humans. Even without the capacity to predict specific effects in detail (which is lacking because of inadequacies in ecological as well as climatological understanding), it is worth noting that:

■ The conditions governing what grows where on land are generally the result of co-evolution of soils, vegetation, and climate. Adjusting to climate change is therefore not just a matter of allowing cropping patterns and forest characteristics to rapidly migrate to a rearranged set of climatic zones; reaching a new equilibrium could take centuries. And where drastic changes in agricultural practices are required to deal with climate change, the capital- and infrastructure-poor developing world will be differentially disadvantaged.

■ Winter is the best pesticide (which is why crop pests and many disease vectors and pathogens are more problematic in the tropics than in temperate zones). This means that warmer winters outside the tropics will be problematic for food production and for human disease.

■ The warmer, wetter conditions that global warming will bring to many of the world's temperate zones will expand the ranges of a variety of diseases (including, quite probably, malaria, cholera, and dengue fever). Industrialised countries' technological and biomedical defences against these diseases may prove less robust than optimists predict, not least because of the continuing emergence of drug-resistant strains.

The conclusions of the IPCC Second Assessment about the consequences of the greenhouse gas–induced warming expected over the 21st century include the following (IPCC, 1996a):

■ Agricultural productivity "is projected to increase in some areas and decrease in others, especially the tropics and subtropics".[22] "Low-income populations depending on isolated agricultural systems, particularly dryland systems in semi-arid and arid regions, are particularly vulnerable to hunger and severe hardship" (p. 6).

■ "As a consequence of possible changes in temperature and water availability under doubled equivalent of CO_2 equilibrium conditions, a substantial fraction (a global average of one-third, varying by region from one-seventh to two-thirds) of the existing forested area of the world will undergo major changes in broad vegetation types—with the greatest changes occurring in high latitudes and the least in the tropics" (pp. 5–6).

■ "Climate change is likely to have wide-ranging and mostly adverse impacts on human health, with significant loss of life...Net climate-change-related increases in the geographic distribution (altitude and latitude) of the vector organisms of infectious diseases (e.g., malarial mosquitoes, schistosome-spreading snails) and changes in the life-cycle dynamics of both vector and infective parasites would, in aggregate, increase the potential transmission of many vector-borne diseases...Increases in non-vector-borne infectious diseases such as cholera, salmonellosis, and other food- and water-related infections also could occur, particularly in tropical and subtropical regions, because of climatic impacts on water distribution, temperature, and microorganism proliferation... [H]otter temperatures in urban environments would enhance both the formation of secondary pollutants (e.g., ozone) and the health impact of certain air pollutants. There would be increases in the frequency of allergic disorders and of cardiorespiratory disorders and deaths caused by various air pollutants".

■ "Climate change and the resulting sea-level rise can have a number of negative impacts on energy, industry, and transportation infrastructure; human settlements; the property insurance industry; tourism; and cultural systems and values".

Nearly all attempts to predict the consequences of greenhouse gas–induced climate change, including those of the IPCC, have confined themselves to addressing the changes associated with roughly a doubling of pre-industrial carbon dioxide concentrations. This has been done so that the results of studies by different investigators would be readily comparable, inasmuch as they were all looking at a similar degree of climate change—not because there is any particular reason to believe that no more than a doubling of pre-industrial carbon dioxide will occur. Indeed, as the next section indicates, the world could end up with carbon dioxide levels three or even four times the pre-industrial value. But the prevalence of studies that look only at the effects of a doubling seems to have led many people to suppose that these are the most that could occur.

In reality, as the few studies of higher levels of warming make plain, the uncertainties and controversies surrounding whether a doubling of atmospheric carbon dioxide would have overwhelmingly negative consequences are of much less importance when one contemplates a quadrupling. A study of quadrupling by one of the main U.S. climate study centres concluded, for example, that the average temperature increases in Northern hemisphere mid-continent regions would be 8–12 degrees Celsius (15–22 degrees Fahrenheit);

that mid-continent soil moisture in summer would fall about 50 percent from 1990s levels; that the sea level rise from thermal expansion alone (not allowing for the melting of any of the Greenland or Antarctic ice sheets) would approach 2 metres; that the North Atlantic thermohaline circulation would shut down completely; and that the July heat index for the southeastern United States would reach 44 degrees Celsius (110 degrees Fahrenheit). The ecological consequences of such changes—and their influence on humans—would be immense.

Greenhouse gas–induced climate change could also affect energy systems, potentially influencing their cost and reliability. The attractiveness of hydropower, windpower, and biomass energy systems, for example, depends on favourable and stable, or at least predictable, climate conditions at their sites over decades. Energy demand is also a function of climate, and changes in temperature, precipitation, wind, and the like will affect it. Thus it is conceivable that climate-change–related reductions in the attractiveness of renewables combined with increases in energy demand could act as positive feedback mechanisms—increasing greenhouse gas emissions faster than they would otherwise because of greater use of fossil fuels.

Alternative energy futures and greenhouse gas emissions

According to the IPCC, in 1990 global emissions of carbon dioxide from fossil fuel burning totalled about 5.9 billion tonnes of contained carbon. (It is customary to keep track of carbon dioxide emissions in terms of their carbon content rather than their total mass, to facilitate comparisons with other stocks and flows in the global carbon cycle, in which carbon may be in a variety of chemical compounds.) Carbon dioxide emissions from tropical deforestation totalled about 1.5 billion tonnes, with an uncertainty of plus or minus 1.0 billion tonnes. The IPCC assumes that rates of tropical deforestation will decline in the 21st century, becoming even smaller relative to fossil fuel carbon dioxide emissions. In 1997 fossil fuel combustion produced about 6.3 billion tonnes of carbon emissions (table 3.6).

The geographic distribution of industrial emissions of carbon—

TABLE 3.6 SOURCES OF INDUSTRIAL CARBON EMISSIONS, 1997 (BILLIONS OF TONNES)	
Combustion of petroleum products	2.70
Combustion of coal	2.40
Combustion of natural gas for energy use	1.20
Cement manufacturing	0.20
Flaring of natural gas	0.05
Total	**6.60**

Source: Authors' calculations based on energy data from BP, 1998; USEIA, 2000.

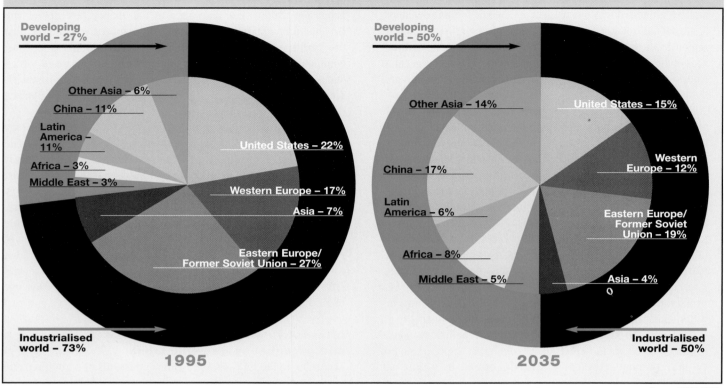

FIGURE 3.9. SOURCES OF INDUSTRIAL CARBON DIOXIDE EMISSIONS, 1995 AND 2035

1995

Developing world – 27%

Other Asia – 6%
China – 11%
Latin America – 11%
Africa – 3%
Middle East – 3%

United States – 22%
Western Europe – 17%
Asia – 7%
Eastern Europe/Former Soviet Union – 27%

Industrialised world – 73%

2035

Developing world – 50%

Other Asia – 14%
China – 17%
Latin America – 6%
Africa – 8%
Middle East – 5%

United States – 15%
Western Europe – 12%
Eastern Europe/Former Soviet Union – 19%
Asia – 4%

Industrialised world – 50%

Source: OSTP, 2000.

that is, emissions from fossil fuel combustion (including flaring of natural gas) and cement manufacturing—is shown in figure 3.9 for 1995 and projects for 2035 under a business-as-usual energy future. In 1995 nearly three-quarters of these emissions came from industrialised countries. Under the business-as-usual scenario, the developing country share will equal that of industrialised countries by 2035. (The cumulative contribution of developing countries to the atmospheric burden of anthropogenic carbon dioxide will remain smaller than that of industrialised countries for some time thereafter, however, and per capita emissions from developing countries will remain smaller than those from industrialised ones for longer still.)

The IPCC analysis and its scenarios for future emissions also take into account the other anthropogenic greenhouse gases—methane, tropospheric ozone, nitrous oxide, and halocarbons—and anthropogenic particulate matter in the atmosphere that partly offsets the heat-trapping effect of the greenhouse gases by screening out incoming sunlight. As noted, the IPCC found that, as of the mid-1990s, the non-carbon dioxide greenhouse gases had added about 75 percent to the heat-trapping effect that would have resulted from the build-up of carbon dioxide alone. But the IPCC's best estimate of the effect of increasing particle concentrations was that these had approximately cancelled out the effect of the increases in non-carbon dioxide greenhouse gases. In one of the six scenarios

developed by the IPCC in 1992, the 'central' scenario, designated IS92a, increases in the effects of atmospheric particles over the next 100 years continue to roughly counterbalance the effects of increases in the non-carbon dioxide greenhouse gases. Thus the net increase in the heat-trapping effect over this period is about what would be expected from the carbon dioxide build-up alone.

The IS92a scenario is very similar to the 'unsustainable' IIASA-WEC (International Institute for Applied Systems Analysis – World Energy Council) A2 scenario presented in chapter 9. Both are based on World Bank 'medium' population projections; the IS92a scenario uses an older median projection in which the world population reaches 11.3 billion by 2100 and the IIASA-WEC uses a newer projection of 10.7 billion by 2100. The IS92a scenario assumes that real economic growth world-wide averages 2.9 percent a year from 1990 to 2025 and 2.0 percent a year from 2025 to 2100, resulting in overall growth of 2.3 percent a year from 1990–2100 compared with 2.5 percent a year in the A2 scenario. Both scenarios assume that the energy intensity of economic activity (energy per unit of real GDP) declines by 1.0 percent a year from 1990–2100 and that the carbon intensity of energy supply (kilograms of carbon emitted in carbon dioxide per unit of energy supplied) decreases by 0.2 percent a year over this period. The result is that global carbon emissions increase in both scenarios from 7.4 billion tonnes a year in 1990 to 20.0 billion tonnes a year in 2100, and cumulative carbon emissions between 1990 and 2100 total 1,500 billion tonnes.

The carbon content of the atmosphere in 2100 under the IS92a and A2 scenarios would be some 1,500 billion tonnes, or about 715 parts per million of carbon dioxide by volume, 2.5 times the pre-industrial level, and still rising steeply. (Only about half of the 1,500 billion tonnes of carbon added between 1990 and 2100 would have remained in the atmosphere, the rest having been taken up by oceans and by vegetation according to the IPCC's carbon cycle model.) This is the scenario for which the IPCC obtained the surface temperature and sea level estimates mentioned above. Because of the thermal lag time of the oceans and the continuing melting of polar ice under warmer conditions, both temperature and sea level would continue to rise after 2100 even if the growth of atmospheric carbon dioxide were halted at that point.

The challenge of stabilising the carbon dioxide content of the atmosphere is illustrated in the IPCC's Second Assessment with emission trajectories that would be able to achieve stabilisation at concentrations ranging from 450–1,000 parts per million by volume (ppmv). (The pre-industrial concentration was about 280 ppmv; today's is 365 ppmv.) These trajectories can be characterised by the cumulative and average emissions they entail between 1990 and 2100 (although what happens after that also matters). The results are summarised in table 3.7.

The IPCC's IS92a scenario and the IIASA-WEC A2 scenario, with cumulative emissions of 1,500 billion tonnes of carbon between 1990 and 2100 and annual emissions of 20 billion tonnes of carbon in 2100, are both above even the highest of these stabilisation trajectories. Such emissions would nearly triple pre-industrial atmospheric carbon content by 2100 and create a situation in which an eventual quadrupling or more could not be avoided no matter what measures were taken thereafter. (These levels are so high as to render irrelevant the current controversies over exactly how severe the climatic consequences of a doubling of atmospheric carbon might be; a quadrupling would transform Earth's climate beyond recognition; see GFDL, 1997.)

To illustrate the challenge associated with reducing emissions to the levels being debated in the context of the United Nations Framework Convention on Climate Change (UNFCCC), consider what the numbers above imply for the stabilisation target for atmospheric carbon dioxide of 550 ppmv, about twice the pre-industrial level. (While there can be no confidence that this level would avoid climate change seriously disruptive of human well-being throughout much of the world, a doubled carbon dioxide target is widely discussed because it is, at least arguably, near the upper limit of what is tolerable and near the lower limit of what seems achievable.) This would require that cumulative emissions between 1990 and 2100 be less than two-thirds those in the IS92a scenario. It would also require that emissions begin to decline after peaking at about 11 billion tonnes of carbon a year around 2030.

This more sustainable development path and the challenge of achieving the transition towards such a path are illustrated by the IIASA-WEC C scenario presented in chapter 9. That scenario leads to the stabilisation of atmospheric carbon concentrations at about 430 ppmv and cumulative emissions of some 540 billion tonnes of carbon from 1990–2100. Perhaps more important, the development path that leads to atmospheric stabilisation of carbon at a relatively benign level also leads to the fulfilment of most of the other criteria for sustainable development discussed in this report.

The difficulty of achieving this goal becomes particularly apparent when one views it in terms of the roles of industrialised and developing countries. In 1990 industrialised countries emitted about 4.5 billion tonnes of carbon from fossil fuel burning (three-quarters of the world total, or 3.6 tonnes per inhabitant of these countries). Developing countries emitted 1.5 billion tonnes (about 0.37 tonnes per capita). In 1992, as part of the UNFCC, industrialised countries agreed to try to limit their carbon emissions in 2000 to 1990 levels (see below). But few are on a track towards achieving this. For example, in 1997 U.S. carbon emissions were about 9 percent higher than in 1990.

Considerably more effort is required. For example, assume that industrialised countries were willing and able to return to their 1990 carbon emissions by 2010—a decade after the initial UNFCCC target (and a performance considerably weaker than called for in the 1997 Kyoto Protocol; see below)—and were also willing and able to reduce these levels by 10 percent a decade thereafter. Even

TABLE 3.7. IPCC SCENARIOS FOR STABILISING CARBON DIOXIDE LEVELS, 2075–2375

To stabilise concentrations at (parts per million by volume)	450	550	650	750	1,000
By about the year	2075	2125	2175	2200	2375
Cumulative emissions in 1990–2100 would need to be in the range of (billions of tonnes of carbon)	550–750	750–1,100	970–1,270	1,090–1,430	1,220–1,610
Average emissions in 1990–2100 would be in the range of (billions of tonnes of carbon per year)	5.7–5.9	7.9–9.0	10.2–10.8	10.0–11.8	12.7
And peak emissions (billions of tonnes of carbon per year)	9.5	11	12.5	13.5	15
In the year	2012	2030	2050	2060	2075

Source: IPCC, 1996b.

then, stabilising atmospheric carbon dioxide concentrations at 550 ppmv would still require that per capita emissions in developing countries not exceed 1 tonne of carbon in the global peak-emissions year of 2030. (This assumes that emissions from deforestation have been eliminated by 2030 and that the population of developing countries is about 7.5 billion at that time, consistent with the 'medium' World Bank projection.) As shown in later chapters, with vigorous promotion of renewables and energy-efficient technologies, such a per capita level could produce much higher living standards.

Even more challenging, given the justifiable economic aspirations of developing countries, the unwillingness of many industrialised countries to take the steps needed to reduce emissions, and the common expectations of all countries to rely heavily on expanded fossil fuel use, is that the per capita emissions of both industrialised and developing countries would need to fall sharply after 2030 to stay on this 550 ppmv stabilisation trajectory. (See chapter 9 for more discussion of carbon emission scenarios, particularly the

C scenario, which achieves the required emissions reduction discussed here.)

International agreements to address global climate change

The UNFCCC is the first binding international legal instrument that deals directly with the threat of climate change. Since its enactment at the 1992 'Earth Summit' in Rio de Janeiro, the convention has been signed by more than 165 states (plus the European Union). It came into force in March 1994.

Signatory countries agreed to take action to realise the goal outlined in article 2 of the convention, namely the "stabilization of greenhouse gas concentrations in the atmosphere at a level that would prevent dangerous anthropogenic interference with the climate system." To achieve this, all parties to the convention, both industrialised and developing, are committed under article 4 to adopt national programs for mitigating climate change; to promote the sustainable management and conservation of greenhouse gas 'sinks' (such as forests); to develop adaptation

---

BOX 3.7. GREENHOUSE GASES AND NATURAL DEBT

Countries take on national debt when they spend money faster than their economies produce it. Building up national debt is essentially a way of borrowing from the country's future earnings. A little national debt can be beneficial, by providing resources so that the economy grows faster than it otherwise might. But a lot of national debt can be quite disruptive. Countries can also take on 'natural debt' by putting pollutants into the environment faster than they are naturally removed. In this way they borrow from the environment's future assimilative capacity.

Humanity has been adding greenhouse gases to the atmosphere faster than they can be naturally removed. As a result the global atmospheric burden of carbon dioxide and other greenhouse gases has been rising. The extra burden of greenhouse gases in the atmosphere above pre-industrial levels is a measure of the global natural debt. Indeed, this natural greenhouse gas debt is the principal driver of climate change, since it determines the extra radiative forcing (warming).

Although most discussions of greenhouse gas control address the current emissions of countries, cumulative emissions (natural debt) are the chief determinant of the impact on the climate. The natural debts of countries differ substantially more than do current emissions, because some countries have been emitting large amounts for much longer than others have. The largest natural debts have been accrued by industrialised countries, which started burning large amounts of fossil fuels early in the 20th century. Some of those greenhouse gases have been removed naturally from the atmosphere, but some

remain because of long residence times. The table below compares the natural debts of a number of countries that together account for 55 percent of the world's population and about 75 percent of global carbon dioxide emissions.

It has been argued that it would be more appropriate to determine a country's

	Current emissions 1996 (tonnes per capita)	Cumulative emissions 1950–96 (tonnes per capita)
United States	5.3	119
Canada	4.2	91
Germany	3.3	87
Russia	3.9	78
United Kingdom	2.7	78
Australia	4.1	70
Sweden	1.7	54
France	1.8	49
Japan	2.4	41
Korea, Dem. Rep.	3.0	32
Korea, Rep.	1.7	16
China	0.6	8
India	0.2	3

Natural debt: Carbon as carbon dioxide remaining in the global atmosphere from fossil fuel combustion

responsibility for reducing emissions based on its natural debt relative to that of other countries rather than on current emissions, since natural debt (cumulative greenhouse gases in the atmosphere) is more closely related to actual climate impact. Such proposals are not welcomed by negotiators for most industrialised countries.

One argument against using natural debt as a measure of responsibility is that it would be unfair. After all, it is argued, the ancestors of today's populations in industrialised countries did not know they were causing a problem by emitting greenhouse gases. Thus today's populations, who did not do the polluting, should not have to pay for past mistakes. This view is partly accounted for in the table, which only shows emissions from 1950. But there are two important counter-arguments:

- Today's rich populations have enjoyed the (considerable) benefits derived from past use of fossil fuels and other greenhouse gas–generating activities and thus should accept the debts that go along with those benefits. It is not a matter of punishment, but one of recognising the debits as well as the credits (the polluter pays principle).
- Saying that if someone did not know they were doing a risky thing that they need not be held responsible is a sure way to encourage people not to make the effort to discover whether their activities might cause problems for future generations. It essentially rewards ignorance. A sustainable world energy system, on the other hand, is one in which cross-generational responsibility is accepted by all.

Source: Smith, 1991a; Hayes and Smith, 1994; Smith, 1997.

strategies; to take climate change into account when setting relevant social, economic, and environmental policies; to cooperate in technical, scientific, and educational matters; and to promote scientific research and information exchange.

Climate change is likely to have wide-ranging and mostly adverse impacts on human health, with significant loss of life.

The UNFCCC also establishes more demanding obligations for industrialised countries, which agreed to try to reduce emissions of carbon dioxide and other greenhouse gases to 1990 levels by 2000. OECD countries are also committed to facilitating the transfer of financial and technological resources to developing countries, beyond those already available through existing development assistance. The convention requires industrialised countries to take the lead in adopting measures to combat climate change, recognising that they are mainly responsible for historic and current emissions of greenhouse gases, and that developing countries will need assistance to meet the treaty's obligations (box 3.7).

The structure provided by the UNFCCC is being built on with additions agreed in a series of conferences of the parties. Most notably:

■ The first conference of the parties, held in Berlin (Germany) in March 1995, focused on the need to reinforce the commitments in article 4 of the UNFCCC with "quantified limitation and reduction" objectives for annex 1 countries after 2000.[24] The mandate did not call for new commitments for developing country parties but only for enhanced efforts at implementing the existing commitments relating to these countries in article 4.

■ The third conference of the parties, held in Kyoto (Japan) in December 1997, produced a protocol to the framework convention codifying commitments for reductions in greenhouse gas emissions after 2000. The protocol commits annex I parties (except Australia, Iceland, New Zealand, Norway, Russia, and Ukraine) to reduce greenhouse gas emissions by 5–8 percent below 1990 levels between 2008 and 2012 and to make "demonstrable progress" towards achieving these commitments by 2005. Overall emissions are to be computed on a net basis, accounting for afforestation, reforestation, and deforestation as well as emissions from energy supply and other industrial activities. (See box 3.7 for a discussion of another approach to measuring a country's greenhouse gas contributions.)

The Kyoto Protocol, having not yet been ratified by the requisite number of nations, is not in force. It has been criticised by some (especially in the United States) as demanding too much too soon of industrialised nations while not requiring anything of developing countries. It has been criticised by others as not requiring enough of anyone, representing only a small 'down payment' on the kinds of emission reductions that will be required over the 21st century to avoid intolerable climate change from greenhouse gases.

Cross-scale impacts

Some types of pollutants are created and create problems at every scale and easily transfer between scales. Aerosols (particulates) are a good example. At the household and community scales, they are probably the chief source of human ill health from energy systems. At the workplace scale, in the form of coal dust for example, they are a principal contributor. At the regional scale, secondary particulates from sulphur and nitrogen gases contribute to ill health and form the basis for acid deposition. At the global scale, they contribute to climate change through local warming or cooling, depending on particle composition and ground characteristics. Overall, it is believed that human-caused aerosols had a net cooling effect during the 20th century, masking some of the warming that would have occurred through greenhouse gas build-up.

The transfer of aerosols from one scale to another is governed by complicated processes involving geography, elevation, wind, moisture, size, composition, and so on. Nevertheless, in general it can be said that reducing emissions at one scale will have impacts at other scales. In most cases these benefits are beneficial. As particulates and their precursors such as sulphur oxides are brought under control because of concerns at other scales, however, greenhouse gas warming may actually become greater than in the immediate past because of the apparent net cooling effect in the atmosphere.

Environmental risk transition

During development, societies tend to push off environmental problems from smaller to larger scales (Smith, 1990, 1997). For energy, household hazards dominate fuel cycles in the poorest parts of the

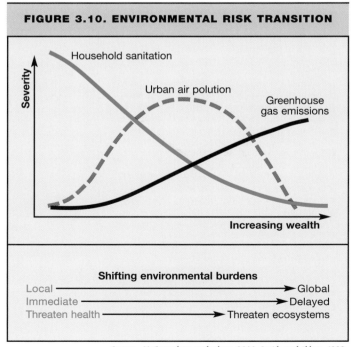

FIGURE 3.10. ENVIRONMENTAL RISK TRANSITION

Source: McGranahan and others, 2000; Smith and Akbar, 1999.

world, while community impacts dominate fuel cycles in middle-income cities through industrial and vehicular pollution. In the richest countries, household and community problems have mostly been pushed off to the global level in the form of greenhouse gases (figure 3.10). In all countries, however, occupational risks per worker-hour tend to be much higher than risk per hour of public exposure. As with other exposures, however, occupational risks also tend to be higher in poorer countries (box 3.8).

The environmental risk transition curves in figure 3.10 should not be considered fixed in the sense that today's developing nations will be forced to go through them in the same way that today's industrialised countries have done. Rather, the curves should be viewed as a management framework by which to judge the progress of development policy. The task in developing countries is to avoid the excesses of the past, to continue to push down the household curve, and to not let the community curve rise out of hand. This might be considered a kind of 'tunnelling' through the curves to avoid climbing over the peaks by applying cleaner, more efficient energy supply and use technologies earlier in the development process than has occurred to date.

Win-win strategies to link environmental improvements at different scales

The most convincing argument for spending resources to reduce current greenhouse gas emissions is that the benefits from reduced impacts of climate change will be greater than the costs. Among the important benefits are avoiding or reducing the direct impacts on human health that might accompany climate change, and avoiding ecosystem effects that could have significant indirect impacts on humanity. Reducing current greenhouse gas emissions could generate long-term health benefits such as fewer malarial mosquitoes, fewer extreme climatic events (including tropical cyclones and heat episodes), shifts in atmospheric composition towards less pollution, reduced impacts on food production, and decreasing refugee populations from reduced sea level rise and other factors (McMichael and others, 1996). Similarly, reduced greenhouse gas emissions could lead to less damage to important ecosystems.

Each step of the causal chain from greenhouse gas emissions to global warming to direct effects on health and ecosystems is not understood with certainty, however. As a result of that uncertainty, many observers are still unconvinced that the potential but distant health and ecosystem benefits justify large spending on greenhouse gas reductions today. Although the consensus scientific opinion (as represented by the IPCC) is that such ill effects are likely if current trends in greenhouse gas emissions continue, scepticism holds back international agreements to significantly alter current greenhouse gas emissions. This is particularly so in developing countries, which must contend with many urgent problems related to human health and welfare. But it also applies to many groups in industrialised countries.

BOX 3.8. THE KUZNETS ENVIRONMENTAL CURVE: FACT OR FALLACY?

An illustration of the environmental risk transition between scales is seen in the figure below, which plots the relationship between urban PM_{10} (particulates smaller than 10 microns in diameter) concentrations and countries' development status as indicated by their UNDP human development index (a function of income, literacy, and life expectancy). Superficially, urban PM_{10} concentrations seem to follow the so-called Kuznets environmental curve—that is, they first rise during development, reach a peak, then decline (Grossman and Kruger, 1994). (The curve is named after the Nobel Prize–winning economist Simon Kuznets, who noted in the 1960s that many countries go through a period of increasing income inequality during development before becoming more equitable.) From the standpoint of the risk transition, however, this curve only addresses the community scale in the form of ambient urban air pollution. It ignores what happens at other scales, which may be more important.

The main concern about particulates is their impact on human health. From a health standpoint, it is not so much urban concentrations that are critical but human exposure, which is a function of not only where the pollution is but also where the people are. Because people spend a lot of

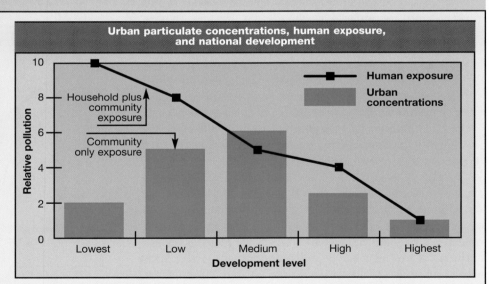

time indoors and in other places close to local sources of pollution, exposure patterns can be quite different from patterns of ambient pollution. Thus, as shown in the figure, because household sources dominate exposure in the poorest countries, the pattern of exposures is quite different than that of urban ambient

concentrations. Instead of rising and then falling, exposures decline continuously—illustrating that the Kuznets curve misses the actual trend, which is that overall risk tends to fall even though community risk rises, because of the shift of household to community impacts (Smith, 1993).

BOX 3.9. WIN-WIN CROSS-SCALE ENVIRONMENTAL STRATEGIES IN CHINA

A recent study found that greenhouse gas reductions resulting from changes in energy use would generally be accompanied by substantial near-term human health benefits in China (Wang and Smith, 1998). But the level of health benefits would vary greatly with the choice of energy technologies and sectors. Shifting from conventional coal-fired power plants to natural gas, for example, has larger health benefits than reducing global warming potential, while shifting from coal power to hydropower results in the same percentage reduction in emissions of health-damaging pollutants and greenhouse gases.

This variation in health benefits is even larger between sectors. The conservative estimates in the study show that the health benefits of a 1 tonne reduction in particulate emissions from household stoves are at least 40 times those from reduction of the same amount from coal-fired power plants. In terms of human health benefits, the choice of energy technologies and sectors in which to conduct greenhouse gas reduction efforts is more important than choice of a particular target for greenhouse gas reduction.

In many developing country households the particulate emissions from burning unprocessed solid fuels (biomass and coal) routinely exceed by an order of magnitude or more the safe levels specified by the World Health Organization. Thus a 15 percent reduction by 2020 in Chinese households' greenhouse gas emissions below the 'business-as-usual' level would avoid more than 100,000 premature deaths a year. Reduced emissions of health-damaging pollutants through household improvements in energy efficiency and changes in the fuel mix would also reduce greenhouse gases. Thus reducing greenhouse gas emissions at the global scale could significantly ease human health impacts at the household scale.

On a national scale, a 15 percent reduction in greenhouse gases below business as usual by 2020 would result in 125,000–185,000 fewer premature deaths in both the power and household sectors, depending on different control pathways (energy efficiency or fuel substitution). This range represents about 1 percent of the total mortality in China

by 2020. Other countries with high household and industrial dependence on solid fuels, such as India, could be expected to see similar benefits.

Acid deposition is increasingly serious in many regions, damaging forests, crops, and aquatic animals. The RAINS-ASIA model (Foell and others, 1995) indicates that large areas in Asia have acidity levels in excess of critical loads due to sulphur deposition, posing significant environmental threats to a variety of ecosystems. The model also projects that sulphur deposition will eventually exceed critical loads by a factor of more than 10 in many parts of Asia as a result of the growing dependence on fossil fuels. This increase will threaten the sustainability of many natural and agricultural ecosystems in the region. The model develops a series of emission control scenarios and shows that energy efficiency and fuel substitution pathways, which are also the main mitigation options for greenhouse gases, can be important instruments for controlling acid-forming emissions.

One approach to resolving this impasse is to promote 'no regrets' scenarios for reducing greenhouse gases. Such scenarios achieve significant near-term benefits for human health and ecosystems in addition to reducing greenhouse gases. Thus such immediate actions can be justified even if climate sensitivity to additional greenhouse gases turns out to be less than is now thought (Repetto and Austin, 1997). Examples of such near-term benefits include the environmental and energy-security advantages that would accrue through less dependence on fossil fuels, and the human welfare benefits that could emerge if an international greenhouse gas control regime were oriented towards assisting economic development and reducing vulnerability among poor populations (Hayes and Smith, 1994).

Among the significant near-term benefits of greenhouse gas reductions are the human health benefits resulting from changes in the efficiency and structure of energy use that would be a large part of most greenhouse gas reduction scenarios. Although fuel cycles have several effects on health and ecosystems—for example, through water pollution, the potential for large accidents, and occupational health and safety—the largest and most sensitive to change are probably those related to pollutant emissions from the processing and burning of fuels. The same combustion processes that produce greenhouse gas emissions such as carbon dioxide and methane also generate local and regional airborne health-damaging and acid-precursor pollutants such as particulates and sulphur oxides. Thus a reduction in greenhouse gases at the global scale, through improvements in energy efficiency and changes in the mix of fuels, can be expected to reduce health-damaging and acid-precursor pollutants as well, potentially bringing immediate environmental improvements at the household, community, and

regional scales. This is a win-win strategy to link environmental improvements between scales.

The potential health benefits from reduced greenhouse gases can be estimated from the global burden of ill health from air pollution. Using airborne particulates as the indicator pollutant, the World Health Organization estimates that air pollution causes 2.7–3.0 million premature deaths a year, or 5–6 percent of global mortality (WHO, 1997). Since most of this pollution comes from the combustion of fossil and biomass fuels, which would be among the main targets of any effort to control greenhouse gases, the potential reduction in health-damaging emissions would seem to be at least as great as the target reduction in greenhouse gas emissions. Arguably it is even greater, however, since switching from dirty, less efficient fuels (such as coal) to cleaner, more efficient fuels (such as natural gas) reduces emissions of health-damaging pollutants even more than greenhouse gas emissions. With greenhouse gas reduction targets on the order of 10–20 percent, the scale of emissions of health-damaging pollutants and associated reduction of ill health could be in the same range or somewhat higher—perhaps a 250,000–750,000 annual reduction in premature deaths world-wide.

To more accurately estimate these near-term health benefits, it is necessary to link each technological option in a particular green-house gas reduction scenario with the accompanying reduction in emissions of health-damaging pollutants. The health impact of these emissions, however, depends on the sector of the economy in which they are taken. This is because the degree of human exposure created by a unit of emissions of health-damaging pollutants depends on where they are released relative to where people spend time, their 'exposure effectiveness'. Thus a tonne of emissions averted in the household or transportation sectors close to where people spend much of the time will generally cause a much greater reduction in human exposure (and improvement in health) than a tonne averted in the industrial or power sectors. An example of such a win-win possibility in China is presented in box 3.9.

On a community scale, more than 1.1 billion people living in urban areas world-wide are exposed to particulate or sulphur dioxide levels in excess of World Health Organization guidelines (Schwela, 1995). These pollutants are released by industrial, household, and transportation energy use. Air pollution is particularly severe in megacities. Again, reducing greenhouse gas emissions by changing energy use and structure can also reduce the particulate and sulphur dioxide emissions that cause severe urban air pollution.

The same principle applies in the cities of the industrialised world, although the scale of absolute benefits is less because air pollution levels are lower. From an economic standpoint, however, there can still be substantial secondary benefits from greenhouse gas controls through associated reductions in health-damaging pollutants, acid precipitation, and the like. The value of these benefits could in many cases rival the costs of the greenhouse gas controls, making a win-win result (Elkins, 1996; Burtraw and Mansur, 1999).

As noted, the near-term health and ecosystem benefits of reducing greenhouse gases provide the opportunity for a true no-regrets reduction policy in which substantial advantages accrue at various scales even if the risk of human-induced climate change turns out to be less than many people now fear. Increases in energy production and end-use efficiency and changes in the mix of fuels can reduce environmental impacts at the household, community, regional, and global scales, while meeting greenhouse gas targets. To achieve these benefits effectively, however, considerations of health and other secondary benefits should be included from the start in designing greenhouse gas control strategies.

This no-regrets strategy also has important implications for emissions trading in the form, for example, of joint implementation and clean development mechanisms. Because the near-term health improvements are local, they accrue almost entirely to the nation in which greenhouse gas control projects are undertaken—unlike the benefits of greenhouse gas reductions, which accrue globally. These large local benefits may provide a significant extra incentive for other developing countries to enter into arrangements in which local greenhouse gas controls are financed externally and the emission credits are shared. Indeed, a greenhouse gas reduction strategy can be consistent with such critical national development objectives as reducing local air pollution, increasing energy efficiency, and improving social equity by providing energy services to remote areas through renewable energy.

The World Health Organization estimates that air pollution causes 2.7–3.0 million premature deaths a year, or 5–6 percent of global mortality.

Assessment methods

A number of methods have been developed to compare the disparate effects of energy systems on a common basis. Here we discuss perhaps the two most common, economic valuation and fuel-cycle analysis. In both cases there is still much uncertainty and some controversy on the fundamental nature of the analyses and on the data inputs required. Thus we present these examples not as definitive, but as illustrative of the type of information they can provide.

How much is clean air worth? Because it generally becomes increasingly expensive to reduce pollution as emission controls tighten, a fundamental question is how much money each bit of emissions control is worth. If the value of averting damage were known, then the degree of control could be set such that the total cost (control cost plus residual damage cost) is minimised. Normally, the cost of control is fairly well known. Similarly, damage is fairly easy to value for simple property destruction, such as corrosion of buildings and reduction of crop yields. But valuing damage to critical ecosystems or human health is not straightforward. As a result there are no universally accepted methods.

Several approaches are used to value human health, including:
- Human capital—the value of lost wages and associated medical costs from illness or injury and premature death.
- Value of statistical life—the imputed value from extrapolating human risk-averting behaviour. For example, if the labour market shows that inducing a worker to accept a job with an additional death risk of 1/1,000 a year requires extra wages of X dollars a year, then X multiplied by 1,000 would equal the value of a lost life.
- Willingness to pay—in which people are asked how much they would be willing to pay to avoid certain risks. These amounts are then extrapolated to find the equivalent value of a life.

In recent years the willingness to pay approach has become more widely used, because it holds more theoretical appeal for economists than other approaches. But beyond the obvious difficulty of finding accurate data, there are three important problems with this approach. First, measured willingness to pay can be quite different for the same issue depending on how the question is phrased, raising doubt about the measure's intrinsic utility. Second, willingness to pay to avoid a certain risk depends on the respondent's knowledge about the risk, which varies dramatically by geography, demography, education, and time, and which is quite difficult to account for in surveys. Finally, although it is clear that willingness to pay varies with income, it is not clear by how much. As people grow richer, their willingness to pay to avoid a given risk generally increases even faster. But this relationship is not clear across different periods and cultures.

Consider some examples of how willingness to pay has been used to value air pollution in developing and industrialised countries. In China, the dirtiest fossil fuel, coal is widely used, its use is expected to grow rapidly in the next few decades, and effective pollution controls are not widely used. A recent study estimated that air pollution cost China about $48 billion in 1995 (7 percent of GDP), including impacts of acid deposition as well as health effects from outdoor and indoor air pollution (World Bank, 1997). The study found that the dominant cost came from health costs for urban residents, some $32 billion (5 percent of GDP). Moreover, it projected that under business-as-usual conditions, pollution-related health costs for urban residents would increase to $98 billion by 2020 at current income levels, or $390 billion (13 percent of GDP) with adjustments to willingness to pay related to growth in income. This is substantially more than the estimated economic damage of greenhouse gas emissions from the same facilities.

China's high pollution-related health costs are partly due to relatively limited pollution controls. Even in countries with relatively extensive pollution controls, however, pollution-related health costs can be high because aggregate energy-related emissions can be high even if emissions per unit of energy provided are low. Moreover, the willingness to pay to avoid pollution damages will be high in high-income countries. And in densely populated regions such as Europe and Japan, large populations are generally exposed to air pollution.

Recent studies in Europe have shown that health impacts dominate the external social costs of pollution, and estimate that the costs of health impacts due to fine particle air pollution are especially high (Rabl and Spadaro, 2000; Spadaro and Rabl, 1998; Spadaro and others, 1998; Krewitt and others, 1999). These economic calculations reflect recent epidemiological studies indicating that fine particles are associated with serious health effects, including premature death (see the section on community scale).

Although considerable uncertainty remains about health impacts from small particles, the economic value of these impacts is expected to be high—at least in densely populated regions of high-income countries, where large populations are exposed to air pollution that can shorten lives by a few months. These populations are willing to pay considerable amounts to avoid this life shortening. Table 3.8 presents recent estimates of the health impacts of coal and natural gas power plants equipped with the best available control technologies. For natural gas combined-cycle plants the only significant health costs are associated with nitrogen oxide emissions, and these costs are relatively low (typically about 5 percent of the electricity generation cost). But for coal the estimated health costs (mostly due to health damage from fine particle air pollutants) are large and comparable to the electricity generation cost. These estimates are quite uncertain, however.

Table 3.9 presents estimates of health costs in France for air pollution from gasoline-fuelled cars equipped with pollution controls and for diesel-fuelled cars. The estimated health impacts, measured per litre of fuel sold, are high (though, as with power generation, quite uncertain), especially for urban driving—about twice the retail price (excluding retail taxes) for gasoline cars and 25 times the retail price for diesel cars. As in China, the economic costs of greenhouse gas emissions from European cars and power plants would seem to be much lower.

These costs will vary significantly by region depending on the mix of rural and urban driving, whether emissions are at ground level or from tall stacks, local and regional population densities, and income, which affects willingness to pay. Applying the results in table 3.9 to developing countries, where per capita income averaged about $2,800 in 1995, the imputed health costs would be 0.1–0.5 times those estimated for France when all other factors are equal, depending on how willingness to pay varies with income.

If willingness to pay continues to increase more rapidly than income, health impacts will become increasingly important for developing countries even if emission controls are put in place. That is because their income and energy consumption levels will rise more rapidly than energy consumption levels, even with emission controls in place. To illustrate, consider the WEC projection

TABLE 3.8. AIR POLLUTANT EMISSIONS AND ESTIMATED HEALTH COSTS FOR EUROPEAN POWER PLANTS EQUIPPED WITH THE BEST AVAILABLE CONTROL TECHNOLOGIES

| Siting | Unit health cost (cents per gram) | | | Emission rate (grams per kilowatt-hour) | | | | Unit health cost (cents per kilowatt-hour) | | | | |
| | | | | Pulverised coal steam-electric | | | Natural gas combined cycle | Pulverised coal steam-electric | | | | Natural gas combined cycle |
	Sulphur dioxide	Nitrogen oxides	PM$_{10}$	Sulphur dioxide	Nitrogen oxides	PM$_{10}$	Nitrogen oxides	Sulphur dioxide	Nitrogen oxides	PM$_{10}$	Total	Nitrogen oxides
Typical	1.0	1.6	1.7	1.0	2.0	0.2	0.1[a]	1.0	3.2	0.3	4.5	0.16
Urban	1.6	2.3	5.1	1.0	2.0	0.2	0.1[a]	1.6	4.6	0.5	6.7	0.23
Rural	0.7	1.1	0.5	1.0	2.0	0.2	0.1[a]	0.7	2.2	0.1	3.0	0.11

Note: These calculations were carried out as part of the European Commission's ExternE Program. Studies under the program have estimated the economic values of health impacts by assessing people's willingness to pay to avoid adverse health effects. The health cost estimates shown are median values; the 68 percent confidence interval is 0.25–4.0 times the median cost. *Source: Rabl and Spadaro, 2000.*

TABLE 3.9. AUTOMOTIVE NITROGEN OXIDE AND PARTICULATE EMISSIONS AND ASSOCIATED PUBLIC HEALTH COSTS IN FRANCE

Fuel and driving environment	Fuel economy (kilometres per litre)	Emission rate (grams per kilometre)		Health costs (dollars)								
				Per gram		Per kilometre			Per litre of fuel		
		Nitrogen oxides	Particulates	Nitrogen oxides	Particulates	Nitrogen oxides	Particulates	Total	Nitrogen oxides	Particulates	Total
Gasoline											
Urban	8.7	0.68	0.017	0.022	2.750	0.015	0.047	0.062	0.13	0.41	0.54
Rural	10.3	0.79	0.015	0.027	0.188	0.021	0.003	0.024	0.22	0.03	0.25
Diesel											
Urban	10.4	0.75	0.174	0.022	2.750	0.017	0.479	0.496	0.17	4.98	5.15
Rural	12.7	0.62	0.150	0.027	0.188	0.017	0.028	0.045	0.21	0.36	0.57

Note: These calculations were carried out as part of the European Commission's ExternE Program. Studies under the program have estimated the economic values of health impacts by assessing people's willingness to pay to avoid adverse health effects. The health cost estimates shown are median values; the 68 percent confidence interval is 0.25–4.0 times the median cost. The gasoline cases are for cars equipped with catalytic converters.

Source: Spadaro and Rabl, 1998; Spadaro and others, 1998.

that in developing countries the number of cars will increase 6-fold between 1990 and 2020 (WEC, 1995). Even if all were gasoline-fuelled cars equipped with three-way catalytic converters, health costs in developing countries would increase to $40–120 billion in 2020, depending on the rate of increase in willingness to pay. If all cars were diesel, health costs would be six times as high. These health cost estimates do not include health impacts associated with buses, trucks, and locomotives.

Health costs might end up being much higher than these estimates because real world emission levels tend to be considerably higher than regulated emission levels (Ross and others, 1995). That happens for a variety of reasons, including that regulated emissions are for well-maintained cars and that regulations tend to be for driving cycles that often do not reflect the way people actually drive.

These high estimated future health costs argue for much tighter emission controls than can be achieved with widely used current technologies. How much additional control will be needed? This is one of the critical questions for providing sustainable transport systems for the world's cities. Nevertheless, despite large uncertainties due to the willingness to pay method as well as to basic understanding of air pollution health effects, it seems safe to conclude that the economic value of air pollution abatement is substantial in developing and industrialised countries alike.

Fuel cycle analysis. Supplying modern energy often involves processes at a chain of facilities that may be quite physically distinct from one another. These processes are usually referred to as 'fuel cycles', although they rarely rely on any cycling. Comparisons based on fuel cycles are useful for organising impact analyses of energy supply and demand.

Consider the fuel cycle supporting the operation of an electric appliance. It may involve a coal mine, coal washery, coal train, coal power plant, and transmission lines, as well as ancillary facilities such as coal tailings piles, washery settling lagoons, and power-plant ash disposal. Each of these facilities has environmental impacts and is, in a sense, 'switched on' whenever the appliance is used even though it may be physically unconnected and thousands of kilometres away. Furthermore, environmental impacts occur not only during normal operations of these facilities, but also during their construction, repair, and dismantling—what is called their life cycle. Even non-fuel energy systems, such as photovoltaic power plants, have fuel cycles and life cycles, including the harvesting, processing, and transport of the materials used to construct the facility.

Comparative risk assessment is one term used for studies of the life-cycle impacts of alternative fuel cycles, such as different ways to produce electric power. Such studies are usually normalised according to an appropriate unit of energy output—for example, impacts may be scaled per kilowatt-hour or per barrel of oil equivalent. The idea is that in this way all the impacts can be fairly compared across alternative energy systems, giving full and consistent information to decision-makers. Such studies first account for insults over the life cycle of each part of the fuel cycle, such as land used, tonnes of pollution released, long-term waste generated, water consumed, and labour required per unit of output. Then most comparative risk assessments try to convert as many insults as possible into impacts with common measures, such as deaths, injuries, illnesses, and financial damage costs. Since the occupational impacts of energy systems can be significant (see the section on workplace scale), often both public and worker risks are determined (box 3.10).

In addition to the methodological and other problems of fuel-cycle analysis and comparative risk assessment mentioned in box 3.10, there are some fundamental concerns with these kinds of comparisons that revolve around this unit of analysis—that is, the production of a certain amount of energy. For occupational impacts, for example, the number of accidents or illnesses per unit of energy output is just as much a measure of labour intensity as of safety.

Indeed, from a societal standpoint, putting many people to work in low-risk activities is much better than employing a few people in high-risk activities. But both may look the same in the comparisons.

In addition, by using energy as the output measure, such analyses reveal little about the impact of such facilities on overall public health, which uses time as the risk denominator. It may be that one way of producing electricity has slightly different public health implications than another, but neither may have much significance overall or, conversely, neither may be acceptable. Entirely different kinds of analyses are needed to evaluate these kinds of questions.

Implications for the future

As noted in the introduction, there has not been space in this chapter to present what is known and suspected about the many environmental insults of different energy systems and the resulting impacts on ecosystems and human health. But we have addressed a large fraction of the most important ones. The central task of this report is to outline the main characteristics of a sustainable energy future. Thus it is appropriate to examine the main categories of insults and impacts discussed in this chapter to see what requirements they impose on such a future.

Household scale

About half of the world's households use solid fuels (biomass and coal) for cooking and heating in simple devices that produce large amounts of air pollution. Because the pollution is released at the times and places where people spend time, the health impact is high, accounting for 4–5 percent of the global burden of disease. The chief ecosystem impact relates to charcoal production and urban fuelwood harvesting, which puts pressure on forests near cities and may account for a few percentage points of global deforestation.

It is difficult to envisage a sustainable energy future in which unprocessed solid fuels remain an important source of energy for a significant fraction of the world's households. Gases, liquids, and electricity are the main clean alternatives. Although today these alternatives mostly derive from fossil fuels, this need not be the case in the future. In the future these alternatives may be made from renewable biomass fuels such as wood and crop residues (see chapters 7, 8, and 10). Indeed, a further criterion for sustainable energy is that any biomass harvested to make household fuels should be done on a renewable basis to ease pressure on forests and other natural ecosystems.

Workplace scale

The harvesting of solid fuels (biomass, coal, uranium) creates the highest risks per energy worker and the largest impacts on the energy workforce world-wide. Risks to coal miners, for example, are many times those for the average industrial worker. To be sustainable, average miner risks will probably have to be lowered to those in the safest mines today.

It is difficult to envisage a sustainable energy future in which unprocessed solid fuels remain an important source of energy for a significant fraction of the world's households.

Community scale

Fuel use is the chief cause of urban air pollution, though there is substantial variation among cities in the relative contributions of vehicles and stationary sources. Diesel-fuelled vehicles, which are more prominent in developing countries, pose a growing challenge to meeting urban health-related pollution guidelines (responsible for about 1 percent of the global burden of disease).

To be sustainable, mean urban air pollution around the world will need to be no greater than what is common in rich countries today—for example, less than 30 micrograms per cubic metre of PM_{10}. An additional requirement for sustainability is that urban ambient ozone levels not rise as vehicle fleets grow. Sufficiently clean power generation by fossil and nuclear sources is technically feasible, although costs are uncertain (see chapter 8). Similarly, hybrid vehicles are substantially cleaner than current types (see box 3.5). Achieving sustainability, however, will probably require moving most of the world's fleet to fuel cells or comparably clean systems by the middle of the 21st century.

Regional scale

The problem of regional atmospheric emissions will not go away quickly. The increasing demand for energy, especially in developing countries, will put heavy pressure on cheap and easily obtainable fossil fuels such as coal and oil. Prospects for constraining increases in regional emissions are better for some pollutants and source types. An ambitious goal for sulphur dioxide emissions, for example, would be a 50 percent reduction world-wide by 2050. This goal could be achieved by reducing the sulphur content of fossil fuels and using emission controls on new, large power plants and industrial facilities. Switching to natural gas in developing countries would also considerably aid the achievement of this goal. Increases in sulphur dioxide emissions in the developing world will be offset by legislatively driven reductions in industrialised countries.

Nitrogen oxide emissions are a bigger problem. The expansion of transportation systems in developing countries will add to the nitrogen oxide burden from industrial production and power generation. Moreover, nitrogen oxides are much harder to control than sulphur dioxide. An ambitious goal would be to stabilise nitrogen oxide emissions at current levels by 2050. Only a major shift away from fossil fuels in all parts of the world or a shift to alternative energy carriers such as hydrogen derived from fossil fuels will enable this goal to be achieved.

Carbon monoxide emissions will likely fall significantly as developing countries move away from biofuels and as automobiles become more efficient world-wide. Emissions of volatile organic compounds from energy sources will likely be reduced, but large increases can be expected from non-energy sources, particularly as the commercial and residential use of solvents increases in the developing world. Holding global emissions of volatile organic compounds to a 20–50 percent increase by 2050 will be a challenge.

BOX 3.10. COMPARATIVE RISK ASSESSMENT USING FUEL-CYCLE ANALYSIS

A number of concerns drive the need to assess the environmental and human health damage associated with electricity production. These include informing utility planning decisions in terms of total social costs, enlightening cost-benefit analyses of pollution mitigation technologies, facilitating formulation of regulatory procedures, and delineating the secondary benefits of reducing greenhouse gas emissions. Attempts to quantify damages incurred by electricity generation technologies date to the 1970s and are known as fuel-cycle analyses or comparative risk assessments. Most fuel-cycle analyses have been undertaken in industrialised countries, but a few have considered electricity production in developing countries (such as Lazarus and others, 1995).

Fuel-cycle analyses attempt to account for all damages caused by physical and chemical processes and activities undertaken to generate electricity from a specific fuel or resource, from fuel acquisition to waste disposal in a steady-state operations approach, or from construction to decommissioning in a facility lifetime approach. Because different insults exert their impacts over different temporal and spatial scales, the geographic extent and time horizon of an analysis must be carefully defined to cover all significant impacts. Contemporary fuel-cycle analyses generally follow a damage function or impact pathway approach whereby dominant impacts are identified; stresses (incremental population exposures to air pollution, occupational hazards, transportation risks) are quantified; stresses are translated to impacts, typically through exposure-response functions or actuarial data; and impacts are quantified and aggregated in terms of the study's chosen metric (ORNL and RFF, 1992; Curtiss and Rabl, 1996). The study design stage entails a number of choices on impacts to be considered (public and occupational health, ecological damage, agricultural losses, material corrosion, visual amenity), temporal and spatial assessment boundaries, models and hypotheses for analysis,

economic parameters such as the discount rate, and the treatment of accident scenarios for which no actuarial data exist (such as expected and worst case).

A fuel-cycle analysis typically results in a list of impacts per unit of output in the form of premature deaths, ecosystem damage, global warming, and the like. To provide a common metric for comparison, many studies then attempt to monetise these impacts. This process introduces substantially more uncertainty and controversy into the process.

Fuel-cycle analyses have typically generated 'total cost' figures in terms of m$ ($0.001) or mECU per kilowatt-hour, with recent (post-1990) European and U.S. estimates ranging from 0.016–80 m$ per kilowatt-hour for coal and from 0.002–23 m$ per kilowatt-hour for nuclear (Rabl and Spadaro, 2000). Given the four orders of magnitude spanned by these fuel chain damage costs, it is clear that they are sensitive to the particular designs and metrics of the studies. Accordingly, interpretation of studies' results requires extensive supplementary information to illuminate, for example, the specific impacts assessed and the study-specific approaches to valuation of life, valuation of non-fatal outcomes, weighting of public and occupational health outcomes, and discount rates. Thus fuel-cycle analysis damage costs cannot stand alone and are difficult to compare, despite the fact that they may superficially appear to be based on comparable metrics (dollars per kilowatt-hour).

Although comparative risk assessment using fuel-cycle analysis cannot yet indicate unambiguous preferences or even readily allow for comparisons between studies, recent studies suggest that public health and occupational health effects dominate the externalities associated with the nuclear fuel chain. Health effects and global warming dominate conventional coal technologies (Rabl and Spadaro, 2000). Biomass as an energy resource is less easily characterised even in terms of dominant impacts because it is highly

dispersed, the nature of its production and use is extremely site-specific, and its associated damages and benefits depend on other local activities such as agriculture (Lazarus and others, 1995). Similarly, hydroelectric utilities elude concise generalisation due to the wide range of sophistication among technologies and the site-specificity of ecological and human health risks. Fuel-cycle analyses yield widely disparate conclusions for solar thermal and dispersed photovoltaic technologies. Some studies, particularly those focusing on operation of energy systems, suggest that these solar technologies confer negligible human health and ecological risks (Rabl and Spadaro, 2000). Other studies assert that the occupational risks and short-term environmental damage associated with solar technologies can exceed those of conventional electricity generation methods (Hallenbeck, 1995; Bezdek, 1993).

Pitfalls associated with fuel-cycle analysis include the use of poorly defined or inconsistent study boundaries, confusion of average and marginal effects, underestimation of the uncertainty associated with quantification of damages, neglect or inadequate treatment of environmental stochasticity, and focus on what is easily quantified rather than on what is actually significant (Koomey, 1990).

A number of outstanding issues remain for streamlining approaches to fuel-cycle analysis. These issues include identifying the functional relations and key parameters defining uncertainty, the variation in damages with key parameters, the degree of accuracy and resolution with regard to atmospheric modelling and receptor distribution (needed to capture the site-specificity of impacts), and the magnitude of error incurred by using 'typical' average values rather than detailed, site-specific data (Curtiss and Rabl, 1996). In addition, metrics used in fuel-cycle analysis to deal with incommensurate impacts—such as the soiling of buildings, crop damage, and human morbidity and mortality—are not uniform between studies.

The faster that clean and efficient vehicles and fuels can replace current vehicles and fuels, the greater will be the reduction in emissions of nitrogen oxides, carbon monoxide, and volatile organic compounds.

It seems that acid deposition world-wide will increasingly become a nitrogen oxide (and possibly an ammonia) problem rather than a sulphur dioxide problem. On balance, reductions in acidification in Europe and North America are likely to continue, but hotspots of damage in the developing world (such as southwestern China) may persist for years and worsen. Regional ozone will increasingly be the biggest problem because of the expected difficulties in mitigating emissions of nitrogen oxides and volatile organic compounds, the two main precursors of ozone. Only small improvements in regional ozone levels may occur in North America and Europe in the next 10–20 years. And considerable deterioration is likely in Asia, Africa, and Latin America, endangering human health and

agricultural production.

Large dams will continue to provide potential for significant benefits and severe environmental impacts, depending on their location and design. For sustainability, much better evaluation will be needed to maximise the benefits and minimise the environmental impacts.

Global scale

Energy systems generate two-thirds of human-caused greenhouse gases. Thus energy use is the human activity most closely linked to the potential for climate change. Climate change is feared to entail significant direct impacts on human health as well as on Earth's ecosystems. As noted, there has been a tendency for environmental problems at the local level to be solved partly by pushing off the impacts to larger scales. Greenhouse gases and their potential for global climate change represent the final and, in many ways, most

A sampling of results from fuel-cycle analyses, which have been used in a variety of contexts, follows:
- An investigation of externalities of electricity production from biomass and coal in the Netherlands suggests that while average private costs for the biomass strategy assessed are projected to be about twice those for coal in 2005, internalisation of external damages and benefits would yield about equal social costs. The most important distinguishing factors between coal and biomass are differences in carbon dioxide emissions and indirect economic effects such as employment (Faaij and others, 1998).
- A comparison of fuel-intensive combustion-based utilities (coal, oil, gas, and biomass), selected renewable energy technologies (solar thermal, photovoltaic, wind, and hydroelectric), and nuclear technologies (light water reactor, fast breeder reactor, and hypothetical fusion reactor) suggests that coal inflicts the greatest delayed occupational health burden (such as disease), with a central estimate of 0.1 fatalities per gigawatt-year of electricity and an upper estimate of about 3 fatalities per GWy(e). Acute occupational risks (such as accidents) posed by combustion technologies are purported to be marginally less than those associated with renewable energy technologies—with central estimates on the order of 1 fatality per GWy(e)—but greater by an order of magni-

tude than those associated with fission technologies and comparable to those for fusion. In the public health domain, with central estimates of about 2 fatalities per GWy(e), coal and oil appear to confer greater delayed mortality burdens by a factor of two (relative to photovoltaic systems) to three or four orders of magnitude (relative to wind, hydroelectric, and nuclear technologies). While acute risks associated with renewable energy technologies are highly uncertain, this study places them as comparable to or somewhat higher than those associated with fuel-intensive combustion technologies, at 0.1–1.0 fatalities per GWy(e) (Fritzsche, 1989).
- A study by the Stockholm Environmental Institute suggests that in terms of greenhouse gas emissions, natural gas is preferred to residual fuel for electricity generation in Venezuela, even under the assumption of relatively high methane emissions through natural gas system losses. In this context the global warming potential per kilowatt-hour of natural gas electricity generation is projected to be 12–27 percent lower than that associated with residual fuel (Lazarus and others, 1995).
- Since the early 1990s several studies have tried to quantify greenhouse gas emissions associated with different fuel cycles (see table below). Some of the variability arises from the different conversion efficiencies of

the technologies assessed—for example, biomass configurations include a wood steam boiler, an atmospheric fluidised bed combustor, and an integrated gasifier combined-cycle turbine. But methodological issues and assumptions associated with activities outside the generation stage account for a large portion of the variability. For example, one study credits product heat from cogeneration cycles for displacing greenhouse gases from gas heating systems (Fritsche, 1992). In this framework the greenhouse gas intensity of biomass can become negative, and that of natural gas fuel cycles can be reduced 50 percent below the next lowest estimate. Among fossil fuels, the greenhouse gas intensity of natural gas is most variable, primarily due to different assumptions about methane emissions during drilling, processing, and transport. For non-fossil fuels, estimates generally span at least an order of magnitude, primarily because of the sensitivity of these cycles to assumptions on the operation life of the facility and the greenhouse gas intensity of the electric and manufacturing sectors on which equipment production depends. In addition, the hydroelectric cycle's greenhouse gas intensity is sensitive to the area of land flooded and, for projects with multiple generating units per reservoir, the boundary of the system considered.

Greenhouse gas emission intensities for selected fuels (grams of carbon dioxide equivalent per kilowatt-hour)								
Conventional coal	Advanced coal	Oil	Gas	Nuclear	Biomass	Photovoltaic	Hydroelectric	Wind
960-1,300	800-860	690-870	460-1,230[a]	9-100	37-166[a]	30-150	2-410	11-75

Note: These estimates encompass a range of technologies and countries as described in Pearce and Bann, 1992; Fritsche, 1992; Yasukawa and others, 1992; ORNL and RFF, 1992–98; Gagnon and van de Vate, 1997; and Rogner and Khan, 1998.

a. Natural gas and biomass fuel cycles were also analysed in cogeneration configurations, with product heat credited for displacing greenhouse gas emissions from gas heating systems. That approach reduced greenhouse gas emissions to 220 grams of carbon dioxide equivalent per kilowatt-hour for natural gas and –400 for biomass (Fritsche, 1992). Other cycles could incorporate cogeneration and be analysed in this manner.

challenging of the stages. Although there are promising technologies for fossil systems that capture and sequester the greenhouse gases resulting from combustion, as well as fossil, nuclear, and solar systems releasing no greenhouse gases, their prospects are not entirely understood (see chapters 7 and 8).

It is difficult to define a sustainable level of greenhouse warming above the natural background. Achieving something akin to the natural background, on the other hand, will not be possible for many centuries, barring major, unprecedented, and unforeseen technical breakthroughs, global catastrophes, or changes in human behaviour. What then, might be considered a workable definition of 'sustainable' for the climate change impacts of the world energy system?

The coming climate change can be considered in two parts: magnitude (total warming) and rate (annual increase). Some types of impacts are more sensitive to one than the other. For example,

sea level rise is more sensitive to magnitude, and ecosystem damage is more sensitive to rate. Perhaps the most worrisome aspect of human-engendered warming, however, is that it threatens to cause warming at rates completely unprecedented in Earth's recent geologic history. The magnitude of potential change is somewhat less unprecedented. Thus it may be reasonable to establish a somewhat less stringent definition of sustainability for greenhouse gas emissions—one that calls for stabilising atmospheric levels as quickly as possible, recognising that the resulting levels (and their warming) will be considerably higher than the natural background.

Achieving stable atmospheric levels during the 21st century will require bringing human greenhouse gas emissions to annual rates substantially below those today. Doing so will not be easy. Indeed, it will require major commitments of resources and political will (see the section on the global scale and chapter 9). The longer such efforts are delayed, the higher and longer will be the eventual stable warming level and accompanying impacts.

Reaching emission levels in 2050 below those in 2000 will probably require annual declines in energy intensity of at least 1.4 percent and in carbon intensity of energy of at least 0.4 percent. With the assumptions in table 9.1, even these major accomplishments would still allow emissions growth of 0.4 percent a year to 22 percent above 2000 emissions by 2050. With such modest growth, however, and 50 years of experience promoting efficient and low-carbon energy sources, it might be possible to achieve emissions below 2000 levels within a few years after 2050.

Cross-scale

There are important opportunities for 'no regrets' strategies that achieve benefits at more than one scale. For example, if greenhouse gas controls are targeted towards reducing solid fuel use in households and in other energy systems with large health impacts (such as vehicle fleets), significant improvements can occur at the local, community, and global scales. Fine particles are generated and have impacts at all scales, so control measures will benefit from integrated approaches. Similarly, the regional impacts from sulphur and nitrogen emissions can be reduced in conjunction with control efforts at the community and global scales. Much additional effort is needed to identify environmental control pathways that optimise these multiple benefits.

Conclusion

Impacts other than those discussed in this chapter need to be considered, particularly in local situations. But if the environmental insults and their ecosystem and health impacts focused on here were controlled as indicated, the world would have moved most of the way towards a sustainable energy system.

Among the other impacts requiring careful consideration are the relationships between energy systems and military, political, and economic security—the subjects of the next chapter. ■

Notes

1. *Insult* is defined here as the physical stressor (such as air pollution) produced by an energy system. *Impact,* in contrast, is defined as the potential negative (or positive) outcome (such as respiratory disease or forest destruction) affecting humanity. As with other useful terms (diagnosis, prognosis, pathology) the term insult is borrowed from medicine, where it is defined as "a generic term for any stressful stimulus, which under normal circumstances does not affect the host organism, but may result in morbidity when it occurs in a background of pre-existing compromising conditions" (Segen, 1992). It has been used in environmental discussions, however, since at least the mid-1970s (see Ehrlich and others, 1977).

2. Modern fuels involve extensive fuel cycles with relevant environmental impacts and energy efficiencies at several points. The air pollution exposures per meal are still lower than that from solid fuels, however.

3. The burden of disease refers to the total healthy life years lost due to this risk factor. It is composed of two parts that are added together: life years lost to deaths and life years lost to diseases and injuries weighted by a severity factor.

4. These include the main gaseous pollutants as well as particulates. For lead emissions, the overall reduction in hazard per vehicle mile was about 75 percent (US Census Bureau, 1996; USEPA, 1996).

5. PM_{10} are particles less than 10 microns (millionths of a meter) in size, which penetrate deeper into the respiratory system than larger particles.

6. The World Commission on Dams, which began deliberating in 1998, is publishing its reports in mid-2000 (WCD, 1999). These will include 8–10 case studies examining social, economic, environmental, energy, financial, managerial, and other aspects plus a database of 150 dams in different countries.

7. This section draws heavily on IPCC (1996a, b). The IPCC was established by the World Meteorological Organization and United Nations Environment Programme in 1988 to assess the scientific, technological, economic, and social aspects of anthropogenic climate change. Some 2,000 scientists and other specialists from more than 40 countries served as authors and reviewers of the 17 volumes of exposition and analysis issued by the IPCC through 1996. The IPCC's first assessment report, completed in late 1990, served as the basis for the negotiations of the United Nations Framework Convention on Climate Change, concluded in 1992 and discussed below.

8. The mean global surface temperature of the Earth is about 15 degrees Celsius (59 degrees Fahrenheit). Without greenhouse gases, it would be −18 degrees Celsius (0 degrees Fahrenheit).

9. Combustion emits water vapour and carbon dioxide in comparable quantities. But the rate of water addition to the global atmosphere by combustion is tens of thousands of times smaller than the rates of addition and removal by evaporation and precipitation. And because the added water remains in the atmosphere only a few days, these human additions cause at most local effects and no long-term build-up. In contrast, the quantity of carbon dioxide added by combustion is only about 10 times smaller than what is added and removed by natural photosynthesis and decomposition, and a large part of the anthropogenic increment remains in the atmosphere for decades. Thus it has time to become uniformly distributed around the globe, irrespective of where it was emitted, and to accumulate over long periods (as long as the sum of the natural and anthropogenic addition rates is greater than the removal rate).

10. There is no net accumulation of carbon dioxide in the atmosphere from combustion of wood and other biomass fuels, as long as new plant growth replaces what is burned. This is because a growing plant removes from the atmosphere exactly as much carbon dioxide as is released when the plant decomposes or burns. When new growth does not replace what is burned or decomposed, as in deforestation, a net addition of carbon dioxide to the atmosphere results. (See the section on greenhouse gas emissions at the household scale, for a discussion of non–carbon dioxide greenhouse gas emissions from incomplete biomass combustion.)

11. Feedbacks are phenomena wherein the consequences of a disturbance act back on its cause, making the disturbance either bigger (positive feedback) or smaller (negative feedback) than it started out.

12. The first and longest-running series of measurements was initiated by Charles Keeling at a monitoring station atop the Mauna Loa volcano on the island of Hawaii.

13. The main such terrestrial 'sinks' for atmospheric carbon are in the Northern hemisphere (see Houghton, 1996; Fan and others, 1998).

14. Particles in the atmosphere exert both cooling and warming effects on the Earth's surface temperature, depending on the characteristics of the specific particles in terms of absorption and scattering of incoming solar and outgoing terrestrial radiation, and on the roles of different particles in cloud formation. Averaged over the globe and the different types of anthropogenic particles, the net effect is cooling.

15. Because particulate matter and its gaseous precursors have much shorter residence times in the atmosphere than any of the major greenhouse gases, its offset of part of the greenhouse effect will shrink in line with declining particulate and precursor emissions.

16. This range corresponds to 0.54–1.08 degrees Fahrenheit, but the two-significant-figure precision resulting from applying the exact conversion (1 degree Celsius = 1.8 degrees Fahrenheit) is illusory. The warming is not uniform, however, being generally greater near the poles than near the equator. And because of the complexity of the heat transfer processes of the climatic system, some regions may get colder even as the globe gets warmer on average.

17. The most sophisticated models demonstrate the fundamental soundness of their representations of global climatic processes by simulating quite accurately the undisturbed climate of the planet in respects such as the variation of geographic patterns of temperature and precipitation with the changes of the seasons.

18. Temperatures would continue to rise thereafter, even in the cases in which the atmospheric concentrations of greenhouse gases had been stabilised by then, because of the climate-response lag time caused by the thermal inertia of the oceans.

19. *Non-linear* means that small disturbances can have large consequences. *Forcing* is the technical term for an externally imposed disturbance, such as a change in greenhouse gas concentrations. An example of a potential positive feedback on global warming from terrestrial ecosystems is that the warming could increase the rate of release of greenhouse gases into the atmosphere from decomposition of dead organic matter in forests and swamps.

20. The discussion here is drawn from a treatment prepared by one of the authors (Holdren) for the report of the Panel on International Cooperation in Energy Research, Development, Demonstration, and Deployment, President's Committee of Advisors on Science and Technology (PCAST, 1999).

21. See IPCC (1996b). Both trends—an increase in rainfall and an increase in the fraction of it occurring in extreme events—have been convincingly documented for the period since 1900 in the United States (Karl and Knight, 1998).

22. The improvements in agricultural productivity foreseen for some regions by the IPCC are due partly to carbon dioxide fertilisation of plant growth, partly to increased water availability from increased precipitation, and partly to technological change. Although the IPCC discusses at length how plant pests and pathogens could prove increasingly problematic in a greenhouse gas–warmed world, these possibilities do not seem to be fully reflected in the productivity projections.

23. This section draws heavily on material written by one of the authors (Holdren) for the report of the Panel on Federal Energy Research and Development, President's Committee of Advisors on Science and Technology (PCAST, 1997).

24. Annex 1 countries, as defined in the UNFCCC, are OECD countries plus the countries of Eastern Europe and some of those of the former Soviet Union (the Baltics, Belarus, Russia, Ukraine).

References

Agarwal, B. 1985. Cold Hearths, Barren Slopes. New Delhi: Allied Pubs.

Akimoto, H., H. Mukai, M. Nishikawa, K. Murano, S. Hatakeyama, C. Liu, M. Buhr, K.J. Hsu, D.A. Jaffe, L. Zhang, R. Honrath, J.T. Merrill, and R.E. Newell. 1996. "Long-range Transport of Ozone in the East Asian Pacific Rim Region." *Journal of Geophysical Research* 101: 1999–2010.

Albright, D., and H.A. Feiveson. 1988. "Plutonium Recycling and the Problem of Nuclear Proliferation." *Annual Review of Energy* 13: 239–65.

American Honda Motor Company. 1999. "Honda Hybrid To Be Called 'Insight'—Will Feature (IMA) Integrated Motor Assist System, Lightweight Aluminum Body Structure." http://www.honda2000.com/insight/press.html

Armstrong, J., and R. Menon. 1998. "Mining and Quarrying." In J.M. Stellman, ed., *Encyclopaedia of Occupational Health and Safety.* 4th ed. Geneva: International Labour Organization.

Arndt, R.L., G.R. Carmichael, D.G. Streets, and N. Bhatti. 1997. "Sulfur Dioxide Emissions and Sectoral Contributions to Sulfur Deposition in Asia." *Atmospheric Environment* 31: 1553–72.

Arthur, E.A., ed. 1997. "Technology Development Examples Applicable to Nuclear Energy and Fuel-Cycle Improvement." Report LA-UR-97-2989. Los Alamos National Laboratory and Sandia National Laboratory, Los Alamos, N.M.

Bascom, R., and others. 1996. "Health Effects of Outdoor Air Pollution." *American Journal of Respiratory Critical Care Medicine* 153: 477–98.

Bezdek, R. H. 1993. "The Environmental, Health, and Safety Implications of Solar Energy in Central Station Power Production." *Energy* 18 (6): 681–85.

Bolin, B. 1998. "The Kyoto Negotiations on Climate Change: A Science Perspective." *Science* 279: 330–31.

Bourke, G. 1988. "Subduing the Sea's Onslaught." *South* (July).

Bower, B.T., and others. 1987. "Guide for Analysis for Integrated Residuals Management." Draft final report. Resources for the Future, Washington, D.C.

BP (British Petroleum). 1998. *BP Statistical Review of World Energy 1998.* London.

Brauer, M., and J. Hisham-Hashim. 1998. "Fires in Indonesia: Crisis and Reaction." *Environmental Science and Technology* 9: 404A–407A.

Braunstein, H.M., and others. 1981. *Biomass Energy Systems and the Environment.* New York: Pergamon Press.

Brimblecombe, P. 1987. *The Big Smoke: A History of Air Pollution in London since Medieval Times.* London: Methuen.

Broecker, W.S. 1997. "Thermohaline Circulation, the Achilles Heel of Our Climate System: Will Man-made CO_2 Upset the Current Balance?" *Science* 278: 1582–88.

Brouwer, I.D. 1994. "Food and Fuel: A Hidden Dimension in Human Nutrition." Diss. Wageningen University, Netherlands.

Burtraw, D., and E. Mansur 1999. "Environmental Effects of SO_2 Trading and Banking." *Environmental Science & Technology* 33 (20): 3489–94.

California Energy Commission. 1998. "Electric Vehicles." http://www.energy.ca.gov/afvs/ev/q_a.html

California Environmental Protection Agency. 1999. "Fuel Cell Electric Vehicles Fact Sheet." Air Resources Board Zero-Emission Vehicles Program. http://www.arb.ca.gov/msprog/zevprog/fuelcell/fcell_fs.pdf

Carpenter, L., and others. 1990. "Health Related Selection and Death Rates in the United Kingdom Atomic Energy Authority Workforce." *British Journal of Industrial Medicine* 47 (4): 248–58.

Carpenter, R.A., and others. 1990. *Environmental Risk Assessment: Dealing with Uncertainty in Environmental Impact Assessment.* Manila: Asian Development Bank.

Chameides, W.L., P.S. Kasibhatla, J. Yienger, and H. Levy. 1994. "Growth of Continental-scale Metro-agro-plexes, Regional Ozone Pollution, and World Food Production." *Science* 264: 74–77.

Charlson, R.J., S.E. Schwartz, J.M. Hales, R.D. Cess, J.A. Coakley, J.E. Hansen, and J. Hoffman. 1992. "Climate Forcing by Anthropogenic Aerosols." *Science* 255: 423–30.

Charpak, G., and R.L. Garwin. 1997. *Feux Follets et Champignons Nucleaires.* Paris: Editions Odile Jacob.

Collier, M., R.H. Webb, and J.C. Schmidt. 1996. "Dams and Rivers: Primer on the Downstream Effects of Dams." Circular 1126. U.S. Geological Survey, Branch of Information Services, Tucson, Ariz., and Denver, Colo.

Crane, M. 1998. "Power Generation and Distribution." In J.M. Stellman, ed., *Encyclopaedia of Occupational Health and Safety.* 4th ed. Geneva: International Labour Organization.

Curren, T., and A. Nixon. 1992. "Current Issue Review: Acid Rain." Library of Parliament, Research Branch, Ottawa, Canada.

Curtiss, P.S., and A. Rabl. 1996. "Impacts of Air Pollution: General Relationships and Site Dependence." *Atmospheric Environment* 30: 3331–47.

Dixon, J.A., and others. 1989. *Dams and the Environment: Considerations in World Bank Projects.* Washington, D.C.: World Bank.

Dohan, M.R., and others. 1974. "The Effect of Specific Energy Uses on Air Pollutant Emissions in New York City." Brookhaven National Laboratory, Upton, NY.

Dunn, S. 1998. "Hydroelectric Power Up Slightly." *In Vital Signs.* New York: Norton and Co.

Dvorak, A.J., and B.G. Lewis. 1978. "Impacts of Coal-fired Power Plants on Fish, Wildlife, and Their Habitats." Argonne National Laboratory, Division of Environmental Impact Studies, Ann Arbor, Mich.

Dynesius, M., and C. Nilsson. 1994. "Fragmentation and Flow Regulation of River Systems in the Northern Third of the World." *Science* 266 (4): 759–62.

Ehrlich, P.R., and others. 1977. *Ecoscience: Population, Resources, Environment.* San Francisco, Calif.: W.H. Freeman.

EIA (Energy Information Administration). 1995. *Electricity Generation and Environmental Externalities: Case Studies.* Washington, D.C.: U.S. Department of Energy.

Elkins, P. 1996. "How Large a Carbon Tax Is Justified by the Secondary Benefits of CO_2 Abatement?" *Resource and Energy Economics* 18: 161–87.

Environment Canada. 1999. "A Primer on Environmental Citizenship." http://www.ns.ec.gc.ca/aeb/ssd/acid/acidfaq.html

Evans, J.S. 1991. "Radiological Health Effects Models for Nuclear Power Plant Accident Consequence Analysis: An Update (1990)." *Nuclear Technology* 94 (2): 204–12.

Faaij, A., and others. 1998. "Externalities of Biomass Based Electricity Production Compared with Power Generation from Coal in the Netherlands." *Biomass and Bioenergy* 14 (2): 125–47.

Fearnside, P. 1995. "Hydroelectric Dams in the Brazilian Amazon as Sources of 'Greenhouse' Gases." *Environmental Conservation* 22(1).

Florig, H.K. 1997. "China's Air Pollution Risks." *Environmental Science and Technology* 31(6): 276A–79A.

Foell, W., M. Amann, G. Carmichael, M. Chadwick, J. Hettelingh, L. Hordijk, and D. Zhao, eds. 1995. *RAINS-ASIA: An Assessment Model for Air Pollution in Asia.* Washington, D.C.: World Bank.

Ford Motor Company. 1998. "1998 Ford Ranger Electric Vehicle Specifications." http://wwwu.ford.com/electricvehicle/rangspecs.html

———. 2000. "Crown Victoria Natural Gas Vehicle Specifications." http://www.ford.com/default.asp?pageid=429

Fritsche, U. 1992. "TEMIS: A Computerized Tool for Energy and Environmental Fuel and Life-Cycle Analysis." Paper presented at an International Energy Agency expert workshop on Life-Cycle Analysis of Energy Systems: Methods and Experience, Paris.

Fritzsche, A.F. 1989. "The Health Risks of Energy Production." *Risk Analysis* 9 (4): 565–77.

Fthenakis, V.M., and others. 1995. "An Assessment of Mercury Emissions and Health Risks from a Coal-Fired Power Plant." *Journal of Hazardous Materials* 44 (2–3): 267–83.

Funk, K., and A. Rabl. 1999. "Electric Versus Conventional Vehicles: Social Costs and Benefits in France." *Transport and Environment* 4 (6): 397–411.

Gagnon, L. 1998. "Greenhouse Gas Emissions from Hydro Reservoirs: The Level of Scientific Uncertainty in 1998." Hydro-Quebec, Montreal.

Gagnon, L., and J.P. van de Vate. 1997. "Greenhouse Gas Emissions from Hydropower." *Energy Policy* 25 (1): 7–13.

General Motors Corporation. 1999. "EV1 Electric: Specs/Pricing." http://www.gmev.com/specs/specs.htm

GFDL (Geophysical Fluid Dynamics Laboratory). 1997. *Climate Impact of Quadrupling Atmospheric CO_2.* National Oceanic and Atmospheric Administration, Princeton, N.J.

Gilinksy, V. 1977. "Plutonium, Proliferation, and Policy." *Technology Review* 79(4): 58–65.

Gleick, P.H. 1992. "Environmental Consequences of Hydroelectric Development: The Role of Size and Type". *Energy* 17:735–47.

Global Toyota. 1999. "Future Vehicles: RAV4 EV." http://www.toyota.com

Gould, J., and T.F. Golob. 1997. "Clean Air Forever? A Longitudinal Analysis of Options about Air Pollution and Electric Vehicles." University of California at Irvine, Institute of Transportation Studies.

Grossman, G., and A. Krueger. 1994. "Economic Growth and the Environment." NBER Working Paper 4634. National Bureau of Economic Research, Cambridge, Mass.

Gupta, N. 1989. "Health Implications of Nuclear Energy." *Economic and Political Weekly* 24 (39): 2166.

Habegger, L.J., and others. 1982. *Direct and Indirect Health and Safety Impacts of Electrical Generation Options.* Vienna: International Atomic Energy Agency.

Haefele, W. 1990. "Energy from Nuclear Power." *Scientific American* 9: 136–44.

Hallenbeck, W.H. 1995. "Health Impact of a Proposed Waste-to-Energy Facility in Illinois." *Bulletin of Environmental Contamination and Toxicology* 54 (3): 342–48.

Hanisch, C. 1999. "Powering Tomorrow's Cars." *Environmental Science and Technology* 33 (11): 458A–62A.

Hayes, P., and K.R. Smith, eds. 1994. *Global Greenhouse Regime: Who Pays?* London and Tokyo: Earthscan and United Nations University Press.

Hiraoka, T. 1994. "Nuclear Electricity Generation by Seawater Uranium. *Journal of the Atomic Energy Society of Japan* 36(7): 644–45.

Holdren, J.P. 1983. "Nuclear Power and Nuclear Weapons: The Connection Is Dangerous." *Bulletin of the Atomic Scientists* 1.

———. 1989. "Civilian Nuclear Technologies and Nuclear Weapons Proliferation." In C. Schaerf, B. Holden-Reid, and D. Carlton, eds., New Technologies and the Arms Race. London: Macmillan.

———. 1992. "The Transition to Costlier Energy." In L. Schipper and S. Meyers, eds., *Energy Efficiency and Human Activity: Past Trends, Future Prospects.* Cambridge: Cambridge University Press.

Holgate, S.T., and others, eds. 1999. *Air Pollution and Health.* San Diego, Calif.: Academic Press.

Holland, M. 1996. "Quantifying the Externalities of Fuel Cycle Activities outside the European Union." Maintenance Note 1 for the ExternE CORE Project, Energy Technology Support Unit. Didcot, Oxfordshire.

Hong Kong Municipal Government. 1999. "Air Pollution Components, Effects and Causes." Planning, Environment, and Lands Bureau. http://www.plb.gov.hk/cleanair/cne.htm

Horii, N. 1999. "Evolution of Energy Demand after China's Economic Reform."

Horne, A. J., and C.R. Goldman. 1994. *Limnology.* New York: McGraw-Hill.

Houghton, J.T., and others, eds. 1994. *Climate Change 1994: Radiative Forcing of Climate Change and an Evaluation of the IPCC IS92 Emission Scenarios.* Cambridge: Cambridge University Press.

Huang, M., Z. Wang, D. He, H. Xu, and L. Zhou. 1995. "Modeling Studies on Sulfur Deposition and Transport in East Asia. *Water, Air and Soil Pollution* 85: 1921–26.

IARC (International Agency for Research on Cancer). 1984. *Carcinogenicity Monographs 1984.*

Ichikawa, Y., and S. Fujita. 1995. "An analysis of Wet Deposition of Sulfate Using a Trajectory Model for East Asia." *Water, Air and Soil Pollution* 85: 1927–32.

ILO (International Labour Organization). 1998. *Yearbook of Labour Statistics.* Geneva.

IPCC (Intergovernmental Panel on Climate Change). 1990. *Climate Change: The IPCC Scientific Assessment.* Cambridge: Cambridge University Press.

———. 1995. *Climate Change 1994: Radiative Forcing of Climate Change.* Cambridge: Cambridge University Press.

———. 1996a. *Climate Change 1995: Impacts, Adaptations, and Mitigation of Climate Change: Scientific-Technical Analyses.* Cambridge: Cambridge University Press.

———. 1996b. *The Science of Climate Change: Summary for Policymakers and Technical Summary of the Working Group I Report.* Cambridge: Cambridge University Press.

Jaffe, D.A., R.E. Honrath, L. Zhang, H. Akimoto, A. Shimizu, H. Mukai. K. Murano, S. Hatakeyama, and J. Merrill. 1996. *Journal of Geophysical Research* 101: 2037–48.

Jenkins, S.A., and others. 1988. "The Impacts of Dam Building on the California Coastal Zone." *California Waterfront Age* (September).

Jennings N.S. 1998. "Mining: An Overview." In J.M. Stellman, ed., *Encyclopaedia of Occupational Health and Safety.* 4th ed. Geneva: International Labour Organization.

Johnson, C.E., and R.G. Derwent. 1996. "Relative Radiative Forcing Consequences of Global Emissions of Hydrocarbons, Carbon Monoxide and Nitrogen Oxide from Human Activities Estimated with a Zonally-Averaged Two-Dimensional Model." *Climatic Change* 34 (3-4): 439–62.

Johnson, F.R., and W. H. Desvousges. 1997. "Estimating Stated Preferences with Rated-pair Data: Environmental, Health, and Employment Effects of Energy Programs." *Journal of Environmental Economics and Management* 34 (1): 79–99.

Karl, T.R., and R.W. Knight. 1998. "Secular Trends of Precipitation Amount, Frequency, and Intensity in the USA." *Bulletin of the American Meteorological Society* 79: 231–41.

Kiehl, J.T., and others. 2000. "Radiative Forcing due to Sulfate Aerosols from Simulations with the National Center for Atmospheric Research Community Climate Model, Version 3." *Journal of Geophysical Research-Atmospheres* 105 (D1): 1441–57.

Kjellstrom, T. 1994. "Issues in the Developing World." In L. Rosenstock and M. Cullen, eds., *Textbook of Clinical Occupational and Environmental Medicine.* Philadelphia, Pa.: W.B. Saunders and Co.

Kjellstrom, T., J.P. Koplan, and R.B. Rothenberg. 1992. "Current and Future Determinants of Adult Ill Health. In R. Feachem and others, eds., *The Health of Adults in the Developing World.* Oxford: Oxford University Press.

Knutson, T.R., R. E. Tuleya, and Y. Kurihara. 1998. "Simulated Increase of Hurricane Intensities in a CO_2-warmed Climate." *Science* 279: 1018–20.

Koomey, J. 1990. "Comparative Analysis of Monetary Estimates of External Environmental Costs Associated with Combustion of Fossil Fuels." University of California, Lawrence Berkeley Laboratory, Applied Science Division.

Kraus, R.S. 1998. "Oil Exploration and Drilling." In J.M. Stellman, ed., *Encyclopaedia of Occupational Health and Safety.* 4th ed. Geneva: International Labour Organization.

Krebs, M. 1999. "Promise, and Pitfalls, of Fuel Cells." *The New York Times,* 2 April, F1.

Kremer, J. 2000. "MOBILE6 and Compressed Natural Gas Vehicles." U.S. Environmental Protection Agency, Office of Mobile Sources, Washington, D.C.

Krewitt, W., T. Heck, A. Truckenmueller, and R. Friedrich. 1999. "Environmental Damage Costs from Fossil Electricity Generation in Germany and Europe." *Energy Policy* 27: 173–83.

Krewitt, W., and others. 1998. "Health Risks of Energy Systems." *Risk Analysis* 18 (4): 377–83.

Lal, M, K. Gauri, and G.C. Holdren. 1981. "Pollutant Effects on Stone Monuments." *Environmental Science and Technology* 15: 386–90.

Lal, M., U. Cubasch, R. Voss, and J. Waszkewitz. 1995. "Effect of Transient Increase in Greenhouse Gases and Sulphate Aerosols on Monsoon Climate." *Current Science* 69: 752–63.

Lazarus, M., and others. 1995. *The SEI/UNEP Fuel Chain Project: Methods, Issues and Case Studies in Developing Countries.* Boston, Mass.: Stockholm Environment Institute–Boston.

Leach, Gerald. 2000. Personal communication.

Leigh, J., P. Macaskill, C. Corvalan, E. Kuosma, and J. Mandryk. 1996. "Global Burden of Disease and Injury Due to Occupational Factors." WHO/EHG/96.20. World Health Organization, Geneva.

Lelieveld, J., and others. 1997. "Terrestrial Sources and Distribution of Atmospheric Sulphur." *Philosophical Transactions of the Royal Society of London Series B-Biological Sciences* 352 (1350): 149–58.

Lerman, Y., A. Finkelstein, and others. 1990. "Asbestos Related Health Hazards among Power Plant Workers." *British Journal of Industrial Medicine* 47 (4): 281–82.

Lew, C.S., and others. 1996. "Use of the Pisces Database: Power Plant Aqueous Stream Compositions." *Water, Air and Soil Pollution* 90: 113–22.

Lovei, M. 1998. *Phasing Out Lead from Gasoline: Worldwide Experience and Policy Implications.* World Bank Technical Paper 397. Washington, D.C.

Lydersen, E., V. Angell, O. Eilertsen, T. Larssen, J. Mulder, I.P. Muniz, H.M. Seip, A. Semb, R.D. Vogt, and P. Aagaard. 1997. "Planning of an Integrated Acidification Study and Survey on Acid Rain Impacts in China." Norwegian Institute for Water Research Report SNO 3719-97. Oslo, Norway.

MacKenzie, J. 1997. *Climate Protection and the National Interest: The Links among Climate Change, Air Pollution, and Energy Security.* Washington, D.C.: World Resources Institute.

Mage, D.R., and O. Zali, eds. 1992. "Motor Vehicle Air Pollution: Public Health Impact and Control Measures." WHO/PEP/92.4. World Health Organization, Geneva.

Mann, M.E., R.S., Bradley, and M.K. Hughes. 1998. "Global-scale Temperature Patterns and Climate Forcing over the Past Six Centuries." *Nature* 392: 779–87.

———. 1999. "Northern Hemisphere Temperatures during the Past Millennium: Inferences, Uncertainties, and Limitations." Geophysical Research Letters (15 March).

Mark, J., J..M. Ohi, and D.V. Hudson, Jr. 1994. "Fuel Savings and Emissions Reductions from Light Duty Fuel Cell Vehicles." NREL/TP-463-6157. National Renewable Energy Laboratory, Golden, Colo.

Matsumoto, S., A. Inaba, and Y. Yanagisawa. 1997. "Technology Assessment of Alternative Fuels by CO_2 Fixation Use in Passenger Cars." *Energy Conversion and Management* 38: S455–60.

McCully, P. 1996. *Silenced Rivers: The Ecology and Politics of Large Dams.* London: Zed Books.

McGranahan, G., and others. 2000. *Citizens at Risk: From Urban Sanitation to Sustainable Cities.* London: Earthscan.

McManus, N. 1998. "Hydroelectric Power Generation." In J.M. Stellman, ed., *Encyclopaedia of Occupational Health and Safety.* 4th ed. Geneva: International Labour Organization.

McMichael, A.J., E. Haines, R. Slooff, and S. Kovats, eds. 1996. "Climate Change and Human Health." Assessment Prepared by a Task Group on behalf of the World Health Organization, World Meteorological Organization, and United Nations Environment Programme. Geneva, Switzerland.

Mendler, C. 1997. "Taking a New Look at Hybrid Electric Vehicle Efficiency." *Automotive Engineering* 105 (2): 67–70.

Mills, W.B., and others. 1998. "Predictions of Potential Human Health and Ecological Risks from Power Plant Discharges of Total Residual Chlorine and Chloroform into Rivers." *Environmental Science & Technology* 32 (14): 2162–71.

Moffit, A. 1998. "Iron and Steel." In J.M. Stellman, ed., *Encyclopaedia of Occupational Health and Safety.* 4th ed. Geneva: International Labour Organization.

Morison, W.G. 1998. "Nuclear Power Generation." In J.M. Stellman, ed., *Encyclopaedia of Occupational Health and Safety.* 4th ed. Geneva: International Labour Organization.

Morris, S.C., and others. 1980. "Health and Environmental Effects of the National Energy Plan: A Critical Review of Some Selected Issues." Brookhaven National Laboratory, Upton, NY.

Moskowits, P.D., M.D. Rowe, and others. 1977. "Workshop Report on Quantifying Environmental Damage from Energy Activities." Brookhaven National Laboratory, National Center for Analysis of Energy Systems, Office of Environmental Policy, Upton, NY.

MRC (Medical Research Council). 1996. *Electrification and Health: The Interface between Energy, Development, and Public Health.* Community Health Research Group. Tygerberg, South Africa.

Murray, C., and A. Lopez, eds. 1996. *Global Burden of Disease. World Health Organization, World Bank, and Harvard School of Public Health.* Cambridge, Mass.: Harvard University Press.

Nakićenović, N., A. Grübler, and A. McDonald, eds. 1998. *Global Energy Perspectives.* Cambridge: Cambridge University Press.

NAPAP (National Acid Precipitation Assessment Program). 1998. *Biennial Report to Congress: An Integrated Assessment. National Science and Technology Council, Committee on Environment and Natural Resources.* Washington, D.C. http://www.nnic.noaa.gov/CENR/NAPAP/NAPAP_96.htm

Nash, L. 1993. "Water Quality and Health." In P.H. Gleick, ed., *Water in Crisis: A Guide to the World's Fresh Water Resources.* New York: Oxford University Press.

National Academy of Sciences. 1994. *Management and Disposition of Excess Weapons Plutonium.* Washington, D.C.: National Academy Press.

———. 1995. *Management and Disposition of Excess Weapons Plutonium: Reactor-Related Options.* Washington, D.C.: National Academy Press.

National Fuel Cell Research Center. 1999. "What Is a Fuel Cell?" http://www.nfcrc.uci.edu/fcinfo/what.htm

National Research Council. 1992. *Nuclear Power: Technical and Institutional Options for the Future. Committee on Future Nuclear Power Development.* Washington, D.C.: National Academy Press.

———. 1998. *Research Priorities for Airborne Particulate Matter.* National Academy of Sciences, Washington, D.C.

Natural Gas Vehicle Coalition. 2000a. "Questions and Answers about Natural Gas Vehicles." http://www.ngvc.org/qa.html

———. 2000b. "The NGV Message: Environmental and Health Benefits." http://www.ngvc.org/ngvmess.html

Neil, D. 1999. "Pump This." *Car and Driver* 44 (10): 110–16.

Nriagu, J.O. 1989. "A Global Assessment of Natural Sources of Atmospheric Trace Metals." *Nature* 338 (6210): 47–49.

———. 1990. "Global Metal Pollution: Poisoning the Biosphere." *Environment* 32 (7): 6–16.

Office of Science and Technology Policy. 2000. *White House Initiative on Global Climate Change,* Washington D.C. www.whitehouse.gov/Initiatives/Climate/greenhouse.html

Olivier, J.G.J., A.F. Bouwman, K.W. Van der Hoek, and J.J.M. Berdowski. 1998. "Global Air Emission Inventories for Anthropogenic Sources of NO_x, NH_3, and N_2O in 1990." *Environmental Pollution* 102: 135–48.

Olivier, J.G.J., A.F. Bouwman, C.W.M. van der Maas, J.J.M. Berdowski, C. Veldt, J.P.J. Bloos, A.J.H. Visschedijk, P.Y.J. Zandveld, and J.L. Haverlag. 1996. "Description of EDGAR Version 2.0." RIVM Report 771060 002. Bilthoven, the Netherlands.

Oppenheimer, M. 1998. "Global Warming and the Stability of the West Antarctic Ice Sheet." *Nature* 393: 325–32.

ORNL and RFF (Oak Ridge National Laboratory and Resources for the Future). 1992. "U.S.-EC Fuel Cycle Study: Background Document to the Approach and Issues." Oak Ridge, Tenn.

———. 1994a. *Estimating Externalities of Coal Fuel Cycles.* Oak Ridge, Tenn.

———. 1994b. *Estimating Externalities of Hydroelectric Fuel Cycles.* Oak Ridge, Tenn.

———. 1994c. *Fuel Cycle Externalities: Analytical Methods and Issues.* Oak Ridge, Tenn.

———. 1995. *Estimating Externalities of Nuclear Fuel Cycles.* Oak Ridge, Tenn.

———. 1996. *Estimating Externalities of Oil Fuel Cycles.* Oak Ridge, Tenn.

———. 1998a. *Estimating Externalities of Biomass Fuel Cycles.* Oak Ridge, Tenn.

———. 1998b. *Estimating Externalities of Natural Gas Fuel Cycles.* Oak Ridge, Tenn.

Osepchuk, J.M. 1996. "Health and Safety Issues for Microwave Power Transmission." *Solar Energy* 56 (1): 53–60.

OTA (Office of Technology Assessment). 1992. *Fueling Development: Energy Technologies for Developing Countries.* OTA-E516. Washington, D.C.: U.S. Government Printing Office.

Page, W.P., and others. 1982. "Direct Monetary Losses to the Agricultural Sector from Coal-fired Electricity Generation and Background: A Regional Analysis." *Energy* 7 (9): 759–68.

PCAST (President's Committee of Advisors on Science and Technology). 1997. "Federal Energy Research and Development for the Challenges of the 21st Century." Office of Science and Technology Policy, Panel on Energy Research and Development, Washington, D.C.

———. 1999. "Powerful Partnerships: The Federal Role in International Cooperation on Energy Innovation." Office of Science and Technology Policy, Panel on International Cooperation in Energy Research, Development, Demonstration, and Deployment, Washington, D.C.

Pearce, D., and C. Bann. 1992. "The Social Costs of Electricity Generation in the U.K." Paper presented at an International Energy Agency expert workshop on Life-Cycle Analysis of Energy Systems: Methods and Experience, Paris.

Penner, J.E., S.J. Ghan, and J.J. Walton. 1991. "The Role of Biomass Burning in the Budget and Cycle of Carbonaceous Soot Aerosols and Their Climate Impact." In J.S. Levine, ed., *Global Biomass Burning: Atmospheric, Climatic, and Biospheric Implications.* Cambridge, Mass.: MIT Press.

Peterson, T.C., K.P. Gallo, J. Lawrimore, T.W. Owen, A. Huang, and D.A. McKittrick. 1999. "Global Rural Temperature Trends." *Geophysical Research Letters* 26: 329–32.

Petrini, C., and P. Vecchia. 1993. "Health Problems Related to High-Power Transmission Lines [in Italian]." *Aei Automazione Energia Informazione* 80 (4): 430–33.

Piccot, S.D., J.J. Watson, and J.W. Jones. 1992. "A Global Inventory of Volatile Organic Compound Emissions from Anthropogenic Sources." *Journal of Geophysical Research* 97: 9897–9912.

Poschen, P. 1998. "Forestry." In J.M. Stellman, ed., *Encyclopaedia of Occupational Health and Safety.* 4th ed. Geneva: International Labour Organization.

Pottinger, I. 1997. "The Environmental Impacts of Large Dams." International Rivers Network. http://www.irn.org/basics/impacts.shtml

Rabl, A. 1998. "Mortality Risks of Air Pollution: The Role of Exposure-response Functions." *Journal of Hazardous Materials* 61 (1–3): 91–98.

Rabl, A. and J.V. Spadaro. 1999. "Damages and Costs of Air Pollution: An Analysis of Uncertainties." *Environment International* 25 (1): 29–46.

———. 2000. "Public Health Impact of Air Pollution and Implications for the Energy System." *Annual Review of Energy and the Environment* 25.

Rabl, A., and others. 1998. "Health Risks of Air Pollution from Incinerators: A Perspective." *Waste Management & Research* 16 (4): 365–88.

Reddy, A.K.N., R.H. Williams, and T.B. Johansson. 1997. *Energy after Rio: Prospects and Challenges.* New York: United Nations Development Programme.

Repetto, R., and D. Austin. 1997. *The Costs of Climate Protection: A Guide for the Perplexed.* Washington, D.C.: World Resources Institute.

Rogner, H.-H. and A. Khan. 1998. "Comparing Energy Options: The Inter-agency DECADES Project." *IAEA Bulletin* 40 (1).

Ross, M., R. Goodwin, R. Watkins, M.Q. Wang, and T. Wenzel. 1995. "Real-World Emissions from Model Year 1993, 2000, and 2010 Passenger Cars." Report prepared for Energy Foundation and U.S. Department of Energy through Lawrence Berkeley Laboratory and Oak Ridge National Laboratory. American Council for an Energy-Efficient Economy, Berkeley, Calif.

Rowe, M.D. 1981. "Human Exposure to Particulate Emissions from Power Plants." Brookhaven National Laboratory, Upton, N.Y.

Rubin, E.S. 1999. "Toxic Releases from Power Plants." *Environmental Science and Technology* 33 (18): 3062–67.

Rudd, J., and others. 1993. "Are Hydroelectric Reservoirs Significant Sources of Greenhouse Gases?" *Ambio* 22 (4).

Saez, R.M., and others. 1998. "Assessment of the Externalities of Biomass Energy, and a Comparison of Its Full Costs with Coal." *Biomass and Bioenergy* 14 (5/6): 469–78.

Saksena, S., and V. Dayal. 1997. "Total Exposures As a Basis for the Economic Valuation of Air Pollution in India." *Energy Environment Monitor* 13 (2): 93–102.

Schwela, D. 1995. "Public Health Implications of Urban Air Pollution in Developing Countries." Paper presented at the Tenth World Clean Air Congress, 28 May–2 June, Erjos, Finland.

Schwela, D., and O. Zali, eds. 1999. *Urban Traffic Pollution.* New York: E & FN Spon.

Segen, J. C. 1992. *The Dictionary of Modern Medicine.* Park Ridge, N.J.: Parthenon.

Seigneur, C., and others. 1996. "Multipathway Health Risk Assessment of Power Plant Water Discharges." *Water Air and Soil Pollution* 90 (1–2): 55–64.

Seip, H., D. Zhao, J. Xiong, D. Zhao, T. Larssen, B. Liao, and R. Vogt. 1995. "Acidic Deposition and Its Effects in Southwestern China." *Water, Air and Soil Pollution* 85: 2301–06.

Shiklomanov, I. 1998. Assessment of Water Resources and Water Availability in the World. *Report for the Comprehensive Assessment of the Fresh Water Resources of the World,* United Nations, New York.

Sims, J. 1994. *Women, Health and Environment: An Anthology.* WHO/EHG/94.11. Geneva: World Health Organization.

Smith, D.R., and A.R. Flegal. 1995. "Lead in the Biosphere: Recent Trends." *Ambio* 24 (1): 21–23.

Smith, K.R. 1990. "Risk Transition and Global Warming." *Journal of Energy Engineering-Asce* 116 (3): 178–88.

———. 1991a. "Allocating Responsibility for Global Warming: The Natural Debt Index." *Ambio* 20 (2): 95–96.

———. 1991b. "Managing the Risk Transition." *Toxicology and Industrial Health* 7 (5–6): 319–27.

———. 1993. "Fuel Combustion, Air Pollution Exposure, and Health: The Situation in Developing Countries." *Annual Review of Energy and Environment* 18: 529–66.

———. 1997. "Development, Health, and the Environmental Risk Transition." In G. Shahi, B.S. Levy, A. Binger, and others, eds., *International Perspectives in Environment, Development, and Health.* New York: Springer Publications.

———. 1998. *The National Burden of Disease from Indoor Air Pollution in India.* Mumbai: Indira Gandhi Institute of Development Research.

———. 2000. "National Burden of Disease in India from Indoor Air Pollution." *Proceedings of the National Academy of Sciences 97.*

Smith, K.R., and S. Akbar. 1999. "Health-damaging Air Pollution: A Matter of Scale." In G. McGranahan and G. Murray, eds., Health and Air Pollution in Rapidly Developing Countries. York, U.K.: Stockholm Environment Institute of York.

Smith, K.R. J.M. Samet, I. Romieu, and N. Bruce. 2000. "Indoor Air Pollution in Developing Countries and ALRI in Children." *Thorax* 55: 518–32.

Smith, K.R., J. Weyant, and J.P. Holdren. 1975. "Evaluation of Conventional Power Systems." University of California at Berkeley, Energy and Resources Program.

Smith, K.R., C. Corvalan and T. Kjellstrom. 1999. "How Much Global Ill-health Is Attributable to Environmental Factors?" *Epidemiology* 10.

Smith, K.R. and others. 2000a., "Greenhouse Gases from Small-scale Combustion Devices in Developing Countries, Phase IIa: Household Stoves in India." EPA-600/R-00-052 U.S. Environmetal Protection Agency, Office of Research and Development, Washington, D.C.

———. 2000b. "Greenhouse Implications of Household Stoves: An Analysis for India." *Annual Review of Energy and Environment* 25: 741–63.

Smithsonian Institution. 1996. "Ocean Planet: Oil Pollution." http://seawifs. gsfc.nasa.gov/OCEAN_PLANET/HTML/peril_oil_pollution.html

Spadaro, J.V., and A. Rabl. 1998. "External Costs of Energy: Application of the ExternE Methodology in France." ARMINES (Ecole des Mines), Paris.

Spadaro, J.V., and others. 1998. "External Costs of Air Pollution: Case Study and Results for Transport between Paris and Lyon." *International Journal of Vehicle Design* 20 (1–4): 274–82.

Spinrad, B. 1983. "Nuclear Power and Nuclear Weapons: The Connection Is Tenuous." *Bulletin of the Atomic Scientists* 2.

Steinbugler, M.M., and R.H. Williams. 1998. "Beyond Combustion: Fuel Cell Cars for the 21st Century." *Forum for Applied Research and Public Policy* 13 (4): 102–07.

Stellman, J.M., ed. 1998. *Encyclopaedia of Occupational Health and Safety.* 4th ed. Geneva: International Labour Organization.

Streets, D.G., G.R. Carmichael, M. Amann, and R.L. Arndt. 1999. "Energy Consumption and Acid Deposition in Northeast Asia." *Ambio* 28: 135–43.

Sweet, W. 1984. "The Nuclear Age: Power, Proliferation, and the Arms Race." *Congressional Quarterly,* Washington, D.C.

Thornton, E.W. 1994. "Health Risks of Energy Saving." *Nature* 372 (6504): 327.

UN (United Nations). 1995. *Framework Convention on Climate Change.* United Nations Conference of the Parties, First Session, Berlin, Germany.

UNECE (United Nations Economic Commission for Europe). 1996. "The State of Transboundary Air Pollution." *Air Pollution Studies* 12. Geneva.

UNEP (United Nations Environment Programme). 1998. *Protecting Our Planet, Securing Our Future.* United Nations Environment Programme, U.S. National Aeronautics and Space Administration, and World Bank.

UNEP and WHO (United Nations Environment Programme and World Health Organization). 1992. *Urban Air Pollution in Megacities of the World.* Blackwell Publishers.

USAEC (U.S. Atomic Energy Commission). 1974. "Comparative Risk-Cost-Benefit Study of Alternative Sources of Electrical Energy." Office of Energy Systems Analysis, Washington, D.C.

U.S. Census Bureau. 1996. *Statistical Abstract of the US: National Data Book.* Washington D.C.: U.S. Department of Commerce.

USDOE (U.S. Department of Energy). 1980. *Nuclear Proliferation and Civilian Nuclear Power: Report of the Non-Proliferation Alternative Systems Assessment Program.* Washington, D.C.: U.S. Government Printing Office.

———. 1995. "Executive Summary: Encouraging the Purchase and Use of Electric Motor Vehicles." Office of Transportation Technologies, Washington, D.C.

———. 1997. *Final Nonproliferation and Arms Control Assessment of Weapons-Usable Fissile Material Storage and Excess Plutonium Disposition Alternatives.* Washington, D.C.

US Energy Information Administration. 2000. *International Energy Annual 1998.* US Department of Energy: Washington D.C.

USEPA (U.S. Environmental Protection Agency). 1994. "Motor Vehicles and the 1990 Clean Air Act." Office of Mobile Sources, Washington, D.C.

———. 1996. *National Air Pollution Emission Trends: 1900–1995.* Washington, D.C.

———. 1997. "Regulatory Impact Analyses for the Particulate Matter and Ozone National Ambient Air Quality Standards and Proposed Regional Haze Rule." Research Triangle Park, N.C.

———. 1998a. "Study of Hazardous Air Pollutant Emissions from Electric Utility Steam Generating Units." Final report to Congress, vol. 1. Washington, D.C.

———. 1998b. "Toyota Prius Hybrid System (THS)." Office of Air and Radiation. http://www.epa.gov/orcdizux/reports/adv-tech/priustst.pdf

———. 1999. "Environmental Effects of Acid Rain." http://www.epa.gov/docs/acidrain/effects/envben.html

van Aardenne, J.A., G.R. Carmichael, H. Levy, D. Streets, and L. Hordijk. 1999. "Anthropogenic NOx Emissions in Asia in the Period 1990–2020." *Atmospheric Environment* 33: 633–46.

Wang, W., and T. Wang. 1995. "On the Origin and the Trend of Acid Precipitation in China." *Water, Air and Soil Pollution* 85: 2295–2300.

Wang, X., and K.R. Smith. 1998. "Near-term Health Benefits of Greenhouse Gas Reductions: A Proposed Method for Assessment and Application to China." WHO/EHG/98.12. World Health Organization, Geneva.

WCD (World Commission on Dams). 1999. "Work Programme in Brief." Cape Town, South Africa. http://www.dams.org

WEC (World Energy Council). 1993. *Energy for Tomorrow's World.* London: Kogan Page.

———. 1995. *Global Transport Sector Energy Demand towards 2020.* London.

Weeks, J.L. 1998. "Health Hazards of Mining and Quarrying." In J.M. Stellman, ed., *Encyclopaedia of Occupational Health and Safety.* 4th ed. Geneva: International Labour Organization.

Wentz, F.J., and M. Schabel. 1998. "Effects of Orbital Decay on Satellite-derived Lower-tropospheric Temperature Trends." *Nature* 394: 661–64.

WHO (World Health Organization). 1994. "Ultraviolet Radiation." *Environmental Health Criteria* 160. Geneva.

———. 1996. "Health Effects of the Chernobyl Accident." WHO/EHG/96.X. Geneva.

———. 1997. "Health and Environment in Sustainable Development: Five Years after the Earth Summit." WHO/EHG/97.8. Geneva.

———. 1998a. "Chrysotile Asbestos." *Environmental Health Criteria* 190. Geneva.

———. 1998b. *Healthy Cities Air Information Management System 2.0.* Geneva.

———. 1999. *Provisional Global Air Quality Guidelines.* Geneva.

Wigley, T.M. 1999. *The Science of Climate Change: Global and U.S. Perspectives.* Arlington, Va.: Pew Center on Global Climate Change.

Wigley, T.M., R.L. Smith, and B.D. Santer. 1998. "Anthropogenic Influence on the Autocorrelation Structure of Hemispheric-mean Temperatures." *Science* 282: 1676–79.

Willrich, M., and T. Taylor. 1974. *Nuclear Theft: Risks and Safeguards.* Cambridge, Mass.: Ballinger.

WMO (World Meteorological Organization). 1995. *Scientific Assessment of Ozone Depletion: 1994.* Geneva.

———. 1999. *Scientific Assessment of Ozone Depletion: 1998.* Geneva.

World Bank. 1992. *World Development Report 1992: Development and the Environment.* New York: Oxford University Press.

———. 1993. *China: Involuntary Resettlement.* Washington, D.C.

———. 1997. *Clear Water, Blue Skies: China's Environment in the New Century.* China 2020 series. Washington, D.C.

WRI (World Resources Institute). 1998. *World Resources Report 1998–99: Environmental Change and Human Health.* New York: Oxford University Press.

Yasukawa, S., and others. 1992. "Life Cycle CO_2 Emission from Nuclear Power Reactor and Fuel Cycle System." Paper presented at an International Energy Agency expert workshop on Life-Cycle Analysis of Energy Systems: Methods and Experience, Paris.

Zhao, D., and J. Xiong. 1988. "Acidification in Southwestern China." In H. Rodhe and R. Herrera, eds., *Acidification in Tropical Countries.* Chichester, U.K.: John Wiley and Sons Ltd.

energy security

CHAPTER 4

Hisham Khatib (Jordan)

LEAD AUTHORS: Alexander Barnes (France), Isam Chalabi (Iraq), H. Steeg (Germany), K. Yokobori (Japan, on behalf of Asia-Pacific Economic Cooperation), and the Planning Department, Organisation of Arab Oil Producing Countries (Kuwait)

The ideas expressed in the chapter are entirely the responsibility of the Convening Lead Author.

ABSTRACT   Energy security—the continuous availability of energy in varied forms, in sufficient quantities, and at reasonable prices—has many aspects. It means limited vulnerability to transient or longer disruptions of imported supplies. It also means the availability of local and imported resources to meet, over time and at reasonable prices, the growing demand for energy. Environmental challenges, liberalisation and deregulation, and the growing dominance of market forces all have profound implications for energy security. These forces have introduced new elements into energy security, affecting the traditionally vital role of government.

In the past, and especially since the early 1970s, energy security has been narrowly viewed as reduced dependence on oil consumption and imports, particularly in OECD and other major oil-importing countries. But changes in oil and other energy markets have altered that view. Suppliers have increased, as have proven reserves and stocks, and prices have become flexible and transparent, dictated by market forces rather than by cartel arrangements. Global tensions as well as regional conflicts are lessening, and trade is flourishing and becoming freer. Suppliers have not imposed any oil sanctions since the early 1980s, nor have there been any real shortages anywhere in the world. Instead, the United Nations and other actors have applied sanctions to some oil suppliers, but without affecting world oil trade or creating shortages. All this points to the present availability of abundant oil supplies at all times, an availability that has been greatly enhanced thanks in large part to technological advances. Moreover, in today's market environment energy security is a shared issue for importing and exporting countries.

Energy security can be ensured through local adequacy—abundant and varied forms of indigenous energy resources. But for countries that face local shortages, as most do, energy security can be enhanced through:

- The ability, of the state or of market players, to draw on foreign energy resources and products that can be freely imported through ports or other transport channels and through cross-boundary energy grids (pipelines and electricity networks). This is increasingly aided by energy treaties and charters and by investment and trade agreements.
- Adequate national (or regional) strategic reserves to address any transient interruption, shortages, or unpredictably high demand.
- Technological and financial resources and know-how to develop indigenous renewable energy sources and domestic power generating facilities to meet part of local energy requirements.
- Adequate attention to environmental challenges.
- Diversification of import sources and types of fuels.

Energy security can also be greatly enhanced by energy conservation and efficiency measures, because reducing energy intensity will reduce the dependence of the economy on energy consumption and imports.

But while all this is very encouraging, new threats to energy security have appeared in recent years. Regional shortages are becoming more acute, and the possibility of insecurity of supplies—due to disruption of trade and reduction in strategic reserves, as a result of conflicts or sabotage—still exists, although it is decreasing. All this points to a need to strengthen global as well as regional and national energy security. This chapter discusses some means and instruments for doing so. ∎

The world has generally seen considerable development and progress in the past 50 years. Living standards have improved, people have become healthier and longer-lived, and science and technology have considerably enhanced human welfare. No doubt the availability of abundant and cheap sources of energy, mainly in the form of crude oil from the Middle East, contributed to these achievements. Adequate global energy supplies, for the world as a whole as well as for individual countries, are essential for sustainable development, proper functioning of the economy, and human well-being. Thus the continuous availability of energy—in the quantities and forms required by the economy and society—must be ensured and secured.

Energy security—the continuous availability of energy in varied forms, in sufficient quantities, and at reasonable prices—has several aspects. It means limited vulnerability to transient or longer disruptions of imported supplies. It also means the availability of local and imported resources to meet growing demand over time and at reasonable prices.

Beginning in the early 1970s energy security was narrowly viewed as reduced dependence on oil consumption and imports, particularly in OECD and other major oil-importing countries. Since that time considerable changes in oil and other energy markets have altered the picture. Suppliers have increased, as have proven reserves and stocks, and prices have become flexible and transparent, dictated by market forces rather than by cartel arrangements. Global tensions and regional conflicts are lessening, and trade is flourishing and becoming freer. Suppliers have not imposed any oil sanctions since the early 1980s, nor have there been any real shortages anywhere in the world. Instead, the United Nations and other actors have applied sanctions to some oil suppliers, but without affecting world oil trade or creating shortages.

All this points to the present abundance of oil supplies. Moreover, in today's market environment energy security is a shared issue for importing and exporting countries. As much as importing countries are anxious to ensure security by having sustainable sources, exporting countries are anxious to export to ensure sustainable income (Mitchell, 1997).

However, although all these developments are very encouraging, they are no cause for complacency. New threats to energy security have emerged in recent years. Regional shortages are becoming more acute, and the possibility of insecurity of supplies—due to disruption of trade and reduction in strategic reserves, as a result of conflicts or sabotage—persists, although it is decreasing. These situations point to a need to strengthen global as well as regional and national energy security (some means for doing this are discussed later in the chapter). There is also a need for a strong plea, under the auspices of the World Trade Organization (WTO), to refrain from restrictions on trade in energy products on grounds of competition or differences in environmental or labour standards.

Environmental challenges to sustainable development are gaining

Energy insecurity and shortages handicap productive activities and undermine consumer welfare.

momentum and have profound implications for energy security, as do the current trends of liberalisation, deregulation, and the growing dominance of market forces. These forces have introduced new elements into energy security, affecting the traditionally vital role of government, as described below. They also have consequences for medium-size companies and individual consumers, who may be tempted by cheap competitive prices and lack of information to sacrifice, sometimes temporarily, supply security.

Energy has always been important to humanity. But its importance is increasing each year. Interruptions of energy supply—even if brief—can cause serious financial, economic, and social losses. Some energy products and carriers have become absolutely essential for modern life and business. Interruption of electricity supply can cause major financial losses and create havoc in cities and urban centres. The absolute security of the energy supply, particularly electricity, is therefore critical. With the widespread use of computers and other voltage- and frequency-sensitive electronic equipment, the quality of supply has also become vital. In the electricity supply industry, a significant share of investment goes into reserve generating plants, standby equipment, and other redundant facilities needed to protect the continuity and quality of supply.

Energy insecurity and shortages affect countries in two ways: they handicap productive activities, and they undermine consumer welfare. Energy insecurity discourages investors by threatening production and increasing costs. Shortages in electricity supplies (as in many developing countries) require more investment for on-site electricity production or standby supplies. For small investors, the cost of operation is increased, since electricity from private small-scale generation is more expensive than public national supplies. Electricity interruptions at home cause consumers great inconvenience, frustration, and loss of productivity, sometimes threatening their well-being.

For any economy, an unreliable energy supply results in both short- and long-term costs. The costs are measured in terms of loss of welfare and production, and the adjustments that consumers (such as firms) facing unreliable fuel and electric power supplies undertake to mitigate their losses. Interruptions in supply may trigger loss of production, costs related to product spoilage, and damage to equipment. The extent of these direct economic costs depends on a host of factors, such as advance notification, duration of the interruption, and timing of the interruption, which relates to the time of day or season and to the prevailing market conditions and demand for the firm's output. These direct costs can be very high. In addition, the economy is affected indirectly because of the secondary costs that arise from the interdependence between one firm's output and another firm's input.

New dimensions and challenges to energy security

Energy security needs to be investigated at several levels: globally, to ensure adequacy of resources; regionally, to ensure that networking and trade can take place; at the country level, to ensure national security of supply; and at the consumer level, to ensure that consumer demand can be satisfied. At the country level, energy security is based on the availability of all energy consumption requirements at all times from indigenous sources or imports and from stocks. Normally in most countries, this is a state responsibility. However, markets in some OECD countries are increasingly shouldering part of this responsibility. To ensure energy security, projections, plans, and supply arrangements should look beyond short-term requirements to medium- and long-term demand as well.

With the increasing deregulation and competition among private and independent suppliers, supply security at the consumer level can become more vulnerable and correspondingly more important in some cases. Consumer demand for energy services can be met by different suppliers competing to deliver different forms of energy at different prices, while the consumer remains unaware of the degree of supply security.

As explained above, environmental challenges, deregulation, and market forces have introduced new players to the energy security scene. This chapter considers energy security at the national (and regional) level as well as consumer security in terms of energy services. In most countries these two levels of security are one and the same. But in some OECD countries, with markets and competition emerging at the consumer level, the two may diverge. The chapter also covers the geopolitical aspects of energy security as well as the limitations of the resource base and other factors that may affect long-term energy security.

Of all energy sources, crude oil and its products are the most versatile, capable of meeting every requirement for energy use and services, particularly in transport. The other fossil fuels, coal and natural gas, are well suited for electricity production and such stationary uses as generation of heat and steam. Coal, increasingly used for electricity production, requires relatively expensive clean technologies, and treatment for liquefaction and gasification to make it more versatile. Natural gas also requires expensive infrastructure, and special treatment to make it useful for transport. Hydropower, newer renewable resources such as wind and photovoltaics, and nuclear energy have limited use beyond electricity production.

Given the versatility of crude oil and its products and the limitations of other energy sources, energy security depends more than anything else on the availability of crude oil in the required amounts (by ship or pipeline) to any importing country in the world. Thus, although energy security has to be interpreted more broadly than in the past, the uninterrupted supply of crude oil in the required amounts and at reasonable prices will continue to be the most important determinant of energy security. Uninterrupted supply—of oil and other forms of energy—includes uninterrupted transit through third countries. As the chapter details later, work is under way, through the Energy Charter Treaty, to improve security for exporters and importers and

Reducing energy intensity will reduce the dependence of the economy on energy consumption and imports.

to promote a favourable climate for investments in upgrading and building new and diversified pipeline routes.

Security of electric power supply

Chronic energy shortages and poor security of the electric power supply trigger long-term adjustments.

If firms expect shortages and unreliable service to persist, they will respond in one or more ways. The most common long-term adjustment by commercial consumers and small industrial firms is to install back-up diesel generator sets. It has been estimated that in many developing countries such standby generation on customer premises accounts for 20 percent or more of the total installed generating capacity (USAID, 1988).

The shortages and inadequate maintenance of the grid also add to poor security. In some developing countries half the public electricity supply is inoperable at any given time. Many manufacturing firms have had to purchase their own generators to meet their demand for electricity. In Nigeria about 92 percent of firms surveyed in the mid-1990s had their own generators. This purchase added to their fixed costs, raised production costs, and tended to discourage new investments. For small firms, the investment in generating capacity represented almost a quarter of their total investment, and for large firms, a tenth (ADB, 1999). Moreover, in many developing countries the electric power system losses (technical and non-technical) are very high, exceeding a quarter of generation in some and as much as half in a few.

Shortages of electric power and supply interruptions are not uncommon, particularly in many developing countries. They occur for two main reasons:

- System inadequacy—shortfalls of delivered electricity under even the best conditions in the electric power system. Such shortfalls, most common in developing countries, usually occur because of an inadequate number of generating facilities capable of meeting peak demand and limitations in the transmission and distribution system, particularly to rural areas.
- Supply insecurity—unreliability of supply due to non-availability of generating plants or breakdowns in the transmission and distribution system. This can occur in varying degrees in any power system in the world.

To ensure system adequacy—the ability of a power system to meet demand and deliver adequate electricity to consumers—requires investment. Most investments in electric power security are meant to reduce the likelihood of shortages and maintain and improve reliability. Most shortages occur as a result of growth in demand, which necessitates expanding generation capacity and strengthening networks. But even with large investments, interruptions are inevitable. And the costs of improving continuity of supply can become very high once a certain level of reliability has been reached.

The function of the electric power system is to provide electricity as economically as possible and with an acceptable degree of security and quality. The economics of electric power security (reliability) involve striking a reasonable balance between cost and quality of service. This balance varies from country to country, and from one category of consumers to another.

To improve supply security, countries invest in redundant facilities. These investments, in reserve generating capacity and other network facilities, normally amount to at least a third of the investments by the electricity supply industry. Low-income developing countries cannot afford such huge investments, leading to supply insecurity. Thus in many developing countries, electricity supplies are enhanced by standby plants on consumer premises. Many industries and commercial outlets have to spend heavily on in-house generation or standby plants to attain a reasonable standard of continuity. This greatly increases the cost of attaining supply security and places an added burden on the limited economic resources of these countries.

Supply interruptions occur not only because of shortages in generating plants or limitations in the grid. They are also attributed to inadequate maintenance due to lack of skilled staff or shortage of spare parts. Attaining a reasonable standard of performance in developing countries' public systems is essential not only to improve electricity supply security but also to limit the wasted resources in standby plants and reserve generating capacity. This can be achieved through proper planning of the system and by investing in training and maintenance rather than only in system expansion.

The cost of insecurity of the electricity system in developing countries varies by country depending on the extent of electrification and quality of the supply. However, in industrialised countries the costs of supply insecurity for non-deferrable economic activities are huge. In the United States it was estimated that these costs might exceed $5 billion a year (Newton-Evans Research Company, 1998). Most of these costs are borne by industrial and commercial consumers (box 4.1).

Routes to enhanced energy security

Energy security can be ensured by local adequacy—abundant and varied forms of indigenous energy resources. In the case of local shortages, which occur in most countries, energy security can be enhanced through:

- The ability, of the state or of market players, to draw on foreign energy resources and products that can be freely imported through ports or other transport channels and through cross-boundary energy grids (pipelines and electricity networks).
- Adequate national (or regional) strategic reserves to address any transient interruption, shortages, or unpredictable surge in demand.
- Technological and financial resources and know-how to develop indigenous renewable sources and power generating facilities to meet part of local energy requirements.
- Adequate attention to environmental challenges.

Energy security can also be enhanced through energy conservation and efficiency measures. Reducing energy intensity will reduce the dependence of the economy on energy consumption and imports.

To achieve energy security requires first of all ensuring global energy adequacy—the existence of enough energy resources, or other prospects, to meet long-term world energy needs.

Energy adequacy

Although energy resources are examined in detail elsewhere in this report (see chapter 5), a quick review is provided here because energy security depends, to a great extent, on the availability of an adequate resource base. The resource base is the sum of reserves and resources. Reserves are occurrences (of all types and forms of hydrocarbon deposits, natural uranium, and thorium) that are known and economically recoverable with present technologies. Resources are less certain, are not economically recoverable with present technologies, or are both. In the future, with advances in technology and geophysics, many of today's resources are likely to become reserves (McKelvey, 1972).

Most of the world's future energy requirements, at least until the middle of the 21st century, will have to be met by fossil fuels (figure 4.1). Many attempts have been made to assess the global fossil fuel resource base. Table 4.1 shows the results of two.

BOX 4.1 VALUING THE COST OF ELECTRICITY SUPPLY SECURITY

The cost of electricity to a consumer—the consumer's valuation of the electricity supply (ignoring consumer surplus)—equals payments for electricity consumed plus the economic (social) cost of interruptions.

Supply insecurity causes disutility and inconvenience, in varying degrees and in different ways, to different classes of consumers—domestic, commercial, and industrial. The costs and losses (L) for the average consumer from supply interruptions are a function of the following:

- Dependence of the consumer on the supply (C).
- Duration of the interruptions (D).
- Frequency of their occurrence during the year (F).
- Time of day in which they occur (T).

That is, $L = C (D^d \times F^f, T^t)$, where d, f, and t are constants that vary from one consumer category to another.

The table shows estimates of the annual cost of electricity supply interruptions for the U.S. economy.

Economic cost of electricity supply interruptions for non-deferrable economic activities the United States, 1997			
Consumer class and average duration of interruption	Cost to consumer per outage (U.S. dollars)	Cost to consumer per lengthy outage (U.S. dollars)	Estimated total annual losses (billions of U.S. dollars)
Residential (20 minutes)	0–20	50–250	0.9–2.7
Commercial (10 minutes)	25–500	5–20 (per minute)	2.9–11.7
Industrial (less than 30 seconds)	200–500 (small plant) 1,000–10,000 (large plant)	5,000–50,000 (per 8-hour day)	1.1–13.5

Note: Assumes nine outages a year for each class of consumer.

Source: Newton-Evans Research Company, 1998.

FIGURE 4.1. SHARE OF FUELS IN GLOBAL ENERGY SUPPLY, 1971–2020

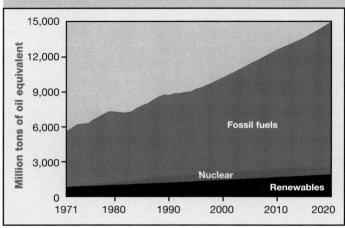

Source: IEA, 1998.

In 1998 world consumption of primary energy totalled almost 355 exajoules, or 8,460 million tonnes of oil equivalent (Mtoe)—7,630 Mtoe of fossil fuels, 620 Mtoe of nuclear energy, and 210 Mtoe of hydropower. To this should be added around 47 exajoules (1,120 Mtoe) of biomass and other renewables, for a total of 402 exajoules (9,580 Mtoe). The huge resource base of fossil and nuclear fuels will be adequate to meet such global requirements for decades to come.

Crude oil

Proven oil reserves have increased steadily over the past 20 years, mainly because oil companies have expanded their estimates of the reserves in already discovered fields. This optimism stems from better knowledge of the fields, increased productivity, and advances in technology. New technologies have led to more accurate estimates of reserves through better seismic (three- and four-dimensional)

exploration, have improved drilling techniques (such as horizontal and offshore drilling), and have increased recovery factors—the share of oil that can be recovered—from 30 percent to 40–50 percent (Campbell and Laherrere, 1998).

Huge amounts of untapped unconventional oil also exist, augmenting conventional oil reserves. Some 1.2 trillion barrels of heavy oil are found in the Orinoco oil belt in Venezuela. And the tar sands of Canada and oil shale deposits of the Russian Federation may contain 300 billion barrels of oil.

The U.S. Geological Survey assessed ultimate oil and gas reserves at the beginning of 1993 (IEA 1998; WEC, 1998). The results, which tally with the World Energy Council (WEC) and International Energy Agency (IEA) figures (see table 4.1), point to ultimate conventional oil reserves of 2,300 billion barrels, with cumulative production until 1993 amounting to 700 billion barrels and unidentified reserves to 470 billion. No shortage of conventional liquid fuels is foreseen before 2020. Any deficiencies after that can be met by the ample reserves of unconventional oil.

Natural gas

The U.S. Geological Survey also assessed ultimate natural gas reserves in 1993 (Masters, 1994). It estimated ultimate reserves at 11,448 trillion cubic feet (11,214 exajoules, or 267 gigatonnes of oil equivalent [Gtoe]), with cumulative production until 1993 amounting to 1,750 trillion cubic feet (1,722 exajoules, or 41 Gtoe). Cumulative world gas production through the end of 1995 was only 17.1 percent of the U.S. Geological Survey's estimate of conventional gas reserves.

Natural gas consumption is projected to grow 2.6 percent a year, mostly as a result of growth in electricity generation in non-OECD countries. Despite this growth, cumulative production is expected to be no more than 41 percent of the U.S. Geological Survey's estimate of conventional gas reserves by 2020. This points to a resource base large enough to serve global requirements for natural gas well into the second half of the 21st century.

TABLE 4.1. GLOBAL ENERGY RESOURCE BASE (EXAJOULES EXCEPT WHERE OTHERWISE INDICATED)

Term	World Energy Council estimates		Institute for Applied Systems Analysis estimates			Consumption
	Proven reserves	Ultimately recoverable	Reserves	Resources	Resource base	1998
Conventional oil	6,300 (150)	8,400 (200)	6,300 (150)	6,090 (145)	12,390 (295)	142.8 (3.4)
Unconventional oil	—	23,100 (550)	8,190 (195)	13,944 (332)	22,050 (525)	n.a.
Conventional gas	5,586 (133)	9,240 (220)	5,922 (141)	11,718 (279)	17,640 (420)	85 (2.0)
Unconventional gas	—	—	8,064 (192)	10,836 (258)	18,900 (450)	n.a.
Coal and lignite	18,060 (430)	142,800 (3,400)	25,452 (606)	117,348 (2,794)	142,800 (3,400)	93 (2.2)
Uranium	3.4 x 10⁹ tonnes	17 x 10⁹ tonnes	(57)	(203)	(260)	64,000 tonnes

— Not available; n.a. Not applicable.
Source: WEC, 1998; IIASA, 1998.
Note: Numbers in parentheses are in gigatonnes of oil equivalent. For definitions of conventional and unconventional resources, see chapter 5.
a. Because of uncertainties about the method of conversion, quantities of uranium have been left in the units reported by the sources.

Coal

Coal is the world's most abundant fossil fuel, with reserves estimated at almost 1,000 billion tonnes, equivalent to 27,300 exajoules, or 650,000 Mtoe (WEC, 1998). At the present rate of production, these reserves should last for more than 220 years. Thus the resource base of coal is much larger than that of oil and gas. In addition, coal reserves are more evenly distributed across the world. And coal is cheap. Efforts are being made to reduce production costs and to apply clean coal technologies to reduce the environmental impact.

Coal demand is forecast to grow at a rate slightly higher than global energy growth. Most of this growth will be for power generation in non-OECD countries, mostly in Asia. Although trade in coal is still low, it is likely to increase slowly over time. Long-term trends in direct coal utilisation are difficult to predict because of the potential impact of climate change policies. Coal gasification and liquefaction will augment global oil and gas resources in the future.

Nuclear energy

Although nuclear energy is sometimes grouped with fossil fuels, it relies on a different resource base. In 1998 nuclear energy production amounted to 2,350 terawatt-hours of electricity, replacing 620 Mtoe of other fuels. Uranium requirements amounted to 63,700 tonnes in 1997, against reasonably assured resources (reserves) of 3.4 million tonnes. Ultimately recoverable reserves amount to almost 17 million tonnes. Considering the relative stagnation in the growth of nuclear power, the enormous occurrences of low-grade uranium, and the prospects for recycling nuclear fuels, such reserves will suffice for many decades.

Renewables

Renewable energy sources—especially hydroelectric power, biomass, wind power, and geothermal energy—account for a growing share of world energy consumption. Today hydropower and biomass together contribute around 15 percent.

Hydroelectric power contributes around 2,500 terawatt-hours of electricity a year, slightly more than nuclear power does. It replaces almost 675 Mtoe of fuels a year, although its direct contribution to primary energy consumption is only a third of this. But it has still more potential. Technically exploitable hydro resources could potentially produce more than 14,000 terawatt-hours of electricity a year, equivalent to the world's total electricity requirements in 1998 (WEC, 1998). For environmental and economic reasons, however, most of these resources will not be exploited.

Still, hydropower will continue to develop. Hydropower is the most important among renewable energy sources. It is a clean, cheap source of energy, requiring only minimal running costs and with a conversion efficiency of almost 100 percent. Thus its annual growth could exceed the growth of global energy demand, slightly improving hydropower's modest contribution towards meeting world requirements.

Techniques for gasification, fermentation, and anaerobic digestion are all increasing the potential of biomass as a sustainable energy source.

Renewable energy sources other than hydro are substantial. These take the form mainly of biomass. Traditional biomass includes fuelwood—the main source of biomass energy—dung, and crop and forest residues. Lack of statistics makes it difficult to accurately estimate the contribution of renewables to the world's primary energy consumption. But it is estimated that the world consumed around 1.20 Gtoe in 1998. About two-thirds of this was from fuelwood, and the remainder from crop residues and dung. Much of this contribution is sustainable from a supply standpoint. But the resulting energy services could be substantially increased by improving conversion efficiencies, which are typically very low.

The contribution of biomass to world energy consumption is expected to increase slightly. It is mainly used as an energy source in developing countries. While energy demand in these countries is steadily increasing, some of the demand is being met by switching from traditional to commercial energy sources.

Biomass energy technology is rapidly advancing. Besides direct combustion, techniques for gasification, fermentation, and anaerobic digestion are all increasing the potential of biomass as a sustainable energy source. The viability of wind energy is increasing as well. Some 2,100 megawatts of new capacity was commissioned in 1998, pushing global wind generating capacity to 9,600 megawatts. Wind power accounted for an estimated 21 terawatt-hours of electricity production in 1999. While that still amounts to only 0.15 percent of global electricity production, the competitiveness of wind power is improving and its growth potential is substantial. Use of geothermal energy for electricity generation is also increasing, with a present generating capacity of more than 8,300 megawatts.

The resource outlook

To summarise, no serious global shortage of energy resources is likely during at least the first half of the 21st century. Reserves of traditional commercial fuels—oil, gas, and coal—will suffice for decades to come. When conventional oil resources are depleted, the huge unconventional oil and gas reserves will be tapped as new extraction and clean generating technologies mature. Coal reserves are also huge: the resource base is more than twice that of conventional and unconventional oil and gas. Clean technologies for coal will allow greater exploitation of this huge resource base, mainly in electricity production, but also through conversion into oil and gas, minimising environmentally harmful emissions.

The uranium resource base is also immense, and it is unlikely, at least in the short term, to be tapped in increasing amounts. The ultimately recoverable uranium reserves will easily meet any nuclear power requirements during this century.

The renewable resource base is also promising. Only part of the global hydro potential has been tapped. Hydropower plants will continue to be built as demand for electricity grows and the economics of long-distance, extra-high-voltage transmission improve. Biomass

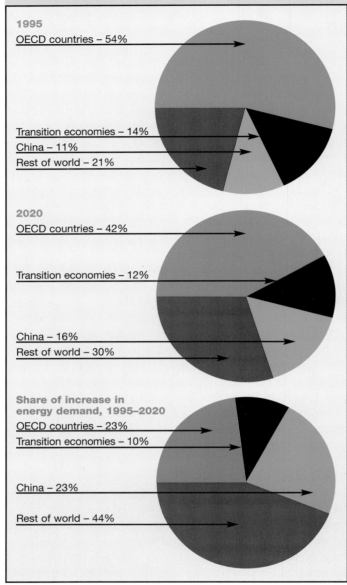

FIGURE 4.2. SHIFTING CONCENTRATION OF WORLD ENERGY DEMAND, 1995–2020

1995
OECD countries – 54%

Transition economies – 14%
China – 11%
Rest of world – 21%

2020
OECD countries – 42%

Transition economies – 12%

China – 16%
Rest of world – 30%

Share of increase in energy demand, 1995–2020
OECD countries – 23%
Transition economies – 10%

China – 23%

Rest of world – 44%

Source: IEA, 1998.

has substantial potential and will continue to be used not only as a traditional fuel but also in increasingly sophisticated ways, through thermochemical and biochemical applications. New renewable sources, particularly wind power, will gradually increase the contribution of renewables to global energy supplies as the economies and technologies of these environmentally attractive sources continue to improve.

In short, the world's energy supplies offer good prospects for energy security in the 21st century. The fossil fuel reserves amount to 1,300 Gtoe and the fossil fuel resource base to around 5,000 Gtoe (see table 4.1), amounts sufficient to cover global requirements throughout this century, even with a high-growth scenario. That does not mean there will be no temporary or structural energy shortages, but as long as the energy resources are being explored and exploited, these shortages will not be due to resource inadequacy.

Supply security

Energy resources are not evenly distributed across the world. Oil in particular, and natural gas to a lesser extent, are concentrated in a few regions. The concentration of oil reserves in the Persian Gulf region has always caused concerns about continuity of supply. Most countries, particularly OECD countries, experienced oil shortages and high prices in the 1970s and early 1980s, with physical disruption in supply leading to economic disruption. Energy importers are anxious not to repeat such experiences.

The oil supply situation has improved significantly since then. OECD countries' share of the energy market is decreasing, while that of developing countries is increasing (figure 4.2). This adds to the security of oil supplies because many developing countries are oil producers or have supply arrangements with producers. OECD countries, which accounted for 70 percent of the energy market in the 1970s, will see their market share fall to less than half by 2010. Technological advance has allowed the discovery and development of new energy reserves and reduced the cost of supplies. It has also helped increase efficiency in energy use, loosening the historically tight link between economic development and energy consumption.

Another major favourable development is the reduction in the sources of conflict that can affect global energy security. The cold war is over, and stability in the Middle East, although still precarious, is improving, with the Arab-Israeli conflict moving towards resolution.

However, some other global developments present both opportunities and new challenges to the energy sector. The policy emphasis on environmentally sustainable development, particularly in OECD countries, has important long-term implications for energy security. And the market liberalisation taking place in most industrialised countries has reduced the state's role in energy security—and increased that of consumers.

Energy security is also important for energy producers and exporters. History shows that oil supply disruptions have negative effects on oil-exporting economies. As consumers in importing economies shift away from oil, the lower demand causes severe economic damage to the exporters. In addition, many oil-exporting countries have recently obtained stakes in downstream operations in importing countries. This involvement in OECD economies will contribute towards energy security, as supply disruptions could mean a loss of business opportunities for both oil exporters and importers.

Causes of supply disruption are not limited to disturbances in production facilities. Disruptions can also occur in the long supply chains, such as serious tanker accidents in the most heavily travelled zones—the Strait of Malacca, for example. Vulnerability to disruption may grow as energy supplies are increasingly delivered through grids (gas pipelines and extra-high-voltage transmission networks). Some of these cross national boundaries and are at least theoretically vulnerable to damage through sabotage and other political disturbances. Terrorist actions could damage liquefied natural gas (LNG) conversion and receiving stations and tankers. But such possibilities are remote. Most energy supplies are delivered under long-term contracts that commit governments to ensuring safe transit and security.

Despite the favourable developments in the energy market, energy security continues to concern planners and strategists in most importing countries. Long-term energy security can be enhanced in several ways:

- Increasing energy independence by fostering and developing local resources (although some may not be economical). Supply security should not be measured solely by energy independence, however. An intelligent supply policy that includes external energy sources can offset many of the drawbacks of dependence and be more economical than a policy that precludes energy imports.
- Diversifying sources of supply and forms of energy used (box 4.2).
- Encouraging international cooperation and agreements among energy-importing countries and between consumer and supplier countries, whether between governments or between companies.
- Investing in and transferring technology to developing countries. Enabling developing countries to develop more energy supplies will enhance the availability of global supplies. Helping these countries increase the efficiency of energy use and improve environmental management will have a similar effect.

> No serious global shortage of energy resources is likely during at least the first half of the 21st century.

- Enhancing and increasing national and regional strategic reserves of crude oil and its products.

Of all the forms of energy, crude oil and its products are still the most important for energy security, because of oil's versatility and because it is the optimal form of energy for the transport sector. Natural gas, because of its affordability and cleanliness, is gaining in importance. Nuclear energy, despite its past promise, faces many difficulties. The security of all these energy forms, as well as coal, is discussed below. Energy intensity is also discussed, because improvements in this area could yield a wider range of benefits for energy security than could providing new sources of energy.

Security of crude oil supply

Over the past 20 years many changes in the oil market have improved the overall security of the energy market. The world economy has become less dependent on oil, as most regions have diversified their energy sources. Oil constituted almost 46 percent of world commercial energy sources in 1973, compared with 40 percent now. There has also been diversification of supply. In the early 1970s the Organization of Petroleum Exporting Countries (OPEC) accounted for more than half the world's oil; today it provides only 42 percent. The world now has 80 oil-producing countries (although very few have the surge capacity needed in emergencies). The oil markets

---

BOX 4.2. FRANCE'S EFFORTS TO ENHANCE ENERGY SECURITY

France has few energy resources and yet is highly industrialised and thus heavily dependent on adequate and reliable energy supplies. Its total energy consumption is estimated at 240 million tonnes of oil equivalent (Mtoe) a year, while domestic primary energy production of oil, gas, and coal amounts to only 8 Mtoe and is declining.

France, which produced half its total energy requirements in the early 1960s, saw its energy self-sufficiency decline sharply by the 1970s, when it produced only 22 percent of its requirements. But through intensive effort and ambitious energy planning, France reversed this trend of increasing dependence on imported energy. Thanks to its advanced technological skills, France was able to undertake an ambitious nuclear energy programme that helped it regain its 50 percent energy self-sufficiency in the late 1980s and to maintain it since.

To enhance its energy security, France pursued the following actions, which take into account its high standard of living, extensive industrialisation, and limited indigenous sources of primary energy:
- Diversification of energy sources and structure of energy use. France significantly reduced its dependence

on imported oil from the Middle East, increased its dependence on gas, mainly from European and Algerian sources, and considerably increased its dependence on domestic electricity produced by nuclear power stations (see the table below).
- Participation in regional cooperation and joint actions, including the International Energy Agency and the Energy Charter Treaty.
- Reduction and rationalisation of demand by improving energy efficiency and encouraging conservation through pricing and taxation, particularly of petroleum products.
- Regional interconnection of gas and electricity networks, helping to mitigate temporary problems in the supply chain.
- Substitution of natural gas and nuclear electricity for petroleum products wherever possible.

By focusing on nuclear energy, France no doubt enhanced its energy security. But it also introduced a new vulnerability into its system. Nuclear power is a viable link in the energy chain as long as it is safe and publicly accepted. With the accidents at U.S., Russian, and Japanese nuclear plants and the growing strength of anti-nuclear

parties in Europe, there is no guarantee that it will remain publicly accepted over the long term.

Energy supply structure in France, 1973 and 1997 (percent)		
Cost	1973	1997
Primary energy		
Coal	14.5	5.6
Oil	66.3	39.7
Gas	7.0	13.1
Primary electricity[a]	7.0	36.6
Renewables[b]	5.2	5.0
Final energy		
Coal	11.0	4.0
Oil	56.4	37.1
Gas	5.5	13.9
Electricity	20.9	39.1
Renewables[b]	6.2	5.9

a. Most primary electricity is from nuclear fuels.
b. Excluding hydroelectricity but including non-commercial uses. *Source: Maillard, 1999.*

have become more like traditional commodity markets (with futures markets), transparent and able to respond quickly to changing circumstances.

Big strides have been made in energy efficiency, gradually reducing the dependence of economic growth on increased oil consumption. Advances in technology have led to discoveries of more oil, reduced the cost of discoveries, and significantly improved the recovery rate, increasing the oil resource base to an estimated 2,300 trillion barrels. World trade has flourished in recent years. In 1998 it was three times that in 1980, and now accounts for 44 percent of global GDP, compared with 39 percent in 1980. Both energy exporters and importers benefit from trade. Most exporters are low-income countries that badly need oil income for development.

Even with the increase in oil-producing countries, the fact remains that almost two-thirds of the world's oil resources are in the Middle East, mostly in the Gulf region (the Islamic Republic of Iran, Iraq, Kuwait, Qatar, Saudi Arabia, and the United Arab Emirates). Although these six countries now account for only 27 percent of global crude oil supplies, they are expected to double their share to 52 percent in 2010. The Middle East, particularly the Gulf region, has not been historically known for political stability and security. But as mentioned, the situation is improving.

OECD countries, which account for almost 80 percent of the world's economic activity and 63 percent of global oil consumption, are particularly dependent on oil imports. All OECD countries are expected to increase their dependence on oil imports over the next few years. Their oil imports, 56 percent of their energy requirements in 1996, are expected to rise to 76 percent in 2020 (table 4.2).

Asia-Pacific countries' crude oil imports are expected to increase to 72 percent of their requirements in 2005 (up from 56 percent in 1993). The Middle East is expected to account for 92 percent of the region's imports, with the Gulf countries the main source of supply. The Gulf region is expected to supply 18 million barrels a day to Asia-Pacific countries in 2010 (figure 4.3), far more than its expected total supplies to Europe and the United States of 12 million barrels a day. That is why oil security, particularly for the major oil-importing countries, and the stability of the Gulf region have such importance to overall energy security and the world economy.

> Despite the favourable developments in the energy market, energy security continues to concern planners and strategists in most importing countries.

This importance will only increase in the future.

Differences between regional requirements and regional supplies will be accentuated in the future. Nowhere will this be more serious than in Asia, particularly among the large oil-consuming countries—China, India, Japan, and the Republic of Korea. Competition for supplies may intensify during emergencies, creating a potential for severe strains among Asian powers. Shortages may tempt some of these countries to project political and even military power to ensure adequate oil supplies. Already some of them—as well as the United States—have increased their naval presence in the Asian and Indian oceans (Jaffe, 1998). And U.S efforts for cooperation and conflict resolution are linked to its military planning and presence in the Gulf region and key oil export sea routes (Kemp and Harkavy, 1997).

Threats to security in oil-exporting countries can be both internal and external. Continued supply from Saudi Arabia is the most important element of energy security. Saudi supplies, now more than 9 million barrels a day, will have to increase to 13–15 million barrels a day in 2010 to meet growing world demand and offset resource depletion in non-OPEC suppliers. By that time the United States will be importing more than 60 percent of its oil. Saudi Arabia has both the potential and the reserves to meet projected demand, but the expansion will call for investment resources from that country as well as the world financial community. For a healthy oil sector, the availability of such financing should be no problem. Over the past few decades the Gulf countries have proved to be stable; continued internal and external stability is crucial to energy security. Disruption of the Gulf oil flow would lead to a deep world-wide recession. This has been presented as one of the gravest threats imaginable to U.S. interests, short of physical attack (David, 1999).

The cost of energy security goes beyond investing in redundant facilities and building pipelines, grids, and strategic reserves. Tremendous military expenditures—both visible and invisible—are required to head off any threats to the flow of oil, particularly from the Gulf countries. These costs cannot be easily computed or ascertained. The enormous expenditures on the 1990–91 Gulf War, totalling several hundred billion dollars, were meant to ensure energy security for major oil importers and the world oil markets in general. The six Gulf Cooperation Council (GCC) states, which control nearly 45 percent of the world's recoverable oil resources, contributed more than $60 billion to the U.S.-led allied offensive to eject Iraqi forces from Kuwait in 1991 (AFP, 1998). The GCC countries' contribution in 1991 exceeded their oil export income in 1998 or 1999. The United States maintains a costly military and naval presence in strategic locations to ensure the uninterrupted flow of GCC oil exports to world markets. At the beginning of 1998, along with the United Kingdom, it assembled large air and naval forces to address perceived threats to the security of oil supply from the Gulf.

Although short-term disruptions in energy supply due to regional

---

TABLE 4.2. OIL IMPORTS AS A SHARE OF TOTAL ENERGY REQUIREMENTS IN OECD COUNTRIES (PERCENT)

OECD country group	1996	2010	2020
North America	45	63	63
Europe	53	74	85
Pacific	90	96	96
Total OECD	56	72	76

Source: IEA, 1998.

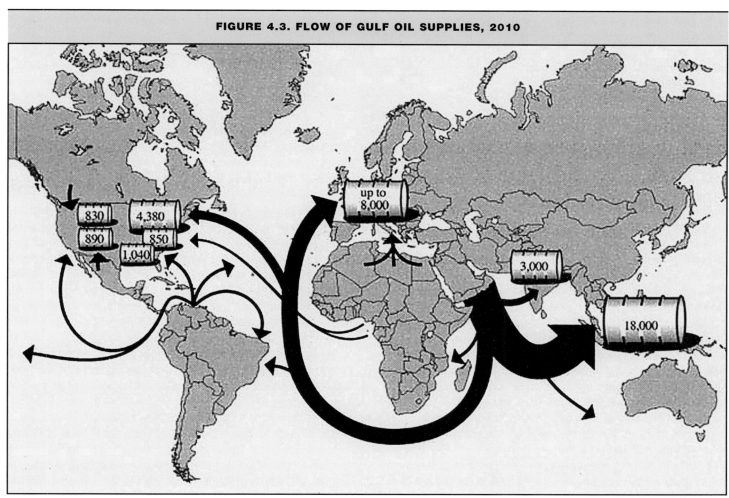

FIGURE 4.3. FLOW OF GULF OIL SUPPLIES, 2010

up to 8,000

830 | 4,380
890 | 850
1,040

3,000

18,000

Source: Kemp and Harkavy, 1997.

conflicts cannot be ruled out, means to overcome such disruptions already exist. The best illustration of this is the minimal effect on oil markets from the Iraqi invasion of Kuwait in 1990. Although 4 million barrels of oil a day dropped out of the market, Saudi Arabia increased its production and restored stability to the oil market and to prices within a few weeks. Instruments for stabilising the oil market are improving year after year—strategic stocks held by oil companies and major importing countries, development and liberalisation of markets, and regional and global energy agreements. And once transport and transit issues are resolved, the Caspian Sea countries' hydrocarbon resources, as a supplement to the North Sea resources, can be added to this list.

Oil stocks: cushioning against supply disruptions. Oil stocks are usually held by oil companies for operational purposes, and by countries and state utilities to provide a cushion against unexpected surges in demand and possible disruptions in imports. Oil companies usually hold stocks that account for 55–65 days of consumption. International Energy Agency members are required to hold emergency oil stocks equivalent to at least 90 days of net imports. The

European Union requires its members—also IEA members—to hold stocks equivalent to at least 90 days of consumption. It is not easy to estimate oil stocks held by developing countries. Because of the cost, their stocks are relatively smaller than those of OECD countries, but can amount to 25–55 days of consumption, which is also typical for oil companies in these countries. Correspondingly, world oil stocks in 1997 were about 5,500 million barrels, equal to 70–80 days of average global consumption. This, at present, is adequate for unexpected transient shortages or temporary interruptions.

With the continued growth of non-OECD oil consumption, oil stocks will function less effectively. Their size relative to the global oil market will decline, since most developing countries do not maintain emergency oil stocks (many cannot afford them). If this trend continues, vulnerability to sudden and substantial oil supply disruptions will increase.

Liberalisation of markets: easing the flow of oil. Another aspect of security is the liberalisation of energy markets in importing countries. Liberalisation and deregulation, coupled with the development of oil futures and forwards markets, mean an easier and more secure flow of oil from exporting to importing countries. Most oil producers are now inviting foreign companies to participate in oil development, which will significantly enhance the security of the oil market. And the strengthening of the World Trade Organization will add further to the security of the energy market.

Although security in terms of flows of oil and gas to importing countries is improving, the security of supply to consumers faces new challenges. Liberalisation, the withdrawal of government responsibility for supply, and competition among private suppliers are creating challenges in securing reliable supply to individual consumers. These are discussed later in detail.

Energy treaties and agreements: enhancing energy security through cooperation. In response to insecurity after the first oil shocks, OECD countries convened a conference in Washington, D.C., in 1974 that led to the establishment of the International Energy Programme (IEP), the founding charter of the International Energy Agency (IEA). To improve energy security, the participating countries pledged to hold oil stocks equivalent to 90 days of net imports. They also developed an integrated set of emergency response measures that included demand restraint, fuel switching, and surge oil production. These measures also included the important provision of stock drawdown and sharing of available supplies in the event of oil supply disruptions involving a loss of 7 percent or more for any member country or for the group (Martin, Imai, and Steeg, 1996).

In 1977 the IEA developed another set of coordinated emergency response measures that allow for a rapid and flexible response to an impending oil security crisis. Also in that year, IEA countries agreed to long-term energy policies and programmes aimed at diversifying resources, employing energy efficiency measures, and developing new energy technologies. And in response to changing circumstances, the IEA updated its policies in a statement of shared goals at its ministerial meeting in 1993.

In 1991, 51 countries signed the European Energy Charter to enhance energy security throughout the Eurasian continent and promote the creation of an open and non-discriminatory energy market. The signatories included the European Communities and their member states, the countries of Central and Eastern Europe, all the members of the Commonwealth of Independent States (CIS), and Australia, Canada, Japan, and the United States. By applying the principles of non-discrimination and market-oriented policies, the charter was aimed at improving energy security, increasing the efficiency of all links in the energy chain, enhancing safety, and minimising environmental impacts.

Three years later, in 1994, all the signatories to the European Energy Charter (except Canada and the United States) signed the Energy Charter Treaty, along with a protocol on Energy Efficiency and Related Environmental Aspects, which entered into force in 1998. Japan and the Central Asian states have since signed the

OECD countries, which account for almost 80 percent of the world's economic activity and 63 percent of global oil consumption, are particularly dependent on oil imports.

Charter Treaty and China is showing increasing interest in it, enhancing its geopolitical scope. The treaty applies to all economic activities related to a broadly defined energy sector. Its main purpose is to promote the creation of an open and non-discriminatory energy market throughout the Eurasian continent (Schuetterle, 1999). The Charter Treaty obligates signatories to encourage and create stable, equitable, and transparent conditions for foreign investors in their countries, stipulates that General Agreement on Tariffs and Trade (GATT) provisions will govern trade in energy materials and products, ensures the transit of energy exports through third countries, and sets out procedures for settling disputes relating to the treaty's provisions.

Also serving to enhance energy security are interregional and intraregional agreements established to foster economic cooperation between member countries, such as Asia-Pacific Economic Cooperation (APEC), which involves 21 economies of Asia, Oceania, and the Americas (box 4.3). Enhancing energy security is one of the aims of APEC, which set up its own Energy Work Group and the Asia Pacific Energy Research Centre (APERC) for this purpose.

No doubt the above-mentioned treaties and arrangements helped to foster energy investments and improve energy security—not only for their members, but also globally—by encouraging sustainable energy policies.

Oil in transport: a special point of vulnerability. The transport sector accounts for half of global oil demand, with heating, electricity generation, industrial processes, and petrochemicals accounting for the rest. Demand for oil in transport is growing rapidly, particularly in aviation. Over the next 20 years demand for oil in transport is expected to grow by 2.3 percent a year, compared with growth in total demand for oil of around 1.9 percent a year. Most of this growth will occur in non-OECD countries, where it is expected to average 3.6 percent a year, with the highest growth projected for China and East and South Asia. Demand in OECD countries, which are already witnessing some saturation in vehicle ownership, is expected to grow at one-third that rate.

In the near term there is no cheap and viable alternative to oil in transport, particularly in private vehicles and aviation (Douaud, 1999). Use of oil for mobility will increase in all countries, as the transport fleet grows and uses exceed improvements in transport efficiency. An interruption in oil supply, however temporary, could cause major disruption to the transport sector and to the world economy.

Oil prices: a source of insecurity. The severe volatility of oil prices in the 1970s and early 1980s contributed to the insecurity in energy markets. The price of oil is the market leader for energy pricing. Gas and coal, because of competition, are priced accordingly.

OPEC has the power to influence oil prices by allocating supply and monitoring and restricting production by its members. With the growing discipline in its ranks, this influence may increase in the future. Moreover, the depletion of non-OPEC oil and future growth in its marginal cost will increase oil prices in the medium and long

BOX 4.3. ASIA-PACIFIC ECONOMIC COOPERATION'S EFFORTS TO ENHANCE ENERGY SECURITY

Asia-Pacific Economic Cooperation (APEC) includes the following member economies in six 'sub-regions':
- The United States.
- Other Americas—Canada, Chile, and Mexico.
- China.
- Other Asia—Hong Kong (China), Japan, Republic of Korea, and Taiwan (China).
- Oceania—Australia, New Zealand, and Papua New Guinea.
- Southeast Asia—Brunei Darussalam, Indonesia, Malaysia, Philippines, Singapore, and Thailand.

In addition, Peru, the Russian Federation, and Viet Nam joined APEC in November 1998.

APEC was formed to foster economic cooperation among its member economies, one aspect of which is energy cooperation and security. APEC economies' energy requirements account for more than half of the world's primary energy supply. The group has rich coal resources, and gas resources almost adequate for its requirements. But it is very short in crude oil resources. By 2010 APEC economies will have to import an estimated 55 percent of their energy requirements. The recent incorporation of Russia, with its enormous gas resources and its oil, has helped alleviate APEC's serious energy security problem. Nevertheless, APEC's significant crude oil shortages are expected to continue. APEC tries to enhance its energy security through the following actions:
- **Encouraging expansion of energy production.** The entry into APEC of Russia, with 40 percent of global gas reserves and 9 percent of oil reserves, should facilitate the development of energy resources in the Asian part of Russia and enhance the supply potential to the growing Asian energy market.

The need for expanded production will lead to more energy development and greater cooperation between APEC economies and other energy-producing economies outside the traditional APEC region. The participation of firms from Asian oil-importing economies in upstream hydrocarbon resource activities will enhance efforts to expand oil and gas production. Similarly, the participation of firms from oil-exporting countries in downstream operations in Asian markets will contribute to the security of energy supply.
- **Allowing more flexible fuel choices.** As a group, APEC economies are heavily biased towards coal use. The main reason is that China, which accounts for a fifth of APEC's requirements, uses coal to meet more than 70 percent of energy demand. Institutional and technological changes to support more flexible choices that are compatible with sustainable development are being considered. Within APEC, nuclear options have been and will be pursued in the Americas and East Asia. In the Americas, however, nuclear power is expected to play a reduced role, while in East Asia nuclear power is expected to expand. In Southeast Asia there is no likelihood that nuclear power will be introduced before 2010.
- **Preparing for energy supply disruptions.** Emergency oil stocks, like those held by members of the International Energy Agency (IEA), are a key element of energy security. With the growth of non-IEA oil consumption, IEA emergency oil reserves will function less effectively, as their size relative to the global market will decline and most non-IEA countries do not maintain emergency oil stocks. If this situation persists, vulnerability to sudden and

substantial oil supply disruptions will grow. The issue of emergency preparedness therefore needs to be examined in a broader context. For this reason the Asia Pacific Energy Research Centre is conducting a study to assess the value of emergency oil stocks in APEC economies.
- **Promoting energy reforms.** The increased competition resulting from regulatory reforms in energy markets promotes energy security in many ways. Yet despite the global trend towards energy sector liberalisation, some APEC economies in Asia still believe that energy security requires maintaining a regulated energy market. Attitudes towards deregulation are gradually softening, however, as long as it does not preclude the state from continuing to play a role when needed to enhance security.
- **Developing transborder energy delivery infrastructure.** APEC economies are examining the feasibility of developing transborder infrastructure. Members of the Association of Southeast Asian Nations (ASEAN) have studied the creation of both gas pipeline networks and electricity grids linking producer and consumer members. In Northeast Asia the concept of a gas pipeline network linking former Soviet economies (Russia and Turkmenistan, for example) with China, the Republic of Korea, and Japan has been discussed. Finally, Russia is promoting the idea of linking electricity grids with neighbouring economies. Besides economic viability, there are many other considerations in such projects: improved regional political stability through cooperation, better use of untapped resources, and increased capacity utilisation, energy supply, and demand diversity.

---

term. Prices will be further increased by the development of the more expensive non-conventional oil, once crude oil supply peaks around 2010. Although short-term price volatility, like that in 1998–2000, cannot be ruled out because of the many factors explained above, oil prices are not expected to be as volatile as in the past. After 2010 gradual, moderate price increases are expected. Many recent predictions have been made of future oil prices. Two of these are given in table 4.3.

Such moderate price increases, along with continuous improvement in energy efficiency, mean that oil prices are unlikely to place a more serious burden on the global economy than they do now. Moreover, the expected improvements in the real price of oil will spur producing countries to enhance and expand their production and provide them with the badly needed financial resources to do so.

Income security for oil-exporting countries. Some countries depend—for income and for development—on energy exports, particularly oil. This group is not limited to the Middle East; it includes a few countries in Sub-Saharan Africa and Latin America.

Nor is this dependence on oil export income restricted to exporting countries; the benefits of oil export income spread to other countries in the region through wage remittances and financial assistance.

In the Gulf countries three-quarters of government revenue is derived from oil exports. Energy exports account for almost two-thirds of government revenue for other countries in the region, such as Algeria, the Islamic Republic of Iran, and Yemen. The dramatic drop in oil prices in 1998 and early 1999 led not only to budgetary problems in many energy-exporting countries, but also

TABLE 4.3. OIL PRICE PROJECTIONS (1997 U.S. DOLLARS PER BARREL)

Source of projections	1997	1998–2010	2015–2020
International Energy Agency	18.50	24.50	26.20
U.S. Department of Energy	18.55	21.30	22.73

Source: IEA, 1998; USDOE, 1998.

to unemployment and significant drops in incomes. Such economic problems were not only restricted to the oil exporters but were also experienced by their neighbours, which depend on revenues from exports of goods and services to the oil-rich countries and on remittances from workers in these countries. For energy-exporting countries, export security is becoming as important as energy import security is to resource-short countries. All this is enhancing the prospects for global energy security.

Dependence on oil exports has an additional implication for exporting countries. These countries, particularly OPEC members, are worried about the possible long-term impact on export demand of policies to mitigate environmental impacts, promote energy efficiency, and increase use of renewable energy sources. Although exaggerated in the short term, the potential impact could pose long-term problems for the countries, adversely affecting their economic and social development. Having met the needs of the global energy sector satisfactorily over the past 25 years, oil-exporting countries are asking for compensation if mitigation actions start to bite. This request is being reviewed in international negotiations. It may be many years before exporting countries' income is affected. Meantime, it is hoped that with international assistance and compensation, they will be able to diversify their income sources and reduce their dependence on oil exports.

Security of natural gas supply

Natural gas is slowly gaining importance in the energy market. Between 1987 and 1997 gas consumption increased from 1,756 giga cubic metres to 2,197, for an annual growth rate of 2.27 percent, compared with 1.47 percent for total primary commercial energy consumption. Over the period until 2020 natural gas demand is expected to grow still faster—at an annual rate of 2.6 percent, compared with 1.9 percent for oil. And natural gas supply, since it is starting from a much lower base than oil supply, is not expected to peak until well beyond 2020 (IEA, 1998).

Internationally traded natural gas accounted for 19 percent of gas consumption in 1997, compared with 44 percent for oil. So, just as for oil, though to a lesser extent, there is a mismatch between the location of gas supply and its consumption. Security of supply is therefore critical. But the physical characteristics of natural gas make ensuring security of supply for gas more complicated than for oil. Crude oil is an eminently fungible commodity, portable by ship, pipeline, road tanker, or even barrel. In contrast, gas requires expensive pipelines or LNG infrastructure. These delivery systems are relatively inflexible: pipelines cannot be moved or built overnight, and LNG, although somewhat portable, still requires an expensive receiving terminal. Crude oil and, more important, refined oil products can be transported to any location that can receive a ship or road tanker. Moreover, gas is difficult to store in significant quantities. The energy content per unit of volume is much lower for gas than for oil. Gas is simply more difficult to handle than liquid. Its storage often depends on the suitability of geological structures, while oil tank farms can be built relatively easily and cheaply. All these factors mean that the solutions used to ensure security of oil supply (storage, diversification of supplies) do not apply as easily to gas.

At its simplest level, gas supply security can mean operational reliability—in other words, that gas flows to the consumer when it is required. In particular, this means meeting consumer needs on days of peak demand, usually in winter. The gas supply system must be configured to give the required flexibility.

Security of supply also involves reducing strategic risk, namely, the risk of a major disruption to supplies caused by, for example, political factors or major technical failure, such as the failure of a high-pressure pipeline. This is an extension of operational security, but of a different order of magnitude. Strategic risk is growing in parallel with the growing share of gas in meeting countries' primary energy requirements. It can be reduced through:

- Interconnectivity, the degree of physical interconnection with other gas systems, an important factor in ensuring strategic security of supply. Interconnectivity is more than simply a guard against potential failure; it also encourages diversity of supply.
- Diversity of supply, which is fundamental to security of supply because it spreads risk. All sources of supply are unlikely to fail at the same time. Countries have often explicitly diversified supply by contracting with several countries. France, for example, buys gas from Algeria, the Netherlands, Norway, and Russia. In recent years there have been a number of spot LNG sales into Europe from LNG suppliers using spare capacity.

Security of supply also entails guarding against long-term risk—ensuring that consuming countries can secure future and additional supplies as their existing supplies are depleted. This represents a challenge, as the bulk of the world's gas reserves are in areas that are far from current markets and also often have a high level of country risk.

Some gas-importing countries, such as France, use long-term strategic storage to guard against significant disruption of supply. Such storage can be in depleted oil or gas fields, aquifers, salt caverns, or other geological structures.

Political risks to gas supplies and security of interregional grids. With the increase in internationally traded natural gas and LNG, political risk to gas supplies and cross-boundary networks will increase. One of the measures taken to reduce political risk is the Energy Charter Treaty, which attempts to provide a legal framework for the transit of hydrocarbons and electricity through pipelines and grids. The treaty prohibits contracting parties from imposing unreasonable charges for the transit of energy or taking unreasonable or discriminatory actions. Most important, in the event of a dispute over transit, transit states may not interrupt or reduce existing transit until the parties have had an opportunity to resolve the dispute using the treaty's dispute resolution mechanisms. As a further aid to international gas trade, the treaty prohibits countries from refusing new transit or new capacity to other treaty signatories solely on the basis of the origin, destination, or ownership of the energy being transported.

Political risk is also an issue for investment in the gas industry. Because of the capital intensity of the industry, a sound investment environment is needed to encourage companies to invest. This requires clear legal, fiscal, and contractual frameworks; transparent regulatory processes; and regulatory certainty. To improve the international investment environment for projects involving the transit of gas as well as oil and electricity across national boundaries, the Energy Charter Conference, an intergovernmental body made up of the 51 states that have signed the Energy Charter Treaty, began in 1999 to elaborate the Multilateral Transit Framework Agreement. The aim is to strengthen the international rule of law on transit issues by further developing the treaty's transit provisions.

With increasing utilisation of gas, lengthy gas pipeline grids across countries and boundaries are becoming familiar. This raises concerns about political and security problems relating to the integrity of the pipeline and continuity of supply—because of possible regional disputes, disagreements among firms, or accidents or sabotage. One of the principal aims of the Energy Charter Treaty is to provide for such contingencies. But not all countries are signatories to the treaty, though the numbers are increasing. However, the treaty provides guidelines (explained above) that non-member countries can incorporate in agreements relating to cross-boundary pipelines. Moreover, the increasing strength of markets, the World Trade Organization regulations, and the increasing interdependence of markets and countries enhance the security of supply from regional gas grids.

Natural gas is an ideal fuel for electricity generation. It is environmentally benign compared with coal and offers the potential for very high efficiencies in combined cycle plants. Like oil, natural gas resources are unevenly distributed across the world, but unlike oil, gas is not easily transportable or tradable. Expensive interregional gas grids are a solution as long as security is guaranteed, an aim of the Multilateral Transit Framework Agreement. Interregional grids provide benefits to all—suppliers, consumers, and transit countries. In addition, the increased security inherent in pipeline systems enhances cooperation among the countries involved.

Satisfying the increasing energy demand in India and South and East Asia may require building a very large interregional pipeline from the Islamic Republic of Iran or the Gulf. This would require not only a huge investment but also a coordinated regional arrangement and guarantees. Such a pipeline could sustainably meet the increasing demand for electrification in parts of Asia that account for more than a third of the world's population and where electricity demand is growing at twice the world average.

Risks to internal security of supply. In addition to the external risks, internal security risks are on the increase. These include the risk of electricity shortages due to increasing dependence on gas in electricity production. This increasing reliance on gas also raises supply security issues because of the possible domino effect in the event of gas supply problems. As a result of an interruption in gas supply to gas-fired power stations, a national grid could find itself short of capacity just as demand is peaking. Such security risks can be reduced, however, through coordination between the gas grid and the electric utilities, by switching combined cycle gas turbines (CCGT) to other fuels in the event of gas shortages, and by diversifying the energy sources for power generation (coal, nuclear, oil, gas, and hydro).

Diversity is more important than origin of supply. The mechanisms for securing diversity can be based on market instruments (payments for reserve capacity) or regulation (requirements for storing a certain number of days' worth of backup fuel supply). The U.S. gas market has shown how the price mechanism can enhance security of supply during less severe shortages. Many power stations burn both fuel oil and natural gas. As gas prices rise and the supply-demand balance tightens, the generators switch to the cheaper fuel, freeing up supply for gas consumers who cannot switch.

Development of national gas markets. Traditionally, international gas trade has been conducted on the basis of long-term (several-year) take-or-pay contracts. Under these contracts, designed to manage risk, the buyer agrees to take a certain volume over a period of time and to pay for that volume regardless of whether it is actually used. In effect, the buyer takes all the volume risk (the risk as to how much gas the end-use market will actually consume). The seller agrees to sell a certain quantity at a price indexed to such factors as the price of competing fuels, the price of electricity, and producer inflation. The seller therefore takes the risk that this price will cover its costs of production and provide a return on its investment. This is completely different from a commodity market, where supply and demand balance at whatever is the market-clearing price.

The 'traditional' take-or-pay system also frequently involved either monopsony or oligopoly buyers such as the European utilities (including the old British Gas and Gaz de France) and the Japanese utilities (Tepco). It has been argued that such a system was the only way to match supply and demand, ensure orderly development of the market, and allow all parties to recoup their investments. The approach has evidently worked: the record on gas supply security in Europe and Japan has been exemplary.

Recently, however, attention has focused on the implications of the liberalisation of gas markets for security of supply. In the United States the natural monopoly aspect of gas supply, gas transport by pipeline, has been separated from the other functions—production, wholesale, and retail. Regulated third-party access has given any gas producer the ability to transport its product to the end market, and any customer the ability to buy gas from any producer or wholesaler. In short, the approach has enhanced U.S. supply security. But the U.S. experience cannot necessarily be applied to other countries.

Long-term take-or-pay contracts do not completely eliminate

Tremendous military expenditures—both visible and invisible—are required to head off any threats to the flow of oil.

political or commercial risks. If a country is unable or unwilling to export its gas reserves for whatever reason, who has legal title to them is irrelevant. What such contracts can do, and have done in the past, is to give the parties a degree of confidence in the viability of a project and help secure financing.

By separating transport from supply, liberalisation, over the long term, will encourage the producers able to supply the market at lowest cost to meet consumers' demand. Moreover, the U.S. experience suggests that as pricing of gas supply and associated services becomes more transparent and explicit, market participants will search for the most cost-effective way of ensuring gas supply. In the United States this has led to greater and more innovative use of storage. The results depend, however, on how the industry structure and regulations evolve—whether dominant players effectively keep out new entrants, for example, or a more level playing field develops.

In summary, while the physical characteristics of gas make supply security problematic, it can nevertheless be enhanced by a variety of mechanisms, enabling gas to continue to play its part in the world's energy balance. Liberalisation of energy markets is not incompatible with supply security, and can arguably enhance it.

Security of coal supply

Coal presents fewer challenges—other than environmental ones—to energy security than do oil and gas. It is abundant and more evenly distributed around the world than oil or gas. It is cheap, and costs are continuously being reduced by competition. The many suppliers and the possibility of switching from one to another mean supply security. The global ratio of coal reserves to production is 225 years; for OECD countries, it is even higher. Coal is still a local fuel, however. International trade in coal is limited, amounting to only 13 percent of production, a smaller share than for gas.

The huge reserves of coal and their even distribution contribute to global energy security. Coal will continue to play a major part in ensuring the energy security of large energy consumers, particularly China (the largest coal consumer), the United States, and South Asia. Over the next few decades the growth in demand for coal is expected to continue to be healthy, exceeding the growth in overall energy demand.

Most of that growth will be for electricity generation, with coal consumption in the electricity sector expected to grow in all regions. But this is also the area where the main security challenge arises, because of the environmental effects of coal use—locally, regionally, and also possibly globally. Coal utilisation is very inefficient, particularly in power generation, where its efficiency is less than 25 percent (Ecoal, 1998). The efficiency of oil and gas in electricity generation is at least 50 percent higher.

For coal to play its deserved role in global energy security, its many detrimental environmental impacts must be addressed. This will require not only clean coal technologies for new plants, but also rehabilitation and refurbishment of existing inefficient plants. And this must happen not only in industrialised countries, but also in developing countries, which are expected to account for most coal

use. All this calls for technology transfer and huge investments, which many developing countries will be unable to afford. Thus technical assistance to developing countries will be essential.

Nuclear energy and energy security

Nuclear energy could continue to add to the energy security of countries short of hydropower and indigenous fossil fuel resources, for several reasons. Uranium resources are widely distributed and abundant world-wide (see chapter 5). Nuclear fuel is cheap: at the price of present long-term uranium supply contracts, the cost of natural uranium per kilowatt-hour is equivalent to an oil price of $0.35 per barrel, so several years' supply could be kept in reserve against possible future supply disruption at a low cost. And the cost of uranium contributes only about 2 percent to the cost of nuclear electricity generation, compared with 40–70 percent for fossil fuels in electricity generation,[1] making the cost of nuclear electricity relatively insensitive to possible future increases in the uranium price.

These considerations played a key part in the decisions of such economies as France, the Republic of Korea, Japan, and Taiwan (China) to launch major nuclear power programmes. In all likelihood, such considerations will also be important determinants in similar decisions by countries with a shortage of indigenous resources and a heavy reliance on imports. Moreover, the fact that nuclear power releases virtually no environmentally damaging emissions of carbon dioxide, sulphur dioxide, and nitrogen oxide could make it an attractive option for many countries seeking technologies leading to reduced greenhouse gas emissions or abatement of local and regional pollution.

In the 1960s and 1970s, particularly after the first oil shock, nuclear power promised to be a viable solution for industrialised countries looking for energy security and cheap power. Largely as a result of investment decisions made in that period, nuclear power has grown to the point where it dominates electricity generation in several industrialised countries, providing about a sixth of global electricity in 1998. But the outlook for nuclear power is not bright. Most of the promise of nuclear energy has evaporated as a result of loss of investor and public confidence in the technology. There is likely to be growth in nuclear power in some Asian countries in the period to 2020 and modest expansion at the global level until 2010. But most projections show nuclear power accounting for a smaller share of global electricity generation in 2020 than today, and many show its absolute contribution staying the same or even shrinking.

The loss of investor and public confidence in nuclear technology is due to concerns about costs, nuclear safety, radioactive waste disposal, and proliferation or diversion (see chapter 8). Until these concerns are adequately dealt with, nuclear energy is unlikely to play an expanding role in enhancing global energy security. The energy security benefits provided by nuclear power might even be diminished if there is another reactor accident involving substantial releases of radioactivity or a proliferation or diversion incident that could be plausibly linked in the public mind to nuclear power.

Recognition that another major accident might not only diminish prospects for nuclear expansion but also trigger demands to shut down existing nuclear plants has catalysed private sector-led efforts, under the auspices of the World Association of Nuclear Operators, to instil a culture of safety in the world's nuclear industry. This situation has also prompted an international effort, led by the International Atomic Energy Agency, to bolster national nuclear regulatory regimes. This effort is embodied in the Convention on Nuclear Safety, adopted by the organisation's members. (For discussion of technological strategies for improving the safety of future reactors, see chapter 8.)

The Nuclear Non-Proliferation Treaty and associated international safeguards and nuclear supplier agreements have been implemented to minimise the nuclear weapons link to nuclear power (Murray, 1995). To date, all but a few states (apart from the five nuclear weapons states recognised in the 1968 Non-Proliferation Treaty, these are India, Israel, and Pakistan) have committed themselves to putting all nuclear material, including the material used for uranium enrichment and reprocessing, indefinitely under safeguard of the International Atomic Energy Agency.

Recent events and concerns about the limitations of existing policies have led various experts to call for further efforts to weaken the nuclear weapons link to nuclear power. But because the risk of proliferation and diversion is not at the forefront of public concerns about nuclear power (and may not be until there is an incident), because national policies in this area differ widely, and because there is much disagreement in the technical community about the best approaches for minimising this risk, there has been less action in this area than there has been in improving reactor safety. Increasing the authority and resources of the International Atomic Energy Agency for monitoring enrichment plants and spent fuel is the principal way immediately available to reduce the proliferation risks associated with existing uranium enrichment and fuel reprocessing capabilities. (For a discussion of institutional strategies for further weakening the nuclear weapons link, see Walker, 1998. For a discussion of future options for weakening this link with advanced technologies, see chapter 8.)

In summary, for the next couple of decades the prospects for enhancing energy security through expansion of nuclear power are not bright at the global level, although they are somewhat better in some Asian countries. In the longer term whether nuclear power can contribute to energy security depends not only on technical and economic considerations to be sorted out by the market, but also on the extent to which the public can be convinced that nuclear power is safe and that wastes can be disposed of safely. It also depends on whether the industry can avoid major accidents and proliferation and diversion incidents, and whether national and international policy-makers and the technical community can reach consensus on what needs to be done to make nuclear energy technology widely acceptable.

If the world economy continues to grow at the expected average rate of 2.7 percent, in 2020 global energy demand will be 45–51 percent higher than in 1998.

Energy intensity

One way to improve energy security in any country is by reducing its energy intensity—the amount of energy required to produce one unit of GDP. The rate of change in energy intensity reflects the overall improvement in energy efficiency as well as structural changes in the economy. Declining rates of energy intensity indicate that economic growth is less tightly linked to increases in energy use.

Energy intensity has improved considerably in industrialised countries. In the United States over the past two centuries it has declined 1 percent a year on average. One unit of GDP now requires only a fifth of the primary energy required 200 years ago (IIASA and WEC, 1998). In the past 15 years energy intensity in the United States has improved 20 percent.

Energy intensity differs depending on the level of economic development. OECD countries generally have an energy intensity that is a fraction of that in developing countries. In 1996 the commercial energy intensity of middle-income developing countries was three times that of high-income countries. This finding remains whether GDP is measured in market dollars or in purchasing power parity (PPP) terms. In most developing countries energy intensity is stagnant or even increasing because these countries are in the early take-off stages of industrialisation, when energy-intensive industries and infrastructure are being established. Moreover, low-income developing countries usually show increasing commercial energy intensity because commercial energy sources are replacing non-commercial fuels.

The prospects for lowering energy intensity are reduced in many developing countries by the proliferation of energy price subsidies and by the use of inefficient and outdated plants and equipment. Generally, however, energy intensity in developing countries is similar to that in industrialised countries when they were at an earlier stage of development.

Economic growth in developing countries has been relatively high in recent years, averaging 2.8 percent a year in the 1990s, compared with 2.1 percent for industrialised countries and 2.3 percent for the world. This trend is likely to continue. If this growth is matched by measures to conserve energy—such as phasing out subsidies and improving environmental awareness—energy security in developing countries is likely to continue to improve as well.

Predicting the future of energy intensity is difficult, particularly for developing countries. In low-income countries energy intensity may increase in the next few years as these countries substitute commercial energy for traditional fuels. But for the world as a whole, energy intensity is likely to improve. Average improvements will range from 0.8 percent to 1.0 percent a year, depending on such factors as environmental awareness and energy prices (IIASA and WEC, 1998). If the world economy continues to grow at the expected average rate of 2.7 percent, energy demand growth will average 1.7–1.9 percent a year. That means that in 2020 global energy demand will be 45–51 percent higher than in 1998. This is a substantial increase. But without the expected efficiency improvements in global energy utilisation, the demand could grow as much as 80 percent.

The potential for efficiency improvements is high in many energy applications (see chapter 6). Some of the most important progress in energy efficiency is that taking place in the conversion of energy to electricity. Modern combined cycle gas turbines burning natural gas have efficiencies approaching 60 percent, and efficiencies of 70 percent are within reach in the foreseeable future. Such efficiencies are more than double the average of 31 percent for the world stock of existing generating plants. As old plants are phased out and new, CCGT-type plants—or the traditional thermal generating plant firing coal at more than 40 percent efficiency—take over, considerable improvements in energy utilisation will gradually occur. In addition, the increased use of electricity as an energy carrier world-wide will further improve energy efficiency. In some applications electricity is more efficient than other forms of energy, and its use is now growing 2.8–3.2 percent a year, a rate more than 50 percent higher than that for primary energy overall (Khatib, 1997). All this will significantly lower energy intensity and thus improve prospects for global energy security.

The environment and energy security

The idea of sustainable development is gaining acceptance on the official level as well as among the public. Sustainable development demands environmental preservation. Energy production and utilisation, particularly in the case of fossil fuels, can be major sources of environmental degradation. These detrimental environmental impacts have a direct bearing on the future of energy—in terms of fuels and the extent of their use—and on energy security. (For a discussion of the environmental impacts of energy use, see chapter 3.)

The United Nations Framework Convention on Climate Change, adopted at the Rio Earth Summit in 1992, and the Kyoto Protocol, signed by more than 160 countries in 1997, call for major reductions of greenhouse gas emissions, which are caused mainly by energy use. Fulfilling the commitments as agreed and at the schedules approved would greatly affect the use of energy resources and could compromise global economic progress. There is a large gap between the commitments and the means for implementation. Targets agreed upon by negotiators were not necessarily implemented by legislators or other policy-makers. Implementation of such targets is hindered not only by cost but also by the need to maintain energy security.

All indications are that fossil fuels will continue to dominate global energy resources for at least the first decades of the 21st century. Moreover, the demand for energy services will continue to increase. Most of the growth will be in developing countries, which can ill afford the high cost of containment measures. It is therefore essential to find means to contain energy-related emissions without compromising energy security.

The environmental effects of energy use occur at the local, regional, and global levels. Local effects consist primarily of heavy hydrocarbons

The increased use of electricity as an energy carrier world-wide will further improve energy efficiency.

and particulate matter (including sulphur flakes) that are deposited within hours and can travel up to 100 kilometres from the source. Regional effects include emissions and effluents, the most important of which are sulphur and nitrogen oxides, which are converted into acids; these acids, which last for a few days in the atmosphere, may travel up to a few thousand kilometres before being deposited, often after crossing boundaries. Global environmental impacts are exemplified by emissions of carbon dioxide and other gases (mainly methane) that have long residence times in the atmosphere.

Local and regional impacts can be addressed by technologies. However, some of these technologies are expensive for developing countries, where growth in the use of low-quality coal will be particularly high. There are no easy answers in dealing with green-house gas emissions. Mitigation and sequestration measures are still to be developed. The most practical solution is to reduce the growth in fossil fuel use by increasing efficiency in energy utilisation.

Enhancing efficiency in energy use not only helps greatly to mitigate emissions; it also improves energy security. But for greater benefits for energy security, energy use should also be made more compatible with the aims of sustainable development through better containment of emissions. Such simple measures as washing coal will rid it of 20–50 percent of its sulphur. Advanced burners and scrubbers remove pollutants and effluent gases from smoke stacks and chimneys. Fuel substitution is another effective measure. A modern CCGT power station, firing gas, will emit only 40 percent as much carbon dioxide as a traditional coal-fired thermal power station. The slow but persistent growth in the use of electricity as an energy carrier will also contribute towards energy security. Besides offering greater efficiency than other forms of energy in many applications, electricity concentrates emissions in a single remote location—the site of the power station—making them easier and cheaper to deal with.

Markets and energy security

Approaches to ensuring energy supply security in the 21st century should differ from past approaches that concentrated on oil substitution. Besides sustainable growth challenges, new approaches need to tackle the new energy security issues raised by market liberalisation.

The enhanced role of markets is tied closely to the process of globalisation. Globalisation, which is still gaining momentum, has encouraged competition and strengthened markets and regional and international trade, particularly for crude oil and oil products, natural gas, and energy services. Globalisation is bringing new opportunities for energy security, such as better access to markets and services and the transfer of technologies that are helping to reduce the cost of energy exploration and expand proven reserves.

International trade in energy resources and services is vital for energy security. The creation of the World Trade Organization in 1995, built on the GATT, is the latest multilateral step towards creating an environment conducive to the exchange of goods and services. It will assist in trade liberalisation and allow countries greater recourse to trade dispute settlement mechanisms. Foreign trade has grown more quickly than the world economy in recent years, a trend that is likely to continue. For developing countries, trade is growing faster than national income, reaching 50 percent of GDP, and a good share of that trade is in energy. The flow of information has become much easier and more transparent, increasing the resources and services available for trade and reducing prices. All this aids greatly in enhancing energy security.

The introduction of a single market in Europe will lead to more competition in energy services and supply of cheaper electricity. Improvements in transport networks and technology are reducing the cost of energy trade. The liberalisation of European gas and electricity markets will initiate major structural changes in European energy enterprises, increasing competition, improving economic performance, and contributing towards fuel diversification and greater energy security (EC, 1999).

In studying the influence of markets, there is a need to distinguish between OECD countries, where free markets prevail, and developing countries, where market liberalisation is still at a very early stage. Security of supply is a public policy objective. But in free markets decisions are made by market players rather than by governments. Markets allow even small and medium-size consumers—as well as suppliers—a say in energy decisions. That requires redefining the political dimension of energy security.

Markets clearly produce benefits for consumers: trade, innovation, cost reduction, technological advances, and better allocation of resources. Moreover, unbundling the supply chain enhances transparency and allows tariffs to reflect real costs. Markets have also taught us a few lessons: they have proven that they can adjust more easily than governments to changing circumstances in the energy market and that it is costly to intervene against the market for an extended period.

Market liberalisation is leaving much of the decision-making to consumers. Are the consumers capable of making the right choices? Or would they choose cheaper options (such as interruptible supply) even if that compromises their energy supply security? This possibility suggests a need for a government role. Moreover, liberalisation will not necessarily cover the entire supply chain. Certain monopolies will remain in transmission and distribution. Governments therefore have a duty to protect consumers at the very end of the supply chain (retail consumers). In addition, the energy market may ignore the interests of other consumer classes, such as remote and isolated consumers. All this necessitates that government continue to be involved in the energy market to a certain extent in almost every country.

The argument applies particularly to the supply side. Energy development entails long-term, capital-intensive investments. Private investors may demand a higher rate of return in a liberalised market than in a government-controlled energy industry. In addition, markets usually look for short-term profits and may therefore forgo diversification of supplies, which is associated with high up-front investment and risk but long-term benefits. How will markets respond to the long-term requirements of sustainable development, which demands heavy investments in research and development?

How can they meet societies' long-term interest in secure supplies at reasonable prices when their interest is mainly in the short term? How can markets respond to an emergency disruption of supply in exporting countries? The division between the production and supply functions does not allow full integration of the security function. Will the energy markets be able to internalise all the costs of security, including political risk?

Having said all that, there are several reasons to believe that regulatory reforms in the energy market that are aimed at enhancing competition would promote energy security. First, as discussed, reforms can lead to increased investment and trade in energy resources, which will, in turn, facilitate expansion of energy production, increase inter-fuel competition, and encourage the construction of trans-boundary energy delivery infrastructure, such as oil and gas pipelines.

Second, also as discussed, the participation in downstream operations by firms from oil-exporting economies, and the participation in upstream operations by firms from oil-importing economies (all of which is facilitated by market liberalisation), will be mutually beneficial and thus increase both exporters' and importers' interest in energy security. In Asia deregulation and other energy sector liberalisation will also promote accelerated growth in energy supplies and a greater sense of energy security.

Third, regulatory reforms will enhance efficiency and effectiveness, even in the area of energy supply emergency response. The IEA's oil supply emergency systems place growing emphasis on drawdowns of oil stocks compared with such measures as demand restraint. The release of oil stocks into the market is more market-oriented than government intervention to restrain demand.

Thus energy sector regulatory reforms could be compatible with or even enhance energy supply security. Governments, while withdrawing from energy investments themselves, need to create a positive climate for trade and investment. With increasing market liberalisation, there is a growing need for governments to monitor private sector actors and deal with market failures. Certain investors might be looking for concentration through mergers and joint ventures, for example, which might conflict with government policy of promoting liberalisation and fostering competition.

In considering the role of markets, the following questions are increasingly asked: Can the important issue of energy security be left entirely to markets? What is the role of the state in ensuring energy security in a liberalised market environment?

The role of the state

Markets are playing an increasingly progressive role in energy. This role is prominent in most OECD countries, modest in some developing countries, and absent in others, where the state remains almost solely responsible for the energy market and the security of supplies and services.

In a globalised market economy, energy security becomes a matter of prices, economic growth rates, and wealth transfers. In an energy (oil) crisis it cannot be assumed that free market conditions will prevail throughout the crisis (Jaffe, 1998). Thus the state still has an important role to play in almost in every country:

- Sending clear signals to markets so that they can be guided by the state's long-term energy policy.
- Continuing to act as a regulator to ensure fair play in the market.
- Ensuring long-term security by making the bold or costly decisions that the market cannot make on its own, such as diversifying fuels and encouraging renewables.
- Preserving the environment and enforcing environmental policies.
- Holding oil stocks for supply security and coordinating with other governments in such arrangements.
- Collecting and disseminating accurate energy market information in the event of emergencies. Left on their own, markets may respond nervously to rumours or distorted information, adding to the confusion and insecurity. Official information systems greatly helped to calm the markets in 1991 following the Gulf war and restored market stability.
- Financing and investing in research and development of new energy technologies and in improving efficiency, and encouraging markets to invest in research and development by offering tax and other incentives.
- Trying to incorporate the 'externalities' (such as long-term assurance of supply, environmental protection, and protection against possible disruptions) in a market-oriented setting.

Structural reforms are helping to foster competition by liberalising markets, but such competition and cost cutting should not be allowed to threaten long-term security of supplies to final consumers. That remains a government responsibility.

Regional cooperation and the growing importance of regional electricity grids and network energies

Use of electricity is growing more rapidly than use of all energy services. Over the next 20 years electricity production is expected to increase by about 3 percent a year, compared with average growth in total energy use of less than 2 percent a year. With this will come growth of electricity grids and regional interconnections. National and regional natural gas networks are also growing as reliance on gas increases because of its price and its environmental attractiveness. All this reflects consumers' growing preference for network energy. Energy security for consumers is thus no longer limited to the availability of resources and geo-political considerations. It is becoming increasingly dependent on markets and competition and on the security of regional networks, a vitally important issue.

Interconnection of neighbouring national grids (electricity and gas networks) into regional grids greatly enhances energy security. It also reduces the cost of supply by taking advantage of differences in peak demand and by allowing a reduction in standby power and reserve generating capacity and the use of cheaper resources. Today regional electricity grids exist not only in Europe but also in many other parts of the world. While the increasing interconnections across borders are providing great benefits to consumers, supply

Markets usually look for short-term profits and may therefore forgo diversification of supplies.

interruptions still occur, mainly because of problems in the local distribution system.

Conclusion

- All indications point to a gradual but steady improvement in energy security in all parts of the world, thanks to technological advances, adequacy of resources, and regional cooperation, energy agencies and treaties, and international trade organisations.
- Present energy security aims go beyond merely ensuring the availability of abundant oil supplies at affordable prices. They also include ensuring long-term energy adequacy in a new economic environment of deregulated and liberalised markets and fostering sustainable development.
- The resource base of fossil fuels is clearly adequate for meeting global energy service requirements well into the second half of the 21st century. But the resources—particularly crude oil and, to a lesser extent, gas—are mismatched between regions and between consuming and producing countries, raising geopolitical questions. Oil resources are heavily concentrated in the Gulf region, a part of the world that has experienced security problems. However, recent trends in energy utilisation and oil technologies are contributing greatly towards stability of supplies and prices in the oil market.
- The world will continue to depend on fossil fuels for decades to come. But these fuels have detrimental impacts on the environment that must be dealt with to achieve sustainable development. This requires promoting clean energy technologies, pursuing energy efficiency, developing renewable forms of energy, and providing technical assistance to developing countries, where most growth in energy use will take place.
- Deregulation and market liberalisation pose questions for energy security and for the future role of the state with respect to energy security. Markets lead to innovation, reduce costs, increase trade, improve allocation of resources, and spur technological development, all of which enhance energy security. Markets also normally pursue short-term objectives, while energy security demands long-term planning, investment, and political will. The state therefore needs to continue to play a role in ensuring national long-term security of supplies and protecting consumers.
- Consumers are gradually opting for energy supplied by grid (electricity and gas). This greatly enhances security of supply, reduces costs, and fosters regional cooperation.
- With energy services increasingly being supplied by electricity, the security of the electric power supply, in terms of both continuity and quality, is becoming paramount. Interruptions, even transient ones, cause serious income and welfare losses for consumers. In many developing countries the security and availability of the electricity supply leave much to be desired, pointing to a need for capital investments. The steady expansion of regional electricity grids, however, is helping to improve the security of electricity supply. ■

Note

1. The total nuclear fuel cycle cost, including enrichment and other fuel processing services, contributes 15–20 percent to the cost of nuclear electricity, but the cost of uranium presently accounts for only about 10 percent of the nuclear fuel cycle cost.

References

ADB (African Development Bank). 1999. *Infrastructure Development in Africa.* Abidjan.

AFP (Agence France-Presse). 1998. "Gulf States Cannot Afford to Finance Another War." *Jordan Times,* 16 February, p. 10.

Campbell, C.J., and J.H. Laherrere. 1998. "The End of Cheap Oil." *Scientific American* 278: 60–65.

David, S.R. 1999. "Saving America from the Coming Civil Wars." *Foreign Affairs* 78: 103–16.

Douaud, A. 1999. "Automotive Fuels." *Oxford Energy Forum* (36): 18–19.

EC (European Commission). 1999. "Economic Foundations for Energy Policy." *Energy in Europe* (special issue, December): 1–170.

Ecoal. 1998. *World Coal Institute* 28(1).

IEA (International Energy Agency). 1998. *World Energy Outlook.* Paris.

IIASA (International Institute for Applied Systems Analysis) and WEC (World Energy Council). 1998. *Global Energy Perspectives.* Edited by Nebojša Nakićenović, Arnulf Grübler, and Alan McDonald. Cambridge: Cambridge University Press.

Jaffe, A. 1998. "The Political, Economic, Social, Cultural and Religious Trends in the Middle East and the Gulf and Their Impact on Energy Supply, Security and Pricing—Energy Security." Rice University, Baker Institute, Houston, Tex.

Kemp, G., and R. Harkavy. 1997. *Strategic Geography and the Changing Middle East.* Washington, D.C.: Brookings Institution Press.

Khatib, H. 1997. *Financial and Economic Evaluation of Projects.* London: Institution of Electrical Engineers.

Maillard, D. 1999. "Energy Security." Ministry of Economy, Finance, and Industry, Paris.

Martin, W., R. Imai, and H. Steeg. 1996. *Maintaining Energy Security in a Global Context.* New York: Trilateral Commission.

Masters, C.D. 1994. *World Petroleum Assessment and Analysis.* Proceedings of the 14th World Petroleum Congress. New York: John Wiley & Sons.

McKelvey, V.E. 1972. "Mineral Resource Estimates and Public Policy." *American Scientist* 60: 32–40.

Mitchell, J.V. 1997. *Will Western Europe Face an Energy Shortage?* Strasbourg: Energy Council of France.

Murray, J. 1995. "Nuclear Non-proliferation: Challenges for the Future." Speech to the Australian Institute of International Affairs, Melbourne, December.

Newton-Evans Research Company. 1998. *Market Trend Digest* (summer). Baltimore.

Schuetterle, P. 1999. Secretary-General of the Energy Charter. Personal correspondence. January.

USAID (U.S. Agency for International Development). 1988. *Power Shortages in Developing Countries: Magnitude, Impacts, Solutions, and the Role of the Private Sector.* Report to U.S. Congress. March. Washington, D.C.

USDOE (U.S. Department of Energy). 1998. *Annual Energy Outlook 1999.* Washington, D.C.

Walker, W. 1998. "Nuclear Power and Nonproliferation." In M. Poireau and A. Zurita, eds., *Nuclear in a Changing World: Proceedings of the European Seminar.* Vol. 2. XII/0318/98.EN. Brussels: European Commission, Directorate-General XII, Science, Research and Development.

WEC (World Energy Council). 1998. *Survey of Energy Resources.* London.

World Bank. 1999. *World Development Report 1999/2000: Entering the 21st Century.* New York: Oxford University Press.

part II

energy resources and technology options

energy resources

CHAPTER 5

Hans-Holger Rogner (Germany)

LEAD AUTHORS: Fritz Barthel (Germany), Maritess Cabrera (Philippines), Andre Faaij (Netherlands), Marc Giroux (France), David Hall (United Kingdom), Vladimir Kagramanian (Russian Federation), Serguei Kononov (Russian Federation), Thierry Lefevre (France), Roberto Moreira (Brazil), R. Nötstaller (Austria), Peter Odell (United Kingdom), and Martin Taylor (United States and United Kingdom)

ABSTRACT A comprehensive account of the world's energy resource endowment is essential for any long-term energy assessment. Energy resources exist in different forms—some exist as stocks and so are exhaustible, others exist as flows and are inexhaustible, and a third form is based on exhaustible stocks that can be leveraged to resemble renewables. Most important, energy resources evolve dynamically as a function of human engineering ingenuity, driven by the desire to supply affordable and convenient energy services. Although the term stocks suggests finiteness (which is ultimately correct), the accessible portion depends on technology and on the future demand for that resource. Resources not demanded by the market are 'neutral stuff'. Demand plus advances in technology and knowledge turn neutral stuff into reserves that are replenished upon use by further advances in technology and knowledge, enabling humans to tap into resources previously beyond reach. But for stocks there will eventually be a limit. In contrast, resources based on annually recurring flows are distinctly different from stocks: harvested prudently, they are renewable. But resources are not an end in themselves, and their attractiveness must be seen in the context of societies' energy service needs, of the technologies that convert resources into energy services, and of the economics associated with their use. This chapter assesses whether long-term energy resource availability could impede sustainable development and, based on a dynamic technology concept, provides a comprehensive account of the world's energy resource endowment. ∎

T his chapter reviews fossil, nuclear, and renewable energy resources. The reserve and resource volumes presented here cover the ranges considered robust by most of the lead authors. The main controversy yet to be resolved concerns the different views on the roles of technology and demand in the long-term availability of a particular resource. Subject to debate is the extent to which reserves can be converted from additional conventional resources with lower geological assurance and from unconventional resources lacking economic attractiveness given current markets and technologies. Natural flows are immense for renewable resources, but the level of their future use will depend on the technological and economic performance of technologies feeding on these flows as well as on possible constraints on their use. The long-term availability of energy resources will likely become more an issue of the degree to which future societies want to balance environmental and economic tradeoffs, control greenhouse gas emissions, and internalise externalities, or of the technological and economic performance of different clean energy conversion technologies, than a question of resource existence.

This chapter examines long-term energy resource availability primarily

Hydrocarbon occurrences become resources only if there is demand for them and appropriate technology has been developed for their conversion and use.

from the perspectives of theoretical maximums, or ultimately recoverable resources. Admittedly, it can be argued that an analysis based on ultimately recoverable resources is irrelevant—hydrocarbon occurrences or natural flows become resources only if there is demand for them and appropriate technology has been developed for their conversion and use. Indeed, energy resources generally should not be scrutinised without reference to the chain extending from the extraction of resources to the supply of energy services—that is, along all the conversion steps to the point of what consumers really want: transportation, communication, air conditioning, and so on. But the assessment in this volume has been structured so that each link of the chain is explored separately. Energy conversion technologies are discussed in chapters 7 (renewable energy technologies) and 8 (advanced fossil and nuclear energy technologies), as well as in chapter 6 (energy efficiency).

Definitions and units

A variety of terms are used to describe energy reserves, and different authors and institutions have different meanings for the same terms. Meanings also vary for different energy sources. The World Energy

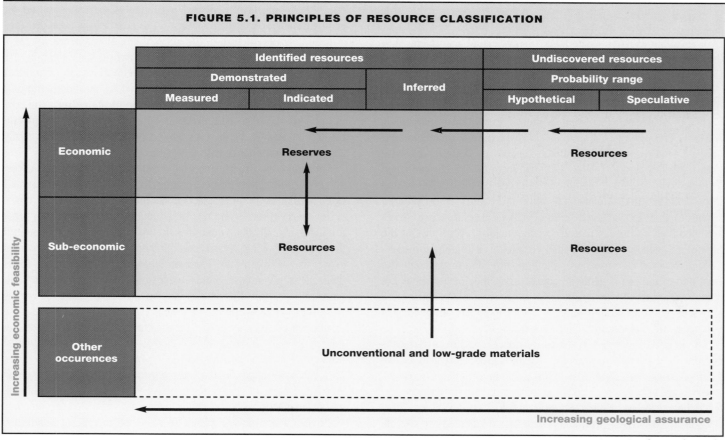

FIGURE 5.1. PRINCIPLES OF RESOURCE CLASSIFICATION

Source: Based on McKelvey, 1967.

Council defines resources as "the occurrences of material in recognisable form" (WEC, 1998). For oil, it is essentially the amount of oil in the ground. Reserves represent a portion of resources and is the term used by the extraction industry. British Petroleum notes that proven reserves of oil are "generally taken to be those quantities that geological and engineering information indicates with reasonable certainty can be recovered in the future from known reservoirs under existing economic and operating conditions" (BP, 1999). Other common terms include probable reserves, indicated reserves, and inferred reserves—that is, hydrocarbon occurrences that do not meet the criteria of proven reserves. Undiscovered resources are what remains and, by definition, one can only speculate on their existence. Ultimately recoverable resources are the sum of identified reserves and the possibly recoverable fraction of undiscovered resources and generally also include production to date. Then there is the difference between conventional and unconventional occurrences (oil shale, tar sands, coalbed methane, clathrates, uranium in black shale or dissolved in sea water), especially the rate at which unconventional resources can be converted into conventional reserves.

To the extent possible, this chapter uses the McKelvey box, which presents resource categories in a matrix with increasing degrees of geological assurance and economic feasibility (figure 5.1). This scheme, developed by the U.S. Bureau of Mines and the U.S. Geological Survey (USGS, 1980), is to some extent also reflected in the international classification system recently proposed by the United Nations.

In this classification system, resources are defined as concentrations of naturally occurring solid, liquid, or gaseous material in or on the Earth's crust in such form that economic extraction is potentially feasible. The geologic dimension is divided into identified and undiscovered resources. Identified resources are deposits that have known location, grade, quality, and quantity or that can be estimated from geologic evidence. Identified resources are further subdivided into demonstrated (measured plus indicated) and inferred resources, to reflect varying degrees of geological assurance. Reserves are identified resources that are economically recoverable at the time of assessment (see the British Petroleum definition, above).

Undiscovered resources are quantities expected or postulated to exist under analogous geologic conditions. Other occurrences are materials that are too low-grade or for other reasons not considered technically or economically extractable. For the most part, unconventional resources are included in 'other occurrences'.

The boundary between reserves, resources, and occurrences is current or expected profitability of exploitation, governed by the ratio of market price to cost of production. Production costs of reserves are usually supported by actual production experience and feasibility analyses, while cost estimates for resources are often inferred from current production experience adjusted for specific geological and geographic conditions.

Technological improvements are continuously pushing resources into the reserve category by advancing knowledge and lowering extraction costs.

For several reasons, reserve and resource quantities and related supply-cost curves are subject to continuous revision. Production inevitably depletes reserves and eventually exhausts deposits, while successful exploration and prospecting add new reserves and resources. Price increases and cost reductions expand reserves by moving resources into the reserve category and vice versa. The dynamic nature of the reserve-resource relationship is illustrated by the arrows in figure 5.1. Technology is the most important force in this process. Technological improvements are continuously pushing resources into the reserve category by advancing knowledge and lowering extraction costs.

The outer boundary of resources and the interface to other occurrences is less clearly defined and often subject to a much wider margin of interpretation and judgement. Other occurrences are not considered to have economic potential at the time of classification. But over the very long term, technological progress may upgrade significant portions to resources.

In 1992 the United Nations Economic Commission on Europe (UNECE) launched an effort to define a generally applicable resource classification scheme with a higher resolution of technical and economic feasibility than the McKelvey box. By adding a third dimension—the level of actual feasibility of extraction based on geological engineering assessments—this new classification provides a more accurate picture of the accessibility of resources. In 1997 the United Nations International Framework Classification for Reserves/Resources—Solid Fuels and Mineral Commodities (UNFC) was completed and recommended by the Economic and Social Council (ECOSOC) for world-wide application. But it will take time for the UNFC to be universally adopted by public and private institutions and for fossil reserves and resources to be consistently reported in compliance with the UNFC.

For renewable energy sources, the concepts of reserves, resources, and occurrences need to be modified. Renewables represent annual flows available, in principle, on an indefinite sustainable basis. Fossil energy reserves and resources, although expanding over time, are fundamentally finite quantities. In this context the annual natural flows of solar, wind, hydro, and geothermal energy and quantities grown by nature in the form of biomass (often referred to as theoretical potentials) would correspond to occurrences. The concept of technical potentials can be used as a proxy for energy resources, while economic potentials correspond to reserves. The distinction between theoretical and technical potentials reflects the degree of use determined by thermodynamic or technological limitations without consideration of practical feasibility or costs. Thus the economic potential is the portion of the technical potential that could be used cost-effectively. In terms of reserves, resources, and occurrences of hydrocarbons, economic and technical potentials are dynamically moving targets in response to market conditions and technology availability and performance.

This chapter reports oil resources in gigatonnes (1 Gt = 10^9 tonnes) and exajoules (1 EJ = 10^{18} joules) using the energy equivalent of 42 gigajoules per tonne of oil equivalent (GJ per toe). Gas resources are reported in tera cubic metres (1 Tm^3 = 10^{12} cubic metres) and converted to EJ using 37 gigajoules per 1,000 cubic metres (GJ per 1,000 m^3). Coal resources are usually reported in natural units, although the energy content of coal may vary considerably within and between different coal categories. The Bundesanstalt für Geowissenschaften und Rohstoffe (Federal Institute for Geosciences and Natural Resources, referred to here as the BGR) in Hannover (Germany) is the only institution that converts regional coal occurrences into tonnes of coal equivalent (1 tce = 29 gigajoules). Thus coal resource data come from the BGR. Uranium and other nuclear materials are usually reported in tonnes of metal. The thermal energy equivalent of 1 tonne of uranium in average once-through fuel cycles is about 589 terajoules (IPCC, 1996a).

Oil reserves and resources

Views on the long-term availability of oil and natural gas continue to spark controversy and debate. One school of thought believes that the best oil fields have already been discovered and that the amount of oil still to be discovered is somewhat limited. The other school regards oil reserves as a dynamic quantity, driven by demand and technological advances. The second school is more optimistic about future hydrocarbon availability.

Ultimately recoverable resources— the static or geologists' view

For many years, world oil reserves have experienced small but steady increases, which implies that the discovery or delineation of new reserves has at least kept pace with production. But many geologists focus on the concept of a quasi-fixed stock of hydrocarbon occurrences that, once production commences, can only decrease. For oil, they argue that few new oil fields have been discovered since the mid-1970s, and that most reserve increases have come from revisions of previously underestimated existing reserves (Hatfield, 1997; Campbell and Laherrere, 1998) and improved recovery techniques. Peak production lags behind peak discovery (of the mid-1960s) by several decades. Larger and more obvious fields are found first, leading to an early peak in discovery and diminishing returns in

TABLE 5.1. ESTIMATED OIL RESERVES

Region	Identified reserves (Masters and others, 1994)		Identified reserves plus 95%[a] (Masters and others, 1994)		Identified reserves plus mode[b] (Masters and others, 1994)		Identified reserves plus 5%[c] (Masters and others, 1994)		Proven recoverable reserves (WEC, 1998)		Proven reserves (BP, 1999)		Total resources from enhanced oil recovery[d]	
	Gigatonnes	Exajoules	Gigatonnes	Exajoules	Gigatonnes	Exajoules	Gigatonnes	Exajoules	Gigatonnes	Exajoules	Gigatonnes	Exajoules	Gigatonnes	Exajoules
North America	8.5	356	14.3	599	17.0	712	23.7	992	4.6	193	4.6	193	13.6	569
Latin America and Caribbean	17.3	724	22.6	946	26.2	1,097	41.6	1,742	19.2	804	19.9	833	23.8	996
Western Europe	5.6	234	6.8	285	7.7	322	11.2	469	2.5	105	2.5	105	3.9	163
Central and Eastern Europe	0.3	13	0.4	17	0.5	21	1.1	46	0.3	13	0.2	8	0.5	21
Former Soviet Union	17.0	712	25.1	1,051	30.6	1,281	49.9	2,089	8.0	335	9.1	381	11.2	469
Middle East and North Africa	87.6	3,668	97.0	4,061	104.6	4,379	126.4	5,292	99.6	4,170	96.8	4,053	59.2	2,479
Sub-Saharan Africa	4.0	167	5.9	247	7.3	306	12.3	515	4.0	167	4.5	188	3.3	138
Pacific Asia	3.1	130	4.1	172	4.8	201	7.3	306	1.5	63	1.5	63	2.1	88
South Asia	1.0	42	1.1	46	1.3	54	1.8	75	0.8	33	0.5	21	0.6	25
Centrally planned Asia	5.1	214	7.8	327	9.8	410	17.9	749	5.4	226	3.4	142	3.7	155
Pacific OECD	0.4	17	0.6	25	0.7	29	1.3	54	0.4	17	0.4	17	0.5	21
Total[e]	150	6,277	186	7,776	210	8,812	295	12,329	146	6,126	143	6,004	123	5,124

Note: Excludes cumulative production to the date of assessment.
a. Identified reserves plus estimates of undiscovered resources with a 95 percent probability of discovery. b. Identified reserves plus estimates of undiscovered resources with a 50 percent probability of discovery. c. Identified reserves plus estimates of undiscovered resources with a 5 percent probability of discovery. d. Includes enhanced recovery of past and future oil production. e. Totals rounded.

exploration: the more that is found, the less is left to find. Fields that are smaller and harder to find and to exploit follow, but eventually the fixed stock will be exhausted. Some 90 percent of current global oil production comes from fields more than 20 years old.

Cumulative production is a good proxy for geological knowledge gained through exploration experience. All these facts leave no room for any conclusion other than that peak production is being approached rapidly. In the 1960s ultimately recoverable resources became a popular concept for quantifying the fixed stock of hydrocarbon occurrences. Ultimately recoverable resources include cumulative production, proven reserves at the time of estimation, and oil remaining to be discovered—in other words, the ultimate oil wealth available to humans. For the past 40 years most estimates of ultimately recoverable resources for conventional oil have ranged from 200–400 gigatonnes. More recently, Campbell and Laherrere (1998) put ultimately recoverable reserves at about 250 gigatonnes, Hiller (1999) at 350 gigatonnes, Edwards (1997) at 385 gigatonnes, Masters and others (1994) at 281–390 gigatonnes, and Odell (1997) at 410 gigatonnes. All these estimates include production to the date of estimation (96–110 gigatonnes).

The debate on the size of ultimately recoverable resources and the time horizon when the depletion midpoint will be reached includes only conventional oil occurrences. Shale oil, tar sands (natural bitumen), and heavy crude oil are considered unconventional oil resources, defined as occurrences that cannot be tapped with conventional production methods for technical or economic reasons or both (Rogner, 1997; Gregory and Rogner, 1998). These resources form a large part of the vast store of hydrocarbons in the Earth's crust and, in the case of oil, have been assessed to be at least as large as conventional oil resources (see below). The existence of unconventional oil and gas is acknowledged by 'fixed stock' analysts, but they are less sanguine about the future technological potential for bringing these resources to market. Technological pessimism and an exclusive focus on conventional oil largely explain the geologists' view that global oil production will reach its peak and mid-depletion point in the near future.

Conventional oil. Table 5.1 reports recent estimates, excluding cumulative production to date, of identified or proven oil reserves and natural gas liquids. All these estimates report reserves at around 1,000 billion barrels of oil (143–150 gigatonnes).

Masters and others (1994) estimate identified reserves on 1 January 1993 to be 150 gigatonnes (6,277 exajoules), only slightly higher than British Petroleum and World Energy Council estimates of proven reserves at the end of 1997.[1] Masters and others also estimate undiscovered oil resources based on a modified Delphi technique

TABLE 5.2. ESTIMATED UNCONVENTIONAL OIL RESERVES AN[...]

Region	Oil shale												Heavy crude oil					
	Identified resources (BGR, 1998)		Total resources (BGR, 1998)		Proven recoverable and estimated additional reserves (WEC, 1998)		Oil in place (BGR, 1998)		Reserves and resources (BGR, 1998)		Future potential recovery (Meyer, 1997)	
	Gigatonnes	Exajoules	Gigatonnes	Exajoules	Gigatonnes	Exajoules	Gigatonnes	Exajoules	Gigatonnes	Exajoules	Gigatonnes	Exajoules
North America	1.1	48	351.6	14,767	217.0	9,114	15.7	659	2.3	96	2.0	82
Latin America and Caribbean	0.3	14	19.4	814	9.6	405	229.3	9,631	59.7	2,509	51.2	2,152
Western Europe	0.5	22	8.9	374	0.0	1	9.8	412	3.7	155	3.2	133
Central and Eastern Europe	1.1	45	2.8	116	0.0	0	0.1	4	0.1	5	0.1	5
Former Soviet Union	4.2	178	9.6	405	6.5	273	0.1	4	19.2	805	16.4	690
Middle East and North Africa	7.6	319	8.1	340	28.0	1,175	45.2	1,898	20.2	847	17.3	726
Sub-Saharan Africa	0.0	0	16.4	690	0.0	0	1.4	59	0.9	39	0.6	27
Pacific Asia	1.0	40	1.0	40	1.7	71	1.1	46	1.5	62	1.4	59
South Asia	0.0	0	0.0	0	0.0	0	1.0	42	0.0	2	0.0	1
Centrally planned Asia	0.6	25	20.0	840	0.0	0	10.8	454	2.6	111	2.3	95
Pacific OECD	3.8	160	44.5	1,870	36.0	1,513	0.0	0	0.0	1	0.0	1
Total	20.3	851	482.3	20,256	298.9	12,552	314.5	13,209	110.3	4,632	94.5	3,971

and geological analogies. Their low estimate (95 percent probability of discovery) brings their total for recoverable conventional oil reserves to 186 gigatonnes (7,771 exajoules). If cumulative production until 1994 of 95 gigatonnes (3,990 exajoules) is added, the total for ultimately recoverable resources is 281 gigatonnes (11,800 exajoules). The medium (mode) estimate of undiscovered resources brings total recoverable oil reserves to 210 gigatonnes (8,812 exajoules) and ultimately recoverable resources to 305 gigatonnes (12,810 exajoules). The high (5 percent probability) estimate of undiscovered resources brings total recoverable oil reserves to 295 gigatonnes (12,329 exajoules) and ultimately recoverable resources to 390 gigatonnes (16,380 exajoules).

In its 1998 survey the World Energy Council reported proven recoverable oil reserves of 146 gigatonnes (6,126 exajoules) and estimates additional recoverable reserves (excluding speculative occurrences) of 28 gigatonnes (1,192 exajoules), for a total of 174 gigatonnes (7,318 exajoules). This compares well with the Masters and others estimate of identified reserves plus 95 percent probability of undiscovered resources of 186 gigatonnes. The oil reserve estimates in table 5.1 reflect the views of geologists on the availability of conventional oil and are consistent with the ultimately recoverable resource estimates presented earlier.

Today only about 35 percent of the oil in place is recovered by primary and secondary production methods. With enhanced oil recovery methods, this rate can be increased to as much as 65 percent of the original oil in place in a reservoir, though at higher extraction costs (BGR, 1995). Thus the application of enhanced oil recovery methods in abandoned fields and new developments increases conventional oil resources.

Table 5.1 shows the potential resources resulting from the use of enhanced oil recovery techniques. Resources are calculated based on an average recovery rate of 35 percent achieved in historical production and used in the delineation of proven recoverable reserves, and an enhanced oil recovery rate of 15 percent, for an overall recovery rate of 50 percent.

Unconventional oil. The vast amounts of unconventional oil occurrences include oil shale, heavy crude oil, and tar sands. Unconventional oil is already economic to exploit in some places, so some is defined as reserves. Further development may depend on higher oil prices, technological developments, and long-term demand for liquid fuels. According to BGR (1998), reserves of unconventional oil could be as high as 245 gigatonnes, substantially exceeding proven reserves of conventional oil (table 5.2).

Oil shale is a sedimentary rock rich in organic matter containing more than 10 percent kerogen. It can be used directly as a fuel in power plants or processed to produce synthetic petroleum products. The kerogen content of oil shale varies widely. According to BGR (1995), only about 1 percent of world resources contains more than 100 litres of oil per cubic metre rock, while 85 percent have less than 40 litres per cubic metre.

Data on oil shale resources are presented in table 5.2. The most recent BGR (1998) estimate of oil shale resources is 482 gigatonnes, down from 920 gigatonnes in the 1995 estimate. WEC (1998) estimates recoverable and estimated additional reserves at 299 gigatonnes. Major oil shale resources are in China, Estonia, the United States, Australia, and Jordan. The large regional differences between the BGR and WEC estimates are likely the result of different definitions.

Because of the high costs of mining and processing, oil shale is produced only in small quantities in China and Estonia. Estonia is the only country with an economy dominated by oil shale as a source of energy and for more than 70 years has been the largest user of oil shale in power generation. Recent production totalled 20 million tonnes of oil shale a year (Hobbs, 1995).

Heavy crude oil is defined as high-viscosity crude oil with a density equal to or less than 20° API (934 kilograms per cubic metre). Extra heavy oil is crude oil with a density equal to or less than 10° API (1,000 kilograms per cubic metre). Unlike tar sands, the viscosity of these hydrocarbons is below 10,000 millipoise (see below). Heavy oil is formed by the degradation of conventional oil in shallow reservoirs.

Recent estimates of heavy oil resources are summarised in table 5.2. BGR (1995) estimates oil in place to be 315 gigatonnes. In BGR (1998), 33 of these are considered reserves and 77 are considered resources, for a total of 110 gigatonnes—well within the range of

Tar sands (natural bitumen)					
Oil in place (BGR, 1998)		Reserves and resources (BGR, 1998)		Proven recoverable and estimated additional reserves (WEC, 1998)	
Gigatonnes	Exajoules	Gigatonnes	Exajoules	Gigatonnes	Exajoules
233	9,786	40.7	1,710	51.7	2,173
190	7,980	33.2	1,395	1.2	49
0	0	0.0	0	0.0	0
0	0	0.0	0	0.0	0
232	9,744	40.5	1,703	0.0	0
0	0	0.0	0	0.0	0
3	126	0.5	22	0.0	0
0	0	0.0	0	0.0	0
0	0	0.0	0	0.0	0
0	0	0.0	0	0.0	0
0	0	0.0	0	0.0	0
658	27,636	115.0	4,830	52.9	2,222

future potential recovery given by Meyer (1997). About half of heavy oil resources are in Venezuela; the former Soviet Union, Kuwait, Iraq, Mexico, and China account for most of the rest.

Meyer (1997) uses the term *unproved reserves* because his estimates include some probable and possible reserves. Quantities stated under undiscovered potential recovery include all resources based on geological and engineering judgement, using a recovery factor of 10 percent.

Some 8 percent of world oil production come from heavy oil reservoirs, with Venezuela, the United States, Canada, Iraq, Mexico, and the former Soviet Union being major producers (BGR, 1998). Due to the nature of heavy oil, enhanced oil recovery methods such as steam flooding and hot water, polymer, and carbon dioxide injection are generally required for its extraction.

Tar sands (natural bitumen) and extra heavy oil are sands or sandstones that contain a large portion of tarry hydrocarbons with a viscosity exceeding 10,000 millipoise. They are formed by thermal metamorphism and biodegradation of conventional oil deposits. The high viscosity of these hydrocarbons requires unconventional extraction methods such as mining with bucket-wheel excavators or in truck and shovel operations. Natural bitumen typically contains large portions of sulphur and trace elements, including vanadium and nickel.

BGR (1998) estimates that 115 of the 658 gigatonnes of tar sands qualify as possible reserves (see table 5.2). Commercial production is limited to the Athabasca tar sand deposits of Alberta (Canada), with a volume of 25 million tonnes in 1998 (WEC, 1998). To reduce the environmental disturbance caused by surface mining, in situ techniques are increasingly used (box 5.1). In addition, new extraction technologies, such as steam-assisted gravity drainage, are being developed to reduce oil viscosity through steam injection (George, 1998). The use of extra heavy oil has commenced in the Orinoco oil belt of Venezuela (BGR, 1998).

Available resources—the dynamic or economists' view

Unlike geologists, who tend to treat resources as an innate component of the physical world, economists view what exists in the Earth's crust as 'neutral stuff' (Odell, 1998) that becomes a resource only if

---

BOX 5.1. ENVIRONMENTAL OBSTACLES TO EXTRACTING UNCONVENTIONAL OIL

The production of unconventional oil and the necessary upgrade to marketable fuels can hurt local environments. Mining, conversion, and upgrading to synthetic crude oil can produce toxic heavy metals and large quantities of solid and acidic liquid and gaseous wastes that need to be contained, cleaned, and disposed of in an environmentally benign manner. This may require stringent environmental controls and new policies for toxic waste disposal. Extracting hydrocarbons from unconventional oils such as tar sands, heavy oils, and oil shale involves very large surface (open-pit or strip) mining and underground mining (room and pillar technique), steam soaking, steam flooding, or in situ combustion. Here the production of tar sand and its upgrading to synthetic crude oil are used to show the potential environmental constraints of large-scale unconventional oil production.

The production of synthetic crude oil from Alberta, Canada's tar sand deposits involves open-pit mining and handling of 5 tonnes of tar sands and overburden per barrel of oil produced (Penner and others, 1982), milling to separate the bitumen from the sand, and upgrading it to commercial quality. Syncrude, a Canadian company, processes 510,000 tonnes of tar sands a day and recovers about one barrel of heavy oil for every 2 tonnes of tar sands processed (Stosur and others, 1998). A hot water process is the most common for extracting oil from the sand. The process is energy-intensive and requires large quantities of hot water. Syncrude operations require 1,400 tonnes an hour of water heated to nearly 500 degrees Celsius. Water is recycled to the maximum extent (90 percent). The remaining materials (tailings) after the bitumen has been extracted (extraction rate some 90 percent) are liquids and sand. Most of the tailings are the excavated overburden rock and rejected sand; both can be stockpiled and used as backfill with little threat to the environment (Stosur and others, 1998).

Things are different for the liquid tailings, which are contaminated with organic and inorganic compounds (sulphur, porphyrins, salts of organic acids) and can seriously damage nearby aquatic ecosystems. The liquid is stored in settling ponds, allowing water to clarify before it is recycled. These ponds are designed as 'zero discharge' basins, and no process-affected water is discharged in running waters. But while tailings sand settles out quickly, the fine-grained materials (silts and clays) and residual bitumen consolidate slowly and can pose a long-term problem and liability. Tailings ponds must be constructed to last several decades and must be guarded against erosion, breaching, and foundation creep until better disposal practices become available (Stosur and others, 1998). New processes such as dry retorting—which generates dry tailings—are expected to minimise the risk of acid drainage from tar sand tailings. Other methods include faster consolidation of fine tailings, detoxification of tailing pond water, and reprocessing of fine tailings (including co-production of minerals and metals).

Spent tar sand (mainly sand, silt, and clay contaminated with the remaining bitumen and caustic compounds) is put in specially designed storage areas to avoid acid drainage or used as fill material in mine reclamation efforts. While the disrupted land area can be considerable, land reclamation is usually imposed on mine operators to limit permanent environmental damage and to return land to a stable, biologically self-sustaining state.

Upgrading operations are the primary source of airborne emissions. Sulphur dioxide, particulates, hydrocarbons, vanadium, and nickel were originally of major concern. In addition, bitumen contains several carcinogenic polycyclic aromatic hydrocarbons (WHO, 1982). Hydrotreaters remove sulphur and nitrogen and produce elemental sulphur as a by-product. Nitrogen is removed as ammonia and used as an under-boiler fuel or for chemical feedstock. Hydrogen sulphide is removed from the by-product fuel gas that fuels parts of the upgrading operations. The synthetic crude oil produced from Alberta's tar sand deposits is 32–33° API with 0.1–0.2 percent sulphur. It contains no residue, while typical conventional crudes have about 8 percent residue.

Stosur and others (1998) estimate that only 15 percent of tar sand resources are suitable for surface mining. The rest would have to be extracted by in situ methods, which minimise land disturbance through multiwell pads and horizontal drilling (Sadler and Houlihan, 1998). To reduce odour and greenhouse gas emissions, care must be taken to collect and reuse or flare the gases generated by the process.

Alberta's tar sand operations indicate that environmental protection is the result of effective environmental regulation and controls, including a balance of resource development and resource conservation and of environmental and socioeconomic policies.

there is a market demand for it. Put differently, "there are huge amounts of hydrocarbons in the earth's crustæ (Adelman and Lynch, 1997), and "estimates of declining reserves and production are incurably wrong because they treat as a quantity what is really a dynamic process driven by growing knowledge" (Nehring, 1998). Improvements in technology—such as three-dimensional seismic surveys and extended-reach drilling—have allowed higher recovery rates from existing reservoirs and the profitable development of fields once considered uneconomic or technically beyond reach, expanding the boundary of reserves and shifting resources into the reserve category.

In addition, economists argue, a distinction between conventional and unconventional occurrences is irrelevant. Today most unconventional occurrences are neutral stuff and will become resources and reserves if there is sufficient demand. In fact, certain unconventional occurrences—heavy oil, tar sands, coalbed methane and gas from aquifers—have already started to 'come in from the margin'. Conventional discoveries previously regarded as uneconomic can now be developed profitably, and recoverable reserves can be increased in fields being developed or under production. In short, economists view oil and gas reserves as a portion of the total hydrocarbon occurrences contained in the Earth's crust, where volumes depend on exploration know-how to locate and evaluate a play (delineated deposit) and on the capability of technology to extract it at an acceptable cost given sufficient demand.

The question of long-term hydrocarbon resource availability, then, is viewed from the perspective of anticipated demand in competitive markets—taking into account technological change and growing knowledge. In the presence of sufficiently large conventional oil reserves there is, at present, no demand for the large-scale use of abundant unconventional oil occurrences (see above). This explains the absence of any significant motivation for a comprehensive and systematic evaluation of these resources or for the development of technology for their economic and environmentally acceptable recovery.

Economists take proven conventional oil reserves of 150 gigatonnes as a point of departure that, based on their definition, can be brought to the market at post-1986 price levels. In addition, economists point to industry expectations that proven reserves will grow 50–70 gigatonnes by 2020 (Shell, 1996). They point out that the oil industry has historically responded to demand by finding and developing reserves, even given the long lead time for this process: since World War II it has taken more than 40 years to move from identifying reserves to producing resources. This is seen as a clear indication that the process of stock replenishment is working effectively.

A bigger role for unconventional oil. Economists also argue that unconventional oil should be viewed as an important element of the oil resource base—and after 2030 it will be a critical complement to conventional oil production in keeping the oil supply curve moving upwards. This long process of the changing supply pattern will be

> The oil industry has historically responded to demand by finding and developing reserves, even given the long lead time for this process.

seamless from the viewpoint of oil producers. From the point of view of users the process will be unimportant, because no essential difference will arise for them merely because of the changing nature of exploitation of oil habitats in the Earth's surface. In precisely the same way, today's oil consumers do not need to consider whether their supply is from shallow or deep horizons, or from onshore or offshore locations.

The ultimate resource base of unconventional oil is irrelevant to the 21st century's energy supply. Occurrences of such oil that are already known and under exploitation can provide the global supply likely to be required in the 21st century. On the other hand, economic or environmental considerations—or both—could convert unconventional resources back to neutral stuff, as has occurred in recent decades with previously designated coal resources.

Costs and technological developments. New technologies for exploring and extracting oil have lowered exploration, development, and production costs while expanding the oil resource base. Further advances in technology must also be expected, resulting in additional reductions in cost. Part of these productivity gains will be offset by the use of more remote, harder-to-access, and smaller deposits. Still, it appears plausible that technological progress will continue to keep production costs in check.[2] The technology learning curve for synthetic crude oil production from tar sands in Alberta is a good example of the impact of technology on production costs. In 1978 a barrel of synthetic crude oil cost about $26 a barrel. By 1996 breakthroughs in the technology for producing and refining bitumen as well as better operating procedures had lowered these costs to $9.60 a barrel (Polikar and Cyr, 1998).

Two developments will likely put upward pressure on prices. The first is the increasing volume of energy that will be demanded in the first half of the 21st century. The second is the significantly increased cash flows required by the international oil industry to sustain enhanced investment in the initial large-scale exploitation of rapidly increasing volumes of unconventional oil and gas. In the 1950s the ability of consumers to secure large volumes of international oil depended on the super-normal profits that the industry was able to generate. More recent breakthroughs for gas in Europe and elsewhere were likewise achieved because of super-normal profitability in the industry. After 2030, following the introduction to global markets of large-scale unconventional hydrocarbons, prices should fall back as the long-run supply prices of the two commodities once again start to decline under conditions of advancing technology and increasing economies of scale (Odell, 1998).

Reconciling the two views

The differences between geologists' (static) and economists' (dynamic) views of oil resources can be partly explained by the way the different schools view unconventional oil. Geologists draw a strict line between conventional oil (the oil they look for) and unconventional oil (the oil that does not fit their template). Although some unconventional oil is being exploited economically, geologists take a conservative view of its long-term commercial viability. In contrast, economists consider irrelevant the dividing line between conventional and unconventional oil. They anticipate a seamless transition from one to the other as long as demand and market prices allow for a profitable return on investment. In that case, unconventional occurrences estimated to exist in the Earth's crust (see table 5.2) would extend the oil age well beyond the mid-21st century. Without demand, the issue of resource availability becomes meaningless and unconventional oil occurrences remain neutral stuff.

A historical review of the most popular guideline for the industry, the ratio of reserves to production, puts into perspective the two schools of thought. This ratio compares known reserves and current production and so measures the temporal reach of exhaustible energy reserves. These ratios typically fluctuate between 20 and 40 years.

But the notion of a reserve-to-production ratio is seriously flawed and, in the past, has led to aberrant conclusions (MacKenzie, 1996). The most erroneous conclusion is that the world will be running out of reserves by the time suggested by the ratio.[3] For oil, ratios of 20–40 years have existed since the early 20th century (figure 5.2). According to this ratio, the world should have run out of oil a long time ago. Instead, driven by economics (in essence, demand for oil), advances in geoscience, and technological progress in upstream production, reserves have been continuously replenished from previously unknown sources (new discoveries) or technologically or economically inaccessible occurrences. Although reserve additions have shifted to more difficult and potentially more costly locations, technological progress has outbalanced potentially diminishing returns.

> New technologies for exploring and extracting oil have lowered exploration, development, and production costs while expanding the oil resource base.

Gas reserves and resources

Unlike oil, gas is not subject to controversy on estimates of ultimately recoverable reserves. Proven reserves are comparable to those of oil but high relative to current and cumulative production. Still, natural gas is often viewed as the poor stepsister of oil. The development of natural gas fields requires large investments in transmission and distribution infrastructure.[4] As a result gas discoveries, especially in developing countries, are often not reported. But this does not imply a lack of gas occurrence—in fact, over the 21st century there is enormous potential for major gas discoveries.

Conventional gas

The most recent estimates of conventional gas reserves come from WEC (1998) for the end of 1996 and BP (1998) for the end of 1998. WEC gives total reserves as 177 Tm^3 (6,534 exajoules) at the end of 1996, 147 Tm^3 (5,450 exajoules) of which were proven recoverable reserves (table 5.3). The rest were additional recoverable reserves. The International Gas Union (IGU, 2000) reports total potentially recoverable reserves as high as 502 Tm^3 (18,390 exajoules).

Reserves have generally increased from survey to survey, reflecting dramatic changes in the economics of gas exploration and recovery. Reservoirs are being added in areas previously thought to have been exhausted, and new reservoirs that were previously overlooked or ignored are now being developed. Over the past 10 years reserve additions averaged 3.7 Tm^3 (134 exajoules) a year, much higher than the 1997 production of 2.2 Tm^3. Ivanhoe and Leckie (1993) note that fewer gas than oil fields are reported in developing regions, probably because gas has a lower economic and utility value, not because there are fewer gas fields.

Enhanced gas recovery using advanced recovery methods—notably hydraulic fracturing aimed at improving the permeability of reservoir rock—can substantially increase natural gas recovery in abandoned fields and newly developed reservoirs. Another, more innovative technique, horizontal air drilling, can also increase gas recovery in depleted gas zones (Elrod, 1997).

Estimates of potential reserves of natural gas resulting from enhanced gas recovery are based on a historical average gas recovery rate of 50 percent and an enhanced recovery rate of 30 percent, for a total recovery factor of 80 percent. Schollnberger (1998) uses similar assumptions in an assessment of possible reserve development through 2100. Global cumulative natural gas production through 1998 totalled 62 Tm^3 (2,276 exajoules). Applying an average recovery factor of 50 percent leads to an original amount of 124 Tm^3. Enhanced gas recovery of 30 percent then enlarges reserves by 37 Tm^3. Likewise, enhanced gas recovery reserves from future production are estimated at 106 Tm^3 using WEC (1998) total recoverable reserves of 177 Tm^3 (see table 5.3). Thus total potential natural gas reserves available from enhanced oil recovery methods are estimated at 143 Tm^3 (5,290 exajoules), an amount only slightly lower than

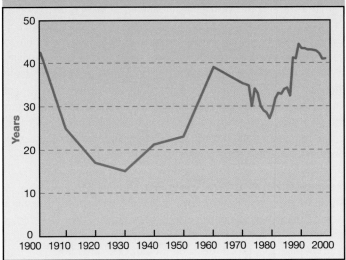

FIGURE 5.2. RATIO OF RESERVES TO PRODUCTION FOR CONVENTIONAL CRUDE OIL, 1900–98

Source: Adapted from BP, 1998.

proven natural gas reserves and almost identical to the potential crude oil reserves expected from enhanced recovery methods.

Unconventional gas

BGR (1995) defines unconventional gas as natural gas derived from reservoirs not exploitable by conventional recovery techniques. Unconventional gas types include coalbed methane, tight formation gas, gas hydrates (clathrates), and aquifer (geopressured) gas. Regional estimates of unconventional gas occurrences in place are provided in table 5.4. The total resource potential exceeds 25,000 Tm^3 (960,000 exajoules).

Coalbed methane. Coalbed methane is a natural gas mixture containing more than 90 percent methane. It occurs primarily in high-rank coal seams from where it can migrate into the surrounding rock strata. Methane contents in coal seams can range from traces to 25 cubic metres per tonne of coal (Davidson, 1995). Regional resources of coalbed methane are genetically associated with the geographic distribution of bituminous coal and anthracite deposits. The former Soviet Union accounts for nearly 50 percent of recoverable resources, centrally planned Asia (including China) has about 20 percent, and North America has 15 percent.

Coalbed methane can be a by-product of underground coal mining

or be produced for the methane exclusively. In fact, coalbed methane is an explosive hazard in underground mining operations and for safety reasons has traditionally been vented with mines' fresh air circulation. Since the 1970s methane captured from underground mining has increasingly been used to supplement local gas supplies. Thus methane capture and use can significantly mitigate greenhouse gas emissions because it avoids the release of methane—a potent greenhouse gas—and may replace fossil fuels with a higher carbon content. For long-term and stable methane supplies from coalbeds, however, dedicated drilling in coalbeds is more important than the methane from active underground coal mines.

Commercial coalbed methane production occurs only in the United States, contributing about 5 percent to natural gas production (BGR, 1998). But pilot projects are under way in a number of other countries, including Australia, China, India, Poland, Russia, Ukraine, and the United Kingdom. Estimates of methane resources range from 85–262 Tm^3 (BGR, 1995, 1998; Rice, Law, and Clayton, 1993). This assessment uses the BGR (1995) estimate of 233 Tm^3 (see table 5.4).

Tight formation gas. Tight formation gas is natural gas trapped in low-permeability reservoirs with in situ permeability of less than 0.1 millidarcy (mD), regardless of the type of the reservoir rock (Law and Spencer, 1993). Production of tight gas requires artificial stimulation

TABLE 5.3. ESTIMATED NATURAL GAS RESERVES

Region	Proven recoverable reserves (WEC, 1998)		Total recoverable reserves (WEC, 1998)		Proven and additional reserves (IGU, 2000)		Proven reserves (BP, 1999)		Enhanced gas recovery	
	Exajoules	Tm^3	Exajoules	Tm^3	Exajoules	Tm^3	Exajoules	Tm^3	Exajoules	Tm^3
North America	252	6.8	389	10.5	2,307	63.0	244	6.6	884	23.9
Latin America and Caribbean	303	8.2	426	11.5	1,556	42.5	298	8.0	306	8.3
Western Europe	181	4.9	300	8.1	436	11.9	177	4.8	306	8.3
Central and Eastern Europe	26	0.7	26	0.7	77	2.1	17	0.5	45	1.2
Former Soviet Union	2,087	56.4	2,583	69.8	5,767	157.5	2,112	56.7	1,923	52.0
Middle East and North Africa	2,076	56.1	2,250	60.8	5,343	149.5	2,065	55.4	1,421	38.4
Sub-Saharan Africa	155	4.2	155	4.2	238	6.5	161	4.3	93	2.5
Pacific Asia	207	5.6	207	5.6	798	21.8	196	5.3	158	4.3
South Asia	63	1.7	63	1.7	377	10.3	54	1.5	50	1.4
Centrally planned Asia	48	1.3	48	1.3	641	17.5	82	2.2	41	1.1
Pacific OECD	56	1.5	89	2.4	850	23.2	47	1.3	62	1.7
Total	**5,450**	**147.3**	**6,534**	**176.6**	**18,390**	**502.2**	**5,454**	**146.4**	**5,290**	**143.0**

TABLE 5.4. ESTIMATED UNCONVENTIONAL NATURAL GAS RESOURCE POTENTIAL IN PLACE

Region	Coalbed methane		Tight formation gas		Gas hydrates		Geopressured gas		Total unconventional gas	
	Exajoules	Tm³	Exajoules	Tm³	Exajoules	Tm³	Exajoules	Tm³	Exajoules	Tm³
North America	2,898	78	518	14	80,575	2,178	109,964	2,972	193,955	5,242
Latin America and Caribbean	0	0	222	6	57,331	1,549	103,341	2,793	160,894	4,348
Western Europe	168	5	222	6	19,806	535	27,861	753	48,057	1,299
Central and Eastern Europe	126	3	37	1	0	0	6,623	179	6,786	183
Former Soviet Union	2,646	72	1,665	45	151,533	4,095	73,667	1,991	229,511	6,203
Middle East and North Africa	0	0	925	25	4,788	129	67,784	1,832	73,497	1,986
Sub-Saharan Africa	42	1	111	3	4,788	129	63,677	1,721	68,618	1,854
Pacific Asia	210	6	148	4	0	0	45,103	1,219	45,461	1,229
South Asia	42	1	37	1	4,788	129	17,427	471	22,294	602
Centrally planned Asia	2,058	56	333	9	0	0	27,824	752	30,215	817
Pacific OECD	420	11	37	1	23,857	645	56,166	1,518	80,480	2,175
Total	**8,610**	**233**	**4,255**	**114**	**347,467**	**9,391**	**599,437**	**16,201**	**959,769**	**25,940**

Source: BGR, 1995, 1998; Rogner, 1997.

techniques—such as massive hydraulic fracturing—to improve reservoir permeability. An advanced technique is horizontal drilling to develop tight gas formations, often in combination with massive hydraulic fracturing. These stimulation methods can achieve gas flow rates two to three times those of conventional vertical wells. In recent years about 3 percent of natural gas production has come from tight gas reservoirs.

Although tight gas reservoirs exist in many regions, only the tight gas resources in the United States have been assessed. The U.S. potential of tight gas resources from tight sandstone and Devonian shale reservoirs is 13.4 Tm³ (BGR, 1995). BGR (1998) applies these U.S. estimates to extrapolate tight gas resource potential for other countries and regions, arriving at a global potential of 114 Tm³ (see table 5.4).

Gas hydrates. IGU (1997) includes some unconventional gas in its definition of additional recoverable reserves—those that are at least of foreseeable economic interest and that may prove technically and economically recoverable with a reasonable level of confidence. This definition appears to exclude gas hydrates (clathrates). IGU (1997) notes that:

> Current scientific inquiries around the world are considering gas hydrates as a potential future supply of natural gas. The hydrates are frozen ice-like deposits that probably cover a significant portion of the ocean floor. The extent of their coverage and the high

methane content of gas hydrates motivate speculation about the gigantic quantities of methane that could become available. At the present time there has been no attractive proposal for a technique to allow this methane to be recovered. Nor has there been any scientific confirmation of the quantities of methane that might be involved. Nevertheless, such investigations might bear fruit at some stage and radically alter current ideas regarding natural gas availability.

The existence of gas hydrates has been confirmed by direct evidence through sampling and by indirect evidence through geochemical and geophysical investigations. Samples have been recovered in 14 parts of the world; indirect evidence has been found in 30 others. Many oceanic occurrences have been inferred based on a special geophysical exploration technique—bottom-stimulating reflection. Resource estimates for gas hydrates are highly uncertain. BGR (1998) reports global clathrate occurrences of more than 9,000 Tm³ (see table 5.4). Other estimates report clathrates as high as 20,000 Tm³ (MacDonald, 1990 a, b; Collet, 1993).

There are no economically attractive technological proposals for recovering methane hydrates (box 5.2). But given their enormous resource potential, it is plausible to expect that extraction methods will eventually be developed if long-term global gas demand warrants clathrate recovery. Research projects are under way in India, Japan, and the United States to examine the viability of gas hydrate recovery (Collet and Kuuskraa, 1998; BGR, 1998).

Aquifer (geopressured) gas. In many parts of the world, natural gas is found dissolved in aquifers under normal hydrostatic pressure, primarily in the form of methane (Marsden, 1993). This unconventional gas is also referred to as hydropressured gas or brine gas. The amount of gas dissolved in underground liquids increases substantially with depth. At depths up to 4,000 metres, 0.5–1.5 cubic metre of gas is dissolved per metre of water in aquifers. This gas factor jumps to 7–20 at depths of 7,000–8,000 metres (BGR, 1995).

Aquifer gas is expected to occur in nearly all sedimentary basins (Marsden, 1993). While no detailed assessment of aquifer gas resources is available, BGR (1998) derives potential aquifer gas in place from the groundwater volume contained in high-permeability sand stones in the hydrosphere. This approach leads to an estimate of 2,400–30,000 Tm³ of geopressured gas in place, with a mean estimate of 16,200 Tm³. In the absence of a more detailed assessment, a practical approach had to be taken in delineating regional resource quantities. The regional breakdown in table 5.4 was obtained by weighting the global mean estimate of gas occurrence in place with regional shares of total sedimentary area.

While these estimates of aquifer gas occurrences are highly speculative, the potential quantities are staggering. Even a future recovery factor of 5 percent implies a resource volume five times the conventional reserves estimates of BP. Aquifer gas is already produced in small quantities from shallow reservoirs in Italy, Japan, and the United States. But in all cases aquifer gas recovery has been motivated by the production of trace elements (such as iodine) rather than by the gas itself.

Coal reserves and resources

Coal deposits can be found in sedimentary basins of various geological ages. Mineable coal deposits require a minimum seam thickness over a sufficiently large area. Coal production occurs in open-pit extraction or underground mining. Coal resource estimates are generally based on drill-hole tests and geological observations. Coal is subdivided into several broadly defined types according to their caloric values. Generally, the types are bituminous coal (including anthracite), sub-bituminous coal, and lignite. For practical purposes, the subdivision is based on energy content, with the value of 16,500 kilojoules per kilogram as demarcation between hard coal (bituminous and high-energy sub-bituminous coals) and soft brown coal (lignite and low-energy sub-bituminous coals).

For almost 200 years coal has provided the basis for energy production as well as iron and steel manufacturing. It also fuelled the industrial revolution of the 19th century. In the 20th century— mainly after World War II—coal lost its leading position to crude oil. But the welfare and economic development of many countries continue to be based on coal. Coal provides about 22 percent of the world energy supply and is the most important fuel for electricity generation. About 40 percent of global electricity is produced in coal-fuelled power stations.

The differences between static and dynamic views of oil resources can be partly explained by the way the different schools view unconventional oil.

Coal will likely contribute substantially to the future world energy supply. Assuming no intervention policies targeted at preventing climate change, projections by IEA (1998c) and Nakićenović, Grübler, and McDonald (1998) show global coal production increasing from 2.4 gigatonnes of oil equivalent (Gtoe) in 1995 to 4.0 Gtoe by 2020. Given its enormous proven reserves, the current rate of coal production could continue well into the future.

The size of coal resources is not a restraining factor to its use throughout the 21st century. Rather, continued coal use will depend on the timely development of production facilities and related infrastructure, given lead times of up to five years for open-cast operations and drift mines. Nevertheless, there is considerable potential for a significant increase in coal production capacity in the short to medium term. Although environmental considerations may limit coal use with current combustion technologies, advanced conversion technology—with carbon abatement and disposal— may create new market opportunities (see chapter 8).

Current resources and reserves

World coal resources in place are estimated at more than 7,400 billion tonnes of coal, or about 4,470 Gtoe (WEC 1998). The recoverable portion is estimated at roughly 500 Gtoe, which corresponds to the amount generally labelled reserves. About

---

BOX 5.2. ARE GAS HYDRATES AN EXPLOITABLE ENERGY RESOURCE?

A gas hydrate is a crystalline cage of water molecules that can trap various gases. Hydrates can form under conditions of high pressure and low temperatures. Methane hydrates exist in polar permafrost and in sediments below the ocean floor where conditions are appropriate. Hydrates will not exist below a depth where the reservoir temperature is too high for their stability. But solid hydrate layers can provide top seals for reservoirs of free methane that can accumulate beneath. Offshore methane hydrate deposits have been identified near the coasts of many countries—including countries (such as Japan) otherwise poor in fossil fuels.

The amount of methane associated with hydrates is highly uncertain, but the quantities are probably far greater than conventional oil and gas resources combined. Estimates of global methane hydrate resources range from 0.1–300 million exajoules (Collet and Kuuskraa, 1998; Max, Pellanbarg, and Hurdle, 1997). How much can be practically and affordably recovered is also highly uncertain (USDOE, 1998). An emerging view is that free gas trapped beneath solid hydrate layers will be easier to recover than gas in hydrates (Max, Pellanbarg, and Hurdle, 1997). Free gas recovery would depressurise the reservoir, leading to hydrate melting at the hydrate– free gas interface and thus to free gas replenishment. The process could continue as long as the hydrate layer remains thick enough to cap the free gas below. Preliminary (though dated) estimates for recovering methane at favourable sites suggest that it might not be significantly more costly than recovering conventional natural gas (Holder, Kamath, and Godbole, 1984). But even if this proves accurate, getting the gas to major markets could often be quite costly because of high transport costs, since hydrate deposits are often far from such markets.

85 percent of the resources in place are classified as bituminous or sub-bituminous (hard) coal; the rest is lignite (soft brown) coal. (Similar proportions apply to reserves.)

Three-quarters of global coal reserves are in Australia, China, India, South Africa, and the United States. Among regions, North America has the largest coal reserves (table 5.5). Substantial reserves are also available in the former Soviet Union and in South Asia. The European share has to be viewed with caution because reserves may soon be declassified to resources (neutral stuff) as production subsidies are eliminated and industry begins to close unprofitable operations.

In 1997 global coal production totalled 2,310 Gtoe, 91 percent of which was hard coal. China was the largest producer of hard coal (31 percent of the world total), followed by the United States (26 percent), India (7 percent), Australia (6 percent), and South Africa (6 percent). All other producers hold shares of less than 5 percent.

Almost 90 percent of world coal production is used domestically. In 1997 the 10 largest coal exporters traded about 500 million tonnes of hard coal. The largest exporter was Australia with a traded share of about 30 percent, followed by the United States with 15 percent.

Projections show global coal production increasing from 2.4 Gtoe in 1995 to 4.0 Gtoe by 2020.

Additional resources

WEC (1998) also provides information on coal resources by type. But because of incomplete country coverage, no regional or global aggregates are given. BGR (1995) estimated global coal resources at 5,000 Gtoe, of which 4,600 Gtoe are hard coal.

In a 1998 update, BGR revised the estimate for additional coal resources in place to 4,300 Gtoe billion, of which about 3,500 Gtoe are additional hard coal resources. The Russian Federation has the largest share—about 2,100 Gtoe of hard coal. About 80 percent of the additional resources in the Russian Federation are in remote areas of Siberia. Large investments for infrastructure and development limit the conversion of these resources into reserves. Because of the large reserves, there is no immediate need for additional investigation of the resource potential world-wide. Estimates of the regional distribution of world total resources (including reserves) are shown in table 5.6.

Summary of fossil resources

Fossil fuel reserves, resources, and additional occurrences are shown relative to cumulative consumption and current (1998) use in table 5.7. For an analysis that extends well into the 21st century and explores the long-term availability of fossil resources, the fossil resource base is the relevant yardstick. The resource base for conventional and unconventional oil and gas is large enough to last comfortably for another 50–100 years—and possibly much longer—essentially at prices not much different from today. This projection assumes that past hydrocarbon productivity gains in the upstream sector can be maintained and that these resources remain in demand.

Tapping into the vast fossil resource base may eventually become a transportation challenge. For one thing, fossil resources are not evenly distributed around the globe. For another, the location of many unconventional oil and, more important, gas occurrences is far from the centres of energy demand. In China and India coal delivery costs (for rail transport) already approach production costs. Transportation logistics and costs may affect the economic attractiveness of remote resource sites. Long-distance and trans-boundary energy transport raises concerns about the security of energy supply (see chapter 4).

The fossil resource data in table 5.7 are also shown in terms of their carbon content. Since the onset of the industrial revolution, 296 gigatonnes of carbon contained in fossil fuels have been oxidised and released to the atmosphere. The resource base represents a carbon volume of some 6,500 gigatonnes of carbon. The 296 gigatonnes of carbon emitted to the atmosphere already raise concerns about climate stability—and humankind has the means to add several times that amount during the 21st century. Fossil resource scarcity will not come to the rescue. Nakićenović, Grübler, and McDonald (1998) indicate that between 1990 and 2100 emissions under the A2 scenario (see chapter 9) of some 1,600 gigatonnes of carbon—

TABLE 5.5. ESTIMATED COAL RESERVES (MILLIONS OF TONNES)

Region	Bituminous (incl. anthracite)	Sub-bituminous	Lignite	Total (exajoules)
North America	115,600	103,300	36,200	6,065
Latin America and Caribbean	8,700	13,900	200	533
Western Europe	26,300	600	47,700	1,178
Central and Eastern Europe	15,400	5,500	10,700	744
Former Soviet Union	97,500	113,500	36,700	4,981
Middle East and North Africa	200	20	0	6
Sub-Saharan Africa	61,000	200	< 100	1,465
Pacific Asia	900	1,600	5,100	10
South Asia	72,800	3,000	2,000	1,611
Centrally planned Asia	62,700	34,000	18,600	2,344
Pacific OECD	48,100	2,000	41,600	1,729
Total	**509,200**	**277,600**	**198,900**	**20,666**

Source: WEC, 1998.

roughly the carbon content of conventional fossil reserves (see table 5.7)—could raise the atmospheric concentration of carbon dioxide to 750 parts per million by volume (ppmv). (Before the industrial revolution, carbon dioxide concentrations were 280 ppmv; today they are 360 ppmv.) The corresponding increase in global mean temperature could be 2.0–4.5 Kelvin.[5]

Since 1973 the tradable price of oil (the 'marker' for competing fuels) has been much higher than the marginal cost of the highest-cost producer, reflecting geopolitics and a lack of competing fuels. Today the highest marginal cost of production is less than $10 a barrel—and in the Gulf it is just $2–3 a barrel (Rogner, 1997; Odell, 1998). Economic rent accounts for the rest of the tradable price. This rent could be reduced if competing fuels—unconventional oil, synliquids from gas or coal, renewable or nuclear energy—could equal the marginal cost of production. Thus the true cost of oil for the entrance of competitors is less than $10 a barrel. This cost level has already been achieved by some producers of unconventional oil and gas—tar sands in Alberta (Chadwick, 1998), heavy oil in Venezuela (Aalund, 1998), coalbed methane in the United States (BGR, 1998). The question then is, can technological advances balance the higher costs of more difficult production? Experience suggests that the answer is probably yes in the long run. But in the Gulf, marginal costs are unlikely to exceed $5–$10 a barrel even in the long term.

One question of interest to many upstream investment planners is, when will the call on unconventional fossil occurrences commence? To some extent it is already here. Alberta's tar sand production started more than 30 years ago and, after some difficulties in the wake of the oil price collapse of 1986, it is now competitive in today's markets. Venezuela's heavy oil has also been produced for many years. Still, the share of unconventional oil—and, for that matter, natural gas—is only about 6 percent of world production.

The future production profile of unconventional oil will be a function of the demand for oil products, the price and availability of

conventional oil, and the cost and availability of oil substitutes. So what are the prospects for future conventional oil production? The answer is by no means conclusive. The February 1998 issue of the *Explorer*, the journal of the American Association of Petroleum Geologists, writes that "it is not comforting that experts disagree on almost every aspect of the world outlook, from annual production to current reserves to projected energy demand…One majority

TABLE 5.6. ESTIMATED COAL RESOURCES (BILLIONS OF TONNES OF COAL EQUIVALENT)

Region	Hard coal	Soft coal/ lignite	Total (exajoules)
North America	674	201	25,638
Latin America and Caribbean	37	2	1,143
Western Europe	337	11	10,196
Central and Eastern Europe	106	14	3,516
Former Soviet Union	3,025	751	110,637
Middle East and North Africa	1	1	58
Sub-Saharan Africa	181	< 1	5,303
Pacific Asia	7	5	352
South Asia	84	1	2,491
Centrally planned Asia	429	35	13,595
Pacific OECD	139	67	6,030
Total	**5,021**	**1,089**	**178,959**

Note: Includes reserves.   *Source: BGR, 1998.*

TABLE 5.7. AGGREGATE FOSSIL ENERGY OCCURRENCES

Type	Consumption 1860–1998		Consumption 1998		Reserves		Resources[a]		Resource base[b]		Additional occurrences	
	Exajoules	Gigatonnes of carbon	Exajoules	Gigatonnes of carbon	Exajoules	Gigatonnes of carbon	Exajoules	Gigatonnes of carbon	Exajoules	Gigatonnes of carbon	Exajoules	Gigatonnes of carbon
Oil												
Conventional	4,854	97	132.7	2.65	6,004	120	6,071	121	12,074	241		
Unconventional	285	6	9.2	0.18	5,108	102	15,240	305	20,348	407	45,000	914
Natural gas[c]												
Conventional	2,346	36	80.2	1.23	5,454	83	11,113	170	16,567	253		
Unconventional	33	1	4.2	0.06	9,424	144	23,814	364	33,238	509	930,000	14,176
Coal	5,990	155	92.2	2.40	20,666	533	179,000	4,618	199,666	5,151	n.a.	
Total	**13,508**	**294**	**319.3**	**6.53**	**46,655**	**983**	**235,238**	**5,579**	**281,893**	**6,562**	**975,000**	**15,090**

a. Reserves to be discovered or resources to be developed as reserves. b. The sum of reserves and resources. c. Includes natural gas liquids.

Source: Compiled by author from tables 5.1–5.6.

opinion emerges: Sometime in the coming century, world-wide production of petroleum liquids will reach a peak and then begin to decline...[but] there is little agreement about when this will happen, and how steep or gradual the decline will be".

Assuming ultimately recoverable conventional oil resources of, say, 400 gigatonnes and a demand development of about 1.5 percent a year, conventional oil production will peak around 2030 (reach the depletion mid-point) with an annual production of 4.4 gigatonnes, up from 3.5 gigatonnes in 1998. Total oil demand, however, would run at 5.8 gigatonnes—implying that unconventional oil will account for 1.4 gigatonnes (Odell, 1998). In other words, unconventional sources will have to be tapped speedily during the first decade of the 21st century. But experience with unconventional oil production shows a long gestation period and high threshold costs of up to $30 a barrel. Most oil price projections for 2010 (which have an extremely poor track record) expect oil prices of $13–$29 a barrel.

Thus accelerated expansion of unconventional oil production (primarily tar sands in Alberta and extra heavy oil in Venezuela and Russia) hinges on:

■ Short-term developments in oil prices.

■ Actual developments in demand.
■ Technological progress in field growth for conventional occurrences.
■ Technological advances in the production of unconventional occurrences.
■ The risk attitude of investors in unconventional production capacity.

Current market prospects for unconventional oil production remain modest at best. But this may change drastically—for example, changing geopolitics could raise oil prices high enough to facilitate investments in unconventional oil. In general, most oil market outlooks project a steady increase in OPEC's share in global oil production.

Reserves and resources of fissile materials

Naturally occurring fissile materials—natural uranium and thorium—can be found in various types of geological deposits. Although they may occur jointly, most uranium and thorium reside in separate deposits. Like fossil occurrences, uranium and thorium are finite in the Earth's crust, and recoverable quantities depend on demand and market conditions, type of deposit, and technology.

During the 1970s, when large increases in uranium demand before the turn of the century were expected, the recovery of low-concentration uranium from seawater was investigated. Although technically feasible, estimated production costs appeared prohibitively high relative to alternatives. More recent research and development indicate that the costs of recovering uranium from seawater have fallen considerably, but are still too high given current and expected market prices for uranium. With the declining demand for uranium, recovery is concentrated on terrestrial deposits where uranium availability is estimated according to different production cost categories—such as recoverable at less than $40 a kilogram, less than $80 a kilogram, and less than $130 a kilogram.

Due to the limited development of thorium-fuelled reactors, little effort has been made to explore and delineate thorium. But reserves and resources are known to exist in substantial quantities.

The resource outlook presented below is based on a 'once-through fuel cycle' of uranium in normal power reactors—that is, 'burner' reactors. But the supply of raw material for reactor fuel is determined not only by uranium presently mined but also by fissile material initially produced for military purposes, which since the mid-1990s has become available for civil use. Reprocessed uranium and plutonium are additional supply sources with the capacity to displace up to 30 percent of the initial demand through recycling.

Uranium reserves

Uranium reserves are periodically estimated by the Organisation for Economic Co-operation and Development's Nuclear Energy Agency (NEA) together with the International Atomic Energy Agency (IAEA), Uranium Institute (UI), World Energy Council (WEC), and numerous national geological institutions. Although these organisations use different reserve and resource definitions, the differences between their estimates are usually insignificant.

TABLE 5.8. REASONABLY ASSURED URANIUM RESOURCES RECOVERABLE AT LESS THAN $80 A KILOGRAM (RESERVES) AND AT $80–130 A KILOGRAM (TONNES OF URANIUM)

Region	< $80 a kilogram[a]	$80–130 a kilogram	Total
North America	420,000	251,000	671,000
Latin America and Caribbean	136,400	5,600	142,000
Western Europe	37,300	53,500	90,800
Central and Eastern Europe	14,000	25,800	39,800
Former Soviet Union	564,300	210,200	774,500
Middle East and North Africa	21,000	8,400	29,400
Sub-Saharan Africa	453,600	96,000	549,600
Pacific Asia	0	16,800	16,800
South Asia	5,000	52,000	57,000
Centrally planned Asia	49,300	65,300	114,600
Pacific OECD	615,000	99,600	714,600
Total	**2,315,900**	**884,200**	**3,200,100**

a. Adjusted for mining and milling losses and production of 1997.

Source: NEA and IAEA, 1997.

Because NEA-IAEA estimates have the widest coverage, the reserves reported in their latest survey are reported here (NEA-IAEA, 1997). The two organisations define as reserves those deposits that could be produced competitively in an expanding market. This category is called reasonably assured resources and includes uranium occurrences that are recoverable at less than $80 a kilogram. (Because of declining market prospects, a number of countries have begun to report estimates of reasonably assured uranium resources at less than $40 a kilogram.[6]) Uranium reserves are estimated at 2.3 million tonnes (table 5.8). These reserves are sufficient to meet the demand of existing and planned nuclear power plants well into the 21st century.

The fission of 1 kilogram of natural uranium produces about 573 gigajoules of thermal energy—some 14,000 times as much as in 1 kilogram of oil. But this is still only a small fraction of the energy potentially available from the uranium; up to 100 times this amount can be derived in a fast neutron reactor (a technology that is well developed but not commercially viable). In today's plants, 22 tonnes of uranium are typically needed to produce 1 terawatt-hour of electricity.

Uranium resources

Uranium resources are classified according to the degree of their geological assurance and the economic feasibility of their recovery. Resources that cost less than $80 a kilogram to recover (that is, reasonably assured resources) are considered reserves. Under higher market price assumptions, reasonably assured resources recoverable at less than $130 a kilogram would also qualify as reserves. Resources beyond these categories have been estimated, but with a lower degree of geological assurance. NEA-IAEA (1997) define two categories of estimated additional resources, EAR-I and EAR-II.[7] Another resource category, speculative resources, is also applied. While reasonably assured resources and EAR-I include known or delineated resources, EAR-II and speculative resources have yet to be discovered (table 5.9). Global conventional uranium reserves and resources total about 20 million tonnes.

In addition, vast quantities of unconventional uranium resources exist, essentially low-concentration occurrences that were of temporary interest when medium-term demand expectations for uranium were thought to exceed known conventional resources. Such unconventional resources include phosphate deposits with uranium concentrations of 100–200 parts per million in sedimentary rocks, and in exceptional conditions more than 1,000 parts per million in igneous rocks. The uranium content of the world's sedimentary phosphates is estimated at nearly 15 million tonnes, more than half of them in Morocco. To date the only way to extract uranium on an industrial basis, demonstrated mainly in the United States, is through recovery from phosphoric acid. This liquid-liquid separation process uses solvent to extract uranium, allowing for the recovery of up to 70 percent of the uranium contained in the ore. Globally, phosphoric acid plants have a theoretical capacity of supplying about 10,000 tonnes

TABLE 5.9. ESTIMATED ADDITIONAL AMOUNTS AND SPECULATIVE RESOURCES OF URANIUM (TONNES OF URANIUM)

Region	Estimated additional amount[a]	Speculative resources
North America	2,559,000	2,040,000
Latin America and Caribbean	277,300	920,000
Western Europe	66,900	158,000
Central and Eastern Europe	90,900	198,000
Former Soviet Union	914,000	1,833,000
Middle East and North Africa	12,000	40,000
Sub-Saharan Africa	852,800	1,138,000
Pacific Asia	5,000	0
South Asia	46,000	17,000
Centrally planned Asia	96,500	3,183,000
Pacific OECD	180,000	2,600,00
Total	**5,100,400**	**12,127,000**

a. Includes reasonably assured resources at extraction costs of $130–260 a kilogram as well as estimated additional resource categories I and II at less than $260 a kilogram. *Source: NEA and IAEA, 1997.*

of uranium a year, provided economic conditions can be met.

Other unconventional uranium resources that have been explored are black shale deposits and granite rocks with elevated uranium concentrations. Although their estimated theoretical resource potential is substantial, exploration and extraction have been limited to experimental scales. The low uranium content and potential environmental challenges associated with the production of these occurrences have led to the termination of all efforts. Another low-concentration source of uranium is the vast amount contained in seawater—about 4.5 billion tonnes at 3 parts per billion, often seen as an eventual 'back-stop' uranium resource (box 5.3).

BOX 5.3 URANIUM FROM SEAWATER

Seawater contains a low concentration of uranium—less than 3 parts per billion. But the quantity of contained uranium is vast—some 4.5 billion tonnes, or 700 times known terrestrial resources recoverable at less than $130 a kilogram. It might be possible to extract uranium from seawater at low cost. Early research in Japan suggested that it might be feasible to recover uranium from seawater at a cost of $300 a kilogram of uranium (Nobukawa and others, 1994). More recent work in France and Japan suggests that costs might be as low as $80–100 a kilogram (Charpak and Garwin, 1998; Garwin, 1999). But these estimates are based on methods used to recover gram quantities of uranium, and unforeseen difficulties may arise in scaling up these methods a million-fold or more. The implications of developing this uranium recovery technology are discussed in chapter 8.

Thorium reserves and resources

Thorium-fuelled burner and breeder reactors were developed in the 1960s and 1970s but fell behind thereafter due to lower than expected market penetration of nuclear power and to a focus on advancing uranium-fuelled nuclear power technologies. Moreover, thorium is not readily useable in a nuclear reactor because the number of neutrons released in each fission makes it difficult to sustain the chain reaction. India has far more thorium than uranium resources, and is attempting to develop the thorium fuel cycle. Important commercial developments of reactors using thorium have not materialised elsewhere. But high-temperature, gas-cooled reactors, like the one in South Africa, could also use a thorium-based fuel cycle. Thorium resources are widely available and could support a large-scale thorium fuel cycle. But given the global availability of inexpensive uranium, thorium-fuelled reactors are unlikely to be significant in resource terms in the next 50 years.

Monazite, a rare-earth and thorium phosphate mineral, is the primary source of thorium. In the absence of demand for rare-earth elements, monazite would probably not be recovered for its thorium content. Other ore minerals with higher thorium contents, such as thorite, would be more likely sources if demand increased significantly. But no thorium demand is expected. In addition, world-wide demand for thorium-bearing rare-earth ores remains low. Thorium disposal is the primary concern in obtaining mining permits for thorium-containing ores. Reserves exist primarily in recent and ancient placer deposits. Lesser quantities of thorium-bearing monazite reserves occur in vein deposits and carbonatites.

Thorium resources occur in provinces similar to those of reserves. The largest share is contained in placer deposits. Resources of more than 500,000 tonnes are contained in placer, vein, and carbonatite deposits.

Global thorium reserves and resources outside the former Soviet Union and China are estimated at 4.5 million tonnes, of which about 2.2 million tonnes are reserves (table 5.10). Large thorium deposits are found in Australia, Brazil, Canada, Greenland, India, the Middle East and North Africa, South Africa, and the United States. Disseminated deposits in other alkaline igneous rocks contain additional resources of more than 2 million tonnes.

Hydroelectric resources

Hydroelectricity, which depends on the natural evaporation of water by solar energy, is by far the largest renewable resource used for electricity generation. In 1997 hydroelectricity generation totalled 2,566 terawatt-hours (IEA, 1999). Water evaporation per unit of surface area is larger for oceans than for land and, assisted by wind, is the principal cause of the continuous transfer of water vapour from oceans to land through precipitation. The maintenance of a global water balance requires that the water precipitated on land eventually returns to the oceans as runoff through rivers.

As with all renewable resources, the amount of water runoff is finite for a defined amount of time but, all else being equal, this finite amount is forever available. By applying knowledge of the hydrological cycle, the world-wide amount of runoff water can be assessed quite accurately. Hydroelectricity is obtained by mechanical conversion of the potential energy of water. An assessment of its energy potential requires detailed information on the locational and geographical factors of runoff water (available head, flow volume per unit of time, and so on).

Because rainfall varies by region and even country, hydro energy is not evenly accessible. Moreover, sizeable hydro resources are often remotely located. As a result of advances in transmission technology and significant capital spending, electricity is being delivered to places far from the generation stations, making energy from water more affordable to more people. Projects considering the connection of electric grids between countries, regions, and even continents have been implemented or are planned (Moreira and Poole, 1993).

Although hydroelectricity is generally considered a clean energy source, it is not totally devoid of greenhouse gas emissions, ecosystem burdens, or adverse socioeconomic impacts (see chapter 3). For comparable electricity outputs, greenhouse gas emissions associated with hydropower are one or two orders of magnitude lower than those from fossil-generated electricity. Ecosystem impacts usually occur downstream and range from changes in fish biodiversity and in the sediment load of the river to coastal erosion and pollution

> Hydro energy is not evenly accessible, and sizeable hydro resources are often remotely located.

TABLE 5.10. ESTIMATED THORIUM RESERVES AND ADDITIONAL RESOURCES (TONNES OF THORIUM)

Region	Reserves	Additional resources
North America	258,000	402,000
Latin America and Caribbean	608,000	702,000
Western Europe	600,000	724,000
Central and Eastern Europe	n.a.	n.a.
Former Soviet Union	n.a.	n.a.
Middle East and North Africa	15,000	310,000
Sub-Saharan Africa	38,000	146,000
Pacific Asia	24,000	26,000
South Asia	319,000	4,000
Centrally planned Asia	n.a.	n.a.
Pacific OECD	300,000	40,000
Total	2,162,000	2,354,000

n.a. Not available.   Source: BGR Data Bank.

(McCulley, 1996). Potentially adverse socio-economic aspects of hydroelectricity include its capital intensity and social and environmental impacts (McCulley, 1996). Capital-intensive projects with long construction and amortisation periods become less attractive in privatising markets. Higher education levels and increasing population densities along river beds substantially raise the socio economic costs of relocation. Local environmental issues require more thorough management than before because modern communications and determined citizen groups can easily turn a remote or local problem into a global issue that can influence international capital and financing markets. Large hydropower projects increasingly encounter public resistance and, as a result, face higher costs.

Integration aspects may increase the competitiveness of hydro-electricity because of its quick response to fluctuations in demand. When hydropower provides spinning reserve and peak supply, this ability allows thermal electric plants to operate closer to their optimal efficiency, lowering fuel costs and reducing emissions from burning fossil fuels. Pump storage might absorb off-peak power or power from intermittent supplies for peak use at a later point.

Theoretical potential

The world's annual water balance is shown in table 5.11. Of the 577,000 cubic kilometres of water evaporating from ocean and land surfaces, 119,000 cubic kilometres precipitate on land. About two-thirds is absorbed in about equal parts by vegetation and soil; the remaining third becomes runoff water. Most of the fraction absorbed by vegetation and soil evaporates again and amounts to 72,000 cubic kilometres. The difference of 47,000 cubic kilometres is, in principle, available for energy purposes.

The amount of inland precipitation varies slightly by continent,

from 740–800 millimetres a year. The two exceptions are South America (1,600 millimetres a year) and Antarctica (165 millimetres). Thus runoff water per unit of land area in South America is at least two times that elsewhere.

Convolution of runoff water volumes with average altitudes allows for the evaluation of theoretical hydropower potential by region (table 5.12). Asia (including Pacific Asia, South Asia, and centrally planned Asia) has the largest potential, because its average altitude of 950 metres is the highest of all continents (except Antarctica, which has an average altitude of 2,040 metres). But average altitudes are insufficient for calculating theoretical hydropower potential—runoff is not evenly distributed across a continent. In addition, seasonal variations in runoff influence theoretical potentials. Estimates of the global theoretical hydroelectricity potential range from 36,000–44,000 terawatt-hours a year (Raabe, 1985; Boiteux, 1989; Bloss and others, 1980; *World Atlas and Industry Guide*, 1998).

The global water balance and regional precipitation patterns may change as a result of climate change. Current models suggest that global precipitation will increase but that regional precipitation patterns will shift. These changes will affect global hydropower potential.

Technical potential

Appraisals of technical potential are based on simplified engineering criteria with few, if any, environmental considerations. Although the technical potential should exclude economic aspects, these appear to be inherent in such appraisals. Evaluation criteria may differ substantially by country and, especially in developing countries, may be quite unsophisticated. Reported technical potentials could be inflated or, because of incomplete assessments, seriously underestimated (Bloss and others, 1980; *International Water Power and Dam Construction*,

TABLE 5.11. ANNUAL WORLD WATER BALANCE

Region	Surface area 10^6 km^2	Precipitation		Evaporation		Runoff[a]	
		Millimetres	Thousands of cubic kilometres	Millimetres	Thousands of cubic kilometres	Millimetres	Thousands of cubic kilometres
Europe	10.5	790	8.3	507	5.3	283	3.0
Asia	43.5	740	32.2	416	18.1	324	14.1
Africa	30.1	740	22.3	587	17.7	153	4.6
North America	24.2	756	18.3	418	10.1	339	8.2
South America	17.8	1,600	28.4	910	16.2	685	12.2
Australia and Oceania	8.9	791	7.1	511	4.6	280	2.5
Antarctica	14.0	165	2.3	0	0.0	165	2.3
Total/average)	149	800	119	485	72	315	47.0
Pacific Ocean	178.7	1,460	260.0	1,510	269.7	-83	-14.8
Atlantic Ocean	91.7	1,010	92.7	1,360	124.4	-226	-20.8
Indian Ocean	76.2	1,320	100.4	1,420	108.0	-81	-6.1
Arctic Ocean	14.7	361	5.3	220	8.2	-355	-5.2
Total/average	361	1,270	458	1,400	505	-130	-47.0
Globe	**510**	**1,130**	**577**	**1,130**	**577**	**0**	**0**

a. Outflow of water from continents into oceans.

Source: UNESC, 1997.

1989; *World Atlas and Industry Guide*, 1998).

Most significant are the differences in theoretical, technical, and economic potential by region, especially for Africa, North America, and the former Soviet Union (figure 5.3).[8] In general, total technical potential has not been fully measured for most developing countries. In Brazil, for example, hydroelectricity is responsible for 96 percent of electricity generation. Of the 260 gigawatts of technical hydropower potential, more than one-third is accounted as estimated. Of that, 32 gigawatts have never been individually analysed (ANEEL, 1999).

Technological advances tend to increase the technical potential and so broaden the prospects for hydropower meeting future electricity requirements. Improvements in the efficiency and utility of turbines for low-head and small hydro sites permit more effective use of a larger number of sites in a less environmentally intrusive manner. Advances in adjustable-speed generation and new large turbines enable the rehabilitation and expansion of existing capacities (Churchill, 1997). Refurbishment of plants has shown that advanced technologies can significantly increase the energy output at essentially unchanged primary water flows (*International Water*

> Large hydropower projects increasingly encounter public resistance and, as a result, face higher costs.

Power and Dam Construction, 1989; Taylor, 1989). In addition, technological improvements enable the use of previously uneconomical potentials and new sites.

But hydroelectric generation is a mature technology for which most components are nearing their practically achievable maximum. As a result further improvements in performance are expected to be modest. Average efficiencies of existing plants are about 85 percent; a 10 percentage point increase would be a major accomplishment.

Economic potential

The economic potential of hydropower is based on detailed economic, social, environmental, geological, and technical evaluations.[9] It is by far the most difficult potential to establish because the financial, environmental, and social parameters that determine it are driven by societal preferences that are inherently difficult to project.

One approach is to use the historically observed fraction of the technical potential used in industrialised countries with extensive hydropower developments. Western Europe has developed 65 percent of its technical hydropower potential, and the United States has developed

TABLE 5.12. THEORETICAL, TECHNICAL, AND ECONOMIC HYDROELECTRIC POTENTIALS, INSTALLED CAPACITIES, AND CAPACITIES UNDER CONSTRUCTION, 1997 (TERAWATT-HOURS UNLESS OTHERWISE INDICATED)

Region	Gross theoretical potential	Technical potential	Economic potential	Installed hydro capacity (gigawatts)	Hydropower production	Hydro capacity under construction (megawatts)
North America	5,817	1,509	912	141	697	882
Latin America and Caribbean	7,533	2,868	1,199	114	519	18,331
Western Europe	3,294	1,822	809	16	48	2,464
Central and Eastern Europe	195	216	128	9	27	7,749
Former Soviet Union	3,258	1,235	770	147	498	6,707
Middle East and North Africa	304	171	128	21	66	1,211
Sub-Saharan Africa	3,583	1,992	1,288	66	225	16,613
Pacific Asia[a]	5,520	814	142	14	41	4,688
South Asia[a]	3,635	948	103	28	105	13,003
Centrally planned Asia	6,511	2,159	1,302	64	226	51,672
Pacific OECD	1,134	211	184	34	129	841
Total	**40,784**	**13,945**	**6,964**	**655**	**2,582**	**124,161**
Total[b]	**40,500**	**14,320**	**8,100**	**660**	**2,600**	**126,000**

a. Several countries in Pacific Asia and South Asia do not publicise their economic potential. As a result the reported economic potentials for the regions are too low—and in South Asia the economic potential is even lower than the electricity generated. b. These are the values listed in the source. They differ from the total in the previous row due to typographical errors and due to the inclusion of estimations for countries for which data are not available.

Source: World Atlas and Industry Guide, 1998.

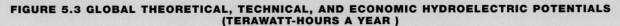

FIGURE 5.3 GLOBAL THEORETICAL, TECHNICAL, AND ECONOMIC HYDROELECTRIC POTENTIALS (TERAWATT-HOURS A YEAR)

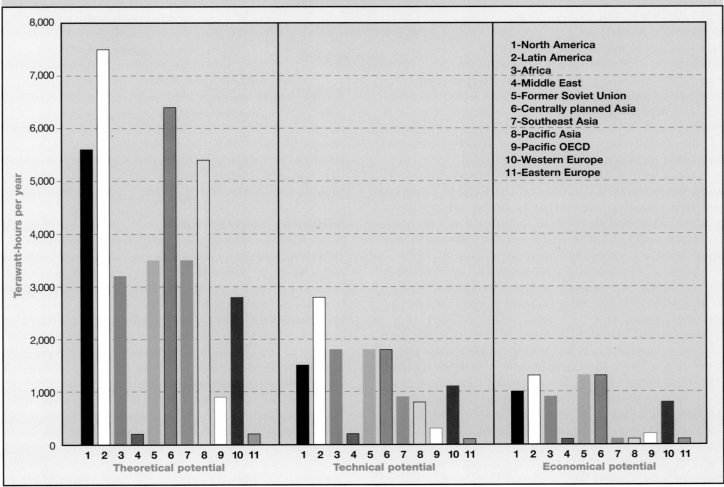

1-North America
2-Latin America
3-Africa
4-Middle East
5-Former Soviet Union
6-Centrally planned Asia
7-Southeast Asia
8-Pacific Asia
9-Pacific OECD
10-Western Europe
11-Eastern Europe

Source: World Atlas and Industry Guide, 1998.

76 percent (*World Atlas and Industry Guide,* 1998). A utilisation rate of 40–60 percent of a region's technical potential is a reasonable assumption and leads to a global economic hydroelectricity potential of 6,000–9,000 terawatt-hours a year. More detailed analysis based on current technological and economic puts the global economic potential at 8,100 terawatt-hours a year (see table 5.12).

Major constraints to hydroelectricity expansion

Physical constraints. Global water runoff is 47,000 cubic kilometres a year, 28,000 cubic kilometres of which is surface runoff and 13,000 of which is stable underground flow into rivers (L'vovich, 1987). Only about three-quarters of the stable underground flow (9,000 cubic kilometres) is easily accessible and economically usable (WRI, 1998). In addition, 3,000 cubic kilometres of useful capacity is available in form of human-made lakes and reservoirs (L'vovich, 1987). Global anthropogenic water withdrawals are about 27 percent of total availability, or 3,250 cubic kilometres a year.

Agriculture accounts for 65 percent of the diverted water, industries for 24 percent, and households and other municipal users for 7 percent, while 4 percent is evaporated from reservoirs (Shiklomanov, 1993).

Water use in agriculture totals 2,300 cubic kilometres a year and is expected to increase with growing food demand. The United Nations projects a 50–100 percent increase in irrigation water by 2025 (Raskin and others, 1997). Most of the projected increase in water demand will occur in developing countries because of rapid growth in population, industry, and agriculture. Water pollution adds enormously to local and regional water scarcity by eliminating large volumes from the available supply. Many developing countries undergoing rapid industrialisation face the full range of modern toxic pollution problems—eutrophication, heavy metals, acidification, and persistent organic pollutants (WHO, 1997).

Globally, water supplies are abundant. But they are unevenly distributed among and within countries. In some areas water withdrawal has reached such dimensions that surface water supplies are shrinking and groundwater reserves are being depleted faster than they can be replenished by precipitation (WHO, 1997). One-third of the world's people live in countries experiencing moderate to high water stress, and that share could rise to two-thirds by 2025 (WRI, 1998). Since 1940 the amount of freshwater used by humans has roughly quadrupled as the world population has doubled (Population Action International, 1997). Another doubling of the world population by 2100 cannot be ruled out. Assuming an upper limit of usable renewable freshwater of 9,000–14,000 cubic kilometres a year, a second quadrupling of world water use appears highly improbable.

In connection with the physical constraints to the use of water for power generation listed above, it should be noted that electricity generation—unlike, say, irrigation and domestic and industrial uses—is a non-consumptive use of water. Under otherwise favourable conditions, such as irrigation at low altitudes, water can be used first to generate power and then for other purposes.

A physical factor needed to develop hydropower economically is the availability of a suitable head. This limitation does not apply to other water uses. This factor is critical in many water-rich but low-lying regions.

Environmental and social constraints. More than 400,000 cubic kilometres of land have been inundated by the construction of dams (Shiklomanov, 1993). These dams generate 2,600 terawatt-hours a year of electricity. Assuming that all flooded areas are used for hydroelectricity, the energy density is 62 megawatt-hours a hectare per year. But hydroelectric plants vary widely in this respect. Goodland (1996) reports on installed capacity, flooded land, and relocated persons for 34 hydroelectric plants, mostly in developing countries. These plants have an average energy density of 135 megawatt-hours a hectare per year. The most land-intensive of them yields 3.5 megawatt-hours a year per hectare of flooded land, but the least land-intensive yields 1.48 million megawatt-hours a year per hectare.

Eleven of the thirty-four plants yield more than 1,800 megawatt-hours a hectare per year (0.205 kilowatt-years per year), the standard for a fixed array photovoltaic plant in sunny areas (see below). Biomass from forests (15 oven dry tonnes a hectare per year) and from crop plantation (10,000 litres of ethanol a hectare per year using sugarcane) have energy densities of about 20 megawatt-hours a hectare per year. Thus hydroelectricity is land-intensive—more so than photovoltaics but less so than biomass plantations.

Hydroelectricity has sparked controversy when large dams with energy densities as low as 0.2 megawatt-hours a hectare per year require large-scale flooding and displace people. Some large dams involve the resettlement of more than 100,000 people (Goodland, 1997). Mandatory resettlement and the boom and bust effects of dam construction on local economies have become contentious social and environmental issues. In the past, resettlement was the responsibility of governments and public utilities involved in the

project. Despite enormous financial expen-ditures and compensation packages, resettlement efforts have had modest success. If private utilities are to finance hydro projects, they will have to take responsibility for dealing with resettlement issues.

National and international cooperation on the development of environmental best practices (such as through working groups on hydropower and the environment in partnership with nongovernmental organisations) may foster public acceptance of hydropower projects. For example, the World Commission on Dams, an independent international commission established in 1998, is reviewing the development effectiveness of large dams and developing internationally acceptable criteria for future decision-making on dams.

Biomass resources

The world derives about 11 percent of its energy from biomass (IEA, 1998b). In developing countries biomass is the most important energy source, accounting for about 35 percent of the total (WEC, 1994). (In the largest developing countries, China and India, biomass accounts for 19 percent and 42 percent of the primary energy supply mix.) But in the world's poorest countries, biomass accounts for up to 90 percent of the energy supply, mostly in traditional or non-commercial forms.[10] This explains why biomass is often perceived as a fuel of the past—one that will be left behind as countries industrialise and their technological base develops.

But biomass resources are abundant in most parts of the world, and various commercially available conversion technologies could transform current traditional and low-tech uses of biomass to modern energy. If dedicated energy crops and advanced conversion technologies are introduced extensively (see chapter 7), biomass could make a substantial contribution to the global energy mix by 2100. Although most biomass is used in traditional ways (as fuel for households and small industries) and not necessarily in a sustainable manner, modern industrial-scale biomass applications have increasingly become commercially available. In 1996 estimates of biomass consumption ranged from 33–55 exajoules (WEC, 1998; IEA, 1998a; Hall, 1997).

Sources

Biomass can be classified as plant biomass (woody, non-woody, processed waste, or processed fuel; table 5.13) or animal biomass. Most woody biomass is supplied by forestry plantations, natural forests, and natural woodlands. Non-woody biomass and processed waste are products or by-products of agroindustrial activities. Animal manure can be used as cooking fuel or as feedstock for biogas generation. Municipal solid waste is also considered a biomass resource.

The annual global primary production of biomatter totals 220 billion oven dry tonnes, or 4,500 exajoules. The theoretically harvestable bioenergy potential is estimated to be 2,900 exajoules, of which 270 exajoules could be considered technically available on a sustainable basis (Hall and Rosillo-Calle, 1998). Hall and Rao

(1994) conclude that the biomass challenge is not availability but sustainable management, conversion, and delivery to the market in the form of modern and affordable energy services. Biomass resources can be converted to chemical fuels or electricity through several routes (see chapter 7).

Two major studies have recently acknowledged the benefits of sustainably produced biomass energy in future energy scenarios. The first is by Shell International Petroleum Company (Shell, 1996), which assessed potential major new sources of energy after 2020, when renewable energies are expected to become competitive with fossil fuels. The Intergovernmental Panel on Climate Change (IPCC, 1996a) has considered a range of options for mitigating climate change, and increased use of biomass for energy features in all its scenarios.

The expected role of biomass in the future energy supply of industrialised countries is based on two main considerations:

- The development of competitive biomass production, collection, and conversion systems to create biomass-derived fuels that can substitute for fossil fuels in existing energy supply infrastructure without contributing to the build-up of greenhouse gases in the atmosphere. Intermittent renewables, such as wind and solar energy, are more challenging to fit into existing distribution and consumption schemes.
- The potential resource base is generally considered substantial given the existence of land not needed or unsuitable for food production, as well as agricultural food yields that continue to rise faster than population growth.

In developing countries an assessment of potential bioenergy development must first address issues ranging from land-use conflicts with food production to health and environmental problems.

Perceptions and problems

Biomass is often perceived as a fuel of the past because of its low efficiency, high pollution, and associations with poverty.

- Biomass is the fuel most closely associated with energy-related health problems in developing countries. Exposure to particulates from biomass or coal burning causes respiratory infections in children, and carbon monoxide is implicated in problems in pregnancy (see chapter 3).

- Biomass fuels are bulky and may have a high water content. Fuel quality may be unpredictable, and physical handling of the material can be challenging. But technologies for biomass fuel upgrading (into pellets or briquettes, for example) are advancing, and the development of dedicated energy crops will also improve fuel standardisation.
- For biomass to become a major fuel, energy crops and plantations will have to become a significant land-use category. Land requirements will depend on energy crop yields, water availability, and the efficiency of biomass conversion to usable fuels. Assuming a 45 percent conversion efficiency to electricity and yields of 15 oven dry tonnes a hectare per year, 2 square kilometres of plantation would be needed per megawatt of electricity of installed capacity running 4,000 hours a year.
- The energy balance is not always favourable. While woody biomass energy output is 10–30 times greater than the energy input, the issue is less clear for liquid fuels derived from biomass (Shapouri, Duffield, and Graboski, 1995). Nevertheless, the use of sugarcane as a source of ethanol yields a very positive balance and is responsible for a net abatement of 9 million tonnes of carbon a year in Brazil (Moreira and Goldemberg, 1999). With the promising development of enzymatic hydrolysis, cellulose can be transformed into ethanol with a very favourable energy balance (PCAST, 1997).
- Large-scale production of biomass can have considerable negative impacts on soil fertility, water and agrochemical use, leaching of nutrients, and biodiversity and landscape. The collection and transport of biomass will increase vehicle and infrastructure use and air-borne emissions.

Technical potential of biomass energy plantations

To estimate future technical biomass potentials, it is necessary to know:
- The amount of land available for biomass plantation.
- The regional distribution of this land and distances to consumption centres.
- The productivity of the land for biomass production, including water availability.
- The environmental implications of biomass production.

TABLE 5.13. TYPES AND EXAMPLES OF PLANT BIOMASS

Woody biomass	Non-woody biomass	Processed waste	Processed fuels
• Trees • Shrubs and scrub • Bushes such as coffee and tea • Sweepings from forest floor • Bamboo • Palms	• Energy crops such as sugarcane • Cereal straw • Cotton, cassava, tobacco stems and roots (partly woody) • Grass • Bananas, plantains, and the like • Soft stems such as pulses and potatoes • Swamp and water plants	• Cereal husks and cobs • Bagasse • Wastes from pineapple and other fruits • Nut shells, flesh, and the like • Plant oil cake • Sawmill wastes • Industrial wood bark and logging wastes • Black liquor from pulp mills • Municipal waste	• Charcoal (wood and residues) • Briquette/densified biomass • Methanol/ethanol (wood alcohol) • Plant oils from palm, rape, sunflower, and the like • Producer gas • Biogas

Source: Adapted from IEA, 1998a.

TABLE 5.14. CURRENT GLOBAL LAND-USE PATTERN

Cropland (arableland and permanent crops)		Forests and woodland		Permanent pastures		Other land		
						Total other land		Land with rainfed cultivation potential
Gha	% of total	Gha	% of total	Gha	% of total	Gha	% of total	Gha
1.5	11	4.2	21	3.4	26	4.0	31	1.6–1.8

Note: Gha stands for billions of hectares. Total land availability is 13.1 billion hectares. *Source: FAO, 1993, 1999; Fischer and Heilig, 1998; WRI, 1998.*

TABLE 5.15. PROJECTED BIOMASS ENERGY POTENTIAL, 2050 (BILLIONS OF HECTARES UNLESS OTHERWISE INDICATED)

1	2	3	4	5	6[a]	7[b]	7[c]
Region	Population in 2050 (billions)	Land with crop production potential in 1990	Cultivated land in 1990	Additional cultivated land required in 2050	Maximum additional area for biomass production	Maximum additional amount of energy from biomass (exajoules)	
Industrialised countries[d]	–	–	0.670	0.050	0.100	17	30
Latin America							
Central and Caribbean	0.286	0.087	0.037	0.015	0.035	6	11
South America	0.524	0.865	0.153	0.082	0.630	107	189
Africa							
East	0.698	0.251	0.063	0.068	0.120	20	36
Central	0.284	0.383	0.043	0.052	0.288	49	86
North	0.317	0.104	0.040	0.014	0.050	9	15
Southern	0.106	0.044	0.016	0.012	0.016	3	5
West	0.639	0.196	0.090	0.096	0.010	2	3
Asia (excl. China)							
Western	0.387	0.042	0.037	0.010	-0.005	0	0
South-central	2.521	0.200	0.205	0.021	-0.026	0	0
East	1.722	0.175	0.131	0.008	0.036	6	11
South-east	0.812	0.148	0.082	0.038	0.028	5	8
China	–	–	–	–	–	2[e]	2[e]
Total[f]	8.296	2.495	0.897	0.416	1.28	226	396
Global biomass energy potential						276[g]	446[g]

a. (6) = (3) – (4) – (5). b. (7) = (6) x 8.5 [oven dry tonnes a hectare per year] x 20 [GJ per oven dry tonne] based on higher heating value (18 GJ per oven dry tonne for lower heating value). The assumptions for biomass productivity may appear on the high side, but they represent technically achievable yields given dedicated research, development, and dissemination. c. (7) = (6) x 15 [oven dry tonnes a hectare per year] x 20 [GJ per oven dry tonne] based on higher heating value (18 GJ per oven dry tonne for lower heating value). d. OECD, Central and Eastern Europe, newly independent states of the former Soviet Union. e. Data are projected values from d'Apote (1998), not maximum estimates. f. Totals in (2), (3), (4), and (5) exclude industrialised countries. g. Includes 50 EJ of current biomass energy generation. *Source: Derived from Fischer and Heilig, 1998; d'Apote, 1998; Nakićenović, Grübler, and McDonald, 1998.*

■ The technical and economic performance of conversion technologies and net energy balance.

Current land-use patterns are shown in table 5.14. Land use is split into cropland, forests and woodland, permanent pastures, and other land. 'Other land' includes uncultivated land, grassland not used for pasture, built-on areas, wastelands, wetlands, roads, barren land, and protected forests. Less than a half of this land (1.6–1.8 billion hectares) can be used for rainfed cultivation, including biomass production (FAO, 1993; Fischer and Heilig, 1998).

Because energy plantations will likely account for 80–100 percent of biomass supply, large-scale use of biomass may compete with land for agriculture and food production. But biomass production for energy purposes should not infringe on food production. By 2100 an additional 1,700 million hectares of land are expected to be needed for agriculture, while 690–1,350 million hectares of additional land would be needed to support biomass energy requirements under a high-growth biomass energy scenario. Hence land-use conflicts could arise.

Land availability. Considerable areas are potentially available for large-scale production of biomass. In tropical countries large areas of deforested and degraded lands could benefit from the establishment of bioenergy plantations. While the theoretical potential of biomass production is one order of magnitude larger than current global energy use, the technical and economic potentials are much smaller. Technical and economic potentials will be determined by numerous factors ranging from current uses of degraded land (which in developing countries is often used by the poor to graze livestock) and land productivity to the economic reach of the land with respect to centres of energy demand.

The United Nations Food and Agriculture Organization's "World Agriculture towards 2010 study (Alexandratos, 1995) assesses potential cropland resources in more than 90 developing countries. In 2025 developing countries will be using only 40 percent of their potential cropland, but with large regional variations. Asia (excluding China, for which data were unavailable) will have a deficit of 47 million hectares, but yields of most food crops are low, and there is great potential for improvement using better genetic strains and management techniques. Modern agricultural technologies have not reached many rural farmers and could boost yields by as much as 50 percent. Whether future productivity gains can avoid a food deficit remains to be seen. Africa currently only uses 20 percent of its potential cropland and would still have 75 percent remaining in 2025. Latin America, currently using only 15 percent of its potential cropland, would have 77 percent left in 2025—land capable of producing nearly eight times its present energy consumption.

Large areas of surplus agricultural land in North America and Europe could become significant biomass production areas. U.S. farmers are paid not to farm about 10 percent of their land, and in the European Union 15 percent of arable farmland can be set aside (amounting to 15–20 million hectares by 2010, and possibly more than 50 million hectares later in the 21st century). In addition to more than 30 million hectares of cropland already set aside in the United States to reduce production or conserve land, another 43 million hectares of cropland have high erosion rates. Another 43 million hectares have wetness problems that could be eased with a shift to perennial energy crops. The U.S. Department of Agriculture estimates that a further 60 million hectares may be idled over the next 25 years.

A projection of these parameters for 2050 is shown in table 5.15. The theoretical and technical potential for biomass energy is about ten times current use (445 exajoules relative to 45 exajoules) and close to current global primary energy use of 402 exajoules a year. But the extent to which this potential can be achieved will depend on numerous factors. These include the share of land allocated to other uses (for example, plantations for timber and pulp), actually achievable specific biomass productivity, technologies for converting biomass to convenient energy services, transport distances, water availability, biodiversity, and the need for fertilisers.

Water resources. The supply of freshwater may become a limiting factor for both food and bioenergy production. Several studies have addressed water issues related to agriculture (FAO, 1999; Fischer and Heilig, 1998; WRI, 1998; Seckler and others, 1998, Falkenmark, 1997).

But water availability for biomass production has not been addressed in great detail. The common view is that "the food needs of the world's rapidly growing population will introduce severe problems, either because the rate of growth will be too rapid for the additional water mobilisation to be met, or because the overall water demands will grow unrealistically high so that they cannot be met" (Falkenmark, 1997, p. 74).

Current and projected water resources, by region, are shown in table 5.16. Two levels of water requirements can be used to estimate water sufficiency. The lowest level of sufficiency is generally considered to be 1,000 cubic metres per capita a year, while the availability of more than 2,000 cubic metres per capita a year makes for a small probability of water shortages (Seckler and others, 1998, Falkenmark, 1997). In addition, a recent study commissioned by the United Nations Commission on Sustainable Development (Raskin and others, 1997) puts the upper limit of sustainable water consumption at 40 percent of available resources.

Even without considering water requirements for biomass production, water shortages (supply below 2,000 cubic metres per capita a year) are possible for about half the world's population as early as 2025. Thus the water constraint for extended biomass production will likely be of importance, especially in the long term (see also the section on physical constraints to hydroelectricity expansion, above).

TABLE 5.16. SUFFICIENCY OF WATER RESOURCES, 1990 AND 2025				
Region	Population in 1990 (millions)	Water resources per capita in 1990 (cubic metres)	Water resources per capita in 2025 (cubic metres)	Supply in 2025 as percentage of available water resources
North America	278	19,370	36,200	6,065
Latin America and Caribbean	433	30,920	200	533
Western Europe	459	10,604	47,700	1,178
Central and Eastern Europe	277	1,902	10,700	744
Former Soviet Union	428	4,561	36,700	4,981
Middle East and North Africa	n.a.	n.a.	0	6
Sub-Saharan Africa	n.a.	n.a.	< 100	1,465
Pacific Asia	405	11,463	5,100	10
South Asia	1,133	4,537	2,000	1,611
Centrally planned Asia	1,252	2,987	18,600	2,344
Pacific OECD	144	8,463	41,600	1,729
Total	**4,809**	**8,497**	**198,900**	**20,666**

n.a. Not available. *Source: Seckler and others, 1998.*

TABLE 5.17. CURRENT AND FEASIBLE BIOMASS PRODUCTIVITY, ENERGY RATIOS, AND ENERGY YIELDS FOR VARIOUS CROPS AND CONDITIONS

Crop and conditions	Yield (dry tonnes a hectare per year)	Energy ratio	Net energy yield (gigajoules a hectare per year)
Short rotation crops (willow, hybrid poplar; United States, Europe)			
• Short term	10-12	10:1	180-200
• Longer term	12-15	20:1	220-260
Tropical plantations (such as eucalyptus)			
• No genetic improvement, fertiliser use, and irrigation	2-10	10:1	30-180
• Genetic improvement and fertiliser use	6-30	20:1	100-550
• Genetic improvement, fertiliser and water added	20-30		340-550
Miscanthus/switchgrass			
• Short term	10-12	12:1	180-200
• Longer term	12-15	20:1	220-260
Sugarcane (Brazil, Zambia)	15-20	18:1[a]	400-500
Wood (commercial forestry)	1- 4	20/30:1	30- 80
Sugar beet (northwest Europe)			
• Short term	10-16	10:1	30-100
• Longer term	16-21	20:1	140-200
Rapeseed (including straw yields; northwest Europe)			
• Short term	4- 7	4:1	50- 90
• Longer term	7-10	10:1	100-170

a. The value in Moreira and Goldemberg (1999)—7.9:1—includes spending on transportation and processing of sugarcane to the final product ethanol.

Source: Biewinga and. van der Bijl, 1996; Hall and Scrase, 1998; IEA, 1994; Kaltschmitt, Reinhardt, and Stelzer, 1996; de Jager, Faaij, and Troelstra, 1998; IPCC, 1996a; Ravindranath and Hall, 1996.

Energy balances and biomass productivity

The energy production per hectare of various crops depends on climatic, soil, and management conditions. Examples of net energy yields—output minus energy inputs for agricultural operations, fertiliser, harvest, and the like—are given in table 5.17. Generally, perennial crops (woody biomass such as willow, eucalyptus, hybrid poplar, miscanthus or switchgrass grasses, sugarcane) perform better than annual crops (which are planted and harvested each year; examples include sorghum and hemp). This is because perennial crops have lower inputs and thus lower production costs as well as lower ecological impacts. Different management situations—irrigation, fertiliser application, genetic plant improvements, or some combination of the three—can also increase biomass productivity, by a factor of up to 10.

In addition to production and harvesting, biomass requires transportation to a conversion facility. The energy used to transport biomass over land averages about 0.5 megajoules per tonne-kilometre, depending on infrastructure and vehicle type (Borjesson, 1996). This means that land transport of biomass can become a significant energy penalty for distances of more than 100 kilometres. But such a radius covers a surface of hundreds of thousands of hectares, and is sufficient to supply enough biomass for conversion facilities of hundreds of megawatts of thermal power.

Transporting biomass by sea is also an option. Sea transport from Latin America to Europe, for example, would require less than 10 percent of the energy input of the biomass (Agterberg and Faaij, 1998). International transport of biomass (or rather, energy forms derived from biomass) is feasible from an energy (and cost) point of view. Sea transport of biomass is already practised: large paper and pulp complexes import wood from all over the world.

Agricultural and forestry residues and municipal waste

Agricultural and forestry residues are the organic by-products from food, fibre, and forest-product industries. Hall and others (1993) estimate the energy contents of these residues at more than one-third of global commercial energy use, of which about 30 percent is recoverable. Limitations arise from the impracticality of recovering all residues and from the need to leave some residues at the site (for fertilisation, for example) to ensure sustainable production of the main product.

Forestry residues obtained from sound forest management do not deplete the resource base. Under sustainable management, trees are replanted, the forest is managed for regeneration to enhance its health and future productivity, or both steps are taken. Energy is just one of the many outputs of forests. One of the difficulties is accurately estimating the potential of residues that can be available for energy use on a national or regional scale.

Municipal solid waste and industrial residues are indirect parts of the biomass resource base. Industrialised countries generate 0.9–1.9 kilograms per capita of municipal solid waste every day. Energy contents range from 4–13 megajoules per kilogram (IPPC, 1996a). Johansson and others (1993) report heating values as high as 15.9 megajoules per kilogram in Canada and the United States. Waste incineration, thermochemical gasification, and biodigestion convert municipal solid waste into electricity, heat, or even gaseous and liquid fuels. Because landfill disposal of municipal solid waste in densely populated areas is increasingly constrained and associated with rising tipping fees, such energy conversion can be profitable. Separating and recycling non-combustible contents.

Municipal solid waste incineration requires tight air pollution abatement due to the generation of complex compounds, some of which—such as dioxins—are carcinogenic (WEC, 1994). Advanced pollution abatement equipment essentially eliminates harmful pollutant emissions (Chen, 1995).

Johansson and others (1993) project that in industrialised countries energy production from urban refuse will reach about 3 exajoules a year by 2025.[11] Data on municipal solid waste in developing countries could not be found, but with rising living standards these same as those in low-income OECD countries. Globally, this could double the potential energy supply from municipal solid waste to 6 exajoules.

Environmental implications of biomass production

Forest energy plantations consist of intensively managed crops of predominantly coppiced hardwoods, grown on cutting cycles of three to five years and harvested solely for use as a source of energy. The site, local, regional, and global impacts of these crops need to be considered. For example, if short-rotation energy crops replace natural forests, the main negative effects include increased risks of erosion, sediment loading, soil compaction, soil organic matter depletion, and reduced long-term site productivity. Water pollution from intensively managed sites usually results from sediment loading, enhanced nutrient concentrations, and chemical residues from herbicides. In contrast, if short-rotation crops replace unused or degraded agricultural land, this reduces erosion, nutrient leaching, and so on.

Developing new crops is a slow and costly process involving many technical and non-technical obstacles (Rosillo-Calle and others, 1996). Farmers have been slow to adopt new crops because of the long-term (more than 15 years) commitment needed. But research and development in Sweden and the United Kingdom have found frost- and pest-resistant clones and generated high yields by using mixed-clone planting and other management practices (Hall and Scrase, 1998).

Soil and nutrients. The abundant use of fertilisers and manure in agriculture has led to considerable environmental problems in various regions. These problems include nitrification of groundwater, saturation of soils with phosphate (leading to eutrophication), and difficulties meeting drinking water standards. In addition, the application of phosphates has increased heavy metal flux to the soil.

The agricultural use of pesticides can affect the health of people as well as the quality of groundwater and surface water—and, consequently, plants and animals. Specific effects depend on the type of chemical, the quantities used, and the method of application. Experience with perennial crops (willow, poplar, eucalyptus) suggests that they meet strict environmental standards. Agrochemical applications per hectare are 5–20 times lower for perennial energy crops than for food crops like cereals (Hall, 1997).

Limited evidence on the soil effects of energy forestry indicates that our understanding of this area is still relatively poor. Current evidence indicates that, with proper practices, forest soil management need not negatively affect physical, chemical, and biological soil parameters. Soil organic matter can improve soil fertility, biology, and physical properties (such as bulk density and water relations).[12] Relative to arable agriculture, energy plantations can improve the physical properties of soil because heavy machinery is used less often and soil disturbances are fewer. Soil solution nitrate can also

In tropical countries large areas of deforested and degraded lands could benefit from the establishment of bioenergy plantations.

be significantly reduced in soils planted with fast-growing trees, as long as nitrogen fertilisers are applied in accordance with the nutrient demands of the trees.

Biological fertilisers may replace chemical nitrogen fertilisers in energy forestry and crops. Biological fertilisation may include:

- Direct planting of nitrogen-fixing woody species and interplanting with nitrogen-fixing trees or ley crops.
- Soil amendments with various forms of organic matter (sewage sludge, wastewater, contaminated groundwater, farmyard manure, green manure).
- Stimulation or introduction of rhizosphere micro-organisms that improve plant nutrient uptake.
- Biological fallow.

Overall, from a nutritional point of view, there is no reason to believe that energy forest plantations will have significant environmental and ecological impacts when proper management practices are applied (Ericson, 1994).

Erosion. Erosion is related to the cultivation of many annual crops in many regions and is a concern with woody energy crops during their establishment phase. Little field data are available for comparison with arable crops. One of the most crucial erosion issues relates to the additional soil stabilisation measures required during the establishment of energy plantations. Growing ground-cover vegetation strips between rows of trees can mitigate erosion as long as competition does not occur.

Changing land use from agricultural production to an energy forest plantation reduces precipitation excess (groundwater recharges) and nutrient leaching. Nitrogen leaching decreases with energy plantations because the standard nutrient supply and the use of animal slurries lead to good uptake efficiencies relative to agricultural production systems. Nitrogen uptake efficiency for arable crops is about 50 percent, for grass 60 percent, and for forest plantations about 75 percent. The losses in these systems are mainly due to leaching and de-nitrification (Rijtman and Vries, 1994).

Another concern relates to possible soil compaction caused by heavy harvesting machinery. But these effects tend to be small to moderate due to the infrequency of forest harvesting (Smith, 1995). Overall, these impacts can be significantly lower than for conventional agriculture. When harvesting peren-nials, soil erosion can be kept to an absolute minimum because the roots remain in the soil. In the United States millions of hectares covered by grasses that fall under the soil conservation programme could provide a promising biomass production area, since biomass production can be combined with soil protection. Another benefit of perennial crops relative to annual crops is that their extensive root system adds to the organic matter content of the soil. Generally, diseases (such as eels) are prevented and the soil gets a better structure.

Many of the environmental and ecological impacts noted thus far can be alleviated with compensating measures. Energy crops are generally more environmentally acceptable than intensive agriculture because chemical inputs are lower and the soil undergoes less disturbance and compaction.

Biodiversity and landscape. Biomass plantations may be criticised because the range of biological species they support is much narrower than is found in natural ecosystems, such as forests. While this is generally true, it is not always relevant. Where plantations are estab-lished on degraded or excess agricultural lands, the restored lands are likely to support a more diverse ecology than before. Moreover, degraded land areas are plentiful: in developing countries about 0.5 billion hectares of degraded land are available (Bekkering, 1992). In any case, it is desirable to restore such land surfaces for water retention, erosion prevention, and microclimate control.

A good plantation design—including set-aside areas for native plants and animals situated in the landscape in a natural way—can avoid problems normally associated with monocultures. The presence of natural predators (such as insects) can also prevent the outbreak of pests and diseases. Altogether, more research and insights on plantations are needed, taking into account local conditions, species, and cultural aspects.

Environmentally motivated responses to biomass production

Management practices are a key factor in the sustainable production and use of biomass. Yet very little is known about managing large-scale energy forest plantations or even agricultural and forestry residues for energy use.[13] The potential adverse environmental effects of large-scale dedicated energy crops and forestry plantations have raised concerns. Considerable effort has gone into investigating these concerns, and much knowledge has been gained (see Tolbert, 1998 and Lowe and Smith, 1997).

As a result good practice guidelines are being developed for the production and use of biomass for energy in Austria, Sweden, the United Kingdom, and the United States, as well as across Europe.

Very little is known about managing large-scale energy forest plantations or even agricultural and forestry residues for energy use.

These guidelines focus on short-rotation coppice and recognise the central importance of site-specific factors and the breadth of social and environmental issues that should be taken into consideration. But given that residues may remain more widely used than energy crops for quite some time, guidelines are urgently needed on when it is appropriate to use residues for energy, what fraction can be used, and how potential environmental advantages can be maximised.

A key message of these guidelines is that site and crop selection must be made carefully, and the crop must be managed sensitively. Energy crops should not displace land uses of high agricultural and ecological value. Consideration needs to be given to the landscape and visibility, soil type, water use, vehicle access, nature conservation, pests and diseases, and public access (ETSU, 1996; Hall and Scrase, 1998). The guidelines also stress the importance of consulting with local people at the early planning stage, and of ongoing community involvement in the development stages. Issues such as changes to the landscape, increased traffic movements, or new employment opportunities in rural areas may prove very significant to local people.

Economics

The production costs of plantation biomass are already favourable in some developing countries. Eucalyptus plantations in Brazil supply wood chips for $1.5–2.0 a gigajoule (Carpentieri, Larson, and Woods, 1993). Based on this commercial experience, Carpentieri, Larson, and Woods (1993) project future biomass (wood chip) production of 13 exajoules a year on 50 million hectares of land. Costs are much higher in industrialised countries (with top values of around $4 a gigajoule in parts of Europe). But in the longer run, by about 2020, better crops and production systems are expected to cut biomass production costs in the United States to $1.5–2.0 a gigajoule for substantial land surfaces (Graham and others, 1995; Turnure and others, 1995).

Biomass costs are influenced by yield, land rent, and labour costs. Thus increases in productivity are essential to reducing biomass production costs. Yields can be improved through crop development, production integration (multiproduct plantation), and mechanisation. Competition for land use should be avoided to minimise inflated land rental rates. Labour costs can be lowered through mechanisation.

Solar energy resources

Solar energy has immense theoretical potential. The amount of solar radiation intercepted by Earth is more than three orders of magnitude higher than annual global energy use (table 5.18). But for several reasons the actual potential of solar energy is somewhat lower:

■ *Time variation.* The amount of solar energy available at a given point is subject to daily and seasonal variations. So, while the maximum solar flux at the surface is about 1 kilowatt per square meter, the annual average for a given point can be as low as

Parameter	Energy
TABLE 5.18 ANNUAL SOLAR ENERGY RECEIVED BY THE EARTH	
Solar energy intercepted by the Earth at ~1.37 kilowatts per square metre	5.5×10^6
Solar energy reflected by the atmosphere back to space at ~0.3 kilowatts per square metre)	1.6×10^6
Solar energy potentially usable at ~1.0 kilowatts per square metre	3.9×10^6
Ratio of potentially usable solar energy to current primary energy consumption (402 exajoules)	~9,000

Source: Author's calculations.

0.1–0.3 kilowatts per square meter, depending on location. For large-scale application of solar energy—more than 5–10 percent of the capacity of an integrated electricity system—the variability of insolation necessitates energy storage or backup systems to achieve a reliable energy supply.

- Geographic variation. The availability of solar energy also depends on latitude. Areas near the equator receive more solar radiation than subpolar regions. But geographic variation can be significantly reduced by using collectors capable of following the position of the sun. Polar regions show a notable increase in irradiance due to light reflection from snow.
- Weather conditions. Weather is another, even stronger, factor influencing the availability of solar energy. Annual average sky clearness may vary by 80–90 percent in locations such as Khartoum (Sudan), Dakar (Bangladesh), Kuwait, Baghdad (Iraq), Salt Lake City (Utah), and by 40–50 percent in Tokyo (Japan) and Bonn (Germany; WEC, 1994). Solar irradiance is often quite diffuse, leading to lower average power densities. Thus large-scale generation of solar energy can require significant land.
- Siting options. While building structures provide interesting local siting possibilities,[14] large-scale solar collectors can be located on land that is not being used—which amounts to about 4 billion hectares (FAO, 1999). Assuming 10 percent of this unused land is allocated for habitation (cities, towns, villages) and infrastructure (roads, ports, railways), some 3.6 billion hectares are available for solar energy.

Large-scale availability of solar energy will thus depend on a region's geographic position, typical weather conditions, and land availability. Using rough estimates of these factors, solar energy potential is shown in table 5.19. This assessment is made in terms of primary energy—that is, energy before the conversion to secondary or final energy is estimated. The amount of final energy will depend on the efficiency of the conversion device used (such as the photovoltaic cell applied). Issues related to energy conversion and its impact on the amount of energy delivered are considered in chapter 7.

This assessment also reflects the physical potential of solar energy. Thus it does not take into account possible technological, economic, and social constraints on the penetration of solar energy except for two different assumptions on available land. The consideration of such constraints is likely to result in much lower estimates—as in WEC (1994), where global solar energy potential in 2020 ranges from 5–230 exajoules a year.

The solar energy potential in table 5.19 is more than sufficient to meet current and projected energy uses well beyond 2100. Thus the contribution of solar energy to global energy supplies will not be limited by resource availability. Rather, three factors will determine the extent to which solar energy is used in the longer run: the availability of efficient and low-cost technologies to convert solar energy into electricity and eventually hydrogen, of effective energy storage technologies for electricity and hydrogen, and of high-efficiency end-use technologies fuelled by electricity and hydrogen.

TABLE 5.19. ANNUAL SOLAR ENERGY POTENTIAL (EXAJOULES)

Region	Minimum	Maximum
North America	181.1	7,410
Latin America and Caribbean	112.6	3,385
Western Europe	25.1	914
Central and Eastern Europe	4.5	154
Former Soviet Union	199.3	8,655
Middle East and North Africa	412.4	11,060
Sub-Saharan Africa	371.9	9,528
Pacific Asia	41.0	994
South Asia	38.8	1,339
Centrally planned Asia	115.5	4,135
Pacific OECD	72.6	2,263
Total	**1,575.0**	**49,837**
Ratio to current primary energy consumption (402 exajoules)	**3.9**	**124**
Ratio to projected primary energy consumption in 2050 (590–1,050 exajoules)	**2.7–1.5**	**84–47**
Ratio to the projected primary energy consumption in 2100 (880–1,900 exajoules)	**1.8–0.8**	**57–26**

Note: The minimum and maximum reflect different assumptions on annual clear sky irradiance, annual average sky clearance, and available land area. *Source: IEA, 1998c; Nakićenović, Grübler, and McDonald, 1998.*

Wind energy resources

Winds develop when solar radiation reaches the Earth's highly varied surface unevenly, creating temperature, density, and pressure differences. Tropical regions have a net gain of heat due to solar radiation, while polar regions are subject to a net loss. This means that the Earth's atmosphere has to circulate to transport heat from the tropics towards the poles. The Earth's rotation further contributes to semi-permanent, planetary-scale circulation patterns in the atmosphere. Topographical features and local temperature gradients also alter wind energy distribution.

A region's mean wind speed and its frequency distribution have to be taken into account to calculate the amount of electricity that can be produced by wind turbines. Wind resources can be exploited in areas where wind power density is at least 400 watts per square metre at 30 metres above the ground (or 500 watts per square metre at 50 metres). Moreover, technical advances are expected to open new areas to development. The following assessment includes regions where the average annual wind power density exceeds 250–300 watts per square metre at 50 metres—corresponding to class 3 or higher in the widely used U.S. classification of wind resources.

TABLE 5.20. ANNUAL WIND ENERGY POTENTIAL

Region	Percentage of land area	Population density (people per square kilometre)	Gross electric potential (thousands of terawatt-hours)	Assessed wind energy potential (exajoules)	Estimated second-order potential (thousands of terawatt-hours)	Assessed wind energy potential, (exajoules)
Africa	24	20	106	1,272	10.6	127
Australia	17	2	30	360	3	36
North America	35	15	139	1,670	14	168
Latin America	18	15	54	648	5.4	65
Western Europe	42	102	31	377	4.8	58
Eastern Europe and former Soviet Union	29	13	106	1,272	10.6	127
Asia (excl. former Soviet Union)	9	100	32	384	4.9	59
Total	**23**		**500**	**6,000**	**53**	**640**

Note: Refers to wind energy with average annual power density of more than 250–300 watts per square metre at 50 metres (resources class 3 and higher in the U.S. classification of wind resources). The energy equivalent in exajoules is calculated based on the electricity generation potential of the referenced sources by dividing the electricity generation potential by a factor of 0.3 (a representative value for the efficiency of wind turbines, including transmission losses), resulting in a primary energy estimate. Totals are rounded.

Source: Grubb and Meyer, 1993.

TABLE 5.21. ESTIMATED ANNUAL WIND ENERGY RESOURCES

Region	Land surface with wind class 3–7		Wind energy resources without land restriction		Wind energy resources if less than 4 percent of land is used	
	Percent	Thousands of square kilometres	Thousands of terawatt-hours	Exajoules	Thousands of terawatt-hours	Exajoules
North America	41	7,876	126	1,512	5.0	60
Latin America and Caribbean	18	3,310	53	636	2.1	25
Western Europe	42	1,968	31	372	1.3	16
Eastern Europe and former Soviet Union	29	6,783	109	1,308	4.3	52
Middle East and North Africa	32	2,566	41	492	1.6	19
Sub-Saharan Africa	30	2,209	35	420	1.4	17
Pacific Asia	20	4,188	67	804	2.7	32
China	11	1,056	17	204	0.7	8
Central and South Asia	6	243	4	48	0.2	2
Total[a]	**27**	**30,200**	**483**	**5,800**	**18.7**	**231**

Note: The energy equivalent in exajoules is calculated based on the electricity generation potential of the referenced sources by dividing the electricity generation potential by a factor of 0.3 (a representative value for the efficiency of wind turbines, including transmission losses), resulting in a primary energy estimate.
a. Excludes China.

Source: WEC, 1994.

Several studies have analysed the global potential of power production using wind. To define technical wind power potential, one needs take into account siting constraints. First-order exclusions may include definite constraints such as cities, forests, difficult terrain, and inaccessible mountain areas. The most important limitations arise from social, environmental, and land-use constraints, including visual and noise impacts, all of which depend on political and social judgements and traditions and may vary by region. Regional estimates of wind electricity potentials (class 3 and above) are summarised in table 5.20.

Grubb and Meyer (1993) estimate the theoretical electricity generation potential of global wind energy resources (class 3 and above) to be 500,000 terawatt-hours a year (see table 5.20). Only about 10 percent of this theoretical potential may be realistically harvested.

WEC (1994) places the global theoretical wind potential at 483,000 terawatt-hours a year (table 5.21). This estimate is based on the assumption that 27 percent of the Earth's land surface is exposed to an annual mean wind speed higher than 5.1 metres per second at 10 metres above ground (class 3 and above), and that this entire area could be used for wind farms. WEC also suggests a more conservative estimate of 19,000 terawatt-hours a year, assuming for practical reasons that just 4 percent of the area exposed to this wind speed can be used for wind farms. (The 4 percent estimate comes from detailed studies of wind power potential in the Netherlands and the United States.)

Geothermal energy resources

Geothermal energy is generally defined as heat stored within the Earth. The Earth's temperature increases by about 3 degrees Celsius for every 100 metres in depth, though this value is highly variable. Heat originates from the Earth's molten interior and from the decay of radioactive materials.

Four types of geothermal energy are usually distinguished:
- Hydrothermal—hot water or steam at moderate depths (100–4,500 metres).
- Geopressed—hot-water aquifers containing dissolved methane under high pressure at depths of 3–6 kilometres.
- Hot dry rock—abnormally hot geologic formations with little or no water.
- Magma—molten rock at temperatures of 700–1,200 degrees Celsius.

Today only hydrothermal resources are used on a commercial scale for electricity generation (some 44 terawatt-hours of electricity in 1997) and as a direct heat source (38 terawatt-hours of heat; Björnsson and others, 1998).

The global potential of geothermal energy is on the order of 140,000,000 exajoules. But a much smaller amount can be classified as resources and reserves (table 5.22). Still, geothermal energy has enormous potential. Even the most accessible part, classified as reserves (about 434 exajoules), exceeds current annual consumption of primary energy. But like other renewable resources (solar energy, wind energy), geothermal energy is widely dispersed. Thus the technological ability to use geothermal energy, not its quantity, will determine its future share. The regional distribution of geothermal energy potential is shown in table 5.23.

Environmental aspects of geothermal energy use relate primarily to gas admixtures to the geothermal fluids such as carbon dioxide, nitrogen, hydrogen sulphides or ammonia and heavy metals such as mercury. The quantities vary considerably with location and temperatures of the feed fluid but are generally low compared to those associated with fossil fuel use. Because the chemicals are dissolved in the feed water which is usually re-injected into the drill holes, releases are minimal.

Ocean energy resources

Four types of ocean energy are known:
- Tidal energy—energy transferred to oceans from the Earth's rotation through gravity of the sun and moon.
- Wave energy—mechanical energy from wind retained by waves.
- Ocean thermal energy—energy stored in warm surface waters that can be made available using the temperature difference with water in ocean depths.
- Salt gradient energy—the energy coming from salinity differences between freshwater discharges into oceans and ocean water.

Tidal energy is the most advanced in terms of current use, with a

TABLE 5.22. ANNUAL GEOTHERMAL POTENTIAL (EXAJOULES)	
Resource category	Energy
Accessible resource base (amount of heat that could theoretically be tapped within a depth of 5 kilometres)	140,000,000
Useful accessible resource base	600,000
Resources (portion of the accessible resource base expected to become economical within 40–50 years)	5,000
Reserves (portion of the accessible resource base expected to become economical within 10–20 years)	500

Source: Palmerini, 1993; Björnsson and others, 1998.

TABLE 5.23. ANNUAL GEOTHERMAL POTENTIAL BY REGION (EXAJOULES)	
Resource category	Energy
North America	26,000,000 •(18.9)
Latin America and Caribbean	26,000,000 •(18.6)
Western Europe	7,000,000 • (5.0)
Eastern Europe and former Soviet Union	23,000,000 •(16.7)
Middle East and North Africa	6,000,000 • (4.5)
Sub-Saharan Africa	17,000,000 •(11.9)
Pacific Asia (excl. China)	11,000,000 • (8.1)
China	11,000,000 • (7.8)
Central and South Asia	13,000,000 • (9.4)
Total	**140,000,000**

Note: Numbers in parentheses are shares of world total.

Source: WEC, 1994; EPRI, 1978.

TABLE 5.24. ANNUAL OCEAN ENERGY POTENTIAL

Resource category	Terawatt-hours	Exajoules
Tidal energy	22,000	79
Wave energy	18,000	65
Ocean thermal energy[a]	2,000,000	7,200
Salt gradient energy[b]	23,000	83
Total	2,063,000	7,400

a. The potential of ocean thermal energy is difficult to assess but is known to be much larger than for the other types of ocean energy. The estimate used here assumes that the potential for ocean thermal energy is two orders of magnitude higher than for tidal, wave, or salt gradient energy. b. Assumes the use of all the world's rivers with devices of perfect efficiency. *Source: WEC, 1994, 1998; Cavanagh, Clarke, and Price, 1993.*

number of commercial plants in operation. Despite notable progress in recent years, the other ocean energy resources are generally not considered mature enough for commercial applications.

The theoretical potential of each type of ocean energy is quite large (table 5.24). But like other renewables, these energy resources are diffuse, which makes it difficult to use the energy. The difficulties are specific to each type of ocean energy, so technical approaches and progress differ as well.

Conclusion

Globally, energy resources are plentiful and are unlikely to constrain sustainable development even beyond the 21st century (tables 5.25 and 5.26). If historical observations are any indication, possible intergenerational equity conflicts on resource availability and costs

will most likely be equilibrated by technological progress. The fossil resource base is at least 600 times current fossil fuel use, or 16 times cumulative fossil fuel consumption between 1860 and 1998. (The resource base does not include methane clathrates and other oil, gas, and coal occurrences, the inclusion of which could quadruple the resource base.)

While the availability and costs of fossil fuels are unlikely to impede sustainable development, current practices for their use and waste disposal are not sustainable (UNCED, 1993). In their natural states, energy resources are environmentally inert (from the perspective of sustainable development). Even mining and production of fossil resources interfere little with sustainable development relative to current pollution emissions and wastes associated with their combustion for the provision of energy services. Thus the economic and environmental performance of fossil, nuclear, and renewable conversion technologies—from resource extraction to waste disposal—will determine the extent to which an energy resource can be considered sustainable.

Relative economic and environmental aspects make up the demand pull for the development of future energy resources. Sociopolitical preferences and policies can appreciably amplify or weaken the demand pull. In many countries, especially transition economies but also several energy-exporting developing countries, the domestic fossil energy resource endowment has yet to be evaluated using market-based criteria. Such evaluations may lead to a substantial revision of readily available reserve volumes and point to unforeseen investments in up-stream operations to raise productivity to international standards.

Energy resources are not evenly distributed across the globe. Although renewables are more evenly distributed and accessible

TABLE 5.25. SUMMARY OF GLOBAL FOSSIL AND FISSILE RESOURSES (THOUSANDS OF EXAJOULES)

Resource	Consumed by end 1998	Consumed in 1998	Reserves	Resources	Resource base[a]	Additional occurrences
Oil	5.14	0.14	11.11	21.31	32.42	45
Conventional	4.85	0.13	6.00	6.07	12.08	
Unconventional	0.29	0.01	5.11	15.24	20.35	45
Gas	2.38	0.08	14.88	34.93	49.81	930
Conventional	2.35	0.08	5.45	11.11	16.57	
Unconventional	0.03	0.00	9.42	23.81	33.24	930
Coal	5.99	0.09	20.67	179.00	199.67	
Fossil total	13.51	0.32	46.66	235.24	281.89	975
Uranium						
Open cycle in thermal reactors[b]	n.e.	0.04	1.89	3.52	5.41	7.1[c]
Closed cycle with fast reactors[d]	—	—	113	211	325	426[b]
Fossil and fissile total[e]	n.e.	0.36	48	446	575	1,400

n.e. Not estimated. — Negligible.
a. Sum of reserves and resources. b. Calculated from the amount in tonnes of uranium, assuming 1 tonne = 589 terajoules (IPCC, 1996a). c. Does not include uranium from seawater or other fissile materials. d. Calculated assuming a 60-fold increase relative to the open cycle, with 1 tonne = 35,340 terajoules. e. All totals are rounded. *Source: Author's calculations from previous chapter tables.*

FIGURE 5.4. GLOBAL ENERGY BALANCE AND FLOWS WITHOUT ANTHROPOGENIC INTERFERENCE

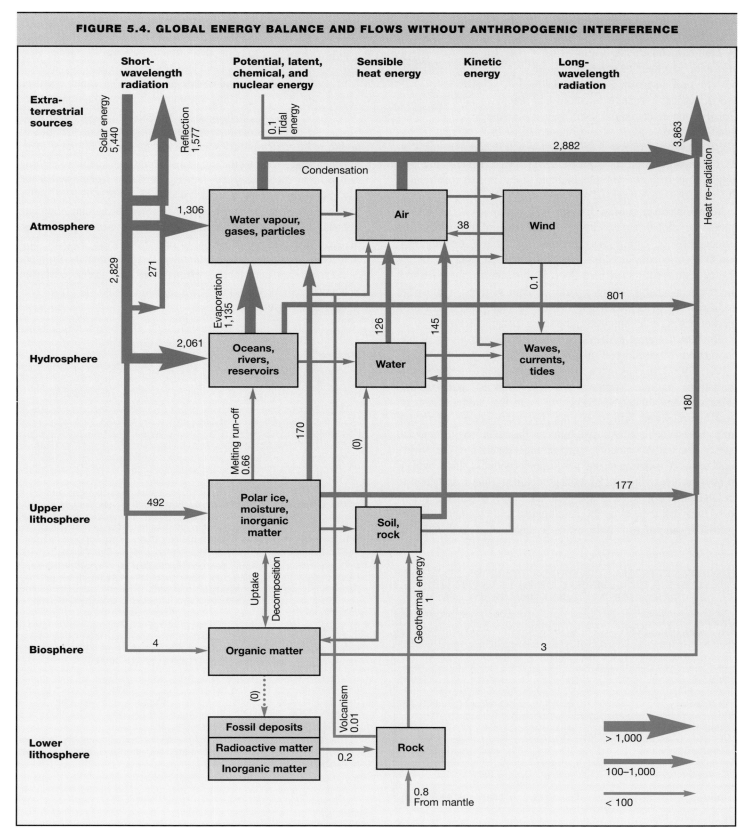

Note: Energy flows are in thousands of exajoules a year. Numbers in parentheses are uncertain or rounded.

Source: Sørensen, 1979.

than fossil and nuclear resources, their economic potential is affected by land-use constraints, variation of availability as a function of latitude (solar power) and location (wind power and hydroelectricity), solar irradiation, and water and soil quality (biomass). Still, renewable energy flows are three orders of magnitude larger than current global energy use (figure 5.4). Their use will depend primarily on the commercialisation of conversion technologies. Similarly, uranium and thorium resources are plentiful and do not pose a constraint to the long-term deployment of nuclear power.

Most long-term energy demand and supply scenarios involve increasing global energy trade, irrespective of the underlying assumptions of energy resource and technology development. Supply security considerations may tilt the balance in favour of one energy resource or set of resources. Supply security improves with the share of energy supplies from national sources. A thorough evaluation of a nation's energy resource endowment based on market criteria is an important step towards supply security.

The world energy system's current dependence on fossil fuel conversion is considered unsustainable by the United Nations (UNDP, 1997). It has often been assumed that fossil resource limitations or the "running out of resources" phenomenon (Meadows and others, 1972) would wean the energy system off fossil sources and bring about the necessary course correction towards sustainable energy development. Based on long-term global energy demand expectations, current understanding of the world's fossil resource endowment, and production economics, this is unlikely to happen before the end of the 21st century. Thus a transition to sustainable energy systems that continue to rely predominantly on fossil fuels will depend on the development and commercialisation of fossil technologies that do not close their fuel cycle through the

> Renewable energy flows are three orders of magnitude larger than current global energy use.

atmosphere.[15] Alternatively, the transition will likely require determined policies to move away from fossil fuels. Large increases in fossil fuel prices as a result of rapid resource depletion are unlikely to drive the transition.

Transitions motivated by factors other than short-term economics usually invoke extra costs that have to be borne by contemporary societies for the benefit of future ones. In either case—making the use of fossil fuels sustainable or shifting to non-fossil energy sources—society must first recognise that the current energy system is unsustainable and that adequate policy measures need to be introduced. These measures may stimulate technological advances and development, change consumer preferences, or both. After all, the existence of enormous fossil, nuclear, and renewable resources is irrelevant unless there is a demand for them and unless technologies for their extraction and sustainable conversion to energy services are commercially available. Otherwise, resources remain 'neutral stuff'. ■

Notes

1. However, Masters and others argue that most major oil-producing countries are reporting as proven reserves what the authors would define as identified reserves (proven plus probable plus possible).

2. Oil production costs and market prices may differ significantly, however. Oil is a highly political commodity with market prices that often have little relation to costs. While economic rationality suggests that the least-cost oil reserves are produced first, this has not been the case, at least since 1973. That gives low-cost and lowest-cost producers quite a bit of leverage in engineering market price instabilities or backing out of high-cost production.

3. The ratio of reserves to production assumes constant demand for a resource as well as constant production over the period suggested by the ratio. In essence, it implies that production will plummet from full output in one year to zero output in another. In reality, production peaks and then declines along a quasi-logistic curve, and supplies will last much longer, though at much lower volumes than suggested by the ratio.

4. Once an investment has been committed for gas export pipelines, it cannot easily be designated for other uses (whereas an oil tanker may be rerouted instantly by a single radio call). Disputes between trading partners may put the investment at risk and lead to disruptions in supply and offtake.

5. Temperature increases as a function of high atmospheric carbon concentrations are highly uncertain. For example, the mean global temperature increase estimated for a doubling of carbon dioxide concentrations ranges from 1.5–4.5 Kelvin (IPCC, 1996b).

6. Uranium reserves as defined by the Uranium Institute are proven and probable reserves (labelled Reserve Class I) at production costs of less than $40 a kilogram, less than $60 a kilogram, and less than $80 a kilogram. WEC (1998) uses the term *proven reserves* for the NEA-IAEA category reasonably assure resources.

7. The Uranium Institute uses for the lesser-known category Reserve Class II. WEC (1998) defines its estimated additional amounts recoverable to correspond to NEA-IAEA EAR I.

8. A detailed and consistent compilation for all countries is not available, and country-specific information is often published without verification. *The International Water Power and Dams Construction Yearbook* (1998) and even the *World Atlas and Industry Guide* (1998) present a few inconsistencies. Nevertheless, a cross-check showed a similar world total for these two sources.

TABLE 5.26. SUMMARY OF THE RENEWABLE RESOURCE BASE (EXAJOULES A YEAR)

Resource	Current use[a]	Technical potential	Theoretical potential
Hydropower	9	50	147
Biomass energy	50	> 276	2,900
Solar energy	0.1	> 1,575	3,900,000
Wind energy	0.12	640	6,000
Geothermal energy	0.6	5,000	140,000,000
Ocean energy	n.e.	n.e.	7,400
Total	56	> 7,600	> 144,000,000

n.e. Not estimated.
a. The electricity part of current use is converted to primary energy with an average factor of 0.385.   *Source: Author's calculations from previous chapter tables.*

9. The consideration of social and environmental aspects suggests that this is the market potential. Because of inconsistencies in the definitions used in different appraisals, here the notion of economic potential is maintained.

10. Non-commercial biomass is difficult to account for accurately or goes unreported. For instance, biomass data for China and India are not included in the WEC statistics.

11. It is assumed that 75 percent of the energy in urban refuse can be recovered and that the waste generation rate per capita is constant over time. Estimates for Canada and the United States are based on a per capita waste generation rate of 330 kilograms a year and a heating value of 15.9 megajoules per kilogram (and a 50 percent recycling rate). Estimates for other OECD countries are based on a per capita waste generation rate of 300 kilograms a year and a heating value of 12.7 megajoules per kilogram.

12. A review of the literature indicates that over time there are few, if any, long-term losses of soil carbon after forest harvesting and reforestation. But substantial losses of soil carbon are reported for systems involving harvesting followed by intensive burning or mechanical site damage. Holistic, life-cycle approaches are required to estimate the contribution of intensive forest management and bioenergy systems to local and global carbon balances.

13. There are exceptions: a lot is known about eucalyptus for charcoal production and sugarcane for ethanol production in Brazil (which tend to follow traditional agricultural and forestry practices). Similarly, there is extensive knowledge about willows for heat power generation in Sweden, where the cultivation of about 16,000 hectares has also borrowed considerably from traditional forestry and agricultural activities.

14. For example, if the performance and costs of solar collectors integrated with buildings are improved, commercial buildings could become local energy production centres. Such integration would enlarge the space available for solar collection and allow buildings to contribute to their energy use.

15. Decarbonisation of fuels (before use) or greenhouse gas abatement (after fuel production or use) and subsequent carbon dioxide disposal could eventually avoid closing the carbon fuel cycle through the atmosphere (see chapters 8 and 11).

References

Aalund, L.R. 1998. "Technology, Money Unlocking Vast Orinoco Reserves." *Oil and Gas Journal Special* 96 (42): 49–50.

Adelman, M.A., and M.C. Lynch. 1997. "Fixed View of Resources Limits Creates Undue Pessimism." *Oil and Gas Journal* 95 (14): 56–60.

Agterberg, A., and A. Faaij. 1998. "Biotrade: International Trade in Renewable Energy from Biomass." In *Proceedings of the 10th European Conference on Biomass for Energy and Industry*. Utrecht University, Department of Science, Technology, and Society, Würzburg, Netherlands.

Alexandratos, N. 1995. "World Agriculture towards 2010 Netherlands". A study by the Food and Agriculture Organization of the United Nations. Chichester: John Wiley & Sons.

ANEEL (Agencia Nacional de Energia Eletrica). 1999. www.aneel.gov.br. Brasilia, Brazil.

Bekkering, T.D. 1992. "Using Tropical Forests to Fix Atmospheric Carbon: The Potential in Theory and Practice." *Ambio* 21: 414–19.

BGR (Bundesanstalt für Geowissenschaften und Rohstoffe [Federal Institute for Geosciences and Natural Resources]). 1995. *Reserven, Ressourcen und Verfügbarkeit von Energierohstoffen 1995 [Availability of Energy Reserves and Resources 1995]*. Hannover, Germany.

———. 1998. *Reserven, Ressourcen und Verfügbarkeit von Energierohstoffen 1998 [Availability of Energy Reserves and Resources 1998]*. Hannover, Germany.

Biewinga, E.E., and G. van der Bijl. 1996. *Sustainability of Energy Crops in Europe: A Methodology Developed and Applied*. CLM 234. Utrecht: Netherlands Centre for Agriculture and Environment.

Björnsson, J., and others. 1998. "The Potential Role of Geothermal Energy and Hydropower in the World Energy Scenario in Year 2020." Paper presented at the 17th Congress of the World Energy Council, 13–18 September, Houston, Tex.

Bloss, W.H., O. Kappelmeyer, J. Koch, J. Meyer, and E. Schubert. 1980. *Survey of Energy Resources*. Hannover, Germany: Federal Institute for Geosciences and Natural Sciences.

Boiteux, M. 1989. "Hydro: An Ancient Source of Power for the Future." *International Water Power and Dam Construction Yearbook*. Sutton, Surrey. England. Buisness Press International.

Borjesson, P. 1996. "Emission of CO_2 from Biomass Production and Transportation in Agriculture and Forestry." *Energy Conversion and Management* 37: 6–8.

BP (British Petroleum). 1998. *BP Statistical Review of World Energy*. London.

———.1999. *BP Statistical Review of World Energy*. London.

Campbell, C.J., and J.H. Laherrere. 1998. "The End of Cheap Oil." *Scientific American* 278 (3): 78–83.

Carpentieri, E., E. Larson, and J. Woods. 1993. "Future Biomass-Based Power Generation in Northeast Brazil." *Biomass and Bioenergy* 4 (3): 149–73.

Cavanagh, J.E., J.H. Clarke, and R. Price. 1993. "Ocean Energy Systems." In T.B. Johansson, H. Kelly, A.K.N. Reddy, and R.H. Williams, eds., *Renewable Energy: Sources for Fuels and Electricity*. Washington, D.C.: Island Press.

Chadwick, J. 1998. "Mining Alberta's Oil Sands." *Mining Magazine* 179 (2): 58–73.

Charpak, G., and R.L. Garwin. 1998. *Feux Follets et Champignons Nucleaires*. Paris: Editions Odile Jacob.

Chen, J. 1995. "The Production of Methanol and Hydrogen from Municipal Solid Waste." MSE Thesis, CEES Report 289. Princeton University, Mechanical and Aerospace Engineering Department, Princeton, N.J.

Churchill, A.A. 1997. "Meeting Hydro's Financing and Development Challenges." In T. Dorcey, ed., *Large Dams: Learning from the Past, Looking at the Future*. Gland, Switzerland: World Conservation Union and the World Bank.

Collet, T.S. 1993. "Natural Gas Production from Arctic Gas Hydrates." U.S. *Geological Survey* 65: 299–311.

Collet, T.S., and V.A. Kuuskraa. 1998. "Hydrates Contain Vast Store of World Gas Resources." *Oil and Gas Journal* 96 (19).

D'Apote, S.L. 1998. "IEA Biomass Energy Analysis and Projections." *In Biomass Energy: Data, Analysis and Trends*. Proceedings of the Organisation for Economic Co-operation and Development and the International Energy Agency conference, 23–24 March, Paris.

Davidson, R.M. 1995. *Coalbed Methane Extraction*. London: International Energy Agency Coal Research.

De Jager, D., A. Faaij, and W.P. Troelstra. 1998. *Cost-Effectiveness of Transportation Fuels from Biomass*. Report prepared for NOVEM (EWAB rapport 9830). Utrecht University, Department of Science, Technology, and Society, Innas B.V., Utrecht, the Netherlands.

Edwards, J.D. 1997. "Crude Oil and Alternative Energy Production Forecasts for the Twenty-first Century: the End of the Hydrocarbon Era." *AAPG Bulletin* 81 (8): 1292–315.

Elrod, J.P. 1997. "Horizontal Air Drilling Increases Gas Recovery in Depleted Zone." *Oil and Gas Journal* 95 (26): 49–63.

EPRI (Electric Power Research Institute). 1978. *Geothermal Energy Prospects for the Next 50 Years*. Palo Alto, Calif.

Ericson, T. 1994. "Nutrient Cycling in Energy Forest Plantations." *Biomass and Bioenergy* 6: 115–21.

ETSU (Energy Technology Support Unit). 1996. *Good Practices Guidelines: Short Rotation Coppice for Energy Production*. Department of Trade and Industry. London: Seacourt Press.

Falkenmark, M.. 1997. "Meeting Water Requirements of an Expanding World." *Phil. Trans. R. Soc. Lond.* B352: 929–36.

FAO (Food and Agriculture Organization of the United Nations) 1993. "Agriculture: Towards 2010." FAO Conference (27th Session), Rome.

———. 1999. "Statistical Databases on the Internet." http://apps.fao.org/cgi-bin/nph-db.pl?subset=agriculture. Rome.

Fischer, G., and G.K. Heilig. 1998. "Population Momentum and the Demand on Land and Water Resources." Report IIASA-RR-98-1. International Institute for Applied Systems Analysis, Laxenburg, Austria.

Garwin, R.L. 1999. Personal communication. September.

George, R.L. 1998. "Mining for Oil." *Scientific American* 278 (3): 84–85.

Goodland, R. 1996. "Distinguishing Better Dams from Worse." *International Water Power and Dam Construction.* Sutton, Surre, England: Buisness Press International.

———. 1997. "Environmental Sustainability in the Hydro Industry: Desegregating the Debate." In T. Dorcey, ed., *Large Dams: Learning from the Past, Looking at the Future.* Gland, Switzerland: World Conservation Union and the World Bank.

Graham, R., E. Lichtenberg, V. Roningen, H. Shapouri, and M. Walsh. 1995. "The Economics of Biomass Production in the United States." In *Proceedings of the Second Biomass Conference of the Americas.* Golden, Colo.: National Renewable Energy Laboratory.

Gregory, K., and H-H. Rogner. 1998. "Energy Resources and Conversion Technologies for the 21st Century." *Mitigation and Adaptation Strategies for Global Change* 3: 171–229.

Grubb, M.J., and N.I. Meyer. 1993. "Wind Energy: Resources, Systems, and Regional Strategies." In Johansson T.B and others, eds., *Renewable Energy: Sources for Fuels and Electricity.* Washington, D.C.: Island Press.

Hall, D.O. 1997. "Biomass Energy in Industrialized Countries: A View of the Future." *Forest Ecology and Management* 91: 17–45.

Hall, D.O., and K.K. Rao. 1994. *Photosynthesis.* Cambridge: Cambridge University Press.

Hall, D.O., and F. Rosillo-Calle. 1998. *Biomass Resources Other than Wood.* London: World Energy Council.

Hall, D.O., and J.I. Scrase. 1998. "Will Biomass Be the Environmentally Friendly Fuel of the Future?" *Biomass and Bioenergy* 15 (4/5): 357–67.

Hall, D O, Rosillo-Calle F, R.H. Williams, and J. Woods. 1993. "Biomass for Energy: Supply, Prospects." In T.B.J. Johansson and others, eds., *Renewable Energy for Fuels and Electricity.* Washington, D.C.: Island Press.

Hatfield, C.B. 1997. "Oil Back on the Global Agenda." *Nature* 387: 121.

Hiller, K. 1999. "Verfügbarkeit von Erdöl [The Availability of Petroleum]." *Erdöl Erdgas Kohle* 115 (2): 50–54.

Hobbs, G.W. 1995. "Energy Minerals. Oil Shale, Coalbed Gas, Geothermal Trends Sized Up." *Oil and Gas Journal* 93 (37).

Holder, G.D., V.A. Kamath, and S.P. Godbole. 1984. "The Potential of Natural Gas Hydrates as an Energy Source." *Annual Review of Energy* 9: 427–45.

IEA (International Energy Agency. 1998a. *Biomass Energy: Data, Analysis and Trends.* Paris.

———. 1998b. *Energy Statistics and Balances of Non-OECD Countries, 1995–1996.* Paris.

———. 1998c. *World Energy Outlook.* Paris

———. 1999. *Key World Energy Statistics from the IEA.* Paris.

IGU (International Gas Union). 1997. *World Gas Prospects: Strategies and Economics.* Proceedings of the 20th World Gas Conference, 10–13 June, Copenhagen, Denmark.

———. 2000. *World Gas Prospects: Strategies and Economics.* Proceedings of the 21st World Gas Conference, 6–9 June, Nice, France.

International Water Power and Dam Construction. 1989. "The Increasing Importance of Power Plant Refurbishment." Sutton, Surrey, England: Business Press International.

———. 1998. *Water Power and Dam Construction Yearbook.* Sutton, Surrey, England: Business Press International.

IPCC (Intergovernmental Panel on Climate Change). 1996a. "Climate Change 1995." In R.T. Watson, M.C. Zinyowera, and R.H. Moss, eds., *Facts, Adaptations and Mitigation of Climate Change: Scientific-technical Analysis. Contribution of Working Group II to the Second Assessment Report of the Intergovernmental Panel on Climate Change.* Cambridge: Cambridge University Press.

———. 1996b. "Climate Change 1995: The Science of Climate Change." In J.T. Houghton, L.G. Meira Filho, B.A. Callander, N. Harris, A. Kattenberg, and K. Maskell, eds., *Contribution of Working Group I to the Second Assessment Report of the Intergovernmental Panel on Climate Change.* Cambridge: Cambridge University Press.

Ivanhoe, L.F., and G.G Leckie. 1993. "Global Oil, Gas Fields, Sizes Tallied, Analyzed." *Oil and Gas Journal* 15: 87–91.

Johansson, T.B., H. Kelly, A. K.N. Reddy, and H. Williams. 1993. "Appendix to Chapter 1: A Renewable-Intensive Global Energy Scenario." In T.B. Johansson, H. Kelly, K.N. Reddy, and R.H. Williams, eds., *Renewable Energy: Sources for Fuels and Electricity.* Washington, D.C.: Island Press.

Kaltschmitt, M., G.A. Reinhardt, and T. Stelzer. 1996. "LCA of Biofuels under Different Environmental Aspects." Universität Stuttgart, Institut für Energiewirtschaft und Rationelle Energieanwendung, Stuttgart, Germany.

Law, B.E., and C.W. Spencer. 1993. "Gas in Tight Reservoirs: An Emerging Major Source of Energy." In *The Future of Energy Gases.* Professional Paper 1570. Reston, Va.: U.S. Geological Survey.

Lowe, A.T, and C.T. Smith. 1997. "Environmental Guidelines for Developing Sustainable Energy Output from Biomass." *Biomass and Bioenergy* 13 (special issue): 187–328.

L'vovich, M.I. 1987. "Ecological Foundations of Global Water Resources Conservation." In D.J. McLaren and B. J Skinner, eds., *Resources and World Development.* Chichester, N.Y.: John Wiley & Sons.

MacDonald, G.J. 1990a. "The Future of Methane as an Energy Resource." *Annual Review of Energy* 15: 53–83.

———. 1990b. "Role of Methane Clathrates in Past and Future." *Climate Change* 16: 247–81.

MacKenzie, J.J. 1996. *Oil As a Finite Resource: When Is Global Production Likely to Peak?* Washington, D.C.: World Resources Institute.

Marsden, S. 1993. "A Survey of Natural Gas Dissolved in Brine." In *The Future of Energy Gases.* Professional Paper 1570. Reston, Va.: U.S. Geological Survey.

Masters, C.D., E.D. Attanasi, and D.H. Root. 1994. *World Petroleum Assessment and Analysis.* Proceedings of the 14th World Petroleum Congress. New York: John Wiley & Sons.

Max, M.D., R.E. Pellanbarg, and B.G. Hurdle. 1997. "Methane Hydrate, a Special Clathrate: Its Attributes and Potential." Report NRL/MR/6101-97-7926. Naval Research Laboratory. Washington D.C.

McCully, P. 1996. *Silenced Rivers: The Ecology and Politics of Large Dams.* London: ZED Books.

McKelvey, V.E. 1967. "Mineral Resource Estimates and Public Policy." *American Scientist* 60: 32–40.

Meadows, C.D., D. Meadows, J. Randers, and W.W. Behrens. 1972. *The Limits to Growth: A Report for the Club of Rome's Project on the Predicament of Mankind.* New York: Universe Books.

Meyer, R.F. 1997. *World Heavy Crude Oil Resources.* Proceedings of the 15th World Petroleum Congress. New York: John Wiley & Sons.

Moreira, J.R., and J. Goldemberg. 1999. "The Alcohol Program." *Energy Policy* 27: 229–45.

Moreira, J. R., and A.D. Poole. 1993. "Hydropower and Its Constraints." In T.B. Johansson H. Kelly, K.N. Reddy, and R.H. Williams, eds., *Renewable Energy: Sources for Fuels and Electricity.* Washington, D.C.: Island Press.

Nakićenović, N., A. Grübler, and A. McDonald, eds. 1998. *Global Energy Perspectives.* Cambridge: Cambridge University Press.

NEA (Nuclear Energy Agency) and IAEA (International Atomic Energy Agency). 1997. *Uranium Resources Production and Demand* ("Red Book"). Paris and Vienna: Organisation for Economic Co-operation and Development.

Nehring, R. 1998. "Knowledge, Technology Improvements Boosting U.S. Upstream Operations." *Oil and Gas Journal* 96 (44): 94–97.

Nobukawa, H., and others. 1994. "Development of a Floating Type System for Uranium Extraction from Seawater Using Sea Current and Wave Power." *Proceedings of the 4th (1994) International Offshore and Polar Engineering Conference.* Cupertino, Calif.: International Society of Offshore and Polar Engineers.

Odell, P.R. 1997. "Oil Reserves: Much More than Meets the Eye." *Petroleum Economist* 64: 29–31.

———. 1998. *Fossil Fuel Resources in the 21st Century.* Vienna: International Atomic Energy Agency.

Palmerini, C.G. 1993. "Geothermal Energy." In T.B. Johansson and others, eds., *Renewable Energy: Sources for Fuels and Electricity.* Washington, D.C.: Island Press.

PCAST (President's Committee of Advisors on Science and Technology), Panel on Energy Research and Development. 1997. *Report to the President on Federal Energy Research and Development for the Challenges of the Twenty-first Century.* Executive Office of the President, Washington D.C.

Penner, S.S., and others. 1982. "Assessment of Research Needs for Oil Recovery from Heavy Oil Sources and Tar Sands." *Energy* 7 (567).

Polikar, M., and T. Cyr. 1998. "Alberta Oil Sands: The Advance of Technology, 1978–1998 and Beyond." In *Proceedings of the 7th UNITAR International Conference on Heavy Crude and Tar Sands.* Paper 1998.002. Beijing, China.

Population Action International. 1997. "Why Population Matters. Population Action International." http://www.populationaction.org/why-pop/graph29.htm

Raabe, I.J. 1985. "Hydro Power: The Design, Use, and Function of Hydro-mechanical, Hydraulic, and Electrical Equipment." VDI-Verlarg, Düsseldorf, Germany.

Raskin, P., P. Gleick, P. Kirschen, G. Pontius, and K. Strzepek. 1997. *Water Futures: Assessment of Long-range Patterns and Problems.* Stockholm: Stockholm Environment Institute.

Ravindranath, N.H., and D.O. Hall. 1996. *Energy for Sustainable Development* 2: 14–20.

Rice, D.R., B.E. Law, and J.L. Clayton. 1993. "Coalbed Gas: An Undeveloped Resource." In *The Future of Energy Gases.* Professional Paper 1570. U.S. Geological Survey. Reston, Va.

Rijtman, P E., and D. Vries. 1994. "Differences in Precipitation Excess and Nitrogen Leaching from Agricultural Lands and Forest Plantations." *Biomass and Bioenergy* 6: 103–13.

Rogner, H-H. 1997. "An Assessment of World Hydrocarbon Resources." *Annual Review of Energy and the Environment* 22: 217–62.

Rosillo-Calle, F., M.E. Rezende, P. Furtado, and D.O. Hall. 1996. *The Charcoal Dilemma. Finding a Sustainable Solution for Brazilian Industry.* London: IT Publications.

Sadler, K., and R. Houlihan. 1998. "Oil Sands Development in Alberta: An EUB Perspective." In *Proceedings of the 7th UNITAR International Conference on Heavy Crude and Tar Sands.* Paper 1998.012. Beijing.

Schollnberger, W.E. 1998. "Gedanken über die Kohlenwasserstoffreserven der Erde. Wie lange können sie vorhalten? [Reflections on Global Hydrocarbon Reserves: How Long Will These Last?]" In J. Zemann, ed., *Energievorräte und mineralische Rohstoffe: Wie lange noch? [Energy Resources and Mineral Resources].* Vienna: Verlag der Österreichischen Akademie der Wissenschaften.

Seckler, D., U. Amarasinghe, D. Molden, R. de Silva, and R. Barker. 1998. *World Water Demand and Supply, 1990 to 2025: Scenarios and Issues.* Research Report 19. Colombo, Sri Lanka: International Water Management Institute.

Shapouri, H., J.A. Duffield, and M.S. Graboski. 1995. *Estimating the Net Energy Balance of Corn Ethanol.* Econ. Res. Serv. Rep. 721. U.S. Department of Agriculture, Washington, D.C.

Shell. 1996. *The Evolution of the World's Energy System.* Group External Affairs, London.

Shiklomanov, I.A. 1993. "World Fresh Water Resources." In P.H. Gleick, ed., *Water in Crisis: A Guide to the World's Fresh Water Resources.* Oxford: Oxford University Press.

Smith, C.T. 1995. "Environmental Consequences of Intensive Harvesting." *Biomass and Bioenergy* 27 (10): 161–79.

Sørensen, B. 1979. *Renewable Energy.* London: Academic Press.

Stosur, G.J., S.L. Waisley, T.B. Reid, and L.C. Marchant. 1998. "Tar Sands: Technologies, Economics, and Environmental Issues for Commercial Production beyond the Year 2000." In *Proceedings of the 7th UNITAR International Conference on Heavy Crude and Tar Sands.* Paper 1998.002. Beijing.

Taylor, J. 1989. "Extending the Operating Life of Hydro Equipment." *International Water Power and Dam Construction Yearbook.* Sutton, Surrey, England. Buisness Press International.

Tolbert, V. 1998. "Environmental Effects of Biomass Crop Production. What Do We Know? What Do We Need to Now?" *Biomass and Bioenergy* (special issue): 1301–1414.

Turnure, J.T., S. Winnett, R. Shackleton, and W. Hohenstein. 1995. "Biomass Electricity: Long-run Economic Prospects and Climate Policy Implications." In *Proceedings of the Second Biomass Conference of the Americas.* Golden, Colo.: National Renewable Energy Laboratory.

UNCED (United Nations Conference on Environment and Development). 1993. *Agenda 21: Resolutions Adopted by the Conference.* Document A/Conf. 151/26/REV.1. New York.

USDOE (United States Department of Energy). 1998. *A Strategy for Methane Hydrates Research and Development.* Office of Fossil Energy, Washington, D.C.

UNDP (United Nations Development Programme). 1997. *Energy after Rio: Prospects and Challenges.* Sustainable Energy and Environment Division, Energy and Atmosphere Programme, New York.

UNEP (United Nations Environment Programme). 1985. "The Environmental Impacts of Exploitation of Oil Shales and Tar Sands." Energy Report Series, ERS-13-85. Nairobi, Kenya.

UNESC (United Nations Economic and Social Council). 1997. "United Nations International Framework Classification for Reserves/Resources." Economic Commission for Europe, Geneva.

USGS (U.S. Geological Survey). 1980. "Principles of a Resource/Reserve Classification for Minerals." U.S. Geological Survey Circular 831.

WEC (World Energy Council). 1994. *New Renewable Energy Resources: A Guide to the Future.* London: Kogan Page Limited.

———. 1998. *Survey of Energy Resources.* 18th ed. London. WEC.

WHO (World Health Organization). 1982. *Environmental Health Criteria 20: Selected Petroleum Products.* Geneva.

———. 1997. *Health and Environment in Sustainable Development: Five Years after the Earth Summit.* Geneva.

Woods, J., and D.O. Hall. 1994. "Bioenergy for Development." FAO Paper 13. Food and Agriculture Organisation, Rome.

World Atlas and Industry Guide. 1998. "Annual Summary." *International Journal on Hydropower and Dams.* Sutton, Surrey: Aqua-Média International.

WRI (World Resources Institute). 1998. *World Resources 1998–99.* Oxford: Oxford University Press.

energy end~use efficiency

CHAPTER 6

Eberhard Jochem (Germany)

LEAD AUTHORS: Anthony Adegbulugbe (Nigeria), Bernard Aebischer (Switzerland), Somnath Bhattacharjee (India), Inna Gritsevich (Russia), Gilberto Jannuzzi (Brazil), Tamas Jaszay (Hungary), Bidyut Baran Saha (Japan), Ernst Worrell (United States), and Zhou Fengqi (China)

CONTRIBUTING AUTHORS: Mohamed Taoufik Adyel (Morocco), John Akinbami (Nigeria), David Bonilla (Japan), Allen Chen (United States), Alexander Kolesov (Russia), Hans Florentin Krause (United States), Wilhelm Mannsbart (Germany), Tim McIntosch (Canada), Louise Metivier (Canada), Folasade Oketola (Nigeria), David Pelemo (Nigeria), Jean Pierre Des Rosiers (France), Lee Schipper (United States), and XiuJian Hu (China)

ABSTRACT Since the 1970s more efficient energy use in OECD countries has weakened or eliminated the link between economic growth and energy use. At the global level just 37 percent of primary energy is converted to useful energy—meaning that nearly two-thirds is lost. The next 20 years will likely see energy efficiency gains of 25–35 percent in most industrialised countries and more than 40 percent in transition economies. Dematerialization and recycling will further reduce energy intensity. Thus energy efficiency is one of the main technological drivers of sustainable development world-wide.

Energy policy has traditionally underestimated the benefits of end-use efficiency for society, the environment, and employment. Achievable levels of economic efficiency depend on a country's industrialisation, motorization, electrification, human capital, and policies. But their realisation can be slowed by sector- and technology-specific obstacles—including lack of knowledge, legal and administrative obstacles, and the market power of energy industries. Governments and companies should recognise innovations that can lower these obstacles. The external costs of energy use can be covered by energy taxes, environmental legislation, and greenhouse gas emissions trading. There is also an important role for international harmonisation of regulations for efficiency of traded products. Rapid growth in demand provides especially favourable conditions for innovations in developing countries—enabling these countries to leapfrog stages of development if market reforms are also in place.

The economic potentials of more efficient energy use will continue to grow with new technologies and with cost reductions resulting from economies of scale and learning effects. Considerations of the second law of thermodynamics at all levels of energy conversion and technological improvements at the level of useful energy suggest further potential for technical efficiency of almost one order of magnitude that may become available during this century. Finally, structural changes in industrialised and transition economies—moving to less energy-intensive production and consumption—will likely contribute to stagnant or lower energy demand per capita in these countries. ■

More efficient energy use
is one of the main options for
achieving global sustainable
development in the
21st century.

T oday more than 400,000 petajoules a year of primary energy deliver almost 300,000 petajoules of final energy to customers, resulting in an estimated 150,000 petajoules of useful energy after conversion in end-use devices. Thus 250,000 petajoules are lost, mostly as low- and medium-temperature heat. Globally, then, the energy efficiency of converting primary to useful energy is estimated at 37 percent. Moreover, considering the capacity to work (that is, the exergy) of primary energy relative to the exergy needed by useful energy according to the second law of thermodynamics, the efficiency of today's energy systems in industrialised countries is less than 15 percent. But energy efficiency can be improved—and energy losses avoided—during the often overlooked step between useful energy and energy services (figure 6.1).

One main goal of energy analysis in the context of sustainable development is to explore ways to reduce the amount of energy used to produce a service or a unit of economic output—and, indirectly, to reduce related emissions. Two questions are key: How tight is the link between final energy use and the energy service in a given end use? And what is the potential for technological and organisational changes to weaken that link in the next 10–20 years? Because the technologies used in different regions differ substantially, the potential for economic efficiency varies. Still, more efficient energy use is one of the main options for achieving global sustainable development in the 21st century.

This chapter focuses on end-use energy efficiency—that is, more efficient use of final energy or useful energy in industry, services, agriculture, households, transportation, and other areas (see figure 6.1). Supply-side energy efficiency (energy extraction, conversion, transportation, and distribution) is treated in chapters 5 and 8. Supply-side efficiency has been the focus of energy investment and research and development since the early 20th century. End-use efficiency has received similar attention only since the mid-1970s, having been proven cheaper in many cases but often more difficult to achieve for reasons discussed below.

Energy efficiency—and indirectly, improved material efficiency— alleviates the conflicting objectives of energy policy. Competitive and low (but full-cost) energy prices support economic development. But they increase the environmental burden of energy use. They also increase net imports of conventional energies and so tend to decrease the diversity of supply. Using less energy for the same service is one way to avoid this conflict. The other way is to increase the use of renewable energies (chapter 7).

Recent trends in energy intensity in countries and regions

A sector's energy use, divided by gross domestic product (GDP), is the starting point for understanding differences in the efficient use of final energy by sector, country, or period. With few exceptions, such analyses have been carried out over long periods only in OECD countries (IEA, 1997a; Morovic and others, 1989; Diekmann and others, 1999). These ratios are instructive for what they say about energy use in different economies at a given point in time. They can also be used to measure changes in energy efficiency and other components of energy use— such as changes in the structure and consumption of a given sector or subsector. Changes in energy efficiency are driven by higher prices, technical improvements, new technologies, cost competition, and energy conservation programmes.

OECD countries

Over the past 30 years every OECD country and region saw a sharp decline in ratios of energy to GDP (figure 6.2; box 6.1).[1] Changes in energy use were distributed unevenly among sectors, however, and only part of the decline was related to increased energy efficiency:

- Industry experienced the largest reductions in ratios of energy to GDP—between 20 and 50 percent. Energy efficiency (if structural change is excluded by holding constant the mix of output in 1990) increased by more than 1 percent a year through the late 1980s, after which lower fuel prices caused a slowdown in improvements (Diekmann and others, 1999). In Japan, the United States, and West Germany the absolute demand for energy by industry dropped about 10 percent because of changes in the mix of products. In other countries structural changes had little impact on energy use.

- Among households, energy requirements per unit of floor area fell modestly, led by space heating. Despite far more extensive indoor heating (with more central heating), in almost all OECD countries energy use was lower in the 1990s than in the early 1970s. (The only notable exception was Japan, where income-driven improvements in heating outweighed savings from added insulation in new buildings and from more efficient heating equipment.) In addition, in most countries the unit consumption of appliances (in kilowatt-hours per year) fell. Increased efficiency outpaced trends towards larger appliances. On the structural side, however, household size continued to shrink, raising per capita energy use. New homes had larger areas per capita and more appliances, continuing an income effect dating from the early 1950s.

- Space heating in the service sector also required less energy—in heat per square metre—in most OECD countries. Electricity use remained closely tied to service sector GDP, but showed little upward trend except where electric heating was important. This outcome may be surprising given the enormous importance of electrification and office automation in the service sector. Over time there is a close relationship between electricity use and floor area.

- In passenger transportation, energy use is dominated by cars and in a few countries (such as the United States) by light trucks. In Canada and the United States in the early 1990s fuel use per

FIGURE 6.1. ENERGY CONVERSION STEPS, TYPES OF ENERGY, AND ENERGY SERVICES: POTENTIALS FOR ENERGY EFFICIENCY

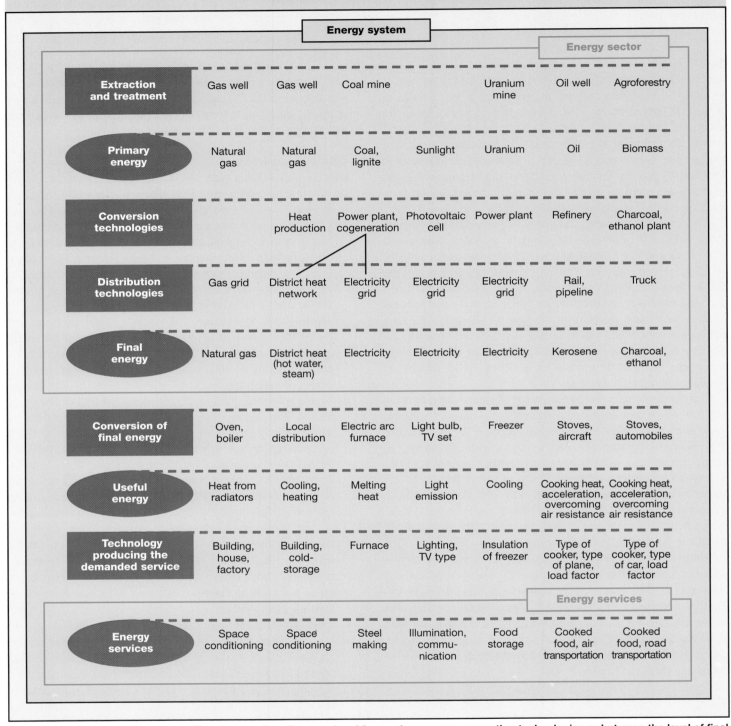

Energy system

Energy sector

Extraction and treatment	Gas well	Gas well	Coal mine		Uranium mine	Oil well	Agroforestry
Primary energy	Natural gas	Natural gas	Coal, lignite	Sunlight	Uranium	Oil	Biomass
Conversion technologies		Heat production	Power plant, cogeneration	Photovoltaic cell	Power plant	Refinery	Charcoal, ethanol plant
Distribution technologies	Gas grid	District heat network	Electricity grid	Electricity grid	Electricity grid	Rail, pipeline	Truck
Final energy	Natural gas	District heat (hot water, steam)	Electricity	Electricity	Electricity	Kerosene	Charcoal, ethanol
Conversion of final energy	Oven, boiler	Local distribution	Electric arc furnace	Light bulb, TV set	Freezer	Stoves, aircraft	Stoves, automobiles
Useful energy	Heat from radiators	Cooling, heating	Melting heat	Light emission	Cooling	Cooking heat, acceleration, overcoming air resistance	Cooking heat, acceleration, overcoming air resistance
Technology producing the demanded service	Building, house, factory	Building, cold-storage	Furnace	Lighting, TV type	Insulation of freezer	Type of cooker, type of plane, load factor	Type of cooker, type of car, load factor
Energy services	Space conditioning	Space conditioning	Steel making	Illumination, communication	Food storage	Cooked food, air transportation	Cooked food, road transportation

Energy services

Potential improvements in energy efficiency are often discussed and focused on energy-converting technologies or between the level of final energy and useful energy. But one major potential of energy efficiency, often not strategically considered, is realised at the level of energy services by avoiding energy losses through new technologies. Such technologies include new building materials and window systems, membrane techniques instead of thermal separation, sheet casting instead of steel rolling, biotechnology applications, and vehicles made of lighter materials such as plastics and foamed metals. Energy storage and reuse of break energy, along with better designs and organisational measures, can also increase energy efficiency.

kilometre by light-duty vehicles was 30 percent below its 1973 level, though by 1995 reductions had ceased (figure 6.3). Reductions ceased relative to person-kilometres because there were only 1.5 people per car in the mid-1990s, compared with more than 2.0 in 1970. Europe saw only small (less than 15 percent) reductions in fuel use per kilometre by cars, almost all of which were offset by a similar drop in load factors. Taxes on gasoline and diesel seem to be the main influence on the average efficiency of the car fleet, with the lowest taxes in the United States (averaging $0.10 a litre) and the highest in France ($0.74 a litre). For air travel, most OECD countries experienced more than a 50 percent drop in fuel use per passenger-kilometre due to improved load factors and increased fuel efficiency. Higher mobility per capita and shifts from trains, buses, and local transport towards cars and air travel, however, counterbalanced the efficiency gains in most countries.

■ Freight transport experienced rather small changes in energy use per tonne-kilometre. Improvements in fuel efficiency were offset by a shift towards trucking. This shift was driven by higher GDP, less shipping of bulk goods by rail and ship, and more lifting of high-value partially manufactured and final goods by trucks and aeroplanes.

In most OECD countries energy intensities fell less rapidly in the 1990s than before. One clear reason—besides higher income—was lower energy prices since 1986 and lower electricity prices (due to the liberalisation of the electricity market in many OECD countries), which slowed the rate of energy efficiency improvement for new systems and technologies.

Eastern Europe and the Commonwealth of Independent States

Relative to OECD countries, the statistical basis for ratios of energy to GDP is somewhat limited in Eastern Europe and the Commonwealth of Independent States.[3] Ratios of primary energy demand to GDP have risen in the Commonwealth of Independent States since 1970 (Dobozi, 1991) but began to decline in many Eastern European countries in the mid-1980s (table 6.1). General shortcomings of central planning, an abundance of energy resources in some countries, a large share of heavy industries, low energy prices, and a deceleration of technological progress have been the main reasons for limited progress (Radetzki, 1991; Dobozi, 1991; Sinyak, 1991; Gritsevich, 1993).

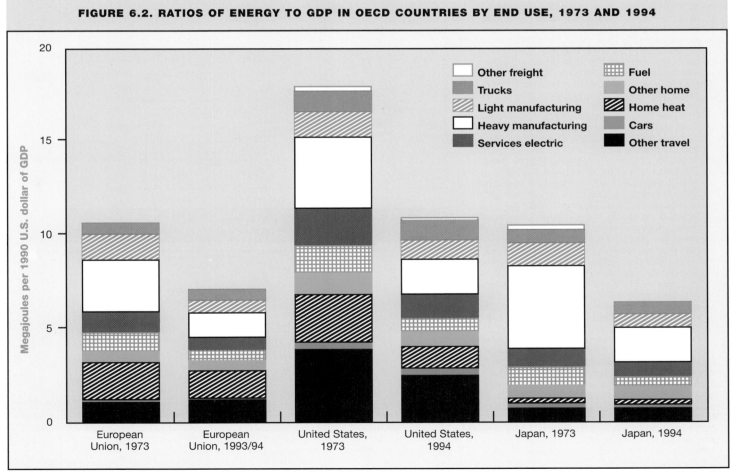

FIGURE 6.2. RATIOS OF ENERGY TO GDP IN OECD COUNTRIES BY END USE, 1973 AND 1994

Note: Measured using purchasing power parity.

Source: Schipper, 1997.

Like ratios of energy to GDP, the production of energy-intensive materials per unit of GDP is falling in almost all industrialised countries (with a few exceptions such as Australia, Iceland, and Russia). Changes in the production of basic materials may affect changes in ratios of energy to GDP. In many OECD countries declining production of steel and primary aluminium is supporting lower ratios of energy to GDP. But production of young, energy-intensive materials—such as polymers substituting for traditional steel or aluminium use—is increasing relative to GDP. In addition, ratios of energy-intensive materials to GDP are increasing slightly in developing countries, almost balancing out the declines in industrialised countries for steel and primary aluminium over the past 25 years.

Dematerialization has different definitions covering the absolute or relative reduction in the quantity of material used to produce a unit of economic output. In its relative definition of tonnes or volumes of material used per unit of GDP, dematerialization has occurred over several decades in many industrial countries. This shift has contributed to structural changes in industry—particularly in energy-intensive areas such as chemicals and construction materials (Carter, 1996; Jaenicke, 1998; Hinterberger, Luks, and Schmidt-Bleek, 1997).

A number of forces are driving dematerialization in industrialised countries (Ayres, 1996; Bernadini, 1993):

- As incomes rise, consumer preferences shift towards services with lower ratios of material content to price.
- As economies mature, there is less demand for new infrastructure (buildings, bridges, roads, railways, factories), reducing the need for steel, cement, non-ferrous metals, and other basic materials.
- Material use is more efficient—as with thinner car sheets, thinner tin cans, and lighter paper for print media.
- Cheaper, lighter, more durable, and sometimes more desirable materials are substituted—as with the substitution of plastics for metal and glass, and fibre optics for copper.
- Recycling of energy-intensive materials (steel, aluminium, glass, paper, plastics, asphalt) contributes to less energy-intensive production. Recycling may be supported by environmental regulation and taxes (Angerer, 1995).
- Reuse of products, longer lifetimes of products (Hiessl, Meyer-Krahmer, and Schön, 1995), and intensified use (leasing, renting, car sharing) decrease new material requirements per unit of service.
- Industrialised countries with high energy imports and energy prices tend to decrease their domestic production of bulk materials, whereas resource-rich developing countries try to integrate the first and second production steps of bulk materials into their domestic industries (Cleveland and Ruth, 1999).

But industrialised countries are also experiencing some of the drivers of increased material use per capita. Increasing urbanisation, mobility, and per capita incomes increase the demand for material-intensive infrastructure, buildings, and products. Smaller households, the increasing importance of suburban communities and shopping centres, and second homes create additional mobility. The move from repair to replacement of products and trends towards throwaway products and packaging work against higher material efficiencies—and, hence, against energy efficiency and sustainable development.

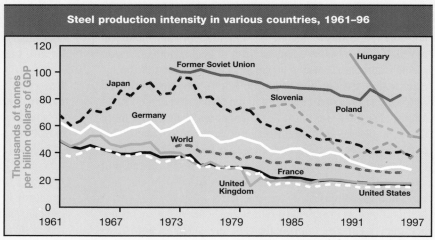

Steel production intensity in various countries, 1961–96

Source: IEA, 1998; Wirtschaftvereinigung Stahl, 1998.

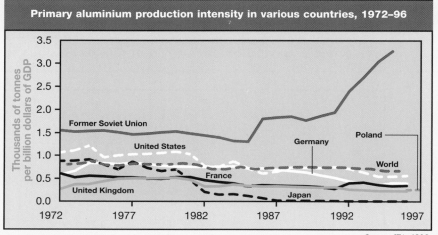

Primary aluminium production intensity in various countries, 1972–96

Source: IEA, 1998.

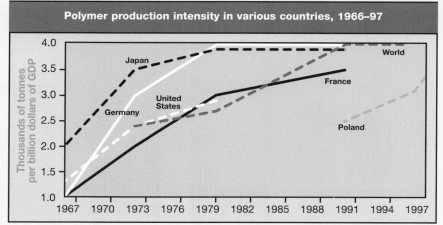

Polymer production intensity in various countries, 1966–97

Note: For the world, includes all plastics. For France, Germany, Japan, and the United States, includes only polyethylene, polypropylene, polystyrene, and polyvinylchloride.

Source: UN, 1999; German Federal Statistical Office; IEA 1998.

Ratios of primary energy to GDP have gone through two phases in these countries, separated by the onset of economic and political reform in the late 1980s and the 1990s. Whereas the ratio increased in Russia, it declined in Armenia, Belarus, Estonia, Kyrgyzstan, Latvia, and Tajikistan. Among the other members of the Commonwealth of Independent States the ratio fluctuated for reasons other than improvements in energy efficiency (IEA, 1997a, 1998). Since 1990 the ratio has declined in most Eastern European countries (see table 6.1).

- In industry, final energy consumption per unit of output fell less than 1 percent a year in Eastern Europe in 1990–97 but increased almost 7 percent a year in Russia (CENEf, 1998).

- Transportation saw few changes in energy use per passenger-kilometre or tonne-kilometre for the two main modes, cars and trucks.

- Among households, small gains in the thermal integrity of buildings could not overcome increasing demands for heating and comfort. Indeed, in the mid-1980s centrally heated Eastern European buildings required 50–100 percent more final energy per unit of area and per degree day (that is, using standardised winter outdoor temperatures) than similar buildings in Western Europe. Moreover, home appliances were often small and inefficient.

In the early 1990s economic reforms began to restructure production and consumption patterns and raise once-subsidised energy prices. In the Baltics, the Czech Republic, Hungary, and Poland this phase led to real declines in ratios of primary energy to GDP as efficiency increased and the structure of manufacturing changed (see table 6.1). Several transition economies also saw lower household fuel use for space and water heating. Such changes were often not related to efficiency, however, and were instead caused by energy shortages, higher energy prices, and related changes in heating behaviour.

Overall, transition economies showed a remarkable contraction in energy use by industry, mostly because of structural changes (Bashmakov, 1997a). But this trend has nearly been outweighed by rapid growth in road transportation and (in some countries) in electricity for appliances and services. Structural changes in industry, integration with global markets, and investments in new processes, buildings, and infrastructure are expected to improve energy efficiency considerably over the next 20 years. These trends will likely help stabilise energy demand despite rising incomes and GDP in these countries.

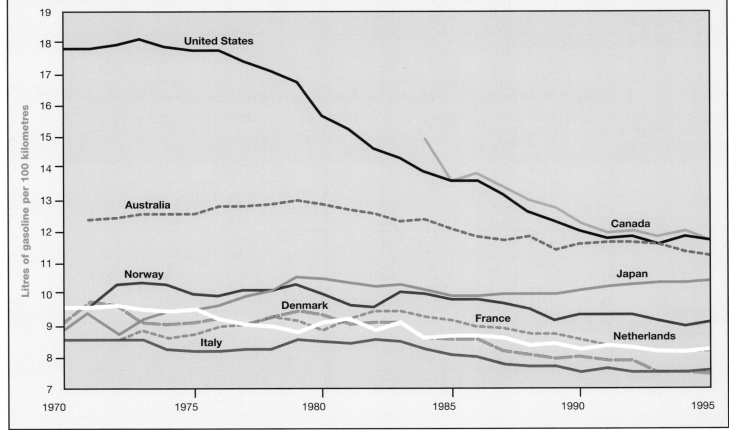

FIGURE 6.3. WEIGHTED AVERAGE OF ON-ROAD AUTOMOBILE GASOLINE AND DIESEL FUEL INTENSITIES IN OECD COUNTRIES, 1970–95

Source: Schipper, 1997.

Developing Asia, Africa, and Latin America

In many developing countries energy use will be driven by industrialisation, urbanisation, increasing road transportation, and increasing personal incomes.[4] Indeed, per capita energy use in developing countries tends to be higher where per capita incomes are higher (in purchasing power parity terms), as in Latin America, India, and Southeast Asia. Wide income disparities in many developing countries are also reflected in energy consumption patterns. Often a small portion of the population accounts for most commercial energy demand. Data limitations hamper careful analysis in many developing countries, however.

Higher-income developing countries (per capita income above $1,200 in 1998 purchasing power parity terms). Energy demand in industry has fallen in most higher-income developing countries, both as a result of higher energy prices in the 1970s and 1980s and open borders to international competition. China has shown the most dramatic developments, but most Latin American and other Asian economies have also shown energy intensity improvements in this sector. In recent years many manufacturers in industrialised nations have moved energy-intensive industries to developing countries, often to take advantage of cheaper labour, less stringent environmental

TABLE 6.1. RATIOS OF PRIMARY ENERGY TO GDP IN TRANSITION ECONOMIES, 1985–96

Region/country	Energy consumption per capita, 1996 (gigajoules)	Megajoules per unit of GDP (1990 purchasing power parity dollars)		
		1985	1990	1995
Commonwealth of Independent States	**135**	**29.8**	**29.4**	**41.4**
Belarus	100			20.5
Russia	170			36.8
Ukraine	127			45.2
Eastern Europe	**89**[a]	**23.9**	**21.8**	**20.9**
Bulgaria	120	36.0	29.7	31.8
Czech Republic	165	23.6	19.6	18.2
Hungary	108	18.3	16.5	16.3
Poland	117	26.5	21.6	19.2
Romania	84	28.5	31.8	25.1
Slovenia[b]	124		12.6	13.8
Former Yugoslavia	53[a]	12.6	14.7	21.4

a. Data are for 1995. b. Based on exchange rates.

Source: IEA, 1997a, Kos, 1999.

TABLE 6.2. RATIOS OF PRIMARY ENERGY TO GDP IN DEVELOPING COUNTRIES, 1975–95

Country or region	Energy consumption per capita, 1996 (gigajoules)	Megajoules per unit of GDP (1990 purchasing power parity dollars)				
		1975	1980	1985	1990	1995
China	36.3[a]	23.4	22.6	17.3	15.0	10.9
India	14.6[a]	7.5	7.8	8.3	8.7	9.2
Indonesia	18.4	3.3	4.2	4.6	5.4	5.4
Argentina	64.1	8.0	8.4	9.2	9.6	9.6
Brazil	61.0[a,b]	4.6	4.6	5.0	5.4	5.9
Mexico	61.4	7.2	8.2	8.5	8.7	8.7
Venezuela	94.0[a]	10.5	11.3	12.6	12.1	12.1
North Africa[c]	29.2	5.4	6.3	7.9	8.8	9.4
Southern Africa[d]	27.4	10.8	11.6	15.2	13.9	14.4
Rest of Africa	2.5	2.6	2.9	2.6	2.6	2.9
Middle East	80.4	8.4	10.9	17.6	20.9	22.6

a. Data are for 1996. b. Includes non-commercial energy. c. Ratios of energy to GDP are for Algeria, Egypt, Libya, Morocco, and Tunisia. d. Ratios of energy to GDP are for Nigeria, South Africa, Zambia, and Zimbabwe.

Source: EC, various years; IEA, 1998.

regulation, and lower overhead and transportation costs. Many of these countries (Brazil, China, India, Indonesia) also need their own basic product industries.

Household appliances, cookers, and water heaters have become more energy efficient in higher-income developing countries. But the rapid acquisition of household devices has far outpaced the impact of greater efficiency.

A similar trend has occurred in the service and public sectors. Buildings in warm higher-income developing countries have increasing rates of air conditioning. Higher lighting levels, increased office automation, and other developments have also contributed to rapidly rising electricity use in this sector (IEA, 1997b).

Transportation accounts for a rising share of energy use in higher-income developing countries. Growing numbers of vehicles, often rising at 1.5 times the rate of GDP growth, have dominated the transportation energy use picture. Many cars and light trucks sold in the developing world have become less fuel intensive. But increased urbanisation and traffic congestion and reduced occupancy have eaten up many of the improvements in vehicle technology.

Overall, more efficient manufacturing does not dominate the increase in ratios of primary energy to GDP in higher-income developing countries (Argentina, Brazil, India, Mexico). Increasing numbers of cars and trucks, electrification of rural areas, and increased energy use by households have played a bigger role (table 6.2). Such energy uses were hardly mature before the 1970s. Motor vehicles and household appliances were far more expensive, in real terms, than they are today. Today such items are less costly and, more important, are often made in developing countries. (China is an exception to this pattern. In 1978, when it initiated economic reform, China exploited economies of scale in manufacturing—such as steel-making—to realise high efficiency improvements in industry and energy.)

Lower-income developing countries (per capita income below $1,200 in 1998 purchasing power parity terms). The situation in lower-income developing countries is somewhat different.

■ When disposable income increases, energy consumption by households in low-income developing countries shifts from traditional to commercial fuels. This trend has significant implications for energy efficiency in households. Since the technical efficiencies of cooking appliances using commercial fuels are higher than those of biomass, composite energy consumption per household tends to fall. A typical example is the move from a fuelwood stove with a technical efficiency of 12–18 percent to a kerosene stove with an efficiency of 48 percent, or to a liquefied petroleum gas stove with an efficiency of 60 percent. On the other hand, the substitution of commercial for traditional fuels raises ratios of energy to GDP, because traditional energy is typically not included when such ratios are calculated. In addition, electrification in rural areas and increasing income and mobility in urbanising areas increase energy use.

■ Most of the technology used by industry in lower-income developing countries is imported from industrialised countries. Thus these

industries should continue to benefit from technological improvements that promote rational energy use (see below). While this is expected to make energy demand fall, the use of obsolete and energy-inefficient technology imported from industrialised countries will drive the specific energy demand of industry.

■ Similarly, the transportation sector should benefit from the global trend towards improving vehicle fuel efficiency. Because lower-income developing countries import vehicles from other countries, the energy intensity of road transport should decrease. But the large share of used vehicles imported by lower-income developing countries is helping to maintain a relatively old car stock with high specific fuel demand.

Energy intensity in lower-income developing countries will largely depend on the interplay between these factors. Although available data (which are patchy at best) show that, for example, Africa's ratio of energy to GDP increased by 1.8 percent a year in 1975–95, that trend may be substantially influenced by the substitution of commercial for non-commercial forms of energy.

Potential benefits of technology transfer

In many cases used factories, machines, and vehicles from industrialised countries are transferred to developing or transition economies, saddling them with inefficient equipment and vehicles for many years.[5] The transfer of energy-efficient equipment and vehicles to developing and transition economies offers an important opportunity for leapfrogging the typical development curves of energy intensity and for achieving sustainable development while maximising know-how transfer and employment opportunities. The transfer of energy-efficient technology represents a win-win-situation for the technology provider and the recipient. Benefits on the receiving end include reduced energy imports, increased demand for skilled workers, job creation, reduced operating costs of facilities, and faster progress in improving energy efficiency. The scope for improving energy efficiency through technology transfer can be seen by comparing energy uses in various industries and countries (table 6.3).

TABLE 6.3. FINAL ENERGY USE IN SELECTED INDUSTRIES AND COUNTRIES, MID-1990S (GIGAJOULES PER TONNE)

Country	Steel	Cement	Pulp and paper
India	39.7	8.4	46.6
China	27.5–35.0	5.9	
United States	25.4	4.0	40.6
Sweden	21.0	5.9	31.6
Japan	17.5	5.0	

Source: Lead authors.

Used equipment and vehicles are traded for lack of capital, lack of life-cycle costing by investors, the investor-user dilemma (see below), and lack of public transportation in developing countries (President's Committee of Advisors on Science and Technology, 1999, p. 4-3; IPCC, 1999b). Thus high efficiency standards for products, machinery, and vechicles in OECD countries will also affect standards in developing and transition economies, particularly for mass-produced and tradable products and for world-wide investments by global players. Opportunities for technology transfer among developing countries will also become more important and should be encouraged. Many of these countries already have well-established domestic expertise and produce goods, technologies, and services suitable for the conditions and climates of other developing countries.

Transition economies

About 40 percent of the fuel consumed in transition economies is used in low-temperature heat supply. Slightly less than half of that heat is directed by district heating systems to residential buildings, public services (schools, kindergartens, hospitals, government agencies), and commercial customers (shops and the like). District heating systems exist in many cities containing more than 20,000 people. In many transition economies a significant share of the building stock (about 20 percent in Hungary) was built using prefabricated concrete panels with poor heat insulation and air infiltration.

Advanced Western technology (automated heat distribution plants, balancing valves, heat mirrors, efficient taps, showerheads, heat-reflecting layers of windows) offers significant potential for more efficient heat use in buildings (Gritsevich, Dashevsky, and Zhuze, 1997). Such technology can save up to 30 percent of heat and hot water and increase indoor comfort. Among the main advantages of Western products are their reliability, efficiency, accuracy, design, and sometimes competitive prices. Some Western companies have launched joint ventures with Eastern European, Ukrainian, and Russian partners or created their own production lines using local workers. In many cases this seems to be a better option than imports, because underemployed factories and human capital may otherwise induce conflicts of interest.

Many transition economies have developed advanced energy-efficiency technology (powder metallurgy, variable-speed drives for super-powerful motors, fuel cells for space stations, plasmic technologies to strengthen working surfaces of turbine blades). Thus the greatest benefits can be gained when domestic technology and human capital and an understanding of local conditions are combined with the best Western technology and practices.

Developing countries

Despite the many positive implications of transferring energy-efficient technology, some major issues need to be addressed to fully exploit the potential benefits to developing countries (UNDP, 1999):

Many developing countries do not have the infrastructure needed to study and evaluate all the technological options that might suit their needs.

■ *Proper technology assessment and selection.* The technology transfer process must help user enterprises evaluate their technological options in the context of their identified requirements (TERI, 1997a). Developing countries are at a great disadvantage in selecting technology through licensing. Companies develop technology mainly to suit their current markets; technology is not necessarily optimised for the conditions in recipient countries. Many developing countries do not have the infrastructure needed to study and evaluate all the technological options that might suit their needs. Moreover, an enterprise trying to sell a technology to a developing country will rarely give complete and unbiased advice. So, there is an urgent need to develop an information support system and institutional infrastructure to facilitate the selection of appropriate technologies. In India, for example, a Technology Development Board was established in 1996 to facilitate the assimilation and adaptation of imported technology (CMIE, 1997).

■ *Adaptation and absorption capability.* Technology transfer is not a one-time phenomenon. The transferred technology needs to be updated from time to time, either indigenously or through periodic imports. Moreover, lack of local capability can result in the transferred technology seldom reaching the designed operational efficiency, and often deteriorating significantly. This raises the need for local capacity building to manage technological change. In a narrower sense, this could be facilitated by policies requiring foreign technology and investment to be accompanied by adequate training of local staff (President's Committee of Advisors on Science and Technology, 1999).

■ *Access to state-of-the-art technology and to capital.* In many cases transferred technology is not state of the art, for several reasons. First, enterprises in industrialised countries need to recover the costs of technology development before transferring the technology to other countries, introducing a time lag in the process. Second, in some developing countries there is a demand lag for the latest technology due to factors such as lack of capital or trained staff. Third, there are inappropriate technology transfers because of the higher costs of acquiring state-of-the-art technology. A lack of capital and strong desire to minimise investment costs have often led developing countries to import obsolete used plants and machinery.

■ *The problems of small and medium-sized enterprises.* Small industrial enterprises account for a large share of energy and technology use in many developing countries. These enterprises may play an important role in the national economy but generally remain isolated from or ignorant of the benefits of technology upgrading. For such enterprises, where off-the-shelf solutions are seldom available, knock-down technology packages from industrialised countries are rarely possible. An important element of technology transfer for this group is proper competence pooling to arrive at appropriate technology solutions.

Again, the situation differs between higher- and lower-income developing countries. Several countries in Latin America and Southeast Asia are producing highly efficient technology and vehicles—electrical motors, refrigerator compressors, cars—through local companies or subsidiaries of multinational companies. Control systems, super-efficient windows, and new materials that improve the thermal insulation of buildings may offer further opportunities for technology transfer to higher-income developing countries (Hagler Bailley Services, 1997).

Types of potential for increased energy efficiency

As noted, the global energy efficiency of converting primary to useful energy is estimated to be 37 percent.[6] But the useful energy needed for a desired energy service will likely fall. Estimated improvements are based on known technologies, expected costs, consumer behaviour, market penetration rates, and policy measures. When considering the potential for increased energy efficiency, it is essential to distinguish between several types of potential, each describing future technological achievements with different time horizons and boundary assumptions (as well as level of analysis in the case of economic potential). This report uses the following definitions (Enquête Commission, 1991; IEA; 1997a; figure 6.4):

- The theoretical potential represents achievable energy savings under theoretical considerations of thermodynamics where energy services (such as air conditioning and steel production) are kept constant but useful energy demand and energy losses can be minimised through process substitution, heat and material reuse, and avoided heat losses (see section below on theoretical potentials after 2020).

- The technical potential represents achievable energy savings that result from implementing the most energy-efficient commercial and near-commercial technology available at a given time, regardless of cost considerations and reinvestment cycles. This can be expressed as a phased-in potential that reflects the total replacement of existing energy-converting and -using capital stocks.

- The market trend potential—or expected potential—is the efficiency improvement that can be expected to be realised for a projected year and given set of boundary conditions (such as energy prices, consumer preferences, and energy policies). The market trend potential reflects obstacles and market imperfections that keep

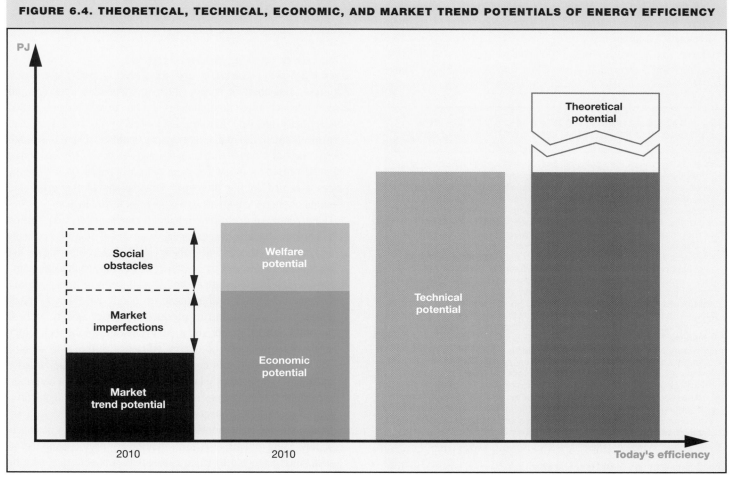

FIGURE 6.4. THEORETICAL, TECHNICAL, ECONOMIC, AND MARKET TREND POTENTIALS OF ENERGY EFFICIENCY

Source: Enquête Commission, 1991.

efficiency potentials from being fully realised (see the section below on obstacles).

■ The economic potential is the energy savings that would result if during each year over the time horizon in question, all replacements, retrofits, and new investments were shifted to the most energy-efficient technologies that are still cost-effective at given energy market prices. It also includes all organisational measures such as maintenance, sensitive operation and control, and timely repairs. The economic potential has subdefinitions depending on the economic perspective being used: the business (or project) perspective, the macroeconomic perspective, or the societal (or welfare-based) perspective (box 6.2). The economic potential implies a well-functioning market, with competition between investments in energy supply and demand. It also assumes that the barriers to such competition have been corrected by energy policies. It is assumed that as a result of such policies, all users have easy access to reliable information about the cost-effectiveness and technical performance of existing and emerging options for energy efficiency. The transaction costs for individual investors, and the indirect costs of policies associated with implementing these options, are assumed to have been lowered to their irreducible minimum.

■ The societal (or welfare-based) potential represents 'cost-effective' savings when externalities are taken into consideration. These

Achieving two benefits of increased energy efficiency—positive economic effects and reduced environmental burden—is called a 'double dividend'.

include damage or avoided damage costs from health impacts, air pollution, global warming, and other ecological impacts, as well as energy-related occupational accidents that accrue to society. This wider definition of cost-effectiveness is the most important for a holistic energy policy that includes energy security and environmental quality (OTA, 1993).

■ Finally, the policy-based achievable potential represents the energy savings that can be realised with various policy instruments or packages of policy instruments. Here field data are used to estimate participation rates and per participant savings in voluntary or standards-based technology programmes. The policy-based achievable potential lies between the market trend potential and the economic potential (which can be influenced by energy taxes).

This chapter focuses on the economic potential. The economic perspective underlying the potentials reported here, however, varies by study. Most current estimates are based on a business (financial) perspective, though there are also hybrids that use a macroeconomic perspective (see box 6.2). Quantitative comparisons between business and macroeconomic efficiency potentials suggest that microeconomic approaches underestimate the cost-effective savings potential (Krause, 1996). Similarly, macroeconomic approaches underestimate cost-effective savings potentials relative to a societal perspective.

The economic potential of energy efficiency by region and sector

Economic potentials of energy efficiency depend on current and foreseeable technology developments and on current and anticipated energy prices (box 6.3). In a world of low energy prices, the potential is relatively small. But high energy prices could be achieved through energy taxes at a national, regional, or global level. The economic potential presented below for each region is based on the energy prices assumed in the literature. Calculations of the economic potential of energy efficiency cover different technologies:

■ The potential of mono-functional and concise energy-converting technology (boilers, heat exchangers, electrical motors) is usually determined by standard profitability calculations comparing the full costs of alternative and statistically relevant conversion technology.

■ Process substitution and new building concepts or transportation systems include other changes in economic efficiency (capital, labour, and so on) and in product or service quality. Here it becomes difficult to talk about the profitability of the technology in the narrow sense of energy efficiency if the new, higher-efficiency technology is considered competitive in the broader sense (as with new catalysts in the production of petrochemicals, separation by membranes instead of energy-intensive distillation, or low-energy houses instead of conventional houses).

■ Branch-specific but technology-clustered energy efficiency potentials of low energy-intensive sectors in industry or the commercial sector are estimated by trend extrapolation of statistical data or by generalisation of calculations made for representative or typified

---

BOX 6.2. DIFFERENT PERSPECTIVES ON THE ECONOMIC POTENTIAL OF ENERGY EFFICIENCY

In all definitions of the economic potential of energy efficiency, the core cost-effectiveness test is the life-cycle cost of providing a given level of energy services. Different definitions of the economic potential arise because of different cost-benefit perspectives. These perspectives influence how costs and financial parameters are defined and whether policy-dependent implementation costs or reductions in external costs are included.

The economic potential at the business level is calculated from the perspective of an individual investor based on engineering and economic life-cycle costs, using a financial perspective. In this narrowest of all definitions, total costs consist of the levelised capital costs of energy efficiency investments plus changes in annual energy and non-energy operation and maintenance costs. Neither the costs of large-scale policy implementation nor the cost savings from policy-induced feedback effects are attached to this potential. The discount rate for evaluating the cost-effectiveness of energy efficiency investments is typically set to reflect the costs of capital of particular sectors, industries, or households. After-tax energy efficiency investments are compared to after-tax average energy prices as projected for each sector or group of energy users.

The macroeconomic potential is based on a more comprehensive accounting of costs and on a different financial perspective. Here the administrative costs of implementing various required policies are included. In addition, energy efficiency investment costs and policy implementation costs are corrected in a forward-looking manner to account for changes in manufacturer pricing strategies, economies of scale, and learning effects.

---

plants or factories. To avoid misinterpretation, data on branch-specific energy efficiency potentials should not include intrabranch structural changes (such as a shift of high value added but low energy-intensive pharmaceuticals to higher shares of total value added in the chemical industry).

These different cost assessments may help explain the differences in certainty about the economic potentials cited below. The data on economic potentials provide projections for 2010 and 2020. This means that where reinvestment cycles last more than 20 years (as with buildings, public transport, and plants of basic product industries), the economic potentials are only partly realised by 2020. The sectors and technological areas discussed in this section were chosen based on the relevance of the efficiency technology and the availability of the literature for the region or country considered.

Deviations from a given economic potential reflect changes in energy prices, economies of scale, or local differences. In many cases the life-cycle cost functions have rather broad minima (such as optimal insulation thickness), which means that there is little risk of overinvesting in energy efficiency or of overestimating the cited potentials.

Western Europe

Industry. Until the early 1990s industry was the largest consumer of final energy in Western Europe.[8] But despite production growth of about 2 percent a year, the final energy demand of Western European industry has hovered near 11,500 petajoules for the past 20 years. Yet industry still holds substantial economic efficiency potential, even in energy-intensive sectors where investment has focused on efficiency improvements to lower high energy costs (Phylipsen, Blok, and Worrell, 1998).

■ De Beer (1998, pp. 75–102) estimates that by 2020 paper mills operating with new pressing and drying techniques, latent heat recovery systems, and a number of minor improvements (closed water circulation, graduated heat recovery) will have 50 percent lower specific heat demand and that investment costs may be lower than for conventional paper-making (table 6.4). The economic efficiency potential of steel-making is less extraordinary, between 13 and 20 percent, and results from thin slab casting, more efficient blast furnaces, and minor improvements in the oxygen steel process by 2020 (Jochem and Bradke, 1996). Similar economic efficiency potential has been described for refineries (Refining Processes, 1998), petrochemical processes (Patel, 1999) and basic organic chemicals (Brewer and Lopez, 1998), construction materials (Rosemann and Ellerbrock, 1998; Ottoboni and others, 1998), glass production (ATLAS, 1997), and the food industry (Jochem and Bradke, 1996).

■ For Dutch light industry, the economic efficiency improvements in 2000 (relative to 1990) are estimated at 30 percent (with a 5 percent discount rate) and 27 percent (with a 10 percent discount rate; Blok and others, 1996; Böde and others, 1999).

■ Baumgartner and Muggli (1996) evaluated the efficiency improvements of cross-cutting technologies in Swiss industry. Savings of 15–35 percent were found for electrical and mechanical

drives over the next 10–15 years (Almeida, Bertoldi, and Leonhard, 1997). Metering, controlling, and optimal regulation can lead to efficiency improvements of up to 15 percent in most industrial processes. Cogeneration in Western Europe still holds economic potential, particularly with the midterm effects of liberalising electricity supply and small cogeneration (ATLAS, 1997; EC, 1999).

Residential. The economic efficiency potential in heating of residential buildings depends—besides regional aspects—on the stock of boilers and their reinvestment cycles, the rate of constructing new buildings, and the rate of refurbishing existing buildings. Condensing boilers are about 10 percent more energy efficient than a new low-temperature boiler and 15–25 percent more efficient than existing boilers (Ziesing and others, 1999). Insulation of building elements, highly efficient window systems, and adequately thick insulation are economic within the cycle of refurbishment (ETSU, 1994). In new buildings, low-energy houses (those with annual heat demand of 50–100 kilowatt-hours per square metre) are now cost-effective due to

---

BOX 6.3. ECONOMIC BENEFITS OF INCREASED ENERGY EFFICIENCY IN END USES—THE UNKNOWN DOUBLE DIVIDEND

Energy consumers benefit when profitable energy efficiency potentials are realised.[7] But the economy also benefits, because saved energy costs can be reallocated, energy imports are replaced (in many countries) by domestically produced energy-efficient products and (energy) services, and labour-intensive branches can grow in industry, construction, and services (instead of capital-intensive energy supply), spurring innovation. Macroeconomic analyses for Germany and the United States show that policies to improve energy efficiency and to shift to advanced technology and less carbon-intensive fuels generate four important benefits for the national economy (Jochem and Hohmeyer, 1992; Laitner, Bernow, and DeCicco, 1998). Such policies:

• Spur economic growth to a small degree (by less than 1 percent of the absolute growth rate of GDP) due to the reallocation of saved energy costs.

• Generate jobs (including entrepreneurial jobs that foster resourceful, self-sufficient, and satisfied workers) for the reasons mentioned above. Net employment increases by 40–60 new jobs per petajoule saved each year.

• Increase exports of high-technology products. In 1976–92 exports of 12 energy-efficient products increased more than 50 percent faster than West Germany's total exports.

• Reduce the environmental and social costs of energy use that were previously uncounted in market transactions for fuel. Such costs may be as high as $0.02 per kilowatt-hour of electricity (Friedrich and Krewitt, 1997) and almost $0.01 per kilowatt-hour of oil product used, not including the impacts of climate change (Hohmeyer, Ottinger, and Rennings, 1997).

Achieving two benefits of increased energy efficiency—positive economic effects and reduced environmental burden—is called a 'double dividend'. Unlike many other employment effects of investment, the jobs created by efficiency investments are not evenly distributed over time. In most cases they are created during the initial period of investment—when wall insulation is installed or investments are made in condensing boilers or high-efficiency window systems. In addition, the regional distribution of net employment becomes more equitable. Employment in the energy supply sector is concentrated in urban and industrial areas, while efficiency involves planners, crafts, trade, and banking in the entire country.

TABLE 6.4. ECONOMIC ENERGY EFFICIENCY POTENTIALS IN WESTERN EUROPE, 2010 AND 2020

Sector and technological area	Economic potential (percent)[a]		Energy price level assumed	Base year	Source
	2010	2020			
Industry					
Iron and steel, coke ovens	9–15	13–20	1994	1995	Jochem and Bradke, 1996; Ameling and others, 1998
Construction materials	5–10	8–15	1997	1997	
Glass production	10–15	15–25	1997	1997	ATLAS, 1997
Refineries	5–8	7–10	1995	1997	*Refining Processes,* 1998
Basic organic chemicals	5–10		1997	1996	Patel, 1999; Brewer and Lopez, 1998
Pulp and paper		50	1996	1997	De Beer, 1998
Investment and consumer goods	10–20	15–25	1994	1995	Jochem and Bradke, 1996; Böde and others, 1999
Food	10–15		1997	1997	Jochem and Bradke, 1996
Cogeneration in industry		10–20	1997	1997	ATLAS, 1997; EC, 1999
Residential					
Existing buildings					
Boilers and burners	15–20	20–25	today's prices	1997	ETSU, 1994; Böde and others,1999
Building envelopes	8–12	10–20	today's prices	1995	Ziesing and others, 1999
New buildings		20–30	today's prices	1995	Altner, Durr, Michelson, 1995
Electric appliances	20–30	35–45	1997	1997	GEA, 1995; ECODROME, 1999; Hennicke and others, 1998; Boardman and others, 1997
Commercial, public, and agriculture					
Commercial buildings	10–20	30	8–13 cts/kWh	1995	Geiger and others, 1999
Electricity	10–25	20–37	4–10 cts/kWh	1997	ECODROME, 1998
Heat		15–25	today's prices	1998	Zeising and others, 1999
Public buildings		30–40	7–15 cts/kWh	1992	Brechbühl, 1992
Agriculture and forestry		15–20	today's prices		Neyer and Strebel, 1996
Horticulture		20–30	today's prices		Arbeitsgemeinschaft, 1992
Decentralised cogeneration		20–30	today's prices	1995	Ravel, 1994
Office equipment		40–50	1995	1995	Aebischer and others, 1996; MACEBUR, 1998; Hallenga and Kok, 1998
Transportation					
Cars	25		today's prices	1995	IPSEP, 1995
Door-to-door integration	4			1995	Zeising and others, 1999
Modal split of freight transport		3[b]		1995	
Trains and railways		20	today's prices	1999	Brunner and Gartner, 1999
Aircraft, logistics	15–20	25–30	today's prices	1998	IPCC, 1999a

a. Assumes a constant structure or use of the sector or technology considered. b. Refers to the final energy use of the entire sector.

better design and low-cost insulation techniques and window sytems (Altner and others, 1995).

The economic efficiency potential of electric appliances in 2010 is best evaluated by comparing the equipment in use with the equipment available on the market. But the market is not homogeneous: a survey of washing machines, dryers, and dishwashers available in the European Union showed minimum:maximum ratios of specific consumption between 1:2.5 for washing machines and 1:4 for condenser tumble dryers (GEA, 1995). Initial costs are sometimes higher for efficient equipment, but life-cycle costs are generally lower. In France a detailed end-use study showed that electricity savings of 40 percent can be achieved by replacing average equipment with the most efficient appliances readily available on the market (Rath and others, 1997; ECODROME, 1998). These results are confirmed by Hennicke and others (1998) and Ziesing and others (1999). Given the relatively short lives of lights and appliances, savings of 33 percent could be achieved in the United Kingdom by 2010 with the widespread adoption of better lights and appliances using known technologies (Boardman and others, 1997).

Service and public sectors. In 1990 office equipment consumed just 3–4 percent of the electricity used in Western Europe's service sector (Aebischer, Schwarz, and Spreng, 1996). But office equipment is the fastest-growing consumer of electricity. About two-thirds of this electricity is used in standby and off modes. Thus easy and cost-effective savings are possible for most equipment (Hallenga and Kok, 1998; MACEBUR, 1998). With the fast increase in the amount of office equipment and its short lives, these improvements could be realised by 2010. Hennicke and others (1998) reports that 27–35 percent of the electricity consumed by Germany's service sector could be saved for $0.043–0.071 a kilowatt-hour.

The economic potential for reducing space and process heat demand in commercial buildings ranges from 15–25 percent (Ziesing and others, 1999; Aebischer and others,1996). The efficiency of heat generation and distribution could be improved by 10–15 percent through reinvestments in boilers, burners, and insulation and control techniques, in some cases by direct process heat generation (avoiding steam and hot water systems), and by engine-driven cogeneration.

TABLE 6.5. ECONOMIC ENERGY EFFICIENCY POTENTIALS IN NORTH AMERICA, 2010

Sector and area	Economic potential (percent)		Energy price level assumed	Base year	Source
	United States[a]	Canada			
Industry			United States: scenario for price developments[b]	United States: 1995	United States: Interlab, 1997; Brown and others, 1998; Romm, 1999
Iron and steel	4– 8	29			
Aluminium (primary)	2– 4				
Cement	4– 8			Canada: 1990	
Glass production	4– 8				
Refineries	4– 8	23	Canada: price scenario by province[c]		Canada: Jaccard and Willis, 1996; Bailie and others, 1998
Bulk chemicals	4– 9	18			
Pulp and paper	4– 8	9			
Light manufacturing	10–18				
Mining	n.a.	7			
Industrial minerals	n.a.	9			
Residential			United States: scenario for price developments	United States: 1995	United States: Interlab, 1997; Brown and others, 1998; OTA, 1992
Lighting	53				
Space heating	11–25				
Space cooling	16			Canada: 1990	
Water heating	28–29		Canada: price scenario		Canada: Bailie and others, 1998
Appliances	10–33				
Overall		13			
Commercial and public			United States: scenario for price developments	United States: 1995	United States: Interlab, 1997; Brown and others, 1998
Space heating	48				
Space cooling	48				
Lighting	25			Canada:1990	Canada: Bailie and others, 1998
Water heating	10–20				
Refrigeration	31		Canada: price scenario		
Miscellaneous	10–33				
Overall	n.a.	9			
Transportation			United States: scenario for price developments	United States: 1997	United States: Interlab, 1997; Brown and others, 1998
Passenger cars	11–17				
Freight trucks	8– 9				
Railways	16–25			Canada: 1990	Canada: Bailie and others, 1998
Aeroplanes	6–11				
Overall	10–14	3	Canada: price scenario		

a. Industrial energy efficiency potentials in the United States reflect an estimated penetration potential under different conditions based on the Interlaboratory Working Group on Energy Efficient and Low-Carbon Technologies (1997). There are no separate estimates available for the economic potential. The economic potential under business-as-usual fuel price developments is estimated at 7 percent in energy-intensive industries and 16 percent in light industries. b. The Inter-Laboratory Working Group study (1997) used price scenarios for 1997–2010 to estimate the potential for energy efficiency improvement, based on the *Annual Energy Outlook 1997* scenario (EIA, 1996). The scenario assumes a 1.2 percent annual increase in oil prices from 1997 levels. c. For comparison; in 2010 light fuel oil prices are $6–8 a gigajoule at the 1999 exchange rate (Jaccard and Willis Energy Services, 1996).

Transportation. Between 1990 and 2010 final energy use by transport may increase by 40 percent in Western Europe if no efficiency potentials are used. About 50 percent of this energy is used by passenger cars and almost 40 percent by road freight. A voluntary agreement concluded by the Association of European Car Manufacturers reflects the potential for energy-efficient car use: in 2008 new cars will be 25 percent more fuel efficient than in 1995. Using taxes and insurance to internalise the external costs of road transport, estimated at $20–70 billion, would increase efficiency by another 7–16 percent.

Relative to road transport, Western Europe's rail transport is about 3 times less energy-intensive for passengers and up to 10 times less energy-intensive for goods. With lighter trains, reduced air drag, and better drive concepts, the specific electricity consumption of rail transport could drop almost 50 percent over

the next 40 years (Brunner and Gartner, 1999). A 25 percent cut in railway freight tariffs due to increased productivity and cross-border harmonisation is expected to induce a shift from road to rail, allowing a 3 percent reduction in final energy use for the transport sector as a whole. Although aeroplanes and related logistics have substantial efficiency potential (IPCC, 1999a), it is not expected to compensate for the growth in air transport mileage.

North America

North America—defined here as Canada and the United States, but not Mexico—has higher energy consumption per capita than any other region.[9] Canada and the United States share several characteristics (large size, low energy prices) but also differ substantially (climate). In both countries recent studies have assessed the potential for increased energy efficiency by 2010. In the United States the Interlaboratory Working Group on Energy-Efficient and Low-Carbon Technologies (1997) assessed the economic potential for efficiency improvement, while a recent follow-up study assesses the potential impact of policies. In Canada a study has assessed several industrial sectors in detail (Jaccard and Willis Energy Services, 1996), while others have assessed the economic potential of sets of technologies in all sectors (Bailie and others, 1998; Brown and others, 1998; Faruqui and others, 1990; OTA, 1991). Both countries are assessing policies to address climate change, and the results may vary from previous studies (table 6.5).

Under the business-as-usual scenario, energy growth in the United States through 2010 would increase energy demand by 26 percent relative to 1990. Two other scenarios address, with progressively stronger measures, the adoption of energy-efficient technologies. The first, the efficiency scenario, assumes that technology-based reductions in energy and carbon emissions become cost-effective and so attractive to the marketplace. The second, the high-efficiency/low-carbon scenario, assumes that the United States makes an even greater commitment to reducing carbon emissions through federal and state programs and policies, as well as active private sector involvement. The high-efficiency/low-carbon scenario assumes that the emission charge is $25 or $50 per tonne of carbon.

Industry. Because of the complexity of industrial processes, the Interlaboratory Working Group did not model from the bottom up using explicit estimates of changes in efficiency expected from the introduction of energy-efficient technologies. Instead, the group used existing models to estimate the potential for increased general investment in industrial energy efficiency, supplemented by examples of a few technologies that have potential throughout the industrial sector (for example, advanced gas turbines and efficient motors). The models single out seven energy-intensive industries that together account for 80 percent of manufacturing energy use. Light manufacturing is considered a separate category.

Under the business-as-usual scenario, manufacturing grows 2.1 percent a year through 2010, divided between energy-intensive industries (1.3 percent a year) and non-intensive industries (2.6 percent a year). Total energy intensity is projected to decline by 1.1 percent a year (Interlaboratory Working Group, 1997).

In the efficiency scenario, industrial energy consumption drops 6.6 percent relative to the business as usual scenario. In the high-efficiency/low-carbon scenario, consumption falls 12.5 percent. Energy efficiency improvements are larger in light industry than in heavy manufacturing because there are more opportunities to adopt energy-efficient-technologies. Energy is a smaller component of overall manufacturing costs, so there is less incentive to adopt new technology than in the past. A recent bottom-up study (Worrell, Martin, and Price, 1999) of energy efficiency potential in the U.S.

iron and steel industry estimates the potential contribution of nearly 50 technologies, and suggests that the potential is twice as high as indicated by the Interlaboratory Working Group study.

Bailie and others (1998) estimate at 8 percent the cost-effective potential for reducing carbon dioxide (CO_2) emissions through increased energy efficiency in Canadian industry. The authors use high discount rates to reflect the market rates of time preference.[10] Jaccard and Willis Energy Services (1996) estimate the economic and technical potential for increased energy efficiency in six major industrial sectors using the same model and a discount rate of 7 percent in assessing the macroeconomic potential (see box 6.2). They find technical potential in 2010 to vary by industry from 8 to 38 percent (relative to 1990), while economic potential varies from 7 to 29 percent. These findings are similar to those for Western Europe (see table 6.4).

Buildings. In the efficiency scenario, buildings use 36.0 exajoules of energy in 2010, compared with 38.0 exajoules in the business as usual scenario. The efficiency scenario assumes that by 2010 buildings will have achieved just over one-third of their cost-effective energy efficiency savings potential of 15 percent (Interlaboratory Working Group, 1997). Energy services cost $11 billion a year less than in the business-as-usual scenario. Costs are lower because the decrease in energy spending that results from installing more efficient technology is larger than the cost of purchasing and installing this technology in buildings. The high-efficiency/low-carbon scenario assumes that nearly two-thirds of the cost-effective energy efficiency savings are achieved by 2010. The result is a larger drop in energy use, to 33.3 exajoules—or by 13 percent relative to the business-as-usual scenario.

Bailie and others (1998) assume that energy efficiency measures are implemented in Canadian buildings. While households show moderate economic potential (13 percent), the economic potential for commercial buildings is limited (9 percent).[11] Although the technical potential is high (Bailie and others, 1998), the assumed high costs and additional office automation lead to smaller economic potentials.

Transportation. The business as usual scenario for U.S. transportation assumes that the passenger car fuel efficiency rate (in litres per 100 kilometres) will improve from 8.55 in 1997 to 7.47 in 2010. But this represents a 1.4 percent annual increase in fuel economy, an improvement that has not been seen in the past without increased fuel mileage standards or higher oil prices. The business-as-usual scenario also assumes that the fuel efficiency of light trucks will not increase. The result is an increase in transportation energy use from 26,000 petajoules in 1997 to 34,000 petajoules in 2010 despite a 10 percent improvement in overall efficiency. Under the efficiency scenario, transportation energy use is 10 percent lower in 2010. Under the high-efficiency/low-carbon scenario, it is 14 percent lower (Interlaboratory Working Group, 1997).

The high-efficiency/low-carbon scenario includes the efficiency scenario assumptions as well as major breakthroughs in fuel cells for light-duty vehicles, large gains in the energy efficiency of aircraft, and an optimistic estimate of the cost of ethanol fuel from biomass. This modelling approach is very different from that taken for buildings, because of the assumption of breakthrough technology in transportation.

Bailie and others (1998), however, estimate an extremely low economic potential for energy efficiency improvement in Canada's transportation sector.[12] The study concentrates on efficiency standards for engines but also includes fuel switching. The baseline scenario assumes large growth in transport demand, dramatically increasing energy demand in Canada between 1990 and 2010. The study finds a large technical potential for efficiency improvement, but the costs of the economic potential are prohibitive. Hence the economic potential is estimated at just 3 percent relative to 2010 baseline energy use.

Japan and Southeast Asia

The literature on energy efficiency potentials in Japan and Southeast Asia is somewhat limited (table 6.6).[13] Although the region has a relatively young capital stock, economic efficiency potentials are still quite high. This is due to intensive technological innovations and relatively high energy prices (Rumsey and Flanagan, 1995a).

Between 1975 and 1995 primary energy demand more than quadrupled, shifting the centre of the energy market from the Atlantic Basin to the Pacific Basin (Fesharaki, 1998). Hence energy efficiency is a paramount policy objective. The Asia Least Cost Greenhouse Gas Abatement Strategy (ADB, GEF, and UNDP, 1998) cites cumulative potentials for 2010 and 2020.

Industry. Goto (1996) estimates industrial energy efficiency improvements through 2010 for several energy-intensive branches in Japan (see table 6.6). The energy savings for iron and steel range from 10–12 percent, for chemicals from 5–10 percent, for cement production from 2–8 percent, and for pulp and paper from 6–18 percent (box 6.4). For Southeast Asia, ADB, GEF, and UNDP (1998), IIEC (1995), Adi (1999), Ishiguro and Akiyama (1995), and the Viet Namese government find that similar savings are possible in 2010 and 2020.

Residential, commercial, and public sectors. The energy savings potential of residential and commercial uses could be untapped with various demand-side management programmes for air conditioning, refrigeration, lighting, and cooling. Some 300–450 petajoules a year could be gained in Japan's residential sector by insulating existing buildings within their reinvestment cycle. IIEC (1995) reports savings of 20–60 percent for electric appliances.

TABLE 6.6. ECONOMIC ENERGY EFFICIENCY POTENTIALS IN JAPAN AND SOUTHEAST ASIA, 2010 AND 2020

Sector and area	Economic potential (percent or petajoules a year)[a]		Energy price level assumed (U.S. cents per kilowatt-hour)	If percent, base year	Source
	Japan 2010	Southeast Asia 2020			
Industry					Japan: Goto, 1996; JISF, 1993
Iron and steel	10–12%		0.2	1990–95	Southeast Asia: Ishiguro and
Cement	2–8%		2–20	1990–95	Akiyama, 1995; ALGAS, 1998,
Chemicals	5–10%		0.4–7.8	1990–95	IIEC, 1995; Adi 1999; Govern-
Pulp and paper	6–18%		1.5–3.3	1990–95	ment of Viet Nam; Nguyen
Electric motors		20%	1998 prices	1995	Thuong, 1998; Aim Project
Total industry		**2,017 PJ**	**1998 prices**	**1998**	Team, 1994
Residential					Kaya and others, 1991; IIEC,
Existing buildings					1995; ALGAS, 1998;
50-100 millimetre insulation	290–450 PJ		2.0–8.5	1995	Wanwacharakul, 1993
Electric appliances	20–60%	20–60%			
Illumination	20–75%	20–60%			
Commercial and public sectors					IIEC, 1995; ALGAS, 1999
Buildings					
50-100 millimetre insulation	240–280 PJ	293 PJ	2–5	1991,92	
Transportation		**2,275 PJ**		**1992**	IIEC, 1995
Compact cars	1.8%		0.044	1990	Japan: Goto, 1996;
Buses	0.2%		0.196	1990	Aim Project Team, 1994
Trucks	2.8%		0	1990	
Compact cargo vehicles	13.7%		0	1990	
Within cities					
Vehicles	7%		0.01–0.06	1990	
Buses, trucks cargo vehicles	14%		0.01–0.06	1990	
Passenger cars	0.3%		0.06	1990	

a. Assuming constant structure or use of the sector or technology considered.

In the commercial and public sectors the same efficiency technology would save 240–280 petajoules a year. Mungwitikul and Mohanty (1997) report electricity savings of 25 percent for office equipment at no additional cost in Thailand.

Transportation. In 1980–95 transport was the largest consumer of energy in Japan and Southeast Asia, with annual growth of 8.8 percent (excluding Viet Nam). Transport energy demand is still increasing because larger vehicles are becoming more popular, while the share of small vehicles in new car sales fell to 60 percent in 1996. Japanese government policy is now aiming to introduce the 'top runner method', setting efficiency standards above the performance standards currently achievable in order to raise vehicle fuel efficiencies. These measures include subsidies for hybrid vehicles, which double fuel efficiencies. Smaller cars are expected to reduce their fuel consumption to 3.0–3.6 litres per 100 kilometres, and one car manufacturer plans to increase efficiency by 25 percent between 1995 and 2005.

Energy policy also attempts to improve the energy efficiency of trains, ships, and planes, upgrading distribution efficiency by promoting railroad transportation, coastal shipping, and public transport. A study on an electric mass transit project under construction in Thailand identified potential savings of 28 petajoules a year. The savings would come from switching to diesel fuel in city buses. The introduction of fuel cells in road vehicles will further improve efficiency after 2010.

Eastern Europe

Economic restructuring is playing a decisive role for the energy system and its efficiency path in Eastern Europe, because the drivers of economic policy are now totally different from those under central planning.[14] Under communist rule a standing ambition for expansion led to a very old capital stock with low energy efficiency for basic industries, buildings, and the energy industry itself. Because the

TABLE 6.7. ECONOMIC ENERGY EFFICIENCY POTENTIALS IN EASTERN EUROPE, 2010

Sector and area	Economic potential (percent)	Energy price level assumed	Base year	Source
Industry				
Pig iron	3	EU, 1995		Ministry of Industry, Poland, 1990
Electric steel	10	EU, 1995		
Hot rolled products	32	EU, 1995		
Ferrous metallurgy	24	EU, 1995		
Electrolytic copper	15	EU, 1995		
Aluminium	24	EU, 1995		National Energy Agency, Bulgaria, 1998
Non-ferrous metals	4	EU, 1995		
Chemical products	31	EU, 1995	1995	
Synthetic fibres	12	EU, 1995		
Building materials	48	EU, 1995		
Cement dry	16	EU, 1995		
Leather, footwear	4	EU, 1995	1995	
Timber, wood industry	5	EU, 1995	1995	
Food industry	23	EU, 1995	1995	
Machine manufacturing	22	EU, 1995	1995	
Construction industry	24	EU, 1995	1995	
Residential				
Existing stock	25	EU, 1995	1995	IEA, 1999
New buildings	30	EU, 1995	1995	
Electric appliances	25	EU, 1995	1995	
Commercial/public				
Heating	25		1995	IEA, 1999
Office equipment	20		1995	
Lighting	40	EU, 1995	1995	
Agriculture				
Heating, drying	22	EU, 1995	1995	IEA, 1999
Electricity	15	EU, 1995	1995	
Transportation				
Cars	20	EU, 1995	1995	IEA, 1999
Public transportation, cities	15	EU, 1995	1995	
Railways	25	EU, 1995	1995	
Air transport	22	EU, 1995	1995	

region started the transition from an extremely weak social and financial position, the economic crisis—an unavoidable element of large-scale restructuring—influences voters (Levine and others, 1991).

As a result governments (who wish to remain in power) are often reluctant to take the restrictive steps needed for economic restructuring in general and energy pricing in particular. Countries starting from a better position (Czech Republic, Hungary, Poland, Slovakia, Slovenia) can take the painful steps earlier. Because statistical systems and aggregation practices differ considerably among transition economies and future developments are uncertain, the data on economic efficiency energy potential in table 6.7 should be viewed only as cautious estimates. The data may be subject to major changes when more empirical data become available.

Industry. Specific energy consumption and related efficiency potentials are related to physical production in energy-intensive industries. The economic potential of other sectors ranges from 4 percent (leather) to 40 percent (building materials) by 2010 (see table 6.7). Available data are from climatically and economically different countries (from Bulgaria to Poland) but most of the figures are similar—reflecting a shared history of Soviet technology and standards.

Residential. Individual heat metering in multifamily houses in Eastern Europe represents an energy efficiency potential of at least 15–20 percent. In panel-built housing estates, individual metering of domestic warm water consumption has already resulted in savings of up to 40 percent where it has been introduced. A programme to improve thermal insulation in these buildings began in the mid-1990s with central support. Thus a 20–30 percent reduction of the heat demand in these buildings can be achieved in the next 10 years.

For 2020 and beyond, specific energy and material demands are expected to be close to the EU average. Economic and technology development in Eastern Europe will likely be carried out through the expansion of multinational companies, integration with the European Union, and globalisation. As a consequence, by 2020 technologies will be in place that are technically and economically acceptable and comparable to EU standards. Exceptions will be some parts of the non-refurbished building stock.

Commercial and public sectors. Improved boilers and heating systems, insulation, high-efficiency window systems, and new lighting systems will contribute to substantial savings in the commercial and public sectors.

Transportation. Although specific energy consumption will likely fall by at least 1 percent a year, the final energy consumed by road transportation will substantially increase due to motorization in Eastern Europe.

Russia and other members of the Commonwealth of Independent States

Members of the Commonwealth of Independent States face very different climates, domestic energy resources, and levels of industrialisation and motorisation.[15] The last extensive studies of economic energy efficiency potentials for the former Soviet Union were performed in the early 1990s (WBNSS, 1999). About 120 technologies and energy-saving measures with potential savings greater than 5.8 petajoules a year were considered, covering all the sectors and assuming the replacement of technology and equipment in use at that time with best-practice, world-class technology (CENEf, 1993). Potential savings were estimated at 21,690 petajoules a year, about 77 percent of

TABLE 6.8. ECONOMIC ENERGY EFFICIENCY POTENTIALS IN RUSSIA AND UKRAINE, 2010

Sector and technological area	Economic potential (percent or petajoules a year)		Energy price level assumed	If percent, base year		Source
	Russia	Ukraine		Russia	Ukraine	
Industry	**3,370–4,980 PJ**	**1,430–2,485 PJ**	1990s price levels of Western Europe	1995	1990	Russia: Federal Ministry of Fuel and Energy, 1998
General	1,524–2,198 PJ			1995		
Metallurgy	733–1,026 PJ	284– 361 PJ		1995	1990	
Iron and steel, coke ovens	132– 161 PJ			1995		Ukraine: ARENA-ECO, 1997; Vakulko/Zlobin, 1997
Construction materials	440 PJ					
Cement	176 PJ			1995		
Refineries	176– 205 PJ	73– 138 PJ[a]		1995	1990	
Basic organic chemicals	176– 322 PJ			1995		
Pulp and paper	176– 322 PJ			1995		
Investment goods industry	322– 469 PJ	247– 249 PJ		1995	1990	
Electricity savings	More than 30%			1997		
Food industries		114– 205 PJ				
Commercial and public sectors and agriculture			1995 price levels of European Union			Bashmakov, Gritsevich, and Sorokina, 1996; ARENA-ECO, 1997; Lapir, 1997
Commercial buildings						
Agriculture	791– 879 PJ	91– 138 PJ		1995	1990	
Horticulture	Up to 3 times			1997		
Residential	**1,905–2,198 PJ**	**475–570 PJ[b]**	1995 price levels of European Union	1995	1990	Bashmakov, Gritsevich, and Sorokina, 1996; ARENA-ECO, 1997
Automated boilers	20–40%			1995		
Existing building stock	20–30%			1995		
New buildings	381– 431 PJ			1995		
Hot water supply	197– 276 PJ			1995		
Transportation	**967–1,172 PJ**	**290–293 PJ**	1995 price levels of European Union	1995	1990	Russia: SNAP, 1999; Russian Federation, Ministry of Transport, 1995
Trains	10–15%			1997		

a. Refineries and chemicals. b. Residential and commercial sectors.

which was considered economical by 2005.

In 1996 Russia and Ukraine—the two largest members of the Commonwealth of Independent States—used 83 percent of the region's primary energy. The most recent estimate of Russia's energy efficiency potential was developed in 1997 (Russian Federation Ministry of Fuel and Energy, 1998). It projects savings of 13,000–15,500 petajoules by 2010; 80 percent of these savings are expected in the end-use sector. The most comprehensive recent evaluation of technological and economic potentials for energy efficiency in Ukraine was undertaken by the Agency for Rational Energy Use and Ecology (ARENA-ECO, 1997).

Industry. The economic efficiency potential of industry in 2010 is about 4,000 petajoules a year (table 6.8). This is equal to about 30 percent of the economic efficiency potential of the entire economy, or more than 30 percent of the projected energy demand for 2010. In ferrous metallurgy, replacing open-heart furnaces with oxygen converters and electric steel furnaces could save 73–88 petajoules a year (box 6.5). Introducing continuous casting on greater scale could save 59–70 petajoules a year. Recycling an additional 10 million tonnes of ferrous scrap would save 290 petajoules a year.

In primary aluminium production it is realistic to cut the use of electric power to 13,200 kilowatt-hours per tonne by using electrolysers of greater capacity and introducing automated control of technological parameters. In the production of building materials the transfer of cement clinker production to dry process in the production of bricks and lime and other related measures may cut energy use by 400 petajoules a year. In the chemical industry, replacing obsolete with modern technology in the production of ammonia, olefines, aromates, alcohols, and the like will not only reduce energy intensity to levels comparable to the best world examples (around 200 petajoules in 2010), it will also improve the product mix.

According to Vakulko and Zlobin (1997), the main directions for rational use of electricity in industrial facilities are: installing electricity metering and control devices, practising power compensation, determining the optimal number of working transformers, and making efficient use of lighting and lighting devices, high-efficiency electric drives, electrothermal devices, welding transformers and units, and converters. Ukraine's energy efficiency potential in industry is similar once adjusted for the smaller country, but are still about 2,000 petajoules a year by 2010 (see table 6.8).

Residential. Better building insulation will reduce heat losses. Overall, by 2010 Russia could save at least 2,000 petajoules a year in its residential sector. Ukraine could save 500 petajoules a year (see table 6.8). Typical for Russian households, a 250–360-litre refrigerator consumes 500–600 kilowatt-hours a year. According to Bashmakov, Gritsevich, and Sorokina (1996), more energy-efficient refrigerators could save up to 175 petajoules a year by 2010. The efficiency measures in this sector and the commercial sector are very similar to those in Russia (installing new metering and control devices, improving insulation of buildings and heating systems).

Transportation. Russia's Ministry of Transport has adopted several programmes to make the transportation system more efficient, safe, and comfortable (SNAP, 1999). In 1995 the ministry introduced a programme aimed at introducing energy-saving vehicles, optimising the structure of the vehicle stock, developing energy-efficient engines, and introducing energy-saving fuels and lubricants (Russian Federation Ministry of Transport 1995). Among other measures, the programme is expected to increase of the share of diesel-fuelled trucks and buses and modernise aeroplanes and helicopters.

Though there is great potential for economic energy savings, these savings will be difficult to achieve. Russia and Ukraine cannot provide the necessary financial support to industry and municipalities. Current investments in energy-saving measures are so low that less than 10 percent of economic energy saving potential is being reached in the Commonwealth of Independent States (Bashmakov, Gritsevich, and Sorokina, 1996). But this is likely to change with the economic recovery of Russia and Ukraine over the next 10 years.

India

With more than 1 billion inhabitants, India is one of the world's biggest emerging economies.[16] In the 50 years since independence the use of commercial energy has increased by ten times, and in 1996/97 was 10,300 petajoules (GOI, Ninth Plan Document, 1996). But per capita energy consumption is only about 15 gigajoules a year (including non-commercial energy)—far below the world average of 65 gigajoules. Given the ever-widening gap between energy supply and demand in India, and the resource constraint impeding large-scale energy generation at source, efficient energy use is an extremely important, cost-effective option. Commercial energy use is dominated by industry (51 percent), followed by transportation (22 percent), households (12 percent), agriculture (9 percent), and other sectors including basic petrochemical products (6 percent).

Industry. Indian industry is highly energy-intensive, with energy efficiency well below that of industrialised countries (see table 6.3). Efforts to promote energy efficiency in such industries could substantially reduce operating costs. About 65–70 percent of industrial energy consumption is accounted for by seven sectors—fertiliser, cement, pulp and paper, textiles, iron and steel, aluminium, and refineries.

TABLE 6.9. ECONOMIC ENERGY EFFICIENCY POTENTIALS IN INDIA, 2010

Sector and technological area	Economic potential (percent or units of energy a year)	Energy price level assumed	If percent, base year	Source
Industry				
Fertiliser	12.6 gigajoules per tonne of NH_3	Today's price		TERI and FAI, 1995
Cement	17%	Today's price	1992	TIFAC, 1992
Electrical	17%			
Thermal	27%			
Pulp and paper	20–25%	Today's price	1994	CII, 1994
Textiles	23%	Today's price	1998	TERI, 1999
Iron and steel	15%	Today's price	1998	TERI, 1996a
Aluminium	15–20%	Today's price	1996	TERI, 1996b
Refineries	8–10%	Today's price	1996	Raghuraman, 1989
Brick-making	15–40%	Today's price	1989	TERI, 1997b
Foundries	30–50%	Today's price	1997	TERI, 1998
Industrial cogeneration	3,500 megawatts (sugar)	Today's price	1997	TERI, 1994
Residential				
Lighting	10–70%	Today's price	1996	TERI, 1997c
Refrigerator	25%	Today's price	1996	TERI, 1997c
Air conditioning	10%	Today's price	1996	TERI, 1997c
Agriculture				
Pump sets	25–55%	Today's price	1995	Kuldip and others, 1995
Transportation				
Two- and three-wheelers	25%	Today's price	1995	IIP, 1995
Cars	7.5–10%	Today's price	1992	TERI, 1992
Trains (diesel)	5–10%	Today's price	1997	TERI, 1997c
Trains (electric)	5–10%	Today's price	1997	TERI, 1997c

The other areas considered for this report are brick-making, foundries, and industrial cogeneration. Potential efficiency improvements are the result of a bundle of feasible and economic energy-saving options, identified through energy and technology audits (table 6.9, box 6.6).

Residential. Energy consumption in India's residential sector varies widely across low-, medium-, and high-income classes in rural and urban areas. Household demand for electricity will likely expand rapidly as urbanisation continues and the availability of consumer durables expands with increasing income. About 40 percent of the electricity used by the sector goes to meet lighting demand, followed by 31 percent for fans and 28 percent for appliances (refrigerators, air conditioners, televisions). The economic potential of efficiency improvements was estimated for lighting (up to 70 percent), refrigerators (25 percent), and air conditioners (10 percent; see table 6.9).

Agriculture. The main areas for conserving energy in agriculture are diesel-fuelled and electric pumps, 16 million of which were in operation in 1991/92. The estimated savings potential of 25–55 percent involves avoiding such common drawbacks as improper selection of pumps and prime movers, improper installation, poor pump characteristics, high friction losses in the valves and the piping system, air inflow in the suction pipe, and improper maintenance and servicing.

Transportation. Transportation accounts for almost half of India's oil product consumption, in the form of high-speed diesel and gasoline

(TERI, 1999). Two major structural aspects of transportation are related to energy efficiency. First, the rail-dominant economy of the 1950s gave way to the road-dominant economy of the 1990s, reaching 81 percent of the sector's energy consumption (TERI, 1997c). Second, inadequate public transport systems and increasing incomes have led to a rapid increase in personalised modes of transport and intermediate public transport, some of which are extremely energy-inefficient.

A large number of two-stroke-engine two-wheelers are used as

BOX 6.6. MORE ENERGY-EFFICIENT FOUNDRIES IN INDIA

Until recently most of India's 6,000 small foundries had conventional cupolas (melting furnaces) with low energy efficiencies and high emissions. In 1998 a new divided-blast cupola and pollution control system were commissioned and fine-tuned. Once various control parameters were optimised, the demonstration cupola was far more energy efficient, with coke savings ranging from 33–65 percent relative to average small-scale foundries in India. Emissions of total suspended particulates are below the most stringent emission norm prevailing in India. In addition, the new cupola has a much reduced oxidation loss for silicon and manganese. This success story outlines an appropriate strategy for small-scale foundries to upgrade to an energy-efficient and environmentally cleaner option. This strategy can be adapted not only to other industry clusters in India, but also to units operating under similar conditions in other countries.

Source: TERI, 1998.

personal vehicles. (In 1996 the number of registered two-wheelers was 23.1 million.) Efficiency improvements of 25 percent are possible for two-stroke engines (two- and three-wheelers). The stringent emission standards proposed for two- and three-wheelers will force manufacturers to switch to four-stroke engines. Efficiency improvements for cars and buses are expected to come primarily from switching from gasoline and diesel to compressed natural gas (TERI, 1992).

The importance of research and development for increasing energy efficiency is still underestimated in India. Spending on research and development increased from 0.35 percent of GNP in 1970 to 0.81 percent in 1994. But this share is still just one-third of the ratio in industrialised countries. Tackling the complex technological problems of the energy sector, particularly end-use efficiencies, will require research and development on a steadily increasing scale.

China

Like India, China is one of the world's main emerging economies, with a population of more than 1.2 billion.[17] In 1996 China's primary energy demand was 44,000 petajoules, or 36 gigajoules per capita. Substantial energy efficiency gains could be realised through intensive investments in the country's productive sectors.

Industry. In 1995 steel and iron industry consumed 3,740 petajoules, accounting for 13 percent of China's final energy use with a performance of 46 percent energy efficiency. Energy consumption per tonne of steel will likely drop from 44 gigajoules in 1995 to 35 gigajoules in 2010, which is a little higher than the level in industrialised countries in the 1970s (table 6.10). The potential efficiency savings in some other energy-intensive branches are higher—construction materials could achieve 20 percent and chemicals up to 30 percent, with particular savings in basic chemicals such as ammonia, sulphate, soda, carbide, and olefine production.

Residential. Since the 1980s domestic energy consumption has increased because of higher living standards and expanded living space. Measures such as preventing heat losses, improving electric appliance efficiency, replacing incandescent lamps with fluorescent lamps, improving stoves and boilers, and using cogeneration will enhance energy efficiency in this sector. In 1995 the average efficiency of China's energy use—as defined by the relationship between useful energy and final energy—was 45 percent in urban areas and 25 percent in rural areas, indicating considerable potential for improvement. By 2010 energy efficiency is expected to reach 50 percent in urban areas and 45 percent in rural areas, close to

TABLE 6.10. ECONOMIC ENERGY EFFICIENCY POTENTIALS IN CHINA, 2010

Sector and area	Economic potential (percent)	Energy price level assumed	Base year	Reference
Industry				
Iron and steel	15-25	Today's price	1995	Hu, 1997
Cement	10-20	Today's price	1995	Hu, 1997
Foundries	8-14	Today's price	1995	Hu, 1997
Pulp and paper	20-40	Today's price	1995	Hu and Jiang, 1997
Textiles	15-28	Today's price	1995	Hu, 1997
Fertiliser	10-20	Today's price	1995	Hu and Jiang, 1997
Aluminium	20	Today's price	1995	Hu and Jiang, 1997
Brick kilns	32	Today's price	1995	Hu and Jiang, 1997
Refineries	5-10	Today's price	1995	Hu and Jiang, 1997
Ethylene	10-30	Today's price	1995	Hu and Jiang, 1997
Calcium carbide	10-22	Today's price	1995	Hu and Jiang, 1997
Sulphate	14-25	Today's price	1995	CIECC, 1997
Caustic soda	10-30	Today's price	1995	CIECC, 1997
Household				
Lighting	10-40	Today's price	1995	CIECC, 1997
Refrigerator	10-15	Today's price	1995	CIECC, 1997
Air conditioner	15	Today's price	1995	CIECC, 1997
Washing machine	15	Today's price	1995	CIECC, 1997
Cooking utensils	20-40	Today's price	1995	CIECC, 1997
Heating equipment	10-30	Today's price	1995	CIECC, 1997
Agriculture				
Motors	10-30	Today's price	1995	CIECC, 1997
Pump sets	20-50	Today's price	1995	CIECC, 1997
Transportation				
Train (diesel)	5-15	Today's price	1995	Hu, 1997
Train (electric)	8-14	Today's price	1995	Hu, 1997
Cars	10-15	Today's price	1995	Hu, 1997
Vessels	10	Today's price	1995	Hu, 1997

levels in industrialised countries in the early 1990s (box 6.7). This means savings of 10–15 percent in urban areas and 80 percent in rural areas. These gains are important because the drivers for energy services will be increasing by 5–18 percent a year.

Other sectors. In 1995 other final energy users in the service sector had an average end-use efficiency of about 40 percent. By 2010 technological progress and technical measures are expected to increase the efficiency level by 5–10 percentage points over 1995, reaching the level of industrialised countries in the early 1990s.

Transportation. Transportation is a large and fast-growing energy-consuming sector, especially for petroleum products (2,640 petajoules in 1995, including public transport). By 2010 energy consumption will almost double, with oil products accounting for 87 percent of transport energy consumption. Relative to other sectors, transportation has a low end-use efficiency of around 30 percent. The main technical measures for increasing efficiency are similar to those elsewhere: increase the share of diesel vehicles, rationalise the weight of cars, speed up road construction and improve its quality; increase the share of electric engines and internal combustion engines on trains, and optimise engines. Better-designed propellers on ships could save 5 percent on ships' fuel consumption. Optimal ship shape energy-saving technology will save 4–10 percent of fuel, and the use of tidal energy another 3–5 percent.

Latin America

Primary energy demand in Latin America grew 2.3 percent a year over the past 20 years, reaching 18,130 petajoules in 1996.[18] The region also contains several emerging economies that are increasing world energy demand. In 1997 Argentina, Brazil, Mexico, and Venezuela used 85 percent of the region's primary energy (EIA, 1999b).

Industry. Four sectors (cement, iron and steel, chemicals, food and beverages) consume 60 percent of industrial energy in Latin America. Iron and steel alone account for 23 percent of industrial energy. Better management of blast furnaces, the injection of gases, and improved processes could reduce energy demand by 10–28 percent (Cavaliero, 1998). Machado and Shaeffer (1998) estimate potential electricity savings of 23 percent in Brazil's iron and steel industry and 11–38 percent in its cement industry (table 6.11). The food and beverage industry and chemical industry have similar efficiency potential (Argentina Secretaria de Energía, 1997; Jannuzzi, 1998).

In Brazil's industrial sector, electrical motors consume 51 percent of electricity, electrochemical processes 21 percent, electrothermal processes 20 percent, refrigeration 6 percent, and lighting 2 percent (Geller and others, 1997 and 1998). In Argentina nearly 75 percent of industrial electricity is used in motors (Dutt and Tanides, 1994) and in Chile it is 85 percent (Valdes-Arrieta, 1993). The Brazilian Electricity Conservation Agency estimates that savings of 8–15 percent are achievable in Brazilian industry based on cost-effective measures such as replacing oversized motors, improving transmission systems, replacing overloaded internal lines and transformers, correcting low

Low-energy houses need only 10–30 percent of the heat per square metre that is used in the average residential building in West Germany.

power factors, and reducing excessive peak loads (box 6.8). Additional savings of 7–15 percent could be achieved by using efficient motors and variable speed drives; improving electrical furnaces, boilers, and electrolytic process efficiencies; and disseminating cogeneration in industry (Geller and others, 1998; Soares and Tabosa, 1996). Recycling the heat surplus or installing more efficient equipment could reduce by 10 percent the amount of electricity used in electric ovens. Similar savings for Argentina have been estimated by Dutt and Tanides (1994) and Argentina Secretaria de Energía (1997).

The significant potential of combined heat and power is under-exploited in most Latin American countries. The potential is great in sectors such as paper and pulp, chemicals, and the alcohol-sugar industry, because they produce industrial residues that can be used to generate a surplus of electricity, which can then be sold to the common grid. Legislation establishing independent power producers is in place, but there are still problems in regulating buy-back rates, maintenance power, and wheeling between industry and electric utilities.

Residential. Annual energy use for cooking is estimated at 5.2 gigajoules per capita, nearly half of which is from firewood (data cover only Argentina, Brazil, Mexico, and Venezuela). The use of biomass (firewood and charcoal) is declining, however, and the use of liquefied petroleum gas and natural gas is on the rise. Because these fuels are more efficient, per capita energy consumption will be 20 percent lower by 2020. During 1990–95 per capita residential electricity use increased by 4–5 percent a year in Brazil and Mexico. Specific savings in electricity use by appliances range from 20–40 percent over the next 10–20 years for several Latin American countries (see table 6.11).

Commercial and public sectors. More efficient energy use in the commercial and public sectors can be achieved by introducing better

---

BOX 6.7. GREEN LIGHT PROGRAMME OF CHINA

China's Green Light Programme is an energy conservation project supported by UNDP and organised and carried out by the State Economic and Trade Commission of China. The programme is designed to increase the use of lighting systems that are highly efficient, long-lasting, safe, and stable. The goal is to save electricity, reduce environmental pollution from power generation, and improve the quality of working and living. The programme has had several achievements:

- **Electricity savings.** During 1995–2000, 300 million compact fluorescent lamps, thin-tube fluorescent lamps, and other high-efficiency illumination products will save 22 terawatt-hours of electricity (as final energy).
- **Reduced emissions.** By 2000 sulphur dioxide emissions will be reduced by 200,000 tonnes and carbon dioxide emissions by 7.4 million tonnes.
- **Establishing the market.** By creating market-driven demand for high-efficiency lighting products, China will minimise spending for the associated gains. Close attention has been given to upgrading energy-efficient products by improving quality standards and certification.

TABLE 6.11. ECONOMIC ENERGY EFFICIENCY POTENTIALS IN LATIN AMERICA, 2010 AND 2020

Sector and area	Economic potential (percent)		Country/ region	Energy price level assumed	Base year	Source
	2010	2020				
Industry						
Electric motors and drives	15–30[a,d]	30	Mexico	0.06–0.09	1996	México Secretaria de Energía, 1997;
Refrigeration	27–42[b]	15–30[c]	Argentina	(elect)[d]	1997	Argentina Secretaria de Energía, 1997;
Process heat	10–20	21–44	Brazil		1997	EIA, 1999a; Geller and others 1998; IIEC,
			Chile	0.01–0.02 (fuels)[b]	1994	1995; Sheinbaum and Rodriguez, 1997
Iron and steel		23[b] (elect)	Brazil		1998	Machado and Shaeffer, 1998; Cavaliero
		28[b] (coke)			1994	1998; Argentina Secretaria de Energía,
		15[a]				1997; EIA, 1999a; IIEC, 1995
		10[d]	Argentina			
			Chile			
Cement		11–38[b] (elect)	Brazil		1998	Machado and Shaeffer, 1998; Sheinbaum and Ozawa, 1998
Food and beverage		20[b]	Brazil		1998	Jannuzzi, 1998; Argentina Secretaria de
		30[a]	Argentina		1998	Energía, 1997; EIA, 1999a; IIEC, 1995
		6[d] (elect)	Chile		1994	
Residential		**20-40 (elect)**	Mexico,		1996	México Secretaria de Energía, 1997;
			Argentina		1997	Argentina Secretaria de Energía, 1997;
			Brazil		1998	EIA, 1999a; Machado and Shaeffer, 1998; Friedmann, 1994
Cooking		24	Latin America		1997	Author's estimate
Electrical appliances	20–25	20–40	Mexico		1996	México Secretaria de Energía, 1997;
			Brazil		1997	Geller and others 1998
Lighting	30–80		Brazil	0.03–0.13	1997	Jannuzzi, 1998; Argentina Secretaria de
			Argentina	(fuels and electricity)[b]	1991	Energía, 1997; EIA, 1999a; Blanc and de Buen, 1994
Refrigeration		35–50	Brazil		1998	Machado and Shaeffer, 1998;
			Argentina			México Secretaria de Energía, 1997
			Mexico		1996	
Commercial and public	**20–40 (elect.)**		Mexico		1996	México Secretaria de Energía, 1997;
			Argentina		1997	Argentina Secretaria de Energía, 1997;
			Chile			EIA, 1999a; IIEC, 1995
Shopping centres		13–38 (elect.)	Brazil		1998	Machado and Shaeffer, 1998
Hotels		12–23	Brazil		1998	Machado and Shaeffer, 1998
Lighting	40		Mexico		1996	México Secretaria de Energía, 1997;
			Brazil		1990	Jannuzzi and others, 1991; Bandala, 1995
Public lighting	21-44[a]		Argentina		1991	Argentina Secretaria de Energía, 1997;
	37[d]		Chile	0.05[d]		EIA, 1999a; IIEC, 1995
Transportation	**25**		Argentina		1998	

Note: Data for Argentina refer to the estimated technical potential. Data for Chile are for 2020; for Brazil, 2020 or 2010, as indicated; for Argentina, 2010 or 1998, as indicated; and for Mexico, 2006. a. Argentina. b. Brazil. c. Mexico. d. Chile.

boilers and maintenance practices as well as small cogeneration. Mexico is implementing building standards, which will accelerate improvements in energy use (Huang and others, 1998). For lighting, air conditioning, and refrigeration, the main electrical end uses, substantial efficiency improvements are possible for most Latin American countries (see table 6.11).

Transportation. About two-thirds of Latin America's transport energy demand is concentrated in Brazil and Mexico, where road transport accounts for 90 percent of the sector's energy consumption. Past improvements in the average specific energy consumption of passenger cars in Mexico (from 491 megajoules per 100 kilometres in 1975 to 423 megajoules in 1990) will likely continue at a similar rate (Sheinbaum, Meyers, and Sathaye, 1994). Mexico's freight transport has seen efficiency improve from 2.47 megajoules per ton-kilometre in 1975 to 1.8 megajoules per ton-kilometre in 1988. Subway systems have not grown at the same rate as passenger demand for travel in Latin America's major cities, the exception being Curitiba, Brazil. In Argentina the Energy Secretariat estimates that 12 petajoules of fuel can be saved each year in passenger and freight transportation (about 25 percent of the transport sector's energy use in 1995; Argentina Secretaria de Energía, 1998f).

Africa

Africa has great potential for energy efficiency savings in industry, households, and transportation, which together account for more than 80 percent of the continent's energy consumption (21 gigajoules per capita in 1996).[19] When assessing the economic efficiency potentials in table 6.12, however, one has to keep in mind the enormous differences in development in Africa and the fact that the literature on this subject is scarce and often dated. South Africa and most North African countries are at more advanced stages of industrialisation and motorisation than the rest of the continent.

TABLE 6.12. ECONOMIC ENERGY EFFICIENCY POTENTIALS IN AFRICA, 2020

Sector and area	Economic potential (percent)	Country	Energy price level assumed	Base year	Source
Industry					
Total industry	15	Zimbabwe		1990	TAU, 1991
	about 30	Zambia		1995	SADC, 1996
	32	Ghana		1991	Davidson and Karekezi, 1991; Adegbulugbe, 1992a
	25	Nigeria		1985	Davidson and Karekezi, 1991; SADC, 1997
	>20	Sierra Leone		1991	Adegbulugbe, 1993
	20	Mozambique			
Iron and steel	7.2	Kenya			Nyoike, 1993
Cement	11.3	Kenya			Nyoike, 1993
	15.4	Ghana		1988	Opam, 1992
	9.8	Kenya			Nyoike, 1993
Aluminium (sec.)	44.8	Kenya			Nyoike, 1993
Refineries	6.3	Kenya			Nyoike, 1993
Inorganic chemicals	19.0	Kenya			Nyoike, 1993
Consumer goods	25	Kenya			Nyoike, 1993
Food	16–24	Mozambique		1993	SADC, 1997
	1–30	Ghana		1988	Opam, 1992
Cogeneration	600 MW	Egypt		1998	Alnakeeb, 1998
Residential					
Electric appliances	20–25	Mozambique	1993	1991	SADC, 1997
	11	South Africa		1995	*Energy Efficiency News,* 1996
Commercial/public/agriculture					
Electricity	20–25	Mozambique	1993	1995	SADC, 1997
	up to 50	Egypt	1998	1998	Alnakeeb and others, 1998
Agriculture/ forestry	12.5	Tanzania (biopower)	1993	1993	
Transportation					
Cars, road system	30	Nigeria		1985	Adegbulugbe, 1992a
Total transport	30	Ethiopia		1995	Mengistu, 1995

Industry. Studies indicate that good housekeeping measures can save substantial amounts of energy in African industries (see table 6.12). Potential energy savings in national industries range from 15–32 percent by 2020. Results from energy audits in Nigeria (of two cement plants, one steel plant, and a furniture manufacturing plant) show potential savings of up to 25 percent. In 28 small- and medium-size industries in Zambia and Zimbabwe the potential savings are between 15 and 30 percent, in Kenyan industries about 25 percent, in nine industrial plants in Egypt about 23 percent, in Ghana 32 percent, and in Sierra Leone more than 20 percent. A more recent analysis carried out in industries in Mozambique indicates an economic electricity saving potential of 20 percent (SADC, 1997). Cogeneration also seems to have unexploited potential—in Egypt four industrial branches could save 600 megawatts by engaging in cogeneration (Alnakeeb, 1998).

Residential. The use of inefficient traditional three-stone fuelwood stoves for cooking, mainly in rural areas, results in considerable energy losses. The end-use efficiency of the stoves ranges from 12–18 percent. Promoting better biomass-cooking stoves and switching to modern fuels would greatly reduce the huge energy losses in this sector. Better cooking stoves could raise efficiency to 30–42 percent in Ghana, Kenya, and Uganda (box 6.9). In urban areas the focus should be on energy-efficient appliances, lighting, and other housekeeping measures for domestic appliances. In lighting a shift from kerosene to incandescent lamps, and from incandescent lamps to fluorescent and compact fluorescent lamps, would increase energy efficiency (see table 6.12).

Transportation. Road transport is the dominant mode in Africa. Nearly all vehicles are imported from overseas, often used cars and trucks. Potential savings are achievable by using roadworthy vehicles and changing policies. Vehicles tend to have low fuel efficiency. The average fuel efficiency in Nigeria is estimated to be about 18 litres of gasoline per 100 kilometres (Adegbulugbe, 1992a). Fuel efficiency is low because the vehicle fleet is old and poorly maintained, because of traffic congestion in most urban centres, and because of bad driving habits. Energy savings of 30 percent could be achieved in the road subsector by shifting from an energy-intensive transport mode to a less energy-intensive public transport system and by adopting traffic management schemes. In Ethiopia and Nigeria the demand for gasoline and diesel could be cut by 30 percent by emphasising public transportation over private automobiles (Adegbulugbe, 1992b; Mengistu, 1995).

The economic potential of energy efficiency—a systemic perspective

The preceding section covered only individual technology for energy conversion and use.[20] But additional—and sometimes major—energy savings can be realised by looking at energy-using systems in a broader sense. Aspects of this systemic view include:

- Optimising the transport and distribution of energy. Commercial energy use is often highly decentralised, yet the energy is produced in central plants; examples include electricity and district heating networks.
- Optimising the location of energy users to avoid transporting goods or people.
- Optimising according the second law of thermodynamics by supplying the suitable form of energy, including heat at the needed temperature and pressure, or by exploiting opportunities for energy cascading.

These concepts are not new. But they are often neglected in the planning of cities and suburbs, industrial sites and areas, airports, power plants, and greenhouses.

Excellent examples of the systemic approach include not only technical systems but also innovations in joint planning and coordinated—or even joint—operation or financing of energy generating, distributing, or using systems (IEA, 1997a):

- A district heating system in Kryukovo, Russia, that supplies almost 10 petajoules of heat was to a large extent manually controlled and monitored. Automated control of substations, remote sensing, and control between substations and the operator working station resulted in savings of 20–25 percent.
- Organising urban mobility is a major challenge for all countries. In areas with rapidly growing populations, planning decisions on residential, industrial, and commercial areas do not adequately consider induced mobility demand and possible modes of transportation. Incentives for car sharing, park-and-ride systems, and parking influence the use of cars and public transportation. In developing countries a lack of capital for subways must not lead to disastrous traffic jams. A possible solution has been realised by the bus system in Curitiba, Brazil (IEA, 1997a, p. 103).
- The adequate use of the exergy of energy carriers is another systemic aspect of energy efficiency. Cogeneration takes many forms: combined gas and steam turbines, gas turbines instead of burners, engine-driven cogeneration, and fuel cells that can supply heat at

the correct levels of temperature and pressure (Kashiwagi, 1999). Excess heat at low temperatures may be used in heat transformers, heat pumps, or adsorption cooling systems. Production processes with high-temperature heat demand can be located in industrial parks surrounded by production processes with lower-temperature heat that can be reused in greenhouses or fish ponds (Kashiwagi, 1995).

These systemic aspects have been investigated less intensively because such systems demand a lot of coordinated planning and action by several actors and institutions. They often also demand changes in legal frameworks and decision-making in companies and administrations. Additional risks have to be managed by new entrepreneurial solutions and insurance services. In many cases, however, the efficiency potentials if such systems may exceed the economic efficiency potentials of individual technologies.

Technical and theoretical potentials for rational energy use after 2020

Many energy economists expect energy demand to increase in industrialised countries, accompanied by a substantial shift to natural gas, nuclear power, and renewables to avoid climate changes caused by energy-related greenhouse gases (chapter 9).[21] Explicitly or implicitly, those expectations assume that substantial cost-effective efficiency improvements will be exhausted within the next 20 years, contributing to new growth in energy demand after some 25 years of stagnation. But applied scientists and engineers have questioned the judgement that feasible improvements in energy efficiency are limited to 30–40 percent (Jochem, 1991; De Beer, 1998; ETSU, 1994; Blok and others, 1996; Kashiwagi and others, 1998). These authors argue that, depending on new technology and scientific knowledge, the long-term technical potential for rational energy use may even exceed 80 percent in the 21st century, driven by efforts to:

- *Increase exergy efficiency* (which today is less than 15 percent, even in industrialised countries) by exploiting the different temperatures of heat streams and using the adequate form of final energy or heat at the needed temperature level.
- *Decrease the level of useful energy* by reducing losses (for example, through insulation or heat recovery) and by substituting energy-intensive processes (such as membrane and absorption technologies instead of thermal separation, thin slab casting of steel instead of rolling steel sheets, new catalysts or enzymes, new bio-technical processes, and inductive electric processes instead of thermal surface treatment).
- *Apply new materials* (new compound plastics, foamed metals, nano-technology applications).
- *Intensify recycling of energy-intensive materials* (increased shares of recycled plastics, aluminium, or flat glass, which still have low recycling rates in most regions).
- *Re-substitute wood, natural fibres, and natural raw materials for energy-intensive plastics* (due to great potential for genetic manip-

ulation of plants and substitution among energy-intensive materials; see box 6.1).

Because of the unbalanced perception between the long-term potential for rational energy use and energy conversion and supply technologies (Jochem, 1991), the huge long-term potential for increasing energy efficiency at the end-use level will likely remain underestimated for some time. Indeed, given the enormous economies of scale in fast-growing national, regional, and global markets, the economic efficiency potentials cited above for 2010 and 2020 may be too small in many cases.

To use as many energy sources as possible, the concept of cascaded energy use must be introduced in the energy conversion and end-use sectors. Cascaded energy use involves fully harnessing the heat produced by fossil fuel combustion (from its initial 1,700°C down to near-ambient temperatures), with a thermal 'down flow' of heat analogous to the downward flow of water in a cascade (Kashiwagi, 1995; Shimazaki and others, 1997). Applications that exploit the full exergetic potential of energy in multiple stages (cascaded) are not common. To exploit the exergetic potential of industrial waste heat, energy transfers between the industrial and residential or commercial sectors are advisable. But low energy prices make it difficult to find economically attractive projects.

For refrigeration, air conditioning, and hot water supply, it is possible to meet most of the heat demand with low-exergy waste heat obtained as a by-product of high-temperature, high-grade primary energy use in heat engines or fuel cells, in a cascaded use of cogeneration. From a thermodynamic viewpoint it is appropriate to combine low-exergy heat sources, such as solar and waste heat, with systems requiring low-exergy heat, such as heating, cooling, and air conditioning.

The level of specific useful energy demand can be influenced by innumerable technological changes without reducing the energy services provided by energy use and without impairing comfort. A few examples demonstrate these almost unconverted possibilities:

- The quality of insulation and air-tightness determine the demand for useful energy in buildings, furnaces, refrigerators and freezers. Low-energy houses need only 10–30 percent of the heat per square metre that is used in the average residential building in West Germany (box 6.12). A cold-storage depot or a refrigerator could be operated by outdoor air in the winter in zones with moderate climate.
- A substantial part of industrial waste heat occurs at temperatures below 50°C. Water adsorption chillers provide a way to recover such heat sources and produce cooling energy (Saha and Kashiwagi, 1997), increasing energy efficiency.
- Catalysts, enzymes, new materials, and new processes will make possible the substitution of many energy-intensive processes. High energy demand to activate chemical reactions, with high-pressure and high-temperature processes, may be rendered unnecessary by new catalysts or biotechnological processes. Membrane processes will use only a small percentage of the useful

energy needed today in thermal separation processes. The production of iron—which today involves energy-intensive sintering and coke-making—will be switched to the new coal metallurgy, with substantial energy savings. Over the long term, the energy-intensive rolling-mill operation of steel-making will be replaced by continuous thin slab casting or even spraying of steel sheets.

■ New materials for cutting edges will improve surface quality, avoiding several machine operations. Lasers will reduce the specific energy demand of metal cutting, and inductive electric processes will save energy in thermal surface treatment. New compound plastics or foamed metals will induce less energy demand in manufacturing and (because of smaller specific weight and reduced losses due to inertia) be used in vehicles and moving parts of machines and engines.

Over the past century energy systems in industrialised countries saw efficiency increase by 1.0–1.5 percent a year. Looking at the theoretical and technical potential of future energy efficiency, a similar increase of 1.0–1.5 percent a year appears possible over the next century. Increases in efficiency will be steadily exhausted by implementing economic efficiency opportunities and steadily fed by implementing technical innovations and cost reductions for energy-efficient technology. This process can be understood as a constant economic efficiency potential of 25–30 percent over the next 20 years, similar to the observation at the energy supply side that the ratio of proven reserves to consumption of oil remains at 30–40 years due to continuous searching for new reserves and technical progress on prospecting, drilling, and production techniques.

Obstacles, market imperfections, and disincentives for efficient energy use

Energy efficiency improvements since the oil shock of 1973 may have done more to redesign energy markets than did changes in conventional energy supply systems.[22] And as noted, such improvements still offer huge opportunities and can contribute to sustainable development in all regions. But given today's levels of energy-related knowledge, decision-making, and power structures, there is much evidence that the great potential for rational energy use will be overlooked by many companies, administrations, and households or deemed purely theoretical or unfeasible.

Of course, it will not be easy to fully achieve economic efficiency potentials, the 'fifth energy resource'. The technologies are decentralised and technologically very different, and increased efficiency is harder to measure than energy consumption. In addition, instead of a dozen large energy supply companies or a few engineering companies in a country, millions of energy consumers have to decide on their energy efficiency investments and organisational measures. The heterogeneity and diversity of energy consumers and manufacturers of energy-efficient equipment contribute to a low perception of the high potential of energy efficiency. Because of this variety and complexity, energy efficiency is not appealing for the media or for politicians (Jochem, 1991).

In theory, given all the benefits of energy efficiency at the microeconomic and macroeconomic levels, a perfect market would invest in, and allocate the rewards from, new energy-efficient technologies and strategies. But in practice, many obstacles and market imperfections prevent profitable energy efficiency from being fully realised (Jochem and Gruber, 1990; Hirst, 1991; IEA, 1997a; Gardner and Stern, 1996; Reddy, 1991). Although these obstacles and market imperfections are universal in principle, their importance differs among sectors, institutions, and regions.

General obstacles

Obstacles to end-use efficiency vary by country for many reasons, including technical education and training, entrepreneurial and household traditions, the availability of capital, and existing legislation. Market imperfections include the external costs of energy use (Hohmeyer, Ottinger, and Rennings, 1997) as well as subsidies, traditional legislation and rules, and traditions, motivations, and decision-making in households, companies, and administrations. Finally, an inherent obstacle is the fact that most energy efficiency investments remain invisible and do not contribute to politicians' public image. The invisibility of energy efficiency measures (in contrast to photovoltaic or solar thermal collectors) and the difficulty of demonstrating and quantifying their impacts are also important. Aspects of social prestige influence the decisions on efficiency of private households—as when buying large cars (Sanstad and Howarth, 1994; Jochem, Sathaye, and Bouille, 2000).

OECD countries. Obstacles to and market imperfections for energy efficiency in end-use sectors have been observed in OECD countries for more than 20 years.[23] While limited, empirical research on the barriers underscores the diversity of individual investors (with thousands of firms, hundreds of thousands of landlords, and millions of consumers in a single country).

Lack of knowledge, know-how, and technical skills and high transaction costs. Improved energy efficiency is brought about by new technology, organisational changes, and minor changes in a known product, process, or vehicle. This implies that investors and energy users are able to get to know and understand the perceived benefits of the technical efficiency improvement as well as evaluate possible risks. It also implies that investors and users have to be prepared to realise the improvement and to take time to absorb the new information and evaluate the innovation (OTA, 1993; Levine and others, 1995; Sioshansi, 1991). But most households and private car drivers, small and medium-size companies, and small public administrations do not have enough knowledge, technical skills, and market information about possibilities for energy savings. The construction industry and many medium-size investment firms face the same problem as small companies on the user's side. Managers, preoccupied with routine business, can only engage themselves in the most immediately important tasks (Velthuijsen, 1995; Ramesohl, 1999). Because energy efficiency reduces a small share of the energy costs of total production or household costs, it gets placed on the back burner.

Lack of access to capital and historically or socially formed investment patterns. The same energy consumers, even if they gain knowledge, often have trouble raising funds for energy efficiency investments. Their capital may be limited, and additional credit may be expensive. Especially when interest rates are high, households and small firms tend to prefer to accept higher current costs and the risk of rising energy prices instead of taking a postponed energy credit (DeCanio, 1993; Gruber and Brand, 1991).

Disparity of profitability expectations of energy supply and demand. The lack of knowledge about energy efficiency among small energy consumers raises their perceptions of risk, so energy consumers and suppliers expect different rates of return on investments (Hassett and Metcalf, 1993). Energy supply companies in countries with monopolistic energy market structures are willing to accept nominal internal rates of return of 8–15 percent (after tax) for major supply projects (IEA, 1987). But for efficiency investments, energy consumers demand—explicitly or without calculating—payback periods between one and five years, which are equivalent to a nominal internal rate of return of 15–50 percent (DeCanio, 1993; Gruber and Brand, 1991). This disparity in rate of return expectations also seems to apply to international loans, putting energy efficiency investments in developing countries at a disadvantage (Levine and others, 1995).

The impact of grid-based price structures on efficient energy use. Grid-based forms of energy play a dominant role in OECD countries. The structure of gas, electricity, and district heat tariffs for small consumers and the level of the load-independent energy charge are important for energy conservation. Tariff structures are designed in two parts to reflect two services—the potential to obtain a certain amount of capacity at any given time, and the delivered energy. The capacity charge plays an important role in profitability calculations for investments where efficiency improvements do not reduce capacity demand, such as inverters on electric engines or control techniques in gas or district heating (IEA, 1991). In addition, in most OECD countries utilities still do not offer time-of-use or seasonal rates to small consumers, which would reward them for using energy during off-peak hours. This, however, may change in fully liberalised electricity and gas markets.

Legal and administrative obstacles. There are legal and administrative obstacles in almost all end-use sectors. They are mostly country specific, and often date back to before 1973, when energy prices were low and declining in real terms and there was no threat of global warming. For most local government authorities the budgeting format is an 'annual budgeting fixation', which means that they cannot transfer funds from the recurrent to the investment budget. With a lot of other urgent needs calling for capital investment, energy efficiency measures are given low priority. The poor perception of public goods adds to the obstacles confronting energy efficiency in developing and transition economies (see below).

Other market barriers. The investor-user dilemma points to the fact that for rented dwellings or leased buildings, machines, or vehicles, there are few incentives for renters to invest in property that they do not own. Similarly, landlords, builders, and owners have few incentives to invest because of the uncertainty of recovering their investment through higher rent (Fisher and Rothkopf, 1989; Golove, 1994). Finally, the quality of delivered energy (as with unstable frequencies or voltages of electricity or impurities in gasoline or diesel) may pose a severe barrier for efficiency investments (electronic control or high efficiency motors).

Additional barriers in transition economies.[24] Transition economies did not experience the sharp increase in world energy prices in the 1970s. As a result opportunities for more efficient energy use were scarcely realised in these countries. Most transition economies suffer from all the barriers described above for OECD countries, as well as from additional market problems stemming from the legacy of central planning. The deep economic and structural crisis during the early years of transition shifted the investment priorities of industrial and commercial companies to short-term decisions, helping them to survive. Technological innovations that increase energy efficiency are hardly considered a priority in many transition economies (Borisova and others, 1997). There are, however, substantial differences among most Eastern European countries and members of the Commonwealth of Independent States.

Unpaid energy bills. The economic crisis in transition economies created special obstacles to investing in energy efficiency, including non-payments and non-monetary payments (barter, promissory notes, and other surrogates by energy consumers, mutual debt clearing between companies). In Georgia less than 30 percent of residential electricity rates were paid in 1994; industrial payments fell to 16 percent, and 25–50 percent of the electricity supply was not accounted or billed (World Bank, 1996; TACIS, 1996). In Russia about 25 percent of generated electricity was not paid for by customers in 1995–97 (BEA, 1998). Industrial and commercial customers covered up to 80 percent of their energy bills using non-monetary and surrogate means (Russian Federation Ministry of Fuel and Energy, 1998). The use of barter is contributing to the neglect of potential reductions in energy costs through efficiency measures. Experience in Eastern Europe, however, demonstrates that cutting customers off from the electricity or gas supply persuades them to pay (box 6.10).

> Because energy efficiency reduces a small share of the energy costs of total production or household costs, it gets placed on the back burner.

BOX 6.10. THE IMPLICATIONS OF TERMINATING ELECTRICITY SUBSIDIES IN HUNGARY

Raising energy prices to cost-covering levels can produce miracles. Until 1997 Hungary spent $5–10 million a year on energy efficiency improvements. In January 1997 energy prices were raised to market-based levels—and in just two years, investments in energy efficiency jumped to $80 million a year. The usual argument against correct energy pricing, that consumers cannot pay the bills, is not proven in Hungary. Just 10 percent of the national energy bill remained unpaid, and that just partly. True, retirees with low incomes have difficulties. But they are not the big consumers with high bills. The problem is a social problem, and has been solved by special payment schemes in the social policy framework of local and national budgets.

Barriers to energy metering. Many energy customers in transition economies are still not equipped with meters and controllers or have simplistic, outdated meters. In particular, residential customers in the Commonwealth of Independent States often have no meters to measure the use of natural gas, heat, and hot water, reflecting a long-held view that heat and fuel are public goods. According to the Russian Federation Ministry of Fuel and Energy (1998), only about 10 percent of heat customers (and no more than 15 percent of hot water and natural gas customers) are equipped with meters. Since 1994, however, significant efforts have been made to manufacture modern meters and controllers and to develop related services (certification, maintenance, and verification) (Minfopenergo, 1996). Meters are far more common in Eastern Europe, because since the 1980s these countries have had to import needed energies in exchange for hard currency.

Lack of cost-based tariffs for grid-based energies. Natural gas, electricity, heat, and hot water are supplied to users in the Commonwealth of Independent States and some Eastern European countries by regional or local energy monopolies with government participation and municipal distribution companies. Energy tariffs are still set by federal and regional energy commissions in most of the Commonwealth of Independent States. In Russia a large portion of customers are subsidised; fuels are of poor quality, expensive, or both; resellers charge excessive costs and receive large profits; detailed information is lacking on the production costs of suppliers; and the decisions of regional commissions do not sufficiently reflect cost considerations, but depend on the political priorities of the local authorities (Vasiliev and others, 1998).

Subsidies. In all Commonwealth of Independent States countries and a few Eastern European countries the grid-based energy supply of residential and agricultural customers is still subsidised. Subsidies are driven by traditional concepts of public goods or social policy. In addition, some groups (war veterans, low income families) pay discounted residential tariffs. In Ukraine the government paid 20 percent of the cost of natural gas for residential customers in 1996 (Gnedoy, 1998). Russian municipalities spend 25–45 percent of their budgets on residential heat subsidies, covering more than half of heat bills (Bashmakov, 1997a).

Subsidised energy prices reduce the economic attractiveness of energy efficiency measures. Cross-subsidies for electric power in the Commonwealth of Independent States distort price signals between groups of customers. For instance, cross-subsidies for residential electricity account for 20–60 percent of prices for industrial customers in different regions of Russia (Moloduik, 1997; Kretinina, Nekrasov, and Voronina, 1998). In principle, this price structure would lead to large investments in efficiency in Russian industry. But non-payment of energy bills prevents that from happening. The case for abolishing electricity subsidies in most Eastern European countries demonstrates that the social aspects of such a pricing policy can be addressed by social policy at the municipality level (see box 6.10).

> Subsidised energy prices reduce the economic attractiveness of energy efficiency measures.

Additional barriers in developing countries. The general obstacles to efficient energy use are sometimes more intense in developing countries than in OECD or transition economies.[25] But there are similarities between subsidies and pricing policies in developing and transition economies. The situation in developing countries may be more complex given the big differences in energy use, income, development, and infrastructure between urban and rural areas in India, China, Latin America, and Africa.

Lack of awareness of potential benefits. The limited awareness of the potential for energy efficiency is the most important obstacle to wide-scale adoption of energy efficiency measures and technologies in developing countries. Limited awareness is a by-product of inadequate information infrastructure to raise awareness of the potential for energy efficiency and of available technologies and proven practices. The media used to raise awareness in most developing countries limit the audience. Awareness campaigns rely on radio, television, and newspapers, which most rural populations—the majority of the population in developing countries—do not have access to. In addition, managers in industry do not have timely information on available efficiency technology (Reddy, 1991), and many producers of end-use equipment are unacquainted with energy-efficient technology and related knowledge.

Many developing countries still lack an effective energy efficiency policy at the national level. Energy supply policies are preferred in most developing countries because of the focus on development policies. This pattern may also be due to the fact that grid-based energy supplies are often owned by national or local governments, a pattern that supports rigid hierarchical structures and closed networks of decision-makers.

Energy supply constraints. In some developing countries, energy supply constraints provide no alternative fuel and technology options for consumers. The limited availability of commercial fuels (petroleum products, electricity) in rural areas impedes switching to more energy-efficient stoves, dryers, and other technologies, posing a major challenge for energy policy (see chapter 10).

Inappropriate energy pricing and cross-subsidies. Energy prices are still below marginal opportunity costs in many developing countries, reflecting the desire of governments to use energy supply to achieve political objectives. Successive governments have upheld energy subsidies over decades, making it politically difficult to raise energy prices to the level of marginal opportunity costs (box 6.11; Nadel, Kothari, and Gopinath, 1991).

Lack of trained staff, operators, and maintenance workers. Insufficient energy workers are an important constraint to the investment and operation of buildings, machines, plants, and transport systems (Suzuki, Ueta, and Mori, 1996).

Lack of capital and import of inefficient used plants and vehicles. Many energy efficiency measures are delayed by a lack of financing. The availability of credit at high interest rates tends to make energy efficiency investments a low priority. In many developing countries there is also a conflict among investment priorities. Growing economies generally favour investments in additional capacity over investments in energy efficiency. This tendency and lack of capital lead to imports of used plants, machinery, and vehicles, aggravating the problem (see the section on technology transfer, above).

Proliferation of inefficient equipment and the desire to minimise initial costs. In the absence of energy labelling schemes and of standards for energy efficiency, energy-inefficient products continue to be manufactured and marketed. Examples include diesel-fuelled irrigation pumps, motors, and transformers. Many users focus on minimising initial costs, with little regard for operating efficiency and life-cycle costs. Thus they tend to opt for cheaper, locally manufactured, inefficient equipment.

Target group-specific and technology-specific obstacles

Many target group–specific and technology-specific obstacles also impede investments in energy efficiency.[26]

Buildings. Lack of information and knowledge is a problem not only among building owners, tenants, and users in *industrialised countries,* but also among architects, consulting engineers, and installers (IEA, 1997a; Enquête Commission, 1991). These groups

have a remarkable influence on the investment decisions of builders, small and medium-size companies, and public authorities. The separation of spending and benefits (or the landlord-tenant dilemma) is common in rented buildings because the owner of a building is not the same as the user (IEA, 1991). This obstacle impedes the adoption of efficient space heating, air conditioning, ventilation, cooling, and lighting equipment in leased buildings and appliances. It is also a problem in the public sector, where schools, sports halls, hospitals, and leased office buildings may have a variety of owners—or where local governments operate and use buildings owned by state or federal governments. Building managers are often not sufficiently trained and do not receive adequate incentives for excellent performance. Planners and architects are often reimbursed based on the total investment cost, not the projected life-cycle cost of the planned building or equipment.

In many *developing countries* building design has been imitated from industrialised countries regardless of different climates, domestic construction materials, and construction traditions. This approach often results in an extremely energy-consuming design for cooling equipment in office buildings in warm developing countries. Houses in higher-income developing countries are often built by the affluent with a view to projecting prestige rather than reflecting economic concerns. Such buildings are generally devoid of energy efficiency aspects. Lack of information on energy-efficient architecture also undermines energy-efficient building standards and regulations. And in countries where such standards and regulations exist, non-compliance is a constraint.

Household appliances and office automation. Residential consumers in *industrialised countries* substantially underinvest in energy-efficient appliances or require returns of 20 to more than 50 percent to make such investments (Sioshansi, 1991; Lovins and Hennicke, 1999). Related obstacles include a lack of life-cycle costing in a culture of convenience, longstanding ties to certain manufacturers, aspects of prestige, and the investor-user dilemma in the case of rented apartments or office equipment.

Low incomes make it difficult for households in *developing countries* to switch from lower efficiency to higher efficiency (but more expensive) devices (improved biomass cook stoves, and liquefied petroleum gas and kerosene stoves). Similarly, fluorescent and compact fluorescent lamps are often not bought due to the lack of life-cycle costing by households.

Small and medium-size companies and public administration. In most small and medium-sized companies, all investments except infrastructure are decided according to payback periods instead of internal interest rate calculations. If the lifespan of energy-saving investments (such as a new condensing boiler or a heat exchanger) is longer than that of existing production plants and machinery and if the payback period is expected to be even for both investments, entrepreneurs expect (consciously or unconsciously) higher profits from energy-saving investments (table 6.13).

Lack of funds is a severe constraint for small and medium-size local governments in many countries. Many communities with high

---

BOX 6.11. DISTORTED ENERGY PRICES RESULT IN BIG LOSSES FOR INDIAN SUPPLIERS

Distorted energy prices are a major obstacle to energy efficiency. In India electricity tariffs vary considerably between states and types of users. The average cost of supply for the country's electricity boards is $0.049 a kilowatt-hour—yet revenue collection averages just $0.037 a kilowatt-hour. Utility losses are mounting and were reported to be $1.49 billion in 1994/95 (GOI, 1995). High commercial losses are mainly caused by the irrational tariff structure, which provides large subsidies to agricultural and domestic uses (see table).

State electricity board	User						
	Domestic	Com-mercial	Agri-culture/ irrigation	Industry	Rail transport	Exports to other states	Average
Haryana	4.7	7.5	1.2	7.5	7.5	3.2	5.3
Himachal Pradesh	1.6	4	1.4	3.5	n.a.	3.5	2.8
Jammu, Kashmir	0.7	1.2	0.2	0.9	n.a.	n.a.	0.8
Kerala	1.4	4.6	0.5	2.4	n.a.	n.a.	2.2
Madhya, Pradesh	1.7	7.3	0.1	7.4	11.8	2.1	5.1
West Bengal	1.9	4.7	0.6	5.9	6.7	n.a.	3.3
Average	2.9	6.7	0.5	6.9	8.5	2.9	4.1

Electricity tariffs in Indian states, 1998 (U.S. cents per kilowatt-hour)

n.a. Not available.

Source: Ministry of Power, Government of India (http://powermin.nic.in/plc72.htm).

unemployment are highly indebted. Making matters worse, municipalities often receive a significant share of their annual budgets through some kind of tax or surcharge on electricity, gas, or district heat sales to their residents, lowering the enthusiasm of local politicians for promoting energy conservation. Finally, in public budget planning, budgets for operating costs are often separate from budgets for investment. Thus possible savings in the operating budget from energy efficiency investments are often not adequately considered in the investment budget.

For small and medium-sized enterprises and communities, installing new energy-efficient equipment is far more difficult than simply paying for energy (Reddy, 1991). Many firms (especially with the current shift towards lean firms) suffer from a shortage of trained technical staff (OTA, 1993) because most personnel are busy maintaining production. In the Netherlands a lack of available personnel was considered a barrier to investing in energy-efficient equipment by one-third of surveyed firms (Velthuijsen, 1995).

Insufficient maintenance of energy-converting systems and related control equipment causes substantial energy losses. Outsiders (external consultants, utilities) are not always welcome, especially if proprietary processes are involved (OTA, 1993). Many companies cannot evaluate the risks connected with new equipment or control techniques in terms of their possible effects on product quality, process reliability, maintenance needs, or performance (OTA, 1993). Thus firms are less likely to invest in new, commercially unproven technology. An aversion to perceived risks is an especially powerful barrier in small and medium-size enterprises (Yakowitz and Hanmer, 1993).

In *transition economies* small companies and local authorities may not be able to afford an energy manager.

In *developing countries* lack of information and technical skills is an enormous problem for small and medium-sized firms, because such firms often account for a large portion of the economy. In addition, the possible disruption of production is perceived as a barrier to investments in energy efficiency. Although such an investment may be economically attractive, unexpected changes in production increase the risk that the investment will not be fully depreciated.

Large enterprises and public administrations. Mechanisms are often lacking to acknowledge energy savings by local administrations, public or private. Public procurement is generally not carried out on the basis of life-cycle cost analysis. Instead, the cheapest bidder gets the contract—and as long as the offered investment meets the project's specifications for energy use, it need not be energy efficient. The industrial sector, where managers are motivated to minimise costs, poses the fewest barriers to energy-efficient investment (Golove, 1994). But DeCanio (1993) shows that firms typically establish internal hurdle rates for energy efficiency investments that are higher than the cost of capital to the firm. This fact reflects the low priority that top managers place on increasing profits by raising energy productivity.

Developing countries often lack sufficient human resources to implement energy efficiency projects and to adequately operate and service them. Thus, even when firms recognise the potential of energy efficiency and want to harness the benefits of energy efficiency measures, they are often hampered by a dearth of skilled staff and consultants and by a lack of competent energy service companies. Capital constrains also impede rational energy use in these countries. Furthermore, low capacity use (sometimes as low as 30 percent; World Bank, 1989) affects efficient energy use by industry. Low capacity use is caused by many factors, including poor maintenance, lack of spare parts and raw materials, and unsuitable scale and design of plants.

These factors are often complicated by the risk-averse management of big firms. This attitude usually stems from resistance to change, limited knowledge on the technical and economic analysis of energy efficiency technology, and a paucity of data on the experiences of previous users of such measures or technology.

Transportation. The transport policies of most countries rarely view transportation as an energy issue. Rather, transportation is considered a driver of economic growth with the development of infrastructure for moving goods and people. This policy is strongly supported by associations of car drivers, the road transport and aviation industries, and vehicle manufacturers. Most countries have no fuel efficiency standards for new vehicles; the exceptions are for cars as in Canada, Japan, and the United States (Bradbrook, 1997) and a recent voluntary agreement among Western European car manufacturers to improve fuel efficiency by 25 percent between 1995 and 2008. In nearly all countries, cars owned by companies or public authorities are often inappropriately powered. Bad driving habits, especially of government- and company-owned vehicles, also impede the rational use of energy in road transportation.

The benefits of fuel efficiency standards are evident from the success of mandatory Corporate Average Fuel Economy (CAFE) standards being introduced in North America (though the standards do not apply to light vehicles). Many voters in *OECD countries* consider driving a car to be an expression of individual freedom. As a result most drivers and politicians do not pay much attention to fuel efficiency.

TABLE 6.13 PAYBACK CALCULATIONS AS A RISK INDICATOR LEAD TO UNDER-INVESTMENT IN PROFITABLE, LONG-LASTING ENERGY EFFICIENCY INVESTMENTS

Payback time requirement (years)	Useful life of plant (years)							
	3	4	5	6	7	10	12	15
2	24%	35%	41%	45%	47%	49%	49.5%	50%
3	0%	13%	20%	25%	27%	31%	32%	33%
4		0%	8%	13%	17%	22%	23%	24%
5			0%	6%	10%	16%	17%	18.5%
6				0%	4%	10.5%	12.5%	14.5%
8	Unprofitable					4.5%	7%	9%

Note: Percentages are annual internal rates of return. Continuous energy saving is assumed over the entire useful life of the plant. Profitable investment possibilities are eliminated by a four-year payback time requirement.

The weak finances of local and national governments in *transition economies* make it difficult to introduce modern public transport systems or to upgrade existing ones. The limited financial resources of households and small companies are the main reason for heavy imports of used cars from Western Europe and Japan.

In *developing countries* road transportation increases mobility without the huge public upfront investment needed for railways, subways, and trams. Thus one major obstacle to improved energy efficiency is the limited number of alternative transport modes. In many developing countries vehicles are either assembled or imported. Economic problems and devaluations of local currencies have driven up vehicle prices. As a result many people and small firms cannot afford new vehicles, so a lot of car buyers opt for imported used vehicles that have been used for several years in the country of origin. Similar problems are being encountered with the pricing of spare parts. In addition, most developing countries lack regulation on regular car inspections. Together these problems have resulted in poor vehicle maintenance that has exacerbated energy inefficiency.

The Intergovernmental Panel on Climate Change report on aviation (IPCC, 1999a) projects a 20 percent improvement in fuel efficiency by 2015 and a 40 percent improvement by 2050 relative to aircraft produced today. Improvements in air traffic management would reduce fuel demand by another 8–18 percent. Environmental levies and emissions trading can help realise these improvements by encouraging technological innovation and reducing the growth in demand for air travel.

Agriculture. Agriculture is the main beneficiary of subsidised electricity in *developing countries.* In some cases electricity is even provided to agricultural consumers free of charge. One major fallout of this approach is the phenomenal growth in electricity consumption by this sector. In the 1980s agriculture consumed 18 percent of India's electricity; by 1994 it consumed 30 percent (CMIE, 1996). Even after accounting for the additional pump sets installed during this period, extremely low electricity prices are one of the main reasons for the increase in the sector's energy intensity.

Cogeneration. Cogeneration has considerable potential in industrial sites and district heating systems. Yet the monopolistic structure of the electricity sector in many countries has led to high prices for maintenance and peak power, rather low buyback rates and costly technical standards for grid connection, and to dumping prices in the case of planning new cogeneration capacity (VDEW, 1997). As a result many auto producers restrict the capacity of the cogeneration plant to their minimum electricity and heat needs, although they may wish to produce more heat by cogeneration. This situation is changing now in countries (such as France) with liberalised electricity markets and regulated or competitive buyback rates.

In *Central and Eastern Europe* centralised district heating remains a widespread solution for heating big housing estates. The economics of centralising the heat supply of a certain area is regarded not as a question of profitability, but a historical fact. But inadequate pricing, inefficient operation, mismanagement, and lack of full use of cogeneration potential are encouraging heat consumers to disconnect from the district heating grid. The easy availability of natural gas, existence of small and medium-size cogeneration units (namely, gas engines and gas turbines), and desire for independence also encourage consumers to disconnect. This tends to make the heat demand density leaner, driving the system in a negative spiral that may end in the economic collapse of many district heating enterprises in transition economies.

The potential for industrial cogeneration is estimated at 20–25 percent of industrial and commercial electricity demand in several *developing countries* (TERI, 1994; Alnakeeb, 1998). India's sugar industry, for instance, generates 3,500 megawatts of bagasse-based cogenerated power. But the full potential of industrial cogeneration in China, India, and Latin America has yet to be realised because of slow progress on power buyback arrangements and the wheeling and banking of cogenerated power by state electricity boards. Although institutional barriers are considered the main obstacle in this regard, limited indigenous capacity to manufacture high-pressure boilers and turbines is also an important barrier, as hard currency is scarce in developing countries (TERI, 1994).

For every obstacle and market imperfection discussed in this section, there are interrelated measures of energy efficiency policy that could remove or reduce them (figure 6.5). But the choice of which policies to pursue must be made with care, because their effectiveness depends on many regional, cultural, and societal circumstances and on the different weights of the obstacles in different regions.

National and international policies to exploit the economic potential of energy efficiency in end-use sectors

Despite the clear warnings of the scientific community (IPCC, 1995) and the commitments made under the Kyoto Protocol, and despite possible reductions in energy costs and the benefits of energy efficiency for employment and economic development (see box 6.3), many scientists and non-governmental organisations (NGOs) feel that "policy makers are still doing too little to use energy efficiency potentials in order to safeguard their citizens and their future" (Lovins and Hennicke, 1999, pp. 7–10; Phylipsen, Blok, and Hendriks, 1999; further citations).[27] These authors ask for more activity in policy areas such as energy efficiency, transportation, and renewables.

Over the past 25 years individual and ad hoc policy measures—such as information, training, grants, or energy taxes—have often produced limited results (Dasgupta, 1999). But integrated energy demand policies—which consider simultaneous obstacles and the interdependence of regulations, consultations, training programmes, and financial incentives—and long-lasting programmes have been relatively successful. Energy demand policy is not only initiated by governments. Companies, utilities, industrial associations, and NGOs may also play an important part.

Low incomes make it difficult for households in developing countries to switch from lower efficiency to higher efficiency (but more expensive) devices.

An integrated energy, transportation, financial, and economic policy is one of the main opportunities for realising the huge economic energy saving potentials not only of individual parts and technologies, but also of a country's energy-using systems. There is a strong need to formulate a long-term strategy that promotes energy efficiency improvements in all sectors of the economy and that takes into account general obstacles, market imperfections, and target group–specific barriers. This section presents the policy initiatives to be taken in different end-use sectors in a linear manner, but such initiatives have to be implemented together to contribute to sustainable development (see figure 6.5). These policies include general policy instruments such as energy taxes, direct tax credits, emissions trading, a general energy conservation law, general education on energy issues in schools, and research and development (see chapter 11). In some cases international cooperation by governments and industrial associations may play an important supporting role.

General policy measures

General policies to promote energy efficiency try to overcome general obstacles and market imperfections. They may also be implemented

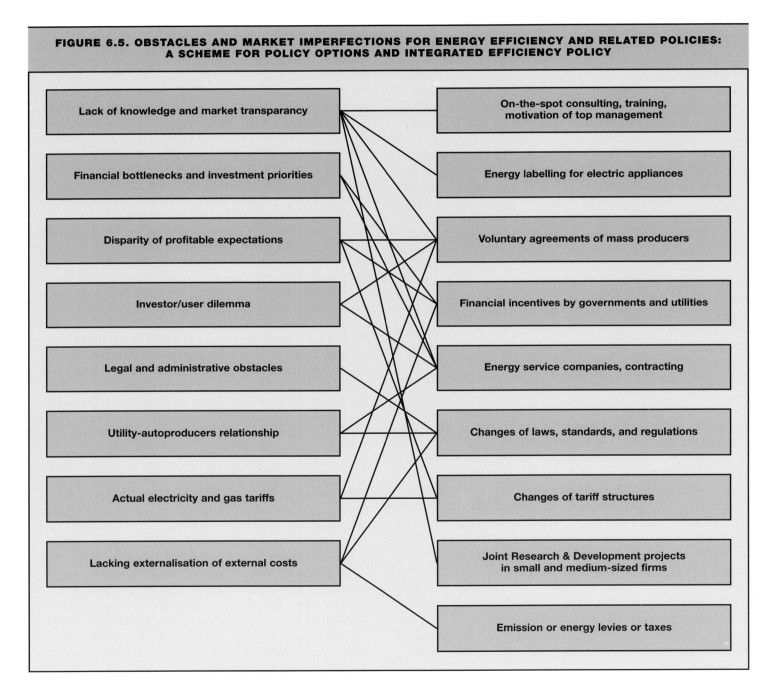

FIGURE 6.5. OBSTACLES AND MARKET IMPERFECTIONS FOR ENERGY EFFICIENCY AND RELATED POLICIES: A SCHEME FOR POLICY OPTIONS AND INTEGRATED EFFICIENCY POLICY

Lack of knowledge and market transparancy

Financial bottlenecks and investment priorities

Disparity of profitable expectations

Investor/user dilemma

Legal and administrative obstacles

Utility-autoproducers relationship

Actual electricity and gas tariffs

Lacking externalisation of external costs

On-the-spot consulting, training, motivation of top management

Energy labelling for electric appliances

Voluntary agreements of mass producers

Financial incentives by governments and utilities

Energy service companies, contracting

Changes of laws, standards, and regulations

Changes of tariff structures

Joint Research & Development projects in small and medium-sized firms

Emission or energy levies or taxes

in the context of broader economic issues, such as shifting the tax burden from labour to non-renewable resources through an ecotax at the national or multinational level (see chapter 11). Or new regulation may be needed to limit the ambiguous impacts of liberalised electricity and gas markets in their transition phase.

The acceptance of such policy measures differs by country and varies over time depending on how much an energy policy objective is violated or in question. Energy efficiency policy was widely accepted in OECD countries in the 1970s and early 1980s, when dependence on oil imports from OPEC countries was high and higher fuel prices had changed cost structures and weakened competitiveness in energy-intensive industries. With declining world energy prices between 1986 and 1999, reduced dependence on energy imports in many OECD countries, and stagnating negotiations on the implementation of the Kyoto Protocol, public interest in energy efficiency policy has fallen in many OECD countries.

By contrast, energy efficiency receives considerable attention from governments, industries, and households in Eastern European countries, in some Commonwealth of Independent States countries without indigenous energy resources, and in many emerging economies facing problems with sufficient and reliable supplies of commercial energy.

Energy conservation laws have been passed in many countries (Australia, Canada, China, Finland, Germany, Japan, Russia, Switzerland, the United States) or are in the process of being passed (India). Such laws are important for establishing a legal framework for sector regulation (building codes, labelling, technical standards for equipment and appliances) and for implementing other measures (energy agencies, financial funds for economic incentives or public procurement). In many countries with federal structures, however, much of the legislative power to enact energy conservation laws rests with individual states— posing problems for compliance and joint action.

Education on energy efficiency issues in primary or secondary schools, along with professional training, raises consciousness and basic knowledge about the efficient use of energy and the most recent technologies.

Direct subsidies and tax credits were often used to promote energy efficiency in the past. Direct subsidies often suffer from a free-rider effect when they are used for investments that would have been made anyway. Although it is difficult to evaluate this effect, in Western Europe 50–80 percent of direct subsidies are estimated to go to free riders (Farla and Blok, 1995). Low-interest loans for energy efficiency projects appear to be a more effective subsidy, although they may have a distribution effect.

Energy service companies are a promising entrepreneurial development, as they simultaneously overcome several obstacles by providing professional engineering, operational, managerial, and financial expertise, along with financial resources. Such companies either get paid a fee based on achieved savings or sign a contract to provide

Energy demand policy is not only initiated by governments. Companies, utilities, industrial associations, and NGOs may also play an important part.

defined energy services such as heating, cooling, illumination, delivery of compressed air, or hot water.

Transition economies. From a policy perspective, efficient energy use creates enormous opportunities in light of huge reinvestments in industry and infrastructure and large new investments in buildings, vehicles, and appliances. In the Commonwealth of Independent States and Eastern Europe increased energy efficiency was made a top political priority in the early and mid-1990s—as with Russia's 1994 National Energy Strategy (IEA, 1995). But according to the Russian Federation Ministry of Fuel and Energy (1998), government support for such activities was less than 8 percent of the planned funding in 1993–97.

Transition economies that were relatively open under central planning (defined as those for whom foreign trade accounted for more than 30 percent of GDP) have had an easier time adjusting to world markets. Multinational companies from Western Europe and other OECD countries maintain their technical standards when building new factories in transition economies. In addition, Eastern European countries are trying to approach (and later, to meet) Western European technical standards as part of their eventual accession to the European Union (Krawczynski and Michna, 1996; Michna, 1994).

Energy efficiency policies developed differently according to the speed of transition and economic growth in these countries. Some elements of efficiency programmes have been quite successful despite economic difficulties: laws, energy agencies, energy auditing of federal buildings. In most transition economies the first energy service companies were established with the support of international institutions. Some industrial enterprises established internal energy monitoring and control, reinforced by incentives and sanctions for particular shops and their management. The results of such activities differed considerably among transition economies, reflecting levels of organisation, human and financial capital, trade experience, foreign investment, energy subsidies, and other factors.

Developing countries. The phasing out of substantial energy subsidies can often be complemented by capacity building, professional training, and design assistance. Utilities in Mexico and Brazil, for example, have been active in demand-side management programmes with cost-benefit ratios of more than 10 to 1 (Dutt and others, 1996). Given the shortage of capital in many developing countries, financial incentives seem to have a large impact on energy efficiency (unlike in OECD countries). An example is China in the 1980s, where such incentives contributed to the remarkable decline in China's industrial energy intensity (Sinton and Levine, 1994).

Sector- and technology-specific policy measures
Given the many obstacles that keep economic energy-saving potential from being realised on a sectoral or technological level, any actor will look for a single instrument that can alleviate all obstacles. For mass products, performance standards are considered an efficient

After the oil shocks of the 1970s, German professional organisations made recommendations for new building standards. In addition, the federal government enacted an ordinance for boiler efficiencies to accelerate the replacement of old boilers by new, more efficient ones. Building codes and boiler standards have since been tightened three times, and regulations on individual heat metering were introduced in the early 1980s. Research and development enabled the new standards to be met. Twenty-five years later, the results are convincing. New buildings are 50–70 percent more efficient, and retrofits have cut energy consumption by 50 percent in Germany (and by at least 30 percent in most Western European countries).

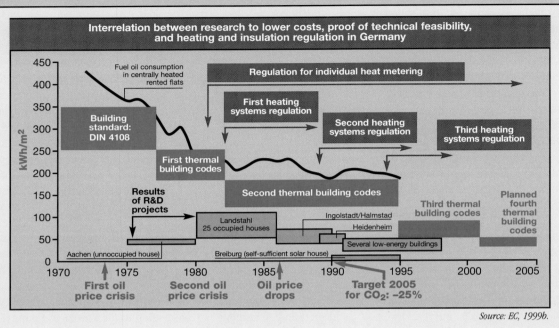

Source: EC, 1999b.

instrument because they can be developed after discussions with scientists, engineers, and industrial associations, manufacturers, and importers. Standards and labelling avoid the need for information, high transaction costs, and dissemination to, consultations with, and training of millions of households, car drivers, and small and medium-size companies (Natural Resources Canada, 1998).

But no single, highly efficient instrument will be available in all cases (as with the refurbishing of buildings or efficiency improvements in industrial plants). In these cases a package of policy measures has to be implemented to alleviate obstacles (see figure 6.5).

Buildings. There seems to be an intellectual barrier between planners and architects for buildings in cold and warm climates, although building codes may offer huge efficiency potential in most countries. Jochem and Hohmeyer (1992) conclude that if comprehensive policy strategies are implemented, governments will discover that the economics of end-use efficiency are far more attractive than is currently believed. A good example is the refurbishing of residential buildings. Homes and apartment buildings consume about 20 percent of final energy in many countries. Refurbishing a building may be primarily an individual event, but its effectiveness depends on such political and social remedies as:

- Advanced education and training of architects, planners, installers, and builders, as carried out in the Swiss 'impulse programme', which has had outstanding results since 1978.
- Information and education for landlords and home owners (particularly on the substitution of energy costs for capital costs).
- Training professional advisers to perform audits and provide practical recommendations. These audits should be subsidised;

otherwise they may be considered too costly by landlords or home owners. Such subsidies have proven cost-effective.

- Investment subsidies tied to a registered energy consultant and a formal heat survey report and minimum energy efficiency level.
- Investment subsidies for specific groups of home owners or multifamily buildings to overcome financial bottlenecks or risks of the investor-user dilemma. The cost-effectiveness of such subsidies has often been overestimated, however.
- Economically justified insulation and window design secured by new building codes that also cover the refurbishing of buildings.
- Research and development to improve building design (low-energy houses, passive solar buildings), insulation material, or windows, or to reduce construction costs.

Energy-saving programs in Denmark, Finland, Germany, Sweden, and Switzerland owe much of their success to this multimeasure approach, which is increasingly being adopted by other countries (box 6.12). The combination of measures has increased capacity in the construction sectors of those countries. Energy labelling for buildings has been introduced in a few OECD countries and is being considered in several others (Bradbrook, 1991). Such labelling provides information on a building's energy costs when it is being rented or bought (Hicks and Clough, 1998). Building standards for cooling have been adopted in Indonesia, Mexico, Singapore, and Thailand. Compliance with building codes is uncertain in many countries, however, because (expensive) controls are lacking (Duffy, 1996).

Household appliances and office automation. Household appliances and office equipment are well suited for technical standards and labelling. Varone (1998) compared instruments used between 1973 and 1997 in Canada, Denmark, Sweden, Switzerland, and the United States to promote energy-efficient household appliances and office equipment. About 20 instruments were identified (table 6.14). Various attempts have been made in the past 10 years to coordinate and harmonise policies at an international level. Some analysts consider international cooperation to be the only real means for inducing a market transformation in office equipment. Varone and Aebischer (1999) prefer to keep a diversity of instruments in different countries—an approach that allows for the testing of new instruments, offers the possibility of testing diverse combinations of instruments, and takes advantage of political windows of opportunity specific to each country (as with the Energy Star Program for office equipment in the United States) (Geller, 1995).

Some *developing countries* (China, India) try to follow OECD policies on technical standards and energy labelling. OECD governments should be aware of this implication (box 6.13).

Small and medium-sized companies and public administrations. Small and medium-sized companies and public administrations are typical targets when several policy measures have to be taken simultaneously: professional training, support for initial consulting by external experts, demonstration projects to increase trust in new technical solutions, energy agencies for several tasks (see above), and soft loans. These companies and administrations are also affected by standards for labelling and for cross-cutting technologies such as boilers and electrical motors and drives (Bradbrook, 1992).

This policy mix seems to be successful for this target group in almost all countries. In Russia and most Eastern European countries, energy agencies are responsible for energy efficiency initiatives in end-use sectors. These agencies are playing an important role, supported by energy service companies that provide financial and technical assistance to realise the identified potentials. Brazil and Mexico have also established national agencies for energy efficiency (see box 6.8). With the privatisation of Brazilian utilities, the new concessionaires are required to spend 1 percent of their revenues (less taxes) on energy efficiency, with 0.25 percent specifically for end-use efficiency measures.

Big enterprises and public administrations. Big enterprises and public administrations have specialised staff and energy managers,

BOX 6.13. FAST TRANSMISSION OF EFFICIENCY PROGRAMMES FROM OECD TO DEVELOPING COUNTRIES: THE CASE OF EFFICIENT LIGHTING

Mexico was the first developing country to implement a large-scale energy-efficient lighting programme for the residential sector. The programme was funded by the Mexican Electricity Commission, ($10 million), the Global Environment Facility ($10 million), and the Norwegian government ($3 million). Between 1995 and 1998 about 1 million compact fluorescent lamps were sold in the areas covered by the programme. Use of the lamps avoided 66.3 megawatts of peak capacity and resulted in monthly energy savings of 30 gigawatt-hours. Given the lifetime of the efficient lamps, the impacts of the programme are expected to last until 2006 (Padilla, 1999).

Economic evaluations show positive returns to households, the power sector, and society. The programme, ILUMEX (Illumination of Mexico), has also helped generate direct and indirect jobs, training and building indigenous capacity to design and implement large-scale efficiency programmes (Vargas Nieto, 1999). Smaller residential energy-efficient lighting programmes have been introduced in other Latin American countries, including Bolivia, Brazil, Costa Rica, Ecuador, and Peru.

but they still need specific policy measures to achieve their economic potential. The government of India occasionally uses expert committees to develop policy recommendations. The reports of the committees include several recommendations to encourage energy efficiency improvements (box 6.14). A 'minister's breakfast' is a key tool for motivating top managers of companies and administrations and for raising awareness of energy efficiency potential. In addition, keynote speakers at the annual meetings of industrial associations can help convey positive experiences with new efficient technologies among the responsible middle managers.

Local governments should consider using life-cycle costs and increasing flexibility between investment and operating budgets. This move may require changes in legislation in some countries.

Transportation. Policies on road transportation may include efficiency standards for vehicles imposed by national governments or technical objectives achieved through voluntary agreements among car manufacturers and importers (Bradbrook, 1994). Similar measures can be taken by aeroplane, truck, and bus manufacturers. High fuel

TABLE 6.14. POLICIES TO INCREASE EFFICIENCY IN ELECTRIC APPLIANCES AND OFFICE EQUIPMENT, VARIOUS OECD COUNTRIES

Area	Canada	Denmark	Sweden	Switzerland	United States
Household appliances	Mandatory labelling (1978) Standards (1992)	Mandatory labelling (1982) Standards (1994)	Mandatory labelling (1976) Technology procurement (1988)	Negotiated target values (1990) Voluntary labelling (1990)	Voluntary labelling (1973) Negotiated target values (1975) Mandatory labelling (1975) Standards (1978) Technology procurement (1992)
Office equipment				Negotiated target values (1990) Quality labelling (1994) Public purchasing (1994)	Quality labelling (1992) Public purchasing (1993)

Source: Varone 1998, p. 143.

taxes in countries with low taxation may support technical progress. A more systemic view relates to several areas of transport systems and policy measures (IEA, 1997a):

■ Subsidies for mobility (such as for daily commuting, national airlines, or public urban transport) increase the demand for transportation, especially road transport, and should be removed where socially acceptable. An untaxed benefit for employees driving a car bought by companies or institutions should also be removed.

BOX 6.14. ENERGY EFFICIENCY POLICY RECOMMENDATIONS BY EXPERT COMMITTEES FOR COMPANIES IN INDIA

Technical and operational measures
• Detailed energy audit should be made mandatory in all large and medium-sized enterprises.
• Potential cogeneration opportunities should be identified and pursued by providing financial assistance
• Energy consumption norms should be set for each industry type and penalties and rewards instituted based on the performance of the industry.

Fiscal and economic measures
• Creation of an energy conservation fund by levying energy conservation taxes on industrial consumption of petroleum products, coal, and electricity.
• Customs duty relief on energy conservation equipment.

Energy pricing
• Energy pricing policies must ensure that sufficient surplus is generated to finance energy sector investments, economical energy use is induced, and interfuel substitution is encouraged.

Industrial licensing, production, and growth
• Before licenses are given to new units, the capacity of existing units and the capacity use factor should be taken into consideration.
• In setting up new units, the technology should be the least energy-intensive option.
• The possibility of using waste heat from power plants by setting up appropriate industries in the vicinity should be considered.

Organisational measures
• The appointment of energy managers in large and medium-sized industries should be mandatory. For small-scale enterprises, a mechanism should be instituted for energy auditing and reporting.

Energy equipment
• Better standards should be set for energy-consuming equipment.
• Restrictions must be placed on the sale of low-efficiency equipment.
• Manufacture of instruments required to monitor energy flows must be encouraged. Imports of such instruments and spare parts should be free of customs duty.

Research and development
• Each industrial process should be reviewed to identify the research and development required to reduce energy consumption.
• Research and development on energy efficiency should be sponsored by the government as a distinct component of the science and technology plan.

Other measures
• Formal training to develop energy conservation expertise should be introduced in technical institutions.
• The government should recognise and honour individuals and organisations for outstanding performance on energy conservation.
• Efforts to raise awareness on energy conservation should be intensified.

Source: Bhattacharjee, 1999.

■ Road user charges and parking charges may reduce driving in cities, cut down on congestion and road accidents, and shift some mobility to public transport. Car sharing also has implications for car use and occupancy levels.

■ It is possible to lower the cost of public transport through automation and international procurement, as is a better organisation of rail freight crossing national borders.

■ In the long term, intelligent city planning that does not divide an urban area by functions and related sections creates substantial potential for reduced mobility.

In *higher-income developing countries* there are concerns that a shift from fuel-efficient to fuel-inefficient transport is threatening the oil security of these countries. To address these concerns, policies should encourage a shift from road transport to subways and rail transport by reducing travel times and increasing the costs of road transportation. These countries should also search for new financing to replace old bus fleets.

Agriculture. Two main issues affect the energy efficiency of agriculture in *developing countries*. The first is related to subsidised electricity tariffs for this sector; the second is the use of highly inefficient prime movers for agricultural pump sets and the ineffective configuration in which they are often used. Increases in electricity tariffs should be accompanied by free consultation by experts and an expansion of credit and savings schemes to help rural people keep their energy costs at an acceptable level. Efficient prime movers and appliances and organisational measures in water use efficiency and irrigation management would help achieve that goal.

Cogeneration. Liberalisation of the electricity market may have different implications for cogeneration in different countries (Jochem and Tönsing, 1998; AGFW, 2000). Earlier obstacles, such as low buyback rates and high rates for maintenance and emergency power, are alleviated by competition. But a legal framework for wheeling and public control seems to be necessary to level the playing field, particularly during the adaptation phase of liberalisation and for small and medium-size cogeneration plants of independent power producers. Lack of expertise and the trend of outsourcing cogeneration plants in industry can be addressed by supporting energy service companies with training, standardised contracts for small units, and deductions on fuels for cogeneration.

Maintaining energy-efficient cogeneration with district heating in *industrialised and transition economies* requires determination, a legal framework, technical and economic skills, and financial resources. Several steps are needed to make or to keep centralised district heating systems competitive:

■ A possibility of switching between fuels (lowering gas prices by switching to storable oil in the coldest 100–200 hours of the winter) and using cheap fuel ('puffer' gas, coal, municipal solid waste, garbage incineration, sewage treatment biogas).

■ Proper and economic sharing of heat generation between centralised heat units and peak load boilers, and an increase in the electricity production planted on the given heat demand by turning to higher parameters in the power-generating cycle (such as combined gas and steam cycles).

- Better performance control of the heating system, variable mass-flow in addition to temperature control in hot water systems, lower temperatures in the heating system, and the use of heat for cooling (through absorption techniques) to improve the seasonal load of the system.
- One-by-one metering and price collection for consumers in transition economies.
- A minimum buyback rate for cogenerated electricity in the adaptation phase of liberalisation (AGFW, 2000).

Such a bundle of measures can assure the competitiveness of other options and the realisation of the huge potential for cogeneration in centralised heating systems.

In *developing countries* a lack of knowledge, capital, and hard currency may constrain cogeneration investments. Thus policy measures and incentives are often needed—and were recommended, for example, by a task force in India in 1993. The Ministry of Non-Conventional Energy Sources launched a national programme promoting bagasse-based cogeneration. The process of agreeing on mutually acceptable buyback rates and wheeling of power by state electricity boards is still under way, but there is hope that the institutional barriers will give way to large-scale cogeneration, particularly in liberalised electricity markets.

International policy measures

The globalisation of many industrial sectors creates enormous potential for improving energy efficiency at the global scale. Harmonising technical standards for manufactured goods offers new opportunities for economies of scale, lowering the cost of energy-efficient products. To avoid the import of energy-inefficient products, governments, associations of importers, and NGOs may consider negotiating efficiency standards for appliances and other mass-produced products imported from industrialised countries. Imported vehicles, used cars, buses, and trucks should not be more than five or six years old (as in Bangladesh and Hungary). Similar rules could be introduced for major imported and energy-intensive plants.

The Energy Charter Protocol on Energy Efficiency and Related Environmental Aspects entered into force in April 1998. The protocol is legally binding but does not impose enforceable obligations on nations to take specified measures. It is a 'soft law' requiring actions such as:
- Formulating aims and strategies for improving energy efficiency and establishing energy efficiency policies.
- Developing, implementing, and updating efficiency programmes and establishing energy efficiency bodies that are sufficiently funded and staffed to develop and implement policies.
- Creating the necessary legal, regulatory, and institutional environment for energy efficiency, with signatories cooperating or assisting each other in this area.

The protocol received significant political support from the EU Environmental Ministers Conference in June 1998. By December 1998,

The globalisation of many industrial sectors creates enormous potential for improving energy efficiency at the global scale.

however, it had only about 40 signatories, mainly Western European countries and transition economies. Thus it has no world-wide support (Bradbrook, 1997).

Commitments to the Kyoto Protocol by Annex B countries are a major driver of energy efficiency, as about 70 percent of these countries' greenhouse gas emissions are related to energy use. Although energy efficiency is a major contributor for achieving the targets of the protocol, there are few references to it in the text of the document. Ratification of the protocol and implementation of the flexible instruments will be important for developing policy awareness in industrialised countries of the substantial potential that improved energy efficiency offers for meeting the objectives.

Better air traffic management will likely reduce aviation fuel burn by some 10 percent if fully implemented in the next 20 years—provided the necessary international regulatory and institutional arrangements have been put in place in time. Stringent aircraft engine emission and energy efficiency regulations or voluntary agreements among airlines can expedite technological innovations. Efforts to remove subsidies, impose environmental levies (charges or taxes), and promote emissions trading could be negotiated at the international level (IPCC, 1999b). These economic policies—though generally preferred by industry—may be highly controversial.

Conclusion

As the long-term potential for energy efficiency reduces useful energy demand and the proceeding levels of energy conversion, future energy policy of most countries and on the international level will have to broaden substantially its scope from energy supply to energy services. This kind of policy will be much more demanding in designing target group–specific and technology-specific bundles of policy measures. But the success of this new policy process will be worth the effort from the economic, social and environmental perspective. ∎

Notes

1. Lee Schipper was the lead author of this section.

2. Eberhard Jochem was the lead author of this box.

3. Inna Gritsevich and Eberhard Jochem were the lead authors of this section.

4. Anthony Adegbulugbe was the lead author of this section.

5. Somnath Bhattacharjee was the lead author of this section.

6. Eberhard Jochem was the lead author of this section.

7. Eberhard Jochem was the lead author of this box.

8. Bernard Aebischer and Eberhard Jochem were the lead authors of this section.

9. Ernst Worrell, Allen Chen, Tim McIntosch, and Louise Metirer were the lead authors of this section.

10. This means that the cost-effective potential is probably equivalent to the microeconomic potential (see the introduction to the section on potential economic benefits).

11. The estimates of the economic potential are based on supply curves for each sector developed by Bailie and others (1998). It is unclear what discount rate was used to estimate the economic potential. Hence we cannot determine if the study estimates a microeconomic or macroeconomic potential (see box 6.2).

12. It is unclear what discount rate was used to estimate the economic potential. In some economic assessments in this report a discount rate of 50 percent is used for investments in the transportation sector.

13. Bidyut Baran Saha and David Bonilla were the lead authors of this section.

14. Tamas Jaszay was the lead author of this section.

15. Inna Gritsevich was the lead author of this section.

16. Somnath Bhattacharjee was the lead author of this section.

17. Fengqi Zhou was the lead author of this section.

18. Gilberto M. Jannuzzi was the lead author of this section.

19. Anthony Adegbulugbe was the lead author of this section.

20. Eberhard Jochem was the lead author of this section.

21. Eberhard Jochem was the lead author of this section.

22. Eberhard Jochem was the lead author of this section.

23. Jean Pierre Des Rosiers was the lead author of this section.

24. Inna Gritsevich and Tamas Jaszay were the lead authors of this section.

25. Somnath Bhattacharjee, Gilberto Jannuzzi, and Fengqi Zhou were the lead authors of this section.

26. Eberhard Jochem was the lead author of this section.

27. Eberhard Jochem was the lead author of this section.

References

ADB (Asian Development Bank), GEF (Global Environment Facility), and UNDP (United Nations Development Programme). 1998. "Asia Least Cost Greenhouse Gas Abatement Strategy." Manila, Philippines.

Adegbulugbe, A.O. 1992a. "The Energy-Environment Nexus: The Role of Energy Efficiency." In *Energy Issues in Nigeria: Today and Tomorrow*. Proceedings of a conference held at the Nigerian Institute of International Affairs, Victoria Island, Lagos.

———, ed. 1992b. "Energy for Tomorrow's World: The Realities, the Real Options and the Agenda for Achievement." *Sub-Saharan Africa Regional Report*. Presented at the 15th World Energy Council Congress, Madrid.

Adegbulugbe, A.O. 1993. "Energy Efficiency in Industry: A Regional Perspective." In S. Karekezi and G.A. Mackenzie, eds., *Energy Options for Africa: Environmentally Sustainable Alternatives*. London: Zed Books.

Adi Cahyono A. 1999. Personal communication. Ministry for Mines and Energy, Indonesia.

Aebischer, B., J. Schwarz, and D. Spreng. 1996. "Perspectives of Energy Demand of the Tertiary Sector: Scenarios I to III, 1990–2030 [in German]." Federal Office of Energy, Bern, Switzerland.

AGFW (Arbeitsgemeinschaft Fernwärme). 2000. "Strategien und Technologien einer pluralistischen Fern- und Nahwärmeversorgung in einem liberalisierten Energiemarkt unter besonderer Berücksichtigung der Kraft-Wärme-Kopplung und erneuerbaren Energien." Studie Kurzzusammenfassung, Frankfurt.

Aim Project Team. 1994. "An Energy Technology Model for Forecasting Carbon Dioxide Emissions in Japan [in Japanese]." Report F-64-94. National Institute for Environmental Studies.

ALGAS, 1998. *Asian Least-Cost Greenhouse Gas Abatement Study*. Tokyo, Japan.

Almeida, A., P. Bertoldi, and W. Leonhard, eds. 1997. *Energy Efficiency Improvements in Electric Motors and Drives*. Berlin: Springer.

Alnakeeb, H. 1998. "Co-generation Potential in Egyptian Industry." Organization for Energy Consumption and Planning, Cairo.

Alnakeeb, H., M. El Gazzar, and M. Emam. 1998. "Demand Side Management of Efficient Lighting: A Case Study of an Administrative Building." Organization for Energy Consumption and Planning, Cairo.

Altner, G., H.-P. Dürr, and G. Michelsen. 1995. *Zukünftige Energiepolitik: Vorrang für rationelle Energienutzung und regenerative Energiequellen [Future Energy Policy Priority for Energy Efficiency and Renewables]*. Bonn: Economica Verlag.

Ameling, D., and others. 1998. "Coke Production Technology in 2000: The State of the Art and New Structures [in German]." *Eisen und Stahl* 118 (11): 55–61.

Angerer, G. 1995. "Auf dem Weg zu einer ökologischen Stoffwirtschaft. Teil I: Die Rolle des Recycling." *GAIA* 4 (2): 77.

Arbeitsgemeinschaft. 1992. "Arbeitsgemeinschaft Amstein & Walthert und Intep AG. Methode zur Optimierung des Elektrizitätsverbrauchs. Sparpotentiale beim Elektrizitätsverbrauch von zehn ausgewählten art-typischen Dienstleistungsbetrieben." Schlussbericht. Bundesamt für Energie, Bern.

ARENA-ECO (Agency for Rational Energy Use and Ecology). 1997. *Ukraine: On the Way to Energy Efficiency*. Kiev, Ukraine.

Argentina Secretaria de Energía. 1997. "Prospectiva del sector eléctrico 1997 [in Spanish]." [http://www.mecon.ar/energia/].

———. 1998a. "Balances energéticos [in Spanish]." [http://energia.mecon.gov.ar/Balances%20/Energeticos/balances.asp].

———. 1998b. "Cogeneración de energía: Analisis sectoriales [in Spanish]." [http://www.mecon.ar/energia/ure/anlisis.htm].

———. 1998c. "Cogeneración de energía en el sector industrial [in Spanish]." [http://energia.mecon.ar/ure/oportunidades.htm].

———. 1998d. "Cogeneración de energía en el sector terciário [in Spanish]." [http://energia.mecon.ar/ure/].

———. 1998e. "Equipos para conservación de alimentos en hogares [in Spanish]." [http://energia.mecon.ar/ure/oportunidades.htm].

———. 1998f. "Uso racional de la energía en el sector transporte [in Spanish]." [http://energia.mecon.ar/ure/anlisis.htm].

ATLAS Report Compendium of Technology Modules. 1997. "Industry: Energy Technology Information Base 1980–2010." European Commission, Brussels.

Ayres, R. 1996. *Industrial Ecology: Towards Closing the Materials Cycle*. London: Edward Elgar.

Bailie, A., B. Sadownik, A. Taylor, M. Nanduri, R. Murphy, J. Nyboer, M. Jaccard, and A. Pape. 1998. "Cost Curve Estimations for Reducing CO₂ Emissions in Canada: An Analysis by Province and Sector." Simon Fraser University, Energy Research Group, Vancouver, Canada.

Bandala, A. 1995. "Importance of the Mexican Lighting Systems in Commerce and Services." Proceedings of the third European Conference on Energy-Efficient Lighting, Newcastle upon Tyne, England.

Bashmakov, I. 1997a. "Heat, Money and Housing Reform." *Energy Efficiency* 14 (January–March).

———. 1997b. "Strengthening the Russian Economy through Climate Change Policies." *Energy Efficiency Bulletin* 17. Centre for Energy Efficiency, Moscow.

Bashmakov, I., I. Gritsevich, and S. Sorokina. 1996. "System of Institutional Measures to Stimulate Energy Efficiency in Russia as Part of the GHG Mitigation Strategy." Report to the Country Study Program. Centre for Energy Efficiency, Moscow.

Baumgartner, W., and C. Muggli. 1996. "Perspectives of Energy Demand of the Industrial Sector: Scenarios I to III, 1990–2030 [in German]." Federal Office of Energy, Bern, Switzerland.

Baxter, L.W. 1995. "Assessment of Net Lost Revenue Adjustment Mechanisms for Utility DSM Programs." Oak Ridge National Laboratory, Oak Ridge, Tenn.

BEA (Bureau of Economic Analysis). 1998. "Survey on Economic Policy in Russia in 1997." Moscow.

Beer, de, Jeroen. 1998. "Potential for Industrial Energy Efficiency Improvement in the Long Term." PhD. diss. University of Utrecht, Netherlands.

Bernadini, R. 1993. "Dematerialization: Long-term Trends in the Intensity of Use of Materials and Energy." *Futures* 25: 431–47.

Bhattacharjee, S. 1999. Personal communication. Tata Energy Research Institute, Mumbai, India.

Blanc, A., and O. de Buen. 1994. "Residential Lighting Efficiency in Mexico: The Road to ILUMEX." In *Proceedings of the ACEEE Summer Study on Energy Efficiency in Buildings.* Asilomar, Calif.: American Council for an Energy-Efficient Economy.

Blok, K., W.C. Turkenburg, W. Eichhammer, U. Farinelli, and T.B. Johansson. 1996. "Overview of Energy RD&D Options for a Sustainable Future." European Commission, Luxembourg.

Böde, U., and others. 1999. "Efficient Energy Use: A Literature Survey [in German]." *BWK* 86 (4): 86–90.

Boardman, B., T. Fawcett, H. Griffin, M. Hinnels, K. Lane, and J. Palmer. 1997. "DECADE: Domestic Equipment and Carbon Dioxide Emissions." University of Oxford, Energy and Environment Program.

Borisova, I., and others. 1997. "Energy Intensity of Russian Economy." *Problems of Forecasting* 6: 11–36.

Bradbrook, A. 1991. "The Development of Energy Conservation Legislation for Private Rental Hosing." *Environmental and Planning Law Journal* 8 (2): 91–1107.

———. 1992. "Energy Conservation Legislation for Industry." *Journal of Energy and Natural Resources Law* 1 (2): 145–63.

———. 1994. "Regulation for Fuel Efficiency in the Road Transportation Sector." *Australian Journal of Natural Resources Law and Policy* 1 (1): 1–31.

———. 1997. "Energy Efficiency and the Energy Charter Treaty." *Environmental and Planning Law Journal* 14 (5): 327–40.

Brechbühl B. 1992. "Energiesparmaßnahmen in Lüftungsanlagen mittels adaptiver Einzelraumregulierung." Proceedings of an international symposium on Energy for Urban Areas, August 25–26, Zürich.

Brewer, W.M., and S.F. Lopez. 1998. "Successful Closed-loop Olefins Plant Optimisation." *Hydrocarbon Processing* 6: 83–89.

Brown, M., M. Levine, J. Romm, and A. Rosenfeld. 1998. "Engineering Economic Studies of Energy Technologies to Reduce Greenhouse Gas Emissions: Opportunities and Challenges." *Annual Review of Energy and the Environment* 23.

Brunner, C.U., and R. Gartner. 1999. Energieeffizienz im Schienenverkehr. Neue Eisenbahnkonzepte senken den Energieverbrauch um 50%. *Bulletin SEV/VSE* 11/99.

CADDET (Centre for the Analysis and Dissemination of Demonstrated Energy Technology). 1997. "International Data on Successfully Demonstrated Energy Efficiency Projects." Sittard, Netherlands.

Carter, A.P. 1996. "The Economics of Technological Change." *Scientific American* 214: 25–31.

Cavaliero, C.K.N. 1998. "Redução das Emissões de CO_2 do Segmento Siderúrgico Nacional através da Injeção de Combustível Auxiliar em Alto Forno: Estudos de Casos na Acesita e Cosipa." Planejamento de Sistemas Energéticos thesis. Universidade Estadual de Campinas (UNICAMP), Faculdade de Engenharia Mecânica, Brazil.

CENEf (Centre for Energy Efficiency). 1993. *Energy Efficiency Potential and Strategy for Russia* [in Russian]. Moscow.

———. 1998. *Russian Energy Picture Statistical Yearbook.* Moscow.

CIECC (China International Engineering Consultant Corporation). 1997. "Comparison between China and Foreign Countries on Unit Energy Consumption of Energy Intensive Industries." State Development Planning Commission, Beijing.

CII (Confederation of Indian Industry). 1994. "Specific Energy Consumption Norm in Indian Pulp and Paper Industry." CII Energy Summit, Madras.

Cleveland, C.J., and M. Ruth. 1999. "Indicators of Dematerialization and the Materials Intensity of Use." *Journal of Industrial Ecology* 3 (3): 15–50.

CMIE (Centre for Monitoring the Indian Economy). 1996. *India's Energy Sector.* Mumbai, India.

———. 1997. "Approach Paper to Ninth Five-year Plan." Mumbai, India.

CODA. 1989. "Household Energy Planning Programme (HEPP)." Uganda, Ministry of Energy, Kampala.

Dadhich P., and B. Bhatia. 1994. "Co-generation—A DSM Option for India." *Energy and Environment Monitor* 10 (1): 27–34.

Dasgupta, N. 1999. "Energy Efficiency and Environmental Improvements in Small Scale Industries: Present Initiatives in India Are Not Working." *Energy Policy* 27 (13): 789–800.

Davidson, O., and S. Karekezi. 1991. "A New Environmentally-Sound Energy Strategy for the Development of Sub-Saharan Africa." AFREPREN, Nairobi, Kenya.

Davidson, O.R., A.M. Al-Shatti, and A.O. Adegbulugbe. 1991. "CO_2 Emissions from Developing Countries: Better Understanding the Role of Energy in the Long Term." Lawrence Berkeley Laboratory Report 30061 UC-350. Berkeley, Calif.

Davis, S. 1997. "Transportation Energy Data Book Edition 17." Oak Ridge National Laboratory, Oak Ridge, Tenn.

DeCanio, S.J. 1993. "Barriers within Firms to Energy-Efficient Investments." *Energy Policy* 21: 906–14.

Diekmann, J., and others. 1999. "Energy Efficiency Indicators: Statistical Bases, Theoretical Foundation, and Basis for Orientation in Policy Practice [in German]." Physica-Verlag, Heidelberg

Dobozi, I. 1991. "Impacts of Market Reforms on USSR Energy Consumption." *Energy Policy* 19 (4): 303–24.

Duffy J. 1996. "Energy Labelling Standards and Building Codes: A Global Survey and Assessment for Selected Developing Countries." International Institute for Energy Conservation, Washington, D.C.

Dutt, G., and C. Tanides. 1994. "Potencial de Uso Eficiente de la Energía Eléctrica: Una Primera Aproximación." Proceedings of Actas de la 17ª Reunión de Trabajo de la Asociación Argentina de Energía Solar, Rosario, Argentina.

Dutt, G., C. Tanides, and M. Brugnoni. 1996. "DSM (Demand-Side Management) y Empresas Distribuidoras en Mercados Desregulados: Possibilidades para Argentina." Proceedings of the International Conference on Electricity Distribution, Buenos Aires, Argentina.

EC (European Commission). 1999a. *Energy in Europe: Energy Outlook 2020.* Special issue. Brussels.

———. 1999b. *Foundations of Energy Policy: Energy in Europe:* Special Issue. Brussels.

———. Various years. *Energy in Europe: Annual Energy Review.* Special issue. Brussels.

ECODROME. 1998. "Etude experimentale des appareils electroménagers à haute éfficacité énergétique places en situation reelle." SAVE programme 4.1031./S/94-093. Auteur Cabinet Olivier Sidler. Partenaire: DGXVII, ADEME, OSRAM, Groupe Brant, Electrolux, Liebher.

EIA (Energy Information Agency). 1996. *Annual Energy Outlook 1997: With Projections to 2015.* DOE/EIA-0383 (97). Washington, D.C.: U.S. Department of Energy.

———. 1999a. "Country Profile: Argentina." [http://www.eia.doe.gov/emeu/cabs/argentna.html].

———. 1999b. "Energy in the Americas." [http://www.eia.doe.gov/emeu/cabs/theamerics].

Enquête Commission (German Bundestag). 1991. *Protecting the Earth: A Status Report with Recommendations for a New Energy Policy.* vol. 2. Bonn: Bonner University Press.

ETSU (Energy Technical Support Unit). 1994. "An Appraisal of UK Energy Research, Development, Demonstration and Dissemination." Her Majesty's Stationery Office, London.

Farla, J.C.M., and K. Blok. 1995. "Energy Conservation Investment Behaviour of Firms: Business as Usual?" In *Proceedings of the 1995 ECEEE Summer Study: Sustainability and the Reinvention of the Government—A Challenge for Energy Efficiency.* Stockholm.

Faruaui, A., M. Mauldin, S. Schick, K. Seiden, and G. Wilder. 1990. "Efficient Electricity Use: Estimates for Maximum Energy Savings." Prepared by Barakat & Chamberlin, Inc. for the Electric Power Research Institute, Palo Alto, Calif.

Fesharaki, F. 1998. "Asia As the Center of Gravity of the World Energy System." *Energy: The International Journal* 19 (4): 85–105.

Fisher, A., and C. Rothkopf. 1989. "Market Failure and Energy Policy." *Energy Policy* 17: 397–406.

Friedmann, R. 1994. "Saving Electricity in Mexican Homes: Potential and Accomplishments to Date." In *Proceedings of the ACEEE Summer Study on Energy Efficiency in Buildings.* Asilomar, Calif.: American Council for an Energy-Efficient Economy.

Friedrich, R., and W. Krewitt. 1997. *Umwelt- und Gesundheitsschäden durch die Stromerzeugung.* Heidelberg/Berlin: Springer.

Gardner, G.T., and P.C Stern. 1996. *Environmental Problems and Human Behaviour.* Needham Heights, Mass.: Allyn and Bacon.

GEA (Group for Efficient Appliances). 1995. *Washing Machines, Dryers and Dishwashers. Final Report.* European Energy Network Working Group. Copenhagen: Danish Energy Agency.

Geiger, B., W. Eichhammer, E. Gruber, D. Köwener, H. Kottmann, W. Mannsbart, U. Mielicke, M. Patel, and D. Saage. 1999. *Energieverbrauch und Energieeinsparung in Handel, Gewerbe und Dienstleistung.* Heidelberg: Physica-Verl.

Geller, H. 1995. *National Appliance Efficiency Standards: Cost-effective Federal Regulations.* Washington D.C.: American Council for an Energy-Efficient Economy.

Geller, H., G. M. Jannuzzi, R. Schaeffer, and M. T. Tolmasquim. 1998. "The Efficient Use of Electricity in Brazil: Progress and Opportunities." *Energy Policy* 26 (11): 859–72.

Geller, H., P. Leonelli, R. Abreu, I. Araújo, and H. Polis. 1997. "Energy-Efficient Lighting in Brazil: Market Evolution, Electricity Savings and Public Policies." In *Proceedings of the Fourth European Conference on Energy-Efficient Lighting.* Copenhagen: International Association of Energy-Efficient Lighting.

German Statistical Office, various years. *Statisches Jahrbuch.* Wiesbaden, Germany.

Gnedoy, N. 1998. "Energy Situation in Ukraine." *Industrial Energy* 5: 10–14.

———. 1983. "Inter Ministerial Working Group Report on Utilisation and Conservation of Energy." New Delhi.

———. 1985. "Report of the Advisory Board on Energy." New Delhi.

———. 1994. "Consultancy Capabilities in Energy Conservation and Management for the Industrial Sector in India." New Delhi.

———. 1995. "State Electricity Boards and Electricity Departments." Planning Commission, Power and Energy Division, New Delhi.

———. 1996. *Ninth Plan Document (1997–2002).* New Delhi.

———. 1997. "Handbook of Industrial Policy and Statistics." Ministry of Industry, Office of the Economic Adviser, New Delhi.

Golove, W. 1994. "Are Investments in Energy Efficiency Over or Under: An Analysis of the Literature." In *Proceedings of the 1994 ACEEE Summer Study on Energy Efficiency in Buildings.* Asilomar, Calif.: American Council for an Energy-Efficient Economy.

Goscomstat of Russia. 1996. *Industry of Russia.* Moscow.

———. 1997. *Russian Statistical Yearbook.* Moscow.

Goto, N. 1996. "Macroeconomic and Sectoral Impacts of Carbon Taxation: A Case Study for the Japanese Economy." In A. Amano, ed., *Global Warming, Carbon Limitation and Economic Development.* National Institute for Environmental Studies and Environment Agency of Japan, Centre for Global Environmental Research, Tokyo.

Goushin, S., and G. Stavinski. 1998. "Case of Implementation of Energy Saving Technologies at Kirishi Refinery Plant 'Kirishinefteorgsyntez'." *Energomeneger* 12: 20–23.

Greene, David, 1998. "Why CAFE Worked." *Energy Policy* 26 (8): 595–613.

Gritsevich, I. 1993. "Energy Conservation Problem under Conditions of Transition to Market Economy." *Economics and Mathematical Methods* 29 (2): 209–16.

Gritsevich, I., Y. Dashevsky, and V. Zhuze. 1997. "Prospects for Western Technologies in Improving District Heating Energy Efficiency in Russia." In *Greenhouse Gas Mitigation: Technologies for Activities Implemented Jointly.* Proceedings of the International Conference on Technologies for Activities Implemented Jointly, May, Vancouver, Canada.

Gruber, E., and M. Brand. 1991. "Promoting Energy Conservation in Small and Medium-sized Companies." *Energy Policy* 279–87.

Hagler Bailly Services, Inc. 1997. "The Energy Efficiency Market in Developing Countries: Trends and Policy Implications." Business Focus Series. U.S. Agency for International Development, Office of Energy, Environment, and Technology, Washington, D.C.

Hallenga, R.J., and I.C. Kok. 1998. "Inventory of Office Equipment Energy Efficiency." Report 98 PO/PRO 606. TNO Institute of Industrial Technology. Delft, Netherlands.

Hassett, K.A., and G.E. Metcalf. 1993. "Energy Conservation Investment: Do Consumers Discount the Future Correctly?" *Energy Policy* 21: 710–16.

Hennicke, P., and others. 1995. "Integrierte Ressourcenplanung." Die LCP-Fallstudie der Stadtwerke Hannover AG. Ergebnisband, Hannover, Germany.

———. 1998. "Interdisciplinary Analysis of Successful Implementation of Energy Efficiency in the Industrial, Commercial and Service Sectors." Final report. Copenhagen, Karlsruhe, Kiel, Vienna, Wuppertal.

Hicks, T.W., and D.W. Clough. 1998. "The ENERGY STAR Building Label: Building Performance through Benchmarking and Recognition." In *Proceedings of the ACEEE Summer Study on Energy Efficiency in Buildings.* Asilomar, Calif.: American Council for an Energy-Efficient Economy.

Hiessl, H., F. Meyer-Krahmer, and M. Schön. 1995. "Auf dem Weg zu einer ökologischen Stoffwirtschaft. Teil II: Die Rolle einer ganzheitlichen Produktpolitik." *GAIA* 4 (2): 89.

Hinterberger, F., F. Luks, and F. Schmidt-Bleek. 1997. "Material Flows versus 'Natural Capital': What Makes an Economy Sustainable?" *Ecological Economics* 23: 1–14.

Hirst, E. 1991. "Improving Energy Efficiency in the USA: The Federal Role." *Energy Policy* 19 (6): 567–77.

Hohmeyer, O., R.L. Ottinger, and K. Rennings, eds. 1997. *Social Costs and Sustainability: Valuation and Implementation in the Energy and Transport Sector.* Berlin/Heidelberg: Springer.

Hu, X. 1997. "Chart for Energy System Network of China and Energy Efficiency Study Report."

Hu, X., and K. Jiang. 1997. "The Structure and Simulation Results Analysis of China AIM Energy Emission Model."

Huang, J., and others. 1998. "A Commercial Building Energy Standard for Mexico." In *Proceedings of the ACEEE Summer Study on Energy Efficiency in Buildings.* American Council for an Energy-Efficient Economy, Asilomar, Calif.

IEA (International Energy Agency). 1987. *Energy Conservation in IEA Countries.* Paris.

———. 1991. *Energy Efficiency and the Environment.* Paris.

————. 1995. *Energy Policies of the Russian Federation.* Paris.

————. 1997a. *Energy Efficiency Initiative.* vol. 1. Paris

————. 1997b. *Energy Efficiency Initiative.* vol. 2. Paris.

————. 1998. *Energy Statistics and Balances of Non-OECD Countries, 1995–1996.* Paris.

————. 1999. *Energy Policies of IEA Countries: Hungary 1999 Review.* Paris.

IIEC (International Institute of Energy Conservation). 1995. *Asian Energy Efficiency Success Stories.* Washington D.C.

IIP (Indian Institute of Petroleum). 1995. *State of the Art Report on Vehicular Pollution.*

Interlaboratory Working Group on Energy Efficient and Low-Carbon Technologies. 1997. "Scenarios of U.S. Carbon Reductions: Potential Impacts of Energy Technologies by 2010 and Beyond." Lawrence Berkeley National Laboratory, Berkeley, Calif.

IPCC (Intergovernmental Panel on Climate Change). 1995. *Second Assessment Report.* Cambridge: Cambridge University Press.

————. 1999a. *Aviation and the Global Atmosphere.* Cambridge: Cambridge University Press.

————. 1999b. *Methodological and Technological Issues in Technology Transfer.* Cambridge: Cambridge University Press.

IPSEP (International Project for Sustainable Energy Paths). 1995. "Negawatt Power: The Cost and Potential of Efficiency Resources in Western Europe." Part 3B in *Energy Policy in the Greenhouse,* vol. II. El Cerrito, Calif.

Ishiguro, M., and T. Akiyama. 1995. *Energy Demand in Five Major Asian Developing Countries: Structure and Prospects.* World Bank Discussion Paper 277. Washington, D.C.

Jaccard, M.K., and Willis Energy Services. 1996. "Industrial Energy End-Use Analysis & Conservation Potential in Six Major Industries in Canada." Natural Resources Canada, Ottawa.

Jaenicke M. 1998. "Towards an End to the 'Era of Materials'? Discussion of a Hypothesis." Forschungsstelle für Umweltpolitik, Berlin.

Jannuzzi, G.M. 1998. "A Sectoral Review of Energy in Brazil: Supply and Demand and Opportunities for Reducing Carbon Emissions." M. Kaplan. Denver, Colorado, Institute for Policy Research and Implementation, Graduate Studies of Public Affairs, University of Colorado at Denver and Câmara de Comércio Brasil-Estados Unidos.

JISF (Japan Iron and Steel Federation). 1993. "Energy Efficient Measures and Energy Reduction in Integrated Steel Mills in Japan [in Japanese]." Tokyo.

Jochem, E., 1991. "Long-Term Potentials of Rational Energy Use—The Unknown Possibilities of Reducing Greenhouse Gas Emissions." *Energy Environment* 2 (1): 31–44.

Jochem, E., and H. Bradke.1996. Energieeffizienz, Strukturwandel und Produktionsentwicklung der deutschen Industrie: IKARUS. Instrumente für Klimagas-Reduktionsstrategien. Abschlußbericht Teilprojekt 6 "Industrie". Jülich: Forschungszentrum Jülich, Zentralbibliothek, Germany.

Jochem, E., and E. Gruber. 1990. "Obstacles to Rational Electricity Use and Measures to Alleviate Them." *Energy Policy* 18 (5): 340–50.

Jochem, E., and O. Hohmeyer. 1992. "The Economics of Near-Term Reductions in Greenhouse Gases." In J.M. Mintzer, ed., *Confronting Climate Change.* Cambridge: Cambridge University Press.

Jochem, E., and E. Tönsing. 1998. "The Impact of the Liberalisation of Electricity and Gas Supply on Rational Energy Use in Germany [in German]." *UWF* 6 (3): 8–11.

Jochem, E., J. Sathaye, and D. Bouille, eds. 2000. *Society, Behaviour, and Climate Change Mitigation.* Kluwer: Dordrecht, Netherlands.

Kashiwagi, T. 1994. "Industrial Energy Efficiency Policies and Programmes." Presented at the International Energy Agency International Workshop, May 26–27, Washington D.C.

————. 1995: "Second Assessment Report of the Intergovernmental Panel on Climate Change." Cambridge: Cambridge University Press.

————. 1999. "The Future Vision of Urban Energy Systems by the Introduction of Polymer Electrolyte Fuel Cell Technology." Osaka Research and Development Forum, Japan.

Kashiwagi T., B.B. Saha, and A. Akisawa. 1998. "Technological Breakthrough for the Environmental Issues in Japan." *Japan Society of Mechanical Engineers News* 9 (1): 3–10.

Kaya, Y., Y. Fujii, R. Matsuhashi, K. Yamaji, Y. Shindo, H. Saiki, I. Furugaki, and O. Kobayashi. 1991. "Assessment of Technological Options for Mitigating Global Warming." Paper presented to the Energy and Industry Subgroup, WG 3 of IPCC, August, Geneva.

Kishimba, M., and F. Musomba. 1996. "Production of Energy from Biomass and Biomass Waste." African Energy Policy Research Network Working Paper 103.

Kos, M. 1999. "Energy Efficiency in Post-Communist Countries." Written communication. Ljubljana, Slovenia.

Krause, F. 1996. "The Costs of Mitigating Carbon Emissions: A Review of Methods and Findings from European Studies." *Energy Policy,* Special Issue on the Second UN IPCC Assessment Report, Working Group III, 24 (10/11): 899–915.

Krawczynski, F., and J. Michna. 1997. "Effektivität westlicher Hilfe im Energiesektor." *Energiewirtschaftliche Tagesfragen* 47(1/2): 23.

Kretinina, Yu., A. Nekrasov, and S. Voronina. 1998. "Energy Price for Population." *Studies on Russian Economic Development* (6): 44–55.

Kuldip, K., and others. 1995. "Energy Conservation in Agricultural Pumping Systems." Proceedings of the National Workshop on Energy Conservation, September 8–9, New Delhi.

Laitner, S., St. Bernow, and J. DeCicco. 1998. "Employment and Other Macroeconomic Benefits of an Innovation-led Climate Strategy for the United States." *Energy Policy* 26 (5): 425–32.

Lapir, M. 1997. "On Energy Saving Activities in the City of Moscow [in Russian]." *Industrial Energy* (9): 7–10.

Levine, M.D., and R. Sonnenblick. 1994. "On the Assessment of Utility Demand-side Management Programs." *Energy Policy* 22.

Levine, M.D., E. Hirst, J.G Koomey, J.E. McMahon, and A.H. Sanstad. 1994. "Energy Efficiency, Market Failures, and Government Policy." Lawrence Berkeley National Laboratory, Berkley, Calif.; and Oak Ridge National Laboratory, Oak Ridge, Calif.

Levine, M.D., J. Koomey, J. McMahin, A. Sanstad, and E. Hirst. 1995. "Energy Efficiency Policies and Market Failures." *Annual Review of Energy and the Environment* 20: 535–55.

Levine, M.D., A. Gadgil, S. Meyers, J. Sathaye, J. Stafurik, and Wilbanks. 1991. "Energy Efficiency, Developing Nations and Eastern Europe." A report to the U.S. Working Group on Global Energy Efficiency, Lawrence Berkeley Lab, Berkeley, Calif.

Livinski, A., 1998. "On Energy Saving Activities in Russia." *Energomeneger* (10): 4–6.

Lovins, A., and P. Hennicke. 1999. "Voller Energie [in German; Full of Energy]." Campus Frankfurt/N.Y.

MACEBUR. 1998. "Energy-Efficient Office Technologies: The One Watt-One Ampere Challenge." European Commission. Contract No XVII/4.1301/s/94-87. Brussels.

Machado, A.C., and R. Shaeffer. 1998. "Estimativa do Potencial de Conservação de Energia Elétrica Pelo Lado da Demanda no Brasil." PROCEL/COPPETEC/ PNUD BRA/93/032, COPPE, Rio de Janeiro.

Mengistu T. 1995. "Energy in the Transport Sector: The Case of Ethiopia." *African Energy Policy Research Network Newsletter* 19.

México Secretaría de Energía. 1997. "Prospectiva Del Sector Eléctrico 1996–2006." Mexico City.

Michna, J., 1994. "Energy Conservation during the Transition Period. Special Issue on Central and Eastern European Energy Policy." *International Journal of Global Energy Issues* 6: 183–90.

Mintopenergo. 1996. "Federal Target Programme of Development of Manufacturing of Certified Metering Devices and System and Equipping Customers in 1996–2000."

Moloduik, V. 1997a. "Main Directions of Restructuring Natural Monopolies in Fuels and Energy Complex." *Energomeneger* 8: 6–8.

———. 1997b. "Problems of Electricity Tariffs Regulation." *Energomeneger* 6: 14–17.

Morovic, T. 1989. *Energy Conservation Indicators II.* Heidelberg, N.Y.: Springer.

Moscow Government. 1997. "Moscow City Energy Saving Programme in 1998–2003." Moscow.

Mungwititkul W., and B. Mohanty. 1997. "Energy Efficiency of Office Equipment in Commercial Buildings: The Case of Thailand." *Energy The International Journal* 22 (7): 673–80.

Nadel, S., V. Kothari, and S. Gopinath. 1991. "Opportunities for Improving End-use Electricity Efficiency in India." American Council for an Energy-Efficient Economy, Washington, D.C.

National Energy Efficiency Agency at the Council of Ministers of Bulgaria. 1998. "National Energy Efficiency Program of Bulgaria." Sofia, Bulgaria.

Natural Resources Canada. 1998. "Energy Efficiency Trends in Canada, 1990 to 1996." Ottawa.

Nelson, K. 1994. "Finding and Implementing Projects that Reduce Waste." In R.H. Socolow, C. Andres, F. Berkhout, and V. Thomas, eds.

Neyer A., and M. Strebel. 1996. "Grundlagenarbeiten für Perspektiven des Energieverbrauchs in Dienstleistungsbetrieben und Landwirtschaft. Schlussbericht. Zürich."

Nikiforov, G. 1998. "On Approaches to Reducing Production Energy Use at MMK." *Energomeneger* (11): 21–23.

Nguyen Thuong. 1998. "Energy Saving Potential in Industry in Vietnam and Climate Friendly Technology." Presented at the First CTI/Industry Joint Seminar on Technology Diffusion in Asia, May, Beijing.

Nyoike, P.M., and Okech, B., 1992. "Energy Management in the Manufacturing Industry—The Case of Kenya." In M.R. Bhagavan and S. Karekezi, eds., *Energy Management in Africa.* London: Zed Books.

Opam M. 1992. "Country Paper on Efficiency and Conservation in Energy Resource Development: The Ghanaian Experience." Energy Sector Workshop, Abidjan, Côte d'Ivoire.

Organización Latino-americana de Energía. 1998. "Energy-Economic Information System (SIEE)." Quito, Ecuador.

OTA (Office of Technology Assessment), U.S. Congress. 1991. *Changing by Degrees: Steps to Reduce Greenhouse Gases.* OTA-0-482. Washington, D.C.: U.S. Government Printing Office.

———. 1992. *Building Energy Efficiency.* OTA-E-518. Washington, D.C.: U.S. Government Printing Office.

———. 1993. "Industrial Energy Efficiency." Washington, D.C.

Ottoboni, and others. 1998. "Efficiency of Destruction of Waste Used in the Co-incineration in the Rotary Kilns." *Energy Conversion and Management* 39 (16–18): 1899–909.

Padilla, A.M. 1999. "Evaluación del Impacto Eléctrico de ILUMEX." In *Proceedings International ILUMEX Seminar.* Puerto Vallarta, Mexico.

Patel, M. 1999. "Closing Carbon Cycles. Carbon Use for Materials in the Context of Resource Efficiency and Climate Change." Dissertation, University of Utrecht, Netherlands.

Phylipsen, D., K. Blok, and Ch. Hendriks. 1999. "A Review of the Stage of Implementation of European Union Policies and Measures for CO_2 Emission Reduction." Report no. 98077. University of Utrecht, Netherlands.

Phylipsen, G.J.M. K Blok, and E. Worrell. 1998. "Handbook on International Comparisons of Energy Efficiency in the Manufacturing Industry." University of Utrecht, Netherlands.

Poland Ministry of Industry. 1990. "Status and Assumptions for Future Development of the Polish Energy Sector in the Years 1990 to 2010." Warsaw.

President's Committee of Advisors on Science and Technology. 1999. "Powerful Partnerships: The Federal Role in International Cooperation on Energy Innovation." Washington, D.C.

Radetzki, M. 1991. "USSR Energy Exports Post-perestroika." *Energy Policy* 19 (4): 291–302.

Raghuraman, V. 1989. "Study Report on Reducing Energy Intensity in Selected Indian Industrial Sectors."

Ramesohl, S., 1999. "Opening the Black Box—What Can Be Learned from Socio-economic Research for Energy Policy Analysis?" In IEA and U.S. Department of Energy, eds., *Proceedings of the International Workshop "Technology to Reduce Greenhouse Gas Emissions: Engineering-Economic Analysis of Conserved Energy and Carbon."* Washington, D.C.

Rath, U., M. Hartmann, A. Präffcke, and C. Mordziol. 1997. "Climate Protection by Reducing the Losses of Electrical Motors [in German]." Research report 204.08 541 UBA-FB 97-071. Umweltbundesamt, Berlin.

Ravel. 1994. Praxislehrstücke, wie Ausgaben für einen rationelleren Stromeinsatz zur lohnenden Investition werden. Bundesamt für Konjunkturfragen, Bern.

Reddy, A.K. 1991. "Barriers to Improvement in Energy Efficiency." *Energy Policy* 19: 953–61.

Reddy, A.K., R.H. Williams, and R.B. Johansson. 1997. *Energy After Rio—Prospects and Challenges.* United Nations Development Programme, New York.

Refining Processes. 1998. "Flow Diagrams and Summary Descriptions Represent Typical Processes Used by Modern Refineries." *Hydrocarbon Processing* 77 (11): 53–114L.

Ritt, A. 1997. "Acme Rolls 0.030 Inch Hot Band." *New Steel* 13 (5).

Romm, J.J. 1999. *Cool Companies—How the Best Businesses Boost Profits and Productivity by Cutting Greenhouse Gas Emissions.* London: Earthscan.

Rosemann, H., and H.G. Ellerbrock. 1998. "Milling Technology of Cement Production [in German]." *ZKG International* 51(2): 51–62.

Rumsey P.R., and T. Flanagan. 1995a. "South East Asian Energy Efficiency Success Stories, Singapore, Malaysia and Indonesia." International Institute for Energy Conservation.

———. 1995b. "Standards and Labelling: The Philippines Residential Air Conditioning Market." International Institute for Energy Conservation.

Russian Federation, Ministry of Fuel and Energy. 1998. "Federal Target Program 'Energy Saving in Russia'." Moscow.

Russian Federation, Ministry of Transport. 1995. "Target Programme 'Fuels and Energy Saving in Transport' [in Russian]."

SADC (South African Development Cooperation). 1996: "Focus on Zambia: Energy Conservation in Zambia." *Energy Management Newsletter* 1 (4).

———.1997. "Focus on Mozambique: Potential for Energy Conservation in Mozambique." *Energy Management Newsletter* 3 (1).

Saha B.B., and T. Kashiwagi. 1997. "Experimental Investigation of an Advanced Adsorption Refrigeration Cycle." *ASHRAE Trans.* 103: 50–57.

Sanstad, A.H., and R.B. Howarth. 1994. "'Normal' Markets, Market Imperfections and Energy Efficiency." *Energy Policy* 22: 811–18.

Schipper, L. 1997. "Indicators of Energy Use and Efficiency: Understanding the Link Between Energy and Human Activity." International Energy Agency and Organisation for Economic Co-operation and Development, Paris.

Sheinbaum, C, and L. Ozawa. 1998. "Energy Use and CO_2 Emissions for Mexico's Cement Industry." *Energy Policy* 23 (9): 725–32.

Sheinbaum, C., and V. Rodríguez. 1997. "Recent Trends in Mexican Industrial Energy Use and Their Impact on Carbon Dioxide Emissions." *Energy Policy* 25 (7–9): 825–31.

Sheinbaum, C., S. Meyers, and J. Sathaye. 1994. "Transportation Energy Used in Mexico." Lawrence Berkeley National Laboratory. LBL-35919. Berkeley, Calif.

Shimazaki Y., A. Akisawa, and T. Kashiwagi. 1997. "A Model Analysis on the Effects of Energy Cascaded Systems." Proceedings of the Thermodynamic Analysis and Improvement of Energy Systems, Beijing.

Sinton, J.E., and M.D. Levine. 1994. "Changing Energy Intensity in Chinese Industry." *Energy Policy* 22: 239–55.

Sinyak, Yu. 1991. "USSR: Energy Efficiency and Prospects." *Energy* 16 (5): 791–815.

Sioshansi, F.P. 1991. "The Myths and Facts of Energy Efficiency." *Energy Policy* 19: 231–43.

SNAP (Strategic National Action Plan). 1999. *Climate Change Action Plan Report to the Country Study Programme.* Moscow.

Soares, J.A., and R.P. Tabosa. 1996. "Motores Elétricos: Uma Análise Comparativa de Mercado e Eficiência." Proceedings: VII Congresso Brasileiro de Energia. Rio de Janeiro, COPPE/UFRJ.

Suzuki Y., K. Ueta, and S. Mori, eds. 1996. *Global Environmental Security.* Berlin: Springer.

TACIS (Technical Assistance for CIS Countries). 1996. "Development of Energy Policy in Georgia." TACIS/92/EG001. Brussels.

Tanides, C., M. Brugnoni, and G. Dutt. 1996. "Characterisation of Residential Electricity Use in Argentina and Implications for Energy Conservation Programmes." Proceedings of the 31st Universities Power Engineering Conference (UPEC 96), Heraklion, Creece.

TAU of SADCC, Energy Sector. 1991. "Experience in Energy Conservation: Zimbabwe Case." Paper presented at the International Seminar on Energy in Africa, Abidjan, Côte d'Ivoire.

TERI (Tata Energy Research Institute). 1992. "State of the Art Report on Use of CNG in the Transport Sector." New Delhi.

———. 1994. "National Programme in Bagasse Based Co-generation." *TERI Energy and Environment Monitor* 10 (1).

———. 1996a. "Research on Energy-intensive Industries in India." New Delhi.

———. 1996b. "Sector Analysis, Aluminium Industry." Prepared for the Energy Efficiency Support Project, New Delhi.

———. 1997a. "Capacity Building for Technology Transfer in the Context of the Climate Change." New Delhi.

———. 1997b. "Report on Small-scale Brick Industry in India." New Delhi.

———. 1997c. "Technical Paper on GHG Mitigation/Abatement Options." New Delhi.

———. 1998. "Action Research Project in Small Scale Foundry Industry." New Delhi.

———. 1999. *TERI Energy Data Directory and Yearbook 1998–99* (TEDDY). New Delhi.

TERI (Tata Energy Research Institute), and FAI (Fertilizer Association of India). 1995. "Development of Oil Consumption Norm for the Fertilizer Industry." New Delhi.

TIFAC (Technology Information Forecasting and Assessment Council). 1992. "Recommendations on Energy Conservation in Cement Industry." Government of India, Department of Scientific and Industrial Research.

Turyareeba, P. 1993. "Mobilizing Local Financial Resources—The Case of Uganda." In S. Karekezi and G.A. Mackenzie, eds., *Energy Options for Africa—Environmentally Sustainable Alternatives.* London: Zed Books.

UN (United Nations). 1999. *Yearbook of Industrial Statistics, 1999.* Vol. II. New York.

UNDP (United Nations Development Programme). 1999. *Energy as a Tool for Sustainable Development for African, Caribbean and Pacific Countries.* New York.

UNFCCC (United Nation Framework Convention on Climate Change).1997. *Horticultural Project in Tyumen. Uniform Report on Activities Implemented Jointly Under the Pilot Phase.* UNFCCC Secretariat, Bonn.

———. 1998. *1998 Annual Energy Review.* Washington, D.C.

Vakulko, A.G., and A.A. Zlobin. 1997. "Energy Saving Measures in Electricity Supply Systems of Industrial Enterprices." *Vestnik Glavgosenergonadzora Rossii* no.1, Moscow.

Valdes-Arrieta, F. 1993. "Saving Energy in Chile: an Assessment of Energy Use and Potential Efficiency Improvements." International Institute for Energy Conservation, Santiago, Chile.

Vargas Nieto, E. 1999. "ILUMEX Project: A General Vision." In *Proceedings International ILUMEX Seminar.* Puerto Vallarta, Mexico.

Varone, F. 1998. "Le choix des instruments des politiques publiques. Une analyse comarée des politique d'efficience énergétique du Canada, du Danmark, des Etats-Unis, de la Suède et de la Suisse." Editions Paul Haupt. Bern, Switzerland.

Varone, F., and B. Aebischer. 1999. "From National Policies to Global Market Transformation: The Challenges of (International) Policy Design." In *Proceedings of the 1999 ECEEE Summer Study "Energy Efficiency and CO2 Reduction: The Dimensions of the Social Challenge"* Paris: ADEME Editions.

Vasiliev, A., and others. 1998. "Improvements of Tariffs Regulations at End-users Energy Markets." *Energomeneger* (11): 12–14 [in Russian].

VDEW (German Electricity Utility Association). 1997. "Stromversorger rüsten sich für den Wettbewerb." *Stromthemen* 7: 1–2.

Velthuijsen, J.W. 1995. "Determinants of Investment in Energy Conservation." SEO, University of Amsterdam, Netherlands.

Wanwacharakul V. 1993. "Reducing CO_2 Emission in Thailand." *Quarterly Environmental Journal,* Thailand Environment Institute 1 (1): 50–65.

WBCSD (World Business Council for Sustainable Development). 1996. "Eco-efficient Leadership for Improved Economic and Environmental Performance." Geneva.

WBNSS (World Bank National Strategy Study). 1999. "Study on Russian National Strategy of Greenhouse Gas Emissions Reduction." Task 4. Moscow.

Wereko-Brobby C. 1993. "Innovative Energy Policy Instruments and Institutional Reform—The Case of Ghana." In S. Karekezi and G.A. Mackenzie, eds., *Energy Options for Africa—Environmentally Sustainable Alternatives.* London: Zed Books.

Werling, E., J. Hall, and D. Meseigeier. 1998. "Lessons Learned in the ENERGY STAR Homes Program." In *Proceedings of the ACEEE Summer Study on Energy Efficiency in Buildings.* Asilomar, Calif.: American Council for an Energy-Efficient Economy.

Wirtschaftvereinigung Stahl. 1998. *Statistical Yearbooks of the Steel Industry* [in German].

World Bank. 1989. *Sub-Saharan Africa: From Crisis to Sustainable Growth.* Washington, D.C.

———. 1993. "Energy Efficiency and Conservation in the Developing World. The World Bank's Role." Policy Paper, Washington, D.C.

———. 1996. *Georgia: Energy Sector Review.* Washington, D.C.

Worrell, E., N. Martin, and L. Price. 1999. "Energy Efficiency and Carbon Emissions Reduction Opportunities in the U.S. Iron and Steel Industry." Lawrence Berkeley National Laboratory, LBNL-41724. Berkeley, Calif.

Yakowitz, H. and R. Hanmer. 1993. "Policy Options—Encouraging Cleaner Production in the 1990s." In: T. Jackson, ed., *Clean Production Strategies.* Boca Raton, Fla.: Lewis Publishers.

Ziesing, H.-J., and others. 1999. "Scenarios and Measures for Mitigating CO2-Emissions in Germany until 2005." In G. Stein and B. Strobel, eds., *Policy Scenarios for Climate Protection* [in German]. Forschungszentrum Jülich, Germany.

renewable energy technologies

CHAPTER 7

Wim C. Turkenburg (Netherlands)

LEAD AUTHORS: Jos Beurskens (Netherlands), André Faaij (Netherlands), Peter Fraenkel (United Kingdom), Ingvar Fridleifsson (Iceland), Erik Lysen (Netherlands), David Mills (Australia), Jose Roberto Moreira (Brazil), Lars J. Nilsson (Sweden), Anton Schaap (Netherlands), and Wim C. Sinke (Netherlands)

CONTRIBUTING AUTHORS: Per Dannemand Andersen (Denmark), Sheila Bailey (United States), Jakob Björnsson (Iceland), Teun Bokhoven (Netherlands), Lex Bosselaar (Netherlands), Suani Teixeira Coelho (Brazil), Baldur Eliasson (Switzerland), Brian Erb (Canada), David Hall (United Kingdom), Peter Helby (Sweden), Stephen Karekezi (Kenya), Eric Larson (United States), Joachim Luther (Germany), Birger Madson (Denmark), E.V.R. Sastry (India), Yohji Uchiyama (Japan), and Richard van den Broek (Netherlands)

ABSTRACT In 1998 renewable energy sources supplied 56 ± 10 exajoules, or about 14 percent of world primary energy consumption. The supply was dominated by traditional biomass (38 ± 10 exajoules a year). Other major contributions came from large hydropower (9 exajoules a year) and from modern biomass (7 exajoules). The contribution of all other renewables—small hydropower, geothermal, wind, solar, and marine energy—was about 2 exajoules. That means that the energy supply from new renewables was about 9 exajoules (about 2 percent of world consumption). The commercial primary energy supply from renewable sources was 27 ± 6 exajoules (nearly 7 percent of world consumption), with 16 ± 6 exajoules from biomass.

Renewable energy sources can meet many times the present world energy demand, so their potential is enormous. They can enhance diversity in energy supply markets, secure long-term sustainable energy supplies, and reduce local and global atmospheric emissions. They can also provide commercially attractive options to meet specific needs for energy services (particularly in developing countries and rural areas), create new employment opportunities, and offer possibilities for local manufacturing of equipment.

There are many renewable technologies. Although often commercially available, most are still at an early stage of development and not technically mature. They demand continuing research, development, and demonstration efforts. In addition, few renewable energy technologies can compete with conventional fuels on cost, except in some niche markets. But substantial cost reductions can be achieved for most renewables, closing gaps and making them more competitive. That will require further technology development and market deployment—and boosting production capacities to mass production.

For the long term and under very favourable conditions, the lowest cost to produce electricity might be $0.01–0.02 a kilowatt-hour for geothermal, $0.03 a kilowatt-hour for wind and hydro, $0.04 a kilowatt-hour for solar thermal and biomass, and $0.05–0.06 a kilowatt-hour for photovoltaics and marine currents. The lowest cost to produce heat might be $0.005 a kilowatt-hour for geothermal, $0.01 a kilowatt-hour for biomass, and $0.02–0.03 a kilowatt-hour for solar thermal. The lowest cost to produce fuels might be $1.5 a gigajoule for biomass, $6–7 a gigajoule for ethanol, $7–10 a gigajoule for methanol, and $6–8 a gigajoule for hydrogen.

Scenarios investigating the potential of renewables reveal that they might contribute 20–50 percent of energy supplies in the second half of the 21st century. A transition to renewables-based energy systems would have to rely on:

■ Successful development and diffusion of renewable energy technologies that become more competitive through cost reductions from technological and organisational developments.

■ Political will to internalise environmental costs and other externalities that permanently increase fossil fuel prices.

Many countries have found ways to promote renewables. As renewable energy activities grow and require more funding, the tendency in many countries is to move away from methods that let taxpayers carry the burden of promoting renewables, towards economic and regulatory methods that let energy consumers carry the burden. ■

R enewable energy sources have been important for humans since the beginning of civilisation. For centuries and in many ways, biomass has been used for heating, cooking, steam raising, and power generation—and hydropower and wind energy, for movement and later for electricity production. Renewable energy sources generally depend on energy flows through the Earth's ecosystem from the insolation of the sun and the geothermal energy of the Earth. One can distinguish:

- Biomass energy (plant growth driven by solar radiation).
- Wind energy (moving air masses driven by solar energy).
- Direct use of solar energy (as for heating and electricity production).
- Hydropower.
- Marine energy (such as wave energy, marine current energy, and energy from tidal barrages).
- Geothermal energy (from heat stored in rock by the natural heat flow of the Earth).

If applied in a modern way, renewable energy sources (or renewables) are considered highly responsive to overall energy

Many renewables technologies are suited to small off-grid applications, good for rural, remote areas, where energy is often crucial in human development.

policy guidelines and environmental, social, and economic goals:

- Diversifying energy carriers for the production of heat, fuels, and electricity.
- Improving access to clean energy sources.
- Balancing the use of fossil fuels, saving them for other applications and for future generations.
- Increasing the flexibility of power systems as electricity demand changes.
- Reducing pollution and emissions from conventional energy systems.
- Reducing dependency and minimising spending on imported fuels.

Furthermore, many renewables technologies are suited to small off-grid applications, good for rural, remote areas, where energy is often crucial in human development. At the same time, such small energy systems can contribute to the local economy and create local jobs.

The natural energy flows through the Earth's ecosystem are immense, and the theoretical potential of what they can produce for human needs exceeds current energy consumption by many times. For example, solar power plants on 1 percent of the world's desert area would generate the world's entire electricity demand today.

TABLE 7.1. CATEGORIES OF RENEWABLE ENERGY CONVERSION TECHNOLOGIES

Technology	Energy product	Application
Biomass energy		
Combustion (domestic scale)	Heat (cooking, space heating)	Widely applied; improved technologies available
Combustion (industrial scale)	Process heat, steam, electricity	Widely applied; potential for improvement
Gasification/power production	Electricity, heat (CHP).	Demonstration phase
Gasification/fuel production	Hydrocarbons, methanol, H_2	Development phase
Hydrolysis and fermentation	Ethanol	Commercially applied for sugar/ starch crops; production from wood under development
Pyrolysis/production of liquid fuels	Bio-oils	Pilot phase; some technical barriers
Pyrolysis/production of solid fuels	Charcoal	Widely applied; wide range of efficiencies
Extraction	Biodiesel	Applied; relatively expensive
Digestion	Biogas	Commercially applied
Wind energy		
Water pumping and battery charging	Movement, power	Small wind machines, widely applied
Onshore wind turbines	Electricity	Widely applied commercially
Offshore wind turbines	Electricity	Development and demonstration phase
Solar energy		
Photovoltaic solar energy conversion	Electricity	Widely applied; rather expensive; further development needed
Solar thermal electricity	Heat, steam, electricity	Demonstrated; further development needed
Low-temperature solar energy use	Heat (water and space heating, cooking, drying) and cold	Solar collectors commercially applied; solar cookers widely applied in some regions; solar drying demonstrated and applied
Passive solar energy use	Heat, cold, light, ventilation	Demonstrations and applications; no active parts
Artificial photosynthesis	H_2 or hydrogen rich fuels	Fundamental and applied research
Hydropower	Power, electricity	Commercially applied; small and large scale applications
Geothermal energy	Heat, steam, electricity	Commercially applied
Marine energy		
Tidal energy	Electricity	Applied; relatively expensive
Wave energy	Electricity	Research, development, and demonstration phase
Current energy	Electricity	Research and development phase
Ocean thermal energy conversion	Heat, electricity	Research, development, and demonstration phase
Salinity gradient / osmotic energy	Electricity	Theoretical option
Marine biomass production	Fuels	Research and development phase

BOX 7.1. LAND USE REQUIREMENTS FOR ENERGY PRODUCTION

Biomass production requires land. The productivity of a perennial crop (willow, eucalyptus, switchgrass) is 8–12 tonnes of dry matter per hectare a year. The lower heating value (LHV) of dry clean wood amounts to about 18 gigajoules a tonne; the higher heating value about 20 gigajoules a tonne. Thus 1 hectare can produce 140–220 gigajoules per hectare a year (LHV; gross energy yield; taking into account energy inputs for cultivation, fertiliser, harvest, and so on, of about 5 percent in total). The production of 1 petajoule currently requires 4,500–7,000 hectares. To fuel a baseload biomass energy power plant of 600 megawatts of electricity with a conversion efficiency of 40 percent would require 140,000–230,000 hectares. Annual production of 100 exajoules (one-quarter of the world's current energy use) would take 450–700 million hectares.

With ample resources and technologies at hand for renewable energy use, the question of future development boils down to economic and political competitiveness with other energy sources. Since the performance and costs of conversion technologies largely determine the competitiveness of renewables, technological development is the key. Still, the World Energy Council, Shell, the Intergovernmental Panel on Climate Change (IPCC), and several UN bodies project a growing role for renewable energy in the 21st century with major contributions from biomass, hydropower, wind, and solar.

A wide variety of technologies are available or under development to provide inexpensive, reliable, and sustainable energy services from renewables (table 7.1). But the stage of development and the competitiveness of those technologies differ greatly. Moreover, performance and competitiveness are determined by local conditions, physical and socioeconomic, and on the local availability of fossil fuels.

All renewable energy sources can be converted to electricity. Since some major renewable energy sources are intermittent (wind, solar), fitting such supplies into a grid creates challenges. This is less of a problem for biomass, hydropower, and geothermal. Only a few of them produce liquid and gaseous fuels as well as heat directly.

Biomass energy

Biomass is a rather simple term for all organic material that stems from plants (including algae), trees, and crops. Biomass sources are therefore diverse, including organic waste streams, agricultural and forestry residues, as well as crops grown to produce heat, fuels, and electricity (energy plantations).

Biomass contributes significantly to the world's energy supply—probably accounting for 45 ± 10 exajoules a year (9–13 percent of the world's energy supply; IEA, 1998; WEC, 1998; Hall, 1997). Its largest contribution to energy consumption—on average between a third and a fifth—is found in developing countries. Compare that with 3 percent in industrialised countries (Hall and others, 1993; WEC, 1994b; IEA REWP, 1999).

Dominating the traditional use of biomass, particularly in developing countries, is firewood for cooking and heating. Some traditional use is not sustainable because it may deprive local soils of needed nutrients, cause indoor and outdoor air pollution, and result in poor health. It may also contribute to greenhouse gas emissions and affect ecosystems (chapters 3 and 10). The modern use of biomass, to produce electricity, steam, and biofuels, is estimated at 7 exajoules a year. This is considered fully commercial, based on bought biomass or used for productive purposes. That leaves the traditional at 38 ± 10 exajoules a year. Part of this is commercial—the household fuelwood in industrialised countries and charcoal and firewood in urban and industrial areas in developing countries. But there are almost no data on the size of this market. If it can be estimated at between 10 percent and 30 percent (9 ± 6 exajoules a year), which seems probable, the total commercial use of biomass in 1998 was 16 ± 6 exajoules.

Since the early 1990s biomass has gained considerable interest world-wide. It is carbon neutral when produced sustainably. Its geographic distribution is relatively even. It has the potential to produce modern energy carriers that are clean and convenient to use. It can make a large contribution to rural development. And its

TABLE 7.2. POTENTIAL CONTRIBUTION OF BIOMASS TO THE WORLD'S ENERGY NEEDS

Source	Time frame (year)	Total projected global energy demand (exajoules a year)	Contribution of biomass to energy demand (exajoules a year)	Comments
RIGES (Johansson and others, 1993)	2025 2050	395 561	145 206	Based on calculation with the RIGES model
SHELL (Kassler,1994)	2060	1,500 900	220 200	Sustained growth scenario Dematerialization scenario
WEC (1994a)	2050 2100	671–1,057 895–1,880	94–157 132–215	Range given here reflects the outcomes of three scenarios
Greenpeace and SEI (Lazarus and others,1993)	2050 2100	610 986	114 181	A scenario in which fossil fuels are phased out during the 21st century
IPCC (Ishitani and Johansson,1996)	2050 2100	560 710	280 325	Biomass intensive energy system development

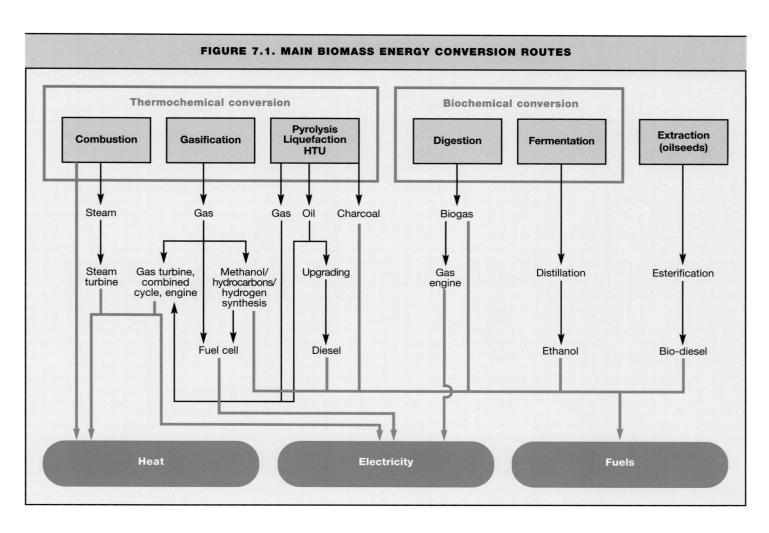

FIGURE 7.1. MAIN BIOMASS ENERGY CONVERSION ROUTES

attractive costs make it a promising energy source in many regions. With various technologies available to convert biomass into modern energy carriers, the application of commercial and modern biomass energy systems is growing in many countries.

The potential of biomass energy

The resource potential of biomass energy is much larger than current world energy consumption (chapter 5). But given the low conversion efficiency of solar to biomass energy (less than 1 percent), large areas are needed to produce modern energy carriers in substantial amounts (box 7.1). With agriculture modernised up to reasonable standards in various regions, and given the need to preserve and improve the world's natural areas, 700–1,400 million hectares may be available for biomass energy production well into the 21st century (Hall and others, 1993; Larson and others, 1995; Ishitani and others, 1996; IIASA and WEC, 1998; Larson, Williams, and Johansson, 1999). This includes degraded, unproductive lands and excess agricultural lands. The availability of land for energy plantations strongly depends on the food supplies needed and on the possibilities for intensifying agricultural production in a sustainable way.

A number of studies have assessed the potential contribution of biomass to the world energy supply (table 7.2). Although the percentage contribution of biomass varies considerably, especially depending on expected land availability and future energy demand, the absolute potential contribution of biomass in the long term is high—from 100–300 exajoules a year. World-wide annual primary energy consumption is now about 400 exajoules.

Biomass energy conversion technologies

Conversion routes to produce heat, electricity, and/or fuels from biomass are plentiful (figure 7.1).

Production of heat. In developing countries the development and introduction of improved stoves for cooking and heating can have a big impact on biomass use (chapters 3 and 10). Especially in colder climates (Scandinavia, Austria, Germany) domestic biomass-fired heating systems are widespread. Improved heating systems are automated, have catalytic gas cleaning, and use standard fuel (such as pellets). The benefit over open fireplaces is considerable, with advanced domestic heaters obtaining efficiencies of more than 70 percent and producing far fewer atmospheric emissions. The present heat-generating capacity is estimated to be more than 200 gigawatts of thermal energy.

Production of electricity. Some features of the main thermochemcial biomass energy conversion routes to electricity and combined heat and power (CHP) are presented in table 7.3. Combustion of biomass to produce electricity is applied commercially in many regions, with the total installed capacity estimated at 40 gigawatts of electricity. The application of fluid bed combustion and advanced gas cleaning allows for efficient production of electricity (and heat) from biomass. At a scale of 20–100 megawatts of electricity, electrical efficiencies of 20–40 percent are possible (van den Broek and others, 1996; Solantausta and others, 1996). Often the electricity is produced along with heat or steam (CHP) in Denmark and Sweden. In Southeast Asia, through the Association of Southeast Asian Nations–European Union COGEN Programme, sawmill factories in Indonesia, Malaysia, and Thailand have cogeneration systems, using wood-waste from the factories.

Co-combustion systems—combining, say, natural gas and coal with biomass—are built in such places as Denmark with the benefits of greater economies of scale and reduced fuel supply risks. Co-combustion of biomass in coal-fired power plants is a popular way to increase biomass-based power generation capacity with minimal investment (chapter 8). Other advantages over coal-based power production are the higher efficiencies (due in most cases to the large scale of the existing power plant) and lower sulphur dioxide (SO_2) and nitrogen oxide (NO_x) emissions (Meuleman and Faaij, 1999).

Large gasification. Gasification technologies can convert biomass into fuel gas, cleaned before its combustion in, say, a gas turbine. Biomass integrated gasification/combined cycle (BIG/CC) systems combine flexible fuel characteristics and high electrical efficiency. Electrical conversion efficiencies of 40 percent (LHV) are possible at a scale of about 30 megawatts of electricity (Consonni and Larson, 1994a, b; Faaij and others, 1997).

Demonstration projects are under way in various countries and for various gasification concepts. In Brazil a project supported by the World Bank and Global Environment Facility will demonstrate a 30 megawatts-electric BIG/CC unit fired with cultivated eucalyptus (Elliott and Booth, 1993). Sweden's first BIG/CC unit, based on pressurised gasification, has several thousands of hours of operational experience. Three other demonstration units around the 6–10 megawatts-electric scale are under way. An atmospheric BIG/CC system is being commissioned in Yorkshire, United Kingdom. In the United States an indirect gasification process is under demonstration at the Burlington power station.

The first generation of BIG/CC systems shows high unit capital costs. Depending on the scale, prices are $2,800–5,000 a kilowatt of electricity. But cost reduction potential is considerable for BIG/CC systems—capital costs might come down to $1,100–2,000 a kilowatt (Williams, 1996; Solantausta and others, 1996; Faaij, Meuleman, and Van Ree, 1998). Co-gasification of biomass, another option, is being applied in the United States and Europe. An interesting alternative for fuel gas produced through biomass gasification is its use in existing (or new) natural gas-fired combined cycles. In this way, economies of scale come with a safe fuel supply (Walter and others, 1998). This option has not been demonstrated yet, but more research is under way.

Small gasification. Small (fixed bed) gasifiers coupled to diesel or gasoline engines (typically for systems of 100–200 kilowatts of electricity with an approximate electrical efficiency of 15–25 percent) are commercially available on the market. But high costs and the need for gas cleaning and careful operation have blocked application in large numbers. Some systems are being applied fairly successfully in rural India and in China and Indonesia (Kaltschmitt and others, 1998; Stassen, 1995).

Biogas production. Anaerobic digestion of biomass has been demonstrated and applied commercially with success in many situations and for a variety of feedstocks–such as organic domestic waste, organic industrial wastes, manure, and sludges. Large advanced systems are developed for wet industrial waste streams and applied in many countries. In India there is widespread production of biogas from

TABLE 7.3. MAIN THERMOCHEMICAL BIOMASS ENERGY CONVERSION ROUTES TO HEAT AND ELECTRICITY

Conversion system	Range	Net efficiency (percent, LHV)	Investment cost (dollars a kilowatt of electricity)
Combustion			
Combined heat and power (CHP)	100 kWe to 1 MWe	60–90 (overall)	
	1–10 MWe	80–99 (overall)	
Standalone	20–100 MWe	20–40 (electrical)	1,600–2,500
Co-combustion	5–20 MWe	30–40 (electrical)	250 plus costs of existing power plant
Gasification			
CHP			900–3,000 (depending on location and configuration)
Diesel	100 kWe to 1 MWe	15–25 (electrical)	
Gas turbine	1–10 MWe	25–30 (electrical)	
BIG/CC	30–100 MWe	40–55 (electrical)	1,100–2,000 (when commercially proven)
Digestion			
Wet biomass materials	Up to several MWe	10–15 (electrical)	5,000

animal and other wastes for cooking, lighting, and power generation (chapter 10).

Digestion has a low overall electric conversion efficiency (roughly 10–15 percent, depending on the feedstock) and is particularly suited for wet biomass materials. Landfills contribute to atmospheric methane emissions. In many situations the collection of landfill gas and its conversion to electricity using gas engines is profitable, and such systems are becoming more widespread (Faaij, Hekkert, and others, 1998).

Production of liquid and gaseous fuels from biomass (bio-oil and biocrude). At temperatures around 500 degrees Celsius in the absence of oxygen, pyrolysis converts biomass to liquid (bio-oil), gaseous, and solid (charcoal) fractions. With flash pyrolysis techniques (fast pyrolysis) the liquid fraction can be up to 70 percent of the thermal biomass input. Bio-oil contains about 40 weight-percent of oxygen and is corrosive and acidic. The oil can be upgraded to reduce the oxygen content, but that has economic and energy penalties. Pyrolysis and upgrading technology are still largely in the pilot phase (Bridgewater, 1998).

Hydrothermal upgrading (HTU), originally developed by Shell, converts biomass at a high pressure and at moderate temperatures in water to biocrude. Biocrude contains far less oxygen than bio-oil produced through pyrolysis, but the process is still in a pre-pilot phase (Naber and others 1997).

Ethanol. Production of ethanol by fermenting sugars is a classic conversion route for sugar cane, maize, and corn on a large scale, especially in Brazil, France, and the United States. Zimbabwe also has a considerable fuel ethanol programme using sugar cane (Hemstock and Hall, 1995). The U.S. and European programmes convert surplus food crops to a useful (by) product. But ethanol production from maize and corn is far from being competitive with gasoline and diesel. Nor is the overall energy balance of such systems very favourable.

An exception is Brazil's PRO-ALCOOL programme, due to the high productivity of sugar cane (Rosillo-Calle and Cortez, 1998). This programme is discussed in some detail later in this chapter. In 1998 world production of ethanol was estimated at 18 billion litres (equivalent to 420 petajoules).

Ethanol can also be produced by the hydrolysis of lignocellulosic biomass, a potentially low-cost and efficient option. Hydrolysis techniques are gaining more development attention, particularly in Sweden and the United States, but some fundamental issues need to be resolved. If these barriers are lowered and ethanol production is combined with efficient electricity production from unconverted wood fractions (such as lignine), ethanol costs could come close to current gasoline prices—as low as $0.12 a litre at biomass costs of about $2 a gigajoule (Lynd, 1996). Overall system conversion efficiency could go up to about 70 percent (LHV).

Esters from oilseeds. Oilseeds, such as rapeseed, can be extracted and converted to esters and are well suited to replace diesel. Substantial quantities of RME (rape methyl esters) are produced in the European Union and to a lesser extent in North America. But RME requires substantial subsidies to compete with diesel. Energy balances for RME systems are less favourable than those for perennial crops (Ishitani and Johansson, 1996), so the net energy production per hectare is low. These balances can be improved if by-products (such as straw) are also used as an energy source.

Methanol, hydrogen, and hydrocarbons through gasification. Production of methanol and hydrogen using gasification technology and traditional syngas conversion processes could offer an attractive conversion route for biomass over the long term. Although such concepts received serious attention in the early 1980s, low oil prices made them unattractive. New technology—such as liquid phase methanol production (combined with electricity generation) and new gas separation technology—offers lower production costs and higher overall conversion efficiencies. With large-scale conversion and the production of both fuel and electricity, methanol and hydrogen from lignocellulosic biomass might compete with gasoline and diesel (Spath and others, 2000; Faaij and others, 1999). In addition, synthetic hydrocarbons and methanol can be produced from syngas using Fischer-Tropsch synthesis (Larson and Jin, 1999a, b).

Environmental impacts of biomass energy systems

Biomass energy can be carbon neutral when all biomass produced is used for energy (short carbon cycle). But sustained production on the same surface of land can have considerable negative impacts on soil fertility, water use, agrochemical use, biodiversity, and landscape. Furthermore, the collection and transport of biomass increases the use of vehicles and infrastructure and the emissions to the atmosphere (Tolbert, 1998; Borjesson, 1999; Faaij, Meuleman, and others, 1998). Seen world-wide, climatic, soil, and socioeconomic conditions set strongly variable demands for what biomass production will be sustainable.

Erosion. Erosion is a problem related to the cultivation of many annual crops in many regions. The best-suited energy crops are perennials, with much better land cover than food crops. And during harvest, the removal of soil can be kept to a minimum, since the roots remain in the soil. Another positive effect is that the formation of an extensive root system adds to the organic matter content of the soil. Generally, diseases (such as eelworms) are prevented, and the soil structure is improved.

Water use. Increased water use caused by additional demands of (new) vegetation can become a concern, particularly in arid and semi-arid regions. The choice of crop can have a considerable effect on water-use efficiency. Some eucalyptus species have a very good water-use efficiency, considering the amount of water needed per tonne of biomass produced. But a eucalyptus plantation on a large area could increase the local demand for groundwater and affect its level. On the other hand, improved land cover generally is good for

Biomass has gained considerable interest worldwide. It is carbon neutral when produced sustainably.

water retention and microclimatic conditions. Thus the impacts on the hydrological situation should be evaluated at the local level.

Agrochemicals. Pesticides affect the quality of groundwater and surface water and thus plants and animals. Specific effects depend on the type of chemical, the quantity used, and the method of application. Experience with perennial crops (willow, poplar, eucalyptus, miscanthus) suggests that they meet strict environmental standards. Compared with food crops like cereals, application rates of agrochemicals per hectare are a fifth to a twentieth for perennial energy crops (Faaij, Meuleman, and others, 1998; Borjesson, 1999).

Nutrients. The abundant use of fertilisers and manure in agriculture has led to considerable environmental problems in various regions: nitrification of groundwater, saturation of soils with phosphate, eutrophication, and unpotable water. Phosphates have also increased the heavy metal flux of the soil. But energy farming with short rotation forestry and perennial grasses requires less fertiliser than conventional agriculture (Kaltschmitt and others, 1996). With perennials, better recycling of nutrients is obtained. The leaching of nitrogen for willow cultivation can be a half to a tenth that for food crops, meeting stringent standards for groundwater protection. The use of plantation biomass will result in removal of nutrients from the soil that have to be replenished in one way or the other. Recycling of ashes is feasible for returning crucial trace elements and phosphates to the soil, already common practice in Austria and Sweden. In Brazil stillage, a nutrient rich remainder of sugar cane fermentation, is returned to sugar cane plantations.

Biodiversity and landscape. Biomass plantations can be criticised because the range of biological species they support is much narrower than what natural forests support (Beyea and others, 1991). Although this is generally true, it is not always relevant. It would be if a virgin forest is replaced by a biomass plantation. But if plantations are established on degraded lands or on excess agricultural lands, the restored lands are likely to support a more diverse ecology.

Degraded lands are plentiful: estimates indicate that about 2 billion hectares of degraded land are 'available' in developing countries (Larson, Williams, and Johansson, 1999; IIASA and WEC, 1998). It would be desirable to restore such land surfaces anyway—for water retention, erosion prevention, and (micro-) climate control. A good plantation design, including areas set aside for native plants and animals fitting in the landscape in a natural way, can avoid the problems normally associated with monocultures, acknowledging that a plantation of energy crops does not always mean a monoculture.

Other risks (fire, disease). Landscaping and managing biomass production systems can considerably reduce the risks of fire and disease. Thus they deserve more attention in coming projects, policies, and research.

Conversion and end use. Conversion of biomass to desired intermediate energy carriers and their use for energy services should meet strict environmental standards as well. Problems that could occur (such as emissions to air) can be easily countered with technology that is well understood and available. Clean combustion of biomass is now common practice in Scandinavia. Gasification allows for cleaning fuel gas prior to combustion or further processing. Care should be paid to small (less than 1 megawatts of thermal energy) conversion systems: technology to meet strict emission standards is available but can have a serious impact on the investment and operational costs of such small systems (Kaltschmitt and others, 1998; Stassen, 1995).

Economics of biomass energy systems

Biomass is a profitable alternative mainly when cheap or even negative-cost biomass residues or wastes are available. To make biomass

TABLE 7.4. MAIN PERFORMANCE DATA FOR SOME CONVERSION ROUTES OF BIOMASS TO FUELS

	RME	Ethanol from sugar or starch crops	Ethanol from lignocellulosic biomass	Hydrogen from lignocellulosic biomass	Methanol from lignocellulosic biomass	Bio-oil from lignocellulosic biomass
Concept	Extraction and esterification	Fermentation	Hydrolysis, fermentation, and electricity production	Gasification	Gasification	Flash pyrolysis
Net energy efficiency of conversion	75 percent based on all energy inputs	50 percent for sugar beet; 44 percent for sugar cane	60–70 percent (longer term with power generation included)	55–65 percent 60–70 percent (longer term)	50–60 percent 60–70 percent (longer term)	70 percent (raw bio-oil)
Cost range, short term[a]	$15–25 a gigajoule (northwest Europe)	$15–25 a gigajoule for sugar beet; $8–10 a gigajoule for sugar cane	$10–15 a gigajoule	$8–10 a gigajoule	$11–13 a gigajoule	n.a.
Cost range, long term[a]	n.a.	n.a.	$6–7 a gigajoule	$6–8 a gigajoule	$7–10 a gigajoule	Unclear

a. Diesel and gasoline production costs vary widely depending on the oil price. Longer–term projections give estimates of roughly $0.25–0.35 a litre, or $8–11 a gigajoule. Retail fuel transport prices are usually dominated by taxes of $0.50–1.30 a litre depending on the country.

Source: Wyman and others, 1993; IEA, 1994; Williams and others, 1995; Jager and others, 1998; Faaij, Hamelinck, and Agterberg, forthcoming.

competitive with fossil fuels, the production of biomass, the conversion technologies, and total bio-energy systems require further optimisation.

Biomass production. Plantation biomass costs already are favourable in some developing countries. Eucalyptus plantations in northeast Brazil supply wood chips at prices between $1.5–2.0 a gigajoule (Carpentieri and others, 1993). Costs are (much) higher in industrialised countries, such as $4 a gigajoule in parts of northwest Europe (Rijk, 1994; van den Broek and others, 1997). But by about 2020, with improved crops and production systems, biomass production costs in the United States could be about $1.5–2.0 a gigajoule for substantial land surfaces (Graham and others, 1995; Turnure and others, 1995; Hughes and Wiltsee, 1995). It is expected for large areas in the world that low-cost biomass can be produced in large quantities. Its competitiveness will depend on the prices of coal (and natural gas), but also on the costs and net returns from alternative, competing uses of productive land.

Power generation from biomass. With biomass prices of about $2 a gigajoule, state of the art combustion technology at a scale of 40–60 megawatts of electricity can result in electricity production costs of $0.05–0.06 a kilowatt-hour (USDOE, 1998b; Solantausta and others, 1996). Co-combustion, particularly at efficient coal-fired power plants, can obtain similar costs. If BIG/CC technology becomes available commercially, production costs could drop further to about $0.04 a kilowatt-hour, especially with higher electrical efficiencies. For larger scales (more than 100 megawatts of electricity) it is expected that cultivated biomass will compete with fossil fuels in many situations. The benefits of lower specific capital costs and increased efficiency certainly outweigh the increase in costs and energy use for transport for considerable distances if a reasonably well-developed infrastructure is in place (Marrison and Larson, 1995a, b; Faaij, Hamelinck, and Agterberg, forthcoming).

Decentralised power (and heat) production is generally more expensive and therefore is better suited for off-grid applications. The costs of gasifier/diesel systems are still unclear and depend on what emissions and fuel quality are considered acceptable. Combined heat and power generation is generally economically attractive when heat is required with a high load factor.

Production of liquid and gaseous fuels from biomass. The economies of 'traditional' fuels like RME and ethanol from starch and sugar crops in moderate climate zones are poor and unlikely to reach competitive price levels. Methanol, hydrogen, and ethanol from lignocellulosic biomass offer better potential in the longer term (table 7.4).

Implementation issues

Modern use of biomass is important in the energy systems of a number of countries (table 7.5). Other countries can be mentioned as well—as in Asia, where biomass, mainly traditional biomass, can account for 50–90 percent of total energy. India has installed more than 2.9 million biomass digesters in villages and produces biogas for cooking—and is using small gasifier diesel systems for rural electrification. Biomass power projects with an aggregate capacity of 222 megawatts have been commissioned in India, with another 280 megawatts under construction (MNCES, 1999). And with tens of millions of hectares of degraded soil, India is involved in wood-for-energy production schemes. Throughout Southeast Asia the interest in modern bio-energy applications has increased in recent years, partly because of the fast-growing demand for power

TABLE 7.5. BIOMASS IN THE ENERGY SYSTEMS OF SELECTED COUNTRIES

Country	Role of biomass in the energy system
Austria	Modern biomass accounts for 11 percent of the national energy supply. Forest residues are used for (district) heating, largely in systems of a relatively small scale.
Brazil	Biomass accounts for about a third of the energy supply. Main modern applications are ethanol for vehicles produced from sugar cane (13–14 billion litres a year) and substantial use of charcoal in steel industry. Government supports ethanol. PRO-ALCOOL is moving towards a rationalisation programme to increase efficiency and lower costs.
Denmark	A programme is under way to use 1.2 million tonnes of straw as well as use forest residues. Various concepts have been devised for co-firing biomass in larger-scale combined heating and power plants, district heating, and digestion of biomass residues.
Finland	Twenty percent of its primary energy demand comes from modern biomass. The pulp and paper industry makes a large contribution through efficient residue and black liquor use for energy production. The government supports biomass; a doubling of the contribution is possible with available resources.
Sweden	Modern biomass accounts for 17 percent of national energy demand. Use of residues in the pulp and paper industry and district heating (CHP) and use of wood for space heating are dominant. Biomass is projected to contribute 40 percent to the national energy supply in 2020.
United States	About 10,700 megawatts-electric biomass-fired capacity was installed by 1998; largely forest residues. Four billion litres per year of ethanol are produced.
Zimbabwe	Forty million litres of ethanol are produced a year. Biomass satisfies about 75 percent of national energy demand.

Source: Kaltschmitt and others, 1998; Rosillo-Calle and others, 1996; Rosillo and Cortez, 1998; NUTEK, 1996; USDOE, 1998a; Hemstock and Hall, 1995.

and because biomass residues from various agricultural production systems are plentiful (box 7.2; Lefevre and others, 1997).

Barriers. Bio-energy use varies remarkably among countries. Varying resource potentials and population densities are not the only reasons. Other barriers hamper implementation:

- *Uncompetitive costs.* The main barrier is that the energy carriers are not competitive unless cheap or negative cost biomass wastes and residues are used. Technology development could reduce the costs of bio-energy. In Denmark and Sweden, where carbon and energy taxes have been introduced, more expensive wood fuels and straw are now used on a large scale. But world-wide, the commercial production of energy crops is almost non-existent. (Brazil is a major exception, having introduced subsidies to make ethanol from sugar cane competitive with gasoline.)

- *The need for efficient, cheap, environmentally sound energy conversion technologies.* Strongly related to costs issues are the availability and the full-scale demonstration of advanced conversion technology, combining a high energy conversion efficiency and environmentally sound performance with low investment costs. Biomass integrated gasifier/combined cycle (BIG/CC) technology can attain higher conversion efficiency at lower costs. Further development of gasification technologies is also important for a cheaper production of methanol and hydrogen from biomass.

- *Required development of dedicated fuel supply systems.* Experience with dedicated fuel supply systems based on 'new' energy crops, such as perennial grasses, is very limited. Higher yields, greater pest resistance, better management techniques, reduced inputs, and further development of machinery are all needed to lower costs and raise productivity. The same is true for harvesting, storage, and logistics.

- *Specific biomass characteristics.* The solar energy conversion

Some 700–1,400 million hectares may be available for biomass energy production well into the 21st century.

efficiency of biomass production is low—in practice less than 1 percent. So, fairly large land surfaces are required to produce a substantially amount of energy. Moreover, biomass has a low energy density. Compare coal's energy density of 28 gigajoules a tonne, mineral oil's 42 gigajoules a tonne, and liquefied natural gas's 52 gigajoules a tonne with biomass's 8 gigajoules a tonne of wood (at 50 percent moisture content). Transport is thus an essential element of biomass energy systems, and transportation distances can become a limiting factor. Another complication is that biomass production is usually bound to seasons, challenging the supply and logistics of a total system. And varying weather conditions affect production year-to-year.

- *Socioeconomic and organisational barriers.* The production of crops based on perennial grasses or short rotation forestry differs substantially from that of conventional food crops. Annual crops provide farmers with a constant cash flow for each hectare of land. For short rotation coppice, however, the intervals between harvests can be 2–10 years, restricting the flexibility of farmers to shift from one crop to another. In addition, bio-energy systems require complex organisations and many actors, creating non-technical barriers.

- *Public acceptability.* Since biomass energy systems require substantial land areas if they are to contribute much to the total energy supply, the needed changes in land-use, crops, and landscape might incite public resistance. And to be acceptable to most people, the ecological impacts of biomass production systems have to be minimal. Increased traffic in biomass production areas might also be seen as a negative.

- *Ecological aspects.* Not much is known about the effects of large-scale energy farming on landscapes and biodiversity. Energy crop plantations have to fit into the landscape both ecologically and aesthetically. And in addition to minimising the environmental impact, attention should be paid to fitting biomass production into existing agricultural systems.

- *Competition for land use.* Competition for land or various land claims may turn out to be a limitation in various regions. Opinions differ on how much (agricultural) land will become available for energy crops (Dyson, 1996; Brown and others, 1996; Gardner, 1996). An accepted principle is that biomass production for energy should not conflict with food production. But given the large potential to increase the productivity of conventional agriculture (Luyten, 1995; WRR, 1992; Larson, Williams, and Johansson, 1999), land's availability is not necessarily a barrier. If conventional agriculture has higher productivity, it will become more profitable—so bio-energy will face even stiffer competition from conventional crops than it does today.

BOX 7.2. INDUSTRIAL USES OF BIO-ENERGY

Two large industrial sectors offer excellent opportunities to use biomass resources efficiently and competitively world-wide: paper and pulp, and sugar (particularly using sugar cane as feed). Traditionally, these sectors use biomass residues (wood waste and bagasse) for their internal energy needs, usually inefficient conversions to low-pressure steam and some power. The absence of regulations to ensure reasonable electricity tariffs for independent power producers make it unattractive for industries to invest in more efficient power generation. But the liberalisation of energy markets in many countries is removing this barrier, opening a window to reduce production costs and modernise production capacity.

Efficient boilers have been installed in many production facilities. Gasification technology could offer even further efficiency gains and lower costs—say, when applied for converting black liquor (Larson and others, 1998). The power generated is generally competitive with grid prices. In Nicaragua electricity production from bagasse using improved boilers could meet the national demand for electricity (van den Broek and van Wijk, 1998).

Strategies. Six areas are essential for successful development and implementation of sustainable and economically competitive bio-energy systems: technologies, production, markets, polygeneration, externalities, and policy.

Technological development and demonstration of key conversion technologies. Research, demonstration, and commercialisation of advanced power generation technology are essential—especially for BIG/CC technology, which can offer high conversion efficiencies, low emissions, and low costs. Another interesting route is producing modern biofuels, using hydrolysis and gasification. Combining biomass with fossil fuels can be an excellent way to achieve economies of scale and reduce the risks of supply disruptions.

More experience with and improvement of biomass production. Local assessments are needed to identify optimal biomass production systems, and more practical experience is needed with a wide variety of systems and crops. Certainly, more research and testing are needed to monitor the impact of energy crops, with particular attention to water use, pest abatement, nutrient leaching, soil quality, biodiversity (on various levels), and proper landscaping. Perennial crops (grasses) and short rotation coppice (eucalyptus, willow) can be applied with minimal ecological impacts.

Cost reduction is essential, though several countries already obtain biomass production costs below $2 a gigajoule. Larger plantations, improved species, and better production systems and equipment can reduce costs further. Another promising way to lower costs is to combine biomass production for energy with other (agricultural or forest) products (multi-output production systems). Yet another is to seek other benefits from biomass production—preventing erosion, removing soil contaminants, and creating recreational and buffer zones.

Creating markets for biomass production, trade, and use. At local and regional scales, the starting phase of getting bio-energy 'off the ground' can be difficult. The supply and demand for biomass need to be matched over prolonged periods. Diversifying biomass supplies can be a key in creating a better biomass market. Flexible conversion capacity to deal with different biomass streams, as well as fossil fuels, is also important. And international trade in bio-energy can buffer supply fluctuations.

Production can also be started in niches. Major examples are the modernisation of power generation in the sugar, in paper and pulp, and in (organic) waste treatment. Regulations—such as acceptable payback tariffs for independent power producers—are essential. Niche markets can also be found for modern biofuels, such as high-value fuel additives, as mixes with gasoline, or for specific parts of a local transport fleet (such as buses). Successful biomass markets are working in Scandinavian countries and in Brazil (boxes 7.3 and 7.4).

Polygeneration of products and energy carriers. To compete with coal (chapter 8), biomass energy may have to follow a polygeneration strategy—coproducing electricity, fuels, fibres, and food from biomass. One example would be the generation of electricity by a BIG/CC plant as well as any fluid that can be produced from the syngas: methanol, dimethyl ether (DME), other

---

BOX 7.3. BRAZIL'S NATIONAL ALCOHOL PROGRAMME

PRO-ALCOOL in Brazil is the largest programme of commercial biomass utilisation in the world. Despite economic difficulties during some of its 25 years of operation, it presents several environmental benefits, reduces import expenditures, and creates jobs in rural areas.

Roughly 700,000 rural jobs in sugar-alcohol are distributed among 350 private industrial units and 50,000 private sugarcane growers. Moreover, the cost of creating a job in sugar-alcohol is much lower than in other industries. But mechanical harvesting could change this.

Despite a small reduction in harvested surface, Brazilian sugar-cane production has shown a continuous increase, reaching 313 million tonnes in the 1998/99 season. Alcohol consumption has been steady, even though almost no new hydrated ethanol powered automobiles are being produced. The decline in consumption from the partial age retirement of this fleet has been balanced by significant growth in the number of automobiles using a blend of 26 percent anhydrous ethanol in gasoline.

Subsidies were reduced in recent years in the southeast of Brazil, where 80 percent of the ethanol is produced, and then fully removed early in 1999. Some government actions—compulsory increases in the amount of ethanol blended in gasoline and special financial conditions for acquisition of new hydrated ethanol powered cars—have favoured producers. Very recently the alcohol price at the pump stations was reduced, triggering the interest of consumers and carmakers in hydrated ethanol cars. Other government policies may include tax reductions on new alcohol cars, 'green' fleets, and mixing alcohol-diesel for diesel motors.

Another promising option is the implementation of a large cogeneration programme for sugar and alcohol. Revenues from electricity sales could allow further reductions in the cost of alcohol production, although it is not yet enough to make it competitive with gasoline in a free market. Even so, production costs continue to come down from learning by doing.

The programme has positive environmental and economic impacts. In 1999 it resulted in an emission reduction of almost 13 mega-tonnes of carbon. And the hard currency saved by not importing oil totals $40 billion over the 25 years since alcohol's introduction.

BOX 7.4. BIOMASS USE IN SWEDEN

Sweden is probably the world leader in creating a working bio-mass market. Its use of biomass for energy purposes—domestic heating with advanced heating systems, district heating, and combined heat and power generation—has increased 4–5-fold in the past 10 years. And the average costs of biomass have come down considerably. Swedish forests have met this growing demand with ease.

The growing contribution of biomass has been combined with a big increase in the number of companies supplying wood and wood products and in the number of parties using biomass. As a result competition has led to lower prices, combined with innovation and more efficient biomass supply systems.

Some 14,000 hectares in short rotation willow plantations have been established. Sweden also imports some biomass, which make up only a small part of the total supply but keep prices low.

Sweden plans to increase the 20 percent share of biomass in the total primary energy supply to 40 percent in 2020, largely by extending and improving the use of residues from production forests and wood processing industries (NUTEK, 1996).

liquids using Fischer-Tropps synthesis (Larson and Jin, 1999a; Faaij and others, 1999). Another could combine biomass and fossil fuels to coproduce modern energy carriers (Oonk and others, 1997).

Internalising external costs and benefits. Bio-energy can offer benefits over fossil fuels that do not show up in its cost—that is, it can offer externalities. Being carbon-neutral is one. Another is the very low sulphur content. A third is that biomass is available in most countries, while fossil fuels often need to be imported. The domestic production of bio-energy also brings macro-economic and employment benefits (Faaij, Meuleman, and others, 1998). It can offer large numbers of unskilled jobs (van den Broek and van Wijk, 1998). It has fewer external costs than (imported) coal and oil (Borjesson, 1999; Faaij, Meuleman, and others, 1998).

Policies. Carbon taxes, price supports, and long-running research and development (R&D) programmes are often central in gaining experience, building infrastructure developing technology, and fostering the national market. Scandinavia and Brazil—and to a somewhat less extent northwest Europe and the United States—show that modernisation is essential for realising the promise of biomass as an alternative energy source (Ravindranath and Hall, 1995). It may even help in phasing out agricultural subsidies.

Conclusion

- Biomass can make a large contribution to the future world's energy supply. Land for biomass production should not be a bottleneck, if the modernisation of conventional agricultural production continues. Recent evaluations indicate that if land surfaces of 400–700 million hectares were used for biomass energy production halfway into the 21st century, there could be no conflicts with other land-use functions and the preservation of nature.

- Bio-energy's current contribution of 45 ± 10 exajoules a year—of which probably 16 ± 6 exajoules a year is commercial—could increase to 100–300 exajoules a year in the 21st century.

- The primary use of biomass for modern production of energy carriers accounts for about 7 exajoules a year. Modern biomass energy production can play an important role in rural development.

- Although developing countries are the main consumers of biomass, the potential, production, and use of biomass in these countries are often poorly quantified and documented.

- Biomass can be used for energy production in many forms. The resource use, the technologies applied, and the set-up of systems will depend on local conditions, both physical and socioeconomic. Perennial crops offer cheap and productive biomass production, with low or even positive environmental impacts.

- Production costs of biomass can be $1.5–2 a gigajoule in many regions. Genetic improvement and optimised production systems—and multi-output production systems, cascading biomass, and multifunctional land use—could bring bio-mass close to the

An accepted principle is that biomass production for energy should not conflict with food production.

(expected) costs of coal.

- A key issue for bio-energy is modernising it to fit sustainable development. Conversion of biomass to modern energy carriers (electricity, fuels) gives biomass commercial value that can provide income and development for local (rural) economies.

- Modernised biomass use can be a full-scale player in the portfolio of energy options for the longer term. The production of electricity and fuels from lignocellulosic biomass are promising options. But they require the development of markets, infrastructure, key conversion technologies (BIG/CC), and advanced fuel production systems.

- Flexible energy systems combining biomass and fossil fuels are likely to become the backbone for low-risk, low-cost energy supply systems.

Wind Energy

Wind energy, in common with other renewable energy sources, is broadly available but diffuse. The global wind resource has been described in chapter 5. Wind energy was widely used as a source of power before the industrial revolution, but later displaced by fossil fuel use because of differences in costs and reliability. The oil crises of the 1970s, however, triggered renewed interest in wind energy technology for grid-connected electricity production, water pumping, and power supply in remote areas (WEC, 1994b).

In recent decades enormous progress has been made in the development of wind turbines for electricity production. Around 1980 the first modern grid-connected wind turbines were installed. In 1990 about 2,000 megawatts of grid-connected wind power was in operation world-wide—at the beginning of 2000, about 13,500 megawatts. In addition, more than 1 million water-pumping wind turbines (wind pumps), manufactured in many developing countries, supply water for livestock, mainly in remote areas. And tens of thousands of small battery-charging wind generators are operated in China, Mongolia, and Central Asia (chapter 10).

The potential of wind energy

The technical potential of onshore wind energy to fulfil energy needs is very large—20,000–50,000 terawatt-hours a year (chapter 5). The economic potential of wind energy depends on the economics of wind turbine systems and of alternative options. Apart from investment costs, the most important parameter determining the economics of a wind turbine system is annual energy output, in turn determined by such parameters as average wind speed, statistical wind speed distribution, turbulence intensities, and roughness of the surrounding terrain. The power in wind is proportional to the third power of the momentary wind speed.

Because of the sensitivity to wind speed, determining the potential of wind energy at a specific site is not straightforward. More accurate meteorological measurements and wind energy maps and handbooks are being produced and (mostly) published, enabling wind project developers to better assess the long-term economic performance of their projects.

In densely populated countries the best sites on land are occupied, and public resistance makes it difficult to realise new projects at acceptable cost. That is why Denmark and the Netherlands are developing offshore projects, despite less favourable economics. Sweden and the United Kingdom are developing offshore projects to preserve the landscape.

Resources offshore are much larger than those onshore, but to be interesting they have to be close to electric infrastructure. A comprehensive study by Germanische Lloyd and Garrad Hassan & Partners (Matthies and others, 1995) concluded that around 3,000 terawatt-hours a year of electricity could be generated in the coastal areas of the European Union (excluding Finland and Sweden). With electricity consumption in those 12 countries at about 2,000 terawatt-hours a year, offshore options should be included in assessments of the potential of wind electricity.

Development of installed wind power

In 1997 the installed wind power was about 7,400 megawatts, in 1998 close to 10,000 megawatts, and in 1999 another annual 3,600 megawatts was installed (BTM Consult, 1999 and 2000). Between 1994 and 1999 the annual growth of installed operating capacity varied between 27 and 33 percent. The electricity generated by wind turbines can be estimated at 18 terawatt-hours in 1998 and 24 terawatt-hours in 1999.

There are 29 countries that have active wind energy programmes. Most of the capacity added in 1998 (2,048 megawatts) was in four countries: for Germany 793 megawatts, for the United States 577 megawatts, for Spain 368 megawatts, and for Denmark 310 megawatts (table 7.6).

Based on an analysis of the national energy policies for the most relevant countries, BMT Consult expects the global installed power to grow to around 30,000 megawatts of electricity in 2004.

Several generic scenarios assess the growth of wind power in the coming decades. One of the most interesting—by BTM Consult for the FORUM for Energy & Development, presented at the COP-4 of the UN-FCCC in Buenos Aires in December 1998—addresses three questions. Can wind power contribute 10 percent of the world's electricity needs within three decades? How long will it take to achieve this? How will wind power be distributed over the world?

Two scenarios were developed. The *recent trends* scenario extrapolates current market development, while the *international agreements* scenario assumes that international agreements are realised. Both scenarios assumed that integrating up to 20 percent of wind power in the grid (in energy terms) would not be a problem with present grids, modern fossil fuel power plants, and modern wind turbines. Analysis of the world's exploitable wind resources, with growth of electricity demand as indicated in the *World Energy Outlook* (IEA, 1995 and 1996), led to the following conclusions:

■ Under the recent trends scenario—starting with 20,000 megawatts by the end of 2002 and assuming a 15 percent cost reduction, and later 12 percent and 10 percent, for each doubling of the accumulated number of installations—10 percent penetration is

TABLE 7.6. INSTALLED WIND POWER, 1997 AND 1998

	Installed megawatts 1997	Cumulative megawatts 1997	Installed megawatts 1998	Cumulative megawatts 1998
Canada	4	26	57	83
Mexico	0	2	0	2
United States	29	1.611	577	2.141
Latin America	10	42	24	66
Total Americas	**43**	**1.681**	**658**	**2.292**
Denmark	285	1.116	310	1.420
Finland	5	12	6	18
France	8	13	8	21
Germany	533	2.081	793	2.874
Greece	0	29	26	55
Ireland	42	53	11	64
Italy	33	103	94	197
Netherlands	44	329	50	379
Portugal	20	39	13	51
Spain	262	512	368	880
Sweden	19	122	54	176
United Kingdom	55	328	10	338
Other Europe	13	57	23	80
Total Europe	**1.318**	**4.793**	**1.766**	**6.553**
China	67	146	54	200
India	65	940	52	992
Other Asia	9	22	11	33
Total Asia	**141**	**1.108**	**117**	**1.224**
Australia and New Zealand	2	8	26	34
Pacific Islands	0	3	0	3
North Africa (incl. Egypt)	0	9	0	9
Middle East	8	18	0	18
Former Soviet Union	1	19	11	19
Total other continents and areas	**11**	**57**	**37**	**83**
Annual installed capacity worldwide	**1.513**		**2.577**	
Cumulative capacity installed worldwide		**7.639**		**10.153**

Note: The cumulative installed capacity by the end of 1998 is not always equal to the 1997 data plus installed capacity during 1998, because of adjustments for decommissioned and dismantled capacity. *Source: BTM Consult, 1999.*

achieved around 2025, and saturation in 2030–35, at about 1.1 terawatt. In this scenario the cost of generating wind electricity would come down to $0.032 a kilowatt-hour (1998 level) on average, ± 15 percent (depending on wind speed, connection costs to the grid, and other considerations).

■ Under the international agreements scenario—with the same starting conditions but a slightly different learning curve—growth is faster and 10 percent penetration is achieved around 2016, with saturation in 2030–35 at about 1.9 terawatts. In this scenario the cost would come down to $0.027 a kilowatt-hour on average, again ± 15 percent.

In this second scenario, the regional distribution of wind power is North America 23 percent, Latin America 6 percent, Europe (Eastern and Western) 14 percent, Asia 23 percent, Pacific OECD 8 percent, North Africa 5 percent, former Soviet Union 16 percent, and rest of the world 5 percent.

Technology developments

Wind turbines become larger. From the beginning of the modern wind energy technology era in the mid-1970s, there has been gradual growth in the unit size of commercial machines. In the mid-1970s the typical size of a wind turbine was 30 kilowatts of generating capacity, with a rotor diameter of 10 metres. The largest units installed in 1998 had capacities of 1,650 kilowatts with rotor diameters of 66 metres. By 1999, 460 units with a generating capacity of 1 megawatt or more were installed world-wide. Turbines with an installed power of 2 megawatts (70 metres diameter) are being introduced in the market, and 3–5 megawatt machines are on the drawing board (table 7.7).

Market demands drive the trend towards larger machines: economies of scale, less visual impacts on the landscape per unit of installed power, and expectations that offshore potential will soon be developed. The average size of wind turbines installed is expected to be 1,200 kilowatts before 2005 and 1,500 kilowatts thereafter. Note, however, that the optimum size of a turbine—in cost, impact, and public acceptance—differs for onshore (nearby as well as remote) and offshore applications.

Wind turbines become more controllable and grid-compatible. The output of stall regulated wind turbines is hardly controllable,

apart from switching the machine on and off. Output varies with the wind speed until reaching the rated wind speed value. As the application of the aerodynamic stall phenomena to structural compliant machines gets more difficult with bigger turbines, blade pitch control systems are being applied to them. For structural dynamics and reliability, a blade-pitch system should be combined with a variable speed electric conversion system. Such systems typically incorporate synchronous generators combined with electronic AC-DC-AC converters.

Modern electronic components have enabled designers to control output—within the operational envelope of the wind speed—and produce excellent power quality. These developments make wind turbines more suitable for integration with the electricity infrastructure and ultimately for higher penetration. These advantages are of particular interest for weak grids, often in rural and remote areas that have a lot of wind.

Wind turbines will have fewer components. For lower costs and greater reliability and maintainability, designers now seek technology with fewer components—such as directly driven, slow-running generators, with passive yaw and passive blade pitch control. In Germany 34 percent of the installed power in 1998 (770 megawatts) was realised with this type of technology.

Special offshore designs are on the drawing board. With the first offshore wind farms in Europe, industrial designers are developing dedicated turbine technologies for large wind farms in the open sea (Beurskens, 2000). Outages onshore can often be corrected quickly so that only a small amount of energy is lost. But offshore the window for carrying out repairs or replacing components is often limited. The high cost of complete installations implies the use of large wind turbines, which will probably have installed powers of 3–6 megawatts. Offshore design features will include novel installation concepts, electricity conversion and transport systems, corrosion protection, and integration with external conditions (both wind and wave loading).

Time to market is becoming shorter than project preparation time. Although there is a temporary shortage of supply of wind turbines in some countries, competition among manufacturers is fierce. One way to become more competitive is to keep implementing innovations and component improvements to reduce cost. Times to market new products are also becoming short (two to three years). As a result, just as the construction of a wind farm commences, the technology is already outdated.

System aspects

Wind turbines deliver energy, but little capacity. Because wind energy is intermittent, wind turbines mainly deliver energy, but little capacity value often 20 percent or less of the installed wind power. And this percentage falls when the penetration of wind turbines increases, requiring even more back-up power for a reliable energy supply. But wind-generated electricity can be transformed from intermittent to baseload power if it is combined with, say, compressed air energy storage. In this way a high capacity factor can be achieved with a

TABLE 7.7. AVERAGE SIZE OF INSTALLED WIND TURBINES, 1992–99

Year	Size (kilowatts)
1992	200
1994	300
1996	500
1998	600
1999	700

small economic penalty, potentially about $0.01 a kilowatt-hour (Cavallo, 1995). This option becomes attractive when wind electricity generation costs fall below $0.03 a kilowatt-hour. It also opens the possibility of exploiting wind resources remote from markets, as in the Great Plains of the United States (Cavallo, 1995) and in inner Mongolia and northwest China (Lew and others, 1998).

Wind power becomes more predictable. Meteorological research on predicting the output of wind farms a few hours in advance has produced computer programs that optimise the operational and fuel costs of regional electricity production parks (Denmark, Germany). This will increase the capacity value of wind power and the value of the electricity produced.

Capacity factors are somewhat adjustable. Some general misconceptions sometimes lead to the wrong decisions or conclusions. The capacity factor (annual energy output/output based on full-time operation at rated power) depends on local winds and wind turbines. By optimising the turbine characteristics to the local wind regime, the capacity factor—now often 20–25 percent—can be optimised without losing too much energy output. But extreme capacity factors—say, 40 percent—automatically means a large loss of potential energy output.

Renewed interest in autonomous systems. In the mid-1980s interest grew in the application of wind turbines in isolated areas without an energy infrastructure. Two systems can be distinguished:
- Hybrid systems, in which a wind turbine operates in parallel with, for example, a diesel set (to save fuel consumption and to decrease maintenance and repairs) or a diesel generator combined with a battery storage unit.
- Standalone units, for charging batteries, pumping water for irrigation, domestic use, watering cattle, or desalination and cooling.

More than 30 experimental hybrid systems have been developed and tested, almost all stopped without a commercial follow up, because of unreliable and expensive components. The interest in hybrid and standalone systems is being revived—initiated by the search for new markets for renewable energy systems and influenced by spectacular improvements in performance and cost for wind turbines and power electronics (box 7.5 and chapter 10). For successful market entry, systems have to be modular, and standards for components and subsystems introduced.

Small battery-charging wind generators are manufactured by the thousand in China, Mongolia, and elsewhere, making them more numerous than larger diameter wind generators. Although their contribution to world energy supply is negligible, their potential impact on the energy needs of rural and nomadic families is significant (as with photovoltaic home systems).

Environmental aspects

Environmental aspects come into play in the three phases of a wind turbine project: building and manufacturing, normal operation during the turbine's lifetime, decommissioning.

Building and manufacturing. No exotic materials or manufacturing processes are required in producing a wind turbine or building the civil works. The energy payback time of a large wind turbine, under typical Danish conditions, is 3 to 4 months (Dannemand Andersen, 1998).

Normal operation. Negative environmental aspects connected to the use of wind turbines are: acoustic noise emission, visual impact on the landscape, impact on bird life, moving shadows caused by the rotor, and electromagnetic interference with radio, television, and radar signals. In practice the noise and visual impact cause the most problems. Acoustic noise emission prevents designers from increasing the tip speed of rotor blades, which would increase the rotational speed of the drive train shaft and thus reduce the cost of gearboxes or generators. Aero-acoustic research has provided design tools and blade configurations to make blades considerably more silent, reducing the distance needed between wind turbines and houses.

The impact on bird life appears to be minor if the turbines are properly located. A research project in the Netherlands showed that the bird casualties from collisions with rotating rotor blades on a wind farm of 1,000 megawatts is a very small fraction of those from hunting, high voltage lines, and vehicle traffic (Winkelman, 1992). In addition, acoustic devices might help prevent birds from flying into rotor blades (Davis, 1995).

During normal operation a wind turbine causes no emissions, so the potential to reduce carbon dioxide emissions depends on the fuel mix of the fossil-fuelled plants the wind turbine is working with. A study by BTM Consult (1999) indicates that in 2025 wind energy could prevent the emission of 1.4–2.5 gigatonnes of carbon dioxide a year.

Decommissioning. Because all components are conventional, the recycling methods for decommissioning the wind turbine are also conventional. Most blades are made from glass or carbon fibre

> *Industrial designers are developing dedicated turbine technologies for large wind farms in the open sea.*

BOX 7.5. HYBRID WIND, BATTERY, AND DIESEL SYSTEMS IN CHINA

Since 1994 the 360 inhabitants of the village of Bayinaobao in Inner Mongolia have been provided with electricity from a hybrid electricity system that employs two 5-kilowatt wind turbines, a battery storage unit, and a diesel generator. In this system the wind turbines provide about 80 percent of the electricity generated. The technology is being developed under a German-Chinese industrial joint venture aimed at transferring the German-developed wind turbine and ancillary technologies. By the time 140 systems have been built, local content should account for about 70 percent of the wind turbine technology, reducing the cost of an imported system by half. Based on the performance of the first unit and the costs projected for components, the electricity from the hybrid system will cost less (up to 22 percent less, at a diesel fuel price of $0.38 a litre) than from the conventional diesel system (Weise and others, 1995).

reinforced plastics, processed by incineration. To replace glass and carbon and close the cycle of material use, wood composites are being applied and biofibres developed.

Economic aspects

The energy generation costs of wind turbines are basically determined by five parameters:

- *Turnkey project cost.* Initial investment costs (expressed in U.S. dollars a square metre of swept rotor area), project preparation, and infrastructure make up the turnkey project costs. The costs of European wind turbines are typically $410 a square metre (machine cost, excluding foundation). Project preparation and infrastructure costs depend heavily on local circumstances, such as soil conditions, road conditions, and the availability of electrical substations. Turnkey costs vary from $460 a square metre to $660 a square metre (with 1 ECU = 1.1 U.S. dollar).

- *Energy output of the system.* The energy output of a wind turbine can be estimated by $E = b \cdot V^3$ kilowatt-hours a square metre, where E is the annual energy output, b is the performance factor, and V is the average wind speed at hub height. The factor b depends on the system efficiency of the wind turbine and the statistical distribution of wind speeds. In coastal climates in Europe a value of 3.15 for b is representative for modern wind turbines and not too far away from the theoretical maximum. On good locations in Denmark, northern Germany, and the Netherlands annual outputs of more than 1,000 kilowatt-hours a square metre are often achieved.

- *Local average wind speed.* In general, local average wind speed should exceed five metres a second at a height of 10 metres to allow economic exploitation of grid-connected wind turbines.

- *Availability of the system.* The technical availability of modern wind farms exceeds 96 percent.

- *Lifetime of the system.* Design tools have improved so much that designing on the basis of fatigue lifetime has become possible. As a result one can confidently use lifetimes of 15–20 years for economic calculations.

For Europe a state-of-the-art reference calculation uses the following values:

Turnkey cost	$600 a square metre
Interest	5 percent
Economic lifetime	15 years
Technical availability	95 percent
Annual energy output	3.15 V³ kilowatt-hours a square metre
O & M costs	$0.005 a kilowatt-hour

If average wind speeds at the hub height range from 5.6–7.5 metres a second, the corresponding electricity production cost is $0.12–0.05 a kilowatt-hour. Because the energy of the wind is proportional to the third power of the wind speed, the economic calculations are very sensitive to the local average annual wind speed.

Figure 7.2 illustrates the cost reductions for electricity generation from wind turbines in Denmark since 1981. But take care in translating these figures to other regions, for the cost of project preparation, infrastructure, and civil works in Denmark is low relative to many other regions. BTM Consult (1999) expects a 35–45 percent reduction in generation costs in the next 15–20 years (figure 7.3).

Implementation issues

Manufacturers and project developers usually identify the following items as serious barriers for efficient implementation of wind turbine projects:

- Fluctuating demand for wind turbines as a result of changing national policies and support schemes.
- Uncertainties leading to financing costs as a result of changing governmental policies.

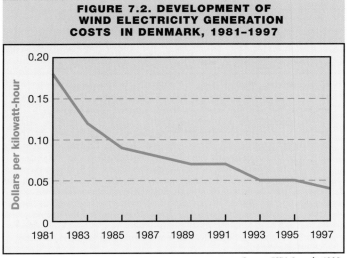

FIGURE 7.2. DEVELOPMENT OF WIND ELECTRICITY GENERATION COSTS IN DENMARK, 1981–1997

Source: BTM Consult, 1999.

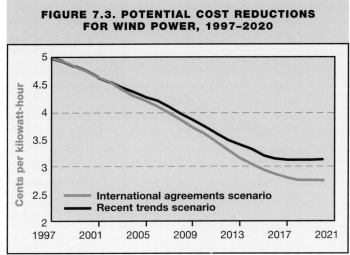

FIGURE 7.3. POTENTIAL COST REDUCTIONS FOR WIND POWER, 1997–2020

Source: BTM Consult, 1999.

- Complicated, time-consuming, and expensive institutional procedures, resulting from a lack of public acceptance, which varies considerably from country to country.
- Project preparation time often longer than the 'time to market' of new wind turbine types.
- Lack of sufficient international acceptance of certification procedures and standards.

Denmark and the United States were the first to introduce an integrated approach to wind energy, encompassing both technical development and the introduction of market incentives. Now more than 25 countries use a great variety of incentives, some very successful and some complete failures. The applied incentive schemes can be grouped in three categories, or in combinations of these categories:

- Fixed tariff systems, such as those of Denmark, Germany, and Spain (favourable payback tariffs are fixed for a period of, say, 10 years).
- Quota or concession systems, such as the Non Fossil Fuel Obligation of England and the systems of France, Ireland, and Scotland (competitive bidding for projects until a set amount of electricity production is realised).
- Other systems to stimulate the application of wind energy, such as tax breaks, carbon taxes, green electricity, and tradable green labels.

With the first schemes, Denmark, Germany, and Spain installed many more wind turbines than countries using other schemes. Elsewhere in Europe, the second system has demonstrated success also (table 7.8). But none of the schemes can be easily translated from one country to another. Legal circumstances and public acceptance may differ completely. Moreover, several incentives have been introduced only recently, and their effectiveness is not yet known.

Under favourable legislation and general acceptance by the public, a fixed tariff system may be quite successful, because it provides financial security to project developers, owners, and financiers. In the long term, however, fixed tariffs will become too expensive to subsidise if they are not modified. As a result the industry might collapse unless the incentive program brings the cost of the technology down. Quota systems based on calls for tenders only once in two or three years may lead to extreme fluctuations in the market growth. Concessions appear interesting for harnessing large, high-quality wind resources in regions remote from major electricity markets (PCAST, 1999). However, very large wind projects for remote wind resources require a different industry structure from today's. Needed are large project developers with deep financial pockets—not wind turbine suppliers. The installation of wind turbines can also increase if individuals, groups of individuals, or cooperatives are allowed to own one or more wind turbines as small independent power producers (IPPs) and to sell electricity to the grid.

It is too early to judge whether tradable green certificates, connected to a quota system, are viable. Marketing green electricity seems to develop successfully only when the public recognises green electricity as a product different from regular electricity, worth the additional costs.

TABLE 7.8. TYPE OF INCENTIVE AND WIND POWER ADDED IN 1998

Type of incentive	Country	Megawatts added	Percentage increase
Fixed tariffs	Denmark	310	28
	Germany	793	38
	Spain	368	72
	Total	**1,471**	**40**
Quota or concession systems	France	8	62
	Ireland	11	21
	United Kingdom	10	3
	Total	**29**	**7**

Conclusion

- The potential of wind energy is large, with the technical potential of generating electricity onshore estimated at 20,000–50,000 terawatt-hours a year.
- When investigating the potential, special attention should go to possibilities offshore. Studies for Europe indicate that the offshore wind resources that can be tapped are bigger than the total electricity demand in Europe.
- The average growth rate of the cumulative capacity over the last six years has been about 30 percent a year, bringing the cumulative installed wind turbine capacity to about 10,000 megawatts at the end of 1998 and about 13,500 megawatts at the end of 1999—and wind energy production to 18 terawatt-hours in 1998 and 24 terawatt-hours in 1999.
- Wind turbines are becoming larger, with the average size installed in 1998 at 600 kilowatts, up from about 30 kilowatts in the mid-1970s. Turbines of megawatt size are being developed and should soon be commercially available.
- Costs have to come down further, requiring development of advanced flexible concepts and dedicated offshore wind energy systems. Cost reductions up to 45 percent are feasible within 15 years. Ultimately wind electricity costs might come down to about $0.03 a kilowatt-hour.
- Although wind-generated electricity is an intermittent resource, it can be transformed to baseload power supply if combined with energy storage. For compressed air energy storage the additional costs may be limited to about $0.01 a kilowatt-hour, opening the possibility of exploiting good wind resources remote from markets.
- The environmental impacts of wind turbines are limited, with noise and visibility causing the most problems, increasing public resistance against the installation of new turbines in densely populated countries.
- Interest in small turbines is being revived for standalone and autonomous systems in rural areas.

Photovoltaic solar energy

Photovoltaic solar energy conversion is the direct conversion of sunlight into electricity. This can be done by flat plate and concentrator systems.

FIGURE 7.4. VARIATIONS IN AVERAGE MONTHLY INSOLATION OVER THE YEAR IN THREE LOCATIONS

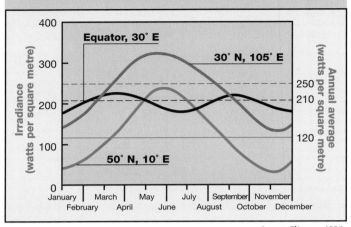

Source: Eliasson, 1998.

TABLE 7.9. POTENTIAL CONTRIBUTION OF SOLAR ENERGY TECHNOLOGIES TO WORLD ENERGY CONSUMPTION ACCORDING TO DIFFERENT STUDIES (EXAJOULES OF ELECTRICITY)

Study	2020–2025	2050	2100
WEC, 1994 a,b	16		
IIASA and WEC, 1998	2–4	7–14	
RIGES, 1993 (solar and wind)	17	35	
Shell, 1996	<10	200	
Greenpeace and SEI, 1993 (solar and wind)	90	270	830
Reference: total world energy consumption	400–600	400–1,200	

An essential component of these systems is the solar cell, in which the photovoltaic effect—the generation of free electrons using the energy of light particles—takes place. These electrons are used to generate electricity.

Characteristics of the source

Solar radiation is available at any location on the surface of the Earth. The maximum irradiance (power density) of sunlight on Earth is about 1,000 watts a square metre, irrespective of location. It is common to describe the solar source in terms of insolation—the energy available per unit of area and per unit of time (such as kilowatt-hours per square metre a year). Measured in a horizontal plane, annual insolation varies over the Earth's surface by a factor of 3—from roughly 800 kilowatt-hours per square metre a year in northern Scandinavia and Canada to a maximum of 2,500 kilowatt-hours per square metre a year in some dry desert areas.

The differences in average monthly insolation (June to December) can vary from 25 percent close to the equator to a factor of 10 in very northern and southern areas (figure 7.4), determining the annual production pattern of solar energy systems. The ratio of diffuse to total annual insolation can range from 10 percent for bright sunny areas to 60 percent or more for areas with a moderate climate, such as Western Europe. The actual ratio largely determines the type of solar energy technology that can be used (non-concentrating or concentrating).

The potential of photovoltaic solar energy

The average power density of solar radiation is 100–300 watts a square metre. The net conversion efficiency of solar electric power systems (sunlight to electricity) is typically 10–15 percent. So substantial areas are required to capture and convert significant amounts of solar energy to fulfil energy needs (especially in industrialised countries, relative to today's energy consumption). For instance, at a plant efficiency of 10 percent, an area of 3–10 square kilometres is required to generate an average of 100 megawatts of electricity—0.9 terawatt-hours of electricity or 3.2 petajoules of electricity a year—using a photovoltaic (or solar thermal electricity) system.

The total average power available at the Earth's surface in the form of solar radiation exceeds the total human power consumption by roughly a factor of 1,500. Calculated per person, the average solar power available is 3 megawatts, while the consumption varies from 100 watts (least industrialised countries) to 10 kilowatts (United States), with an average of 2 kilowatts. Although these numbers provide a useful rough picture of the absolute boundaries of the possibilities of solar energy, they have little significance for the technical and economic potential. Because of differences in the solar energy supply pattern, energy infrastructure, population density, geographic conditions, and the like, a detailed analysis of the technical and economic potential of solar energy is best made regionally or nationally. The global potential is then the sum of these national or regional potentials.

The *economic* potential of solar energy, a matter of debate, depends on the perspectives for cost reduction. In the recent past several scenario studies have assessed the potential application of solar energy technologies (IIASA and WEC, 1998; WEC, 1994a,b; Johansson and others, 1993a; Shell, 1996; Greenpeace and SEI, 1993). They provide a picture of different views on the potential penetration of solar energy in the 21st century (table 7.9).

The *technical* potential of photovoltaics has been studied in some detail in several countries. In densely populated countries with a well-developed infrastructure, there is an emphasis on applications of grid-connected photovoltaic systems in the built environment (including infrastructural objects like railways and roads). These systems are necessarily small- or medium-sized, typically 1 kilowatt to 1 megawatt.[1] The electricity is generated physically close to the place where electricity is also consumed. In less densely populated countries there is also considerable interest in 'ground-based' systems, generally larger than 1 megawatt. The area that would be required to generate an average electrical power equal to the total present human power consumption—assuming 10 percent plant efficiency and an insolation of 2,000 kilowatt-hours per square metre a year—is roughly 750 x 750 square kilometres. In countries or rural regions with a weak or incomplete grid infrastructure, small standalone systems and modular electric systems may be used for electrification of houses or village communities.

Photovoltaic market developments

Between 1983 and 1999 photovoltaic shipments grew by just over 15 percent a year (figure 7.5). In 1998 around 150 megawatts of solar cell modules were produced, in 1999 nearly 200 megawatts. In 1998 cumulative production was around 800 megawatts. Probably about 500 megawatts, perhaps 600 megawatts, of this production was in operation in 1998, generating about 0.5 terawatt-hours a year. In 1993–98 operating capacity increased by roughly 30 percent a year.

In 1990–94 the market share of solar home systems and village power systems was 20 percent (based on power volume).

Grid-connected systems accounted for 11 percent, with the rest for water pumping, communication, leisure, consumer products, and the like (EPIA and Altener, 1996). In 1995–98 the relative importance of grid-connected systems increased to 23 percent (Maycock, 1998).

Current status and future development of photovoltaic solar cells and modules

The major component of photovoltaic solar energy systems is the solar module, normally a number of solar cells connected in series. The efficiency of an ideal photovoltaic cell is about 30 percent at most (for a single cell under natural sunlight). Higher efficiencies can be achieved by stacking cells with different optical properties in a tandem device, by using concentrator cells, or by combining these two. The efficiency of practical solar cells is determined by several loss mechanisms. An overview of efficiencies achieved through 1999 for different cells and modules is given in table 7.10.

Solar cells and their corresponding modules can be divided into two main categories: wafer-type and thin-film. Wafer-type cells are made from silicon wafers cut from a rod or ingot, or from silicon

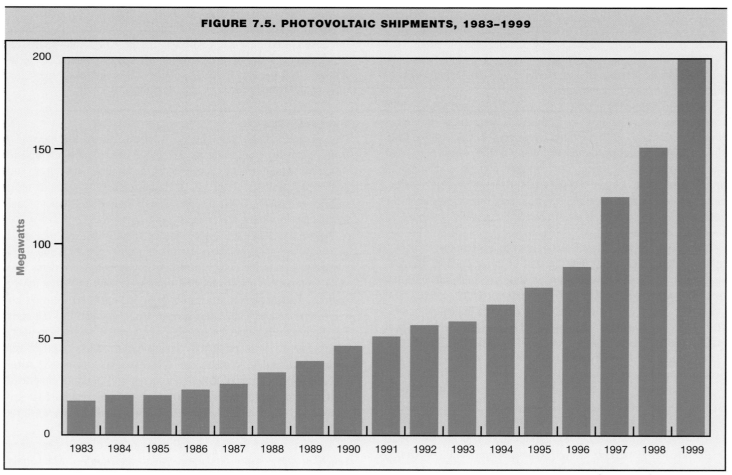

FIGURE 7.5. PHOTOVOLTAIC SHIPMENTS, 1983–1999

Source: Based on a Maycock, 1998; PVIR, 1999.

TABLE 7.10. IMPORTANT PHOTOVOLTAIC SOLAR CELL AND MODULE TECHNOLOGIES

Technology	Symbol	Characteristic	Record efficiency laboratory cells (percent)	Typical efficiency commercial flat-plate modules (percent)
Single crystal silicon	sc-Si	Wafer-type	24	13–15
Multi-crystalline silicon	mc-Si	Wafer-type	19	12–14
Crystalline silicon films on ceramics	f-Si	Wafer type	17	(8–11)
Crystalline silicon films on glass		Thin film	9	
Amorphous silicon (including silicon-germanium tandems)	a-Si	Thin film	13	6–9
Copper-indium/gallium-diselenide	CIGS	Thin film	18	(8–11)
Cadmium telluride	CdTe	Thin film	16	(7–10)
Organic cells (including dye-sensitised titanium dioxide cells)		Thin film	11	
High-efficiency tandem cells	III-V	Wafer-type and thin film	30	
High-efficiency concentrator cells	III-V	Wafer-type and thin-film	33 (tandem) 28 (single)	

Note: Numbers in parentheses are results from pilot production or first commercial production.   *Source: Green and others, 1999.*

ribbons. Thin-film cells are deposited directly onto a substrate (glass, stainless steel, plastic). For flat-plate applications, the individual cells are connected in series to form a module. Solar cells for concentrator systems are mounted in a one-dimensional or two-dimensional optical concentrator.

For the technologies in table 7.10, sc-Si, mc-Si, and a-Si are fully commercial, with the first two taking 85 percent of the 1998 commercial market, and the third 13 percent. (PVIR, 1999). CIGS and CdTe are emerging commercial technologies, whereas f-Si and one form of crystalline silicon films on glass appear to be in a pilot production phase. Organic cells are still in a laboratory stage, though dye-sensitised titanium dioxide cells are considered for near-term indoor applications. High-efficiency cells are used in concentrator systems.

It is still too early to identify winners or losers among the photovoltaic technologies under development or in production. There is reasonable consensus that thin-film technologies generally offer the best long-term perspective for very low production cost. But crystalline silicon wafer technology also still has a huge potential for cost reduction through economies of scale and technological improvements. This perspective recently triggered major investments in new production capacity. So it is not yet clear when thin films will become dominant in the photovoltaics market.

The conversion efficiency of commercial modules should increase steadily over the next decades (irrespective of the technology). For the medium term (2010) the efficiency is likely to be about 12–20 percent (Maycock, 1998), and for the longer term (beyond 2020) possibly 30 percent or even somewhat more (EUREC Agency, 1996). Note, however, that this is based on an evaluation of what

is physically possible, not on what could be done technologically at low cost. Moreover, it is not expected that these high efficiencies can be obtained by simple extrapolation of today's commercial technologies. It is not very likely that modules with the lowest manufacturing cost per watt have the highest efficiency.

System aspects

Photovoltaic system components. To make use of the electricity from photovoltaic cells and modules, one has to build a complete system, also comprising electronic parts, support structures, and sometimes electricity storage. It is customary to use the term balance-of-system (BOS) for the sum of system components and installation excluding modules.

Type and size of photovoltaic systems. Photovoltaics can be used in a wide variety of applications, from consumer products and small standalone units for rural use (such as solar home systems and solar lanterns) to grid-connected rooftop systems and large power stations. Typical system size varies from 50 watts to 1 kilowatt for standalone systems with battery storage, from 500 watts to 5 kilowatts for rooftop grid-connected systems, and from 10 kilowatts to many megawatts for grid-connected ground-based systems and larger building-integrated systems. Of these market segments, rural electrification for sustainable development and building-integrated systems (as forerunners of large-scale implementation) are expected to grow rapidly because of concentrated marketing efforts and financial incentives.

Need for storage. Because photovoltaic modules offer an intermittent source of energy, most standalone systems are equipped with battery storage (usually a lead-acid battery) to provide energy during the night or during days with insufficient sunshine. In some cases batteries store energy during longer periods. When using grid-connected photovoltaic systems, the grid serves as 'virtual storage': electricity fed into the grid by photovoltaics effectively reduces the use of fuel by power plants fired by coal, oil, or gas.

Performance ratio of photovoltaic systems. It is of great practical importance to be able to predict the actual energy that a photovoltaic system of a certain size feeds into the grid. But that requires reliable information on the insolation in the plane of the system, on the system power under standard test conditions, and on the system losses. For simplicity, all system losses in grid-connected photovoltaic systems are taken together in the performance ratio, which is the ratio of the time-averaged system efficiency to the module efficiency under standard conditions. For grid-connected photovoltaic systems the state-of-the-art performance ratio, now typically 0.75–0.85, could increase to 0.9 in the longer term. For state-of-the-art standalone systems the typical performance ratio is 0.6.

Environmental aspects

Environmental life-cycle analysis. Solar technologies do not cause emissions during operation, but they do cause emissions during manufacturing and possibly on decommissioning (unless produced entirely by 'solar breeders'). With the industry growing, there is now considerable interest in environmental aspects of solar technologies. Environmental life-cycle analyses of photovoltaic systems and components (Alsema and Nieuwlaar, 1998) are already leading to the development of different materials and processes in the manufacturing of photovoltaic modules (see Tsuo and others, 1998). An example is developing water-based pastes instead of pastes based on organic solvents for screen printing. In addition, several recycling processes have been developed for off-spec or rejected modules.

Energy payback time. One of the most controversial issues for photovoltaics is whether the amount of energy required to manufacture a complete system is smaller or larger than the energy produced over its lifetime. Early photovoltaic systems were net consumers of energy rather than producers. In other words, the energy payback time of these systems was longer than their lifetime. This situation has changed and modern grid-connected rooftop photovoltaic systems now have payback times much shorter than their (expected) technical lifetime of roughly 30 years (Alsema, Frankl, and Kato, 1998) (table 7.11).

For grid-connected ground-based systems the energy payback time of the balance of system is longer than for rooftop systems, because of materials used in foundation and support. The energy payback time, now three to nine years, will decrease to one to two years.

For standalone photovoltaic systems with battery storage (such as solar home systems) the situation is less favourable than for grid-connected systems, because of the long energy payback time associated with the (lead-acid) battery. At an insolation of 2,000

kilowatt-hours per square metre a year, the energy payback time of modern solar home systems is now seven to 10 years (Alsema and Nieuwlaar, 1998). This number may come down to roughly six years, of which five are due to the battery. Since the technical lifetime of a battery in a photovoltaic system is usually five years or less, the direct effectiveness of (present generation) solar home systems for the reduction of greenhouse gas emissions is a matter of debate.

Carbon dioxide mitigation potential. The carbon dioxide mitigation potential of photovoltaics can be roughly inferred from the data on energy payback time, assuming that emissions of greenhouse gases (SF_6 and CF_4) related to photovoltaic cell and module production are effectively minimised. As an example, a photovoltaic system with an energy payback time of two years at 1,500 kilowatt-hours per square metre a year and a technical lifetime of 30 years (ratio 1:15) will produce 15 kilowatt-hours of electricity without emissions for each kilowatt-hour of electricity 'invested' in manufacturing. Specific carbon dioxide emissions are therefore fifteen times lower than those of the relevant fuel mix—the mix used in supplying the total photovoltaics industry chain with energy.

Materials availability. The crystalline silicon photovoltaics industry has so far used off-grade material from the semiconductor industry as its feedstock. Very fast growth of the crystalline silicon photovoltaics industry would require dedicated production of 'solar grade' silicon (Bruton and others, 1997). Although several processes for solar grade silicon have been developed to a laboratory scale, none has been taken into commercial production. It is expected, however, that new feedstock can be made available in time if necessary. The availability of some of the elements in thin-film photovoltaic modules (like indium and tellurium) is a subject of concern. There apparently are no short-term supply limitations, but the match between demand from the photovoltaics industry and world market supply may become an issue at very large (multiple gigawatts a year) production levels (Johansson and others, 1993b). CdTe and CIGS may therefore be valuable bridging technologies (Andersson, 1998).

TABLE 7.11. ESTIMATED ENERGY PAYBACK TIME OF GRID-CONNECTED ROOFTOP PHOTOVOLTAIC SYSTEMS (YEARS)

	State of the art	Near to medium term (<10 years)	Long term
Modules			
Crystalline silicon	3–8	1.5–2.5	<1.5
Thin film	2–3	0.5–1.5	<0.5
Balance of system	<1	0.5	<0.5
Total system			
Crystalline silicon	4–9	2–3	<2
Thin film	3–4	1–2	<1

Note: Based on an insolation of 1,500 kilowatt-hours per square metre a year.
Source: Alsema, Frankl and Kato, 1998.

Health. Of special concern is the acceptance of cadmium-containing photovoltaic modules. The cadmium content of CdTe (and CIGS) modules appears to be well within limits for safe use (Alsema and Nieuwlaar, 1998). And production processes can fulfil all applicable requirements. But political and public acceptance is not automatic. Therefore, there are efforts to eliminate cadmium from CIGS modules even at the cost of a reduced efficiency. Also a closed cycle for reclaiming and recycling of disposed CdTe modules has been developed (Bohland and others, 1998).

Economic aspects

Photovoltaic system cost. The turnkey cost of a photovoltaic system is determined by the module cost and by the balance-of-system (BOS) costs, which contains the cost of all other system components, electrical installation costs, and costs associated with building integration, site preparation, erection of support structures, and so on. The turnkey price is generally 20–40 percent higher than the *cost*.

In 1998 photovoltaic module prices were $3–6 a watt, depending on supplier, type, and size of order (Maycock, 1998; IEA PVPS, 1998). The prices of complete photovoltaic systems vary widely with system type and size, and from country to country (Thomas and others, 1999; IEA PVPS, 1998). But $5–10 a watt for grid-connected systems and $8–40 a watt for standalone systems are considered representative today.

The future cost and price reduction of photovoltaic modules and systems can be evaluated in two ways. The first is by detailed analysis of manufacturing costs for a specific technology as function of technology improvements and innovations—and of production volumes. The second is by general analysis of photovoltaic markets and industries, using a learning curve approach. (Note that the second approach deals with prices rather than costs.)

■ *Approach 1.* For crystalline silicon technologies, the manufacturing cost of solar cell modules can be reduced from the present $3–4 a watt down to $1.5–2 a watt in the short term and to around $1

It is still too early to identify winners or losers among the photovoltaic technologies under development or in production.

a watt in the longer term. For thin films (a-Si, CdTe, and CIGS), the module costs are expected to fall to $1–1.5 a watt in the short term, $0.5–1 a watt in the longer term (Carlson and Wagner, 1993; Bruton and others, 1997; Little and Nowlan, 1997; Maycock, 1998). EUREC Agency (1996, p.84) even mentions module costs as low as $0.30 a watt. The corresponding prices are again 20–40 percent higher.

The balance-of-system costs for rooftop and ground-based grid-connected systems are now typically $2–6 a watt. Improvements and economies of scale in power electronics, integration in the building process, and standardisation will enable reductions to $1–2 a watt in the short term, $0.5 a watt in the longer term. The turnkey system cost is therefore expected to decrease to $2–4 a watt in the short to medium term and to $1.0–1.5 a watt in the longer term. Ultimately (after 2015) system costs around or even below $1 a watt are foreseen (Johansson and others, 1993b; WEC, 1994b; Böer, 1998), resulting in prices of roughly $1 a watt (table 7.12). For such extremely low prices it is necessary to use very cheap modules with high efficiencies (15–30 percent), to reduce area-related balance of system costs.

■ *Approach 2.* An evaluation of the development of photovoltaic (mostly module) costs and prices using a learning curve can be found in IIASA and WEC (1998), Maycock (1998), ECN (1999b), and elsewhere. For 1975–97 the learning rate has been roughly 20 percent: prices have been reduced by 20 percent for each doubling of the cumulative sales. When the technology and market mature, as for gas turbines, the learning rate may fall to 10 percent (IIASA and WEC, 1998). It is not clear, however, whether this will apply to photovoltaics as well, since the range for all industries is 10–30 percent and the value for the semiconductor industry is roughly 30 percent (ECN, 1999a). Here it is assumed that the learning rate stays at 20 percent—and that this rate applies to the total system price, not just to the module price.

In 1998 cumulative sales were roughly 800 megawatts. Production was about 150 megawatts. At growth of 15 percent a year (the average over the past 15 years; IEA PVPS, 1998), annual sales will double every five years—to about 3 gigawatts a year in 2020, when cumulative sales would be 25 gigawatts. As a result prices will have fallen in 2020 to a third of the 1998 level. With far more optimistic growth of 25 percent a year, annual sales would be 20 gigawatts a year in 2020, and cumulative sales 100 gigawatts. Prices will then have fallen to a fifth of the 1998 level.

Table 7.13 gives an overview of the cost estimates using a learning curve approach, for a learning rate of 20 percent (historic value). Results for a low learning rate of 10 percent are given for comparison. The projections using a learning curve approach show a somewhat slower decrease than those based on evaluations of photovoltaic production technologies. Note, however, that new technologies based on the use of thin-film solar cells can follow a different (lower) learning curve than the sum of all technologies.

TABLE 7.12. POSSIBLE COSTS OF GRID-CONNECTED PHOTOVOLTAIC SYSTEMS, BASED ON DIFFERENT EVALUATIONS OF PHOTOVOLTAIC PRODUCTION TECHNOLOGIES (APPROACH 1) (1998 DOLLARS PER WATT)

Element	1998	Short term (to 2005)	Medium term (2005–15)	Long term (after 2015)
Modules	3–4	1–2	0.5–1.0	≤ 0.5
Balance of system	2–6	1–2	0.5–1.0	≤ 0.5
Turnkey systems	5–10	2–4	1–2	≤ 1.0

Note: Prices are 20–40 percent higher than costs.

Photovoltaic electricity costs. Electricity costs are determined by turnkey system costs, economic lifetime (depreciation period), interest rates, operation and maintenance costs (including possible replacement of components), electricity yields of the system (a function of insolation and thus of geographic location), insurance costs, and so on (table 7.14).

Implementation issues

Since the cost of photovoltaic electricity is now well above that of electricity from the grid, photovoltaics are implemented through two distinct paths. One is market development of commercial high-value applications. The second is stimulating the installation of grid-connected systems. Both paths are generally supported through government and international aid programs.

The first path deals mainly with standalone photovoltaic systems and (more recently but to less extent) with small grid-connected systems for private use. The photovoltaics industry has survived the past decades by actively developing niche markets in telecommunication, leisure, lighting, signalling, water-pumping, and rural electrification. The rural market is now being actively pursued as potentially huge, since an estimated 2 billion people in developing countries do not have access to a grid (see chapter 10).

Photovoltaics are often a viable alternative for bringing small amounts of electricity (less than 1 kilowatt-hour a day) to end users. More than 300,000 solar home systems (typically 50 watts) have been installed over the past 10 years, only a very modest step towards true large-scale use (Böer, 1998). In addition a large number of even smaller systems has been sold. This rural market cannot be judged by the total peak power of the systems (300,000 x 50 watts = 15 megawatts). Even if all 2 billion people were to own a 100 watt photovoltaic system, this would contribute less than 1 exajoule of electricity to the world's energy consumption. Instead, it is the large number of people involved that is significant—and even more that photovoltaics provide light, radio, television, and other important services to them.

A major barrier for rapid growth and very widespread use is the lack (in most countries) of properly developed financing schemes and the infrastructure for distribution, after-sales service, and so on. Financing is essential because few of those 2 billion people can pay cash of $400 for a system. But some can pay a smaller amount, or even a monthly rate of a few dollars up to tens of dollars. This widely acknowledged problem has two solutions. The first is the full commercial development of very small photovoltaic systems to meet basic needs and be paid for in cash (mainly photovoltaic lanterns and other lighting systems in the range of 5–20 watts). The second is financing schemes using a down payment and monthly fees of roughly $5–20 a lease, or fee-for-service (Böer, 1998).

For grid-connected systems it is important to distinguish between small and medium-sized decentralised systems (typically 500 watts to 1 megawatt) integrated in the built environment and large ground-based, central systems (typically greater than 1 megawatt). Decentralised

integrated systems have some advantages over central ground-based ones. Their balance of system costs are generally lower. And they have more technical and non-technical possibilities to increase their competitiveness.

Photovoltaic market development through government programs in industrialised countries (IEA PVPV, 1998) applies mainly to systems integrated in the built environment. The aim of these programs is to boost the development and application of photovoltaic technology as an essential step towards future large-scale use. They provide market volume to the photovoltaics industry to achieve economies of scale and experience with a completely new

TABLE 7.13. POSSIBLE EVOLUTION OF TYPICAL COSTS OF GRID-CONNECTED PHOTOVOLTAIC SYSTEMS USING A LEARNING CURVE (APPROACH 2)

	1998	Medium term (2010)		Long term (2020)	
Average annual market growth rate (percent)	15 (1983–98)	15	25	15	25
Annual sales (gigawatts)	0.15	0.8	2	3	20
Cumulative sales (gigawatts)	0.8	6	11	25	100
Turnkey system price (1998 dollars per watt) at a learning rate of 20 percent	5–10	2.7–5.3	2.2–4.3	1.7–3.3	1 –2
Turnkey system price (1998 dollars per watt) at a learning rate of 10 percent	5–10	3.7–7.4	3.4–6.8	3.0–5.9	2.4–4.8

TABLE 7.14 ELECTRICITY COST AS A FUNCTION OF COST, ECONOMIC LIFETIME, AND ELECTRICITY YIELD OF PHOTOVOLTAIC SYSTEMS (DOLLARS A KILOWATT-HOUR)

Turnkey system cost (dollars a watt)	Economic lifetime (years)	Electricity yield (kilowatt-hours a year per kilowatt of installed capacity)	
		750	1,500
5 (lower limit 1998)	10	1.00–1.22	0.51–0.61
	25	0.61–0.87	0.31–0.44
1 (long term)	10	0.12–0.24	0.10–0.12
	25	0.12–0.17	0.06–0.09

Note: Operation and maintenance and insurance costs are 2 percent of the annual system cost. The interest rate is 5–10 percent.

BOX 7.6 SELECTED NATIONAL AND INTERNATIONAL PHOTOVOLTAIC PROGRAMMES

Japan. In 1994 the Japanese government adopted the New Energy Introduction Outline, with targets for renewable energy technologies, including photovoltaics. The aim is to install 400 megawatts of (mainly residential grid-connected) photovoltaic systems by 2000 and 4,600 megawatts by 2010 (Luchi, 1998). The program is based on gradually decreasing subsidies (starting at 50 percent) and net metering.

United States. The Million Solar Roofs program aims to install 1,000,000 solar hot water systems and photovoltaic systems by 2010 (IEA PVPS, 1998; Böer, 1998). The trend is from demonstrations and tests towards market-centred projects with funding primarily from the private sector. The program works by creating partnerships between communities, federal agencies, and the Department of Energy (Rannels, 1998).

Germany. The 100,000 Roofs program (300–350 megawatts in 2005) is dedicated to grid-connected photovoltaic systems. Private investments in photovoltaics are stimulated by interest-free loans and a subsidy of 12.5 percent (Photon, 1999b). In addition, the government decided recently to pay nearly 1 deutsche mark a kilowatt-hour to owners of photovoltaic systems, financed by a small increase of electricity rates.

Italy. The 10,000 Rooftops program aims to install 50 megawatts by around 2005 (Garrozzo and Causi, 1998). With a focus on building small- and medium-sized integrated, grid-connected photovoltaic systems, funding may be mixed public (75 percent) and private (25 percent).

European Union. The target for photovoltaics is an installed capacity of 3 gigawatts by 2010. This has been translated into a Million Roofs program to install 500,000 grid-connected photovoltaic systems on roofs and facades in the Union and to export another 500,000 village systems for decentralised electrification in developing countries (EC, 1997; EC, 1999; IEA PVPS, 1998).

Indonesia. In 1998 the installed capacity of photovoltaic systems in Indonesia was 5 megawatts. A new strategy has been developed to enhance the use of renewable energy technologies, especially photovoltaics. Some characteristics of this strategy are: establish renewable energy non-governmental organisations, prepare renewable energy product standards, run demonstration projects in partnership with the private sector, provide training, disseminate information, strengthen international cooperation, and institute policy development and regulation.

India. With a total installed capacity of about 40 megawatts of photovoltaic systems, India has among the world's largest national programs in photovoltaics. The five-year national plan 1997–2002 envisages a deployment of 58 megawatts in addition to the 28 megawatts installed as of 1997. Exports of 12 megawatts are also foreseen. Government-sponsored programs include installing solar lanterns and other lighting systems—and electrifying villages and grid-connected power plants. Subsidies are available to rural users (Sastry, 1999).

South Africa. Shell Renewables Ltd. and Eskom are investing $30 million in rural solar power development in South Africa from 1999 until 2001. This venture should provide standalone photovoltaic units to about 50,000 homes presently without electricity at a cost of about $8 a month (see chapter 10).

Kenya. Kenya has a high penetration rate of household photovoltaic systems. In 1999 more than 80,000 systems were in place and annual sales are about 20,000 systems. The market operates without significant external aid or support (see chapter 10).

World Bank. The World Bank has become very active in developing financial schemes and programs for rural electrification in developing countries (Photon, 1999a). An example is the photovoltaic Market Transformation Initiative. The Bank's activities, fully integrated on a national level, mainly aim at removing barriers and building capacity. Generally, the approach is not to stimulate photovoltaics through subsidies for system hardware, but to facilitate commercial operations fitted to the local circumstances.

way of sustainable (decentralised) electricity generation. Clearly, this policy-driven market depends on public support and high expectations for photovoltaics as a major electricity source for the future.

A variety of instruments can achieve a self-sustained market: rate-based measures (favourable feed-in tariffs), fiscal measures, investment subsidies, soft loans, building codes. Another instrument is the removal of barriers related, say, to building design and material use. In addition to these incentives, the added value of photovoltaics—like aesthetics in building integration, combining electricity generation and light transmission, and generating part or all of one's own electricity consumption—are used in marketing photovoltaics. Green electricity and green certificates for the use of renewables are also expected to be important in the further development of a self-sustained market for grid-connected systems. They enable selling electricity from photovoltaics (or other renewables) to environmentally conscious electricity consumers.

Several countries have set targets or formulated programs for renewable energy technologies, specifically solar (box 7.6). In countries with a well-developed electricity infrastructure, the long-term aim is to achieve a substantial contribution to the electricity generation from solar energy. In developing countries and countries with a less-developed electricity infrastructure, efforts are focused on the large-scale implementation of smaller standalone solar photovoltaic systems. In these cases the dissemination of solar energy is a tool for social and economic development.

Space-based solar energy

A very different approach to exploiting solar energy is to capture it in space and convey it to the Earth by wireless transmission. Unlike terrestrial capture of solar energy, a space-based system would not be limited by the vagaries of the day-night cycle and adverse weather—and so could provide baseload electricity (Glaser and others, 1997).

In space the maximum irradiance (power density) is much higher than on Earth—around 1,360 watts per square metre—and is nearly constant. This energy can be captured and converted to electricity just as it can on Earth, as is done routinely to power spacecraft. The elements of such a space-based solar energy system would include:

- Satellites in geosynchronous or other orbits designed as large solar collectors.
- Power conditioning and conversion components to turn the electricity generated by the photovoltaic arrays into radio frequency form.
- Transmitting antennas that form one or more beams directed from the satellites to the Earth.
- Receiving antennas on Earth that collect the incoming radio frequency energy and convert it into useful electricity. Such a device is called a rectenna (for rectifying receiving antenna). The power yield from typical rectennas at low to middle latitudes would be on the order of 30 megawatts per square kilometre.
- Power conditioning components to convert the direct current output from the rectenna to alternating current for local use.

As with any solar source, space-based energy would not contribute to greenhouse gas emissions during operation. The high launch rate required to place a space-based energy system could affect the Earth's atmosphere, however. The effects of power transmission to the ground need to be assessed for at least three factors: influences on the atmosphere (particularly the ionosphere on the way down), inference between the wireless power transmission and communications or electronic equipment, and the effects of the transmitted beam on life forms. Estimates and some experiments indicate that these effects might be small.

Very preliminary estimates suggest that a cost target of $0.05 per kilowatt-hour may ultimately be achievable for a mature space-based solar energy system (Mankins, 1998). But several important issues must be addressed:

- A number of key technologies require maturation.
- The cost of access to space must be substantially lowered.
- Safety and environmental concerns must be resolved.
- Optimal designs for space-based solar systems need to be established.
- Orbital slots for collecting platforms and frequencies for power transmission need to be obtained.

Conclusion

- Since 1983 the average growth rate of photovoltaic module shipments has been 15 percent a year. In 1998 the production was 150 megawatts, and in 1999, about 200 megawatts. In 1998 the cumulative production was around 800 megawatts, with the operating capacity probably about 500 megawatts, perhaps 600 megawatts. The growth of operating photovoltaic capacity in the last five years can be estimated at roughly 30 percent a year.
- Since 1975 the learning rate (cost reduction as function of cumulative production) has been roughly 20 percent. In 1998 turnkey costs of grid-connected photovoltaic systems were $5–10 a watt. In the future these costs may come down to about $1 a watt.
- Today photovoltaics generally cannot compete with conventional power plants in grid-connected applications. Photovoltaic electricity production costs are about $0.3–1.5 a kilowatt-hour, depending on solar insolation, turnkey costs, depreciation periods, and interest rates. Under favourable conditions and at favourable sites, the lowest cost figure may come down to $0.05-0.06 a kilowatt-hour.
- It remains uncertain whether and when photovoltaics will compete with fossil fuels on a large scale. This mainly depends on the development of photovoltaics, on the price development of coal and natural gas, and on possibilities for (or policies on) carbon dioxide removal at low cost.
- Supplying less than 1 percent of the world's energy consumption, photovoltaic systems can play a major role in rural electrification by reaching many of the 2 billion people in developing countries who do not have access to electricity.
- There appear to be no invincible technical problems for solar energy to contribute much to the world's energy supply. What matters

Photovoltaics are often a viable alternative for bringing small amounts of electricity (less than 1 kilowatt-hour a day) to end users.

are policy developments and the market position of fossil fuels and other energy sources.

Solar thermal electricity

Solar radiation can produce high-temperature heat, which can generate electricity. The most important solar thermal technologies to produce electricity—concentrating—use direct irradiation. Low cloud areas with little scattered radiation, such as deserts, are considered most suitable for direct-beam-only collectors. Thus the primary market for concentrating solar thermal electric technologies is in sunnier regions, particularly in warm temperate, sub-tropical, or desert areas. About 1 percent of the world's desert area used by solar thermal power plants would be sufficient to generate today's world electricity demand. Here we will assess the current status and future development of solar thermal electricity (STE) technologies.

The potential of solar thermal electricity

STE is probably 20 years behind wind power in market exploitation. In 1998 operating STE capacity was about 400 megawatts of electricity, with annual electricity output of nearly 1 terawatt-hour. New projects in mind mount to a maximum of 500 megawatts of electricity, and it is probable that 2,000 megawatts of installed capacity will not be reached until 2010 (the capacity wind reached in 1990). Because STE costs are dropping rapidly towards levels similar to those obtained by wind, STE may grow in a manner somewhat similar to wind. If the growth rate is 20–25 percent after 2010, this installed STE capacity would be 12,000–18,000 megawatts of electricity by 2020. If annual growth rate then averages 15 percent a year, the result would be 800–1,200 gigawatts of electricity by 2050. The Cost Reduction Study for Solar Thermal Power Plants, prepared for the World Bank in early 1999 (Enermodal, 1999), concludes that the large potential market of STE could reach an annual installation rate of 2,000 megawatts of electricity. In the foregoing scenario this rate is reached between 2015 and 2020. Advanced low-cost STE systems are likely to offer energy output at an annual capacity factor of 0.22 or more. So, the contribution of STE would be about 24–36 terawatt-hours of electricity by 2020 and 1,600–2,400 terawatt-hours by 2050.

Solar thermal electricity market developments

STE technologies can meet the requirements of two major electric power markets: large-scale dispatchable markets comprising grid-connected peaking and baseload power, and rapidly expanding distributed markets including both on-grid and remote applications.

Dispatchable power markets. Using storage and hybridisation capabilities (integration of STE with fossil fuel power plants), dispatchable solar thermal electric technologies can address this market. Currently offering the lowest-cost, highest-value solar electricity available, they have the potential to be economically competitive with fossil energy in the longer term. With continuing development success and early implementation opportunities, the electricity production cost of dispatchable STE systems is expected to drop from $0.12–0.18 a kilowatt-hour today to about $0.08–0.14 a kilowatt-hour in 2005 and to $0.04–0.10 a kilowatt-hour thereafter.

In this market there is a huge existing global capacity of fossil fuel plant, much of it coal, available for low solar-fraction retrofit as a transition strategy. Coal-fired plants tend to be much larger individually than solar thermal standalone plants (600–1,200 megawatts of electricity compared with 5–80 megawatts), and usable land around coal-fired plants is restricted. Any solar retrofit to a typical coal-fired plant will supply only a small percentage of its total electricity output. But around the world, there are hundreds of such fossil fuel plants in good insolation areas, many with sufficient adjacent land area to accommodate a solar field of the size of the current largest STE units of about 80 megawatts. This market could account for a large fraction of the 12,000–18,000 megawatts by 2020 in the scenario above.

Distributed power markets. The majority of these applications are for remote power, such as water pumping and village electrification, with no utility grid. In these applications, diesel engine generators are the primary current competition. The STE technology appropriate for smaller distributed applications is the dish/engine system. Each dish/engine module (10–50 kilowatts of electricity) is an independent power system designed for automatic start-up and unattended operation. Multiple dish/engine systems can be installed at a single site to provide as much power as required, and the system can readily be expanded with additional modules to accommodate future load growth. The systems can be designed for solar-only applications, easily hybridised with fossil fuels to allow power production without sunlight, or deployed with battery systems to store energy for later use.

The high value of distributed power (more than $0.50 a kilowatt-hour for some remote applications) provides opportunities for commercial deployment early in the technology development. The technology enhancements needed to achieve high reliability and reduce operation and maintenance costs are understood. With continuing development, the electricity production costs of distributed STE system are expected to drop from $0.20–0.40 a kilowatt-hour today to about $0.12–0.20 a kilowatt-hour in 2005 and to $0.05–0.10 a kilowatt-hour in the long run.

STE projects, ranging from about 10 kilowatts to 80 megawatts of electricity, have been realised or are being developed in Australia, Egypt, Greece, India, Iran, Jordan, Mexico, Morocco, Spain, and the United States (box 7.7).

Market entry strategy. Three phases can be distinguished in an STE market entry strategy:

- *Solar field additions.* Small solar fields can be integrated into combined cycle and coal or fuel oil-fired power plants for $700–1,500 per kilowatt installed.
- *Increased solar share.* With increasing fossil fuel prices or compensation premiums for carbon dioxide avoidance as well as solar field cost reductions, the share of solar can be increased to about 50 percent in solar-fossil hybrid power stations.
- *Thermal energy storage.* With further improvement in the cost-benefit ratio of STE, thermal energy storage will further substitute for the need of a fossil back-up fuel source. In the long run, baseload operated solar thermal power plants without any fossil fuel addition are in principle possible, and clean bio-energy back-up is also feasible.

Figure 7.6 presents an outlook on the market introduction of STE technologies and the associated reduction in electricity generation costs as presented by SunLab (1999).

Solar thermal electricity technologies

Five distinct solar thermal electric conversion concepts are available, each with different operating and commercial features. Two non-concentrating technologies—solar chimney and solar pond—are not included in this brief description of emerging solar thermal power concepts, because they lack significantly sized pilot and demonstration test facilities.

All concentrating solar power technologies rely on four basic key elements: collector/concentrator, receiver, transport/storage, and power conversion. The collector/concentrator captures and concentrates solar radiation, which is then delivered to the receiver. The receiver absorbs the concentrated sunlight, transferring its heat energy to a working fluid. The transport/storage system passes the fluid from the receiver to the power conversion system. In some solar thermal plants a portion of the thermal energy is stored for later use. As solar thermal power conversion systems, Rankine, Brayton, Combined, and Stirling cycles have been successfully demonstrated.

BOX 7.7. COMMERCIAL SOLAR THERMAL ELECTRICITY DEVELOPMENTS NOW UNDER WAY

Australia. Under the Australian Greenhouse Office (AGO) Renewable Energy Showcase Programme, a 13 megawatt-thermal compact linear fresnel reflector (CLFR) demonstration unit will be installed in 2001, retrofitted to an existing 1,400 megawatts-electric coal-fired plant in Queensland (Burbridge and others, 2000). It is expected to offer the solar electricity from this first commercial project as green power at a price below $0.09 a kilowatt-hour. A 2 megawatts-electric demonstration unit, using paraboloidal dish technology, has also been announced for installation in 2001, retrofitted to a gas-fired steam generating plant (Luzzi, 2000).

Greece. On the island of Crete, the private venture capital fund Solar Millennium—together with Greek and European industrial partners—has established the first solar thermal project company (THESEUS S.A.) and submitted an application for licensing a 52 megawatt-thermal solar thermal power plant with 300,000 square metres of parabolic trough solar field.

Spain. New incentive premiums for the generation of renewable electricity in 1999 caused Spanish companies such as Abengoa, Gamesa, and Ghersa to engage in solar thermal technologies and to establish various project companies (Osuna and others, 2000).

United States. Green electricity and renewable portfolio policies of various states have revived the interest of such industrial firms as Bechtel, Boeing, and Dukesolar in the further development of STE technologies.

Global Environment Facility. In 1999 the Global Environmental Facility approved grants for the first solar thermal projects in Egypt, India, Mexico, and Morocco—about $200 million in total. The proposed Indian plant uses integrated gas combined cycle and solar thermal (Garg, 2000).

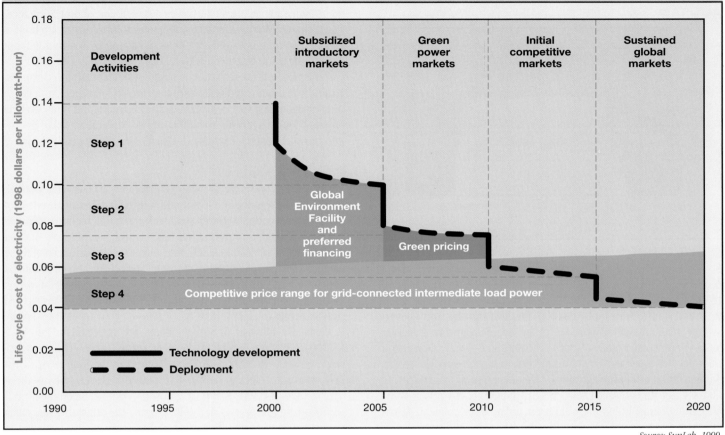

FIGURE 7.6 MARKET INTRODUCTION OF SOLAR THERMAL ELECTRICITY TECHNOLOGIES WITH INITIAL SUBSIDIES AND GREEN POWER TARIFFS, 1990–2020

Source: SunLab, 1999.

An inherent advantage of STE technologies is their unique ability to be integrated with conventional thermal plants. All of them can be integrated as a solar boiler into conventional thermal cycles, in parallel with a fossil-fuelled boiler. They can thus be provided with thermal storage or fossil fuel back-up firm capacity without the need for separate back-up power plants and without stochastic perturbations of the grid (figure 7.7). The potential availability of storage and ability to share generation facilities with clean biomass suggest a future ability to provide a 100 percent replacement for high capacity factor fossil fuel plant when needed.

Parabolic trough systems. The parabolic trough (solar farm) consists of long parallel rows of identical concentrator modules, typically using trough-shaped glass mirrors. Tracking the sun from east to west by rotation on one axis, the trough collector concentrates the direct solar radiation onto an absorber pipe located along its focal line. A heat transfer medium, typically oil at temperatures up to 400 degrees Celsius, is circulated through the pipes. The hot oil converts water to steam, driving the steam turbine generator of a conventional power block.

With 354 megawatts-electric of parabolic trough solar electric

generating systems connected to the grid in southern California since the mid-1980s, parabolic troughs are the most mature STE technology (Pilkington, 1996). There are more than 100 plant-years of experience from the nine operating plants. The plants range in size from 14–80 megawatts of electricity. Until the end of 1998, 8 terawatt-hours of solar electrical energy had been fed into the Californian grid, resulting in sales revenues of more than $1,000 million. The technology is under active development and refinement to improve its performance and reduce production costs.

Central receiver/power tower. The solar central receiver or power tower is surrounded by a large array of two-axis tracking mirrors—termed heliostats—reflecting direct solar radiation onto a fixed receiver located on the top of the tower. Within the receiver, a fluid transfers the absorbed solar heat to the power block where it is used to heat a steam generator. Water, air, liquid metal, and molten salt have been tested as fluids.

Advanced high-temperature power tower concepts are now under investigation, heating pressurised air to more than 1,000 degrees Celsius to feed it into the gas turbines of modern combined cycles. In Barstow, California, a 10 megawatts-electric pilot plant

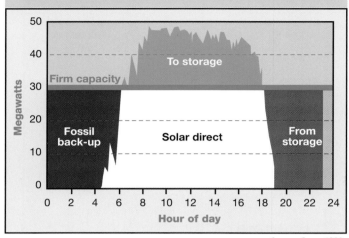

FIGURE 7.7. WITH MINIMAL FOSSIL BACK-UP AND THERMAL ENERGY STORAGE, SOLAR CAPACITY IS TRANSFORMED INTO FIRM CAPACITY

Source: Geyer, 1999.

(Solar One) operated with steam from 1982–88. After modification of the complete plant in 1996, it operated as Solar Two for a few thousand hours, with molten salt as the heat-transfer and energy-storage medium, delivering power to the electricity grid on a regular basis (Pacheco and others, 2000). The net solar-electric conversion efficiency was 8 percent. Solar Two has demonstrated, through storage, the feasibility of delivering utility-scale solar power to the grid 24 hours a day, if necessary (Kolb, 1998). In parallel, European activities have demonstrated the volumetric air receiver concept, where the solar energy is absorbed on fine-mesh screens and immediately transferred to air as the working fluid (Buck and others, 2000).

Dish/engine power plants. Parabolic dish systems consist of a parabolic-shaped point focus concentrator in the form of a dish that reflects solar radiation onto a receiver mounted at the focal point. These concentrators are mounted on a structure with a two-axis tracking system to follow the sun. The collected heat is often used directly by a heat engine, mounted on the receiver. Stirling and Brayton cycle engines are currently favoured for decentralised power conversion. Central Rankine cycles are being studied for large fields of such dishes where the receiver does not contain a heat engine.

Several dish/engine prototypes have operated successfully in the last 10 years, including 7–25 kilowatts-electric units developed in the United States. But there has not yet been a large-scale deployment. In Spain six units with a 9–10 kilowatts-electric rating are operating successfully. Australia has demonstrated a 400 square metre, 10 kilowatts-electric 'big dish' at the Australian National University in Canberra (Luzzi, 2000). Work is proceeding to develop a dish plant of 2–3 megawatts- electric attached to an existing fossil fuel power plant.

Advanced systems under development. Compact linear fresnel reflector (CLFR) technology has recently been developed at the University of Sydney in Australia. Individual reflectors have the option of directing reflected solar radiation to at least two towers.

This additional variable in reflector orientation provides the means for much more densely packed arrays. The CLFR concept, intended to reduce costs in all elements of the solar thermal array, includes many additional features that enhance system cost and performance. The technology aims only at temperatures suitable for steam boilers and pre-heaters, with the view that superheating is a minor input and can be done by other fuels.

Fuels. Long-term research is under way in Australia, Germany, Israel, Switzerland, and elsewhere to produce solar fuels for a range of uses, including fuel cells for electricity production. This work is targeted towards the thermochemical conversion of solar energy into chemical energy carriers (hydrogen, synthesis gas, metals).

Economic aspects

The Cost Reduction Study for Solar Thermal Power Plants (Enermodal, 1999) has assessed the current and future cost competitiveness of STE with conventional power systems for two STE technologies: the parabolic trough and the molten salt central receiver system. Two approaches were used to assess the future cost performance of these technologies: an engineering approach based on known technical improvements and cost reductions from commercialisation, and a learning (experience) curve approach. The two approaches yielded similar results.

Costs per kilowatt of trough plants are expected to fall from $3,000–3,500 a kilowatt in the near term (for a 30 megawatts-electric plant) to $2,000–2,500 a kilowatt in the long term (for a 200 megawatts-electric plant). For central receiver systems these figures are $4,200–5,000 a kilowatt in the near term and $1,600–1,900 a kilowatt in the long term. The attainable net solar-to-electric conversion efficiencies of these systems are expected to be 13–16 percent in the near term and 18–20 percent in the long term. Operation and maintenance costs can decrease from about $0.025 a kilowatt-hour in the near term to about $0.005 a kilowatt-hour in the long term.

If the cost of electricity from conventional power plants stays constant over the next 20 years, the solar levelised energy cost (LEC) can be calculated to fall to less than half of current values—from $0.14–0.18 a kilowatt-hour to $0.04–0.06 a kilowatt-hour. At this cost, the potential for STE power plants to compete with Rankine cycle plants (coal, gas, or oil fired) can be promising. The solar LEC for the tower is calculated to be less than for the trough because of the use of thermal storage. If troughs were equipped with storage as well, the same advantage would probably be found. It can thus be concluded that 24-hour power does not increase the total generating costs. If a credit of $25–40 a tonne were included for reduced carbon dioxide emissions, STE power may have an even lower LEC than coal-fired Rankine plants.

Environmental and social aspects

Carbon dioxide emission savings. A solar boiler can supply 2,000 to 2,500 full load hours per year to a steam cycle. With STE technologies, each square meter of solar field can produce up to 1,200 kilowatt-hours of thermal energy a year—or up to 500 kilowatt-hours of electricity a year. Taking into account a thermal plant carbon dioxide emissions of 0.4–0.8 kilograms a kilowatt-hour electric, there results a cumulative saving of up to 5–10 tonnes of carbon dioxide per square metre of STE system over its 25-year lifetime (Pilkington, 1996).

Impact on fossil fuels consumption. The embodied energy of a STE plant is recovered after less than 1.5 years of plant operation (Lenzen, 1999). STE systems can preserve fossil energy or biomass resources. Taking into account an average conventional thermal power plant efficiency of 40 percent, there results a cumulative saving of about 2.5 tonnes of coal per square metre of solar field over its 25-year lifetime.

Land use. Land use is sometimes cited as a concern with renewables. If renewables are to contribute to energy production on a global scale, sufficient areas have to be available in suitable locations. Most solar thermal power plants need about 1 square kilometre of area for 60 megawatts of electricity capacity, although STE technologies like CLFR (see above) might reduce this by a factor or 3 or so (Mills and Morrison, 2000a, b).

Domestic supply of equipment and materials. The higher up-front cost of solar thermal power stations results from the additional investment into the STE equipment and erection. Most of this equipment and most of the construction materials required can be produced domestically. The evaluation of the domestic supply capability of selected countries indicates national supply shares ranging from 40 percent to more than 50 percent of the total project value. This supply share can be increased for subsequent projects (Pilkington, 1996).

Labour requirements. The erection and operation of the nine STE power plants in California indicate current labour requirements. The last 80 megawatts-electric plants showed that during the two-year construction period, there is a peak of about 1,000 jobs. Operation of the plant requires about 50 permanent qualified jobs (Pilkington, 1996).

Conclusion

- In the sunbelt of the world, solar thermal power is one of the candidates to provide a significant share of renewable clean energy needed in the future.
- STE is now ready for more widespread application if we start more intensified market penetration immediately; its application is not strongly restricted by land area or resource limitations.
- The STE technology appropriate for smaller remote power production is the dish/engine power plant. For grid-connected applications, technologies such as the parabolic trough system and the central receiver/power tower are applied.
- The installed STE capacity, now about 400 megawatts of electricity, may grow to 2,000 megawatts of electricity in 2010—and to 12,000–18,000 megawatts of electricity in 2020. An annual growth rate of 15 percent after 2020 would yield 1,600–2,400 terawatt-hours a year by 2050.

- Small solar fields can be integrated into fossil fuel power plants at relatively low costs. With improvement of the cost-benefit ratio of STE, the solar share in hybrid solar/fossil power plants may increase to about 50 percent. Thermal energy storage will be able to further substitute for the need for a fossil back-up fuel. In the long run, baseload-operated solar thermal power plants without any fossil fuel addition are now technically proven.
- STE is the lowest-cost solar electricity in the world, promising cost competitiveness with fossil fuel plants in the future—especially if assisted by environmental credits. Electricity production costs of grid-connected STE systems may come down from $0.12–0.18 a kilowatt-hour today to $0.04–0.10 a kilowatt-hour in the long term. In remote areas, the production costs of distributed systems may come down from $0.20–0.40 a kilowatt-hour today to $0.05–0.10 a kilowatt-hour in the long term.

Low-temperature solar energy

The easiest and most direct application of solar energy is the direct conversion of sunlight into low-temperature heat—up to a temperature of 100 degrees Celsius. In general, two classes of technologies can be distinguished: passive and active solar energy conversion. With active conversion there is always a solar collector, and the heat is transported to the process by a medium. With passive conversion the conversion takes place in the process, so no active components are used.

In this section the main focus is on active conversion, for which a broad range of technologies is available. The best known is the solar domestic hot water system. Another technology in the building sector is the solar space heating system. Such a system can be sized for single houses or for collective buildings and district heating. Similar technologies can be applied in the industrial and agricultural sector for low-temperature heating and drying applications. Heating using solar energy can also be achieved by heat pumps. Finally, there are technologies to use solar energy for cooling and cooking purposes.

Low-temperature solar energy potential and market developments

The world's commercial low-temperature heat consumption can be estimated at about 50 exajoules a year for space heating and at about 10 exajoules a year for hot water production. Low- and medium-temperature heat (up to 200 degrees Celsius) is also used as process heat, in total about 40 exajoules a year. Almost any low-and medium-temperature heat demand can be met at least partially with solar energy. One of the drawbacks for this application is the mismatch between availability of sunlight and demand for heating. Therefore nearly any solar heating system contains a storage unit.

The solar domestic hot water system (SDHW) is the most important application for low-temperature solar heat at this moment. In 1994 some 7 million SDHWs had been installed world-wide. In 1994 the total installed collector area of SDHWs and other solar energy systems was about 22 million square metres (Morrison, 1999) and in 1998 about 30 million square metres. This can be expressed as an installed capacity of around 18,000 megawatts. The total amount of heat generated by these solar energy systems can be estimated roughly at 50 petajoules a year. This is only 0.5 percent of the potential of around 10 exajoules a year. Table 7.15 provides an overview of the annually produced and total installed glazed collector area.

In Europe the market rapidly expanded after 1994. In 1996 about 700,000 square metres were produced, mainly in Germany (330,000 square metres) and Austria (230,000 square metres). The European Solar Industry Federation expects annual growth of around 20 percent (ESIF, 1996). In 1998 sales in Europe were probably on the order of 1 million square metres. In the United States the market has declined—the amount of collector area sold

in SDHW systems decreased from 1.1 million square metres in 1984 to around 80,000 square metres in 1998 (Morrison, 1999). The market collapsed in 1986 because the federal R&D funding and tax credits ended abruptly. In China production is increasing rapidly. In Japan the market is increasing after a collapse in 1987 (ESIF, 1996). For different regions, growth of 10–25 percent a year is foreseen. In 2010 the installed collector area could be 150 million square metres.

Another important technology is the electric heat pump. Driven by electricity, this pump can withdraw heat from a heat source and raise the temperature to deliver the heat to a process (such as space heating). Tens of millions of appliances have been installed that can be operated as heat pumps, while most of them can also be operated as cooling devices (air conditioners). Whether the application of these machines results in net fuel savings depends on the local situation, taking into account aspects such as the performance of the heat pump, the reference situation, and characteristics of the electricity source. A lack of data makes it impossible to determine the net contribution of heat pumps to the energy supply.

Low-temperature solar energy technologies and systems

Solar domestic hot water systems. The solar domestic hot water system (SDHW) consists of three components: a solar collector panel, a storage tank, and a circulation system to transfer the heat from the panel to the store. SDHW systems for household range in size, because of differences in hot water demands and climate conditions. In general price/performance analysis will be made to size the solar hot water system and to investigate the optimum solar fraction (contribution of solar energy in energy demand). The results show a general dependence on the climate. The SDHW systems in Northern and Central Europe are designed to operate on a solar fraction of 50–65 percent. Subtropical climates generally achieve solar fractions of 80–100 percent. Table 7.16 indicates typical characteristics of applied systems in various climate zones in Europe.

Pump/circulation systems are generally used in climate zones with a serious frost and overheating danger. These systems either use the drain-back principle (the fluid drains from the collector if there is no solar contribution) or an antifreeze additive in the collector fluid. In countries with a warmer climate, natural circulation systems are mostly used. Almost all collectors installed are of the flat plate type. But in China in 1997 about 2 million evacuated tube collectors (about 150,000 square metres of collector area) were produced (Morrison, 1999). These are double-walled concentric glass tubes, of which the enclosed space is evacuated.

In regions with high solar irradiation, the use of SDHW systems may result in solar heat production costs ranging from $0.03–0.12 a kilowatt-hour. In regions with relatively low solar irradiation, the costs may range from $0.08–0.25 a kilowatt-hour. In many areas these costs can be competitive with electricity prices—but in most cases not with fossil fuel prices. Further cost reductions are therefore required.

■ One approach is the use of complete prefabricated systems or kits, leaving no possibility to make changes in the system design,

TABLE 7.15. MAJOR SOLAR COLLECTOR MARKETS, 1994 (THOUSANDS OF SQUARE METRES)

Economy	Total glazed collector area installed	Glazed collector area produced
Australia	1,400	140
China	1,500	500
India	500	50
Israel	2,800	300
Japan	7,000	500
Taiwan, China	200	90
United States	4,000	70
Europe	4,700	500
Austria	400	125
Cyprus	600	30
France	260	18
Germany	690	140
Greece	2,000	120
Portugal	200	13
World	~ 22,000	~ 2,200

Source: Based on Morrison, 1999.

TABLE 7.16. CHARACTERISTICS OF SOLAR DOMESTIC HOT WATER SYSTEMS IN EUROPE

Feature	Northern Europe	Central Europe	Mediter-ranean
Collector area (square metres)	3–6	3–5	2–4
Storage capacity (litres)	100–300	200–300	100–200
Annual system performance (kilowatt-hours per square metre)	300–450	400–550	500–650
Installed system costs (dollars per square metre)	400–1,000	400–1,000	300–600[a]
Common system type	Pump/circulation	Pump/circulation	Thermo-syphon

a. In countries like Israel and Turkey this figure can be even lower.

thus simplifying the installation work and reducing both the hardware and the installation cost.

- Another approach, in Northern Europe, is the development of solar thermal energy markets on a large scale, to reduce production, installation, and overhead costs. As demonstrated in the Netherlands, large projects can reduce the installed system price by 30–40 percent relative to the price of individually marketed systems.

- Cost reductions can also be achieved by further development of the technology (including integration of collector and storage unit). As a result of these approaches, solar heat production costs may come down 40–50 percent (TNO, 1992).

SDHW systems are commonly produced from metals (aluminium, copper, steel), glass and insulation materials. In most designs the systems can easily be separated into the constituent materials; all metals and glass can be recycled. The energy payback time of a SDHW system is now generally less than one year (van der Leun, 1994).

Large water heating systems. Solar thermal systems can provide heat and hot water for direct use or as pre-heated water to boilers that generate steam. Such large water heating systems find widespread use in swimming pools, hotels, hospitals, and homes for the elderly. Other markets are fertiliser and chemical factories, textile mills, dairies, and food processing units. Substantial quantities of fossil fuels or electricity can be saved through their use. But the installed collector area is rather low—around a tenth of the total installed area. It is especially low in the industrial sector, mainly because of low fossil fuel costs and relatively high economic payback times of solar systems. India provides tax benefits through accelerated depreciation on such commercial systems and also has a programme to provide soft loans to finance their installation. Within these systems about 400,000 square metres of collector area has been installed in India (TERI, 1996/97). The costs per kilowatt-hour of large water heating systems are now somewhat less than SDHW energy costs. And in the long term these costs can be reduced, probably about 25 percent, mainly by mass production.

Solar space heating. Total world space heating demand is estimated at 50 exajoules a year. In northern climates this demand can be more than 20 percent of total energy use. Mismatch between supply and demand limits the direct contribution of solar thermal energy to the space heating of a building to a maximum of 20 percent in these regions. If seasonal storage of heat is applied, solar fractions of up to 100 percent are achievable (Fisch, 1998). Space heating systems are available as water systems and as air heating systems, with air heating systems generally cheaper. Water-based systems are usually solar combi-systems that supply domestic hot water and space heating.

Seasonal storage has mainly been applied in demonstration projects, showing its technological feasibility. The technologies are divided into large and small systems. For large systems (storage for more than 250 houses) the insulation is not so important, and duct storage or aquifer storage is possible. For small systems storage of heat in an insulated tank is the only solution to date. More advanced concepts— such as chemical storage of heat— have been proven on a laboratory scale. Storage of cold from the winter to be used in the summer has proven to be profitable, if aquifers are available in the underground.

District heating. Solar energy can also be applied for district heating. Providing hot water and space heat, several of these systems, using a central collector area, have been realised in Denmark, Germany, and Sweden. They reach similar solar fractions as single house systems: 50 percent for hot water production and 15 percent for the total heat demand (hot water plus space heating). Some of these systems have been combined with a seasonal storage increasing the solar fraction to 80 percent for the total heat demand.

Heat pumps. Heat pumps can generate high-temperature heat from a low-temperature heat source. Working in the opposite direction the same appliance can also be used as a cooling device. In fact most heat pumps are air conditioners that are also suitable for heating purposes. Tens of millions of these appliances have been installed world-wide. In colder climates there is a market for heat pumps for heating only. In Europe in 1996 around 900,000 of these pumps were installed (Laue, 1999), and the market is growing at about 10 percent a year (Bouma, 1999).

Energy (mostly electricity) is needed to operate the heat pump. Typically the heat energy output is two to four times the electrical energy input. The low-temperature heat input can come directly or indirectly from the sun. For example, with ground-coupled heat pump systems, the surface can be seen as a cheap solar collector— and the ground beneath it as a storage system from which the low-temperature heat can be extracted. Today, however, most systems extract heat from the open air. Different systems have been tested using solar collectors as a heat source. Because heat pumps can work with low temperatures, the collectors can be cheap.

No general statement can be made about the contribution of heat pumps to savings in fossil fuel consumption and environmental emissions. But by further improving the performance of the heat pump and by using electricity from renewable sources (hydro, wind, photovoltaics), this contribution will be definitely positive.

Solar cooling. About 30 million air conditioners are sold each year (Nishimura, 1999). Cooling with solar heat seems an obvious application, because demand for cooling and supply of solar heat are in phase. The technologies available are absorption cooling, adsorption cooling, and desiccant cooling. A standard, single-effect absorption chiller can be driven with temperatures around 90 degrees Celsius. This can be generated with standard flat plate solar collectors. Different systems have been designed and tested, but their economics turned out to be poor. As a result this field of applications has been disregarded over the last 10 years. Recently some newer cooling cycles have become available, the solar collector performance has improved, and collector prices have gone down. So solar cooling may become a feasible option (Henning, 1999).

Passive solar energy use has become an attractive option for heating and cooling buildings because of the development of new materials and powerful simulation tools.

Solar cooking. About half the world's cooking uses firewood as the fuel, with the other half based on gas, kerosene, or electricity. In some regions cooking energy requirements place a great pressure on biomass resources while also causing considerable inconvenience and health effects to users in the collection and burning of biomass (see chapter 3). Considering that these regions also have significant levels of solar radiation, it would appear that cooking provides a significant and beneficial impact.

China and India are among several countries promoting the use of solar cookers. A simple box-type cooker and a parabolic concentrating type cooker are among the common models deployed. Efforts have also been made to develop solar cookers for institutional use. In India some 450,000 box type cookers have been installed. The world's largest solar cooking system—capable of preparing meals for 10,000 persons twice a day—was installed in 1999 in Taleti in Rajasthan, India (TERI, 1996/97; MNCES, 1999). In China some 100,000 concentrator-type cookers have been deployed (Wentzel, 1995).

Solar cooking devices have certain limitations and can only supplement, not replace conventional fuels. A home that uses a solar cooker regularly can save a third to a half of the conventional fuel that is used for cooking. The economic payback time is usually between 2–4 years. The large-scale use of solar cookers, however, will also require some adjustment by users.

Solar crop drying. The drying of agricultural products requires large quantities of low-temperature heat—in many cases, year round. Low-cost air-based solar collectors can provide this heat at collection efficiencies of 30–70 percent (Voskens and Carpenter, 1999). In Finland, Norway, and Switzerland hay drying is already an established technology. By 1998 more than 100,000 square metres of air collectors for drying purposes had been installed.

In developing countries 60–70 percent of grain production (as estimated by the Food and Agriculture Organisation) is retained at the farmer level, and crop drying is effected predominantly by exposure to direct sunlight (sun drying). In industrialised countries crops are typically dried in large fossil-fuelled drying systems, operating at relatively high temperatures with a high throughput of material. If a solar dryer is used in place of sun drying, there will not be any energy savings, but the solar dryer will achieve higher throughput of material, better quality of material, and lower loss of material (to

pests or theft). Air-collector-type solar dryers have the most potential in replacing fuel-fired dryers for crops dried at temperatures less than 50 degrees Celsius (table 7.17).

The technology for solar crop drying is available, and its application can be economically viable. Market introduction of these technologies will thus be the next step, but that will require training and demonstration projects targeted at specific crops and specific potential users and regions.

Passive solar energy use. The application of passive solar principles can contribute significantly to the reduction of (active) energy demands for heating, cooling, lighting, and ventilating buildings. Some of these principles (Boyle, 1996) are :
- Be well insulated.
- Have a responsive, efficient heating system.
- Face south.
- Avoid overshading by other buildings.
- Be thermally massive.

The principles have to be considered in relation to the building design process, because they have a direct effect on the architectural appearance of the building, on the level of comfort (heat, cold, light, ventilation), and on people's experience of the building. Nowadays a number of techniques can diminish energy demands with passive means:
- *Low-emission double-glazed windows.* In cold climates these windows keep out the cold while allowing the solar radiation to pass. In summer the windows can be shaded, and heat is kept outside.
- *Low-cost opaque insulation material and high insulating building elements.* These elements can keep out the heat as well as the cold.
- *Transparent insulation material.* This material can be used to allow day-lighting while keeping out the cold or heat.
- *High-efficiency ventilation heat recovery.*
- *High-efficiency lighting systems and electrical appliances with automatic control.* These can bring down the internal heat gain, reducing the cooling load. Advanced daylight systems can lead to 40 percent reduction of the energy use for lighting purposes.

By carrying out detailed simulation studies, the energy demand of a building can be optimised, without affecting comfort (Hastings, 1994). It has been estimated that 13 percent of the heat demand of buildings is covered by passive solar energy use. For optimised buildings this fraction can go up to 30 percent without major investments (Brouwer and Bosselaar, 1999). Because of the development of better materials and powerful simulation models, passive use of solar energy is becoming the number one consideration for heating and cooling buildings.

Implementation issues

In many countries incentive programmes help to stimulate the further development and application of low-temperature solar energy systems, improving their performance and reducing economic and other barriers. In countries where government stimulation is lacking, it is often the economic attractiveness of the system or environmental conscience that motivates people to install these systems.

In many cases energy companies, especially utilities, have stimulated the use of solar thermal energy. Motivated by environmental action

TABLE 7.17. WORLD PRACTICAL POTENTIAL ESTIMATION FOR SOLAR CROP DRYING (PETAJOULES A YEAR)

Type of drying	Low	High
< 50 degrees Celsius	220	770
> 50 degrees Celsius	40	110
Sun dried	420	650
Total	680	1,530

Source: ESIF, 1996; Voskens and Carpenter, 1999.

programs, demand-side management programs, or a desire to diversify and serve new markets, these companies have taken over a significant part of the effort to get the solar water systems to the market. They support these projects by active marketing, by financial contributions, or by offering the possibility to rent or lease a system (IEA Caddet, 1998).

Conclusion

- Low-temperature solar thermal technologies can contribute many exajoules to the annual heat demand. Today this contribution is limited to about 50 petajoules a year (excluding heat pumps and passive solar energy use).
- World-wide, about 7 million solar hot water systems, mainly SDHW systems, have been installed. In many regions their dissemination strongly depends on governmental policy, mainly because of the relatively high heat-production costs ($0.03–0.20 a kilowatt hour). They can, however, compete with electric hot water systems.
- The costs of installed solar hot water systems in moderate climate zones may be reduced 25–50 percent by further technology development and/or mass production and installation.
- Active solar systems for space heating with seasonal storage are mainly in a demonstration phase.
- Passive solar energy use has become an attractive option in heating and cooling buildings, because of the development of new materials and powerful simulation tools.
- Electric heat pumps for space heating are especially attractive in countries where electricity is produced by hydropower or wind energy. In other countries a net contribution to the energy supply is achieved only if they have a high performance factor.
- Solar drying of agricultural crops is in many cases a viable technological and economical option. The next step is market introduction.
- Solar cooking provides a significant beneficial impact. Many hundreds of thousands of solar cooking devices have been sold, but they have limitations and can only supplement conventional fuel use.

Hydroelectricity

There is a general view that hydroelectricity is the renewable energy source par excellence, non-exhaustible, non-polluting, and more economically attractive than other options. And although the number of hydropower plants that can be built is finite, only a third of the sites quantified as economically feasible are tapped.

Hydropower plants emit much less greenhouse gas than do thermal plants. Greenhouse gas emissions of hydropower are caused by the decay of vegetation in flooded areas and by the extensive use of cement in the dam construction. Unfortunately, there are local impacts of the use of rivers, social as well as ecological, and they are gaining importance as people become aware of how those impacts affect living standards.

Most renewable sources of energy hydroelectricity generation are capital intensive but have lower operational costs than thermal and nuclear options. The high initial cost is a serious barrier for its growth in developing countries where most of the untapped economic potential is located.

The potential of hydroelectricity

Chapter 5 provides extensive information on the theoretical and technical potential of hydroelectricity. An overview is given in table 7.18, which also presents the economically feasible potential, estimated at 8,100 terawatt-hours a year.

In 1997 total installed hydroelectric capacity was about 660 gigawatts, of which about 23 gigawatts were small scale (plant capacity of less than 10 megawatts). About a fifth of the world electricity supply, hydroelectricity produced 2,600 terawatt-hours (*World Atlas,* 1998), of which about 3.5 percent (about 90 terawatt-hours) was in small hydroelectric plants.

In some regions (North America, Western Europe, Pacific OECD countries) more than 65 percent of the economically feasible potential is already in use. In others (Sub-Saharan Africa, centrally planned Asia, India) less than 18 percent of the potential is in use (see table 7.18). In Latin America and the Caribbean nearly 44 percent of the economically feasible potential is already tapped. Since the OECD operational capacity is at 80 percent of the economic potential, most experts believe this value to be an upper limit for capacity installation.

In 1997 the hydro capacity under installation was 125 gigawatts. Assuming these plants will have the same average capacity factor as the units already in operation (45 percent), this represents another 490 terawatt-hours a year, or 6 percent of the economically feasible potential. This will push the hydroelectricity production in the first years of the 21st century to at least 3,000 terawatt-hours a year. By the middle of this century that could grow to 6,000 terawatt-hours a year (IIASA and WEC, 1998; Johansson and others, 1993a).

In 1997 developing countries had a total installed capacity of 262 gigawatts, soon to grow to about 364 gigawatts (see table 7.18). In 1997 the 70 major developing countries were responsible for 225 gigawatts of installed capacity (*World Atlas,* 1998). In 1989–97 these 70 countries' installed capacity increased by 40 gigawatts, or about 22 percent (2.5 percent a year),[2] much less than the 5.7 percent a year growth forecast by Moore and Smith (1990). The significant slowdown in the construction of hydroelectric plants in developing countries, compared with 1970–90 (Moore and Smith, 1990; Churchill, 1994), can mainly be explained by shortages of capital and difficulties in finding financing abroad.

Hydroelectric technology development

Technologies to reduce dam construction and power generation costs. Hydroelectricity generation is usually regarded as a mature technology, unlikely to advance. That may be so for the efficiency and cost of conventional turbines, where the large number of units constructed has led to an optimised design. But for small-scale hydropower, there is room for further technical development. Examples include the use of variable speed turbines at low heads, induction generators, electronic control and telemetry, submersible turbo-generators, new materials, and the further development of innovative turbines (EUREC Agency, 1996; Schainker, 1997).

On dam construction, there has recently been further progress, especially with roller compacted concrete (RCC) dams. The lower cement content and the mechanised placing of the concrete yield a relatively low unit cost of around $30–40 per cubic metre of dam body, less than half the price of conventional placed concrete. Due to the rapid concrete placement with the RCC technique, dams can grow by 60 centimetres a day, making it possible to build a 200-metre high dam in less than a year (Oud and Muir, 1997). With RCC dams, river diversion during construction is often in-river, rather than by diversion tunnels, saving time and money. The RCC technology has made many dams feasible that previously appeared economically unattractive (Oud and Muir, 1997). For smaller structures, dams with geo-membrane lining (up to 80 metres high) and inflatable rubber weirs (up to 15 metres high) are becoming acceptable alternatives to concrete weirs and low rock-fill or earth-fill dams.

Other parts of the operational system, such as spillways, are now better understood, allowing the use of higher specific discharges per meter width of the spillway chute, saving on cost (Oud and Muir, 1997). Tunnel-boring machines are becoming more attractive. Underground water conduits are attractive because they do not disturb the landscape (Oud and Muir, 1997). Power houses and control rooms are being designed to cut costs and manufacturing time of hydroelectric equipment.

The present installed system cost ranges from $1,000–1,500 a kilowatt for the most favourable sites. In practice cost figures of $3,000 a kilowatt and higher are also found. There are some expectations that technology advances can reduce costs, but in small amounts since the present technology is well optimised. With low investment costs and favourable financing conditions (interest 6 percent a year and 30 years for payment), generation costs for an average capacity factor of 45 percent is $0.04–0.06 a kilowatt hour. At higher capacity factors and with longer payback times, lowest generations costs of about $0.02 a kilowatt hour are found. Because the plant is usually placed far from the point of electricity use, investment can also be required for transmission, perhaps adding another $0.01 per kilowatt-hour.

For small-scale hydropower, the unit cost is expected to be higher than for large-scale hydro. But with the choice of very favourable sites, the use of existing administrative structures and existing civil works for flood-control purposes, avoiding the use of cofferdams during installation, and refurbishing of old sites, electricity production costs may come down from $0.04–0.10 a kilowatt-hour to $0.03–0.10 a kilowatt-hour.

Technologies to reduce social and ecological impacts. Considering the criticism of hydropower production, especially when large dams are built, modern construction tries to include in the system design several technologies that minimise the social and ecological impacts. Some of the most important impacts are changes in fish amount and fish biodiversity, sedimentation, biodiversity perturbation, water quality standards, human health deterioration, and downstream impacts (see also chapter 3).

■ *Changes in fish amount and fish biodiversity.* Technologies are being pursued to preserve subsistence and commercial fish production as well as fish biodiversity. Further R & D is being recommended to achieve a quantitative understanding of the responses of fish to multiple stresses inside a turbine and to develop biological performance criteria for use in advanced turbine design (National Laboratory, 1997). Inclusion of passage facilities, such as fish ladders (Goodland, 1997), are becoming a necessity for renewing dam operational contracts in the United States. In tropical countries, where such technology is not useful, electric luring of fish into containers or elevators, as carried out in Yacyreta (between Argentina and Paraguay), may be a solution (Goodland, 1997). Because most new dams will be built in tropical countries, it is necessary to carry out extensive studies to identify new or rare species and determine if they can live in adjacent rivers not slated for damming (Goodland, 1997).

■ *Sedimentation.* Sedimentation increases strongly when catchments are developed. Another possibility is the sporadic filling of the reservoir with large amount of land due to land slide or due to some exceptional flood (Goodland, 1997). Such problems can be minimised through watershed management, debris dams, sediment bypassing, sediment flushing, sediment sluicing, sediment dredging, and using reservoir density currents.

■ *Biodiversity perturbation.* Conservation of biodiversity demands, at the least, no net loss of species. This requires complete knowledge of what is present before the dam is built, which is difficult. The main conservation measures have become site selection and selection of reservoir size. In practice, the conservation of onsite biodiversity depends on not flooding large areas, particularly intact habitats such as tropical forests, and on conserving an offset in perpetuity (Goodland, 1997).

■ *Water quality.* Initially water quality is mainly disturbed by the large amount of biomass left in the flooded area and by filling the reservoir. This can be mitigated by removing biomass and by filling the reservoir at a moderate rate. After filling, thermal stratification frequently occurs in reservoirs with a long water residence time (full seasons cycle) and water depths of more than 10 metres. Reservoir stratification can release water of colder or warmer temperatures than the river would experience without a dam, with positive or negative impacts on the river fishery. It can be minimised through (1) changes in inlet structure configuration, (2) in-reservoir de-stratification, (3) multilevel outlet works for mitigation of downstream effects, and (4) positive mixing and aeration by fountain jets or compressed air. But sufficient knowledge is not yet available, and further R&D is recommended (National Laboratory, 1997).

■ *Human health deterioration.* Reservoirs can cause epidemics of three water-related diseases: malaria, schistosomiasis, and Japanese B encephalitis. The proliferation of malaria and encephalitis

Only a third of the sites quantified as economically feasible for hydro-electricity production are tapped.

can be avoided with chemicals and chemotherapy. But resistance of mosquitoes and *Plasmodium* protozoan parasite makes malaria increasingly expensive to control. Schistosomiasis is better controlled by chemotherapy.

■ *Downstream impacts.* Downstream social impacts can exceed upstream resettlement upheavals, and they deserve more attention than is common nowadays. Cessation of annual fertile silt and moisture deposition leads to declining yields, grazing impairment, fish and wildlife decline, and erosion at the mouth of the river, due to the reduction in suspended particles that replace the land normally washed out by the ocean. In addition, the decline in water availability and agricultural yields increases the competition for water and other scarce resources. Furthermore, the construction of a dam forces people who are long adapted to cyclical floods to switch suddenly to rainfed livelihoods (Goodland, 1997). Some of these issues can be mitigated through off-takes at various levels to allow for flexibility of the water temperature in accord with downstream needs, and others through measures that reduce reservoir stratification, including local mixing and shorter water residence time.

System aspects

To even out annual seasonal flow, dams are erected and land areas flooded. Since the flows vary from year to year, every attempt to increase the reliability of the water supply increases the flooded area, and that increase is exponential for reliability above 70 percent (Moreira and Poole, 1993). Another alternative to increase system reliability and reduce cost is hydropower complementation, based on the notion that different river basins can be wire connected, letting a higher flow in one basin compensate for low flow in the other. Hydrologic diversity usually involves large geographic distance, but on either side of the equator distances are modest (Moreira and Poole, 1993).

A third alternative is to use hydroelectricity to store intermittent renewable energy. Storage energy, to ensure reliable, high quality service, will provide for increased renewable use and system stabilisation with distributed generation. Areas of importance include pumped hydro (Schainker, 1997). Further research is recommended to examine the benefits and costs of coupling hydropower to renewable energy storage needs (PCAST, 1997).

TABLE 7.18. HYDROELECTRIC THEORETICAL, TECHNICALLY FEASIBLE, AND ECONOMICALLY FEASIBLE POTENTIAL AS WELL AS INSTALLED AND UNDER INSTALLATION CAPACITY IN 1997, BY REGION (TERAWATT-HOURS A YEAR UNLESS OTHERWISE NOTED)

Region	Gross theoretical potential	Technically feasible potential	Econo-mically feasible potential	Installed hydro capacity (gigawatts)	Installed hydro capacity in developing countries (gigawatts)	Production from hydro plants	Hydro capacity under construction (gigawatts)	Hydro capacity under construction in developing countries (gigawatts)
North America	5,817	1,509	912	141.2	0	697	0.9	0
Latin America and Caribbean	7,533	2,868	1,199	114.1	114.1	519	18.3	18.3
Western Europe	3,294	1,822	809	16.3	16.3	48	2.5	2.5
Central and Eastern Europe	195	216	128	9.1	9.1	27	7.7	7.7
Former Soviet Union	3,258	1,235	770	146.6	16.5	498	6.7	3.9
Middle East and North Africa	304	171	128	21.3	0	66	1.2	0.03
Sub-Saharan Africa	3,583	1,992	1,288	65.7	0	225	16.6	0
Centrally planned Asia	6,511	2,159	1,302	64.3	64.3	226	51.7	51.7
South Asia[a]	3,635	948	103	28.5	28.5	105	13.0	13.0
Pacific Asia[a]	5,520	814	142	13.5	13.5	41	4.7	4.7
Pacific OECD	1,134	211	184	34.2	0	129	0.8	0
World total	**40,784**	**13,945**	**6,965**	**654.8**	**262.3**	**2,581**	**124.1**	**101.8**
World total[b]	**~40,500**	**~14,320**	**~8,100**	**~660**		**~2,600**	**~126**	

a. Several South Asian and other Pacific Asian countries do not release their economically feasible potential. As a result economically feasible potential for these regions are too low, and in one case for South Asia are even lower than the electricity generated. b. These are the values quoted in the source. They differ from the world total in the previous row mainly due the inclusion of estimates for countries for which data are not available.   *Source: World Atlas, 1998.*

Environmental and social impacts

The average energy density of hydro-electricity generation shows thatt significant amounts of land have been flooded for this purpose (see chapter 5). If new plants will keep the average energy density (optimistic, since the best sites have already been used), some extra 50 million hectares of land will be flooded to make available two-thirds of the economic potential. This figure may not look so high relative to the land required for biomass energy production, but river surroundings are the most densely inhabited areas in rural regions. Several other environmental impacts in the flooded area can be minimised by convenient choosing of sites where it is possible to store large water volumes in a small area, such as canyons.

With a responsibility to preserve the environment, the overall cost of producing hydropower is increasing. As the hydropower industry moves towards an open market, it is a challenge to figure out how it will survive marginal cost pricing. Some operators with high costs could also find themselves in a restructured environment with old and insufficient generating plant. In the United States several dams associated with power production are being decommissioned, mainly because they disturb commercial fishing or impose a significant onus for biodiversity (Koch, 1996).

A well-understood impact is caused by displacing inhabitants from the flooded area, and mitigating it can represent a significant cost for the project. Some estimates put the displacement cost per person at about six times the annual per capita gross national product (Besant-Jones, 1995)—and others as high as $25,000 per family. Displacing 100,000 inhabitants can add $2 billion to the project cost, enough to make it unfeasible. Strong criticism is always to be expected for hydro projects requiring the relocation of a great number of people. Of utmost importance here is building trust between the people affected by resettlement, the developer, and the authorities; people must know and feel that they matter and that they are taken seriously.

Economic and financial aspects

Hydropower plants are more capital intensive than thermal plants. Historically, hydroelectricity in the developing world has been financed predominantly from public or guaranteed funding. The World Bank has financed about 110 hydroelectric power projects in 50 developing countries, ranging from 6.6 megawatts to 2,240 megawatts, with a combined generating capacity of about 35 gigawatts.

Reliable global data on trends in hydro financing are not available. But World Bank data show a market decline in its lending for hydro—from 3.4 percent to 2.5 percent of the approximately $20 billion it lends annually. There is no doubt that environmental pressures on the Bank (and other multilateral agencies) account for some of this decline (Briscoe, 1998).

In the past few years with the emerging privatisation of the electric sector in developing countries, private capital flows have increased dramatically (Briscoe, 1998). Private activity in infrastructure, previously concentrated in East Asia and Latin America, is now expanding in Eastern Europe and Central Asia, South Asia, and Sub-Saharan Africa. Private infrastructure investment can grow much more, since it accounted for only about 15 percent of all infrastructure investment in developing countries in 1996. Even so, the private sector sees substantial risks, some inherent in the degree to which each hydro project (unlike thermal projects) has to be tailored to specific hydrological, geographic, and geological conditions.

In addition, hydropower project costs have tended to exceed estimates substantially. A World Bank review of 80 hydro projects completed in the 1970s and 1980s indicate that three-fourths had final costs in excess of budget. Costs were at least 25 percent higher for half the projects and 50 percent or more for 30 percent of the projects. Costs were less than estimated on 25 percent of projects (Bacon and others, 1996). Major reasons for such cost increases were unexpected geologic conditions, funding delays, and resettlement problems (Churchill, 1997).

It is essential that the hydro industry comes to grips with the poor record of cost estimation and project implementation. This record has caused the financial community to regard hydro project as riskier than in the past, raising the cost of capital and pricing many hydro projects out of the market. Inadequate resource exploration and site investigation is one reason for the cost and schedule overruns. Governments can solve this by initiating careful resource and site investigations at an early stage using public money. They can recover these costs from the project developer as part of an authorisation or tendering procedure.

It is much easier to involve the private sector in smaller projects, of 40–400 megawatts, where hydropower plants are accepted as environmentally benign if they are run-of-the river, incorporate high head, and are on tributaries to the big rivers (Briscoe, 1998). For larger projects there has been, and will be, little private sector financing unless there is substantial involvement of governments and bilateral and multilateral agencies (Briscoe, 1998).

Conclusion

- Hydropower contributes about 20 percent to the electricity supply, about a third of its potential. The supply of hydroelectricity may grow from 2,600 terawatt-hours a year in 1997 (of which about 3.5 percent from small-scale hydropower) to 3,000 terawatt-hours in the first years of the 21st century and to 6,000 terawatt-hours a year in 2050.
- Hydropower is a clean energy source with many technical advantages over thermal and nuclear plants: operating reserves, spinning reserves, load following services, voltage control, and cold start capability. Some of these characteristics help in aggregating intermittent sources of electricity to the existing system.
- The electricity production cost of large hydroelectricity plants is $0.02–0.08 a kilowatt-hour, with new reductions from technology development offset by the need to mitigate social and environmental

Modern construction of dams tries to include technologies that minimize the social and ecological impacts.

effects. For small hydroelectricity plants, the electricity production cost may come down from $0.03–0.10 a kilowatt-hour to $0.04–0.10 a kilowatts-hour in the long term.

- Improvements and efficiency measures are needed in dam structures, turbines, generators, substations, transmission lines, and environmental mitigation technology to sustain hydropower's role as a clean, renewable energy source. Of utmost importance is building trust between the people affected by resettlement, the developer and the authorities—to address the criticisms regarding social and environmental impacts.
- The emerging liberalisation and privatisation in the electric sector in most industrialised countries may reduce investments in new hydropower plants since they are more capital intensive and riskier than thermal plants.

Geothermal energy

Geothermal energy has been used for bathing and washing for thousands of years, but it is only in the 20th century that it has been harnessed on a large scale for space heating, industrial energy use, and electricity production. Prince Piero Ginori Conti initiated electric power generation with geothermal steam at Larderello in Italy in 1904. The first large municipal district heating service started in Iceland in the 1930s.

Geothermal energy has been used commercially for some 70 years, and on the scale of hundreds of megawatts, 40 years, both for electricity generation and direct use. Its use has increased rapidly in the past three decades—at about 9 percent a year in 1975–95 for electricity and at about 6 percent a year for direct use. Geothermal resources have been identified in more than 80 countries, with quantified records of geothermal use in 46.

The potential of geothermal energy

Exploitable geothermal systems occur in several geological environments. High-temperature fields used for conventional power production (with temperatures above 150° C) are largely confined to areas with young volcanism, seismic, and magmatic activity. But low-temperature resources suitable for direct use can be found in most countries. The ground source heat pump has opened a new dimension in using the Earth's heat, as these pumps can be used basically everywhere.

Geothermal use is commonly divided into two categories—electricity production and direct application. In 1997 world-wide use of geothermal energy amounted to about 44 terawatt-hours a year of electricity and 38 terawatt-hours a year for direct use (table 7.19). A new estimate of world geothermal potential shows the useful accessible resource base for electricity production to be some 12,000 terawatt-hours a year (Björnsson and others, 1998). Since only a small fraction of the geothermal potential has been developed, there is ample space for accelerated use of geothermal energy for electricity generation in the near future.

The scope for direct use of geothermal energy is even more plentiful, as the useful accessible resource base is estimated to be 600,000 exajoules, which corresponds to the present direct use of geothermal energy for some 5 million years (Björnsson and others, 1998). With both ample resources and a relatively mature technology at hand, the question of future development of geothermal energy use boils down to economic and political competitiveness with other energy sources on the markets in different countries.

Recent developments

Electricity production. The growth of the total generation capacity in 1990–98 was about 40 percent (table 7.20), with the largest additions in the Philippines (957 megawatts), Indonesia (445 megawatts), Japan (315 megawatts), Italy (224 megawatts), Costa Rica (120 megawatts), Iceland (95 megawatts), the United States (75 megawatts), New Zealand (62 megawatts), and Mexico (43 megawatts). The most

TABLE 7.19. ELECTRICITY GENERATION AND DIRECT USE OF GEOTHERMAL ENERGY, 1997

Region	Electricity generation			Direct use		
	Installed capacity (giga-watts-electric)	Total production		Installed capacity (giga-watts-thermal)	Total production	
		Terawatt-hours (electric)	Percent		Terawatt-hours (thermal)	Percent
European Union	0.75	3.8		1.03	3.7	
Europe, other	0.11	0.5		4.09	16.1	
Total Europe	0.86	4.3	10	5.12	19.8	52
North America	2.85	16.2		1.91	4.0	
Latin America	0.96	6.9				
Total Americas	3.81	23.1	53	1.91	4.0	10
Asia	2.94	13.0	30	3.08	12.2	32
Oceania	0.36	2.9	6	0.26	1.8	5
Africa	0.05	0.4	1	0.07	0.4	1
World total	8.02	43.8	100	10.44	38.2	100

Source: Based on Stefansson and Fridleifsson, 1998.

TABLE 7.20. INSTALLED GEOTHERMAL ELECTRICITY GENERATION CAPACITY (MEGAWATTS OF ELECTRICITY)

Country	1990	1995	1998
Argentina	0.7	0.7	0
Australia	0	0.2	0.4
China	19	29	32
Costa Rica	0	55	120
El Salvador	95	105	105
France (Guadeloupe)	4	4	4
Guatemala	0	0	5
Iceland	45	50	140
Indonesia	145	310	590
Italy	545	632	769
Japan	215	414	530
Kenya	45	45	45
Mexico	700	753	743
New Zealand	283	286	345
Nicaragua	70	70	70
Philippines	891	1,191	1,848
Portugal (Azores)	3	5	11
Russia	11	11	11
Thailand	0.3	0.3	0.3
Turkey	20	20	20
United States	2,775	2,817	2,850
Total	**5,867**	**6,798**	**8,239**

Source: Based on IGA, 1999.

progressive of these countries, the Philippines, with 22 percent of its electricity generated with geothermal steam, plans to add 580 megawatts to its installed capacity in 1999–2008 (Benito, 1998). Other countries generating 10–20 percent of their electricity with geothermal are Costa Rica, El Salvador, Kenya, and Nicaragua.

The participation of private operators in steam field developments through BOT (build, operate, and transfer) and BOO (build, own, and operate) contracts and through JOC (joint operation contracts) have significantly increased the speed of geothermal development in the Philippines (Vasquez and Javellana, 1997) and Indonesia (Radja, 1997; Aryawijaya, 1997). And several developing countries are considering the participation of private operators.

The electricity generation cost is variable—commonly around $0.04 a kilowatt-hour for modern, cost-effective plants, but ranging from $0.02–0.10 a kilowatt-hour. The installed system costs may range from $800–3,000 a kilowatt-hour. With cost reductions and under favourable conditions the cost can come down to $0.01–0.02 a kilowatt-hour.

Direct use of geothermal energy. Direct application of geothermal energy can involve a wide variety of end uses, such as space heating and cooling, industry, greenhouses, fish farming, and health spas. It uses mostly existing technology and straightforward engineering. The technology, reliability, economics, and environmental acceptability of direct use of geothermal energy have been demonstrated throughout the world.

Compared with electricity production from geothermal energy, direct use has several advantages, such as much higher energy efficiency (50–70 percent compared with 5–20 percent for conventional geothermal electric plants). Generally the development time is much shorter, and normally much less capital investment is involved. And possible for high- and low-temperature geothermal resources, direct use is much more widely available in the world. But it is more site specific for the market, with steam and hot water rarely transported long distances from the geothermal site. The longest geothermal hot water pipeline in the world, in Iceland, is 63 kilometres.

The production costs for direct use are highly variable, but commonly under $0.02 a kilowatt-hour. The production costs might range from $0.005–0.05 a kilowatt-hour (thermal energy), and the turnkey investments costs from $200–2,000 a kilowatt.

The two countries with the highest energy production (Japan and Iceland) are not the same as the two with the highest installed capacities (China and the United States), because of the variety in the load factors for the different types of use (table 7.21).

Lund (1996) has recently written a comprehensive summary on the various types of direct use of geothermal energy. Space heating is the dominant application (33 percent). Other common applications are bathing/swimming/balneology (19 percent), greenhouses (14 percent), heat pumps for air conditioning and heating (12 percent), fish farming (11 percent), and industry (10 percent).

Heat pump applications. Geothermal energy previously had considerable economic potential only in areas where thermal water or steam is found concentrated at depths less than 3 kilometres, analogous to oil in commercial oil reservoirs. This has changed recently with developments in the application of ground source heat pumps—using the Earth as a heat source for heating or as a heat sink for cooling, depending on the season. These pumps can be used basically everywhere.

Switzerland, not known for hot springs and geysers, shows the impact geothermal heat pumps can have—generating about 230 gigawatt-hours a year in 1994 (Rybach and Goran, 1995). In the United States, at the end of 1997, more than 300,000 geothermal heat pumps were operating nation-wide in homes, schools, and commercial buildings for space heating and cooling (air conditioning), providing 8–11 terawatt-hours a year of end-use energy according to different estimates.

Geothermal heat pumps are rated among the most energy-efficient space conditioning equipment available in the United States. Reducing the need for new generating capacity, they perform at greater efficiencies than conventional air source heat pumps used for air conditioning. Several electric utilities have introduced financial incentive schemes by encouraging house owners to use groundwater heat pumps for space cooling and heating purposes and thus reducing the peak loads on their electric systems. The Geothermal Heat Pump Consortium has established a $100 million 6-year program to increase the geothermal heat pump unit sales from 40,000 to 400,000 annually, which will reduce greenhouse gas emissions by 1.5 million metric tonnes of carbon equivalent annually (Pratsch, 1996). A third of the funding comes from the U.S. Department of Energy and the Environmental Protection Agency, two-thirds from the electric power industry. Financial incentive schemes have also been set up in Germany and Switzerland.

Potential market developments

Some 80 countries are interested in geothermal energy development, of which almost 50 now have quantifiable geothermal use. A worldwide survey (Fridleifsson and Freeston, 1994) showed that the total investments in geothermal energy in 1973–92 were about $22 billion. In 1973–82 public funding amounted to $4.6 billion, private funding to $3 billion. In 1983–92 public funding amounted to $6.6 billion, private funding to $7.7 billion. Of special interest, private investment in geothermal rose by 160 percent from the first decade to the second, while public investments rose by 43 percent, showing the confidence of private enterprises in this energy source and demonstrating its commercial viability.

Extrapolations of past trends show the long-term prognosis for potential development. In 1975–95 the growth of the installed capacity for electricity generation world-wide was about 9 percent a year. If this rate continues for another 25 years, the installed capacity would be 25 gigawatts of electricity in 2010 and 58 gigawatts of electricity in 2020 (table 7.22). The annual electricity generation shown in table 7.22 is based on the assumption that the use factor will be similar to that in 1997 (Stefansson and Fridleifsson, 1998). In 1990–98 the annual growth was close to 4 percent a year, not 9 percent. So, new incentives are needed to realise this scenario.

The average growth in the direct use of geothermal energy can be estimated at about 6 percent a year in the past decade. With annual growth rate of 6 percent in the near future, the installed capacity would be around 22 gigawatts of thermal energy in 2010 and 40 gigawatts of thermal energy in 2020 (see table 7.22). This is not taking into account the rapid development of ground-based heat pumps in recent years. In a matter of some years, this sector has grown from infancy to 1,400 megawatts of thermal energy in the United States alone. Development is also fast in Switzerland, Germany, and Sweden. The forecast for direct use therefore might be somewhat pessimistic.

The U.S. Department of Energy's Office of Geothermal Technologies recently identified five strategic goals for geothermal energy as a

TABLE 7.21. GEOTHERMAL ENERGY PRODUCTION WITH DIRECT USE IN COUNTRIES WITH MORE THAN 40 MEGAWATTS-THERMAL INSTALLED CAPACITY

Country	Installed capacity (gigawatts-thermal)	Heat production (terawatt-hours a year)
Japan	1.16	7.50
Iceland	1.44	5.88
China	1.91	4.72
United States	1.91	3.97
Hungary	0.75	3.29
Turkey	0.64	2.50
New Zealand	0.26	1.84
France	0.31	1.36
Italy	0.31	1.03
Germany	0.31	0.81
Georgia	0.25	n.a
Serbia	0.09	0.67
Russia	0.21	0.67
Romania	0.14	0.53
Switzerland	0.19	0.42
Slovak Rep.	0.08	0.38
Sweden	0.05	0.35
Tunisia	0.07	0.35
Bulgaria	0.10	0.35
Israel	0.04	0.33
Macedonia FYR	0.08	0.15
Poland	0.04	0.14

Source: Based on Stefansson and Fridleifsson, 1998.

TABLE 7.22. POTENTIAL DEVELOPMENT OF THE INSTALLED CAPACITY AND ENERGY PRODUCTION FROM GEOTHERMAL SOURCES IN THE FORM OF ELECTRICITY AND DIRECT USE OF HEAT, 1997–2020

Year	Gigawatts-electric	Terawatt-hours (electric)	Gigawatts-electric	Terawatt-hours (thermal)
1997	8.0	43.8	10.4	38.20
2010	24	134	22	81
2020	58	318	40	146

preferred alternative to polluting energy sources (USDOE OGT, 1998), including:

- Supply the electric power needs of 7 million U.S. homes (18 million people) from geothermal energy by 2010.
- Expand direct uses of geothermal resources and application of geothermal heat pumps to provide the heating, cooling, and hot water needs of 7 million homes by 2010.
- Meet the basic energy needs of 100 million people in developing countries by using U.S. geothermal technology to install at least 10 gigawatts by 2010.

Environmental aspects

Geothermal fluids contain a variable quantity of gas—largely nitrogen and carbon dioxide with some hydrogen sulphide and smaller proportions of ammonia, mercury, radon, and boron. The amounts depend on the geological conditions of different fields. Most of the chemicals are concentrated in the disposal water, routinely re-injected into drill holes, and thus not released into the environment. The concentrations of the gases are usually not harmful, and the removal of such gases as hydrogen sulphide from geothermal steam is a routine matter in geothermal power stations where the gas content is high. The range in carbon dioxide emissions from high-temperature geothermal fields used for electricity production in the world is 13–380 grams a kilowatt-hour, less than for fossil fuel power stations. Sulphur emissions are also significantly less for geothermal than fossil fuel electric power stations.

The gas emissions from low-temperature geothermal resources are normally only a fraction of the emissions from the high-temperature fields used for electricity production. The gas content of low-temperature water is in many cases minute—in Reykjavik, Iceland, the carbon dioxide content is lower than that of the cold groundwater. In sedimentary basins, such as the Paris basin, the gas content may be too high to be released. In such cases the geothermal fluid is kept at pressure within a closed circuit (the geothermal doublet) and re-injected into the reservoir without any degassing. Conventional geothermal schemes in sedimentary basins commonly produce brines that are generally re-injected into the reservoir and thus never released into the environment. The carbon dioxide emission from these is thus zero.

Conclusion

- Geothermal energy has been used commercially for 70 years, both for electricity generation and direct use, with use increasing rapidly in the past three decades. In 1975–95 the growth rate for electricity generation was about 9 percent a year and in recent years about 4 percent a year. For direct use it was about 6 percent a year.
- For the 46 countries with records of geothermal use the electricity generated was 44 terawatt-hours of electricity and the direct use 38 terawatt-hours of thermal energy in 1997, and 45 terawatt-hours of electricity and 40 terawatt-hours of thermal energy in 1998.
- Assuming world-wide annual growth to average 9 percent a year through 2020, the electricity production may reach about 130 terawatt-hours in 2010 and about 310 terawatt-hours in 2020. Assuming the annual growth rate for direct use to continue at 6 percent, the energy production may reach about 80 terawatt-hours in 2010 and about 140 terawatt-hours in 2020.
- Recent developments in the application of the ground source heat pump opens a new dimension in the scope for using the Earth's heat. Heat pumps can be used basically everywhere and are not site-specific, as conventional geothermal resources are.
- Geothermal energy, with its proven technology and abundant resources, can make a significant contribution towards reducing the emission of greenhouse gases. But it requires that governments implement policies and measures to improve the competitiveness of geothermal energy systems with conventional energy systems.

Marine energy technologies

The oceans, covering more than two-thirds of the Earth, represent an enormous energy resource containing vastly more energy than the human race could possibly use. The energy of the seas is stored partly as kinetic energy from the motion of waves and currents and partly as thermal energy from the sun. (Chapter 5 summarises the nature and scale of the ocean energy resource.)

Although most marine energy is too diffuse and too far from where it is needed to be economically exploited, in special situations it can be effectively captured for practical use. Tidal energy needs the more extreme tidal ranges or currents. Wave energy needs to be exploited in places with a higher-than-average wave climate. Ocean thermal energy conversion needs as large a temperature difference as possible between the surface waters and the water near the seabed. Such requirements tend to limit the use of the resource to certain areas of coastline offering the coincidence of a suitably intense resource and a potential market for the energy. This makes many published estimates of enormous global marine energy resources academic.

The potential and technology of marine energy

The main marine energy resources can be summarised, in order of maturity and use, as:

- Tidal barrage energy.
- Wave energy.
- Tidal/marine currents.
- Ocean thermal energy conversion (OTEC).
- Salinity gradient/osmotic energy.
- Marine biomass fuels.

Exploiting salinity gradients and the cultivation of marine biomass are not discussed because their exploitation seems a long way from any practical application, though new research might clarify their potential.

> Not until the 20th century has geothermal energy been harnessed on a large scale for space heating, industrial energy use, and electricity production.

Tidal barrage energy. The rise and fall of the tides creates, in effect, a low-head hydropower system. Tidal energy has been exploited in this way on a small scale for centuries in the form of water mills. The one large modern version is the 240 megawatt-electric La Rance scheme, built in France in the 1960s, the world's largest tidal barrage, using a conventional bulb turbine. A handful of smaller schemes have also been built.

Numerous studies have been completed for potentially promising locations with unusually high tidal ranges, such as the Bay of Fundy in Canada and the 7-gigawatt scheme for the Severn Estuary in the United Kingdom. But most schemes of this kind have proved to be extremely large and costly. The proposed Severn Barrage scheme—which the U.K. government decided not to pursue—would have involved the use of 216 turbo-generators, each nine metres in diameter and 40 megawatts in capacity. The load factor would have been around 23 percent, the cost an estimated $12 billion (Boyle, 1996).

The combination of high costs, major environmental impact, and poor load factors makes this technology generally unattractive, but there may be occasional niche applications for it in the future in especially favourable locations.

Wave energy. Energy can be extracted from waves. As an example, in deep water off the northwest coast of Scotland (one of the more intense wave climates in the world) the average energy along the prevailing wave front can be 70 kilowatts a metre (or more). Closer inshore this falls to an average of around 20 or 30 kilowatts a metre, and along the shoreline to about 10 kilowatts a metre or less. The energy availability is thus sensitive to the distance from the shoreline (ETSU/DTI, 1999).

Wave energy remains at an experimental stage, with only a few prototype systems actually working. All of the few existing systems that have run for more than a few hours are shoreline devices (built into the shore). Total grid-connected wave power is less than 1 megawatt, consisting of several small oscillating water column devices in China, India, and the United Kingdom (YY, 1998). A new generation of larger devices is under development, due to be installed notably in the Azores (Pico) and Japan, as well as in the countries mentioned earlier. The world's wave energy capacity will increase to a few megawatts in the next few years.

If wave energy is to become an important contributor to future energy needs, it will need to move further offshore into deeper water where there are larger and much more energetic waves. This will require a quantum leap in the size and nature of the systems used. Systems capable of surviving under such difficult conditions have not yet been demonstrated, so it is likely to take a decade or more before wave energy can even start to make a contribution to world energy needs (Fraenkel, 1999). Eventually, however, it seems likely to contribute as much as 100 terawatt-hours a year for Europe, and perhaps three times that for the world.

The general immaturity of wave energy technology is illustrated by the variety of solutions proposed for exploiting it. No real consensus has yet emerged as to the 'best' way to convert energy from waves into electricity. Wave energy conversion systems can be classified as:

- Shoreline devices (mounted on the shore).
- Near-shoreline devices (usually installed on the seabed in water less than 20 metres deep).
- Offshore or deep-water devices (usually floating devices moored in deep water with highly energetic wave conditions).

The most popular shoreline device is the oscillating water column (OWC), a large chamber that has a free opening to the sea, encloses an air volume, and is compressed by the wave pressure. A duct between the chamber and the outside atmosphere allows air to be drawn in and out of the chamber as a result of the variation of pressure caused by incoming waves. An air-turbine system, installed in the duct, generates electricity from this reversing air flow.

Most near-shore wave energy converters are designed to be deployed in lines parallel to the shoreline to intercept the wave energy. Another concept is the point absorber, which can occupy a small space yet capture the energy from a larger area surrounding it using resonance effects. Studies show that such arrays can be highly efficient (Randlov and others, 1994). In the longer term other large floating devices, such as the Salter Duck, which relies on modules that rock in response to wave action, will convert the higher power levels available farther offshore.

Tidal and marine current energy. Tidal and marine current energy is the most recent of the marine energy resources to be seriously studied, with most work in the 1990s. The results show that large-scale energy generation from currents requires a totally submerged turbine—and, to be reliable, offshore large, robust systems are required that are only now becoming technically feasible.

In most places the movements of seawater are too slow—and the energy availability is too diffuse—to permit practical energy exploitation. But there are locations where the water velocity is speeded up by a reduction in cross-section of the flow area, such as straits between islands and the mainland, around the ends of headlands, and in estuaries and other such topographical features. As with wind energy, a cube law relates instantaneous power to fluid velocity. So a marine current of 2.5 metres a second (5 knots), not an unusual occurrence at such locations, represents a power flux of about 8 kilowatts a square metre. The minimum velocity for practical purposes is around 1 metre a second (2 knots), about 0.5 kilowatts a square metre. The main siting requirement is thus a location having flows exceeding about 1.5 metres a second for a reasonable period (Fraenkel, 1999; IT Power, 1996).

Data on marine currents are sparse. A major study by the European Commission evaluating the tidal current resource for 106 locations around Europe estimated an exploitable resource from just those sites of 48 terawatt-hours a year (IT Power, 1996). The U.K. government recently came up with an estimate of about 320 megawatts of installed capacity for the United Kingdom by 2010 (ETSU/DTI, 1999). There is potential at known United Kingdom locations to install several gigawatts of tidal turbines. The worldwide potential is obviously much larger.

All that has been done so far is the short-term demonstration of small experimental model systems in the sea, the largest so far being

TABLE 7.23. CURRENT STATUS OF MARINE RENEWABLE ENERGY TECHNOLOGIES

Technology	Maturity	Load factor (percent)	Installed capital cost (dollars per kilowatt)	Unit cost of electricity (dollars per kilowatt-hour)
Tidal barrage	Virtually abandoned	20–30	1,700–2,500	0.08–0.15
Wave–shoreline OWC	Experimental	20–30	2,000–3,000	0.10–0.20
Wave–near shoreline OWC	Commercial 2002–05	25–35	1,500–2,500	0.08–0.15
Wave–offshore – point absorber	Commercial 2010 or later	30–60	2,500–3,000	0.06–0.15
Tidal current turbine	Commercial 2005–10	25–35	2,000–3,000	0.08–0.15
OTEC	Commercial 2005–10	70–80	Unclear	Unclear

only 15 kilowatts, at Loch Linnhe in Scotland in 1994. A Japanese university successfully ran a 3-kilowatt turbine on the seabed off the Japanese coast for some 9 months, and a floating system of about 5 kilowatts was demonstrated in Australian waters. Work is under way to develop and install the first grid-connected tidal current turbine, rated at 300 kilowatts, during 2000.

The various turbine rotor options generally coincide with those used for wind turbines. The two main types are the horizontal axis, axial-flow turbine (with a propeller type of rotor) and the cross-flow or Darrieus turbine, in which blades rotate about an axis perpendicular to the flow. The more promising rotor configuration seems to be the conventional axial flow rotor.

The maximum flow velocity tends to be near the sea's surface, so marine current turbine rotors ideally need to intercept as much of the depth of flow as possible, but especially the near-surface flow. Options for securing a rotor include mounting it beneath a floating pontoon or buoy, suspending it from a tension leg arrangement between an anchor on the seabed and a flotation unit on the surface, and seabed mounting (feasible in shallow water, but more difficult in deeper water). Floating devices have the problem of providing secure anchors and moorings. Seabed-mounted devices seem more straightforward to engineer. One option is a mono-pile set into a socket drilled into the seabed, which seems the most cost-effective solution, just as it is for offshore wind turbines.

Ocean thermal energy conversion. Exploiting natural temperature differences in the sea by using some form of heat engine, potentially the largest source of renewable energy of all, has been considered and discussed for the best part of 100 years (Boyle, 1996). But the laws of thermodynamics demand as large a temperature difference as possible to deliver a technically feasible and reasonably economic system. OTEC requires a temperature difference of about 20 degrees Celsius, and this limits the application of this technology to a few tropical regions with very deep water. Two main processes are used for power production from this source, both based on the Rankine (steam/vapour) cycle:

- The open cycle system flash evaporates warm seawater into vapour (at reduced pressure) and then draws it through a turbine by condensing it in a condenser cooled by cold seawater.
- The closed cycle system uses warm seawater to boil a low-temperature fluid, such as ammonia, which is then drawn through a turbine by being condensed in a heat exchanger with cold seawater and then recycled back to the boiler by a feed pump.

Offshore OTEC is technically difficult because of the need to pipe large volumes of water from the seabed to a floating system, the huge areas of heat exchanger needed, and the difficulty of transmitting power from a device floating in deep water to the shore (SERI, 1989). A few experimental OTEC plants have been tested, notably in Hawaii, but do not seem to offer economic viability. Consequently, OTEC is not likely to make a major contribution to the energy supply in the short to medium term. Shoreline OTEC, however, could be more readily developed and applied economically than devices floating in deep waters.

The latest thinking is that OTEC needs to be applied as a multi-purpose technology: for example, the nutrient-rich cold water drawn from the deep ocean has been found to be valuable for fish-farming. In addition, the cold water can be used directly for cooling applications in the tropics such as air conditioning (NREL, 1999). If OTEC takes off, it is likely to be with energy as a by-product.

Economic aspects

Because of limited experience with the marine renewables, it is difficult to be certain how economic they will be if developed to a mature stage. There is experience (albeit limited) with tidal barrages, but their failure to take off speaks for itself. A rough indication of the relative unit costs of some offshore technologies is given in table 7.23 (Fraenkel, 1999). Several of these options are already competitive in the context of niche markets, such as island communities using conventional small-scale diesel generation, which typically can cost from $0.10 to as much as $0.50 a kilowatt-hour.

Environmental aspects

Offshore environmental impacts for marine energy technologies tend to be minimal. Few produce pollution while in operation. One exception is tidal barrages, where the creation of a large human-made seawater lake behind the barrage has the potential to affect fish and bird breeding and feeding, siltation, and so on. Another exception is OTEC, which may cause the release of carbon dioxide from seawater to the atmosphere.

The main issues, however, tend to be conflicts with other users of the seas—for fishing, marine traffic, and leisure activities. Of these, fishing is perhaps the main potential area of conflict. None of the technologies discussed seems likely to cause measurable harm to fish or marine mammals. But some—such as marine current turbines and wave power devices—may need small fishery exclusion zones to avoid entanglement with nets.

Implementation issues

Numerous legal hurdles await developers of offshore technologies in gaining licenses and permissions from the many marine agencies charged by governments with overseeing the environment, navigation, fisheries, and so on. Most of the marine renewable energy technologies are immature and not well developed, facing difficult engineering problems and higher-than-usual financial risks due to the high overheads of running experimental systems at sea. If these technologies are to develop at a reasonable speed to make a significant contribution to clean energy generation, they will need much greater support for RD&D. In the end the power to make marine renewable energy technologies succeed (or fail) lies largely with governments.

Conclusion

- Energy is in the seas in prodigious quantities. The question is whether it can be tapped, converted to a useful form, and delivered cost-effectively in comparison with other methods of energy generation. Several technologies show reasonable prospects for doing so.
- Tidal barrages have been tried in a limited way and abandoned as uneconomic, largely because they are very low-head hydro power plants with unusually high civil costs and an unusually poor load factor.
- Wave energy is beginning to see success with shoreline systems, but has yet to be effectively demonstrated on any scale near shore, let alone offshore, where most of the energy is found.
- Marine current energy is only just starting to be experimented with, but because it involves less technical risk than wave energy (conditions are less extreme), it promises to develop relatively quickly.
- OTEC, experimented with extensively, shows most promise as a multipurpose process (energy with cooling, nutrients for fish-farms, and/or potable water from seawater). Shoreline OTEC may possibly be more readily developed and economically applied than devices floating in deep waters.
- The two remaining known options—exploiting salinity gradients and cultivating marine biomass—seem a long way from any practical application.

Wave energy remains at an experimental stage, with only a few prototype systems actually working.

System aspects

Rapid changes in the energy sector, liberalisation of energy markets and the success of new technologies such as the combined cycle gas turbine offer challenges to the integration of renewable energy technologies into energy supply systems. They also lead to new issues at the system level.

System aspects come into play when there are many relatively small energy generation units, both renewable and conventional. The issues discussed here focus on electricity because of the instant response of electricity. Few thermal and fuel networks experience these issues because of their storage capacity.

With the rapid increase in the number of small generators connected to distribution networks at low and medium voltages, these networks need to handle more two-way flows of electricity, requiring decentralised intelligent control systems and local storage systems to increase reliability.

Trends in the energy sector

The energy sector is undergoing rapid change because of the following trends:

- World-wide restructuring of utilities and liberalisation of energy markets.
- Greater choice for large and small customers.
- Customer interest in green pricing and the emerging trade in green certificates.
- Technological innovations in efficiency, demand-side management, transport and distribution, electronic power handling, and generation.

These trends directly or indirectly affect the electricity system. Patterson (1999) describes how the global electricity industry is in confusion, how long-accepted ground rules for technology, fuels, ownership, operation, management, and finance are changing by the day. The traditional shape of the electricity system is based on two pillars: large remote power stations generating centrally controller synchronised alternate current, and a monopoly franchise to finance, build, and operate the system.

Technical innovations, such as the gas turbine and advanced power electronics, are undermining the first pillar. Institutional innovation and price competition are undermining the second. In effect liberalisation and new technological development are democratising the system by decentralising it. And suddenly direct current, favoured by Edison, is discussed again, not least because it fits rather better into the micro-applications of computer chips and electronics (FT, 1998).

These trends are also summarised in the concept of the distributed utility, based on the principle that the economies of scale for large generation units are replaced by the economies of numbers in producing large quantities of small units: wind, photovoltaics, fuel cells, internal combustion engines, small gas turbines, and storage systems (Weinberg, 1995; Ianucci and others, 1999). The concept involves both energy efficiency and demand-side management measures at the customers' end, as well as distributed generation and distributed storage in the networks. For the customer it implies, in principle, lower energy prices, new and better services, and new products. Market studies in the United States indicate that in the traditional vertically integrated utility, distributed generation and storage could serve 20–40 percent of U.S. load growth. If the existing load could be served by distributed generation through replacement or retirement of central station generation, the potential is even greater (Ianucci and others, 1999).

Characteristics of renewable energy systems

From a system point of view, a distinction should be made between intermittent renewable energy sources (wind, solar photovoltaic) and those with a more stable and controllable output (hydro, biomass). The intermittent ones deliver primarily energy but only limited capacity, whereas the more stable ones deliver both. Note, however, that an intermittent resource can be transformed to baseload power supply if it is combined with an energy storage system.

Characterising the typical intermittent sources are capacity factors with values often a third or less of those of conventional systems. (The capacity factor is defined as the ratio of year-averaged system power to the rated system power.) In energy output per installed kilowatt, each year conventional power plants produce 4,000–7,000 kilowatt-hours per kilowatt of installed capacity, wind plants generally produce 2,000–2,500, and solar photovoltaic plants produce 750–1,500. The network should be designed to absorb that peak capacity and to provide electricity reliably when the intermittent sources are not available.

The renewable sources with an inherently stable output can, from a system point of view, be treated as conventional units: hydro and biomass-powered units, as well as OTEC and wave power. Hybrid solar thermal power stations co-fired with natural gas (or biofuels) are also regarded as conventional.

Electrical system design

Today's electrical system is designed for one-way traffic from the large generating unit through the transmission and distribution network to the customers. With the advent of smaller generating units distributed throughout the network, two-way traffic becomes more important and requires a rethinking of the network's design. New analytical tools are being developed for this purpose, and innovations in power electronics are becoming more important (Verhoeven, 1999). This is true for transmission lines where high voltage direct current cables (equipped with power electronics at both ends) are preferred for bulk power transport. For medium-and low-voltage lines, power electronics are important in voltage conditioning, preventing voltage dips, and reactive power compensation. The electricity network should become more flexible, facilitating co-operation between generators, storage, and efficient energy consuming systems. In short, the intelligent network of the future

> *Most studies confirm that an intermittent renewable energy contribution up to 10–20 percent can easily be absorbed in electricity networks.*

will be able to 'talk' to its connected systems (Verhoeven, 1999).

The effect of decentralised systems on the reliability of the network is of prime concern to the network operators. Studies by KEMA for the Dutch electricity system indicate that by introducing decentralised generators and storage systems (close to the customers) the reliability of the network can increase significantly. Where new grids are to be installed, the grid can become 'thinner' and built with less redundancy. And the transmission and distribution networks can become simpler because of intelligent control systems (Vaessen, 1997).

Model studies by the Pacific Northwest Laboratory confirm that distributed utility (DU) generation will have a significant impact on bulk transmission system stability at heavy penetration levels (Donelly and others, 1996). By locating DU technologies at points of critical loading, utilities may be able to defer upgrades of transmission and distribution facilities. Many utilities have already had operating experience with DU generation, and such local issues such as protection, interaction with distribution automation schemes, and reactive power control have been successfully resolved. Questions remain on how these resources, along with dispatchable generation and storage, interact with each other as their penetration increases.

Grid integration of intermittent renewables

The amount of intermittent power that can be connected to a grid without problems of grid reliability or quality depends on many factors. Locally problems can occur quite soon when feeding substantial intermittent power (more than 100 kilowatts) into the low-voltage grid at one point. But it has been shown that penetration as high as 40 percent can be achieved for wind turbines (feeding into the medium-voltage grid). This is a subject for further investigation. Most studies confirm that an intermittent renewable energy contribution up to 10–20 percent can easily be absorbed in electricity networks. Higher penetration rates may require adequate control or such measures as output limiting or load shedding. Another approach could be to increase the flexibility of the electricity system by means of gas turbines. Penetration values up to 50 percent are possible for large systems with reservoir-based hydropower units (Grubb and Meyer, 1993; Kelly and Weinburg, 1993).

Intermittent renewables and energy storage

Large penetration of intermittent renewable energy technologies would become much easier with some cheap form of large-scale electricity storage, than the virtual storage. At present, however, any other form of electricity storage than the virtual storage offered by conventional plants to the grid seems unattractive.

In the Netherlands several studies in the 1980s analysed the possibilities of large pumped storage systems (storage capacity of 10–30 gigawatt-hours, discharge capacity of 1,500–2,000 megawatts-electric), both above ground and below ground, based on water or compressed air. Estimated investment costs ranged from $1,000 to

$2,000 million (EZ, 1988). The studies were initiated partly because of the (then) estimated limited allowable penetration ratios for wind power into the grid. With the insight that higher penetration ratios were possible, and because of the high investment costs, the immediate interest in storage evaporated.

Schainker provides estimates for the capital costs of electricity storage (Schainker, 1997; PCAST, 1999). Compressed air systems appear to be fairly attractive, both for 2-hour and 20-hour storage options (table 7.24). In Germany the Huntorf power plant near Bremen, commissioned in 1978, used compressed air as a storage medium for the compression part of the gas-turbine cycle. With cheap electricity, the air was stored in off-peak hours, to be used during peak hours as on input to the gas-turbine, co-fired with natural gas.

As noted, wind-generated electricity can be transformed from an intermittent resource to a baseload power supply if combined with compressed air energy storage (CAES), adding probably $0.01 a kilowatt-hour to the wind electricity production costs (Cavallo, 1995).

Value of renewables

For standalone systems, the value of renewables is often the value of the service. Examples are lighting, heating, cooling, cooking, pumping, transportation, and telecommunication. How this value should be evaluated is determined by the minimum cost of any equivalent alternative energy source or technology.

For grid-connected electricity systems, the value of renewables can be defined in different ways: avoided fuel, capacity, and maintenance costs; avoided electricity consumption costs; buy-back rate; and non-financial benefits (Turkenburg, 1992).

The avoided fuel costs in the conventional system usually represent the lowest possible value (typically $0.02–0.05 a kilowatt-hour). Renewables also have a capacity value, though this may be small for intermittent technologies (Alsema and others, 1983; van Wijk and others, 1992). For solar energy systems used for peak shaving (such as peaks due to air conditioning) or grid support, the value of photovoltaic power may be substantially higher than the value of base-load power.

Avoided costs of electricity consumption refer to the situation where a renewable energy system is connected to the grid by a bidirectional kilowatt-hour meter. By definition, the value then becomes equal to the costs (tariffs) of normal electricity. In many countries this is in the range of $0.10–0.25 a kilowatt-hour for small users (IEA PVPS, 1997)

In the buy-back rate method, the value of renewables can be lower or higher than that of energy from the grid. It is lower if an intermediate rate between avoided fuel costs and electricity tariffs is used, as is often the case (IEA PVPS, 1997). It can be higher if a high value is given to the fact that it is green electricity. In some areas (parts of Germany) buy-back rates are based on true costs of renewables and may be as high as about $0.5 a kilowatt-hour for photovoltaics.

Finally, the value of renewables for the owners of a system may partly be non-financial, such as the mere fact that they cover (part of) their own consumption in an independent and clean way. Obviously this cannot be easily expressed in financial terms.

Conclusion

■ Current trends in the energy sector favour the emergence of distributed utilities, where growing numbers of relatively small renewable and conventional supply systems can be integrated, thanks to local intelligent control systems supported by local storage systems. When properly planned they can even improve the reliability of the networks, but continued research is required in such areas as network modelling.

TABLE 7.24. OVERVIEW OF CAPITAL COSTS FOR ELECTRICITY STORAGE (1997 DOLLARS)

Technology	Component capital cost		Total capital cost	
	Discharge capacity (dollars per kilowatt)	Storage capacity (dollars per kilowatt-hour)	2-hour storage (dollars per kilowatt)	20-hour storage (dollars per kilowatt)
Compressed air Large (350 megawatts) Small (50 megawatts) Above ground (16 megawatts)	350 450 500	1 2 20	350 450 540	370 490 900
Conventional pumped hydro	900	10	920	1,100
Battery (target, 10 megawatts) Lead acid Advanced	120 120	170 100	460 320	3,500 2,100
Flywheel (target, 100 megawatts)	150	300	750	6,200
Superconducting magnetic storage (target, 100 megawatts)	120	300	720	6,100
Supercapacitors (target)	120	3,600	7,300	72,000

Source: PCAST, 1999.

- A fundamental change is taking place in the way electricity networks will be managed and used in the near future, thanks to the liberalisation of energy markets and the success of new technologies such as combined-cycle gas turbines and power electronics. The energy sector is moving away from the centralised massive supply of kilowatt-hours into supplying decentralised tailored services to its customers.

- Penetration ratios of renewable energy systems realised without loss of supply security are around 10–20 percent or higher, depending on the characteristics of the total system. High penetration rates can be achieved with advanced power electronics, steadily improving weather prediction methods, availability of hydropower plants, and integration of storage systems.

- The value of energy carriers produced by renewable sources depends on local circumstances. In practice figures are $0.02–1.00 a kilowatt-hour.

Policies and instruments

New renewable energy technologies are trying to make a way into different markets, often in competition with other options to fulfil the demand for energy services. Contrary to assumptions in the 1970s and 1980s, shortages of oil and gas due to resource constraints are not expected in the nearest decades. And coal resources are very large. Increasing fossil fuel prices driven by resource constraints are not also expected in the nearest decades. So a transition to renewables-based energy systems must largely rely on:

- Successful continuing development and diffusion of renewable energy technologies that become increasingly competitive through cost reductions from technological and organisational development.

- Political will to remove various barriers to the deployment of renewables and internalise environmental costs and other externalities that permanently increase fossil fuel prices.

As many countries have demonstrated, a variety of incentive mechanisms can promote the development and use of renewable energy sources:

- The cost of competing conventional energy.
- Financing and fiscal policy.
- Regulation.
- Getting started new technologies.

Cost of competing conventional energy

Reduce subsidies. Subsidies for conventional energy are pervasive and reduce the competitiveness of renewables (chapter 12). They have often proved to be difficult to remove.

Internalise environmental costs. From a theoretical point of view, carbon dioxide taxes would be the simplest and most consistent method for internalising the costs of mitigating climate change. Similarly, taxes can be used to internalise other environmental costs associated with fossil fuels or external costs associated with nuclear

> The value of renewables for the owners of a system may partly be non financial, as they cover (part of) their own consumption in an independent and clean way.

power. Although the magnitude of the environmental cost for various energy supply alternatives is debated, they are relatively lower for renewable energy.

Markets in many cases adapt quite rapidly to substantial changes in relative prices. Swedish carbon taxes are a case in point. The new energy and carbon taxes introduced in the early 1990s made bio-energy the least expensive fuel for heat production. Boilers are relatively flexible regarding fuel choice, and the market share of bio-energy in district heat production in Sweden increased from 9 percent (3.6 terawatt-hours) in 1990 to 30 percent (13.7 terawatt-hours) in 1998.

In general, however, this approach has not been particularly successful. Politically, it is difficult to gain acceptance for the large rise in energy prices that this approach could entail. At the national policy level, an important objection is the negative effect on the competitive position of domestic industries. A system of tradable emission permits or high taxes on marginal carbon dioxide emissions might circumvent this problem.

Financing and fiscal policy

Subsidies. Subsidies to stimulate the market penetration of renewables may be seen as the second-best solution to taxes—that is, relative prices are manipulated by subsidising what is desirable rather than taxing what is undesirable. Subsidies can take different shapes: investment subsidies (which give little incentive to actually produce), production subsidies (which may be perceived as unreliable and subject to change), and various indirect subsidies through preferential tax treatment, depreciation rules, and the like (see below). System benefit charges, such as the fossil fuel levy, are increasingly popular mechanisms to finance a subsidy for renewable energy through shifting the economic burden from taxpayers to consumers.

Financing. Financing arrangements are particularly important to renewable energy projects, which are often capital intensive, with many factors making their financing more expensive than for more traditional power investment (Wiser and Pickle, 1997). These factors include real and perceived project risks, the small size of renewable energy industry and many renewable energy projects, and dependence on unpredictable government policies to promote renewable energy.

The right choice of financing schemes (private, corporate, participation, project, and third party), ownership (single, corporate, participation, project finance, and third party) and legal entities (personal, partnership, corporation, and co-operation) can have a decisive impact on the economic viability of a project (Langniss, 1999). In developing countries, financing adapted to local needs and tradition—such as through revolving funds—has proven important in the diffusion of small renewable energy technologies, such as household photovoltaic systems (Gregory and others, 1997). Coping with the demand put on financing by the specific characteristics of renewables is an important challenge for international and other financial institutions.

Taxation. As noted, general and specific tax rules can work for or against renewable energy. Preferential tax treatment, tax exemption, accelerated depreciation, and other approaches can promote renewable energy. The Netherlands, for example, is moving away from using direct subsidies to supporting renewables through a variety of tax incentives. As for other policies and measures, tax mechanisms must be carefully designed to avoid undesirable consequences such as low incentives for project performance, as in the California wind rush, which also disrupted the Danish wind industry when tax incentives where removed (Wiser and Pickle, 1997). Experiences were similar in the initial years of wind power development in India (Mathews, 1998a, b).

Market approaches. Increasing consumer willingness to pay a premium for renewable energy can generate the higher revenues that may be needed to recover production costs. This approach is spreading fast through the increased marketing of environmental labelling and green pricing, notably in North America and Europe. Retail competition and the subsequent need for suppliers to diversify and become more customer oriented is an important driving force, an outcome of the commercial impulse to diversify and add value to basic products. Labelling can be done by a credible independent third party, such as an non-governmental organisation or government agency. In some cases electricity suppliers offer production-specified electricity, such as guaranteed annual average deliveries of wind electricity. The willingness to pay of large electricity users is likely to be low or nil, and green pricing may result only in modest additions of renewable energy. It can, however, nurse a market for new renewable technologies.

Regulation

The focus of most regulatory approaches to promote renewables has been the electricity sector. Regulation has also been used to introduce alternative transportation fuels, notably blending in ethanol with gasoline. Mechanisms to promote renewables through regulatory approaches can be categorised as obligations to buy and obligations to supply. Regulation in other domains can also have an influence.

Obligations to buy. Obligations to buy generally stipulate under what rules independent power producers get access to the grid and economic compensation for delivered electricity. This approach is commonly used in monopoly markets to ensure access for independent power producers with renewable energy. Regulated access and prices reduce transaction costs. Prices are usually based on avoided costs to the utility, and the principles by which these are calculated are important for the outcome. Obligations to buy may be complicated to maintain in liberalised electricity markets with competition between suppliers. The obligation to buy under the U.K. Non Fossil Fuel Obligation has been complemented with a mechanism for reimbursing electricity companies for the extra cost incurred.

Obligations to supply. Renewable portfolio standards can be used as an alternative to, or in combination with, system benefit charges to promote renewable electricity. A renewable portfolio standard imposes an obligation on all electricity suppliers to include a stipulated fraction of renewable electricity in their supply mix. This obligation is sometimes combined with a system for renewable energy credits to facilitate trade of renewable electricity between suppliers. Renewable portfolio standards are being implemented or discussed in Europe and in several states in the United States. Voluntary or negotiated agreements are sometimes used as an alternative to regulation.

Regulation in other domains. Regulation and policies in other sectors or domains (agricultural policy, land-use planning), or the lack thereof, often inflict serious constraints or barriers to the use of renewable energy. For bio-energy, the prospects generally depend heavily on forestry and agricultural policy. In temperate regions a prime option for bio-energy is short rotation forests on agricultural land. But establishing an energy plantation means committing the land to one use for many years or even decades. In contrast, agricultural subsidies tend to change frequently, deterring most farmers from making this commitment.

A lack of regulation can also hinder exploitation. For example, the exploration and exploitation of such natural resources as minerals or fossil fuels are usually regulated through legislation and involve selling or giving concessions. The absence of corresponding regulation for wind concessions, which would secure the rights to a resource, can be a barrier to commercial investments in exploration and exploitation (Brennand, 1996). Consequently, coherence should be sought between regulation in the renewable energy area and in other domains.

Getting new technologies started

Widespread diffusion of new renewable energy technology also depends on a successful chain of research, development, deployment, and cost reduction before a technology is commercially viable. Once that stage is reached, success also depends on availability of information about the resources, technologies, and institutional, organisational, and technical capabilities to adopt a technology to local conditions. This complex process, called the energy technology innovation pipeline, includes research, development, demonstration, buying down the cost of innovative energy technologies along their learning curves, widespread deployment, and involving of a range of actors (PCAST, 1999).

Research and development spending and priorities. In many areas, including the energy sector, the private sector under-invests in RR&D relative to the public benefits that could be realised from such investments, motivating public support for energy R&D. There are several examples of how electricity and gas sector restructuring is resulting in cutbacks on energy R&D and a shift to projects with short-term commercial benefits (PCAST, 1999). Government spending on energy R&D is collected and reported by the International Energy Agency for OECD countries (IEA, 1998). Between 1986 and 1996 the total reported annual energy R&D spending decreased by 19 percent, from about $11.0 billion to about $9.0 billion (1996 prices). But in the same period spending on energy conservation R&D increased by 64 percent to about $1.0 billion (1996 dollars) while spending on renewables R&D increased marginally from $700 million in 1986 to $720 million in 1996.

Demonstration and cost-reduction strategies. Demonstrations are necessary to test new energy-technology manufacturing (such as solar photovoltaics or fuel cells) and energy conversion facilities (such as integrated biomass gasification combined cycle plant)—and to prove their technical and economic viability. The private sector may find it difficult to build demonstration plants for various reasons—high capital requirements, required rates of return, high risk, and difficulties to appropriate the long-term benefits. Thus, public support is needed when clear public benefits can be associated with the technology.

In recent years, more attention has been going to the phase between demonstrations and commercial competitiveness. For essentially all technologies and production processes, a substantial amount of experience or learning results from their application, which in turn reduces costs. For various products and processes a 0–30 percent reduction in costs has been observed with each doubling of cumulative

Increasing consumers' willingness to pay a premium for renewable energy can generate the higher revenues that may be needed to recover production costs.

production (Neij, 1999). This phenomenon—called the experience curve or learning curve—has motivated private firms to use forward pricing. That is, they initially sell products below production cost under the expectation that learning effects will drive down costs and that profits will be generated later. But for renewable energy, it may be difficult for an individual firm to recover the costs of forward pricing. Here public financial support in combination with other measures can be key to success. In the wind industry in Denmark, a combination of subsidies, physical planning, wind turbine certification, and the like has produced in a thriving industry with a 50 percent share of the world market (see chapter 12).

Building capacity for widespread deployment. Although a technology may be competitive, its widespread deployment also depends on a range of other factors. A new technology may face a range of barriers to its widespread application. These include high perceived risk, high transaction and information costs, uncertainty about resource availability, and low technical and institutional capabilities to handle this new

TABLE 7.25. CURRENT STATUS OF RENEWABLE ENERGY TECHNOLOGIES

Technology	Increase in installed capacity in past five years (percent a year)	Operating capacity, end 1998	Capacity factor (percent)	Energy production 1998	Turnkey investment costs (U.S. dollars per kilowatt)	Current energy cost of new systems	Potential future energy cost
Biomass energy							
Electricity	≈ 3	40 GWe	25–80	160 TWh (e)	900– 3,000	5–15 ¢/kWh	4–10 ¢/kWh
Heat[a]	≈ 3	> 200 GWth	25–80	> 700 TWh (th)	250– 750	1–5 ¢/kWh	1–5 ¢/kWh
Ethanol	≈ 3	18 bln litres		420 PJ		8–25 $/GJ	6–10 $/GJ
Wind electricity	≈ 30	10 GWe	20–30	18 TWh (e)	1,100– 1,700	5–13 ¢/kWh	3–10 ¢/kWh
Solar photovoltaic electricity	≈ 30	500 MWe	8–20	0.5 TWh (e)	5,000–10,000	25–125 ¢/kWh	5 or 6–25 ¢/kWh
Solar thermal electricity	≈ 5	400 MWe	20–35	1 TWh (e)	3,000– 4,000	12–18 ¢/kWh	4–10 ¢/kWh
Low-temperature solar heat	≈ 8	18 GWth (30 mln m²)	8–20	14 TWh (th)	500– 1,700	3–20 ¢/kWh	2 or 3–10 ¢/kWh
Hydroelectricity							
Large	≈ 2	640 GWe	35–60	2,510 TWh (e)	1,000– 3,500	2-8 ¢/kWh	2-8 ¢/kWh
Small	≈ 3	23 GWe	20–70	90 TWh (e)	1,200– 3,000	4–10 ¢/kWh	3–10 ¢/kWh
Geothermal energy							
Electricity	≈ 4	8 GWe	45–90	46 TWh (e)	800– 3,000	2–10 ¢/kWh	1 or 2–8 ¢/kWh
Heat	≈ 6	11 GWth	20–70	40 TWh (th)	200– 2,000	0.5–5 ¢/kWh	0.5–5 ¢/kWh
Marine energy							
Tidal	0	300 MWe	20–30	0.6 TWh (e)	1,700– 2,500	8–15 ¢/kWh	8–15 ¢/kWh
Wave	—	exp. phase	20–35	—	1,500– 3,000	8–20 ¢/kWh	—
Current	—	exp. phase	25–35	—	2,000– 3,000	8–15 ¢/kWh	5–7 ¢/kWh
OTEC	—	exp. phase	70–80	—	—	—	—

a. Heat embodied in steam (or hot water in district heating), often produced by combined heat and power systems using forest residues, black liquor, or bagasse.

technology. Taxes, financing, fiscal policy, legislation, and regulation are important to address such barriers and have been discussed above.

Information and transaction costs can be the target of specific government initiatives. For example, responsibility for mapping natural resources should lie with the government. Transaction costs can be reduced by simplified permitting procedures, physical planning, use of standardised contracts, and clear regulation for suppliers of electricity and fuels from renewables. Information costs for new technologies and risk may be effectively reduced through a government testing and certification procedure. Governments, as key sponsors of the educational system in most countries, also have an obligation and an opportunity to support education and continuing education for practitioners.

Conclusion

Renewable energy sources supply 56 ± 10 exajoules a year (12–16 percent) of total world energy consumption (400 ± 10 exajoules in 1998). The supply is dominated by traditional biomass (probably 38 ± 10 exajoules a year), mostly firewood used for cooking and heating, especially in developing countries in Africa, Asia, and Latin America. A major contribution is made by large hydropower (about 9 exajoules a year). Another major contribution, estimated at 7 exajoules a year, comes from primary biomass used in modern energy conversion processes. The contribution from all other renewables (small hydropower, geothermal, wind, solar, and marine energy) is about 2 exajoules a year.

Of the total biomass energy supply, 16 ± 6 exajoules a year is estimated to be commercial. The total primary energy supply from renewable sources in 1998 used commercially can be estimated at 27 ± 6 exajoules. It is estimated that in 1998 new renewable energy sources—modern bio-energy, small hydropower, geothermal energy, wind energy, solar energy and marine energy—supplied 9 exajoules (about 2 percent).

The enormous potential of renewable energy sources can meet many times the world energy demand. They can enhance diversity in energy supply markets, contribute to long-term sustainable energy supplies, and reduce local and global atmospheric emissions. They can also provide commercially attractive options to meet specific needs for energy services, particularly in developing countries and rural areas, create new employment opportunities, and offer opportunities to manufacture much of the equipment locally (IEA, 1997). A brief overview of the many technologies to exploit them is presented in table 7.25.

A number of factors will have to be overcome to increase the market deployment of renewable energy technologies (IEA, 1997). Many technologies are still at an early stage of development. Their technological maturity will demand continuing research, development, and demonstration. Few renewable energy technologies can compete with conventional fuels on a strict cost basis, except in some niche markets in industrialised countries and in non-grid applications in developing countries. Clearly, the cost of production has to come down. As this chapter shows, substantial cost reductions can be achieved for most technologies, closing gaps and making renewables increasingly competitive (see table 7.25). This requires further technology development and market deployments and an increase in production capacities to mass-production levels.

Scenario studies investigating the potential contribution of renewables to global energy supplies indicate that this contribution might range from nearly 20 percent to more than 50 percent in the second half of the 21st century. We conclude that it is unclear what role renewables will play. Much will depend on the development of fossil-fuel energy supplies and the regulatory environment, especially for greenhouse gases (Eliasson, 1998). Contrary to assmp- tions in the 1970s and 1980s, shortages of oil and gas due to resource constraints are not expected in the nearest decades, and coal resources are very large. Therefore, apart from production and distribution constraints, substantially increasing fossil fuel prices driven by resource constraints are not expected in the nearest decades. In addition, advanced technology developments might allow fossil fuel use with greatly reduced atmospheric emissions (see chapter 8).

A transition to renewables-based energy systems would have to rely largely on successful development and diffusion of renewable energy technologies that become increasingly competitive through cost reductions resulting from technological and organisational development—and on the political will to internalise environmental costs and other externalities that permanently increase fossil fuel prices. Different technologies vary widely in their technological maturity, commercial status, integration aspects, and so on. Policies aimed at accelerating renewable energy must be sensitive to these differences. As renewable energy activities grow and ever more extensive funding is required, many countries are moving away from methods that let taxpayers carry the burden of promoting renewables, towards economic and regulatory methods that let energy consumers carry the burden. ■

Notes

1. The capacity of a photovoltaic cell, module, or system is defined as the generating capacity at an irradiance of 1,000 watts a square metre (spectrum AM 1.5) and a cell temperature of 25 degrees Celsius.

2. This figure is obtained by comparing the 1989 installed potential of the 70 developing countries (185 gigawatts) from Moore and Smith (1990) and the value for 1997 (225 gigawatts) obtained from table 7.18.

References

Alsema, E.A., A.J.M. van Wijk, and W.C. Turkenburg. 1983. "The Capacity Credit of Grid-Connected Photovoltaic Systems." In *Proceedings of the 5th EC PV Solar Energy Conference.* Reidel, Dordrecht, Netherlands.

Alsema, E.A., and E. Nieuwlaar, eds. 1998. "Environmental Aspects of PV Power Systems": *Progress in Photovoltaics—Research and Applications.* Vol. 6, no 2.

Alsema, E.A., P. Frankl, and K. Kato. 1998. "Energy Pay-back Time of Photovoltaic Energy Systems: Present Status and Prospects." In J. Schmid and others, eds., *Proceedings of the Second World Conference and Exhibition on PV Solar Energy Conversion.* Report EUR 18656 EN. Brussels.

Andersson, B.A. 1998. "Materials, Availability, and Waste Streams for Large Scale PV." In *Proceedings of the BNL/NREL Workshop on PV and the Environment.* Keystone, Colo.

Aryawijaya, R. 1997. "Government Regulations on Geothermal Development and Environmental Protection in Indonesia." In *Proceedings of the NEDO International Geothermal Symposium.* Sendai, Japan.

Bacon, R.W., J.E. Besant-Jones, and J. Heidarian. 1996. *Estimating Construction Costs and Schedules—Experience with Power Generation Projects in Developing Countries.* World Bank Technical Paper 325, Energy Series. Washington, D.C.

Benito, F.A. 1998. "The Role of Government in Philippine Geothermal Energy Development." Paper presented at the 20th Anniversary Geothermal Workshop of the United Nations University Geothermal Training Programme, Reykjavik, Iceland.

Besant-Jones, J. 1995. "Attracting Finance for Hydroelectric Power." Finance, Private Sector, and Development Energy Note 3. World Bank, Washington, D.C.

Beurskens, H.J.M. 2000. "Offshore Wind Turbine Systems in Europe." Paper presented to the Workshop Technische Machbarkeit der Windenergienutzung im Offshore der Nordsee, Kiel, Germany.

Beyea, J., J. Cook, D. Hall, R. Socolow, and R. Williams. 1991. *Towards Ecological Guidelines for Large-scale Biomass Energy Development: Executive Summary.* National Aubudon Society, Princeton University, N.J.

Björnsson, J., I.B. Fridleifsson, T. Helgason, H. Jonatansson, J.M. Mariusson, G. Palmason, V. Stefansson, and L. Thorsteinsson. 1998. "The Potential Role of Geothermal Energy and Hydro Power in the World Energy Scenario in Year 2020." In *Proceedings of the 17th WEC Congress.* Houston, Tex.

Böer, K.W., ed. 1998. *Advances in Solar Energy.* Vol. 12. Boulder, Colo.: American Solar Energy Society.

Bohland, J., T. Dapkus, K. Kamm, and K. Smigielski. 1998. "Photovoltaics as Hazardous Materials; the Recycling Solution." In J. Schmid, and others, eds., *Proceedings of the Second World Conference and Exhibition on PV Solar Energy Conversion.* Report EUR 18656 EN. Brussels.

Borjesson, P. 1999. "Environmental Effects of Energy Crop cultivation in Sweden—I: Identification and Quantification, and II: Economic Evaluation." *Biomass and Bioenergy* 16 (2): 137–70.

Bouma, J. 1999. "Heat Pump Market in Europe." In *Proceedings 6th IEA Heat Pump Conference.* Berlin.

Boyle, G., ed. 1996. *Renewable Energy: Power for a Sustainable Future.* Oxford: Oxford University Press.

Brennand, T. 1996. "Concessions for Wind Farms: A New Approach to Wind Energy Development." Report prepared for Council for International Co-operation on Environment and Development, Working Group on Energy Strategies and Technologies, Beijing.

Bridgewater, A.V. 1998. "The Status of Fast Pyrolysis of Biomass in Europe." In *Proceedings of the 10th European Biomass Conference and Technology Exhibition.* Wurzburg, Germany.

Briscoe, J. 1998. "The Financing of Hydropower, Irrigation and Water Supply Infrastructure in Developing Countries." Paper prepared for the United Nations Commission on Sustainable Development, New York.

Brouwer, L.C., and L. Bosselaar. 1999. "Policy for Stimulating Passive Solar Energy in the Netherlands." In *Proceedings of the Northsun 1999 Conference.* Edmonton, Canada.

Brown, L.R., J. Abramovitz, C. Bright, C. Flavin, G. Gardner, H. Kane, A. Platt, S. Postel, D. Roodman, A. Sachs, and L. Starke. 1996. *State of the World: A World Watch Institute Report on Progress toward a Sustainable Society.* New York: World Watch Institute.

Bruton, T.M., and others. 1997. "A Study of the Manufacture at 500 MWp p.a. of Crystalline Silicon Photovoltaic Modules. In *Proceedings of the 14th European PV Solar Energy Conference.* Bedford, United Kingdom: H.S. Stephens & Ass.

BTM Consult. 1999: *International Wind Energy Development: World Market Update 1998.* Denmark.

———. 2000. Personal communication. 15 February. Denmark.

Buck, R., E. Lupert, and F. Teelez. 2000. *Proceedings of the 10th SolarPACES International Symposium of Solar Thermal Concentrating Technologies, Solar Thermal 2000.* March 8–10, Sydney.

Burbidge, D., D. Mills, and G. Morrison. 2000. "Stanwell Solar Thermal Power Project." In *Proceedings of the 10th SolarPACES International Symposium of Solar Thermal Concentrating Technologies, Solar Thermal 2000.* March 8–10, Sydney.

Carlson, D.E., and S. Wagner. 1993. "Amorphous Silicon Photovoltaic Systems." In T.B. Johansson, H. Kelly, A.K.N. Reddy, R.H. Wiliams, and L. Burnham, *Renewable Energy: Sources for Fuels and Electricity.* Washington, D.C.: Island Press.

Carpentieri, E., E. Larson, and J. Woods. 1993. "Future Biomass-based Power Generation in North-East Brazil." *Biomass and Bioenergy* 4 (3): 149–73.

Cavallo, A.J. 1995. "High-Capacity Factor Wind Energy Systems." *Journal of Solar Energy Engineering* 117: 137–43.

Churchill, A. A. 1994. "Meeting Hydro's Financing and Development Challenges." *Hydro Review World Wide* 2 (3): 22.

Churchill, A. A. 1997. "Meeting Hydro's Financing and Development Challenges." In T. Dorcey, ed., *Proceedings of the Workshop Large Dams: Learning from the Past, Looking at the Future.* IUCN, World Conservation Union, and World Bank Group; Gland, Switzerland; Cambridge, United Kingdom; and Washington, D.C.

Consonni, S. and E.D. Larson. 1994a. "Biomass-gasifier/Aeroderivative Gas Turbine Combined Cycles, Part A: Technologies and Performance Modelling." Part B: Performance calculations and economic assessment." Paper prepared for the Eighth Congress and Exposition on Gas Turbines in Cogeneration and Utility, Industrial, and Independent Power Generation, October 25–27, Portland, Or.

———. 1994b. "Biomass-gasifer/Aeroderivative Gas Turbine Combined Cycles. Part B: Performance Calculations and Economic Assessment". Paper prepared for the Eighth Congress and Exposition on Gas Turbines in Cogeneration and Utility, Industrial, and Independent Power Generation, October 25–27, Portland, Or.

Dannemand Andersen, P. 1998. *Wind Power in Denmark: Technology, Policies and Results.* Roskilde, Denmark: Riso National Laboratory.

Davis, E. 1995. "Device Developed for Bird Protection." *EPRI Journal* March/April.

Donelly, M.K., J.E. Dagle, and D.J. Trudnowski. 1996. "Impacts of Distributed Utility on Transmission System Stability." *IEEE Transactions on Power Systems* 11 (2): 741–46.

Dyson, T. 1996. "Population and Food, Global Trends and Future Prospects." Global Environmental Change Programme, New York.

EC (European Commission). 1997. "Community Strategy and Action Plan for Renewable Energy Sources." White Paper, Brussels.

———. 1999. "Electricity from Renewable Energy Sources and the International Electricity Market." Working Paper, Brussels.

ECN (Energieonderzoek Centrum Nederland) 1999a. Data Collected for the Shell/Novem/ECN Solar Panel. Personal communication with C.J.J. Tool, Netherlands Energy Research Foundation, Petten, Netherlands.

———. 1999b. T*he Role of Renewable Energy in the Netherlands until 2020* (in Dutch). Netherlands Energy Research Foundation, Petten, Netherlands.

Eliasson, B. 1998. *Renewable Energy: Status and Prospects.* Växjö, Sweden: ABB Environmental Affairs.

Elliott, P., and R. Booth. 1993. *Brazilian Biomass Power Demonstration Project.* London: Shell International.

Enermodal. 1999. "Cost Reduction Study for Solar Thermal Power Plants." Paper prepared for World Bank. Enermodal Engineering, Ontario. [www.eren.doe.gov/sunlab/Frame4.htm].

EPIA and Altener. 1996. *Photovoltaics in 2010.* Brussels: Office for Official Publications of the European Commission.

ESIF (European Solar Industry Federation) 1996. *Sun in Action.* Brussels: European Commission.

ETSU (Eldergy Technology Support Unit) and DTI (Department of Trade and Industry) 1999. *New and Renewable Energy: Prospects in the UK for the 21st Century—Supporting Analysis.* Harwell.

EUREC Agency. 1996. *The Future for Renewable Energy: Prospects and Directions.* London: James & James.

EZ (Ministerie van Economische Zaken) 1988. *Storage of Electricity in the Netherlands: Feasible and Acceptable?* (in Dutch). The Hague: Netherlands Ministry of Economic Affairs.

Faaij, A., B. Meuleman, and R. van Ree. 1998. "Long-Term Perspectives of BIG/CC Technology, Performance and Costs." Utrecht University, Deptartment of Science, Technology and Society, and Netherlands Energy Research Foundation, Petten, Netherlands.

Faaij, A., B. Meuleman, W. Turkenburg, A. van Wijk, A. Bauen, F. Rosillo-Calle, and D. Hall. 1998. "Externalities of Biomass Based Electricity Production Compared to Power Generation from Coal in the Netherlands." *Biomass and Bioenergy* 14 (2): 125–47.

Faaij, A., C. Hamelinck, and A.E. Agterberg. Forthcoming. *Long-term Perspectives for Production of Fuels from Biomass: Integrated Assessment and RD&D Priorities.*

Faaij, A., C. Hamelinck, E. Larson, and T. Kreutz. 1999. "Production of Methanol and Hydrogen from Biomass via Advanced Conversion Concepts." In R.P. Overend and E. Chornet, eds., *Proceedings of the 4th Biomass Conference of the Americas.* Oxford: Elsevier Science.

Faaij, A., M. Hekkert, E. Worrell, and A. van Wijk. 1998. "Optimization of the Final Waste Treatment System in the Netherlands." *Resources, Conservation and Recycling* 22: 47–82.

Faaij, A., R. van Ree, L. Waldheim, E. Olsson, A. Oudhuis, A. van Wijk, C. Daey Ouwens, and W. Turkenburg. 1997. "Gasification of Biomass Wastes and Residues for Electricity Production." *Biomass and Bioenergy* 12 (6): 387–407.

Fisch, M.N. 1998. "A Review of Large-Scale Solar Heating Systems in Europe." *Solar Energy* 63 (6): 355–66.

Fraenkel, P.L. 1999. "New Developments in Tidal and Wavepower Technologies." In *Proceedings of the Silver Jubilee Conference: Towards a Renewable Future.* Conference C73 of the Solar Energy Society, May 13–15, Brighton, U.K.

Fridleifsson, I.B., and Freeston, D. 1994. "Geothermal Energy Research and Development." *Geothermics* 23: 175–214.

FT (Financial Times). 1998. "Transforming Electricity."*Financial Times Energy World.* 11: 4–8.

Gardner, G. 1996. "Shrinking Fields: Cropland Loss in a World of Eight Billion." World Watch Paper 131. New York.

Garg, S. 2000. "Manthania Integrated Combined Cycle Project (status note on the 140MW first ISCC project)." In *Proceedings of the 10th SolarPACES International Symposium of Solar Thermal Concentrating Technologies, Solar Thermal 2000.* March 8–10, Sydney.

Garozzo, M, and S. Li Causi. 1998. "The Italian 10,000 Rooftops Program." In J. Schmid and others, eds., *Proceedings of the Second World Conference and Exhibition on PV Solar Energy Conversion.* Report EUR 18656 EN. Brussels.

Glaser, P.E., and others. 1997. *Solar Power Satellites: A Space Energy System for Earth.* Chichester, UK: John Wiley and Sons.

Goodland, R. 1997. "Environmental Sustainability in the Hydro Industry: Disaggregating the Debate." In T. Dorcey, ed., *Proceedings of the Workshop on 'Large Dams: Learning from the Past, Looking in the Future.'* IUCN, World Conservation Union, and World Bank Group; Gland, Switzerland; Cambridge, United Kingdom; and Washington, D.C.

Graham, R. E. Lichtenberg, V. Roningen, H. Shapouri, and M. Walsh. 1995. "The Economics of Biomass Production in the United States." In *Proceedings of the Second Biomass Conference of the Americas.* Portland, Or.

Green, M.A., K. Emery, K. Bücher, D.L. King, and S. Igaru. 1999. "Solar Cell Efficiency Tables (Version 13)." *Progress in Photovoltaics: Research and Applications* 7: 31–37.

Greenpeace and SEI (Stockholm Environment Institute). 1993. *Towards a Fossil Free Energy Future.* Boston: SEI.

Gregory, J., S. Silveira, A. Derrick, P. Cowley, C. Allinson, and O. Paish. *1997 Financing Renewable Energy Projects, a Guide for Development Workers.* London: Intermediate Technology Publications.

Grubb, M.J., and N.I. Meyer. 1993. "Wind Energy: Resources, Systems and Regional Strategies." In T.B. Johansson, H. Kelly, A.K.N. Reddy, R.H. Wiliams, and L. Burnham, *Renewable Energy: Sources for Fuels and Electricity.* Washington, D.C.: Island Press.

Hall, D.O. 1997. "Biomass Energy in Industrialized Countries: A View of the Future." *Forest Ecology and Management* 91: 17–45.

Hall, D.O., F. Rosillo-Calle, R.H. Williams, and J. Woods. 1993. Biomass for Energy: Supply Prospects. In Johansson, T.B, H. Kelly, A.K.N. Reddy, R.H. Wiliams, and L. Burnham, Renewable Energy: Sources for Fuels and Electricity. Washington, D.C.: Island Press.

Hastings, S.R., ed. 1994. *Passive Solar Commercial and Institutional Buildings.* New York: Wiley and sons.

Hemstock, S.L., and D.O. Hall. 1995. "Biomass Energy Flows in Zimbabwe." *Biomass and Bioenergy* 8 (3): 151–73.

Henning, H.M. 1999. "Economic Study of Solar Assisted Cooling Systems." Bericht TOS1-HMH-9905-E01, Fraunhofer Institute ISE, Freiburg, Germany.

Hughes, E.E., and G.A. Wiltsee. 1995. "Comparative Evaluation of Fuel Costs from Energy Crops." In *Proceedings of the Second Biomass Conference of the Americas.* Portland, Or.

Ianucci, J., S. Horgan, J. Eyer, and L. Cibulka. 1999. "Distributed Utility Perspectives." White Paper prepared for the International Energy Agency Renewable Energy Working Party, DU Associates, Livermore, Ca.

IEA (International Energy Agency). 1994. *Biofuels.* Energy and Environment Policy Analysis Series, Organisation for Economic Co-operation and Development and IEA, Paris, France.

———. 1995. *World Energy Outlook.* Paris: IEA and Organisation for Economic Co-operation and Development.

———. 1996. *World Energy Outlook.* Paris: IEA and Organisation for Economic Co-operation and Development.

———. 1997. *Key Issues in Developing Renewables.* Paris: IEA and Organisation for Economic Co-operation and Development.

———. 1998. E*nergy Policies of IEA Countries, 1998 Review.* Paris.

———. 1998. *Proceedings of the Conference on Biomass Energy: Data, Analysis and Trends.* March 23–24, Paris.

IEA (International Energy Agency), CADDET Centre for Renewable Energy. 1998. *Opportunities for Large-scale Purchase of Active Solar Systems.* ETSU, Harwell, U.K.

IEA (International Energy Agency), PVPS (Photovoltaic Power Systems). 1997. *Photovoltaic Power Systems in Selected IEA Member Countries.* Paris.

———. 1998. *Trends in PV Power Applications in Selected IEA Countries between 1992 and 1997.* Report IEA PVPS 1–06. Paris.

IEA (International Energy Agency), REWP (Renewable Energy Working Party). 1999. *The Evolving Renewable Energy Market.* Netherlands: Novem, Sittard.

IGA (International Geothermal Association). 1999. [http://www.demon.co.uk/geosci/igahome.html].

IIASA (International Institute for Applied Systems Analysis) and WEC (World Energy Council). 1998. *Global Energy Perspectives.* Cambridge: Cambridge University Press.

Ishitani, H., and T.B. Johansson, eds. 1996. "Energy Supply Mitigation Options." In R.T. Watson and others, eds., *Climate Change 1995: Impacts, Adaptations and Mitigation of Climate Change: Scientific-Technical Analyses.* Intergovernmental Panel on Climate Change. Cambridge: Cambridge University Press.

IT Power Ltd. 1996. "The Exploitation of Tidal Marine Currents." Tecnomare SpA, Report EUR 16683 EN. European Communities, Office for Official Publications, Luxembourg.

Jager, D. de, A. Faaij, and W.P. Troelstra. 1998. *Cost-effectiveness of Transportation Fuels from Biomass.* ECOFYS. Utrecht University, Department of Science, Technology and Society, Innas B.V, Delft.

Johansson, T. B., H. Kelly, A. K. N. Reddy, and R. Williams. 1993a. "Renewable Fuels and Electricity for a Growing World Economy: Defining and Achieving the Potential." In T. B. Johansson, H. Kelly, A.K.N. Reddy, R.H. Wiliams, and L. Burnham, *Renewable Energy: Sources for Fuels and Electricity.* Washington, D.C.: Island Press.

Johansson, T.B, H. Kelly, A.K.N. Reddy, R.H. Wiliams, and L. Burnham, eds. 1993b. *Renewable Energy: Sources for Fuels and Electricity.* Washington, D.C.: Island Press.

Kaltschmitt, M., C. Rosch, and L. Dinkelbach, eds. 1998. "Biomass Gasification in Europe." Stuttgart University, Institute of Energy Economics and the Rational Use of Energy, Stuttgart, Germany.

Kaltschmitt, M., G.A. Reinhardt, and T. Stelzer. 1996. "LCA of Biofuels under Different Environmental Aspects." Stuttgart University, Institut für Energiewirtschaft und Rationelle Energieanwendung, Stuttgart, Germany.

Kassler, P. 1994. "Energy for Development." Shell Selected Paper. Shell International Petroleum Company, London.

Kelly, H., and C. Weinberg. 1993. "Utility Strategies for Using Renewables." In T. B. Johansson, H. Kelly, A.K.N. Reddy, R.H. Wiliams, and L. Burnham, *Renewable Energy: Sources for Fuels and Electricity.* Washington, D.C.: Island Press.

Koch, A., 1996: "Playing the Electricity Market." *International Water Power and Dam Construction Yearbook.* Sutton, Surrey, England: British Press International.

Kolb, G.J. 1998. "Economic Evaluation of Solar-only and Hybrid Power Towers Using Molten-salt Technology." *Solar Energy* 62 (1): 51–61.

Langniss, O., ed. 1999. "Financing Renewable Energy Systems." Report to the European Commission, German Aerospace Center, Stuttgart, Germany.

Larson, E.D., and H. Jin. 1999a. "Biomass Conversion to Fisher-Tropsch Liquids: Preliminary Energy Balances." In R.P. Overend and E. Chornet, eds., *Proceedings of the 4th Biomass Conference of the Americas.* Oxford: Elsevier Science.

———. 1999b. "A Preliminary Assessment of Biomass Conversion to Fischer-Tropsch Cooking Fuels for Rural China." In R.P. Overend and E. Chornet, eds., *Proceedings of the 4th Biomass Conference of the Americas.* Oxford: Elsevier Science.

Larson, E.D., C.I. Marrison, and R.H. Williams. 1995. "Mitigation Potential of Biomass Energy Plantations in Developing Regions." Princeton University, Center for Energy and Environmental Studies, Princeton, N.J.

Larson, E.D., R.H. Williams, and T.B. Johansson. 1999. "Future Demands on Forests as a Source of Energy." Princeton University, Center for Energy and Environmental Studies, Princeton, N.J.; and United Nations Development Programme, New York.

Larson, E.D., S. Consonni, and T. Kreutz. 1998. "Preliminary Economics of Black Liquor Gasifier/Gas Turbine Cogeneration at Pulp and Paper Mills." Paper prepared for the 43rd ASME gas turbine and aeroengine congress, exposition, and users symposium, June 2–5, Stockholm.

Laue, H.J. 1999. "Heat Pumps, Status and Trends in Europe." In *Proceedings 6th IEA Heat Pump Conference.* Berlin.

Lazarus, M.L., L. Greber, J. Hall, C. Bartels, S. Bernow, E. Hansen, P. Raskin, and D. von Hippel. 1993. "Towards a Fossil Free Energy Future, The Next Energy Transitions: A Technical Analysis for Greenpeace International." Stockholm Environmental Institute and Boston Center.

Lefevre T., J. Todoc, and G. Timilsina. 1997. "The Role of Wood Energy in Asia; Wood Energy Today and Tomorrow (WETT)." Regional Studies, FAO-working paper FOPW/97/2. Food and Agriculture Organization of the United Nations, Rome.

Lenzen, M. 1999. "Greenhouse Gas Analysis of Solar-thermal Electricity Generation." *Solar Energy* 65 (6): 353–68..

Lew, D., R.H. Williams, S. Xie, and S. Zhang. 1998. "Large-Scale Baseload Wind Power in China." *Natural Resources Forum* 22 (3): 165–84.

Little, R.G., and M.J. Nowlan. 1997. "Crystalline Silicon Photovoltaics: The Hurdle for Thin Films." *Progress in Photovoltaics: Research and Applications* 5: 309–15.

Luchi, M. 1998. "An Empirical Analysis of Consumer Decision Making Processes on Setting up Residential PV Systems." In J. Schmid and others, eds., *Proceedings of the Second World Conference and Exhibition on PV Solar Energy Conversion.* Report EUR 18656 EN. Brussels.

Lund, J.W. 1996. "Lectures on Direct Utilization of Geothermal Energy." Report 1996–1. United Nations University, Geothermal Training Programme, Reykjavik, Iceland.

Luyten, J.C. 1995. "Sustainable World Food Production and Environment." Research Institute for Agrobiology and Soil Fertility, Report 37. Agricultural Research Department, Wageningen, Netherlands.

Luzzi, A. 2000. "Showcase Project: 2 MW Demonstration Sole Thermal Power Plant." In *Proceedings of the 10th SolarPACES International Symposium of Solar Thermal Concentrating Technologies, Solar Thermal 2000.* March 8–10, Sydney.

Lynd, L.R. 1996. "Overview and Evaluation of Fuel Ethanol from Lignocellulosic Biomass: Technology, Economics, the Environment and Policy." *Annual Review of Energy and the Environment* 21: 403–65.

Mankins, J.C. 1998. "Power from Space: A Major New Energy Option?" Paper 4.1.16. Presented at the Proceedings of the 17th Congress of the World Energy Council. Houston, Tex.

Marrison, C.I., and E.D. Larson. 1995a. "Cost versus Scale for Advanced Plantation-based Biomass Energy Systems in the US." In *Proceedings of the EOA Symposium on Greenhouse Gas Emissions and Mitigation Research.* June 27–29, Washington, D.C.

———. 1995b. "A Preliminary Estimate for the Biomass Energy Production Potential in Africa for 2025." *Biomass and Bioenergy* 10 (5–6): 337–51.

Mathews, N. 1998a. "Changes for the Better on the Way." *Wind Power Monthly* 14 (5): 26–27.

———. 1998b. "Tax Evasion Scam Linked to Wind." *Wind Power Monthly* 14 (3): 26.

Matthies, H.G. and others. 1995. *Study of Offshore Wind Energy in the EC.* Brekendorf, Germany: Verlag Natürliche Energien.

Maycock, P.D. 1998. *Photovoltaic Technology, Performance, Cost and Market Forecast: 1975–2010,* Version 7. Warrenton, Va.: Photovoltaic Energy Systems.

Meuleman, B., and A. Faaij. 1999. *Overview of Co-combustion Options for Coal Fired Power Plants.* Utrecht University, Deptartment of Science, Technology and Society, Netherlands.

Mills, D., and G. Morrison. 2000a. "Compact Linear Fresnel Reflector Solar Thermal Power Plants." *Source* 68 (3): 263–83.

———. 2000b. "Stanwell Solar Thermal Power Project."

MNCES (Ministry of Non-Conventional Energy Sources). 1999. *Annual Report 1990–2000.* Government of India.

Moore, E. A., and G. Smith. 1990. "Capital Expenditures for Electric Power in Developing Countries in the 1990s." Energy Series Paper, no. 21. World Bank, Washington, D.C.

Moore, T. 2000. "Renewed Interest for Space Solar Power." *EPRI Journal* (spring): 7–17.

Moreira, J. R., and A. D. Poole. 1993. "Hydropower and Its Constraints." In T. B. Johansson, H. Kelly, A.K.N. Reddy, R.H. Wiliams, and L. Burnham, *Renewable Energy: Sources for Fuels and Electricity.* Washington, D.C.: Island Press.

Morrison, G.L. 1999. "Packaged Solar Water Heating Technology, Twenty Years of Progress." In *Proceedings of the Solar World Congress.* Jerusalem.

Naber, J.E., F. Goudriaan, and A.S. Louter. 1997. "Further Development and Commercialisation of the Small Hydro-thermal Upgrading Process for Biomass Liquefaction." In *Proceedings of the Third Biomass Conference of the Americas.* Montreal.

National Laboratory. 1997. "Technology Opportunities to Reduce U.S. Greenhouse Gas Emissions – Appendix B – Technology Pathways Characteristics." Prepared for the U.S. Department of Energy [http://www.ornl.gov/climatechange].

Neij, L. 1999. "Dynamics of Energy Systems, Methods of Analysing Technology Change." Ph.D. diss., Lund University, Lund Institute of Technology, Sweden.

Nishimura, T. 1999. "Heat Pumps: Status and Trends in Asia and the Pacific." In *Proceedings of the 6th Heat Pump Conference.* Berlin.

NREL (National Renewable Energy Laboratory). 1999. [http://www.nrel.gov/otec].

NUTEK. 1996. *Energy in Sweden 1995.* Stockholm.

Oonk, H., J. Vis, E. Worrell, A. Faaij, and J.W. Bode. 1997. "The Methahydro Process: Preliminary Design and Cost Evaluation." TNO Report R 97/214. TNO Institute of Environmental Sciences, Energy Research and Process Innovation, Apeldoorn, Netherlands.

Osuna, R., V. Fernandez, M. Romero, and M. Blanco. 2000. "PS 10: A 10 Solar Power Evaluation Program." In *Proceedings of the 10th SolarPACES International Symposium of Solar Thermal Concentrating Technologies, Solar Thermal 2000.* March 8–10, Sydney.

Oud, E., and T.C. Muir. 1997. "Engineering and Economic Aspects of Planning, Design, Construction and Operation of Large Dam Projects." In T. Dorcey, ed., *Proceedings of the Workshop on 'Large Dams: Learning from the Past, Looking at the Future.'* IUCN, World Conservation Union, and World Bank Group; Gland, Switzerland; Cambridge, U.K. and Washington, D.C.

Pacheco, J., H. Reily, G. Kolb, and C. Tyner. 2000. "Summary of the Solar Two Test and Evaluation Program." In *Proceedings of the 10th SolarPACES International Symposium of Solar Thermal Concentrating Technologies, Solar Thermal 2000.* March 8–10, Sydney.

Patterson, W. 1999. *Transforming Electricity: The Coming Generation of Change.* Royal Institute of International Affairs. London: Earthscan.

PCAST (President's Committee of Advisors on Science and Technology). 1997. "Report to the President on Federal Energy Research and Development for the Challenges of the Twenty-first Century." Executive Office of the President of the United States, Panel on Energy Research and Development, Washington, D.C.

———. 1999. *Powerful Partnerships: The Federal Role in International Cooperation on Energy Innovation.* Executive Office of the President of the United States, Panel on International Cooperation in Energy Research, Development, Demonstration and Deployment, Washington, D.C.

Photon. 1999a. "The End of a Dream." *Photon* 1–99: 20–21.

———. 1999b. "World Ideas for PV Financing." *Photon* 1–99: 16–19.

Pikington. 1996. *Status Report on Solar Thermal Power Plants.* Cologne: Pikington Solar International.

Pratsch, L.W. 1996. "Geothermal, a Household Word by the Year 2000." *GRC Bulletin* 25: 25–31.

PVIR (Photovoltaic Insider's Report). 1999. *Photovoltaic Insider's Report.* 18 (2): 6.

Radja, V. 1997. "Strategy for Geothermal Energy Development in Indonesia Facing the Year 2000." In *Proceedings of NEDO International Geothermal Symposium.* Japan.

Randlov and others. 1994. "Final Report for JOULE Wave Energy Preliminary Actions." CEC DGXII, Brussels.

Rannels, J.E. 1998. Implementation and Financing for President Clinton's Million Solar Roofs Initiative. In J. Schmid and others, eds., *Proceedings of the Second World Conference and Exhibition on PV Solar Energy Conversion.* Report EUR 18656 EN. Brussels.

Ravindranath, N.H., and D.O. Hall. 1995. *Biomass, Energy and Environment: A Developing Country Perspective from India.* Oxford: Oxford University Press.

Rijk, P. 1994. *The Costs and Benefits of Willow (Salix) in Short Rotation for Niche Energy Markets in The Netherlands.* Agricultural Economics Institute (LEI-DLO), The Hague.

Rosillo-Calle, F., and L.A.B. Cortez. 1998. "Towards Pro-Alcool II: A Review of the Brazilian Bioethanol Programme." *Biomass and Bioenergy* 14 (2): 115–24.

Rosillo-Calle, F., M.A.A. de Rezende, P. Furtado, and D.O. Hall. 1996. *The Charcoal Dilemma: Finding a Sustainable Solution for Brazilian Industry.* Biomass Users Network. London: Intermediate Technology.

Rybach, L., and H.L. Goran. 1995. "Swiss Geothermal Energy Update." In *Proceedings the World Geothermal Congress 1995.*

Sastry, E.V.R. 1999. Personal communication. Ministry of Non-Conventional Energy Sources, Government of India.

Schainker, R.B. 1997 "Presentation to the PCAST Energy R&D Panel." Electric Power Research Institute, July 14. Palo Alto, Ca.

SERI (Solar Energy Research Institute). 1989. *Ocean Thermal Energy Conversion: An Overview.* SERI/SP-220-3024. Golden, Colo.

Shell. 1996. *The Evolution of the World's Energy Systems.* Shell International, Group External Affairs, London.

Solantausta, Y., T. Bridgewater, and D. Beckman. 1996. *Electricity Production by Advanced Biomass Power Systems.* Espoo, Finland: VTT Technical Research Centre of Finland.

Spath, P., M. Mann, and W. Amos. 2000. "Comparison of Gasification Technologies for Converting Biomass to Hydrogen." Paper prepared for the First World Conference on Biomass and Industry, June 5–9, Seville, Spain.

Stassen, H.E. 1995. *Small Scale Biomass Gasification for Heat and Power Production: A Global Review.* World Bank Technical Paper 296, Energy Series. Washington, D.C.

Stefansson, V., and I.B. Fridleifsson. 1998. "Geothermal Energy: European and World-wide Perspective." Paper presented at expert hearing on assessment and prospects for geothermal energy in Europe. Parliamentary Assembly of the Council of Europe, Sub-Committee on Technology Policy and Energy, Strasbourg, France.

SunLab. 1999. "Parabolic Trough Technology Roadmap." http://www.eren.doe.gov/sunlab/TechOverview.htm

TERI. (Tata Energy Research Institute). 1996/97. *TERI Energy Data Directory and Yearbook.* New Delhi.

Thomas, G.T., H.N. Post, and R. DeBlasio. 1999. "Photovoltaic Systems: An End-of-Millennium Review." *Progress in Photovoltaics: Research and Applications* 7: 1–19.

TNO. 1992. *Aandachtspunten voor componentenonderzoek en alternatieve zonneboilerconcepten.* TNO B-92-0969. Delft, Netherlands.

Tolbert, V., ed. 1998. "Environmental Effects of Biomass Crop Production: What Do We Know, What Do We Need to Know?" *Biomass and Bioenergy* 14 (4): 301–414.

Tsuo, Y.S., J.M. Gee, P. Menna, D.S. Strebkov, A. Pinov, and V. Zadde. 1998. "Environmentally Benign Silicon Solar Cell Manufacturing." In J. Schmid and others, eds., *Proceedings of the Second World Conference on PV Solar Energy Conversion.* Report EUR 18656. Brussels.

Turkenburg, W.C. 1992. "On the Potential and Implementation of Wind Energy." In *Proceedings of the European Wind Energy Conference.* Vol. 2. Amsterdam: Elsevier.

Turnure, J.T., S. Winnett, R. Shackleton, and W. Hohenstein. 1995. "Biomass Electricity: Long Run Economic Prospects and Climate Policy Implications." In *Proceedings of the Second Biomass Conference of the Americas.* Portland, Or.

U.S. DOE (Department of Energy). 1998a.. *Renewable Energy Annual.* Washington, D.C.

———. 1998b. *Renewable Energy Technology Characterizations.* Office of Utility Technologies, Washington, D.C.

U.S. DOE (Department of Energy), OGT (Office of Geothermal Technologies). 1998. *Strategic Plan for the Geothermal Energy Program.* Washington, D.C.

Vaessen, P. 1997. "The Influence of Decentral Generation on Reliability (in Dutch). " Hidde Nijland Symposium. Den Bosch, Netherlands.

van den Broek, R., and A. van Wijk. 1998. "Electricidad a partir de eucalipto y bagazo en ingenios azucareros de nicaragua: costos, aspectos macroeconomicos y medioambientales." Documento de trabajo FOPW/99/2. Food and Agriculture Organization of the United Nations, Rome.

van den Broek, R., A. Faaij, and A. van Wijk, 1996. "Biomass Combustion Power Generation Technologies." *Biomass and Bioenergy* 11 (4): 271–81.

van den Broek, R., A. Faaij, A.J.M. van Wijk, T. Kent, M. Bulfin, K. Healion, and G. Blaney. 1997. "Willow Firing in Retrofitted Irish Power Plants." *Biomass and Bioenergy* 12 (2): 75–90.

van der Leun, C. "Environmental Aspects of Material Use of SDHW Systems" (in Dutch). Utrecht, Netherlands: Ecofys.

Wijk, A.J.M. van, N. Halberg, and W.C. Turkenburg. 1992. "Capacity Credit of Wind Power in the Netherlands." *Electric Power Systems Research* 23 (3): 189–200.

Vasquez, N.C., and S.P. Javellana. 1997. "Present and Future Geothermal Development in the Philippines." In *Proceedings of the NEDO International Geothermal Symposium.* Sendai, Japan.

Verhoeven, S. 1999. "Two-way Traffic in the Electricity Grid and the Role of Power Electronics (in Dutch)." Paper presented at the STT Symposium Rapid Current: The Next Wave of Electrical Innovation, February 25, The Hague, Netherlands.

Voskens, R.G.J.H., and S. Carpenter. 1999. "Potential for Solar Drying in the World." Enermodal engineering, Canada / Ecofys, The Netherlands.

Walter, A., M.R. Souza, and R.P. Overend. 1998. "Preliminary Evaluation of Co-firing Biomass (Sugar-Cane Residues) and Natural Gas in Brazil." State University of Campinas, Mechanical Engineering College, Energy Division, Brazil; and National Renewable Energy Laboratory, Golden, Colo.

WEC (World Energy Council). 1994a. *Energy for Toworrow's World.* London: Kogan Page.

———. 1994b. *New Renewable Energy Resources: A Guide to the Future.* London: Kogan Page.

———. 1998. *Survey of Energy Resources 1998.* London.

Weinberg, C. 1995. "A New Age for Electricity: Integrating Technology into Business and Strategy." UNIPEDE (International Union of Producers and Distributors of Electric Energy), International Electrical Research Exchange, Monte-Carlo, Monaco.

Weise, E., R. Klockner, R. Kniehl, Ma Shenghong, and Qin Jianping. 1995. "Remote Power Supply Using Wind and Solar Energy: A Sino-German Technical Co-operation Project." In *Proceedings of the Beijing International Conference on Wind Energy.* Beijing.

Wentzel, M. 1995. "Solar Cooking: Problems, Perspectives and Possibilities." In *Proceedings Solar World Congress.* Harare, Zimbabwe.

Williams, R.H., and E.D. Larson. 1996. Biomass Gasifier Gas Turbine Power Generating Technology." *Biomass and Bioenergy* 10 (2–3): 149–66.

Williams, R.H., E.D. Larson, R.E. Katofsky, and J. Chen. 1995. "Methanol and Hydrogen from Biomass for Transportation, with Comparisons to Methanol and Hydrogen from Natural Gas and Coal." Princeton University, Centre for Energy and Environmental Studies, Princeton, N.J.

Winkelman, J.E. 1992. "De invloed van de SEP proef-windcentrale te Oosterbierum op Vogels: Aanvaringsslachtoffers." RIN-rapport 92/2. DLO-instituut voor Bos-en Natuuronderzoek, Arnhem, Netherlands.

Wiser, R., and Pickle S. 1997. "Financing Investments in Renewable Energy: The Role of Policy Design and Restructuring." Report LBNL-39826. Lawrence Berkeley National Laboratory, Environmental Energy Technologies Division, Calif.

World Atlas. 1998. 1998 World Atlas and Industry Guide. International Journal on Hydropower and Dams. Aqua-Media International, Sutton, U.K.

WRR (Wetenschappelijke Raad voor het Regeringsbeleid). 1992. *Ground for Choices: Four Perspectives for the Rural Areas in the European Community.* The Hague: Sdu uitgeverij.

Wyman, C.E., R.L. Bain, N.D. Hinman, and D.J. Stevens. 1993. "Ethanol and Methanol from Cellulosic Biomass." In T.B. Johansson J.H. Kelly, A.K.N. Reddy, R.H. Wiliams, and L. Burnham, *Renewable Energy: Sources for Fuels and Electricity.* Washington, D.C. Island Press.

YY. 1998. *Proceedings: Third European Wave Power Conference.* September–October, Patras,Greece.

advanced energy supply technologies

CHAPTER 8

Robert H. Williams (United States)

CONTRIBUTING AUTHORS: Matthew Bunn (United States), Stefano Consonni (Italy), William Gunter (Canada), Sam Holloway (United Kingdom), Robert Moore (United States), and Dale Simbeck (United States)

ABSTRACT	**Fossil energy technologies.** Sustainability principles indicate that fossil energy technologies should evolve towards the long-term goal of near-zero air pollutant and greenhouse gas emissions—without complicated end-of-pipe control technologies. Near-term technologies and strategies should support this long-term goal.

The technological revolution under way in power generation—where advanced systems are replacing steam turbine technologies—supports this long-term goal. Natural-gas-fired combined cycles offering low costs, high efficiency, and low environmental impacts are being chosen wherever natural gas is readily available. Cogeneration is more cost-effective and can play a much larger role in the energy economy if based on gas turbines and combined cycles rather than on steam turbines.

Reciprocating engines and emerging microturbine and fuel cell technologies are strong candidates for cogeneration at smaller scales. Coal gasification by partial oxidation with oxygen to make syngas (mainly carbon monoxide, CO, and hydrogen, H_2) makes it possible to provide electricity through integrated gasifier combined cycle plants with air pollutant emissions nearly as low as for those plants using natural gas combined cycles. Today power from integrated gasifier combined cycle cogeneration plants can often compete with power from coal steam-electric plants in either cogeneration or power-only configurations.

Although synthetic liquid fuels made in single-product facilities are not competitive, superclean syngas-derived synthetic fuels that are produced in polygeneration facilities making several products simultaneously may soon be. Syngas can be produced from natural gas by steam reforming or other means or from coal by gasification with oxygen. Expanding markets for clean synthetic fuels are likely to result from toughening air pollution regulations. Synthetic fuels produced through polygeneration will be based on natural gas, if it is readily available. In natural-gas-poor, coal-rich regions, polygeneration based on coal gasification is promising.

The barriers to widespread deployment of advanced cogeneration and polygeneration systems are mainly institutional. Most such systems will produce far more electricity than can be consumed on site, so achieving favourable economics depends on being able to sell coproduct electricity at competitive prices into electric grids. Utility policies have often made doing so difficult, but under the competitive market conditions towards which electric systems are evolving in many regions, cogeneration and polygeneration systems will often fare well.

Near-term pursuit of a syngas-based strategy could pave the way for widespread use of H_2 as an energy carrier, because for decades the cheapest way to make H_2 will be from fossil-fuel-derived syngas. Syngas-based power and H_2 production strategies facilitate the separation and storage of carbon dioxide from fossil energy systems, making it possible to obtain useful energy with near-zero emissions of greenhouse gases, without large increases in energy costs. Successful development of fuel cells would, in turn, facilitate introduction of H_2 for energy. Fuel cells are getting intense attention, because they offer high efficiency and near-zero air pollutant emissions. Automakers are racing to develop fuel cell cars, with market entry targeted for 2004–10.

Other advanced technologies not based on syngas offer some benefits relative to conventional technologies. But unlike syngas-based technologies, such options pursued in the near term would not offer clear paths to the long-term goal of near-zero emissions without significant increases in costs for energy services.

Nuclear energy technologies. World-wide, nuclear energy accounts for 6 percent of energy and 16 percent of electricity. Although it dominates electricity generation in some countries, its initial promise has not been realised. Most analysts project that nuclear energy's contribution to global energy will not grow and might decline in the near future. Nuclear power is more costly than originally expected, competition from alternative technologies is increasing, and there has been a loss of public confidence because of concerns relating to safety, radioactive waste management, and potential nuclear weapons proliferation.

Because nuclear power can provide energy without emitting conventional air pollutants and greenhouse gases, however, it is worth exploring whether advanced technologies might offer lower costs, restore public confidence in the safety of reactors, assure that nuclear programmes are not used for military purposes, and facilitate effective waste management.

In contrast to Chernobyl-type reactors, the light water reactors (LWRs) that dominate nuclear power globally have had a good safety record, though this has been achieved at considerable cost to minimise the risk of accidents.

The potential linkage between peaceful and military uses of nuclear energy was recognised at the dawn of the nuclear age. Steps taken to create a non-proliferation regime through treaties, controls on nuclear commerce, and safeguards on nuclear materials have kept peaceful and military uses separate. But if there is to be a major expansion of nuclear power, stronger institutional and technological measures will be needed to maintain this separation both for proliferation by nations and theft of weapons-usable materials by subnational groups.

Reactor vendors now offer several evolutionary LWRs with improved safety features and standardised designs, and there is some ongoing work on new reactor concepts.

Limited supplies of low-cost uranium might constrain LWR-based nuclear power development after 2050. Plutonium breeder reactors could address the resource constraint, but keeping peaceful and military uses of nuclear materials separate would be more challenging with breeders. Other possibilities for dealing with the resource constraint are extraction of uranium from seawater and thermonuclear fusion. There are many uncertainties regarding such advanced technologies, and all would take decades to develop.

Radioactive waste by-products of nuclear energy must be isolated so that they can never return to the human environment in harmful concentrations. Many in the technical community are confident that this objective can be met. But in most countries there is no consensus on waste disposal strategies. The current stalemate regarding waste disposal clouds prospects for nuclear expansion. ■

The arguments for marginal, incremental change are not convincing—not in this day and age. The future, after all, is not linear. History is full of sparks that set the status quo ablaze. —Peter Bijur, chief executive officer and chairman, Texaco, keynote speech to 17th Congress of World Energy Council, Houston, 14 September 1998

This chapter discusses advanced energy supply technologies with regard to their potential for facilitating the widespread use of fossil and nuclear energy sources in ways consistent with sustainable development objectives.[1] In each case the current situation is described, goals for innovation are formulated in the context of these objectives, near-term and long-term technology options are discussed in relation to these goals, and illustrative cost estimates are presented for options with reasonably well-understood costs.*

ADVANCED FOSSIL ENERGY TECHNOLOGIES

Fossil fuel supply considerations as a context for fossil energy innovation

Fossil energy technology development will be strongly shaped by energy supply security concerns and environmental challenges.

The emerging need for oil supplements in liquid fuel markets

Oil, the dominant fossil fuel, accounted for 44 percent of fossil fuel use in 1998. Although there is no imminent danger of running out of oil (chapter 5), dependence on oil from the Persian Gulf, where remaining low-cost oil resources are concentrated, is expected to grow. For example, the U.S. Energy Information Administration projects in its reference scenario that from 1997–2020, as global oil production increases by nearly 50 percent, the Persian Gulf's production share will increase from 27 to 37 percent (EIA, 1999a). This increase suggests the need to seek greater supply diversity in liquid fuel markets to reduce energy supply security concerns (chapter 4).

In addition, growing concerns about air quality are leading to increased interest in new fuels that have a higher degree of inherent cleanliness than traditional liquid fuels derived from crude oil, especially for transportation applications. To meet growing fluid fuel demand in the face of such constraints, some combination of a shift to natural gas and the introduction of clean synthetic fuels derived from various feedstocks (natural gas, petroleum residuals, coal, biomass) is likely to be needed to supplement oil during the next 25 years.

The oil crises of the 1970s catalysed major development efforts for synthetic fuels. For example, U.S. President Jimmy Carter's administration supported a synfuels programme that involved large government-supported commercialisation projects. Most such projects failed because the technologies were rendered uneconomic by the collapse of world oil prices in the mid-1980s. But, as will be shown, emerging synfuel technologies generally have better environmental characteristics and, when deployed through innovative multiple-energy-product (poly-generation) strategies, reasonably good economic prospects, even at relatively low oil price levels. Moreover, the private sector, rather than the government, is taking the lead in advancing these new technologies. The government's role has shifted from managing demonstration projects to supporting research and development that enables private-sector-led commercialisation and to helping remove institutional barriers to deployment.

Entering the age of gas

For natural gas, the cleanest, least-carbon-intensive fossil fuel, ultimately recoverable conventional resources are at least as abundant as for oil (chapter 5). Although the global consumption rate for gas is about half that for oil, the abundance of natural gas and its economic and environmental attractiveness have led it to play a growing role.[2] Since 1980 the share of natural gas in the global energy economy has grown, while oil and coal shares have declined. Wherever natural gas supplies are readily available, the natural-gas-fired gas-turbine–steam-turbine combined cycle (NGCC) has become the technology of choice for power generation, in which applications it is typically both the cleanest and least-costly fossil fuel option. As will be shown, clean natural-gas-derived synthetic fuels also have good prospects of beginning to compete in liquid fuels markets.

For developing countries, the huge investments needed for natural gas infrastructure (pipelines, liquid natural gas facilities) are daunting. But NGCC plants might be built as targeted initial gas users, using the revenues to facilitate infrastructure financing.

Alternatives to conventional gas might be needed to meet the growing demand for fluid fuels in 2025–50. Options include synthetic fluid fuels derived from coal and various unconventional natural gas resources (chapter 5).

Unconventional natural gas resources associated with methane hydrates are especially large, although the quantities that might be recoverable and delivered to major markets at competitive costs are highly uncertain (chapter 5). There is little private sector interest in better understanding the magnitude and cost dimensions of the methane hydrate resource, because conventional natural gas supplies

---

* Life-cycle costs are presented for an assumed 10 percent real (inflation-corrected) cost of capital (discount rate), neglecting corporate income and property taxes. Neglecting such taxes is appropriate in a global study such as this report, partly because tax codes vary markedly from country to country, and partly because such taxes are transfer payments rather than true costs. Moreover, such capital-related taxes discriminate against many capital-intensive technologies that offer promise in addressing sustainable development objectives. Including such taxes, annual capital charge rates—including a 0.5 percent a year insurance charge—are typically 15 percent for a plant with a 25-year operating life, in comparison with 11.5 percent when such taxes are neglected (U.S. conditions).

are abundant on time scales of interest to business.

An understanding of methane hydrate issues is important for decisions on near-term research and development priorities related to unconventional gas resource development versus coal synthetic fuels development. For this reason—as well as the theoretical potential of the hydrate resource and the attractions of natural gas as an energy carrier—the U.S. President's Committee of Advisors on Science and Technology has urged international collaborative research and development in this area, building on embryonic efforts in India, Japan, and Russia (PCAST Energy Research and Development Panel, 1997; PCAST Panel on ICERD[3], 1999).

The drawbacks and attractions of coal

Coal use is declining in most industrialised countries other than the United States, where use is expected to grow slowly. World-wide, coal use is expected to grow as fast as oil use, with much of the growth accounted for by China, whose global share might increase from 30 percent today to nearly 50 percent by 2020 (EIA, 1999a).

For coal, the dirtiest, most carbon-intensive fossil fuel, global resources are abundant (chapter 5). Coal is generally less costly than other fossil fuels. Substantial productivity gains have been made for coal production in both Australia and the United States (Williams, 1999b). Such gains can be expected in other regions once energy market reforms are put in place. Productivity gains have caused coal prices in the United States to decline by a factor of 2 since the early 1980s, to a level half that for natural gas.

During the next 20 years, a 20 percent rise in the price of natural gas and a 30 percent drop in the price of coal are expected in the United States (EIA, 1998a), leading to growth in the price ratio to 3.5. In Europe coal prices are not as low as in the United States, but even there the average price of coal imported into the European Union fell by more than a factor of 2 between 1983 and 1995 (Decker, 1999).

Although many regions are moving away from coal, this chapter shows that there are reasonable prospects that improved technology could propel a shift back to coal by making it feasible to provide from coal, at attractive costs, energy systems characterised by near-zero emissions of both air pollutants and greenhouse gases. Concerted efforts to develop and commercialise such technologies are desirable in light of the strategic importance of coal to coal-rich countries where conventional oil and natural gas resources are scarce (for example, China and India).

Setting goals for advanced fossil energy technologies

Designing advanced fossil energy technologies to be compatible with sustainable development requires that:

- Fossil energy be widely affordable.
- Fossil energy help satisfy development needs not now being met.
- Energy supply insecurity concerns be minimised.
- Adverse environmental impacts be acceptably low.
- For the longer term, emissions of carbon dioxide (CO_2) and other

greenhouse gases be sufficiently low to meet the objectives of the United Nations Framework Convention on Climate Change (UNFCC, 1992).[3]

If fossil fuels are to play major roles in facilitating sustainable development, all these objectives must be met simultaneously—which is impossible with today's technologies. Thus there is a need for substantial research, development, demonstration, and deployment programmes aimed at launching advanced, sustainable fossil energy technologies in the market. Because resources available to support energy innovation are scarce (and the fossil energy community must share these scarce resources with the end-use energy efficiency, renewable energy, and nuclear energy communities), criteria should be established for the long-term goals of the innovation effort. In addition, alternative technological strategies should be assessed with regard to their prospects for meeting these goals. This section introduces sustainable development goals for advanced fossil energy technologies. Later sections discuss the prospects for meeting these goals with alternative clusters of technologies.

The objective of making energy widely affordable is satisfied for most consuming groups with existing fossil energy technologies, which tend to be the least costly energy supplies. Addressing other sustainability objectives simultaneously will tend to increase costs. However, advanced technologies can help contain costs when these other objectives are also pursued. Moreover, as will be shown, new approaches to organising energy systems so that multiple products are made in a single facility—polygeneration strategies—can also lead to lower energy costs. The fossil energy technologies with the greatest potential to meet environmental goals are especially well-suited to polygeneration.

A key aspect of the objective of satisfying unmet energy needs for development involves giving the poor—especially the rural poor in developing countries—access to clean, modern energy carriers. Clean cooking fuels and electricity to satisfy basic needs are particularly important (chapters 2, 3, and 10). Advanced fossil energy technologies can help address these needs. Innovations in synthetic fuel technology, together with the attractive economics associated with deploying such technologies in polygeneration configurations, make the prospects for clean synthetic fuels much brighter today than they have been.

Some of the most promising synthetic fuels (such as dimethyl ether, or DME) are attractive energy carriers for serving both cooking fuel and transportation markets. The revolution in power-generating technology and the market reforms that are making small-scale power generation (reciprocating engines, microturbines, fuel cells) increasingly attractive economically in grid-connected power markets can also be deployed in remote rural markets, many of which are not currently served by grid electricity. Even in such markets where fossil fuels are not readily available, these systems can be adapted for use with locally available biomass resources in rural areas (Mukunda, Dasappa, and Srinivasa, 1993; Kartha, Kruetz, and Williams, 1997; Henderick, 1999; Henderick and Williams, 2000). Likewise,

The most formidable challenges facing the fossil energy system are likely to be achieving near-zero emissions of air pollutant and CO_2 emissions.

clean synthetic fuels for cooking can also be derived from biomass (Larson and Jin, 1999). Fossil energy technology advances have made biomass applications feasible for both small-scale power generation and synthetic cooking fuel production.

To a large extent, the objective of minimising energy supply insecurity concerns can be addressed with advanced fossil energy technologies by pursuing opportunities to diversify the supply base for fluid fuels. Especially promising are opportunities to make synthetic fluid fuels through polygeneration strategies—using petroleum residuals, natural gas, and coal as feedstocks as appropriate, depending on local resource endowments. And for the longer term, successful development of methane clathrate hydrate technology could lead to improved energy security for a number of economies that heavily depend on imported hydrocarbons but have large off-shore hydrate deposits (such as India, Japan, Republic of Korea, and Taiwan, China).

The objective of making adverse environmental impacts acceptably low requires addressing the question: how low is low enough? Among environmental impacts, air pollution effects are especially important, for developing and industrialised countries alike. Moreover, adverse health impacts of air pollution tend to dominate overall air pollution impacts (chapter 3).

For many developing countries, the cost of the environmental damage caused by air pollution is high even though per capita energy consumption is low—mainly because pollution controls are largely lacking.[4] Costs from air pollution are also high for industrialised countries with strong pollution controls,[5] not only because of much higher energy consumption but also because the cost of uncontrolled emissions grows much faster than energy consumption, given that economists measure these costs on the basis of willingness to pay to avoid these damages (chapter 3).[6] Tables 8.1 and 8.2 show that even low estimates of these damage costs are significant relative to typical direct economic costs (direct costs are $0.03–0.04 a kilowatt-hour for electricity and $0.20–0.30 a litre for transport fuels) for both coal power plants and for automobiles, but are low for modern natural gas power plants.[7]

Here it is assumed that a major long-term goal for advanced fossil energy technology that is implicit in the objective of making adverse environmental impacts acceptably low is near-zero air pollutant emissions—without the need for complicated and costly end-of-pipe control technologies. 'Near-zero emissions' is taken to mean emissions so low that residual environmental damage costs are a tiny fraction of the direct economic cost of energy. 'Long-term'

TABLE 8.1. EMISSION RATES FOR AND ESTIMATED COSTS OF ENVIRONMENTAL DAMAGE FROM AIR POLLUTANT EMISSIONS OF FOSSIL FUEL POWER PLANT (LOW VALUATION FOR TYPICAL EUROPEAN CONDITIONS)

Primary air pollutant	Emission rate (grams per kilowatt-hour)			Low estimate of costs of environmental damages (dollars per thousand kilowatt-hours)[a]				Environmental damage costs relative to NGCC
	SO_2	NO_x	PM_{10}	SO_2	NO_x	PM_{10}	Total	Total
Average U.S. coal steam-electric plant, 1997	6.10[b]	3.47[b]	0.16[c]	15.9	13.9	0.7	30.5	82
New coal steam-electric plant with best available control technology[d]	0.46	0.87	0.15[c]	1.2	3.5	0.6	5.3	14
Coal IGCC plant[e]	0.075	0.082	0.0025	0.20	0.33	0.01	0.54	1.5
NGCC plant[f]	—	0.092	—	—	0.37	—	0.37	1.0

a. Environmental damage costs from power plant air pollutant emissions are assumed to be 25 percent of the median estimates of Rabl and Spadaro (2000) for typical power plant sitings in Europe. (The Rabl and Spadaro calculations were carried out under the European Commission's ExternE Programme. Nearly all the estimated costs of environmental damages are associated with adverse health impacts; the economic values of health impacts were estimated on the basis of the principle of willingness to pay to avoid adverse health effects.) Rabl and Spadaro considered a wide range of pollutants, but the only significant damage costs were from SO_2, NO_x, and PM_{10}, for which their median estimates of damage costs (in dollars per kilogram) were $10.44, $16.00, and $17.00. Damage costs at 25 percent of the median estimates of Rabl and Spadaro (equivalent to one standard deviation below the median) are assumed, to put a conservatism into the calculation to reflect the scientific uncertainty. b. Average emission rates in 1997 for U.S. coal plants, whose average efficiency was 33 percent (EIA, 1998b). c. In 1990 PM_{10} emissions from U.S. electric utility coal power plants amounted to 245,000 tonnes (Spengler and Wilson, 1996) when these plants consumed 17.1 exajoules of coal (EIA, 1998b), so the PM_{10} emission rate was 14.34 grams per gigajoule—the assumed emission rate for all steam-electric cases in this table. d. It is assumed that the new coal steam-electric plant is 35.5 percent efficient; that the coal contains 454 grams of sulphur per gigajoule (1.08 percent sulphur by weight), the average for U.S. coal power plants in 1997 (EIA, 1998b); that SO_2 emissions are reduced 95 percent, a commercially feasible rate; and that the NO_x emission rate is 86 grams per gigajoule—achievable with advanced low-NO_x burners that will be commercially available shortly; e. It is assumed that the coal integrated gasifier combined cycle (IGCC) plant is 43.8 percent efficient, based on use of steam-cooled gas turbines (see table 8.4); that the emission rates equal the measured values for the Buggenum coal IGCC plant (Netherlands): 10.0 and 0.3 grams per gigajoule of coal for NO_x and particulates, respectively, as well as 99 percent sulphur recovery (data presented by Co van Liere, KEMA, at the Gasification Technologies Conference in San Francisco, 17–20 October 1999); and that the coal contains 454 grams of sulphur per gigajoule. f. It is assumed that the natural gas combined cycle (NGCC) plant is 54.1 percent efficient, based on use of steam-cooled gas turbines (see table 8.4); and that the NO_x emission rate is 9 parts per million on a dry volume basis (at 15 percent O_2), corresponding to an emission rate of 0.092 grams per kilowatt-hour.

TABLE 8.2. EMISSION RATES FOR AND ESTIMATED COSTS OF ENVIRONMENTAL DAMAGE FROM AIR POLLUTANT EMISSIONS OF AUTOMOBILES (LOW VALUATION FOR TYPICAL FRENCH CONDITIONS)

Fuel and driving environment	Fuel economy (kilometres per litre)	Emission rate (grams per kilometre)		Low estimate of costs of environmental damages, EU conditions[a] (dollars)							
				Per kilogram		Per thousand kilometres of driving			Per thousand litres of fuel consumed		
		NO_x	PM	NO_x	PM	NO_x	PM	Total[b]	NO_x	PM	Total[b]
Gasoline[c]											
Urban[d]	8.7	0.68	0.017	5.5	690	3.7	11.7	16.6	32	102	144
Rural[d]	10.3	0.79	0.015	6.8	47	5.4	0.71	7.3	56	7.3	75
Diesel											
Urban[d]	10.4	0.75	0.174	5.5	690	4.1	120	125	43	1250	1300
Rural[d]	12.7	0.62	0.150	6.8	47	4.2	7.1	12.5	53	90	159

a. Environmental damage costs from automotive air pollutant emissions are assumed to be 25 percent of the median estimates presented in Spadaro and Rabl (1999) and Spadaro and others (1998)—calculations carried out under the European Commission's ExternE Programme. Nearly all the estimated costs of environmental damages are associated with adverse health impacts; the economic values of health impacts were estimated on the basis of the principle of willingness to pay to avoid adverse health effects. Damage costs at 25 percent of the mean estimates in these studies (equivalent to one standard deviation below the median) are assumed, to put a conservatism into the calculation to reflect the scientific uncertainty. b. Total costs per kilometre include, in addition to costs associated with NO_x and PM emissions, costs associated with emissions from CO, volatile organic compounds (VOC), SO_2, and benzo-a-pyrene (BaP). c. For a gasoline internal combustion engine car equipped with a catalytic converter. d. Urban cost estimates are for driving around Paris, where the average population density is 7,500 per square kilometre. Rural costs estimates are for a trip from Paris to Lyon, for which the average density of the population exposed to the automotive air pollution is 400 per square kilometre.

is defined as 2015 and beyond. Thus the goal of near-zero emissions is a target for energy innovation (research, development, demonstration, early deployment) rather than a near-term regulatory goal. There are five readily identifiable reasons for setting such an ambitious goal for emissions.

First, air pollution damage costs are associated largely with small-particle pollution, for which there appears to be no threshold below which the pollution is safe (chapter 3). Second, the trend has been towards continually more stringent controls on emissions in industrialised countries, both as a result of improved knowledge of adverse impacts and of increasing societal demands for cleaner air as incomes rise. But meeting air quality goals by continually ratcheting up the required end-of-pipe controls has proven very costly—both because the cost of reducing emissions by the next increment tends to increase sharply with the level of reduction, and because the continual technological change required to keep up with evolving regulatory goals can be very costly when there is not enough time between changes in regulations to recover the cost of the last incremental improvement before the next one must be made.

Third, regulations calling for ever tighter end-of-pipe controls on emissions are sometimes not nearly as effective in meeting air quality goals as they are supposed to be, as is illustrated by the wide gap between actual emission levels and regulated emission levels for U.S. cars—a gap that has been projected to increase in the future, as regulations tighten (table 8.3).[8] Fourth, even for developing countries, the long-term near-zero emissions goal makes sense, because much of the energy technology that will be put into place in the period 2015–25 will still be operating decades later when incomes and societal desires for clean air will be high.[9] And fifth, there are promising technological options for converting the near

zero emissions goal into reality. For example, managers of the U.S. Department of Energy's fossil energy programme have enough confidence in this idea to have created a new programme that seeks to develop new fossil energy technologies by 2015 that are characterised, among other things, by near-zero air pollutant emissions, as well as zero solid and liquid waste discharges.[10]

The challenge of setting goals with regard to the objective of preventing dangerous anthropogenic interference with the climate system is complicated by the fact that there is not yet agreement in the global community as to the level at which atmospheric CO_2 should be stabilised. However, the level that is eventually decided on is likely to be far below the level to which the world would evolve for an energy system that would follow a business-as-usual path. The IS92a scenario of the Intergovernmental Panel on Climate Change might be considered a business-as-usual energy future (IPCC, 1995). In this scenario the CO_2 emission rate grows from 7.5 gigatonnes of carbon (GtC) in 1990 (6.0 GtC from fossil fuel burning plus 1.5 GtC from deforestation) to 20 GtC in 2100. By way of contrast, stabilisation at twice the pre-industrial CO_2 level (550 parts per million by volume, a target favoured by various groups) would require reducing annual fossil energy emissions to 5.5 GtC by 2100. Stabilisation at 450 parts per million by volume (up from 360 parts per million by volume today) would require emissions falling to about 2.5 GtC by 2100 (DOE, 1999).

Many believe that coping adequately with the challenge of climate change will require major shifts to renewable energy sources, nuclear energy sources, or both. Although such shifts might be desirable for a variety of reasons, climate change concerns do not necessarily require a major shift away from fossil fuels. To be sure, the dimensions of the challenge are such that the deep reductions in CO_2 emissions that might be required during the next 100 years cannot be achieved only by making efficiency improvements in fossil energy conversion, however desirable energy efficiency improvements might be. But energy efficiency improvement is not the only option for reducing CO_2 emissions from fossil fuels. The energy content of these fuels can also be recovered while preventing the release of CO_2 into the atmosphere—for example, by separating out the CO_2 and sequestering it in geological formations or in the deep ocean.

There is growing optimism in the scientific and technological communities that fossil energy systems can be made compatible with a world of severely constrained greenhouse gas emissions (Socolow, 1997). This optimism is reflected in new fossil energy research and development programmes (for example, in Japan, Norway, and the United States) that aim to achieve near-zero emissions from fossil energy systems. As will be shown, even with some already developed technologies it appears feasible to achieve deep reductions in CO_2 emissions without large increases in fossil energy costs. Although uncertainties regarding storage security and potentially adverse environmental impacts (especially for ocean sequestration) must be resolved before a high degree of confidence can be assigned to this option, there is growing scientific confidence that the potential for sequestering CO_2 is vast.

How can such considerations be used to frame goals for advanced fossil energy technologies that are consistent with the UN Framework Convention on Climate Change, when global society has not yet decided what goal is needed? In light of the long lead times required to bring new technologies to market at large scales, and considering that energy research and development is cheap insurance for addressing the climate change challenge (PCAST Energy Research and Development Panel, 1997), it is assumed here that a major element of the overall fossil energy innovation effort should be to develop the capacity to achieve deep reductions in CO_2 and other greenhouse gases. Thus, if global society eventually decides that deep reductions are needed, the fossil energy community will be prepared to respond with advanced technologies and strategies. As with air pollution, the goal of reducing greenhouse gas emissions to near zero is a target for capacity development through technological innovation over the long term, rather than for near-term regulations.

Of the challenges facing the fossil energy system in moving towards sustainable development, the most formidable are likely to be near-zero emissions of air pollutants and CO_2. Consequently, these two challenges are given the greatest emphasis in the following sections.

Technologies and strategies for moving towards near-zero emissions

This section describes fossil energy technologies and strategies that offer considerable promise to meet all the sustainable development criteria set forth in the previous section, including, for the longer term, the especially daunting criteria of near-zero emissions of both air pollutants and greenhouse gases. Near-zero emissions could be achieved in the long term if the dominant energy carriers were electricity and hydrogen (H_2). The importance of having H_2 as an option complementing electricity as an energy carrier is discussed in box 8.1.

Here technologies are first discussed for power generation and then for synthetic fuels production. Key near-term strategies to hasten the widespread use of these technologies are cogeneration (combined heat and power) and polygeneration, which entails the simultaneous production of various combinations of synthetic fuels, electricity, process heat, and chemicals. Cogeneration and polygeneration offer favourable economics that can facilitate the industrial development of energy production technology based on synthesis gas (a mixture of gases consisting mainly of CO and H_2), which will subsequently be called syngas. Syngas is a key intermediate energy product that makes it possible to make many clean final energy products from fossil fuels—including, for the longer term, H_2.

TABLE 8.3. ESTIMATED COSTS OF ENVIRONMENTAL DAMAGE FROM NO_X EMISSIONS OF AUTOMOBILES (LOW VALUATION FOR TYPICAL FRENCH CONDITIONS, ASSUMING U.S. REGULATED AND ESTIMATED ACTUAL EMISSION LEVELS)

Model year	NO_X emission rate (grams per kilometre)		Estimated environmental damage cost (dollars per thousand kilometres, low estimate, French conditions; 55 percent urban + 45 percent rural driving, so that average cost = $6.1 per kilogram)[a]		New car fuel economy (kilometres per litre)	Estimated environmental damage costs (dollars per thousand litres of gasoline)	
	Regulated level	Estimated actual level[b]	Emissions at regulated level	Estimated actual emissions		Emissions at regulated level	Estimated actual emissions
1993	0.62	1.1	4	7	11.8	45	79
2000	0.25	0.8	2	5	11.9	18	58
2010	0.12	0.5	1	3	12.8	9	39

a. Low estimates of the costs of environmental damages for NO_X emissions from gasoline-powered automobiles operated under French conditions (from table 8.2): $5.5 per kilogram for urban areas and $6.8 per kilogram for rural areas. For regions other than France, costs at the same per capita GDP levels will scale roughly according to the regional population density. b. From Ross, Goodwin, and Watkins, 1995.

BOX 8.1. THE STRATEGIC IMPORTANCE OF HYDROGEN AS AN ENERGY CARRIER

For the long term, it is desirable that the energy system be based largely on inherently clean energy carriers. Like electricity, during its use hydrogen (H_2) generates zero or near-zero emissions of air pollutants and CO_2. And, as for electricity, it can be produced from fossil fuels as well as from non-carbon-based primary energy sources through various processes characterised by near-zero emissions of air pollutants and CO_2 (see the section below on enhancing prospects for H_2).

The importance of having H_2 as well as electricity as an inherently clean energy carrier stems from the difficulty of using electricity efficiently and cost-effectively in some important markets such as transportation. In principle, near-zero emissions could be realised throughout the energy economy with electricity, which accounts for a third of global CO_2 emissions from burning fossil fuels. In practice, however, for most applications electricity use is limited mainly to systems that can be supplied with electricity relatively continuously from stationary sources, because of the difficulties that have been encountered in evolving suitable cost-competitive electricity storage technologies.

Consider that although the zero-emissions mandate for cars in California was focused initially on developing battery-powered electric cars, the goal of producing light-weight, low-cost batteries with adequate range between rechargings has proven an elusive technological challenge; this difficulty is one of the factors that has resulted in refocusing much of the zero-emission-vehicle quest on fuel cells, with the expectation that ultimately fuel cell vehicles will be fuelled with H_2. Although storing H_2 onboard vehicles is more difficult than storing liquid fuels, providing enough low-cost storage capacity to reduce refuelling rates to acceptable levels for consumers is a far less daunting challenge for H_2 than for electricity.

More generally, development of near-zero-emitting H_2 energy systems is desirable because modellers expect, under business-as-usual conditions, major continuing high demand levels for fluid (liquid and gaseous) fuels and high levels of CO_2 emissions associated with fluid fuels production and use. Consider, for example, the reference IS92a scenario (IPCC, 1995). Although electricity's share of worldwide secondary energy consumption grows from 15 percent in 1990 to 28 percent in 2100, the fluid fuel share is only slightly less in 2100 than in 1990 (57 versus 64 percent) in the IS92a scenario.

Moreover, because of the projected rapidly growing importance of synthetic fuels after 2050, fluid fuel production accounts for 60 percent of IS92a's 20 GtC of total energy-related CO_2 emissions in 2100, up from 47 percent of the 6 GtC of total energy-related CO_2 emissions in 1990. Thus, even if electricity generation could be made 100 percent free of CO_2 emissions by 2100 (through a shift of projected fossil electric generation to some mix of renewable energy, nuclear energy, and decarbonised fossil energy), emissions in 2100 would still be double those of 1990 (even though CO_2-neutral biomass produced at a rate equivalent to more than half of total primary energy use in 1990 provides a third of total synthetic fuels in 2100).

Having available H_2 as well as electricity provided by production systems with near-zero emissions would provide society with the capacity to achieve, in the longer term, deep reductions in CO_2 emissions from the fluid fuel sectors as well as from the electric sector, and thereby help make it possible to limit the CO_2 level in the atmosphere to twice the pre-industrial level or less in response to climate change concerns.

Advanced technologies for power generation and cogeneration

Promising advanced power generation and cogeneration technologies for the near (less than 5 years) to medium (5–15 years) term include natural-gas-fired gas-turbine-based technologies, coal integrated gasifier combined cycle (IGCC) technologies, small engines suitable for distributed cogeneration applications, and various fuel cell technologies.

Natural-gas- and gas-turbine-based technologies. The pace of technological change has been brisk for gas turbines,[11] to the point where efficiencies are now comparable to those for coal steam-electric plants, even though turbine exhaust gas temperatures are high. To avoid wasting exhaust gas heat, gas turbines used in central-station power plants for purposes other than meeting peak loads are typically coupled through heat recovery steam generators to steam turbines in gas turbine–steam turbine combined cycles.

Table 8.4 presents cost and performance characteristics of two NGCC units: a 50 percent efficient* Frame 7F unit (commercially available) equipped with air-cooled gas turbine blades and a 54 percent efficient Frame 7H unit (available in 2000 or after) equipped with steam-cooled turbine blades.[12] In competitive power markets, installed costs of NGCCs have fallen to less than $500 per kilowatt-electric. For typical U.S. and European fuel prices, modern NGCCs can provide electricity at lower cost and about 60 percent less CO_2 emissions per kilowatt-hour than coal steam-electric plants (see table 8.4).

Thermal nitrogen oxide (NO_x) generated in the combustor by oxidising nitrogen from the air at high flame temperatures is the only significant air pollutant arising from NGCC operation. But even in areas with tight regulations on NO_x emissions,[13] modern NGCCs are often able to meet regulatory requirements without having to install costly end-of-pipe controls, by premixing fuel and air for the combustor and thereby avoiding high flame temperatures. With this technology, NO_x emissions per kilowatt-hour are only 10 percent of those for coal steam-electric plants equipped with the best available control technology, and overall costs of pollution damages from NGCCs are one-fourteenth of those for coal plants equipped with the best available control technology (see table 8.1).

Opportunities for innovation are not exhausted. One option is to eliminate entirely the relatively capital-intensive steam turbine in a so-called Tophat® cycle that involves heating air exiting the compressor with turbine exhaust heat and spray intercooling during compression (van Liere, 1998). By injecting a mist of fine water particles into the compressor to cool the air during compression (using hot water produced from turbine exhaust heat), compressor work requirements are greatly reduced, and net turbine output and efficiency are increased.[14]

One study applying the Tophat® concept to a redesign of a modern aeroderivative gas turbine estimated that the gas turbine output would increase from 47 to 104 megawatts-electric, the efficiency would increase from 36.5 to 52.2 percent (almost to the level for the 400-megawatt-electric Frame 7H NGCC; see table 8.4), and NO_x emissions would be substantially reduced. The capital cost per kilowatt-electric for such a unit is expected to be less than for NGCCs (van Liere, 1998).[15]

In addition, during the next 10 years, system efficiencies might increase further to levels of nearly 60 percent, as technological advances make it possible for turbine inlet temperatures to move up to about 1,500 degrees Celsius, and various cycle configurations (for example, reheating and intercooling) are exploited (Chiesa and others, 1993).

---

*Efficiencies in this chapter are expressed on a higher heating value (HHV) basis unless explicitly indicated otherwise.

TABLE 8.4. PERFORMANCE, GENERATION COSTS, AND CO₂ EMISSION RATES FOR ALTERNATIVE CONVENTIONAL FOSSIL FUEL POWER PLANTS

Performance, costs, and emission rates[a]	Pulverised coal steam-electric plant with flue gas desulphurisation	Coal integrated gasifier combined cycle (IGCC) plant		Natural gas combined cycle (NGCC) plant	
		Air-cooled turbine	Steam-cooled turbine	Air-cooled turbine	Steam-cooled turbine
Plant capacity (megawatts)	500	500	400	506	400
Efficiency (percent, higher heating value [HHV] basis)	35.5	40.1	43.8	50.2	54.1
Installed capital cost (dollars per kilowatt)	1090	1320	1091	468	445
Generation cost components (dollars per thousand kilowatt-hours)					
Capital charges[b]	17.9	21.7	17.9	7.7	7.3
Fixed operation and maintenance	2.3	2.8	3.0	2.3	2.3
Variable operation and maintenance	2.0	2.0	2.1	1.5	1.5
Fuel					
Typical U.S. fuel price[c]	10.1	9.0	8.2	19.4	18.0
Typical European fuel price[c]	17.2	15.3	14.0	22.9	21.3
Total generation cost (dollars per thousand kilowatt-hours)					
Typical U.S. fuel price[c]	32.3	35.5	31.2	30.9	29.1
Typical European fuel price[c]	39.4	41.8	37.0	34.4	32.4
CO₂ emission rate (grams of carbon per kilowatt-hour)[d]	238	210	193	98	91

a. Plant capacities, installed capital costs, operation and maintenance costs, and plant efficiencies are from Todd and Stoll (1997). Combined cycle plants with air-cooled and steam-cooled gas turbine blades involve use of General Electric Frame 7F (commercial) and Frame 7H (near commercial) gas turbines, respectively.
b. Capital charges are calculated assuming a 10 percent discount rate, a 25-year plant life, and an insurance rate of 0.5 percent a year, and neglecting corporate income taxes, so that the annual capital charge rate is 11.5 percent. It is assumed that all power plants are operated at an average capacity factor of 80 percent.
c. For the United States: coal and natural gas prices of $1.00 and $2.70 per gigajoule, respectively (average prices projected by the U.S. Energy Information Administration for electric generators in 2010; EIA, 1998a). For Europe: prices for electric generators of $1.70 per gigajoule for coal (average for OECD countries in 1997) and $3.20 per gigajoule for natural gas (average for Finland, Germany, Netherlands, and United Kingdom for 1997). d. The carbon contents of coal and natural gas are assumed to be 23.4 kilograms of carbon per gigajoule and 13.7 kilograms of carbon per gigajoule, respectively.

If there are opportunities for using steam (for example, in support of an industrial process), hot gas turbine exhaust gases can be used to produce this steam in cogeneration configurations. Combined cycles can also be used for cogeneration—for example, by installing a back-pressure steam turbine instead of a condensing steam turbine with the gas turbine. With a back-pressure turbine, the high-quality steam produced from the gas turbine exhaust heat is first used to produce some electricity, and subsequently the lower quality steam discharged in the steam turbine exhaust is used for process applications. For such a system the ratio of produced electricity to process steam is higher than for a simple cycle gas turbine (figure 8.1).

Cogeneration is especially important in the near term for rapidly industrialising countries. Because these countries are in the early stages of building their infrastructure, their process-heat-intensive, basic-materials-processing industries are growing rapidly. Rapidly growing steam loads represent important resource bases for cogeneration, so that these industries have the potential of becoming major providers of clean, cost-competitive power. In this context, cogeneration systems employing gas turbines and combined cycles equipped with back-pressure turbines provide several times as much electricity per unit of process steam as systems based on simple back-pressure turbines (figure 8.1). These and other cogeneration technologies characterised by high output ratios of electricity to steam (for example, reciprocating internal combustion engines and fuel cells) make it

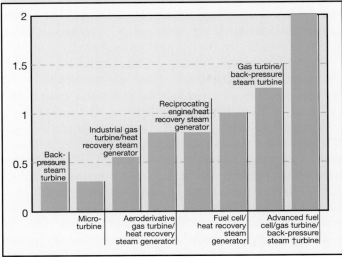

FIGURE 8.1. OUTPUT RATIOS OF POWER (KILOWATTS-ELECTRIC) TO HEAT (KILOWATTS-THERMAL) FOR ALTERNATIVE COGENERATION TECHNOLOGIES

Note: Ratios are for systems producing 10 bar steam. All steam turbines are back-pressure steam turbines with no steam condenser.

Source: Simbeck, 1999b.

TABLE 8.5. COGENERATION VERSUS SEPARATE PRODUCTION OF ELECTRICITY AND STEAM USING NATURAL GAS COMBINED CYCLES

Rates of activity and costs	Separate production facilities for electricity and steam			Cogeneration facility
	Electricity	Steam	Total	
Power generation rate (megawatts-electric)	400	—	400	400
Process steam production rate, 10-15 bar (megawatts-thermal)	—	400	400	400
Natural gas input rate (terajoules per hour)	2.66	1.77	4.43	3.48
First Law efficiency (percent)	54.1	81.1	64.9	82.8
CO_2 emission rate (tonnes per hour)	132	88	220	172
Capital investment (millions of dollars)	166	48	214	194
Energy production cost (dollars per thousand kilowatt-hours) Capital Operation and maintenance (4 percent of capital cost per year) Fuel Credit for cogenerated steam (at $14.7 per thousand kilowatt-hours of steam)	 6.8 2.4 18.0 —	 2.0 0.7 12.0 —	 — — — —	 8.0 2.8 23.5 -14.7
Total (net) production cost (dollars per thousand kilowatt-hours)	27.2	14.7	—	19.6
Annual cost of energy (millions of dollars)	76.3	41.2	117.5	55.0+41.2
Cost of CO_2 emissions avoided (dollars per tonne of carbon)	—	—	—	-$232

Note: Based on calculations by Dale Simbeck, SFA Pacific. Engineering and contingencies and general facilities are each 10 percent of process capital equipment costs. The annual capital charge rate is 11.5 percent. The natural gas price is $2.70 per gigajoule (see note c, table 8.4). The annual average capacity factor equals 80 percent. The combined cycle plant assumed for both power only and cogeneration applications is the unit with steam-cooled gas turbine blades analysed in table 8.4.

possible for cogeneration to play a far greater role in power generation than is feasible with steam-turbine technology.[16]

An example of cogeneration with NGCC technology and equal quantities of electric and steam power is described in table 8.5. For this system, the fuel required is a fifth less and the net cost of electricity is a quarter less per kilowatt-hour than for electricity and heat production in separate facilities. Moreover, net costs for CO_2 emissions reduction are strongly negative at −$230 per tonne of carbon relative to costs for systems that produce these products singly!

Cogeneration systems based on combined cycles and other high electricity and steam output ratio technologies will typically lead to far more electricity generated than the host factory can consume (Williams, 1978). Entrepreneurs will not be motivated to deploy such technologies unless they are able to sell into the grid electricity produced at fair market rates. Existing electric-sector policies in many countries discourage such sales—for example, electric companies often will not purchase cogenerated power at market rates or will charge exorbitant fees for back-up service. But other countries have adopted policies encouraging cogeneration. In competitive power markets, cogenerators would typically do well (see table 8.5).

A final note: NGCC economic and environmental benefits in power and cogeneration markets are so attractive that countries with constrained natural gas supplies (such as China and India) should consider introducing NGCC plants as anchor users for natural gas

supplies that might be introduced transnationally, using NGCC power generation and cogeneration revenues to underwrite pipeline and other gas infrastructure costs.

Oxygen-blown coal gasification and integrated gasifier combined cycle technologies. Gasification technology makes it possible to extend to coal the economic, thermodynamic, and environmental benefits of combined cycles in the form of IGCC power plants. Gasifiers can be oxygen-blown (O_2) or air-blown. All commercial units are O_2-blown, although some systems based on air-blown units are being demonstrated. The focus here is on systems with O_2-blown gasifiers; systems with air-blown gasifiers are discussed below.

Since the demonstration of IGCC technology with the 94-megawatt-electric Coolwater Project in southern California (1984–89), there has been much progress relating to its commercialisation. Table 8.6 lists five large commercial-scale coal IGCC plants around the world that produce electricity or electricity and steam (cogeneration), as well as nine other large commercial projects that involve gasification of petroleum residues to coproduce electricity with H_2, syngas, or steam.[17] If all the syngas capacity in these 14 plants (9,825 megawatts-thermal) were dedicated to power generation, the equivalent electric generating capacity would be about 5,300 megawatts-electric.

Pollutant emission levels for coal IGCCs can be nearly as low as for NGCCs—much less than for coal steam-electric plants.

Environmental damage costs associated with emission levels equivalent to those measured at the Buggenum plant in the Netherlands are less than 2 percent of such costs for average coal-fired power plants in the United States and about 10 percent of such costs for coal steam-electric plants equipped with the best available control technology (see table 8.1). Deep reductions in emissions are feasible because pollutants are recovered in concentrated form from the fuel gas (syngas) leaving the gasifier—undiluted by the large amounts of nitrogen from combustion air that are present in flue gases, from which air pollutants are recovered for conventional power plants.

IGCC technology also offers solid waste management advantages. Most direct combustion processes recover sulphur from flue gases as a nonmarketable wet scrubber sludge or as a dry spent sulphur sorbent (the by-product gypsum can be marketed). For such systems, solid wastes are more difficult to handle and market or dispose of, and volumes to be managed are two to three times those for IGCC systems, which recover a marketable elemental sulphur by-product.[18]

The cost of electricity for IGCC technology is somewhat higher than for coal steam-electric plants (compare Frame 7F IGCC and steam-electric plant costs in table 8.4)—when credit is not given

Growing concerns about air quality are leading to increased interest in new fuels that have a higher degree of inherent cleanliness than traditional liquid fuels derived from crude oil.

for the environmental benefits, which would probably tip the balance decisively in favour of IGCC (see table 8.1). New turbine technology based on the use of steam-cooled turbine blades (Frame 7H technology) could tip the balance slightly in favour of IGCC, even without environmental credits (see table 8.4). But the direct economic benefits are likely to be too small to convince users to shift from familiar technology to any new technology, with all the attendant risks associated with its adoption. The user will take such risks only if forced to (for example, by environmental regulations) or because the economic benefits would be decisive.

O_2-blown coal gasification probably has a better chance of being launched in the market through applications other than power-only—for example, cogeneration. Table 8.7 illustrates the advantages offered by IGCC-based cogeneration. For this system, fuel requirements are reduced one fifth and the net electricity generation cost is reduced one fourth relative to electricity and steam production in separate facilities (as in the corresponding natural gas case—see table 8.5).

Of course, cogeneration strategies can also be pursued with conventional steam turbine technology. However, as illustrated by the calculation in table 8.8 for the same levels of electricity and

TABLE 8.6. LARGE COMMERCIAL GASIFICATION-BASED PROJECTS INVOLVING ELECTRICITY AS PRODUCT OR COPRODUCT

Location	Plant owner	Technology	Syngas out (megawatts-thermal)	Feedstock(s)	Product(s)	Start-up year
Spain	Repsol and Iberola	Texaco	1,654	Vacuum residues	Electricity	2004
Italy	SARLUX srl	Texaco	1,067	Visbreaker residues	Electricity, H_2	2000
Italy	ISAB Energy	Texaco	982	ROSE asphalt	Electricity, H_2	1999
France	Total France, EdF, and Texaco	Texaco	895	Fuel oil	Electricity, H_2	2003
Netherlands	Shell Nederland Raffinaderij BV	Shell	637	Visbreaker residues	Electricity, H_2	1997
Czech Republic	SUV and EGT	Lurgi Dry Ash	636	Coal	Electricity, steam	1996
United States	Public Service of Indiana	Destec	591	Bituminous Coal	Electricity	1995
Spain	Elcogas SA	PRENFLO	588	Coal, petcoke	Electricity	1997
United States	Motiva Enterprises LLC	Texaco	558	Fluid petcoke	Electricity, steam	1999
Italy	API Raffineria de Ancona S.p.A.	Texaco	496	Visbreaker residues	Electricity	1999
Netherlands	Demkolec BV	Shell	466	Bituminous Coal	Electricity	1994
United States	Tampa Electric Company	Texaco	455	Coal	Electricity	1996
United States	Exxon USA Inc.	Texaco	436	Petcoke	Electricity, syngas	2000
Singapore	Esso Singapore Pty. Ltd.	Texaco	364	Residual oil	Electricity, H_2	2000

Source: Simbeck and Johnson, 1999.

process steam generation as in the IGCC case,[19] the fuel savings rate (5 percent) and the reduction in the net cost of electricity (9 percent) are far less than for the IGCC case. Moreover, a comparison of tables 8.7 and 8.8 shows that although there is little difference in efficiency and cost for IGCC and ultrasupercritical steam turbine technologies in producing electricity only, IGCC technology is a markedly better performer in cogeneration applications.

Once gasification technology is established in the market, a continuing stream of innovations can be expected to improve performance and reduce costs—because there are many opportunities (van der Burgt, 1998; Holt, 1999a). One way innovation will take place is by relatively passively incorporating continually improving gas turbine designs into IGCC systems—the benefits of which are illustrated by the shift from air-cooled to steam-cooled gas turbine blades in table 8.4. And if Tophat® turbines are developed (see above), such systems used with gasified coal would be both less capital-intensive and more energy-efficient than current IGCC systems—for example, van der Burgt and van Liere (1996) estimate that with such cycles overall efficiency would increase to about 50 percent.

Specific IGCC-related improvements might also be made. For example, new gasifiers are needed that are well suited for coals with high ash content (typical of many coals in China, India, and South Africa) and for low-rank coals (which are abundant world-wide; see chapter 5), because commercially available entrained-flow gasifiers are not well suited for such coals. Fluidised-bed gasifiers are good candidates for these coals; such gasifiers would also be better suited for handling most biomass and waste as co-feedstocks than are entrained-flow gasifiers. Such technology, in the form of the High Temperature Winkler gasifier, was demonstrated with brown coal at a plant in Berrenrath, Germany, where the syngas was used to produce methanol (Simbeck and others, 1993). An IGCC project based on the High Temperature Winkler gasifier for coal fines has been proposed for construction in the Czech Republic (Holt, 1999b).

One research and development focus is technology to clean gases at high temperatures to reduce thermodynamic losses associated with thermal cycling of gases exiting the gasifier.[20] Such technology is being pursued largely because it is necessary for successful development of IGCC systems based on air-blown gasifiers and advanced pressurised fluidised-bed combustion systems (see below). However, hot gas clean-up is not necessary for IGCC systems with O_2-blown gasifiers. The technology is challenging (especially to realise the low emission levels achievable with present cold-gas cleanup), and potential economic benefits are modest even if positive, especially because coal prices are low and declining (Simbeck, 1995; Williams, 1999b).

Despite coal IGCC technical successes, there are few opportunities for deploying the technology in the industrialised world, where electricity demand is growing slowly, and where the NGCC is the technology of choice wherever there is a need for new power supplies and natural gas is available. The best potential opportunities for IGCC technology are in China and other developing countries where natural gas is not readily available and rapid growth in coal use is expected. There, IGCC technology could have enormous positive impacts in reducing local and regional air pollution, while substantially improving efficiencies and reducing greenhouse gas emissions. To make initial deployment of IGCC technology economically interesting to such countries, the first installations might be in cogeneration or polygeneration (see below) configurations. As in the case of NGCC cogeneration, the key to unlocking the cogeneration potential offered by IGCC technology is policies that make competitive electricity prices available to these producers for the electricity they wish to sell into electricity grids.

Small engines for cogeneration (reciprocating engines and microturbines). IGCC cogeneration technologies are suitable for deployment at scales of hundreds of megawatts; NGCC cogeneration technologies can be deployed at scales from a few up to hundreds of megawatts. But many small factories, commercial buildings, and apartment buildings would be good candidates for clean, gas-based cogeneration if appropriate technologies were available at scales from less than 100 kilowatts-electric to a few megawatts. Both reciprocating engines and microturbines show promise as near-term technologies for cogeneration at such scales.

From June 1997 through May 1998, world-wide sales of reciprocating engines for stationary power markets totalled about 5,100 units (9.6 gigawatts-electric of total capacity)—a gain of five times from 10 years earlier (Wadman, 1998). More than half of the units will be for continuous service.[21] Although most units will use oil, 13 percent will use natural gas or will be capable of using dual fuels. Gas applications might expand markedly under increasingly competitive power market conditions.

For spark-ignited engines, shifting to natural gas involves significant de-rating. Compression-ignition engines can also be converted to gas, either by adding a spark plug or by using a liquid spark—a small amount of diesel fuel for ignition. The latter approach is preferable with regard to both first cost and efficiency. Compression-ignition engines with liquid sparks bring to natural gas applications the low cost and high efficiencies of these engines, with much less de-rating. Recent advances have reduced liquid spark requirements for dual-fuel engines to 1 percent of system fuel requirements for larger engines. Such engine generator sets are commercially available at scales of 1–16 megawatts-electric with lower heating value (LHV) efficiencies of 39–42 percent.

Prices for both spark-ignited and dual-fuel engine generator sets (for equipment only) for the capacity range under 1 megawatt-electric typically lie in the range $425–600 per kilowatt-electric—prices that do not include the costs for heat recovery equipment for cogeneration. Operation and maintenance costs for reciprocating engines are typically significantly higher than for combustion turbines. Reciprocating engines can be used for cogeneration by recovering

TABLE 8.7. COGENERATION VERSUS SEPARATE PRODUCTION OF ELECTRICITY AND STEAM USING COMBINED CYCLE AND COAL GASIFICATION TECHNOLOGIES

Rates of activity and costs	Separate production facilities for electricity and steam			Cogeneration plant
	IGCC plant	Industrial boiler	Total	
Power generation rate (megawatts-electric)	400	—	400	400
Process steam production rate, 10-15 bar (megawatts-thermal)	—	400	400	400
Coal input rate (terajoules per hour)	3.20	1.65	4.85	3.88
First Law efficiency (percent)	45.1	87.2	59.4	74.3
CO_2 emission rate (tonnes per hour)	274	142	416	333
Capital investment (millions of dollars)	453	197	650	537
Annual energy production cost (millions of dollars per year) Capital Operation and maintenance (4 percent of capital cost per year) Fuel Total annual energy cost	52.19 18.12 22.44 92.75	22.69 7.88 11.57 42.14	74.88 26.00 34.01 134.89	61.86 21.48 27.21 110.55
Specific cost of energy (dollars per thousand kilowatt-hours) Gross cost Credit for steam coproduct Net cost	For power: 33.1 — 33.1	For steam: 15.0 — 15.0	— — —	For power: 39.4 -15.0 24.4

Note: Based on calculations by Dale Simbeck, SFA Pacific. Engineering plus contingencies are 10 percent of process capital equipment costs; general facilities are 10 percent of process capital equipment costs. The annual capital charge rate is 11.5 percent. The coal price is $1.00 per gigajoule (see note c, table 8.4). The annual average capacity factor is 80 percent. Both the stand-alone integrated gasifier combined cycle (IGCC) power plant and the cogeneration plant use a Destec O_2-blown coal gasifier coupled to a combined cycle with steam-cooled gas turbine blades.

TABLE 8.8. COGENERATION VERSUS SEPARATE PRODUCTION OF ELECTRICITY AND STEAM USING STEAM TURBINE AND PULVERIZED COAL COMBUSTION TECHNOLOGIES

Rates of PCC activity and costs	Separate production facilities for electricity and steam			Cogeneration plant
	PCC power plant	Industrial boiler	Total	
Power generation rate (megawatts-electric)	400	—	400	400
Process steam production rate, 10-15 bar (megawatts-thermal)	—	400	400	400
Coal input rate (terajoules per hour)	3.39	1.65	5.04	4.68
First Law efficiency (percent)	42.4	87.2	57.1	61.6
CO_2 emission rate (tonnes per hour)	291	142	433	402
Capital investment (millions of dollars)	453	197	650	612
Annual energy production cost (millions of dollars per year) Capital Operation and maintenance (4 percent of capital cost per year) Fuel Total annual energy cost	52.19 18.12 23.77 94.08	22.69 7.88 11.57 42.14	74.88 26.00 35.34 136.22	70.50 24.48 32.82 127.8
Specific cost of energy (dollars per thousand kilowatt-hours) Gross cost Credit for steam coproduct Net cost	For power: 33.6 — 33.6	For steam: 15.0 — 15.0	— — —	For power: 45.6 -15.0 30.6

Note: Based on calculations by Dale Simbeck, SFA Pacific. Engineering plus contingencies are 10 percent of process capital equipment costs, as are general facilities. The annual capital charge rate is 11.5 percent. The coal price is $1.00 per gigajoule (see note c, table 8.4). The average capacity factor is 80 percent. The pulverized coal combustion (PCC) plant is an ultrasupercritical unit for the stand-alone power plant and a sub-critical unit for the cogeneration plant.

both high-quality heat from the engine exhaust and low-quality heat from the engine jacket cooling water. Like gas turbines and combined cycles, reciprocating engines are attractive for such applications because of their high electricity-heat output ratios (see figure 8.1). Some reciprocating engine vendors offer complete cogeneration package systems. Very small-scale systems (under 100 kilowatts-electric) sell in the United States for $1,500–2,000 per kilowatt-electric. The engines for such systems last only 3–4 years, but replacement engines cost only $75 per kilowatt-electric.

Air pollutant emissions, especially NO_x, are a concern. Uncontrolled gas engines produce significant CO and non-methane hydrocarbon emissions; however, relatively low-cost oxidation catalytic converters can control such emissions. Most lean-burning, spark-ignited natural gas engines and micro-liquid-spark, dual-fuel engines can achieve NO_x emission of 1.4 grams per kilowatt-hour (100 parts per million by volume at 15 percent O_2)—about 15 times the emission rate for large modern NGCCs with state-of-the-art NO_x controls (see table 8.1). Some vendors now offer systems with half this level of emissions but at an energy efficiency penalty of about 1 percentage point. In some areas (for example, many parts of the United States), NO_x emission regulations will severely limit deployment of reciprocating engines for stationary power markets at scales from 100 kilowatts-electric to 2 megawatts-electric.

Operation of reciprocating engines on town gas (that is, syngas) is also feasible and would be an especially attractive option for natural-gas-poor, coal-rich regions. There town gas could be produced from coal at centralised facilities along with syngas for other poly-generation activities and piped up to 30 kilometres to various distributed cogeneration facilities. The air quality benefits of such gas-based technologies relative to direct coal combustion would be especially important in countries such as China, where coal is used for heating in small, inefficient boilers equipped with little or no air pollution control equipment. However, such systems would not be pollution free. Air emission concerns would be similar to those for reciprocating engines operated on natural gas, except that NO_x emissions might be higher because of higher adiabatic flame temperatures.

Reciprocating engines can also be adapted to small-scale operations in rural areas using either biogas (from anaerobic digesters) or producer gas generated by thermochemical gasification of biomass (see Mukunda, Dasappa, and Srinivasa, 1993; chapters 7 and 10).

Efforts under way to improve reciprocating engine markets for stationary power include the five-year Advanced Reciprocating Engine Systems (ARES) programme—being carried out by a consortium of U.S. manufacturers, the U.S. Department of Energy, the Gas Research Institute, and the Southwest Research Institute. ARES is targeting development of an advanced gas engine with an efficiency of 50 percent (LHV basis) and a NO_x output of 5 parts per million by volume (including catalytic aftertreatment if necessary).

There is growing confidence among scientists that underground sequestration of CO_2 will prove to be a major option for mitigating climate-change risks.

The microturbine is a gas turbine just entering the market for applications at scales less than 100 kilowatts-electric. Its development recently got a boost as a result of its being chosen as a cruise missile engine. One vendor has already launched the technology in the market, and several other aerospace firms are getting ready to market it for stationary power applications. Promoters project that it will do well in new highly competitive distributed power markets (Craig, 1997).

The system involves a low-pressure ratio (3 to 4) gas turbine and compressor mounted on a single shaft.[22] The most promising models available are air cooled and have variable speed generators (the output of which is rectified and converted electronically to the alternating-current line frequency), no gear-box, no lubricating oil requirements, and only one moving part. Turbine blades are not cooled, turbine inlet temperatures are modest (840 degrees Celsius), but engine speeds are high—80,000 revolutions a minute or more. Conversion efficiencies with natural gas fuelling are 25 percent (LHV basis) at full power output—far less than for large reciprocating engines but comparable to reciprocating engine generator set efficiencies at scales of tens of kilowatts-electric. Efficiency falls off at part load—to 75 percent of the efficiency at full output when output falls to a third of the peak level (Campanari, 1999).

Although electric efficiencies are not especially high, the technology offers four attractive features:
- Potentially low capital costs in mass production, because of the simple design.
- Low maintenance costs—probably considerably lower than for reciprocating engines, because of the low combustion temperature and the simple design's expected higher reliability.
- Suitability for cogeneration, because all waste heat is of high quality, in the form of hot (230–270 degrees Celsius) air.
- The possibility of low NO_x emissions without stack gas controls.[23]

The microturbine faces competition from both reciprocating engines and fuel cells. Maintenance and air quality issues will be important in determining the outcome of competition with reciprocating engines. At scales of hundreds of kilowatts-electric, it will be very difficult for microturbines to compete in efficiency with reciprocating engines. Moreover, if the ARES programme meets its NO_x emissions reduction target, the competition from reciprocating engine technology will be strong at all sizes for which such emissions can be realised.

At the small scales (under 100 kilowatts-electric) that are the focus for market development, the major competition will be from fuel cells—for example, the proton exchange membrane (PEM) fuel cell (see below). Fuel cells will be more efficient in producing electricity from natural gas and will have lower air pollutant emissions. But microturbines will be better performers in providing heat for cogeneration than PEM fuel cells, for which the waste heat quality is low. And microturbines will probably be valued more by utilities as peaking units than PEM fuel cells operated on natural gas, which cannot so readily be dispatched to serve peaking needs.

Microturbines could have great appeal in markets where low-cost gaseous fuels are available—for example, producer gas derived from low-cost crop residues in rural areas of developing countries (chapter 10). They also appear to be well suited for use as bottoming cycles for hybrid cycles that employ pressurised molten carbonate or solid oxide fuel cells as topping cycles (Campanari, 1999; Kartha, Kreutz, and Williams, 1997).

Fuel cells for stationary power and cogeneration. The fuel cell converts fuel into electricity electrochemically, without first burning it to produce heat (Kartha and Grimes, 1994). Fuel cells have attractive features for electricity markets characterised by increasing competition and environmental regulations: high thermodynamic efficiency, low maintenance requirements, quiet operation, zero or near-zero air pollutant emissions without exhaust-gas controls, and high reliability. Fuel cells are likely to be economically viable even in small-scale (100 kilowatts-electric or less) applications. Its properties make it possible to site systems in small, unobtrusive generating facilities close to end users.

Such distributed power sources make cogeneration designs economically attractive and offer the potential of reducing capital outlays for electricity transmission and distribution equipment (Hoff, Wenger, and Farmer, 1996). Low-temperature phosphoric acid fuel cells (PAFCs) and proton exchange membrane fuel cells (PEMCs) are well suited for combined heat and power applications in small- to medium-scale commercial and residential buildings, providing domestic hot water and space heating and cooling (Little, 1995; Dunnison and Wilson, 1994). Developers of high-temperature molten carbonate fuel cells (MCFCs) and solid-oxide fuel cells (SOFCs) target medium- to large-scale industrial applications.

The PAFC, developed largely in Japan and the United States, is the only commercial fuel cell. Several hundred PAFC power plants (mostly 200-kilowatt-electric natural-gas-fuelled units) are operating. Accumulated experience has demonstrated that fuel cell power plants can be made to operate reliably. Costs are high, however, and whether they can be reduced enough with volume production to make the PAFC widely competitive is uncertain.

Because of recent technological advances, substantial U.S., European, and Japanese activities are seeking to accelerate commercialisation of the PEMFC for residential and commercial building cogeneration markets (Dunnison and Wilson, 1994; Little, 1995; Lloyd, 1999) as well as for transportation (see below). Several companies are developing residential PEMFC combined heat and power systems (Lloyd, 1999). Ballard Generation Systems plans to begin selling 250-kilowatts-electric system for commercial buildings by 2003–04; Plug Power is focussing on smaller (less than 35-kilowatt-electric) units and plans to install the first residential units by 2001.[24] In initial applications it is expected that most systems would use mainly existing natural gas infrastructure and, like PAFCs, process natural gas at the point of use in an external fuel processor into an H_2-rich gas the fuel cell can use.

The best chances for making small fuel cells competitive are in markets that value electricity highly (for example, in residential or other buildings, where produced electricity must be less costly than the retail rate) and where fuel cell waste heat can be used effectively. Space heating and cooling markets are not well matched to PEMFC capabilities; space heating demand is seasonal with enormous variation in the heating season; and the operating PEMFC temperature (80 degrees Celsius) is too low to use waste heat for heat-driven air conditioners.

However, domestic hot water demand often provides a good match—demand is fairly level year-round, and the PEM operating temperature is well suited for domestic hot water. Especially promising opportunities are where the fuel cell is sized to meet the demand for domestic hot water, so that very little waste heat is discarded. If the PEMFC size were increased to meet a larger fraction of the electrical load, it would become more and more difficult to compete, because more and more of the waste heat would have to be discarded, reducing the credit (per kilowatt-hour of electricity) for waste heat utilisation.

The economic prospects are best for apartment buildings, hotels, and hospitals, where a centralised building-scale PEM fuel cell system serves power and hot water needs throughout. It would be more difficult for such systems to compete at the level of single-family dwellings for currently expected PEMFC economies of scale (Kreutz and Ogden, 2000).

The high operating temperatures for MCFCs (600–650 degrees Celsius) and SOFCs (1,000 degrees Celsius) make them well suited for cogeneration, including applications that use the waste heat to operate heat-driven air conditioners. They also offer the option of using directly natural gas or syngas derived through gasification from coal or other feedstocks without an external fuel processor—because these gases can be reformed (using waste heat from fuel cell operation) and shifted on the anode into an H_2-rich gas the fuel cell can easily use—leading, potentially, to higher efficiency, simplified operation, and increasing reliability. (But having an external reformer offers the flexibility of being able to switch relatively easily to operation on alternative fuels.)

The two principal vendors for MCFCs have been Energy Research Corporation and MC Power. Energy Research Corporation units operate at atmospheric pressure with internal reforming; MC Power units operate at pressure but with an external reformer. A 1.8-megawatt-electric demonstration plant based on Energy Research Corporation technology was built and operated on natural gas beginning in April 1996 in Santa Clara, California; a peak efficiency of 40 percent was achieved. Because of various difficulties, the unit was operated for only 4,000 hours and was dismantled in March 1997. In March 1999 Energy Research Corporation put into operation a 250-kilowatt-electric demonstration unit at its Danbury, Connecticut, headquarters. In 1997 MC Power operated a 250-kilowatt-electric cogeneration unit at the Naval (now Marine Corps) Mirimar Air Station in San Diego, California. Unable to raise new funding for research and development, MC Power went out of business in March 2000.

SOFCs offer the potential for high efficiency, low cost, and potentially long operating lifetimes (Bakker, 1996). The main uncertainties concern manufacturing costs and durability in operation as a result of the fact that SOFCs are made of ceramics. Although the cost of the materials in the ceramics is inherently low ($7–15 per kilowatt-electric; Goldstein, 1992), fabrication of ceramics is difficult and costly. Moreover, there are risks that the ceramic components will develop cracks during operation as a result of thermal cycling.

Siemens Westinghouse, the leading SOFC developer, has focussed on a tubular design and has deployed seven fully integrated, automatically controlled, packaged SOFC systems as experimental field units. The largest of these is a 100-kilowatt-electric natural-gas-fuelled cogeneration system deployed in the Netherlands in early 1998. The system has realised extremely low pollutant emissions—0.2 parts per million by volume of NO_x and undetectable levels of sulphur dioxide (SO_2), CO, and unburned hydrocarbons (Veyo, 1998).

The tubular design facilitates manufacture and realisation of properly operating seals, but it is uncertain how low costs can become in mass production. Planar designs that operate at lower temperatures (800 degrees Celsius)[25] seem promising with regard to both high efficiency (55–70 percent on natural gas, LHV basis) and capital cost in mass production ($700–800 per kilowatt-electric at a scale of 500 kilowatts-electric; Chen, Wright, and Krist, 1997). But such designs require considerable more research and development.

In the 1970s and 1980s it was expected that high-temperature fuel cells would eventually be able to compete with conventional power generating technologies at a wide range of scales—including large central-station power plants as well as cogeneration plants of all sizes. But the enormous success of gas turbines and combined cycles dampened the prospects for large-scale fuel cell applications during the early 1990s—when it became apparent that the marginal efficiency gains offered by fuel cells over combined cycles would not be able to justify the expected higher capital costs—except in small-scale operations (1 megawatt-electric or less). However, since the early 1990s two developments have once more brightened the prospects for high-temperature fuel cells for larger-scale installations.

The first is a hybrid concept that offers both higher efficiency and lower capital cost. A hybrid would be made up of a high-temperature fuel cell topping cycle and a gas turbine or a steam turbine or gas turbine–steam turbine combined cycle bottoming cycle. A high-temperature fuel cell operated on natural gas or syngas will utilise only 80–90 percent of the gas energy. The chemical energy remaining in the hot anode exhaust gases can be burned to generate more electricity in a bottoming cycle. Modelling carried out at the Electric Power Research Institute indicates that a 56 percent efficient natural-gas-fuelled SOFC combined with a regenerative gas turbine bottoming cycle could lead to a system efficiency of 71 percent (Bakker, 1996)—efficiencies well above the levels that can be realised with gas turbine–steam turbine combined cycles. Because the cost per kilowatt-electric of the bottoming cycle will typically be less than the than the cost per kilowatt-electric for the fuel cell itself, the overall capital cost for the hybrid will be less than for a pure-bred fuel cell.

The second new development is related to the fact that pressurised high-temperature fuel cells offer an option for low-cost CO_2 recovery and disposal as a response to climate change concerns. The concept is related to the fact that CO_2 is available at high partial

---

BOX 8.2. DEEP OCEAN SEQUESTRATION OF ANTHROPOGENIC CARBON DIOXIDE

The ocean, containing 40,000 gigatonnes of carbon (relative to 750 GtC in the atmosphere), represents the largest potential sink for anthropogenic CO_2; disposing in the ocean of an amount of CO_2 that would otherwise lead to a doubling of the atmosphere's content would thus increase the ocean concentration by less than 2 percent. On a 1,000-year time scale, more than 90 percent of today's anthropogenic emissions will be transferred to the oceans through a slow, natural process. The basic idea of ocean sequestration of CO_2 is to inject CO_2 directly into the deep ocean to accelerate this process and reduce both peak atmospheric CO_2 concentrations and their rate of increase.

For a large fraction of injected CO_2 to remain in the ocean, injection must be at great depths. This is because CO_2 would be a gas above 800 metres and a liquid below 800 metres. Liquid CO_2 is negatively buoyant relative to ordinary seawater only below 3,000 metres. Liquid CO_2 is negatively buoyant relative to seawater saturated with CO_2 only below 3,700 metres. And at injection depths of about 500 metres or more, a CO_2-seawater mixture (depending on the relative compositions) can lead to formation of a CO_2 hydrate, which is about 10 percent denser than seawater.

A consensus is developing that the best near-term strategy would be to discharge CO_2 at depths of 1,000–1,500 metres, which can be done with existing technology. A major uncertainty that requires more research for clarification relates to the sequestration efficiency (the fraction of the CO_2 that remains in the ocean) of injection at such depths (see, for example, Brewer and others, 1999). Another approach, aimed at maximising sequestration efficiency, is to inject liquid CO_2 into a deep sea-floor depression, forming a stable deep lake at a depth of 4,000 metres—an approach that is technologically challenging with current technology. A simple and feasible but very costly option is to release dry ice from a surface ship. Another approach is to create a dense CO_2-seawater mixture at a depth of 500–1,000 metres and cause it to form a sinking-bottom gravity current—an approach that has raised many environmental impact concerns.

On a global scale, both climate change and other environmental impacts of ocean disposal (for example, increased ocean acidity) are positive. But on a local scale, there are considerable environmental concerns arising largely as a result of the increased acidification near the points of injection—for example, impacts on non-swimming marine organisms residing at depths of 1,000 metres or more.

Japan has the world's most active ocean sequestration research programme, led by the Research Institute of Innovative Technology for the Earth and the Kansai Environmental Engineering Centre, and funded at an annual level of more than 10 million dollars.

Although the deep ocean has been the most-discussed option for CO_2 disposal, much more research is needed to better understand the security, costs, and environmental impacts of various ocean disposal schemes (Turkenburg, 1992). In addition, the viability of ocean storage as a greenhouse gas mitigation option hinges on social and political as well as technical, economic, and environmental considerations. The public is generally cautious regarding ocean projects.

Source: Herzog, 1999b.

pressure in the anode exhaust of pressurised SOFCs or MCFCs in highly concentrated form. To illustrate, consider operation of a pressurised SOFC on syngas (mainly CO and H_2) derived from coal through O_2-blown gasification. Both the CO and the H_2 react in the anode directly with O_2 (transported across the electrolyte from the cathode as an oxygen ion) to form CO_2 and H_2O. If the 10–20 percent of the unconverted CO and H_2 exiting the anode is then burned in O_2 for use in a bottoming cycle,[26] the gaseous product will be a mixture of CO_2 and H_2O, from which the H_2O can easily be removed by cooling and condensation. Moreover, if the bottoming cycle is a steam turbine, the CO_2 can be recovered for disposal at relatively high pressure, leading to low costs for further pressurising the CO_2 to the level needed for disposal. Recognising the value of this strategy, Shell announced in July 1999 plans to develop and market with Siemens Westinghouse SOFC technology capable of disposing of CO_2 in this manner.[27]

Decarbonisation and carbon dioxide sequestration strategies for power generation systems. Because of climate change concerns, increasing attention has been given in recent years to strategies for extracting energy from fossil fuels without releasing CO_2 into the atmosphere. The issues involved concern the capacity, security, and cost of alternative CO_2 disposal options and the costs of separating the CO_2 from fossil energy systems and preparing it for disposal.

The options for CO_2 sequestration include both the deep ocean and geological reservoirs. Although ocean disposal has received the most attention (box 8.2), large uncertainties in its prospects (Turkenburg, 1992) have led to a shift of focus in recent years to give more attention to geological (underground) storage of CO_2, in depleted oil and natural gas fields (including storage in conjunction with enhanced oil and gas recovery), in deep coal beds (in conjunction with coal bed methane recovery), and in deep saline aquifers.

CO_2 injection for enhanced oil recovery (Blunt, Fayers, and Orr, 1993), enhanced gas recovery (van der Burgt, Cantle, and Boutkan, 1992; Blok and others, 1997), and enhanced recovery of deep coal bed methane (Byrer and Guthrie, 1999; Gunter and others, 1997; Stevens and others, 1999; Williams, 1999a) might become profitable focuses of initial efforts to sequester CO_2. Enhanced oil recovery using CO_2 injection is well-established technology; one project that began in 2000 in Saskatchewan, Canada, is injecting yearly up to 1.5 million tonnes of CO_2, which is transported 300 kilometres to the injection site from a synthetic natural gas plant in North Dakota (see below).

Sequestration in depleted oil and gas fields is generally thought to be a secure option if the original reservoir pressure is not exceeded (van der Burgt, Cantle, and Boutkan, 1992; Summerfield and others, 1993). One estimate of the prospective global sequestering capacity of such reservoirs associated with past production plus proven reserves plus estimated undiscovered conventional resources is 100 GtC for oil fields and 400 GtC for gas fields

A fierce global competition is underway to accelerate the development of fuel cell vehicles.

(Hendriks, 1994). Other estimates are as low as 40 GtC for depleted oil fields and 90 GtC for depleted gas fields, plus 20 GtC associated with enhanced oil recovery (IPCC, 1996a). The range is wide because reservoir properties vary greatly in their suitability for storage, and because oil and gas recovery may have altered the formations and affected reservoir integrity. Much of the prospective sequestering capacity will not be available until these fields are nearly depleted of oil and gas.

Deep aquifers are much more widely available than oil or gas fields. Such aquifers underlie most sedimentary basins, the total areas of which amount to 70 million square kilometres (two-thirds onshore and one-third offshore), more than half the 130-million-square-kilometre land area of the inhabited continents. Some sedimentary basins offer better prospects for CO_2 storage than others (Hitchon and others, 1999; Bachu and Gunter, 1999). To achieve high storage densities, CO_2 should be stored at supercritical pressures (more than about 75 times atmospheric pressure), which typically requires storage at depths greater than 800 metres. The aquifers at such depths are typically saline and not effectively connected to the much shallower (typically less than 300-metre) sweet-water aquifers used by people. If aquifer storage is limited to closed aquifers with structural traps, the potential global sequestering capacity is relatively limited—about 50 GtC (Hendriks, 1994), equivalent to less than 10 years of global CO_2 production from burning fossil fuel at the current rate.

However, if structural traps are not required for effective storage, potential aquifer storage capacity might be huge; estimates range from 2,700 GtC (Omerod, 1994) to 13,000 GtC (Hendriks, 1994). For comparison, estimated remaining recoverable fossil fuel resources (excluding methane hydrates) contain about 5,600 GtC (see table 5.7). A growing body of knowledge indicates that many large horizontal open aquifers might provide effective storage[28] if the CO_2 is injected far enough from reservoir boundaries that it dissolves in the formation water or precipitates out as a mineral as a result of reactions with the surrounding rock before migrating more than a few kilometres towards the basin boundaries (Bachu, Gunter, and Perkins, 1994; Gunter, Perkins, and McCann, 1993; Socolow, 1997). The relatively new idea that large horizontal aquifers can provide effective sequestration has contributed to growing confidence among scientists that underground sequestration of CO_2 will prove to be a major option for mitigating climate-change risks (Holloway, 1996; Socolow, 1997; PCAST Energy Research and Development Panel, 1997).

Experience with aquifer disposal will be provided by two projects involving injection into nearby aquifers of CO_2 separated from natural gas recovered from CO_2-rich gas reservoirs. One is a Statoil project begun in 1996 to recover 1 million tonnes of CO_2 a year from the Sleipner Vest offshore natural gas field in Norway

(Kaarstad, 1992). The second, which will commence in 10 years, will involve the recovery of more than 100 million tonnes a year (equivalent to 0.5 percent of total global emissions from fossil fuel burning) from the Natuna natural gas field in the South China Sea (71 percent of the reservoir gas is CO_2) (IEA, 1996).

Extensive historical experience with underground gas storage contributes to the growing scientific confidence in the reliability of geological reservoirs for storing CO_2. And regulations that have been evolving for underground gas storage provide a good basis for defining the issues associated with formulation of regulations for CO_2 storage (Gunter, Chalaturnyk, and Scott, 1999).

More research, field testing, modelling, and monitoring are needed to narrow the uncertainties relating to CO_2 storage in geological reservoirs. From a policy perspective, it is particularly important to understand better potential effective storage capacities on a region-by-region basis so that energy and environmental planners will have a better understanding of the overall potential for fossil fuel decarbonisation with CO_2 sequestration as an option for dealing with climate change. Getting such important information is not likely to be especially costly. For example, Stefan Bachu of the Alberta Research Council

has estimated that obtaining a reasonable estimate of the geological CO_2 storage capacity of Canada would cost $14 million (Gunter, 1999). The cost is relatively low because geological surveys have collected an enormous amount of relevant data during the past 100 years, and many more relevant data from industrial sources are available from regulatory bodies.

Public acceptability issues are paramount. Fuel decarbonisation with CO_2 sequestration is unfamiliar to most people as a strategy for dealing with the climate change challenge. What will public attitudes be? The scientific community has a major responsibility to inform the public debates on the various issues relating to safety and environmental impacts. Much can be learned from both natural events (Holloway, 1997) and from the extensive historical experience with use of CO_2 injection for enhanced oil recovery and with underground gas storage (Gunter, Chalaturnyk, and Scott, 1999). But more research is needed to clarify the issues.

An optimistic note on which to end this discussion: in the sections that follow, it will be shown that those advanced fossil energy technologies offering the potential for CO_2 disposal at the least costs are also characterised by near-zero emissions of air pollutants.

TABLE 8.9. ALTERNATIVE TECHNOLOGIES FOR REDUCING CO_2 EMISSIONS FROM 400-MEGAWATT-ELECTRIC COAL PLANTS

Technology	Efficiency (percent, HHV)	Capital cost (dollars per kilowatt)	Generation cost (dollars per thousand kilowatt-hours)	O_2 requirements (tonnes per hour)	CO_2 emissions (grams of carbon per kilowatt-hour)	Cost of avoiding CO_2 emissions (dollars per tonne of carbon)
Ultrasupercritical pulverised coal steam turbine plant						
Reference, CO_2 vented	43.1	1,114	33.0	0	196	—
CO_2 recovery from flue gasses	34.3	1,812	52.2	0	36.8	134
O_2 firing, CO_2 recovery from flue gasses	32.0	1,661	52.8	339	0	111
Pressurised fluidised-bed combustion plant						
Reference, CO_2 vented	43.1	1,114	33.0	0	196	—
O_2 firing, CO_2 recovery from flue gasses	35.4	1,675	51.6	307	0	104
Integrated gasifier–combined cycle plant						
Reference, CO_2 vented	45.9	1,114	32.5	80	184	—
Cold CO_2 recovery from synthesis gas	36.1	1,514	47.9	108	23.9	96
Warm CO_2 recovery from synthesis gas (advanced technology)	41.5	1,466	44.5	94	20.4	73
H_2-O_2 Rankine cycle plant: Cold CO_2 recovery from synthesis gas (advanced technology)	40.5	1,622	48.4	259	6.1	90
Solid oxide fuel cell (SOFC) plant						
H_2-fueled SOFC–gas turbine–steam turbine plant, warm CO_2 recovery from synthesis gas (advanced technology)	45.7	1,461	43.3	85	19.1	65
SOFC–steam turbine plant, CO_2 recovered from anode exhaust burned with O_2 (advanced technology)	44.3	1,427	43.1	114	6.8	60

Note: Based on calculations by Dale Simbeck, SFA Pacific. Engineering and contingencies are 10 percent of process capital equipment costs; general facilities are 10 percent of process capital equipment costs. The annual capital charge rate is 11.5 percent. The coal price is $1.00 per gigajoule. The annual average capacity factor is 80 percent. All options involving CO_2 separation and disposal include the cost of compressing the separated CO_2 to 135 bar plus a cost of $5 per tonne of CO_2 ($18 per tonne of carbon) for pipeline transmission and ultimate disposal.

People are likely to be more willing to accept fuel decarbonisation with CO_2 sequestration as a major energy option if the technology also offers near-zero emissions than if they view it as a way to sustain a dirty energy system—away from which they would rather evolve.

Table 8.9 presents performance and cost calculations (developed in a self-consistent manner across options) for eight alternative technologies and strategies for CO_2 removal and disposal for coal-fired power systems—variants of calculations developed earlier by Simbeck (1999c). Four options are based on current or near-term (before 2005) technologies. The other four (labelled advanced technology) require considerable technological development. The H_2-O_2 Rankine cycle plant involves producing H_2 through coal gasification and burning it with O_2 in a Rankine cycle—a technology proposed by Westinghouse researchers (Bannister and others, 1996; Bannister, Newby, and Yang, 1997, 1998). The turbine in this system looks like a gas turbine in the high-pressure stages but a steam turbine at the condensing end—because the combustion of H_2 in O_2 leads to the production of only steam. If there were a market for the turbine used in this system, it could probably be developed in 2010–20. The SOFC options require commercialisation of SOFC power technology, which developers expect to take place before 2010. The two warm gas recovery options require the development of relatively challenging advanced gas separation technologies, which could be commercial by 2015.

The CO_2 separation and disposal options are compared with three reference technologies for power generation without CO_2 removal and disposal: an ultrasupercritical steam-electric plant (see below), a pressurised fluidised-bed combustion plant (see below), and an IGCC plant (the Frame 7H option described in table 8.4). Identical capital costs are assumed for these reference plants: Not only is this a reasonable approximation, but also this assumption helps clarify cost differences for CO_2 separation and disposal among alternatives.[29] The cost of avoided CO_2 emissions for each case is calculated relative to the least costly option in the table (the reference IGCC case, with CO_2 venting).

The first CO_2 recovery option involves CO_2 scrubbing from the stack gases of an ultrasupercritical steam-electric plant using an amine solution (flue gas scrubbing). The cost of avoiding CO_2 emissions and the power generation cost penalty are relatively high ($134 per tonne of carbon and $0.020 per kilowatt-hour), largely because of the high cost penalties associated with recovering CO_2 from the stack gases, where its concentration and partial pressure are low (15 percent and 0.15 bar, respectively).

The second option uses atmospheric pressure O_2 rather than air as oxidant, and recycles the separated CO_2 back to the ultra supercritical steam plant combustor. This strategy greatly increases the partial pressure of CO_2 in the flue gas. Cost penalties are comparable to those for flue gas recovery because of the large quantities of costly O_2 required. The third option is for a pressurised fluidised-bed

combustion unit that uses pressurised O_2 as the oxidant instead of pressurised air. This further increases the CO_2 partial pressure in the flue gas and reduces CO_2 removal costs; however, because pressurised O_2 is more costly than O_2 at atmospheric pressure, the savings relative to the ultrasupercritical steam-electric cases is modest.

The five remaining options—which have avoided CO_2 emission costs that are much lower than for the first three—are for systems involving O_2-blown gasifiers. The first, cold CO_2 recovery from synthesis gas for IGCC plants, is based on existing CO_2 recovery technology. This option starts with gasification to produce syngas (mainly CO and H_2). The syngas is reacted with steam in shift reactors to convert CO into H_2 and CO_2. Subsequently, CO_2 is separated out for disposal, and the H_2-rich fuel gas is burned in the gas turbine combustor.[30] This option has the least cost penalties of all the near-term options ($96 per tonne of carbon and $0.015 per kilowatt-hour). The low cost is realised largely because, when CO_2 is recovered from the shifted syngas in an IGCC, its concentration is high (33 percent), as is its partial pressure (more than 10 bar). The advanced technology option labelled warm CO_2 recovery from synthesis gas for IGCC plants, could—if successfully developed—reduce avoided CO_2 emission costs by a fourth relative to the cold gas recovery option. For the advanced technology option labelled cold CO_2 recovery from synthesis gas for an H_2-O_2 Rankine cycle, the H_2-O_2 turbine capital cost is expected to be relatively low, and the efficiency of converting H_2 into electricity high. However, the system requires large quantities of costly O_2. As a result this system would not improve on the least costly current technology option—cold CO_2 recovery from synthesis gas for an IGCC plant.

The last two entries depend on the successful development of SOFC technology. The penultimate entry also depends on the success of warm-gas separation technology. The last entry is the least costly of the advanced technology options—involving recovery of CO_2 at pressure from the anode exhaust (see above). This technology would provide electricity from coal with only 3 percent of the CO_2 emissions for the conventional coal steam-electric plant at a generation cost of $0.043 per kilowatt-hour, for an avoided CO_2 emission cost of $60 per tonne of carbon.[31] This is about $0.01 per kilowatt-hour more than the cost of electricity from a coal-fired power plant today with no CO_2 removal and sequestration. This is consistent with findings by a group at the Massachusetts Institute of Technology (MIT) Energy Laboratory that, with advanced IGCC technology (expected to be commercially available by 2012), the cost penalty for decarbonisation and sequestration would be less than $0.01 per kilowatt-hour (Herzog, 1999a).

An implicit assumption for these calculations is that a new coal plant is the least costly option—for example, the calculations are appropriate for coal-rich, natural-gas-poor countries. If natural gas were available, the cost of CO_2 emissions avoided by CO_2 recovery and disposal at a coal plant would typically be higher. Table 8.10

TABLE 8.10. THE COST OF ELECTRICITY FROM COAL AND NATURAL GAS WITH AND WITHOUT CO_2 SEQUESTRATION, BASED ON NEAR-TERM TECHNOLOGIES

Rates of activity and costs	USC steam[a]	Natural gas-fired combined cycle[b]			Coal IGCC[b]	
CO_2 sequestered?	No	No	Yes	Yes	No	Yes
CO_2 separation method	—	—	FGS[c]	NG→H_2[c]	-	Syngas→H_2
Efficiency (percent, HHV basis)	43.1	54.0	45.7	42.2	45.9	36.1
Emission rate (grams of carbon per kilowatt-hour)	196	90	15.7	11.6	184	23.9
CO_2 disposal rate (grams of carbon per kilowatt-hour)	—	—	91	104	—	210
Capital cost (dollars per kilowatt)	1,114	416	907	918	1,114	1,514
Generation cost[d] (dollars per thousand kilowatt-hours)						
Capital	18.30	6.83	14.90	15.08	18.30	24.87
Operation and maintenance	6.35	2.37	5.17	5.24	6.35	8.64
Fuel	8.35•P_C	6.67•P_{NG}	7.88•P_{NG}	8.53•P_{NG}	7.84•P_C	9.97•P_C
CO_2 disposal (at \$5 per tonne of CO_2)[e]	—	—	1.66	1.90	—	4.38
Total generation cost[f]	24.65+8.35•P_C	9.20+6.67•P_{NG}	21.73+7.88•P_{NG}	22.22+8.53•P_{NG}	24.65+7.84•P_C	37.89+9.97•P_C
at 1998 U.S. fuel prices	34.6	23.8	39.5	41.5	34.0	49.8
at 2020 U.S. fuel prices	32.0	29.7	45.9	48.4	31.6	46.7
Avoided CO_2 emissions cost, relative to same technology without separation and disposal (dollars per tonne of carbon, for 2020 U.S. fuel prices)[g]	—	—	219	236	—	96
Electricity cost (dollars per thousand kilowatt-hours), for 2020 U.S. fuel prices and \$219 tax per tonne of carbon	74.9	49.3	49.3	51.0	71.8	51.9

a. For a 400-megawatt-electric, pulverised-coal, ultrasupercritical steam-electric plant; see table 8.9. b. Based on an analysis developed in Simbeck (1999c); coal IGCC technologies are the same as for reference and cold CO_2 recovery cases in table 8.9. c. FGS = flue gas scrubber; for NG→H_2 case, natural gas (NG) is converted to H_2 using an O_2-autothermal reformer. d. Annual capital charge rate = 11.5 percent; annual operation and maintenance cost = 4 percent of capital cost; P_C = coal price, P_{NG} = natural gas price (dollars per gigajoule). e. To account for pipeline transmission and ultimate disposal costs. f. For 1998: P_C = \$1.19 per gigajoule; P_{NG} = \$2.26 per gigajoule, average U.S. prices for electric generators (EIA, 1999b). For 2020: P_C = \$0.88 per gigajoule; P_{NG} = \$3.07 per gigajoule, average U.S. prices projected for electric generators in the Energy Information Administration's reference scenario (EIA, 1998a). g. Avoided cost = (generation cost with sequestration minus generation cost without sequestration) divided by (emissions without sequestration minus emissions with sequestration).

presents calculations, also based on Simbeck (1999c), that illustrate the situation for near-term (before 2005) technology when NGCCs and coal IGCCs are competing, and emission reductions of 90 percent are considered for both. The IGCC option is the IGCC with cold CO_2 recovery from table 8.9. For NGCCs, two CO_2 separation-and-disposal options are considered. The least costly option involves scrubbing CO_2 from flue gases.

Even though removal of twice as much CO_2 per kilowatt-hour is required for the IGCC case, the cost penalty per kilowatt-hour of CO_2 separation and disposal is not greater than for the NGCC case. This counterintuitive result arises because scrubbing CO_2 from NGCC *flue gases* is more capital- and energy-intensive than recovering CO_2 from IGCC *fuel gas*. H_2 could also be made from natural gas by reforming. But as shown, with current technology doing so would not be less costly than scrubbing flue gas, because the gain in

reduced cost by avoiding the flue gas scrubber would be offset by the added costs for reformer and shift reactors.[32]

One result of the analysis shown in table 8.10 is that—for the CO_2 recovery-and-disposal cases and 2020 U.S. fuel prices—the costs of generating electricity from natural gas and coal are about the same (\$0.046–0.047 per kilowatt-hour). The findings of Herzog (1999a)—who considered improvements in the technologies relative to the cases presented in table 8.10 and which he projected would be commercial by 2012—indicate that this cost parity between coal and natural gas systems is likely to hold even when technological improvements are taken into account for natural gas as well as coal technologies.[33]

The last row in table 8.10 shows the electric generating costs with a carbon tax high enough to induce NGCC power generators (as well as coal IGCC power generators) to separate and dispose of CO_2.

This tax ($220 per tonne of carbon) is 2.3 times the carbon tax needed if there were no competition from natural gas. The cost of power generation (including the carbon tax) would be $0.05 per kilowatt-hour for all options except coal plants without CO_2 separation and disposal. With the advanced technologies considered by Herzog (1999a), the carbon tax needed to induce CO_2 recovery and disposal for NGCC plants would be less ($170 versus $70 per tonne of carbon for coal IGCC plants).

The technologies considered here for CO_2 recovery and disposal do not exhaust the possibilities. A class of advanced technologies that offers considerable promise of increasing system efficiency and reducing CO_2 removal costs for both natural gas and coal power systems involves using inorganic membranes that are highly permeable to H_2 but not other gases. If such membranes were applied to natural gas combined cycles, they might make it possible to carry out simultaneously steam reforming, water gas shifting, and H_2 separation in a single vessel. Continuous H_2 removal by the membrane might make it feasible to carry out reforming reactions at temperatures low enough that gas turbine exhaust heat could be used to provide the needed heat (Moritsuka, 1999). (The application of such technologies to coal systems is discussed below.)

Advanced fuels for transportation and other applications

This section discusses the prospects for using advanced fuels to satisfy the sustainable development objectives of keeping fuels affordable, increasing energy security, and evolving towards near-zero emissions of both air pollutants and greenhouse gases. The focus here is mainly on transport fuels that can be derived from syngas, with some reference to synthetic cooking fuels. (The prospects for synthetic fuels derived by direct coal liquefaction are discussed in the next section below.) This discussion of transport fuels is presented in the context of the associated vehicle technologies and the challenges posed by various fuel-vehicle combinations.

Oxygenated fuels: the current focus. U.S. fuel improvement efforts have focussed on reducing levels of benzene (an extremely carcinogenic aromatic compound) in gasoline and on adding oxygenates such as methyl tertiary butyl ether (MTBE) to gasoline to reduce CO emissions and inhibit photochemical smog formation, while maintaining octane ratings that would otherwise fall as a result of lead removal. Although oxygenates are effective in reducing CO emissions and maintaining octane rating, they offer negligible benefits in reducing atmospheric ozone formation (Calvert and others, 1993).

MTBE derived from methanol (MeOH) is widely added to gasoline in volumetric quantities up to 15 percent to help control CO emissions. About 30 percent of the U.S. population lives in areas where MTBE is in regular use; U.S. production levels reached more than 6 million tonnes in 1995. But MTBE use in the future is likely to be severely limited. In July 1999 the U.S. Environmental Protection Agency announced that it would act to greatly reduce the use of MTBE in reformulated gasoline, and in December 1999 the California Air Resources Board banned the use of MTBE in reformulated gasoline in California beginning in 2003.

The shift from MTBE is taking place not only because its air quality benefits appear to be marginal, but also because it is extremely soluble and persistent in water, and humans may be experiencing prolonged exposure to it through tap water. Although it is not especially harmful to humans at typical exposure levels, it imparts a bitter taste and solvent-like odour to water that it contaminates—and human taste and odour thresholds are extremely low (40 parts per billion). MTBE enters drinking water through leaks in gasoline tanks or spills into surface water or groundwater. Although tank leaks also release benzene and many other aromatic and non-aromatic compounds, MTBE tends to migrate faster than other contaminants and is likely to be at the leading edge of a travelling plume (Stern and Tardiff, 1997).

Alcohols. Alcohols (methanol and ethanol) have attracted considerable interest as alternative automotive fuels, especially in Brazil and the United States. The production from biomass of ethanol through biological processes and methanol through thermochemical processes that begin with thermochemical gasification are discussed in chapter 7.

MeOH can be produced from any carbonaceous feedstock through processes that begin with syngas production—for example, from natural gas through steam reforming, from coal through O_2-blown gasification, or from biomass through steam gasification (Williams and others, 1995). Nearly all MeOH is produced from low-cost sources of natural gas, which are often available at remote sites where a natural gas pipeline infrastructure has not been established. Because MeOH is an easily transported liquid, its production from remote gas sources provides a means of exploiting such resources. Most MeOH is used as a chemical feedstock. Its use as a fuel has mainly been for MTBE manufacture. In addition, modest amounts have been used directly in blends with gasoline for cars. With conventional technology, the cost of making it from coal is much greater than from natural gas, because the added capital cost for gasification generally cannot be adequately compensated for by the lower cost of coal relative to natural gas.

Although the use of alcohol fuels in vehicles with internal combustion engines can lead to reduced oil dependence, it is now generally believed that alcohol fuels—especially when blended with gasoline and used in flexible-fuel internal combustion engine vehicles—offer little or no air quality advantages other than lower CO emissions (Calvert and others, 1993). Moreover, reformulated gasoline can meet or surpass the air pollution reductions of alcohol-gasoline blends (CTOFM, 1991). With MeOH, CO emissions would be reduced, and emissions of volatile organic compounds would be less problematic than for gasoline. NO_x emissions would probably not be reduced, however. Ethanol offers fewer air quality benefits than MeOH and may produce more ozone per carbon atom (Calvert and others, 1993).

Emissions from alcohol-fuelled fuel cell vehicles would be a tiny fraction of the emissions from gasoline-fuelled internal combustion engine vehicles. Moreover, the use of alcohols in fuel cell vehicles would lead to marked improvements in fuel economy relative to their use in internal combustion engine vehicles. Several auto manufacturers plan to launch fuel cell vehicles in the market using MeOH as fuel (see below).

If MeOH were to become widely used as an energy carrier for transportation, a concern is its toxicity through direct ingestion, absorption through the skin, or ingestion as a result of drinking methanol-contaminated groundwater.[34] Detailed risk assessments indicate that toxicity is not likely to be a significant concern in routine use, although it might be problematic for accidents involving large spills (Health Effects Institute, 1987). In the case of groundwater contamination, risks are generally much less than for MTBE, because in most situations MeOH would degrade quickly. But oil companies—having been burned by recent decisions to ban MTBE after having made enormous investments in MTBE production, and concerned about liability issues relating to MeOH's toxicity—might be reluctant to make major investments in MeOH, especially if there are promising non-toxic, clean alternative fuels.

The need for a policy framework for transport fuels and engines. The discussions of MTBE and alcohol fuels highlight the lack of a coherent, consistent policy framework for developing advanced fuels and engines for transportation. Closely related to these discussions is the emerging view that environmental regulations are not focussed on the most important pollutants.

Recent studies indicate that by far the greatest costs associated with health impacts arising from transport-related air pollutant emissions are those from fine particles (chapter 3)—both those emitted from vehicles directly and nitrate particles formed in the atmosphere from NO_x emissions. Spadaro and Rabl (1998) estimate that relative to the costs associated with fine particles the health costs posed by CO emissions are negligible, and health costs associated with ozone formation are modest (see table 8.2). It thus appears that concerns about NO_x and particulate emissions will shape future technological choices for fuels and engines.

Besides the lack of a properly focused environmental policy, low oil prices and gasoline taxes also provide no market incentive in the United States for fuel-efficient cars. There the trend has been towards an increasing market share of fuel-guzzling sport utility vehicles—exacerbating concerns about energy supply security and emissions of air pollutants and CO_2.

One auspicious development from Japan is recent commercialisation of a gasoline-fuelled car powered by a hybrid of an internal combustion engine and a battery. This hybrid offers fuel economy twice that of conventional cars with internal combustion engines. Their high efficiency and the fact that they can be operated most of the time near their optimal operating points make it feasible to achieve much lower emissions with gasoline hybrids than with conventional internal combustion engine vehicles.

Advanced hybrid vehicles are being developed under the U.S. Partnership for a New Generation of Vehicles (PNGV), a government-industry initiative that seeks to develop production-ready prototypes that will get 80 miles a gallon (34 kilometres a litre) by 2004 (NRC, 1998). Because this goal is three times the fuel economy of existing cars, emphasis is being given to hybrids based on compression ignition engines (specifically, compression-ignition direct-injection, or CIDI, engines), which are more fuel efficient than spark-ignited hybrids. The CIDI hybrid and the fuel cell car (see below) are the leading contenders to meet PNGV goals for the car of the future.

But the ambitious PNGV research and development programme is not complemented by incentives to introduce such fuel-efficient vehicles into the market. Moreover, unlike the situation with gasoline hybrids, there is no strong air quality driver for advancing CIDI hybrids. To the contrary, air pollution mitigation challenges are far more daunting for compression-ignition than for spark-ignited engines (see table 8.2). In early 2000 DaimlerChrysler introduced a prototype CIDI hybrid car developed under the PNGV that got 72 miles a gallon (30.6 kilometres a litre). Although this car met the air quality standards in effect in 1993, when the PNGV was launched, the current design cannot meet the standards that will be in effect in 2005, when such cars might first be produced on a commercial basis.

There is also a need for better coordination between development activities for fuels and engines. There are needs not only for new fuels but also new engines that are optimised for these fuels.

Syngas-derived fuels for compression-ignition engines and other applications. Compression-ignition engines play major roles in transport, where they are used for buses, trucks, and trains, and in some regions (such as Europe) for cars as well. Such engines are especially important for developing and transition economies, where in 1996 diesel fuel accounted for half of all transport fuel (relative to a fifth in the United States; EIA, 1999a). The efficiency benefits offered by these engines will be even more important in the future as transport demand grows. For example, the World Energy Council's 1995 market rules scenario projects that the number of cars will grow by six times between 1990 and 2020 in developing and transition economies, from 95 million to 580 million (WEC, 1995). Both improved engines and improved fuels will be needed to help mitigate the challenges that such growth poses for energy supply security, air quality, and greenhouse gases.

CIDI engines are promising advanced technologies for improving efficiency, especially when used in hybrid vehicles. Concerns about CIDI hybrids include high costs and whether they will be able to meet expected tougher regulatory goals for NO_x and particulate emissions. In its fourth review of the PNGV, the U.S. National Research Council urged the PNGV to consider shifting emphasis in its CIDI research to non-hybrid versions, in light of the high costs of hybrids (NRC, 1998).

Among the leading candidate fuels for addressing the challenges posed by compression-ignition engines are synthetic middle distillates (SMDs) and dimethyl ether (DME). SMDs are straight-chain hydrocarbon fuels (paraffins and olefins) produced through the Fischer-Tropsch (F-T) process. The F-T process begins with the production of syngas from a carbonaceous feedstock—for example, from natural gas through steam reforming or partial oxidation, or from coal through O_2-blown gasification and even from biomass through gasification.

SMDs are well suited for use in compression-ignition engines, in part because of their high cetane numbers.[35] Moreover, they contain no benzene, other aromatic compounds, or sulphur. Measurements have shown 13–37 percent reductions in particulate emissions and 6–28 percent reductions in NO_x emissions relative to operation on diesel fuel (Sirman, Owens, and Whitney, 1998; Schaberg and others, 1997; Norton and others, 1998). Even greater reductions would be likely if the engines were optimised for use with these fuels, including exhaust gas aftertreatment as well as engine modifications.

The well-established F-T technology for making SMDs can be used with either natural gas or coal as feedstock. Near-term activities will be focussed on use of low-cost supplies of natural gas. Despite high production costs, Shell's small, natural-gas-based Malaysian SMD plant (12,500 barrels a day; see below) made money by selling SMDs for making blends with ordinary diesel fuel to enable compression-ignition engines to meet the tough air pollution standards in California and by selling high-value coproducts (for example, waxes) in niche markets.[36]

Efforts to reduce costs will involve building larger plants. For example, Exxon is considering building a large (50,000–100,000 barrels a day) SMD plant in Qatar as a strategy for developing that country's vast low-cost gas supplies (Fritsch, 1996; Corzine, 1997). Reducing costs will also involve pursuing polygeneration strategies (see the next section).

Another candidate fuel for compression ignition engines is DME, an oxygenated fuel that can be produced from any carbonaceous feedstock by a process that begins, as in the case of MeOH and SMDs, with syngas production. Today DME is produced (150,000 tonnes a year) mainly to provide a replacement for chlorofluoro-carbons as a propellant in aerosol spray cans. Not only does DME not harm the ozone layer (it degrades quickly in the troposphere), but it is non-toxic and non-carcinogenic.

For compression ignition engine applications, DME offers a high cetane number and the potential to achieve low emissions without tailpipe emission controls. Because DME has no carbon-carbon bonds, soot emissions from its combustion are zero. In addition, NO_x emissions can be substantially less than with ordinary diesel fuel. Truck engine emission tests show that NO_x emission are down 55–60 percent and particle emissions are down 75 percent relative to diesel fuel. Residual particle emissions appear to come from the lubricating oil (Fleisch and Meurer, 1995).

DME has also been identified as an especially promising clean cooking fuel (Chen and Niu, 1995). Its wide availability in developing countries could dramatically mitigate the horrendous air pollution

health impacts from burning biomass and coal for cooking (chapters 3 and 10). The main drawback of DME is that at atmospheric pressure it boils at –25 degrees Celsius, so it must be stored in moderately pressurised (9-bar) tanks (much as liquid petroleum gas, which boils at –42 degrees Celsius, is stored). Thus infrastructure challenges would be more demanding in shifting to DME than in shifting to SMDs. But this is not a show-stopper.

Today DME is produced by catalytic dehydration of MeOH and is thus more costly than MeOH. However, an advanced single-step process under development by Haldor Topsoe would make it possible to make DME from natural gas at higher efficiency and less cost than for MeOH. Haldor Topsoe and Amoco have estimated that if DME were produced in large plants in areas with low-cost natural gas, it could be produced at costs not much higher than comparable diesel prices, taking into account the environmental benefits of DME (Hansen and others, 1995). Also promising is the outlook for DME production in polygeneration systems (see below).

It is very likely that fuel strategies will have to be complemented by engine strategies to realise needed low levels of emissions from compression-ignition engines. The possibilities include the use of high-pressure fuel injectors, of catalytic converters to reduce the soluble organic fraction of the particulates, and of particulate traps positioned in the engine exhaust stream—along with some means of burning off the collected particulate matter, most of which is soot (Walsh, 1995; 1997). One new twist is that new engines and exhaust controls being developed to dramatically reduce the mass concentration of particles, in response to tightening air quality regulations, seem to give rise to larger number concentrations (Kittelson, 1998; Bagley and others, 1996; Kruger and others, 1997; Mayer and others, 1995).[37] The larger number concentrations might be problematic because of growing concerns about health impacts of small particle pollutants—although the public health implications of this emissions shift are unclear because of the paucity of data.

Although there are many promising technological opportunities to reduce emissions from compression-ignition engines, it is not clear if advanced fuel and engine technological strategies will be adequate to address air quality challenges fully. The fuel cell is a competing technology for addressing these challenges (see below).

Polygeneration strategies for synthetic fuels production. Just as cogeneration can lead to improved economics relative to production of electricity and process steam in separate facilities (see tables 8.5 and 8.7), so can synthetic fuel production economics be improved by polygeneration—including as coproducts various combinations of electricity, steam, town gas, and chemicals. Especially promising are strategies that coproduce electricity and synthetic fuels from syngas in once-through processes—in which syngas is passed once through a reactor to produce synthetic fuel, and the unconverted syngas is burned to produce electricity in a combined cycle.

Once-through processes are well matched to new liquid-phase

TABLE 8.11. TRIGENERATION VERSUS SEPARATE PRODUCTION OF METHANOL AND COGENERATION USING COAL GASIFICATION TECHNOLOGY

Rates of activity and costs	Separate production facilities for MeOH and cogeneration			Trigeneration plant
	MeOH plant	Cogeneration plant	Total	
Power generation rate (megawatts-electric)	—	400	400	400
Process steam production rate, 10-15 bar (megawatts-thermal)	—	400	400	400
Methanol production rate (megawatts-thermal)	400	—	400	400
Coal input rate (terajoules per hour)	2.46	3.88	6.34	6.46
First Law efficiency (percent)	58.6	74.3	68.1	66.9
CO_2 emission rate (tonnes per hour)	211	333	544	555
Capital investment (millions of dollars)	379	537	916	700
Annual energy production cost (millions of dollars per year) Capital Operation and maintenance (4 percent of capital cost per year) Fuel Total annual energy cost	43.66 15.16 17.25 76.07	61.86 21.48 27.21 110.55	105.52 36.64 44.46 186.62	80.64 28.00 45.30 153.94
Specific cost of energy (dollars per thousand kilowatt-hours) Gross cost Credit for steam coproduct Credit for electricity coproduct Net cost	For MeOH: 27.1 — — 27.1 ($0.12 per litre)	For power: 39.4 -15.0 — 24.4	— — — —	For MeOH: 54.9 -15.0 -24.4 15.5 ($0.07 per litre)

Note: Based on calculations by Robert Moore (formerly Air Products), building on Dale Simbeck's analysis in table 8.7 for a gasification-based cogeneration plant, assuming Air Products' liquid-phase reactor for MeOH production. Engineering plus contingencies and general facilities are each 10 percent of process capital equipment costs. The annual capital charge rate is 11.5 percent. The coal price is $1 per gigajoule (see note c, table 8.4). The annual average capacity factor is 80 percent.

TABLE 8.12. QUADGENERATION VERSUS SEPARATE PRODUCTION OF TOWN GAS AND TRIGENERATION USING COAL GASIFICATION TECHNOLOGY

Rates of activity and costs	Separate production facilities for towngas and trigeneration			Quadgeneration plant
	Towngas plant	Trigen plant	Total	
Power generation rate (megawatts-electric)	—	400	400	400
Process steam production rate, 10-15 bar (megawatts-thermal)	—	400	400	400
Methanol production rate (megawatts-thermal)	—	400	400	400
Syngas production rate (megawatts-thermal)	400	—	400	400
Coal input rate (terajoules per hour)	1.89	6.46	8.35	8.36
First Law efficiency (percent)	76.0	66.9	69.0	68.9
CO_2 emission rate (tonnes per hour)	163	555	718	718
Capital investment (millions of dollars)	228	700	928	783
Annual energy production cost (millions of dollars per year) Capital Operation and maintenance (4 percent of capital cost per year) Fuel Total annual energy cost	26.27 9.12 13.25 48.64	80.64 28.00 45.30 153.94	106.91 37.12 58.55 202.58	90.20 31.32 58.63 180.15
Specific cost of energy (dollars per thousand kilowatt-hours) Gross cost Credit for steam coproduct Credit for electricity coproduct Credit for MeOH coproduct Net cost	For town gas: 17.3 — — — 17.3 ($4.80 per gigajoule)	For MeOH: 54.9 -15.0 -24.4 — 15.5 ($0.07 per litre)	— — — — —	For town gas: 64.2 -15.0 -24.4 -15.5 9.3 ($2.60 per gigajoule)

Note: Based on calculations by Robert Moore (formerly Air Products), building on Dale Simbeck's analysis in table 8.7 for a gasification-based cogeneration plant, assuming Air Products' liquid-phase reactor for MeOH production. Engineering plus contingencies and general facilities are each 10 percent of process capital equipment costs. The annual capital charge rate is 11.5 percent. The coal price is $1 per gigajoule (see note c, table 8.4). The annual average capacity factor is 80 percent.

reactors. With conventional gas-phase reactors, relatively low conversions are achieved in a single syngas pass through the reactor, so that syngas is usually recycled to achieve higher conversions using recycling equipment that is typically capital- and energy-intensive. New liquid-phase reactors—which involve bubbling syngas through a column of heavy oil in which catalysts appropriate to the desired conversion are suspended—offer outstanding heat removal capability in controlling highly exothermic reactions and can achieve high conversions in a single pass, making recycling less attractive and once-through conversion more attractive.

To illustrate polygeneration based on coal-derived syngas, table 8.11 presents calculations for the coproduction of 400 megawatts each of MeOH, electricity, and process steam (trigeneration) from coal by adding extra syngas production capacity to the system described in table 8.7 for the cogeneration of 400 megawatts each of electricity and process steam. Table 8.12 presents calculations for the coproduction of 400 megawatts each of town gas, MeOH, electricity, and process steam (quadgeneration) from coal by adding still more syngas production capacity to the system described in table 8.11.[38] Costs for MeOH produced in liquid-phase reactors through once-through processes have been extensively analysed (Drown and others, 1997), and the technology is relatively well developed.[39]

Consider first the trigeneration system (see table 8.11). In contrast to the cogeneration system (see table 8.7) from which it is evolved, trigeneration does not lead to further fuel savings, but capital cost savings are large. Values assumed for coproducts are $0.0150 a kilowatt-hour for steam (its cost in a stand-alone boiler) and $0.0244 a kilowatt-hour for electricity (its cost in gasification-based cogeneration). Thus the incremental cost for methanol is $0.07 a litre ($4.30 a gigajoule)—compared with $0.012 a litre for MeOH produced from coal in a stand-alone plant. This MeOH cost is less than the average U.S. refinery (wholesale, untaxed) gasoline price in 1997 ($5.10 a gigajoule).

In the quadgeneration example, extra syngas is produced as town gas for distribution by pipelines to nearby users—for example, small-scale cogeneration facilities based on compression-ignition reciprocating engines with pilot oil (see above). Note that, whereas producing 400 megawatts of town gas in a dedicated gasification facility would cost $4.80 a gigajoule, the cost of adding an extra 400 megawatts of syngas capacity for town gas purposes at a trigeneration plant would cost instead $2.60 a gigajoule, because of the scale economy effect. For comparison, the average 1997 U.S. city-gate price of natural gas was $3.30 a gigajoule.

The trigeneration and quadgeneration calculations illustrate the importance of building large, centralised, coal-syngas-based production systems to serve distributed markets for the products. The synthetic liquid fuels produced can be readily transported to vast markets of remote users. Likewise, the electricity coproduct can serve large markets if the polygenerator is able to sell the electricity coproduct into the electric grid at market rates. In contrast, the extra syngas produced as town gas can be transported economically only up to distances of 10–30 kilometres from the production facility. But even in this case, the markets served could be large if the centralised coal conversion plant were located near cities where large numbers of small factories, commercial buildings, and apartment buildings could be served.

Urban siting for these facilities can be considered for gasification-based coal conversion systems because of the very low levels of air pollutant emissions that can be realised (see table 8.1). The major restriction imposed by the market for the strategy illustrated in tables 8.7, 8.11, and 8.12 is that the process steam demand is defined by the needs of the host and is thus very site-specific, with limited overall market opportunity. Thus the coproduction of process steam should be considered an important initial market for helping to launch coal gasification technology in the market rather than a large, unconstrained market opportunity. Polygeneration strategies will often make economic sense, even without the benefit of the process steam coproduct.

Coal-based polygeneration strategies will be especially important for coal-rich, natural-gas-poor countries like China. Although most polygeneration activity relating to syngas production is taking place in industrialised countries, it is also getting under way in some developing countries (table 8.13—and table 8.6 above). Consider that—although China has deployed no modern O_2-blown gasifiers in the power sector—it is already using many such gasifiers in the chemical process industries.[40] Such industries might provide better homes for launching IGCC technologies on the market in China and many other countries than would the electric power industry as it now exists.

Simbeck and Johnson (1999) point out that gasification-based polygeneration is being carried out in some countries without subsidy at refineries and chemical plants, because the economics are inherently attractive. They also point out that polygeneration based on gasification of refinery residues will often be more attractive economically than for coal. Such residues often have high sulphur content and are priced low. Moreover, capital costs tend to be lower—for example, because solids handling, crushing, and feeding systems are not needed. In addition, the generally lower levels of ash in heavy oils means less fouling of syngas coolers, so that lower cost designs might be employed (Todd and Stoll, 1997). Yet much of the technology is the same as for coal, so that this early experience will be helpful in buying down the cost of the technology as experience accumulates, making the technology increasingly attractive for coal as well.

In contrast to the use of large-scale polygeneration systems for improving the economics of coal-based synthetic fuels, the focus for natural-gas-based polygeneration is likely to be on making synfuels production more attractive at small scales—by enabling the production of easy-to-transport liquid fuels from remote, small-scale sources of cheap natural gas.

To illustrate, consider the economics of the coproduction of F-T liquids and electricity from natural gas using liquid-phase reactors in a once-through process. Choi and others (1997) found that such systems producing about 8,800 barrels a day of liquids—plus 84

TABLE 8.13. LARGE COMMERCIAL GASIFICATION-BASED PROJECTS THAT DO NOT GENERATE ELECTRICITY

Location	Plant owner	Technology	Syngas out (megawatts-thermal)	Feedstock(s)	Product(s)	Start-up year
South Africa	Sasol-II	Lurgi Dry Ash	4,130	Sub-bituminous coal	F-T liquids	1977
South Africa	Sasol-III	Lurgi Dry Ash	4,130	Sub-bituminous coal	F-T liquids	1982
United States	Dakota Gasification Company	Lurgi Dry Ash	1,545	Lignite, refinery residues	Synthetic natural gas	1984
Malaysia	Shell MDS Sdn. Bhd.	Shell	1,032	Natural gas	Middle distillates	1993
Germany	Linde AG	Shell	984	Visbreaker residues	Methanol, H_2	1997
South Africa	SASOL-I	Lurgi Dry Ash	911	Sub-bituminous coal	F-T liquids	1955
United States	Unspecified	Texaco	656	Natural gas	MeOH, CO	1979
Taiwan, China	Chinese Petroleum Corp.	Texaco	621	Bitumen	H_2, CO	1984
Germany	Hydro Agri Brunsbüttel	Shell	615	Heavy vacuum residues	NH_3	1978
Germany	VEBA Chemie AG.	Shell	588	Vacuum residues	NH_3, MeOH	1973
Czech Republic	Chemopetrol a.s.	Shell	492	Vacuum residues	NH_3, MeOH	1971
Brazil	Ultrafertil S.A.	Shell	451	Asphalt residues	NH_3	1979
China	Shanghai Pacific Chemical Corp.	Texaco	439	Anthracite coal	MeOH, town gas	1995
China	Shanghai Pacific Chemical Corp.	IGT U-Gas	410	Bituminous coal	Fuel gas, town gas	1994
India	Gujarat National Fertilizer Corp.	Texaco	405	Refinery residues	NH_3, MeOH	1982
Portugal	Quimigal Adubos	Shell	328	Vacuum residues	NH_3	1984

Source: Simbeck and Johnson, 1999.

megawatts-electric of by-product power from remote gas—would be able to provide liquid fuels at a cost competitive with liquid fuels derived from $19 a barrel crude oil, assuming that the by-product electricity is sold for $0.03 a kilowatt-hour. The authors also found that such a plant would be competitive with a F-T plant employing recycling technology producing five times as much synfuels output. Thus, as long as crude oil prices do not plunge much below $20 a barrel, gas liquids derived from natural gas through liquid-phase reactor technology in once-through configurations are likely to be cost-competitive.

The benefits of this technology are related not just to the product price but also to natural gas resource development prospects. The total plant cost (including the cost of an 84-meagwatt-electric combined cycle power plant) estimated by Choi and others (1997) is $415 million. This is in contrast to capital requirement per plant of $2–4 billion for a typical liquid natural gas (LNG) facility. Thus the investment hurdle is far less for a once-through F-T liquids plus power plant than for an LNG plant. Moreover, the proven gas reserves required per site for an F-T plant amounts to only 1 exajoule, relative to 6–8 exajoules for an LNG facility.

Thus F-T technology makes it feasible to exploit much smaller

remote gas fields than is feasible for LNG. Of course, this strategy requires that there be markets for the electricity coproduct, and many remote gas fields are not near transmission networks. However, the costs of building transmission lines to deliver baseload electricity to demand centres might often be economically attractive (requiring much less investment than for energy-equivalent gas infrastructure) given the low generation cost, particularly if outputs of several small fields in the region could be combined for long-distance transmission at scales on the order of 1 gigawatt-electric.

Air Products is also developing liquid-phase reactor technology for DME production (Peng and others, 1997; Peng and others, 1998). As in the case of MeOH and F-T liquids production, liquid-phase reactor technology used in conjunction with once-through process is expected to make DME production from natural gas economically attractive at relatively small scales.

There needs to be continuing research and development on all these liquid-phase reactor synthetic fuels technologies—especially on DME, which has attractive attributes but is the least developed of the technologies described here. But the main barriers to the deployment of these technologies are institutional rather than technological: Their economic viability depends on the ability of the polygenerator to sell the electricity coproduct into the electricity grid at a fair market price. Reforms to promote more competition in power markets will be helpful in nurturing the development of syngas-based synthetic fuels technology.

Hydrogen and the quest for near-zero emissions. The strategic importance of having an energy system for the long term in which H_2 is a major clean energy carrier has been noted (see box 8.1). No CO_2 or air pollutants are emitted during use when H_2 is consumed in fuel cells. If H_2 is burned in gas-turbine-based power plants, the only air pollutant is NO_x (formed by oxidation of N_2 in air); but these NO_x emissions can be controlled to very low levels by lean combustion strategies or by injecting steam or water into the combustor or compressor air stream of suitably designed power plants.[41]

When H_2 is made electrolytically by decomposing water from renewable or nuclear electric sources, CO_2 and pollutant emissions associated with H_2 manufacture and thus life-cycle CO_2 emissions are also zero or near zero. When H_2 is made from a fossil fuel, life-cycle pollutant emissions are also very low,[42] although CO_2 emissions from H_2 manufacture can be high. However, for large, centralised H_2 production facilities, CO_2 can be generated as a nearly pure by-product that can be disposed of (for example, in a geological reservoir) at modest cost. Even if this CO_2 had to be disposed of in aquifers (where there is no credit for enhanced resource recovery) that are as far away as 500 kilometres from production sites, the cost of disposal based on current technology would be less than $50 a tonne of carbon (Williams, 1999b). If the H_2 so produced were a competitive energy carrier (which is not the case today), the cost of CO_2 emissions avoided would approach this disposal cost—which is less than the least avoided cost for the coal electric generation technologies described in table 8.9.

Concerns are often raised about H_2 safety. In this regard, H_2 is better than other fuels in some ways, worse in other ways, and in still other ways just different (Ringland, 1994). However, H_2 can be used safely if procedures are followed that respect its physical and chemical properties (box 8.3). Such theoretical considerations are buttressed by extensive experience with residential town gas (typically 50 percent H_2), which was widely used in the United States until the 1940s and in Europe until the 1960s, and is still used in China and South Africa.

The manufacture of H_2 from a fossil fuel begins with syngas production—the mostly costly step in the overall process. Thus, if the world pursues the syngas-based energy technologies described in previous sections, it would be embarked on a path that would facilitate a transition to H_2.

The dominant commercial H_2 production technology is reforming of natural gas. H_2 can also be made through gasification of any carbonaceous feedstock (Williams and others, 1995), including coal, heavy oils, biomass, or municipal solid waste (Larson, Worrell, and Chen, 1996), or through electrolysis of water using renewables (for example, hydropower, wind, or solar; Ogden and Williams, 1989), nuclear energy, or other power sources. Until fossil fuel prices are far higher than at present, electrolytic approaches for producing H_2, now and in the future, will tend to be much more costly than making H_2 from natural gas, coal, or other fossil fuels—even when the added costs of CO_2 sequestration are taken into account (Williams,1998; IPCC, 1996a).[43]

Technology for producing H_2 from fossil fuels is well established commercially. Although H_2 is currently used only in niche applications as an energy carrier (for example, for the U.S. National Aeronautics and Space Administration's space shuttle launches), it is widely used in oil refining and the chemical process industries. H_2 is produced commercially in the United States at a rate of 8.5 million tonnes a year (Moore and Raman, 1998) or 1.2 exajoules a year (1.25 percent of U.S. energy consumption). Several large-scale polygeneration plants have been or are being built around the world for the coproduction of H_2 and electricity from petroleum residues through gasification (see table 8.6).

Such projects reflect the rapid growth (10 percent a year) in demand for H_2 at refineries, as a result of cleaner transportation fuel mandates and requirements for processing heavier crudes. The major obstacle to widespread deployment of H_2 as an energy carrier is the fact that H_2 is not competitive in energy markets. There are two ways this situation might change: the emergence of H_2-using technologies that put a high market value on H_2, and H_2 production technologies that reduce its cost—the prospects for which are reviewed in the next two sub-sections.

Enhancing the prospects for H_2 with fuel cell vehicle technology. Successful commercialisation of fuel cell vehicles would give H_2 a high market price, because H_2 fuel cell vehicles would typically be much more fuel efficient that internal combustion engine vehicles with the same performance and would offer substantial air quality benefits.[44] Although H_2 storage onboard vehicles is challenging,

---

BOX 8.3. HYDROGEN SAFETY

Hydrogen is widely perceived to be an unsafe fuel, because it burns or detonates over a wider range of mixture with air than other fuels, and very little energy is required to ignite H_2 mixed with the minimum amount of air needed to completely burn it. Although H_2 is flammable in air over a wide range of mixtures, when used in unconfined spaces (as will be typical in transport applications), the lower limits for flammability and detonability matter most. In this regard, H_2 is comparable to or better than gasoline. Gasoline and natural gas can also be easily ignited with low-energy ignition sources such as electrostatic discharges—like those that result from a person walking across a rug. Moreover, in dilute mixtures with air, the ignition energy for H_2 is essentially the same as for methane. In another regard, H_2 has an advantage over gasoline: In case of a leak in an unconfined space, H_2 will disperse quickly in the air because of its buoyancy, whereas gasoline will puddle.

An important safety issue for H_2 is leaks—prevention, detection, and management, particularly in confined spaces. Areas where H_2 is stored and dispensed have to be well ventilated; because of H_2's buoyancy, this means providing vents at the highest points in ceilings. Considering all these issues, a major study of H_2 safety (Ringland, 1994) concluded that "H_2 can be handled safely, if its unique properties—sometimes better, sometimes worse, and sometimes just different from other fuels—are respected."

BOX 8.4. HYDROGEN STORAGE FOR MOTOR VEHICLES

Storing H_2 onboard motor vehicles is challenging because of H_2's low volumetric energy density. With current technology, the least costly option is compressed gas (typically at 350 atmospheres; James and others, 1996), for which the storage density is less than one-tenth gasoline's.

Volumetric storage densities do not have to equal that of gasoline to make H_2 storage manageable—in part because of the high fuel economies of fuel cell vehicles. An H_2 fuel cell car that meets the PNGV fuel economy goal (2.94 litres per 100 kilometres or 80 miles a gallon, gasoline-equivalent) would require 240 litres of compressed H_2 storage capacity for a 680-kilometre (425-mile) range between refuellings, compared to 64 litres for a typical gasoline ICE car (9.4 litres per 100 kilometres, or 25 miles a gallon fuel economy). A prototype H_2 fuel cell van introduced in 1997 by Daimler Benz involved storing H_2 cylinders in an under-the-roof compartment; a car with a PNGV fuel economy and a 680-kilometre range might use three such cylinders, each 110 centimetres long and 32 centimetres in diameter.

In comparison with gaseous storage, storage volumes could be reduced by half with metal hydrides, but storage system weight would increase several times, and costs would be much higher. H_2 liquefaction could reduce storage volumes to a third of those for compressed H_2 but would require consuming electricity equivalent to a third of the H_2 (higher heating value basis), and boil-off (typically 1.5–2 percent a day) makes this option wasteful for private cars that are typically used an hour a day or less.

H_2 storage using carbon nanofibres is under development through alternative approaches (Chambers and others, 1998; Chen and others, 1999; Liu and others, 1999; Dresselhaus, Williams, and Ecklund, 1999). It offers the potential for dramatically improving performance—some options are even able to store H_2 at relatively high energy densities near atmospheric pressure and ambient temperatures. Successful development of one or more of these technologies might make storing H_2 in fuel cell vehicles no more difficult than storing gasoline in gasoline internal combustion engine cars.

problems seem to be surmountable with existing technologies, and some promising advanced options could plausibly make H_2 storage no more challenging for fuel cell vehicles than gasoline storage is today for internal combustion engine vehicles (box 8.4).

A fierce global competition is under way to accelerate the development of fuel cell vehicles (Steinbugler and Williams, 1998; Appleby, 1999). Nearly all major auto manufacturers have produced test vehicles (table 8.14). Several automakers have set goals to introduce fuel cells into the automotive market during 2003–10. Developmental efforts are focused on PEM fuel cells. Industrial interest is motivated largely by the prospect that fuel cell vehicles will have zero or near-zero emissions, without tailpipe emission controls. The air quality benefits provide a powerful rationale for developing fuel cells for a wide range of vehicles, including buses, trucks, locomotives, and small two-and three-wheeled vehicles (which account for much of the air pollution in cities of the developing world; PCAST Panel on ICERD[3], 1999), as well as cars—the focus of fuel cell vehicle development in industrialised countries.

Under a zero-emission-vehicle (ZEV) technology-forcing policy to meet its air quality goals, the state of California has mandated that 10 percent of new cars sold in the state be ZEVs by 2003. Initially, the battery-powered electric vehicle (BPEV) was the focus of efforts to meet the mandate. Although there have been some significant advances (for example, in electric drive-train technology), the BPEV is no longer the only focus of ZEV developmental efforts; the technological challenges of overcoming the problems of long battery recharging times, modest vehicle ranges between rechargings, and high costs have proven formidable. The ZEV mandate has also been catalytic in stimulating industrial interest in fuel cell vehicles as an alternative technology that offers good prospects for addressing the shortcomings of the BPEV.

Although the natural fuel for fuel cell vehicles is H_2, many efforts aimed at commercialising fuel cell vehicles are emphasising H_2 production onboard the car from either MeOH or gasoline, because an H_2 refuelling infrastructure is not yet in place. MeOH and gasoline are liquid fuels that are easily stored and transported. Processing MeOH onboard cars is easier and has been successfully demonstrated. Processing gasoline is more difficult, requiring higher temperatures, but gasoline offers the clear advantage that no new fuel infrastructure is needed. Detailed modelling has shown that MeOH and gasoline fuel cell vehicles would be a third less fuel efficient than H_2 fuel cell vehicles but still more fuel efficient than gasoline-fuelled internal combustion engine vehicles (Ogden, Kreutz, and Steinbugler, 1998).

Although fuel cell vehicles might be launched on the market using MeOH or gasoline, an H_2 fuel cell vehicle would be less costly to own and operate—largely because of expected lower capital and maintenance requirements. Even if fuel cell vehicles are launched with gasoline or MeOH, an internal market pressure subsequently would develop that would encourage a shift to H_2 as soon as an H_2 infrastructure could be put in place (Steinbugler and Williams, 1998; Ogden, Kreutz, and Steinbugler, 1998). By the time fuel cell vehicles account for a large enough fraction of the market to justify the infrastructure investments, a plausible scenario for supplying the needed H_2 would be to establish near each major city one or more large facilities for making H_2 from some mix of natural gas, refinery residues, coal, municipal solid waste, and biomass. These facilities should be large enough to justify economically sequestration of the separated CO_2 but sufficiently close to vehicle refuelling stations that only relatively modest-scale H_2 pipeline networks would be needed to distribute the H_2 to users (Williams, 1999b).

With such an infrastructure in place, fuel cell vehicles could then offer transportation services with zero or near-zero emissions of CO_2 (as well as air pollutants). The added cost to consumers for sequestering the separated CO_2 would amount to less than $0.002 per kilometre of driving (less than 1 percent of the cost of owning and operating a car), assuming current H_2 production technology for coal and natural gas (Kaarstad and Audus, 1997) and fuel cell vehicles having the target gasoline-equivalent fuel economy for the U.S. PNGV (80 mpg, or 2.94 litres per 100 kilometres).

The potential for reducing CO_2 emissions with H_2 fuel cell vehicles depends on how fast the technology penetrates the market. Even the most optimistic scenarios project capturing a fourth of the new car market by 2025—which implies displacing only a tenth of all cars by that time. If all fuel cell cars were fuelled with H_2, and the separated CO_2 were sequestered, global CO_2 emissions would be only 0.1 GtC less than under business-as-usual conditions. Such considerations illustrate the long periods required for new technologies to have major impacts—and underscore the importance of launching accelerated development initiatives for technologies that offer major public benefits, so that they can have significant impacts 25 years in the future.

Can fuel cell vehicles compete? The leading North American developer of PEM fuel cell fuels has said in press releases that PEM fuel cells will be competitive in transport applications when production volumes reach 250,000–300,000 fuel cell vehicle engines a year, which the company expects well before 2010. Some studies in the public domain also project that mass-produced fuel cell vehicles can be competitive (Thomas and others, 1998a, b). Although the economics of fuel cell vehicle technology are still very uncertain, no intrinsic costs of PEM fuel cell materials or fabrication are so obviously high as to preclude mass-produced fuel cell vehicles from being competitive. The fuel cell's inherent simplicity (for example, no moving parts) and mild operating conditions (80 degrees Celsius) relative to internal combustion engine vehicles also suggest substantial cost reduction opportunities.

It will not be easy for the fuel cell vehicle to displace the internal combustion engine vehicle, an entrenched, mature technology. Moreover, as noted, internal combustion engine technology is still being improved. Japanese automakers have already introduced clean spark-ignited internal combustion–electric hybrids that offer twice the fuel economy of conventional internal combustion engine vehicles. It will be difficult for gasoline fuel cell vehicles to compete with these hybrids, because the two sets of vehicles will have comparable efficiencies, and it is always difficult for a new technology to displace an old one—unless it offers enormous advantages.

The air pollution issue will be centre stage during the competition between fuel cell and hybrid internal combustion engine vehicles to be car of the future. Meeting air quality goals will be especially challenging for hybrids involving compression-ignition engines (NRG, 1998). Moreover, Ross and others (1995) estimate that there will be a growing gap between actual life-cycle emissions and regulated emissions for internal combustion engine vehicles with spark-ignited engines (see table 8.3).

Hybrids fueled with H_2 would pose significant competition for H_2 fuel cell vehicles in the race to zero emissions. NO_x would be the only significant pollutant emission for H_2 hybrids; because ultra-

TABLE 8.14. FUEL CELL TEST VEHICLES AROUND THE WORLD

| Year | Company | Fuel storage | Fuel cell power system | | | Range (kilometres) |
			Power output (kilowatts)	Auxiliary power	Vehicle type	
1993	Ballard	Pressurised H_2	120	No	Bus	160
1994	DaimlerChrysler	Pressurised H_2	54 net	No	Necar I (van)	130
1996	DaimlerChrysler	Pressurised H_2	50 net	No	Necar II (van)	250
1996	Toyota	Metal hydride	20	Pb battery	Car	250
1997	Ballard	Pressurised H_2	205 net	No	Bus	400
1997	DaimlerChrysler	MeOH (onboard reformer)	50	No	Necar III (car)	Greater than 400
1997	Mazda	Metal hydride	20	Ultra-capacitor	Car	170
1997	DaimlerChrysler	Pressurised H_2	190 net	No	Nebus (bus)	250
1998	Renault	Liquid H_2	30	Ni-MH battery	Station wagon	400
1998	Opel	MeOH (onboard reformer)	50 (motor)	Ni-MH battery	Minivan	-
1999	DaimlerChrysler	Liquid H_2	70	No	Necar IV (car)	400
1999	Ford	Pressurised H_2	75	No	Car	96
1999	Nissan	MeOH (onboard reformer)	10	Li-ion battery	Station wagon	—
1999	Honda	Metal hydride	60	Ni-MH battery	Car	—
1999	Honda	MeOH (onboard reformer)	60	Ni-MH battery	Station wagon	—
2000	General Motors	Chemical hydride	75	Ni-MH battery	Car	800

Source: Various fuel cell vehicle newsletters.

lean combustion is feasible with H_2 fueling, NO_x emissions of hybrids can be controlled to low levels. However, such hybrids would be less fuel efficient than H_2 fuel cell vehicles and thus more costly to operate. The economic winner of this race to zero emissions depends on what relative vehicle costs turn out to be when vehicles are mass produced.

Despite the many uncertainties, there is growing private sector confidence in the prospects for making fuel cell vehicle technology competitive, as indicated by substantial auto industry investment levels and growing attention being paid to the technology also by the oil industry (API, 1999).[45] Making fuel cell vehicles competitive in the near term requires accelerated commercialisation, because current costs are high, and large production volumes are needed to bring costs down quickly. (Fuel cells—like many other new technologies—are expected to be well described by learning curves for which costs decline 10–30 percent for each cumulative doubling of production; Rogner, 1998; Lipman and Sperling, 1999.) Recognising this, one industrial consortium for fuel cell vehicle development—automakers DaimlerChrysler, Ford, and Mazda, and fuel cell developer Ballard Power Systems—has bullishly set an ambitious goal of selling 40,000 fuel cell cars a year by 2004.

Enhancing prospects for hydrogen with advanced hydrogen production technologies. H_2 might eventually be able to compete in fuel cell vehicle markets using current H_2 production technologies. But new H_2 production technologies are needed to enable H_2 to compete in applications such as stationary power generation, for which H_2 fuels cells do not offer major efficiency advantages over conventional fossil energy technologies. There are many opportunities.

One set of opportunities involves integrating CO_2 removal into production processes in creative ways—for example, coproduction of H_2 and F-T liquids from natural gas to reduce costs by avoiding the need for a costly air separation plant.[46] Advanced gas separation technologies warrant focussed attention, especially for separating CO_2 and H_2.[47] One innovative technology receiving development support from the U.S. Department of Energy involves cooling the pressurised gaseous mixture (mainly CO_2 and H_2) exiting the water-gas shift reactors to less than 10 degrees Celsius, then bubbling the gases through a water column. Under appropriate conditions the H_2 passes through but the CO_2 is converted into a CO_2 clathrate hydrate that is heavier than water and easily removed. With this technology it might be possible to substantially reduce the energy and capital costs of CO_2 removal and disposal (Spenser, 1999; Spencer and Tam, 1999).

Another promising set of options involves using inorganic membrane reactors to simultaneously drive the water-gas shift reaction towards maximum H_2 yield and separate the H_2 and CO_2. Williams (1999b) points out that using such reactors offers the potential for making H_2 from coal (without CO_2 sequestration) at costs that approach typical natural gas prices for electricity producers in the United States, with CO_2 sequestration costs adding \$1.00–1.50 a gigajoule. At such costs, coal-derived H_2 with sequestration of the separated CO_2 could be an economically attractive option even for central-station power generation in a greenhouse gas emissions-constrained world.

In one variant of this concept, the Parsons Group has proposed a plant design to make H_2 from coal that involves separating H_2 from CO_2 at high temperatures using porous ceramic membranes. Substantial cost reductions are projected relative to conventional methods for making H_2 from coal (Parsons Infrastructure and Technology Group, 1998; Badin and others, 1999). But Williams (1999b) suggests that attention be given instead to carrying out the gas separations at much lower temperatures than proposed by the Parsons Group, to avoid the formidable technological difficulties of high-temperature processes. Operation of membrane reactors at lower temperatures increases the number of technological options for gas separation, including especially promising non-porous composite metal membrane technologies that can provide H_2 of high purity— important for applications involving PEM fuel cells, which are poisoned by CO at low (10 parts per million by volume) concentrations.

If methane hydrates could be exploited at large scales (chapter 5), ways would eventually be needed to extract the energy without releasing the separated CO_2 into the atmosphere, to prevent a greenhouse disaster.[48] One way this might be accomplished is to make H_2 from the methane using steam reforming and leave behind in nearby reservoirs the by-product CO_2 as CO_2 clathrate hydrates (PCAST Energy Research and Development Panel, 1997), which are stable under pressure and temperature conditions similar to those for methane hydrates. Indeed, sub-seabed disposal of CO_2 in the form of clathrate hydrates has been proposed as a major option for effectively disposing of CO_2 generated in fossil energy systems (Koide and others, 1997).

Alternatively, H_2 could be extracted through methane thermal decomposition to produce H_2 and carbon black (Steinberg and Cheng, 1989), an endothermic process. If some of the produced H_2 is burned to provide the needed heat, the process would be CO_2-emissions free, and the net H_2 energy yield would still be more than 50 percent of the energy content of the original methane. Although this conversion would have much less than the 80–85 percent efficiency that can be achieved with conventional reforming technologies, methane thermal decomposition might prove interesting if there are unforeseen obstacles (political or technical) to large-scale CO_2 sequestration (carbon black is easier to store than CO_2).

Other near-term advanced fossil energy technologies

Besides the advanced technologies described above that are consistent with all sustainable development goals, other near-term advanced fossil energy technologies—for both power generation and synthetic fuels production—offer improved performance relative to today's technologies but would not be consistent with all sustainable development goals. In particular, they would not provide a good basis for moving over the longer term towards near-zero pollutant and CO_2 emissions. Yet some of them might become important in limited applications.

Power generation

Other candidate advanced coal-based power-generating technologies include ultrasupercritical coal steam-electric plants, IGCC plants that employ air-blown gasifiers, and pressurised fluidised-bed combustion (PFBC).

Ultrasupercritical coal steam-electric plants. A typical modern coal steam-electric plant with flue gas desulphurisation has 35.5 percent efficiency (see table 8.4), a level that has changed little since the 1950s. Attention has recently been given to opportunities to achieve higher efficiencies by using advanced alloys that make it possible to increase peak steam temperatures and pressures to ultrasupercritical steam conditions and by deploying efficiency-boosting cycle configurations (for example, double reheating, which increases efficiency by increasing the average temperature at which heat is added to the cycle). For example, ELSAM of Denmark has built a 400-megawatt-electric ultrasupercritical, coal steam-electric plant with an announced efficiency of 47 percent (Kjaer, 1993).[49] This project should be watched closely to see if operators can avoid the high forced outage rates that plagued earlier attempts to operate steam-electric plants under ultrasupercritical conditions. Increased forced outage risk will be more important under future competitive market conditions than in the past, when most electric companies had a guaranteed rate of return on investment.

One limitation of the technology is that it is not nearly as well suited as the IGCC for cogeneration. The low electricity-heat output ratio characteristic of steam cycles using back-pressure turbines (see figure 8.1) limits the overall cost reduction potential, as well as the overall power-generating and fuel-saving potentials from cogeneration based on this technology (compare tables 8.7 and 8.8). In addition, the cogeneration operating mode is typically not cost-effective for systems that involve steam reheating.[50]

Achieving ultra-low air pollutant emissions will be much harder than for IGCC plants with O_2-blown gasifiers, because contaminants to be removed are in flue gas volumes 40–60 times larger than for the pressurised fuel gases from which pollutants are removed in IGCC plants. In addition, although ultrasupercritical steam plants release a fifth less CO_2 per kilowatt-hour than conventional steam-electric plants, achieving deep reductions in CO_2 emissions requires approaches that involve removing CO_2 from flue gases, which is much more costly than for IGCC plants with fuel gas decarbonisation equipment (see table 8.9).

Coal IGCC technology based on air-blown gasification. Although commercial coal IGCC technology is based on O_2-blown gasifiers, the research and development community is interested in developing systems based on air-blown gasifiers—motivated largely by a desire to eliminate the air separation plant.[51] Interest in air-blown gasification in turn has driven interest in research and development on warm gas clean-up technologies that could reduce the thermal losses from cooling down the gas exiting the gasifier for clean-up and heating it up again for combustion.[52]

> Government support for innovation is needed—particularly for long-term research, and for early deployment of new technologies.

Development of warm gas clean-up is proving to be difficult.[53] But even if these difficulties were eventually overcome, broadly based comparisons of O_2- and air-blown gasifier-based systems (Simbeck, 1995) show that O_2-blown gasifiers are usually preferred for coal.[54] The advantage of avoiding the need for O_2 is offset by disadvantages of air-blown gasifier systems, considering only direct costs. First, because of the lower heating value of the gas, an air-blown gasifier requires twice the gasifier volume as does an O_2-blown gasifier—important in light of the capital intensity of gasifiers. Second, for gasifiers operated at comparable temperatures, the sensible heat of the raw gas leaving an air-blown unit is typically 50–60 percent more than for an O_2-blown gasifier, which implies a significant increase in the duty of the raw gas cooler—one of a gasification plant's more costly items.

In addition, seven strategic considerations amplify the relative benefits of O_2-blown systems. First, O_2-blown gasification facilitates an evolutionary strategy in which gas turbines and combined cycles are fired first with natural gas and converted later to coal as natural gas prices rise—a difficult option for air-blown gasifiers without major system modifications and technical risk. Second, air-blown units are less able to exploit advances in gas turbine technology that enable higher turbine inlet temperatures and higher efficiencies.[55] Third, with air-blown gasification, polygeneration strategies (see above) other than cogeneration of process heat and electricity are not practical. Fourth, warm-gas clean-up is essential for favourable system economics with air-blown gasifiers, but merely an option that offers higher efficiency for systems with O_2-blown gasifiers—the benefit of which must be traded off against capital cost, reliability, and environmental considerations. Fifth, if warm-gas clean-up can be made commercially viable, environmental benefits would be less for air-blown systems, because dilution of the contaminants with N_2 makes achieving the same levels of air pollutant emissions reduction more costly than for O_2-blown systems. Sixth, achieving deep reductions in CO_2 emissions with IGCCs equipped with air-blown gasifiers would require flue gas CO_2 recovery approaches that are much more costly than are fuel gas recovery approaches for O_2-blown systems (see table 8.9). Seventh, successful development of air-blown gasifier-based systems would not make a major contribution in moving towards near-zero emissions in the long term, while the O_2-blown gasifier is the key near-term technology that would enable this evolutionary strategy.

Pressurised fluidised-bed combustion. PFBC is an advanced technology evolved from atmospheric pressure fluidised-bed combustion (AFBC) technology, which is already on the market (with both bubbling- and circulating-bed variants).[56]

A review of AFBC technology is helpful in understanding PFBC. Although not more energy-efficient than pulverised coal plants, AFBC plants make it possible to use a wide range of coals and other fuels in a single combustor. One manifestation of this fuel flexibility is the ability to cofire coal units with biomass, a common practice in Scandinavia (Saviharju, 1995). This practice makes it possible both to realise the economies of larger-scale conversion for biomass than are typically feasible with dedicated biomass units and to reduce the AFBC unit's air pollutant and greenhouse gas emissions (as a result of the typically low sulphur and nitrogen contents of biomass feedstocks and their CO_2 emissions neutrality). (This flexibility to accommodate biomass is also provided by fluidised-bed gasification technologies.)

At the low operating temperatures of AFBC plants, thermal NO_x emissions are considerably less than for pulverised coal plants, although about 10 percent of nitrogen in coal can be converted to NO_x (Pillai, 1989). For some coals and in areas with tight regulations on emissions, NO_x control equipment is needed. Up to 90 percent sulphur removal can be accomplished by adding limestone or dolomite to the bed; higher removal rates are theoretically possible but impractical because of the large quantities of limestone and dolomite needed and consequent high solid waste disposal rates. AFBC sulphur removal technology is practically restricted to use with relatively low-sulphur coals and for meeting regulatory requirements calling for relatively modest sulphur removal. The high pH of the waste (because of free lime, accounting for a third of limestone-related wastes) might cause the waste to be classified as hazardous in some areas and thus be subject to especially stringent disposal regulations. Moreover, waste utilisation strategies are difficult because potentially useful products (such as gypsum) are intimately mixed with other wastes.

When a fluidised-bed combustor is pressurised to 10–15 atmospheres, electricity can be produced by feeding the combustion-product gases to a gas turbine after clean-up and using the turbine exhaust gases to produce steam in a heat recovery boiler that drives a steam turbine. Such PFBC technology thus makes higher efficiency possible with a combined cycle, while reducing boiler size. Early PFBC units have 37–40 percent efficiencies. Improved designs, such as ABB Carbon's design with an ultrasupercritical double-reheating PFBC boiler and steam turbine, can achieve 43 percent efficiency.

PFBC and IGCC based on O_2-blown gasifiers are the leading competing advanced coal power technologies. The main PFBC advantages are fuel flexibility (as for AFBC) and simplicity—because PFBC uses one reactor (combustor) relative to two (gasifier and combustor) for IGCC—which might give PFBC a near-term cost advantage. A major PFBC limitation is that, unlike the IGCC, it cannot take advantage of continuing advances in gas turbine technology, because the turbine inlet temperature is fixed at the bed temperature, which is far below the state of the art for modern gas turbines. Future systems might be able to exploit gas turbine technology advances,[57] although they would not be simpler than IGCC systems and thus would lose the original appeal of the PFBC concept and current designs. Efficiencies of 45–48 percent are being targeted. As in the case of air-blown IGCC technology, successful development of warm gas clean-up technology is key to achieving high performance with future PFBC systems. Like

AFBC, PFBC is limited mainly to use with low-sulphur coals, because of solid waste disposal issues; PFBC typically generates more solid waste per unit of fuel consumed than AFBC.

The higher efficiencies offered by PFBC can lead to reduced CO_2 emissions—for example, a 43 percent efficient unit equipped with an ultrasupercritical double-reheat PFBC boiler and steam turbine would have a fifth less CO_2 emissions than a typical new 35.5 percent efficient pulverised coal plant. But achieving deep reductions in CO_2 emissions would require approaches that involve removing CO_2 from flue gases, which are more costly than for IGCC plants with fuel gas decarbonisation equipment (see table 8.9). In addition, unlike most combustion systems, greenhouse gas emissions from fluidised-bed combustion units can be significantly greater than emissions from fuel carbon. A powerful additional greenhouse gas is nitrous oxide (N_2O), which is produced efficiently from nitrogen in coal at the low operating temperatures of fluidised beds.[58]

Measurements of N_2O in AFBC exhaust gases (de Soete, 1993) correspond to a 5–25 percent increase in CO_2-equivalent greenhouse gas emissions relative to CO_2 emissions from coal burning. Sub-bituminous coals and lignite generally produce less N_2O than bituminous coals, and circulating fluidised beds tend to produce more N_2O than bubbling beds, possibly because of the longer residence times for the former (de Soete, 1993). Reducing N_2O emissions from AFBC units will be technologically challenging. For PFBC systems, N_2O emission data are relatively scant. Measurements at the Swedish Värtan PFBC cogeneration plant (Dahl, 1993) show that emissions vary markedly with operating conditions. From these measurements, it is estimated that when NO_x control technologies are not deployed, the CO_2-equivalent emissions of N_2O emissions are 3–10 percent of CO_2 emissions from coal burning. In addition, when NH_3 injection is used for NO_x control, the CO_2-equivalent emissions are 5–18 percent of CO_2 emissions from coal burning.

Although it is a significant improvement over conventional pulverised coal and AFBC technologies, PFBC technology is limited for the longer term by constraints similar to those for ultrasupercritical pulverised coal steam plants and IGCCs using air-blown gasifiers. For applications involving cogeneration of process heat and electricity, characteristic PFBC electricity-heat output ratios are much less than those for IGCC technologies (because of the relatively minor role played by the gas turbine in PFBC units), so that cogeneration economics would tend to be less favourable than for IGCC systems. And, as for conventional ultrasupercritical pulverised coal steam-electric plants, energy-efficient PFBC designs that employ steam reheat cycles are generally poor candidates for cogeneration. Moreover, PFBC systems cannot exploit the syngas-based polygeneration opportunities feasible with O_2-blown gasification.

Whether PFBC can meet its long-term goals depends critically on success with warm-gas cleanup; comments relating to warm-gas clean-up for PFBC versus IGCC with O_2-blown gasifiers would be similar to those presented above for warm-gas clean-up for IGCC with air-blown gasifiers versus IGCC with O_2-blown gasifiers. Perhaps the most fundamental shortcoming of PFBC technology is that, as for ultrasupercritical steam technology and IGCC technology with air-blown gasifiers, it is not a stepping stone along the path to near-zero emissions for coal.

Liquid fuels production through direct liquefaction of low-quality feedstocks

An alternative to the indirect liquefaction technology that provides syngas-derived synthetic fuels from carbonaceous feedstocks (see above) is direct coal liquefaction, which involves adding H_2 to coal in a solvent slurry at elevated temperatures and pressures. Direct liquefaction was commercialised in Germany and Japan to provide liquid fuels during World War II, when coal-derived gasoline levels reached 75,000 barrels a day (Simbeck, Dickenson, and Moll, 1981). Interest in the technology virtually disappeared when low-cost Middle Eastern oil became available in the 1950s but was revived during the oil crises of the 1970s, when several pilot and demonstration projects were carried out. Interest almost disappeared again with the collapse of the world oil price in the mid-1980s. Today the technology is again being considered as an option for making synthetic fuels in natural-gas-poor regions such as China.[59]

An advantage often claimed for direct liquefaction is that overall conversion efficiencies are higher than for indirect liquefaction (Stiegel, 1994). However, to the extent that potential efficiency gains relative to indirect liquefaction can be realised, this is largely due to the fact that direct liquefaction plants produce liquids that are aromatic-rich and thus require less H_2 than typical fuels derived through indirect processes (Simbeck, Dickenson, and Moll, 1981). But here an improvement in efficiency would represent a step backwards for environmental management, because new environmental regulations aim to propel a shift to inherently cleaner fuels—for example, recent U.S. regulations limit aromatic contents of transport fuels.

A review of direct coal liquefaction technology by a panel convened by U.S. President Bill Clinton to advise him on energy research and development needs (PCAST Energy Research and Development Panel, 1997) found that the technology:
- Offered no advantages relative to indirect liquefaction.
- Would lead to liquid fuels that generate twice as much CO_2 as petroleum-based fuels.
- Would provide no obvious path to achieving deep reductions in CO_2 emissions over the long term at low cost—in contrast to syngas-based strategies, which can evolve to the point where H_2 is a major energy carrier with low-cost sequestration of the separated CO_2.

Because of such considerations, the panel recommended that the U.S. Department of Energy terminate federal research and development funding for direct coal liquefaction. The panel also recommended that the freed-up resources be used to support research and development on syngas-based technologies that are consistent with a technological evolution over the longer term to near-zero emissions for fossil fuels.

The arguments set forth here favouring indirect over direct liquefaction apply to other low-quality feedstocks as well as coal—for example, tar sands and heavy crudes, which are far more abundant than conventional oil and natural gas resources (chapter 5). Such feedstocks could be used to produce cleaner fuels through indirect liquefaction, and ultimately H_2 with sequestration of the separated CO_2, thereby helping to realise the long-term goal of near-zero emissions for fossil fuels.

Conclusion

The fossil energy system can evolve in ways consistent with sustainable development objectives if public policies guide a high rate of innovation toward super-clean fossil energy technologies. On the basis of present knowledge, it is possible to identify and describe advanced fossil energy technologies that meet sustainable development objectives at reasonable cost.

The trend towards the growing use of natural gas is making clean energy more widely available at attractive prices. But the move to gas in the context of an increasingly competitive energy industry is also making innovation difficult. To stimulate the needed innovation, policy-makers could set long-term goals for advanced fossil energy technologies, including near-zero emissions of both air pollutants and greenhouse gases. They could also enact policies with incentives to motivate the private sector to develop and deploy technologies that would lead the fossil energy system towards a future consistent with sustainable development objectives.

Key technologies needed to bring about such a fossil energy future are advanced gas turbines, fuel cells, advanced syngas production technologies, and inorganic membranes for gaseous separations. The private sector is fully capable of carrying out most of the needed research and development for all such technologies. But government support for innovation is needed—particularly for long-term research, for which private sector incentives are especially weak, and for early deployment of new technologies that offer major public benefits related to sustainable development (PCAST Panel on ICERD[3], 1999).

Major roles for developing countries (where most fossil energy demand growth will take place) in the innovation process are also needed to ensure that innovations are tailored to developing country needs (PCAST Panel on ICERD[3], 1999). Government also could play a role in guiding and facilitating new infrastructure development—for example, for natural gas delivery systems in the near term and H_2 delivery systems in the long term. Both the energy innovation process and infrastructure-building activities have strong international dimensions and highlight the importance of fostering international collaborations—for example, through industrial joint ventures (PCAST Panel on ICERD[3], 1999).

Reforms that encourage competitive power markets could help put industry on a path to fossil energy with near-zero emissions by helping launch syngas-based polygeneration activities that provide clean synthetic fuels for transportation, cooking, and other applications, along with electricity and process steam.

Two sets of research and development issues stand out for a long-term fossil energy strategy. One concerns the effectiveness, safety, and capacity for CO_2 disposal. A better scientific and technical understanding of these issues, on a region-by-region basis, would help policy-makers decide how much climate-change mitigation resources to commit to this strategy relative to other options, such as renewable or nuclear energy. The other concerns the prospects for energy recovery from methane hydrates. A better scientific and technical understanding of this resource, on a region-by-region basis, would help policy-makers decide how to allocate resources for long-term fossil energy research and development (for example, how to allocate between coal and methane hydrate options). Getting answers to both sets of questions would require expenditures of public resources, because private sector interest is weak as a result of the long-term nature of the questions. But in both cases, the required expenditures are likely to be modest.

An uncertainty regarding the strategy outlined here—guiding the fossil energy system towards widespread fuel decarbonisation with CO_2 sequestration—is whether the public will find large-scale sequestration acceptable. The public has to be convinced that sequestration will be safe and effective. Broad public participation in activities related to decarbonisation and sequestration should be encouraged—for example, a wide range of stakeholder groups should have roles in reviewing scientific studies, demonstration projects, and planning activities. The fact that the least costly technologies for CO_2 disposal also offer near-zero emissions of air pollutants should help gain public confidence. The public will want to know the trade-offs, in relative costs and side effects, among fossil, renewable, and nuclear options for realising the goal of near-zero emissions, and also the trade-offs between pursuing near-zero emissions and not doing so.

ADVANCED NUCLEAR ENERGY TECHNOLOGIES

Nuclear power dominates electricity production in several countries[60] and is making substantial contributions to global energy: At the 1998 level of installed nuclear capacity of 349 gigawatts-electric, nuclear power provided 16 percent of world-wide electricity (IAEA, 1999). Although there is likely to be modest expansion until 2010, most projections are that the nuclear share of electricity generation will be less in 2020 than today. And many projections envisage that nuclear power's absolute contribution in electricity will be no more than today and might even be less.[61]

The regional outlook has more contrasts.[62] For industrialised countries, which accounted for 81 percent of nuclear generating capacity in 1997, the U.S. Energy Information Administration (EIA) projects that nuclear capacity in 2020 will be 44, 75, and 100 percent of the capacity in 1997 for its low-growth, reference, and high-growth scenarios. The projected reductions in capacity in industrialised countries reflect the expectation that nuclear plants retired at the ends of their useful lives will not be replaced, although utilities in several countries are considering plant life extensions. For Eastern Europe and the countries of the former Soviet Union (which accounted for 13 percent of global nuclear capacity in 1997), the EIA projects that, for these same scenarios, capacity in 2020 will be 26 gigawatts-electric less, 6 less, and 24 more than in 1997. For developing countries (which accounted for 6 percent of global nuclear capacity in 1997), the EIA projects capacity increases for the respective scenarios of 10, 34, and 67 gigawatts-electric, with most of the expansion in Asia.

There is a nuclear power stalemate in many regions, in part because the technology is much more costly than was originally projected—a problem exacerbated by low fossil fuel prices, growing numbers of new competing technologies, and increasingly competitive market conditions world-wide in the electric power industry. In addition, the prospects for continuing and expanding the contribution of nuclear power to the world energy supply have been clouded by concerns related to safety, radioactive waste management, and nuclear weapons proliferation and diversion. All these issues have led to a loss of public confidence in nuclear technology.

Rationale for reconsidering the nuclear option

If ways can be found to make nuclear power widely acceptable, it could help address problems posed by conventional fossil energy technologies—especially health impacts of air pollution and climate change arising from CO_2 build-up in the atmosphere. Considering the chain of activities for nuclear power production (including mining operations, nuclear fuel conversion, nuclear power plant operation, decommissioning, transportation, and waste disposal), recent analysis carried out under the European Commission's ExternE Program estimated that the total cost of environmental damage (local, regional, and global impacts integrated during a period of up to 100,000 years) is about $0.003 per kilowatt-hour when evaluating future impacts with a zero discount rate (Rabl and Spadaro, 2000).[63] This is far less than the environmental damage costs of coal steam-electric plants with the best available control technologies, but (considering the margin of error in these estimates) is comparable to damage costs of modern natural gas combined cycle and coal IGCC plants (see table 8.1).

These externality cost comparisons for nuclear and fossil energy systems are incomplete, however. The calculations do not take into account costs associated with the potential diversion of nuclear materials to weapons purposes or wars triggered by concerns about access to energy or water supplies, which are inherently difficult to quantify in economic terms. For nuclear power, greenhouse gas emissions are zero, a benefit (also inherently difficult to quantify) that must also be taken into account in comparing nuclear and fossil energy technologies.

As an aid in thinking about potential roles for nuclear energy in mitigating climate change, consider two alternative scenarios:

- A high-growth scenario that extrapolates the EIA's high-growth scenario to 2100, with nuclear capacity increasing to 1,000 gigawatts-electric by 2050, 3,000 by 2075, and 6,500 by 2100.[64]
- A low-growth scenario that extrapolates the EIA's low growth scenario to zero nuclear capacity by 2050.

The greenhouse gas mitigation benefit of the high-growth relative to the low-growth scenario would be reductions in CO_2 emissions of 225 GtC during the next 100 years if coal power were displaced and 110 GtC if natural gas power were displaced[65]—reductions equivalent to 16 percent and 8 percent of emissions during the period under a business-as-usual future.[66] This calculation shows that, for nuclear energy to make a significant contribution to coping with climate change, nuclear capacity must be increased by at least an order of magnitude during the next 100 years.

The need for advanced technologies

It is desirable to see if acceptable solutions can be found to the economic, safety, proliferation and diversion, and waste management concerns that presently constrain the prospects for further nuclear deployment.[67] Solutions are desirable both because nuclear energy can potentially contribute to solving the major problems posed by conventional fossil energy technologies and because of uncertainties associated with the prospects of other advanced energy-supply options (both the advanced fossil technologies described above and the renewable technologies described in chapter 7). Emphasis here is on technological strategies and the kinds of research and development that offer promise in making the nuclear option more attractive. However, socio-political considerations are also discussed.

The sociopolitical context

Identification of promising technologies for future nuclear power is complicated by the lack of consensus in the broader community of stakeholders (utilities, governments, publics, scientists, engineers) on goals for nuclear energy innovation and ways to address the goals. At the root of these difficulties is the fact that the issues cannot be resolved in narrow technical and economic terms. Perceptions of costs, safety, proliferation and diversion impacts, and risks in waste management matter as much as engineers' calculations.

To illustrate, consider that although most experts believe waste disposal is the least challenging problem facing nuclear energy and

Most projections are that the nuclear share of electricity generation will be less in 2020 than today.

is soluble, many in the general public regard waste disposal as the most daunting challenge. Public concerns about managing wastes for the very long term thus have focused attention in the technical community on waste mitigation strategies that could radically shorten the time required to keep waste under surveillance (for example, nuclear waste separation and transmutation proposals)—relatively costly strategies that some experts believe would exacerbate proliferation and diversion concerns without gaining many benefits. As long as there are such seemingly fundamental disagreements, nuclear energy innovation efforts will remain unfocused.

The analysis of technologies and strategies that follows is based largely on technical considerations. But the reader should bear in mind that bringing about a 'nuclear renaissance' would require more than just doing the right research and development. Because—after an ambitious start—nuclear power has lost its lustre, the barriers to its revival are probably higher than if the technology were entirely new. Nuclear power may never again be seen as "a welcome sign that the modern age is dawning; it can at best hope to be tolerated. Therefore, nuclear power must have a substantial advantage if it is to be used" (Lidsky, 1991). And new nuclear technology must appeal not only to experts but also to the public.

Nuclear electricity costs

Nuclear fuel costs are low relative to fossil fuel costs. For example, in 1998 the average fuel cost for nuclear power in the United States was $0.0054 per kilowatt-hour (Ryan, 1999)—a third that for coal steam-electric power and a fourth that for natural gas combined cycles in Europe (see table 8.4). But operation and maintenance costs and capital costs have been high for nuclear plants. Operation and maintenance costs have been declining somewhat in recent years as a result of competitive pressures but are high relative to operation and maintenance costs for fossil fuel plants. For example, in 1998 operation and maintenance costs for U.S. nuclear plants averaged $0.014 per kilowatt-hour (Ryan, 1999)—more than three times the operation and maintenance cost for U.S. coal or natural gas plants (see table 8.4). Operation and maintenance costs have been high for nuclear plants largely because of the large operating staff—typically 800–900 for a large 1,100-megawatt-electric power station. Staffing requirements are high, to a large degree because of the need to operate the plants within current regulatory guidelines designed to ensure safety.

A recent survey of electricity generation costs in 18 countries found that installed capital costs for new nuclear power plants around the world are $1,700–3,100 per kilowatt-electric (Paffenbarger and Bertel, 1998),[68] much higher than for typical new fossil energy plants. Despite such high capital costs, the study found that, for new plants, nuclear power would be less costly than coal- or natural-gas-based power in two countries—China and France.

The costs of alternatives to nuclear power are fast-moving targets in many regions. Privatisation is taking place in many countries where the power sector was once dominated by parastatal energy companies, and the trend is towards more competition in power markets, where competitive new smaller-scale technologies have ended the historical natural monopoly status of electricity generation. As noted, the natural gas combined cycle has become the technology of choice for thermal power generation where natural gas is readily available. Where competitive conditions are strong, costs have been coming down, even for mature technologies such as pulverised coal steam-electric plants—for example, by a fourth in the United States from 1992–95 (Stoll and Todd, 1996).

Moreover, since the early 1980s the average price of coal for electric companies in the United States has fallen by a factor of 2 in real (inflation-adjusted) terms, and the average coal price is expected to fall a further 30 percent by 2020, to $0.90 a gigajoule (EIA, 1999a). In Europe fossil energy prices are not as low as in the United States, but even there prices have been falling; from 1983–95 the average prices for coal and natural gas imported into the European Union fell from 55 to 65 percent (Decker, 1999). Such intensifying competition from fossil fuels can be expected to spread to more and more regions undergoing electric industry restructuring.

Quantification of the external costs of today's fossil energy plants would improve the economics of nuclear power. But these benefits will not be so great with various advanced fossil energy technologies: Fossil energy technologies now coming onto the market can provide electricity with very low emissions of local and regional air pollutants. Moreover, as discussed above, even the climate change benefits offered by nuclear power likely will face stiff competition from advanced coal systems that involve fuel decarbonisation and CO_2 sequestration. Thus direct economic costs will continue to be important in determining the future of nuclear power. If nuclear power is to become economically viable once again, innovations will be needed that can provide electricity at costs competitive with other future near-zero-emission energy technologies. Moreover, this has to be done in ways that are consistent with meeting concerns about nuclear safety, proliferation and diversion, and radioactive waste disposal.

Nuclear safety

If substantial quantities of the radionuclides produced in nuclear reactors are released to the environment, the result can be considerable damage—not just the direct impacts on people and the environment but also the indirect impacts on the viability of the industry itself. The loss-of-coolant accident at Three Mile Island shook investor confidence in nuclear power, even though radioactive material releases to the environment were minimal. As a result of the Chernobyl accident, the public has little confidence that nuclear power is safe.

For nuclear energy to qualify as a sustainable energy option, concerns regarding safety, waste disposal, and proliferation must be addressed in ways that enable it to compete on an economic basis.

Unlike Chernobyl-type reactors, the light water reactors (LWRs) that dominate nuclear power around the world have had a remarkably good safety record. But LWR accidents can happen. The Three Mile Island accident stimulated numerous improvements in reactor safety. Detailed calculations indicate that, for current U.S. reactors, the probability of core damage is less than 10^{-4} per reactor per year, and the probability of significant radioactive releases is a tenth as large (Fetter, 1999). But this record has been achieved at a high cost for a complex technology to minimise serious accident risk, and the technology is unforgiving of error.[69]

Advanced reactors are likely to be significantly safer. Two approaches to safety are used in advanced reactor designs. One is aimed at improving the technology in an evolutionary manner with the present defence-in-depth approach to safety, which provides redundancy or multiple levels of active interventions by equipment and operators to prevent fuel damage—and, even if fuel is damaged, to prevent the release of significant quantities of radioactivity to the environment. Although enough redundancy can reduce the probability of failure to arbitrarily small values, sceptics can always claim that not all events leading to accidents can be imagined, so that the probabilities used in probabilistic risk assessment are not accurate (Spiewak and Weinberg, 1985). Such systems depend on proper operation and maintenance of reactors, which cannot always be assured.[70]

The complexity of active safety systems also can tempt workers to ignore regulations they believe to be overly conservative (as was the case at Chernobyl). And finally, complex systems can make it difficult to achieve the goal of reducing capital and operation and maintenance costs. An alternative approach to safety is to identify and develop technologies that offer a high inherent degree of safety without the need for complicated, capital-intensive safety controls—often called passive safety systems. If passive systems can be developed and made to work effectively, they offer the potential to address safety and cost challenges simultaneously. Lidsky (1991) argues that new reactor technologies have to be not only safe but demonstrably safe, because "the public has lost faith in all experts and has little trust in probabilistic risk assessments".

Nuclear proliferation and diversion

The knowledge needed to design and fabricate fission bombs is available to almost every nation. For many years, lack of access to nuclear explosive materials,[71] not lack of knowledge, has been the main technical barrier to the spread of nuclear weapons capability. The essence of the potential nuclear weapons link to fission power (box 8.5) is that this technology provides the possibility of obtaining this missing ingredient, in the form of either uranium-enrichment capability or plutonium extractable from spent reactor fuel through chemical reprocessing. Access to such materials makes it easier for additional countries to acquire nuclear weapons (Holdren, 1989).

In the future, as sub-national criminal groups become more sophisticated, the related threat that these too might acquire nuclear bombs or radiological weapons by misusing nuclear energy technologies may grow in importance (Willrich and Taylor, 1974; Leventhal and Alexander, 1987; LLNL, 1998).

Are proliferation and diversion resistant technologies needed? A multifaceted effort is required to minimise the motivations for proliferation: control commerce in sensitive facilities, equipment, and materials; detect any misuse of such facilities or equipment or diversion of materials; and intervene where necessary to prevent an errant nation or sub-national criminal group from acquiring nuclear weapons. The main approach to addressing these challenges has been the Nuclear Non-Proliferation Treaty and associated international safeguards and nuclear supplier agreements (box 8.6). These deterrents are more significant than ever before: A nation-state deciding to launch a nuclear weapons programme today would need to find motivation sufficient to offset the penalties of discovery, the possibilities that the enterprise might not succeed, and costs that might be prohibitive.

The issue of how to deal in the future with the risk that nuclear materials in civilian nuclear power programmes will be used for weapons purposes is a focus of debate. One view is that this risk can be adequately addressed by a system of institutional controls, building on the historical success of the Nuclear Non-Proliferation Treaty (Walker, 1999). Others argue that if the role of nuclear energy were to expand substantially (for example, to the extent that nuclear power could have a significant role in mitigating climate change risks), the requirements imposed on institutional measures such as safeguards would increase significantly. Thus, it is argued, research and development is needed to see if the inherent resistance of nuclear energy systems to proliferation can be increased, thereby lessening the intensity of reliance on institutional measures alone to reduce proliferation risks (Bunn, 1999; Feiveson, 1999; Williams and Feiveson, 1990; PCAST Energy Research and Development Panel, 1997; PCAST Panel on ICERD3, 1999).[72]

Clearly, additional countries can acquire nuclear weapons if they want them badly enough to openly abrogate the Nuclear Non-Proliferation Treaty or to take their chances that a clandestine weapons programme will not be detected. And such countries can do this whether or not civilian nuclear energy technology is available to them as a partial basis for their weapons effort. It appears that the steps taken to strengthen the non-proliferation regime in recent years have significantly increased the difficulty, cost, and detectability of such efforts to produce nuclear weapons.

Looking to the future, the key proliferation and diversion issue is how to minimise the temptations and advantages that nuclear programmes may offer potential proliferator states and sub-national groups—that is, how to minimise any contribution of nuclear energy to the rate at which additional states or groups seek to acquire and succeed in acquiring nuclear weapons.

The sections below explore the prospects for reducing proliferation and diversion risks with advanced technologies, which could be especially important in a world where nuclear power is developed on a scale far larger than at present.[73] Two approaches to proliferation and diversion resistance are considered. One involves systems in which plutonium and other weapons-usable materials are never separated from spent fuel, the radioactivity of which deters proliferation and diversion efforts. These systems build on the fact that contemporary light-water reactors using low-enriched uranium in a once-through

---

BOX 8.5. NUCLEAR WEAPONS PROLIFERATION RISKS POSED BY NUCLEAR ENERGY TECHNOLOGIES

Nuclear explosives can be made both from highly enriched uranium and plutonium, including plutonium produced in civilian nuclear power plants. Although there are complications in weapon design, fabrication, and maintenance when reactor-grade instead of weapons-grade plutonium is used, these do not add substantially to those that must be faced when using any nuclear-explosive material for making weapons, according to individuals and groups with authoritative knowledge of nuclear weapons technology (Holdren, 1989; Mark, 1993; CISAC, 1994, 1995). Reactor-grade plutonium can be used to construct devastating nuclear weapons at all levels of technical sophistication (DOE, 1997). So that the dangers of reactor-grade plutonium will not continue to be misunderstood, in recent years the U.S. Department of Energy (custodian of the world's most sophisticated knowledge base on the subject) has made this point clear in unclassified reports and has allowed those with DOE nuclear-weapon security clearances to make explicit statements about it in other forums. Especially relevant points are made in the following quotations:

> The difficulties of developing an effective design of the most straight forward type are not appreciably greater with reactor-grade plutonium than those that have to be met for the use of weapons-grade plutonium. (Mark, 1993)

> Using reactor-grade rather than weapons-grade plutonium would present some complications. But even with relatively simple designs such as that used in the Nagasaki weapon—which are within the capabilities of many nations and possibly some subnational groups—nuclear explosives could be constructed that would be assured of having yields of at least 1 to 2 kilotons. With more sophisticated designs, reactor-grade plutonium could be used for weapons having considerably higher minimum yields. (CISAC, 1994)

> At the other end of the spectrum, advanced nuclear weapon states such as the United States and Russia, using modern designs, could produce weapons from reactor-grade plutonium having reliable explosive yields, weight, and other characteristics generally comparable to those of weapons made from weapons-grade plutonium. (DOE, 1997)

Although there are more direct ways for a country to acquire nuclear bombs than from its commercial nuclear energy facilities (for example, centrifuges for uranium enrichment and special reactors dedicated to plutonium production), the acquisition of nuclear explosive materials is made easier if the requisite technical skills and infrastructure are already in place through a nuclear power programme. The existence or prospect of commercial nuclear power in a country, moreover, provides a legitimating cover for nuclear activities that, without electricity generation as their manifest purpose, would be considered unambiguously weapons-oriented and thus potentially subject both to internal dissent and external sanctions and counter-measures. Feiveson (1978) points out that even countries that initially have no intention of acquiring nuclear weapons might later be more likely to acquire them, under altered internal or external political circumstances, because their having a nuclear power programme has made it easier to do so.

BOX 8.6. INSTITUTIONAL MECHANISMS ADDRESSING PROLIFERATION RISKS OF NUCLEAR ENERGY

International efforts to stem the spread of nuclear weapon capabilities have been more successful than almost anyone at the beginning of the nuclear era dared to hope. Rather than the dozens of nuclear weapon states once predicted, today only eight states are believed to have nuclear weapons capabilities, a number that has not increased for more than 10 years. Indeed, South Africa has provided the first case of genuine nuclear disarmament—a state that had full control over its own arsenal of nuclear weapons and agreed to give them up entirely. The international regime that has achieved this result includes both political elements designed to convince states that acquiring nuclear weapons is not in their interest, and technical elements designed to increase the detectability, difficulty, and cost of nuclear weapons acquisition. The foundation of this regime is the Nuclear Non-Proliferation Treaty, which now has 187 parties—more than the United Nations Charter. The civilian nuclear energy programmes of all of these besides the five nuclear-weapon states recognised by the treaty are subject to 'full scope' IAEA (International Atomic Energy Agency) safeguards designed to verify their commitments not to acquire nuclear weapons.

Several parts of the non-proliferation regime are designed to address the nuclear weapons proliferation risks posed by civilian nuclear energy programmes. The most fundamental part is IAEA safeguards, which allow international verification of the peaceful use of all nuclear materials in non-nuclear-weapons states (OTA, 1995). In the aftermath of the post–Gulf War revelation of Iraq's large-scale clandestine nuclear weapons programme, and the failure of previous IAEA monitoring and inspections to detect it, IAEA safeguards are being substantially strengthened, with new measures designed not only to verify that nuclear material

at declared sites is not misused, but also to help ferret out activities that may be taking place at secret sites (Hooper 1997). Other critically important institutional measures to reduce the risk of proliferation include the international system of controls on exports of technologies that could be used for nuclear weapons programmes, as well as programmes to ensure that all potentially weapons-usable nuclear material is secure and accounted for—and so cannot be stolen for use in nuclear weapons by proliferating states or terrorist groups.

But confidence in the future effectiveness of the non-proliferation regime in general, and the barriers to use of nuclear-energy technologies for proliferation in particular, cannot be unconditional or complete. The non-proliferation regime itself is imperilled by the recent efforts in this direction by Iraq and the Democratic People's Republic of Korea, and by the failure of the recognised nuclear-weapons states (above all, Russia and the United States) to move more decisively, in the aftermath of the cold war, towards fulfilling their legal obligation under Article VI of the Nuclear Non-Proliferation Treaty to negotiate in good faith towards nuclear disarmament (Barletta and Sands, 1999). The extensively documented case of Iraq, in particular, demonstrates that eternal vigilance is required to prevent states from clandestinely acquiring critical technologies despite the existence of export controls on them.

Moreover, the safeguards implemented by the IAEA—which include monitoring of records and on-site inspections at reactors and fuel-cycle facilities, along with the broader measures beginning to be implemented in the aftermath of the Gulf War—at best only provide assurance that diversion of nuclear materials to weaponry will be detected. These safe-

guards are not intended to prevent such diversion, or to prevent theft of these materials by sub-national groups. (Protection against theft is the province of individual states; there are no binding international standards governing the adequacy of such protection, and levels of protection vary world-wide from excellent to grossly inadequate.) Even detection of diversion or theft is not completely assured, both because of limitations on the resources being provided to the IAEA and because of the intrinsic difficulty of the task of safeguarding nuclear materials, particularly when large quantities of weapons-usable nuclear material are being processed in bulk.

This difficulty has been recognised since the dawn of the nuclear era. Addressing the adequacy of international inspections for the purpose of preventing nuclear proliferation, the Acheson-Lillienthal Report that formed the basis of the Baruch Plan for international control of nuclear weapons (submitted to the UN by the United States in 1946) stated that "there is no prospect of security against atomic warfare in a system of international agreements to outlaw such weapons controlled only by a system which relies on inspection and similar police-like methods. The reasons supporting this conclusion are not merely technical but primarily the inseparable political, social, and organizational problems involved in enforcing agreements between nations, each free to develop atomic energy but only pledged not to use bombs...So long as intrinsically dangerous activities may be carried on by nations, rivalries are inevitable and fears are engendered that place so great a pressure on a systems of international enforcement by police methods that no degree of ingenuity or technical competence could possibly cope with them" (Lillienthal and others,1946).

---

fuel cycle that leaves the plutonium mixed with fission products in spent fuel are the most prominent operational example of a relatively proliferation-and-diversion-resistant fuel cycle. An improved variant of this approach is advanced once-through reactor and fuel cycle technologies for which the quantities of weapons-usable materials available in spent fuel are reduced—thereby reducing incentives to mine spent fuel for weapons-usable materials. A completely different approach is to convert nuclear energy to electricity and hydrogen in large international energy parks at which weapons-usable materials are maintained under tight international control and to distribute these carriers to distant consumers. The next subsection discusses proliferation and diversion issues associated with nuclear fuel reprocessing and plutonium recycling for today's civilian nuclear power technology.

Nuclear fuel reprocessing and plutonium recycling. Several countries have begun commercial-scale reprocessing to recover plutonium along with unused uranium from spent fuel (with

intentions to dispose of the separated radioactive wastes in geologic repositories at a future date) and to recycle plutonium in mixed-oxide uranium-plutonium (MOX) fuel for LWRs. These activities make the nuclear weapons proliferation risk a more serious concern than when LWRs fuelled with low-enriched uranium are operated on once-through fuel cycles.

Commercial LWR fuel-reprocessing systems have been established in France (at La Hague), Russia (Chelyabinsk-Ozersk), and the United Kingdom (Windscale-Sellafield).[74] These facilities are nodes of a global nuclear fuel management system in which spent fuel is sent from reactors to reprocessing plants, and the separated constituents (uranium, plutonium, radioactive wastes) are to be returned (eventually) to the fuel owners.[75] These three sites are reprocessing fuel from about 150 reactors operating in nine countries (Berkhout, 1998).

Reprocessing facilities now handle a fourth of the spent fuel discharged from power reactors. The rest is in interim storage, either targeted for eventual geological disposal in canisters designed for direct disposal without reprocessing, or (for the majority of the material outside Canada and the United States) pending a decision on whether to go to geological storage or reprocessing. Today 20 tonnes of plutonium is being separated from spent fuel annually world-wide; by the end of 1995, 180 tonnes had been separated from civilian nuclear reactor spent fuel—18 percent of the total plutonium discharged from these reactors (Albright, Berkhout, and Walker, 1997). Some of the recovered plutonium and uranium mixed with fresh uranium (MOX fuel) is being used as fuel for LWRs. The challenge of managing the growing stockpile of separated civilian plutonium (the total quantity separated less the amount used as fuel in plutonium recycling, about 180 tonnes world-wide as of 2000) parallels the problem of managing the growing quantity of separated surplus military plutonium produced by dismantling excess nuclear weapons in the aftermath of the cold war, now approaching 100 tonnes in Russia and the United States combined (PCAST Panel on ICERD[3], 1999).

Although it reduces uranium requirements for power generation, the reprocessing-recycling option does not compete in economic terms with once-through use of low-enriched uranium fuel in LWRs,[76] reflecting the fact that it has become clear that the world has large, low-cost reserves of uranium (chapter 5). Yet reprocessing and recycling activities continue for a number of reasons: sunk capital costs, government subsidies, long-term contracts signed when uranium seemed scarcer and costlier, reluctance to throw away the energy content of unrecycled plutonium and uranium, perceptions that reprocessed wastes are easier to manage than spent fuel, and lack of alternatives to reprocessing as a means of removing spent fuel from reactor sites in the short term (PCAST Panel on ICERD[3], 1999).

Nuclear waste disposal

The radioactive by-products of fission must be isolated from the human environment to the extent that they can never return in concentrations that could cause significant harm. Spent fuel removed from a reactor is first stored for at least a few years in cooling pools at the reactor site. After the very short-lived fission products have decayed, the fuel can:

■ Remain in the pools (if they have sufficient capacity).
■ Be stored on-site in dry casks (which provide a safe and economic alternative for storage for several decades).
■ Be transported to an away-from-reactor storage site (either pools or dry casks).
■ Be transported to a reprocessing plant or a geologic disposal facility.

In many cases efforts to expand long-term storage capacity on-site or particularly to establish large away-from-reactor stores not associated with reprocessing or disposal sites have encountered public opposition, leaving some utilities in doubt as to where to put their spent fuel as their cooling ponds fill up.

Eventually, the spent fuel will either be reprocessed, and the high-level wastes sent to a long-term storage site, or it will be encapsulated in suitable canisters and sent directly to a long-term disposal site.

Safe ways of storing wastes for periods up to 1 million years may be required. For the first hundred years of the required isolation period, the radioactivity and heat of these wastes are dominated by fission products. After several hundred years, the major concerns are the very-long-lived transuranics (various isotopes of plutonium, neptunium, and Americium) and long-lived iodine and technetium fission products.

There is a consensus among states using nuclear energy that deep geologic disposal in mined repositories is the best currently available approach for disposal of nuclear wastes.[77] And most experts believe that geologic repositories can be designed to be safe (NEA, 1999). However, to date, no country has yet disposed of any spent fuel or high-level waste in such a repository.

Because wastes are concentrated, disposal cost is not a significant issue. In the United States, for example, utilities are charged only $0.001 per kilowatt-hour for management and disposal of their spent fuel (2–3 percent of generation cost). Detailed calculations suggest that this will be fully adequate to finance that portion of the cost of the nuclear waste disposal programme attributable to civilian spent fuel (DOE, 1998). Costs would be higher for small countries if repositories were established there to accommodate only their own wastes.

Public and political opposition to waste disposal has delayed efforts to open targeted repositories in some countries. There have also been technical problems. But long-term waste disposal should not be an intractable problem from a technical perspective. Even if some wastes eventually leak from repositories, problems would be manageable because of the small storage space required.

For example, storage density limits for spent LWR fuel at Yucca Mountain, Nevada, are 41 square metres per megawatt-electric of nuclear generating capacity for a power plant operated for 30 years (Kadak, 1999). At this storage density, the area required for storing all radioactive waste generated during the 21st century for the global high-nuclear-growth scenario above is 270 square kilometres. Suppose that a waste-isolation land area 10 times as large is purchased at a cost of $100,000 per hectare to be maintained in perpetuity with no human intrusion. The required land area is 0.003 percent of the continental land areas. The cost of the land would be $0.0009 per kilowatt-hour generated (2 percent of generation cost) for a 10 percent discount rate, or $0.00002 per kilowatt-hour (0.05 percent of generation cost) for a 0 percent discount rate, assuming in both cases that the land is paid for in 2000.

Because the areas required are modest, it is not necessary for every country to develop its own repository. Globally, only a small number of sites is needed. Restricting storage to a small number of favourable sites around the world would be attractive for various reasons (McCombie, 1999a, b; McCombie and others, 1999; Miller and others, 1999), including realisation of scale economies, the potential for optimising the prospects for achieving demonstrable safety, and various additional reasons discussed below.

Although coping with the radioactive waste problem seems manageable from a technical perspective, a technical fix by itself is *not a solution: A real solution has many non-technical features as well (see below).*

Must spent fuel be reprocessed for radioactive waste disposal? At one time, it was thought by some that reprocessing is needed to safely dispose of radioactive wastes. However, the International Fuel Cycle Evaluation, carried out from 1977–79 to consider the commercial use of plutonium, concluded that spent fuel itself could be safely disposed of in a waste repository (STATS, 1996). This conclusion has been strengthened by subsequent intensive investigations of spent fuel disposal in several countries (for example, Finland, Sweden, and the United States).

Nevertheless, both public opposition to interim away-from-reactor storage sites and delays in opening long-term waste repositories are causing great difficulties for utilities, because storage pools at reactor sites are fast approaching capacity. In some countries (not the United States, which has abandoned civilian reactor fuel repossessing), nuclear utilities have been forced into reprocessing as a de facto interim waste management strategy. But reprocessing does not solve the waste disposal problem—it merely buys time and transforms the spent fuel management problem into several other problems associated with plutonium disposition: management of high-, medium-, and low-level wastes at reprocessing plants; management of transuranic wastes at plutonium fuel fabrication plants; and, eventually, decommissioning wastes from these plants (plus residual spent-fuel disposal, if plutonium is not recycled indefinitely).

Should long-lived wastes be separated and transmuted? The challenge of storing the very-long-lived components of radioactive wastes has led to various separations and transmutation (S&T) proposals for separating out the hazardous, long-lived components and transmuting them by neutron bombardment to form nuclides that would be either stable or radioactive with much shorter half-lives. The Committee on Separations Technology and Transmutation Systems (STATS) was formed by the U.S. National Research Council at the request of the U.S. Department of Energy to evaluate alternative S&T options for addressing such issues and assess their implications for nuclear waste management.

The STATS committee investigated several alternative reactor and particle accelerator systems. It found that, although S&T might be technically feasible for some of the options studied, the need for permanent long-term storage would remain. Many decades to centuries would be required to reduce the radioactivity to the low levels specified by S&T proponents as their objective, and disposal costs would increase substantially (STATS, 1996).[78] Moreover, it is unlikely that the modest reduction in waste-disposal risk for the long term (which is already very small) would outweigh the high costs and increased near-term accident and proliferation risks that would be associated with S&T (Fetter, 1999). The most active programmes in this area are those of France, Japan, Russia, Sweden, and the United States.

Towards geological disposal. As noted, the focus world-wide for

> Effectively addressing nuclear concerns probably requires advanced technologies as well as improved institutional risk management strategies.

long-term disposal is on geologic repositories. All concepts rely on multiple barriers provided by the storage canisters, the backfill material used to surround the canisters in the storage rock, and the rock itself. Test results suggest that corrosion-resistant containers may be able to keep nearly all the waste contained for thousands of years.

There have been setbacks, though not always for scientific and technical reasons; public and political opposition has sometimes slowed technical progress. In the United States, public acceptability considerations led Congress to choose the Yucca Mountain site in sparsely populated Nevada, even though technically it may not be an especially good site (Fetter, 1999).[79]

Advances in waste disposal science and technology have been rapid in Sweden, where the decision to phase out nuclear power facilitated a societal consensus on a waste disposal programme (Gillena, 1994). Swedish researchers are developing a scheme to put spent fuel in copper-clad steel canisters to be embedded in bentonite clay in a granite monolith 600 metres underground at a site near the sea; they anticipate a million-year canister lifetime for the site's reducing conditions (Whipple, 1996). Should the storage canisters eventually leak, surrounding backfill material and rock would inhibit movement of leaked wastes to the surface.

The widely shared judgement of the technical community that long-term storage can be made safe is based on careful assessments of safety and environmental impacts that take into account both waste characteristics and the properties of all barriers involved. Several extensive safety assessments have been carried out in OECD countries. Potential radiation exposures have been calculated to be close to zero for periods of 100,000 years for all scenarios and sites considered; for longer periods, the risks are so small as to impose very small additional externality costs, even if there is no discounting for these uncertain remote future events.[80]

Technical uncertainties need further study.[81] But none is likely to be a show-stopper. Moreover, there is time to resolve technical issues because, from a technical perspective, there is no urgency to move wastes from interim to permanent long-term storage sites. In fact, delay for a period of 50 years would not only buy time to improve scientific understanding of long-term storage issues and storage technology, but would also facilitate waste disposal by reducing required heat removal rates as a result of radioactive decay of fission products. Delaying long-term waste disposal would probably require establishing secure storage sites (which might be the same as the long-term disposal sites) for spent fuel for part of this cooling off period; but, as recent experience has shown, this will not be easily accomplished in the political arena.

Will spent fuel repositories become plutonium mines? A final technical waste disposal issue relates to the concern that, if radioactive wastes are stored as spent fuel rather than reprocessed wastes, repositories might one day be mined as sources of low-cost plutonium for nuclear weapons. The Committee on International Security and

Arms Control of the U.S. National Academy of Sciences has identified general proliferation hazards associated with spent fuel management, including the issue of mining waste repositories for plutonium recovery, as an area warranting continued research "at the conceptual level" (CISAC, 1994).

Peterson (1996) has argued that, after a hundred years or so, the costs of clandestine tunnelling into spent fuel repositories to recover plutonium would be less than the costs for conventional dedicated facilities to acquire plutonium. In examining this issue, Lyman and Feiveson (1998) found that the range of conditions under which repository mining would look attractive relative to other means of acquiring plutonium is narrow. Although safeguards would be needed in perpetuity, the measures needed to deter mining need not involve expensive and intrusive inspections but could focus on containment and surveillance procedures, including remote monitoring by satellites. And the safeguard management challenge would be greatly facilitated if there were only a small number of repositories around the world.

Perspective on radioactive waste disposal. The most important unresolved issues relating to radioactive waste disposal are political rather than technical. Providing adequate disposal capacity for nuclear wastes has been and is likely to continue to be fraught with political controversy.

The world would be better off if secure, internationally managed, interim, away-from-reactor storage sites could be set up for spent fuel, even for periods of 50 years before activating any permanent repository. If such interim storage capacity were to become available, fewer and fewer utilities would be willing to pay the extra near-term costs of reprocessing, and the reprocessing industry would slowly be competed out of business. Yet the world is not moving in this direction. As noted by Häckel (1997):

> The historical record of the past decades is littered with the acronyms of defunct proposals for an internationalised back end fuel cycle…Not only have these not materialised; it appears that at the back end of the fuel cycle internationalisation is actually on the retreat…Stalemate and procrastination seem to be a general phenomenon of fuel cycle policy everywhere.

O'Neill (1998) identifies several factors as inhibiting the development of an international spent fuel management regime or regimes: widespread political and public opposition to siting of storage facilities (which would be heightened in a country faced with the prospect of becoming the world's nuclear dumping ground) and to transport radioactive substances within countries and across borders; differences in national interests and practices (for example, it is unlikely that most states with existing reprocessing capacity will give it up); sovereignty concerns; compliance, information gathering, and dissemination issues (states need assurances that if they comply, others will too, with appropriate verification provisions); and the long time horizons involved (for example, even interim storage sites would have to outlast not only political lives but the actual lifetimes of most political leaders).

O'Neill offers no easy answers to this stalemate but suggests an evolutionary strategy focussing initially on regional rather than global arrangements, because states in a geographic region are more likely to share common norms (although, of course, animosities can also be intense at the regional level). And although both interim and permanent disposal face political opposition, there are probably fewer obstacles to the former.

Advanced nuclear generating options for the immediate future

In what follows, near-term advanced nuclear generating technology options are described, focussing on advanced LWR and fuel cycle technologies, and the pebble bed modular reactor. No attempt is made to be comprehensive; rather, the intent is to use these examples to illustrate what advanced technologies offer to address the challenges posed by current nuclear technologies.

Advanced light water reactors

Can LWR technology improvements help in addressing the challenges facing current technologies? Simpler plant designs and shorter plant construction periods would help bring down costs. Improved safety designs could help restore public confidence in nuclear power. And more proliferation-resistant designs would reduce proliferation and diversion risks.

Evolutionary advanced light water reactors. In recent years the main nuclear reactor vendors have developed modified LWRs that offer both improved safety and lower cost than LWRs now in use (NRC, 1992; CISAC, 1995; Kupitz and Cleveland, 1999).[82] These modified LWRs build on more than 40 years of experience with LWR technology to provide technological improvements in standardised designs, for which there can be a high degree of confidence that performance and cost targets will be met. All of the modified LWRs use active but simplified safety systems, and some have some passive safety features.

One reactor in this category is the Westinghouse AP600, a 600-megawatt-electric pressurised water reactor (PWR). The design is simpler than existing PWRs; and it is modular, with about half the capacity of most existing PWRs—which allows some components to be factory-built and assembled faster on-site at lower cost than for plants that are entirely field-constructed. The AP600 is expected to be safer than existing PWRs, able to be constructed in 3 years, and cost about 15 percent less than existing PWRs of the same capacity (NPDP, 1998). In late 1999 the AP600 received design certification from the U.S. Nuclear Regulation Commission.

Also in this category are the ABB/Combustion Engineering System 80+ and the GE Advanced Boiling Water Reactor (ABWR); both received design certification from the U.S. Nuclear Regulatory Commission in 1997. The System 80+ is a large (1,350-megawatt-electric) unit, for which the estimated core damage frequency is 2.7 times 10^{-6}, two orders of magnitude lower than for its predecessor. The ABWR has as a design objective a core damage frequency of less than 10^{-6} and a target capital cost that is 20 percent less than for BWRs previously built in Japan (NPDP, 1998). Two ABWRs are now operating in Japan. Two more are under construction in Japan and also in Taiwan (China).

In Europe a Framatome-Siemens joint venture and a group of 'nuclear' German utilities have developed the European pressurised water reactor (EPR), a 1,750-megawatt-electric system designed to specifications endorsed by utilities in Europe—with hoped-for economies of scale at this large unit size. The EPR is being offered on the international market.

Shifting light water reactors to a denatured uranium-thorium fuel cycle. If the advanced LWRs described above were operated on low-enriched uranium in once-through fuel cycles, they would be as proliferation and diversion resistant as existing LWRs, with fission products in spent fuel deterring plutonium removal by would-be proliferators and diverters. But because plutonium inventories build up quickly (200 kilograms a gigawatt-electric per year)—posing a significant proliferation hazard if the plutonium is separated by reprocessing, and conceivably making spent fuel at reactors or in off-site storage potential targets for proliferation and diversion—attention has been given recently to LWRs operated on a denatured uranium-thorium once-through fuel cycle that is more proliferation-diversion-resistant even than current LWRs operated on a once-through fuel cycle (Gasperin, Reichert, and Radkowsky, 1997; Herring and MacDonald, 1998).

Although it would not differ markedly from current LWR technology with regard to capital cost and safety, the LWR operated on a denatured uranium-thorium once-through fuel cycle would produce less transuranic wastes than current LWRs. Most important, it would have proliferation and diversion resistant features relating to both plutonium and uranium. Only a fifth as much plutonium would be generated in spent fuel as in an LWR fuelled with low-enriched uranium. Moreover, the plutonium would contain a significant amount of Pu-238, which generates heat that makes weapon manufacture more difficult. In this cycle the U-233 is bred from thorium denatured by the U-238, at enrichment levels such that this uranium cannot be used to make weapons without further enrichment; moreover, the uranium contains gamma-emitting daughters of U-232, which makes weapon manufacture more difficult.[83]

The technology is not diversion-proof. Reliable nuclear weapons could be made by many nations from both plutonium and uranium that could be recovered from spent fuel by relatively straightforward chemical means.[84] In the hands of terrorists or an unsophisticated country, the recovered plutonium could be used to make weapons with yields of 1 or 2 kilotons. These reservations notwithstanding, this system would be more proliferation-resistant than a conventional LWR operated on slightly enriched uranium, because incentives for recovering weapons-usable material from spent fuel would be less.

Yet discussion of the specifics of this particular technology shows that setting goals for proliferation and diversion resistance will not be easily accomplished. This is because trade-offs must be taken into account in considering the weapons potential of the plutonium and uranium materials involved.

There seem to be reasonably good prospects for making reactors demonstrably safe while simultaneously reducing costs.

The pebble bed modular reactor. For decades, a different approach to nuclear fission based on moderating the reactor with graphite and cooling it with helium (rather than using water for both purposes in LWRs) has been under development in several countries. These high-temperature gas-cooled reactors (HTGRs) typically involve large numbers of tiny uranium fuel pellets encased in layers of carbon, silica, or both (designed to contain the fission products from the reaction). These pellets are generally pressed into larger fuel elements, which are either encased in solid graphite blocks or circulate through the reactor core in a so-called pebble bed system.[85]

Modern HTGRs are designed to be passively safe, offering the potential to avoid many of the complex, expensive safety systems used in LWRs. Moreover, HTGR concepts are being explored that would have lifetime cores—that is, they would be installed, switched on, and the operators would not have to do anything about fuelling or de-fuelling for the life of the reactor. In combination, it is hoped that such features could lead to lower costs and improved safety. In what follows, design and performance issues for the pebble bed modular reactor (PBMR) are discussed to illustrate the possibilities that might be offered by HTGR technology.

The key to enhanced safety for the PBMR is a design that ensures that the highest temperature in the reactor core—under any conceivable operating or accident condition—never exceeds the 1,600 degrees Celsius operating limit of the fuel. This requirement limits the thermal output for a single module to 250 megawatts-thermal and the electrical output to 100 megawatts-electric—a factor of 10 smaller than for a typical LWR. The viability of the technology depends, among other things, on being routinely able to produce high-quality fuel particles and pebbles. There have been problems in the past in particle design and manufacturing, leading to release of radioactivity from the particles (NRC, 1992). In addition, the direct helium gas turbine cycle required with the PBMR is undemonstrated for a nuclear plant and requires substantial engineering (CISAC, 1995).

The spent fuel of the PBMR would be high-burn-up material in many tiny spheres, making it a comparatively unattractive source from which to recover weapons-usable material. Moreover, the PBMR and other HTGR variants could be operated on a denatured uranium-thorium once-through fuel cycle that would have the same proliferation and diversion resistance features as an LWR operated on this fuel cycle (Feiveson, von Hippel, and Williams, 1979).

The PBMR's extraordinarily low power density[86] (a key safety feature) and modest scale will tend to drive up its specific cost (dollars per kilowatt-electric). But developers hope that these diseconomies will be offset at least partially by cost-saving opportunities—including design simplicity and system modularity that facilitate standardisation and realisation of mass production economies with a high fraction of the construction taking place in factories. Use of a closed-cycle helium gas turbine instead of a steam turbine for energy conversion assists in this objective, because this turbine's specific cost is lower and less scale-sensitive than the LWR's steam turbine.

Eskom, the South African utility attempting to develop the technology (Nicholls, 1998), is targeting a capital cost of $1,000 per kilowatt-electric under mass production conditions for a power plant made up of a block of 10 100 MW_e modules. This is far less than the costs of $1,700–3,100 per kilowatt-electric that characterise today's LWRs (Paffenbarger and Bertel, 1998). Despite the good prospects for cost cutting as a result of the PBMR's attractive features (such as passive safety, modularity, and the relative scale insensitivity of the helium turbine's capital cost), this is an aggressive cost target, considering the high capital cost for the reactor itself that is inherent in its low power density—which requires, for example, very large and costly reactor vessels that can withstand high operating pressures. An MIT group investigating the PBMR estimates a capital cost about twice that estimated by Eskom (NPPDP, 1998). Earlier independent estimates of the capital cost of other HTGR systems, such as the General Atomics system developed in the United States, tended to be consistently higher than the costs of LWRs, because of the low power density of the HTGR concept (NRC, 1992).

The technology is at too early a developmental stage to ascertain which of these estimates is closer to what can be expected in a commercial product. If the MIT estimate turns out to be close to the mark, the cost of electricity from this plant (table 8.15) would be about the same as for an coal integrated gasifier–solid oxide fuel cell–steam turbine power plant with CO_2 separation and sequestration (see table 8.9). If the cost turns out to be closer to the Eskom estimate, the direct economic balance would tip in favour of the PBMR. In such circumstances, other factors such as public attitudes towards waste disposal could be important determinants in the race between nuclear and fossil technologies to near-zero emissions.

In contrast to the approach being taken for advanced LWR development—an activity that is well advanced; involves making only incremental, evolutionary changes relative to existing LWRs; and can build on a well-established industrial base—industrial activity relating to HTGRs is embryonic. No HTGR has yet been economically competitive. Nevertheless, the concept illustrates reasonable prospects for achieving at least the goal of demonstrable safety.

Nuclear energy for the long term

Uranium resource constraints might someday become important determinants of nuclear technology development. For the global high-nuclear-growth scenario discussed above, cumulative uranium requirements to 2050 with current technology are 3 million tonnes—less than reasonably assured resources recoverable at less than $130 a kilogram, so that resource constraints are not important in this period. But cumulative uranium requirements to 2100 for this scenario are close to the estimated 20 million tonnes of conventional uranium resources (including 12 million of speculative resources; chapter 5).

Thus, sometime after 2050, technology that can address the resource constraint challenge might have to become available under high-nuclear-growth conditions. Can advanced technologies address this potential constraint while simultaneously satisfying cost, safety, and proliferation and diversion concerns? In light of prospective long research and development gestation times and the need to make rational near-term research and development resource allocation decisions regarding post-2050 deployment options, it is important for this report to address this question. Five options are considered: conventional plutonium fast breeder reactors; alternative breeder concepts; extracting uranium from seawater; large-scale, internationalised nuclear energy parks; and thermonuclear fusion.

Conventional plutonium fast breeder reactors

Until the mid-1970s, it was thought that uranium was scarce. Therefore, it was expected that the LWR would be a stop-gap technology to provide start-up fuel for the fast breeder reactor (FBR), which by 1990 would overtake the LWR as the technology of choice for new plants (Lidsky and Miller, 1998).[87]

The LWR makes use of only 0.5 percent of the fission energy stored in natural uranium—primarily that in the fissile (chain-reacting) isotope U-235, which accounts for only 0.7 percent of natural uranium. The FBR would alleviate this constraint by transmuting a large fraction of the abundant fertile isotope U-238 through neutron capture into fissile isotopes of plutonium—making it possible to extract 50–100 times as much energy from a kilogram of uranium as the LWR. Among FBR options, particular attention was given to the liquid-metal (sodium) cooled fast breeder reactor (LMFBR), which offered the potential of being an effective fuel factory that could produce excess plutonium—adequate not only to sustain itself but also to serve as seed stock for a rapidly growing fleet of similar reactors.

The LWR-FBR vision has not materialised, and the prospects that

TABLE 8.15. TWO ESTIMATES OF THE ELECTRICITY GENERATION COST FOR THE PEBBLE BED MODULAR REACTOR (DOLLARS PER THOUSAND KILOWATT-HOURS)

Cost component	Estimate based on Eskom parameters[a]	Estimate based on MIT parameters[b]
Capital[c]	16.4	34.2
Operation and maintenance[d]	4.1	4.1+0.6[e]
Fuel	3.8	3.8
Total	24.3	42.7

Note: Estimates are for a 1,000 megawatt-electric plant made up of 10 100-megawatt-electric modules.
a. Data are from Nicholls, 1998. b. Data are from Kadak, 1999. c. For an annual capital charge rate of 11.5 percent and an 80 percent capacity factor. The unit capital cost estimated by Eskom and MIT analysts are $1,000 and $2,090 per kilowatt-electric, respectively. d. The staffing requirement for the plant is estimated to be 80 persons by Eskom (Nicholls, 1998) and 150 persons by MIT analysts (Andy Kadak, private communication, 8 September 1999). e. The $0.6 per thousand kilowatt-hours component of the cost is for decommissioning (Kadak, 1999).

it ever will are not bright. Although a few countries have FBR development programmes (China, France, India, Japan, Russia), these programmes are in virtual stasis. Most countries have abandoned once-ambitious programmes as a result of unpromising economics and a much brighter global outlook for uranium supplies (chapter 5) than when FBR programmes were originally put in place.[88] By the late 1970s it had become clear that FBR unit capital costs (dollars per kilowatt) would be much higher than for LWRs and that costs for fabricating MOX LWR fuel and FBR fuel would be far higher than previously projected. Life-cycle cost comparisons made at that time showed that the FBR could not compete with the LWR at then-projected uranium prices (Feiveson, von Hippel, and Williams, 1979). And now, with expectations that relatively low-cost uranium resources are far more abundant than was thought 20 years ago, it appears that the need for an FBR or alternative uranium-saving technology will not materialise before 2050, and possibly long after that (STATS, 1996).

Alternative breeder concepts

If uranium scarcity concerns should one day force a shift to breeder reactors, it would be desirable to have technologies that are simultaneously demonstrably safe and cost competitive and much more proliferation and diversion resistant than conventional liquid-sodium-cooled plutonium fast breeder reactors, which involve reprocessing spent fuel and recycling recovered plutonium in fresh reactor fuel.[89]

One set of such technologies is metal-cooled fast reactors, for which plutonium is never separated from fission products. One variant of the concept under investigation is a metal-cooled fast reactor using lead or a lead-bismuth eutectic instead of sodium as the liquid metal coolant (Filin and others, 1999, Hill and others, 1999; Lopatkin and Orlov, 1999; Orlov and others, 1999; Zrodnikov and others, 1999), building on Russian work carried out on lead-bismuth-cooled reactors for submarine applications.[90] Spent fuel reprocessing technology for these reactors would be designed to extract most fission products for waste disposal but leave 1–10 percent of the fission products plus plutonium and most transuranics in the reprocessed fuel that is returned to the reactor. The radiation hazard from residual fission products and transuranics would deter would-be proliferators and diverters.

Some natural or U-235-depleted uranium would be added to reprocessed fuel as source material to generate more plutonium in the reactor; the reactor would be designed to produce from uranium as much plutonium as it consumes.[91] A high level of burn-up of transuranics and long-lived fission products in the spent fuel could be achieved with repeated recycling and appropriate reprocessing technology—without the need for separate burners for transuranics and long-lived fission-products. Moreover, reprocessing plants might be co-sited with reactors, to eliminate proliferation and diversion risks associated with the transport of spent and reprocessed fuel. A modest-scale (100-megawatt-electric) version with a lifetime (15-year) sealed core has been proposed for developing country applications (Hill and others, 1999).[92]

Although this liquid metal reactor technology would deal effectively with the uranium supply constraint challenge and be more proliferation and diversion resistant than conventional plutonium breeder reactors, the reactors would have very large plutonium inventories—for example, 8–9 tonnes for a large 1,200-megawatt-electric design (Filin and others, 1999) and 2.5 tonnes for a small 100-megawatt-electric unit with a lifetime reactor core (Hill and others, 1999).[93] Although the system would be designed so that plutonium would never be fully separated from spent fuel, such systems would provide their operators with extensive knowledge of, experience with, and facilities for chemical processing of intensely radioactive spent fuel, which could provide the basis for moving quickly to separating plutonium for a weapons programme should a decision be made to do so.

Moreover, for safeguards, either new measurement technologies would have to be developed to allow accurate material accounting for the intensely radioactive material involved in these fuel cycles, or almost complete reliance would have to be placed on containment and surveillance measures rather than material accounting. Hence, although such systems would certainly have higher inherent proliferation resistance than traditional reprocessing and recycling approaches involving fully separated, weapons-usable plutonium, the overall proliferation risks that might result from widespread deployment of these technologies across the globe are likely to be the focus of considerable debate in the technical community, should large-scale deployment ever seem a realistic possibility.[94]

Other alternative breeder concepts include molten salt thermal breeder reactors that would integrate continuous reprocessing for removal of fission products with reactor operations (Tinturier, Estève, and Mouney, 1999) and various particle-accelerator-based reactor concepts. Each seems to have one or more attractive features relative to conventional breeder reactor concepts, but all are technologies whose relative merits regarding cost, safety, proliferation-diversion risk, and waste disposal are the subject of intense debate in the technical community (NRC, 1992; CISAC, 1995).

Extracting uranium from seawater

If low-cost uranium resources are much more abundant than indicated by conventional uranium resource estimates (chapter 5), even high nuclear growth to 2100 and beyond could be realised with proliferation and diversion resistant once-through fuel cycles. The recovery of uranium from seawater is one promising option for extending uranium resources; preliminary estimates of recovery costs are $100–300 per kilogram (chapter 5). Although the high estimated recovery cost is more than 10 times the current uranium price, it would contribute just $0.004 per kilowatt-hour to the cost of electricity for an HTGR operated on a once-through denatured uranium-thorium fuel cycle[95]—equivalent to the fuel cost for an oil-fired power plant burning oil priced at $2.50 a barrel!

Recovery of 15 percent of the uranium in seawater could support the year 2100 nuclear capacity level (6,500 gigawatts-electric) in the high-growth scenario (discussed above) for 1,000 years using such once-through reactor-fuel-cycle technologies. The key unresolved question is whether production of uranium from seawater could be carried out at acceptable cost at scales large enough to support a significant fraction of the world's nuclear capacity.

Large-scale, internationalised nuclear energy parks

If development of advanced proliferation- and diversion-resistant nuclear energy systems proves to be an elusive goal and the world opts for large-scale use of reprocessing and recycling technologies with substantial proliferation and diversion vulnerabilities, it might become necessary to cluster all the sensitive facilities—enrichment plants, reactors, reprocessing plants, fuel fabrication plants—in large, heavily guarded nuclear parks under international control to reduce the proliferation and diversion risks of nuclear fission. Electricity produced in such parks could be made available even to remote users through direct-current transmission lines. In addition, with reactors operated at suitably high temperatures (for example, high-temperature, gas-cooled reactors), hydrogen might also be produced as an energy carrier for world-wide energy commerce—initially perhaps by steam-reforming natural gas and ultimately with advanced thermal cycles that would use nuclear heat to extract hydrogen from water (Marchetti, 1976; Miyamoto and others, 1999; Scott and Hafele, 1990; Wade and Hill, 1999).

There is no doubt that this is technically feasible and would reduce proliferation and diversion dangers substantially. Much more questionable, however, is whether it is politically realistic to expect all the world's countries to place major components of their electricity supplies under international control—and to agree on the administrative arrangements for doing so.

Thermonuclear fusion

Another nuclear energy option for the very long term is thermonuclear fusion, based on exploiting the energy recovered in fusing light elements (for example, deuterium and tritium) rather than fissioning uranium or plutonium. The resources upon which fusion would depend—lithium and deuterium in seawater—are virtually inexhaustible.

How fusion compares with fission with regard to reactor safety, radioactive waste management, and proliferation and diversion risks depends on how the technology is developed. But relative to today's LWRs, it offers considerable promise, for three reasons (PCAST Fusion Review Panel, 1995). First, with regard to safety, population exposures to radiation from worst-case accidents are 100 times smaller than those from worst-case fission accidents. Second, with respect to radioactive waste hazards, those from fusion (on the basis of the most meaningful of indices combining volume, radiotoxicity, and longevity) can be expected to be at least 100 times and perhaps 10,000 or more times smaller than those from fission. Third, with regard to nuclear weaponry, electricity supply systems based on fusion would be less likely than fission systems to contribute to nuclear weapons capabilities acquisition by sub-national groups and, if designed appropriately, could be easier to safeguard against clandestine fissile material production by governments.

> The essence of the potential nuclear weapons link to fission power is that this technology provides the possibility of obtaining access to nuclear explosive materials.

Despite these advantages, it is still unclear whether fusion will eventually become a commercial energy technology. Even if technical goals can be realised, fusion is not expected to become an option for commercial energy applications before 2050 (PCAST Fusion Review Panel, 1995).

The outlook for addressing the challenges

Can the challenges related to nuclear power—cost, safety, proliferation and diversion, and waste management—all be adequately addressed with advanced technologies to make it widely acceptable? This question cannot be fully answered at this time—in part because consensus has not been reached on goals for technological innovation, and in part because the answer does not depend only on technical considerations.

Clarification of goals is needed to facilitate the development of a focussed nuclear energy innovation effort. The market, ideally with external costs internalised, will determine the competitiveness of future nuclear technologies, so that cost goals for the technology will have to be adjusted over time to respond to the changing competition. Although this uncertainty is common to all technologies, the intrinsic high investment cost required to bring new nuclear technologies to market makes this a continuing difficult challenge for nuclear power. Among externality concerns, consensus might converge on a goal of demonstrable safety (Lidsky, 1991).

However, goals relating to proliferation and diversion resistance and waste management require considerable clarification. There is a strong technical case that LWRs operated on once-through fuel cycles are more proliferation and diversion resistant than today's reprocess-recycle technologies, but beyond that there is little agreement in the technical community as to the relative merits of alternative advanced concepts. For waste management, goals need to be better defined, not only to include various non-technical considerations but also to ensure that proliferation and diversion resistance goals are not compromised.

There seem to be reasonably good prospects for making reactors demonstrably safe while simultaneously also reducing cost—although this must be demonstrated, through appropriate research, development, and dissemination. This leaves proliferation and diversion and waste management—issues that also involve cost considerations. How much more proliferation and diversion resistant advanced nuclear technologies can be made relative to LWRs operated on once-through fuel cycles is unclear—as is the potential for maintaining even this degree of resistance in the future, when uranium might be much scarcer than it is today. But at least for the immediately future, there are no economic obstacles to making reactors at least as resistant to proliferation and diversion as LWRs operated on once-through fuel cycles.

A promising option for sustaining the proliferation and diversion resistance of reactors operated on once-through fuel cycles seems to be extraction of uranium from seawater. Because the technology probably will not be needed at least until sometime after 2050, there is no urgency to develop the technology. However, a critical near-term need is assessment of the feasibility of the concept at large scale to provide a more informed basis for prioritising research and development on alternative nuclear technologies for the long term.

Waste management is probably a technically soluble problem, but it is unclear whether promising technical fixes can be made broadly acceptable to the public. S&T technologies for burning transuranics and long-lived fission products will probably get considerable research and development support as an option for addressing the waste disposal challenge—in large part because many people have little confidence in human capabilities to adequately manage waste risks for the long periods required (O'Neill, 1998)—even though S&T technologies are probably not necessary to adequately protect the public in the very long term. In a world where overall research and development investment funds are limited, such investments could limit funds available for other needed nuclear research and development activities.

In summary, for nuclear energy to qualify as a sustainable energy option, concerns regarding safety, waste disposal, and proliferation and diversion must be addressed in ways that enable nuclear energy to compete on an economic basis. Effectively addressing these concerns to enable a large expansion of nuclear power probably requires advanced technologies, as well as improved institutional risk management strategies.

Although it is possible to envision sets of nuclear technologies and management strategies that might fulfil the requirements for sustainability, decisions on future nuclear power will be made largely at the political level rather than on narrow technical and economic grounds. Gaining broad public support for nuclear power is not simply a matter of better educating the public on the issues, which is what many in the nuclear industry believe is needed most. The industry should also seek to better understand public concerns.[96] The industry must recognise that a stable political consensus on nuclear goals and strategies is needed to bring about a nuclear-intensive energy future. The industry should also consider opening up the nuclear decision-making process to diverse interest groups, so that a well-informed public could ensure that its concerns are addressed every step of the way (Bunn, 1999).

During the next 20 years there might be enough nuclear plant orders (mainly in Asia) and business opportunities associated with maintaining existing plants to keep the nuclear industry from collapsing. But taking into account expected plant retirements, this period will probably be characterised by little if any net nuclear power expansion world-wide. The industry might consider this de facto moratorium on net expansion as a window of opportunity for confidence-building, through which it could seek to convince the public and investors that concerns about cost, safety, proliferation and diversion, and waste disposal can be dealt with effectively.

The number one priority on the confidence-building agenda is to reach a broad consensus on waste disposal policy. To get this consensus requires that industry engage effectively all stakeholder groups, including those ideologically opposed to nuclear power. Whether the needed deal-making is feasible or not is unknowable at this time, but not implausible. For example, as a strategy to deal with its strongest critics, industry leaders might consider becoming vocal supporters of public-sector-supported renewable energy and energy efficiency programmes in exchange for broad support for sensible nuclear waste management strategies and policies—in effect, giving the renewable and energy efficiency communities the opportunity (during the moratorium) to show whether they can deliver on what they hope for.[97]

If the energy innovation effort in the near term emphasises improved energy efficiency, renewables, and decarbonised fossil energy strategies,[98] the world community should know by 2020 or before much better than now if nuclear power will be needed on a large scale to meet sustainable energy goals. With broad support for a sensible waste management strategy, the nuclear industry would be far better positioned to take off again at that time than if it were to continue dealing with its critics in a more confrontational manner.

In parallel with such confidence-building, the industry might consider strategies to prioritise the nuclear energy innovation effort. The first steps might include exploratory research and development (which is quite inexpensive relative to building large-scale demonstration projects) aimed at better clarifying the options.[99] These steps could be followed by efforts to reach consensus within the technical community regarding priorities, so that the industry would be well prepared to move ahead if the world community eventually decides that large-scale nuclear power is needed to meet sustainable energy goals. ■

> Although coping with the radioactive waste problem seems manageable from a technical perspective, a technical fix by itself is not a solution.

Notes

1. Major reviewers for this chapter were Harry Audus (United Kingdom), Tim Brennand (United Kingdom), Ramon Espino (United States), Richard Garwin (United States), Chris Hendriks (Netherlands), Olav Kaarstad (Norway), Larry Lidsky (United States), Marvin Miller (United States), Larry Papay (United States), Jefferson Tester (United States), and Maarten van der Burgt (Netherlands).

2. Because methane is a powerful greenhouse gas (chapter 3), getting climate change benefits from shifting to natural gas requires minimising gas leakage from the entire gas system.

3. The Convention on Climate Change seeks to "achieve stabilisation of the greenhouse gas concentration in the atmosphere at a level that would prevent dangerous anthropogenic interference with the climate system. Such a level should be achieved within a time frame sufficient to allow economic systems to adapt naturally to climate change, to ensure that food production is not threatened, and to enable economic development to proceed in a sustainable manner" (UNFCC, 1992).

4. For example, the World Bank (World Bank, 1997) has estimated that in 1995 air pollution damages in China cost $48 billion, or 7 percent of GDP; see chapter 3.

5. In a study carried out under the auspices of the European Commission's ExternE Programme, Krewitt and others (1999) estimated that for the European Union (EU-15) the total cost of environmental damages arising from air pollutant emissions of fossil fuel power plants in 1990 was $70 billion, or more than $0.06 per kilowatt-hour of electricity generated; 97 percent of this cost is related to health—mostly fine-particle air pollution.

6. Uncontrolled emissions increase roughly in proportion to oil plus coal consumption, which in turn grows roughly in proportion to GDP. Assuming, as economists often do, that the willingness to pay to avoid health damages from air pollution increases as (GDP/P), it follows that the cost of health damages from uncontrolled emissions increases roughly as $P \bullet (GDP/P)^2$, where P = population.

7. The cost estimates presented in tables 8.1 and 8.2, like the estimates in Krewitt and others (1999), were developed under the ExternE Programme of the European Commission.

8. This gap exists for a variety of reasons—for example, regulated emission levels are for well-maintained cars, and regulations tend to be for driving cycles that often do not adequately reflect the way people actually drive cars (Ross, Goodwin, and Watkins, 1995).

9. To illustrate the challenge of addressing air quality goals as economies evolve, consider a simple model of a hypothetical average developing country that grows from its 1990 state, in which per capita GDP (GDP/P) = $2,300 (1990 dollars, purchasing power parity basis—the average for all developing countries in 1990) and there are no air pollutant emission controls in place, to a future state where per capita GDP is 7.2 times higher (GDP/P = $16,400, the average for countries belonging to the Organisation for Economic Co-operation and Development, or OECD, in 1990—a level that could be realised in 100 years with a sustained 2 percent per year GDP/P growth rate). Suppose also that in this period per capita consumption of coal plus oil also increases 7.3 times, from the actual average level in 1990 for developing countries to the 1990 level for OECD countries, and that without controls pollutant emissions increase in proportion to coal plus oil consumption levels. Without pollution controls and taking into account an expected doubling of population in this period, health damage costs would increase about 100 times (2 x 7.2 x 7.3; assuming, as most economists do, that the willingness to pay to avoid pollution damages increases in proportion to per capita GDP). Thus end-of-pipe controls that reduce emissions by 99 percent would be required to keep damage costs in dollar terms to a level no greater than in 1990.

10. For example, the U.S. Department of Energy's Vision 21 Program (Clean Energy Plants for the 21st Century) seeks—in addition to achieving near-zero pollution emissions with advanced technology—reduced CO_2 emissions through both efficiency improvements and development of the capability to reduce CO_2 emissions to zero or near zero by means of CO_2 capture and sequestration. A complementary new DOE programme is carbon sequestration—a research and development effort aimed at developing carbon sequestration technologies to the point of deployment, so that these sequestration technologies will be ready to be deployed (if and when needed).

11. Efficiencies have been rising continually in conjunction with increasing turbine inlet temperatures, which have been rising at an average rate of 13 degrees Celsius a year for the past 30 years (Chiesa and others, 1993), as a result of more heat-resistant materials being used for turbine blades and improved turbine blade cooling technologies.

12. On a lower heating value (LHV) basis, the efficiencies of the Frame 7F and Frame 7H are 56 and 60 percent, respectively.

13. Some regulations require controlling NO_x emissions to less than 10 parts per million, dry volume basis (at 15 percent O_2)—relative to typical uncontrolled emissions for natural-gas-fired systems of 125 parts per million.

14. In a typical gas turbine, two-thirds of the output of the turbine is needed to drive the compressor.

15. Spray intercooling has been applied to an existing gas turbine (without major modification) in a commercial product (McNeely, 1998). But this unit involves only 1–3 percent of the maximum feasible water injection rate.

16. The electricity generating potential through combined heat and power in a particular industry is the heat load times the characteristic output ratio of electricity to heat for the cogenerating technology.

17. These large syngas projects that involve electricity as a product or coproduct are part of a recent global inventory of syngas projected compiled by Simbeck and Johnson (1999) that involves 161 real and planned commercial-scale projects with a combined syngas production capacity of 60,880 megawatts-thermal. Many of these are polygeneration projects that involve the coproduction of various combinations of products—for example, electricity, steam for process, chemicals, town gas; and many of the projects are in the petroleum refining and chemical industries. About 44 percent of the productive capacity is based on coal; much of the rest is based on the use of low-cost petroleum refinery residues.

18. As an IGCC-based power industry grows, the benefit of by-product sulphur sales per kilowatt-hour will eventually decline when the sulphur supplies exceed demand, so that sulphur prices will fall.

19. For the cogeneration systems described in tables 8.7 and 8.8, condensing and extraction turbines rather than back-pressure turbines are needed; otherwise the ratio of electricity to heat production would be less than 1 to 1. (In condensing and extraction systems, some of the steam is bled from the turbine at the pressure appropriate for the process, and the rest of the steam is used to produce more power and then condensed; for the steam that is condensed, there is no cogeneration fuel-saving benefit.) The fraction of the steam that must be condensed is much greater in the steam turbine case than in the IGCC case, because of the much lower electricity-heat output ratios for steam turbines relative to combined cycles (see figure 8.1).

20. At present, gases exiting the gasifier at temperatures of 1,000 degrees Celsius or more are cooled to about 100 degrees Celsius to facilitate cleaning the gas of particulates and sulphur and nitrogen compounds. Then the cleaned gas is heated up to the turbine inlet temperature of 1,300 degrees Celsius or more.

21. Most of the rest will be used for standby service.

22. Because the temperature of the turbine exhaust is higher than that of the air exiting the compressor, the turbine exhaust heat is often recovered to preheat the air exiting the compressor before it is delivered to the combustor, so that moderate efficiencies are achievable despite the low pressure ratio.

23. Less than 0.24 grams per kilowatt-hour (9 parts per million by volume at 15 percent O_2) for the 28-kilowatt-electric Capstone Model 330 using a non-catalytic staged combustion system.

24. Ballard is a joint venture involving Ballard Power Systems, General Public Utilities International, and GEC Alsthom. Plug Power is a joint venture involving Mechanical Technologies, Inc., Detroit Edison, and General Electric.

25. An operating temperature in the range 700–800 degrees Celsius enables an efficiency increase of about 10 percent without compromising fuel flexibility and the process advantages offered by SOFCs operated at 1,000 degrees Celsius. A reduced operating temperature also leads to greater choice of electrode materials and reductions in system cost and complexity (Goldstein, 1992).

26. Oxygen would be needed for coal gasification, in any case.

27. Shell intends to use the technology in conjunction with its own oil and gas operations—including use of the separated CO_2 for enhanced oil recovery (SIEP, 1998).

28. To be effective in sequestering CO_2, aquifers need not be leak free. Lindeberg (1997) modelled CO_2 sequestration for injection during a 25-year period into aquifers for which there is an open boundary or fracture 8,000 metres from the injection well and showed that, if such aquifers

have high permeability, some of the injected CO_2 would eventually escape. Assuming all CO_2 associated with future fossil fuel consumption (7,000 GtC) as projected in the IPCC's IS92a scenario (IPCC, 1995) is injected into such aquifers, Lindeberg estimated for the worst (leakiest) case that a fifth of the injected CO_2 would eventually leak out but would do so slowly over many centuries at climatically inconsequential rates—with leakage peaking in 3100 at 2 GtC per year; in contrast, if the same amount of CO_2 were released to the atmosphere during fossil fuel combustion, emissions would increase until they peak at 30 GtC a year in about 2150 and subsequently decline as fossil fuel resources are depleted.

29. All cases include costs to pressurise CO_2 to 135 bar plus a CO_2 disposal cost of $18 per tonne of carbon (equivalent to $5 per tonne of CO_2).

30. The calculation presented is an updated calculation for this decarbonisation of fuel gas strategy originally advanced by Blok, Hendriks, and Turkenburg (1989) and van der Burgt, Cantle, and Boutkan (1992); also see Chiesa and Consonni (1998).

31. This is for disposal near the CO_2 separation site or for disposal with some credit for enhanced resource recovery. If the separated CO_2 had to be transported 500 kilometres to a remote aquifer for disposal, with no credit for enhanced resource recovery, the avoided cost would increase about another $10 per tonne of carbon (Williams, 1999b).

32. The system described in table 8.10 (based on Simbeck, 1999c) involves an autothermal reformer that uses steam and O_2 for reforming natural gas. Audus, Kaarstad, and Singer (1999) describe a system that instead uses steam and air for reforming, thereby avoiding the cost for air separation; their estimate of the CO_2 recovery cost penalty is less than two-thirds of the estimate in table 8.10. Simbeck (1999c) also estimates costs for autothermal reforming with steam and air but finds the cost to be higher than for reforming with steam and O_2, because savings from avoiding the cost of an air separation unit are more than offset by higher costs for downstream components that arise because the fuel gas is diluted with nitrogen from air.

33. For the advanced technology (2012) cases considered by Herzog (1999a), the lower heating value (LHV) efficiencies with CO_2 recovery and disposal are 55.6 percent for the NGCC case and 42.4 percent for the coal IGCC case, compared to 50.8 percent and 37.2 percent for the corresponding cases presented in table 8.10. The corresponding busbar costs in the Herzog analysis with 2020 U.S. fuel prices are $0.045 per kilowatt-hour for the NGCC case and $0.044 per kilowatt-hour for the coal IGCC case. (To put the Herzog analysis on the same basis as the present analysis, Herzog's annual capital charge rate was changed from 15 to 11.5 percent, the capacity factor was increased from 75 to 80 percent, and a CO_2 transport-and-disposal cost—not taken into account by Herzog—of $5 per tonne of CO_2 was included .)

34. A litre of water contaminated with MeOH would contain a fatal dose if it were 2–7 percent MeOH by weight.

35. The cetane number is a measure of a fuel's ability to auto-ignite. A high cetane number is desirable for candidate fuels for compression-ignition engines because it shortens ignition delay, lowering premixed burning and resultant NO_x emissions and noise. High octane fuels have low cetane numbers, and fuels with high cetane numbers have low octane ratings.

36. This plant commenced operations in 1993 but was shut down in late 1997 by an explosion at the air separation plant (from the build-up of small particles taken in from the air—apparently as a result of the prolonged haze that had blanketed the entire South Asian region in late 1997). The plant is scheduled to reopen in 2000, after repairs are completed.

37. These increased emissions of especially small particles appear to arise as a result of controlling soot particle emissions—which dominate the mass of particulate emissions—using current technology. Removing soot particles thereby removes nucleating agents on which these tiny particles would otherwise condense or adsorb; these very small particles seem to come from ash in the lubricating oil (Abdul-Khalek and others, 1998).

38. The calculations presented in tables 8.11 and 8.12 are based on well-established cost estimates and cost-scaling exponents for each of

the many components of these systems. However, it is assumed in these calculations that each component (for example, the coal gasifier) can be built in a single train to the required capacity. The maximum sizes of single-train components that are commercially available today are less than the capacities associated with many of the components for the polygeneration systems presented in these tables. To the extent that multiple trains instead of single trains would have to be used for practical systems, the cost savings would be less than indicated in tables 8.11 and 8.12. But these tables illustrate the value of evolving towards systems based on large single-train systems and thus represent good targets for development.

39. Air Products and Eastman Chemicals tested liquid-phase MeOH production technology in a process development unit at LaPorte, Texas, which was designed to produce 6,900 litres per day and which operated for 7,400 hours. Following this, a commercial-scale plant (designed to produce 288,000 litres per day) went into operation in January 1997, at Kingport, Tennessee, under the U.S. Department of Energy's Clean Coal Technology Program, to demonstrate the technology during a period of 4 years of expected plant operation.

40. In China more than 20 Texaco gasifiers are operating, under construction, or on order for the production of chemical fertiliser, MeOH, town gas, or oxochemicals. In addition, 6 Shell gasifiers and at least 1 Lurgi gasifier are being used to produce ammonia (NH_3) from coal.

41. Water or steam injection would probably not be pursued for gas turbine and steam turbine combined cycles because these options would reduce efficiency. However, the technique would be appropriate for low-capital-cost systems that use steam or water injection for efficiency augmentation—such as intercooled steam-injected gas turbines (Williams and Larson, 1989) or, for water injection, Tophat® cycles (van Liere, 1998).

42. Consider H_2 manufacture from coal—a process that begins with O_2-blown coal gasification, which is also the first step in processing coal for IGCC plants. Just as pollutant emissions from coal IGCC plants are almost as low as from NGCC plants (see table 8.1), pollutant emissions from H_2 production plants are expected to be very low. Pollutant emissions per unit of coal consumed would tend to be lower than for IGCC plants, because gases exiting the gasifier must be cleaned to a higher degree to protect catalysts in downstream processing equipment from damage by contaminants such as sulphur. Catalyst protection requirements are often more stringent than regulatory requirements for air pollutant emissions.

43. For example, it is estimated that at a future (optimistic but plausible) photovoltaic electricity price of $0.027 per kilowatt-hour, the cost of photovoltaic-derived H_2 would be $17 per gigajoule (IPCC, 1996a). For comparison, the cost of making H_2 from natural gas and coal today, including the cost of storing the separated CO_2 underground, is $6 per gigajoule for natural gas and $11 per gigajoule for coal (Kaarstad and Audus, 1997). With advanced fossil-energy conversion technologies that are likely to be available by the time a photovoltaic electricity price of $0.027 per kilowatt-hour is reached, fossil-energy-derived H_2 costs with CO_2 sequestration would be less (Williams, 1999b). (Even credit for the by-product O_2 generated in electrolytic processes would not help much; such a credit would amount to only about $0.60 per gigajoule of electrolytic H_2 ($20 per tonne of O_2) assuming an installed cost of $21.60 per tonne of O_2 per day for an air liquefaction plant).

44. An H_2 fuel cell car would typically be three times more fuel-efficient than a conventional gasoline internal combustion engine car of comparable performance. This efficiency gain arises because, while the efficiency of an internal combustion engine declines with decreasing load (so that the efficiency of driving a car, averaged over all driving conditions, is a modest 15 percent), the efficiency of a fuel cell increases as the load decreases (so that the efficiency at average part-load conditions is a high 50 percent).

45. Some indicators of the level of industrial effort to develop fuel cell vehicles: by the end of 1999 the four largest Japanese manufacturers had spent $546 million on fuel cell development. Honda has announced plans to spend up to $500 million on fuel cell research and development during the next five years. DaimlerChrysler has spent $300 million on fuel cells and expects that it will have spent $1.4 billion by 2004, when it starts producing engines for fuel cell vehicles.

46. For F-T liquids production, syngas with an H_2 to CO ratio of 2 is needed. Because steam reforming instead gives a ratio of 3 ($CH_4 + H_2O \rightarrow CO + 3H_2$), syngas is typically made through partial oxidation ($CH_4 + 1/2 O_2 \rightarrow CO + 2H_2$), which gives the right ratio but requires an expensive air separation plant. When some CH_4 is instead used to produce H_2, the CO_2 by-product can be used for doing some CO_2 reforming ($CH_4 + CO_2 \rightarrow 2CO + 2H_2$), along with steam reforming, to get the right overall ratio, thereby avoiding the need for an air separation plant.

47. The process of making H_2 from syngas (mainly CO and H_2) involves reacting the CO with steam (in water-gas shift reactors) to produce H_2 and CO_2. With current technology, this is followed by the use of capital- and energy-intensive equipment to separate the H_2 and CO_2.

48. As indicated in chapter 5, global methane clathrate hydrate occurrences have an energy content of 780,000 exajoules (table 5.7) and a carbon content of 12,000 GtC (table 5.8). If half of this resource could ultimately be recovered and burned along with 5,000 GtC of fossil energy reserves and resources (table 5.8), and if half the released CO_2 stayed in the atmosphere, the atmospheric CO_2 level would be eight times higher than at present.

49. The announced efficiency is on an LHV basis, and the design is for once-through processes using cold seawater under wintertime conditions for northern Europe and does not include energy penalties for pollution control. Correcting to the norm of 40 millibar (29 degrees Celsius) of the International Standards Organization for once-through cooling with steam condensation, accounting for fuel consumption requirements for air pollution control equipment that would lead to low levels of SO_2 and NOx emissions, and converting to a higher heating value basis (the norm for this report), the efficiency would be about 43 percent (see entry in the first row of table 8.9).

50. Because cogeneration systems involving condensing heat transfer are less costly than those requiring steam cooling, reheat steam cycles (which deliver superheated steam) are typically not attractive (Kovacik, 1996).

51. The air separation plant contributes $150 per kilowatt-electric to the capital cost of an IGCC plant and requires 12 percent of gross power output for operations (Simbeck, 1999a).

52. Advanced clean-up technologies being pursued operate at 500–600 degrees Celsius, well below the temperatures of gases exiting the gasifiers—so that the process is described as warm rather than hot.

53. The U.S. Department of Energy–supported demonstration project aimed at proving warm gas clean-up for IGCCs with air-blown gasification (a 100-megawatt-electric Pinon Pine IGCC Power Project in Nevada that was put into service in early 1997) had sustained operating runs of less than 13 hours as of June 1999 (Motter, 1999).

54. But air-blown gasifiers are well-suited for biomass IGCCs (Simbeck and Karp, 1995; Williams and Larson, 1993); low sulphur and nitrogen contents of typical feedstocks make biomass a good candidate for warm-gas cleanup. In addition, scale economies make air separation costly at the relatively small scales of most biomass power applications.

55. Heating up the extra mass of N_2 in combustion leads to lower peak flame temperatures for air-blown units.

56. In fluidised-bed combustion, fuel is burned in a bed of fuel and other materials that behaves like a fluid, as a result of a gas passing upwards through the bed fast enough to support fuel and other particles but not so fast as to transport particles out of the bed. Typically 2–3 percent of the weight of the bed material is coal.

57. Second-generation technology, which is entering the pilot and demonstration phases, will employ a coal pyrolyser to produce, from some of the coal input, fuel gas that is burned in a gas turbine combustor so as to increase the turbine inlet temperature of the gases delivered to the gas turbine.

58. Still another source of greenhouse gas emissions arises because all carbon in the limestone added to an AFBC unit for sulphur removal (limestone is typically added at two or more times the rate theoretically required for sulphur removal) is released as CO_2 at levels that could be significant for high-sulphur coals. The problem is less for PFBC units, which can be designed to suppress CO_2 emissions from the quantities of limestone present in the bed at levels in excess of the theoretical amounts needed for sulphur removal. In both cases these extra CO_2 emissions are not significant in practice because the use of high-sulphur coals is not practical for fluidised-bed combustion units.

59. The need for H_2 arises from the H-C ratio of 2 for today's hydrocarbon fuels, relative to 0.8 for coal.

60. In 1996, more than 75 percent in France and Lithuania, and more than 50 percent in Belgium and Sweden.

61. The reference scenario of the Energy Information Administration (EIA) of the U.S. Department of Energy is that nuclear capacity will be 311 gigawatts-electric in 2020; the low-growth and high-growth EIA scenarios for 2020 project 179 and 442 gigawatts-electric of nuclear capacity, respectively (EIA, 1999a). The most recent forecast of the International Atomic Energy Agency (IAEA) is that nuclear capacity in 2020 will be 305–582 gigawatts-electric, with its share in total power generation falling by then to 10–14 percent (IAEA, 1999).

62. There is a considerable range in nuclear forecasts for individual countries. For Japan in 2010, the EIA (1999) projects 39.6–54.8 gigawatts-electric, with a reference value of 47.5 gigawatts-electric—relative to 43.9 in 1997. In contrast, the official (Ministry of Trade and Industry) projection for Japan in 2010 is 70 gigawatts-electric (Matsuoka and Hiranuma, 1998); others project 55–60 gigawatts-electric or less (Hard, 1997; Hagen, 1998). For China in 2010, the EIA (1999a) projects 8.7–11.5 gigawatts-electric, with a reference value of 11.5 gigawatts-electric—up from 2.2 in 1997. The Chinese National Nuclear Corporation has projected a total installed capacity of 20 gigawatts-electric by 2010; however, this might not be achieved, as a result of both overall excess electric generating capacity and the high costs of nuclear expansion.

63. The Rabl and Spadaro damage cost estimates include consideration of severe reactor accidents, for which they assumed a reactor core melt probability of 10^{-5} per year with a release of 1 percent of the radioactivity in the core in an accident—corresponding to the reference accident scenario used by French national safety authorities. According to the authors, the calculations assume "a mature and stable political system, with strict verification of compliance with all regulations."

64. This scenario involves net new nuclear generating capacity being added at an average rate of 62 gigawatts-electric per year during the next 100 years, and, if nuclear plants last 40 years, a corresponding average rate of nuclear plant construction (including replacement capacity) of 115 gigawatts-electric per year. For comparison, the nuclear capacity in the most nuclear-intensive IIASA-WEC scenario (A3) is 6,000 gigawatts-electric in 2100 (chapter 9).

65. Assuming 50 percent efficient coal plants and 60 percent efficient natural gas plants.

66. Cumulative CO_2 emissions for the IPCC's IS92a scenario are 1,500 GtC, 1990–2100; or 1,420 GtC, 2000–2100 (IPCC, 1995).

67. This gloom-hope perspective on the prospects for nuclear power is widely shared by governments. In the text agreed to by government delegations at the final plenary session for Working Group II of the IPCC's second assessment report, it is stated that "nuclear energy could replace baseload fossil fuel electricity generation in many parts of the world if generally acceptable responses can be found to concerns such as reactor safety, radioactive waste transport and disposal, and nuclear proliferation" (IPCC, 1996b). Similarly, the Energy Research and Development Panel of U.S. President Clinton's Committee of Advisors on Science and Technology concluded: "Several problems cloud fission's potential as an acceptable power source today and into the future: disposal of radioactive waste; concern about nuclear weapons proliferation; concern about safe operation of plants; and noncompetitive economics…Given the projected growth in global energy demand…and the need to stabilize and then reduce GHG emissions, it is important to establish fission energy as an acceptable and viable option, if at all possible…Therefore, R&D is needed to solve the problems" (PCAST Energy Research and Development Panel, 1997).

68. Assuming a 10 percent discount rate, the value assumed in assessing all technologies in chapter 8. For a 5 percent discount rate, this report projected costs of $1,400–2,800 per kilowatt-electric (Paffenbarger and Bertel, 1998).

69. The high cost and complexity of the LWR are related in part to its high power density—ironically the reason it was originally chosen for submarine use!

70. For example, the former chairman of the Atomic Energy Board of India was warned that the safety status of nuclear energy installations in India is far below international standards, and that in the absence of an independent regulatory body this has serious implications for public safety (Gopalakrishnan, 1999).

71. Nuclear-explosive materials are those that can sustain a fission chain reaction based on fast neutrons, which is the requirement for making a nuclear bomb. The two principal nuclear-explosive materials are mixtures of uranium isotopes that contain more than 20 percent of the fissile isotopes U-233 and U-235; and all mixtures of plutonium isotopes, except those containing a high proportion of Pu-238 (see CISAC, 1995).

72. The importance of complementing institutional measures with technological strategies was underscored recently by Evgeniy Adamov, the Russian minister of atomic energy, who has expressed the view that the risk of diversion of nuclear material is one of the key problems of the non-proliferation regime, and therefore, "no matter how efficient the inspection and safety regime in different countries may be, it is necessary to pass on to a different kind of technological cycle in nuclear energy that has built into it a mechanism to prevent the development of weapons-grade materials" (press conference transcript, 25 November 1998).

73. On the institutional side, continuing efforts are under way to strengthen the international safeguard system, export controls over key technologies, and security systems designed to prevent the theft of weapons-usable nuclear materials. Much more remains to be done in each of these areas, however—particularly because the collapse of the Soviet Union has greatly weakened controls over technologies, information, and materials in the former Soviet states. In the case of the international safeguards regime, the IAEA is critically in need of more resources, having been on a near-zero-real-growth budget even while taking on substantial new responsibilities, and the IAEA also requires strong political support to effectively implement the new safeguard measures agreed to in recent years. R&D is also needed to improve safeguard technologies, including those designed to detect clandestine nuclear activities from kilometres away and those to account more accurately for plutonium in spent fuel and in bulk processing (as occurs during reprocessing and plutonium fuel fabrication), as well as highly enriched uranium in bulk processing. For a detailed discussion of institutional strategies for reducing proliferation risks associated with nuclear power, see Walker (1999).

74. In addition, India has a small pilot reprocessing plant at Tarapur and has recently put into operation a second reprocessing plant at Kalpakkam. And Japan has a small reprocessing plant at Tokai Mura (currently shut down). Under the Carter administration, the United States abandoned plans for fuel reprocessing and plutonium recycling as a result of both nuclear proliferation concerns and poor prospective economics. Since 1990 the Russian reprocessing plant has been running at a modest fraction of its rated capacity; some of its non-Russian clients have shifted from a spent fuel reprocessing strategy to a direct spent fuel disposal strategy, and Russian reactor operators are failing to pay their bills (Berkhout, 1998).

75. For the Russian Federation's reprocessing plants, the situation is somewhat more complex. There does not appear to be a requirement for plutonium return. Older contracts do not appear to require return of high-level wastes; high-level waste return appears to be required by at least some interpretations of Russian law, but the law is being ignored.

76. At today's low uranium market price of $25 per kilogram (equivalent to an oil price of less than $0.30 per barrel), the purchase of uranium contributes to the cost of nuclear electricity less than $0.0005 per kilowatt-hour. A 1994 study estimated that the levelised fuel cost for the once-through LWR fuel cycle is 14 percent less than for the reprocessing cycle (NEA, 1994). A more recent analysis found reprocessing and plutonium

recycling to be much less attractive economically and estimated that uranium prices would have to increase by six times before reprocessing and recycling would be economic (Fetter, Bunn, and Holdren, 1999).

77. A variety of other possibilities have been considered over the years and might still be pursued someday as alternatives to repositories, including disposal in the seabed, in miles-deep drilled boreholes, in space, and the like.

78. This cost assessment is consistent with a Framatome assessment that a particle-accelerator-based system that would transmute minor transuranics and long-lived fission products would not be competitive in electricity generation with LWRs (Valée, 1999).

79. For example, it has been recently discovered that water moves through the mountain much faster than had been thought, and thermal inclusions have been identified that may (or may not) suggest upwellings of water in the not very distant past.

80. During a period of 500,000 to 1 million years, the most exposed community 30 kilometres from Yucca Mountain (if that site becomes a U.S. nuclear waste repository) may have exposure from groundwater that is comparable to background radiation. However, only a tiny fraction of the population would be so exposed.

81. For example, recent measurements challenge the widely held technical view that the greatest long-term waste disposal hazards arise not from transuranics but from long-lived fission products. The relative lack of concern about transuranics arises from the belief that even if storage canisters eventually lose their integrity, the transuranics will not dissolve readily in reservoir groundwater because they are quite insoluble relative to long-lived fission products under both oxidising and reducing conditions. Thus, except where there would be human intrusion into the repository, the main doses to humans after long periods would be from the long-lived fission products Tc-99 and I-129, which are soluble and thus can move through groundwater pathways (STATS Committee, 1996). But recently, trace plutonium contamination was discovered in sub-surface waters in Nevada that can be unambiguously identified as having come from a nuclear weapons test 30 years earlier at the Nevada test site 1.3 kilometres from the point where the plutonium contamination was found. This measurement (Kersting, 1999) and related tracer experiments (McCarthy, Sanford, and Stafford, 1998) suggest that sub-micron-scale colloidal particles are the carriers of plutonium through groundwater. In addition, it has recently been shown that water, even at ambient temperatures, can further oxidise PuO_2 into forms for which more than 25 percent of the Pu ions exist in states that are far more soluble (Haschke, Allen, and Morales, 2000). Although these findings do not prove that such mechanisms will provide significant exposure pathways from nuclear weapons test sites or radioactive waste disposal sites, they do show that concerns about long-term waste disposal are made up of technical as well as political elements (Honeyman, 1999; Madic, 2000).

82. Vendors of heavy water reactors are also developing evolutionary advanced designs, with features similar to those being incorporated into evolutionary advanced light water reactor designs.

83. U-233, like U-233 and Pu-239, is a fissile material from which nuclear weapons can be readily made.

84. Relatively pure U-233 might be obtained by extracting chemically from spent fuel the Pa-233 precursor of U-233 before the Pa-233 (with a 27-day half-life) has a chance to decay (Glaser, 1998). Glaser (1998) also points out that if a would-be had access to relatively modest-scale uranium enrichment capacity, weapons-grade uranium could be produced from both the U-233 and the U-235 in the denatured fuel, because most of the separative work required to produce weapons-grade uranium from natural uranium has already been carried out.

85. The type of HTGR involving fixed graphite blocks has been the focus of considerable effort in several countries (including construction and operation of prototype reactors with varying degrees of success); an international consortium including France, Japan, the Russian Federation, and the United States is developing a next-generation modular design of such a system, with the idea of possibly constructing a prototype in the Russian federation. The pebble bed variant of the HTGR has been

the focus of development in several countries (including construction and operation of an early prototype in Germany some years ago), and a pebble bed modular reactor is now the focus of an embryonic international effort led by Eskom, the electric utility of South Africa, with particiaption from German experts and MIT, among others.

86. Less than 4.5 megawatts per cubic metre, relative to 100 megawatts per cubic metre for an LWR.

87. The nuclear LWR-FBR nuclear vision was epitomised by the US Atomic Energy Commissions' 1973 projection that by 2000 the United States would get half its electric power from 400 FPRs and 600 LWRs.

88. The United States abandoned the 300-megawatt-electric Clinch River Breeder Reactor demonstration project in 1983, after spending $7 billion, and cancelled the follow-on Integral Fast Reactor in 1994. The United Kingdom completed an FBR prototype in 1974 but shut it down in 1994, after abandoning plans for construction of a follow-up full-scale demonstration project. France completed the 300-megawatt-electric Phenix prototype FBR in 1973 and $5 billion full-sized, 1,200-megawatt-electirc Super Phenix in 1985. Although the Phenix has been relatively trouble free, the Super Phenix has been shut down for long periods as a result of sodium leaks and related safety issues, and the French government recently announced that the Super Phenix will be dismantled. Germany completed an FBR progamme; a sodium coolant accident at the Monju prototype FBR in 1995 has put the Japanese FBR programme largely on hold, although some variant of the plutonium FBR remains a major objective of Japanese nuclear energy policy (Hori and others, 1999). The Russian Federation operates the world's only remaining commercial-scale breeder (the BN-600 at Beloyarsk) and has the world's only remaining plans for near-term construction of additional commercial breeders (the BN-800), but construction of these has been stopped for many years for lack of funds. The BN-350 breeder reactor in Kazakhstan was recently closed, with no plans for replacement.

89. Consider implications for plutonium management if the world nuclear industry evolves according to the high-nuclear-growth scenario given above, with 6,500 gigawatts-electric of installed nuclear capacity in 2100. Suppose also that, by that time, uranium resource constraints will have led to a decision to introduce conventional plutonium recycling. Each one-gigawatt-electric power plant under such circumstances would discharge in its spent fuel 10^3 kilograms of plutonium each year that would be recovered via reprocessing and used in fresh fuel. The amount of plutonium circulating in global commerce would be 6.5 million kilograms per year. The amount of plutonium needed to make a nuclear weapon is less than 10 kilograms. Because of the daunting institutional challenges associated with preventing significant quantities of this plutonium from being diverted to weapons purposes, it would be desirable to have available more proliferation-and-diversion-resistant nuclear technologies that would not be so difficult to manage institutionally.

90. Two ground-based reactor test facilities were constructed, and eight nuclear submarines powered with lead-bismuth-cooled reactors were built (Crodnikov and others, 1999).

91. In constrast to conventional plutonium breeders, for which plutonium production targets are greater than plutonium consumption rates.

92. The reactor for the proposed system would be compact (with a core volume of 6.8 cubic metres). The reactor core would be sealed so that individual fuel assemblies could not be removed. The entire sealed core could be delivered as a unit to the power plant site and returned to the factory at the end of its useful life.

93. High security would have to be provided to deter theft of sealed reactor cores during transport to (as well as from) deployment sites.

94. It would take 10–15 years to develop and build an experimental reactor and 20 years before a demonstration unit could be put into operation (Orlov and others, 1999). Thus, even with a dedicated effort, deployment could not take place for decades.

95. Assuming a 1970s-vintage version of this technology, for which the uranium fuelling requirements (with a tails assay of 0.1 percent U-235 at the uranium enrichment plant) are estimated to be 13.5 times 10^{-6} kilograms per kilowatt-hour, which is 64 percent of the uranium fuelling required for an LWR (Feiveson, von Hippel, and Williams, 1979).

96. To this end, Bunn (1999) sees the need for independent research by social and political scientists on the roots of public attitudes on nuclear technology.

97. Such a strategy was suggested by Lidsky and Cohn (1993).

98. In contrast to the situation for the renewables and energy efficiency communities, those seeking expanded roles for fossil fuels in a greenhouse-gas-constrained world probably do not need political support from the nuclear industry to get a fair chance to prove whether or not decarbonised fossil energy strategies are viable.

99. This strategy was also suggested by Lidsky and Cohn (1993).

References

Abdul-Khalek, I.S., D.B. Kittelson, B.R. Graskow, and Q. Wei. 1998. "Diesel Exhaust Particle Size: Issues and Trends." SAE Technical Paper 980525. Prepared for Society of Automotive Engineers International Congress and Exposition, 23–26 February, Detroit, Mich.

Albright, D., F. Berkhout, and W. Walker. 1997. *Plutonium, Highly Enriched Uranium 1996: World Inventories, Capabilities, and Policies.* Oxford: Oxford University Press for Stockholm International Peace Research Institute.

Appleby, A.J. 1999. "The Electrochemical Engine for Vehicles." *Scientific American* 280 (7): 74–79.

API (American Petroleum Institute). 1999. *Fuel Choices for Fuel Cell Powered Vehicles.* Washington, D.C.

Audus, H., O. Kaarstad, and G. Skinner. 1999. "CO_2 Capture by Pre-Combustion Decarbonization of Natural Gas." In B. Eliasson, P. Riemer, and A. Wokaun, eds., *Greenhouse Gas Control Technologies: Proceedings of the 4th International Conference on GHG Control Technologies.* Amsterdam: Pergamon.

Bachu, S., and W.D. Gunter. 1999. "Storage Capacity of CO_2 in Geological Media in Sedimentary Basins with Application to the Alberta Basin." In B. Eliasson, P. Riemer, and A. Wokaun, eds., *Greenhouse Gas Control Technologies: Proceedings of the 4th International Conference on GHG Control Technologies.* Amsterdam: Pergamon.

Bachu, S., W.D. Gunter, and E.H. Perkins. 1994. "Aquifer Disposal of CO_2: Hydrodynamic and Mineral Trapping." *Energy Conversion and Management* 35: 269–79.

Badin, J.S., M.R. DeLallo, M.G. Klett, M.D. Rutkowski, and J.R. Temchin. 1999. "Decarbonized Fuel Production Facility: A Technical Strategy for Coal in the Next Century." Paper presented at Gasification Technologies Conference, 17–20 October, San Francisco, Calif.

Bagley, S.T., K.J. Baumgard, L.D. Gratz, J.H. Johnson, and D.G. Leddy. 1996. "Characterization of Fuel and Aftertreatment Device Effects on Diesel Emissions." Research Report 76. Health Effects Institute, Cambridge, Mass.

Bakker, W. 1996. "Advances in Solid-Oxide Fuel Cells." *EPRI Journal* 21 (5): 42–45.

Bannister, R.L., D.J. Huber, R.A. Newby, and J.A. Pattenbarger. 1996. "Hydrogen-Fueled Combustion Turbine Cycles." ASME Paper 96-GT-247. Presented at the International Gas Turbine and Aeroengine Congress and Exhibition, 10–13 June, Birmingham, U.K.

Bannister, R.L., R.A. Newby, and W.-C. Yang. 1997. "Development of a Hydrogen-Fueled Combustion Turbine Cycle for Power Generation." ASME Paper 97-GT-14. Presented at the International Gas Turbine and Aeroengine Congress and Exhibition, 2–5 June, Orlando, Fla.

———. 1998. "Final Report on the Development of a Hydrogen-Fueled Combustion Turbine Cycle for Power Generation." ASME Paper 98-GT-21. Presented at International Gas Turbine and Aeroengine Congress and Exhibition, 2–5 June, Stockholm.

Barletta, M., and A. Sands, eds. 1999. *Nonproliferation Regimes at Risk.* Monterey, Calif.: Monterey Institute for International Studies, Center for Nonproliferation Studies.

Berkhout, F. 1998. "The International Civilian Reprocessing Business." University of Sussex, Science Policy Research Unit, Brighton, UK.

Berkhout, F., A. Diakov, H. Feiveson, H. Hunt, E. Lyman, M. Miller, and F. von Hippel. 1993. "Disposition of Separated Plutonium." *Science and Global Security* 3: 161–213.

Blok, K., C. Hendriks, and W. Turkenburg. 1989. "The Role of Carbon Dioxide Removal in the Reduction of the Greenhouse Effect." Paper presented at the International Energy Agency–Organisation for Economic Co-operation and Development Expert Seminar on Energy Technologies for Reducing Emissions of Greenhouse Gases, 12–14 April, Paris.

Blok, K., R.H. Williams, R.E. Katofsky, and C.A. Hendriks. 1997. "Hydrogen Production from Natural Gas, Sequestration of Recovered CO_2 in Depleted Gas Wells and Enhanced Natural Gas Recovery." *Energy* 22 (2–3): 161–68.

Blunt, M., F.J. Fayers, and F.M. Orr Jr. 1993. "Carbon Dioxide in Enhanced Oil Recovery." *Energy Conversion and Management* 34 (9–11): 1197–1204.

Brewer, P.G., G. Friederich, E.T. Peltzer, and F.M. Orr Jr. 1999. "Direct Experiments on the Ocean Disposal of Fossil Fuel CO2." *Science* 284: 943–45.

Bunn, M. 1999. "Enabling a Significant Future for Nuclear Power: Avoiding Catastrophes, Developing New Technologies, and Democratizing Decisions—and Staying away from Separated Plutonium." Paper presented at Global '99: Nuclear Technology—Bridging the Millennia, International Conference on Future Nuclear Systems, 29 August–3 September, Jackson Hole, Wyo.

Byrer, C.W., and H.D. Guthrie. 1999. "Coal Deposits: Potential Geological Sink for Sequestering Carbon Dioxide Emissions from Power Plants." In B. Eliasson, P. Riemer, and A. Wokaun, eds., *Greenhouse Gas Control Technologies: Proceedings of the 4th International Conference on GHG Control Technologies.* Amsterdam: Pergamon.

Calvert, J.G., J.B. Heywood, R.F. Sawyer, and J.H. Seinfeld. 1993. "Achieving Acceptable Air Quality: Some Reflections on Controlling Vehicle Emissions." *Science* 261: 37–45.

Campanari, S. 1999. "Full Load and Part-Load Performance Prediction for Integrated SOFC and Microturbine Systems." Paper presented at International Gas Turbine and Aeroengine Congress and Exhibition, 7–10 June, Indianapolis, Ind.

Chambers, A., C. Park, R.T.K. Baker, and N.M. Rodriguez. 1998. "Hydrogen Storage in Graphite Nanofibers." *Journal of Physical Chemistry* B 102: 4253–56.

Chen, P., X. Wu, J. Lin, and K.L. Tan. 1999. "High H_2 Uptake by Alkali-Doped Carbon Nanotubes under Ambient Pressure and Mode-rate Temperatures." *Science* 285: 91–93.

Chen, T.-P., J.D. Wright, and K. Krist. 1997. "SOFC System Analysis." Paper presented at the Fuel Cells Review Meeting, 26–28 August, Morgantown, W.Va.

Chen, Z.H., and Y.Q. Niu. 1995. *Mei Hua Gong* 2: 31.

Chiesa, P., and S. Consonni. 1998. "Shift Reactors and Physical Absorption for Low CO2 Emission IGCCs." Paper presented at ASME Turbo Expo 98, June, Stockholm, Sweden.

Chiesa, P., S. Consonni, G. Lozza, and E. Macchi. 1993. "Predicting the Ultimate Performance of Advanced Power Cycles Based on Very High Temperature Gas Turbine Engines." ASME Paper 93-GT-223. Presented at the International Gas Turbine and Aeroengine Congress and Exposition, 24–27 May, Cincinnati, Ohio.

Choi, G.N., S.J. Kramer, S.S. Tam, J.M. Fox, N.L. Carr, and G.R. Wilson. 1997. "Design/Economics of a Once-Through Fischer-Tropsch plant with Power Co-Production." Paper presented at the Coal Liquefaction and Solid Fuels Contractors Review Conference, 3–4 September, Pittsburgh, Penn.

CISAC (Committee on International Security and Arms Control of the National Academy of Sciences). 1994. *Management and Disposition of Excess Weapons Plutonium.* Washington, D.C.: National Academy of Sciences.

———. 1995. *Management and Disposition of Excess Weapons Plutonium: Reactor-Related Options.* Washington, D.C.: National Academy of Sciences.

Collett, T., and V. Kuuskraa. 1998. "Hydrates Contain Vast Store of World Gas Resources." *Oil and Gas Journal,* 11 May.

Corzine, R. 1997. "Gas into Liquid Gold." *Financial Times,* 4 July, p. 17.

Craig, P. 1997. "The Capstone Turbogenerator as an Alternative Power Source." ASME Paper 97092. American Society of Automotive Engineers, Warrendale, Pa.

CTOFM (Committee on Tropospheric Ozone Formation and Measurement, National Research Council). 1991. *Rethinking the Ozone Problem in Local and Regional Air Pollution.* Washington, D.C.: National Academy of Sciences.

Dahl, Anders. 1993. "Operation Experience of the PFBC Plant in Värtan, Stockholm." In Lynn Rubow, ed., *Proceedings of the 1993 International Conference on Fluidized Bed Combustion,* vol. 2. New York: American Society of Mechanical Engineers.

Decker, Manfred. 1999. Personal communication. European Commission, 9 September.

de Soete, G. 1993. "Nitrous Oxide Emissions from Combustion and Industry; Chemistry, Emissions, and Control [in French]." *Revue de L'Institut Français du Petrole* 48 (4).

DOE (U.S. Department of Energy). 1997. "Nonproliferation and Arms Control Assessment of Weapons-Usable Fissile Material Storage and Excess Plutonium Disposition Alternatives." Report DOE/NN-007. Washington, D.C.

———. 1998. "Nuclear Waste Fund Fee Adequacy: An Assessment." Report DOE/RW-0509. Office of Civilian Radioactive Waste Management, Washington, D.C.

———. 1999. "Carbon Sequestration R&D Program Plan: FY 1999–FY 2000." Washington, D.C.

Dresselhaus, M.S., K.A. Williams, and P.C. Eklund. 1999. "Hydrogen Adsorption in Carbon Materials." *MRS Bulletin* 24 (11): 45–50.

Drown, D.P., E.C. Heydorn, R.B. Moore, E.S. Schaub, D.M. Brown, W.C. Jones, and R.M. Kornosky. 1997. "The Liquid Phase Methanol (LPMEOHTM) Process Demonstration at Kingsport." Paper presented at the Fifth Annual DOE Clean Coal Technology Conference, 7–9 January, Tampa, Fla.

Dunnison, D.S., and J. Wilson. 1994. "PEM Fuel Cells: A Commercial Reality." In *A Collection of Technical Papers: Part 3, 29th Intersociety Energy Conversion Engineering Conference.* Washington, D.C.: American Institute of Aeronautics and Astronautics.

EIA (U.S. Energy Information Administration). 1998a. *Annual Energy Outlook 1999, with Projections Through 2020.* DOE/EIA-0383(99). Washington, D.C.: U.S. Department of Energy.

———. 1998b. *Electric Power Annual 1997,* Volume II. DOE/EIA-0348(97)/2. Washington, D.C.: U.S. Department of Energy.

———. 1999a. *International Energy Outlook 1999, with Projections through 2020.* DOE/EIA-0484(99). Washington, D.C.: U.S. Department of Energy.

———. 1999b. *Monthly Energy Review.* DOE/EIA-0035(99/04). Washington, D.C.: U.S. Department of Energy.

Feiveson, H.A. 1978. "Proliferation-Resistant Nuclear Fuel Cycles." *Annual Review of Energy* 3: 357–94.

———. 1999. "Expanding Nuclear Power in a Greenhouse World." Paper presented at Global '99: Nuclear Technology—Bridging the Millennia, International Conference on Future Nuclear Systems, 29 August–3 September, Jackson Hole, Wyo.

Feiveson, H.A., F. von Hippel, and R.H. Williams. 1979. "Fission Power: An Evolutionary Strategy." *Science* 203: 330–37.

Fetter, S. 1999. "Climate Change and the Transformation of World Energy Supply." Stanford University, Center for International Security and Cooperation, Stanford, Calif.

Fetter, S., M. Bunn, and J.P. Holdren. 1999. "The Economics of Reprocessing versus Direct Disposal of Spent Nuclear Fuel: Short-Term and Long-Term Prospects." Paper presented at Global '99: Nuclear Technology—Bridging the Millennia, International Conference on Future Nuclear Systems, 29 August–3 September, Jackson Hole, Wyo.

Filin, A.I., V.V. Orlov, V.N. Leonov, A.G. Sila-Novitskij, V.S. Smirnov, and V.S. Tsikunov. 1999. "Design Features of BREST Reactors; Experimental Work to Advance the Concept of BREST Reactors; Results and Plans." Paper presented at Global '99: Nuclear Technology—Bridging the Millennia, International Conference on Future Nuclear Systems, 29 August–3 September, Jackson Hole, Wyo.

Fleisch, T.H., and P.C. Meurer. 1995. "DME: The Diesel Fuel for the 21st Century?" Paper presented at the AVL Conference on Engine and Environment 1995, Graz, Austria.

Fritsch, P. 1996. "Exxon Project to Expand Use of Natural Gas." *Wall Street Journal,* 30 October, p. A3.

Gasperin, A., P. Reichert, and A. Radkowsky. 1997. "Thorium Fuel for Light Water Reactors—Reducing Proliferation Potential of Nuclear Power Cycle." *Science and Global Security* 6: 265–90.

Gillena, E. 1994. "Science Friction: How Technology, Time, and Concilation Could End the Bitter War over Nuclear Waste." *Nukem* (November): 4–19.

Glaser, A. 1998. "The Thorium Fuel Cycle: A Noteworthy Gain in Proliferation Resistance?" Paper presented at the Tenth International Summer Symposium on Science and World Affairs, 14–21 July, Boston.

Goldstein, R. 1992. *Solid Oxide Fuel Cell Research at EPRI.* Technical Brief. Palo Alto, Calif.: Electric Power Research Institute.

Gopalakrishnan, A. 1999. "Issues of Nuclear Safety." *Frontline,* 26 March.

Gunter, W.D. 1999. Personal communication. 5 October.

Gunter, W.D., R.J. Chalaturnyk, and J.D. Scott. 1999. "Monitoring of Aquifer Disposal of CO2: Experience from Underground Gas Storage and Enhanced Oil Recovery." In B. Eliasson, P. Riemer, and A. Wokaun, eds., *Greenhouse Gas Control Technologies: Proceedings of the 4th International Conference on GHG Control Technologies.* Amsterdam: Pergamon.

Gunter, W.D., T. Gentzix, B.A. Rottenfusser, and R.J.H. Richardson. 1997. "Deep Coalbed Methane in Alberta, Canada: A Fuel Resource with the Potential of Zero Greenhouse Emissions." *Energy Conversion and Management* 38: S217–22.

Gunter, W.D., E.H. Perkins, and T.J. McCann. 1993. "Aquifer Disposal of CO_2-Rich Gases: Reaction Design for Added Capacity." *Energy Conversion and Management* 34: 941–48.

Häckel, E. 1997. "Internationalization of the Back End of the Nuclear Fuel Cycle: Problems and Prospects." Paper resented at the IAEA Symposium on the Nuclear Fuel Cycle and Reactor Strategies: Adjusting to Realities, 3–6 June, Vienna.

Hagen, R.E., 1998. "Asia's Nuclear Power Disparity: Glowing Promises, Dismal Performance." Paper presented at the International Symposium on Energy Future in the Asia-Pacific Region, 27–28 March, Honolulu, Hawaii.

Hansen, J.B., B. Voss, F. Joensen, and I.D. Siguroardottir. 1995. "Large-Scale Manufacture of Dimethyl Ether—A New Alternative Diesel Fuel from Natural Gas." Paper presented at the International Congress and Exhibition of Society of Automotive Engineers, 27 February–2 March, Detroit, Mich.

Hard, R.J. 1997. "Will the Nuclear Scales Balance?" *Nukem Market Report* (November): 11.

Haschke, J.M., T.H. Allen, and L.A. Morales. 2000. "Reaction of Plutonium Dioxide with Water: Formation and Properties of PuO_2+x." *Science* 287 (5451): 285–87.

Health Effects Institute. 1987. *Automotive Methanol Vapors and Human Health.* Cambridge, Mass.

Henderick, P. 1999. "An Assessment of Biomass-Powered Microturbines and the Potential for Applications in Rural China." M.S. thesis. Princeton University, Department of Mechanical and Aerospace Engineering and Center for Energy and Environmental Studies, Princeton, N.J.

Henderick, P., and R.H. Williams. 2000. "Trigeneration in a Northern Chinese Village Using Crop Residues." *Energy for Sustainable Development* 4 (3): 12–28.

Hendriks, C.A. 1994. "Carbon Dioxide Removal from Coal-Fired Power Plants." Ph.D. thesis, Utrecht University, Department of Science, Technology, and Society, Utrecht, Netherlands.

Herring, J.S., and P.E. MacDonald. 1998. "Characteristics of a Mixed Thorium-Uranium Dioxide High-Burnup Fuel." Idaho National Engineering and Environmental Laboratory, Idaho Falls, Ida.

Herzog, H., 1999a. "The Economics of CO_2: Separation and Capture." Paper presented at the Second Dixie Lee Ray Memorial Symposium, August, Washington, D.C. Available at http://web.mit.edu/energylab/www/hjherzog/publications.html

———. 1999b. "Ocean Sequestration of CO_2: An Overview." In B. Eliasson, P. Riemer, and A. Wokaun, eds., *Greenhouse Gas Control Technologies: Proceedings of the 4th International Conference on GHG Control Technologies.* Amsterdam: Pergamon.

Hill, R.N., J.E. Cahalan, H.S. Khalil, and D.C. Wade. 1999. "Development of Small, Fast Reactor Core Designs Using Lead-Based Coolant." Paper presented at Global '99: Nuclear Technology—Bridging the Millennia, International Conference on Future Nuclear Systems, 29 August–3 September, Jackson Hole, Wyo.

Hitchon, B., W.D. Gunter, T. Gentzis, and R. Bailey. 1999. "Sedimentary Basins and Greenhouse Gases: A Serendipitous Association." *Energy Conversion and Management* 40: 825–43.

Hoff, T.E., H.J. Wenger, and B.K. Farmer. 1996. "Distributed Generation: An Alternative to Electricity Investments in System Capacity." *Energy Policy* 24 (2): 137–47.

Holdren, J. P. 1989. "Civilian Nuclear Technologies and Nuclear Weapons Proliferation." In C. Schaerf, B. Holden-Reid, and D. Carlton, eds., *New Technologies and the Arms Race.* London: Macmillan.

Holloway, S., ed. 1996. *The Underground Storage of Carbon Dioxide.* Report prepared for Joule II Programme of Commission of the European Communities, Contract JOU2 CT92-0031, Brussels.

———. 1997. "Safety of Underground Disposal of Carbon Dioxide." *Energy Conversion and Management* 38: S241–45.

Holt, N. 1999a. "Comments on the DOE Vision 21 Program with Particular Reference to Gasification and Associated Technologies." Paper presented to the Committee on Research and Development Opportunities for Advanced Fossil-Fueled Energy Complexes of National Research Council, 30 June, Washington, D.C.

———. 1999b. "What's in the Pipeline? New Projects and Opportunities." Paper presented at the Gasification Technologies Conference, 17–20 October, San Francisco, Calif.

Honeyman, B.D. 1999. "Colloidal Culprits in Contamination." *Nature* 397: 23–24.

Hooper, R. 1997. "Strengthened Safeguards: Insight into the IAEA's Strengthened Safeguards System." *IAEA Bulletin* 39 (4).

IAEA (International Atomic Energy Agency). 1999. *Energy, Electricity, and Nuclear Power Estimates for the Period Up to 2020.* Reference Data Series 1. Vienna.

IEA (International Energy Agency). 1996. "CO_2 Capture and Storage in the Natuna NG Project." *Greenhouse Issues* 22: 1.

———. 1998. *Carbon Dioxide Disposal from Power Stations.* IEA Greenhouse Gas Programme, http://www.ieagreeen.org.uk

IPCC (Intergovernmental Panel on Climate Change). 1995. "Climate Change 1994: Radiative Forcing of Climate Change and an Evaluation of the IPCC Emissions Scenarios." In J.T. Houghton, L.G. Meira Filho, J. Bruce, Hoesing Lee, B.A. Callander, E. Haites, N. Harris, and K. Maskell, eds., *Reports of Working Groups I and III of the IPCC, Forming Part of the IPCC Special Report to the First Session of the Conference of Parties to the UN Framework Convention on Climate Change.* Cambridge: Cambridge University Press.

———. 1996a. "Energy Supply Mitigation Options." In R.T. Watson, M.C. Zinyowera, R.H. Moss, eds., *Climate Change 1995: Impacts, Adaptations and Mitigation of Climate Change: Scientific-Technical Analyses.* Second Assessment Report of IPCC. Cambridge: Cambridge University Press.

———. 1996b. "Summary for Policymakers: Scientific-Technical Analyses of Impacts, Adaptations, and Mitigations of Climate Change." In R.T. Watson, M.C. Zinyowera, and R.H. Moss, eds., *Climate Change 1995: Impacts, Adaptations and Mitigation of Climate Change: Scientific-Technical Analyses.* Second Assessment Report of IPCC. Cambridge: Cambridge University Press.

James, B.D., G.N. Baum, F.D. Lomax, C.E. Thomas, and I.F. Kuhn. 1996. "Comparison of Onboard Hydrogen Storage for Fuel Cell Vehicles." In *Direct Hydrogen-Fueled Proton-Exchange Membrane (PEM) Fuel Cell System for Transportation Applications.* Final report prepared for Ford Motor Company under Prime Contract DE-AC02-94CE50389. Washington, D.C.: U.S. Department of Energy.

Kaarstad, O. 1992. "Emission-Free Fossil Energy from Norway." *Energy Conversion and Management* 33 (5–8): 781–86.

Kaarstad, O., and H. Audus. 1997. "Hydrogen and Electricity from Decarbonised Fossil Fuels." *Energy Conversion and Management* 38: S431–42.

Kadak, A.C. 1999. "The Politically Correct Reactor." Massachusetts Institute of Technology, Nuclear Engineering Department, Cambridge, Mass.

Kartha, S., and P. Grimes. 1994. "Fuel Cells: Energy Conversion for the Next Century." *Physics Today* (November): 54–61.

Kartha, S., T.G. Kreutz, and R.H. Williams. 1997. "Small-Scale Biomass Fuel Cell/Gas Turbine Power Systems for Rural Areas." Paper presented at the Third Biomass Conference of the Americas, 19–24 August, Montreal.

Kersting, A.B. 1999. "Migration of Plutonium in Ground Water at the Nevada Test Site." *Nature* 39 (7): 56–59.

Kittelson, D.B. 1998. "Engines and Nanoparticles." *Journal of Aerosol Science* 29 (5–6): 575–88.

Kjaer, S. 1993. "The Future 400 MW ELSAM Units in Aalborg and Skaerbaek, Denmark." *VGB Kraftwerkstechnik* 73 (11): 803–10.

Koide, H., J. Shindo, Y. Tazaki, M. Iljima, K. Ito, N. Kimura, and K. Omata. 1997. "Deep Seabed Disposal of CO_2: The Most Protective Storage." *Energy Conversion and Management* 38: S253–58.

Kovacik, J.M. 1996. "Cogeneration Application Considerations." GE Power Generation, General Electric Company, Schenectady, N.Y.

Kreutz, T., and J. Ogden. 2000. "Prospective Performance and Economics of Residential Cogeneration Using Natural Gas-Fueled PEMFC Power Systems." Presented at the 11th Annual U.S. Hydrogen Meeting, 29 February–2 March, Vienna, Va.

Krewitt, W., T. Heck, A. Truckenmueller, and R. Friedrich. 1999. "Environmental Damage Costs from Fossil Electricity Generation in Germany and Europe." *Energy Policy* 27: 173–83.

Kruger, M., H. Luders, B. Luers, R. Kayfmann, W. Koch, and T. Kauffeldt. 1997. "Influence of Exhaust Gas Aftertreatment on Particulate Characteristics of Vehicle Diesel Engines [in German]." *Motortechnische Zeitshrift* 58.

Kupitz, J., and J. Cleveland. 1999. "Overview of Global Development of Advanced Nuclear Power Plants, and the Role of the IAEA." International Atomic Energy Agency, Vienna.

Larson, E.D., and Jin Haiming. 1999. "A Preliminary Assessment of Biomass Conversion to Fischer-Tropsch Cooking Fuels for Rural China." Paper prepared for the Fourth Biomass Conference of the Americas, 29 August–2 September, Oakland, Calif.

Larson, E.D., E. Worrell, and J.S. Chen. 1996. "Clean Fuels from Municipal Solid Waste for Fuel Cell Buses in Metropolitan Areas." *Resources, Conservation, and Recycling* 17: 273–98.

Leventhal, P., and Y. Alexander, eds. 1987. *Preventing Nuclear Terrorism.* Lexington, Mass.: Lexington Books.

Lidsky, L. 1991: "Nuclear Power in a World with Options." Paper presented at Symposium on (R)Evolutionary Reactor Types, Ultra-Centrfuge Nederland N.V., 29 May, Almelo, Netherlands.

Lidsky, L., and S.M. Cohn. 1993. "What Now? An Examination of the Impact of the Issues Raised. A Response to the Presentation by R.H. Williams, 'The Outlook for Renewable Energy'." In *Proceedings of the 2nd MIT International Conference on the New Generation of Nuclear Power Technology.* Cambridge, Mass.: Massachusetts Institute of Technology.

Lidsky, L., and M.M. Miller. 1998. "Nuclear Power and Energy Security: A Revised Strategy for Japan." Massachusetts Institute of Technology, Center for International Studies, Cambridge, Mass.

Lilienthal, D.E., C.I. Barnard, J.R. Oppenheimer, C.A. Thomas, and H.A. Winne. 1946. A Report on the International Control of Atomic Energy. Report prepared for Secretary of State's Committee on Atomic Energy. Washington, D.C.: U.S. Government Printing Office.

Lindeberg, E. 1997. "Escape of CO_2 from Aquifers." *Energy Conversion and Management* 38: S235–40.

Lipman, T.E., and D. Sperling. 1999. "Forecasting the Costs of Automotive PEM Fuel Cell Systems Using Bounded Manufacturing Progress Functions." Paper presented at the IEA International Workshop on Experience Curves for Policy Making: The Case of Energy Technologies, 10–11 May, Stuttgart.

Little, A.D. 1995. *Fuel Cells for Building Cogeneration Application—Cost/Performance Requirements and Markets.* Final report prepared for Building Equipment Division, Office of Building Technology, U.S. Department of Energy. Springfield, Va.: National Technical Information Service.

Liu, C., Y.Y. Fan, M. Liu, H.T. Cong, H.M. Cheng, and M.S. Dresselhaus. 1999. "Hydrogen Storage in Single-Walled Carbon Nanotubes at Room Temperature." *Science* 286: 1127–29.

LLNL (Lawrence Livermore National Laboratory). 1998. *Comparative Analysis of Approaches to Protection of Fissile Materials.* Proceedings of a Workshop held 28–30 July 1997, Stanford, Calif. Document Conf. 97-0721. Livermore, Calif.: Lawrence Livermore National Laboratory.

Lloyd, A.C. 1999. "The Power Plant in your Basement." *Scientific American* 280 (7): 80–86.

Lopatkin, A.V., and V.V. Orlov. 1999. "Fuel Cycle of BREST-1200 with Non-Proliferation of Plutonium and Equivalent Disposal of Radioactive Waste." Paper presented at Global '99: Nuclear Technology—Bridging the Millennia, International Conference on Future Nuclear Systems, 29 August–3 September, Jackson Hole, Wyo.

Lyman, E.S., and H.A. Feiveson. 1998. "The Proliferation Risks of Plutonium Mines." *Science and Global Security* 7: 119–28.

McCarthy, J.F., W.E. Sanford, and P.L. Stafford. 1998. "Lanthanide Field Tracers Demonstrate Enhanced Transport of Transuranic Radionuclides by Natural Organic Matter." *Environmental Science and Technology* 32 (24): 3901–08.

McCombie, C. 1999a. "Multinational Repositories: A Win-Win Disposal Strategy." Paper presented at ENS Topseal '99 Conference, October, Antwerp, Belgium.

———. 1999b. "A Prospective Global Solution for the Disposal of Unwanted Nuclear Materials." Paper presented at the ICEM Conference, Nagoya, Japan.

McCombie, C., G. Butler, M. Kurzeme, D. Pentz, J. Voss, and P. Winter. 1999. "The Pangea International Repository: A Technical Overview." Paper presented at the WM99 Conference, March, Tucson, Ariz.

McNeely, M. 1998. "Intercooling for LM6000 Gas Turbines." *Diesel & Gas Turbine Worldwide* (July–August): 42–45.

Madic, C. 2000. "Towards the End of PuO_2's Supremacy." *Science* 287 (5451): 243–44.

Marchetti, C. 1976. "Hydrogen and Energy Systems." *International Journal of Hydrogen Energy* 1: 3–10.

Mark, J.C. 1993. "Explosive Properties of Reactor-Grade Plutonium." *Science and Global Security* 4: 111–28.

Masters, C.D., E.D. Attanasi, and D.H. Root. 1994. "World Petroleum Assessment and Analysis." Paper presented at the Fourteenth World Petroleum Congress, Stavanger, Norway.

Matsuoka, J., and H. Hiranuma.1998. "Nuclear Industry and Human Resources in Japan." Paper presented at the International Symposium on Energy Future in the Asia-Pacific Region, 27–28 March, Honolulu, Ha.

Mayer, A., H. Egli, H. Burtscher, J. Czerwinski, and H. Gehrig. 1995. "Particle Size Distribution Downstream Traps of Different Design." SAE Paper 950373. Society of Automotive Engineers, Warrendale, Pa.

Miller, I., J. Black, C. McCombie, D. Pentz, and P. Zuidema. 1999. "High-Isolation Sites for Radioactive Waste Disposal: A Fresh Look at the Challenge of Locating Safe Sites for Radioactive Repositories." Paper presented at the WM99 Conference, March, Tucson, Ariz.

Miyamoto, Y., S. Shizawa, M. Ogawa, and K. Hada. 1999. "Development Program on Hydrogen Production at JAERI (Japan Atomic Energy Research Institute)." Paper presented at Global '99: Nuclear Technology—Bridging the Millennia, International Conference on Future Nuclear Systems, 29 August–3 September, Jackson Hole, Wyo.

Moore, R.B., and V. Raman. 1998. "Hydrogen Infrastructure for Fuel Cell Transportation." *International Journal of Hydrogen Energy* 23 (7): 617–20.

Moritsuka, H. 1999. "Hydrogen Decomposed Turbine Systems for Carbon Dioxide Recovery." In B. Eliasson, P. Riemer, and A. Wokaun, eds., *Greenhouse Gas Control Technologies: Proceedings of the 4th International Conference on GHG Control Technologies.* Amsterdam: Pergamon.

Motter, J.W. 1999. "Operational Experience with the 100 MW Pinon Pine IGCC Project: Lessons Learned, and Outlook for the KRW Air-Blown Gasification Technology with Hot-Gas Cleanup." Paper presented at the Seventh Clean Coal Technology Conference—21st Century Coal Utilization: Prospects for Economic Viability, Global Prosperity and a Cleaner Environment, 22–24 June, Knoxville, Tenn.

Mukunda, H., S. Dasappa, and U. Srinivasa. 1993. "Wood Gasification in Open-Top Gasifiers—The Technology and the Economics." In T.B. Johansson, H. Kelly, A.K.N. Reddy, and R.H. Williams, eds., *Renewable Energy: Sources for Fuel and Electricity.* Washington, D.C.: Island Press.

Nakićenović, N., A. Grübler, and A. McDonald, eds. 1998. *Global Energy Perspectives.* Cambridge: Cambridge University Press.

NEA (Nuclear Energy Agency of the Organisation for Economic Co-operation and Development). 1994. *The Economics of the Nuclear Fuel Cycle.* Paris.

———. 1999. *Progress Towards Geologic Disposal of Radioactive Waste: Where Do We Stand: An International Assessment.* Issy-les-Moulineaux, France.

Nicholls, D.R. 1998. *Status of the Pebble Bed Modular Reactor.* South Africa: Eskom.

Norton, P., K. Vertin, B. Bailey, N.N. Clark, D.W. Lyons, S. Goguen, and J. Eberhardt. 1998. "Emissions from Trucks Using Fischer-Tropsch Diesel Fuels." SAE Paper 982526. Society of Automotive Engineers, Warrendale, Pa.

NPPDP (Nuclear Power Plant Design Project). 1998. "A Response to the Environmental and Economic Challenge of Global Warming: Phase I: Review of Options and Selection of Technology of Choice." Massachusetts Institute of Technology, Cambridge, Mass.

NRC (National Research Council). 1992. *Nuclear Power: Technical and Institutional Options for the Future.* Washington, D.C.: National Academy Press.

———. 1998. *Review of the Partnership for a New Generation of Vehicles: Fourth Report.* Prepared by the Standing Committee to Review the Research Program of the Partnership for a New Generation of Vehicles. Washington, D.C.: National Academy Press.

Ogden, J.M., T.G. Kreutz, and M. Steinbugler. 1998. "Fuels for Fuel Cell Vehicles: Vehicle Design and Infrastructure Issues." SAE Technical Paper 982500. Prepared for the International Fall Fuels and Lubricants Meeting and Exposition, 19–22 October, San Francisco, Calif.

Ogden, J.M., and R.H. Williams. 1989. *Solar Hydrogen: Moving Beyond Fossil Fuels.* Washington, D.C.: World Resources Institute.

Ormerod, W. 1994. *The Disposal of Carbon Dioxide from Fossil Fuel Power Stations.* IEA/GHG/SR3. Cheltenham, U.K.: IEA Greenhouse Gas Research and Development Programme.

O'Neill, Kate. 1998. *(Not) Getting to 'Go': Recent Experience in International Cooperation over the Management of Spent Nuclear Fuel.* BCSIA Discussion Paper 98-22. Harvard University, Kennedy School of Government, Cambridge, Mass.

Orlov, V., V. Leonov, A. Sila-Novitski, V. Smirnov, V. Tsikunov, and A. Filin. 1999. "Nuclear Power of the Coming Century and Requirements of the Nuclear Technology." Paper presented at Global '99: Nuclear Technology—Bridging the Millennia, International Conference on Future Nuclear Systems, 29 August–3 September, Jackson Hole, Wyo.

OTA (U.S. Office of Technology Assessment). 1995. *Nuclear Safeguards and the International Atomic Energy Agency.* Report OTA-ISS-615. Washington D.C.: U.S. Congress.

Paffenbarger, J.A., and E. Bertel. 1998. "Results from the OECD report on International Projects of Electricity Generating Costs." Paper presented at IJPGC 98: International Joint Power Generation Conference and Exhibition, 24–26 August.

Parsons Infrastructure and Technology Group, Inc. 1998. "Decarbonized Fuel Plants Utilizing Inorganic Membranes for Hydrogen Production." Paper presented at the Twelfth Annual Conference on Fossil Fuels Materials, 12–14 May, Knoxville, Tenn.

PCAST (U.S. President's Committee of Advisors on Science and Technology) Fusion Review Panel. 1995. The *U.S. Program of Fusion Energy Research and Development.* Washington, D.C.

PCAST Energy Research and Development Panel. 1997. *Federal Energy Research & Development for the Challenges of the 21st Century.* http://www.whitehouse.gov/WH/EOP/OSTP/html/ISTP_Home.html

PCAST Panel on ICERD3 (Panel on International Cooperation in Energy Research, Development, Demonstration, and Deployment). 1999. *Powerful Partnerships: The Federal Role in International Cooperation on Energy Innovation.* http://www.whitehouse.gov/WH/EOP/OSTP/html/ISTP_Home.html

Peng, X.D., B.A. Toseland, and P.J.A. Tijm. 1998. "Kinetic Understanding of the Chemical Synergy under LPDMETM Conditions—Once-Through Applications." Paper presented at the Fifteenth International Symposium on Chemical Reaction Engineering, 13–16 September, Newport Beach, Calif.

Peng, X.D., B.A. Toseland, A.W. Wang, and G.E. Parris. 1997. "Progress in Development of PPMDE Process: Kinetics and Catalysts." Paper presented at the Coal Liquefaction and Solid Fuels Contractors Review Conference, 3–4 September, Pittsburgh, Penn.

Peterson, P.F. 1996. "Long-Term Safeguards for Plutonium in Geologic Repositories." *Science and Global Security* 6: 1–29.

Pillai, K.K. 1989. "Pressurized Fluidized Bed Combustion." In T.B. Johansson, B. Bodlund, and R.H. Williams, eds., *Electricity: Efficient End-Use and New Generation Technologies, and Their Planning Implications.* Lund, Sweden: Lund University Press.

Rabl, A. and J.V. Spadaro. 2000. "Public Health Impact of Air Pollution and Implications for the Energy System." *Annual Review of Energy and the Environment* 25 (in press).

Ringland, J.T. 1994. *Safety Issues for Hydrogen-Powered Vehicles.* Albuquerque, N.M.: Sandia National Laboratories.

Rogner, H.-H. 1998. "Hydrogen Technologies and Technology Learning Curve." *International Journal of Hydrogen Energy* 23 (9): 833–40.

Ross, M., R. Goodwin, R. Watkins, M.Q. Wang, and T. Wnnzel. 1995. *Real-World Emissions from Model Year 1993, 2000, and 2010 Passenger Cars.* Report prepared for Energy Foundation and U.S. Department of Energy, through Lawrence Berkeley Laboratory and Oak Ridge National Laboratory. Berkeley, Calif.: American Council for an Energy-Efficient Economy.

Ryan, M.L. 1999. "Fuel Costs Taking More of O&M Budget: Even As Costs Drop, Efficiency Rises." *Nuclear Fuel* 24 (14): 1–10.

Saviharju, K. 1995. "Combined Heat and Power Production." Background paper prepared for Working Group II of IPCC's Second Assessment Report. In VTT Research Notes. Espoo, Finland.

Schaberg, P., and others 1997. "Diesel Exhaust Emissions Using Sasol Slurry Phase Distillate Fuels." SAE Paper 972898. Society of Automotive Engineers, Warrendale, Pa.

Scott, D.S., and W. Hafele. 1990. "The Coming Hydrogen Age: Preventing World Climatic Disruption." *International Journal of Hydrogen Energy* 15 (10): 727–37.

SIEP (Shell International Exploration and Production, B.V.). 1998. "Doing It the Gentle Way: Producing Electricity from Hydrocarbons without CO2." SIEP 98-5039. Research and Technical Services, London.

Simbeck, D. 1995. "Air-Blown versus Oxygen-Blown Gasification." Paper presented at the Institution of Chemical Engineers Conference on Gasification: An Alternative to Natural Gas, 22–23 November, London.

———. 1999a. Personal communication. July.

———. 1999b: "Perspective on the Future of Distributed Generation—Hype or Reality?" Paper presented at the Energy Frontiers International Conference on Distributed Generation: Microturbines & Fuel Cells, 4–5 May, Orcas Island, Wash.

———. 1999c. "A Portfolio Selection Approach for Power Plant CO2 Capture, Separation, and R&D Options." In B. Eliasson, P. Riemer, and A. Wokaun, eds., *Greenhouse Gas Control Technologies: Proceedings of the 4th International Conference on GHG Control Technologies.* Amsterdam: Pergamon.

Simbeck, D., R. Dickenson, and J. Moll. 1981. "Coal Liquefaction: Direct versus Indirect—Making a Choice." *Oil and Gas Journal* (4 May): 254–68.

Simbeck, D., and H.E. Johnson (SFA Pacific). 1999: "Report on SFA Pacific Gasification Database and World Market Report." Paper presented at the 1999 Gasification Technologies Conference, 17–20 October, San Francisco, Calif.

Simbeck, D., and A.D. Karp. 1995. "Air-Blown versus Oxygen-Blown Gasification—An Honest Appraisal." Paper presented at Alternate Energy '95: Council on Alternate Fuels, 3 May, Vancouver, Canada.

Simbeck, D., N. Korens, F.E. Biasca, S. Vejtasa, and R.L. Dickenson. 1993. "Coal Gasification Guidebook: Status, Applications, and Technologies." Final report TR-102034. Electric Power Research Institute, Palo Alto, Calif.

Sirman, M., E. Owens, and K. Whitney. 1998. "Emissions Comparison of Alternative Fuels in an Advanced Automotive Diesel Engine." Interim report TFLRF 338. Prepared for U.S. Department of Energy by U.S. Army TARDEC Fuels and Lubricants Research Facility. Southwest Research Institute, San Antonio, Tex.

Socolow, R.H., ed. 1997. "Fuels Decarbonization and Carbon Sequestration: Report of a Workshop by the Members of the Report Committee." PU/CEES Report 302. Princeton University, Center for Energy and Environmental Studies, Princeton, N.J. Available at http://www.princeton.edu/~ceesdoe

Spadaro, J.V, and A. Rabl. 1998. "Social Costs and Environmental Burdens of Transport: An Analysis Using Two Case Studies in France." Ecole des Mines, Centre d'Energetique, Paris.

Spadaro, J.V, A. Rabl, E. Jourdain, and P. Coussy. 1998. "External Costs of Air Pollution: Case Study and Results for Transport between Paris and Lyon." *International Journal of Vehicle Design* 20: 274–82.

Spengler, J., and R. Wilson. 1996. "Emissions, Dispersion, and Concentration of Particles." In R. Wilson and J. Spengler, eds., *Particles in Our Air: Concentrations and Health Effects.* Cambridge, Mass.: Harvard University Press.

Spenser, D. 1999. "Integration of an Advanced CO2 Separation Process with Methods of Disposing of CO2 in Oceans and Terrestrial Deep Aquifers." In B. Eliasson, P. Riemer, and A. Wokaun, eds., *Greenhouse Gas Control Technologies: Proceedings of the 4th International Conference on GHG Control Technologies,* Interlaken, Switzerland, 30 August–2 September. Amsterdam: Pergamon.

Spenser, D., and S.S. Tam. 1999. "An Engineering and Economic Evaluation of a CO2 Hydrate Separation for Shifted Synthesis Gas." Paper presented at the Pittsburgh Coal Conference, October, Pittsburgh, Penn.

Spiewak, I., and A.M. Weinberg. 1985. "Inherently Safe Reactors." *Annual Review of Energy* 10: 431–62.

STATS (Committee on Separations Technology and Transmutation Systems, National Research Council). 1996. *Nuclear Wastes: Technologies for Separations and Transmutation.* Washington, D.C.: National Academy Press.

Steinberg, M., and H.C. Cheng. 1989. "Modern and Prospective Technologies for Hydrogen Production from Fossil Fuels." *International Journal of Hydrogen Energy* 14 (11): 797–820.

Steinbugler, M.M., and R.H. Williams. 1998. "Beyond Combustion. Fuel Cell Cars for the 21st Century." *Forum for Applied Research and Public Policy* (winter): 102–07.

Stiegel, G. 1994. "Indirect Liquefaction." Paper presented to the Committee on Strategic Assessment of DOE's Coal Program of the National Academy of Sciences, 14 January, Washington, D.C.

Stern, B.R., and R.G. Tardiff. 1997. "Risk Characterization of Methyl Tertiary Butyl Ether (MTBE) in Tap Water." *Risk Analysis* 17 (6): 727–43.

Stevens, S.H, V.A. Kuuskraa, D. Spector, and P. Riemer. 1999. "Enhanced Coalbed Methane Recovery Using CO2 Injection: Worldwide Resource and CO2 Injection Potential." In B. Eliasson, P. Riemer, and A. Wokaun, eds., *Greenhouse Gas Control Technologies: Proceedings of the 4th International Conference on GHG Control Technologies.* Amsterdam: Pergamon.

Stoll, H., and D.M. Todd. 1996. "Competitive Power Generation Costs for IGCC." Paper presented at the EPRI Gasification Technologies Conference, 2–4 October, San Francisco, Calif.

Summerfield, I.R., S.H. Goldhorpe, N. Williams, and A. Sheikh. 1993. "Costs of CO2 Disposal Options." In *Proceedings of the International Energy Agency Carbon Dioxide Disposal Symposium.* Amsterdam: Pergamon.

Thomas, C.E., B.D. James, F.D. Lomax, Jr., and I.F. Kuhn, Jr. 1998a. "Integrated Analysis of Hydrogen Passenger Vehicle Transportation Pathways." Draft final report prepared by Directed Technologies, Inc. under Contract AXE-6-16685-01. U.S. Department of Energy, National Renewable Energy Laboratory, Golden, Colo.

———. 1998b. "Societal Impacts of Fuel Options for Fuel Cell Vehicles." SAE Technical Paper 982496. Prepared for International Fall Fuels and Lubricants Meeting and Exposition, 19–22 October, San Francisco, Calif.

Tinturier, B., B. Estève, and H. Mouney. 1999. "Innovative Concepts: An EDF Viewpoint." Paper presented at Global '99: Nuclear Technology—Bridging the Millennia, International Conference on Future Nuclear Systems, 29 August–3 September, Jackson Hole, Wyo.

Todd, D.M., and H. Stoll. 1997. "Integrated Gasification Combined Cycle: The Preferred Power Technology for a Variety of Applications." Paper presented at Power-Gen Europe '97, June, Madrid.

Turkenburg, W.C. 1992. "CO2 Removal: Some Conclusions." *Energy Conversion and Management* 33 (5–8): 819–23.

UNFCCC (United Nations Framework Convention on Climate Change). 1992. "United Nations Framework Convention on Climate Change." Convention text, UNEP/WMO Information Unit of Climate Change (IUCC) on behalf of the Interim Secretariat of the Convention. IUCC, Geneva.

Valée, A.M. (Framatome). 1999. "Nuclear Reactors for the Future." Paper presented at Global '99: Nuclear Technology—Bridging the Millennia, International Conference on Future Nuclear Systems, 29 August–3 September, Jackson Hole, Wyo.

van der Burgt, M.J. 1998. "IGCC Cost Reduction Potential." Paper presented at EPRI-GTC Gasification Technologies Conference, October, San Francisco, Calif.

van der Burgt, M.J., J. Cantle, J., and V.K. Boutkan. 1992. "Carbon Dioxide Disposal from Coal-Based IGCCs in Depleted Gas Fields." Energy Conversion and Management 33 (5–8): 603–10.

van der Burgt, M.J., and C. van Liere. 1996. "Applications of the 'Tophat'® Cycle in Power Generation." Paper presented at Gasification Technologies Conference, 2–4 October, San Francisco, Calif.

van Liere, J.. 1998. The Tophat® Cycle. Available at http://users.bart.nl/~jvliere/tophat.htm

Veyo, S.E. 1998. "Tubular SOFC Power System Operational Experience." Paper presented at the Fuel Cell Seminar: Fuel Cells—Clean Energy for Today's World, 16–19 November, Palm Springs, Calif.

Wade, D.C., and D.J. Hill. 1999. "Requirements and Potential Development Pathways for Fission Energy Supply Infrastructures of the 21st Century: A Systems Viewpoint." Paper presented at Global '99: Nuclear Technology—Bridging the Millennia, International Conference on Future Nuclear Systems, 29 August–3 September, Jackson Hole, Wyo.

Wadman, B. 1998. "A Very Good Year for Power Generation." Diesel & Gas Turbine Worldwide (October): 46–54.

Walker, W. 1999. "Nuclear Power and Non-Proliferation." In M. Poireau and A. Zurita, eds, Nuclear in a Changing World: Proceedings of the European Seminar, vol. 2. European Commission, Directorate General XII—Science, Research, and Development. Luxembourg: Office of Official Publications of the European Communities.

Walsh, M.P. 1995. "Global Trends in Diesel Emissions Control: A 1995 Update." SAE Technical Paper 950149. Presented at SAE International Congress and Exposition, 27 February–2 March, Detroit, Mich.

———. 1997. "Global Trends in Diesel Emissions Control: A 1997 Update." SAE Technical Paper 970179. Presented at SAE International Congress and Exposition, 24–27 February, Detroit, Mich.

WEC (World Energy Council). 1995. Global Transport Sector Energy Demand Towards 2020. London.

Whipple, C.G. 1996. "Can Nuclear Waste Be Stored Safely at Yucca Mountain?" Scientific American 274 (6).

Williams, R.H. 1978. "Industrial Cogeneration." Annual Review of Energy 2: 313–56.

———. 1998. "Fuel Decarbonization for Fuel Cell Applications and Sequestration of the Separated CO_2." In Robert U. Ayres, ed., Eco-restructuring: Implications for Sustainable Development. Tokyo: United Nations University Press.

———. 1999a. "Hydrogen Production from Coal and Coal Bed Methane, Using Byproduct CO_2 for Enhanced Methane Recovery and Sequestering the CO_2 in the Coal Bed." In B. Eliasson, P. Riemer, and A. Wokaun, eds., Greenhouse Gas Control Technologies: Proceedings of the 4th International Conference on GHG Control Technologies. Amsterdam: Pergamon.

———. 1999b. "Towards Zero Emissions for Coal: Roles for Inorganic Membranes." In Proceedings of the International Symposium Towards Zero Emissions: the Challenge for Hydrocarbons. Milan: EniTecnologie, Eni Group.

Williams, R.H., and H.A. Feiveson. 1990. "Diversion-Resistance Criteria for Future Nuclear Power." Energy Policy (July–August): 543–49.

Williams, R.H., and E.D. Larson. 1989. "Expanding Roles for Gas Turbines in Power Generation." In T.B. Johansson, B. Bodlund, and R.H. Williams, eds., Electricity: Efficient End-Use and New Generation Technologies, and Their Planning Implications. Lund, Sweden: Lund University Press.

———. 1993. "Advanced Gasification-Based Power Generation." In T.B. Johannson, H. Kelly, A.K.N. Reddy, and R.H. Williams, eds., Renewable Energy: Sources for Fuels and Electricity. Washington, D.C.: Island Press.

Williams, R.H., E.D. Larson, R.E. Katofsky, and J. Chen. 1995. "Methanol and Hydrogen from Biomass for Transportation." Energy for Sustainable Development 1 (5): 18–34.

Willrich, M., and T. Taylor. 1974. Nuclear Theft: Risks and Safeguards. Cambridge, Mass.: Ballinger.

World Bank. 1997. Clear Water, Blue Skies: China's Environment in the New Century. China 2020 series. Washington, D.C.

Zrodnikov, A.V., V.I. Chitaykin, B.F. Gromov, G.I. Toshinsky, U.G. Dragunov, and V.S. Stepanov. 1999. "Application of Reactors Cooled by Lead-Bismuth Alloy in Nuclear Power Energy." Paper presented at Global '99: Nuclear Technology—Bridging the Millennia, International Conference on Future Nuclear Systems, 29 August–3 September, Jackson Hole, Wyo.

part III
are sustainable futures possible?

energy scenarios

CHAPTER 9

Nebojsa Nakićenović (Austria)

LEAD AUTHORS: Tom Kram (Netherlands), Alexj Makarov (Russian Federation), Bent Sørensen, (Denmark), Keiichi Yokobori (Japan), and Zhou Fengqi (China)

CONTRIBUTING AUTHORS: Yasumasa Fujii (Japan), Jeffrey Stewart (United States), and John Weyant (United States)

ABSTRACT   Energy scenarios provide a framework for exploring future energy perspectives, including various combinations of technology options and their implications. Many scenarios in the literature illustrate how energy system developments will affect the global issues analysed in part 1 (chapters 1–4). Some describe energy futures that are compatible with sustainable development goals, such as improved energy efficiencies and the adoption of advanced energy supply technologies. Sustainable development scenarios are also characterised by low environmental impacts (local, regional, global) and equitable allocation of resources and wealth.

The three cases of alternative global developments presented in this chapter suggest how the future could unfold in terms of economic growth, population trends, and energy use. The challenge is formidable. For example, by 2100, 6–8 billion additional people—significantly more than the world population today—will need access to affordable, reliable, flexible, and convenient energy services. All three cases achieve this, through different energy system developments, but with varying degrees of sustainability.

A middle-course reference case (B) includes one scenario and is based on the direction in which the world is headed. Assuming continued moderate economic growth and modest technological improvement, this scenario leads to adverse environmental impacts, ranging from regional acidification to climate change. Thus—although it is a substantial improvement over the current situation—this scenario falls short of achieving a transition towards sustainable development. The other two cases and their variants lead to higher levels of economic development with vigorous improvement of energy technologies. They both—especially the ecologically driven case (C)—also result in a transition towards sustainable development.

Case A includes three scenarios with high economic growth throughout the world. One of them, A3, achieves some sustainable development goals through rapid economic growth in conjunction with a shift towards more environmentally benign energy technologies, including a significant role for clean fossil, renewables, and nuclear energy. The other two lead to a higher dependence on carbon-intensive fossil fuels, resulting in high energy-related emissions—and so are unsustainable.

Case C includes two ecologically driven scenarios with high growth in developing countries (towards being rich and 'green'). One of them, C1, assumes a global phaseout of nuclear energy by 2100. The other, C2, does not. Both assume that carbon and energy taxes will be introduced to promote renewables and end-use efficiency improvements—rather than to reduce other taxes in industrialised regions.

The considerable differences in expected total energy consumption among the scenarios reflect varying approaches to addressing the need for energy services in the future and demonstrate that policy matters. Increases in research, development, and deployment efforts for new energy technologies are a prerequisite for the achievement of the three scenarios that have characteristics of sustainable development. Significant technological advances will be required, as well as incremental improvements in conventional energy technologies. In general, scenarios A3, C1, and C2 require significant policy and behavioural changes in the next few decades to achieve more sustainable development paths. Taken together, these changes, which are described in more detail in part 4 (chapters 11 and 12), represent a clear departure from a business-as-usual approach.

Another crucial prerequisite for achieving sustainability in the scenarios is near-universal access to adequate and affordable energy services and more equitable allocation of resources. Finally, environmental protection—from indoor pollution to climate change—is an essential characteristic of sustainable development in the scenarios. The resolution of these future challenges offers a window of opportunity between now and 2020. Because of the long lifetimes of power plants, refineries, and other energy-related infrastructure investments, there will not be sufficient turnover of such facilities to reveal large differences among the alternative scenarios presented here before 2020. But the seeds of the post-2020 world will have been sown by then. Although choices about the world's future energy systems are now relatively wide open, they will narrow by 2020, and development opportunities, such as achieving sustainability, might not be achievable later if forgone today. ■

sustainable development has become a synonym for desirable transitions into the new millennium. This is often reflected in energy scenarios that consider conditions for achieving sustainable development. Because energy systems change slowly, energy scenarios have long time horizons—often extending more than 100 years into the future. These long time periods are needed to formulate transitions to sustainable development paths. And because energy is also an important prerequisite for sustainability, there is a large body of literature on energy scenarios that describe sustainable development paths.

This chapter assesses that literature and summarises the main driving forces of future energy developments and their implications. The objective of the chapter is to link—through global scenarios—the energy options presented in part 2 (chapters 5–8) with the salient energy issues presented in part 1 (chapters 1–4), thereby illustrating the conditions for sustainable futures. Three global scenarios (A3, C1, and C2) are considered that to varying degrees lead towards sustainability. All of them require polices and measures in the near future to accomplish the envisaged transition, and none is compatible with current trends. They are compared with a third reference scenario (B) that also outlines positive future developments but lacks many of the characteristics of sustainability. This scenario is more consistent with current developments and trends. These three scenarios have been developed jointly by the International Institute for Applied Systems Analysis (IIASA) and the World Energy Council (WEC) and are presented here to represent a wider literature on reference and sustainable development scenarios (IIASA-WEC, 1995; Morita and Lee, 1998; Nakićenović, Grübler, and McDonald, 1998; Nakićenović, Victor, and Morita, 1998).

What are scenarios and how are they used for energy assessments?

Scenarios are images of alternative futures. Scenarios are neither predictions nor forecasts. Each scenario can be interpreted as one particular image of how the future could unfold. Scenarios are useful tools for investigating alternative future developments and their implications, for learning about the behaviour of complex systems, and for policy-making.

Energy systems are complex, their behaviour may be uncertain and is not always well understood, and information on them is often incomplete. Frequently scenarios are the best tool for understanding alternative energy developments and their implications. In scientific energy assessments, scenarios are usually based on an internally consistent, reproducible set of assumptions or theories about the key relationships and driving forces of change, which are derived from our understanding of both history and the current situation. Often such energy scenarios are formulated with the help of formal models. More than 400 quantitative energy scenarios are documented in the database developed by Morita and Lee (1998).

Formal models cannot, however, capture all aspects of energy

Each scenario can be interpreted as one particular image of how the future could unfold.

systems. Some aspects of energy perspectives can only be appreciated through intuition and are best communicated by images and stories. Thus scenarios are sometimes less quantitative and more descriptive, and in a few cases do not involve any formal analysis and are expressed in qualitative terms. Energy scenarios can also involve components of both; they sometimes have a narrative part, often called a "storyline", and a number of corresponding quantitative scenarios for each storyline. Some scenarios are primarily narrative and qualitative, even if actual numbers are used for illustrative purposes. This is often the case with energy scenarios that prescribe the achievement of sustainability and thus make particularly strong assumptions about the future.

Scenarios are not value free, and can often be divided into two broad groups: descriptive and normative. Descriptive scenarios are evolutionary and open-ended, and explore paths into the future without any preconceived endpoint. Normative (or prescriptive) scenarios are explicitly values-based and teleological, and explore the routes to desired or undesired endpoints (utopias or dystopias). The distinction between the two groups is not always clear (Nakićenović and others, 2000). For instance, two of the three scenarios from the International Institute for Applied Systems Analysis and World Energy Council (IIASA-WEC) that are considered here describe how many conditions of sustainability could be achieved by the end of the 21st century but also contain many normative elements that illustrate polices and measures that would be required to change current trends.

Alternative development paths and how they are reflected in scenarios

The starting point for any analysis of energy development is a prospective look into the future. Because it is impossible to predict future energy developments, an important purpose of alternative energy scenarios is to analyse possible global and regional developments for periods of a century or more so that their implications for sustainable development can be assessed. For now, these long-term energy scenarios are the best way to integrate demographic, economic, societal, and technological knowledge with our understanding of ecological systems and environmental implications. As an integration tool, scenarios also allow a role for intuition, analysis, and synthesis. By developing scenarios, researchers can analyse future determinants of energy requirements and compare them to supply availabilities, financing, environmental constraints, and other salient factors and driving forces. Long-term scenarios can provide a framework for a 'retrospective view from the future' and for assessing near-term measures to achieve sustainable and other desirable development paths.

The traditional method of formulating scenarios first involves developing a 'business-as-usual' baseline that essentially assumes that things will not change in the future; then 'policy' cases starting from the baseline are developed. But it is becoming increasingly evident that it is next to impossible to formulate future developments that do not include any change in comparison with today; namely, futures that capture the business-as-usual course of events. In fact, even though energy futures are unpredictable, one thing that appears almost certain is that the future will be different from today. In addition, it is virtually impossible to imagine future developments that can avoid changes. Within a century, for example, two technological discontinuities could occur, along with a major shift in societal values and perhaps a change in the balance of geopolitical power. Thus there is a growing literature on alternative scenarios that map a wide range of future possibilities. The hope is that, by mapping alternative development scenarios, it will be possible to identify a wider range of differing courses of action. These alternative scenarios are tools for capturing different relationships and the evolution of factors that determine future energy trajectories and spatial patterns.

It is important to realise that such approaches depend on assessments of the driving forces of energy futures and the relationships among them, ranging from population developments to technological change. Usually a very small subset of alternative scenarios can be identified that will lead to sustainability. The driving forces in these scenarios must be consistent with the concept of sustainability. For example, such scenarios should not have dangerously high environmental impacts or inequitable resource allocation.

Such approaches also allow for the unfolding of different futures. Differing scenarios, while sharing similar outcomes, might have varying mixes of the same characteristics. For example, different economic development paths might lead to similar global energy requirements by the middle of the 21st century. A world with high population and relatively low levels of development might have almost the same total energy needs as a world with low population and high levels of affluence. But the latter clearly would offer more possible choices for achieving sustainability.

Energy scenarios for sustainable development

To assess what kinds of development will ultimately be sustainable, one must have a global perspective and a very long time horizon covering periods of at least a century. Chapters 1–4 amply illustrate that access to affordable energy services is a crucial prerequisite for sustainable development. At the same time, energy use is also a main cause of environmental degradation at all scales and thus can impede achieving sustainability. (Often a higher degree of equity in the world is also included in the concept of sustainable development.)

Sustainable development is an elusive concept. It is often easier to define those development paths that are not sustainable than those that are. In many ways, this is the advantage of the concept. It has sufficient clarity to identify which development paths do not lead to a sustainable future, and it offers flexibility while being prescriptive. Sustainable energy scenarios are often designed to offer policy guidance on managing, for example, an orderly transition from today's energy system, which relies largely on fossil fuels, towards an energy system

Sustainable futures usually are not considered to be achievable with current policies and prevailing development trends.

more compatible with sustainable development in all its dimensions (Goldemberg and others, 1988).[1]

All sustainable futures are in some sense positive and have some normative elements. In all of them the world develops equitably with relatively low environmental impacts.

Sustainable energy scenarios sometimes include strong assumptions about desirable futures; because they prescribe how such futures can be achieved, they are normative. In such normative approaches, sustainable futures usually are not considered to be achievable with current policies and prevailing development trends, but rather often depend on a fundamental change or a major paradigm shift.

Brief review of the literature on energy scenarios

The construction of scenarios to investigate alternative future developments under a set of assumed conditions dates far back in history. Scenarios were and continue to be one of the main tools for dealing with the complexity and uncertainty of future challenges.

The first scenarios were probably used to plan military operations. Scenarios now are being increasingly used in business enterprises and for many other commercial purposes. Perhaps most famous in the literature is the use of scenarios by the Shell Group in the wake of the so-called oil crisis to plan its corporate response strategies (Schwartz, 1991). Today scenarios are quite widespread and are found in all kinds of enterprises around the world. Many are quantitative; this is often the case for enterprises in the energy sector. Some of them also include considerations of sustainability. Recently the World Business Council for Sustainable Development presented a set of scenarios that was developed in collaboration with 35 major corporations (WBCSD, 1998).

During the past 30 years a number of global studies have used scenarios as a tool to assess future paths of energy system development. One of the first global studies to employ scenarios for this purpose was conducted by IIASA during the late 1970s (Häfele, 1981). Another influential series of scenarios that included the assessment of sustainable development was formulated by the World Energy Council (WEC, 1993). The Intergovernmental Panel on Climate Change (IPCC) has used scenarios since its inception to assess greenhouse gas emissions and climate change. In 1992 it developed a set of very influential scenarios that gave a detailed treatment of energy sector developments. The set includes six scenarios called IS92, three of which describe futures that include characteristics of sustainable development (Pepper and others, 1992; Leggett, Pepper, and Swart, 1992).

A growing number of global studies consider futures with radical policy and behavioural changes to achieve sustainable development (Goldemberg and others, 1988). One of the first global scenarios to focus on achieving sustainable development was formulated by Greenpeace (Lazarus and others, 1993). Another among the first global energy scenarios with characteristics of sustainable development describes a transition to renewable energy futures (Johansson and others, 1993). In its second assessment report, the IPCC also considered a range of global energy scenarios, based on some elements of the IS92 set, with varying degrees of sustainability (Ishitani and others, 1996).

In more recent studies, sustainable development scenarios are usually included among other alternative futures. This class of sustainable scenarios can be characterised by low environmental impacts at all scales and more equitable allocation of resources and wealth relative to current situations. Recently the Global Scenario Group presented a set of three scenarios that received considerable attention (Raskin and others, 1998). These scenarios were based on elaborate narratives describing alternative futures, including some that are decisively sustainable. The set of scenarios developed by the WBCSD also includes narratives and describes alternative development paths, some of which include strong emphasis on sustainable development (WBCSD, 1998).

There is also a large literature of global energy scenarios that serve as a reference for showing that, under business-as-usual conditions, many of the developments crucial for the achievement of sustainability would not be realised. For example, the *World Energy Outlook,* regularly published by the International Energy Agency (IEA, 1998), is very influential. Many of these global energy scenarios are limited to developments during the next 20–30 years and do not go far enough into the future to assess all crucial aspects of sustainable development, such as climate change. But they often are very relevant to issues such as the conditions for meeting the carbon emissions targets specified in the Kyoto Protocol under the United Nations Framework Convention on Climate Change (UNFCCC, 1992).

The literature on sustainable energy scenarios is large, and this brief review cannot give a comprehensive account. The IPCC has developed a database that includes a number of global energy scenarios that can be characterised as describing sustainable development (Morita and Lee, 1998). This database, which includes more than 400 global and regional scenarios, illustrates that the literature is quite rich; thus not all scenarios can be described in this chapter. (In the following sections dealing with such scenario driving forces as economic development, some of the comparisons use scenarios from the database.)

The IPCC, in its recent *Special Report on Emissions Scenarios,* considers 40 scenarios that include a large number of sustainable futures (Nakićenović and others, 2000). This set of scenarios is unique in a number of respects—it was developed using six different models, it covers a wide range of alternative futures based on the scenarios in the literature, it includes narrative descriptions of alternative futures, and it has been reviewed extensively.

Here some of the conditions for achieving a transition towards sustainable development will be illustrated with the three scenarios developed by IIASA and WEC. These will then be contrasted to a reference case that captures many positive future developments but cannot be characterised as leading to sustainability. These scenarios cover a wide range of possible future developments and are representative of the scenario literature. Where appropriate, other scenarios will be drawn upon to illustrate the conditions and implications of sustainable development.

Three energy scenarios for the 21st century

IIASA and WEC undertook a five-year joint study published as *Global Energy Perspectives* (Nakićenović, Grübler, and McDonald, 1998). The objectives of the study were to integrate near-term strategies through 2020 with long-term opportunities to 2100; analyse alternative future developments; ensure consistency and reproducibility with a unified methodological framework using formal models and databases; incorporate a dynamic treatment of technological change; and harmonise regional aspirations with global possibilities. The study centres on three cases of future social, economic, and technological development for 11 world regions.

The three cases unfold into six scenarios of energy system alternatives. Together they span a wider range of alternative future developments and driving forces. The three cases are designated as A, B, and C. Case A includes three variant scenarios and reflects a high-growth future of vigorous economic development and rapid technological improvements. One of its variants (A3) includes many characteristics of sustainable and equitable development. Case B represents a middle course, with intermediate economic growth and more modest technological improvements. Case C is ecologically driven (with two variants: C1, with new renewables and a phaseout of nuclear energy by 2100; and C2, with renewables and new nuclear); it incorporates challenging environmental and energy taxes to simultaneously protect the environment and transfer wealth from North to South to enhance economic equity. This approach leads to lower energy use but high overall growth, especially in the South. Case C illustrates most vividly the conditions for achieving a high degree of sustainability and equity in the world. Table 9.1 gives an overview of the three cases and their six scenarios of energy development. Full documentation is available in the published study report (Nakićenović, Grübler, and McDonald, 1998) and at the study Website (http://www.iiasa.ac.at/cgi-bin/ecs/book_dyn/bookcnt.py).

These scenarios received a wide review that included about 100 leading energy experts. They incorporate both a top-down approach based on an integrated set of energy, economic, and environmental models to initially develop the set of scenarios, and a bottom-up evaluation of the regional perspectives provided by the 11 review groups. This set of scenarios will be used to illustrate to what extent the concepts of sustainable development are captured across the scenarios. They have been chosen because they cover a wide range of alternative future developments and are quite representative of the recent scenario literature. Again, where appropriate, reference will be given to other scenarios from the literature.

Three of the six scenarios will be used to illustrate alternative conditions for achieving transitions of energy systems towards sustainability. Table 9.2 provides a number of indicators that may be used to characterise the achievement of sustainable development in energy scenarios and shows how the three scenarios selected for

TABLE 9.1. SUMMARY OF THREE ENERGY DEVELOPMENT CASES IN 2050 AND 2100 COMPARED WITH 1990

		Case A High growth	Case B Middle growth	Case C Ecologically driven
Population (billions)	1990 2050 2100	5.3 10.1 11.7	5.3 10.1 11.7	5.3 10.1 11.7
Gross world product (trillions of 1990 dollars)	1990 2050 2100	20 100 300	20 75 200	20 75 220
Gross world product (annual percentage change)	1990–2050 1990–2100	**High** 2.7 2.5	**Medium** 2.2 2.1	**Medium** 2.2 2.2
Primary energy intensity (megajoules per 1990 dollar of gross world product)	1990 2050 2100	19.0 10.4 6.1	19.0 11.2 7.3	19.0 8.0 4.0
Primary energy intensity improvement rate (annual percentage change)	1990–2050 1990–2100	**Medium** –0.9 –1.0	**Low** –0.8 –0.8	**High** –1.4 –1.4
Primary energy consumption (exajoules)	1990 2050 2100	379 1,041 1,859	379 837 1,464	379 601 880
Cumulative primary energy consumption, 1990–2100 (thousands of exajoules)	Coal Oil Natural gas Nuclear energy Hydropower Biomass Solar energy Other Global total	8.9 – 30.7 27.6 – 15.7 18.4 – 28.7 6.2 – 11.2 3.7 – 4.2 7.4 – 14.3 1.8 – 7.7 3.0 – 4.7 94.0 – 94.9	17.5 15.3 15.8 10.5 3.6 8.3 1.9 4.3 77.2	7.1 – 7.2 10.9 12.2 – 12.9 2.1 – 6.2 3.6 – 4.0 9.1 – 10.1 6.3 – 7.4 1.4 – 2.2 56.9
Energy technology cost reductions (through learning)	Fossil Non-fossil	**High** **High**	**Medium** **Medium**	**Low** **High**
Energy technology diffusion rates	Fossil Non-fossil	**High** **High**	**Medium** **Medium**	**Medium** **High**
Environmental taxes (excluding carbon dioxide taxes)		**No**	**No**	**Yes**
Sulphur dioxide emissions (millions of tonnes of sulphur)	1990 2050 2100	58.6 44.8 – 64.2 9.3 – 55.4	58.6 54.9 58.3	58.6 22.1 7.1
Carbon dioxide emission constraints and taxes		**No**	**No**	**Yes**
Net carbon dioxide emissions (gigatonnes of carbon)	1990 2050 2100	6 9 – 15 6 – 20	6 10 11	6 5 2
Cumulative carbon dioxide emissions (gigatonnes of carbon)	1990–2100	910 – 1,450	1,000	540
Carbon dioxide concentrations (parts per million by volume)	1990 2050 2100	358 460 – 510 530 – 730	358 470 590	358 430 430
Carbon intensity (grams of carbon per 1990 dollar of gross world product)	1990 2050 2100	280 90 – 140 20 – 60	280 130 60	280 70 10
Investments in energy supply sector (trillions of 1990 dollars)	1990–2020 2020–50 2050–2100	15.7 24.7 93.7	12.4 22.3 82.3	9.4 14.1 43.3
Number of scenarios		3	1	2

The three cases unfold into six scenarios of energy system alternatives: three case A scenarios (A1, ample oil and gas; A2, return to coal; and A3, non-fossil future), a single case B scenario (middle course), and two case C scenarios (C1, new renewables; and C2, renewables and new nuclear). Some of the scenario characteristics, such as cumulative energy consumption, cumulative carbon dioxide emissions, and decarbonisation, are shown as ranges for the three case A and two C scenarios.

Source: Nakićenović, Grübler, and McDonald, 1998.

this assessment fare in comparison with each other. The middle-course scenario (B) was chosen to serve as a reference baseline because it was designed to represent a future characterised by incremental and gradual changes. In fact, this scenario would represent a major improvement in the global energy system and its use, but it does fall short of fulfilling many indicators of the sustainability suggested in table 9.2. The other two scenarios shown in table 9.2 (A3 and C1) describe futures that include characteristics of sustainability. The third scenario (C2), which can also be characterised along the same lines, includes continuous reliance on nuclear energy, in contrast to the other ecologically driven scenario, which has a global nuclear phaseout by 2100 (C1). Neither the A3 nor the C1 scenario, however, is compatible with current trends and developments, so both would require new policy initiatives and measures directed towards achieving sustainable development. Even so, neither of the scenarios ranks very high on all 13 indicators of sustainability considered in table 9.2. At the same time, table 9.2 indicates that, among the spectrum of energy futures considered here, C1 represents the energy future that is the most compatible with sustainable development.

Scenario A3 envisions a future with impressive technological improvements and subsequent high degrees of economic development, a structural shift first towards natural gas and then towards renewable and nuclear energy options, and very high levels of energy efficiency. Environmental impacts are therefore quite low in this future. Equity is achieved through rapid development, with today's developing regions achieving a high level of affluence by the end of the 21st century. The development gap narrows, increasing equity in the world. This scenario also includes characteristics of sustainability. This is achieved primarily through vigorous development (without active redistribution of income). Rapid technological and economic development allows access to an ever-expanding resource base with decreasing energy and material intensities, and a radical decline in adverse environmental impacts. However, it requires a paradigm shift and a host of new policies.

The ecologically driven case C scenario presents a rich and 'green' future and represents a fundamentally different development path. It includes both substantial technological progress and unprecedented international cooperation centred explicitly on environmental protection and international equity—it includes a high degree of environmental protection at all scales, from indoor air pollution to climate, with active redistribution of wealth and very high levels of energy efficiency and conservation. It fulfils most of the other criteria associated with sustainable development (see table 9.2), such as increasing equity, both in an economic and ecological sense, among regions and countries. Thus it can be considered to lead to sustainable development. For example, it incorporates a challenging, broad portfolio of environmental control technologies and policies, such as emissions standards and caps, incentives to encourage energy producers and consumers to use energy more efficiently and carefully, 'green' taxes (levied on energy and carbon), international environmental and economic agreements, and technology transfer.

TABLE 9.2. CHARACTERISTICS OF SUSTAINABILITY IN THREE ENERGY DEVELOPMENT SCENARIOS IN 2050 AND 2100 COMPARED WITH 1990

Indicator of sustainability	1990	Scenario A3	Scenario B	Scenario C1
Eradicating poverty	Low	Very high	Medium	Very high
Reducing relative income gaps	Low	High	Medium	Very high
Providing universal access to energy	Low	Very high	High	Very high
Increasing affordability of energy	Low	High	Medium	Very high
Reducing adverse health impacts	Medium	Very high	High	Very high
Reducing air pollution	Medium	Very high	High	Very high
Limiting long-lived radionuclides	Medium	Very low	Very low	High
Limiting toxic materials[a]	Medium	High	Low	High
Limiting GHG emissions	Low	High	Low	Very high
Raising indigenous energy use	Medium	High	Low	Very high
Improving supply efficiency	Medium	Very high	High	Very high
Increasing end-use efficiency	Low	High	Medium	Very high
Accelerating technology diffusion	Low	Very high	Medium	Medium

a. For this row only, the qualitative indicators are not based on quantitative features of the scenarios, but were specified by the authors on the basis of additional assumptions.

The case C scenario also reflects substantial resource transfers from industrialised to developing countries to spur growth and eradicate poverty. These transfers include stringent international environmental taxes and incentives, which recycle funds from industrialised countries (members of the Organisation for Economic Co-operation and Development, or OECD) to developing countries. Specifically, it is assumed that energy and carbon taxes are applied universally, albeit at different rates and timing, and that the tax revenues are used to promote development. In the scenario, this means that the proceeds from these taxes in OECD countries are recycled as resource transfers to developing countries and are earmarked for the development of energy infrastructure, clean technologies, efficiency, and conservation. Because this scenario requires a fundamental paradigm shift from current socioeconomic, technological, and environmental development trends, new policies would be required to achieve the future it describes. Thus the transition towards more sustainable development paths in both cases C and A3 would require a host of new policies to promote the diffusion of advanced technologies, reliable and affordable access to energy for all, free trade, vigorous economic growth, and reduced emissions at all scales. These findings are consistent with chapter 12, where it is stated that new policies would be required to achieve more sustainable development.

The three cases have a number of common features. All provide for substantial social and economic development, particularly in the developing world, and all give much wider access to reliable, affordable energy throughout the world. During the 21st century, as affluence increases throughout the world, the current distinction between developing and industrialised regions will become less and less appropriate in the scenarios considered here. All the scenarios provide for improved energy efficiencies and environmental compatibility, and hence for associated growth in both the quantity and quality of energy services.

The task is indeed daunting. Nearly 2 billion people, or a third of the world's population, lack access to adequate, affordable, clean, and convenient energy services such as electricity (chapter 2). The current disparities in energy use mirror the disparities in access to affordable energy services and in the distribution of wealth—the richest 20 percent of the world's population uses 55 percent of final, primary energy, while the poorest 20 percent uses only 5 percent. Exclusion from modern energy services is generally associated with poverty and environmental degradation.

Although it is true that about two-thirds of the global population, or about 4 billion people, are now connected to electricity and that great progress has been achieved, the challenge ahead is formidable; a simple calculation illustrates its magnitude. In addition to the 2 billion people today who still need to be connected to energy distribution or decentralised systems and endowed with sufficient purchasing power to be able to afford modern energy services, two to three times as many people are likely to be added to the global population during the new century. This means that 6–8 billion people would need to be provided with the access to affordable, clean, flexible, and convenient energy services during the 21st century, a number larger than the current world population. All scenarios considered here achieve this transition—to a varying extent and through different energy system developments. Some of them do so while fulfilling some of the criteria of sustainable development as well (see the conclusion to this chapter).

In all three cases the structure of final energy develops towards greater flexibility, quality, and environmental compatibility, and energy intensities improve steadily. To facilitate comparisons among the three cases, all share the same central demographic baseline assumption, in which global population grows to 10 billion people by 2050 and to nearly 11.7 billion by 2100. This is higher than the current medium projections of about 10.4 billion in 2100 by the World Bank, United Nations, and IIASA (box 9.1). This means that 6–8 billion additional people would achieve access to adequate energy services in all three cases.

Economic development and equity

Economic development and growth are fundamental prerequisites for achieving an increase in living standards and equity in the world. It is therefore not surprising that assumptions about economic development are among the most important determinants of energy scenarios. At the same time, economic growth prospects are among the most uncertain determinants of scenarios.

Economic and social development has many dimensions, and a number of indicators have been devised to assess progress and setbacks in human development. The United Nations Development Programme defines development as the furthering of human choices (UNDP, 1997). Arguably, choices are only possible once basic human

---

BOX 9.1. DEMOGRAPHIC TRANSITION AND POPULATION GROWTH

Population is one of the driving forces of future energy requirements. Today there are three main sources of global population projections: the United Nations (UN, 1998), World Bank (Bos and Vu, 1994), and IIASA (Lutz, Sanderson, and Scherbov, 1997).

Most central population projections lead to a doubling of global population by 2100, to about 10 billion, compared with 5.3 billion in 1990. In recent years the central population projections for 2100 have declined somewhat but are still in line with a doubling by 2100. For example, the latest UN (1998) medium-low and medium-high projections indicate a range of between 7.2 and 14.6 billion people by 2100, with the medium scenario at 10.4 billion. The IIASA central estimate for 2100 is also 10.4 billion, with 95 percent probability that world population would exceed 6 billion and be lower than 17 billion (Lutz, Sanderson, and Scherbov, 1997).

Thus the population assumptions in the IIASA-WEC scenarios are higher (11.7 billion in comparison with 10.4 billion) but still consistent with recent population projections (see figure 9.3). It should be noted that the population projections used in most scenarios that describe sustainable development paths appear to have the same range as for all other scenarios in the literature. This implies that population policies are apparently not considered appropriate for achieving sustainability, nor is energy seen as an appropriate instrument for achieving the population transition, at least across most of the scenarios in the literature (see chapter 2).

needs for food, shelter, health care, and education have been met. Eradication of poverty is essential for achieving sustainability and human development in general. Beyond the satisfaction of basic needs, the issue of what constitutes development involves many cultural, social, and economic factors that inherently involve questions of values, preferences, and policies.

Income is not an end in itself, but rather a means of enabling human choices—or foreclosing them, in the case of poverty. Therefore per capita income (usually measured by per capita GDP) has been widely used to indicate the degree of economic development. In many instances this is closely correlated (as lead or lag indicator) with other indicators and dimensions of social development, such as mortality, nutrition, and access to basic services.

Although future rates of economic development are highly uncertain, in all three cases of economic development considered in the IIASA-WEC study, future economic and energy markets move to today's developing countries. The rate and timing of this transition varies across the three cases, but the overall direction of change is the same. Along with population growth, the economic catch-up of developing to industrialised countries implies a long-term shift in the geographic focus of economic activities.

Currently the situation is fundamentally different. OECD countries produce and consume close to 80 percent of global economic output (measured by gross world product), while they account for less than 20 percent of global population. These disparities are illustrated in figure 9.1, which shows the size of 11 world regions in proportion to their 1990 GDP (at market exchange rates and 1990 prices). In 1990 the economic map of the world was very different from geographic maps (Mercartor projections)—it was highly distorted as a result of disparities among regions. Most developing regions were barely discernible relative to Japan, Western Europe, and North America. In figure 9.1, for example, compare the size of Japan in 1990 with that of China or the Indian subcontinent.

For 2050 and 2100, the economic maps shown in figure 9.1 correspond to case B, the middle-course scenario of the IIASA-WEC study that is the most cautious with respect to the speed of the developing world's economic catch-up. Nonetheless, over the long term economic maps begin to resemble the geographic maps with which all of us are familiar. This means two things. First, economic catch-up, even in relative terms, is a century-long process and one of the greatest human challenges. Some regions may forge ahead, but in the aggregate developing countries will require more than 50 years to approach the income levels that OECD countries had in the 1960s or 1970s. Second, with long-term development and catch-up (in relative but not absolute terms), economic, as well as energy market, growth will be primarily in the developing world.

In figure 9.1, between 1990 and 2100 the world economy increases in size 10 times, from $20 trillion to $200 trillion (1990 dollars; or $24 trillion to $240 trillion in 1998 dollars). This leads to more equitable

The richest 20 percent of the world's population uses 55 percent of final, primary energy, while the poorest 20 percent uses only 5 percent.

distribution of economic activities geographically, but the gap in per capita income remains very large. Therefore, in this scenario, in many parts of the world local difficulties will persist and, despite rapid economic development, adequate energy services may not be available to every citizen even 100 years from now. Higher rates of economic development are required to narrow the gap more substantially.

This is illustrated in table 9.3, which compares per capita income for the three cases (A, B, and C) for the 11 world regions. Cases A and C include the three more sustainable scenarios (A3, C1, and C2). The table shows that in case B only half of today's developing regions will achieve the 1990 income levels of OECD countries by 2100, whereas this is the case for most of the regions in the other three scenarios (A3, C1, and C2). The attainment of this higher degree of economic catch-up is, however, fundamentally different for the three more sustainable scenarios. In A3 this is achieved primarily through economic growth that results from liberalised markets, free trade, and high investment rates, whereas in C1 and C2 it is achieved through a substantial redistribution of wealth (from industrialised to developing countries and possibly from rich to poor) with a strong focus on maintaining environmental enmities. All three futures are more equitable than reference case B, leading to much higher economic development in the world. Gross world product increases by a factor of 11–15 in A3, C1, and C2, to $220–300 trillion (1990 dollars; $270–370 trillion in 1998 dollars) by 2100.

A comparison of these three cases of economic development shows considerable uncertainty about future per capita GDP growth rates and about the effectiveness of different policy measures in reducing the relative income gap between today's industrialised and developing countries. The range across the scenarios is consistent with earlier reviews of economic growth assumptions for long-term scenarios by Nordhaus and Yohe (1983), Grübler (1994), Manne and Richels (1994), and Alcamo and others (1995). For instance, in the scenarios reviewed in Alcamo and others (1995), and Grübler (1994), per capita annual GDP growth rates typically are 1–3 percent for 1990–2100. On the basis of an average per capita income of $4,000 in 1990, global per capita GDP could range from $10,000–100,000 by 2100. Such uncertainties become amplified by regional disparities, in particular future productivity growth in developing countries.

The great inherent uncertainty of future economic development prospects is reflected in the wide range of economic development paths assumed in the scenarios from the literature. The further one looks into the future, the higher is the uncertainty. By 2100 the range is between 3 (IS92c scenario, Pepper and others, 1992) and 30 times (FUND/EMF, modeller's choice scenario, Tol, 1995) the 1990 level (Nakićenović, Victor, and Morita, 1998). Thus the scenarios give a range of $60–$700 trillion, with a median of $240 trillion (1990 dollars; $290 trillion in 1998 dollars). These figures

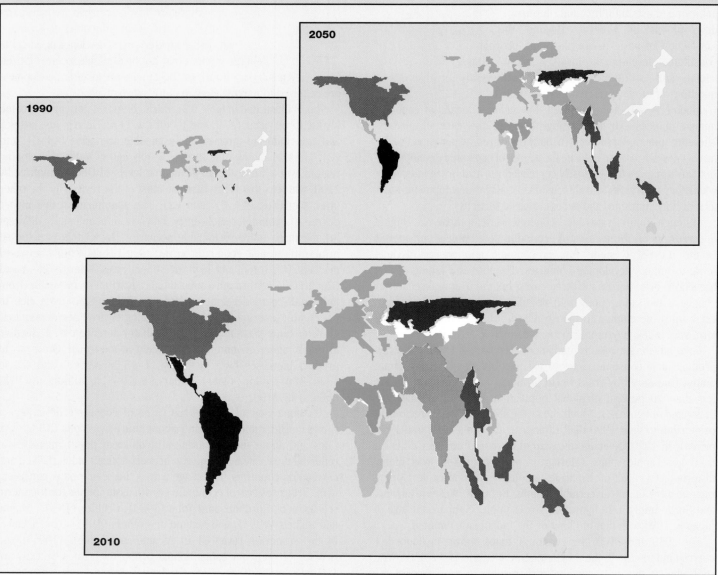

FIGURE 9.1. THE CHANGING GEOGRAPHY OF ECONOMIC WEALTH FOR THE MIDDLE-COURSE (CASE B) SCENARIO IN 2050 AND 2100 RELATIVE TO 1990

2050

1990

2010

The areas of world regions are proportional to their 1990 levels of GDP, expressed at 1990 market exchange rates.

Source: Nakićenović, Grübler, and McDonald, 1998.

translate into an annual growth rate variation of 1.1–3.2 percent, and a median growth rate of 2.1 percent. Future economic growth rates therefore are generally assumed to be lower than those of historical experience.

It is important to note that by 2100 the global scenarios that represent sustainable development are mostly above the median of about $240 trillion (1990 dollars). Assuming a central population projection of 10 billion people by 2100, the median growth path translates into about $24,000 (1990 dollars; $29,000 in 1998 dollars) average per capita gross world product, or roughly the current per

capita income level in more affluent industrialised countries. Thus economic growth rates are high for the scenarios that achieve sustainability, indicating that economic development is a prerequisite for both higher equity and lower environmental impacts. This tendency is also reflected in the three more sustainable scenarios in the IIASA-WEC study relative to the reference case.

Improvement of energy intensities

In all three cases economic development outpaces the increase in energy, leading to substantially reduced energy intensities. As technologies progress, and as inefficient technologies are replaced by more efficient ones, the amount of primary energy needed per unit of GDP—the energy intensity—decreases. In some developing regions the intensity of commercial energy initially increases as traditional, less efficient forms are replaced by commercial energy, but total energy intensity decreases in these cases as well. All other factors being equal, the faster economic growth, the higher the turnover of capital and the greater the increase in energy intensity.

In the scenarios, improvements in individual technologies were varied across a range derived from historical trends and literature on future technology characteristics. When combined with the economic growth patterns of the different scenarios, the average annual overall global reduction in energy intensity varies from about 0.8 percent, in line with historical experience, to 1.4 percent. These figures bracket the long-term average annual rate for industrialised countries during the past 100 years of about 1 percent, and cumulatively lead to substantial energy intensity decreases across all scenarios (figure 4 in the overview). Efficiency improvements are significantly higher in some regions, especially for shorter periods of time.

These differences in global developments across the scenarios are reflected in even larger regional variations. The East Asian 'miracle' of double-digit average growth during the early 1990s has been interrupted recently, but prospects for continued sound growth are good for the coming decades. The transition economies of Central Asia, the Russian Federation, and Eastern Europe have undergone a period of profound change and reform, reflected in a deep recession and economic decline during the 1990s. The prosperous economies of Western Europe have focused on reducing the high unemployment that accompanied low growth rates.

The IIASA-WEC scenarios start in the base year 1990 and were developed between 1992 and 1998, so that the actual trends of past years can be compared with initial developments in the long-term scenarios. Figure 9.2 shows the energy intensity improvement rates for six regions for the three cases of economic development relative to historical trends (figure 4 in the overview). They range from vigorous reduction of about 4 percent a year for China and other centrally planned economies in Asia to a (temporary) increase in energy intensities in the transition economies of Eastern Europe, Central Asia, and the former Soviet Union. The scenario trajectories provide an excellent anticipation of short-term developments during the 1990s, especially for the transition economies. All scenarios assume that the next few decades will be characterised by successful reform and restructuring in all transition economies, leading to sustained investment in the energy sector and economic development that will be reflected in long-term increases in energy intensities.

In addition to the energy intensity improvements, rates of technological change and available energy resources also vary consistently across the scenarios. For example, high rates of economic growth are associated with rapid technological advance, ample resource availability, and high rates of energy intensity increase. Conversely low rates of

TABLE 9.3 PER CAPITA GDP FOR THE 11 WORLD REGIONS IN 1990 AND IN THE THREE IIASA-WEC CASES IN 2050 AND 2100 (THOUSANDS OF 1990 DOLLARS, MEASURED AT MARKET EXCHANGE RATES)

Region	1990	2050			2100		
		A	B	C	A	B	C
Sub-Saharan Africa	0.5	1.6	1.0	1.2	11.0	6.3	11.4
Centrally planned Asia and China	0.4	7.0	3.4	5.4	21.2	12.8	15.4
Central and Eastern Europe	2.4	16.3	7.8	8.0	52.7	29.0	21.8
Former Soviet Union	2.7	14.1	7.5	7.1	49.3	26.8	20.2
Latin America	2.5	8.3	7.1	7.4	27.8	20.1	21.0
Middle East and North Africa	2.1	5.6	4.0	4.1	13.8	11.0	12.9
North America	21.6	54.5	45.8	38.8	108.7	77.0	59.2
Pacific OECD	22.8	58.7	45.8	42.8	111.0	74.6	62.9
Other Pacific Asia	1.5	12.2	7.9	10.2	29.6	18.8	23.7
South Asia	0.3	2.0	1.3	1.8	15.3	10.0	14.8
Western Europe	16.2	45.9	37.1	32.9	93.5	63.9	53.7
World	**4.0**	**10.1**	**7.2**	**7.5**	**26.4**	**17.3**	**19.0**

Note: Three scenarios are shown; middle-course case B is compared with the three more sustainable scenarios, A3, C1, and C2, which are characterised by higher economic growth, greater equity, and substantially lower environmental impacts. All case A scenarios (A1, A2, and A3) share the same type of economic development, as do the case C scenarios (C1 and C2). *Source: Nakićenović, Grubler, and McDonald, 1998.*

economic growth result in a more limited expansion of energy resources, lower rates of technological innovation in general, and lower rates of decrease in energy intensities.

Primary energy requirements and supply

Future rates of economic development are among the most important determinants of energy demand in the long term.[2] The IIASA-WEC study spans an increase in global energy needs in the range of 1.5–3 times by 2050, and 2–5 times by 2100. Taken together, energy requirements are envisaged to increase at lower rates than economic growth. This means that energy intensity is presumed to decline across all scenarios. By 2100 it falls to between 80 and 20 percent of 1990 levels. This translates into annual declines of between 0.8 percent and more than 1.5 percent, with a median of about 1 percent. Thus the lowest future energy intensity improvements of 0.8 percent a year are in line with the historical experience of industrialised countries.

Figure 9.3 shows a wide range of alternative future primary energy requirements for the three scenarios. The energy needs for reference case B are in the middle, about tripling by 2100. This development is bracketed by the three more sustainable scenarios. A3 indicates substantially higher energy needs resulting from more rapid economic growth, despite much higher energy intensity. It nevertheless includes important characteristics of sustainability because it leads to a substantially higher degree of economic equity with lower environmental impacts at all scales. C1 (as well as C2) leads to the lowest energy requirements of all scenarios, to about a doubling by 2100, resulting from efficiency improvements and conservation; it is marked by a higher degree of economic equity and very low environmental impacts.

For comparison, figure 9.3 also shows the highest and lowest energy demand trajectories from the literature (Morita and Lee, 1998). The range of future energy requirements across the scenarios is

FIGURE 9.2. PRIMARY ENERGY INTENSITIES FOR 6 REPRESENTATIVE REGIONS OUT OF THE 11 WORLD REGIONS, 1970–96, AND IN THREE CASES, 1990–2020

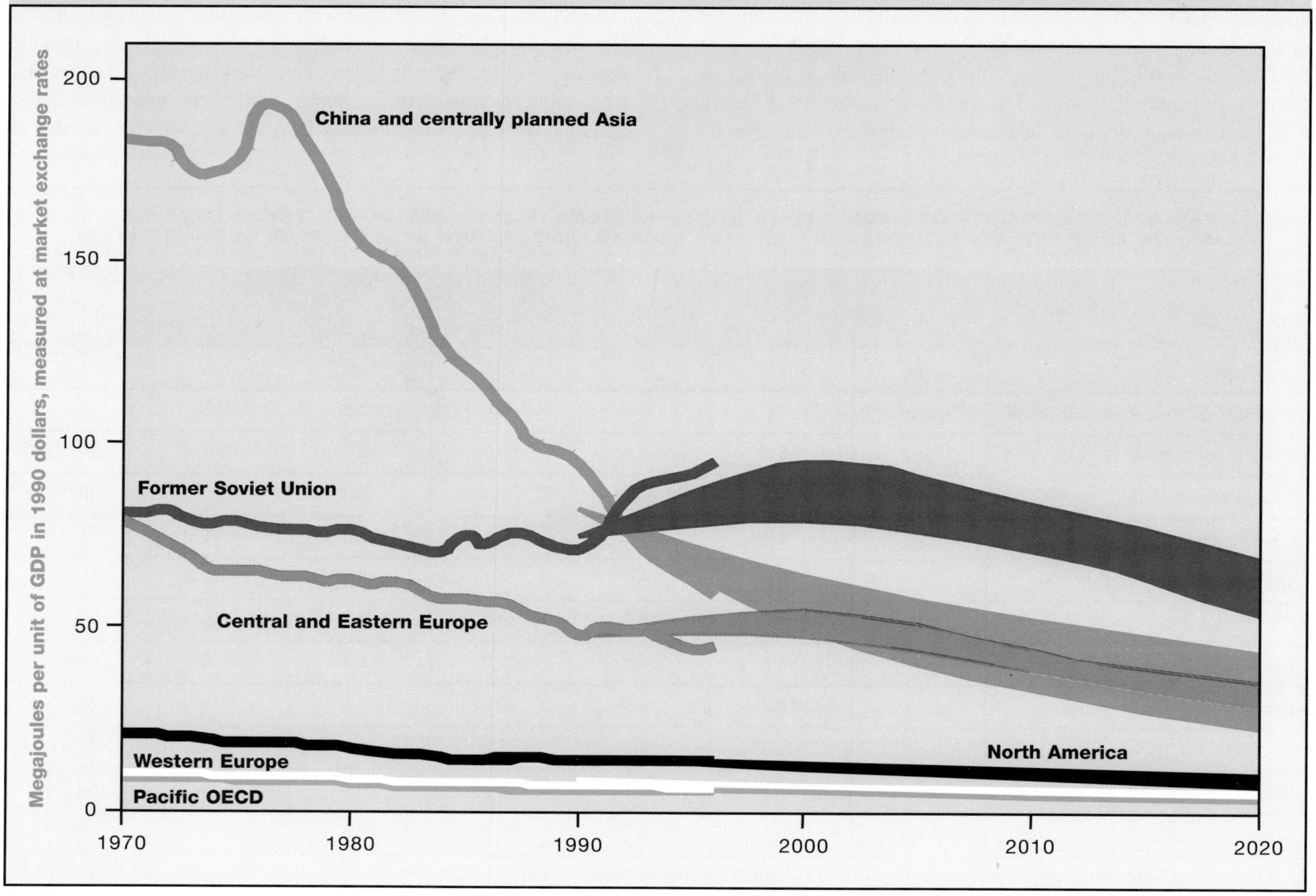

Source: Nakićenović, Grübler, and McDonald, 1998.

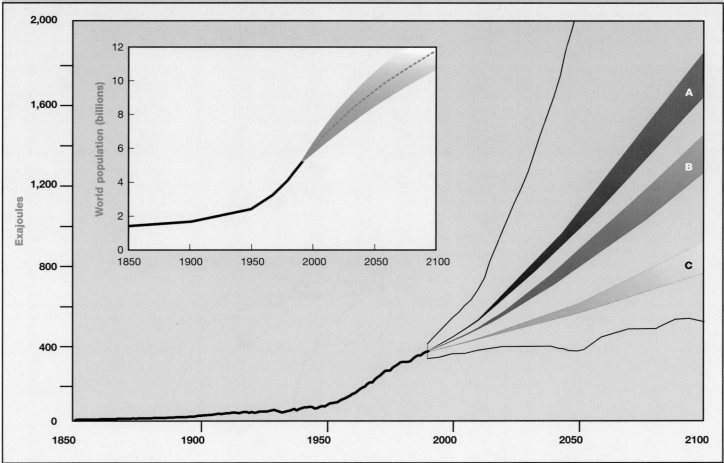

FIGURE 9.3 GLOBAL PRIMARY ENERGY REQUIREMENTS, 1850–1990, AND IN THREE CASES, 1990–2100

The figure also shows the wide range of future energy requirements for other scenarios in the literature. The vertical line that spans the scenario range in 1990 indicates the uncertainty across the literature of base-year energy requirements. The insert shows global population growth, 1850–2000, and projections to 2100. *Source: Nakićenović, Grübler, and McDonald, 1998; Morita and Lee, 1998; Nakićenović, Victor, and Morita, 1998; Bos and Vu, 1994.*

indeed large, from a decline in the lowest scenario to an increase of 10 times in the highest. In absolute terms, the increase by 2100 in primary energy requirements—in comparison with 379 exajoules in 1990—is expected to range from a moderate increase, to 500 exajoules, to almost 3,200 exajoules. The highest energy requirements correspond to an annual growth rate of 2 percent, exactly in line with historical experience (since 1850; see figure 9.3). Also in line with historical experience, many scenarios project a growing demand for fossil energy, even if relative shares might be declining relative to alternative sources of energy. This again emphasises the need for continuing improvement in all energy efficiencies, including clean fossil fuels. The three IIASA-WEC scenarios cover a significant part of the full range of primary energy consumption spanned by other scenarios in the literature.

Finally, the inset in figure 9.3 shows the global population projections common to all IIASA-WEC scenarios. C1 leads to roughly constant per capita primary energy consumption during the 21st century and

describes a transition towards more equity and lower environmental impacts. But it assumes implementation of challenging policies, such as world-wide energy and carbon taxes, that will change current development trends. In contrast A3 leads to a higher increase—by 2.5 times—in per capita energy requirements, but it shows that vigorous structural change of the energy system towards decarbonisation can lead to low environmental impacts, even in conjunction with very high levels of economic development and energy needs. The high rates of decarbonisation are, however, not sufficient to offset increased energy demand, so the total carbon emissions with A3 are substantially higher than those with C. Reference case B indicates energy needs in the median range relative to the other two alternatives (A and C) and the scenario literature in general, but it falls short of the transitions described in the other three more sustainable alternatives.

Alternative structures of future energy systems are capable of meeting this growing demand for higher-quality energy end use and services. Despite all the variations the scenarios look quite similar

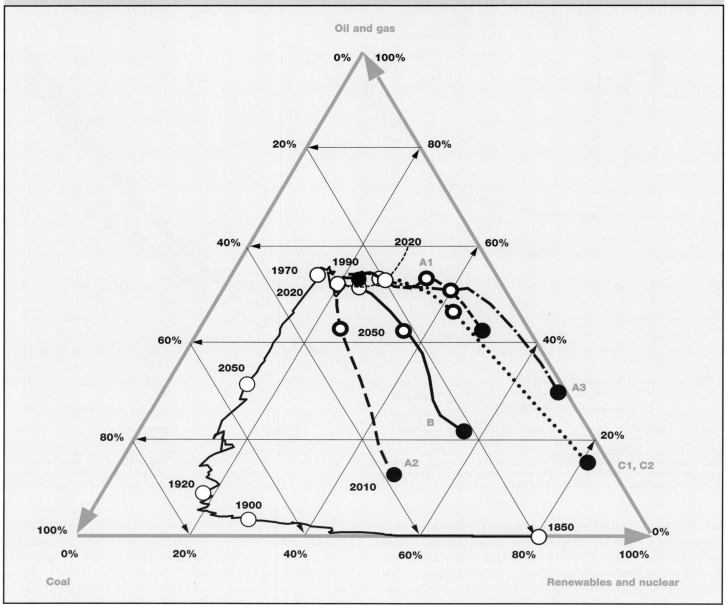

Shares are measured against the grid lines with percentages shown on the three axes; see text for explanation of the figure.

Source: Nakićenović, Grübler, and McDonald, 1998.

through 2020, and all still rely on fossil fuels. But after 2020 the scenarios diverge, and the energy transitions of the three more sustainable scenarios undergo a similar degree of structural change in the energy system.

The roles of different primary energy sources, which vary across the six scenarios, contribute to this divergence. Some continue to be fossil fuel intensive; others envisage stronger shifts towards alternative sources such as renewables or nuclear power. The geophysical availability of energy resources is not a major constraint, even though currently estimated conventional oil and gas reserves would soon be depleted across most of the scenarios. Instead the availability of energy resources and the rates at which they are converted into reserves are a function of the envisaged development strategies in the scenarios. Part of the divergence in the structures of energy systems depends on policy choices and development strategies. For example, the two case C scenarios that assume strong international cooperation focused on environmental protection through energy and carbon taxes rely much less on fossil fuel than do the other scenarios. Figure 9.4 illustrates this long-term divergence in the structures of energy systems across the scenarios.

Each corner of the triangle in figure 9.4 represents a hypothetical situation in which all primary energy is supplied by a single energy source: oil and gas on the top, coal on the lower left, and renewables and nuclear energy on the lower right. Nuclear energy and renewables are grouped together because they are in principle the non-fossil energy alternatives available in the longer term. The illustration shows the historical development of the global energy system starting in the 1850s, when most primary energy needs were met by traditional (renewable) sources of energy, such as wood and animal power, which in some cases are still harnessed in an unsustainable manner—contributing to about 10 percent of deforestation and other adverse impacts (chapters 3, 5, and 7).

The first transition in the historical development of the global energy system, which lasted about 70 years, from 1850 to 1920, involved the substitution of coal for traditional energy sources. The share of traditional non-fossil energy sources declined from about 80 to 20 percent during this period, while the share of coal increased from 20 to more than 70 percent. The next transition has also lasted about 70 years, from 1920 to the present. It involves the substitution of oil and gas for coal. The share of coal has declined to about 30 percent, while the share of oil and gas has increased to about 50 percent.

Figure 9.4 illustrates alternative development paths in the structure of the energy system that might characterise the next transition. Scenarios branch out after 2020. Some become coal intensive, such as reference case B and high-growth A2. Others are more renewable and nuclear intensive, such as the more sustainable A3 and ecologically driven C1 and C2. All the scenarios eventually lead to a partial shift from fossil fuels to other sources of energy; however, they follow alternative development paths. As the paths spread out, they form diverging future developments. To some extent they are mutually exclusive.

Most of the divergence after 2020 will depend on technological developments and industrial strategies implemented between now and then. Which energy sources in 2020 will best match the more flexible, more convenient, cleaner forms of energy desired by consumers? Which firms will have made the investments in research and development that will give them a technological edge? And which will have refocused their operations away from merely providing tonnes of coal or kilowatt-hours of electricity and towards offering better energy services to consumers?

The answers to these questions will be determined between now and 2020. Near-term investment decisions and efforts in technology research and development will determine which of the alternative development paths will dominate the post-2020 period. For example, the scenarios have the same assumptions about fossil and nuclear energy resources and renewable energy potentials (chapter 5). But their use differs across the scenarios, and these differences tend to be amplified after 2020. Because of the long lifetimes of infrastructure, power plants, refineries, and other energy investments, there will not be a sufficiently large turnover of such facilities to reveal large differences in the scenarios before 2020. But the seeds of the post-2020 world will have been sown by then. Figure 9.4 illustrates that the achievement of a more sustainably structured energy system should be seen as a cumulative, evolutionary process: It needs to be initiated early to allow for the long time constants required for fundamental transitions, such as a shift to cleaner fossil fuels, renewables, and possibly nuclear energy.

Long-term global energy futures are no longer seen as being geologically preordained. The imminent resource scarcity forecast in the 1970s did not materialise. With continued exploration efforts and technological progress, accessible and affordable reserves have increased, and this trend is likely to continue. After 2020 all scenarios move away from their current reliance on conventional oil and gas. As mentioned, the currently estimated conventional oil and gas reserves do not reach much into the post-2020 periods in any of the scenarios (chapter 5). This transition progresses relatively slowly in scenario A1, where oil and gas are plentiful. In the more sustainable scenarios, A3, C1 and C2, it progresses more rapidly because of faster technological progress towards cleaner fossil energy systems (A3) or because energy and environmental policies favour non-fossil alternatives (C1 and C2).

An ecologically driven clean-fossil version of case C is also conceivable. Such a third C variant (C3) would incorporate most of the environmentally compatible fossil energy conversion system together with decarbonisation and carbon removal and storage. But such a scenario was not developed, for two reasons. First, A3 already includes clean and efficient fossil energy technologies, along with some carbon removal and its use for enhanced oil recovery. Thus limited carbon removal and sequestration occur for economic reasons and are competitive with other options for enhanced oil recovery. But additional carbon removal, although technically possible, is expensive and thus would require introducing carbon taxes or emissions limits. In A3 cumulative carbon emissions are about 1,000 gigatonnes for 1990–2100. Thus that amount of carbon— about 50 percent more than now in the atmosphere—would need to be stored. Disposal in geological reservoirs is possible; however, the amounts involved are gigantic, and affordable disposal and storage systems still need to be developed (chapter 8). Second, the advantage of an ecologically driven clean-fossil version of case C would basically be very similar to A3 but would have the advantage of requiring storage of much less carbon, but still a very large amount, comparable to the current carbon dioxide in the atmosphere.

In scenario A2 and reference case B, the transition away from oil and gas includes an important contribution from coal, whose long-

The achievement of a more sustainably structured energy system needs to be initiated early to allow for the long time constants required for fundamental transitions to cleaner fuels.

term market share after 2050 is 20–40 percent. Nonetheless little of this coal is used directly. Instead it is converted to high-quality energy carriers (electricity, liquids, and gases) demanded by high-income consumers after 2050. Thus very different resource and technological options can be drawn upon to meet the cleaner energy being demanded by more and more affluent consumers world-wide.

Technological dynamics and structural change
Technology is the key determinant of economic development and is essential for raising standards of living and for easing humanity's burden on the environment (Grübler, 1998b). Because technological progress is based on human ingenuity, it is thus a human-made resource that is renewable—as long as it is nurtured. But this nurture has a price. Innovation, especially the commercialisation of novel technologies and processes, requires continual investments of effort and money in research, development, and demonstration (RD&D). Technology diffusion, in turn, depends on both RD&D and learning by doing. Some advanced technologies important in the scenarios—such as hydrogen production, distribution, and end use—would be radical innovations that are not likely to result from incremental improvement of current technologies. And without investment and experience, there can be no long-term technological improvement, either through incremental or radical change.

Innovation and technology diffusion require both that opportunities are perceived and that the entrepreneurial spirit exists to pursue them. Long-term scenarios cannot forecast future technological 'winners' or 'losers', but they can indicate areas of technological opportunity. Figure 9.5 illustrates the global market potential in the IIASA-WEC scenarios for four classes of energy technologies: new end-use energy devices (efficient lighting, heat pumps), power plants, synfuel production (from biomass, coal, and natural gas), and energy transport, transmission, and distribution infrastructure. For each of the four classes of technologies, the minimum, maximum, and average market potential for the six scenarios are shown in 2020, 2050, and 2100.

Across the wide variation in possible energy developments depicted in the scenarios, the importance of energy infrastructure grows persistently. Even in the sustainable, low-demand scenarios of case C (C1 and C2), energy infrastructure delivers at least 400 exajoules a year by 2050. By the end of the century it averages 800 exajoules a year across all scenarios, reaching close to 1,600 exajoules a year in the highest scenarios. The markets for power sector technologies also grow substantially, with a wide spread between the maximum and minimum scenarios. By 2050 the annual range is 120–560 exajoules (energy delivered). Part of this spread is due to uncertainties about demand growth, but part arises from energy end-use innovations in the form of new, on-site decentralised electricity generation technologies, such as photovoltaics or fuel cells. The potential for decentralised systems in the long term outgrows

Long-term scenarios cannot forecast future technological 'winners' or 'losers', but they can indicate areas of technological opportunity.

that of the power sector. The most important customers for energy technologies would no longer be a limited number of utility managers but rather millions of energy consumers world-wide. Synfuels also emerge in the long term as a major technology market. An orderly transition away from conventional oil and gas translates into large technology markets for synliquids, syngas—and, in the long term, increasing shares of hydrogen produced from both fossil fuels (coal and natural gas) and renewables (biomass). By 2100 the global synfuels market could be at least 160 exajoules a year, comparable to the current global oil market.

As noted above, technological progress has a price—it requires continual investment in RD&D. All the technological improvements in the scenarios that are reflected in the expansion of all technology categories shown in figure 9.5 presume steady RD&D investment. Given the importance of strategic investment in RD&D, it is a cause for concern that energy-related RD&D expenditures are currently declining in most OECD countries. Evidently upfront RD&D expenditures are increasingly viewed as too expensive in markets where maximising short-term shareholder value takes precedence over longer-term socioeconomic development and environmental protection.

The important conclusion from this analysis of IIASA-WEC scenarios is that far-reaching technological improvements (chapters 6–8) are central to the transition towards sustainable development and thus need to be developed and disseminated throughout the energy system—including to decentralised systems and end users. Perhaps this is not surprising because end use is the least efficient part of the whole energy system. These possible developments have two important implications. First, they weaken the argument for extensive RD&D investment in large, sophisticated, 'lumpy', inflexible technologies such as fusion power and centralised solar thermal power plants. Improvements in end-use technologies, through which millions, rather than hundreds, of units are produced and used, are more amenable to standardisation, modularisation, and mass production, and hence to benefit from learning-curve effects (resulting in cost reductions and performance improvements). Second, institutional arrangements governing final energy use and supply are critical. The deregulation, reregulation, and liberalisation of electricity markets can create incentives in this direction; service packages can be tailored to various consumer preferences, especially because traditional consumers can sell electricity back to the grid. But liberalisation could discourage long-term RD&D by emphasising short-term profits.

The structure of final energy requirements
In virtually all energy scenarios in the literature, economic growth outpaces the increase in energy consumption, leading to substantial reductions in energy intensities and efficiencies. This is to a large extent due to technological change and structural changes towards less materials-intensive, more knowledge-intensive activities. As individual technologies are developed and enter the marketplace,

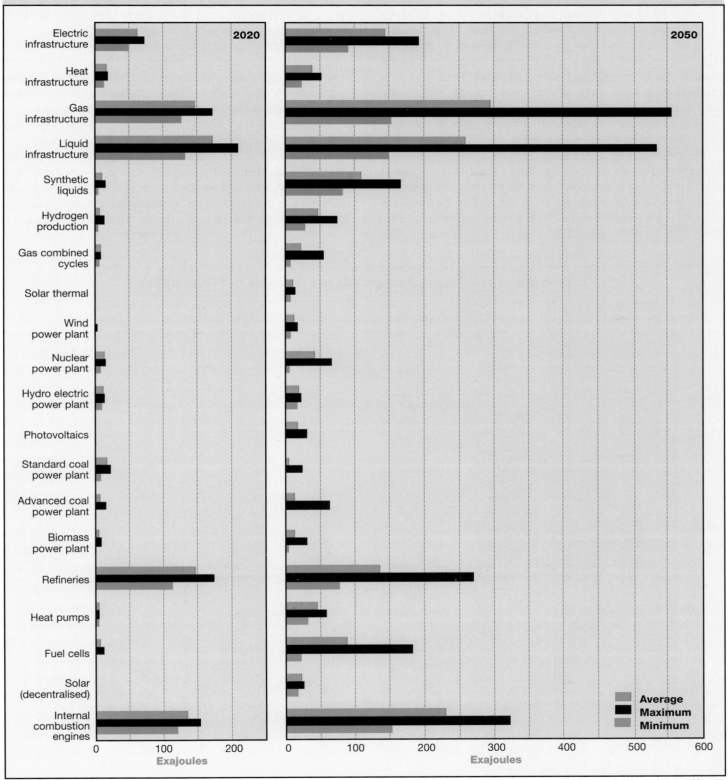

FIGURE 9.5. GLOBAL MARKET POTENTIALS FOR POWER PLANTS, SYNFUEL PRODUCTION, NEW END-USE ENERGY DEVICES, AND ENERGY INFRASTRUCTURE ACROSS SIX SCENARIOS, 2020 AND 2050

Source: Nakićenović, Grübler, and McDonald, 1998.

inefficient technologies are replaced by more efficient ones, and the structure of the energy-supply system and patterns of energy services change. These factors reduce the amount of primary energy needed per unit of final energy delivered to end users, as well as final energy per unit energy service. With all other factors being equal, the faster economic growth, the higher the rate of technological change, the higher the turnover of capital, and the greater the decline in energy intensity and improvement of energy efficiency. These long-term relationships between energy efficiency and economic development are reflected in the majority of scenarios in the literature and are consistent with historical experience across a range of alternative development paths in different countries.

The scenarios cover a wide range of energy supply possibilities to meet growing energy requirements, from a tremendous expansion of coal production to strict limits on it, from a phase-out of nuclear energy to a substantial increase in its use. Yet all the variations explored in the alternative scenarios match the continuing need for more flexible, more convenient, cleaner forms of energy. This means that all energy is increasingly converted into quality carriers such as electricity, liquids, and energy gases. For example, the direct end use of solids by final consumers disappears by 2050. Solid energy sources are more and more converted into liquids and gird-oriented energy carriers such as energy gases and electricity.

Thus despite all the variations in major driving forces of energy end use across a wide range of scenarios, the pattern of final energy use is remarkably consistent across many scenarios that describe sustainable energy development. Figure 9.6 illustrates the convergence in the structure of final energy for the IIASA-WEC scenarios.

As shown in figure 9.6, all six scenarios portray a pervasive shift from energy being used in its original form, such as traditional direct uses of coal and biomass, to elaborate systems of energy conversion and delivery. This shift continues in all cases, leading to ever more sophisticated energy systems and higher-quality energy carriers. A second profound transformation is the increasing delivery of energy by dedicated transport infrastructure, such as pipelines and electric networks. This development enhances trade possibilities and

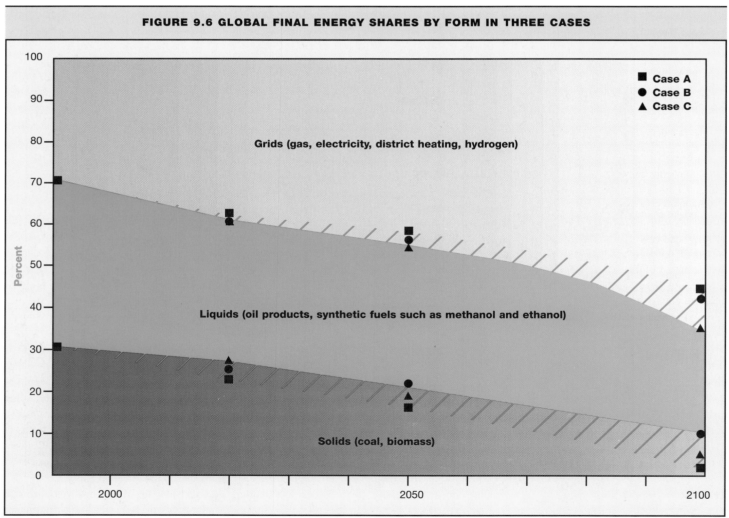

FIGURE 9.6 GLOBAL FINAL ENERGY SHARES BY FORM IN THREE CASES

- ■ Case A
- ● Case B
- ▲ Case C

Grids (gas, electricity, district heating, hydrogen)

Liquids (oil products, synthetic fuels such as methanol and ethanol)

Solids (coal, biomass)

Percent

2000 2050 2100

Solids include direct delivery to end users. Overlapping areas indicate variations across the cases.

Source: Nakićenović, Grübler, and McDonald, 1998.

promotes similar end-use patterns across regions with fundamentally different primary energy supply structures. Third, changes in final energy patterns reflect the changes in economic structure presented in the scenarios. As incomes increase, the share of transport, residential, and commercial applications also increases.

These converging final energy patterns yield substantial quality improvements in the energy (and energy services) delivered to the consumer. Quality improvements are measured by two indicators: fuel-mix-induced efficiency gains and the carbon intensity of final energy. The efficiency of final energy use improves as the final energy carrier portfolio changes in the direction of higher-quality fuels. The effect is an improvement via inter-fuel substitution of 20–30 percent. The actual end-use efficiency gains are of course much larger, for they are mostly driven by technological change in end-use devices (cars, light bulbs, and so on). The main points are that more efficient end-use devices will require higher-quality fuels, and there is a high degree of congruence across all six scenarios. Thus whereas primary energy supply structures and resulting carbon intensities diverge in the IIASA-WEC scenarios, those of final energy converge. The decarbonisation trend of final energy relative to primary energy is also faster across all the cases.

These energy developments are characteristic of many sustainable scenarios. The use of non-commercial final energy generally disappears, while industrial and transport energy shares generally grow, largely due to an enormous increase in industrial production and mobility in developing countries. In industrialised regions, however, residential and commercial energy needs generally grow faster than those for industry. Growth of mobility, especially in developing regions, is one of the pervasive changes across all the scenarios. Even in industrialised countries, transport energy requirements grow faster than any other final energy use. The share of final energy for transportation increases from one-fifth today to a third in the case A scenarios and to a quarter in the case C scenarios. The increase is more modest in C scenarios because of their orientation towards public rather than individual transport and towards partial replacement of mobility through communication. With high levels of affluence and leisure, new services and new activities emerge that shift final energy requirements away from materials- and energy-intensive production. The demographic changes associated with ageing and single-person households reinforce this trend in such scenarios.

As noted, some scenarios describe less-intensive mobility and urbanisation developments. This is true for the case C scenarios that foresee a stronger shift towards decentralised energy systems and reliance on local solutions. Final energy needs in the residential and commercial sector increase to more than half of all final energy after 2050. Mobility and materials-intensive production are replaced by communication and services, resulting in lower material and energy intensities. This leads to significant differences across regions and scenarios in the end-use devices that are used and in

how they are used (that is, lifestyles), even when differences in total final energy demand are small. This points to an important but still poorly understood and thus weak interaction between lifestyles and energy services. An illustration is given in the IIASA-WEC study, which contrasts the three high-growth A scenarios for Latin America with the ecologically driven C scenario for Western Europe. Both regions have a strong tradition of detailed analyses of energy end use and associated lifestyle changes (Goldemberg and others, 1988; Schipper and Meyers, 1992; IEA, 1993).

Temporal and spatial scales of scenarios

Energy scenarios in the literature cover a wide range of time horizons, from 10–20 to more than 100 years. Sustainable energy scenarios usually have long time horizons. The inertia of energy systems is high, so it takes decades before a shift away from reliance on fossil energy sources can be achieved in sustainable scenarios. Major exceptions are some of the recent studies of policies and measures for meeting the carbon emission targets specified in the Kyoto Protocol (UNFCCC, 1992). The protocol calls for the reduction of emissions in industrialised countries (so-called Annex I under the UNFCCC) by about 5 percent relative to the base year 1990 during the 2008–12 period (UNFCCC, 1997). A number of scenarios in the literature (such as IEA, 1998) focus on this time period and on achieving emission reductions. Some of these scenarios would presumably lead to sustainable development in the long run, assuming that structural change towards clean fossil and non-fossil energy continues.

Generally, however, most scenarios that describe sustainable development have long time horizons, usually extending for 100 years. They make up an important share of all long-term energy scenarios. They share a number of features with other long-term scenarios that are significantly different from those of short-term scenarios. In general the longer the time horizon, the lower the likely growth rates of driving forces and energy need. This tendency is probably linked to the fundamental difference between short- and long-term scenarios. Short-term scenarios are often national or regional and frequently describe energy options that may be overly optimistic from a global perspective. In contrast long-term scenarios are often global and focus on possibilities that might be more limited than regional expectations.

The variability and uncertainty of regional and global scenarios also tend to increase with higher temporal and spatial resolutions. Thus over longer periods and larger areas, developments tend to average out, leading to lower variations and uncertainties. If this is generally true, then it means that the future is more open at higher scales of spatial and temporal resolution, requiring a larger portfolio of alternative scenarios to cover the range of possibilities.

Spatial phenomena are therefore important for developing and interpreting scenarios. For example, many scenario environmental impacts require a detailed regional resolution. Many environmental phenomena require that scenario driving forces, energy use, and emissions be gridded with a very high spatial resolution. Very few scenarios and modelling approaches are based on a fine geographic scale. Thus, for a number of reasons, national or regional spatial scales are not always ideal for energy scenarios. But such scenarios are rare due to many unresolved methodological issues. With current methodological approaches, energy-related spatial phenomena are more difficult to capture on the global scale than evolution in time.

There are, of course, exceptions. Recent scenarios by Sørensen, Kuemmel, and Meibom (1999) have high geographic resolution for driving forces as well as energy use patterns (box 9.2). The scenarios highlight the uneven geographic distribution of economic activities, resources, and energy patterns—and also bring new insights into energy trade implications, energy infrastructure, and transport. For example, the scenarios that rely on clean fossil fuel and safe nuclear energy options entail trade and transmission of energy in much the same pattern as today. This situation has important implications for economic development in energy-importing countries that may have lower economic growth relative to other scenarios with more self-sufficient domestic provision of energy. The scenarios demonstrate that focusing on decentralised, renewable energy sources with low energy densities would make it difficult to match energy demand growth in some parts of the world by 2050. In contrast scenarios that also rely on centrally produced renewable energy create supply in excess of demand and through trade foster robust energy systems and low adverse environmental impacts (Sørensen, Kuemmel, and Meibom, 1999).

The legacy of past generations

Energy scenarios explore the future and rarely look at the past. But the dynamics of history matter for future developments. This is especially relevant to scenarios that achieve sustainability for future generations. Equity often plays an important role in such considerations.

This is in stark contrast to our common history. Both in the past and today, a small minority of the global population accounts for most economic activity, materials use, and mobility, just to mention a few driving forces of energy use. Thus most energy is consumed by a relatively small, affluent part of the global population that lives in industrialised countries; this 20 percent of the population enjoys about 80 percent of gross world product (see figure 9.1) and more than 60 percent of global energy consumption. Historically, today's affluent part of the global population has consumed about 80 percent of fossil energy. Its many benefits from this consumption include enormous economic development. But many of the adverse environmental and other impacts of this cumulative energy consumption have been shared with the rest of the world.

Most sustainable energy scenarios envisage a fundamental change in the future from today's inequitable distribution of benefits and adverse impacts. The scenarios use various methods to implement policies to move global development towards sustainability. For example, the IIASA-WEC case C scenarios assume revenue-neutral energy and carbon dioxide taxes whose proceeds enhance international collaboration and resource transfers from industrialised to developing regions. This situation may appear unrealistic from the current

---

BOX 9.2. SPATIAL SCENARIO OF ENERGY END USE

Sørensen, Kuemmel, and Meibom (1999) give an example of an energy scenario that emphasises demand-side management, high levels of energy efficiency, and conservation while attaining high levels of global prosperity. It assumes that average energy technology efficiency in 2050 will correspond to the best current rates. This results in total global energy end-use demand of about 220 exajoules in 2050. The scenario is thus characterised by relatively low energy requirements relative to the increase in per capita energy use. The energy available to the end user today is only about 12 percent of primary energy, and the challenge is to increase this fraction. The resulting energy requirements are roughly half those in the IIASA-WEC case C scenarios. Population assumptions are about the same. Sørensen, Kuemmel, and Meibom (1999) base their scenario on UN median population projections (UN, 1996) and UN increasing urbanisation estimates (UN, 1997).

A unique feature of the scenario is a very high geographic resolution (using the middle scenario of UN, 1996), increasing urbanisation (UN, 1997), and an increase from today's per capita energy use by an average factor of 2.7. GNP growth is larger because of the de-coupling of economic and energy growth, and the distribution of this growth across regions is not even (because a higher growth rate is assumed for today's poor regions). Figure below shows the 'gridded' total energy delivered to end users in 2050.

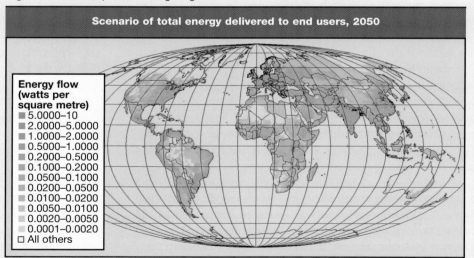

Scenario of total energy delivered to end users, 2050

Energy flow (watts per square metre)
- 5.0000–10
- 2.0000–5.0000
- 1.0000–2.0000
- 0.5000–1.0000
- 0.2000–0.5000
- 0.1000–0.2000
- 0.0500–0.1000
- 0.0200–0.0500
- 0.0100–0.0200
- 0.0050–0.0100
- 0.0020–0.0050
- 0.0001–0.0020
- All others

Note: Includes energy for air conditioning, process heat, stationary mechanical energy, electric energy, energy for transportation, and energy in food. The average energy demand is about 23 gigajoules per capita, or three times the amount made useful at the end use today.

Source: Sørensen, Juemmel, and Meibom, 1999.

---

perspective, but it was necessary to achieve both rapid development of poor regions and environmental protection. Another example is the so-called B1 family of sustainable scenarios (developed by different modelling approaches) for the IPCC *Special Report on Emissions Scenarios* (Nakićenović and others, 2000) that all achieve equity through a host of policy and behavioural changes in the world, along with improvements of environmental compatibility at all scales (De Vries and others, 2000). Thus sustainable energy scenarios require challenging changes.

The role of policies

Sustainable energy scenarios usually assume or imply a host of measures to achieve their goals, from a transition from fossil energy sources to adoption of environmentally friendly behaviour patterns. The policies include market-based and regulatory mechanisms as well as assumed changes in human behaviour (chapter 12). Regulatory standards, taxes, and emissions trading schemes are comparatively easy to implement in scenarios developed using formal models. But it is much more difficult to determine what measures would be required to achieve the behavioural and institutional changes called for in such scenarios. One example from recent IPCC scenarios is given here for illustrative purposes (Nakićenović and others, 2000).

The IPCC B1 scenario family includes many characteristics of sustainable development. Its storyline or narrative description calls for extensive changes (for further details see the Website at http://sres.ciesin.org; http://www.ipcc.ch; http://www.iiasa.ac.at/Research/TNT/Draft/Publications/publications.html; De Vries and others, 2000; Nakićenović and others, 2000; and Nakićenović, 2000). The storyline assumes a high level of environmental consciousness and institutional effectiveness. Consequently environmental quality is high because most of the potentially negative environmental aspects of rapid development are anticipated and dealt with effectively at local, national, and international levels. For example, transboundary air pollution (acid rain) is basically eliminated in the long term. Land use is carefully managed to counteract the impacts of activities that could damage the environment. Cities are compact and designed for public and non-motorised transport, and suburban developments are tightly controlled. Strong incentives for low-input, low-impact agriculture, along with maintenance of large areas of wilderness, contribute to high food prices with much lower levels of meat consumption.

These proactive local and regional environmental measures and policies also lead to relatively low energy requirements and low emissions, even in the absence of explicit interventions directed at conserving energy or mitigating climate change. The IPCC B1 world invests a large part of its gains in more efficient resource use ('dematerialisation'), greater equity, stronger social institutions, and increased environmental protection. A strong welfare net prevents social exclusion on the basis of poverty. But the storyline also considers

> Most sustainable energy scenarios envisage a fundamental change in the future from today's inequitable distribution of benefits and adverse impacts.

that counter-currents may develop, and in some places people may not conform to the main social and environmental intentions of the mainstream in this scenario family. Massive income redistribution and presumably high taxes may adversely affect the functioning of world markets. Environmental protection could become an issue in some parts of the world. This all illustrates how achieving sustainable development is a very difficult task—even in scenarios—as new policies play out in relation to other driving forces.

Other examples of strong policies can be seen in nearly all sustainable development scenarios. The "Transformed World" of Hammond (1998), based on the "Great Transitions" of Gallopin and others (1997), stresses the role of global technological innovation in addition to enlightened corporate actions, government policies, and empowerment of local groups. In the "Shared Space" of the Millennium Institute (Glenn and Gordon, 1997), resources are shared more equitably for the benefit of all and the safety of humanity. The Shell "Sustainable World" (1996, 1998) and the WBCSD (1998) "Geopolity" and "Jazz" also examine sustainable futures.

Implications of sustainable energy scenarios

The divergence among the three cases described in this chapter reflects different assumptions for a number of driving forces of future development, such as demographic changes and economic growth. Assumptions about future technological change are the most important determinants of how the scenarios unfold. These assumptions include the effectiveness of RD&D and the direction and rate of technological diffusion (including lock-in effects and learning curves). Future capital investments and financing are also crucial determinants of future energy development, as are global energy trade patterns. Finally the impact of environmental changes at local, regional, and global levels will also drive change and energy developments.

RD&D trends and requirements and technological diffusion

The development of clean, efficient, affordable, reliable energy systems is a common characteristic of most sustainable energy scenarios. An important prerequisite for such future technology developments is sufficient investment in RD&D. But this alone is not a guarantee for success. Radically new technologies need to be introduced into the marketplace and (if successful) need to be pervasively diffused to contribute to sustainability. Incremental improvement of existing technologies is likely to fall short of changing technoeconomic paradigms, as is foreseen in the three scenarios characterised by sustainability. In fact, all these scenarios rely on pervasive diffusion, over a long time period, of new technoeconomic systems in the energy system—from a combination of advanced, highly efficient energy extractions, to conversion and end-use technologies, to new, clean energy carriers such as hydrogen.

These technology needs for achieving sustainability are in stark contrast to recent developments. RD&D efforts have increased substantially in most OECD countries. But energy-related RD&D has declined in all of them except Japan and Switzerland. In share of GDP, energy-related efforts may have declined by as much as 10 percent a year on average in OECD countries. It has been argued that this decline in public RD&D funding is more than compensated for by private sources as a consequence of recent energy privatisation and liberalisation. But the tentative evidence indicates that this is not necessarily true for investments in radical new technologies, and that private-sector energy RD&D focuses more on incrementally improving technologies and may be declining. For example, private energy-related RD&D has fallen by nearly a third in the United States during the past five years, while RD&D in other sectors has increased (chapter 12).

Finally, it has been claimed that the deployment of new energy technologies has occurred at an unprecedented rate in recent years despite the declines in RD&D funding. This is supposed to indicate that there are plenty of funds available for attractive new technologies. Perhaps this is true, but many of the energy technologies that have been deployed successfully in recent years—from combined-cycle gas turbine to horizontal drilling—were developed long ago, when RD&D funding was plentiful. There also have been important spillovers from other sectors; for example, the development of gas turbines benefited from enormous progress on both military and civilian jet engines. But new competitive pressures have probably contributed to price declines and wide diffusion of these technologies.

A strong conclusion for a whole range of sustainable scenarios is that a substantial increase in RD&D for new energy technologies is needed. Otherwise most clean, efficient fossil and renewable technologies may not reach competitiveness with traditional options. Significant improvements in these technologies are required as traditional technologies improve as well. This is not, however, an appeal to return to the types of exclusively public expenditure programs on energy RD&D of past decades. The paradigm has shifted now towards a balance between publicly and privately funded basic research and towards far more reliance on incentives to promote private RD&D and market applications, for example through tax and regulatory incentives for innovation.

These kinds of advances in knowledge and technology are likely to be as important for achieving a sustainable future as they were for explaining the productivity growth in today's industrialised countries. In the original study by Solow (1956) it was estimated that 87 percent of per capita productivity growth was due to technological change (the remainder was attributed to increases in capital inputs). The contribution of technical progress to pollution abatement is even greater: as the chapters on energy technology (7 and 8) and the economy (11) show, innovations in pollution control can often cut emissions by 95 percent, and potentially completely in some cases.

Technological diffusion occurs over a long period of time, from a new technology's first introduction to its pervasive adoption.

Advances in knowledge thus do not simply contribute to economic development in general but also help achieve a higher degree of affluence, equity, and environmental compatibility.

Economic growth theory suggests that different capital and labour productivities across countries lead to different productivity growth rates and hence to conditional convergence across economies. As Rostow (1990) explained, the "poor get richer and the rich slow down". This relative convergence of the poor and rich stems from the assumption of diminishing returns on capital. Additional convergence potentials may accrue for economies with a higher ratio of human to physical capital. In terms of a functional relationship for future developments, therefore, per capita GDP growth rates are expected (all other things being equal) to be higher for economies with low per capita GDP levels. Notwithstanding many frustrating setbacks like the recent 'lost decade' for economic catch-up in Africa and Latin America, empirical data indicate that the convergence theorem holds. The evidence put forward by Barro (1997) and Barro and Sala-I-Martin (1995), based on the experience of some 100 countries in 1960–85, shows per capita GDP growth rates as a function of GDP per capita levels after accounting for all other salient influencing variables (such as education, inflation, terms of trade, and institutional factors).

Many sustainable scenarios have in common this kind of relative economic convergence and catch-up between today's developing and industrialised regions in the next 100 years. The successful diffusion of new technologies and different consumption patterns are therefore important prerequisites for achieving sustainability in such scenarios.

With a few notable exceptions (for example, the scenario developed by Lazarus and others, 1993, and the case C scenarios presented in the IIASA-WEC study), the challenge of exploring conditions for closing the income gap between developing and industrialised regions appears to be a fundamental challenge for scenarios that describe sustainable development. Differential economic growth rates can close a part of this gap; the other part needs to be closed through additional measures ranging from accelerated rates of technological diffusion to more equitable income and resource distribution. For example, the C scenarios incorporate a challenging, broad portfolio of environmental control technologies and policies, including incentives to encourage energy producers and consumers to use energy more efficiently and carefully, 'green' taxes (levied on energy and carbon), international environmental and economic agreements, and technology transfer.

Case C reflects substantial resource transfers from industrialised to developing countries, which spur growth and eradicate poverty. Specifically, C assumes that energy and carbon taxes are applied universally, albeit at different rates and timing, and are revenue neutral. The proceeds from these taxes in OECD countries are recycled as resource transfers to developing countries and are used to promote energy infrastructure, clean technologies, efficiency, and conservation. Such transfers help solve part of the scenarios' development problem, which is fundamental for a sustainable world. Solving the other part of the problem entails revitalising international programs to address world poverty. These poverty alleviation aspects of achieving sustainability are implicit in the scenarios—and include investment in energy and environmental ends, but more important in education, health, security against natural disasters, and so forth.

Capital requirements and financing

Capital investment is crucial for energy development. Both the overall development of and structural changes in energy systems result from investments in plant, equipment, and energy infrastructure. Because adequate and affordable energy supplies are critical for economic growth, any difficulties in attracting capital for energy investment can slow economic development, especially in the least developed countries, where 2 billion people have yet to gain access to commercial energy services. And—although energy investment accounts for only a small share of the global capital market—the availability of the capital needed for a growing energy sector cannot be taken for granted but depends on prices and regulations that permit investors to earn rates of return that are competitive with other opportunities offered by international capital markets. This is especially the case for sustainable development paths, which require high levels of investment in new technologies and conservation measures that may not be initially competitive with their traditional counterparts.

Capital markets have been growing faster than total GDP for quite some time, and this trend is unlikely to change. Present annual global energy investments are approximately 7 percent of international credit financing of about $3.6 trillion (Hanke, 1995). With capital markets growing relative to GDP, and assuming largely stable future energy investment ratios, capital market size does not appear to be a limiting factor for energy sector finance today and is not likely to be one across a wide range of scenarios.

Very few scenarios in the literature give a detailed account of energy-related investments. Even fewer describe investments that will promote sustainable energy futures. Thus estimates of global capital requirements for energy development are often based on back-of-the-envelope calculations of aggregate energy investment indicators for several major energy-consuming countries that have been extrapolated to the rest of the world. These estimates tend to be highly influenced by present market realities and short-term market expectations and necessarily incorporate a number of ad hoc (and not necessarily consistent) assumptions about the relationship between income growth and energy requirements.

For example, if energy intensities are assumed to increase, capital requirements will, other things being equal, differ significantly from scenarios in which energy intensities decline. Investments are likely to grow faster than GDP in the former case and slower than GDP in the latter. Capital estimates also depend greatly on the assumed costs of different technologies, including infrastructure, and the projected energy mix. As a result, comparisons among estimates of

future investment requirements must recognise that each reflects a set of assumptions consistent with a specific energy-economy-environment scenario.

The IIASA-WEC scenarios provide a comprehensive assessment of energy-related investment requirements on the basis of detailed bottom-up cost calculations for the entire energy sector, extending from resource extraction (such as coal mining and oil exploration) through development and production to delivery of energy products to final consumers. The estimates of energy investments do not include, however, those required to achieve more efficient services or structural changes that lead to greater efficiencies. Each technology—an oil platform, gas pipeline, liquefied natural gas (LNG) terminal, electricity generating plant, district heat grid, and so forth—is characterised by a set of technoeconomic parameters, one of which is investment cost in dollars per unit of installed capacity. These costs are then aggregated into the total investment requirements for the entire energy sector. But because these cost estimates were derived during the 1990s (for the base year 1990), they do not reflect more recent changes, such as declines in energy costs.

A conclusion consistent across all six IIASA-WEC scenarios is that the capital requirements of the energy sector will be extremely large relative to current standards, but will not be infeasible. During the next 30 years capital requirements across the scenarios are estimated to be $12–17 trillion, measured at market exchange rates and 1998 dollars (or $10–15 trillion in 1990 dollars; this is to be compared with 1990 gross world product of about $20 trillion; see table 9.1). (In 2000–20, investment requirements are estimated to be $9–$13 trillion, 1998 dollars.) Figure 9.7 shows this range of cumulative

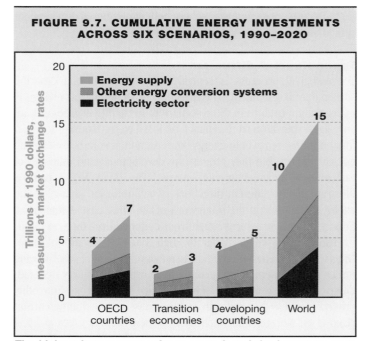

FIGURE 9.7. CUMULATIVE ENERGY INVESTMENTS ACROSS SIX SCENARIOS, 1990–2020

The highest investments refer to case A and the lowest to case C scenarios. *Source: Nakićenović, Grübler, and McDonald, 1998.*

global energy investment requirements between 1990 and 2020. They are desegregated into investments in the electricity sector, other energy conversion systems, and energy supply (extraction, upgrading, transmission, and distribution) for three major world regions; table 9.1 shows the cumulative investments for 2020–50 and 2050–2100. Note that capital requirements are lowest for the case C scenarios that describe sustainable development paths. These scenarios' relative advantage of substantially lower energy financing requirements is an important indicator of the high economic value of energy efficiency and conservation. But the costs of energy end-use changes are not included in the assessment.

As a share of GDP, global energy investments range from 1.5 to 1.9 percent across the scenarios. This is in line with historical norms: During the early 1990s investment averaged just over 1 percent of global GDP (ranging from $240–280 billion a year). In the scenarios they are highest in the transition economies of Europe and Asia, where they range up to 7–9 percent of GDP. These high investment needs are a legacy of the high energy intensity of the former centrally planned economies and recent declines in investment that went along with economic recession. The result is a substantial need to reconstruct and upgrade energy infrastructure. Another important aspect of future energy investment is that the share of developing regions rises sharply, from today's 25–30 percent to 42–48 percent, and these regions become the largest capital investment market in all scenarios.

Overall, energy investments in the scenarios decrease as a share of GDP throughout the world. But the challenge will be that an increasing fraction of capital requirements will need to be raised from the private sector, where energy needs will face stiffer competition and return-on-investment criteria. Also most investments must be made in developing countries, where both international development capital and private investment capital are often scarce.

Technological diffusion

Technological progress is central to all scenarios that describe sustainable development. The direction of technological change is of crucial importance in these scenarios. To varying degrees they all envisage a transition from reliance on fossil energy sources to clean fossil options, renewable energy sources, and in some cases to safe nuclear energy. But they require the development and diffusion of radical new technoeconomic systems. The IIASA-WEC scenarios illustrate this by different directions of technological change in the energy system within the framework of the three case A scenarios. Energy systems structures range from continued reliance on fossil-intensive development paths to high rates of decarbonisation. Otherwise the scenarios share the same development of other driving forces such as population, economic growth, and energy demand. Clearly the fossil-intensive scenarios do not meet sustainability criteria—unless they radically reduce emissions, including carbon removal and storage. Other implications of these alternative technological development paths are equally important. This illustrates that the direction of technological change can be as important for achieving

sustainable development as all other driving forces combined.

Technological diffusion occurs over a long period of time, from a new technology's first introduction to its pervasive adoption. For energy technologies diffusion time may range from 10–20 years all the way to 100 years. For example, the diffusion of motor vehicles or air conditioning systems usually takes 10–20 years. In contrast, the diffusion of new energy systems consisting of numerous individual technologies, such as a shift to renewable sources, might take almost 100 years. A principal conclusion of many sustainable energy scenarios is that the long-term transition to new energy technologies will largely be determined by technological choices made in the next 10–30 years. There is a need to anticipate technical characteristics—such as performance, cost, and diffusion—of new energy technologies such as photovoltaics, hydrogen production, and fuel cells; the long-term diffusion, transfer, and performance of these technologies depends on near-term RD&D and investment policies and decisions. If new technologies are not developed through dedicated RD&D efforts, they will not be diffused and will not be available when needed. Diffusion is an endogenous process. This illustrates path dependence in technological diffusion; because there is a virtual lock-in to the development path formed by many individual, related decisions, other possibilities are excluded (for example, see Grübler, 1998b).

These lock-in effects have two implications. First, early investments and early applications are extremely important in determining which technologies—and energy resources—will be most important in the future. This means that there needs to be an early investment in sustainable technologies if the sustainable development path is to be achieved. Second, learning and lock-in make technology transfer more difficult. This means that—in this context—the difference between diffusion and transfer disappears; they are parts of the same process. Successfully building and using computers, cars, and power plants depends as much on learning through hands-on experience as on design drawings and instruction manuals. And a technology that is tremendously productive when supported by complementary networks of suppliers, repair workers, training programs, and so forth, and by an infrastructure that has co-evolved with the technology, will be much less effective in isolation.

Technology costs and performance—including energy efficiency in particular—improve with experience, and there is a common pattern to such improvements for most technologies. This pattern of increasing returns to diffusion and transfer is important for the transition to sustainable energy futures, and it needs to be incorporated more explicitly into the scenarios.

In case A, there are substantial learning-curve effects for all new, and currently marginal, energy production and conversion technologies. These developments are consistent with the technological perspectives given in chapters 7 and 8. Thus there are considerable advances in hydrocarbon exploration, extraction, and conversion, carbon removal and storage, renewable and nuclear electricity generation, and hydrogen and biofuel production and conversion. For case B, the learning-curve effects are also substantial, especially for new, environmentally desirable technologies. But they lag on average 30 percent behind those in case A, which is consistent with the less concentrated RD&D efforts in case B. For case C, learning-curve effects by design favour low-carbon fossil and renewable technologies. These technologies benefit from improvements equal to those in case A. All other technologies develop as in case B.

International energy trade and security

Generally a lot of trade takes place in the scenarios, ranging from capital goods to energy. Energy-related trade in capital goods includes plant and equipment—required, for example, for the adoption of environmentally friendly technologies. So not only trade in energy is important in the scenarios. An analysis of the energy trade flows implied by the scenarios reveals a general decline in the share of primary energy (equivalent) that is traded world-wide. Currently about 18 percent of global primary energy is traded among the main world regions (as defined in the IIASA-WEC study). This is in close agreement with the true country-by-country figure

for 1990 of about 19 percent (Nakićenović, Grübler, and McDonald, 1998). Crude oil and oil products are currently dominant, accounting for 78 percent of global energy trade; coal accounts for 13 percent and natural gas for 9 percent. By 2050 primary energy traded declines to between 11 and 16 percent. In comparison, oil and gas imports to Western Europe were about 34 percent of primary energy consumption in 1990, and oil imports to North America were about 16 percent of primary energy consumption the same year. But absolute volumes continue to increase in the scenarios—up to a factor of 2.5 for case A and a factor of 1.7 for case B. The increase in case C is much lower, at 10–40 percent. Energy trade in case C is limited primarily to sustainable energy forms (such as biomass, methanol, ethanol, and to a lesser degree hydrogen) and actually shrinks beyond 2050. This indicates that even in case C scenarios world trade in oil and gas continues to increase, despite a shift towards stronger reliance on renewable energy sources throughout the new century.

FIGURE 9.8. OIL EXPORT QUANTITIES, PRICES, AND REVENUES FOR THE MIDDLE EAST AND NORTH AFRICA, 1963–96, AND IN SIX SCENARIOS, 2010–2050

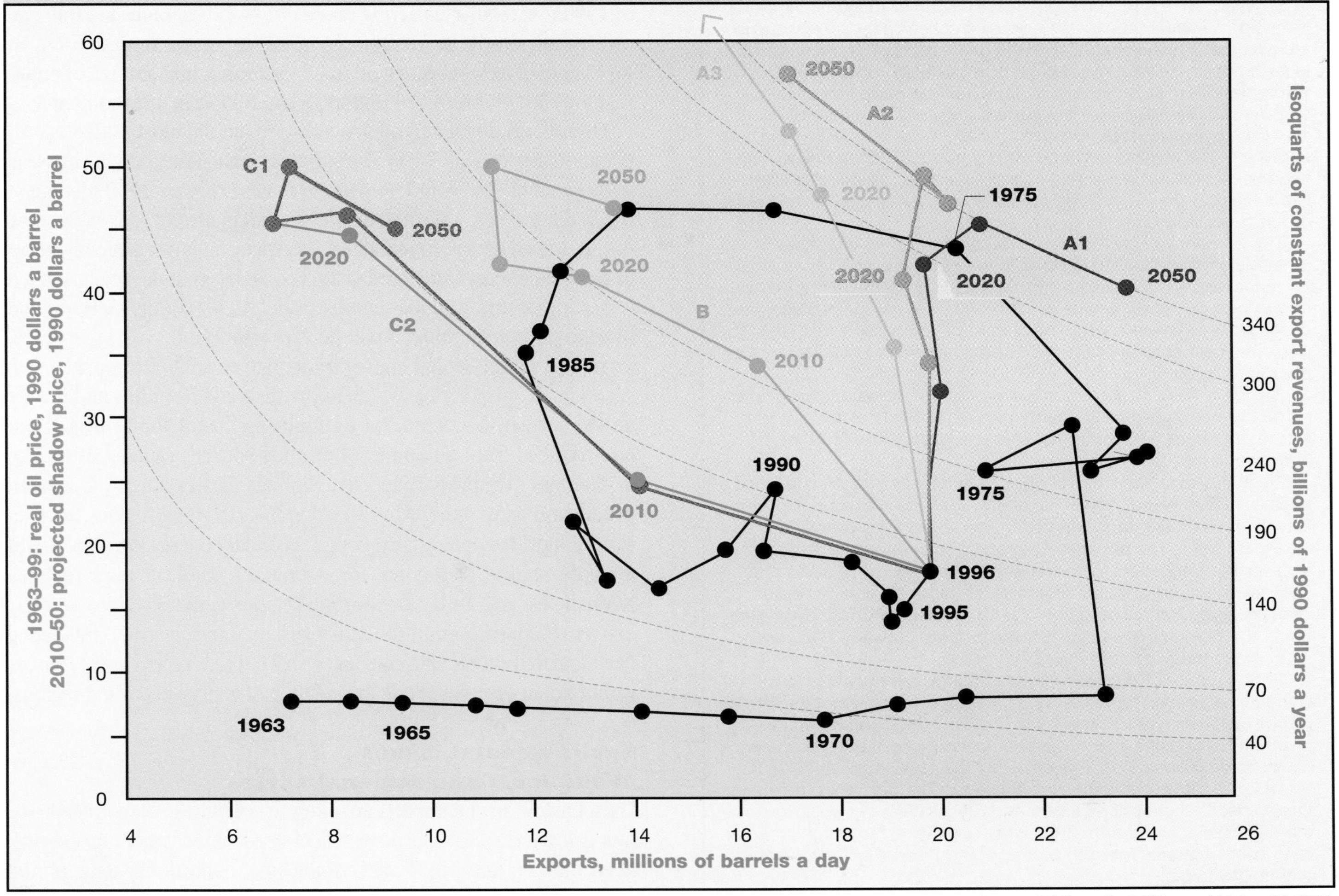

Source: Nakićenović, Grübler, and McDonald, 1998.

The overall geopolitical shift in energy use from industrialised regions to today's developing regions across all scenarios is also reflected in energy trade. In 1990 OECD imports accounted for 84 percent of international energy trade. By 2020 OECD-country shares drop to 55 percent in case C and 65 percent in case B, and by 2050 to 10 percent in case C and 34 percent in case A. This shift is likely to erode the current position of OECD countries as the dominant energy buyers. Conversely import security concerns, which traditionally have been strong in import-dependent Western Europe and Japan, will increasingly be shared by today's developing regions (chapter 4). Concerns about absolute import needs will also grow in developing countries in comparison with OECD countries.

The prospects for oil-exporting regions are bright in the long run

across all scenarios, and, at least through 2050, oil revenue is unlikely to be below $170 billion (in 1998 dollars) a year in the Middle East and North Africa. But there are differences among the three cases, as shown in figure 9.8. In case C, environmental policies reduce fossil fuel (that is, taxes and regulation) demand and cause declining exports, but rising export prices keep revenue constant. In cases A and B, technological change and the speed at which reserves are replenished from the resource base (chapter 5) determine export prices, export volumes, and revenues. In case A, greater technological progress than in case B enables higher export at slightly elevated export prices, and long-term revenues may exceed $360 billion (in 1998 dollars) annually. The slower the rate of technological change, the more important the price component becomes in revenue generation. Export volumes slip as reserves are replenished more slowly, prices rise, and revenues vary as a function of the scenario-specific oil substitution possibilities. Long-term export revenues for the region exceed $360 billion a year in case A and are at least $240 billion a year in case B, and thus are substantially higher than at present.

Another potential exporter of fossil energy is the former Soviet Union, where natural gas will be the principal energy export (box 9.3). Gas exports from this region increase for all scenarios, from 4 exajoules in 1990 to a relatively narrow range of 11–12 exajoules in 2020 and diverge afterwards across the scenarios, as shown in figure 9.9. By 2050 annual exports range up to 27 exajoules, and annual revenues reach $150 billion (1990 dollars; $180 billion in 1998 dollars).

Overall, crude oil and oil products remain the most traded energy commodities through 2050. The spread is quite large, ranging between 77 percent in case A and 33 percent in case C. After 2050 methanol, piped natural gas, LNG, and to a lesser extent also hydrogen become the key traded energy commodities. Electricity, an important component of regional energy trade, and is thus considered in the scenarios but is not important in global energy trade. As noted above, trade and investment in technologies will be very important.

In general the global energy trade pattern shifts from primary to secondary energy forms, which improves trade flexibility and lowers energy security concerns. For example, methanol and hydrogen can be produced from a number of primary sources ranging from coal to biomass (chapters 7 and 8). Biofuels and eventually hydrogen production leave more value added in the exporting regions than the export of primary energy. Exporting secondary energy forms becomes a staple source of income for a number of developing regions. Nevertheless oil- and gas-exporting regions generally increase their export revenues even in the more sustainable scenarios, indicating that improved energy efficiency and a shift towards other energy sources would not necessarily erode the position of energy-exporting regions.

Environmental issues at the local and regional scales

Local environmental impacts are likely to continue to take precedence over global change in the achievement of sustainable energy developments. According to the IIASA-WEC study, the natural capacity of the environment to absorb higher levels of pollution is also likely to

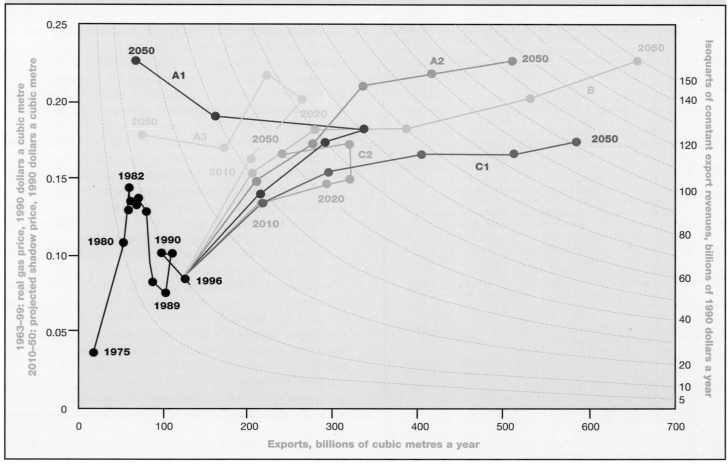

FIGURE 9.9. NATURAL GAS EXPORT QUANTITIES, PRICES, AND REVENUES FOR THE FORMER SOVIET UNION, 1975–96, AND IN SIX SCENARIOS, 2010–2050

Source: Nakićenović, Grübler, and McDonald, 1998.

become a limiting factor on the unconstrained use of fossil fuels. This also appears to be the case in many other sustainable energy scenarios. Increasing income would also lead to a higher demand for cleaner energy end uses in rural areas world-wide. This includes a shift away from cooking with wood and coal in inefficient traditional open fireplaces. Such a change would reduce indoor pollution levels, currently estimated to be 20 times higher than in industrialised countries.

A particularly urgent environmental problem in densely populated metropolitan areas is the high concentration of particulate matter and sulphur dioxide. Here cleaner fuels, such as natural gas, and active abatement measures will be required. Regional air pollution could also prove problematic, especially in the rapidly growing, densely populated, coal-intensive economies of Asia. In the booming cities of China and Southeast Asia, high levels of air pollution must be addressed with appropriate measures (box 9.4).

According to the findings of the IIASA-WEC study, one of the scenarios (A2), with a high dependence on coal (assuming no abatement measures), would result in high sulphur dioxide emissions

and significant regional acidification, causing key agricultural crops in the region to suffer acid deposition 10 times the sustainable level before 2020. Figure 9.10 shows excess sulphur deposition above critical loads in Asia for the unabated A2 scenario. According to this scenario, emissions could triple in Asia by 2020, and ambient air quality in South and East Asia could deteriorate significantly in both metropolitan and rural areas. Sulphur deposition would reach twice the worst levels ever observed in the most polluted areas of Central and Eastern Europe (for example, in the so-called black triangle between the Czech Republic, Germany, and Poland). Of critical importance for economically important food crops in Asia is that unabated sulphur emissions would cause critical loads to be exceeded by factors of up to 10. As a result severe losses in crop production could occur over large areas of Asia. In contrast to this dire outlook of possible consequences of unabated sulphur emissions in coal-intensive A2, A3 and C are relatively benign, leading to some, but not alarming, excess emissions in the future; perhaps more important, by the middle of the 21st century global sulphur emissions

BOX 9.4. ENERGY SCENARIOS FOR CHINA

Five scenarios are considered for China. The first is a baseline scenario; the other four illustrate different strategies to achieve more sustainable development from a regional perspective (Zhou, 1999).

The baseline scenario is intended to represent a practical, feasible fulfilment of future energy demand with low risk. It is assumed that GDP will expand by 22.7 times between 1990 and 2050, while energy demand will increase relatively modestly by about 1.7 times during the same period. This is due to vigorous improvement of energy intensities in combination with rapid economic growth. The future energy supply in the baseline scenario continues to be dominated by coal, however, with substantial technology and efficiency improvements. The main limitations and concerns are related to potential adverse environmental impacts. In particular, this coal-intensive baseline scenario is likely to lead to air pollution and energy-related emissions that substantially exceed acceptable levels. This is the main reason for the formulation of alternative development paths that fulfil the development objectives of China, but with substantially lower adverse environmental impacts.

The four sustainable scenarios explore alternative measures and policies to reduce the environmental burden of energy. The first scenario focuses on strengthening energy conservation. It is estimated that the energy conservation potential, if fully utilised, could reduce energy demand in China by 12 percent relative to the baseline by 2050. The second alternative scenario focuses on adoption of clean coal technologies. The main advantage of this scenario is that it would allow for the use of large domestic coal resources while curbing air pollution and sulphur emissions. But it would still lead to high carbon dioxide emissions. The third scenario focuses on renewable energy sources as replacements for coal. The fourth scenario focuses on nuclear energy, including breeder reactors, as a replacement for coal.

Combinations of these alternative scenarios were also considered, resulting in a substantial decrease in the ultimate share of coal to below 40 percent by 2050. Nevertheless coal remains the most important energy source across all these alternatives. Thus one of the conclusions is that a high priority should be placed on developing and diffusing clean coal technologies—in addition to conservation—in the four more sustainable scenarios. This strategy could lead to mitigation of 40 percent of future sulphur emissions (for example, in the second alternative scenario, at relatively modest increases in investment requirements, sulphur emissions decline from 23.7 million tonnes in 1995 to 13.5 millions tonnes in 2050). The energy conservation scenario had the advantage of low financing requirements and the lowest carbon dioxide emissions—but at the expense of a 60 percent increase in sulphur emissions. In contrast the clean coal scenario achieves a 40 percent reduction of sulphur emissions but has the highest carbon dioxide emissions. The renewable and nuclear energy scenarios lead to reductions in emissions at all scales, but the reductions in sulphur and carbon dioxide are not very large (10 percent and 20 percent), while the investment costs are very high.

would be reduced to well below current levels.

People world-wide already suffer from local and regional air pollution, and both governments and individuals are taking steps to improve the situation. These actions are part of the drive towards higher efficiencies and cleaner fuels and may also contribute to the shift towards a more sustainable development path. They also have the positive spin-off effect of reducing carbon emissions and possible global warming, although that is not their principal motivation.

Consequently emissions of sulphur aerosol precursors portray very dynamic patterns in time and space in most sustainable energy scenarios, in contrast to the development in many reference scenarios

(see figure 9.10). A detailed review of long-term global and regional sulphur emission scenarios is given in Grübler (1998a). Most recent scenarios recognise the significant adverse impacts of sulphur emissions on human health, food production, and ecosystems. As a result scenarios published since 1995 generally assume various degrees of sulphur controls to be implemented in the future and are thus substantially lower than previous projections. Other developments, such more sulphur-poor coals and clean fossil technologies and a shift towards renewables and natural gas in scenarios A3 and C, help promote substantial additional emissions reductions as ancillary benefits.

A related reason for lower sulphur emission projections is the recent tightening of sulphur-control policies in OECD countries that continue to dominate global emissions, such as the amendments to the U.S. Clean Air Act and implementation of the Second European Sulphur Protocol. These legislative changes were not yet reflected in previous long-term emission scenarios, as noted in Alcamo and others (1995) and Houghton and others (1995). The median from newer sulphur-control scenarios is consequently significantly lower relative to the older scenarios, indicating a continual decline in global sulphur emissions.

Scenarios A3 and C include a host of environmental control measures that help reduce emissions of sulphur dioxide and other pollutants. This is consistent with most of the scenarios that lead to a long-term, sustainable decline of particulate and sulphur levels, which would return emission levels to those of 1900. As a general pattern, global sulphur emissions do rise initially in recent scenarios, but eventually decline even in absolute terms after 2050. The spatial distribution of emissions changes markedly, generally from OECD regions to rapidly developing regions in Asia, and varies across scenarios.

In the sustainable IIASA-WEC scenarios (A3 and C), emissions in OECD countries continue their recent declining trend, reflecting a tightening of control measures. Emissions outside OECD countries, most notably in Asia, initially rise and then decline, resembling the current trend in OECD emissions. The reductions are especially pronounced in the C scenarios because of a virtual transition to the post-fossil era by 2100, essentially eliminating sulphur emissions. A3 leads to substantial sulphur declines, even though it has the same economic growth prospects as A2. There are many reasons. First, clean coal technologies, such as gasification, remove sulphur as an inherent property of the conversion process. Then there is a shift in fossil energy supply to low sulphur-grade coals, higher shares of natural gas, and later to non-fossils as well. Over the long term sulphur emissions decline in both scenarios throughout the world, but the timing and magnitude vary.

Climate change: land use and other global issues

One important implication of the varying pattern of particulate and sulphur emissions across the scenarios is that the historically important, but uncertain, negative radiative forcing of sulfate aerosols may decline in the very long run (Hulme, 1997; chapter 3). This means that the current cooling effect on the climate that results from the emissions of particulates and sulphur aerosols would diminish, causing additional, spatially different patterns of climate change. This view is also confirmed by the model calculations reported in Subak, Hulme, and Bohn (1997), Nakićenović, Grübler, and McDonald (1998), Nakićenović (2000), Smith and others (forthcoming), and Wigley (1999) and is based on recent long-term greenhouse gas and sulphur emission scenarios. This means that precursors of air pollution and acidification at the local and regional levels have an important role in global climate change. But emissions of greenhouse gases such as carbon dioxide continue to be the main source of climate warming.

Cumulative future CO_2 emissions are in the first approximation indicative of potential climate change (chapter 3). Carbon dioxide emissions are the major anthropogenic source of climate change, and energy is the most important source of CO_2 emissions. A number of energy scenarios in the literature account for the emissions of other greenhouse gases and thus provide a more complete picture of possible implications for climate change. For simplicity, only energy-related sources of CO_2 emissions are evaluated here.

Figure 9.11 shows the CO_2 emissions of the six IIASA-WEC scenarios superimposed on the emissions range of the energy scenarios from the literature. The range is very wide by 2100, from more than seven times current emissions to almost none for scenarios that assume a complete transition away from fossil energy. The emission profiles are different across the range of scenarios. Most portray a continuous increase throughout the 21st century, whereas the sustainable scenarios generally have lower, more dynamic emission profiles. Some of them curve through a maximum and decline.

For the scenarios in the literature, the distribution of emissions by 2100 is very asymmetrical and portrays a structure resembling a trimodal frequency distribution: those with emissions of more than 30 gigatonnes of carbon (20 scenarios), those with emissions of 12–30 gigatonnes of carbon (88 scenarios), and those with emissions of less than 12 gigatonnes of carbon (82 scenarios). Most of the scenarios in this lowest cluster are situated at 2–9 gigatonnes of carbon; this cluster appears to include many of the sustainable energy scenarios, and the second and third clusters most likely include only a few of them. The lowest cluster may have been influenced by many analyses of stabilising atmospheric concentrations, for example at 450 and 550 parts per million by volume (ppmv), in

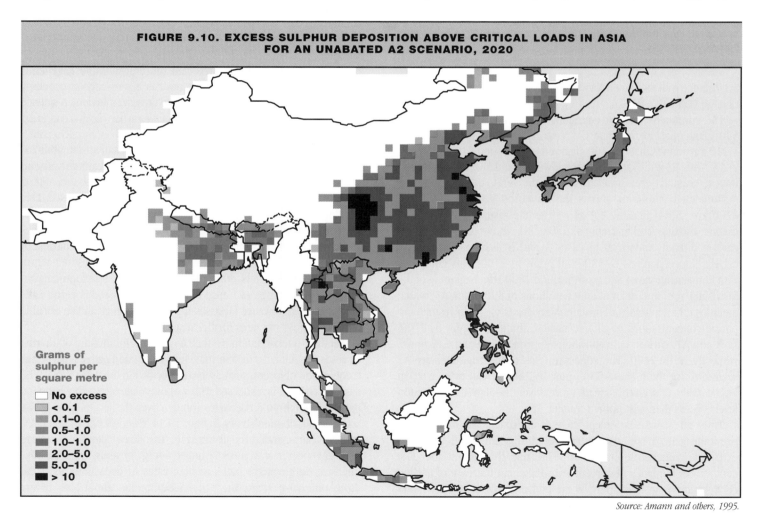

FIGURE 9.10. EXCESS SULPHUR DEPOSITION ABOVE CRITICAL LOADS IN ASIA FOR AN UNABATED A2 SCENARIO, 2020

Grams of sulphur per square metre

- No excess
- < 0.1
- 0.1–0.5
- 0.5–1.0
- 1.0–1.0
- 2.0–5.0
- 5.0–10
- > 10

Source: Amann and others, 1995.

FIGURE 9.11. GLOBAL CARBON EMISSIONS FROM FOSSIL FUEL USE, 1850–1990, AND IN SIX SCENARIOS, 1990–2100

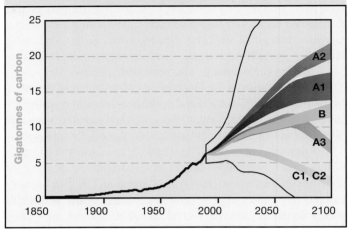

For each scenario, the range shows the difference between gross and net emissions. Gross emissions are actual carbon dioxide released into the atmosphere. Net emissions include deductions for carbon absorption (through biomass regrowth and sequestration). The figure also shows the wider range of emissions for 190 scenarios in the literature. The vertical line that spans the scenario range in 1990 indicates the uncertainty across the literature of base-year carbon emissions.

Source: Nakićenović, Grübler, and McDonald, 1998; Morita and Lee, 1998.

accordance with the United Nations Framework Convention on Climate Change (UNFCCC, 1992).

The cumulative carbon emissions between 1990 and 2100 are 540 gigatonnes in the case C scenarios, 1,000 gigatonnes in B, 1,210 gigatonnes in A1, 1,450 gigatonnes in A2, and 910 gigatonnes in A3. Thus A3 and C have both the lowest cumulative emissions and lowest annual emissions towards the end of the century. Accumulated emissions across the scenarios between 1990 and 2100 are shown in table 9.1 as well as the resulting atmospheric carbon dioxide concentrations. Table 9.1 shows that the rising carbon dioxide emissions in cases A and B lead to atmospheric carbon concentrations of 530–730 ppmv in 2100. This compares with concentrations of 280 ppmv around 1800 (the beginning of the fossil-fuel age) and current concentrations of 370 ppmv. A3, which includes characteristics of sustainability, leads to the lowest atmospheric concentrations of all A scenarios, about 530 ppmv by 2100. In B and A1, carbon concentrations approach 590 and 620 ppmv, respectively, by 2100. The concentrations of the coal-intensive A2 scenarios are the highest, 730 ppmv by 2100, about twice current levels. Only C scenarios lead to relatively benign concentration levels of less than 450 ppmv (chapter 3).

Thus all scenarios except case C approach the doubling of pre-industrial carbon concentrations. And again in all scenarios except C, concentrations continue to rise throughout the 21st century. On the basis of current knowledge, an increase of carbon concentrations to 600 ppmv by the end of the 21st century could lead to an increase in the mean global surface temperature of about

2.5 degrees Celsius, assuming the mean climate sensitivity and with an uncertainty range of 1.5–4.5 degrees Celsius (chapter 3).

The C scenarios are the only ones in which carbon concentrations stabilise by 2100, reflecting their ambitious emission reduction profile, from 6 gigatonnes in 1990 to 2 gigatonnes in 2100. After peaking at about 450 ppmv around 2080, carbon concentrations slowly begin to decline as natural sinks absorb excess carbon dioxide. The carbon cycle models indicate that the emissions reduction to about 2 gigatonnes of carbon a year (or about a third to at most half the current global emissions) is an essential prerequisite for eventually achieving stabilisation of atmospheric concentrations. This is the reason why all other scenarios, including A3, result in continuously increasing concentrations over the time horizon (although A3 is consistent, with stabilisation at 550 ppmv in the 22nd century, assuming that the emissions would further be reduced to about 2 gigatonnes of carbon a year).

Even with its ambitious emission reduction measures, C's atmospheric carbon concentrations rise by up to 90 ppmv during the 21st century. This increase is about equal to the concentration rise since the onset of industrialisation until today (from 280 to 370 ppmv during the past 200 years). Thus even in C, some climate change appears inevitable: perhaps 1.5 degrees Celsius (with an uncertainty range of 1.0–2.5 degrees Celsius) in increased global mean surface temperature. This illustrates both the legacy of our past dependence on fossil fuels and the considerable lead times required for an orderly transition towards a zero-carbon economy and sustainable development paths. It also illustrates the long residence time of carbon in the atmosphere. Some of the carbon dioxide emissions from Watt's first steam engine are still airborne.

Both IIASA-WEC scenarios with characteristics of sustainability, C and A3, are situated within the lowest cluster with emissions found in the literature, at 2–9 gigatonnes of carbon by 2100. Thus they appear to cover the range of future emissions associated with sustainable development quite well—their range excludes only the most extreme emission scenarios found in the literature. This leads to a substantial overlap in emission ranges across different scenarios. In other words a similar quantification of the driving forces that are all consistent with various concepts of sustainable development can lead to a wide range of future emissions. Because this result is of fundamental importance for assessing climate change and sustainable development, it warrants further discussion.

Another interpretation is that a given combination of driving forces is not sufficient to determine future emission paths. A particular combination of forces, such as those specified in the three IIASA-WEC case A scenarios, is associated with a whole range of possible emission paths. These three A scenarios jointly cover the largest part of the scenario distribution shown in figure 9.11. But only one of them, A3, can be characterised as sustainable. The three scenarios explore different specific structures of future energy systems, from carbon-intensive development paths to high rates of decarbonisation. All three otherwise share the same assumptions about the driving forces. This indicates that different structures of the energy system can lead to basically the same variation in future emissions as can be generated by different combinations of the other main driving forces—population, economic activities, and energy consumption levels—with basically the same structure of the energy system. The implication is that decarbonisation of energy systems—the shift from carbon-intensive to less carbon-intensive and carbon-free sources of energy—is of similar importance as other driving forces in determining future emission paths.

Figure 9.12 shows the degree of decarbonisation achieved in the scenarios relative to historical trends and the range observed in scenarios from the literature. Carbon intensity of primary energy is shown as an indicator of decarbonisation. The carbon intensity improves across all IIASA-WEC scenarios, but is especially pronounced in the three with characteristics of sustainability, C1, C2, and A3. Sustained decarbonisation requires the development and successful diffusion of new technologies. An important implication of the varying

The long-term transition to new energy technologies will largely be determined by technological choices made in the next 10–30 years.

interplay of the main scenario driving forces is that investments in new technologies during the coming decades might have the same magnitude of influence on future emissions as population growth, economic development, and levels of energy consumption taken together. Thus high or low emissions can be associated with a range of social and economic scenarios; the distinguishing feature of the low emissions and low pollution scenarios is that the policies and technologies are in place to reduce emissions. But countries will be better placed to implement climate-friendly policies if development, in its broadest sense, is successful.

Furthermore decarbonisation also means that other environmental impacts tend to be lower (Nakićenović, 1996). Thus the energy systems structure of IIASA-WEC scenario A3 is one of the main determinants of its sustainability. In contrast, C scenarios require fundamental changes that encompass energy end use as well. In many ways the

FIGURE 9.12. GLOBAL CARBON INTENSITY OF PRIMARY ENERGY, 1850–1990, AND IN SIX SCENARIOS, 1990–2100, RELATIVE TO THE SCENARIOS FROM THE LITERATURE AND THE IPCC IS92 SCENARIOS

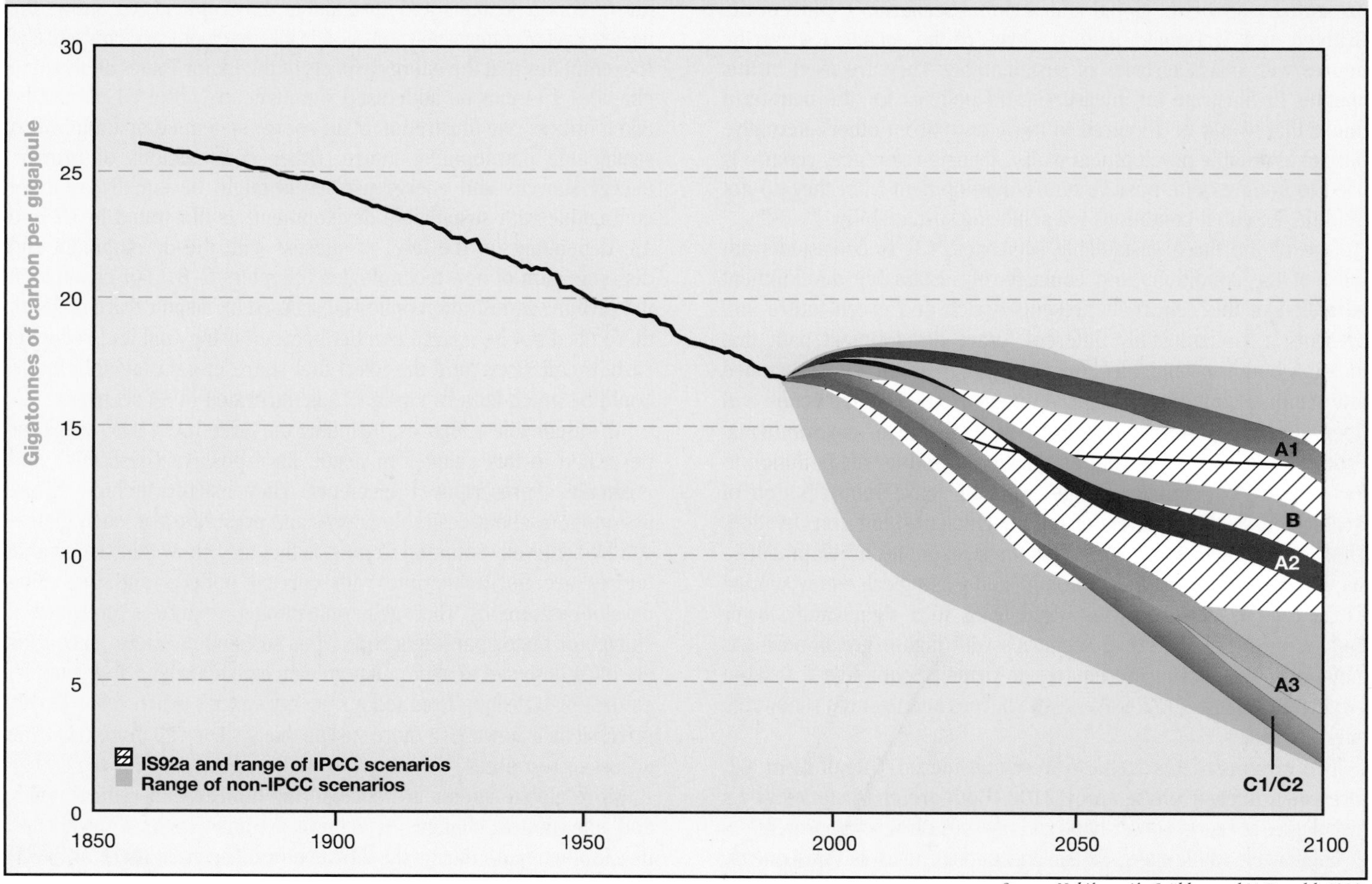

Source: Nakićenović, Grübler, and McDonald, 1998.

transitions in the structures of the energy systems described by the scenarios cannot be seen in isolation from the overall development path towards sustainability. Other scenarios presented in the IIASA-WEC study do not appear to be consistent with the characteristics of sustainability given in table 9.2. This result suggests that the future direction of technological change in the energy system is not only important for reducing the dangers of climate change but can also help nudge the overall development path in the direction of sustainability.

Conclusion

Scenarios are frequently used to assess sustainable development paths. Sustainable futures often are easier to illustrate when they are compared with other scenarios that contradict some of the conditions for achieving sustainability. This is one of the reasons that, in recent studies, sustainable scenarios are usually included among alternative futures. This class of sustainable scenarios can be characterised by low environmental impacts at all scales and more equitable allocation of resources and wealth relative to the current situations and other alternative future energy developments. Recently IIASA and WEC presented a set of six global and regional scenarios (Nakićenović, Grübler, and McDonald, 1998). Three of the scenarios describe futures with characteristics of sustainability. They are used in this chapter to illustrate the measures and policies for the near-term future that would be required to move away from other alternative but unsustainable development paths. A single reference scenario is used to outline quite positive future developments, but they do not fulfil the essential conditions for achieving sustainability.

One of the three sustainable scenarios, C1, is consistent with most of the conditions and concepts of sustainable development advanced in this report. It presents a rich and green future and presents a fundamentally different future development path that includes both substantial technological progress and unprecedented international cooperation centred on environmental protection and international equity—it includes a high degree of environmental protection at all scales, from eradication of indoor air pollution to low impacts on climate change, with an active redistribution of wealth and very high levels of energy efficiency and conservation. Thus it fulfils most of the criteria for sustainable development—such as increasing both economic and ecological equity among world regions and countries—and leads to a significantly lower impact on the climate than scenarios with higher greenhouse gas emissions This scenario requires a virtually complete transition away from reliance on fossil energy sources and towards renewable energy sources.

Two variants of this scenario were considered. One of them, C2, foresees a nuclear phaseout by 2100. Both are characterised by a high degree of energy conservation and vigorous efficiency improvements throughout the whole energy system and among end users. Consequently total energy requirements are relatively low relative to the high levels of affluence and quality of life, especially in today's developing regions. The achievement of such a future is indeed challenging, and ranges from devising new RD&D policies to bringing to market new energy technologies, to imposing energy and carbon taxes as incentives for improving energy efficiency and conservation and increasing the shift away from fossil fuels.

The second scenario that includes characteristics of sustainability, A3, is fundamentally different in nature and quite similar to the reference scenario except in the future structure of the energy system. Thus environmental protection and higher levels of affluence are achieved less through changes in levels of energy end use and structure and more through a dedicated decarbonisation of the energy system. Again efficiency improvements are important, and clean fossils such as natural gas are foreseen as gaining much larger shares of global energy needs, along with renewable sources of energy—all contributing towards decarbonisation. Decarbonisation is in part also achieved through more sophisticated energy conversion and processing that includes carbon removal along with more conventional pollutants.

These scenarios illustrate different levels of compatibility between future energy systems and sustainable development. C1 shows the highest level of compatibility with sustainable development characteristics. It exemplifies that the energy aspects of the major issues analysed in chapters 1–4 can be addressed simultaneously. But C1 should be taken only as one illustration of an energy system compatible with a sustainable development future. Other combinations of primary energy sources and energy use levels might be equally or more compatible with sustainable development, as illustrated by C2 and A3, depending on the level of success with the development and dissemination of new technologies (chapters 6–8). For example, if the carbon sequestration options discussed in chapter 8 are realised, there need not be a large conflict between using coal and reducing carbon emissions, and the fossil fuel share in a sustainable future could be much larger than in C1, as illustrated in A3 scenario.

All sustainable scenarios, including the three IIASA-WEC scenarios described in this chapter in detail, have positive (desirable) and normative (prescriptive) elements. They usually include strong assumptions about desirable futures and prescribe how such futures can be achieved. Common to most is that they show that sustainable futures are not achievable with current policies and prevailing development trends. Their achievement often requires a fundamental change or major paradigm shift. Thus sustainable energy scenarios are often designed to offer policy guidance on managing, for example, an orderly transition from today's energy system, which relies largely on fossil fuels, towards a more sustainable system with more equitable access to resources.

More global studies are considering futures with radical policy and behavioural changes to achieve a transition to a sustainable development path during the 21st century. The great merit of RD&D policies, diffusion, and the adoption of new technologies associated with market-based instruments for environmental change is that radical developments often proceed gradually from seemingly moderate policies, leading to major improvements over time. But they require continuity over decades so that the cumulative effects of moderate polices can result in radical change. These are some of the crucial characteristics of the three IIASA-WEC scenarios that lead towards sustainable development.

Another central feature of these three scenarios is that adequate provision of energy services and more equitable allocation of resources are crucial for achieving sustainability. At the same time, energy use is a main cause of environmental degradation at all scales and so can inhibit the achievement of sustainability. Thus environmental protection—from indoor pollution to climate change—is an essential element of sustainable development in these scenarios. Rapid development and clean, efficient energy are complementary elements of most of the scenarios. The resolution of these future challenges offers a window of opportunity between now and 2020. Because of the long lifetimes of power plants, refineries, and other energy investments, there is not a sufficient turnover of such facilities to reveal large differences among the alternative scenarios presented here before 2020, but the seeds of the post-2020 world will have been sown by then.

The choice of the world's future energy systems may be wide open now. It will be a lot narrower by 2020, and certain development opportunities that are forgone now might not be achievable later. There may well be environmental irreversibilities, but technical changes may still take place, and it is a question of whether they will be too late rather than whether they will occur at all. Perhaps more important is the question of development initiatives directed at eradicating poverty, disease, and illiteracy in the world, and whether they will be timely and sufficient to offset currently inadequate efforts. The achievement of sustainable development dictates a global perspective, a very long time horizon, and immediate policy measures that take into account the long lead times needed to change the system. ∎

Notes

1. Table 9.2 provides a number of indicators that can be used to characterise the achievement of sustainable development in energy scenarios and shows how the three scenarios selected for this assessment fare relative to one another.

2. Energy prices are an important determinant in the short to medium term. But in the long term, technology and policy are more important determinants, although important feedback mechanisms do exist—for example, in the form of induced technical change. As a result future levels of energy demand can vary widely, even for otherwise similar scenario characteristics, in terms of population and level of economic development.

References

Alcamo, J., A. Bouwman, J. Edmonds, A. Grübler, T. Morita, and A. Sugandhy. 1995. "An Evaluation of the IPCC IS92 Emission Scenarios." In Houghton, J.T., L.G. Meira Filho, J. Bruce, Hoesung Lee, B. A. Callander, E. Haites, N. Harris, and K. Maskell, eds., *Climate Change 1994: Radiative Forcing of Climate Change and An Evaluation of the IPCC IS92 Emission Scenarios.* Cambridge: Cambridge University Press for the Intergovernmental Panel on Climate Change.

Amann, M., J. Cofala, P. Dörfner, F. Gyarfas, and W. Schöpp. 1995. "Impacts of Energy Scenarios on Regional Acidifications." In WEC Project 4 on Environment, Working Group C, Local and Regional Energy Related Environmental Issues. London: World Energy Council.

Barro, R.J. 1997. *Determinants of Economic Growth.* Cambridge, Mass.: MIT Press.

Barro, R.J., and X. Sala-I-Martin. 1995. *Economic Growth.* New York: McGraw-Hill.

Bos, E., and M.T. Vu. 1994. *World Population Projections: Estimates and Projections with Related Demographic Statistics,* 1994-1995 Edition. Washington, D.C.: World Bank.

De Vries, B., J. Bollen, L. Bouwman, M. den Elzen, M. Janssen, and E. Kreileman. 2000. "Greenhouse Gas Emissions in an Equity-, Environment- and Service-Oriented World: An IMAGE-Based Scenario for the Next Century." *Technological Forecasting & Social Change* 63 (2–3).

Gallopin, G., A. Hammond, P. Raskin, and R. Swart. 1997. *Branch Points.* PoleStar Series Report 7. Boston: Stockholm Environment Institute Boston Center.

Glenn, J.C., and T.J. Gordon, eds. 1997. "State of the Future: Implications for Actions Today." American Council for the United Nations University, Millennium Project, Washington, D.C.

Goldemberg, J., T.B. Johansson, A.K. Reddy, and R.H. Williams. 1988. *Energy for a Sustainable World.* New Delhi: Wiley Eastern.

Grübler, A. 1994. "A Comparison of Global and Regional Energy Emission Scenarios." WP-94-132. International Institute for Applied Systems Analysis, Laxenburg, Austria.

———. 1998a. "A Review of Global and Regional Sulfur Emission Scenarios." *Mitigation and Adaptation Strategies for Global Change* 3 (2–4): 383–418.

———. 1998b. *Technology and Global Change.* Cambridge: Cambridge University Press.

Hammond, A. 1998: *Which World? Scenarios for the 21st Century, Global Destinies, Regional Choices.* London: Earthscan.

Häfele, W., ed. 1981. *Energy in a Finite World: A Global Systems Analysis.* Cambridge, Mass.: Ballinger.

Hanke, T. 1995. "Die Märke spielen verrückt [in German]." *Die Zeit* 18: 33.

Houghton, J.T., L.G. Meira Filho, J. Bruce, Hoesung Lee, B. A. Callander, E. Haites, N. Harris, and K. Maskell, eds. 1995. *Climate Change 1994: Radiative Forcing of Climate Change and an Evaluation of the IPCC IS92 Emissions Scenarios.* Cambridge: Cambridge University Press for the Intergovernmental Panel on Climate Change.

Hulme, M. 1997. "Comment on the First Draft of the Sulfur Discussion Paper." Climate Research Unit, University of East Anglia, Norwich, U.K.

IEA (International Energy Agency). 1993. *Cars and Climate Change.* Paris: Organisation for Economic Co-operation and Development.

———. 1998. *World Energy Outlook.* Paris: Organisation for Economic Co-operation and Development.

IIASA-WEC (International Institute for Applied Systems Analysis and World Energy Council). 1995. *Global Energy Perspectives to 2050 and Beyond.* Laxenburg, Austria: International Institute for Applied Systems Analysis.

Ishitani H., T.B. Johansson, S. Al-Khouli, H. Audus, E. Bertel and others. 1996. "Energy Supply Mitigation Options." In R.T. Watson, M.C. Zinyowera, and R.H. Moss, eds., *Climate Change 1995—Impacts, Adaptation and Mitigation of Climate Change: Scientific Analysis.* Cambridge University Press for the Intergovernmental Panel on Climate Change.

Johansson, T.B, H. Kelly, A.K.N. Reddy, and R.H. Williams. 1993. "Renewable Fuels and Electricity for a Growing World Economy: Defining and Achieving the Potential." In T.B. Johansson, H. Kelly, A.K.N. Reddy, and R.H. Williams, ed., *Renewable Energy: Sources for Fuels and Electricity.* Washington, D.C.: Island Press.

Kram, T., K. Riahi, R.A. Roehrl, S. van Rooijen, T. Morita, and B. de Vries. 2000. "Global and Regional Greenhouse Gas Emissions Scenarios." *Technological Forecasting & Social Change* 63 (2–3).

Lazarus, M.L., L. Greber, J. Hall, C. Bartels, S. Bernow, E. Hansen, P. Raskin, and D. von Hippel. 1993. *Towards a Fossil Free Energy Future: The Next Energy Transition.* Technical Analysis for Greenpeace International. Boston: Stockholm Environmental Institute Boston Center.

Leggett, J., W.J. Pepper, and R.J. Swart. 1992. "Emissions Scenarios for IPCC: An Update." In J.T. Houghton, B.A. Callander, and S.K. Varney, eds., *Climate Change 1992: The Supplementary Report to the IPCC Scientific Assessment.* Cambridge: Cambridge University Press for the Intergovernmental Panel on Climate Change.

Lutz, W., W. Sanderson, and S. Scherbov. 1997. "Doubling of World Population Unlikely." *Nature* 387 (6635): 803–05.

Makarov, A.A. 1999. "Newly Independent States of the Former Soviet Union." Paper prepared for the World Energy Assessment. United Nations Development Programme, New York.

Manne, A., and R. Richels. 1994. "The Costs of Stabilizing Global CO_2 Emissions: A Probabilistic Analysis Based on Expert Judgements." *Energy Journal* 15 (1): 31–56.

Morita, T., and H.-C. Lee. 1998. "IPCC SRES Database, Version 0.1, Emission Scenario." Database prepared for IPCC Special Report on Emissions Scenarios, http://www-cger.nies.go.jp/cger-e/db/ipcc.html

Nakićenović, N. 1996. "Freeing Energy from Carbon." *Daedalus* 125 (3): 95–112.

———. 2000. "Greenhouse Gas Emissions Scenarios." *Technological Forecasting & Social Change* 65 (3).

Nakićenović, N., A. Grübler, and A. McDonald, eds. 1998. *Global Energy Perspectives.* Cambridge: Cambridge University Press.

Nakićenović, N., N. Victor, and T. Morita. 1998. "Emissions Scenarios Database and Review of Scenarios." *Mitigation and Adaptation Strategies for Global Change* 3 (2–4): 95–120.

Nakićenović, N., J. Alcamo, G. Davis, B. de Vries, J. Fenhann, and others. 2000. *Special Report on Emissions Scenarios by the Intergovernmental Panel on Climate Change.* Cambridge: Cambridge University Press for the Intergovernmental Panel on Climate Change.

Nordhaus, W.D., and G.W. Yohe. 1983. "Future Paths of Energy and Carbon Dioxide Emissions." In W.A. Nierenberg, ed., *Changing Climate: Report of the Carbon Dioxide Assessment Committee.* Washington, D.C.: National Academy Press.

Pepper, W.J., J. Leggett, R. Swart, J. Wasson, J. Edmonds, and I. Mintzer. 1992. "Emissions Scenarios for the IPCC. An Update: Assumptions, Methodology, and Results. Support Document for Chapter A3." In J.T. Houghton, B.A. Callandar, and S.K. Varney, eds., *Climate Change 1992: Supplementary Report to the IPCC Scientific Assessment.* Cambridge: Cambridge University Press for the Intergovernmental Panel on Climate Change.

Raskin, P., G. Gallopin, P. Gutman, A. Hammond, and R. Swart. 1998. *Bending the Curve: Toward Global Sustainability.* Report of the Global Scenario Group, PoleStar Series Report 8. Stockholm: Stockholm Environment Institute.

Rostow, W.W. 1990. *The Stages of Economic Growth.* 3rd edition. Cambridge: Cambridge University Press.

Schipper, L., and S. Meyers. 1992. *Energy Efficiency and Human Activity: Past Trends, Future Prospects.* Cambridge: Cambridge University Press.

Schwartz, P. 1991. *The Art of the Longview: Three Global Scenarios to 2005.* New York: Doubleday.

Shell International Ltd. 1996. *The Evolution of the World's Energy Systems.* The Hague: Shell International.

———. 1998. *People and the Environment: The 1997 Shell International Exploration and Production Health, Safety and Environment Report.* The Hague: Shell International.

Smith, S.J., T.M.L. Wigley, N. Nakićenović, and S.C.B. Raper. Forthcoming. "Climate Implications of Greenhouse Gas Emissions Scenarios." *Technological Forecasting & Social Change.*

Solow, R. 1956. "A Contribution to the Theory of Economic Growth." *Quarterly Journal of Economics* 70: 56–94.

Sørensen, B., B. Kuemmel, and P. Meibom. 1999. "Long-Term Scenarios Global Energy Demand and Supply." IMFUFA [Department of Studies in Mathematics and Physics and their Functions in Education, Research and Applications], Roskilde University, Roskilde, Denmark.

Subak, S., M. Hulme, and L. Bohn. 1997. *The Implications of FCCC Protocol Proposals for Future Global Temperature: Results Considering Alternative Sulfur Forcing.* CSERGE Working Paper GEC-97-19. Centre for Social and Economic Research on the Global Environment, University of East Anglia, Norwich, U.K.

Tol, R.S.J. 1995. "The Climate Fund Sensitivity, Uncertainty, and Robustness Analyses." W-95/02, Institute for Environmental Studies, Climate Framework. Vrije Universiteit, Amsterdam.

UN (United Nations). 1996. *Annual Populations 1950–2050: The 1996 Revision.* New York: UN Population Division (data on diskettes).

———. 1997. *United Nations Commission on Population and Development, Thirteenth Session, Report of the Secretary General on Progress on Work in the Field of Population in 1996.* New York: United Nations.

———. 1998. *World Population Projections to 2150.* New York: Population Division, UN Department of Economics and Social Affairs.

UNDP (United Nations Development Programme). 1997. *Human Development Report 1997.* Oxford: Oxford University Press.

UNFCCC (United Nations Framework Convention on Climate Change). 1992. "United Nations Framework Convention on Climate Change." UNEP/WMO Information Unit of Climate Change (IUCC) on behalf of the Interim Secretariat of the Convention. IUCC, Geneva.

———. 1997. "Kyoto Protocol to the United Nations Framework Convention on Climate Change." FCCC/CP/L7/Add.1, 10 December 1997. United Nations, New York.

WBCSD (World Business Council for Sustainable Development). 1998. "Exploring Sustainable Development." Geneva.

Wigley, T.M.L. 1999. "The Science of Climate Change. Global and U.S. Perspectives." PEW Center on Global Climate Change, Arlington, Va.

WEC (World Energy Council). 1993. *Energy for Tomorrow's World.* London: Kogan Page.

Zhou, F. 1999. "China's Future Energy Scenario Analysis." Paper prepared for the World Energy Assessment. United Nations Development Programme, New York.

rural energy in developing countries

CHAPTER 10

José Goldemberg (Brazil)

LEAD AUTHORS: Amulya K.N. Reddy (India), Kirk R. Smith (United States), and Robert H. Williams (United States)

ABSTRACT Supplying modern energy services to the 2 billion people who still cook with traditional solid fuels and lack access to electricity is probably one of the most pressing problems facing humanity today. The amount of energy needed to satisfy the basic needs of rural populations around the world is relatively small, and appropriate technologies are available. However, widening access to modern energy services is limited by the extreme poverty found particularly in the least developed countries.

Living standards in rural areas can be significantly improved by promoting a shift from direct combustion of biomass fuels (dung, crop residues, and fuelwood) or coal in inefficient and polluting stoves to clean, efficient liquid or gaseous fuels and electricity. Although consumers tend to shift to these modern, higher-quality energy carriers as their incomes rise and the carriers become more affordable, the process is slow. Yet a shift to such carriers can reduce the damage to human health and the drudgery associated with continued reliance on inefficient, polluting solid fuels.

This chapter describes experience with and prospects for improving the technologies used to cook with biomass in several countries, as well as the development of clean, non-toxic cooking fuels. Progress in rural electrification—using both centralised, grid-based approaches and small-scale, decentralised technologies—is also described.

Technological developments alone, however, will not improve access or promote greater equity. New institutional measures are also needed, including financing to cover the initial capital costs of devices and equipment. Energy initiatives will be most successful when integrated with other policies that promote development. And because local populations will ultimately use, maintain, and pay for energy services, they should be involved in making decisions about energy systems. ▪

The lack of adequate energy services in rural areas of developing countries has social dimensions (chapter 2) as well as serious environmental and health effects (chapter 3). Many of these problems are exacerbated by the almost exclusive reliance of rural populations in most areas on traditional fuels coupled with simple technologies characterised by low energy efficiency and harmful emissions. This chapter thus focuses on technological opportunities, as well as other strategies, for delivering adequate, affordable, cleaner energy supplies to rural areas.

The second half of the 20th century witnessed a strong urbanisation trend and the emergence of megacities (those containing more than 10 million people) in most developing countries. Between 1970 and 1990 the share of people living in cities grew from 28 to 50 percent. But while the rural population relatively decreased during this period, the absolute number of people living in rural areas increased to 3 billion. Despite this, rural development often remains low on government agendas because of increasing demands of growing, politically and economically dominant urban populations. Thus the explosive growth of cities makes it difficult for policy-makers to give rural development the attention it deserves.

The dispersed character of rural populations and their low commercial energy consumption result in poor capacity utilisation efficiency for transmission and distribution systems and other energy infrastructure. Extending an electric grid to a few households in a rural setting can result in energy costs of up to $0.70 per kilowatt-hour, seven times the cost of providing electricity in an urban area (World Bank, 1996). Thus conventional approaches to extending energy infrastructure are economically inefficient, for both public and private providers—which is another reason the energy problems of rural populations are given low priority by governments.

Because the poor people in rural areas lack access to electricity and modern fuels, they rely primarily on human and animal power for mechanical tasks, such as agricultural activities and transport, and on the direct combustion of biomass (wood, crop residues, dung) for activities that require heat or lighting. Human energy is expended for household work (gathering and preparing biomass for fuel, fetching water, washing clothes), agriculture, and small industry. Biomass fuels are typically used for cooking (which dominates inanimate energy consumption in most warm regions), space heating, heating water for bathing, and meeting some industrial heating needs. Kerosene is used predominantly for lighting, and to a small extent in rural industry. Although much of the world's rural population has no access to electricity generation, many have small battery-operated devices such as radios and flashlights.

Rungs on the energy ladder

Large amounts of human energy are spent gathering fuelwood in many parts of the world, and the burden tends to fall more heavily on women and children.[1] Although there are exceptions, history has generally shown that when alternatives are available and affordable, consumers opt for more modern energy carriers. As incomes rise and opportunities for using better technologies become available, consumer preferences shift to more efficient, convenient, cleaner energy systems as they become more affordable. That is, consumers move up the energy ladder (chapter 3). This involves a shift to modern energy carriers or to more convenient and energy-efficient conversion devices.

For cooking and other heating purposes, the lowest rungs on the energy ladder involve use of dung or crop residues, with fuelwood, charcoal, kerosene, and liquefied petroleum gas (LPG) or natural gas representing successively higher rungs. For lighting, the lowest rung is represented by fire, followed in turn by liquid-fuelled (such as kerosene) lamps, gas lanterns, and electric bulbs. To do mechanical work, consumers shift from human and animal energy to diesel fuel and electricity as soon as they become available, because they are almost always more cost-effective. Often a synergy between modern energy carriers and more efficient end-use devices occurs.

One of the aims of this chapter is to explore the technological, economic, social, and institutional prospects for more rapidly introducing modern energy carriers into rural areas—which would allow households to move quickly to the top of the energy ladder, ideally skipping (leapfrogging) some of its rungs. Accelerating the introduction of modern energy, then, is a key strategy for promoting sustainable development in rural areas of developing countries. Principally, it involves providing:

- Clean liquid or gaseous fuels for cooking, and electricity for lighting and other basic household amenities.
- Liquid fuels and electricity to mechanise agriculture.
- Electricity sufficiently low in cost to attract industrial activity to rural areas (thereby providing well-paying jobs and helping to stem migration to urban settlements).

It is desirable to skip rungs and advance to the highest rungs on the energy ladder wherever feasible.[2] But because the 2 billion rural poor live in many different circumstances, a complete range of approaches need to be explored, and those that work best in each set of circumstances need to be encouraged. Appropriate public policies should be implemented to accelerate the process and reduce human suffering.

Satisfying basic human needs with modern energy carriers requires relatively small amounts of energy in absolute terms. In regions that do not require space heating, final household energy requirements for satisfying basic needs are estimated to be about 2,000 kilocalories per capita per day, or 0.1 kilowatt per capita in average power provided (80 percent for cooking and 20 percent for electricity; Reddy, 1999). The cooking needs of the 2 billion people not served by modern fuels correspond to about 120 million tonnes of oil equivalent of LPG a year—which equals 1 percent of global commercial energy consumption or 3 percent of global oil consumption. This is less than is currently lost flaring natural gas in oil fields and refineries.

Thus commercial energy requirements for satisfying basic needs

FIGURE 10.1. EFFICIENCY OF STOVES WITH COMMERCIAL AND NON-COMMERCIAL FUELS

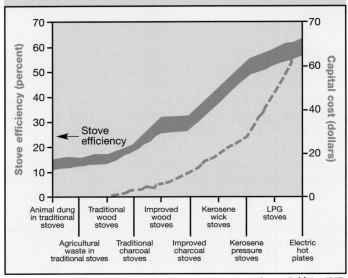

Source: Baldwin, 1987.

in rural areas are truly modest. Yet provision of even these modest amounts of energy to rural areas would offer the potential for enormous increases in amenities, particularly if these modern energy carriers were coupled with energy-efficient end-use devices.[3]

Progress in delivering modern energy to rural areas has been slow. But as will be shown, technical options to provide rural people with access to convenient, affordable energy services are commercially available (or nearly so). This is particularly the case in regions where modern energy carriers, such as biogas or producer gas, can be derived from local biomass and where gathering biomass feedstock can provide opportunity for income generation. The challenge of making modern energy available to the very poorest households is primarily institutional, notwithstanding the economic costs and risks inherent in developing and disseminating untried systems. New financial mechanisms and other innovative policy approaches are needed, as discussed below.

Fuels in rural areas: climbing the energy ladder

The oldest human energy technology, the home cooking fire, persists as the most prevalent fuel-using technology in the world. For much of the world's population, household fuel demand makes up more than half of total energy demand. The energy ladder (discussed briefly above and in chapter 3) is used here as a framework for examining the trends and impacts of household fuel use. As figure 10.1 illustrates, the fuel-stove combinations that represent rungs on the ladder tend to increase in cleanliness, efficiency, and controllability. Conversely, capital cost and dependence on centralised fuel cycles also tend to increase with movement up the ladder.

Shortages of local wood supplies combined with institutional and economic constraints on petroleum-based fuels often lead to household

BOX 10.1. COMPARISON OF STOVE PROGRAMMES IN CHINA AND INDIA

China	India
The programme focused on areas with the greatest need and selected pilot counties with biomass fuel deficits.	The programme was implemented country-wide, resulting in dispersion of effort and dilution of financial resources.
Direct contracts between the central government and the county bypassed much bureaucracy. This arrangement generated self-sustaining rural energy companies that manufacture, install, and service stoves and other energy technologies.	The programme administration was cumbersome, moving from the centre to the state level, then to the district, and finally to the *taluka,* where the stove programme is just one of many national efforts being implemented locally by the same people.
Local rural energy offices run by provincial governments are in charge of technical training, service, implementation, and monitoring for the programmes. These efforts are separately funded and relatively independent.	Lack of a strong monitoring plan was a severe weakness in early programmes. Some improvement has occurred through assignment of the task to university-based technical backup units. Coverage is still incomplete, however.
Stoves are not only suitable for fuel savings and reduction of household smoke, but also are designed for convenience and attractiveness, highlighting the lessons learned from problems in early programmes that stressed only fuel savings.	India has made a wide variety of attempts to integrate efficiency and convenience, which have suffered from the top-down structure of the programme.
Stove adopters pay the full cost of materials and labour. The government helps producers through stove construction training, administration, and promotion support.	Stove adopters pay about half the cost of stoves; the government pays the rest. As a result the producer's incentive to construct stoves is oriented towards the government.
Emphasis has been on long-lived stoves made of ceramic or metal and otherwise designed to be a significant household asset for a number of years.	Many of the stoves have been made from local materials and by villagers without artisanal skills, resulting in short lifetimes in day-to-day household use.

Source: Smith and others, 1993; Barnes and others, 1993; Ramakrishna, 1991a, b.

coal use, which is widespread in Eastern Europe, China, and South Africa. Coal has a higher energy density than wood and so is easier to store. Coal's high energy density also makes it cost-effective to ship over longer distances than wood to efficiently supply urban or rural markets. In these senses, coal is similar to other household fossil fuels. Unlike kerosene and gas, however, coal often represents a decrease in cleanliness relative to wood. Like wood, another solid fuel, coal is difficult to use efficiently in household appliances.

Climbing the energy ladder for cooking can be accomplished using commercially available technologies such as improved cooking stoves and kerosene or LPG. As discussed below, biogas and producer gas are almost at the point of commercialisation, and additional and cleaner advanced technologies for meeting cooking needs are under development.

Improved cooking stoves

Since about 1980, several hundred programmes around the world have focussed on developing and disseminating improved biomass cooking stoves in the villages and urban slums of the developing world. These programmes have ranged in size from the introduction of a few hundred stoves by local non-governmental organisations to huge national efforts in China and India that have affected millions of households. The programmes seek to accelerate the natural trend for people to move towards cleaner, more efficient devices when they are available and affordable.

Such programmes have had mixed success. Some have disseminated many improved stoves with significant lifetimes. Others have not. The failures, however, represent progress along a learning curve, and more recent programmes have tended to have higher success rates. In this regard, it is instructive to compare the two largest initiatives, those of China and India (box 10.1).

Over the past 20 years, perhaps 90 percent of world-wide installations of improved cooking stoves occurred in China. From 1982–99 the Chinese National Improved Stoves Programme reported the installation of improved stoves in more than 175 million rural households. These were mainly biomass stoves used for cooking. But in the northern states of China, where temperatures drop during the winter, dual-use stoves for cooking and heating were included. In China improved stoves are affordable, and the government contribution is low. An improved stove in China costs about 85 yuan ($10), and the government contributes an average of 4.2 yuan per stove ($0.84). Part of the success of the programme is attributed to the attention— including well-publicised national competitions and awards—given to improved stove design.

The Indian programme, initiated in 1983, is called the National Programme on Improved Chulhas (cooking stoves). So far, nearly 30 million stoves have been disseminated. A mix of portable (without chimneys) and fixed designs have been approved. The government subsidises at least half of the costs of the stoves, which amounts to 200 rupees ($4.50) per stove. Although dissemination has been impressive, follow-up surveys suggest that less than one-third of the improved stoves are still in use. Some reasons given for discontinuing use are that the stoves did not really save energy, did not eliminate smoke, or broke down. Other surveys found that adopters felt that stoves were consuming less energy and producing less smoke. The mixed perceptions indicate differing levels of success in implementation.

Several lessons can be learned from the two programmes. The greater success in China can be attributed to programme design and implementation, including the factors described in box 10.1. Both programmes now face pressure to reduce subsidies in a more market-based approach. In addition, although both programmes now incorporate monitoring for energy efficiency, neither includes evaluations of the smoke-exposure benefits.

The cooking needs of the 2 billion people not served by modern fuels correspond to about 1 percent of global commercial energy consumption or 3 percent of global oil consumption.

Another commonly cited example of success is the introduction of a more efficient ceramic charcoal cooking stove, the *jiko*, developed in Kenya. At least 700,000 such stoves are now in use in that country, in more than 50 percent of urban homes and in about 16 percent of rural homes. About 200 small-scale businesses and artisans produce more than 13,000 stoves each month. Both the stove itself and the general programme for disseminating it have been adapted for use in a number of other African nations (table 10.1).

The process of research, development, demonstration, and commercialisation that led first to the improved jiko and then to other high-efficiency stoves was seeded by international and local development funds (in contrast to the Indian and Chinese programmes, which were almost entirely organised and funded domestically). Most important, policy-makers decided not to directly subsidise the production and dissemination of these stoves but to provide support to designers and manufacturers.

Because the stoves were relatively expensive ($15) and their quality was highly variable, sales were slow at first. But continued research and increased competition among manufacturers and vendors spurred innovations in both the materials used and the methods of production. An extensive marketing network for those stoves is flourishing, and prices have fallen to $1–3, depending on size, design, and quality. This outcome is consistent with the learning curve theory, whereby the price of a new technology decreases by a uniform amount (often about 20 percent) for each doubling of cumulative sales (chapter 12).

Part of the success of the jiko, however, is due to its use of a relatively high-quality fuel, charcoal. It is much easier to design simple stoves with high energy efficiency for use with such low-volatility solid fuels relative to those that use the unprocessed biomass that is the main source of household energy in the world's

TABLE 10.1. NUMBER OF IMPROVED STOVES DISSEMINATED IN EAST AND SOUTHERN AFRICA, 1995

Country	Urban	Rural	Total
Kenya	600,000	180,000	780,000
Tanzania	54,000	n.a.	54,000
Uganda	52,000	n.a.	52,000
Ethiopia	23,000	22,000	45,000
Rwanda[a]	30,000	n.a.	30,000
Sudan	27,000	1,400	28,400
Zimbabwe	11,000	10,000	21,000
Burundi[a]	20,500	n.a.	20,500
Somalia[a]	15,400	n.a.	15,400

n.a. – Not available.
a. Civil strife has significantly affected stove programmes and reduced the number of improved stoves in use. *Source: Karekezi and Ranja, 1997.*

villages. Charcoal stoves are also inherently less polluting than those burning unprocessed biomass, and thus do not incorporate chimneys. Like other low-volatility solid fuels—such as some coals—charcoal produces fewer health-damaging particles and gases than wood, but it does produce substantial carbon monoxide. Households relying on such low-volatility fuels, therefore, risk overnight carbon monoxide poisoning, which annually causes thousands of deaths world-wide.

In addition, the process of making charcoal from wood is often quite inefficient, leading to heavy pressure on forests in much of Africa to supply urban areas. The inefficiency of charcoal kilns means that the charcoal fuel cycle is probably the most greenhouse-gas-intensive major fuel cycle in the world, even when the wood is harvested renewably, and often it is not. Thus charcoal could not be a sustainable rural energy option in the long run, unless its supply system were to be drastically altered.

Even the best biomass stoves available today do not greatly reduce the health-damaging pollution from biomass combustion, although they may put it outside through well-operating chimneys or hoods. This is certainly better than releasing the smoke inside; but in densely populated villages and slums, it can lead to heavy neighbourhood pollution. Thus even nearby households using clean (or no!) fuels may suffer from high levels of exposure. Therefore, because of health concerns—unless truly clean-burning biomass stoves can be developed at reasonable costs—in many areas, improved stoves are probably not sustainable in the long run. They may continue to play an important interim role in improving the quality of life of the rural and urban poor; but as concluded in chapter 3, the long-term goal should be to eliminate household use of unprocessed solid fuels.

Kerosene and LPG actually produce fewer greenhouse gas emissions per unit of energy service than biomass fuels used in traditional ways.

Kerosene and liquefied petroleum gas

In countries that achieved successful rural development during the past 50 years, kerosene and then LPG replaced biomass fuels. Figure 10.2 shows the changing household fuel picture in the Republic of Korea as rural development proceeded in the 1960s. At the start of the period, wood was the chief fuel, but 15 years later it had been replaced almost entirely by petroleum-based fuels. Similar transitions have occurred in other regions as well. Natural gas and town gas (made from coal) have continuing important roles in urban development (but rarely in rural areas, because of pipeline transmission requirements).

As consumers climb the energy ladder, kerosene is usually the first modern fuel to be used, because it is more easily transported and stored than LPG. However some countries—notably China—have restricted the availability of kerosene, thereby encouraging the direct movement to LPG. Kerosene, although substantially superior to biomass in efficiency and cleanliness, is not as desirable as LPG, which burns nearly without pollution in comparison with fuels on lower rungs. Of course, liquid and gaseous fuels pose other risks: For LPG, the most important are fires and explosions; in the case of kerosene, children may suffer poisoning due to careless household storage. Experience has shown, however, that these risks are lower than those posed by biomass fuels.

LPG must be distributed in pressurised canisters that, along with the stove, involve significant up-front investments by households. In addition, both LPG and kerosene require a stable, reliable distribution system running from the refinery to neighbourhood distributors, something that does not exist in many parts of the developing world. The combination of these two factors often prevents LPG from being used by many households that could otherwise afford its daily cost. Indeed, in many developing-country cities, the daily cost of LPG would be less than the cost of shipping biomass from rural areas. Lack of capital for the stove and canister and poor supply reliability, however, prevent households from shifting to LPG.

Despite these problems, LPG programmes have been very successful in most of Latin America, particularly in Brazil, where LPG has replaced all other fuels for cooking—even in many remote rural areas. The main reason for this success was a very dependable system of distribution and replacement of LPG canisters.

A study in Hyderabad, India, found that the simple measure of stabilising LPG supplies by the local government encouraged many urban households to shift to LPG. This is a policy without fuel subsidies that saves money for households and has a beneficial impact on the environment (Barnes and others, 1994). If users have a first-cost constraint, the programme should provide low-interest loans towards initial costs. Subsidies to help households meet the up-front costs for equipment such as stoves and canisters are much more acceptable policies than subsidising fuel. Fuel subsidies alone tend to divert use of fuel to industry, transport, and households that already have stoves, making the subsidies very costly, economically inefficient ways to help the poor.

FIGURE 10.2. POST-BIOMASS ENERGY TRANSITION IN THE REPUBLIC OF KOREA, 1965–80

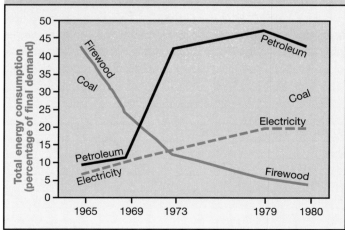

Source: Baldwin, 1987.

Because fossil fuels such as kerosene and LPG are non-renewable and their combustion contributes to greenhouse-gas emissions, some may question their role in sustainable energy strategies. However, the quantity of LPG needed to support cooking for the current unserved population of 2 billion is trivial at the global level (see above). Moreover, kerosene and LPG actually produce fewer greenhouse gas emissions per unit of energy service than biomass fuels used in traditional ways (chapter 3).

Nevertheless, instead of relying on fossil fuels with substantial new infrastructure requirements, it is sometimes desirable to produce clean fuels that can be used efficiently from local biomass resources. Biogas and producer gas systems, as well as advanced technology options such as synthetic LPG or dimethyl ether (DME), appear promising in the longer term.

Biogas for cooking

Biogas, a clean-burning methane-rich fuel gas produced through anaerobic digestion (bacterial action in a tank without air) of suitable biomass feedstocks, is the only biomass-derived modern energy carrier for household applications with which there is widespread experience. Biogas can be generated from cattle dung and animal wastes, and with substantially more difficulty, from some crop residues. Although these feedstocks are frequently used directly as cooking fuel, in most areas they are not preferred fuels and are used only when wood is not available. Biogas systems offer multiple benefits. The digester-effluent is usually a good fertiliser, and, if connected to latrines, biogas plants can provide valuable sanitation services. For cooking and other thermal household tasks, it is simple and reasonably efficient to use the gas directly in conventional low-pressure gas burners. Biogas can also provide lighting when used in mantle lamps.

In societies where suitable feedstocks are readily available, small family-sized biogas digesters were thought to have considerable potential. A number of countries initiated programmes—China and India on a large scale. Results have been mixed, especially in the early stages. China's efforts resulted in the construction of 7 million household-scale digesters from 1973–78. But quality control and management problems resulted in a large number of failures. More recently, coordinated efforts have focused on regions thought to be most promising for the technology. Service organisations and biogas services stations have been established. By 1994, 5 million domestic plants were operating satisfactorily. India's experience has been on a slightly smaller scale, but the numbers are still impressive—by the end of 1998, almost 2.8 million domestic plants were installed. India's Ministry of Non-Conventional Energy Sources has identified a potential for 12 million digesters.

Biogas experience in Africa has been on a far smaller scale and has been generally disappointing at the household level. The capital cost, maintenance, and management support required have been higher than expected. Moreover, under subsistence agriculture, access to cattle dung and to water that must be mixed with slurry has been more of an obstacle than expected. However, possibilities are better where farming is done with more actively managed livestock and where

dung supply is abundant—as in rearing feedlot-based livestock.

The initial enthusiasm for biogas has thus been somewhat dampened by experience. Because of its requirement for relatively large amounts of animal dung, the niche for household biogas plants is likely to remain small. Poor families do not have access to enough dung, and better-off families with sufficient animals often prefer to purchase fuel and fertiliser rather than spend time gathering dung and managing the often-temperamental digesters. Even so, in the right social and institutional context, and with appropriate technical expertise, the potential for biogas remains significant. These conditions seem to have been achieved in the Biogas Support Programme in Nepal through an innovative financial scheme (box 10.2).

Producer gas for cooking

An alternative to biogas is producer gas, a mixture consisting largely of carbon monoxide, hydrogen, and nitrogen. Producer gas is generated in a thermochemical conversion process through partial oxidation in air of biomass feedstocks (Stassen, 1995). The basic principles of generating producer gas have been known since the 18th century. Producer gas derived from biomass has been used for domestic and industrial heating purposes, for cooking, for stationary power, and for motor vehicle applications. (During World War II more than a million gasifier-powered vehicles helped to keep basic transport systems running in Europe and Asia.)

During periods of peace and wide availability of cheap, more convenient fossil fuels, interest in biomass-derived producer gas has been low. The energy crises of the 1970s rekindled interest in producer gas technology, but interest waned again with the collapse of world oil prices in the mid-1980s. Once again, there is growing interest in technology for making producer gas from biomass for cooking, heating, and electricity generation. Power generation applications of producer gas are discussed later in this chapter. Here the focus is on domestic cooking.

Part of the reason for renewed interest in producer gas technology is increasing concern about the adverse health effects of indoor air pollution caused by biomass and coal burned for domestic cooking and heating (chapter 3) and the large role that producer gas used in gas-burning stoves could play in reducing this pollution—the air pollution from these stoves is nearly zero. In typical agricultural regions, the energy generation potential from producer gas is greater than that from biogas, because crop residues tend to be more abundant than dung.[4] And whereas biogas generation is often the preferred energy conversion technology for making use of the energy content of dung, producer gas generation is a far easier approach for exploiting the energy content of crop residues.

In addition, because it is a chemical rather than biological process, producer gas manufacture is not sensitive to ambient temperature, greatly increasing the potential geographic extent of its application. Another reason for renewed interest in biomass-derived producer gas in China is a severe new air pollution problem caused by the burning of crop residues in fields—a consequence of the rising affluence of farmers (see the annex to this chapter). This problem is forcing a search for new productive uses of crop residues.

Several Chinese provinces are making efforts to convert residues into producer gas in centralised village-scale gasifiers and to distribute the cooking gas by pipes to households. For example, the Shangdong Academy of Sciences has developed crop residue gasifiers and centralised

> Subsidies to help households meet the up-front costs for equipment such as stoves and canisters are much more acceptable policies than subsidising fuel.

gas supply system technology for cooking gas applications, and 20 such village-scale gasification systems are operating in the province (Dai and Lu, 1998). Monitoring and assessment of a village experience in Shangdong Province (case 1 in the annex) shows that current technology has considerable consumer appeal and would be highly competitive if the gas were properly priced. The technology for making producer gas from crop residues promises to be widely deployable for cooking applications, and thus to largely solve the indoor air pollution problem caused by stoves that burn biomass or coal.

One problem posed by current gasifiers used in China is that they produce substantial tars (condensable hydrocarbons that are scrubbed from the gas before delivery to consumers). If disposed of without adequate treatment to groundwater or surface water, these tar wastes would pose significant water pollution problems. Moreover, the option of using crop residues or producer gas for cooking will not solve the air pollution problem in China that arises from burning excess crop residues in the field. The producer gas option is about twice as efficient as direct combustion in providing cooking services, so that only about half as much residue is required for cooking relative to direct-combustion stove systems.[5] At the national level, use of just 60 percent of all crop residues potentially available for energy purposes would be adequate to meet all rural cooking needs.

In addition, the producer gas cooking option poses another public health risk: Typically, about 20 percent of producer gas is carbon monoxide—of which accidental leaks into houses can be lethal. Although some hydrocarbon impurities in the gas impart an odour to producer gas that is usually noticed before a lethal dose is inhaled, occasional accidents are inevitable. Therefore (as discussed below), safe, clean, advanced technological options for producing cooking fuel from biomass should be the focus of research and development.

Rural electrification

Electricity is at the top of the energy ladder and is highly efficient and convenient for some specialised cooking appliances, such as rice cookers and microwave ovens. But for many years to come, electricity is unlikely to be practical for general cooking in most rural areas of the developing world. Nevertheless, for lighting, communication, refrigeration, and motor applications, electricity is essential for a satisfactory quality of life. Moreover, electricity is key to improving agricultural productivity through mechanisation and is essential for many rural industrial activities. Considerable progress has been made in rural electrification programmes designed to extend electricity services to isolated villages (table 10.2).

The centralised approach

Between 1970 and 1990, 800 million people in rural areas gained access to electricity. Yet of the 3 billion people living in rural areas of developing countries in 1990, 2 billion were still without access to electricity. This global total masks significant variations between

TABLE 10.2. GLOBAL POPULATION AND ACCESS TO ELECTRICITY, 1970–90 (MILLIONS OF PEOPLE)

Country	1970	1980	1990
World population	3,600	4,400	5,300
Rural population	2,600	3.000	3,200
With access to electricity[a]	610	1,000	1,400
Without access to electricity	2,000	2,000	1,800
Percentage of rural population with access	23	33	44

a. Access includes people living in villages connected to power lines. This does not necessarily mean that most households are hooked up to electricity.

Source: Davis, 1995.

regions and countries. In particular, China's rapid electrification programme—through which 365 million rural residents gained access to electricity from 1970–90—significantly increased the world total. If China were excluded, current access levels would drop from 44 to 33 percent, or exactly the level of 1980.[6]

The distinction between access to electricity by villages and households should also be noted. India, for example, has an ambitious rural electrification programme, targeting agricultural end use. But while 80 percent of villages have electricity, less than 50 percent of households can afford it.

Several studies highlight an important point for economic success: electrification cannot by itself ensure economic development. It is a necessary but insufficient condition. Electrification works best when overall conditions are right for rural income growth and when it is complemented by social and economic infrastructure development—such as rural water supplies, health programmes, primary and secondary education, and regional and feeder roads. Thus rural electrification contributes to but is not a substitute for other rural development measures.

Rural electrification programmes have typically concentrated on connecting villages and remote areas to a national grid—often owned and operated by a public utility. The tendency has been to extend the grid incrementally, reaching towns and settlements in order of increasing capital costs. Thus remote areas with small populations are likely to be the last to receive electricity. Moreover, many rural areas face high transmission and distribution costs, for several reasons:

- The capacity of power lines is inefficiently used because of low population.
- Densities and demand levels are low.
- Villages may have very peaky (undiversified) demand profiles.
- Line losses tend to be high.

In addition, incremental extension of the grid (rather than extension optimised to minimise losses) causes lines to be strung haphazardly, resulting in greater losses.

The decentralised approach

Because of the problems of supplying grid electricity for small, scattered, peaky loads, decentralised electricity generation is becoming more attractive. With decentralised systems, the high costs of transmission and distribution networks can be avoided. But small-scale, decentralised solutions face other barriers. The decentralised generation technologies discussed below are diesel-engine generator sets, small-scale hydropower, photovoltaics, wind, and small-scale biopower using producer gas. No attempt is made to be comprehensive on the technological opportunities for decentralised electricity generation. Instead, the discussion illustrates key features of different technologies, highlighting advantages and drawbacks for rural development needs.

Diesel-engine generator sets. Diesel generators are common in many remote settlements, either for a single user or as part of a local distribution network. Such systems may be operated by a power utility or, more commonly, by private enterprises. Rural hospitals, government offices, and police stations in remote areas typically have their own diesel generators.

Diesel sets with capacities of 50–500 kilowatts of electricity are widely used in rural Latin America and Asia but have only recently been disseminated in Africa. The electricity produced by diesel sets typically costs $0.30 a kilowatt-hour—two to three times the cost of electricity from grids in urban areas but still cost-effective relative to grid extension. (This cost is typical of the Amazonia region of Brazil, where there are 900 diesel sets with a total generating capacity of 391 megawatts.) The high costs of maintenance and of transporting diesel fuel and lubricating oil to remote places make electricity fairly expensive.[7] Despite these costs, electricity is typically highly valued by local populations because of the enormous improvements in living standards that it brings (box 10.3). But while high-cost electricity may be acceptable for satisfying basic needs in households and for some agricultural and cottage industry applications, lower costs are needed to attract a greater job-generating industrial base to rural areas.

Small-scale hydropower. Small-scale hydropower is a locally available resource that in some regions can be exploited to deliver electricity or mechanical power (for pumping water and other applications) to rural areas. The resource potential for small-scale hydropower is discussed in chapter 5; its technology, costs, and future prospects are discussed in chapter 7. Here the focus is on current activities and the prospects for using small-scale hydropower to address rural development needs.

Small-scale hydropower technology, which is being pursued in about 100 countries, is often divided into three categories: micro hydro (less than 100 kilowatts), mini hydro (100–1,000 kilowatts), and small hydro (1–30 megawatts). By the end of 1994 China alone had 6,000 small-scale hydropower stations with a total installed capacity of 15,650 megawatts, supplying 49 terawatt-hours of electricity (Qui and others, 1996)—29 percent of hydroelectric power generation and nearly 8 percent of rural electricity consumption (Deng and others, 1996). In 1989 China accounted for about 38 percent of world-wide small hydropower (23.5 gigawatts), at which time more than 130 companies manufactured equipment specifically for plants with capacities ranging from 10 kilowatts to more than 10 megawatts. Of the 205 turbines ordered world-wide in 1989, the size distribution was micro hydro, 15 percent; mini hydro, 57 percent; and small hydro, 28 percent (Moreira and Poole, 1993). In China and Viet Nam even sub-kilowatt systems have been sold for household electrification. Such turbines are installed at the end of hose-pipes, with somewhat unreliable but serviceable results. However, the potential market for such systems is limited by the availability of water resources.

On a somewhat larger scale, hydropower plants of 50 kilowatts and more can be used to electrify communities or small regions by establishing mini grids. Costs are highly variable (chapter 7), depending on the site topography, proximity of the site to the main load area, and hydrological conditions.

Small-scale hydropower has one drawback: it is almost always obtained from run-of-river plants that lack the reservoir capacity to store water. Consequently, severe seasonal variations in power output may occur, depending on a site's hydrology. Thus the long-term viability of small-scale hydropower may depend on backup electricity that is supplied either locally or through the grid (Moreira and Poole, 1993).

Photovoltaics. Photovoltaic technology is cost-effective in providing electricity to rural areas at the very smallest scales (typically less than 100 watts) in areas with no access to grid electricity and where electricity demand is characterised by such low levels and infrequency that even diesel electricity cannot compete (see chapter 7 for details about photovoltaic technology and its economics in such applications). The potential for photovoltaic technology to support rural development arises from the fact that it can be used for household lighting, radios, and television sets, and to refrigerate medicines at rural clinics.

In 1999 global photovoltaic sales totalled 200 megawatts, 10 percent of which was for off-grid applications in rural areas of developing countries. One important obstacle to wider rural deployment of photovoltaic technology is the limited financing available for such small systems (see section below on the time horizon for technological options). Kenya has the world's highest penetration rate of household photovoltaic systems, with more than 80,000 systems in place and annual sales of 20,000 systems. Fifty local and fifteen international importers, assemblers, installers, and after-sales providers serve this market, which developed without significant aid, subsidies, or other support. Although the current market is strong, there is still a tremendous need to standardise equipment, as well as improve batteries, lighting fixtures, and electronic ballasts used in integrated household photovoltaic systems. In addition, possible credit arrangements need to be studied, as do the relative advantages of leasing a system rather than purchasing it.

In 1999 South Africa's power utility, Eskom, entered into a joint venture with Shell Solar Systems to provide 50,000 homes with photovoltaic systems in areas where grid connection is not considered feasible. This three-year programme contributes to a market that is

---

BOX 10.3. DIESEL ENGINES IN A MULTIPURPOSE PLATFORM PROJECT IN MALI

In Mali a project is under way to introduce, by 2003, 450 multipurpose platforms to provide, at the village scale, mechanical power and electricity through diesel engines to 10 percent of the country's rural population. At least two-thirds of these platforms will be coupled to water and electricity distribution networks. By 2003 rural access to electricity is expected to be more than 3 percentage points higher than urban access. Although the project is based on the use of diesel fuel oil, it is envisaged that in the future pourghere nut oil or some other liquid biofuel will be used.

The engine selected for this project is a 1950s-vintage slow diesel engine (a Lister engine, from India). This engine was chosen because of its low initial capital cost; low prices for its spare parts; its ability to operate without damage on the relatively low-quality diesel fuel typically available in villages; its ease of operation, maintenance, and repair by local artisans (blacksmiths, mechanics, carpenters); and the availability of a network of sellers and servicers for it throughout much of Mali.

It is intended that the engine in a typical platform would power various types of equipment, such as a cereal mill, husker, alternator, battery charger, pump, welder, and carpentry machine. Thus the platforms would reduce many rural women's burdensome tasks (fetching water, grinding cereal); offer them income-generating opportunities and management experience; and, as they become more economically independent, help them improve their social status. Because so many activities would be supported by the platforms, their economic and social benefits would be felt at multiple levels, resulting in an overall empowerment of women. In the pilot phase of the project (1996–98), during which 45 platforms with 14 water or electricity networks

were installed, the platforms' availability stimulated the creation, development, and modernisation of artisanal activities in participating villages. The platforms are being operated and maintained on a cost-recovery basis by private enterprise.

By design, the acquisition of a multipurpose platform is a demand-driven process. The initial request has to be made by a recognised, registered women's association at the grass-roots level. International donors are subsidising equipment costs (including the engine, mill, de-huller, alternator, battery charger, and building) at up to $1,500 per module. In situations where the supply of electricity and running water is requested, the contribution of the international donor can be increased by up to $10,000 per module. An equity contribution of at least 50 percent is required of the women's associations. Operation and maintenance costs are borne entirely by beneficiaries.

The mechanical work provided by the engines costs about $0.25 per kilowatt-hour (see table). Notably, more than 70 percent of the cost is for diesel fuel and lubricating oil, which must be imported into the region. If the mechanical work were converted to electricity, the added cost associated with the generator and conversion losses would increase the electricity cost to at least $0.30 per kilowatt-hour. If liquid biofuels produced in the region eventually could be substituted for imported oil, the region's balance of payments would be improved, although costs would probably not be reduced much or at all, because liquid biofuels tend to be more costly than petroleum fuels.

Although this project is interesting in revealing consumer wants, it is in its initial phase of implementation, and only experience will supply information on real costs. Nevertheless,

the project shows that there are attractive alternatives to grid extension, that rural electrification does not necessarily mean grid electrification, that decentralised electrification is a serious option, and that entrepreneur-driven participatory development is crucial.

Cost of mechanical work for a diesel engine, Mali multipurpose platform		
Cost	Dollars per year	Dollars per kilowatt-hour
Capital[a]	131	0.018
Fuel[b]	1,140	0.138
Maintenance		
Every 100 hours		
Lubricating oil	158	0.022
Other	36	0.005
Every 500 hours	179	0.025
Every 1,000 hours	104	0.015
Every 1,500 hours	74	0.010
Total	1,820	0.233

a. For an 8-horsepower (6-kilowatt) Indian Lister diesel engine with a 7-year plant life costing $600 (excluding the cost of a generator) and operated 1,500 hours a year at 80 percent of rated capacity, on average, so that the annual average capacity factor is 13.7 percent. Assuming a 12 percent discount rate, the capital recovery factor is 21.9 percent a year.

b. For a diesel fuel price of $0.44 a litre and an engine efficiency of 30 percent (higher heating value basis).

Source: Mali and UNDP, 1999.

believed to exceed 2 million households. Customers pay a monthly rate to lease and use the equipment, which allows a reasonable rate of return to Eskom.

Still another approach to reach a greater portion of low-income rural people was adopted by Soluz. This company developed a system to lease small photovoltaic battery systems to provide high-quality electric services at an affordable price while offering a positive financial return to its investors. In 1993, with assistance from the Rockefeller Foundation, Soluz conducted a pre-feasibility study for a solar electricity delivery company and construction of a company prototype for 200 rural homes in the Dominican Republic. The company installs standalone photovoltaic battery systems on or near rural homes yet retains ownership of the systems. The photovoltaic systems provide lighting and access to information services (through radio and television). Users make regular payments, as determined in the lease agreement, and the company is responsible for maintaining the systems.

In Central America customers pay a monthly fee of $15–20, depending on the size of the photovoltaic system leased. The company has an on-time collection rate exceeding 90 percent. Many customers are small businesses, for whom the provision of high-quality energy services contributes to increased profitability.

But even where appropriate financing is made available, the poorest households often cannot afford photovoltaic systems (box 10.4). In considering measures to support photovoltaic programmes for rural areas, it is important to pay particular attention to the poorest households and to strategies to make the technology available to them.

Although significant in improving the quality of life in rural areas, without major cost reductions, photovoltaic technology will be limited mainly to remote household and other small-scale applications and will not be able to compete in the provision of electricity for manufacturing or even most cottage industrial applications.

Household-scale wind turbines (of about 100 watts) offer benefits to wind-rich regions similar to those offered by domestic photovoltaic systems.

Wind. There are two promising ways to exploit wind power to meet rural energy needs. The first is household units that provide electricity at scales where neither grid power nor mini-grid power from diesel units is cost-effective. The second is village-scale wind-battery-diesel hybrid systems (using wind turbines with capacities typically of 5–100 kilowatts).

Household-scale wind turbines (of about 100 watts) offer benefits to wind-rich regions similar to those offered by domestic photovoltaic systems. Such turbines have been developed, produced, and deployed, for example, in China, mostly in the Inner Mongolian Autonomous Region. The dispersion of houses in this region of low population density (18 people per square kilometre) makes household wind systems a viable option for providing electricity. In Inner Mongolia an estimated 130,000 small-scale (mostly 50–200 watt) wind energy systems have been installed, providing electricity for lighting, radios, television, and small appliances to more than 500,000 people, mostly rural herdsmen (about one-third of the population). About 89,000 of these systems are operating routinely, producing from 8.7 megawatts of installed capacity about 15.7 gigawatt-hours a year (Wu, 1995).

The success of the Chinese programme was achieved through careful planning and the creation of an effective regional and local infrastructure for manufacturing, sales, maintenance, and training. This included the development of a market for individual household systems through various subsidy mechanisms. The government of Inner Mongolia also recognised and allowed for the long gestation period and sustained support needed to create a thriving local industry. The project has also led to technology transfers at many levels—between Inner Mongolia and local, regional, and national organisations within China, as well as with other countries. Replicating the programme would require enough institutional capacity to support such ventures.

Where rural households are clustered in villages far from electric grids that are served instead by diesel-engine generator sets, an alternative option is to deploy wind turbines in wind-diesel or wind-battery-diesel hybrid configurations, which have been installed in many parts of the world (Baring-Gould and others, 1999). In regions where diesel fuel is costly, these hybrid systems can lead to lower electricity costs and less air pollution than conventional diesel-engine generator sets.

Unlike the household-scale wind turbines being developed in China, however, many components of these hybrid systems are based on technology developed in industrialised countries, and costs of imported systems are often prohibitive. But if these systems can be mass produced in developing countries under arrangements—such as international industrial joint ventures—that are conducive to technology transfer, substantial cost reductions are possible (see chapter 7 for an example).

Small-scale biopower using producer gas. Biomass-derived producer gas (see above) can be used to make electricity at scales

---

BOX 10.4. EQUITY ISSUES RELATING TO PHOTOVOLTAIC TECHNOLOGY FOR RURAL AREAS IN INDIA

Of the 79 million rural households in India without electricity (out of a total of 114 million rural households), 7, 17, and 75 percent of households could afford, respectively, 37-watt (four-light), 20-watt (two-light), and 10-watt (one-light) photovoltaic systems with Grameen-type financing (five-year loans at 12 percent interest with a 15 percent down payment; see box 10.7). Thus it appears that the poorest 25 percent of households cannot afford any photovoltaic purchase, even with financing.

But such findings, which are based on willingness-to-pay considerations, might be overly simplistic. The availability of lighting might be exploited to earn extra income that could make a photovoltaic system affordable for even the poorest household. If, for example, a poor Indian household could weave two extra baskets a night by the light made available by a 10-watt photovoltaic system, the technology would become affordable.

Source: Reddy, 1999; Hande, 1999.

---

comparable to those associated with diesel-engine generator sets. The potential benefits are:

- The capacity to use locally available biomass as fuel instead of oil imported into the region.
- Lower electricity generation costs than with diesel.
- Increased rural income generation, and possibly rural industrialisation, as a result of the lower electricity cost.

The reciprocating compression-ignition (diesel) engine is the main commercially viable engine available for these applications.[8] When producer gas is used with such engines, it must be supplemented with a pilot oil to assist ignition because mixtures of producer gas and air do not auto-ignite at the pressures and temperatures realised when the gas is compressed. As a result producer gas can typically displace about 70 percent of diesel fuel consumption. When operated with producer gas in the dual-fuel mode, diesel-engine generators have somewhat lower efficiencies and rated capacities (typically about 20 percent lower than when operating on pure diesel fuel).

Producer gas must meet far higher standards for reciprocating engine operation than for cooking or heating (domestic or industrial) applications. The main problem is the propensity of tars formed in the gasifier to condense on downstream surfaces, causing problems such as the sticking of engine gas intake valves. Most early gasifiers generated so much tar that adequate gas clean-up for engine operation was impractical, and tar removal would significantly reduce the potential for power generation from a given amount of biomass feedstock. But in recent years, gasifiers have been developed (notably in India) that generate tars at levels that make engine operation on producer gas acceptable (Kartha and Larson, 2000).

Biomass-derived technology for producer gas, reciprocating-engine generators is commercially ready. In India, for example, the Ministry of Non-Conventional Energy Sources has supported development efforts that have led to technically sound gasifier-engine systems and trial implementation of more than 1,600 such systems with a total installed capacity of more than 28 megawatts (Kartha and Larson, 2000). For engines operated on producer gas and pilot oil, fuel costs are typically much lower than for conventional diesel systems. But capital, operation, and maintenance costs are higher (see table A10.1).

In fact, the savings derived from diesel replacement have to pay for the extra initial capital cost as well as the extra operation and maintenance costs incurred for the gasifier. The technology can be cost-effective, either where diesel fuel costs are very high (for example, $0.35–0.40 a litre or more, as is often the case for extremely remote regions) or, with efficient capital utilisation, in regions where diesel fuel prices are more moderate. If the diesel fuel price is $0.25 a litre, a typical system must be operated at full capacity for 3,000 hours a year to break even with a conventional diesel system. About 6,000 hours of annual operation are needed to realise a cost savings of 25 percent (see table A10.1). It is desirable to seek opportunities for such high rates of capacity utilisation because consumers are

Historically, electric utilities have discouraged independent power producers from selling electricity into grids, but this situation is changing as electricity markets are becoming more competitive.

likely to be more motivated to adopt the technology if they can realise substantial cost savings. Unfortunately, achieving high rates of capital utilisation is often difficult because local electricity demand is typically low and sporadic but peaky, with very little electric load diversity.

A promising strategy for launching a producer gas, engine-generator technology industry would be to focus initially on market opportunities where the technology could be deployed in large numbers in baseload configurations. This requires that two conditions be satisfied. Biomass supplies have to be adequate for fuelling baseload plants, and the demand for electricity has to be adequate to justify baseload operation. Strong candidate regions for doing this are agricultural regions of China where crop residues are abundant and where grid connections exist (87 percent of the rural population in China is grid-connected), so that electricity generated in excess of local needs can be sold into the grid (Li, Bai, and Overend, 1998). Historically, electric utilities have discouraged independent power producers from selling electricity into grids, but this situation is changing as electricity markets are becoming more competitive (chapter 12).

New technologies that might be commercialised in the near term (5–10 years) offer the potential for electricity generation at costs significantly lower than with current technology. One promising new technology is the microturbine, which might be deployed with essentially the same gasifiers that have been developed to provide producer gas for use with diesel dual-fuel engine generator sets.

Microturbines are gas turbines designed for operation at scales of 50–250 kilowatts of electricity, with electric efficiencies (lower heating value) of 25–30 percent for larger units. Microturbines were originally developed for military and aerospace applications and are now offered by several companies for applications in distributed power and cogeneration markets, mainly for use with natural gas or diesel fuel. Developers expect microturbine use to grow rapidly for such applications in regions where there is competition in electricity markets (chapter 8). The technology appears to be readily adaptable for use with biomass-derived producer gas (Henderick, 2000).

Microturbines are less complex (some variants have only one moving part) than reciprocating engines. They can be fuelled with producer gas without de-rating and without loss of efficiency relative to operation on natural gas or diesel fuel. Most important, they need no costly pilot oil (Henderick, 2000). In regions where crop residues or other low-cost biomass feedstocks are readily available, there are reasonably good prospects that the technology could become widely competitive in grid-connected applications (Henderick and Williams, 2000). Case 2 in the annex describes a potential application of the technology to the trigeneration of cooking gas, electricity, and space heating through district heating in a hypothetical village in northern China.

To illustrate the aggregate potential of this technology, consider that in China, 376 million tonnes of crop residues a year are potentially available for energy purposes.[9] Committing these residues to trigeneration (case 2 in the annex) could provide enough cooking gas for 230 million people (27 percent of China's rural population) plus 270 terawatt-hours a year of electricity (equivalent to 30 percent of coal power generation in China in 1997) plus hot water for space heating in regions where it is needed (for example, in regions with cold winters).

Several public policy initiatives could facilitate the creation of a viable industry for small-scale biopower technologies. One important measure would be to eliminate or phase out diesel fuel subsidies that exist in many regions. Another would be market reforms that facilitate the sale of electricity into electric grids, coupled with incentives to encourage the extension of electric grids to more rural areas. Notably, the commercial availability of competitive baseload biopower technology could profoundly influence the economics of extending electric grids to rural areas. In contrast to the poor capacity utilisation (and hence poor economics) of transmission-distribution lines sending electrons from centralised power plants to rural areas, high capacity factors (and thus more favourable economics) could be realised if electrons instead flowed to urban centres from baseload village-scale biopower plants.

Finally, demonstration projects are needed to prove the viability of new technological concepts for biopower. Projects are needed for biopower systems based on gasification of alternative crop residue feedstocks, for which tar production rates are higher than for wood chips (Henderick and Williams, 2000). Such projects could involve the use of commercially established diesel dual-fuel engine technologies. Demonstrations are also needed of microturbines in producer gas applications. If carried out together with the above institutional reforms, these projects could lead to commercially viable microturbine-based products for biopower applications in the near term (2005–10).

Leapfrogging to new rungs on the energy ladder

The previous sections have shown that existing and near-term energy technologies have great potential for improving the quality of life in rural areas. But advanced technologies have residual problems that might need to be addressed. For instance, fuels such as LPG are highly desirable for cooking, but making LPG widely available requires considerable infrastructure for distribution, and finding ways to make LPG affordable to the poorest households is a major challenge. Moreover, because LPG is derived from petroleum—a commodity for which price swings can be substantial, as recent experience has shown—price spikes are likely to be burdensome for lower-income households that depend on LPG for their cooking needs.

Local manufacture of clean cooking fuels (such as biogas and producer gas derived from biomass feedstocks) is a strategy for addressing the fuel-infrastructure challenges and price volatility concerns posed by exclusive reliance on LPG. This strategy also provides opportunities for addressing the needs of the very poorest house-holds, because the need to gather typically dispersed biomass feedstocks (such as dung for biogas or crop residues for producer gas) and deliver them to the conversion facility can sometimes make it possible for the poor to monetise their labour and thereby earn income to help pay for these clean cooking fuels (case 2 in the annex).

But today's available gaseous cooking fuel technologies have limitations. Biogas technologies, though well suited for use with dung feedstocks, are not easily applied to crop residues, which tend to be much more abundant. And a persistent concern about producer gas is that it contains carbon monoxide, accidental leaks of which might lead to fatalities. Odourants added to producer gas could greatly reduce the risk of poisoning, but accidents are difficult to avoid completely.

Advanced technologies can make it possible to manufacture synthetic cooking fuels from biomass that are non-toxic as well as clean. A promising approach is to adapt to biomass some of the technologies being developed for fossil fuels—specifically, syngas-based fluid fuels (chapter 8). Strong candidates are synthetic LPG (SLPG) and dimethyl ether (DME), which can be made from any carbonaceous feedstock by catalytic synthesis from syngas (a gaseous mixture consisting largely of carbon monoxide and hydrogen). SLPG (like petroleum-derived LPG, a mixture of propane and butane) and DME are superclean, non-toxic cooking fuels that are gaseous at ambient conditions but can be stored and delivered to consumers as liquids in moderately pressurised canisters. These fuels can be produced from crop residues or other biomass feedstocks through thermochemical gasification to produce the needed syngas. (Case 3 in the annex discusses the potential offered by such technologies for rural regions of China rich in crop residues.)

In addition to the toxicity advantages offered by SLPG and DME, both fuels could be readily transported in canisters by truck or donkey cart to remote, scattered households. Producer gas, by contrast, is a viable option primarily for villages in which houses are clustered closely enough to make pipe transport economically viable. Thus SLPG and DME extend the scope of the cooking fuel markets that could be served relative to producer gas. DME is also a potentially strong low-polluting synthetic fuel for diesel-engine vehicle applications (chapter 8) and might be used as tractor fuel, thereby facilitating the mechanisation of agriculture.

Neither SLPG nor DME is currently produced for fuel applications, but either fuel derived from biomass feedstocks could probably be brought to market readiness by 2010–15 if there were sufficient market interest and a focused development effort. Because neither SLPG nor DME is currently on the market anywhere in the world, a shift from the use of current low-quality fuels to either might be described as jumping to entirely new rungs at the top of the energy ladder (technological leapfrogging).

The time horizon for technological options

Chapters 6–8 and this chapter show that there are abundant opportun-ities for technological change relating to rural energy. Technological change is desirable to the extent that it serves development needs. Rural development planners can help shape the course of technological change for desirable options, taking into account the time horizons required for development and implementation—demanding more of the longer-term options in addressing societal needs. Options that warrant focussed attention in the near term (that is, implementation in the next 5 years) as alternatives to current technology should offer the potential for immediate improvement. For the medium term (5–15 years), planners should emphasise technologies that can potentially achieve dramatic improvements relative to current technology. To the extent that technologies realisable in the medium term fall short of performance consistent with sustainable development goals, policy-makers should also encourage for the long-term (15–30 years) technologies that are fully consistent with sustainable development goals.

It is also wise to have a balanced portfolio with a combination of near-, medium-, and long-term options, to ensure a continuing flow of improved technologies into rural energy markets. Successes with near-term improvements can help win political support for the development of longer-term options. Some important technological options for rural energy in the near, medium, and long terms are summarised in table 10.3.

Accelerating rural energy development

The preceding sections show that there are many technological opportunities for implementing the goals set forth at the start of this chapter: providing clean liquid or gaseous fuels for cooking and electricity for lighting and other basic household amenities, and making bulk electricity available at low cost for mechanising rural agriculture and promoting rural industrialisation.

Both centralised and decentralised energy technologies and strategies can make contributions to reaching these ends. But new strategies and policies are needed to increase access to these modern energy services and to make modern energy services widely affordable. Coordinated efforts that include the active participation of rural people can accelerate the process.

Integrated rural development

Making modern energy services more readily available is a necessary but insufficient condition for rural development. To be most effective, certain forms of energy (such as grid-based electricity) should be introduced into rural areas only after, or along with, other development inputs or infrastructure components. To achieve this integration, it is essential that there be horizontal communication among all agencies involved in rural development.

Many rural development activities—agriculture, transport, water supply, education, income generation, health care—have energy requirements. Yet the ministries and departments responsible for these activities rarely coordinate or cooperate with the ministry of energy, or with one another, to arrive at the most rational, integrated solution

TABLE 10.3. SOME NEAR-, MEDIUM-, AND LONG-TERM TECHNOLOGICAL OPTIONS FOR RURAL ENERGY

Energy source or task	Present	Near term	Medium term	Long term
Source Electricity	Grid or no electricity	Natural gas combined cycles, biomass-based generation using gasifiers coupled to internal combustion engines, photovoltaic, small wind, small hydroelectric for applications remote from grids	Biomass-based generation using gasifiers coupled to micro-turbines and integrated gasifier combined cycles, mini grids involving various combinations of photovoltaic, wind, small hydroelectric, batteries	Grid-connected photovoltaic and solar thermal, biomass-based generation using gasifiers coupled to fuel cells and fuel cell/turbine hybrids
Fuel	Wood, charcoal, dung, crop residues	Natural gas, LPG, producer gas, biogas	Syngas, DME	Biomass-derived DME with electricity coproduct
Cogeneration (combined heat and power)		Internal combustion engines, turbines	Microturbines and integrated gasifier combined cycles	Fuel cells, fuel cell/turbine hybrids
Task Cooking	Woodstoves	Improved woodstoves, LPG stoves, biogas	Producer gas, natural gas and DME stoves	Electric stoves, catalytic burners
Lighting	Oil and kerosene lamps	Electric lights	Fluorescent and compact fluorescent lamps	Improved fluorescent and compact fluorescent lamps
Motive power	Human- and animal-powered devices	Internal combustion engines, electric motors	Biofueled prime movers, improved motors	Fuel cells
Process heat	Wood, biomass	Electric furnaces, cogeneration, producer gas, NG/solar thermal furnaces	Induction furnaces, biomass/solar thermal furnaces	Solar thermal furnaces with heat storage

to their energy needs. Decentralisation of rural energy planning may help achieve this. But optimising the allocation of development resources requires attention at the central government planning level as well. In the many places where integrated rural development has been pursued, the availability of affordable modern energy supplies has proven to be a catalyst for economic and social transformation.

The provision of affordable financial services for rural people has long been a prime component of rural development strategies. Originally, these strategies focussed on concessional loans to farmers. More recently, however, this approach has been replaced by much wider financing for rural activities, with lower transaction costs. By creating rural financial markets and integrating them with general financial markets, it may be possible to mobilise substantial domestic savings as the main capital resource for rural people—and to reduce their dependence on concessional outside funds. Where urban-biased financial policies have inhibited the creation of effective rural financial institutions, new policies and strategies should seek to integrate rural and urban financial services and thus promote the greatest financial efficiency and lowest credit costs for rural people.

Involving rural people (particularly women) in decision-making

Above all, planning for rural energy development should have a decentralised component and should involve rural people—the customers—in planning and decision-making. And special attention should be devoted to involving women, because they bear the burden of traditional energy systems and are likely to be the greatest beneficiaries of improved systems. A major driving force for the move towards decentralisation has been the recognition of the limited extent to which benefits have flowed to rural people from the investments already made. More active involvement of rural people (particularly women) and their institutions in identifying rural energy problems, and in formulating and implementing plans to overcome them, would result in more efficient, rational use of resources and more equitable sharing of the benefits of development.

Decentralisation of rural energy planning is wise for other reasons as well. Rural energy systems are based primarily on biomass, a local energy resource. Although historically this has involved direct combustion of biomass for cooking or heating (as this chapter has shown), clean, convenient, modern energy carriers can also be derived from biomass. Consequently, an assessment of the demand and supply flows and of desirable interventions must all also occur on the same geographic scale. Through their superior knowledge of the local situation, local people—women in particular—can be integral parts of the solution.

Strategies for expanding access to modern energy services

Often, policies ensuring that supplies—even from centralised production sources—are reliable and stable can promote the use of modern energy carriers. The Hyderabad, India, example (see above) shows that by the simple expedient of stabilising LPG supplies, the local government was able to encourage many households to shift from biomass to LPG for cooking.

For rural electrification through grid extension, rural cooperatives seem to be a viable alternative to grid extension by the large parastatals that have dominated power generation in developing countries. In Bangladesh financial and technical failures of public power utilities in 1980 led to a government-supported take-over of its parastatals by rural electrification cooperatives. Now numbering 45, the cooperatives have engineered a rapid expansion of grid-based rural electricity supply that serves 1.6 million consumers—as many as the public sector in urban areas. Power outages have fallen dramatically, while revenue collection has improved from 91 to 98 percent, despite higher tariffs. Most important, the cooperatives have fostered an alternative structure to meet a demand that was previously unexpected in such a poor country. They have also demonstrated that consumers have considerable interest in getting access to electricity and are willing to pay for reliable service.

More effective electric grid extension measures can also help promote the wider availability of electricity from local biomass sources by making village-scale biopower-generating technology more attractive to investors. Grid access would make it possible to operate biopower plants as baseload units, thereby increasing capacity utilisation and reducing generation costs per kilowatt-hour. Grid access would enable rural populations to sell into the grid electricity produced in excess of local needs—until local rural industrial capacity could be increased to more fully use the electricity produced this way (case 2 in the annex). Thus a promising new approach would be to couple grid extension in regions rich in crop residues (or other suitable biomass resources) to measures that encourage village-scale biopower generation.

This strategy would also make investments in grid extension more attractive. The availability of baseload biopower on these grids would enhance grid capacity utilisation and make transmission costs per kilowatt-hour much lower than when electrons instead flow from large central power plants to rural areas to serve small, scattered, peaky rural electrical loads.

Policies that make grid access possible are needed to facilitate the launch of such baseload biopower technologies on the market. Policies promoting increasing competition in electricity generation would be helpful. But consideration also has to be given to the fact that, when any new technology is introduced, its cost is higher than that of the established technology it would replace. That remains the case until enough new plants have been built to buy down the cost of the new technology along its learning curve to prospective market-clearing price levels (chapter 12).

One way to pursue technology cost buydown in a competitive electricity market is to require that each electricity provider include in its portfolio a small but growing fraction provided by biopower or other renewable energy supplies. This requirement would be imposed during a transitional period as new renewable energy industries are being launched on the market. Power generators could either produce this renewable electricity themselves or purchase renewable energy credits that are sold in a credit trading market. Experiments with this mechanism are being conducted in the United States (where it is called a renewable portfolio standard) and in Europe (where it is called green certificate markets). The concept has great promise for developing countries.

A major challenge in extending energy services to rural areas is to find and pursue the least costly mix of energy options (centralised and decentralised, fossil and renewable, end-use efficiency improvements) for a particular region. This might be achieved, for example, through concessions for both cooking fuels and electricity. Concessions grant the exclusive right to provide energy services in exchange for the obligation to serve all customers in the region. They offer the advantage of being able to reduce transaction costs greatly in serving large numbers of small customers, relative to other mechanisms. Concessionaires ought to have the flexibility to choose the least costly combinations of technologies in meeting their obligations. The rural energy concessions recently introduced in Argentina illustrate how the concept might work (box 10.5).

BOX 10.5. A CONCESSION SCHEME FOR RURAL ENERGY DEVELOPMENT IN ARGENTINA

Argentina recently began implementing an innovative rural energy plan to encourage private sector involvement in rural energy services. To begin with, the programme targets eight provinces with 1.4 million people and 6,000 facilities without access. In each province, private companies bid for the right to provide electricity to the people and to the schools, medical centres, drinking water facilities, and other public facilities without access. Solar photovoltaic panels, small wind turbines, micro hydropower, and diesel-driven generators compete on a least-cost basis.

Preliminary analyses show that in most cases renewable technologies will be competitive with diesel generators. A large share of household supply will be through solar photovoltaic home systems. Total investment for all provinces amounts to $314 million, with a 55 percent subsidy from provincial, federal, and World Bank funds to cover initial capital investments. The winning bids will be those seeking the lowest government subsidy per energy hook-up.

In 1996 two concessions were awarded in Jujuy and Salta provinces. In Jujuy, after solving some initial problems with the tariff structure proposed in the bidding papers, 500 of 2,000 new users are now served through renewable sources, and a programme to supply 550 additional users through solar home systems is in progress. By 1998 solar systems were installed in 220 schools in Salta province, which aims to achieve full coverage of public service electrification (including schools and first-aid medical centres) in 2000.

In April 1999 a $30 million loan from the World Bank and a $10 million subsidy from the Global Environment Facility were approved. These funds will help finance the national government's share of subsidies for the first eight provinces to adopt the programme, as well as overcome barriers to the use of renewable energies. Concessions to provide electric power to significant portions of the population within three years were granted in the next six provinces to adopt the programme in late 1999 and early 2000. Eventually, all rural Argentine provinces will participate in the programme.

Source: Covarrubias and Reiche, 2000.

Strategies for making modern energy services affordable

Although policies aimed at widening access to modern energy services are necessary, they are often insufficient to deliver modern energy services to all rural residents. Modern energy technologies are useful only to those who can afford to adopt them. Even the more affluent rural households typically cannot afford to purchase photovoltaic systems, which may be the only plausible electrification option for scattered rural households. Moreover, the very poorest households are unable to pay for even less capital-intensive modern energy options. And such households are the majority in the poorest countries: 37 of the countries listed in the World Bank's *World Development Report 1998/99* had a 1997 GDP per capita below $500 (unadjusted for purchasing power parity).

Historically, energy price subsidies have been used extensively to promote wider use of modern energy carriers. But energy price subsidies are problematic. The welfare objective embodied in such subsidies is often not realised because of their diversion to unintended uses. Typically, there is a disproportionate exploitation of the subsidies by the more affluent, who could afford to pay unsubsidised prices. Such subsidies help explain the poor financial conditions of many parastatal energy companies, and have made continued expansion of energy supplies difficult (chapter 12). Energy price subsidies should be a policy of last resort to deliver modern energy services to rural areas.

When attempting to increase the level of energy services provided, a central question is: what is affordable? There is frequent mention of affordability, but there has been no rigorous quantification of this concept. One might argue that a consumer's current energy expenditures—for example, on kerosene for lighting—are a good indicator of what that consumer is prepared to spend for electric lighting. In some cases, however, the consumer is prepared to spend more for a new technology if it is safer or more convenient.

Policy reforms to make capital resources more readily available for small-scale rural energy investments would be especially helpful in making modern energy affordable to small rural consumers. Various microfinance schemes are being tried (box 10.6), and some are proving quite successful. When the poor have access to microfinance, they are no longer beneficiaries of government and donor largesse but clients with assets, whose preferences and needs must be respected. Microfinance has demonstrated success not only in providing access to energy services for poor households, but also in generating income and alternative economic activities. Microfinance is facilitating access to affordable modern energy technologies for which many people are willing to pay the full cost.

Poor Indian households that currently buy kerosene for lighting could afford electric lighting if energy-efficient fluorescent bulbs were used (Reddy, 1999). An appropriate microfinance scheme could make investment in fluorescent lights a viable option, even for poor households, if total spending on electricity plus debt servicing was less than maximum household spending on energy (about 15 percent). The combination of modern technology and microfinance can thus widen the window of opportunity. Because of the capital-intensive nature of photovoltaic and other renewable energy technologies,

At the smallest scales, many sustainable energy technologies (including small-scale wind and hydropower supplies and photovoltaics for homes) cost a few hundred dollars. Buying them outright is impossible for most rural households in developing countries. But an important minority of households, communities, and small businesses can afford to buy them with credit. The main obstacle to serving this crucial market is the reluctance of banks to manage numerous small loans and to lend without collateral or other guarantees against loan defaults. A variety of innovative approaches are being used to overcome this obstacle:

- **Financing through dealers.** Banks transfer the collateral problem from the end user to dealers by lending to dealers, who in turn lend to purchasers using payment schemes compatible with their income. Dealers must bear the financial risk along with technical risks. This system is best suited to large, relatively high-income rural markets.
- **Financing through energy service companies.** These companies can replace dealers as the financing intermediary. Companies typically require greater efforts to establish higher funding levels, because they provide a more comprehensive installation and back-up service to clients.
- **Revolving funds (with grant support).** A bank takes on the risk of operating a revolving loan fund, usually with start-up capital provided by a grant.
- **Loan aggregation through cooperatives.** To avoid the high costs of servicing many small loans, prospective borrowers form a community association (or enlarge the functions of an existing village or farmer cooperative). Banks lend to the cooperative or lease the energy systems but retain ownership of the equipment in case of payment defaults.
- **Concessional funding for public sector objectives.** The government contracts and pays a local company to provide energy services that meet development objectives, such as photovoltaic lighting for schools. This provides entry capital for the company to offer credit and expand its business to other local markets, such as photovoltaics for households, health clinics, and community centres.
- **Payment for energy services.** Payment for outputs, such as irrigation and drinking water, have been used to fund the recurrent operation and maintenance costs of small-scale energy systems. These cost streams are usually hard to fund, or remain unfunded, when loans target the capital cost.

Most of these approaches demand high levels of local participation and so take time to mature. Participation must start at the concept development stage, so that local people can decide which schemes and parameters are most appropriate.

Source: EC and UNDP, 1999.

In 1996 the Grameen Bank of Bangladesh, a microlending agency with more than 1,000 branches and 2 million members, initiated a programme of loans for photovoltaic home systems to serve those without access to electricity. The loans are administered by a non-profit rural energy company, Grameen Shakti, and call for a small down payment.

Grameen Shakti's first initiative has been a 1,000-unit project to understand better a number of important issues concerning household photovoltaic systems. These include:
- Technical performance of these systems in rural Bangladesh.
- Acceptance of the systems by the poor.
- Income-generating potential of light in the evening.
- Affordability, factoring in technical improvements and economies of scale.
- The training, monitoring, and evaluation expertise that would be required to replicate this project if it proves successful.

Grameen Shakti expects that 100,000 photovoltaic systems will be operating in rural Bangladeshi homes in 2000. The bank plans to expand this service by offering small loans for wind power and biogas plants. Demonstration projects are under way to determine the most appropriate financing packages for these technologies.

that facilitate the formation of such joint ventures and steer them towards the provision of energy services for rural areas (chapter 12).

The very poorest households may need higher incomes as well as microfinance to afford modern energy supplies and end-use devices. Increasing the incomes of the rural poor through macroeconomic policies is an especially daunting challenge and takes a long time. But energy policies that facilitate the introduction of low-cost electricity generation for rural industrialisation could effectively promote income generation.

Especially promising are the possibilities for electricity generation from low-cost crop residues in agriculture-intensive regions. Moreover, village-scale, crop-residue-based biopower technologies offer the possibility of near-term income from gathering biomass and delivering it to conversion facilities. This could help the poor pay for modern energy supplies without having to wait for rural industrialisation opportunities to materialise (case 2 in the annex). A key to making such income-generating activities viable seems to be the opportunity to sell into the grid electricity produced in excess of local needs (see the section above on small-scale biopower).

Pursuing all the above strategies might still leave the very poorest households in some areas unable to afford convenient energy services. If so, subsidies may still be needed. As noted, to stimulate the use of new technologies (such as fluorescent light bulbs), one-time equipment subsidies are preferable to continued price subsidies.

To sum up, sustainable development implies that modern energy carriers need to be made affordable to satisfy the basic needs of all rural residents. Policies are needed that will make pursuing this objective profitable. If a subsidy is needed, it might be provided as an integral part of a new social contract that creates highly competitive conditions in the energy sector (a key element of ongoing energy reforms), complemented by the establishment of a public benefits fund financed with wire and pipe charges imposed on electricity, oil, and gas providers to protect the public interest under new

microfinance schemes are especially important to promote their widespread dissemination (box 10.7).

Microfinance by itself is no panacea, however. Two other factors limit the affordability of energy services: the high costs of imported energy products (including high inherent costs and inefficient procurement of small quantities) and the low incomes of the very poorest households. But international industrial joint ventures that manufacture modern energy technology with gradually increasing domestic content can, over time, reduce costs relative to the cost of the same technology if imported (Weise and others, 1995; see also the case study of wind-diesel hybrid technology in China in chapter 7). Such cost reductions lead to expanded market opportunities, which lead to further cost reductions resulting from higher production volumes. The keys to success in creating this kind of virtuous cycle of cost reduction and market expansion are policies competitive market conditions (see chapter 12 for a discussion of public benefits funds). Specifically, some fund revenues could subsidise the basic energy needs.

This public benefits fund strategy could be made entirely consistent with a shift to greater reliance on market forces to more efficiently allocate resources. If, for example, an energy concession proved to be the preferred way to deliver modern energy services to a particular rural area, and if the concession was awarded competitively, market forces would be brought into play to find the least costly mix of energy technologies with the least amount of subsidy to satisfy the concessionaire's obligation to provide modern energy services to all.

Conclusion

Between 1970 and 1990 rural electrification from grids brought electricity to 800 million additional people. In addition, in the past 20–30 years a number of innovative schemes have been developed to commercialise improved cooking stove, biogas, and producer gas systems; photovoltaics; wind; and so on—with the result that several hundred million people have improved their access to energy. Perhaps as many as 600 million people have benefited from these innovations. Yet despite these efforts to improve energy services to rural areas, the population without access to such services has stayed about the same: 2 billion.

The task is daunting but not hopeless. Technologies can be deployed immediately or in the near term to improve energy services for rural areas. These technologies will lead to dramatic advances in the quality of life for rural populations. These advances can

Through their superior knowledge of the local situation, local people—women in particular—can be integral parts of the solution.

be achieved at costs that are within the means of governments and beneficiaries. They also require quite modest increases in the magnitudes of total energy supplied to the countries involved. They offer attractive options for decision-makers seeking quick political pay-offs before the next popular judgement of their performance. Even more exciting is the possibility of interesting new technologies that might be developed and exploited. All such possibilities would enable rural populations to climb up the energy ladder, leapfrog to higher rungs on the ladder, or even reach new rungs that could be added near the top of the ladder.

New policies are needed to bring the top of the energy ladder within reach of all rural people. Past efforts to deliver modern energy to rural areas have often been ineffective and inefficient. Some recent programmes are showing good results, but more promising new approaches need to be tested to determine if they can address poverty, equity, environmental, and public health concerns in the context of the ongoing global restructuring of energy industries. Much can be done towards these ends without resorting to large subsidies if competitive market conditions are fostered and complemented by measures to protect the public interest. Subsidies should be reserved for situations in which new strategies alone cannot make modern energy widely available. Even then, fuel price subsidies should be avoided if basic needs can be addressed by alternatives, such as subsidised purchases of energy-efficient equipment. Sound policies to accelerate the wide availability of modern energy services in rural areas could lead to even more dramatic improvements in the rural quality of life without creating large demands on public treasuries. ■

ANNEX **Case studies of crop-residue-derived modern energy carriers in China**

In densely populated countries that are largely self-sufficient in food production and are prolific generators of crop residues, thermo-chemical gasification of crop residues can provide an attractive means of providing both clean cooking fuel and electricity or combined heat and power (CHP) to satisfy basic human needs and generate additional electricity in support of income generation and rural industrialisation. Prospects in this regard are here illustrated by three case studies for China that illustrate the prospects for providing:

■ With existing technology, residue-derived producer gas as a clean cooking fuel at the village scale.
■ With medium-term (5–10 year) technology, cooking gas plus CHP at the village scale, with residue-derived producer gas.
■ With long-term (10–20 year) technology, both electricity suitable for rural industrialisation and a synthetic fluid fuel for cooking (synthetic LPG or DME derived from synthesis gas; see chapter 8) that is safe as well as clean.

There are three reasons to focus on China in studying this approach to making modern energy carriers widely available in rural areas.

First, China satisfies the criteria of being densely populated, self-sufficient in food, and a prolific generator of crop residues. About 376 million tonnes a year (about half the total residue generation rate) are potentially available for energy; the rest is used for paper-making, forage, or returned to the fields to sustain soil quality (Li, Bai, and Overend, 1998). The energy content of these residues is equivalent to 15 percent of the coal energy use in China in 1998.

Second, China has a severe new air pollution problem caused by the burning of crop residues in the field at harvest time, a consequence of the rising affluence of farmers. Traditionally, in poor agricultural communities of China, residues were fully utilised for heating, cooking, and other purposes. But as incomes have risen, growing numbers of farmers have become less willing to gather residues from the fields and store them for use throughout the year—preferring instead to buy coal briquettes or LPG as needed. As a result, excess crop residues that do not readily decay (because they dry out too quickly) for incorporation into the soils have been burned off in the fields to avoid insect infestation problems. The resulting air pollution has been severe—often even closing airports near harvest time. As a response, the government in 1999 banned burning crop residues near airports, railroads, and highways. The ban will be difficult to enforce, however, unless alternative productive uses of residues can be found.

Third, a key to providing low-cost electricity from crop residues as a coproduct of cooking gas is being able to produce baseload electricity and to sell electricity produced in excess of local needs into the electric grid. In most developing countries, this is not yet feasible because few rural communities are hooked up to grids. But in China, 87 percent of rural households are connected, in comparison with an average of about 33 percent for all other developing countries. Thus China stands out as a strong candidate country for launching small-scale biopower technologies in the market.

Case 1. Cooking with producer gas generated at the village scale

With technology currently available in China, it is feasible to provide clean cooking gas derived from crop residues at the village scale through partial oxidation in air, as illustrated by recent experience in Shangdong Province.[10]

In May 1996 a village-scale crop residue gasification system serving village households with producer gas for cooking went into operation in Tengzhai village (216 households, 800 people), Huantai County, Shangdong Province (the second village-scale gasification system installed in the province), using an atmospheric pressure, air-blown, downdraft gasifier developed by the Energy Research Institute of the Shangdong Academy of Sciences. Researchers at the institute also carried out detailed socio-economic studies of the implications of the technology and of costs in relation to benefits.

The gasifier requires 0.25 tonnes of crop residue per capita to meet the annual cooking needs of villagers. About 12 percent of the residues generated by the village's wheat and corn crops are adequate to meet all its cooking energy requirements. Researchers estimated that, with the producer gas cooking system, cooking time for housewives is reduced from 3.0 to 1.5 hours a day.

In a survey of 30 randomly selected households, the researchers found that this technology was regarded as being as good as or better than coal or LPG (the major technologies displaced) with regard to price, convenience, reliability of supply, environmental impact, and working intensity of housewives (all the issues investigated in the survey) by 97.5 percent or more of all households surveyed for each issue.

The total capital cost for the entire project (with an expected 10-year project life) was 378,000 yuan ($47,000, or $220 a household), a third of which was provided by a government subsidy. The producer gas is sold to villagers at a price that is a third of the market price for LPG on an equivalent-cooking-service-provided basis.[11] At this selling price, the project is not cost-effective, even with the capital subsidy. However, if the gas selling price were raised to two-thirds of the equivalent market price for LPG, the technology would be cost-effective without any capital subsidy, generating an internal rate of return of 17 percent. At this higher gas price, the annual cost of cooking fuel per household would be 360 yuan ($45) a year, about 25 percent less than the fuel cost for cooking with coal.

Case 2. Combined heat and power systems using producer gas generated at the village scale

Although desirable as a way to make an affordable, clean, convenient cooking fuel available to villagers, the strategy described above will not solve the air pollution problem caused by burning excess residues. However, using residues in excess of what are needed to make cooking gas power generation or CHP could solve the problem.

This case discusses the prospects for improving village living conditions through the 'trigeneration' of cooking gas, hot water for space heating, and electricity from a village-scale gasifier that converts crop residues (corn stalks) into producer gas (Henderick and Williams, 2000). The system is designed to satisfy all cooking needs in the village with a clean gas, plus meet all village electricity needs, plus generate much more electricity for sale into the grid, plus generate hot water through waste heat recovery at the biopower plant for distribution to village households through a district heating system that would satisfy all space-heating needs (especially important in Jilin Province, where winters are very cold). For specificity, the analysis is for a hypothetical 100-household village (400 residents) in Jilin Province, where about half the residue generated could potentially be exploited for energy purposes at a rate of about 6.5 tonnes a household per year (Cao and others, 1998).

With currently available biopower technology, electricity could be produced at the least cost with diesel-engine generator sets operated in dual-fuel mode, using producer gas as the primary fuel, plus pilot diesel fuel for ignition purposes (see the section in the main text of the chapter on small-scale biopower using producer gas). Because this technology is more capital-intensive than conventional diesel technology (table A10.1), a high level of capital utilisation (high capacity factor) is often required to reach economically attractive generation costs. Local electricity demand in poor rural areas is often inadequate to make the required high capacity factors feasible. If electricity could be sold into the electric grid, high capacity factors could often be realised.

A microturbine providing 75 kilowatts of electricity, a second-generation small-scale biopower technology (see the section on small-scale biopower using producer gas), was selected for the detailed design of a village trigeneration system. The microturbine is a technology for which the potential generating cost using low-cost residues is low enough (see table A10.1) to make the technology quite attractive for selling electricity into the grid. The energy balance for the village trigeneration system based on the use of this microturbine is shown in figure A10.1.

The estimated initial investment (base case) for the system is $1,800 a household, a third of which is for gas and for infrastructure to pipe hot water. It is assumed that the infrastructure investment is covered by a loan from the government at 6 percent interest, and that the rest of the investment is covered by equity capital provided

TABLE A10.1 COSTS OF ELECTRICITY WITH ALTERNATIVE ENGINE-GENERATORS FUELLED WITH DIESEL OIL AND/OR PRODUCER GAS DERIVED FROM CROP RESIDUES

System type[a]	Diesel engine		Spark-ignition engine	Microturbine
	Diesel only	Dual-fuel[b]		
Engine-generator set				
Equipment lifetime (years)[c]	6	6	6	10
Rated power output (kilowatts)	80	100	160	80
De-rated power output (kilowatts)[d]	80	80	80	80
Thermal efficiency, lower heating value (percent)[e]	34	27	21	28
Installed equipment cost (dollars per rated kilowatt)[f]	181	181	362	350
Installed equipment cost (dollars per de-rated kilowatt)	181	226	724	350
Present value of lifecycle capital investment for the engine-generator set (dollars per de-rated kilowatt)[g]	330	413	1,320	463
Total system (including building plus gasifier plus gas clean-up)[h]				
Initial cost (dollars per de-rated kilowatt)[i]	243	680	1,280	850
Present value of lifecycle capital investment for the total system (dollars per de-rated kilowatt)[j]	392	960	1,970	1,070
Operating costs				
Diesel fuel (dollars per hour, at full power output)[k]	5.48	1.65	0	0
Crop residues (dollars per hour, at full power output)[l]	0	0.39	0.66	0.50
Lubricating oil (dollars per hour, at full power output)[m]	0.21	0.42	0.42	0
Labour (dollars per hour during operation, at full power output)[n]	0.12	0.23	0.23	0.23
System maintenance (dollars per year)[o]	1,500	2,800	2,800	3,300
Levelised life-cycle electricity generation cost (cents per kilowatt-hour)				
Total capital cost	0.92	2.26	4.63	2.51
Diesel fuel	6.85	2.06	0	0
Biomass	0	0.49	0.83	0.62
Lubricating oil	0.26	0.53	0.53	0
Maintenance	0.34	0.62	0.62	0.73
Labour	0.16	0.33	0.33	0.33
Total (cents per kilowatt-hour)	**8.5**	**6.3**	**6.9**	**4.2**

a. All costs are in 1998 U.S. dollars. All systems are designed for an electrical output capacity of 80 kilowatts of electricity, and operation at 65 percent average capacity factor, so that annual electricity generation is 456,000 kilowatt-hours. Costs are calculated for a 12 percent real discount rate and a system lifetime of 20 years, so that the capital recovery factor is 0.134. b. Dual fuel refers to operation on producer gas plus pilot oil. It is assumed that producer gas displaces 70 percent of the diesel fuel required for standard operation on diesel fuel only. c. It is assumed that reciprocating internal combustion engines have 6-year (34,000-hour) lifetimes. The 10-year (57,000-hour) lifetime for the microturbine is an estimate by Honeywell. d. Relative to operation on diesel fuel, a diesel engine operated on producer gas plus pilot oil is typically de-rated 20 percent. For spark-ignited engines operated on producer gas, a 50 percent de-rating relative to operation on gasoline is typical. There is no de-rating penalty for microturbines operated on producer gas (Henderick, 2000). e. The assumed efficiencies (producer gas to electricity) for internal combustion engines converted to run on producer gas (21 percent for spark-ignition engines and 27 percent for diesel engines) are representative (Reed and Das, 1988). For the microturbine, 28 percent is representative of Honeywell's 75-kilowatt model (their target is 30 percent). The overall conversion efficiency (crop residue to electricity) is obtained by multiplying these efficiencies by the 70 percent gasifier efficiency. f. The diesel engine capital cost is from Mukunda and others (1993). The spark-ignition engine is assumed to be an industrial gas engine, for which the capital cost is typically twice that of a diesel (McKeon, 1998). Honeywell product literature (1998) estimates year 2003 installed equipment cost at $350–450 a kilowatt for its 75-kilowatt microturbine. g. Present value of the life-cycle capital investment includes the installed equipment cost plus future replacements during the 20-year life cycle, less equipment salvage value at 20 years. h. On the basis of Mukunda and others (1993), capital costs for gasification and gas clean-up are assumed to be $1,160 for the gasifier, $8,700 for the cooling and cleaning system, $11,600 for a control system, and $5,800 for a building ($1,740 if diesel only). For the microturbine, an additional fine filtration cleaning unit costing $20 a kilowatt is assumed. i. The total initial cost includes a 20 percent increment over the installed equipment cost to allow for engineering and contingencies. j. During the 20-year life cycle, the gasifier is replaced three times (6-year life), and the clean-up and control systems are replaced once (10-year life), while the building requires no replacement (Mukunda and others, 1993). k. The cost of diesel fuel is assumed to be $0.25 a litre. l. For rural Jilin Province, China, the cost of gathering corn stalks from the field and delivering them to the trigeneration facility modelled in Henderick and Williams (2000) is estimated to be 45 yuan a tonne ($0.33 a gigajoule), on the basis of data for the province provided by Cao and others (1998). m. On the basis of Mukunda and others (1993), lubricating oil requirements are assumed to be 1.36 grams a kilowatt-hour for dual-fuel engines; for spark-ignition engines the same value is assumed, and half this rate is assumed for conventional diesel engines; microturbines require no lubricating oil. Also on the basis of Mukunda and others (1993), the lubricating oil cost is assumed to be $3.50 a litre ($3.87 a kilogram). n. On the basis of Mukunda and others (1993) for rural India, during the 65 percent of the time the engine is assumed to be operating at full output, labour costs are $0.23 an hour (4 rupees an hour) for two workers for dual-fuel systems—assumed to be the same for spark-ignition engines and microturbines. Labour costs at half this rate are assumed for conventional diesel engines. In addition, it is assumed that these labour cost rates are applicable for 14 hours a week during downtime, for maintenance, preparation, and so on. o. On the basis of Mukunda and others (1993), annual maintenance costs are estimated as fixed percentages of installed building and equipment costs (not including engineering and contingencies) for the diesel, dual-fuel, and microturbine cases. The assumed percentage for diesel and dual-fuel engines is 10 percent; that for microturbines is assumed to be 8 percent. The assumed percentage for the building, gasifier, and gas clean-up is 5 percent; for the control system, 2 percent. It is assumed that the maintenance costs for the spark-ignited engine case are the same as for the dual-fuel engine case.

Source: Based on Henderick and Williams, 2000.

either by an independent power producer or by a villager-owned corporation. (Village corporation financing is plausible because the required capital is equivalent to less than three years of the average savings rate—38 percent of income in 1998—for Jilin's rural population.) For the village corporation option, the average net cash flow to villagers (income from crop residue sales plus revenues to the corporation minus expenses of the corporation) is adequate to cover all expenditures on energy by the villagers for the 20-year life of the system.[12]

The low-interest government loan for piping infrastructure might be justified as a cost-effective measure for avoiding the health costs of indoor air pollution associated with burning solid fuels for cooking and heating. For the hypothetical village, the annual health damage costs avoided would be $4,800 (assuming the average per capita value for all rural China; World Bank, 1997), more than three times the cost savings to the villagers, as a result of having debt instead of equity financing for piping.

Poor households that own no crop residues might earn income to cover energy expenditures by being paid by rich farmers to remove crop residues from their fields (for example, to enable them to comply with the ban on field burning of residues); residue recovery from the farmland of less than five average households would enable a poor household to earn enough income to cover all energy expenditures.

Case 3. Coproduction at industrial-scale of synthetic liquid petroleum gas and electricity from crop residues

The trigeneration technology described above could be improved if the cooking fuel provided were safe as well as clean (for example, producer gas contains carbon monoxide, so the risk of leaks poses a danger). This might be realised through the coproduction, at industrial scales, of electricity and synthetic liquid petroleum gas (SLPG) or dimethyl ether (DME)—synthetic fuels well suited for cooking, the use of which would involve no risk of carbon monoxide poisoning.

A preliminary design of a plant that would convert grain crop residues into SLPG and electricity using a once-through Fischer-Tropsch liquids plant coupled to a biomass integrated gasifier combined cycle (IGCC) plant has been carried out (Larson and Jin, 1999) at plant scales appropriate for Jilin Province, the corn belt of China, which produced 15 million tonnes of corn in 1995 (13 percent of the country's total). The technology would build on advances that are being made for liquid-phase syngas reactors that are being developed for the coproduction of synthetic liquid fuels and electricity from fossil fuel feedstocks (chapter 8).

The design involves 10-megawatt-electric biomass IGCC plants producing SLPG as a coproduct (250 barrels of crude oil equivalent a day). For the corn crop residue densities characteristic of Jilin, residues would have to be gathered from cornfields within a 11-kilometre radius to meet feedstock needs at the plant. Such plants could convert 15 percent of the biomass feedstock to electricity and 28 percent to LPG. Preliminary estimates are that the SLPG produced this way in rural Jilin might be competitive with conventional LPG, once biomass IGCC technology is established in the market (Larson and Jin, 1999). As discussed in chapter 7, biomass IGCC technology has advanced to the point where it is now being demonstrated in various parts of the world, building on the experience that has already brought coal IGCC technology to commercial readiness (chapter 8).[13]

If the technology could be used with all the 376 million tonnes of crop residues per year potentially available for energy purposes in China, it could provide 1.4 exajoules a year of SLPG along with 210 terawatt-hours a year of electricity. This much LPG could meet—in the form of a super-clean fuel—the cooking needs of 560 million people (about 70 percent of the rural population projected for 2010), while generating electricity at a rate equivalent to the output of 2.5 Three Gorges power plants (the Three Gorges plant's output is 18 gigawatts of electricity). And whereas the electricity from the Three Gorges plant would have to be transmitted long distances to most customers, this residue-generated electricity would be

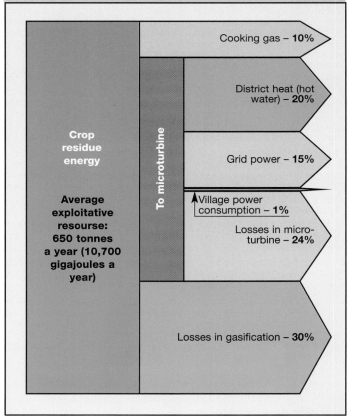

FIGURE A10.1. ENERGY BALANCE FOR A TRIGENERATION SYSTEM BASED ON THE USE OF PRODUCER GAS DERIVED FROM CROP RESIDUES IN A HYPOTHETICAL 100-HOUSEHOLD VILLAGE, JILIN PROVINCE, CHINA

Crop residue energy

Average exploitative resourse: 650 tonnes a year (10,700 gigajoules a year)

To microturbine

Cooking gas – 10%

District heat (hot water) – 20%

Grid power – 15%

Village power consumption – 1%

Losses in microturbine – 24%

Losses in gasification – 30%

Source: Henderick and Williams, 2000.

produced in 3,400 power plants (each with output of 10 megawatts of electricity), which would typically be located close to the consumers they serve.

As in the case of the village-scale trigeneration system described above, with this technology the very poorest households could pay enough for electricity and clean cooking fuel to satisfy their basic needs by gathering residues from the fields of rich farmers and delivering the residues to the energy conversion plants, thereby monetising their labour.

DME, which is expected to be easier to manufacture as a synthetic fuel than SLPG, would have similar properties as a cooking fuel. Although the technology for making DME is not as far advanced as that for SLPG, either option could probably be commercially ready by 2010–15 with a concerted development effort. The Institute of Coal Chemistry at the Chinese Academy of Sciences is investigating prospects for making DME from coal for cooking fuel applications (Niu, 2000). ■

Notes

1. The amount of time varies widely depending on the availability of biomass. Surveys have shown that in some regions, women spend close to an hour a day collecting firewood, and could spend more than two hours a day in areas where fuels are scarce (World Bank, 1996).

2. As discussed in the next section, many of the technologies associated with the intermediate rungs on the ladder pose greater development challenges than technologies associated with the top rungs.

3. For a family of five, 0.08 kilowatts per capita consumption for cooking is equivalent to 21 kilograms of LPG per month. Assuming that 30 percent of the 0.02 kilowatts per capita of electricity is consumed to support community activities, the remaining electricity would be adequate to support six compact fluorescent light bulbs used for four hours a day in addition to a television for two hours a day plus a refrigerator-freezer with the average energy efficiency projected for new U.S. units in 2001.

4. For example, in China the energy content of crop residues is twice that of animal excrement on large and medium-size farms, and the fraction of crop residues recoverable for energy purposes (about half the total generation rate) is equivalent in terms of contained energy to about 20 percent of China's coal consumption rate (Li and others, 1998; Su and others, 1998).

5. Gasifiers are about 70 percent efficient in converting biomass energy into gas energy, and producer gas stoves are about 50 percent efficient. Thus the overall efficiency of converting biomass into heat energy used in cooking is about 35 percent, which is double or more the efficiency of typical biomass stoves.

6. In China the number without access to electricity in 1996 was only 110 million, less than 13 percent of China's rural population (Dai, Liu, and Lu, 1998).

7. Lubricating oil can contribute as much to the generation cost as natural gas fuel contributes to the generation costs of a modern large combined-cycle power plant—compare tables 10.3 and 8.4.

8. If spark-ignited instead of compression-ignited engines were used for power generation, the need for diesel fuel could be eliminated entirely. But such engines are less efficient and more capital intensive than diesel engines, and they must be de-rated more (about 50 percent relative to operation on gasoline) than compression-ignition engines. As a result or are often not competitive (Henderick and Williams, 2000).

9. This is about half the total residue generation rate. The rest is used for paper-making, forage, or returned to the fields to sustain soil quality (Li, Bai, and Overend, 1998).

10. This case is based on Dai and Lu (1998), Dai and Sun (1998), and Dai, Liu, and Lu (1998).

11. The market price for LPG in the village is 3.3 yuan per kilogram ($8.30 per gigajoule).

12. It is assumed that villagers are paid $0.33 a gigajoule for residues delivered to the conversion facility. It is also assumed that gas is sold for $6 a gigajoule (somewhat less than the LPG price) and hot water is sold for $5 a gigajoule (lower than the gas price to discourage gas burning for heat), and that electricity is sold to villagers for $0.10 a kilowatt-hour (the price they would otherwise pay for grid electricity) and to the grid for $0.05 a kilowatt-hour.

13. Demonstration projects include a Global Environment Facility–sponsored, 30-megawatt-electric IGCC project in northeast Brazil (chapter 7).

References

Baldwin, S.F. 1987. "Biomass Stoves: Engineering Design, Development, and Administration." Arlington, Va.: Volunteers in Technical Assistance.

Baring-Gould, E.I, C.D. Barley, L. Flowers, P. Lilienthal, and M. Shirazi. 1999. "Diesel Minigrid Retrofits: Technical and Economic Aspects." National Renewable Energy Laboratory, Golden, Colo.

Barnes, D.F., K. Openshaw, K.R. Smith, and R. van der Plas. 1993. "The Design and Diffusion of Improved Cookstoves." *The World Bank Research Observer* 8(2): 119–41.

———. 1994. *What Makes People Cook with Improved Biomass Stoves? A Comparative International Review of Stove Programmes.* World Bank Technical Paper 242. Washington, D.C.

Cao, J., and others (Planning Committee of Jilin Province). 1998. "Evaluation of Biomass Energy Supply and Utilization Technology Prospect in Jilin Province." In *Proceedings of Workshop on Small-Scale Power Generation from Biomass.* Beijing: Working Group on Energy Strategies and Technologies, China Council for International Cooperation on Environment and Development.

Covarrubias, A. and K. Reiche. 2000. "A Case Study on Exclusive Concession for Rural Off-Grid Service in Argentina." In *Energy Services for the World's Poor.* Energy Sector and Development Report 2000. World Bank, Washington, D. C.

Dai, L., and Z. Lu. 1998. "Biomass Gasification System for Central Gas Supply." In L. Dai, J. Li, and R. Overend, eds., *Biomass Energy Conversion Technologies in China: Development and Evaluation.* Report prepared by the Energy Research Institute of the State Development Planning Commission of China and National Renewable Energy Laboratory of the United States. Beijing: China Environmental Science Press.

Dai, L., and L. Sun. 1998. "The Development and Assessment of Biomass Gasification Conversion Technology Fed by Crop Straw." In L. Dai, J. Li, and R. Overend, eds., *Biomass Energy Conversion Technologies in China: Development and Evaluation.* Report prepared by the Energy Research Institute of the State Development Planning Commission of China and National Renewable Energy Laboratory of the United States. Beijing: China Environmental Science Press.

Dai, L., X. Liu, and Z. Lu. 1998. "Analysis of Users of Biomass Gasification System of Central Gas Supply." In L. Dai, J. Li, and R. Overend, eds., *Biomass Energy Conversion Technologies in China: Development and Evaluation.* Report prepared by the Energy Research Institute of the State Development Planning Commission of China and the National Renewable Energy Laboratory of the United States. Beijing: China Environmental Science Press.

Davis, M. 1995. "Institutional Frameworks for Electricity Supply to Rural Communities: A Literature Review." Energy and Development Research Centre, University of Cape Town, Cape Town, South Africa.

Deng, K., S. Gu, and W. Liu. 1996. "Rural Energy Development in China." *Energy for Sustainable Development* 3 (September): 31–36.

EC (European Commission) and UNDP (United Nations Development Programme). 1999. *Energy As a Tool for Sustainable Development for African, Caribbean and Pacific Countries.* Brussels.

Hande, H. 1999. Personal communication. Solar Electric Light Company.

Henderick, P.M. 2000. "An Assessment of Biomass-Powered Microturbines and the Potential for Applications in Rural China." Report 322. Princeton University, Center for the Energy and Environmental Studies, Princeton, N.J.

Henderick, P.M., and R.H. Williams. 2000. "Trigeneration Using Crop Residues for a Northern Chinese Village." *Energy for Sustainable Development* 4 (October).

Kammen, D. M. 1999. "Bringing Power to the People." *Environment* 41 (5): 10–41.

Karekezi, S., and T. Ranja. 1997. *Renewable Energy Technologies in Africa.* London: African Energy Policy Research Network and Stockholm: Environment Institute and Zed Books. Stockholm.

Kartha, S., and E.D. Larson. 2000. *A Bioenergy Primer: Roles for Modernized Biomass Energy Systems in Promoting Sustainable Development.* Report prepared for the Energy and Atmosphere Programme, Sustainable Energy and Environment Division. New York: United Nations Development Programme.

Kashyap, A. 2000. Personal communication. Rockefeller Foundation, New York.

Larson, E.D., and H. Jin. 1999. "A Preliminary Assessment of Biomass Conversion to Fischer-Tropsch Cooking Fuels for Rural China." In R.P. Overend and E. Chornet, eds., *Biomass—A Growth Opportunity in Green Energy and Value-Added Products.* Volume 1 of the Proceedings of the 4th Biomass Conference of the Americas. Oxford: Pergamon.

Li, J., J. Bai, and R. Overend, eds. 1998. *Assessment of Biomass Resource Availability in China.* Report prepared by the Energy Research Institute of the State Development Planning Commission of China and National Renewable Energy Laboratory of the United States. Beijing: China Environmental Science Press.

Li, J., A. Zhou, J. Bai, and Z. Su. 1998. "Study on the Availability of Straw and Stalk Resources in China." In J. Li, J. Bai, and R. Overend, eds., *Assessment of Biomass Resource Availability in China.* Report prepared by the Energy Research Institute of the State Development Planning Commission of China and National Renewable Energy Laboratory of the United States. Beijing: China Environmental Science Press.

Mali, Republic of, Ministry of Industry, Trade, and Handicraft; and UNDP (United Nations Development Programme). 1999. "Overcoming Rural Women's Poverty with the Multipurpose Platform." Bamako and New York.

McKeon, M. 1998. Personal communication. Dealership representative, Catapillar Inc.

Mendis, Matthew S. 1999. Personal communication. Alternative Energy Development, Inc.

Moreira, J.R., and A.D. Poole. 1993. "Hydropower and Its Constraints." In T.B. Johannson, H. Kelly, A.K.N. Reddy, and R.H. Williams, eds., *Renewable Energy: Sources for Fuels and Electricity.* Washington, D.C.: Island Press.

Mukunda, H.S., S. Dasappa, and U. Shrinivasa. 1993. "Open-Top Wood Gasifiers." In T.B. Johannson, H. Kelly, A.K.N. Reddy, and R.H. Williams, eds., *Renewable Energy: Sources for Fuels and Electricity.* Washington, D.C.: Island Press.

Natarajan, I. 1999. "Social Cost Benefit Analysis of the National Programme on Improved Chulha in India." Paper presented at the United Nations Food and Agriculture Organization's Regional Wood Energy Development Program meeting on Wood Energy, Climate, and Health, October, Phuket, Thailand.

Niu, Y. 2000. "Dimethyl Ether: Clean Fuel in the 21st Century." Paper presented at the Workshop on Polygeneration Strategies Based on Oxygen-Blown Gasification, convened by the Working Group on Energy Strategies and Technologies, China Council for International Cooperation on Environment and Development, 11–12 May, Beijing.

Qui, D., L. Yan, and H. Zhang. 1996. "Status Review of Sources and End-uses of Energy in China." *Energy for Sustainable Development* 3 (September): 7–13.

Ramakrishna, J. 1991a. "India Country Review." Report of the East-West Center Global Review of Improved Cookstoves. Prepared for the World Bank's Energy Sector Management Assistance Program, Washington, D.C.

———. 1991b. "Results and Analyses of the Global Survey of Improved Cookstoves." Report of the East-West Center Global Review of Improved Cookstoves. Prepared for the World Bank's Energy Sector Management Assistance Program, Washington, D.C.

Reddy, A.K.N. 1999. "Goals, Strategies, and Policies for Rural Energy." *Economic and Political Weekly* 34 (49): 3435–45.

Reed, T.B., and A. Das. 1988. *Handbook of Biomass Downdraft Gasifier Engine Systems.* SERI/SP-271-3022. Solar Energy Research Institute, Golden, Colo.

Smith, K.R., S. Gu, K. Huang, and D. Qiu. 1993. "100 Million Improved Stoves in China: How Was It Done?" *World Development* 21(6): 941–61.

Stassen, H.E. 1995. *Small-Scale Biomass Gasifiers for Heat and Power: A Global Review.* World Bank Technical Paper 296. Washington, D.C.

Su, Z., J. Li, J. Bai, and Z. Huang. 1998. "Research on Availability of Excrement Resources on Large and Medium-Size Domestic Animal Farms in China." In J. Li, J. Bai, and R. Overend, eds., *Assessment of Biomass Resource Availability in China.* Report prepared by the Energy Research Institute of the State Development Planning Commission of China and National Renewable Energy Laboratory of the United States. Beijing: China Environmental Science Press.

WEC-FAO (World Energy Council and United Nations Food and Agriculture Organization). 1999. *The Challenge of Rural Energy Poverty in Developing Countries.* London.

Weise, E., R. Klockner, R. Kniehl, Ma Shenghong, and Qin Jianping. 1995. "Remote Power Supply Using Wind and Solar Energy: A Sino-German Technical Cooperation Project." In *Proceedings of the Beijing International Conference on Wind Energy.* Beijing: Organizing Committee of the Beijing International Conference on Wind Energy '95.

World Bank. 1996. *Rural Energy and Development: Improving Energy Supplies for Two Billion People.* Washington, D.C.

———. 1997. *Clear Water, Blue Skies: China's Environment in the New Century.* China 2020 series. Washington, D.C.

———. 1999. *World Development Report 1998/99: Knowledge for Development.* New York: Oxford University Press.

Wu, L. 1995. "Inner Mongolia: One of the Pioneers of Chinese Wind Power Development." In *Proceedings of the Beijing International Conference on Wind Energy.* Beijing: Organizing Committee of the Beijing International Conference on Wind Energy '95.

Yao, X. 1999. "Wood: Biomass Use and Emissions in China." Paper presented at the United Nations Food and Agriculture Organization's Regional Wood Energy Development Program meeting on Wood Energy, Climate, and Health, October, Phuket, Thailand.

part IV
where do we go from here?

energy and economic prosperity

Dennis Anderson (United Kingdom)

ABSTRACT Energy demand in developing countries will rise enormously as per capita incomes and populations grow. By reference to the situations of people without access to modern energy forms, the chapter shows why energy is an economic 'good', and thus why energy supplies will need to be expanded to meet emerging demands if living standards are to be improved and developing countries are to achieve prosperity. Energy demand in industrialised countries is also likely to remain strong, notwithstanding—and to some extent, because of—continuing gains in the efficiency with which energy is produced and used. Both energy resources and financial resources are amply available to meet market needs.

But will solving the 'pollution problem' from energy use prove too costly from an economic perspective? There is no evidence that it will, and most assessments point to the likelihood of an improvement, not a deterioration, in economic prospects with enlightened environmental policies. Technologies are now available for addressing the most serious forms of local and regional pollution from fossil fuel use, at costs that are small relative to the costs of energy supplies. So there is every reason to be sanguine in this respect. In fact, developing countries are in a position to address their local and regional pollution problems at a far earlier phase of development than were the industrialised countries before them—within the first third of this century if they wish. Furthermore, there are highly promising options for addressing global warming in the long term—renewable energy, hydrogen-related technologies and fuel cells, for example—which could be developed through enlightened research, development, and demonstration policies.

Much therefore will depend on energy and environmental policies. In reviewing the ground rules for such policies, the chapter shows that the aims of developing countries for achieving economic prosperity and of industrialised countries for improving theirs are fully consistent with those of simultaneously meeting rising world energy demand and realising a low-pollution future. ∎

> Modern energy forms are often viewed as economic 'bads'. In fact, they are an economic good, capable of improving the living standards of billions of people.

Despite rising energy taxes, demand-side interventions, and supply shortages in many countries, world consumption of commercial energy continues to rise. The increase averages 1.5 percent a year, or 150–200 million tonnes of oil equivalent energy (6.5–8.5 exajoules) a year—an amount equivalent to two-thirds of the annual energy consumption in France or the United Kingdom. Developing countries in Asia, Latin America, the Middle East, and Africa account for most of this growth (table 11.1). In North America, Europe, and Japan energy markets have matured and aggregate growth is low; in the transition economies of the former Soviet Union and Central and Eastern Europe consumption has declined substantially with economic recession and restructuring.

The reasons for the rapid growth of consumption in developing regions are well known. Income elasticities of demand for energy are high, and as per capita incomes grow people want their energy needs met—just as people in industrialised countries did before them. Nearly 2 billion people are without access to modern energy forms such as electricity and gas, while average consumption levels of the 2 billion people who do have access are barely one-fifth of those in the economies of the Organisation for Economic Co-operation and Development (OECD). With population growth, perhaps as many as 6 billion more people will require access to modern forms of energy over the next half century. With successful economic growth—and especially with catch-up in the developing regions—world economic product is set to rise 10-fold or more

this century, much as it did in the industrialised countries in the last century. Large increases in world energy demand thus lie ahead in any scenario of economic success. (For further details see the scenarios for the growth of populations, economic output, and energy use in chapter 9.)

This chapter provides an economic perspective on the questions posed by the prospective increases in consumption:

■ How important is meeting emerging energy demand to the achievement of economic prosperity in all regions of the world in this century? What of the 2 billion people still without access and the demands of new populations—how are their demands to be met, and what would be the economic and environmental consequences of failing to meet them?

■ What will be the impact on economic growth of meeting the environmental challenges discussed in chapter 3?

■ How, and under what conditions, will market liberalisation, the changing role of government, and globalisation of the energy industry—all inter-related developments—help to meet the challenges of achieving energy market growth, extending services to unserved populations, and solving the environmental problem?

■ Modern energy forms are often viewed ad economic 'bads.' In fact, they are an economic good, capable of improving the living standards of billions of people.

Energy consumption and economic well-being

Notwithstanding the historical importance of modern energy forms in raising economic output, they are often viewed as economic 'bads' not 'goods'—a view that has gathered force in recent years and is the source of much confusion in energy and environmental policies. In some countries energy use is under attack not only from environmental groups but also from finance ministries who see high energy taxes as a means of simultaneously raising revenues (which of course they do) and reducing pollution (at most a secondary effect).

In fact, modern energy forms are an economic good, capable of improving the living standards of billions of people, most of all the billions of people in developing countries who lack access to service or whose consumption levels are far below those of people in industrialised countries. It is the pollution arising from energy production and use that is the economic bad, not energy use itself.[1] This distinction, however elementary, is not trivial. Technologies are available, emerging, or capable of being developed that can solve the pollution problem at a small fraction of the overall costs of energy supplies. The more policies recognise the distinction, the more likely will we be able to meet rising world energy demands with greatly reduced pollution. Furthermore, once the benefits of pollution abatement are taken into account, economic output and well-being are likely to be higher not lower.

No country has been able to raise per capita incomes from low levels without increasing its use of commercial energy. In industrialised

TABLE 11.1. PRIMARY ENERGY CONSUMPTION BY REGION, 1987 AND 1997 (EXAJOULES)

Region	1987	1997	Total increase	Annual percentage increase
United States and Canada	86	101	15	1.7
Europe	74	76	2	0.2
Former Soviet Union	58	38	−20	−4.1
South and Central America (including Mexico)	15	20	5	3.4
Middle East	10	15	5	4.6
Africa	8	11	3	3.0
Asia and Pacific (including Japan)	64	101	37	4.8
Total	315	362	47	1.5

Note: Converted at the rate of 1 billion tonne of oil equivalent energy = 43.2 exajoules.

Source: BP, 1998.

TABLE 11.2. PER CAPITA INCOMES AND CONSUMPTION OF COMMERCIAL ENERGY FOR SELECTED DEVELOPING AND INDUSTRIALISED COUNTRIES, MID-1990S

Country	Per capita income, 1995	Per capita consumption of commercial energy, 1994 (gigajoules)[a]
India	340	10
Ghana	390	4
China	620	28
Egypt	790	25
Brazil	3,640	30
Korea, Rep. of	9,700	125
United Kingdom	18,700	158
United States	26,980	327
Germany	27,510	173

a. Converted at the rate of 1 kilogram of oil equivalent = 0.0418 gigajoules.

Source: World Bank, 1997.

countries demand for fossil fuels has expanded more than 50-fold (in energy units) since 1860. Horsepower per worker in industry and agriculture has grown commensurately and contributed to enormous increases in labour productivity. Cross-sectional data show unequivocal correlations between the use of energy and power and the quality of life (see figure 1 and table 1 in the overview). A similar pattern is evident in comparisons of per capita consumption levels of commercial energy in selected developing countries with those in industrialised countries (table 11.2).

These are, of course, simple correlations that leave open the questions of how much energy actually contributes to economic well-being and how much energy per person is needed to achieve a satisfactory standard of living. These questions are considered below, first with reference to people without access to modern energy supplies in developing countries today and then to people in industrialised countries before modern energy supplies were widely available.

The transition from traditional to modern energy sources

Alongside the nearly 2 billion people in developing countries who lack access to electricity and modern fuels[2] are some 1.3 billion people—more than twice the populations of the United States and the European Union combined—who were newly served with electricity during 1970–95. Large regions of the developing world are not standing still, and technical progress is making the transition from traditional to modern fuels possible at a much earlier phase of development than was the case for industrialised countries. In the United States the transition from 90 percent dependence on wood fuels to virtually none took 70 years (1850–1920), by which time average per capita income was nearly $5,000 (in 1997 prices).[3] In

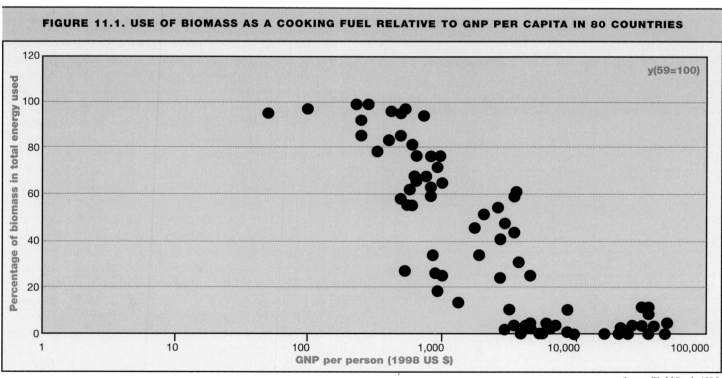

FIGURE 11.1. USE OF BIOMASS AS A COOKING FUEL RELATIVE TO GNP PER CAPITA IN 80 COUNTRIES

Source: World Bank, 1996.

the Republic of Korea the transition was substantially complete by 1980, when average per capita income was about $3,000. For developing countries today the transition to modern fuels tends to be nearly complete when per capita incomes are in the range $1,000-2,000 (World Bank, 1996; figure 11.1).

Technical progress and lower costs. Why is this transition taking place at lower incomes? The main reasons are that modern energy forms are more abundant and the costs of energy are much lower than they were when today's industrialised countries were making the transition. Electricity was not available a century ago, when per capita incomes in the now-industrialised countries were five times those in South Asia and Sub-Saharan Africa today. When electrification began, the costs, at $1.7 a kilowatt per hour (in 1997 prices), were 20 times today's costs (World Bank, 1992). Natural gas and liquefied petroleum gas (LPG) were also unavailable. Lebergott (1993, pp. 106-107) notes that, notwithstanding the massive increase in energy consumption in the United States in the 20th century, as families began to heat and later to cool every room in the house, U.S. consumers spent no more on heating and cooling their homes in 1990 than they did in 1900: "Despite all the factors driving up expenditures for fuel, …. they actually spent less than 3 percent [of their incomes]— compared to 3 percent in 1900. The explanation? Persistent productivity advance by businesses that mined fuel and produced electricity". These productivity advances were made possible, in part, by public policies that permitted the energy companies and utilities to earn good returns on their investments (this point is developed further in the section on liberalisation and globalisation).

The importance of per capita income growth. Although modern energy forms contribute appreciably to economic welfare, they are not affordable until incomes rise above a certain threshold (see figure 11.1). Technical progress and falling costs are lowering this threshold, but ultimately income growth is what matters. Countries that have been able to raise productivity and incomes on a broad basis—through good macroeconomic management, trade, and investment in human and physical resources—have been able to extend service most rapidly.

The benefits of service extension

At the same time, improving access to modern energy forms yields appreciable economic and health benefits.

Savings in time and labour in the home. As the World Bank's (1996) report on rural energy and development noted, when wood fuels are scarce, the time people spend collecting fuel is time they cannot devote to productive activities. Recent surveys in Nepal show that women spend up to 2.5 hours a day collecting fuel wood and fodder in areas where wood fuels are scarce.

The saving in time and labour, however, extends far beyond the saving arising from the displacement of fuel wood. It includes the economic convenience of modern energy forms and the advances they make possible, including hot and running water, washing machines, refrigeration, food and crop processing, extension of the day through electric lighting, and an array and diversity of other uses in homes,

industry, and commerce too numerous to list here. Table 11.3 illustrates this point with a few comparative statistics for a developing and an industrialised country. Lebergott (1993, p. 112) comments:

From 1620 to 1920, the American washing machine was a house-wife. As late as 1920 the family laundry took about seven hours a week. The typical housewife washed some 40,000 diapers for her four children.4 Lacking running water, she carried 9,000 gallons [40 tons] of water into the house each year, then boiled most of it. And she relied on a scrub board, not a washing machine.

The heavy reliance on family labour to provide for the most basic of energy needs—for cooking food and, in many climates, keeping the family warm—is an immense opportunity cost to the family. When used for pumping, modern energy forms also improve access to water. In developing countries today a family of six people consuming 30 litres of water per person per day (a low level of consumption, about one-fifth to one-tenth of that consumed in industrialised countries) will fetch and carry by hand around 35 tons of water a year from wells and hand-pumps, often over appreciable distances.[5] Surveys of low income families consistently reveal the economic importance of the saving in family labour made possible by substituting fossil for wood fuels and of the contribution modern energy forms may make, among other things, to improving access to water.[6]

Reductions in pollution and improvements in health. The switch to modern fuels reduces the level of indoor pollution by several orders of magnitude, eliminating a major health risk now afflicting billions of people (see chapter 3). A study of air pollution in developing countries found air pollution levels from biomass combustion at several multiples of the World Trade Organisation (WHO) peak guidelines: 6 times greater for Zimbabwe, 11 times for China, 5 to 34 times for Kenya (daily average), 9 to 38 times for Nepal, 1 to 39 times for Papua New Guinea, and 16 to 90 times for India (a 15 minute peak) (Smith 1988). Fitting stoves with flues lowers pollution levels to well within WHO guidelines and leads to considerable gains in efficiency as well.

TABLE 11.3. APPLIANCE USE IN HOUSEHOLDS WITH ELECTRICITY IN INDONESIA AND THE UNITED STATES, 1987 (PERCENTAGE OF HOUSEHOLDS)

Appliance	Indonesia (low-income households)	U.S. households
Lighting	100	100
Television	31	100
Irons	21	—
Refrigerator	1	100
Washing machine	—	73
Air conditioning	0	62

— Not available.   Source: World Bank, 1996, and Lebergott, 1993.

TABLE 11.4. POPULATIONS SIZE AND ESTIMATED PER CAPITA CONSUMPTION OF COMMERCIAL ENERGY BY COUNTRY GROUP, 1998

Energy form and country group	Estimated commercial energy consumption	Population (millions)
Primary energy	gigajoules per person	
• OECD	230	900
• Countries of the former Soviet Union	125	300
• Developing countries	23	4,800
Peak electricity demand	killowatt hours per person	
• OECD	1.8	900
• Countries of the former Soviet Union	0.9	300
• Developing countries	0.2	4,800

Note: Consumption estimates are based on statistics for 1992 and OED projections, assuming a 55 percent load factor for electricity demands. Population estimates are based on World Bank projections from 1992.

Source: OECD, 1995, for consumption; World Bank, 1992, for population.

Reductions in environmental damage. The transition to modern fuels *reduces* pressures on forests and land, and thus on watersheds and groundwater resources and even on biodiversity. The dangers of flash flooding are also reduced. By some estimates the consumption of wood, crop residues, and animal dung for cooking fuels amounts to 1,000 million tons of oil equivalent energy a year, more than three times the coal mined in Europe in a single year and twice that mined in the United States and China in a year (World Bank, 1996). The same amount of useful heat could be produced with only 100 million tons of LPG (in oil equivalent units) or 200 million tons of kerosene, which is equal to only 3 percent of world oil and gas consumption.

Gains in energy efficiency. Thus the transition to modern fuels can lead to large gains in energy efficiency. LPG and kerosene are just two woodfuel substitutes that result in large efficiency gains. The use of biogas from agricultural residues leads to similarly large gains. It is not surprising, therefore, though the point is often overlooked, that a rise in commercial energy use among the poorest people in the world *reduces* their energy demand, a pattern that

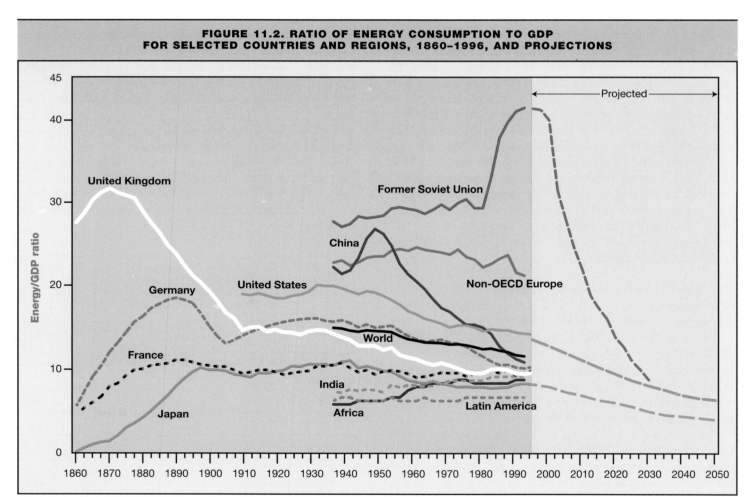

FIGURE 11.2. RATIO OF ENERGY CONSUMPTION TO GDP FOR SELECTED COUNTRIES AND REGIONS, 1860–1996, AND PROJECTIONS

Note: Energy consumption is measured in megajoules; GDP in 1990 U.S. dollars in purchasing power parity. Pre-1961 GDP calculations are based on exchange rates. Energy data exclude energy from biomass.

Source: IEA, 1997, 1998; CEC 1996; Chandler, and others, 1990; ISI 1999

continues until incomes reach quite high levels—in the case of Brazil, for example, to somewhere between 2 and 5 times the minimum wage (see figure 3 in the overview; chapter 10 provides further data on the efficiency of the alternative fuels for cooking).

Energy use forecasts and energy efficiency

In light of the contribution of modern energy forms to higher incomes and greater economic well-being, the expansion of supplies should be welcomed from both economic and commercial viewpoints. Energy markets are potentially very large and are set to grow for most of the century. Recall that per capita consumption levels of commercial energy and electricity in developing countries are barely one-tenth of those in OECD countries, while their populations are over five times larger (table 11.4). The energy scenarios presented in chapter 9 point to an increase in the world's consumption of commercial energy over this century of roughly 2.5 to 5 times today's levels.

Forecasts of long-term energy demands vary considerably with assumptions about the growth of per capita incomes and populations.[7] They also vary with assumptions about future gains in energy efficiency. The assumptions about energy efficiency gains warrant further discussion because of their impact on assessments of the amount of energy required to support economic production and provide for people's energy needs.

It has been widely observed that the energy intensity of an economy (the ratio of energy consumption to GDP) rises during the early and middle phases of economic development, when the industrialisation and 'motorisation' of economies are strong, and then peaks and declines as the less energy-intensive service sector begins to occupy a larger share of economic activity (figure 11.2).[8] The later a country industrialises, the lower its peak energy intensity because of intervening improvements in the efficiency of energy conversion processes—especially for electricity generation—and energy use. This pattern has held for more than a century, as a comparison of the experiences of the United Kingdom, Germany, the United States, France, and Japan shows (see figure 11.2). Developing regions are exhibiting the same pattern. (Exceptions are economies in transition, which have experienced abnormally high energy intensities historically, but which are now expected to decline with new investment and gains in energy efficiency.) A number of engineering and economic studies have shown that the possibilities for further gains in energy efficiency are far from exhausted, such that we can expect a continual lowering of the peak intensity as more countries become developed.[9]

Such improvements in energy efficiency mean that developing countries are likely to need less energy to produce a unit of GNP and to meet consumer needs per unit of income than was the case for the industrialised countries. How much less is controversial, because of ambiguities in the evidence and oversimplifications in both the engineering and economic models of energy consumption. However, no empirically based study has shown that developing countries can achieve prosperity without very large increases in demand for energy, even with strong assumptions about improvements in energy efficiency.

Ambiguities in the evidence and shortcomings in methods

Another perspective on the links between income growth and energy consumption is provided by economic estimates of income elasticities of energy demand. These show a rising trend as per capita income grows from very low levels and then a declining trend at high income levels (table 11.5). The income effect is weak among the most impoverished people in the world—whose main initial demands, as incomes begin to rise, are for meeting such basic needs as food, safe water, and improved health services—but becomes very strong as incomes rise above a certain threshold. Recall figure 11.1, which shows that once income moves into the $1,000–$2,000 range, substitution from biofuels to modern energy proceeds as rapidly as income growth permits. The income effect is also strong in the industrialisation phase of development, but it then begins to decline as markets mature, falling to a low value at high income levels, such as those of the OECD economies in the 1970s and 1980s.

An intriguing estimation result in table 11.5 is the *negative* per capita income elasticity in the highest income range. Judson, Schmalensee, and Stoker (1999) caution that this estimate may not be statistically significant, commenting that it is "more likely to reflect some sort of isolated measurement problem than a real economic phenomenon. We are on balance fairly confident that beyond per capita incomes of $1,500 or so (in 1985 dollars), there is a tendency of the economy-wide income elasticity of demand for energy to fall with per-capita income, but the evidence for a negative income elasticity at high income levels is, in this sample, less than compelling".

Yet engineering studies also point to the possibility of a decline in energy demand per capita at high income levels even as per capita incomes increase. As energy markets become satiated at high income levels, long-term improvements in the efficiency of energy use may more than offset any further increases in demand

TABLE 11.5. VARIATION IN PER CAPITA INCOME ELASTICITIES OF DEMAND FOR COMMERCIAL ENERGY WITH PER CAPITA INCOMES

Income (1985 U.S. dollars in purchasing power parity)	Income elasticity
≤ 823	0.219
823–1430	1.098
1,430–2,545	1.400
2,545–4,249	0.784
4,249–8,759	0.394
≥ 8,759	–0.312

Source: Judson, Schmalensee, and Stoker, 1999.

arising from income growth.[10] The effects are complex, and it is not surprising that the study by Judson, Schmalenensee, and Stoker (1999) is inconclusive. Economic models have so far not been able to capture the effects in a satisfactory way.

There are five effects on energy demand that need to be considered: income, price, population, energy efficiency as a means of *reducing* energy demand for a particular purpose, and energy efficiency as a means of reducing the price of energy and thereby *raising* energy demand (sometimes called the rebound effect). These effects can be summed up in the simplified model of energy demand growth:

$$e = \gamma.g - \beta.p\{x\} - x + n$$

where e is growth of per capita energy demand; g is growth of per capita income; p is growth of prices; n is population growth; x is the growth of what is sometimes called the autonomous energy efficiency index; γ is the income elasticity of demand for energy; and β is the numerical value of the price elasticity. The notation $p\{x\}$ summarises the fifth effect, of price as a function of—and generally declining with—energy efficiency.

Most energy demand studies using econometric techniques have not attempted to estimate x, the rate of improvement in the autonomous energy efficiency index. The review by Grubb and others (1993, p.453) sums up the uncertainties. First they note the wide range—from less than 0.5 percent to more than 1.5 percent a year—in x. They then add:

> We cannot suggest a definite value for this parameter, but it is important to understand it. The parameter has been badly misnamed: it is a measure of all non-price-induced changes in gross energy-intensity—which may be neither autonomous nor concern energy efficiency alone. It is not simply a measure of technical progress, for it conflates at least three different factors. One indeed is *technical developments*…. another is *structural change,* i.e., shifts in the mix of economic activities…. The third is *policy-driven uptake of more efficient technologies*…. [Emphasis in original.]

Compounded over a century, the 1 percentage point difference in estimates of the autonomous energy efficiency index results in a 2.7-fold difference in energy demand projections and helps to explain the large differences in the scenarios of energy demand developed in chapter 9.

Energy efficiency as a beneficial stimulus to energy use

Environmental studies frequently argue for improvements in energy efficiency as a means of reducing environmental damage. There are, however, two dangers in placing too much reliance on this argument. One is that improving energy efficiency, by lowering costs and prices, may also increase demand (the rebound effect noted above).[11] The second is that the argument neglects an important

Per capita consumption levels of commercial energy and electricity in developing countries are barely one-tenth of those in OECD countries.

economic benefit of energy efficiency: it makes energy more affordable and accessible to consumers, which is especially important today for developing countries.[12]

Consider the following examples. The efficiency of motive power rose from less than 1 percent for the early steam engines of Newcomen and Smeaton in the 18th century and 5 percent with the invention of the stream condenser by Watt later in the century to 20 percent for gasoline and diesel engines and 40 percent for electric motors today (after allowing for losses in electric power stations). This was a 40-fold increase over two centuries. It is conceivable that without such efficiency improvements the industrial revolution—and the unprecedented increase it brought about in per capita incomes in the industrial economies in the past two centuries—might not have taken place.

Or consider lighting. The efficiency in lumens per watt rose 20-fold following the displacement of kerosene by electric incandescent lamps and then another 5-fold with the invention of fluorescent lamps in the 1930s. These improvements help explain the massive growth in commercial lighting over the past half century. Another socially important example, mentioned earlier, is the contribution of modern fuels to the efficiency of cooking and heating devices in the homes. These were a primary cause of the movement away from traditional fuels and of improvements in the economic well-being of billions of people.

To take a final example, the conversion efficiency of power stations fired by fossil fuels rose from around 3 percent at the beginning of the 20th century to more than 50 percent for combined-cycle gas-fired power stations today (Anderson, 1993). This improvement has contributed to a 20-fold drop in the costs of electricity since 1900, stimulated industrial expansion, and brought the benefits of electricity consumption to more than 3 billion people in the world today. Numerous other examples could be cited, from commercial heating (insulation, heat pumps, double glazing, energy management systems, combined heat and power) and air conditioning to refrigeration and industrial processes.

In sum, the main benefits of improvements in energy efficiency are that they make modern energy services more affordable and accessible by reducing the energy required for any particular purpose and thereby reducing costs. It is only in the high-income economies that there is some suggestion that per capita energy use might eventually decline as incomes grow and energy needs become satiated. In developing countries, however, demand is set to grow substantially, even allowing for—and to some extent because of—improvements in energy efficiency, in any scenario of economic success.[13]

Reconciling increased energy consumption and environmental protection

Two important issues that arise in any discussion about meeting growing energy demand are: What will be the environmental impact, and can the impact be ameliorated at an affordable cost for developing countries? To answer these questions we need to distinguish between local and regional pollution on the one hand and global pollution from greenhouse gases on the other. For local and regional pollution the technologies are well developed, based on 40 years of operational experience in industrialised countries. For global warming the required technologies, while promising, are at a much earlier phase of development and use and raise different issues for policy.

Reducing local and regional pollution

Studies have estimated high social costs of pollution from energy production and use in developing countries (Lvovsky and Hughes, 1999; Lovei, 1995; Downing, Ramankutty, and Shah, 1997). The costs of pollution in cities are especially high:

■ Marginal damage costs per ton of local pollutants vary greatly across sources and locations and are much higher for small (low-stack) sources because of the dispersion pattern.

■ For some fuel uses the marginal damage costs are as high as producer and retail prices—or even higher.

■ Diesel-powered vehicles and small stoves or boilers burning coal, wood, or oil impose the highest social costs per ton of fuel.

■ Sulphur deposition levels are already at 5–10 grams per square meter per year in the industrial areas of Indonesia, Malaysia, the Philippines, and Thailand, and at more than 18 grams in China. By comparison, deposition levels in the most heavily polluted parts of the industrialised world—the black triangle of Central and Eastern Europe—are about 15 grams.

■ Local health effects dominate the damage costs. Lead blood levels during the early 1990s were 25 micrograms per decilitre in Mexico City and Budapest, 30 in Cairo, and 40 in Bangkok,

TABLE 11.6. RELATIVE POLLUTION INTENSITIES AND COSTS OF SELECTED LOW-POLLUTING TECHNOLOGIES FOR ENERGY PRODUCTION AND USE (INDEX = 100 FOR ALL HIGH-POLLUTING TECHNOLOGIES)

Source and pollutant	Low-polluting technology	Costs as share of supply or user costs (percent)[a]	Nature of low-polluting alternatives
Electricity generation (coal) Particulate matter Sulphur dioxide Nitrogen oxides	<0.1[b] 0–0.5 5–10	<0–≈2[b] 5 5	Natural gas; electrostatic precipitators, bag-house filters, flue gas desulphurization, integrated coal gasification combined-cycle technologies, and fluidised bed combustion (for coal); low nitrogen oxides combustion and catalytic methods.
Motor vehicles Gasoline engines Lead Carbon monoxide Nitrogen oxides Volatile organic compounds Diesel engines Particulate matter Nitrogen oxides	0 5 20 5 ≈10–20 ≈40	≈4–5 share of lifetime cost of vehicle fuel and equipment costs, for gasoline and diesel engines	Unleaded/reformulated fuels; catalytic converters.Improved fuel injection, engine design, maintenance. and 'proper' fuel use; catalytic converters.
Traditional household fuels (wood and dung) in low income countries Smoke (particulate matter, carbon monoxide, and sulphur)	<0.01	<0[d]	Gas, kerosene.
Carbon dioxide emissions from combustion of fossil fuels Electricity (developing countries) Electricity (developed countries) Liquid fuel substitutes	0 0 0	≈0–≈20[e] ≈30–50	Advanced solar energy, wind, and other renewable energy technologies for power generation; biomass for liquid fuels and power generation; hydrogen from renewable energy sources and fuel cells for power generation and vehicles.

Note: Except for carbon dioxide all the estimates are based on technologies and practices commonly in use.
a. Net private marginal costs are used because some technologies and fuels have benefits that go beyond their environmental benefits—use of gas as a domestic and industrial fuel is an example. Such investments are routinely justified in terms of their economic convenience or productivity relative to the alternatives, without reference to their environmental benefits, however important. b. Negative costs arise if gas is available for power generation as a substitute for coal. c. High emissions (especially of particulate matter) in developing countries stem very much from ageing vehicles, poor maintenance, and improper use of fuels (for example, kerosene instead of diesel). d. In urban areas and where traditional fuels are scarce, modern fuels are generally cheaper to use once the costs of household labour are taken into account, in part because of their higher energy efficiency (see chapter 10) and their convenience and savings in time (see discussion in text). e. Estimates are much lower for developing countries than for the northern industrialised countries because solar insolation is two to three times greater in developing regions and its seasonal fluctuation is one-third less. Estimates are of long-term costs.

Source: ADB, 1991, and Charpentier and Tavoulareas, 1995 for electricity; Faiz, Weaver, and Walsh, 1996, for motor vehicles; Smith, 1993, for traditional fuels. Anderson and Chua, 1999, review the engineering economic literature, and Kiely, 1997, provides an introductory text on technologies; both have ample bibliographies.

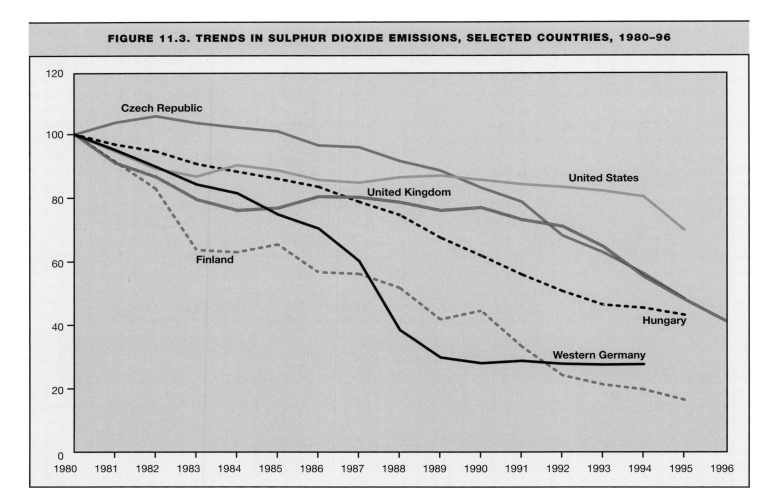

FIGURE 11.3. TRENDS IN SULPHUR DIOXIDE EMISSIONS, SELECTED COUNTRIES, 1980–96

Source: Data from OECD, 1997; U.S. EPA, 1997; and U.K. Department of Environment, Transport, and the Regions National Air Quality Archive (http://www.aeat.couk/netcen/airqual/).

well above the 2 micrograms per decilitre in the United States (reflecting an eightfold decline over the preceding 15 years).

There are several options for substantially reducing local and regional pollution loads over the long term. This is evident both from the experience of industrialised countries (table 11.6) and from comparisons of pollution loads in industrialised and developing countries (figure 11.3). Given the time required to incorporate low-polluting options in new investments and to replace the old capital stock, however, pollution is likely to rise before it falls. But the experiences of industrialised countries also shows that there is little doubt that major reductions of local and regional pollution from energy use could be achieved in the long term with supportive policies.

Low-polluting technologies, in wide use in industrialised countries, have led to appreciable reductions in smog, acid deposition, and emissions of lead, particulate matter, and volatile organic compounds; and although energy consumption per capita is an order of magnitude *higher* than in developing countries, local and regional pollution is an order of magnitude or more *lower* or (in the case of acid deposition) headed in that direction. (See chapter 3 for a full discussion of pollution loads in the industrialised and developing countries.)

The costs of controlling local and regional pollution are small relative to the total costs of energy supply or use. If coal is used as the principal fuel in electricity generation, the costs of pollution abatement range from 2 percent of supply costs for particulate matter (the most environmentally damaging of pollutants) to 5–10 percent for acid deposition. If gas is used as the principal fuel, the costs of pollution abatement are negative once allowance is made for the higher thermal efficiencies and lower capital costs of the power plant. For motor vehicle emissions the absolute cost of abatement, including the cost of catalytic converters, is estimated at less than $0.04–0.15 per gallon of fuel consumed. Similarly, supplying modern fuels to households in place of traditional fuels significantly reduces both indoor and local pollution (see chapter 3) and, except in remote communities, the costs of energy supplies as well.

Simulations of the effects of introducing abatement policies for reducing acid deposition in Asia illustrate the potential of innovation for enabling developing countries to address environmental problems at an earlier phase of their development than did industrialised countries (Anderson and Cavendish, 1999; figure 11.4). Studies that assume that environmental problems will not be addressed until the per capita incomes of the main emitters in the region (China and India) approach those of industrialised countries when they began to address acid deposition in the 1970s (about $10,000[14]) put that date at half a century from now for China and nearly a century from now for India, even under optimistic growth rate assumptions. When the simulations are run under the assumption that countries in Asia take advantage of new methods of sulphur dioxide abatement that have emerged in recent years, including coal desulphurization and the use of gas for power generation (now a rapidly growing possibility in East Asia), the results clearly show the opportunity for solving the problem much earlier with greatly reduced pollution loads. Downing, Ramankutty, and Shah (1997), in a study of acid deposition in Asia, come to similar conclusions; so do the scenarios in chapter 9.

The relatively low costs of pollution control suggest that the required financing can be generated through policies that allow prices to reflect the marginal costs of supply, including the costs of

For some fuel uses the marginal damage costs are as high as producer and retail prices—or even higher.

pollution control — the central goal of internalising externalities in market prices. Simulation studies consistently show that the extra investments would not only become self-financing, but would over time be offset by efficiency gains in the industry as a result of new thermal efficiencies in power plants, improvements in plant availabilities, reductions in distribution losses, and gains in managerial efficiency from liberalisation and improved forms of regulation (Cavendish and Anderson, 1994; World Bank, 1992). Thus while subsidies should not be necessary to finance investments in reducing local or regional pollution, environmental regulation and taxation would be.

In addition, experience in industrialised countries has shown that there are good economic returns to such investments through improvements in people's health and reduced damage to natural resources (chapter 3). In a review of U.S. experience, Davies and Mazurek (1998, p. 148) conclude that:

The macroeconomic effects of pollution control and regulation are generally modest. Regulation has had some adverse effects

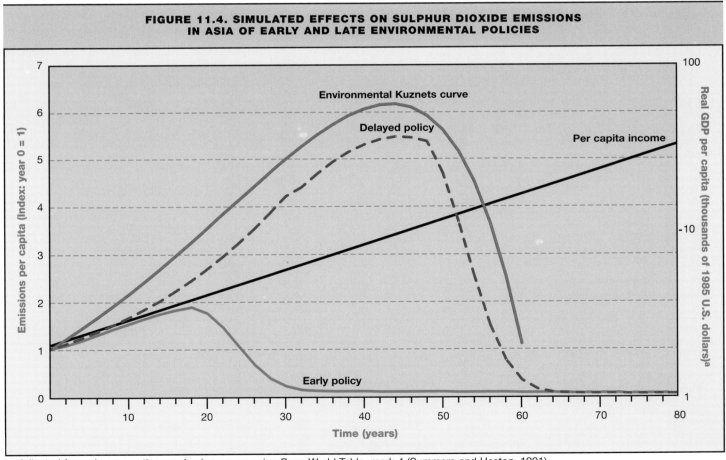

FIGURE 11.4. SIMULATED EFFECTS ON SULPHUR DIOXIDE EMISSIONS IN ASIA OF EARLY AND LATE ENVIRONMENTAL POLICIES

a. Adjusted for real comparative purchasing power using Penn World Table, mark 4 (Summers and Heston, 1991).

Source: Anderson and Cavendish, 1999; Selden and Song, 1994, for the environmental Kuznets curve.

on GDP growth, but most economists think that the effect has been relatively small, and the negative effect fails to take into account most of the benefits of regulation.... When looked at as a whole, U.S. environmental progress has made economic sense. It can be shown that benefits exceed costs in a great number of cases.

In developing countries the net effects on growth should be even greater, since their environmental priorities in the energy sector include the elimination of smoke, emissions of particulate matter, lead in fuels, and the indoor air pollution and damage to soils and forests arising from the use of traditional fuels. Thus there is no reason from an economic perspective why developing countries cannot adopt ambitious policies for reducing local and regional pollution from energy production and use. The technologies and practices are now available that should, if the 'right' policies are put in place, enable developing countries to reduce such sources of environmental damage at a much earlier phase of development than was the case for industrialised countries.

Mitigating global warming

The other energy-related environmental concern is global warming. For understandable reasons developing countries have been reluctant to commit themselves to emission reduction targets for greenhouse gasses. The costs of mitigation are thought to be too high, and there is some resistance to the notion that developing countries should not use fossil fuels to further economic development, as the industrialised countries did in the 19th and 20th centuries.

Yet developing countries may stand to benefit unexpectedly over the long term from international policies on climate change, particularly from the use of the renewable energy technologies now emerging from the energy research, development, and demonstration (RD&D) programmes of the industrial countries. In fact, some countries, such as Brazil, China, and India, have themselves begun to put resources into the development of renewable energy. The development and use of renewable energy have also become a focal point of the Global Environment Facility, the financing arm of the United Nations Framework Conventions on Climate Change and Biodiversity. What makes the technologies promising is the abundance of renewable energy resources and the falling costs being brought about by technical progress. (For more detailed information about renewable potentials and technologies, see chapters 5 and 7.)

Abundant renewable energy resources. The Earth receives a yearly energy input from the sun equal to more than 10,000 times the world's consumption of commercial energy. Solar insolation varies from 2,000 kilowatt hours per square metre to more than 2,500 a year over vast areas of developing countries, from 800 to 1,700 in Europe, and from 1100 to over 2,500 in the United States. Photovoltaic systems and solar-thermal power stations

TABLE 11.7. USE AND COMPARABLE COST OF SELECTED RENEWABLE ENERGY TECHNOLOGIES, 1998

Technology	Average cost (U.S. cents per kilowatt hour unless otherwise indicated)	Comments
Wind (electric power)	5–13	Costs declined fivefold from 1985 to 1995.
Biomass Electric power Ethanol	5–15 $2–3/gallon ($15–25 gigajoule)	Steam cycle of 25 megawatts Brazil data. Declined by factor of three since 1980s.
Photovoltaic systems Insolation, 2500 kilowatt hours/square metre Insolation, 1500 kilowatt hours/square metre Insolation, 1000 kilowatt hours/square metre	20–40 35–70 50–100	Based on costs of $5–10/peak watt. Costs have declined 50-fold since 1975, 5-fold since 1980, 2-fold since 1990. Medium- and long-term storage a major issue. With battery storage, cost of $8–40/ peak watt in off-grid, stand-alone applications are commonly reported; see chapter 7.
Thermal solar (electric power)	10–18	Parabolic troughs. Latest vintages, around 1990, in high insolation areas only.)
Geothermal	3–10	Costs vary greatly with location.
Gas-fired, combined-cycle power plant	3–5	Higher figure is for liquefied natural gas.
Grid supplies Off-peak Peak Average, urban areas Average, rural areas	2–3 15–25 8–10 15 to >70	Depends on spikiness of peak Rural areas in developing countries

Note: All figures are rounded. Estimates are adjusted to 10 percent discount rates.

Source: Based on the author's interpretations of the following reviews, of more than 500 papers and studies: Mock, Tester, and Wright, 1997, on geothermal; Larson, 1993, on biomass; Ahmed, 1994, on solar and biomass; Gregory, 1998, on several technologies, including fossil fuels; World Bank, 1996, on renewable energy and grid supplies in rural areas; and chapter 7 of this report. Refer to those sources for details and qualifications.

are capable of converting 10–15 percent—15–30 percent with further development—of the incident solar energy into electricity.

In theory, all of the world's primary energy requirements of 8 gigatons of oil equivalent a year could be met on an area of land equal to about 0.25 percent of the land now under crops and permanent pasture.[15] There is thus no significant land constraint on the use of solar energy. The main issue is cost. Other renewable energy technologies, such as biomass and wind power for electricity generation, have greater land intensities than solar energy; they have already attracted significant investment.[16]

Encouraging technical progress and falling costs. The relative costs of fossil fuels and renewable energy can be assessed only within broad limits, even assuming reasonable stability of fossil fuel prices (table 11.7). The estimates shown indicate why niche markets have emerged for renewable energy in favourable locations: geothermal, wind, biomass for power generation; solar thermal in areas of high insolation; and photovoltaic systems for off-grid markets and for distributed generation when there is a good co-incidence of solar peak and demand peak. Renewable energy installations (excluding hydropower) generate about 30,000 megawatts world-wide. While small relative to the world's generating capacity (more than 3 million megawatts), this experience has provided good information on the costs and reliability of renewable energy technologies.

Two factors, often neglected, are also important to cost calculations. One is the comparative advantage developing countries may have in using renewable energy. Solar insolation, for example, is two to three times greater than in the northern regions of industrialised countries, and seasonal swings are much lower. For this reason developing countries may enjoy a five-to-one cost advantage in using direct solar technologies. The second factor concerns differences between average and marginal costs. In off-peak times the marginal cost of grid supplies may be one-quarter to one-third the average cost, while in peak times marginal costs can be as much as two to five times higher than average costs—or even more. This differential has been obscured in many countries by the common practice of average cost pricing and, too often, by subsidies. But when there is a good co-incidence between solar peaks and demand peaks, there is an economic case for using photovoltaic systems for distributed generation. Better efficiency in the level and structure of prices will also be needed to provide proper incentives for solving the problem of intermittence in renewable energy supplies. Differential pricing, with high peak and low off-peak rates, provides the ideal incentive. Such pricing structures have already emerged at the bulk supply level in some countries with liberalised electricity markets (the United Kingdom is a prominent example).

Energy research, development, and demonstration. But we need to go beyond the (undoubtedly important) principle of 'getting prices right' for commercial investment and to revisit the case for technology development policies. Most member countries of the

Developing countries may enjoy a five-to-one cost advantage in using direct solar technologies.

International Energy Agency have such policies in one form or another, aimed at developing new alternatives to fossil fuels. International economic co-operation to foster trade, investment, and the diffusion of know-how in these technologies has also begun to emerge, albeit on a small scale considering the task in hand (see section on liberalisation and globalisation).

The principal example of international co-operation is the Global Environment Facility. The marketable permit systems and other flexibility mechanisms of the Joint Implementation and Clean Development Mechanism, if implemented, will be important extensions of these initiatives. But while public support for commercialisation and international co-operation has been growing, energy RD&D programmes in OECD countries have declined precipitously in the past 20 years. Many question whether they have declined too far, considering the severity of environmental problems and the competition from fossil fuels (see box 11.1 for a discussion of energy research and development).

Cost uncertainties and scenarios of carbon emissions. Notwithstanding the promise of renewable energy, the uncertainties remain appreciable. The future use of renewable energy will depend on its costs relative to the costs of fossil fuels and on taxes and regulation of carbon emissions. Minor changes in assumptions about the effects of innovation on costs, when extrapolated over long periods, lead to large differences in estimates of the energy supply mix, as do differences in assumptions about climate change policies.

It is possible (and many people hold this view) that renewable energy will remain confined to niche markets in the absence of climate change policies. It is also possible (and many others hold this view) that with further innovations and scale economies in manufacturing and marketing, renewable energy will eventually meet a substantial share of the world's energy needs.

Uncertainties about the costs of non–fossil fuel technologies and different assumptions about climate change policies are the main reasons why scenarios of carbon emissions differ so greatly. Industry scenarios (for example, Kassler's 1994 report for the Royal Dutch Shell group of companies) and the recent lower emission scenarios of the International Panel on Climate Change (Nakićenović, Victor, and Morita, 1998) show carbon emissions rising from 6 gigatons of carbon a year today to a peak of 10 gigatons by the middle of the century and then declining to low levels by the end of the century. These scenarios also allow for the emergence of other non–fossil fuel technologies and for technological surprise.

These results can be reproduced using elementary simulation models. The results of one such simulation for a developing country are shown in figure 11.5. They contrast the emissions associated with the country's early introduction of climate change policies with those that would arise if the country were to wait until its per capita income began to approach that of industrialised countries today, a projected delay of roughly half a century. Note the long lags before the full effects of the policies are felt, a (further) delay that arises from the scale of the problem of replacing fossil fuels in the energy supply mix and the longevity of investments in energy supplies from fossil fuels.

There is a wide range in costs for the early policy scenario. Significant investment would be required in the early decades, as is clear from the data in table 11.7 and from the report of the President's Committee of Advisers on Science and Technology noted in box 11.1. However, the costs in the long term may well prove to be small or negative. When the full probability distributions for the parameters representing the effects of technical progress on costs are included in the analysis, it can be shown that there is a significant chance of

a technological and an economic surprise arising, so that alternatives might become less expensive than fossil fuels for a large number of applications. This outcome is consistent with the findings of the industry scenarios (Kassler, 1994). We cannot say with certainty that such a favourable outcome will materialise, and it may well be that a transition to renewable energy will eventually require a permanent and significant tax or regulation on the use of fossil fuels. But reflecting on the technological developments and reductions in the costs of energy over the past century, who could say with confidence that the scope for innovation in alternatives to fossil fuels is exhausted or that addressing climate change is unlikely to yield a technological or an economic surprise?

BOX 11.1. HAS PUBLIC SUPPORT FOR ENERGY RESEARCH AND DEVELOPMENT DECLINED TOO FAR?

Public support for energy research, development, and demonstration (RD&D) programmes in OECD countries has declined considerably since 1985: by 80 percent in Germany, 75 percent in Italy, 50 percent in Canada, and 10 percent in Japan (where, as in France, nuclear power occupies the bulk of the budget) and the United States (IEA 1997a). Recent public energy RD&D expenditures in International Energy Agency (IEA) countries are about $8.5 billion a year. About 55 percent of spending goes for nuclear power and 40 percent for renewable energy and conservation.

In most countries the cuts were made across the board and equally applied. The cuts were motivated in part by market liberalisation, whose aim was to shift the onus for innovation to the private sector, and in part by competing demands on public revenues for social sector programmes. The decline in public support for RD&D also reflects discouragement with state-selected programmes supported by direct state expenditures in the period from around 1950 to 1990.

Following a major re-assessment of the approach over the past 15 years, public policies in several OECD economies are now moving towards a complex mix of incentives based on:
- Regulatory requirements for private industry to develop technologies with low carbon emissions.
- Technology-neutral tax incentives for the development of low carbon technologies.
- Marketable permit and related systems, such as the proposed programmes of Joint Implementation and the Clean Development Mechanism.
- Special financing facilities such as the Global Environment Facility that blend their own concessionary or grant finance with the hard finance of the multilateral development banks and industry to achieve a softer financial blend for innovative environmental projects.

These are all clearly more market-oriented

initiatives that avoid the problems encountered previously under state-directed programmes. The main issue is whether the incentives provided today are sufficient in light of the emerging environmental problems and the continuing competition from fossil fuels.

The U.S. President's Committee of Advisers on Science and Technology (1999, p. ES-5) concluded that they are not. "[U.S. federal RD&D programmes] are not commensurate in scope and scale with the energy challenges and opportunities the twenty-first century will present….especially…in relation to the challenge of responding prudently and cost-effectively to the risk of global climatic change from society's greenhouse gas emissions". Yet on a per capita basis U.S. RD&D programmes on non-fossil and non-nuclear technologies are among the largest in the OECD (see figure).

What are the alternatives to providing

incentives for RD&D? The costs of the non-fossil components of energy RD&D programmes are about $2.3 per ton of carbon emitted in IEA countries including nuclear power and less than $1 per ton excluding nuclear power. Economic estimates of the carbon taxes required to address the climate change problem are much larger, at five to several hundred dollars per ton.[1] When uncertainties are large, as they are in the case of developing technological alternatives in response to a highly uncertain problem such as global warming, it is a good policy, well supported by the principles of economic analysis, to invest in options that reduce uncertainties and costs.

1. "The World Bank Global Carbon Initiative", attachments to a published speech by James D. Wolfensohn to the UN General Assembly, June 25, (available from the World Bank Global Environment, Washington D.C.).

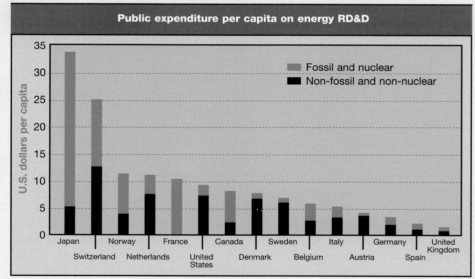

Public expenditure per capita on energy RD&D

Legend:
- Fossil and nuclear
- Non-fossil and non-nuclear

(y-axis: U.S. dollars per capita, 0 to 35)

Countries: Japan, Switzerland, Norway, Netherlands, France, United States, Canada, Denmark, Sweden, Belgium, Italy, Austria, Germany, Spain, United Kingdom

Note: This figure understates the actual level of public RD&D in energy related matters since RD&D in some sectors—in transport and building sectors in particular—also has a large bearing on the development of energy-efficient technologies and practices. *Source: IEA 1997a.*

FIGURE 11.5. SIMULATED EFFECTS OF ENVIRONMENTAL POLICY ON CARBON DIOXIDE EMISSIONS FOR A DEVELOPING COUNTRY

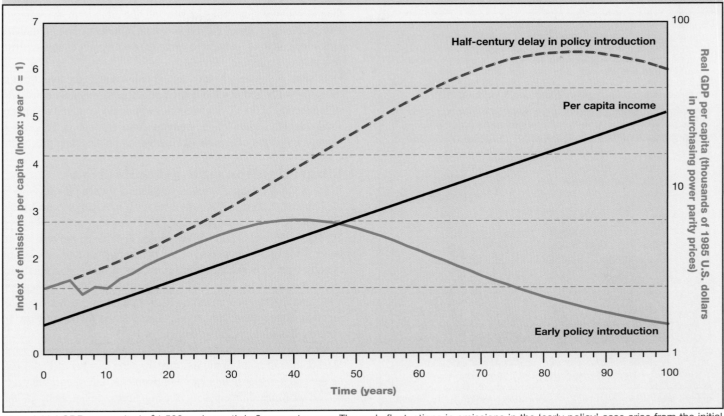

Note: Initial GDP per capita is $1,500 and growth is 3 percent a year. The early fluctuations in emissions in the 'early policy' case arise from the initial price effects on demand.
Source: Special run by the author using the model described in Anderson and Cavendish, 1999.

Competition from fossil fuels and lessons from the history of nuclear power. In addition to the above-mentioned uncertainties, competition from fossil fuels continues to increase. Estimates of fossil fuel reserves are far greater today than they were 40 years ago, when nuclear power programmes were being initiated. Estimates for the 1955 UN Atoms for Peace Conference put proven reserves at 480 gigatons of oil equivalent and ultimately recoverable reserves at 2,300 (United Nations, 1955)—respectively one-quarter and one-twelfth of current estimates. With the convenience of hindsight, we now know that the underlying premise of the nuclear power programmes that were being advocated at the time—that fossil fuels would be severely depleted by the first half of the 21st century—was wrong, as were two other assumptions: that growing pressures on reserves would increase the costs of fossil fuels, while technical progress would lower those of nuclear power.

In fact, the opposite happened. Except during the oil price shocks of the 1970s, real oil prices have consistently been in the $10-20 per barrel range (in 1995 dollars) for 120 years, despite huge increases in demand. The prices of coal and natural gas (per unit of energy) have generally been even lower than those of oil (BP 1996).[17] Low costs were made possible not only by continued

discoveries, but also by technological progress in exploration and production and throughout the downstream industries. In addition, continued technological progress in the electricity industry reduced both the capital and the fuel costs of generation from fossil fuels. In the 1950s the thermal efficiencies of new fossil fuel–fired stations were 30–35 percent; today they are around 45 percent for new coal-fired plant and 55 percent for gas-fired plant.

Technological progress and discoveries of reserves thus reduced the costs of power generation from fossil fuels relative to nuclear power. The history of oil and gas is replete with predictions of rapidly depleting reserves and rising prices.[18] In addition, there are promising options for hydrogen production from natural gas and for coal bed methane in which carbon dioxide is re-injected in coal beds for enhanced methane recovery (on a closed, non-net-carbon-emitting cycle), used for enhanced oil recovery, or sequestered deep in saline aquifers (see chapter 8). In sum, non–fossil fuel technologies, including the emerging renewable energy technologies, will continue to face intense competition from fossil fuels for many years ahead.

Nevertheless, from an economic perspective the evidence allows for an optimistic conclusion: technologies are emerging that should

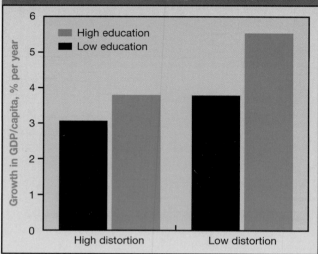
enable the virtual elimination of carbon emissions from energy use should the need arise. This is so even if the higher energy demand scenario (scenario A) in chapter 9 were to materialise. The estimated incremental costs of abating carbon emissions are modest in relative terms: most studies put them at 1–6 percent of world economic product to achieve 50–60 percent abatement by the middle of the next century and 2–8 percent of world product by the end of

the century.[19] Even at the higher end these estimates would amount to less than two year's growth of world product over a 50 year period and four year's growth over a century. They would shave less than 0.1 percentage point a year off the long-term growth rate (which averages about 2 percent a year in industrialised countries and more than 4 percent a year in developing countries with progressive economic policies).

In sum? A scenario of low carbon emissions in the long term is technologically and economically achievable and is fully consistent with the goals of developing countries achieving economic prosperity (and enjoying higher levels of energy consumption) in the present century, and of the industrialised countries improving their prosperity.

Liberalisation and globalisation

In the past half century successive multilateral rounds of reductions in the barriers to trade and foreign investment have led to considerable increases in the level and globalisation of economic activity. Between 1971 and 1995, as world GDP expanded at almost 3 percent a year, international trade increased at 5.6 percent a year and now stands at more than 22 percent of world economic product. Foreign direct investment expanded even more rapidly, at 12 percent a year between 1980 and 1996, encouraged by liberalisation and privatisation of formerly state-owned companies. It accounted for more than 10 percent of total domestic investment in 1995.

What are the implications of globalisation for the energy industry? Market liberalisation in the industry over the past two decades can be seen as a response to a range of problems and opportunities:

- The growing difficulties of raising finance (especially in the electricity sector), a consequence of high levels of government intervention and subsidies.
- The growing difficulties of the public sector in providing for the financial losses of the state-owned industries.
- Deteriorating service levels in many countries, reflected in frequent black-outs and brown-outs.
- The need to reduce losses and cost inefficiencies.
- The increasing transparency of costs and investment decisions, in the electricity, nuclear power, and coal industries in particular, which led to increased questioning of the cost-efficiency of public investments in the industry.
- The rapid growth of energy markets in developing regions and related opportunities for trade and investment in all energy sectors—electricity, coal, gas, and oil.
- New opportunities for trade and investment in high-efficiency technologies, such as combined-cycle power plants, brought about by the growth of world gas reserves.

But as the world economy has become more integrated, there are fears that the rapid growth of trade and investment will have two undesirable side effects. The first is that the most impoverished people will be left out of the process of economic growth and development—only higher income groups will benefit—and inequality, poverty, and social conflict will intensify. The second is that there will be deleterious effects on the environment.

These fears are not unfounded. But they rest on the (perhaps less commonly articulated) assumption that complementary policies will not be put in place to achieve growth on a broad basis and to protect the environment. It is not possible to predict reliably whether such policies will be pursued, but we do know that the effects will be profound one way or the other. (See box 11.2 for a discussion of the influence of just one policy variable, investment in education, that has been shown to be crucial for improving growth and reducing poverty.)

If complementary policies are in place, the rate of economic growth and development on a broad basis will be appreciably higher under liberalisation. Environmental policies and a range of other policies—health and population, agricultural extension, vocational training, physical infrastructure, and social infrastructure, including a regulatory framework for industry and commerce[20]—are also complementary to the growth process. No policy of market liberalisation can succeed without them.

On the environmental front there has already been a substantial response by the energy industry. Trade and foreign investment—in environmental as in other technologies—are ideal conduits for technology transfer and a means of enabling developing countries to address their local and regional environmental problems at a much earlier phase of development than industrialised countries did. The new forms of regulation that are accompanying liberalisation of energy markets also provide an opportunity for incorporating investment incentives for the development and commercialisation of environmentally friendly technologies (renewable energy, hydrogen and fuel cells).

The problem of access will be more of a challenge. Providing modern energy services to perhaps 6 billion new customers must be one of the primary goals of the energy industry in this century. But it is clear from the range of complementary policies that are needed for market liberalisation to work that the industry cannot accomplish this alone. All markets in open societies function within a framework of laws, legislation, standards, and public and private information services designed to improve the clarity, integrity, and equity of economic transactions. This framework is the 'ghost in the machine'. Without it the risks of investment rise for any industry attempting to address the problem of access by investing in low-income markets, and without it sustained income growth in these markets will also be more difficult to achieve.

While there is much evidence to show that liberalisation should facilitate service extension, progress will need to be monitored. There is a danger that the industry may concentrate on the easier, more established markets in urban areas where demand growth is high. Some financial or regulatory incentives may be required to address the problem. While the evidence is still ambiguous, it is noticeable in the electricity sector that private investment in liberalised markets has so far been concentrated either in greenfield investments in power generation or in the acquisition of assets, with relatively little investment in the expansion of distribution (table 11.8).

While it is possible that these investments in assets are a prelude to service expansion and extension, service extension is too important to rest solely on unmonitored assumptions. There will thus be a need for independent oversight both of the industry and of the regulatory process. Ground rules for regulation (discussed in the concluding section) will not only need to concentrate on the usual goals of monopoly avoidance and economic efficiency, but also on the problems of widening public access to energy services.

Conclusion: economic perspectives on policy

Over the next half century the energy industry will need to reach another 6 billion people or more (depending on population growth), while meeting the rising demands of the 4 billion already served. It will need to do this while substantially reducing local and regional pollution levels, particularly in developing regions, where the task of pollution abatement has hardly begun, and while developing new technologies and practices for reducing global carbon emissions and other greenhouse gases in the long term.

Several lessons of experience and ground rules for policy can be derived from a large number of studies that have reviewed energy and environmental policies:

The extension of modern energy supplies to people currently without them cannot be accomplished by the industry acting in isolation, but will depend also on the quality of development policies. Income growth is the main determinant of people's ability to afford and use modern energy forms. If development policies fail to promote economic growth on a broad basis, attempts by the energy industry to widen access will have limited success. If development policies are progressive, the industry (and its regulators) can be confident that markets will emerge in low-income as well as higher income communities to meet emerging demand and so will improve the social and economic situation of billions of people.

The liberalisation of energy markets, which experience has

TABLE 11.8. PRIVATE INVESTMENT IN DEVELOPING COUNTRY POWER SECTORS, 1994-98

Type of activity	Capacity financed (gigawatts)	Investment (billions of U.S. dollars)
Greenfield	36	46
Privatisation	26	14
Distribution	0	58
Total	62	117

Source: Martin, 1999, who comments that the greenfield investments are mainly in generation.

shown to be fundamental for the efficient growth of the industry, is also crucial for widening access. The liquefied petroleum gas (LPG) market in Brazil illustrates this point. By 1991 it served nearly 90 percent of the population. As a cooking fuel LPG is 10 times more energy efficient than wood fuel and several thousand times less polluting. In Brazil it is supplied entirely by private enterprise. The only times investment and progress towards the extension of LPG service suffered were when the government heavily regulated its price and distribution (Reis, 1991). The World Bank (1996) reports a similar experience in Hyderabad, India. As a consequence of liberalisation of the energy markets, LPG use expanded from the richest 10 percent of households in 1980 to more than 60 percent of households in the early 1990s, even as the population doubled.

Providing modern energy services to perhaps 6 billion new customers must be one of the primary goals of the energy industry in this century.

The goals of liberalisation extend to trade and foreign investment in energy technologies and services. Enabling trade and foreign investment in energy technologies and services will allow the energy industry to apply its considerable financial, technical, and managerial resources to improving and extending energy supplies. Trade and foreign investment are also ideal conduits for the transfer of efficient end-use and environmentally improved technologies.

Economic efficiency provides a good basis for regulation. It points to a range of indicators for assessing an industry's performance. It requires regulators to look at measures of cost and price efficiency, at environmental performance (since the persistence of undesirable external costs is a source of economic inefficiency), and at the industry's efforts to extend service. The following are some ground rules for the electricity industry; parallel ones can be developed for gas:

■ *Price efficiency.* Prices reflect the level and structure of the marginal costs of supply, differentiated by time of day, season, and voltage levels (an outcome of pool pricing and supply competition in liberalised markets). Marginal costs include the costs of compliance with environmental policy.

■ *Subsidies.* These are avoided, with financially minor but socially important exceptions, and are not such as to undermine the financial performance of the industry. They are also unnecessary, since the industry has long been capable of financing its own expansion—including the expansion of service to new consumers—through retained earnings and recourse to capital markets. Exceptions may be 'lifeline' rates for household consumers with low levels of consumption, allowances for the higher fixed costs of the extension of service to new areas, and investments in RD&D projects.

■ *Cost efficiency.* Typical yardsticks are the costs and efficiencies of thermal plant relative to known international best-practice standards, reserve plant margins, electrical losses, and plant availability factors.

■ *Quality of service.* Probabilities of loss of load and brown-outs are good indicators of service quality.

■ *Widening access.* The portion of the population served by grid

or off-grid schemes is monitored and used as a measure of progress towards the goal of providing universal service.

■ *Commercialisation policies for environmental innovation.* New forms of arm's length regulation following market liberalisation provide opportunities for establishing new forms of incentives for the development and commercialisation of environmentally friendly technologies. These include competitive bidding processes and incentives for private investment. The modularity of many of the emerging technologies means that the financial risks are small, especially relative to those of the nuclear power industry in the 1950s to the 1970s.

Taxing energy is not an effective instrument of environmental policy, notwith-standing many claims to the contrary The case for energy taxes has long been widely accepted on the grounds that they are an efficient form of taxation—they raise revenues without, it is thought, seriously distorting economic activity. The case for imposing additional energy taxes on environmental grounds, however, is not well founded. Such taxes increase revenues while having negligible effects on pollution. If pollution is to be reduced, there is no substitute for taxing or regulating pollution directly.

There is no reason, from either a technological or an economic standpoint, why the world cannot enjoy the benefits of both high levels of energy use and a better environment. Technological and managerial options are already available or capable of being developed that would substantially solve both local and global environmental problems from energy use at costs that may be large in absolute terms but are small relative to the long-run costs of energy supplies. Reducing local pollution is likely to raise rather than diminish economic output because of the attendant reduction in external costs. This conclusion should be especially heartening to developing countries, whose energy consumption will rise substantially as they strive to achieve economic prosperity.

In light of the promise of new, 'environmentally friendly' energy technologies on the one hand, and of emerging environmental problems on the other, there is a good case for revisiting the role of technology policies, including public support for RD&D. There is ample evidence of market-led technical progress in the energy industry: reductions in the costs of off-shore oil and gas exploration, improvements in the thermal efficiencies of power plant and reductions in the costs of electricity supply, reductions in power plant lead-times, and the ability to develop technologies for reducing pollution by orders of magnitude, to note a few.

Yet many people have argued, in response to concerns about climate change—and governments in the OECD countries are, by and large, accepting the arguments—for public or regulatory support for the industry to develop new non–fossil fuel technologies, based on renewable energy and fuel cells and hydrogen. Such policies, which differ in detail and scale but not in intent between countries, hold the potential for economic and technological surprise. These areas are fertile ground for industry RD&D—areas that the industry might otherwise have ignored because of the abundance of fossil fuel reserves.

In view of the climate change problem, energy technology development and commercialisation programmes for climate friendly technologies also need to become more outward looking and international in scope. Developing countries especially need to become engaged in the development and use of such technologies. Aside from bilateral initiatives there are three complementary instruments of policy well suited to this purpose: the Global Environment Facility, the financing arm of the Framework Conventions on Climate Change and Biodiversity; Joint Implementation and the Clean Development Mechanism, which, if ratified, will enable companies to reduce carbon emissions through foreign investment when (as it often will be) it is cheaper to do so abroad than in the home country; and regulatory and tax policies to provide financial incentives for the early development and use of non–fossil fuel options in developing countries. There are now many examples in the OECD countries to show that such policies can be pursued in market-oriented ways without compromising the financial integrity of the industry.

Financial analysis consistently shows that, under enlightened regulation, the energy industry is capable of mobilising the financial resources required to expand services and address environmental problems through a mix of internal cash generation and recourse to the financial markets. As the report of the World Energy Council (WEC 1997, p. iv) concludes: "global capital resources in principle are more than adequate to meet any potential demands coming from the energy sector. These demands are unlikely to exceed 3-4 percent of global output, the same proportion that has prevailed over past decades", a period of rapid industry expansion similar to that of the trajectory in the high-growth scenario (Scenario A) in chapter 9. The same conclusion applies to the provision of finance to meet the cost of solving local and regional environmental problems. These costs are unlikely to exceed more than 5–10 percent of the costs of supply, and any increase in costs is likely to be more than offset by gains in efficiency. Pollution should be greatly abated and the costs of energy supplies should fall. The financial requirements of the RD&D effort required to develop new non–fossil fuel technologies are also likely to be relatively small.

The main financial problem ahead could be posed by the capital requirements of developing countries. But if this materialised, it would be a self-inflicted problem. As the World Energy Council (WEC 1997, p. iv) further argues, "Contrary to popular belief, savings rates in many developing countries are double those of the US and generally one third greater than those of Europe or Japan". A large proportion of the required finance could be generated internally, with the remainder coming from international capital markets, which should in a favourable economic environment find investments in energy among the most attractive of options. The key is to offer a system of arm's length regulatory policies that allow investors to enter energy markets and to earn good rates of return while enabling the industry to extend service and reduce pollution.

Notwithstanding an immense literature on the subject of energy and the environment, four propositions remain needlessly controversial and a source of much confusion, not least among the policy-making community. They are that:

■ Local, regional, and global pollution arising from energy production and use can be virtually eliminated through technological substitution towards low-polluting forms of energy. With the important but partial exception of carbon dioxide abatement, where significant RD&D and commercialisation efforts for new technologies are merited, alternative fuels and technologies are already available or emerging.

■ Thanks to developments in pollution prevention and control, most stemming from recent policies in industrialised countries, developing countries can aspire to eliminate major forms of pollution at a far earlier phase of development—in most cases in the first third of this century—than the industrialised countries before them.

■ The costs would not be large in relative terms and could be financed internally through the application of standard instruments of environmental policy.

■ A low pollution future is fully consistent with higher levels of energy use in developing countries and the achievement of economic prosperity on a broad basis. A low pollution future is also consistent with high levels of energy use in industrialised countries, provided that efforts to develop the required technologies and practices continue.

In workshops and though other forums we need to debate such propositions further, to show just what enlightened policies might accomplish.

Notes

1. See glossary for definition of terms.

2. This figure, reported in World Bank (1996), was compiled and presented initially by Zihong Ziang in an unpublished research note for the World Bank. Ziang surveyed energy statistics from a large number of reports in the World Bank's files. Figure 3.1 in chapter 3 provides a regional breakdown of the estimate of unserved populations.

3. See Lebergott (1993, table II.16, p 107), World Bank (1996, p 39-40), and Pearson (1994).

4. Explaining this statistic, Lebergott footnotes: "As of 1990, a yearly estimate of 4,420 cloth diapers per child, plus 8,060 gallons of water to rinse and wash them and 2.5 years in diapers" appears in a survey by Arthur D. Little Inc.

5. The estimates from a survey by Whittington, and others. (1994) on water vending in Ukunda, Kenya. are based on an unpublished survey undertaken by water supply engineers in Lagos in 1986 in connection with a World Bank project; the average distance over which the water was carried was a quarter of a mile.

6. Recent surveys of rural families in countries as diverse as Colombia, Jordan, Nepal, and Ukraine on their preferences for cooking fuels yielded identical results: the preferred fuel was gas or LPG, followed by kerosene and then wood. But the actual choice depended crucially on availability and costs (with costs varying immensely with the accessibility of the village and the quality of roads). Where wood was locally abundant, low- (but not high-) income families would use it until local resources were depleted. I thank the following students for undertaking surveys on preferences of rural people: Mike Hugh (in Jordan), Paras Gravouniotis (Nepal), Ernesto Salas (Colombia) and Nick Fraser (Ukraine) on field trips to these countries. The results are available in UNDP files.

7. Forecasts are reviewed in IPCC (1995 a, b) and Nakicenovic, Victor, and Morita (1998), which summarise more than 300 projections of world energy demand and carbon emissions.

8. I thank Eberhard Jochem for this figure and comments on it.

9. See Schipper and Meyers (1992); U.S. Congress (1995 a, b); Watson, Zinyowera, and Moss (1996); WEC (1993); and IPCC (1995); chapter 6 provides further evidence and an ample bibliography.

10. As discussed below, the annual rate of improvement in energy efficiency is thought to be in the range of 0.5 to 1.5 percent a year. If the latter figure holds, or even a figure of 1 percent a year, then an economy whose per capita income elasticity has declined to the 0.25 to 0.5 range and whose long-term growth rate is 2–3 percent a year could easily enter a period in which the long-term trend in energy demand is negative.

11. The actual effect on demand depends on two factors: the effects on costs and prices, and the price elasticities. The change in demand (D) following a change in price (P) is given by $DD/D = aDP/P$, where a is the price elasticity. Suppose energy efficiency reduces energy needs for a given application by a factor of 2, but also reduces the costs by the same amount; if the price elasticity is -0.5, demand will fall by only 0.5 x 0.5, or 25 percent, not by half as predicted by engineering calculations, which neglect the point that the number of applications commonly rise following a reduction of price. Overall, since energy demand is fairly price inelastic, the prevailing consensus is that energy efficiency will lower energy demands relative to prevailing trends. However, the effect is smaller than often thought, and much depends on the price elasticity for the particular application. Also important, of course, are the prices of the appliances.

12. In this respect it is lamentable that a commonly used index of environmental damage is energy consumption, when as argued earlier energy is a good not a bad, and the essential task for environmental policy is to abate the pollution from energy use not energy use itself.

13. For values of $\gamma = 1.0$, $g = 4$, $n = 2$, $x = 1.5$ (the higher limit), for example, and neglecting for now any declines in the costs and prices of energy brought about by further improvements in energy efficiency, the long-term growth rate would still be more than 4 percent a year in developing regions, with demands doubling every 15 to 18 years.

14. In 1985 prices. In these studies of the environmental Kuznets curves, per capita incomes are based on real comparative purchasing power data provided from the Penn World Tables (mark 4; Summers and Heston, 1991). Such data point to significantly higher real incomes in developing countries than are provided in national income data converted at official exchange rates. The environmental Kuznets curve (the inverted U-shaped hypothesis) is controversial and was never put forward by the late Simon Kuznets himself. As a device for predicting future trends in pollution, it has been discredited.

15. In practice, rooftops and desert areas would be used for the direct solar technologies, such that there would be little or no competition for arable lands arising from these technologies.

16. Visual intrusion is often a serious problem with wind and is now leading several European countries to move to introduce 'offshore' wind farms.

17. The prices per British thermal unit (Btu) were $3.20 for oil, $1.50–2.50 for gas, and $1.50 for coal in 1995, with the price of gas varying with region. The figure

for coal is based on a conversion factor of 27 million Btu per tonne.

18. See Odell (1998), who draws attention to past errors of under-estimating the capacity of the fossil fuel industry to discover new reserves and lower costs, and the moral to be drawn from this.

19. See Weyant (1993) and Grubb, and others (1993). Estimates vary with assumptions about the rate of progress in the development of non-carbon technologies. As noted earlier, these estimates are conservative and fail to consider the possibilities of the innovation leading to technologies with costs lower than those of fossil fuels. So the ranges are actually from < 0.0 to the upper estimates cited here.

20. For an earlier assessment of the effects of social and economic policies on growth, see Harberger (1984). The World Bank's *World Development Reports* provide several syntheses of the effects of social and economic policies on the growth and distribution of per capita incomes and contain ample bibliographies.

References

Adelman, M.A. 1997. "My Educaton in Mineral (especially Oil) Economics." *Annual Review of Energy and the Environment* . 22: 13–46

Ahmed, K. 1994. *Renewable Energy Technologies: a Review of the Status and Costs of Selected Technologies.* World Bank Technical Paper 240: Energy Series. Washington, D.C.

Anderson, D. 1993. "Energy Efficiency and the Economics of Pollution Abatement." *Annual Review of Energy and the Environment* 18: 291–318.

Anderson, D., and W. Cavendish. 1999. "Dynamic Simulation and Environmental Policy Analysis: Beyond Comparative Statics and Environmental Kuznets' Curves." Imperial College Centre for Energy Policy and Technology, London.

Anderson, D., and S. Chua. 1999. "Economic Growth, Trade, Liberalisation, Foreign Investment and the Environment—A Review, with Special Reference to the Abatement of Air and Water Pollution in Developing Regions." Oxford University, Institute of Economics and Statistics, Oxford.

ADB (Asian Development Bank). 1991. *Environmental Considerations in Energy Development.* Manila.

BP (British Petroleum). 1996. B*P Statistical Review of World Energy.* London.

———. 1998. *BP Statistical Review of World Energy.* London.

Cavendish, W., and D. Anderson. 1994. "Efficiency and Substitution in Pollution Abatement." *Oxford Economic Papers* 46: 774–99.

CEC (Commission of European Community). 2000. 1999 Annual Energy Review. *Energy in Europa.* Special Issue. Brussels.

Charpentier, J.-P., and E.S. Tavoulareas. 1995. Clean Coal Technologies for Developing Countries. World Bank Technical Paper 286: Energy Series. Washington, D.C.

Davies, J.C., and J. Mazurek. 1998. *Pollution Control in the United States.* Washington, D.C.: Resources for the Future.

Downing, R.J., R. Ramankutty, and J.J. Shah. 1997. *Rains Asia: An Assessment Model for Acid Deposition in Asia.* Washington, D.C.: World Bank.

Faiz, A., C.S. Weaver, and M.P. Walsh. 1996. *Air Pollution from Motor Vehicles: Standards and Technologies for Controlling Emissions.* Washington, D.C.: World Bank.

Gregory, K. 1998. "Energy Resources." Intergovernmental Panel on Climate Change Special Report on Emission Scenarios.

Grubb, M., J. Edmunds, P. ten Brink, and M. Morrison. 1993. "The Costs of Limiting Fossil-fuel CO2 Emission: A Survey and Analysis." *Annual Review of Energy and the Environment* 18: 397–478.

Harberger, A.C.E. 1984. *World Economic Growth: Case Studies of Developed and Developing Nations.* San Francisco: Institute for Contemporary Studies.

IEA (International Energy Association). 1997a. *Energy Policies of IEA Countries.* Paris.

———. 1997b. *Energy Statistics and Balances of Non-OECD Countries.* Paris.

———. 1998. *Balances of OECD Countries 1995–1996.* Paris

———. 1999. *Balances of Non-OECD Countries 1996–1997.* Paris

———. 2000. *Balances of OECD Countries 1997–1998.* Paris

IPCC (Intergovernment Panel on Climate Change). 1995a. *Climate Change 1995. Impacts, Adaptations and Mitigation of Climate Change: Scientific-Technical Analyses.* Cambridge: Cambridge University Press.

———. 1995b. *Economic and Social Dimensions of Climate Change. Contribution of Working Group III to the Second Assessment Report of the Intergovernmental Panel on Climate Change.* Cambridge: Cambridge University Press.

Judson, R.A., R. Schmalensee, and T.M. Stoker. 1999. "Economic Development and the Structure of the Demand for Commercial Energy." *Energy Journal* 20 (2): 29–57.

Kassler, P. 1994. "Energy for Development." Shell Selected Papers. Shell Group of Companies, London.

Kiely, G. 1997. *Environmental Engineering.* London: McGraw-Hill.

Larson, E.D. 1993. "Technology for Electricity and Fuels from Biomass." *Annual Review of Energy and the Environment* 18: 567–630.

Lebergott, S. 1993. *Pursuing Happiness: American Consumers in the Twentieth Century.* Princeton, New Jersey: Princeton University Press.

Lovei, M. 1995. "Why Lead Should Be Removed from Gasoline." World Bank Environment Dissemination Note. World Bank, Washington, D.C.

Lvovsky, K., and G. Hughes. 1999. "Environmental Costs of Fuel Use in Developing Countries." World Bank, Washington, D.C.

Martin, F. 1999. "Taking Stock of Progress: the Energy Sector in Developing Countries. Financial Reform." In World Bank, ed., *Energy and Development Report.* Washington, D.C.: World Bank.

Mock, J.E., J.W. Tester, and M.P. Wright. 1997. "Geothermal Energy from the Earth: Its Potential Impact as an Environmentally Sustainable Resource." *Annual Review of Energy and the Environment* 22: 305–56.

Nakicenovic, N., N. Victor, and T. Morita. 1998. "Emissions Scenarios Database and Review of Scenarios." *Mitigation and Adaptation Strategies for Global Change* 3: 95–120.

Norberg-Bohm, V. Forthcoming. "Technology Commercialization and Environmental Regulation: Lessons from the U.S. Energy Sector." In J. Hemmelskamp, K. Rennings, and F. Leone, eds., Heidelberg: Physica-Verlag, Springer.

Odell, P.R. 1998. *Fossil Fuel Resources in the 21st Century.* Vienna: International Atomic Energy Agency.

OECD (Organisation for Economic Co-operation and Development). 1995. *World Energy Outlook.* Paris.

———. 1997. *Statistical Compendium 1997* (CD-Rom). Paris: OECD.[

Pearson, P.J.G. 1994. "Energy, Externalities and Environmental Quality: Will Development Cure the Ills It Creates?" *Energy Studies Review* 6 (3): 199–216.

Reis, M.S. 1991. *LPG In Brazil: 50 Years of History.* São Paulo: Sindicato Nacional das Empresas Distribuidoras de Gas Liqufeito do Petroleo.

Selden, T.M., and D. Song. 1994. "Environmental Quality and Development: Is There a Kuznets Curve for Air Pollution Emissions?" *Journal of Environmental Economics and Management* 27 (2): 147–62.

Schipper, Lee, and Stephen Meyers. 1992. *Energy Efficiency and Human Activity: Past Trends, Future Prospects*. Cambridge: Cambridge University Press.

Smith, K. 1988. "Air Pollution: Assessing Total Exposure in Developing Countries." *Environment* 30 (10): 16–35.

Smith, K.R. 1993. "Fuel Combustion, Air Exposure, and Health: the Situation in Developing Countries." *Annual Review of Energy and the Environment* 18: 529–66.

Summers, R., and A. Heston. 1991. "The Penn World Table (Mark 5): An Expanded Data Set of International Comparisons, 1950–1988." *Quarterly Journal of Economics* 56: 327–69.

United Nations. 1955. *Peaceful Uses of Atomic Energy.* International Conference on the Peaceful Uses of Atomic Energy. Geneva: United Nations.

U.S. Congress, Office of Technology Assessment. 1995. *Renewing Our Energy Future.* Washington, D.C.: Government Printing Office.

U.S. EPA (United States Environmental Protection Agency), U.S. Office of Air Quality Planning and Standards. 1997. *National Air Pollutant Emission Trends, 1900-1996: National Emission Trends (NET) Data Base.* N.C.: Research Triangle Park

U.S. President's Committee of Advisers on Science and Technology. 1999. *Powerful Partnerships: The Federal Role in International Cooperation on Energy Innovation.* Washington, D.C.

Watson, Robert T., Marufu Zinyowera, and Richard H. Moss. 1996. "Technologies, Policies and Measures for Mitigating Climate Change." IPCC Technical Paper 1. Nairobi: United Nations Environment Programme.

Weyant, J.P. 1993. "Costs of Reducing Global Carbon Emissions." *Journal of Economic Perspectives* 7 (4): 27–46.

Whittington, D., D.T. Lauria, D.A. Okun, and X. Mu. 1994. "Water Vending in Developing Countries: A Case Study of Ukunda, Kenya." In R. Layard and S. Glaister, eds., *Cost-Benefit Analysis.* Cambridge: Cambridge University Press.

World Bank. 1991. *World Development Report 1991: The Challenge of Development.* New York: Oxford University Press.

———. 1992. *World Development Report 1992: Development and the Environment.* New York: Oxford University Press.

———. 1996. *Rural Energy and Development: Meeting the Energy Needs of Two Billion People.* Washington, D.C.

———. 1997. *World Development Report 1997: The State in a Changing World.* New York: Oxford University Press.

WEC (World Energy Council). 1993. *Energy for Tomorrow's World—the Realities, the Real Options and the Agenda for Achievement.* London: St. Martin's Press.

———. 1997. *Financing the Global Energy Sector—The Task Ahead.* London: World Energy Council.

energy policies for sustainable development

CHAPTER 12

Michael Jefferson (United Kingdom)

MAJOR REVIEWERS: John Baker (United Kingdom), Richard Balzhiser (United States), Gerald Doucet (Canada), Anton Eberhard (South Africa), Howard Geller (United States), Eberhard Jochem (Germany), Hisham Khatib (Jordan), Derek Osborn (United Kingdom), Lee Solsbery (United States), R. Vedavalli (India), and Robert H. Williams (United States)

ABSTRACT The scenarios described in chapter 9 indicate that changes are needed if energy systems are to promote sustainable development. The key challenges are expanding access to affordable, reliable, and adequate energy supplies while addressing environmental impacts at all levels. Policies can support sustainable development by:

- Delivering adequate and affordable energy supplies—including liquid and gaseous fuels for cooking and electricity for domestic and commercial use—to unserved areas.
- Encouraging energy efficiency.
- Accelerating the use of new renewables.
- Widening the diffusion and use of other advanced energy technologies.

With the right policies, prices, and regulations, markets can achieve many of these objectives. But where markets do not operate or where they fail to protect important public benefits, targeted government policies, programmes, and regulations are justified when they can achieve policy goals.

The broad strategies to encourage sustainable energy systems are straightforward. But they require wider acknowledgement of the challenges we face and stronger commitment to specific policies. The strategies include:

- Making markets work better by reducing price distortions, encouraging competition, and removing barriers to energy efficiency.
- Complementing energy sector restructuring with regulations that encourage sustainable energy.
- Mobilising additional investments in sustainable energy.
- Accelerating technological innovation at every stage of the energy innovation chain.
- Supporting technological leadership by transferring technology and building human and institutional capacity in developing countries.
- Encouraging greater international cooperation.

The challenge of sustainable energy includes crucial enabling roles for governments, international organisations, multilateral financial institutions, and civil society—including local communities, business and industry, non-governmental organisations (NGOs), and consumers. Partnerships will be required, based on integrated and cooperative approaches and drawing on practical experience. A common denominator across all sectors and regions is setting the necessary framework conditions and ensuring that public institutions work effectively and efficiently with the rest of society to achieve sustainable development.

Energy can be a powerful tool for sustainable development. But redirecting its power to work towards that goal will require major policy changes within the overall enabling framework. Unless those changes occur within the next few decades—and are begun without further delay—many of the opportunities now available will be lost or the costs of their eventual realisation (where possible) greatly increased. Either way, the ability of future generations to meet their needs would be gravely compromised. ■

A t the core of any sustainable energy strategy is a vision for improving the provision and use of energy so that it contributes to sustainable development. For that to happen, policies must widen access to reliable and affordable modern energy supplies and reduce the negative health and environmental impacts related to energy use. Increased energy supplies and more efficient allocation of resources for sectoral investment will also be required to support economic development. The key requirement is that steps be taken to make markets work more effectively, or to help build energy markets where they do not exist.

A competitive market is the most efficient allocator of resources and is capable of providing high levels of consumer service and satisfaction. Thus a key element of a sustainable energy strategy should be to strive for, and to maintain, competitive market conditions. But the market alone cannot be expected to meet the needs of the most vulnerable groups, to protect the environment, to ensure energy security in the face of politically motivated disruption, and to support other public goods, such as basic research that underpins the innovation and diffusion of new technologies. In general, however, given the proper framework set by government—with competitive pricing and effective regulation—markets can achieve many of the objectives of sustainable energy.

Where markets still fail to protect public benefits, targeted

The market alone cannot be expected to meet the needs of the most vulnerable groups, to protect the environment, to ensure energy security, and to support other public goods.

government interventions are indicated. The need should depend on whether government intervention will produce the desired results. Government interventions tend to be less efficient than market approaches and often have unintended consequences at odds with their original aims.

Moreover, the introduction of sound policies does not prevent backsliding. For these reasons there is a need to adopt a pluralistic approach, to try different approaches, to learn from the experiences of other countries, and to be prepared to adjust policies in light of lessons learned domestically and internationally.

Chapter 9 shows, through energy scenarios, that our world needs to change direction if the goal of sustainable development is to be achieved. Change takes time. Economic, social, and political obstacles must be overcome. The life cycle of some investments is long, and change cannot always be readily accelerated. New, environmentally friendly technologies cannot be summoned out of thin air in the quantities and in the places required. There is inertia in behaviour and consumption patterns. There is reluctance to pay now for uncertain, or even probable, future benefits. Widespread public awareness and support need to go hand in hand with sound political leadership and policy-making if successful change is to come about. Our world does not seem ready to change in the direction and to the extent required. But unless an early start is made on

TABLE 12.1. DEFINING GOALS, STRATEGIES, POLICIES, AND POLICY INSTRUMENTS

Term	Definition	Example
Goal	Overarching aim or framework	Sustainable development
Strategies	Broad paths to reach a goal	Using energy provision and use to foster sustainable development
Policies	Courses of action to implement strategies	Making markets work more effectively by: • Restructuring the energy sector • Attracting private capital • Phasing out subsidies for conventional energy supply and consumption • Internalising externalities • Strengthening regulations • Supporting energy sector innovation • Accelerating the deployment of sustainable energy technologies • Promoting energy efficiency • Building institutional and human capacity in sustainable energy • Improving international cooperation and linkages between trade and the environment
Policy instruments	Specific measures used	• Efficiency standards • Public procurement policies • Voluntary agreements • Appliance labelling • Externality taxes and incentives (such as carbon taxes and early retirement incentives for older, less efficient, more polluting energy-using devices) • Fuel switching • Obligation to buy energy from renewable sources • Obligation to supply energy from renewable sources • Systems benefit charges (otherwise known as public benefits funds) • Supporting research and development demonstration projects • Lowering the cost of new technologies for more rapid deployment

BOX 12.1. THE NEED FOR A NEW ENERGY PARADIGM

Traditional paradigm	Emerging paradigm
Energy considered primarily as a sectoral issue	Greater consideration of social, economic, and environmental impacts of energy use
Limitations on fossil fuels	Limitations on the assimilative capacity of the earth and its atmosphere
Emphasis on expanding supplies of fossil fuels	Emphasis on developing a wider portfolio of energy resources, and on cleaner energy technologies
External social and environmental costs of energy use largely ignored	Finding ways to address the negative externalities associated with energy use
Economic growth accorded highest priority (even in prosperous economies)	Understanding of the links between economy and ecology, and of the cost-effectiveness of addressing environment impacts early on
Tendency to focus on local pollution	Recognition of the need to address environmental impacts of all kinds and at all scales (local to global)
Emphasis on increasing energy supply	Emphasis on expanding energy services, widening access, and increasing efficiency
Concern with ourselves and our present needs	Recognition of our common future and of the welfare of future generations

changing direction, the delay will almost certainly result in additional costs even where change is still possible—and various long-term development paths are likely to get blocked off (WEC, 1995; Nakićenović, Grübler, and McDonald, 1998).

Policy goals and challenges

The policies considered here are targeted towards addressing the needs of people who do not have access to modern energy carriers, making energy supplies more reliable and encouraging the more efficient use of energy, and accelerating the development and wider deployment of new renewable technologies and clean and safe advanced fossil fuel technologies.[1] Clean, efficient, and safe technologies are either under-exploited or need to be developed. But such technologies have the potential to address the health and environmental problems associated with conventional fossil fuel technologies.

The broad policies to encourage sustainable energy systems are straightforward. But taken together and implemented effectively, they would represent a significant departure from current practices. They are largely aimed at harnessing market efficiencies to achieve sustainable development. They include, under the broad heading of

making markets work better:

- Energy sector restructuring, where this is not already taking place.
- Attracting private capital.
- Phasing out subsidies for conventional energy supply and consumption.
- Internalising externalities, such as health and environmental impacts.
- Promoting energy efficiency.
- Supporting energy sector innovation and the wider and accelerated use of sustainable energy technologies.
- Building institutional and human capacity in sustainable energy.
- Introducing wider-ranging and more effective regulatory measures, to improve market operations and their public benefits.
- Achieving more effective international cooperation, as well as closer links between multilateral trade and environmental measures.

Table 12.1 provides the framework for the overarching policy goal of sustainable development, along with supporting strategies, policies, and instruments that would help markets work better.

Changes are occurring around the world in all the above directions, but on neither a wide enough basis nor at a rapid enough pace given the scale and range of the challenges to sustainable development. Without an appropriate sense of urgency, it becomes difficult to muster the political will and public support to take the needed actions. This report is one attempt to convey how much is at stake—and how soon action is needed to initiate what will be a long process of change before sustainable energy development (in both the static and dynamic senses) can be securely acknowledged.

Even though there is not yet a widely shared sense of urgency about the need to shift to a sustainable energy path, many sustainable energy policy instruments enjoy widespread support. These include efforts to raise the efficiency and quality of energy services (heat for cooking and warmth, cooling, lighting, mobility and motive power) and to put in place social policies that address the plight of people who cannot afford energy services. Similarly, where local environmental conditions have deteriorated to an unacceptable level, communities often find alternative ways of doing things.

The greatest challenge comes when society is asked to move from addressing tangible current needs to taking actions to manage environmental resources for the future and for the sake of future generations. Taking such actions in the face of competing short-term interests will require a major reorientation in the approach to energy and energy services. What is required is a new global consensus, essentially the evolution of a new energy paradigm aligned with the goal of sustainable development (box 12.1). This, in turn, needs to be reflected in national, local, and individual perspectives and priorities.

For such a shift to occur, the sustainability debate will need to move to centre stage, accompanied by much higher public awareness, information, and commitment. If public support for sustainable energy development is not forthcoming, it will be extremely difficult to implement many of the policies discussed here.

The findings so far

Chapters 2–4 show that energy is far more than a sectoral issue—it cuts across many aspects of sustainable development and is vitally connected to economic prosperity, social well-being, environmental issues, and security. The expansion of choices that the wider availability and higher quality of energy services can make possible is a fundamental aspect of human development. But modern energy services are currently beyond the reach of about one-third of the world's people. And for development to be sustainable, the demand for affordable energy services must be met in ways that protect human health and the local, regional, and global environment, as well as provide reliable supplies.

Chapters 5–8 indicate that technical progress has helped identify ample energy resources—fossil fuel, renewable, and nuclear—to support future economic and social development. Thus the availability of energy resources is not likely to be a serious problem in the next century. The critical challenge is finding ways to use these resources at reasonable costs and in ways that do not damage the environment. The health and environmental implications of meeting the world's energy demands suggest that energy technologies with near-zero emissions will eventually be required to ensure sustainability. Technologies are already available to increase the use of renewable energy sources and improve energy end-use efficiencies. Emerging innovations offer the potential to use conventional sources of energy (fossil fuels being the most significant) in ways that are cleaner, more efficient, safer, flexible, and affordable.

Chapters 9 and 10 demonstrate that the current mix of energy sources, energy infrastructure, and energy end-use applications is not efficient enough, diverse enough, or clean enough to deliver the energy services required during this century in a sustainable fashion. Incremental improvements are occurring—such as the rapid deployment of efficient combined cycle gas turbines for electricity generation, and wider use of renewables and other environmentally friendly technologies. But the scenarios described in chapter 9 show that a huge increase in the scale, pace, and effectiveness of policy initiatives and measures will be required to change course to a sustainable path. In the absence of such changes, sustainable energy development is unlikely to be achieved.

Defining the goals of policy

Chapter 1 provides a definition of sustainable development. The importance of the Brundtland Commission's definition was that it balanced the need to address current realities and priorities—of poverty, deprivation, and inequity—with the needs of future generations and the desirability of maintaining resources and biological diversity.[2] Chapter 9 also addresses the idea of sustainability, using a series of indicators.

The concept of sustainability was discussed further at the Earth Summit (officially known as the United Nations Conference on Environment and Development) held in Rio de Janeiro in 1992 and in one of the summit's main outputs, Agenda 21 (particularly in chapter 9; UN, 1992). The 1997 report of the UN Secretary-General

> A huge increase in the scale, pace, and effectiveness of policy initiatives and measures will be required to change course to a sustainable path

on progress achieved since the Earth Summit states that the secretariats of the organisations of the UN system believe that sustainable development "should continue to provide an 'overarching' policy framework for the entire spectrum of UN activities in the economic, social and environmental fields at the global, regional and national levels"(clause 139; see Osborn and Bigg, 1998).

The same report, however, points to major gaps in international discussions of certain economic sectors—namely, energy, transport, and tourism. With energy arguably being the most critical link between the environment and development, the tensions between the legitimate needs of developing countries for socioeconomic development and the health and pollution issues arising from the use of conventional fuels have been inadequately addressed. More focused analysis and action are required, including efforts that enable developing countries to acquire the energy they need for their development while reducing their dependence on carbon-based fuels (clause 129).

The UN Secretary-General's report recognises the plight of the more than 2 billion people with little or no access to commercial energy supplies (clause 11), and identifies poverty eradication throughout the world as a priority for sustainable development (clause 120). The report emphasises the need for an integrated approach and for better policy coordination at the international, regional, and national levels. It points out that since the Earth Summit the debate has focused on the complementarities between trade liberalisation, economic development, and environmental protection (clause 50). Technology partnerships and arrangements to stimulate cooperation between governments and industry at the national and international levels are needed (clause 135). But the report claims that there has been notable progress on industry-government partnerships and on the development of innovative policy instruments—with greater consideration by governments of cost-efficiency and effectiveness—and environmentally efficient technologies (clauses 89 and 90).

The report considers the increase in regional trading arrangements to be another positive feature (clause 10). The increase in private capital flows in the 1990s (particularly relatively stable foreign direct investments) is highlighted (clause 101), but this is qualified by the fact that these mainly went to a relatively small number of developing countries (clause 13). Indeed, many countries and people have failed to share in the development and growth since the Earth Summit. Debt burdens have hampered the development potential of many low-income countries. Official development assistance from industrialised countries has generally been a grave disappointment for potential recipients. And technology flows to developing countries have "not been realized as envisaged at [the Earth Summit]" (clause 105). Limited progress has been made with economic instruments intended to internalise environmental costs in the prices of goods and services (clause 134). The report soberly pronounces that "much needs to be done to ensure that sustainable development is understood by decision makers as well as by the public", and states that there is a need for adequate communications strategies (clause 118).

The Programme for the Further Implementation of Agenda 21, adopted by the UN General Assembly Special Session in June 1997, echoes many of these sentiments (Osborn and Bigg, 1998). It recognises that overall trends for sustainable development were worse than five years earlier (clause 4). It dwells at greater length on the need to strengthen cooperation and coordination between relevant UN institutions, and states that there is a particular need to make trade and the environment mutually supportive within a transparent, rule-based multilateral trading system. The programme argues that national and international environmental and social policies should be implemented and strengthened to ensure that globalisation has a positive impact on sustainable development (clause 7). The programme recognises that fossil fuels "will continue to dominate the energy supply situation for many years to come in most developed and developing countries" and calls for enhanced international cooperation—notably in the provision of concessional finance for capacity development and transfer of the relevant technology, and through appropriate national action (clause 42). The programme also recognises the need for international cooperation in promoting energy conservation and improving energy efficiency, expanding renewable energy use and research, and developing and disseminating innovative energy-related technology (clause 45).

To advance towards sustainable patterns of production, distribution, and use of energy at the intergovernmental level, the programme states that the UN Commission on Sustainable Development will discuss energy issues at its ninth session in 2001, with preparations beginning two years in advance. The commission was established to review progress in the implementation of Agenda 21, advance global dialogue, and foster partnerships for sustainable development. The programme sponsored by the UN General Assembly Special Session recognised that the commission had catalysed new action and commitments, but that much remained to be done.

Indeed, the informed study by Osborn and Bigg (1998) concludes that there was a gulf between the rhetoric offered by many world leaders who addressed the UN General Assembly Special Session in June 1997 and the more 'prosaic' document that was agreed in their name. The authors also found that public attention and political will to tackle these issues constructively and cooperatively seemed to have diminished since the Earth Summit. In particular, industrialised countries—with a few exceptions—had failed to deliver on their promise to make new and additional resources available to developing countries to enable them to handle their development in a more sustainable way. But the authors noted that the UN Commission for Sustainable Development and the UN Department of Economic and Social Affairs had "been able to make some significant improvements

The critical challenge is finding ways to use energy resources at reasonable costs and in ways that do not damage the environment.

in the five years since Rio, and to give sustainable development a key role in the whole structure of UN bodies" (pp. 19–20).

Many of the themes and comments made during the deliberations on sustainable development, including the finding that "overall energy trends remain unsustainable" (clause 10), are still applicable. Sustainable energy policies proceed by consideration of, and agreement on, the basic strategy and its purpose—to contribute to sustainable development, introduce policies aimed at implementing the strategy, and implement policy instruments (see table 12.1).

Responding to the challenge of widening access

Drawing on the objectives identified by the Brundtland Commission (WCED, 1987)—itself drawing on earlier studies—and from commitments made at subsequent UN conferences, the first priority of energy policy should be to satisfy the basic needs of the one-third of the world's people without modern energy services. While the scale of this challenge seems enormous, it may not be as great as is commonly perceived. For example, the primary energy required to satisfy the cooking needs of 2 billion people—by providing access to relatively clean modern cooking fuel—has been estimated at 5 exajoules a year, or less than 1.5 percent of world commercial energy consumption. The electricity required to satisfy basic needs is also relatively small (see chapter 10). In fact, relatively high levels of energy services could theoretically be provided to those currently relying on traditional fuels without major increases in primary energy consumption. That could happen if sufficient emphasis were given to making modern energy carriers and energy-efficient conversion technologies widely available.

Absolute poverty is the fundamental obstacle to widening access. The world's poorest 1.3 billion people live on less than $1 a day and consume only 0.2 tonnes of oil equivalent per capita, mostly as biomass. The only way to foster the necessary investments in situations where poverty precludes the normal operation of energy markets is a combination of a major increase in transfers from industrialised to developing countries and a determined effort to mobilise the often substantial potential of domestic savings in developing countries. Providing every person in the world with a minimum of 500 kilowatt-hours of electricity in 2020 would require additional investment of $30 billion a year between 2000 and 2020 (WEC, 2000). If industrialised countries were to fulfil their agreed commitment to allocate 0.7 percent of their GDP to official development assistance (instead of their recent performance of about 0.2 percent, on average), this additional sum would be readily available.

But official development assistance is expected to continue to be inadequate as long as there are concerns that recipients are using the funds for other purposes—such as military conflicts, payments into private bank accounts, and prestige projects of doubtful value to the community at large. As South African President Thabo Mbeki put it in his New Year's 2000 address: "We must say enough is enough—we have seen too many military coups, too many wars. We have had to live with corruption. We have seen our continent being marginalised." The improper use of official development assistance is also likely to inhibit the creation and satisfactory performance of the institutions needed to encourage the accumulation and sound use of domestic savings. For official development assistance and the successful mobilisation of domestic savings, it seems essential that all parties firmly commit to ensuring that funds are used for sustainable development projects in energy and other fields. Otherwise it will be difficult to break the vicious circle that exists in too many needy countries.

Access to affordable commercial energy is necessary but insufficient for rural development, and is most effective when integrated with other rural development activities to improve water supply, agriculture, and transport. Key components of the overall strategy for widening access, discussed in more detail in chapter 10, include:

- Improving access to modern, efficient cooking fuel. This is important both to reduce the time and effort spent using traditional fuels and cooking devices, and to reduce the environmental impacts at the household level, which have particularly pernicious effects on women.

- Making electricity available both to satisfy basic needs and to support economic development. Even small amounts of electricity can greatly improve living standards and facilitate income-generating activities, not least in rural areas (see chapter 10). Historically, most needed electricity has been provided through grid extension. Most rural electrification projects have been the result of cooperative efforts and public loans. The main barriers have been private monopolies (which, with few exceptions, regarded rural electrification as unacceptably costly; see Hughes, 1983 and Nye, 1990), government support for state-owned monopolies (which undermine the efforts of rural cooperatives; Smallridge, 1999), and public interventions in private and cooperative efforts marked by incompetence, vacillation, and disregard for the needs of investors and the value of investments already made (Poulter, 1986; Hannah, 1979). But historically, as today, there are examples of successful public-private partnerships. Some rural electrification projects have been subsidised by urban electricity users, but this appears to have been of modest significance. More encouraging are the demonstrable benefits of shifting the responsibility for rural electrification to private cooperatives (as in Bangladesh since 1980), establishing effective partnerships (as with Eskom in South Africa for grid extension to urban and rural customers and for off-grid solar photovoltaic power), breaking up inefficient monopolies, and introducing new regulatory frameworks. (For the historical record on these developments, see Ballin, 1946; Bowers, 1982; Hannah, 1979; Hughes, 1983; Nye, 1990; Parsons,1939; Poulter,1986; Schlesinger,1960; Shapiro, 1989; and Smallridge, 1999.) Local circumstances should always be taken into account, however. Between 1970 and 2000 the number of rural residents in developing countries with access to electricity jumped by 1.1 billion (chapter 10). Yet the number without access seems to have remained much the same in 2000 as in 1990—1.8 billion (Davis, 1995). The main reason is that rural population growth

greatly exceeded electrification in South Asia and Sub-Saharan Africa (World Bank, 1996). Extending grid-based electricity supplies in rural areas can cost seven times as much as in urban areas, where load densities are low. And even where rural load densities are high, the cost is likely to be 50 percent higher than in urban areas (World Bank, 1996). Thus decentralised, smaller-scale solutions are being sought. Since 1987 more rural households in Kenya have received electric lighting from an unsubsidised solar photovoltaic programme than from the heavily government-subsidised rural electrification programme.

- Addressing the challenges of growing urban populations. Large urban populations in some developing countries result in large numbers of people living a marginal existence, suffering from widespread poverty and uncertain employment and incomes. In the1990s more than 30 percent of the urban population in many developing countries lived below the national poverty line. More than 400 million urban residents of developing countries lack electricity. Whereas 46 percent of the world's population was urban in 1996, by 2030 the share is projected by the UN to reach 60 percent. Africa's urban population, which was about 250 million in 1996, may reach 850 million by 2030. In Latin America the figure is expected to rise from 350 million to 850 million; in Asia from 1.25 billion to 2.75 billion. Much of the increase is anticipated to come from a rural exodus propelled by population growth, poverty, and lack of employment opportunities. Growing urban population will also be a major factor, occurring largely among the poorer sections of the community. (All these projections may have to be modified if the ravages of AIDS prove higher than currently anticipated.) Whereas grid connection will be a relatively attractive option for extending electricity supplies to urban dwellers, affordability will be a major issue. The experiences of Eskom in South African townships and Electropaulo in São Paulo, Brazil, indicate that well-designed schemes and partnerships can make a major contribution to addressing these challenges.

- Providing decentralised options. This is gaining greater attention in the search for ways to increase access to electricity in rural areas, and more options are becoming available. Options for decentralised electricity generation include diesel-engine generator sets (recently beginning to be deployed in Sub-Saharan Africa), mini-hydropower, photovoltaics (being deployed in Botswana, Kenya, Mozambique, and South Africa, as well as in numerous Asian and Latin American countries), windpower (India's windpower capacity reached 1,077 megawatts at the end of 1999, and China's reached 300 megawatts, up 34 percent from the end of 1998), and small-scale biomass gasifier engine-generator sets (see chapter 10). There have been problems with system reliability, and the need for guaranteed performance standards has been highlighted in a number of project evaluations—especially for solar home systems. Lack of sufficient capital to purchase equipment, and costs of imported equipment (especially where import duties and value added taxes are levied, and where the 1997–99 East Asian financial crisis had a devastating impact on foreign exchange rates), have also been recurring issues. Microturbines (using natural gas or diesel fuel) are believed to have considerable potential (chapters 8 and 10). Liquefied petroleum gas (LPG), heating oil (both kerosene and fuel oil), and biogasifiers using anaerobic fermentation technologies (China is a world leader in this field) are other decentralised options. When used in stoves for cooking, LPG, biogas, and kerosene are several times more efficient than wood (see figure 10.1) and are friendlier to the local environment. Among the conditions for success of these alternatives to traditional fuels are good marketing and after-sales service (including the necessary infrastructure), and the avoidance of inhibiting price caps and regulation (see chapter 11 for details on experiences with LPG markets in Brazil and India). A coordinated institutional approach and community participation are also required.

- Financing rural energy. Rural residents often pay more for commercial fuels (kerosene, LPG, diesel, gasoline) than do urban dwellers. They often need help meeting the high initial costs of switching to energy carriers (including the devices required for their use) that are higher on the energy ladder, and ultimately less expensive. By providing people with access to credit, rapid service improvements can often be obtained at relatively low cost and without resorting to subsidies (which are often counterproductive).

- Developing new institutional structures and partnerships for providing rural energy services. New institutional forms will be required to deliver rural energy services in ways that are consistent with the more competitive conditions to which energy systems are evolving. One option would be to issue rural energy concessions that oblige concessionaires to serve, in the least costly ways, all rural residents with clean cooking fuels and electricity at levels adequate to meet basic needs. Efforts have been made to support relevant schemes by providing financial help to systems dealers and suppliers and to participating banks; dealers and suppliers in turn offer instalment plans to users. The results have been mixed. (After an encouraging start, for instance, Indonesia's Solar Home Systems Project ran into difficulties starting in 1997, after the onset of the Asian financial crisis, and was terminated in 2000). Nevertheless, the need for innovative systems is clear, given the shift from conventional energy carriers with relatively few actors and large supply-side structures to new systems with a multitude of small, scattered installations manufactured, distributed, marketed, and operated by numerous individuals or small firms. In this context it is interesting to note that more than 10 million people borrow from microfinance programmes world-wide, although this remains a young industry (World Bank, 1999c, p. 128).

Improving environmental acceptability

Given the degree to which human civilisation has already altered the planet, environmental protection is no longer a luxury. Rather, it is critical to maintaining the health of the ecosystems on which we all depend. Minimising the adverse environmental impacts of energy use is essential for sustainable development. Thus much of this chapter deals with how environmental acceptability can and should be improved, by incorporating environmental costs into markets, by improving end-use efficiency, and by spurring the development of new technologies with fewer adverse impacts.

Chapters 2 and 3 provide compelling evidence on why the adverse environmental impacts of energy use must be reduced if human living standards and prospects are to be improved. Indoor pollution, transport emissions, other urban pollution (including precursors to tropospheric ozone formation, which has a radiative forcing effect), and acid deposition have been highlighted in this report as pressing problems. Gains have been recorded in industrialised countries, with some indicators of air, water, and land showing improvement past degradation, along with lower emissions of sulphur, lead, and particulates. But most of these gains are corrections of past practices. A much cheaper approach for countries in early stages of development would be to leapfrog directly to the cleanest modern technologies possible, thereby avoiding the mistakes of today's industrialised countries. A number of technology options that combat local and regional pollution also mitigate global climate change. Because all countries stand to gain from this, encouraging technological leapfrogging and leadership in developing countries should be a major focus for international cooperation.

In addition to local and regional pollution, threats to the global environment are arousing growing concern. Energy use associated with the combustion of fossil fuels is the main source of anthropogenic greenhouse gas emissions, which are widely believed to be damaging the global climate (chapter 3) and threatening further temperature rises. There are, however, some promising technological options that can mitigate climate change (chapter 8). (Global climate change is addressed in greater detail below, in the section on more effective cooperation.)

Many, but by no means sufficient, initiatives are being taken to improve environmental acceptability. These include:
- The introduction of better cooking stoves to reduce indoor pollution (chapters 2, 3, and 10).
- Energy efficiency measures (see chapter 6 and section below on raising energy efficiency).
- Efforts to encourage new renewable energy deployment (as in Argentina, Botswana, Brazil, China, Costa Rica, Denmark, the Dominican Republic, Finland, Germany, Honduras, India, Indonesia, Kenya, Mexico, Morocco, the Philippines, South Africa, Spain, Swaziland, Sweden, the United Kingdom, and the United States; see also chapters 7 and 10).
- Cleaner fossil fuel provision and use (as with coal washing, sulphur abatement, and reduced particulate emissions in China and India).

> Competition may be hampered by too few players or too few new entrants, or by market distortions that give advantages to some players.

■ Carbon sequestration (such as injecting separated carbon dioxide into depleted oil and natural gas formations, and into subsea aquifers under the North Sea; or diverting recaptured carbon dioxide from coal-fired electricity generating plants.

Making markets work better

Markets are more effective than administered systems in providing innovative and affordable products, securing needed finance and investment, and achieving consumer satisfaction (box 12.2). Markets mainly operate through competition and price signals, and thus have a built-in ability to adjust to changes in supply and demand. They encourage learning through continuous provision of relevant information and choices. A recurring message of this report is that, within the energy sector, market processes are preferable to 'command and control' approaches. To the extent possible, policy initiatives should focus on helping markets operate more effectively and more widely.

Markets never work perfectly, however. Competition may be hampered by too few players or too few new entrants, or by market distortions that give advantages to some players. In many countries competition is relatively new in the energy sector or has not been introduced. Yet even if markets were working well in these respects, they are widely regarded as unable to address issues of equity, and externalities of

---

BOX 12.2. WHY ELECTRICITY SUPPLIES ARE UNRELIABLE WHEN MARKETS ARE DISCOURAGED FROM FUNCTIONING

In many places, especially in developing and transition economies, markets work poorly. As a result electricity supplies are highly unreliable and have high attendant costs.

In addition to the 2 billion people who rely on traditional fuels for cooking, about as many suffer from highly unreliable supplies. World Bank data on transmission and distribution losses in many developing and some transition economies reflect this. Frequent blackouts and brownouts can be life-threatening and result in severe economic losses and social disruption. Large Nigerian companies spend about 10 percent of their capital investment on standby generators. In smaller companies standby generators account for nearly 30 percent of capital investment. Such diversion of investments imposes a heavy cost on businesses and their customers (ADB, 1999).

Among the reasons for unreliable, inefficient, and low-quality service are:
- Lack of competition (usually due to the predominance of inefficient monopolies).
- Lack of investment (reflecting difficulties in agreeing on adequate returns or in retaining or repatriating earnings).
- Poor maintenance.
- Competing financial priorities (most governments are now unwilling to provide investment capital for energy projects to state-owned companies).
- Lack of the discipline of competition, which fosters economic efficiency.
- Low priority accorded to customer service.

By introducing competition, improving regulation, imposing penalties for non-performance, offering higher and more secure returns to investors, and exposing inefficiency and corruption, considerable progress can be made in achieving reliable supplies. In essence, this means making markets work better and ensuring that competition is effective.

---

health and the environment, unless market reforms include measures to address the public benefits concerns associated with these issues.

Markets often fail to support sustainable energy systems because of the short-term horizons of business and investor decision-making (which takes into account interest and discount rates and perceived risks) relative to the long-term challenges of sustainable energy development. Government initiatives often have a short-term orientation as well. New regulations may be required to ensure fair competition and advance public benefits, including meeting the needs of vulnerable customers, protecting the environment, and facilitating the deployment of innovative energy technologies that help in the pursuit of sustainability goals. This section discusses policies that can make markets work better to deliver sustainable energy. The rest of the chapter deals with targeted policies needed to deal with gaps that markets, under current conditions, do not fill.

An 'uneven playing field' is one of the biggest barriers to the widespread implementation of sustainable energy strategies. This means that some competitors enjoy an unfair advantage, true competition is not occurring, new entry is inhibited, and market forces cannot operate effectively. In the energy sector, markets and prices are distorted by widespread subsidies for fossil fuels (often introduced to benefit the poor or to encourage growth, but frequently achieving neither goal effectively) and by a failure to account for externalities. If subsidies were phased out, and externalities fully reflected in energy prices, market forces could achieve many of the aims of sustainability.

Internalising externalities

Free market prices do not reflect the full social and environmental costs resulting from commercial and industrial activities. Since it does not receive these pricing 'signals', on its own the market will not lead to optimal investments from a societal perspective. Including social and environmental externalities in energy prices is, in principle, an elegant way to address many issues of sustainability. But in the real world it proves difficult, for practical and political reasons. Finding ways to figure externalities into energy prices is problematic because there is no consensus on how to measure their costs (for a more detailed discussion of cost-accounting externalities that affect health and the environment, see chapter 3). These costs are substantial but, as chapter 11 emphasises, not insuperable.[3]

Environmental economists have been proposing appropriate techniques for many years (such as willingness to pay to avoid and willingness to accept environmental intrusion at a negotiated or estimated price; or hedonistic pricing). Chapter 7 argues that, in principle, carbon dioxide taxes are the simplest and most consistent method for internalising the cost of mitigating climate change. Others favour a mix of energy and carbon taxes as a way to curb a wider variety of energy-linked externalities. One advantage of a mix of taxes—which could include taxes on hydropower and biomass as well as fossil fuels—is that it would encourage end-use efficiency for all energy users and reflect the wider range of adverse social and

BOX 12.3. CARBON TAXES

A carbon tax is a charge on each fossil fuel proportional to the quantity of carbon emitted when that fuel is burned. Carbon taxes have often been advocated as a cost-effective instrument for reducing emissions.

Carbon taxes (and emission taxes in general) are market-based instruments because, once the administrative authority has set the tax rates, emissions-intensive goods will have higher market prices, lower profits, or both. As a result market forces will spontaneously work in a cost-effective way to reduce emissions. More precisely, taxes have two incentive effects. A direct effect, through price increases, stimulates conservation measures, energy efficient investments, fuel and product switching, and changes in the economy's production and consumption structures. An indirect effect, by recycling the fiscal revenues collected, reinforces the previous effects by shifting investment and consumption patterns.

In addition to emission and carbon taxes, other taxes affect emissions from energy use, though this may not be their stated intention. For example, carbon emissions are already implicitly taxed in most countries—even in those that do not have explicit carbon taxes. The implicit carbon tax is the sum of all taxes on energy, including taxes on energy sales (excise duties). Because such taxes are not proportional to carbon content, their efficiency is impaired as carbon taxes. There are three other problems with carbon taxes—their impacts on competitiveness, on the distribution of the tax burden, and on the environment.

The impact on competitiveness is the main perceived obstacle to the implementation of carbon taxes. Yet empirical studies on carbon and energy taxes seem to indicate that they do not have a significant impact on either losses or gains.

On the distributive impacts of carbon and energy taxes, empirical studies (almost entirely confined to industrialised countries) indicate that there is an expectation that carbon taxes will be regressive. But available studies are almost equally divided between those that support this expectation and those that do not.

As far as environmental impacts are concerned, empirical studies evaluating the reductions of carbon dioxide emissions resulting from carbon taxes are rather limited. Moreover, the reduction in local pollution associated with a decrease in fossil fuel consumption represents an additional benefit from carbon taxes, but it is not always mentioned and studied in detail. However, carbon dioxide is not the only greenhouse gas that can be emitted as a result of human activities, nor is it the only one emitted in energy use. All anthropogenic greenhouse gases should, in principle, be encompassed in policy measures, by levying taxes proportional to their estimated global warming potentials.

The introduction of and adjustments to carbon taxes can be greatly facilitated by starting with a small levy along with the announcement that the tax will be gradually increased by specified increments at specified intervals. This approach gives energy users time to adjust their patterns of investment and use of energy-using devices to less carbon-intensive and more efficient ones, minimising economic disruption.

Carbon taxes are an interesting policy option, and their main negative impacts can be compensated through the design of the tax and the use of the generated fiscal revenues. Consideration can also be given to shifting the imposition or collection of such taxes from downstream (consumers or importing governments) to upstream (producers or exporting governments) to offset the implied diversion of income that would otherwise result, in keeping with article 4.8 (h) of the UN Framework Convention on Climate Change.

Source: Baranzini, Goldemberg, and Speck, 2000.

environmental impacts implied by different forms of energy. Various countries have introduced policies aimed at integrating externalities into energy prices. For example, six Western European countries (four of them in Scandinavia, which has a higher tolerance for taxes for social purposes than most countries) have introduced taxes on carbon emissions or fossil fuels along revenue-neutral lines.[4] The United Kingdom plans to introduce a climate change levy on industry in April 2001—but with relief for the heaviest emitters (the details have been greatly changed from those originally announced due to lobbying by interested parties)—and a sliding-scale emissions charge on company-owned vehicles in April 2002. Proposals for a carbon tax have been tabled in Switzerland. These countries already have implicit carbon taxes on gasoline exceeding \$100 per tonne of carbon dioxide (Baranzini, Goldemberg, and Speck, 2000, table 1). Residential energy consumption generally escapes such tax innovations, undermining their effectiveness. The industrial sector in OECD countries has demonstrated significant emission reductions over many years but continues to be the target for emissions reduction taxation. As a general rule, however, the heaviest emitters attract the greatest relief.

Box 12.3 discusses the dynamics and economic implications of carbon taxes in greater detail. An alternative approach is greenhouse gas emissions trading—nationally (along the lines of sulphur dioxide emissions permit trading in the United States) or internationally (as proposed in article 17 of the Kyoto Protocol). This alternative is frequently preferred by those who dislike new taxes or who are sceptical that revenue authorities will use revenues for their intended purposes. There are numerous examples of revenues from road vehicle taxes, intended to expand and upgrade road infrastructure, being diverted for general public spending. A recent example comes from the Netherlands, where revenues from a fuel tax introduced in 1988 were initially earmarked for environmental spending—but in 1992 the fuel tax was modified and revenues were no longer earmarked (Baranzini, Goldemberg, and Speck, 2000).

The logic has also been questioned of exempting energy or emission taxes on raw materials processing and heavy industrial energy activities involving high emissions, as is now widely the case. If the real objective is to reduce emissions, then full imposition of energy or emission taxes on the heaviest emitters can be expected to make a major contribution to achieving that goal. It may encourage early and major shifts in the use of certain materials and products, and in attitudes and behaviour, needed to effect emission reductions but which exemptions are likely to frustrate. In pursuing such an intellectually rigorous policy, steps may need to be taken to discourage relocation of heavily emitting activities ('carbon leakage'), including barriers in international trade rules to the import and use of the resulting materials and products to ensure global benefits.

Phasing out subsidies to conventional energy

A second issue to consider in achieving true competition is the significant subsidies for conventional energy that still exist in many economies—industrialised, transition, and developing. These publicly supported subsidies may be granted to producers, consumers, or both, and can take various forms. Their common feature is that they distort market signals and, hence, consumer and producer behaviour.

Although subsidies are being cut in many countries, they are still believed to account for more than $150 billion a year in public spending (excluding the transport sector; see World Bank, 1997c; Hwang, 1995; Larsen and Shah, 1992 and 1995; Michaelis, 1996; de Moor, 1997; Myers, 1998; Ruijgrok and Oosterhuis, 1997).

Russia slashed fossil fuel subsides by about two-thirds between 1991 and 1996. China is also phasing out fossil fuel subsidies. They have already been cut by 50 percent and now effectively remain only on coal, at a much lower rate. (Moreover, between 1997 and early 2000 China closed more than 50,000 coal mines, so recent policy initiatives and economic conditions have resulted in a significant fall in carbon dioxide emissions from coal combustion.) As explained in chapter 11, conventional energy subsidies have been found to be financially unsustainable as well as largely counterproductive—because they often do not go to the most needy, and generally prolong inefficiency and harmful emissions throughout the energy chain.

In many countries subsidies for conventional energy coexist with incentives for conservation and new renewable energy development. Some subsidies may be partially hidden—as with preferential tax rates on domestic fuel and power use, incentives to use private motor vehicles (such as free or subsidised fuel and parking), and fiscal measures that have the least impact on the heaviest users. In addition to working at cross-purposes to the aims of sustainable development, subsidies often impose a substantial financial burden, especially in developing countries. The under-pricing of electricity in developing countries was estimated to result in annual revenue shortfalls of more than $130 billion by the early 1990s (World Bank, 1996).

Some countries ostensibly maintain energy subsidies to help poor people. But other approaches may be more effective, particularly since subsidies intended to help the poorest people often deliver the most benefits to richer and heavier users. Investing in insulation for homes, for instance, could achieve the same result as subsidising heating fuel for the poor. But investing in insulation would have additional and longer-lasting social benefits (reducing greenhouse gases, creating jobs). Innovative credit schemes can be more cost-effective than subsidies in terms of extending energy services to the rural poor. In general, subsidies to reduce kerosene or electricity prices benefit richer and heavier users. For example, diesel subsidies to better-off farmers may cause excessive pumping of water for irrigation, seriously lowering the water table. Agricultural electricity tariffs in India have long caused particular concern, being at times little more than 3 percent of those in Bangladesh and only 6–15 percent of those in a number of other Asian countries (World Bank, 1996).

If carefully designed, however, schemes providing the very poorest members of society with a small quantity of electricity (say, 50 kilowatt-hours per household per month) free of charge or at a very low cost offer a workable and effective way of helping poor people (see chapter 6). This approach has worked well in São Paulo, Brazil, where Electropaulo (the local electricity utility) and the city authorities agreed in 1979 to

Six Western European countries have introduced taxes on carbon emissions or fossil fuels along revenue-neutral lines.

bill consumers a subsidised flat rate for minimal monthly consumption of 50 kilowatt-hours. By the late 1980s electricity consumption per shack had increased to 175 kilowatt-hours a month—and many of the dwellings and the quality of service had improved, with an array of social benefits (Boa Nova and Goldemberg, 1998). In addition, well-designed temporary subsidies may be needed to speed sustainable energy innovations to the point of commercialisation, after which time the subsidies should be phased out (see chapter 11 and the section below on the rationale for public policy support).

Regulatory options for restructured energy sectors

Recent and ongoing changes in the electricity and natural gas sectors are altering the long-accepted ground rules for ownership, operation, management, and financing of utilities. For several decades, energy supply systems were regarded as being necessarily large to achieve economies of scale and support massive capital investments. This view encouraged the idea that energy supply systems required the creation and support of natural monopolies, that duplication was economically inefficient, and that the public interest could be protected only by state-owned and -operated monopolies. Over the years subsidies proliferated, biases in favour of large and highly visible projects became evident, innovation stalled (often reflecting an unwillingness to access the best available technologies from elsewhere), management was found wanting, external finance became problematic (due to inefficiency and administrative interventions), and strains on government budgets escalated. The assumption that electricity generation and distribution were a natural monopoly—whether publicly or privately controlled—eventually began to be revisited, and industrialised and developing countries alike have begun to restructure their energy sectors to encourage competition and improve economic efficiency.

One major problem facing policy-makers in a number of developing countries, especially in Sub-Saharan Africa and some Southeast Asian countries, is that options for liberalisation suffer from several constraints. Breaking up a public monopoly often results in substitution by a private monopoly. Domestic savings and investment institutions either do not exist or are inadequate for requirements. And external finance is difficult to attract. Any monopoly is likely to create problems of poor efficiency, choice, and quality of service, so strict regulations need to be put in place and the monopoly broken up or subjected to competition from new entrants wherever possible. External support may be needed for capacity building that focuses on institutional creation and reform. Political stability and a welcoming investment regime are the usual means by which external finance is best attracted. Studies of World Bank projects show that where the macroeconomic fundamentals of low inflation, limited budget deficits, and openness to trade and financial flows are adhered to, projects are more successful. But projects also require the participation of beneficiaries and the support of governments (World Bank, 1999d).

The encouragement of competition and efficiency is leading to a widening of the playing field and a decentralisation of systems, allowing the forces of competition to work more effectively. Introducing competition in the energy sector tends to lower costs and increase consumer satisfaction. At the same time, competitive pressures can make it more difficult for energy suppliers to support public benefits (such as clean air or research, development, and deployment) through cross-subsidies or other means. The introduction and effective implementation of consistent policies and measures for market players can, however, provide the opportunity for balancing efficiency and supporting other public benefits.

By itself energy market restructuring may not help achieve the long-term vision compatible with sustainable energy policies and their successful application. For instance, market liberalisation and privatisation are claimed to have slowed rural electrification in Latin America—although this judgement appears speculative given that liberalisation and privatisation were only just getting under way in Latin America by 1997 (OLADE, 1997). Restructuring is unlikely to encourage the promotion of energy forms with high front-end costs—such as current nuclear power technologies and large hydropower schemes. In Argentina and Brazil market reform is expected to encourage natural gas at the expense of electricity generated by large hydropower schemes, raising greenhouse gas emissions. In the United Kingdom market liberalisation and privatisation have encouraged natural gas over nuclear energy. (The same pattern is expected in Germany.)

The market reform process, however, provides a window of opportunity for introducing reforms that facilitate the introduction of sustainable energy technologies. Energy market restructuring should also serve as a reminder that a number of public benefits were not addressed in the non-competitive electricity and gas sectors in many countries. (The situation was often different in the downstream oil sector.)

Although energy sector liberalisation tends to make energy services more affordable (though there have been some countries where this has not been the case), it requires the establishment of a regulatory framework to foster other public benefits. The basic characteristics of energy sector liberalisation include:

- Industry restructuring, most often involving the unbundling of vertically integrated activities to permit power to be transported and traded by more independent entities.
- The active promotion of competition and private sector cooperation.
- Deregulation and reduction of barriers to new entry.
- Commercialisation (or corporatisation) of state-owned entities and, increasingly, their privatisation.
- Industry restructuring, most frequently involving the unbundling of vertically integrated activities to permit power to be transported and traded by more independent entities.

Achieving greater energy efficiency generally requires less investment than does new generation.

- The establishment of a regulatory framework.

Unlike liberalisation, privatisation may not be necessary to make energy markets more efficient. In Norway, for example, most electric utilities are publicly owned (more than half by municipalities and some 30 percent by the state). But since the 1990 Energy Act, there has been a transition to a fully deregulated market at both the generation and retail levels, allowing individual producers and customers to act as independent sellers and buyers. The system uses negotiated bilateral agreements, maximum five-year futures contracts negotiated on a weekly basis, spot market purchases with market-determined prices fixed for the next 24 hours, and instant market purchases for delivery with as little as 15 minutes' notice (York, 1994). However, Norway is the most frequently cited instance where electricity prices have risen for consumers since liberalisation.

Unbundling of vertically integrated activities has widely been regarded as essential for competition. For instance, competition among electricity generators and suppliers (including energy service companies) has usually been introduced for large industrial customers, then spread gradually to households. The separation of transmission and distribution networks from providers (generators and suppliers) has also generally marked a major redefinition of electric utilities. Finally, retail competition may be marked by service providers seeking to bundle together various services—taking advantage of the databases and information technology at their disposal (initiatives that regulators tend to watch carefully lest earlier dominant positions are abused).

While restructuring has, by and large, contributed to lower energy costs, it is not clear how good a job it will do in protecting all desired public benefits. For that to occur effectively, it may be useful for policy-makers to work with the private sector to develop regulatory measures to advance public benefits in the context of a restructured, global, and more competitive environment. Some countries are taking advantage of the window of opportunity opened by restructuring to consider various funding mechanisms associated with energy use to pursue public benefits. Options include regulatory measures to allow prices to reflect the level and structure of the marginal cost of supply, including the costs of compliance with environmental policies. This, in turn, would allow industry to attract finance and to earn satisfactory returns on investments, including the investments required to comply with environmental policies.

Regulations could also require companies to report on progress with the extension of supplies to unserved populations, in much the same way that progress with environmental protection is monitored. But it is clear from Norway's experience that, whether market reforms involve privatisation or continued public ownership, they are unlikely to protect or advance public benefits unless accompanied by specific regulatory measures to that end. In framing policy to cover this wider range of objectives, it is likely to remain important that the primary duty of competition regulators is to maintain and further competition. In many countries there is also a need to find ways of financing extensions of energy carriers to areas not currently considered attractive to private investors.

Two types of policy initiatives have recently been introduced by some countries to address the public benefits issue (apart from programmes to raise energy efficiency and reduce local and regional pollution):

- Measures to support renewable energy development by obliging utilities to buy or sell a minimum proportion of energy from renewable sources.
- Systems benefits charges (also known as a public benefits fund), which raise revenue from a 'wires charge' that is then used for public goods programmes such as assisting energy use by low-income households or promoting energy efficiency, renewable energy, and research and development.

One of the most successful examples of an obligation to buy, in terms of capacity created, is Germany's windpower development programme, introduced under its 1991 Electricity Feed Law. (However distribution utilities raised strong objections to the premium prices they had to pay—which they were not permitted to pass on to consumers—and the resulting financial burden. The law was modified in 2000 to permit costs to be passed on.) By the end of 1999 Germany's windpower capacity stood at 4,444 megawatts, up from 2,875 megawatts at the end of 1998.

In the United Kingdom a non-fossil fuel obligation (which in its early years overwhelmingly went to subsidise nuclear power, and proved rather disappointing in expanding windpower capacity) is not being retained. Instead, a renewables obligation is requiring licensed electricity suppliers to supply customers with a specified proportion of their supplies from renewable sources. A cap will be placed on the maximum price paid for renewables, to minimise the impact on consumer prices, and suppliers will be permitted to fulfil their obligation through the purchase of 'green certificates'. Concern has been expressed, however, about the limited penalties for non-compliance implied. The U.K. government hopes to raise the renewable energy component of electricity supply from 2.5 percent today to 5 percent by the end of 2003, to 10 percent by 2010 (DETR, 2000). There are widespread concerns about the feasibility of these targets and non-compliance, given the low share of 'green' electricity in the United Kingdom relative to most other EU member countries (Runci, 1998).

Denmark has successfully pursued a renewables obligation for utilities, to the point that windpower capacity stood at nearly 1,740 megawatts at the end of 1999 and a successful international business in wind turbines had been achieved. Power market reforms introduced in 1999 will, however, move Denmark to a programme of both renewables portfolio standards and systems benefits charges.

In the United States renewables portfolio standards have obliged electricity suppliers to include a stipulated proportion of renewables-based electricity in their supply mix. The U.S. experience, for instance with windpower development, has been mixed. But in 1999 there was a surge in U.S. windpower capacity, from 1,770 to 2,500 megawatts. The extension of the Federal Production Tax Credit to January 1, 2002, is expected to help maintain rapid expansion of windpower capacity. Buyers have also been signing up for green power in increasing numbers—particularly in California, where customer incentives were funded by the state's restructuring legislation. These incentives were so successful that by late 1999 steps had to be taken to reduce the subsidy before the state ran out of funds. The best-known programme of systems benefits charges also exists in California, where it was introduced in 1996. (The wires charge on electricity entering California's transmission and distribution system is $0.003 a kilowatt-hour, or about 3 percent of the average tariff.) The Clinton administration proposed making such a scheme— a public benefits fund—applicable throughout the United States under an electricity restructuring bill.

In Brazil new concessionaires following privatisation are required to spend 1 percent of their (after-tax) revenues on energy conservation—and 0.25 percent specifically on end-use measures. These requirements will provide considerable support to PROCEL, Brazil's national electricity conservation programme.

In summary, key regulatory options to encourage sustainable energy include:

- Measures to widen competition—for example, by guaranteeing independent power producers access to power grids and giving energy service companies opportunities to bid on supply contracts.
- Allowing prices to reflect marginal costs of supply.
- Obligations to serve specific regions in return for exclusive markets (concessionaire arrangements).
- Obligations to buy (such as renewables portfolio standards, which help bring down the cost of clean new technologies).
- Creating a public benefits fund (for example, through a wires charge) to support wider access, or the development and diffusion of sustainable energy technologies.
- Energy efficiency and performance standards.
- Reporting requirements to ensure transparency.

Raising energy efficiency

From a societal perspective, achieving greater energy efficiency generally requires less investment than does new generation, and it means fewer energy-related environmental externalities. From an individual perspective, it can mean significant savings over the long term. Why, then, do energy efficiency measures not achieve their cost-effective potential, even in market economies? As noted, markets do not work perfectly, and market barriers for energy efficiency measures are many, including:

- Lack of information, technical knowledge, and training.
- Uncertainties about the performance of investments.
- Lack of capital or financing possibilities.
- High initial and perceived costs of more efficient technologies.
- High transaction costs.
- Lack of incentives for maintenance.
- Differential benefits to the user relative to the investor (for example, when monthly energy bills are paid by the renter rather than by the property owner).

■ Consumer patterns and habits (such as inertia, convenience, and prestige).

As shown in chapter 6, large reductions in primary energy requirements can be made cost-effectively using current technologies to provide energy services. Even greater savings can be realised using advanced technologies. Seeking to capture the full economic potential for energy efficiency improvements is desirable in order to benefit from the lower cost of providing energy services, to free economic resources for other purposes, to reduce adverse environmental impacts, and to expand fuel mix flexibility.

Evidence suggests that more than 60 percent of the primary energy initially recovered or gathered is lost or wasted in the various stages of conversion and use. More than 60 percent of this loss or waste occurs at the end-use stage (Nakićenović, Grübler, and McDonald, 1998); hence the importance of the discussion in chapter 6. In a similar exercise for the Intergovernmental Panel on Climate Change, almost 71 percent of primary energy was calculated as wasted or 'rejected' (Watson, Zinyowera, and Moss, 1996). Furthermore, there is even greater theoretical potential for energy efficiency that goes beyond the first law of thermodynamics (to the concept of exergy) and that suggests global end-use efficiency is only 3.0–3.5 percent (WEC, 1993).

Raising the efficiency with which energy is provided and used is a common objective for energy specialists and policy-makers, and is a strategy that can work synergistically with each of the other strategies discussed here. Raising energy efficiency, especially at the point of end use, eases the apparent conflict between energy as a public good and the negative impacts of energy use. It may also be a more politically realistic way of achieving reductions in energy consumption than persuading individuals to change consumption patterns. It is frequently suggested that in richer, market-driven societies, changes in attitude and behaviour would greatly reduce energy consumption. In principle this is true. But it is extremely difficult to get people to change their life styles. Desired results may be more readily obtained by lowering primary energy consumption significantly while maintaining the quantity and quality of energy services provided—namely, through energy efficiency improvements. Ideally, a two-pronged approach should be adopted.

Clear energy-using appliance labelling schemes are an important first step in providing information on energy efficiency, and on the efficiency of other resource use where appropriate (as with water use in washing machines and dishwashers). Tighter performance standards together with labelling can greatly enhance the energy efficiency of end-use appliances such as refrigerators, washing machines, and videocassette recorders. Tighter performance standards and measures to discourage avoidable use can greatly improve the energy efficiency and environmental performance of motor vehicles. A number of countries would claim to engage in demand-side management, a term used in the U.S. electricity sector, to provide a comprehensive approach to raising energy efficiency. A more piecemeal approach has been the reality. Moreover, few countries are applying consistent and pervasive standards in road transportation.

Western Europe, with high taxes and duties on gasoline (and in some cases carbon taxes) and widespread emission controls, comes closest to a consistent and effective policy framework. The often-cited Corporate Average Fuel Economy (CAFE) standards applied to light-duty vehicles in the United States since 1975 made a major contribution to fuel economy until the late 1980s (reinforced by a tax on 'gas guzzlers' in the 1980s) and encouraged conservation. But these achievements were undermined in the 1990s by the growing popularity of sports utility vehicles and people carriers with size and fuel consumption characteristics that place them in the category of trucks. (In the Ford Excursion, Chevrolet Suburban, and Dodge Durango, for example, fuel consumption of about 12 miles a gallon is not unusual.)

A number of developing countries are taking steps to raise end-use efficiency in building, lighting, and appliance uses. In the early 1980s China introduced an energy efficiency programme (including financial incentives) that is the largest such programme ever launched in a developing country. Overall energy intensity fell 50 percent between 1980 and 1987, helped by this programme—although, even with steady gains since, intensity remains much higher than in industrialised and many developing countries. Some countries are using energy audits to raise efficiency in industrial, commercial, and governmental uses of energy; Egypt has been doing so since 1985. A growing number of developing countries are deploying labelling schemes and efficiency standards. Brazil's PROCEL programme (introduced in 1986), Mexico's CONAE programme (introduced in 1989), and more recent programmes in the Republic of Korea and the Philippines offer significant examples. Thailand's main energy efficiency scheme is funded by customers through a levy. In a five-year project, initial targets have already been greatly exceeded for lighting, refrigerators, and air conditioning. The key elements are educating consumers and labelling appliances, and the Thai utility (EGAT) has played a key role in both elements (see also the final section of chapter 6, on policy measures).

In several transition economies in Central and Eastern Europe and in the Russian Federation (along with Denmark and Finland) efforts to increase energy efficiency have, in principle, long been enhanced by district heating systems. During the 1990s numerous efforts were made to upgrade these systems, in some cases with the support of energy service companies. But it has been difficult to attract the necessary investment and to have confidence that end-use efficiency will be maximised. A major barrier is getting individual apartments metered, largely because of the costs of installing individual meters. This has resulted in buildings continuing to be metered as a single unit, which gives residents of individual apartments less incentive to cut their use of heat and power. But many transition economies have taken more general efforts to raise energy efficiency, including through lower subsidies and higher prices. One example is Poland, where GDP increased 32 percent in 1990–98 but primary energy consumption fell 23 percent.

There are a number of ways of addressing the 'least first-cost' barrier and other barriers to ensuring that energy efficiency is accorded higher priority in decision-making. One is through voluntary agreements intended to ensure that business and industry are

BOX 12.4. IMPROVING ENERGY EFFICIENCY AND REDUCING EMISSIONS IN THE TRANSPORT SECTOR

A discussion of energy efficiency policy options would not be complete without reference to the transport sector. The on-road fuel intensities of automobiles in Australia, Canada, and the United States remain high relative to those in Western Europe. Automobile fuel intensity is also somewhat higher in Japan and rose between 1985 and 1995 (see figure 6.3).

Light-duty vehicle energy use is highly sensitive to changes in vehicle use and fuel efficiency. A sensitivity analysis conducted for the United States and Canada in a World Energy Council (WEC) report on global transportation anticipates that by 2020 light-duty vehicle energy use could be 300–512 million tonnes of oil equivalent (mtoe)—a difference of more than 40 percent (Eads and Peake, 1998). Perhaps even more important for global energy use by the transport sector is whether the developing world follows the U.S. pattern of relatively high light-duty vehicle fuel intensity and vehicle use, or the pattern of Western Europe. The WEC sensitivity analysis showed that if the latter course were pursued, global light-duty vehicle energy demand could be 350 mtoe, or 27 percent below the base case projection—and only 27 mtoe above the 1995 level. This would imply a savings of 300 million tonnes of global carbon emissions in 2020 relative to the base case projection. Most analysts believe that higher fuel prices reduce vehicle use and encourage motorists to purchase more fuel-efficient vehicles. Gasoline taxes in Western Europe range from about $2.50 to more than $4.00 a gallon.

The WEC study did not explore the longer-term potentials of alternative fuels in general or of fuel cells in particular. Although fuel cells could begin entering the transport market by 2010, the impact at the global level will be modest by 2020. Beyond 2020, however, there is considerable potential for major change.

There are also close links between transport and urban and rural planning. An obvious planning option is to design urban systems to maximise the accessibility of efficient collective transport modes (as was done in the often-cited example of Curitiba, Brazil, although further development is increasing strains even there). Another option is to discourage out-of-town developments that impel more personal vehicle use and undermine the viability of urban and suburban centres. Similarly, planning systems can discourage piecemeal development in rural areas that increases use of personal motorised vehicles and road freight.

In 1995 road freight accounted for 30 percent of global transport energy demand, and that share is expected to rise in the next few decades. Among the policy options for containing that change are maintaining or increasing the shares of rail transport and water-borne freight. That requires policy measures to improve rail and shipping infrastructure, and subsequent measures to discourage road transport for competing routes and journeys, especially in urban areas. Air passenger transport, which accounted for 8 percent of global transport energy demand in 1995, is expected to increase its share sharply through 2020. The WEC report on global transport included a base case projection of energy demand growing at nearly 4 percent a year, increasing air passenger energy demand to 13 percent of the transport total. Policy-makers will wish to consider the many implications of this expansion both at ground level and in the air, not least because of the complex interactions between the environment and aircraft flying at high speeds in or close to the lower stratosphere. Airfares do not reflect the many environmental costs of air travel.

Transport policy options include:
- Raising vehicle fuel efficiency and lowering use, thereby reducing light-duty vehicle fuel intensity—particularly in Australia, Canada, Japan, and the United States.
- Applying full-cost pricing and rigorous emission and fuel efficiency standards on all vehicles, with specific policies targeting unnecessarily high fuel use (for example, from four-wheel drive vehicles used by urban motorists and from low-occupant journeys by 'people carriers').
- Encouraging the introduction and deployment of advanced transportation technologies that offer high efficiency, low emissions, and opportunities for fuel diversification.
- Promoting alternative fuels, including investments in fuel delivery infrastructure.
- Adjusting fuel prices to achieve the above goals.
- Encouraging a shift to Western European (rather than U.S.) driving patterns in developing countries.
- Improving effectiveness and consistency of urban and rural planning.
- Promoting bus and rail use and supporting related infrastructure.
- Facilitating pedestrian and pedal-cycle journeys.
- Maintaining rail and water-borne modal shares for freight transport.
- Monitoring passenger aircraft use for land-use and other environmental impacts.

Even after new technologies for greater efficiency and more pollution control are introduced, they take years to achieve full market penetration. (It takes 15 years for a full turnover of stock in OECD countries, and substantially longer in developing countries.) Thus policy actions initiated now will take years to have a significant effect on the environment.

---

proactively involved. As has been seen in Germany, the Netherlands, and the United States, voluntary agreements by and with business and industry can pay considerable dividends—provided that participants genuinely support the initiative and do not seek it as a means of avoiding actions that would otherwise have been required under regulatory approaches. In assessing the likely viability of voluntary agreements, importance is usually placed on the local political and cultural climate of industry-regulator relationships (Wallace, 1995). A second approach is through tighter public procurement policies. Public procurement policies can prioritise more efficient buildings and end-use devices, but few countries have taken this very far or formally. The scope for change is large. Since 1993, for example, the U.S. Energy Star labelling scheme has raised the energy efficiency of computer hardware with considerable success and increasing international collaboration.

A third approach was adopted by the National Board for Industrial and Technical Development (NUTEK, replaced in 1998 by the Swedish National Energy Agency). The board convened consumers to learn about their needs in terms of efficient appliances. By indicating the existence of a market for such appliances, this effort encouraged producers to satisfy those needs with equipment of improved efficiency and performance. Significant results were achieved for refrigerators and freezers, lighting, windows, heat pumps, and washing machines.

There is considerable further potential for taking a sectoral approach to raising the efficiency of energy use. One such area is construction materials and building design. Since 1978 Switzerland has gone to great lengths to ensure that architects, builders, and materials suppliers are aware of the issues at stake. Building design competitions can also be used to heighten awareness. The transport sector poses particular challenges, and has an evident need for clearly focussed policy responses (box 12.4; see also chapter 6).

Mobilising investments in sustainable energy

Cumulative global energy investments required in 1990–2020 are estimated at $9–16 trillion. The lower figure reflects a major drive towards energy efficiency and new renewables, as in case C in chapter 9. The higher figure reflects the challenges of meeting the higher-growth case A. At constant 1990 prices these figures imply energy investments of $300–550 billion a year, which is within the range of current investment levels. The lower investments estimated for case C offer an important rationale for aiming for this rich and green future, rather than towards the higher-growth case A (assuming the estimates are robust).

The investments required to achieve case C represent less than 10 percent of recent global domestic investment (estimated at more than $6 trillion in 1997) and would be much less than 10 percent of total global investment over 2000–20. Thus the amounts are not large relative to the finance available for investment, either internationally or as implied by the high domestic savings ratios in many developing countries.[5] The challenge, then, is not so much to conjure the capital into existence, but to mobilise what already exists. But this challenge has been described as severe—particularly in developing countries, because of political instability, an absence of reliable savings and investment institutions, the wariness of savers and investors, unreliable legal procedures, and the high incidence of political and administrative intervention (WEC, 1997). In some countries corruption is also a problem (World Bank, 1997d, ch. 6). All these features are liable to have an adverse impact on access to credit for parastatal energy companies, international corporations, domestic private enterprises, and individual consumers.

Many developing country governments, in particular, still need to allocate sufficient public funds to meet investment needs, attract sufficient funds from elsewhere, and underwrite energy activities. Many countries have problems accessing capital for political or institutional reasons (or both), and poor and needy developing countries, as well as a significant number of transition economies, are among the weakest in terms of political stability and institutional frameworks. In some of these countries political risks, absence of the necessary institutional frameworks and effective legal remedies, and prevalence of arbitrary interventions pose powerful barriers to investment and successful project completion. The result, as the programme adopted by the UN General Assembly Special Session in June 1997 recognises, is that "conditions in some of these countries have been less attractive to private sector investment and technological change slower, thus limiting their ability to meet their commitments to Agenda 21 and other international agreements" (clause 21).

Several industrialised countries have developed bilateral insurance schemes to address the problems of political risk and non-performance, although in many instances at a considerable financial cost for the scheme and for taxpayers in the investing country. The Multilateral Investment Guarantee Agency (part of the World Bank Group) provides long-term investment guarantees against political risks in Eastern Europe and Central Asia. The role of this agency has been questioned in some quarters. But there have been suggestions that a multilateral global energy fund should be created to cover political risks and facilitate needed energy projects. Experience suggests that some fairly straightforward conditions need to be met for successful project realisation with or without political risk infrastructure, and they are not confined to the energy sector (box 12.5).

Thus financing remains a daunting challenge for many of the countries and areas that need sustainable energy systems the most. Public investments are increasingly difficult to finance as governments respond to pressures to balance budgets. Market reforms and the creation of functioning legal frameworks (which include not only laws but also strong and fair judicial systems to enforce them) are moving slowly in many countries. Businesses, households, and small communities may wish to carry out projects that are too small to attract standard bank lending, so financial incentives and credit arrangements may be important for project viability. More extensive use of private initiatives, cooperative schemes, and public-private partnerships will be required, and new forms of partnership considered, to sustain long-term investment programmes designed to deliver energy to rural areas (see chapter 10). Investors should be encouraged to work with governments and financial institutions to extend commercial energy services to populations in developing countries as rapidly as possible.

A major challenge will be to find ways to facilitate the widespread deployment of new, clean, and efficient energy technologies in developing and transition economies. One suggestion is that this task become the main energy-related activity of the World Bank, since the main traditional energy activity of the Bank—financing conventional energy projects—cannot easily be justified under the reformed market conditions to which most developing countries are evolving. (Under such conditions the World Bank would compete for financing contracts with commercial banks, which will be fully capable of providing the needed capital.) It has also been suggested

---

BOX 12.5. CONDITIONS CONDUCIVE TO ATTRACTING FOREIGN DIRECT INVESTMENT IN THE ENERGY SECTOR (AND OTHERS)

- Political and economic stability, to provide reasonable predictability and reduce the risk of non-performance.
- A functioning legal framework, including currency convertibility, freedom to remit dividends and other investment proceeds, and a stable domestic savings and investment regime.
- A regulatory regime that promotes competition and efficiency and that, once created by government, is independent of and protected from arbitrary political intervention.
- Necessary physical infrastructure.
- Availability of, or capacity to supply from elsewhere, technical skills, goods and services, and a trained and trainable workforce.
- Availability of all the above to all companies and investors through law and general practice, without the need for recourse to special deals or treatment or discretionary decisions by elected officials or bureaucrats.

Source: WEC, 1997.

that the Global Environment Facility (GEF) allocate more resources to capacity and institution building, as part of the improvements in the disbursement of funds called for in UN documents (see Osborn and Bigg, 1998, pp. 112 and 173). In June 1997 the UN General Assembly Special Session pointed out the need for the GEF implementing agencies—UNDP, the United Nations Environment Programme, and the World Bank—"to strengthen, as appropriate and in accordance with their respective mandates, their co-operation at all levels, including the field level" (clause 79; see Osborn and Bigg, 1998, p. 173).

Earlier in the year the UN Secretary-General had recognised UNDP's Capacity 21 Programme as "an effective catalyst and learning mechanism to support capacity-building for sustainable development" (clause 108; see Osborn and Bigg, 1998, p. 114), and in June 1997 the UN General Assembly Special Session asked UNDP to give this priority attention through, among other things, the Capacity 21 Programme (clause 99; see Osborn and Bigg, 1998, p. 180). In May 1999 a strategic partnership between UNDP and GEF was agreed and a start made on producing a comprehensive approach for developing the capacities needed at the country level to meet the challenges of global environmental action. This has become the Capacity Development Initiative (CDI), which will have three stages: assessment of capacity development needs (a questionnaire for this purpose was being evaluated in April 2000), strategy development to meet identified needs, and action plans for GEF. So far the focus appears to have been on biodiversity, desertification, and climate change because these are the three most relevant UN conventions in existence. But consideration should be given to specific consideration of energy capacity development needs.

The World Bank has been active in promoting capacity building over a wide area of activities, including the Global Knowledge Partnership and its knowledge management system, both of which are relevant to promoting advanced energy technologies (World Bank, 1999c). In addition, institutional arrangements such as the Clean Development Mechanism proposed under the Kyoto Protocol could help disseminate clean new energy technologies in developing countries.

Multilateral agencies have been criticised for their expensive, time-consuming, and complicated procedural requirements—yet these agencies are often the only source available for financing rural electrification and renewable energy projects in emerging markets. In addition, the smaller size of these projects often means that they cannot receive the allocation of staff from the agencies, which focus on large power projects (usually fossil-fuelled). Financing procedures are usually geared towards large national projects, and place costly burdens on smaller renewable energy projects. Review standards may be more stringent and time-consuming for small renewable projects, with innovative technologies, than for well-defined large fossil fuel plants. It has been suggested that a fast-track process for one stop financing be instituted for renewable energy projects. The process should incorporate a short review period, a restricted number of financing participants with a team leader, agency teams assigned

Financing procedures are usually geared towards large national projects, placing costly hurdles on smaller renewable energy projects.

to projects from beginning to end, standard project agreements for renewable projects, and a closing schedule agreed at the outset (Bronicki, 2000). This would help reduce transaction costs and project costs, provide more energy services sooner, and foster more efficient and cost-effective financing operations of multilateral agencies.

Attracting private capital

Encouraging private investment in the supply of sustainable energy carriers to developing countries is essential for two reasons. First, many governments no longer wish (and may not be able) to provide the needed capital investment (see above). Second, multilateral and other official lending institutions are unlikely to provide more than 15 percent of the funding required for energy investments over the next few decades (WEC, 1997, p. 75).

Thus a high priority should be placed on the types of reform required to attract both domestic and foreign private capital at the country level. Foreign direct investment by private companies is an important and growing share of net resource flows to developing countries. Official development assistance fell by about 20 percent (in real terms) during the 1990s, and represents a shrinking fraction of net resource flows. In 1997 official development assistance represented only about 15 percent of net resource flows to developing countries, down from 43 percent in 1990. In contrast, foreign direct investment expanded rapidly in the 1990s. In 1998 foreign direct investment rose 39 percent, to $644 billion. Of this, $165 billion went to developing countries (UNCTAD, 1999).

But most foreign direct investment—70 percent in 1998 (World Bank, 1999c)—goes to just 10 countries, rather than to the much larger number in serious need. In 1997 the main recipients were China (31 percent), Brazil (13 percent), and Mexico (7 percent). Nevertheless, the World Bank (1999a, p. 47) has reported that foreign direct investment is less volatile than other forms of capital inflows. For instance, during the 1990s foreign direct investment was less volatile than commercial bank loans or total portfolio flows (World Bank, 1999d, p. 37). This is in keeping with the findings of the UN Secretary-General's report of January 1997 and the UN General Assembly Special Session programme of June 1997 (see above, in the section on policy goals; Osborn and Bigg, 1998).

In many ways the history of the oil and gas industries illustrates how private enterprise, working within an established system of concessions around the world, has been able to attract significant and sufficient capital investments to fund energy exploration, production, and distribution. In many countries these functions have been carried out through public-private partnerships. Private-private joint ventures are also common, and have led to efficient operation and transfer of technologies.

In many countries the conditions for attracting foreign direct investment are unlikely to be met in the near future (see box 12.5). In such cases public-private partnerships may offer an alternative structure to encourage foreign investment in energy projects. In a public-private partnership the two sides bring a wider range of concerns and capabilities to the table. Given a competitive framework, private sector participation will tend to increase economic efficiency. The public sector, on the other hand, has an obligation to protect other public benefits. The combination can increase the political acceptability of conditions that lead to private investment. Adequate returns and tolerable risks are, however, a precondition for private investment. In some institutional arrangements—such as joint ventures between publicly and privately owned corporations—the best of both sides may be harnessed. Examples exist in Argentina, the Dominican Republic, Honduras, Mexico, the Philippines, and South Africa.

Tapping other sources of funding

Where private financing is not available, developing countries must turn to other sources. Domestic policies, as well as the broader policy environment in which financing and lending decisions are made, will have an impact on the ability of developing countries to finance sustainable energy initiatives.

For example, financing at reasonable interest rates is often critical for the successful diffusion of end-use energy efficiency and renewable energy measures. Innovative credit schemes are facilitating the adoption of off-grid household solar photovoltaic systems in many developing countries, with mixed results. Multilateral development banks have contributed to many of these programs, as in India and Indonesia. Although much has been made of the need for microcredit—with Bangladesh's Grameen Bank the most often-cited example of a microcredit institution—the availability of funds falls far short of needs. Few microcredit schemes operate specifically to finance sustainable energy projects. Since 1974 the Grameen Bank has successfully loaned money in small amounts to many people (particularly women) for economic and social development purposes. And in recent years Grameen Shakti (Energy) has been lending money for modern energy schemes—solar photovoltaic and windpower— though it still operates on a small scale. Still, with more than 10 million people now benefiting from microcredit facilities for all purposes, there is potential for making greater use of such schemes in promoting sustainable energy development.

Historically, the vast majority of energy loans from development banks went to large-scale hydropower, fossil fuel, and traditional energy infrastructure projects. Very little funding was devoted to energy efficiency or smaller-scale renewable energy technologies. Recently, however, the development banks have begun to shift the balance of their activities. In 1994–97 the World Bank approved $1.2 billion in loans for energy end-use efficiency projects, efficiency improvements in district heating systems, and non-traditional renewable energy projects. This is equivalent to about 7 percent of World Bank energy loans during this period (World Bank, 1999c). Furthermore, the Bank had another $1.5 billion in energy efficiency

and renewable energy loans scheduled for approval in 1998–2000. This is a positive trend.

The Asia Alternative Energy Program (ASTAE) within the World Bank provides a useful model for promoting energy efficiency and renewable energy technologies. ASTAE's mission is to give greater priority to such projects and technologies within the Bank's activities in Asia. Major loans have been approved for China, India, Indonesia, and other countries in the region, in many cases together with grant funding from GEF or bilateral donors for training, capacity building, and market development. By the end of 1998 ASTAE had helped develop and obtain approval for 24 projects involving $750 million in World Bank loans and GEF grants (ASTAE, 1998).

GEF was created to help developing countries pay the incremental costs of technologies with significant global environmental benefits. But to date GEF has operated largely on an ad hoc project-by-project basis. GEF is starting to work systematically on some advanced energy technologies—for example, through its fuel cell programme and photovoltaic market transformation initiative. But closer links between GEF and the private sector will be required to broaden such initiatives.

New forms of international public finance have been suggested as ways of addressing the declining share of official development assistance to developing countries and promoting sustainable development. A variety of proposals have been put forward for raising revenue for these purposes, ranging from an international carbon tax to charges for using the global commons. The suggested advantage of such taxes is their potential to raise large sums of money automatically— that is, without continuous funding cycles and voluntary commitments. Their disadvantage, as seen by the main revenue-raising authorities and taxpayers, is lack of control over how the money is spent and dissent over its allocation.

This raises the sensitive subject of conditionality in official development assistance and other financial and technology transfers. Where finance provided for sustainable development has been (or is being) used for other purposes, there may be legitimate grounds for donors to apply ex ante or ex post conditions to additional finance. To encourage flows of the funding needed for sustainable development, this topic needs to be discussed more openly between developing and industrialised countries. Initiatives such as the erasure of the external debt obligations of heavily indebted poor countries could include rules on future funding and credit allocation that foster efficient and environmentally friendly energy technologies.

Some other relatively new options have had trouble achieving their objectives because of reluctance by governments and bureaucracies to establish and maintain mutually satisfactory conditions. In recent years many developing countries have tried to introduce privately financed electrification projects by guaranteeing markets to independent power producers in exchange for new generating capacity. In this they have followed an approach based on experience in the United States, following the Public Utility Regulatory Policy Act of 1978. But the conditions that made independent power producers attractive in the United States have changed. With the opening of the U.S. electricity market, many utilities are unwilling to sign long-term power purchase agreements (WEC, 1997).

A number of projects involving independent power producers in various countries have run into problems for the following reasons:
- Authorities failing to allow market-based prices.
- Poor credit ratings of agencies contracting to purchase the power.
- Exposure to political risks.
- Excessive debt-equity ratios.
- Inability to raise sufficient equity.
- High foreign exchange risks.
- Efforts by the authorities to control rates of return.

The East Asian financial crisis of 1997–99 created additional obstacles to the introduction of independent power producers. Since then, however, interest has revived in such producers.

Build-own-transfer (BOT) and build-own-operate-transfer (BOOT) schemes have also been attempted, with varying success. In such projects a developer owns the plant for a limited period, after which the asset is transferred to a utility (usually under government control and ownership). Because the plant is usually planned to have no residual value to the investor at the end of the fixed period, the returns on the investment in the early years, and the price of electricity from the plant, will have to compensate. This makes BOT and BOOT schemes relatively costly and complicated options. Moreover, an independent power producer's investment in such schemes is unmarketable, so risks cannot be spread, shares cannot be sold, and an opportunity to develop local capital markets is lost (WEC, 1997). Where BOT and BOOT schemes do take off successfully, it is usually due to the provision of government guarantees, which are essentially a form of public procurement and credit. Such schemes can have the benefits of putting projects in place, using modern technology, and building local capacity. But their relative costliness and complexity remain a barrier, and the time limitation can inhibit capacity building.

Following the scope for joint implementation of policies and measures between parties to the UN Framework Convention on Climate Change, introduced under the convention's article 4.2(a), more than 130 projects have been brought forward, although the issue of crediting has not been resolved. (This led to the introduction of the phrase 'activities implemented jointly'—without crediting— at the first conference of the parties to the convention in 1995.) The Kyoto Protocol seeks to take this further with projects that supplement domestic action, especially under the Clean Development Mechanism and in keeping with the sorts of action consistent with article 2 of the protocol (for example, promoting efficiency, new and renewable forms of energy, carbon dioxide sequestration technologies, and advanced and innovative environmentally sound technologies).

Encouraging technological innovation for sustainable energy development

Chapter 5 shows that limited energy resources are not expected to constrain development. But meeting the demands of sustainability will require major improvements in the efficiency of energy use, a much higher reliance on renewable energy technologies, and cleaner and safer fossil fuel technologies. While much can be accomplished through the wider deployment of commercial technologies, new technologies are also needed. Chapters 6–10 point out that while new technologies hold great promise, their development and diffusion is not occurring quickly enough or at a large enough scale to meet the challenges of sustainability. Thus there is a need to accelerate the energy innovation process through all effective means, including appropriate public policies where these can be identified.

The energy innovation chain has four stages: research and development (R&D), demonstration, early deployment, and widespread dissemination. Each stage has distinct requirements, faces barriers, and involves policy options for seeking to overcome those barriers. These characteristics are summarised in table 12.2 and described in more detail in the remainder of this section.

While there is widespread agreement on the need for a smooth transition through all links in the chain, different observers have different opinions about the problems. Researchers active at the beginning of the chain, whether or not reliant on external grants and contracts, may highlight the dangers of bottlenecks in the early part of the chain. Those who are more market-oriented—being engaged in the development and sale of products using the resulting technologies—are likely to focus on the severe barriers to widespread dissemination, and the desirability of gaining higher priority for sustainable energy technologies, with which this chapter is primarily concerned.

In considering policy initiatives to support energy R&D, some profound issues need to be addressed. For instance, a school of thought believes, based on a careful review of U.S. experience, that government support has often been profoundly inconsistent with successful R&D projects (such as photovoltaics), causing the projects to suffer from "highly unstable annual budgets" (Cohen and Noll, 1991, p. vii). On the other hand, some unsuccessful projects (such as the Clinch River Breeder Reactor) "have continued to receive support long past the time when the project was clearly destined to fail, because of inflexibilities in project design and political imperatives" (p. vii). This school of thought has concluded that "these problems are inherent in long-term, risky investments by the government, and thus constitute an argument for favouring generic research activities rather than large-scale commercialization projects" (p. vii). In this view R&D programmes are more likely to succeed the less fragmented is responsibility for them across agencies and Congressional committees (Cohen and Noll, 1991).

Additional lessons can be learned from the U.S. federal programme intended to make synthetic fuels from coal. Cohen and Noll and their colleagues identified three main reasons for failure that are liable to be replicated in future government programmes for energy R&D. The first is the risk that government makes decisions based on short-run circumstances and point projections from very speculative projections, or knee-jerk reactions. Second, cost estimates are liable to demonstrate their proponents' ubiquitous optimism about undeveloped processes. Third, the synthetic fuels programme demonstrated the difficulty of government support for long-term commercial development—an expensive development programme was required but needed a strong, stable coalition of political interests to support it and substantial benefits for lobbying interests such as the industry, technology providers, or consumers. The programme did not have such sustained support. Many observers believe that the first two reasons for failure arise only when there is an effort to substitute government (taxpayer) funding for private risk capital in commercialisation projects. The U.S. experience has important parallels in some other industrialised countries. Ideally, therefore, a smooth transition through the energy innovation chain should be aimed at, and government support should focus on generic research.

Understanding the energy innovation chain

Before they can reach commercial readiness, new energy technologies, building designs, and infrastructure need several years to decades (depending on the technology) for research, development, and demonstration. And once they become commercially ready, these technologies typically require decades of market growth to achieve major market shares (Grübler, 1998). The juxtaposition of such long lead times against the urgency of moving towards sustainable development goals underscores the need for smooth and, where needed, accelerated progress along the energy innovation chain for promising technologies. The practical implementation of this perceived need nevertheless has to take into account:

■ The time profiles of capital stock turnover (which vary according to the type of capital item under review) and the extent to which economic and political barriers may constrain the pace of turnover.

■ The significance of fundamental research relative to incremental R&D.

■ The amount being spent on energy R&D under its various subheadings—and the cases where it can reliably be claimed that more should be spent on environmentally sound technologies or on areas where growth rates (and therefore capital stock expansion or turnover) are fastest.

Most ongoing innovative activity is for incremental improvements in technologies (such as combined cycles) already established in the market. Where there has been substantial progress with radically new technologies, it has, in a number of high-profile and important instances (such as gas turbine and nuclear technologies), been based on past government-supported activities for which support has subsequently declined. Although some radically new technologies will be needed to meet sustainability goals during the 21st century (along with wider application of already well-developed environmentally friendly ones), it is uncertain which will prove to be the most affordable, convenient, safe, and environmentally benign. Chapter 11 points out that when uncertainties are large, it makes economic sense to invest in creating options and reducing uncertainties and costs. Policies that encourage technological innovation also open the door for unexpected side benefits.

Clean and efficient end-use energy technologies are somewhat different. These can often be developed and marketed over much shorter periods because they involve briefer re-investment cycles, and thus greater opportunities for short-term change. Control techniques, appliances, production machinery, and automobiles offer such opportunities. Here public policies that focus on incentives, including stable macroeconomic fundamen-tals (which promote innovation under competitive conditions), may be appropriate.

The arguments in favour of accelerating the introduction of inher-

TABLE 12.2. THE ENERGY INNOVATION CHAIN FOR SUSTAINABLE ENERGY TECHNOLOGIES

	Research and development (laboratory)	Demonstration (pilot to market)	Early deployment (technology cost buy-down)	Widespread dissemination (overcoming institutional barriers and increasing investment)
Key barriers	• Governments consider R&D funding problematic • Private firms cannot appropriate full benefits of their R&D investments	• Governments consider allocating funds for demonstration projects difficult • Difficult for private sector to capture benefits • Technological risks • High capital costs	• Financing for incremental cost reduction (which can be substantial) • Uncertainties relating to potential for cost reduction • Environmental and other social costs not fully internalised	• Weaknesses in investment, savings, and legal institutions and processes • Subsidies to conventional technologies and lack of competition • Prices for competing technologies exclude externalities • Weaknesses in retail supply financing and service • Lack of information for consumers and inertia • Environmental and other social costs not fully internalised
Policy options to address barriers	• Direct public funding (national or international) • Tax incentives • Incentives for collaborative R&D partnerships	• Direct national or international support for demonstration projects • Tax incentives • Low-cost or guaranteed loans • Temporary price guarantees for energy products of demonstration projects	• Temporary subsidies through tax incentives, government procurement, or competitive market transformation initiatives	• Phasing out subsidies to established energy technologies • Measures to promote competition • Full costing of externalities in energy prices • 'Green' labelling and marketing • Concessions and other market-aggregating mechanisms • Innovative retail financing and consumer credit schemes • Clean Development Mechanism (see text)

Source: Adapted from PCAST, 1999.

ently clean and safe energy-converting and energy-using technologies are often as relevant for developing countries as for industrialised ones. For that reason it is desirable to extend the scope of energy R&D so that a significant fraction is directed to meeting the needs of the developing world, which will account for most of the world's incremental energy requirements (see chapter 9). Major shifts will almost certainly be required globally, because today nine OECD countries account for more than 95 percent of the world's publicly supported energy R&D (Dooley and Runci, 1999a). Simply importing advanced technologies from industrialised countries—even if affordable—is unlikely to suffice, although adjustments based on local conditions and practices may be possible. New energy technologies should be tailored to the resource endowments and specific needs and capabilities of developing countries. Optimising new technologies for developing needs will require significant developing country participation in the energy innovation process.

Although there is much ongoing technological advance,[6] public investment in energy innovation has been falling. In a few countries private spending on energy R&D is low and may be falling as well. In the United States in 1981–96, the energy sector's R&D intensity was extremely low and falling relative to many other sectors (Margolis and Kammen, 1999). This contrasted with a 5 percent annual increase in overall private U.S. investment in R&D in the 1990s (Dooley, 1999b).

But there is also evidence suggesting that private spending on energy R&D has been stable or rising in other countries—such as Finland, Germany, and Japan. A U.K. Department of Trade and Industry survey found that R&D spending by the world's top 300 international companies rose 13 percent in 1997 and 12 percent in 1998, to $254 billion (The Financial Times, 25 June 1999). The oil and gas sectors strongly increased R&D spending in 1996–98, as did most of the leading engineering companies associated with energy. No international comparison was available for electricity, but the same source found that U.K. electricity R&D was 8 percent higher in 1998 than in 1997.

Where spending on energy R&D has fallen off, much of the decline represents decreased funding for nuclear technologies and standard fossil fuel technologies. Some of this funding is now going to advanced cleaner fossil fuel research and carbon sequestration. Funding for renewables has been relatively flat (although this may—and in some cases does—mask large increases in some subsectors, such as solar in Japan). Funding for energy efficiency programmes has been consistently increasing. Even in the United States, widely portrayed as the epitome of collapsing spending on energy R&D, real federal spending on energy efficiency R&D rose 8 percent a year in the 1990s, and real federal spending on renewable energy R&D rose about 1 percent a year (Dooley, 1999b). But the evidence requires careful analysis, as discussed in more detail in the annex to this chapter.[7] Nevertheless, there is concern that spending on energy innovation, from both private and public sources, may prove inadequate relative to the challenges confronting the world in the 21st century (see PCAST, 1997 and 1999; Margolis and Kammen, 1999; and Dooley and Runci, 1999a).

One dilemma is how to distinguish between R&D inputs and R&D outputs. Outputs may not flow readily from inputs and may change over time (for instance, due to improvements in computer hardware and software). Another challenge is to account accurately for the R&D outsourcing by mature companies to specialised firms (as anticipated by Stigler, 1968). Furthermore, policy, institutional, and financial barriers inhibit the pace and pattern of technical diffusion. Hence the contention that market conditions are of overwhelming importance.

Although demonstration plants and early production units are often much more costly per unit of installed capacity than plants based on existing technology, the unit cost of manufactured goods tends to fall with cumulative production experience. This usually happens rapidly at first but tapers off as the technology matures—a relationship called an experience curve when it accounts for all production costs across an industry (figure 12.1). Early investments can 'buy down' the costs of new technologies along their experience curves to levels where the technologies may be widely competitive. The three technologies in figure 12.1 have progress ratios of about 0.8, which is close to the historical median for many industries.

Successfully demonstrated technologies that are radically different from existing technologies are typically much more costly than established alternatives. Thus it may be desirable to promote investments aimed at lowering their costs to competitive levels. Strategies are required for overcoming policy, institutional, and end-user financial barriers to the wide dissemination of new sustainable energy technologies that are both proven and cost-competitive. The entire innovation process can be stalled if any link in this chain is weak. Conversely, the existence of strong market demand (pull) can overcome weaknesses earlier in the chain.

The rationale for public policies in support of energy innovation

Schumpeter (1942) pointed out that successful innovators are rewarded with temporary monopoly control over what they have created, and there is an extensive literature on the relatively high returns achievable on R&D spending. Despite these broadly supportive background conditions, there is concern in some quarters that innovation rests on a few players—while imitators who incur few R&D costs prevent the main R&D investors from enjoying the full benefits of their efforts (the 'free rider' problem). This concern has led to the claim that spending on energy R&D is suboptimal.

In other quarters the concern about free riders is principally regarded as a restatement of the nature of innovation, not a justification for public policy intervention. Further action may be more readily

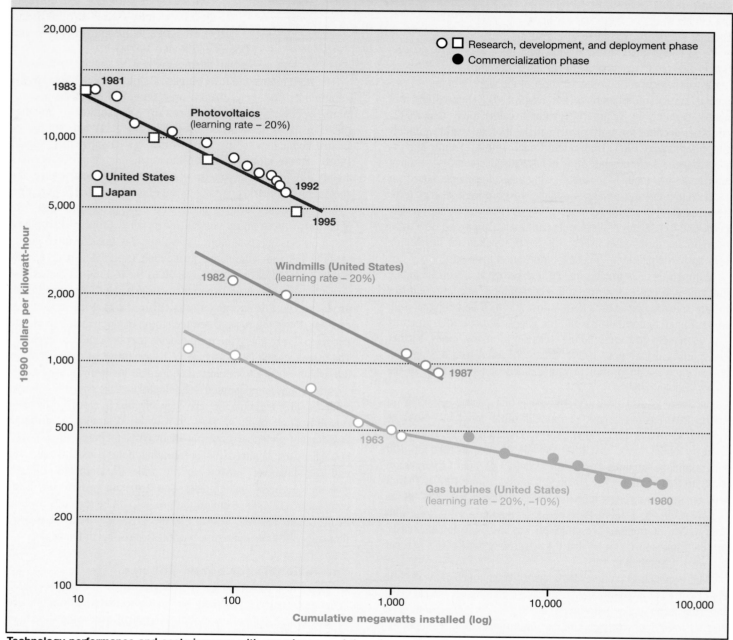

FIGURE 12.1. EXPERIENCE CURVES FOR PHOTOVOLTAICS, WINDMILLS, AND GAS TURBINES IN JAPAN AND THE UNITED STATES

○ □ Research, development, and deployment phase
● Commercialization phase

Photovoltaics (learning rate – 20%)

○ United States
□ Japan

Windmills (United States) (learning rate – 20%)

Gas turbines (United States) (learning rate – 20%, –10%)

1990 dollars per kilowatt-hour

Cumulative megawatts installed (log)

Technology performance and costs improve with experience, and there is a pattern to such improvements common to many technologies. The specific shape depends on the technology, but the persistent characteristic of diminishing costs is termed the 'learning' or 'experience' curve. The curve is likely to fall more sharply as technologies first seek a market niche, then full commercialisation, because lower costs become increasingly important for wider success.

Source: Nakićenović, Grübler, and McDonald, 1998.

justified on other policy grounds, such as the desirability of incentives to encourage specific courses of action. Such incentives can be directed at areas where spending is considered suboptimal. But since it can be countered that moving from the current situation implies opportunity costs, it follows that claims of current suboptimality may be judgmental. Where there has been a major move away from R&D

spending on nuclear power and less advanced fossil fuel technologies, towards R&D spending on renewable energy, advanced fossil fuel and carbon sequestration technologies, and energy efficiency—as has happened recently in some countries—this may reflect widespread political and public opinion. In any event, the key issue may be that it is not so much R&D spending in preferred subsectors that is lacking, but diffusion of the preferred technologies that is found problematic for a variety of reasons.

Those actively engaged in or responsible for corporate R&D often dispute claims that private R&D spending is inadequate, and severely constrained by the free-rider problem, on the grounds that they need to—and do—invest in R&D to keep up with competitors and survive. There are many examples within and outside the energy sector where this is the case. But there may also be a grey area where energy companies might gain from making additional R&D expenditures, particularly with a view to using successful results in their daily operations, but are reluctant to move ahead of competitors if extra costs are going to be incurred and competitive gains eroded more quickly than expected returns can justify. The wide range of corporate R&D spending between innovative engineering companies, on the one hand, and energy service providers, on the other, may reflect these differing views.

More cogently, firms may not invest adequately in R&D when innovation is needed to reduce costs not reflected in market prices (such as environmental costs). Public investment in R&D, as well as policies that stimulate private investment in R&D related to sustainable energy goals, may be warranted where there is good reason to believe that private efforts are falling short.

In general, private efforts seem most likely to fall short in long-term research (see chapter 8), where returns may be expected to be particularly uncertain and deferred (and investments open-ended and potentially large). This approach may be entirely rational for private efforts, yet it may not advance the public good. In such cases government support for innovation may be desirable. In the context of using energy provision and use to move towards sustainable development in the long run, government support is potentially of great significance.

There is considerable debate about the appropriate role for government in supporting activities downstream of R&D that involve potential commercial products. One widely held view is that such activities should be left entirely to the private sector. But as noted, the private sector tends to focus its energy innovation investments on incremental changes to existing technologies for which initial prices for new products are not much higher than for existing products (and might even be less). For this and other reasons, some recent studies recommend a major government role in these areas for energy products anticipated to provide significant benefits that are not adequately reflected in market prices (PCAST, 1999; Duke and Kammen, 1999).

There is no guarantee, however, that such government involvement will produce the benefits sought. Indeed, there is a risk—in this as in other public policy areas—that as a result of lobbying for research spending (the technology 'pork barrel'; see Cohen and Noll, 1991 and Savage, 1999, among others), there may be wasteful diversion of taxpayer funds from more urgent or productive uses. Such diversion occurs despite numerous past failures from government interventions of this kind, as indicated at the start of this section.

Policy options for promoting technological innovation

Research and development. Options for government support of R&D include grants and contracts, tax incentives to encourage private R&D, and incentives for national and international collaborations involving various combinations of private firms, universities, and other research institutions.

Demonstration projects. Demonstration efforts to prove technical viability at a near-commercial scale are generally costly, risky, and difficult to finance. The public sector has a poor track record in picking winners; its support for demonstration has rarely led to successful commercial products.[8] The most successful demonstration efforts have been those in which the government role has been limited to setting performance and cost goals and to providing some financial support. The private sector, meanwhile, takes responsibility for technological choices in addressing these goals and shoulders a major share of the needed investment.

Buying down costs. For some radically new energy technologies intended to meet sustainable development goals, public subsidies may be needed and justifiable to facilitate private sector–led efforts aimed at buying down technology costs. Many industrialised and some developing countries offer financial incentives to stimulate new renewable energy development. The need for subsidies is especially great where external costs are not fully internalised in energy prices.

Public resources for technology cost buy-down should be allocated according to criteria focused on maximising societal returns on these scarce funds. Incentives should:

- Encourage lower technology costs through all possible means—including competition, economies of scale in production, economies of learning through accumulated experience, and gains from making marginal technological improvements as cumulative production grows.
- Have sunset provisions that limit their duration.
- Be restricted to emerging technologies that offer major public benefits not fully valued in market prices, that have steep learning curves, and that have good prospects for market penetration after the subsidies have been phased out.

To spread and reduce risks, buy-down programmes can be designed to support portfolios of new clean energy technologies.

Competitive market transformation initiatives should be given close attention for two reasons. First, they offer cost-savings potential. Second, ongoing energy market reforms provide an opportunity for introducing policy measures that would make technology buy-down easier. Examples of competitive market transformation initiatives include the U.S. Renewable Portfolio Standard, Germany's former Feedstock Law, and the recently abandoned U.K. Non-Fossil Fuel Obligation (see above). As noted in the next section, focused attention should be given to cost buy-down initiatives in developing countries.

Widespread deployment. Even after successful buy-down, new energy technologies being pursued for sustainable development benefits often face significant institutional barriers to widespread deployment. The removal of such barriers—for example, the sorting out of patent issues, or support for domestic savings institutions—is an important public policy objective.

Many of the market reforms discussed in the section on making markets work better (removing subsidies, internalising externalities) will facilitate widespread deployment of some new clean energy technologies. Such reforms will be especially helpful in accelerating the deployment of the new cogeneration and polygeneration options discussed in chapter 8. In addition, green energy labelling and energy marketing are made possible by market reforms that enable consumers to choose their energy suppliers.[9]

One important set of policy issues relates to scale. Some promising new clean energy technologies are small-scale and modular, offering attractive economics through their potential for low cost through mass production and their potential for deployment near users, where market values are high. But deployment of such technologies, which includes both efficient end-use technologies and small-scale production technologies, faces barriers at both the consumer and producer levels.

As discussed in the section on raising energy efficiency, users of small-scale technologies often lack information on product availability, costs, and benefits and face barriers to financing. For providers of energy services from small-scale technologies, a major challenge is overcoming the high transaction costs that often characterise small-scale systems. Policies to encourage economies of scope and scale would be helpful in this regard.

Economies of scale might be exploited through policies that facilitate the development of industries that are able to exploit commercially—through the introduction of innovative products and services—efficiency standards, renewables portfolio standards, 'green certificate' markets, energy labelling of mass-produced products, and cooperative procurement. Energy service companies that provide consumers with a broad range of energy services—whether on their own or through franchises or concessions—may also emerge (see also chapter 10). Franchises and concessions should be issued competitively, under contracts that require winners to meet strict societal obligations (often, the obligation to serve all consumers in the franchise or concession territory) in exchange for monopoly rights. A long history of cooperative ventures to promote rural electrification (for example, in Argentina, Canada, and Europe) offers a model for supporting the diffusion of small-scale technology (see the section above on widening access). Two off-grid solar photovoltaic joint ventures in South Africa, between Eskom and Shell and British Petroleum/Amoco, are other successful models.

A note of caution about new technologies and innovation policies. Societies hope and expect that new technologies will liberate humans and enhance the environment—and this is often the case. But not all technologies provide the benefits sought or intended. Technology can be a source of environmental damage as well as a remedy (Grübler, 1998). Perverse consequences may follow from what were intended as benign interventions (Jewkes, Sawers, and Stillerman, 1958). Experience highlights the virtues of caution, the need for open and multiple processes, and the desirability of taking nothing for granted.

In pursuing new technologies, the risks and liabilities of potential negative outcomes should be addressed fundamentally and holistically, so that actions relating to better understanding and avoiding or mitigating potential adverse side effects are made an integral part of the innovative process. A key element of a strategy to minimise the risks of adverse unforeseen consequences should be to take a portfolio approach to technology development (that is, 'don't put all your eggs in one basket'). The preceding chapters show the rich diversity of technological opportunities for pursuing sustainable development goals.

Moreover, long-term research on promising technologies is usually cheap insurance in pursuing sustainable development (Schock and others, 1999). And because many of the more promising technologies for achieving sustainable development objectives are small-scale and modular (fuel cells, efficient building and automobile design, photovoltaic systems), it should be feasible to construct commercial technology portfolios that are not too costly. Such considerations also underscore the importance of energy strategies that emphasise more efficient use of energy. With lower energy demands, society gains greater flexibility in choosing among advanced energy supply options and can avoid major commitments to those that appear to pose greater risks.

Even where there is clear evidence that public spending on energy R&D has fallen or remained static, this may not indicate a need for increased public spending. It may reflect shifting priorities or the need for a change in priorities—away from unrewarding programmes or those insufficiently geared to sustainable development. Public policies, like markets, should be in a continuous process of evaluation and change with the intention of learning from others and striving to do better: employing a pluralistic approach, not seeking monolithic social ends (Popper, 1961 [addenda to 1945]).

Still, the considerations in this section suggest that it may be desirable to seek new public-private partnerships for accelerating sustainable energy technology innovation in the 21st century. In partnership with the private sector, governments may seek to define broad objectives and timetables for appropriate technological innovation consistent with sustainable development, and back up these objectives with appropriate incentives. The private sector would necessarily play the main role in exploring the main technological choices and making the investments needed to meet these objectives. The option of carrying out demonstration projects under international auspices should also be explored, along with innovative ways of financing such projects.

Encouraging technological innovation in developing countries

Instead of following the example of today's industrialised countries, developing countries have the opportunity to leapfrog directly to modern, cleaner, and more energy-efficient alternatives. Some developing countries are well-positioned—from the standpoint of their rapidly growing energy demands, nascent infrastructure, and natural resource endowments—to reap the benefits of technological leapfrogging. In some cases developing countries may even be able to adopt emerging new technologies with near-zero emissions—resolving the seemingly inherent conflict between environmental protection and economic development.

There are many developing country examples of technological leapfrogging. One of the most familiar is the widespread adoption of cellular telephones, which has eliminated the need for overhead telephone line infrastructure as a precondition for the diffusion of telephone technology. There are some notable examples of developing countries being the first to adopt new technologies, including energy-related technologies. The following advanced iron-making technologies are among them: direct reduction using natural gas (Mexico), modern charcoal-based iron-making (Brazil), and first-generation smelt reduction technology (South Africa). In addition, China is a world leader in biogas technology. And Brazil led the world in the production and use of biomass-derived ethanol as a transport fuel, although this initiative has received less public support in recent years.

Opportunities for technological leadership
Leapfrogging over some of the historical steps in the technological development of today's industrialised countries is a widely accepted principle. But conventional wisdom cautions against developing countries taking the lead in commercialising technologies not widely used elsewhere. Because developing countries face so many pressing needs (see chapter 2), the argument goes, they cannot afford to take the many risks associated with technological innovation. There is reason to modify this view in some situations.

First, developing countries in general—and rapidly industrialising countries (Brazil, China, India, Indonesia, South Africa) in particular—are becoming favourable theatres for innovation. Most developing countries are experiencing rapid growth in the demand for energy services, a necessary condition for successful technological change. Moreover, many rapidly industrialising countries have large internal markets and are moving towards the development of strong domestic capital markets and market reforms, including energy market reforms, that will provide more favourable investment climates. In many cases these countries also have a large cadre of suitably trained engineers and others who can contribute to technological advance.

Second, developing countries need new technologies different from those of industrialised countries. For example, most developing countries are in the early stages of infrastructure development. They have enormous demands for basic materials and need innovative technologies that will facilitate infrastructure development. In industrialised countries, by contrast, the demand for basic materials is reaching the saturation point, and there is little need for fundamentally new technologies for basic materials processing.

Third, early deployment of advanced energy generation and use technologies that are inherently low polluting offers advantages in coping with the growing environmental problems that are rapidly becoming major concerns in developing countries, and where end-of-pipe solutions are inherently costly and likely to become more burdensome as regulations tighten. This is an important consideration for most developing countries, where regulations for environmental management are at a very early stage.

Fourth, local manufacturing could lead to larger domestic markets and opportunities for export growth. Lower wage costs, at least in the early stages of economic development, could contribute to cost competitiveness. All these factors suggest that new sustainable energy technologies could reach competitive levels if substantial early deployment opportunities are pursued in developing countries.

In addition, substantial benefits may arise from combining local customs and practices with new technologies, processes, and materials. Vernacular architecture, long suited to local climatic conditions and culture, may be intrinsically superior to imported designs and materials, yet open to benefits from better processes and materials. Cooking and space heating devices may be similarly open to local reconfiguration.

Supporting demonstration and diffusion
Beyond the widely applicable remarks already offered on policies supportive of energy innovation (see the section on the rationale for public policy support), a few additional considerations apply specifically to demonstration and cost buy-down projects in developing countries. Demonstration projects will be needed in many developing countries because technologies developed elsewhere should be tailored to host country needs. In addition, some of the needed technologies—such as biogas- and biomass-derived gaseous and liquid cooking fuels and small-scale biomass power generating technologies (see chapter 10)—are unlikely to be developed and demonstrated elsewhere. Yet financing such projects in developing countries is difficult, not only because of the high costs and technological risks involved, but also because it is difficult to get support from industrialised country governments or international agencies.

Focused attention should also be given to possibilities for technology cost buy-down projects in developing countries. Otherwise, large volumes of new equipment based on old, polluting technologies are likely to be installed in these countries and locked in place for decades to come. Moreover, the rapid growth in energy demand in these countries offers an opportunity to buy down technology costs more quickly than in the relatively slow-growing markets of industrialised countries. Broad-based financial support and risk-sharing strategies are likely to be key for both demonstration and cost buy-down projects.

In the absence of proactive measures, barriers to international trade may have to be resorted to, in order to impede imports of less efficient and dirtier technologies, and to provide preferences for more efficient and cleaner technologies. Environmental treaties using trade measures date back to 1881, when steps were taken to prevent the international transfer of phylloxera in vines. Recent examples include CITES, which constrains trade in listed species and products; the UN agreement on conserving and managing straddling fish stocks and highly migratory fish stocks; and the Montreal Protocol, which requires signatories to ban imports of ozone-depleting substances from non-signatories not in compliance with the protocol. The World Bank has outlined the reasons multilateral trade measures, but not unilateral ones, may be justified to help tackle global environmental problems—provided they can be made effective (World Bank, 1999d). And in June 1997 the UN General Assembly adopted proposals to make trade and the environment mutually supportive. If trade measures were used wisely and well in international environmental agreements, they could facilitate technological leapfrogging.

International industrial collaboration

Economic globalisation and ongoing market and institutional reforms are attracting more private capital to developing countries, as reflected in the sharp increase in private investment in these countries (especially net foreign direct investment). In contrast, the drop in official development assistance from OECD countries suggests that the adverse environmental consequences accompanying industrialisation in developing countries are unlikely to be corrected by aid unless there is a huge turnaround from the declines of the 1990s. This implies that the private sector should be looked to in order to fill the vacuum. The fact that legal rights to and experience with most advanced and new technologies exist in the private domain needs to be acknowledged and suitably compensated for (possibly by industrialised governments in support of technology transfer) if the vacuum is to be filled. Making industrialisation an instrument for sustainable development could prove an important means of addressing these problems (Wallace, 1995).

International industrial collaboration could provide a means to exploit the potential cost advantages of early deployment of state-of-the-art sustainable energy technologies in some rapidly industrialising countries. Such collaboration could also foster the development of such technologies to the point that developing countries become world leaders and even exporters of such technologies. Among alternative approaches to industrial collaboration, the international joint venture is especially promising for technology transfer (STAP and GEF, 1996).

In principle, private sector–led technology transfer holds considerable appeal. But some developing country policy-makers believe that payments for technology are beyond their means and that international technology transfer contributes little to technological development in the recipient economy. Through empirical research on factors affecting energy-saving technical changes in Thailand's energy-intensive industrial firms, Chantramonklasri (1990) has shown that such problems can be reduced if measures are taken to promote "active technological behaviour" by technology-importing firms. He points out that effective technological development requires complementing the acquisition of capital goods, services, and operational know-how with the acquisition of system-related knowledge.

This includes the basic technological principles involved, the various technical and managerial skills and experience needed to use the acquired system effectively, and initiatives to improve the system incrementally in light of local conditions and needs.

The research shows that the greater is the stock of technological capabilities within and around technology-importing firms, the greater are the increments to that stock that can be acquired in industrial collaborations. Chantramonklasri finds that with active intervention and interaction, a virtuous circle can lead to gains in technological capacity and industrial productivity. Firms that fail to take actions that enable them to enter the virtuous circle will be left in a vicious circle of technological dependence and stagnation.

Towards a supportive policy framework

As discussed, developing and transition economies can increase economic efficiency by introducing reforms that price energy rationally, promote competition in energy markets, and strengthen domestic capital markets. Such market reforms also facilitate energy technology transfer and energy technology innovation generally. Along with relatively rapid growth in the demand for energy services, these reforms can create strong markets in these countries and encourage the provision of energy technologies that are well suited to domestic needs.

The market reform process provides a window of opportunity for simultaneously introducing reforms that facilitate the introduction of innovative sustainable energy technologies. The process may be enhanced by governments setting goals that define the performance characteristics of qualifying sustainable energy technologies (for example, by specifying efficiency and air pollution emission characteristics). The setting of these goals can be complemented by credible regulatory or other policy mechanisms that favour sustainable energy technologies in energy market choices.

Policy-makers should also consider introducing institutional reforms that facilitate the formation of international joint ventures and other international collaborative efforts to encourage sustainable energy technology transfer and innovation. Where such reforms are conducive to greater political stability, more straightforward transactions, and fewer arbitrary interventions, they are likely to prove especially supportive of technological innovation and diffusion. Bilateral and multilateral financing and assistance agencies could usefully be encouraged to be more open to supporting energy technology innovation that is consistent with sustainable development goals.

Capacity and institution building

Capacity and institution building are needed if sustainable energy technologies are to fulfil their potential in contributing to the sustainable energy development of developing and many transition economies. Programmes should build on the experience of the World Bank and UNDP (such as UNDP's Capacity 21 Programme, cited above) and on the experience gained in numerous developing countries (Farinelli, 1999).

One priority is training aimed at providing expertise for staffing companies that will produce, market, install, and maintain sustainable energy technologies. This need has been underscored by evidence that higher technical and managerial skills among staff of host country partners in international industrial collaborations improve prospects for successful technology transfer and innovation (Chantramonklasri, 1990). Technological capability can also be raised by establishing regional institutes that provide training in the basic skills of technology management. Such institutes are likely to be more effective if they enjoy close links to energy technology user groups.

Public agencies and private research institutes in industrialised countries could also help build capacity for sustainable energy development in developing and some transition economies, by helping to form and staff parallel institutions in these countries to assist local policy development and technology assessment. Regional and national programmes and centres for renewable energy and energy efficiency promotion in Brazil, China, India, and Eastern Europe could serve as models. Such agencies and research institutes can help provide independent assessments of alternative technology and policy choices, and can explore strategies for overcoming barriers inhibiting large-scale implementation of sustainable energy technologies.

There is also scope for coordinated initiatives between specialised consultancies, companies, and local communities.[10] These ideas do not imply, however, that specialists in industrialised countries have achieved the desired results of sustainable energy development, and that they can now apply their efforts elsewhere. This is not the case, and it would be condescending even if it were. The challenges remain global.

Moving towards more effective cooperation

In recent decades there has emerged a growing sense that many of the issues facing today's world cross national boundaries—and that national policies and measures are insufficient to address them. This is particularly the case for resource exploitation, support for the needy, and environmental issues with cross-boundary impacts. A view is emerging that internationally harmonised measures are becoming increasingly necessary to improve performance standards, reduce adverse environmental impacts of human activities, and accelerate change in the directions widely desired.

To do so successfully, however, requires careful evaluation, adequate funding, and appropriate conditionality on spending to ensure that it conforms to its intended purpose. As set out in numerous UN documents, and agreed to by all the parties to them, industrialised countries have undertaken to take the lead in this endeavour, not least by supporting the transfer of technology, finance, and know-how to developing and transition economies. Although international cooperation in these matters is still in its infancy, many consider the pace of progress unsatisfactorily slow relative to the scale and nature of the problems facing our world.

In June 1997 the UN General Assembly Special Session noted the increasing need for better coordination at the international level as well as for continued and more concerted efforts to enhance collaboration among the secretariats of international organisations in the UN system and beyond (clause 117; see Osborn and Bigg, 1998, p. 185). Along those lines, the UN Commission for Sustainable Development was asked to establish closer interaction with a range of international institutions and to strengthen its interaction with and encourage inputs from a range of social actors (clause 133; Osborn and Bigg, 1998, p. 189).

More recently, the roles of the International Monetary Fund and the World Bank have come under scrutiny, particularly in the contexts of whether their resources are sufficiently targeted on improving the development performance of the poorest countries and on the criterion of sustainable development. Where existing jurisdictions are not sufficiently broad or institutions do not move quickly and effectively enough to meet policy goals or allay public concerns, consideration should be given to institutional reform or the creation of new institutions.

Issues that fall into multiple jurisdictions require coordinated international action. These include international trade disputes, transnational efficiency and performance standards for equipment and appliances, international aviation and marine bunkers, and transit corridors for energy transport (pipelines, tankers, and grids).

The World Trade Organization (WTO), created in 1995 to succeed the General Agreement on Tariffs and Trade (GATT) after completion of the Uruguay Round of international trade negotiations, has a mandate to expand multilateral trade. It operates by policing the multilateral trade system and by seeking to resolve trade disputes through 'independent' dispute panels. Widely regarded as a vehicle for globalisation, its activities have been criticised by special interest groups who see globalisation as a threat—to trade unions, environmental protection, and local cultural values and customs.

The WTO meeting in Seattle, Washington, in December 1999, intended to start a new round of trade liberalisation, turned into a "fiasco" according to *The Economist* (4 December 1999). The same magazine recognised the following week that this was "only the latest and most visible in a string of recent NGO [non-governmental organisation] victories". The official outcome of Seattle was that the effort to start a new round of trade negotiations was "suspended". Criticism continues of what are claimed to be the WTO's unwieldy structure, arcane procedures, and numerous festering disputes.

Yet free international trade is of great importance to developing countries—by 1999, 134 countries had joined the WTO (World Bank, 1999d)—and to the welfare of poor people. There is a vast literature on the links between trade and increased incomes for the poor as well as the relatively rich. WTO critics are particularly vocal on the need to link free international trade with new initiatives on employment standards (which risk undermining the competitiveness of developing countries and protecting jobs in industrialised countries) and the environment. They are also usually highly critical of the role of major companies involved in international business.

The International Labour Organization plays a key role in employment conditions. There are various environmental initiatives under UN auspices (through the United Nations Environment Programme, United Nations Framework Convention on Climate Change, and so on). The United Nations Conference on Trade and Development (UNCTAD) has been concerned since 1964 with improving the prospects for developing countries' trade. This could be accomplished by better coordinating international action on multilateral trade, including a closer link to the needs of sustainable development. The WTO could play a significant role in promoting sustainable energy development in general, and technology leapfrogging in particular, by developing supportive multilateral trade measures. This discussion is in line with the need perceived by the UN General Assembly Special Session in June 1997 to make trade and the environment mutually supportive.

International initiatives on international aviation and marine bunkers are proceeding slowly. In both cases users and beneficiaries are not paying the full costs of operations. In international aviation, costs should capture the impacts of flight on the lower stratosphere and upper atmosphere, of emissions and noise at lower levels, and of infrastructure requirements on the ground (Penner and others, 1999). In international maritime movements, the full effects of emissions and spills should be captured in costs and the onus for reductions and removal should be placed firmly on the operators. Increasingly stringent standards should be imposed, especially for sea-going vessels in which multihull construction and high maintenance standards may not be readily detectable.

Under the aegis of the UN Framework Convention on Climate Change, the International Civil Aviation Organization and the International Maritime Organization have been asked to report on greenhouse gas emissions associated with international aviation and marine bunkers. The environmental impacts of these emissions go beyond global climate change, however.

Cooperative efforts to ensure supply security

Supply security is a concern related to availability, the functioning of markets, and the need for international cooperation. A priority issue for national and international policy in 1971–85 (especially during the crises of 1973–74 and 1978–80), it has slipped down the list of priorities. As discussed in chapters 4 and 5, the world has huge geological resources of fossil fuels, along with considerable potential for energy from non-fossil fuels. It is usually in the interest of producers to keep supplies flowing smoothly. A common view is that there will be ample oil and natural gas available, that it will be supplied at low prices, and that if financial flows are inadequate, it will mainly be exporters of oil and natural gas who suffer. This perception is applicable at least to the foreseeable future—the first 20 years of this century.

An alternative view should not be overlooked, however. The number of people dependent on imported oil and natural gas is likely to more than double by 2020 from the nearly 3 billion in 1990. Political unrest, economic frustration, or simply misjudgement about the potential gains from supply disruption could increase over the period. Despite the physical availability of energy sources, precautionary strategies to maintain supply security continue to have merit (see chapter 4; IEA, 1998; EC, 1999). These include:

■ Encouraging open international trade systems.
■ Maintaining harmonious international diplomacy.
■ Considering different allocations of tax revenues between upstream and downstream governments (along the lines of 'compensation' for fossil fuel producers and exporters as indicated in article 4.8 (h) of the UN Framework Convention on Climate Change).
■ Diversifying supply sources (widening the geographic range of suppliers and maintaining adequate storage facilities and inventories of oil and natural gas).
■ Expanding indigenous supplies of non-fossil fuels, provided there are no severely adverse consequences.

In the meantime, fluctuating OPEC production levels may cause large price fluctuations—as with the tripling of crude oil prices in 1999. Market responses have included rising prices of gasoline and of oil products for heating. By March 2000 gasoline prices at the pump had risen above $2 a gallon in many parts of the United States, once again raising questions about 'gas guzzling' vehicles and encouraging the use of public transport. This experience has again demonstrated the potential value of market prices in the promotion of sustainable development.

The Energy Charter Treaty is a potentially useful example of broad international action that encourages its signatories to afford comparable treatment of energy markets, with special protocols being negotiated on energy transit, energy efficiency, and other matters (see also chapter 4). Originally put forward in 1990 as the European Energy Charter, the Energy Charter Treaty was signed in 1994 by some 50 countries, including most OECD countries, all the republics of the former Soviet Union, and the countries of Central and Eastern Europe.

Despite the charter's purpose of facilitating energy trade and investment between the signatory countries, and general recognition of the need for this, the charter has a long way to go before it becomes meaningful in practical terms. The reasons partly lie in the legal and administrative weaknesses and complexities in most transition economies. Moreover, the charter imposes no enforceable obligations on its signatories. Nevertheless, such an approach could in principle be used more broadly to address the significant shift needed to achieve sustainable energy.

A number of regional unions and associations could promote sustainable energy development. More than 80 regional trading arrangements came into force between 1990 and 1998 (World Bank, 1999d). The Mercosur customs union created by Argentina, Brazil, Paraguay, and Uruguay in 1991 (the final protocol was signed in 1994) is one example, with an emphasis on regional cooperation and the abolition of tariffs. Other organisations in other regions (including several in the Mediterranean Basin) could perform a similar role. Especially in Africa, there is a perceived need for progress on this front. One goal of such regional arrangements could be to promote cross-border interconnections for electricity distribution and gas pipeline networks, to widen access to these fuels.

International cooperation on climate change

The challenge of sustainable development presents significant opportunities for international cooperation. The 1992 Earth Summit was a particular landmark. Tangible outcomes from it include the Rio Declaration, Agenda 21, and international conventions on climate change, biodiversity, and desertification.

The most detailed convention framework is the UN Framework Convention on Climate Change (box 12.6). The Kyoto Protocol is a potentially useful further development—if industrialised countries take effective action to curb their greenhouse gas emissions and supplemental action is taken to implement the Kyoto mechanisms. But progress in implementing the provisions of the Convention on Climate Change has been slower than the threat and likely impacts

of global climate change suggest are desirable. Agreement on many issues is proving elusive, including realistic emission targets, speedy and effective introduction of new mechanisms, emphasis on the priority of domestic action by all industrialised country parties, and genuine acceptance of legally binding agreements. Yet all these elements seem to have been agreed to in principle by the parties to the convention.

Despite international concern, the UN Framework Convention on Climate Change and its aims, and the Kyoto Protocol and its targets, many industrialised countries continue to increase their greenhouse gas emissions, especially of carbon dioxide (table 12.3). Data for 1999 suggest that carbon dioxide emissions from fossil fuel combustion rose 2 percent in Canada and the United States (though against a backdrop of even faster real GDP growth). The three original OECD Pacific economies (Australia, Japan, and New Zealand) also increased their carbon dioxide emissions by almost 2 percent. By contrast, the 15 members of the European Union saw emissions drop 0.5 percent from 1998. Reductions in China's carbon dioxide emissions from coal burning—which first became apparent in

---

BOX 12.6. THE MONTREAL PROTOCOL AND THE UN FRAMEWORK CONVENTION ON CLIMATE CHANGE: CONTRASTING EXAMPLES OF INTERNATIONAL COOPERATION

The 1987 Montreal Protocol (and subsequent amendments and tightening)—which curbs the production and use of stratospheric ozone-depleting substances—is the most successful recent initiative for international cooperation. Except for a few outstanding issues (such as the continued production and smuggling of these substances), this initiative was agreed to with unprecedented speed and has proven increasingly effective.

The speed and outcome of the UN Framework Convention on Climate Change and its subsequent agreements are far less certain, even though the framework is solid. As a way of drawing lessons from the success of the Montreal Protocol, it may be useful to consider some of the factors that contributed to it, relative to similar elements in the effort on climate change.

In terms of the pace of international action on climate change, the first point is key. Many public statements are predicated on the assumption that climate change is problematic

only over the long term. They tend to underestimate how much climate change is believed to have already occurred (even taking into account natural variability) and how long it will take for atmospheric concentrations of greenhouse gases to cease rising.

According to scientists and informed commentators, the situation calls for greater urgency. Mean surface temperature levels have risen by about 0.8 degrees Celsius since the 1890s. The 20th century warming (in 1910–45 and 1976–99) was the fastest in more than 800 years. The 1976–99 warming converts to a centennial rate of change of almost 2 degrees Celsius.

Perhaps of greater significance, the atmospheric concentration of carbon dioxide (currently about 368 parts per million by volume, or ppmv) is considerably higher than at any time in at least 400,000 years—and perhaps for 15 million years. It is already more than 30 percent higher than the pre-industrial level (280 ppmv)

of the early 1800s. Given what is firmly known about the science of the greenhouse effect, this is disturbing. The most optimistic and environmentally driven scenarios suggest atmospheric carbon dioxide concentrations peaking around 2060 at about 430 ppmv, and falling only slowly over the next 50 years, with global surface temperature rising by about 1.5 degrees Celsius. Even this increase could have significant local and regional impacts.

But there is a real risk of much greater temperature increases, with severe consequences, if atmospheric concentrations of the key greenhouse gases continue on the upward path of recent decades. For 10 years the Intergovernmental Panel on Climate Change has maintained its view that global anthropogenic carbon dioxide emissions need to be cut by at least 60 percent from their 1990 level in order to eventually stabilise atmospheric concentrations at their 1990 level of 353 ppmv (Houghton, Jenkins, and Ephraums, 1990).

Montreal Protocol	Convention on Climate Change
A widely acknowledged and immediate (as well as long-term) threat to human well-being, with clear identification of human causation.	Dispute over the scale, urgency, and human causation of climate change—although in principle the convention regards scientific uncertainties as irrelevant to the need for precautionary measures.
A widely available range of alternatives for use in industry (a result of extensive research and development in both industrialised and developing countries).	Alternatives to fossil fuels and clean fossil fuel technologies are still emerging. Their widespread availability and affordability will require further support.
Support from crucial industry players.	Industry has been receiving mixed signals and has sent mixed signals (especially some sections of U.S. industry), and there are many players.
Industrialised countries willing to financially support programmes for reducing ozone-depleting substances in developing countries.	Multilateral and bilateral support for pilot projects, but without crediting and after considerable opposition from many developing countries.

1997—were even more marked, dropping by more than 5 percent in 1999. This progress is exceptional, and may not be long-lasting. The policies, measures, and technologies that would permit the lowering of future trajectories of developing country emissions are not being put in place quickly enough.

Once frameworks have been established through intergovernmental negotiation, signature, and ratification, actual progress relies on genuine cooperation. Politics and short-term manoeuvres need to give way to seeking the most cost-effective and technically feasible means of accelerating progress towards the agreed goals. One problem is that commitments entered into by negotiators are not always enacted by lawmakers, which complicates the timely pursuit and achievement of goals relating to sustainable development. For this reason, new mechanisms are needed and should be given practical trial without delay. If such mechanisms prove effective, early movers could be given tangible rewards. Short action plans could accelerate performance. Achievement of commitments could be enhanced by legally binding penalties for non-performance.

Where divisions and delaying tactics exist, the underlying problem of lack of societal commitment, political support, or agreement within the national government may need to be addressed separately. The preferred option in such circumstances is to gain the support of other social actors—from business and industry, local communities and municipal governments, and environmental and other socially concerned non-governmental organisations (NGOs).

The Clean Development Mechanism and Joint Implementation articles (12 and 6, respectively) of the Kyoto Protocol, negotiated in 1997 under the UN Framework Convention on Climate Change, offer potentially important opportunities to increase investments in developing and transition economies, respectively, in sustainable energy. The complex nature of climate change negotiations and the uncertainties surrounding the issue mean that effective introduction of such instruments may not come about for many years (though some people

TABLE 12.3. CHANGES IN CARBON DIOXIDE EMISSIONS FROM FOSSIL FUEL USE, 1990–99 (PERCENT)

Area	Change
Canada andthe United States	+12.7
Latin America	+23.3
European Union	+0.8[a]
Central and Eastern Europe/CIS Republics	−35.8
Middle East	+62.7
Africa	+21.9
Asia and the Pacific (excl. Australia, Japan, New Zealand)	+34.8
Total OECD (excl. Hungary, Rep. of Korea, Mexico, Poland)	+10.8
Developing countries	+34.3
World	+7.6

a. If not for major reductions in Germany (−13.5 percent) and the United Kingdom (nearly −8 percent), this figure would be much higher.

Source: Jefferson, 2000.

hope that real implementation may follow quickly from the Sixth Conference of the Parties to the Climate Convention, or COP-6, in November 2000). Meanwhile, a growing number of people in the industrialised world's business and industry community have already developed plans to participate in relevant projects drawing on the mechanisms that have been tabled, especially in the Kyoto Protocol, and are experimenting with emissions trading under article 17 of the protocol.

In 1999 a World Energy Council pilot project (strongly supported by Asea Brown Boveri) identified nearly 400 projects in some 80 countries expected to avert 720 million tonnes of carbon dioxide by 2005. (The project also identified another 91 potential or planned projects that could avert an additional 139 million tonnes of carbon dioxide.) Although many of these projects may not be additional to what might otherwise have occurred, they indicate that a substantial—though insufficient—effort is under way.

For several years, and especially since the Earth Summit, companies and their senior executives associated with the World Business Council for Sustainable Development have been promoting actions and investments consistent with sustainable energy development, including climate change mitigation, under an eco-efficiency programme. The European Business Council for a Sustainable Energy Future is one of several regional and national business associations that have been promoting sustainable energy development in general and climate change responses in particular. In Latin America the regional chapter of the World Business Council for Sustainable Development has been very active. More recently, the Pew Center on Global Climate Change has brought together major international corporations (Dow, DuPont, British Petroleum/Amoco, Royal Dutch/Shell Group) to take voluntary steps to reduce their greenhouse gas emissions and raise energy efficiency. These endeavours could usefully be extended to smaller companies and to the particular challenges and opportunities facing developing and transition economies.

Intergovernmental and international institutions have made efforts to take forward the mechanisms set down in the Kyoto Protocol. Potentially one of the most significant recent funding initiatives, in terms of possible scale and geographic range, is the World Bank's Prototype Carbon Fund, launched in January 2000. Involving four governments and nine companies (six of them Japanese electric utilities), the fund raises money from both the public and private sectors. (Governments pay $10 million to participate, companies pay $5 million.) The fund will be used to finance projects aimed at reducing greenhouse gas emissions in developing countries. Participating countries will receive emission credits from the World Bank in line with the emission reductions achieved by the projects.

Although some observers have questioned whether the World Bank is the most appropriate body to conduct this task, it does encourage public-private cooperation, relevant projects, early action, and rewards to early movers. Still, it will be important to ensure the commercial viability of projects so that wider and faster diffusion of sustainable energy technologies can be attained, and to gain general agreement on credits awarded.

Overall, however, more—and more rapid—work is needed to implement cost-effective precautions in line with the UN Framework Convention on Climate Change. Three features of the Programme for the Further Implementation of Agenda 21, adopted by the UN General Assembly Special Session in June 1997, stand out as having met with an inadequate response:

■ International cooperation on implementing chapter 9 of Agenda 21, particularly in technology transfer to and capacity building in developing countries—which are also essential for the effective implementation of the UN Framework Convention on Climate Change (clause 53; see Osborn and Bigg, 1998, p. 161).

■ Progress by many industrialised countries in meeting their aim to return greenhouse emissions to 1990 levels by 2000 (clause 48; see Osborn and Bigg, 1998, p. 160).

■ The need to strengthen systematic observational networks to identify the possible onset and distribution of climate change and assess potential impacts, particularly at the regional level (clause 54; see Osborn and Bigg, 1998, p. 161).

Widening the involvement in sustainable energy development

A critical mass of general public support will be needed for major changes to take place and the pursuit of sustainable development to occur. Here the role of NGOs could prove increasingly influential and beneficial, building on their contributions in the 1990s (for example, at the Earth Summit and at the series of conferences taking place on climate change). Some observers have expressed concern that rivalry between NGOs (in part to secure public support and attract funding) could be self-defeating. There has also been concern that NGOs may supplant the role of national governments, with negative as well as positive consequences.

NGOs can nevertheless be expected to play an increasingly important role in bringing the issues discussed in this chapter to a wider audience, in mobilising opinion, and in emphasising the importance of bearing in mind local conditions and cultures—in part through their huge network of contacts. Policy development is likely to benefit from bringing better-informed NGOs to the centre of policy formulation and application. For this to succeed, however, national and intergovernmental institutions will have to genuinely interact and consult in a two-way process.

The same is true for other social actors, whether they be local authorities, business and industry, educational institutions, the scientific community, the media, the young and the old, men and women—all with their particular perspectives and needs. In June 1997 the UN General Assembly Special Session recognised the importance of all these groups (for example, in clauses 11 and 28). But both in the programme it adopted for the further implementation of Agenda 21 and in this chapter, two points may stand out above all others. The first is the need to invigorate a genuine new

> A critical mass of general public support will be needed for major changes to take place and the pursuit of sustainable development to occur.

global partnership. The second is the need to provide adequate and predictable financial resources to developing countries, where private capital flows and an environment conducive to their continuation and expansion are of paramount importance if sustainable development is to be achieved.

Conclusion

In essence, sustainable development means widening the choices available to humans alive today, and to at least the next few generations. A shift in the direction of energy systems and policies along the lines described in this chapter—towards greater emphasis on end-use efficiency, renewable energies, and low-emission technologies—is necessary for achieving that goal. It is impossible to know in advance the precise combination of policies and policy instruments that will work under different conditions, and the costs and benefits of emerging technologies. But the broad strategies put forward here provide an indication of the way forward. There is also a sufficient variety of policies from which to begin to gauge the more likely successes.

The ongoing liberalisation and restructuring of energy markets and sectors offer an important window of opportunity in which to make many of the needed changes. Growing energy demands in the developing world provide further impetus to make changes sooner rather than later. Energy systems generally take decades to change. If we fail to initiate changes now, it will become more difficult and more costly to undertake them at some later date (WEC, 1995; Nakićenović, Grübler, and McDonald, 1998).

The policies likely to encourage energy systems that will support sustainable development, as discussed in this chapter, are founded on the underlying aim of making markets work better. Additional investments in environmentally friendly technologies will be required, as will encouragement of the innovation and diffusion of sustainable energy technologies. Successful implementation of these policies requires improving the costing and pricing of energy carriers and services, as well as specific regulations to raise efficiency and reduce pollution, in order to ensure greater and wider public benefits.

Making markets work better

Policies that reduce market distortions (that is, level the playing field) would give sustainable energy—new renewable sources, energy efficiency measures, new technologies with near-zero emissions—a considerably better market position relative to conventional energy sources. Market distortions can be reduced by phasing out permanent direct and indirect subsidies to conventional energies and energy use in all end-use sectors, by including social and environmental costs in prices, and by introducing appropriate regulation, taxes, or financial incentives.

Another way of making markets work better is to complement ongoing market reform with regulations that support sustainable energy. A number of the obstacles to greater energy end-use efficiency are the result of market imperfections or barriers. Options to overcome these barriers include voluntary or mandatory standards for appliances, vehicles, and buildings; labelling schemes to better inform consumers; technical training in new energy efficiency technologies and their maintenance; and credit mechanisms to help consumers meet higher first costs.

The ongoing liberalisation and restructuring of energy markets and sectors offer an important window of opportunity in which to make many of the needed changes.

Mobilising additional investments in sustainable energy

Incentives may be needed to encourage private companies to invest in sustainable energy or to defray the risks associated with such investments. International funding sources may also need to play a greater role in the least developed countries, especially those where the overall conditions that attract business are lacking and joint efforts are required to improve those conditions. Supportive financial and credit arrangements (including many microcredit arrangements already in existence) will be needed to introduce commercial energy to those excluded from markets, especially in rural areas.

For decentralised provision of modern energy services, capital costs may best be met from a mix of local equity capital (communal or private) and loans from banks or other conventional credit organisation at commercial rates. There may be a role for industrialised country governments in backing loans with guarantees, on mutually acceptable criteria. Subsidies, with 'sunset' clauses for environmentally sustainable technologies, may help. Above all, a one-stop approach from agencies specialising in the financing of rural electrification and renewable energy schemes would be beneficial—especially in overcoming the barriers associated with current time-consuming and costly procedures. The scale of such arrangements will need to be massively expanded to achieve the required results. The principles of good governance—including stability, probity, and the rule of law—are also significant for the promotion of investment.

Encouraging technological innovation

Currently applied technologies are not adequate to deliver the energy services that will be needed in the 21st century and simultaneously protect human health and environmental stability. Adequate support for a portfolio of promising advanced and new technologies is one way to help ensure that options will be available as the need for them becomes more acute. Direct government support is one option, but the historic record is somewhat discouraging and suggests that support for generic research rather than large-scale commercialisation is likely to be more fruitful. Other ways to support technological innovation, while still using competition wherever possible to keep down costs, include tax incentives, collaborative R&D ventures, government and industry procurement policies, 'green labelling' schemes, public benefits charges, and market transformation initiatives.

Supporting technological leadership and capacity building in developing coutries

Because most of the projected growth in energy demand will occur in the developing world, innovation and leadership in energy technologies could be highly profitable for some developing countries in economic, environmental, and human terms. But they will need assistance with technology diffusion (including transfers), financing, and capacity building. Much of this support will need to be led by the private sector, by private-public partnerships, or both.

Consideration could be given on a multilateral basis to providing preferential treatment for international trade in cleaner and more efficient technologies and products, within international trading arrangements that could be adjusted more clearly towards sustainable energy development. Wider use of green labelling schemes and harmonised regulations and standards would help. International industrial collaboration offers a way for the private sector to gain markets while fostering the migration of new technologies to developing countries. Public agencies, private research institutes, and regional institutes that provide training in technological management are additional possibilities for further technology sharing and capacity building. Coordinated institutional approaches are required for capacity building, effective market functioning, technology diffusion and financing, and successful international initiatives. Community participation can also play an important role in promoting these policies.

Encouraging greater international cooperation

Ongoing globalisation means that ideas, finances, and energy flow from one country to another. In this context, isolated national actions are no longer likely to be the only or the most effective option. Two key areas in which harmonisation could be helpful are environmental taxes and efficiency standards. The need for concerted action on energy is also clear from the major international conventions that emerged from the Earth Summit—particularly the UN Framework Convention on Climate Change. Although the basic principles and many more detailed articles of that convention encourage sustainable energy development, and should provide an excellent framework for future progress, implementation has been slow relative to the urgency of achieving greater sustainability.

The challenge of sustainable energy includes crucial enabling roles for governments, international organisations, multilateral financial institutions, and civil society, including the private sector, NGOs, and individual consumers. Partnerships will be required, based on more integrated and cooperative approaches, and drawing on a range of practical experience. A common denominator across all sectors and regions is setting the right framework conditions and making public institutions work effectively and efficiently with the rest of society and economic actors in reaching beneficial and shared objectives.

Used safely and wisely, energy can make a powerful contribution to sustainable development. Redirecting its power to work towards the overarching goal of sustainability, however, will require major policy changes within an enabling overall framework. Poverty, inequity, inefficiency, unreliable service, immediate environmental priorities, lack of information and basic skills, and absence of needed institutions and resources require that changes be made. Unless truly significant changes begin to take place within the next 20–30 years, many of the opportunities now available will be lost, the possibilities for future generations diminished, and the goal of sustainable development unrealised. The ninth session of the UN Commission for Sustainable Development provides an opening in which to galvanise consensus on the energy and transportation issues discussed in this chapter. The special session of the UN General Assembly in 2002 is a further opportunity to pursue ways in which the broader international policy framework can be more supportive of sustainable energy goals. ■

ANNEX   Trends in research and development funding

It is widely held that R&D expenditures on sustainable energy technologies are too low and falling. This annex examines R&D trends in more detail. As discussed in box A12.1, however, because of the way the data are collected, categorised, and compared, the accuracy of the figures cited here and elsewhere is difficult to assess.

Private sector spending on energy research and development

Private sector spending on energy R&D, based on U.S. data, is believed to have been low as a share of sales over a long period. In recent years U.S. utilities appear to have invested just 10 percent as much as U.S. industries overall. But whereas most major electric utilities and oil and gas companies in OECD countries spend less than 1 percent of sales on R&D, the main research-oriented firms servicing broader energy technology needs (such as Asea Brown Boveri and Siemens) invest 8–30 times as much. Still, spending on energy R&D generally seems low relative to the 7 percent of GDP represented by retail spending on energy in countries that are members of the International Energy Agency.

On the other hand, in several countries with relatively detailed and reliable data on private sector spending on energy R&D—such as Finland, Germany, and Japan—it is clear that there have been significant overall increases in recent years. Part of the explanation is that during the 1990s these countries saw sharp increases in R&D spending on renewables, energy efficiency, and advanced cleaner fossil fuel technologies. The progress of private sector spending on energy R&D in Japan, as provided in a major report prepared in 2000 (Ito 2000), is distinctly more upbeat than others have reported (Dooley, 1999a). Although private sector spending on energy R&D in Canada has remained flat in real terms since the early 1980s, this masks a decline in fossil fuel R&D on the one hand, and an increase in energy efficiency, fuel cell, climate change technology, and electricity R&D on the other. There is no evidence of a decline in utilities' spending on R&D in Norway and Sweden (Haegermark, 2000). In Germany private sector R&D has assumed an increasing role while government R&D has fallen. In Austria, although there have been considerable variations in recent years, industrial spending on renewable energy—particularly biomass—rose sharply in 1996–98 (Faninger, 2000).

Thus there are strongly contrasting experiences. The reported decline in private sector energy R&D in the United States is seemingly shared by Italy, Spain, and the United Kingdom. There can be no doubt that spending on nuclear R&D collapsed in many countries during the 1990s. In the United Kingdom spending on energy R&D is estimated to have fallen by some 40 percent in the gas and electricity industries following privatisation, and by 55 percent in the coal and oil sectors. But the position on renewable energy and energy efficiency R&D is not so dismal even in the latter countries. And due to increasing R&D productivity benefits arising from improving information technology, it has been claimed that even where spending has declined, productivity may have increased.

There is no way of knowing with confidence what level of spending on energy R&D is optimal, or even sufficient for short-term needs.

BOX A12.1. INTERPRETING DATA ON RESEARCH AND DEVELOPMENT

There are several reasons for caution when considering the energy R&D data presented in this annex—or almost any such data. First, there is no universally accepted definition of energy R&D (although it should include basic and applied research, feasibility testing, and small-scale deployment). Detailed classifications are rarely provided for data series and are not comparable between series. Even in the United States the only official surveys of private industry spending on energy R&D—the National Science Foundation annual surveys—provides only a "most cursory" definition of energy R&D, and "there is no way of knowing what kinds of energy technologies are being developed by industry through looking at this data set" (Dooley, 1997, appendix I, p. 1). The surveys exclude energy R&D conducted by non-profit organisations (recourse has been made to the Electric Power Research Institute and Gas Research Institute to try to remedy this omission). The situation is even less clear in other OECD countries.

Second, distortions arise because of a failure to use a common currency basis. For example, since market exchange rates rather than purchasing power parities are used, it has been claimed that R&D spending by Japan is inflated relative to that by the United States (Dooley, 2000).

Third, aggregate data often exclude most military-related R&D spending and ancillary benefits (such as the development of jet engines for military purposes and their impact on combined-cycle gas turbines). Thus the data are misleading.

Fourth, comparison of R&D spending over time is complicated by increases in the productivity of R&D spending—due, for example, to the use of better data processing hardware and software.

Two firm conclusions can be drawn from this catalogue of problems. The first is that even official government statistics and international comparisons thereof should be handled with extreme care. The second is that the quality of data needs to be improved to permit sound comparisons over time and among countries and technologies if it is to form a basis for policy.

Although R&D spending by the oil sector seems to have been low, this did not prevent major gains in exploration and enhanced recovery—including cost reductions—in recent years. Similarly, low R&D spending by gas and electric utilities does not seem to have blocked a rapid shift to combined-cycle gas turbines for electricity generation. Nevertheless, it is widely believed that long-range R&D spending has fallen as a share of total R&D spending in the energy sector in several countries. This outcome is attributed to the emphasis the private sector places on incremental improvements to existing technologies and products relative to basic research.

Public sector spending on energy research and development

Since the mid-1980s aggregate public support for energy R&D has fallen steadily in OECD countries (table A12.1). About 80 percent of the decline, however, has occurred in the United States. And declining R&D for nuclear technologies are of the same broad order of magnitude—$4 billion.

In other countries, by comparison, the declines have generally been marginal in value terms, though sometimes large in percentage terms, with nuclear R&D bearing the brunt of the decline. Japan saw a 20 percent increase in overall energy R&D spending between 1980 and the mid-1990s. Although a small fall occurred in total public sector energy R&D spending between 1995 and 1997, the actual falls were confined to nuclear power, coal, and the conservation and storage of electric power—there were rises in all other energy R&D categories. A sharp decline in public sector energy R&D occurred during the 1990s in the United Kingdom, particularly after the Department of Energy was abolished in 1992 and its remaining R&D

responsibilities were handed over to the Department of Trade and Industry (which focuses on the commercial deployment of existing technologies). Declines have also occurred in Italy and Spain. In Germany federal spending on energy R&D has fallen somewhat, but inclusion of lander expenditures results in near stability. Stability or expansion of public spending can be observed in Denmark and Finland. In Switzerland, although there was a slight decline in overall government spending on energy R&D between 1994 and 1997, spending on renewable energy R&D remained stable. In Austria government spending on energy R&D rose steadily through the 1990s. Between 1993 and 1998 spending on renewable energy R&D rose 200 percent. Spending on nuclear fusion R&D was, perhaps surprisingly, higher in 1998 than in 1993. Fossil fuels and conservation were the only areas exhibiting a declining trend (Faninger, 2000). However, it should be noted that the United States and Japan are by far the heaviest public sector spenders on energy R&D.

Among member countries of the International Energy Agency, public sector spending on R&D for energy conservation was generally higher in the 1990s than in the 1980s, and public spending on R&D for renewable energy sources remained fairly static in the decade to 1997. It is worth noting that although EU spending on nuclear fission R&D fell by more than 50 percent between 1988 and 1998, spending on energy efficiency and renewables R&D more than doubled between 1993 and 1996 (from less than $100 million a year to more than $200 million), and has been running in excess of $200 million since. Even public spending on R&D for fossil fuels fell sharply only between 1994 and 1997—a rather short period on which to base a story of general and sustained decline. Public and private R&D spending on coal and natural gas has tended to increase, particularly

TABLE A12.1. REPORTED RESEARCH AND DEVELOPMENT BUDGETS AND GDP IN IEA COUNTRIES, 1983–97 (BILLIONS OF 1998 U.S. DOLLARS EXCEPT WHERE OTHERWISE INDICATED)

Year	Fossil energy	Nuclear fission	Nuclear fusion	Energy conser-vation	Renewables	Other	Total Billions of dollars	Total Percentage of GDP	GDP (trillions of 1998 dollars)
1983	1.61	6.13	1.39	0.82	1.03	1.09	12.07	0.158	7.64
1984	1.52	5.85	1.41	0.73	1.02	1.01	11.53	0.147	7.87
1985	1.49	6.66	1.46	0.75	0.87	1.06	12.28	0.137	8.99
1986	1.49	5.96	1.33	0.64	0.67	0.96	11.05	0.102	10.82
1987	1.33	4.63	1.26	0.67	0.62	1.07	9.58	0.075	12.71
1988	1.44	3.94	1.18	0.56	0.62	1.24	8.98	0.065	13.85
1989	1.30	4.38	1.09	0.49	0.57	1.39	9.21	0.063	14.72
1990	1.74	3.96	1.06	0.54	0.58	1.21	9.09	0.056	16.23
1991	1.48	3.93	0.95	0.62	0.63	1.42	9.04	0.052	17.41
1992	1.02	3.29	0.92	0.59	0.68	1.32	7.82	0.045	17.43
1993	1.04	3.19	1.00	0.69	0.70	1.44	8.06	0.042	19.13
1994	1.06	3.06	0.96	0.96	0.63	1.43	8.09	0.040	20.07
1995	0.90	3.23	0.97	1.05	0.68	1.39	8.22	0.037	22.44
1996	0.84	3.17	0.86	0.98	0.60	1.38	7.83	0.035	22.14
1997	0.69	3.04	0.83	0.94	0.59	1.43	7.52	0.034	21.99

Source: IEA, 1999.

for clean fuel technologies and carbon sequestration. EU spending on cleaner energy systems (including cleaner fossil fuels) has increased in recent years and is now around $140 million a year.

There is little evidence on energy R&D spending in developing countries, and with two or three exceptions it is likely that spending has been modest. One exception is South Africa, where energy R&D spending by the Department of Minerals and Energy fell during t0he 1990s (Cooper, 2000). ■

Notes

1. Renewable technologies, in the context of this chapter, include modern bio-energy, small hydropower and solar, wind, and geothermal technologies. They exclude large hydropower and estuarine barrage. Large-scale biomass productivity, however, has the potential to undermine biodiversity as well as generate serious adverse visual impacts.

2. The Brundtland Comission is formally known as the World Commission on Environment and Development; see WCED (1987).

3. Abatement of carbon dioxide in specific projects—such as the separation and injection of emissions from Norway's offshore Sleipner Field—has resulted from a $50 a tonne carbon tax levied by the Norwegian government on offshore carbon dioxide emissions. Another project indicates carbon dioxide abatement costs of $28–52 per tonne of carbon (Barland, 1999).

4. Revenue-neutral taxes are new taxes that result in a corresponding reduction of other taxes. While overall government revenues do not increase, the change in the tax regime might have other societal effects.

5. According to World Bank estimates, domestic savings ratios in developing countries often exceed 20 percent of GDP.

6. Examples include advanced oil and gas recovery, combined cycle gas turbine innovations, and integrated gasifier combined cycles. Among new renewable technologies, windpower is already economically competitive in many wind-rich regions; photovoltaic technologies are competitive in applications remote from utility grids and are on the verge of becoming competitive at retail price levels in grid-connected, building-integrated applications; low-polluting internal combustion engine/battery-powered hybrid cars that are twice as fuel-efficient as conventional cars have recently become available; fuel cell cars are being developed that would be three times as fuel-efficient as today's cars; and information technologies are being exploited to improve many energy-producing and energy-consuming technologies.

7. Comparing R&D data from various sources is complicated by the fact that there is no universally accepted definition of energy R&D. Because of other distortions, described more fully in the annex, even official government statistics and international comparisons must be analysed carefully.

8. Many U.S. commentators point to the failure of synfuel projects, which were predicated on high energy prices continuing through the 1980s. Few specialists took a contrary view, and the best-known exception had been overly confident in the 1970s that OPEC and consumer interests would fail to keep up crude oil prices (Adelman, 1972 and 1995). These stances were never wholly accepted in Europe, where sharp oil price rises in the late 1970s were anticipated by 1976—along with the assumption that relapse would follow thereafter (Jefferson, 1983).

9. A shortcoming of relying on green pricing to facilitate widespread deployment of clean energy technologies is that there may be a free-rider problem: those who are unwilling to pay more for green energy enjoy the environmental benefits that come from green energy purchases by those who are willing to pay more (Rader and Norgaard, 1996). One way to avoid this is to give a tax deduction on existing carbon dioxide or other energy taxes, as in the Netherlands.

10. A number of international frameworks can be drawn on to support this approach, such as the International Standards Organization (ISO) 14001 introduced in 1996 and for which the 1992 Earth Summit provided the impetus, the Eco-Management and Audit Scheme introduced by the EU Commission in 1995, and the Global Reporting Initiative now under development.

References

ADB (African Development Bank). 1999. *African Development Report 1999*. Oxford: Oxford University Press.

Adelman, M.A. 1972. *The World Petroleum Market*. Baltimore, Md.: Johns Hopkins University Press for Resources for the Future.

———. 1995. *The Genie out of the Bottle: World Oil since 1970*. Cambridge, Mass.: MIT Press.

ASTAE (Asia Alternative Energy Program). 1998. "The World Bank Asia Alternative Energy Program (ASTAE) Status Report #6." World Bank, Washington, D.C.

Austin, D. 1998. "Contributions to Climate Change: Are Conventional Metrics Misleading the Debate?" *Climate Notes*. World Resources Institute, Washington, D.C.

Ballin, H.H. 1946. *The Organisation of Electricity Supply in Great Britain*. London: Electrical Press.

Baranzini, A., J. Goldemberg, and S. Speck. 2000. "A Future for Carbon Taxes." *Ecological Economics* 32 (3): 395–412.

Barland, K. 1999. "CO_2 Capture and Disposal." In *Technology Assessment in Climate Change Mitigation: Report of the IPIECA Workshop*. London: International Petroleum Industry Environmental Conservation Association.

Boa Nova, A.C., and J. Goldemberg. 1998. "Electrification of the Favelas in São Paulo, Brazil." Universidade de São Paulo, Brazil.

Bowers, B. 1982. *A History of Electric Light and Power*. London: Peter Peregrinus.

Boyle, G. 1996. *Renewable Energy: Power for a Sustainable Future*. Oxford: Oxford University Press.

Brack, D., ed. 1998. *Trade and Environment: Conflict or Compatibility?* London: Earthscan for the Royal Institute of International Affairs.

Brenton, T. 1994. *The Greening of Machiavelli: The Evolution of International Environmental Politics*. London: Earthscan for the Royal Institute of International Affairs.

Broadman, H.G., ed. 1998. *Russian Trade Policy Reform for WTO Accession*. World Bank Discussion Paper 401. Washington, D.C.

Bronicki, L.Y. 2000. "Financing of Private Renewable Energy Projects." In A.A.M. Sayigh, ed., *World Renewable Energy Congress VI, Part III*. Oxford: Elsevier.

Bruce, J.P., H. Lee, and E.F. Haites, eds. 1996. *Climate Change 1995: Economic and Social Dimensions of Climate Change*. Cambridge: Cambridge University Press for the Intergovernmental Panel on Climate Change.

Chantramonklasri, N. 1990. "The Development of Technological and Managerial Capability in the Developing Countries." In M. Chatterji, ed., *Technology Transfer in the Developing Countries*. London: Macmillan.

Cohen, L.R., and R.G. Noll. 1991. "The Technology Pork Barrel." Brookings Institution, Washington, D.C.

Cooper, C. 2000. Personal communication. Director, South African Energy Association, Melville, South Africa.

Cowan, R.S. 1997. *A Social History of American Technology*. New York: Oxford University Press.

Darnell, J.R., and M. Jefferson, eds. 1994. *New Renewable Energy Resources: A Guide to the Future*. London: Kogan Page.

Davis, M. 1995. "Institutional Frameworks for Electricity Supply to Rural Communities: A Literature Review." University of Cape Town, Energy and Development Research Centre, South Africa.

DETR (Department of Environment, Transport, and the Regions). 2000. "Climate Change: Draft UK Programme." London.

Dodds, F., ed. 1997. *The Way Forward: Beyond Agenda 21*. London: Earthscan.

Dooley, J.J. 1997. "US National Investment in Energy R&D: 1974–1996." PNNL-11788. Battelle Memorial Institute, Pacific Northwest National Laboratory, Richland, Wash.

———. 1999a. "Energy Research and Development in Japan." PNNL-12214. Battelle Memorial Institute, Pacific Northwest National Laboratory, Richland, Wash.

———. 1999b. "Energy Research and Development in the United States." PNNL-12188. Battelle Memorial Institute, Pacific Northwest National Laboratory, Richland, Wash.

———. 2000. "A Short Primer on Collecting and Analyzing Energy R&D Statistics." PNNL-13158. Battelle Memorial Institute, Pacific Northwest National Laboratory, Richland, Wash.

Dooley, J.J., and P.J. Runci. 1999a. "Adopting a Long View to Energy R&D and Global Climate Change." PNNL-12115. Battelle Memorial Institute, Pacific Northwest National Laboratory, Richland, Wash.

———. 1999b. "Energy Research and Development in Germany." PNNL-12207. Battelle Memorial Institute, Pacific Northwest National Laboratory, Richland, Wash.

Dooley, J.J., P.J. Runci, and E.E.M. Luiten. 1998. "Energy in the Industrialized World: Retrenchment and Refocusing." PNNL-12061. Battelle Memorial Institute, Pacific Northwest National Laboratory, Richland, Wash.

Dore, J., and R. De Bauw. 1995. "The Energy Charter Treaty: Origins, Aims and Prospects." Royal Institute of International Affairs, London.

Duke, R.D., and D.M. Kammen. 1999. "The Economics of Energy Market Transformation Initiatives." *The Energy Journal* 20 (4): 15–64.

Eads, G.S., and S. Peake. 1998. "Global Transport and Energy Development: The Scope for Change." World Energy Council, London.

EC (European Commission). 1999. "Energy in Europe: Economic Foundations for Energy Policy." The Shared Analysis Project, Luxembourg.

Eliasson, B. 1998. "The Road to Renewables: Energy Technologies for the Post-Kyoto World." *World Energy Council Journal* (July): 38–44. London.

Emsperger, W. 2000. Personal communication. Siemens, Power Generation Division, Erlangen, Germany.

Engelman, R. 1998. "Profiles in Carbon: An Update on Population, Consumption and Carbon Dioxide Emissions." Population Action International, Washington, D.C.

EPRI (Electric Power Research Institute). 1999. "Electricity Technology Roadmap: Powering Progress—1999 Summary and Synthesis." Palo Alto, Calif.

Evans, M.1999. "Energy Research and Development in Italy." PNNL-13071. Battelle Memorial Institute, Pacific Northwest National Laboratory, Richland, Wash.

Faninger, G. 2000. Personal communication. University of Klagenfurt, Institute for Interdisciplinary Research and Continuing Education, Austria.

Farinelli, U., ed. 1999. *Energy As a Tool for Sustainable Development for African, Caribbean and Pacific Countries.* European Commission and UNDP. New York: United Nations.

Forsyth, T. 1999. *International Investment and Climate Change: Energy Technologies for Developing Countries.* London: Royal Institute of International Affairs and Earthscan.

Fry, A. 1997. "Business and Climate Change: Case Studies in Greenhouse Gas Reduction." International Chamber of Commerce and World Business Council for Sustainable Development, Kyoto, Japan.

Goldemberg, J., and T. Johansson, eds. 1995. *Energy as an Instrument for Socio-economic Development.* New York: UNDP.

Goldemberg, J., and W. Reid, eds. 1998. *Issues and Options: The Clean Development Mechanism.* New York: UNDP.

———. 1999. *Promoting Development while Limiting Greenhouse Gas Emissions: Trends and Baselines.* New York: UNDP and World Resources Institute.

Goldemberg, J., T.B. Johansson, A.K.N. Reddy, and R.H. Williams. 1988. *Energy for a Sustainable World.* New Delhi: J. Wiley.

Grubb, M., C. Vrolijk, and D. Brack. 1999. "The Kyoto Protocol: A Guide and Assessment." Royal Institute of International Affairs, London.

Grübler, A. 1996. "Time for a Change: On the Patterns of Diffusion of Innovation." *Daedalus: The Journal of the American Academy of Arts* 125 (3): 19–42.

———. 1998. *Technology and Global Change.* Cambridge: Cambridge University Press.

Haegermark, H. 2000. Personal communication. Vice President, Elforsk, Stockholm, Sweden.

Hannah, L. 1979. *Electricity before Nationalization.* London: Macmillan.

———. 1982. *Engineers, Managers and Politicians.* London: Macmillan.

Heede, R., R. Morgan, and S. Ridley. 1985. "The Hidden Costs of Energy: How Taxpayers Subsidize Energy Development." Center for Renewable Resources, Washington, D.C.

Hippel, E. von. 1988. *The Sources of Innovation.* Oxford: Oxford University Press.

Houghton, J.T., G.J. Jenkins, and J.J. Ephraums, eds. 1990. *Climate Change: The IPCC Scientific Assessment.* Cambridge: Cambridge University Press.

Hughes, T.P. 1983. *Networks of Power: Electrification in Western Society, 1880–1930.* Baltimore, Md.: Johns Hopkins University Press.

Hwang, R. 1995. "Money down the Pipeline: Uncovering the Hidden Subsidies to the Oil Industry." Union of Concerned Scientists, Cambridge, Mass.

IEA (International Energy Agency). 1997a. *Energy Efficiency Initiative.* vols. 1 (*Energy Policy Analysis*) and 2 (*Country Profiles and Case Studies*). Paris.

———. 1997b. *IEA Energy Technology R&D Statistics: 1974–1995.* Paris.

———. 1997c. *The Link between Energy and Human Activity.* Paris.

———. 1998. *World Energy Outlook.* Paris.

Ito, F. 2000. Personal communication. Secretary General, Japan Energy Association, Tokyo.

Jefferson, M. 1983. "Economic Uncertainty and Business Decision-Making." In J. Wiseman, ed., *Beyond Positive Economics?* London: Macmillan.

———. 1996. "Climate Change 1995: The IPCC Second Assessment Report Reviewed." Report 5. World Energy Council, London.

———. 1998a. "After Buenos Aires: A World Looking to Business and Industry for Help?" *Geopolitics of Energy* 20 (11). Canada Energy Research Institute, Calgary, Alberta.

———. 1998b. "Instruments for Mitigating Climate Change." Report 10. World Energy Council, London.

———. 1998c. "The Kyoto Conference and Protocol." Report 8. World Energy Council, London.

———. 2000. "Carbon Dioxide Emissions from 1990 to 1999: What's Been Happening?." *Ecoal* 35 (September). World Coal Institute, London.

Jevons, W.S. 1965 [1906]. *The Coal Question.* 3rd ed. New York: A.M. Kelley.

Jewkes, J., D. Sawers, and R. Stillerman. 1958. *The Sources of Invention.* London: Macmillan.

Johnson, S.P. 1993. *The Earth Summit: The United Nations Conference on Environment and Development (UNCED).* London: Graham and Trotman.

Landes, D.S. 1969. *The Unbound Prometheus: Technological Change and Industrial Development in Western Europe from 1750 to the Present.* Cambridge: Cambridge University Press.

———. 1998. *The Wealth and Poverty of Nations: Why Some Are So Rich and Some So Poor.* London: Little, Brown.

Larsen, B., and A. Shah. 1992. "World Fossil Fuel Subsidies and Global Carbon Emissions." World Bank, Washington, D.C.

———. 1995. "Global Climate Change, Energy Subsidies, and National Carbon Taxes." In L. Bovenberg and S. Cnossen, eds., *Public Economics and the Environment in an Imperfect World.* Boston, Mass.: Kluwer.

Leggett, J. 1999. "The Carbon War: Dispatches from the End of the Oil Century." London: Allen Lane/Penguin Press.

Levy, H. 1968 [1909]. *Monopolies, Cartels and Trusts in British Industry.* 1st German ed. London: F. Cass.

Littlechild, S.C. 2000. "Privatisation, Competition and Regulation." Institute of Economic Affairs, London.

Loh, J. 1998. *Living Planet Report.* Gland, Switzerland: World Wildlife Fund International.

Lovei, M., and C. Weiss. 1998. *Environmental Management and Institutions in OECD Countries: Lessons from Experience.* World Bank Technical Paper 391. Washington, D.C.

Lovins, A.B. 1996. "Negawatts: Twelve Transitions, Eight Improvements and One Distraction." *Energy Policy* (April).

Luiten, E.E., and K. Blok. 1999. "Energy Research and Development in the Netherlands." PNNL-12177. Battelle Memorial Institute, Pacific Northwest National Laboratory, Richland, Wash.

Luoma, H. 2000. Personal communication. VTT Energy, Jyvaskyla, Finland.

Lutz, W.L. 1997. *The Future Population of the World: What Can We Assume Today?* London: International Institute for Applied Systems Analysis and Earthscan.

Maddison, A. 1995. *Monitoring the World Economy 1820–1992.* Paris: Organisation for Economic Co-operation and Development.

Margolis, R.M., and D.M. Kammen. 1999. "Underinvestment: The Energy Technology and R&D Policy Challenge." *Science* 285 (30 July): 690–92.

Marshall, Lord. 1998. *Economic Instruments and the Business Use of Energy.* London: H.M. Treasury.

Michaelis, L. 1996. *Reforming Coal and Electricity Subsidies.* Paris: Organisation for Economic Co-operation and Development.

Mintzer, L.M., and J.A. Leonard. 1994. *Negotiating Climate Change: The Inside Story of the Rio Convention.* Cambridge: Cambridge University Press.

Mitchell, C. 1998. "Renewable Energy in the U.K.: Policies for the Future." Council for the Protection of Rural England, London.

Moisan, F. 1998. "Energy Efficiency Policies and Indicators." World Energy Council, London.

Moor, A.P.G. de. 1997. "Perverse Incentives." Earth Council, San José, Costa Rica.

Mowery, D.C., and N. Rosenberg. 1998. *Paths of Innovation: Technological Change in 20th Century America.* Cambridge: Cambridge University Press.

Munasinghe, M., and R. Swart. 2000. "Climate Change and Its Linkages with Development, Equity, and Sustainability." Intergovernmental Panel on Climate Change, Geneva, Switzerland.

Muraki, S. 1998. "Industry's Technical Initiatives Towards Climate Change Mitigation." Report 9. World Energy Council, London.

Myers, N., with J. Kent. 1998. "Perverse Subsidies." International Institute for Sustainable Development, Washington, D.C.

Nakićenoviić, N., A. Grübler, and A. McDonald, eds. 1998. *Global Energy Perspectives.* Cambridge: Cambridge University Press for International Institute for Applied Systems Analysis and World Energy Council.

Nye, D.E. 1990. *Electrifying America: Social Meanings of a New Technology, 1880–1940.* Cambridge, Mass.: MIT Press.

———. 1998. *Consuming Power: A Social History of American Energies.* Cambridge, Mass.: MIT Press.

Obermair, G. 2000. Personal communication. Secretary General, Austrian National Committee, World Energy Council, Vienna, Austria.

OLADE (Organización Latinoamericana de Energia). 1997. *Energy and Sustainable Development in Latin America and the Caribbean.* Quito, Ecuador.

O'Riordan, T., and J. Jaeger. 1996. *Politics of Climate Change: A European Perspective.* London: Routledge.

Osborn, D. 1998. "Towards Earth Summit III in 2002." Millennium Paper 1. United Nations Environment and Development, London.

Osborn, D., and T. Bigg. 1998. *Earth Summit II: Outcomes and Analysis.* London: Earthscan. (Contains UN Secretary-General's Report of January 1997 and Programme for the Further Implementation of Agenda 21, approved by UNGASS in June 1997.)

Parsons, R.H. 1939. *The Early Days of the Power Station Industry.* Cambridge: Cambridge University Press.

Patterson, W.C. 1990. "The Energy Alternative." Boxtree/Channel 4, London.

———. 1999. *Transforming Electricity: The Coming Generation of Change.* London: Royal Institute of International Affairs and Earthscan.

PCAST (President's Committee of Advisors on Science and Technology). 1997. *Federal Energy Research and Development for the Challenges of the Twenty-first Century.* Washington, D.C.

———. 1999. *Powerful Partnerships: The Federal Role in International Cooperation on Energy Innovation.* Washington, D.C.

Pearce, D.W., and others. 1996. "Government Subsidies with Unintended Environmental Effects." CSERGE, London and Norwich.

Penner, J.E., D.H. Lister, D.J. Griggs, D.J. Dokken, and M. McFarland, eds. 1999. *Aviation and the Global Atmosphere.* A Special Report of IPCC Working Groups 1 and 3. Cambridge: Cambridge University Press for the Intergovernmental Panel on Climate Change.

Piscitello, E.S., and V.S. Bogach. 1998. *Financial Incentives for Renewable Energy Development.* World Bank Discussion Paper 391. Washington, D.C.

Popper, K.R. 1945, with addenda in 1961 and 1965. *The Open Society and Its Enemies.* London: Routledge and Kegan Paul.

———. 1972 [1963]. *Conjectures and Refutations: The Growth of Scientific Knowledge.* London: Routledge and Kegan Paul.

Poulter, J.D. 1986. *An Early History of Electricity Supply.* London: Peter Peregrinus.

Rader, N.A., and R.B. Norgaard. 1996. "Efficiency and Sustainability in Restructured Electricity Markets: The Renewables Portfolio Standard." *The Electricity Journal* 9 (6): 37–49.

Reddy, A.K.N., R.H. Williams, and T.B. Johansson. 1996. *Energy after Rio: Prospects and Challenges.* New York: UNDP.

Romm, J.J. 1999. *Cool Companies: How the Best Businesses Boost Profits and Productivity by Cutting Greenhouse Gas Emissions.* Washington, D.C.: Island Press.

Ruijgrok, E., and F. Oosterhuis. 1997. "Energy Subsidies in Western Europe." Greenpeace International, Amsterdam.

Runci, P. 1998. "After Kyoto: Are There Rational Pathways to a Sustainable Global Energy System?" Paper presented at the Aspen Institute's Energy Policy Forum, Washington, D.C.

———. 1999. "Energy Research and Development in the European Union." PNNL-12218. Battelle Memorial Institute, Pacific Northwest National Laboratory, Richland, Wash.

———. 2000a. "Energy Research and Development in Canada." PNNL-13233. Battelle Memorial Institute, Pacific Northwest National Laboratory, Richland, Wash.

———. 2000b. "Energy Research and Development in the United Kingdom." PNNL-13234. Battelle Memorial Institute, Pacific Northwest National Laboratory, Richland, Wash.

Sabugal Garcia, S. 2000. Personal communication. Director, Engineering Research and Development, Grupo ENDESA, Madrid, Spain.

Savage, J.D. 1999. *Funding Science in America: Congress, Universities, and the Politics of the Academic Pork Barrel.* Cambridge: Cambridge University Press.

Schipper, L., and S. Meyers with R.B. Howarth and R. Steiner. 1992a. *Energy Efficiency and Human Activity: Past Trends, Future Prospects.* Cambridge: Cambridge University Press.

———. 1992b. "World Energy: Building a Sustainable Future." Stockholm Environment Institute, Stockholm.

Schlesinger, A.M. 1960. *The Politics of Upheaval.* Boston, Mass.: Houghton Mifflin.

Schock, R.N., W. Fulkerson, M.L. Brown, R.L. San Martin, D.L. Greene, and J. Edmonds. 1999. "How Much Is Energy Research and Development Worth as Insurance?" *Annual Review of Energy and the Environment* 24: 487–512.

Schumpeter, J.A. 1942. *Capitalism, Socialism and Democracy.* New York: Harper.

Shapiro, D.L. 1989. *Generating Failure: Public Power Policy in the Northwest.* Lanham, Md.: University Press of America.

Smallridge, C.G. 1999. "Rural Energy and Development: A Study of Canadian Rural Electrification." C.G. Smallridge & Associates, Ottawa, Canada.

Sørensen, B., B. Kuemmel, and P. Meibom. 1999. "Long-term Scenarios for Global Energy Demand and Supply." Tekst. 359. Roskilde Universitets Center, Denmark.

Stahel, C. 2000. Personal communication. Swiss Energy Council, Berne, Switzerland.

STAP (Scientific and Technical Advisory Panel) and GEF (Global Environment Facility). 1996. "International Industrial Collaboration for Accelerated Adoption of Environmentally Sound Energy Technologies in Developing Countries." Nairobi, Kenya.

STAPPA (State and Territorial Air Pollution Program Administrators) and ALAPCO. 1999. "Reducing Greenhouse Gases and Air Pollution: A Menu of Harmonized Options—Final Report." Washington, D.C.

Stigler, G.J. 1968. *The Organization of Industry.* Holmwood, Ill.: Richard D. Irwin.

Strickland, C., and R. Sturm. 1998. "Energy Efficiency in World Bank Power Sector Policy and Lending: New Opportunities." *Energy Policy* 26 (11): 873–84.

Swiss Office Federale de l'Energie. 1999. *Plan directeur de la recherche energetique de la Confederation, 2000–2003.* Berne.

Taylor. R.P., and V.S. Bogach. 1998. *China: A Strategy for International Assistance to Accelerate Renewable Energy Development.* World Bank Discussion Paper 388. Washington, D.C.

Thomas, C. 1992. "The Environment in International Relations." Royal Institute of International Affairs, London.

UN (United Nations). 1992. *Earth Summit Agenda 21: The United Nations Programme of Action from Rio.* New York.

UNCSD (United Nations Commission on Sustainable Development). 1997. "Critical Issues and Policies for Sustainable Development: Energy, Transport, Water." E/CN.17/1997/17/Add.1. Available at http://www.un.org/esa/sustdev/csd.htm

UNCTAD (United Nations Conference on Trade and Development). 1999. *World Investment Report 1999: Foreign Direct Investment and the Challenge of Development.* New York and Geneva.

UNDP (United Nations Development Programme). 1999. *Human Development Report 1999.* New York.

USDOE (U.S. Department of Energy). 1998. *Technological Opportunities to Reduce U.S. Greenhouse Gas Emissions.* A Report by National Laboratory Directors. Washington, D.C. (Together with "Appendix B: Technology Pathways Characterization—Working Document.")

Wallace, D. 1995. *Environmental Policy and Industrial Innovation: Strategies in Europe, the US and Japan.* London: Royal Institute of International Affairs and Earthscan.

———. 1996. *Sustainable Industrialization.* London: Royal Institute of International Affairs and Earthscan.

Watson, R.T., M.C. Zinyowera, and R.H. Moss. 1996. *Climate Change 1995: Impacts, Adaptation and Mitigation of Climate Change: Scientific-Technical Analysis.* Cambridge: Cambridge University Press for the Intergovernmental Panel on Climate Change.

Watson, R.T., and others, eds. 1998. *The Regional Impacts of Climate Change: An Assessment of Vulnerability.* Cambridge: Cambridge University Press for the Intergovernmental Panel on Climate Change.

WCED (World Commission on Environment and Development). 1987. *Our Common Future.* Oxford: Oxford University Press.

WEC (World Energy Council). 1992. *15th WEC Congress Conclusions and Recommendations.* Madrid.

———. 1993. *Energy for Tomorrow's World.* London: Kogan Page and New York: St. Martin's Press.

———. 1995. *16th WEC Congress Conclusions and Recommendations.* Tokyo.

———. 1997. *Financing the Global Energy Sector: The Task Ahead.* London.

———. 1998a. *The Benefits and Deficiencies of Energy Sector Liberalisation.* Three volumes. London.

———. 1998b. *17th WEC Congress Conclusions and Recommendations.* Houston, Tex.

———. 1999. *The Challenge of Rural Energy Poverty in Developing Countries.* London.

———. 2000. "Energy for Tomorrow's World—Acting Now!" Atalink Projects, London.

Williams, Robert H. 1998. "A Technological Strategy for Making Fossil Fuels Environment and Climate Friendly." World Energy Council Journal (July): 59–67. London.

World Bank. 1994. *A Survey of Asia's Energy Prices.* Technical Paper 248. Washington, D.C.

———. 1996. *Rural Energy and Development: Improving Energy Supplies for Two Billion People.* Washington, D.C.

———. 1997a. *Clear Water, Blue Skies: China's Environment in the New Century.* China 2020 series. Washington, D.C.

———. 1997b. *Expanding the Measure of Wealth: Indicators of Environmentally Sustainable Development.* Washington, D.C.

———. 1997c. *World Development Indicators 1997.* Washington, D.C.

———. 1997d. *World Development Report 1997: The State in a Changing World.* New York: Oxford University Press.

———. 1998. *Financing Decentralized Renewable Energy: The Right Mix.* Washington, D.C.

———. 1999a. *Natural Gas: Private Sector Participation and Market Development.* Washington, D.C.

———. 1999b. *Global Development Finance: Analysis and Summary Tables.* Washington, D.C.

———. 1999c. *World Development Report 1998/99: Knowledge for Development.* New York: Oxford University Press.

———. 1999d. *World Development Report 1999/2000: Entering the 21st Century.* New York: Oxford University Press.

WRI (World Resources Institute). 1998. *World Resources: A Guide to the Global Environment, 1998–1999.* Washington, D.C.

York, D.W. 1994. "Competitive Electricity Markets in Practice: Experience from Norway." *The Electricity Journal* 7 (5): 48–55.

part V
further information and reference material

annexes

TABLE A1. ENERGY CONVERSIONS*

To:	Terajoule (TJ)	Gigacalorie (Gcal)	Megatonne oil (equiv) (Mtoe)	Million British thermal units (Mbtu)	Gigawatt-hour (GWh)
From:	**Multiply by:**				
Terajoule (TJ)	1	238.8	2.388×10^{-5}	947.8	0.2778
Megatonne oil (equiv) (Mtoe)	4.1868×10^4	10^7	1	3.968×10^7	11,630
Million British thermal units (Mbtu)	1.0551×10^{-3}	0.252	2.52×10^{-8}	1	2.931×10^{-4}
Gigawatt-hour (GWh)	3.6	860	8.6×10^{-5}	3,412	1

* IEA figures. Additional conversion figures available at http://www.iea.org/stat.htm

TABLE A2. UNIT PREFIXES

k	kilo (10^3)
M	mega (10^6)
G	giga (10^9)
T	tera (10^{12})
P	peta (10^{15})
E	exa (10^{18})

TABLE A3. ASSUMED EFFICIENCY IN ELECTRICITY GENERATION (FOR CALCULATING PRIMARY ENERGY)

Type of power	Assumed efficiency
Nuclear power	.33
Hydroelectric	1.00
Wind and solar	1.00
Geothermal	.10

TABLE A4. UNIT ABBREVIATIONS

EJ	Exajoule
GJ	Gigajoule
Gtoe	Giga tonnes oil equivalent
GWe	Giga Watt electricity
GWth	Giga Watt thermal
ha	Hectare
km^2	Square kilometre
kWh	Kilo Watt hour
Mtoe	Million tonnes oil equivalent
MWe	Mega Watt electricity
PJ	Petajoule
t	Tonne
TWh	Tera Watt hour

Energy is defined as the ability to do work and is measured in joules (J), where 1 joule is the work done when a force of 1 newton (N) is applied through a distance of 1 metre. (A newton is the unit of force that, acting on a mass of one kilogram, increases its velocity by one metre per second every second along the direction in which it acts.) Power is the rate at which energy is transferred and is commonly measured in watts (W), where 1 watt is 1 joule per second. Newton, joule, and watt are defined in the International System of Units. Other units used to measure energy are tonnes of oil equivalent (toe; 1 toe equals 41.87×10^9 J) and barrels of oil equivalent (boe; 1 boe equals 5.71×10^9 J), used by the oil industry; tonnes of coal equivalent (tce; 1 tce equals 29.31×10^9 J), used by the coal industry; and kilowatt-hour (kWh; 1 kWh equals 3.6×10^6 J), used to measure electricity. See also annex A, which provides conversion factors for energy units.)

Studies on national, regional, and global energy issues use a variety of technical terms for various types of energy. The same terminology may reflect different meanings or be used for different boundary conditions. Similarly, a particular form of energy may be defined differently. For example, when referring to total primary energy use, most studies mean *commercial energy*—that is, energy that is traded in the marketplace and exchanged at the going market price. Although non-commercial energy is often the primary energy supply in many developing countries, it is usually ignored. Non-commercial energy includes wood, agricultural residues, and dung, which are collected by the user or the extended family without involving any financial transaction. Because there are no records and a lack of data on actual use, most energy statistics do not report non-commercial energy use. Estimates of global non-commercial energy use range from 23-35 exajoules a year. In contrast, wood and other biomass sold in the marketplace is reported as solids (often lumped together with coal) and becomes part of commercial energy.

Traditional energy is another term closely related to non-commercial energy. This term generally refers to biomass used in traditional ways—that is, in the simplest cooking stoves and fireplaces—and is often meant as a proxy for inefficient energy conversion with substantial indoor and local air pollution. But traditional does not always mean non-commercial: wood burned in a kitchen stove may have been bought commercially and be reflected in commercial data. Estimates of biomass used in traditional ways range from 28-48 exajoules per year.

The term *modern* (or *new*) *renewables* is used to distinguish between traditional renewables used directly with low conversion technology and renewables using capital-intensive high-tech energy conversion such as solar, wind, geothermal, biomass, or ocean energy to produce state-of-the-art fuels and energy services.

Another issue concerns the heating value of chemical fuels assumed in statistics and analyses. The difference between the higher heating value (HHV) and the lower heating value (LHV) is that the higher heating value includes the energy of condensation of the water vapour contained in the combustion products. The difference for coal and oil is about 5 percent and for natural gas 10 percent. Most energy production and use are reported on the basis of the lower heating value.

Yet another source of inconsistency comes from different conversion factors to the primary energy equivalent of electricity generated by hydropower, nuclear, wind, solar, and geothermal energy. In the past, non-combustion-based electricity sources were converted to their primary equivalents by applying a universal conversion efficiency of 38.5 percent. More recently, hydropower, solar, and wind electricity in OECD statistics are converted with a factor of 100 percent, nuclear electricity with 33 percent, and geothermal with 10 percent.

The quality of data differs considerably between regions. Statistical bureaus in developing countries often lack the resources of their counterparts in industrialised countries, or data are simply not collected. Countries of the former Soviet Union used to have different classifications for sectoral energy use. Data reported by different government institutions in the same country can differ greatly, often reflecting specific priorities.

The composition of regions also varies in statistical compendiums and energy studies. At times, North America is composed of Canada and the United States—but it might also include Mexico. Except where otherwise noted, the following countries joined the Organisation for Economic Co-operation and Development (OECD) in 1961: Australia (1971), Austria, Belgium, Canada, the Czech Republic (1995), Denmark, Finland (1969), France, Germany, Greece, Hungary (1996), Iceland, Ireland, Italy, Japan (1964), Korea (1996), Luxembourg, Mexico (1994), the Netherlands, New Zealand (1973), Norway, Poland (1996), Portugal, Spain, Sweden, Switzerland, Turkey, the United Kingdom, the United States. Depending on when the data was collected, OECD data may or may not include the Czech Republic, Hungary, the Republic of Korea, Mexico, or Poland.

Finally, a word on the efficiency of energy conversion. Energy efficiency is a measure of the energy used in providing a particular energy service and is defined as the ratio of the desired (usable) energy output to the energy input. For example, for an electric motor this is the ratio of the shaft power to the energy (electricity) input. Or in the case of a natural gas furnace for space heating, energy efficiency is the ratio of heat energy supplied to the home to the energy of the natural gas entering the furnace. Because energy is conserved (the first law of thermodynamics), the difference between the energy entering a device and the desirable output is dissipated to the environment in the form of heat. Thus energy is not consumed but conserved. What is consumed is its quality to do useful work (as described by the second law of thermodynamics).

What this means is that a 90 percent efficient gas furnace for space heating has limited potential for further efficiency improvements. While this is correct for the furnace, it is not the case for delivering space heat. For example, a heat pump operating on electricity extracts heat from a local environment—outdoor air, indoor exhaust air, groundwater—and may deliver three units of heat for one unit of electrical energy to the building, for a coefficient of performance of 3. Not accounted for in this example, however, are the energy losses during electricity generation. Assuming a modern gas-fired combined cycle power plant with 50 percent efficiency, the overall coefficient of performance is 1.5—still significantly higher than the gas furnace heating system. ■

TABLE C.1. PRIMARY ENERGY USE PER CAPITA BY REGION, 1971–97

Region	1971 (gigajoules)	1980 (gigajoules)	1985 (gigajoules)	1990 (gigajoules)	1997 (gigajoules)	Change, 1990–97 (percent)	Change, 1971–97 (percent)	Annual growth rate, 1990–97 (percent)	Annual growth rate, 1971–97 (percent)
North America	266	276	258	263	272	3.7	2.4	0.5	0.3
Latin America	36	42	39	40	47	15.4	27.7	2.1	3.6
OECD Europe[a]	118	134	134	137	141	3.3	19.9	0.5	2.6
Non-OECD Europe[b]	76	108	112	108	84	-21.8	10.6	-3.4	1.5
Former Soviet Union	135	178	192	195	129	-33.9	-4.2	-5.7	-0.6
Middle East	35	61	72	77	95	23.9	175.9	3.1	15.6
Africa	23	26	27	27	27	0.1	17.1	0.0	2.3
China	20	25	28	32	38	18.8	93.6	2.5	9.9
Asia[c]	15	17	19	21	26	18.9	66.3	2.5	7.5
Pacific OECD[d]	94	113	117	142	174	23.2	85.1	3.0	9.2
World total	**62**	**69**	**69**	**70**	**70**	**-0.1**	**12.5**	**0.0**	**1.7**
Memorandum items OECD countries	161	177	173	181	194	7.0	20.4	1.0	2.7
Transition economies	124	165	177	180	121	-32.4	-2.0	-5.4	-0.3
Developing countries	20	25	27	29	34	16.0	66.2	2.1	7.5

a. Includes Czech Republic, Hungary, and Poland. b. Excludes the former Soviet Union. c. Excludes China. d. Includes Republic of Korea. *Source: IEA, 1999a.*

TABLE C.2. ELECTRICITY USE PER CAPITA BY REGION, 1980–96 (KILOWATT-HOURS)

Region	1980	1985	1990	1996
North America	8,986	9,359	20,509	11,330
OECD	5,686	6,277	7,177	8,053
East Asia	243	314	426	624
South Asia	116	157	228	313
Sub-Saharan Africa	444	440	448	439
Middle East	485	781	925	1,166
China	253	331	450	687
Transition economies	2,925	3,553	3,823	2,788
Least developed countries[a]	74	66	60	83
World	**1,576**	**1,741**	**1,927**	**2,027**

a. As defined by the United Nations. *Source: World Bank, 1999.*

TABLE C.3. ELECTRICITY DISTRIBUTION LOSSES BY REGION, 1980–96 (PERCENT)

Region	1980	1985	1990	1996
North America	6.9	6.8	7.0	7.6
OECD	7.6	6.8	7.2	6.4
East Asia	8.4	8.8	8.2	10.1
South Asia	19.4	19.1	18.8	18.7
Sub-Saharan Africa	9.2	8.6	8.8	9.6
Transition economies	8.4	8.9	8.4	11.0
Least developed countries[a]	11.0	15.8	20.3	20.9
World	**8.3**	**8.0**	**8.3**	**8.5**

a. As defined by the United Nations. *Source: World Bank, 1999.*

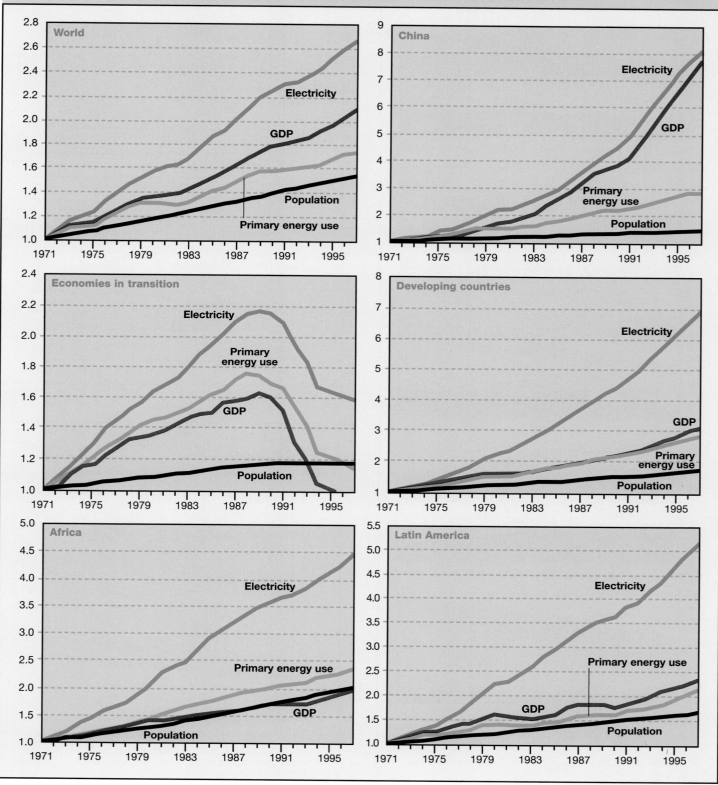

FIGURE C.1. CHANGES IN GDP, POPULATION, PRIMARY ENERGY USE, AND ELECTRICITY USE BY REGION, 1971–97 (INDEX: 1971=1)

Source: IEA, 1999a.

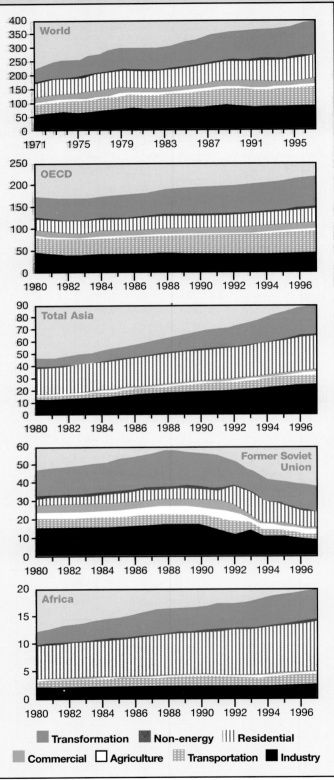

FIGURE C.2. ENERGY USE BY SECTOR IN SELECTED REGIONS, 1980–97 (EXAJOULES)

Transformation ■ Non-energy ⦀ Residential
Commercial □ Agriculture ▦ Transportation ■ Industry

Source: IEA, 1999a.

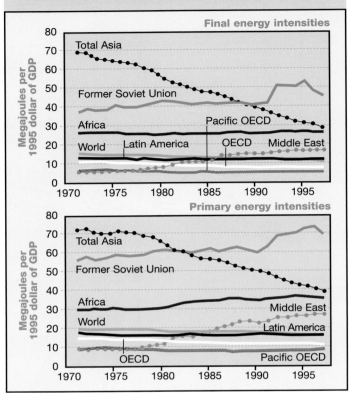

FIGURE C.3. DEVELOPMENT OF PRIMARY AND FINAL ENERGY INTENSITIES BY REGION, 1971–1997

Source: IEA, 1999a.

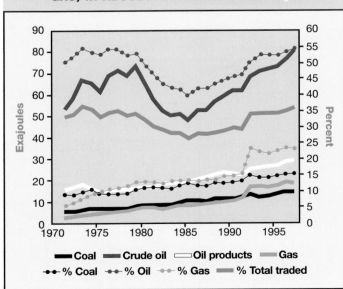

FIGURE C.4. GLOBAL TRADE IN CRUDE OIL, OIL PRODUCTS, COAL, AND NATURAL GAS, IN ABSOLUTE AND RELATIVE TERMS

■ Coal ▦ Crude oil □ Oil products ■ Gas
●— % Coal ●— % Oil ●— % Gas ▬ % Total traded

Note: Total traded shows share of total specific fuel use that is traded, that is total traded energy/primary energy.

Source: BP, 1999, IEA, 1999a, World Bank, 1999.

FIGURE C.5. MAJOR OIL IMPORTERS AND EXPORTERS, 1980–98

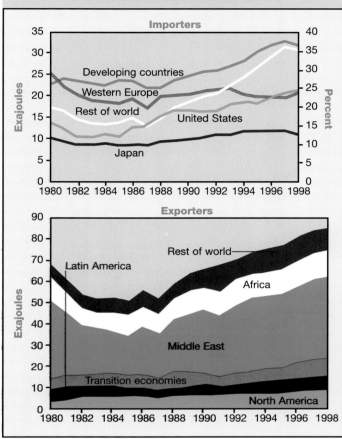

Source: BP, 1999.

FIGURE C.7. ENERGY TAXES IN SELECTED COUNTRIES, 1998

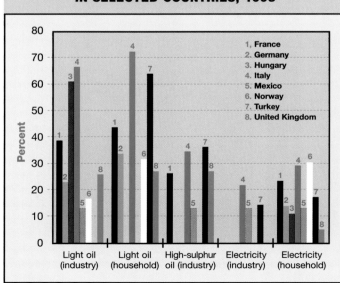

1, France
2, Germany
3, Hungary
4, Italy
5, Mexico
6, Norway
7, Turkey
8, United Kingdom

Source: IEA, 1999b.

FIGURE C.6. GROSS FOREIGN DIRECT INVESTMENT AND DOMESTIC AND FOREIGN FINANCING BY REGION, 1980–97

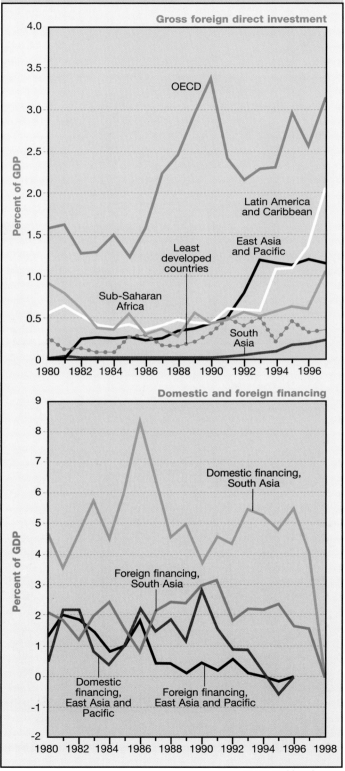

Source: World Bank, 1999.

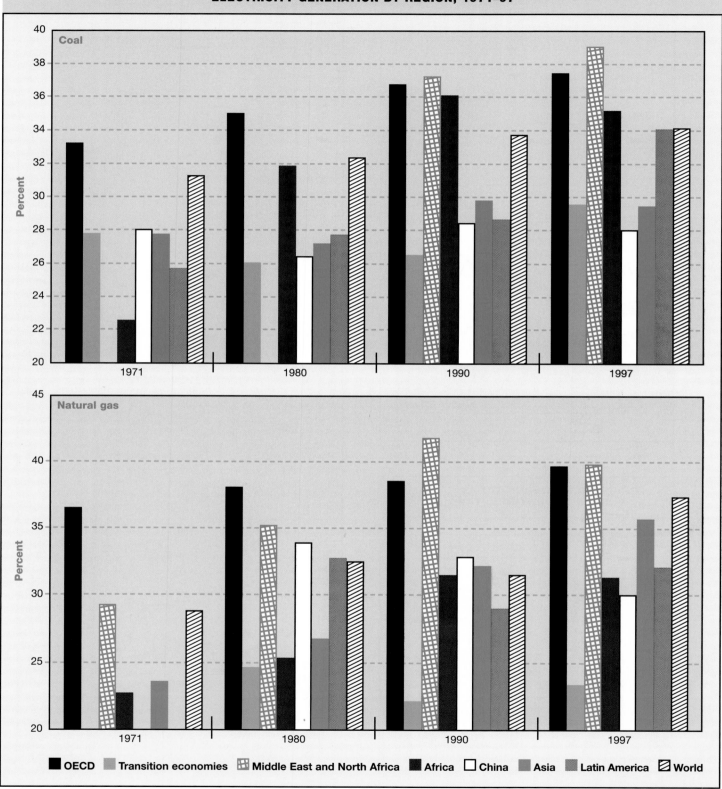

FIGURE C.8. EFFICIENCY OF COAL-FUELLED AND NATURAL GAS-FUELLED ELECTRICITY GENERATION BY REGION, 1971–97

Coal

Natural gas

■ OECD ■ Transition economies ▦ Middle East and North Africa ■ Africa □ China ■ Asia ■ Latin America ▨ World

Source: Adapted from IEA, 1999a.

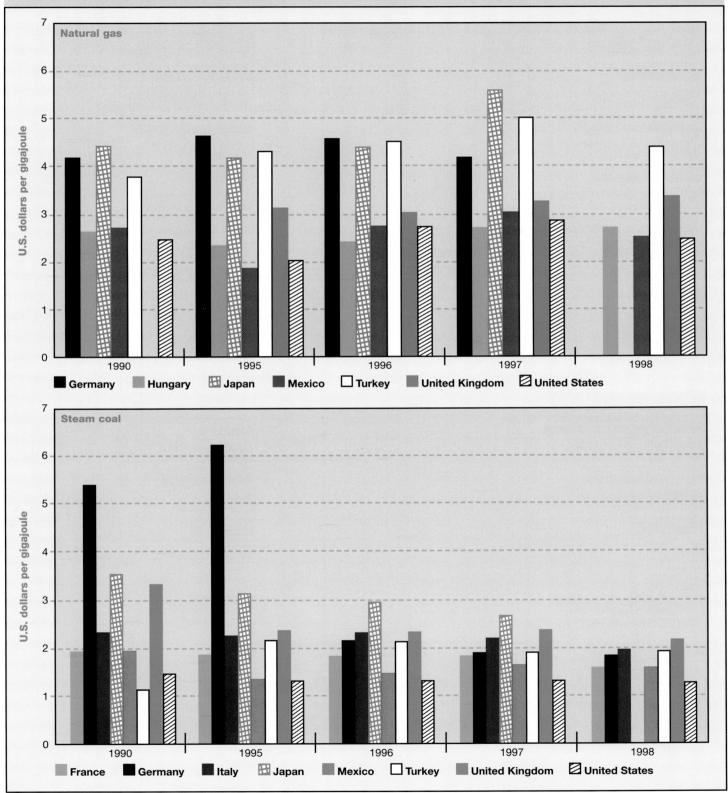

FIGURE C.9. NATURAL GAS AND STEAM COAL PRICES FOR ELECTRICITY GENERATION BY REGION, 1990–98

Natural gas

Legend: Germany, Hungary, Japan, Mexico, Turkey, United Kingdom, United States

Steam coal

Legend: France, Germany, Italy, Japan, Mexico, Turkey, United Kingdom, United States

Source: IEA, 1999b.

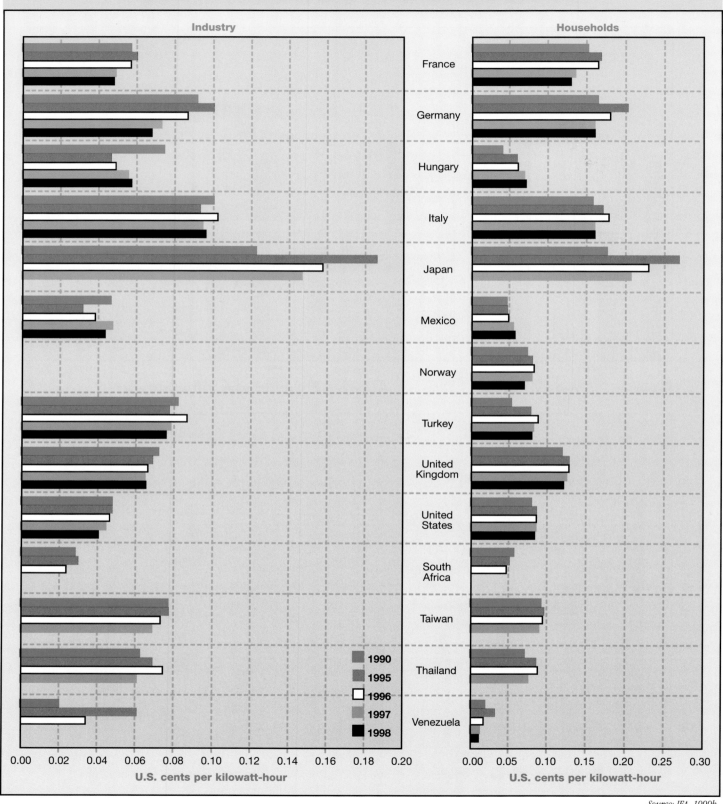

FIGURE C.10. ELECTRICITY PRICES IN SELECTED COUNTRIES, 1990-98

Industry

Households

France
Germany
Hungary
Italy
Japan
Mexico
Norway
Turkey
United Kingdom
United States
South Africa
Taiwan
Thailand
Venezuela

- 1990
- 1995
- 1996
- 1997
- 1998

U.S. cents per kilowatt-hour

U.S. cents per kilowatt-hour

Source: IEA, 1999b.

FIGURE C.11. OIL PRODUCT PRICES IN SELECTED COUNTRIES, 1990–98

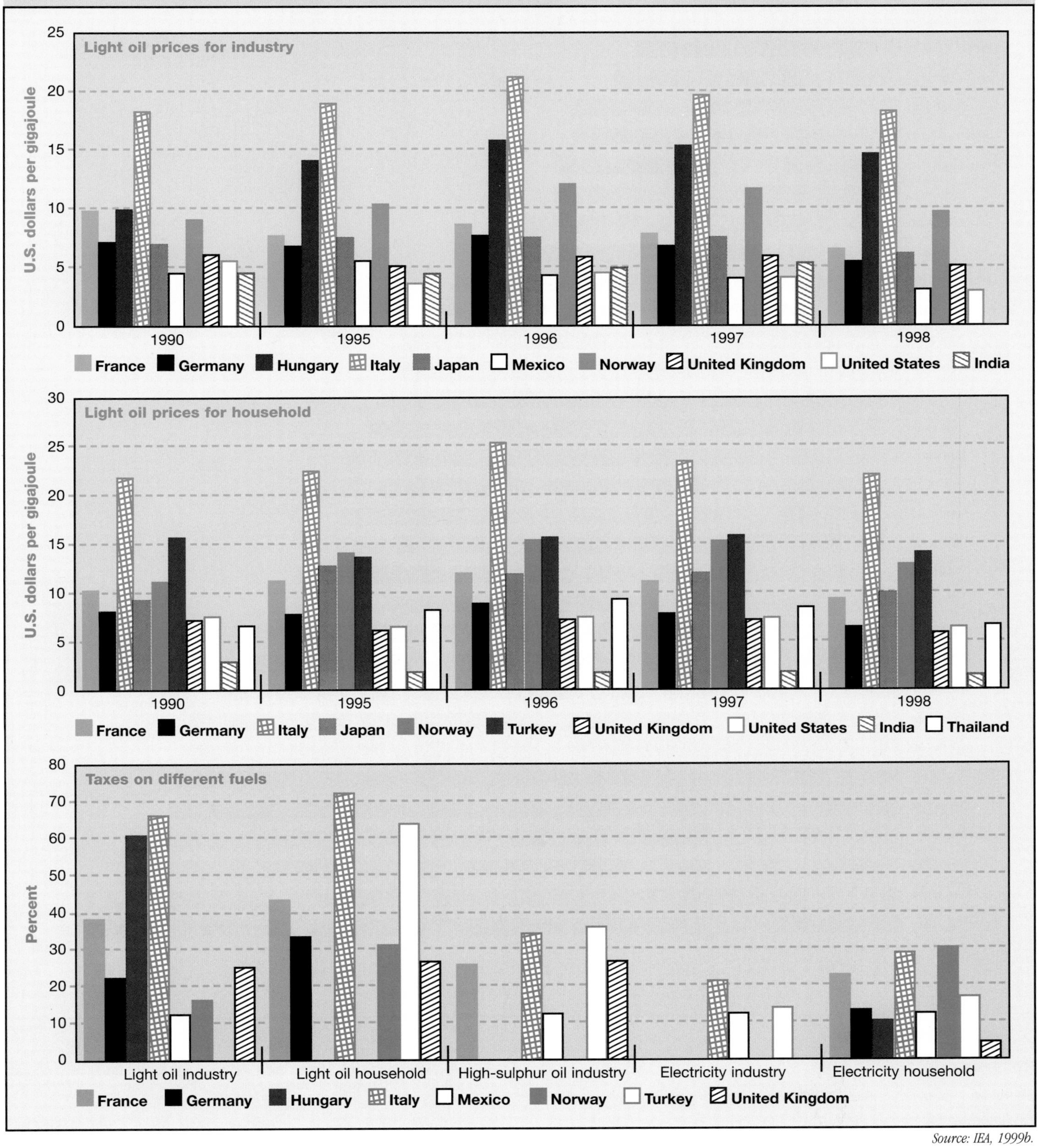
Light oil prices for industry
U.S. dollars per gigajoule
25
20
15
10
5
0
1990
1995
1996
1997
1998
France
Germany
Hungary
Italy
Japan
Mexico
Norway
United Kingdom
United States
India
Light oil prices for household
U.S. dollars per gigajoule
30
25
20
15
10
5
0
1990
1995
1996
1997
1998
France
Germany
Italy
Japan
Norway
Turkey
United Kingdom
United States
India
Thailand
Taxes on different fuels
Percent
80
70
60
50
40
30
20
10
0
Light oil industry
Light oil household
High-sulphur oil industry
Electricity industry
Electricity household
France
Germany
Hungary
Italy
Mexico
Norway
Turkey
United Kingdom

Source: IEA, 1999b.

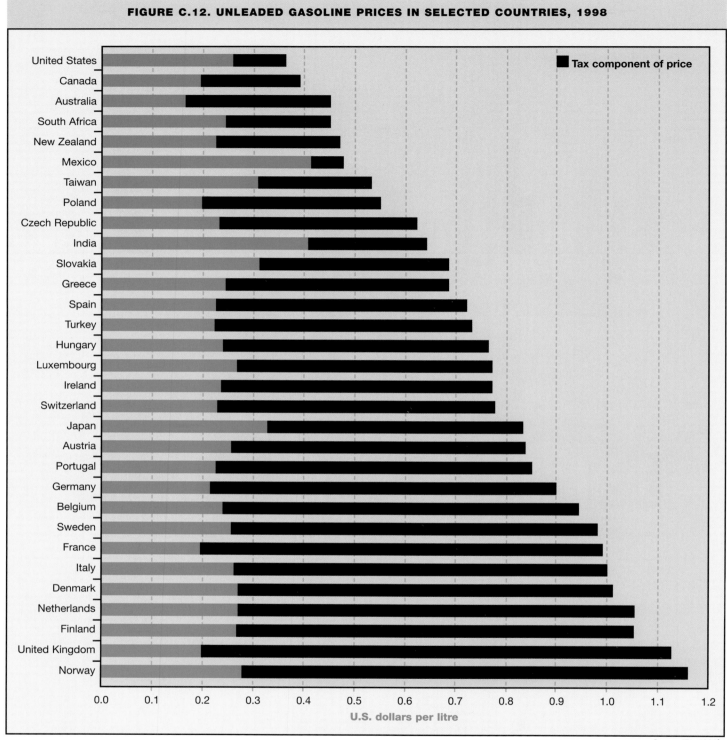

FIGURE C.12. UNLEADED GASOLINE PRICES IN SELECTED COUNTRIES, 1998

■ Tax component of price

U.S. dollars per litre

Source: IEA, 1999b.

References

BP (British Petroleum). 1999. *BP Statistical Review of World Energy.* London.

IEA (International Energy Agency). 1999a. *Energy Balances.* Organisation for Economic Co-operation and Development. Paris.

————. 1999b. *Energy Prices and Taxes.* Quarterly statistics (second quarter). Organisation for Economic Co-operation and Development. Paris.

World Bank. 1999. *World Development Indicators 1999.* CD-ROM. Washington, D.C.

The fossil energy used in 1998 contained about 6.5 gigatonnes of carbon, down slightly from 1997. The slight reduction was caused by the economic crisis in East Asia, which curbed energy use in this fast-growing region, and China's closure of inefficient and coal-intensive heavy industry enterprises. All this carbon essentially ends up in the atmosphere in the form of carbon dioxide, the inevitable by-product of any combustion process involving hydrocarbon fuels.

The energy sector emitted about 2.8 gigatonnes of carbon during the extraction and conversion of primary energy to fuels and electricity, and during transmission and distribution to final use. The rest, about 3.7 gigatonnes of carbon, was emitted at the point of end use. Included are 0.4 gigatonnes of carbon embodied in durable hydrocarbon-based materials and products such as plastics, asphalt, lubricants, and pharmaceuticals. Although these materials do not necessarily contribute to carbon emissions in the year they are statistically accounted for as energy or non-energy use, most materials manufactured from hydrocarbons are eventually oxidised to carbon dioxide.

Carbon is also released from the combustion of biomass. Annual net emissions from biomass conversion are difficult to determine and depend on the extent to which the biomass use is truly renewable. The information presented here assumes that biomass-based energy services are renewable and so do not result in net additions to atmospheric concentrations of carbon dioxide.

Box D.1 reports the range of carbon emission factors found in the literature and the IPCC factors used to calculate the past and current carbon emissions shown in figure D.1. Global carbon

BOX D.1. CARBON DIOXIDE EMISSION FACTORS

Carbon dioxide emissions are measured in units of elemental carbon. For example, in 1998 global carbon dioxide emissions were 6.5 gigatonnes (billion tonnes) of carbon. In the literature carbon dioxide emissions are often reported as the mass of the carbon dioxide molecules (1 kilogram of carbon corresponds to 3.67 kilograms of carbon dioxide).

Carbon emission factors for some primary energy sources (kilograms of carbon per gigajoule)			
Source	Heating value	OECD and IPCC, 1995	Literature range
Wood	HHV LHV		26.8–28.4 28.1–29.9
Peat	HHV LHV	28.9	30.3
Coal (bituminous)	HHV LHV	25.8	23.9–24.5 25.1–25.8
Crude oil	HHV LHV	20.0	19.0–20.3 20.0–21.4
Natural gas	HHV LHV	15.3	13.6–14.0 15.0–15.4

Note: HHV is the higher heating value, LHV is the lower heating value. The difference is that the higher heating value includes the energy of condensation of the water vapour contained in the combustion products (see annex A). *Source: IPCC, 1996.*

FIGURE D.1. CARBON EMISSIONS BY REGION, 1965–98

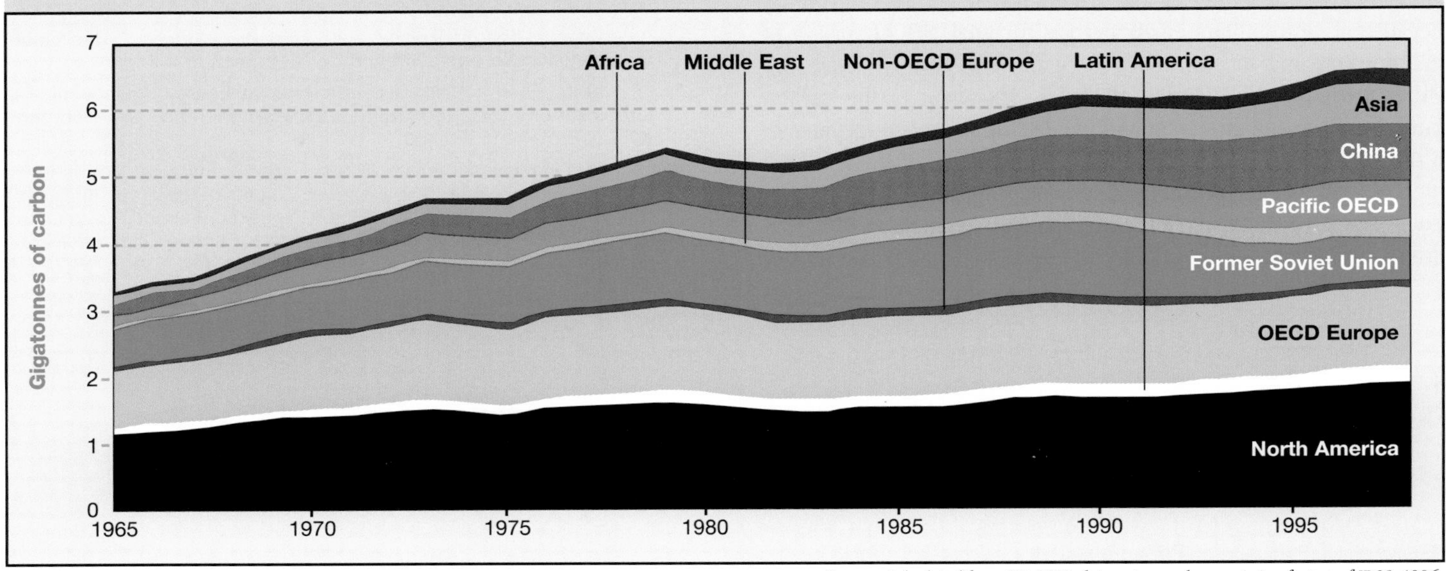

Source: Calculated from BP, 1999 data using carbon emission factors of IPCC, 1996.

FIGURE D.2. GLOBAL CARBON EMISSIONS, CARBON EMISSIONS PER CAPITA, AND DECARBONISATION OF THE ENERGY SYSTEM AND OF ECONOMIC PRODUCTION, 1971–97

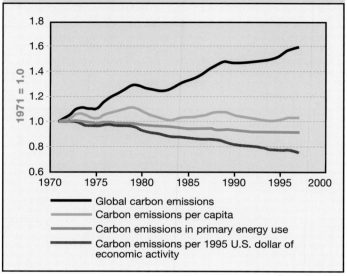

Legend:
- Global carbon emissions
- Carbon emissions per capita
- Carbon emissions in primary energy use
- Carbon emissions per 1995 U.S. dollar of economic activity

Source: IEA, 1999.

TABLE D.1. CARBON EMISSIONS PER CAPITA BY REGION, 1975–97 (TONNES OF CARBON)

Region	1975	1980	1985	1990	1995	1997
North America[a]	4.84	4.96	4.54	4.54	4.55	4.70
OECD Europe	2.42	2.59	2.41	2.35	2.26	2.29
Pacific OECD[b]	2.06	2.19	2.14	2.52	2.86	3.02
Non-OECD Europe	1.71	2.05	2.10	1.99	1.45	1.44
Former Soviet Union	3.16	3.47	3.53	3.50	2.36	2.15
Latin America	0.53	0.57	0.50	0.53	0.57	0.63
Middle East	0.78	1.13	1.34	1.41	1.62	1.73
Asia[c]	0.15	0.18	0.20	0.25	0.31	0.34
China	0.35	0.42	0.50	0.59	0.72	0.73
Africa	0.21	0.25	0.29	0.28	0.28	0.28
World	1.14	1.21	1.16	1.17	1.13	1.15

a. Includes Mexico. b. Includes the Republic of Korea. c. Excludes China.

Source: Calculated from IEA, 1999 energy data and IPCC carbon emission factors (see box D.1).

emissions effectively doubled between 1965 and 1998, corresponding to an average increase of 2.1 percent a year—not surprisingly, a mirror image of the fossil fuel–dominated global energy use. Since 1990 the average rate of increase has slowed to 0.7 percent a year, not because of carbon emission mitigation efforts but because of the economic collapse of the former Soviet Union and the financial crisis in East Asia. Although figure D.1 clearly identifies industrialised countries as the main source of carbon emissions, it also shows the growing emissions from developing countries.

The carbon intensity (carbon per unit of primary energy) of the global energy system fell by 0.3 percent a year in the 20th century because of substitutions of oil and gas for coal, the expansion of hydropower, and the introduction of nuclear power. Figure D.2 shows carbon intensities for 1971–97. The drop in the carbon intensity of the energy system and the decline in the energy intensity of economic production have reduced the carbon intensity of GDP by 1 percent a year. Carbon emissions per capita have not changed much since 1971. In 1997 the average carbon intensity was 16.3 grams of carbon per megajoule, the carbon intensity per unit of

economic activity was 258 grams of carbon per 1995 U.S. dollar, and carbon emissions per capita were 1.15 tonnes.

Regional carbon emissions per capita vary considerably around the average of 1.15 tonnes. In 1997 the average North American emitted 4.70 tonnes of carbon, while the average African emitted just 0.28 tonnes—6 percent of the North American's emissions (table D.1). ■

References

BP (British Petroleum). 1999. *BP Statistical Review of World Energy*. London.

IEA (International Energy Agency). 1992. *Energy Balances.* Organisation for Economic Co-operation and Development, Paris.

———. 1999. *Energy Balances.* International Energy Agency of the Organization for Economic Cooperation and Development (OECD/IEA). Paris, France.

IPCC. 1996. *Primer.* In Climate Change 1995 - Impacts, Adaptations and Mitigation of Climate Change: Scientific-Technical Analyses. R.T. Watson, M.C. Zinyowera, R.H. Moss, eds., Second Assessment Report of the Intergovernmental Panel on Climate Change (IPCC). Cambridge University Press, Cambridge and New York, 879 pp.

editorial board

Brief biographies of Editorial Board members

Dennis Anderson is a Professor and the Director of the Imperial College Centre of Energy Policy and Technology, London, and a visiting Professor at the University College, London. Anderson holds degrees in economics from the London School of Economics (1967) and in engineering from the University of Manchester (1963). He is a Research Associate at the Oxford University Centre for the Study of African Economies and a Member of St. Antony's College. A former Senior Economist for the World Bank and Chief Economist for Shell, Anderson has published several works on rural energy and development, economic and environmental interactions, and climate change technology. His current research interests include economic and environmental interactions, energy pricing and regulation, and development policy. ■

Safiatou Franciose Ba-N'Daw is a former Minister of Economic Infrastructure in the Ministry of Energy of Côte d'Ivoire. She holds an M.Sc. in Economic Sciences from the University of Abidjan, studied statistics at Georgetown University, Washington, D.C., and received an MBA from Harvard University. She is also a Certified Public Accountant. Ba-N'Daw has worked as Financial Analyst for the World Bank, and has extensive experience in the development of small and medium-sized businesses in Hungary, Turkey and Tunisia. She has served as Senior Financial Specialist with the Central Bank of Pakistan and the Government of Pakistan on the development of financial institutions in that country. She also worked on financial issues in Sri Lanka until her promotion to the Ministry of Energy. ■

John W. Baker, Chairman of the World Energy Council from 1995-98, currently serves as the Deputy Chairman of Celltech Group, a pharmaceuticals company, and is a non-executive director for several other companies. He is also a member of the Education Standards Task Force and the Welfare to Work Task Force for the British Government. An arts graduate of Oxford University, he spent ten years dealing with transport policy and finance, and another decade in the field of urban renewal and public housing. In 1979 he moved into the energy sector to become the Corporate Managing Director of the Central Electricity Generating Board, and later led the man-agement of the UK electricity privatisation and restructuring programme. He was Chief Executive Officer of National Power since its establishment in 1990, then serving as its Chairman from 1995 to 1997. ■

JoAnne DiSano is the Director of the Division for Sustainable Development for the UN Department of Economic and Social Affairs. DiSano has a degree in psychology and sociology from the University of Windsor, Ontario, and a Masters of Education from Wayne State University (U.S.). Before joining the United Nations, she held several senior management positions with the Government of Canada, culminating in her work with the Department of Arts, Sport, the Environment, Tourism and Territories, where she served as the First Assistant Secretary, Environment and Conservation Policy Division,

and as Deputy Executive Director, Environment Strategies Directorate. From 1996 to 1998, DiSano was the Deputy Head of the Environment Protection Group of that department. She has also held positions with the Canadian Employment and Immigration Commission and the Treasury Board in Ottawa. ■

Gerald Doucet is the Secretary General of the World Energy Council, a position he has held since September 1998. A graduate of Ottawa University, with a Masters in Economics from Carlton University, Doucet worked for the Government of Canada in various economic and policy roles from 1967-1981. He then joined the Retail Council of Canada as Senior Vice President, and in 1988 he became the Agent General for Ontario in Europe for the Province of Ontario. From 1992 to 1994 he served as President and a Founding Director of the Europe-Canada Development Association, and from 1994 – 98 as President and CEO of the Canadian Gas Association. ■

Emad El-Sharkawi is chairman of the Egyptian National Committee of the World Energy Council, vice-chair of WEC's executive assembly for Africa, general coordinator for UN-financed energy projects in Egypt, and advisor to numerous energy organizations and commissions. He has a post-graduate diploma in electrical power engineering from King's College, University of Durham, and a Ph.D. in electrical power systems from the University of Manchester. After supervising engineering projects in Egypt early in his career, he taught and led research on electrical power systems and energy at universities in Iraq. Returning to Egypt, El-Sharkawi joined the Ministry of Electricity and Energy and later the Nuclear Power Plants Authority as Manager of Technical Affairs (1977-78). Since that time he has supervised many renewable energy programmes in Egypt and served as a member of the country's specialised councils on energies. In 1986 he was named Chairman of the Board of Directors for the Egyptian Electricity Authority. El-Sharkawi has co-authored many papers on energy and systems planning, and his efforts in the field of energy led to his election to the Royal Swedish Academy for Engineering Sciences. ■

José Goldemberg is a member of the Brazilian Academy of Sciences and the Third World Academy of Sciences. Trained in physics at the University of Saskatchewan (Canada) and the University of Illinois, Goldemberg holds a Ph.D. in Physical Sciences from the University of São Paulo. During his long academic career, he has taught at the University of São Paulo (where he also served as Rector from 1986–89), Stanford University, and the University of Paris (Orsay). He was a Visiting Professor at Princeton University in 1993–94, at the International Academy of the Environment in Geneva in 1995, and at Stanford University in 1996–97. He served the Federal Government in Brazil as Secretary of State of Science and Technology in 1990–91, Minister of Education in 1991–92, and Acting Secretary of State of the Environment in 1992. The author of several books and technical papers, Goldemberg is an internationally respected expert on nuclear physics, the environment, and energy.

In 1991 Goldemberg was the co-winner of the Mitchell Prize for Sustainable Development, and in 1994 he was honoured with the establishment of the José Goldemberg Chair in Atmospheric Physics at Tel Aviv University. In 2000, he was awarded the Volvo Environmental Prize, along with three of his colleagues on the World Energy Assessment. ■

John P. Holdren is the Teresa and John Heinz Professor of Environmental Policy and Director of the Program on Science, Technology, and Public Policy in the John F. Kennedy School of Government, and a Professor of Environmental Science and Public Policy in the Department of Earth and Planetary Sciences at Harvard University. Trained in engineering and plasma physics at MIT and Stanford, from 1973–96 Holdren co-founded and co-led the interdisciplinary graduate programme in energy and resources at the University of California, Berkeley. He is a member of the President's Committee of Advisors on Science and Technology (PCAST) and has chaired PCAST panels on protection of nuclear bomb materials, the U.S. fusion-energy R&D program, U.S. energy R&D strategy for the climate-change challenge, and international cooperation on energy. He is also a member of the U.S. National Academy of Sciences (NAS) and National Academy of Engineering (NAE), Chairman of the NAS Committee on International Security and Arms Control, and Chairman of the NAS/NAE Committee on U.S.-India Cooperation on Energy. ■

Michael Jefferson runs a consulting firm, Global Energy and Environment Consultants, in the United Kingdom. A graduate of the Universities of Oxford and the London School of Economics, Jefferson has worked extensively in the private sector, from merchant banking to head of oil supply strategy and planning for Europe at the Royal Dutch/Shell Group of Companies. In 1990 Jefferson was seconded to the World Energy Council (WEC) as Deputy Secretary General, and he later became director of studies and policy development for WEC. He is the author of numerous books and articles related to energy and climate change, including *Energy for Tomorrow's World* (written for a WEC commission in 1993). He was a lead author and contributing author for the Intergovernmental Panel on Climate Change (IPCC) Second Assessment Report, a member of the drafting team for the IPCC's Synthesis Report, and an IPCC peer review editor for the Third Assessment Report. He is technical coordinator and lead consultant to the G8 Renewable Energy Task Force. He also participated in the UNDP report, *Energy after Rio*, written in 1997. ■

Eberhard Jochem is the Senior Scientist at the Fraunhofer Institute of Systems and Innovation Research (Karlsruhe, Germany) and Co-director of the Centre for Energy Policy and Economics (Zurich, Switzerland). Jochem holds degrees in chemical engineering (Aachen, 1967) and economics (Munich, 1971), and a Ph.D. in technical chemistry (Munich, 1971). He was a research fellow at Munich University and Harvard University. As an internationally acknowledged expert in systems analysis, technical and socio-economic research, and policy evaluation, Jochem is a member of several national and international scientific organizations and advisory committees, including the IPCC Bureau and the Enquête Commission on "Sustainable Energy, Liberalization, and Globalization" of the German Parliament. He presented lectures at the universities in Karlsruhe and Kassel until 1999 and since then in Zurich and Lausanne, Switzerland. He is a member of the Editorial Advisory Board of *Energy Environment* and *Climate Policy*. ■

Thomas B. Johansson, who is on leave from the University of Lund in Sweden, is the Director of the Energy and Atmosphere Programme of the Bureau for Development Policy of UNDP. Johansson, who holds a Ph.D. in nuclear physics from the Lund Institute of Technology, is International Co-Chairman of the Working Group on Energy Strategies and Technologies of the China Council for International Cooperation on Environment and Development. He has served as Convening Lead Author, Energy Supply Mitigation Options (Working Group IIA of the Intergovernmental Panel on Climate Change); Vice-Chairman, UN Committee on New and Renewable Sources of Energy and on Energy for Development; Chairman, UN Solar Energy Group for Environment and Development; and Director of Vattenfall, the Swedish State Power Board. He is has authored or co-authored numerous books and articles including *Energy after Rio; Renewable Energy: Sources for Fuels and Electricity; Electricity-Efficient End Use and New Generation Technologies and their Planning Implications;* and *Energy for a Sustainable World.* Along with three other members of the editorial board, he was awarded the Volvo Environment Prize in 2000. ■

Hisham Khatib, an engineer and economist, serves as honorary Vice Chairman of the World Energy Council, as a member of the Roster of Experts for the Global Environment Facility's Scientific and Advisory Panel, and as the Advisory Editor to the *Utilities Policy* and *Energy Policy* journals (U.K.) and the *Natural Resources Forum* (U.S.). Khatib received an M.Sc. from the University of Birmingham, and a Ph.D. in electrical engineering from the University of London, where he also received a B.Sc. in economics. Khatib has more than 40 years' experience in matters relating to electricity, energy, water, and environmental issues. He has consulted to the United Nations, UNDP, UNEP, Global Environment Facility, UNIDO, World Bank, Arab Fund, Islamic Development Bank, and many other regional and international development agencies. Khatib also served as Minister of Planning, Minister of Water and Irrigation, and Minister of Energy and Mineral Resources for the government of Jordan. He is the author of two books, *Economics of Reliability in Electrical Power Systems* and *Financial and Economic Evaluation of Projects,* and of more than 100 articles and papers. In 1998 he was honoured with the "Achievement Medal" of the Institution of Electrical Engineers. ■

Kui-Nang Mak has been chief of the Energy and Transport Branch of the Division for Sustainable Development, UN Department of Economic and Social Affairs (DESA) since 1990. He holds a M.Sc. in electrical engineering from the University of Illinois, where he has completed all requirements except dissertation for a Ph.D. in electrical engineering; an I.E. degree in industrial economics and management from Columbia University and a Certificate from the Executive Programme on Climate Change and Development from Harvard University. He has worked for the United Nations since 1975, acting as an Economic Affairs Officer specializing in energy for DESA from 1978 to 1990. He is the author of several papers and reports on global energy issues, particularly on international cooperation and financing. His professional affiliations include serving as a member of the Sub-Committee on International Practices, Institute of Electrical and Electronics Engineers; a member of the Committee on Cleaner Fossil Fuel Systems of the World Energy Council; and an advisor for the China Coal Preparation Association. ■

Nebojsa Nakićenović is the Project Leader of the Transitions to New Technologies Project at the International Institute for Applied Systems Analysis (IIASA). He is also the Convening Lead Author of the Special Report on Emissions Scenarios by the Intergovernmental Panel on Climate Change, and Guest Professor at the Technical University of Graz. Nakićenović holds bachelor's and master's degrees in economics and computer science from Princeton University and the University of Vienna, where he completed his Ph.D. He also received an *honoris causa* Ph.D degree in engineering from the Russian Academy of Sciences. Before joining IIASA, Nakićenović worked with the Research Centre (Karlsruhe, Germany) in the field of nuclear materials accountability. He is the author or co-author of many scientific papers and books on the dynamics of technological and social change, economic restructuring, mitigation of anthropogenic impacts on the environment, and response strategies to global change. Nakićenović has been Associate Editor of the *International Journal on Technological Forecasting and Social Change* and of the *International Journal on Energy,* and he serves as an advisor to many groups, including the United Nations Commission on Sustainable Development. Currently, his research focuses on the diffusion of new technologies and their interactions with the environment. ■

Anca Popescu is the Director of the Institute of Power Studies and Design in Romania. Popescu holds a B.Sc. in electrical engineering and a Ph.D. University in high-voltage technique from the Bucharest Polytechnic. An expert in energy policy, integrated resources planning, and power sector development and investment planning, she has served as a scientific and technical expert to the UN Framework Convention on Climate Change and was the Chief Scientific Investigator on the role of nuclear power plants in greenhouse gas emission reductions in Romania in a study sponsored by the International Atomic Energy Agency. The author of numerous papers on energy planning, policy, and development, Popescu has also served as a guest lecturer at Bucharest Polytechnic University and at the National Electricity Company Training Centre. ■

Amulya Reddy was President of the International Energy Initiative until April 2000. Reddy received his Ph.D. in applied physical chemistry from the University of London in 1958. From 1970–91 he was a professor at the Indian Institute of Science, in Bangalore, India, and was a visiting Senior Research Scientist at the Center for Energy and Environmental Studies at Princeton University in 1984. From 1990–93, Reddy was a member of the Scientific and Technical Advisory Panel of the Global Environment Facility. He has also been a member of the Energy Research Group of the International Development Research Centre in Canada; the Economic and Planning Council, Government of Karnataka; and a member of the Panel of Eminent Persons on Power for the Minister of Power, India. He is the author of more than 250 papers, and co-author and editor of several books on energy, rural technology, and science and technology policy. Reddy was awarded the Volvo Environmental Prize for 2000, along with three other members of the World Energy Assessment editorial board. ■

Hans-Holger Rogner is the Head of the Planning and Economic Studies Section in the Department of Nuclear Energy in the International Atomic Energy Agency. He holds an industrial engineering degree and a Ph.D. in energy economics from the Technical University of Karlsruhe. He specialised in applying systems analysis to long-term energy demand and supply issues and in identifying technologically and economically feasible paths to sustainable energy systems. At the International Atomic Energy Agency, Rogner's activities focus on sustainable energy development and technology change. He contributes to UN efforts targeted at Agenda 21, including combating climate change. ■

Kirk R. Smith is Professor of Environment Health Sciences, Associate Director for International Programs at the Center for Occupational and Environment Health, and Deputy Director of the Institute for Global Health at the University of California, Berkeley. Smith holds a Ph.D. and M.P.H. in biomedical and environmental health sciences from Berkeley. He has been a Senior Fellow at the East-West Center's Program on Environment (Honolulu), and was the founding head of the East-West Center's Energy Program (1978-1985). Smith is the author of more than 200 articles and 7 books, sits on the boards of 7 international scientific journals, and is advisor to the governments of several developing countries on environment. He is also a member of the India-U.S. Academies of Science Energy/ Environment Program and of the World Health Organisation's Comparative Risk Assessment and Air Quality Guidelines committees. In 1997, he was elected to the US National Academy of Sciences. ■

Wim C. Turkenburg is Professor and Head of the Department of Science, Technology, and Society at Utrecht University. He is also a member of the Council on Housing, Physical Planning, and Environment of the Netherlands, Vice Chairperson of the UN Committee on Energy and Natural Resources for Development (UN-CENRD), and Chairperson of the Subcommittee on Energy of the

UN-CENRD. He studied physics, mathematics, and astronomy at Leiden University and the University of Amsterdam, and received his Ph.D. in science and mathematics from the University of Amsterdam in 1971. Turkenburg is an expert on energy, the environment, and systema analysis. He is author or co-author of many articles on renewables (wind energy, photovoltaics, biomass energy), energy efficiency improvement, cleaner use of fossil fuels (decarbonization technologies), and energy and climate change. He has been member of a number of national and international boards, committees and working groups on energy, energy research, and energy and environmental policy development, serving inter alia the International Solar Energy Society, the World Energy Council, the Intergovernmental Panel on Climate Change, and the Government of the Netherlands. ▪

Francisco Lopez Viray is the Secretary of Energy in the Philippines, and chairs its subsidiary agencies, including the National Power Corporation, the Philippine National Oil Company, and the National Electrification Administration. Viray holds an M.Sc. in electrical engineering from the University of the Philippines and a Ph.D. in engineering from West Virginia University. His extensive career has included advisory and research positions on a number of energy and power planning projects. A specialist in the areas of power system engineering, computer applications in engineering and energy planning and management, Viray has received several citations and awards, including the ASEAN Achievement Award in Engineering, and the Outstanding Professional in Electrical Engineering from the Professional Regulation Committee of the Philippines. ▪

Robert H. Williams is a Senior Research Scientist at Princeton University's Center for Energy and Environmental Studies, with a Ph.D. in physics from the University of California, Berkeley (1967). He served on two panels of the President's Committee of Advisors on Science and Technology: the Energy R&D Panel (1997), as chair of its Renewable Energy Task Force; and the International Energy Research, Development, Demonstration, and Deployment Panel (1999), as chair of its Energy Supply Task Force. Since 1993 he has been a member of the Working Group on Energy Strategies and Technologies of the China Council for International Cooperation on Environment and Development. He was a member of the Scientific and Technical Advisory Panel for the Global Environment Facility and chaired its Climate and Energy Working Group (1995-1998). He has written many articles and coauthored several books on a wide range of energy topics. He is recipient of the American Physical Society's Leo Szilard Award for Physics in the Public Interest (1988), the U.S. Department of Energy's Sadi Carnot Award (1991) for his work on energy efficiency, and a MacArthur Foundation Prize (1993). In 2000, along with three other members of the World Energy Assessment editorial board, he received the Volvo Environmental Prize. ▪

glossary

Selected terminology

Acid deposition: fallout of substances from the atmosphere (through rain, snow, fog or dry particles) that have the potential to increase the acidity of the receptor medium. They are primarily the result of the discharge of gaseous sulphur oxides and nitrogen oxides from the burning of coal and oil e.g. in electricity generation, smelting industries and transport. "Acid rain" is the result of the combination of these gases in the air with vapor. Acidifying deposition can be responsible for acidification of lakes, rivers and groundwater, with resulting damage to fish and other components of aquatic ecosystems, and for damage to forests and other harmful effects on plants. (Note: precipitation is naturally acid as a result of the absorption of carbon dioxide from the atmosphere.)

Agenda 21: a comprehensive plan of action to be taken globally, nationally and locally in every area in which human impacts on the environment. It was adopted by more than 175 governments at the UN Conference on Environment and Development in 1992 (also known as the Rio Earth Summit).

Animate energy: energy derived from human or animal power.

Anthropogenic emissions: the share of emissions attributed to human activities.

API degree: the American Petroleum Institute has adopted a scale of measurement for the specific gravity of crude oils and petroleum products that is expressed in degrees.

Biofuels: fuels obtained as a product of biomass conversion (such as alcohol or gasohol).

Biomass: organic, non-fossil material oil of biological origin, a part of which constitutes an exploitable energy resource. Although the different forms of energy from biomass are always considered as renewable, it must be noted that their rates of renewability are different. These rates depend on the seasonal or daily cycles of solar flux, the vagaries of climate, agricultural techniques or cycles of plant growth, and may be affected by intensive exploitation.

Biogas: a gas composed principally of a mixture of methane and carbon dioxide produced by anaerobic digestion of biomass.

Breeder reactor: a reactor which produces a fissile substance identical to the one it consumes and in greater quantity than the one it has consumed, that is, it has a conversion ratio greater than unity.

Business-as-usual: the projected future state of energy and economic variables in the event that current technological, economic, political, and social trends persist.

Capacity building: developing skills and capabilities for technology innovation and deployment in the relevant government, private-sector, academic, and civil institutions.

Carbon sequestration: the capture and secure storage of carbon that would otherwise be emitted or remain in the atmosphere, either by (1) diverting carbon from reaching the atmosphere; or (2) removing carbon already in the atmosphere. Examples of the first type are trapping the CO_2 in power plant flue gases, and capturing CO_2 during the production of decarbonised fuels. The common approach to the second type is to increase or enhance carbon sinks.

Carbon tax: a levy exacted by a government on the use of carbon-containing fuel for the purpose of influencing human behavior (specifically economic behavior) to use less fossil fuels (and thus limit greenhouse gas emissions).

Carbon sinks: places where CO_2 can be absorbed, such as forests, oceans and soil.

Clean Development Mechanism (CDM): is one of four 'flexibility' mechanisms adopted in the Kyoto Protocol to the UN Framework Convention on Climate Change. It is a cooperative arrangement through which certified greenhouse gas emission reductions accruing from sustainable development projects in developing countries can help industrialized countries meet part of their reduction commitments as specified in Annex B of the Protocol.

Cogeneration: see combined heat and power

Combined cycle plant: electricity generating plant comprising a gas-turbine generator unit, whose exhaust gases are fed to a waste-heat boiler, which may or may not have a supplementary burner, and the steam raised by the boiler is used to drive a steam-turbine generator.

Combined heat and power (CHP) station: also referred to as a cogeneration plant. A thermal power station in which all the steam generated in the boilers passes to turbo-generators for electricity generation, but designed so that steam may be extracted at points on the turbine and/or from the turbine exhaust as back-pressure steam and used to supply heat, typically for industrial processes or district heating.

Commercial energy: energy that is subject to a commercial transaction and that can thus be accounted for. This contrasts to non-commercial energy, which is not subject to a commercial exchange, and thus difficult to account for in energy balances. The term non-commercial energy thus is technically distinct from traditional energy, but in practice they are often used interchangeably.

Commission on Sustainable Development (CSD): was created in December 1992 to ensure effective follow-up of the United Nations Conference on Environment and Development, to monitor and report on implementation of the agreements at the local, national, regional and international levels.

Compressed natural gas (CNG): natural gas stored under pressure in cylinders and used as fuel for automotive engines.

Cost buy-down: the process of paying the difference in unit cost (price) between an innovative energy technology and a conventional energy technology in order to increase sales volume, thus stimulating cost reductions through manufacturing scale-up and economies of learning throughout the production, distribution, deployment, use, and maintenance cycle.

Developing countries: generally used in this report to refer to the countries that are members of the Group of 77 Countries and China.

Digester: a tank designed for the anaerobic fermentation of biomass.

Dimethyl ether (DME): an oxygenated fuel that can be produced from any carbonaceous feedstock by a process that begins with syngas production.

Discount rate: the annual rate at which the effects of future events are reduced so as to be comparable to the effect of present events.

Economies in transition: national economies that are moving from a period of heavy government control toward lessened intervention, increased privatization, and greater use of competition.

Energy innovation chain: the linked process by which an energy-supply or energy-end-use technology moves from its conception in theory and the laboratory to its feasibility testing through demonstration projects, small-scale implementation and finally large-scale deployment.

Energy intensity: ratio between the consumption of energy to a given quantity, usually refers to the amount of primary or final energy consumed per unit of gross domestic or national product.

Energy efficiency: the amount of utility or energy service provided by a unit of energy (U/E), which can be used as a measure of energy efficiency in end-use applications. An increase in energy efficiency enables consumers to enjoy an increase in utility or energy service for the same amount of energy consumed or to enjoy the same utility of energy services with reduced energy consumption, $U = (U/E) E$. The usual situation is one in which an increase in energy efficiency (U/E) boosts both energy use and the utility derived from each unit of energy consumed.

Energy payback/time: the time of exploitation of an energy installation, necessary for recuperating all the energy consumed in its construction and operation during the projected lifespan of the installation.

Energy sector restructuring and reform: encouraging market competition in energy supply (often by transfer of ownership from the public to the private sector), while removing subsidies and other distortions in energy pricing and preserving public benefits.

Energy services: the utility of energy is often referred to by engineers as *energy services,* although that term can be confusing since units vary between applications and sometimes are not defined at all. For example, lumens is a natural unit in lighting services, and Thomas Edison proposed charging for lumens rather than kilowatt hours when electricity was first used for lighting; for practical reasons he eventually settled on charging by the kilowatt hour instead. James Watt charged for his steam engines not by their motive power, but by the difference in the costs of fuel he and his customers saved when they substituted his engine for their old one. However, when the utility or 'services' provided by energy are felt through a hot shower, chilled drinks, refrigerated food, a comfortably warm or cool house, increased transport miles, or labour saved in washing and ironing or in producing an innumerable array of industrial goods and services, it is only practicable to charge for energy in energy units.

Environmental taxes (ecotaxes): levies on products or services collected to account for environmental impacts associated with them.

Ethanol (ethyl alcohol): alcohol produced by the fermentation of glucose. The glucose may be derived from sugary plants such as sugar cane and beets or from starchy and cellulosic materials by hydrolysis. The ethanol may be concentrated by distillation, and can be blended with petroleum products to produce motor fuel.

Exergy: the maximum amount of energy that can be converted into any other form or energy under given thermodynamic conditions; also known as availability of work potential.

Externalities: benefits or costs resulting as an unintended byproduct of an economic activity that accrue to someone other than the parties involved in the activity. While energy is an economic 'good' that sustains growth and development and human well-being, there are by-products of energy production and use that have an undesirable effect on the environment (economic 'bads'). Most of these are emissions from the combustion of fossil fuels.

Final energy: is the energy transported and distributed to the point of final use. Examples include gasoline at the service station, electricity at the socket, or fuelwood in the barn. The next energy transformation is the conversion of final energy in end-use devices, such as appliances, machines, and vehicles, into useful energy, such as work and heat. Useful energy is measured at the crankshaft of an automobile engine or an industrial electric motor, by the heat of a household radiator or an industrial boiler, or by the luminosity of a light bulb. The application of useful energy provides energy services, such as a moving vehicle, a warm room, process heat, or illumination.

Foreign direct investment (FDI): is net inflows of investment to acquire a lasting management interest (10 percent or more of voting stock) in an enterprise operating in an economy other than that of the investor. It is the sum of equity capital, reinvestment of earnings, other long-term capital, and short-term capital as shown in the balance of payments. Gross foreign direct investment is the sum of the absolute values of inflows and outflows of foreign direct investment recorded in the balance of payments financial account. It includes equity capital, reinvestment of earnings, other long-term capital, and short-term capital. Note that this indicator differs from the standard measure of foreign direct investment, which captures only inward investment.

Fuel cells: devices that enable chemical energy to be converted directly into electrical energy without the intervention of the heat engine cycle, in which electrical power is produced in a controlled reaction involving a fuel, generally hydrogen, methanol or a hydrocarbon.

Fuelwood: wood and wood products, possibly including coppices, scrubs, and branches, bought or gathered, and used by direct combustion.

Global Environment Facility (GEF): a financial institution that provides grants and concessionary financing to developing countries and economies-in-transition for projects and activities that provide global benefits in four topical areas: climate change; biological diversity; international waters; and stratospheric ozone. The GEF was established for the purpose of implementing agreements stemming from the 1992 UN Conference on Environment and Development including the UN Framework Convention on Climate Change. The World Bank Group is one of the three implementing agencies for the GEF, together with the United Nations Development Program and the United Nations Environment Program.

Green pricing: labelling and pricing schemes that allow consumers to pay a premium for environmentally friendly services and products if they choose.

Greenfield investment: starting up an entirely new plant, in contrast to rebuilding an older one.

Greenhouse Gases (GHGs): heat-trapping gases in the atmosphere that warm the Earth's surface by absorbing outgoing infrared radiation and re-radiating part of it downward. Water vapour is the most important naturally occurring greenhouse gas, but the principal greenhouse gases, whose atmospheric concentrations are being augmented by emission from human activities are carbon dioxide, methane, nitrous oxide, and halocarbons.

Grid extension: extending the infrastructural network that supplies energy, such as transmission wires for electricity.

Gross National Product (GNP): total production of goods and services by the subjects of a country at home and abroad. In national income accounting, it is a measure of the performance of the nation's economy, within a specific accounting period (usually a year).

Higher heating value (HHV): quantity of heat liberated by the complete combustion of a unit volume or weight of a fuel in the determination of which the water produced is assumed completely condensed and the heat recovered. Contrast to lower heating value.

Industrialized countries: for purposes of this report, this term refers primarily to high-income OECD countries. While many transitional economies are also characterized by a high degree of industrialization, they are often considered and discussed separately because of their specific development requirements.

Infrastructure: the physical structures and delivery systems necessary to supply energy and end-users. In the case of power plants, the infrastructure is the high-tension wires needed to carry the electricity to consumers; in the case of natural gas, it is the pipeline network; in the case of liquid fuels, it is the fueling stations.

Intergovernmental Panel on Climate Change (IPCC): a multilateral scientific organization established by the United Nations Environment Programme (UNEP) and the World Meteorological Organization to assess the available scientific, technical, and socio-economic information in the field of climate change and to assess technical and policy options for reducing climate change and its impacts.

Irradiance: the quantity of solar energy falling per area of plane surface and time.

Kyoto Protocol (to the UN Framework Convention on Climate Change): contains legally binding emissions targets for industrialized (Annex I) countries for the post-2000 period. Together they must reduce their combined emissions of six key greenhouse gases by at least 5% by the period 2008-2012, calculated as an average over these five years. The Protocol will enter into force 90 days after it has been ratified by at least 55 Parties to the Climate Change Convention; these Parties must include industrialized countries representing at least 55% of this group's total 1990 carbon dioxide emissions. See also Clean Development Mechanism.

Leapfrogging: moving directly to most cleanest, most advanced technologies possible, rather than making incremental technological progress.

Liberalisation: the doctrine that advocates the greatest possible use of markets and the forces of competition to co-ordinate economic activity. It allows to the state only those activities which the market cannot perform (e.g. the provision of public goods) or those that are necessary to establish the framework within which the private enterprise economy cannot operate efficiently (e.g. the establishment of the legal framework on property and contract and the adoption of such policies and anti-monopoly legislation).

Lifecycle cost: the cost of a good or service over its entire lifetime.

Light water reactor (LWR): a nuclear reactor in which ordinary water, as opposed to heavy-water, or a steam/water mixture is used as reactor coolant and moderator. The boiling water reactor (BWR) and the pressurized water reactor (PWR) are examples of light water reactors.

Liquefied natural gas (LNG): natural gas made up mainly of methane and ethane and which, generally to facilitate its transport, has been converted to the liquid phase by having its temperature lowered.

Liquefied petroleum gas (LPG): light hydrocarbons, principally propane and butane, which are gaseous under normal conditions, but are maintained in a liquid state by an increase of pressure or lowering of temperature.

Lower heating value (LHV): quantity of heat liberated by the complete combustion of a unit volume or weight of a fuel in the determination of which the water produced is assumed to remain as a vapour and the heat not recovered. Contrast to higher heating value.

Macroeconomic: pertaining to a study of economics in terms of whole systems, especially with reference to general levels of output and income and to the interrelations among sectors of the economy.

Marginal cost: the cost of one additional unit of effort. In terms of reducing emissions, it represents the cost of reducing emission by one more unit.

Marginal cost pricing: a system of setting the price of energy equal to the marginal cost of providing the energy to a class of consumer.

Market barriers: conditions that prevent or impede the diffusion of cost-effective technologies or practices.

Market penetration: the percentage of all its potential purchasers to which a good or service is sold per unit time.

Market potential (or currently realizable potential): the portion of the economic potential for GHG emissions reductions or energy-efficiency improvements that could be achieved under existing market conditions, assuming no new policies and measures.

Methanol (methyl alcohol): alcohol primarily produced by chemical synthesis but also by the destructive distillation of wood. Methanol is regarded as a marketable synthetic motor fuel.

New renewables: used in this report to refer to modern bio-fuels, wind, solar, small hydropower, marine and geothermal energy. Geothermal energy cannot be strictly considered renewable, but is included for practical reasons.

Nitrogen oxides (NO$_x$): oxides formed an released in all common types of combustion at high temperature. Direct harmful effects of nitrogen oxides include human respiratory tract irritation and damage to plants. Indirect effects arise from their essential role in photochemical smog reactions and their contribution to acid rain problems.

Nuclear fuel cycle: a group of processes connected with nuclear power production; using, storing, reprocessing and disposing of nuclear materials used in the operation of nuclear reactors. The closed fuel cycle concept involves the reprocessing and reuse of fissionable material from the spent fuel. The once-through fuel cycle concept involves the disposal of the spent fuel following its use in the reactor.

Opportunity cost: the cost of an economic activity foregone by the choice of another activity.

Organisation for Economic Co-operation and Development (OECD): a multilateral organization of 29 industrialized nations, producing among them two-thirds of the world's goods and services. The objective of the OECD is the development of social and economic policies and the coordination of domestic and international activities.

Pollution associated with energy use. This is usually measured as pollution per unit of energy use, or $P = (P/E)E$. Modern methods of pollution control and emerging energy technologies are capable of reducing the ratio P/E—and thus P—to very low levels, sometimes to zero. This means that if environmental policies focus on P rather than E, there is no reason why high levels of energy use (and the utility derived from it) cannot be enjoyed and pollution virtually eliminated in the long term, a process known as delinking environmental concerns from energy use.

Primary energy is the energy that is embodied in resources as they exist in nature: chemical energy embodied in fossil fuels (coal, oil, and natural gas) or biomass, the potential energy of a water reservoir, the electromagnetic energy of solar radiation, and the energy released in nuclear reactions. For the most part, primary energy is not used directly but is first mined, harvested or converted and transformed into electricity and fuels such as gasoline, jet fuel, heating oil, or charcoal.

Public Benefits Fund (PBF): a financial mechanism created to serve the greater public interest by funding programs for environment and public health, services to the poor and disenfranchised, energy technology innovation, or other public goods not accounted for by a restructured energy sector.

Purchasing power parity (PPP): GDP estimates based on the purchasing power of currencies rather than on current exchange rates. Such estimates are a blend of extrapolated and regression-based numbers, using the result of the International Comparison Program. PPP estimates tend to lower per capita GDPs in industrialized countries and raise per capita GDPs in developing countries.

Research and development (R&D): the first two stages in the energy innovation chain. R, D & D refers to demonstration projects as well.

Reserves: those occurrences of energy sources or mineral that are identified and measured as economically and technically recoverable with current technologies and prices (see chapter 5).

Resources: those occurrences of energy sources or minerals with less certain geological and/or economic/technical recoverability characteristics, but that are considered to become potentially recoverable with foreseeable technological and economic development (see chapter 5).

Revenue neutral taxes: governmental levies placed on certain goods or services that replace other taxes and thus do not add to total revenues collected, but rather attempt to change behaviours.

Scenario: a plausible description of how the future may develop based on analysis of a coherent and internally consistent set of assumptions about key relationships and driving forces (e.g. rate of technology changes, prices). Note that scenarios are neither predictions nor forecasts.

Standards/performance criteria: a set of rules or codes mandating or defining product performance (e.g. grades, dimensions, characteristics, test methods, rules for use).

Structural changes: changes in the relative share of GDP produced by the industrial, agricultural or services sectors of an economy; or, more generally, systems transformations whereby some components are either replaced or partially substituted by other ones.

Subsidies: publicly supported cost reductions that may be granted to producers and consumers – directly, through price reductions, or in less visible forms, through tax breaks, market support or inadequate metering.

Sulphur oxides (SO$_x$): oxides produced by the combustion of fossil fuels containing sulphur. Sulphur oxides, the most widespread of which is sulphur dioxide, a colorless gas having a strong and acrid odor, are toxic at a given concentration for the respiratory system and gave harmful effects on the environment, in particular on buildings and vegetation. They contribute to the acid rain problem.

Sustainable energy: as the term is used in this document, is not meant to suggest simply a continual supply of energy. Rather it means environmentally sound, safe, reliable, affordable energy; in other words, energy that supports sustainable development in all its economic, environmental, social and security dimensions.

Syngas: a gaseous mixture composed mainly of carbon monoxide and hydrogen and synthesized from a carbonaceous feedstock such as coal or biomass. It is used as a building block for the production of synthetic liquid fuels. Syngas-based systems can make it possible to extract energy services from carbonaceous feedstocks with very low levels of pollutant or greenhouse gas emissions.

Transitional economies: see economies in transition

Unproven reserves: the estimated quantities, at a given date, which analysis of geologic and engineering data indicates might be economically recoverable from already discovered deposits, with a sufficient degree of probability to suggest their existence. Because of uncertainties as to whether, and to what extent, such unproven reserves may be expected to be recoverable in the future, the estimates should be given as a range but may be given as a single intermediate figure in which all uncertainties have been incorporated. Unproven reserves may be further categorized as probable reserves or possible reserves.

United Nations Framework Convention on Climate Change (UNFCCC): a major global convention adopted in 1992 that establishes a framework for progress in stabilizing atmospheric concentrations of greenhouse gases at safe levels. It directs that "such a level should be achieved within a time-frame sufficient to allow ecosystems to adapt naturally to climate change, to ensure that food production is not threatened and to enable economic development to proceed in a sustainable manner". It also recognizes the right of developing countries to economic development, their vulnerability to the effects of climate change, and that rich countries should shoulder greater responsibility for the problem.

United Nations Conference on Environment and Development (UNCED): also known as the Rio Earth Summit. The first of a series of major United Nations conferences on global issues that were convened in the 1990s.

World Bank Group: a multilateral, United Nations affiliated lending institution which annually makes available roughly $20 billion in loans to developing countries, mainly but not exclusively for large scale infrastructure projects. The World Bank Group comprises five agencies: the International Bank for Reconstruction and Development, the International Development Association, the International Finance Corporation (IFC), the Multilateral Investment Guarantee Agency (MIGA), and the International Centre for Settlement of Investment Disputes (ICSID). The World Bank Group raises capital from both public sources and financial markets.

contributors

World Energy Assessment
Advisory Panel and peer reviewers

A n initial draft of the World Energy Assessment formed the basis for the first round of peer review at an Advisory Panel meeting that took place in July, 1999 in Geneva. Based on comments from working groups at that meeting, as well as comments received from hundreds of experts around the world, a second draft was prepared.

The second draft of the report was circulated to the Advisory Panel, energy experts, governments and NGOs by mail and via a website. With input from that second round of comments, as well as from careful scrutiny by the Editorial Board, the final versions of the chapters were produced. A list of Advisory Panel members and peer reviewers appears below.

Advisory Panel

Mohamad Ali Abduli, Ministry of Energy, Iran

Mohammed Taoufik Adyel, Ministère de l'Energie et des Mines, Morocco

Jassim Al-Gumer, Organization of Arab Petroleum Exporting Countries, Kuwait

Hani Alnakeeb, Organization for Energy Planning, Egypt

Boris Berkovski, United Nations Educational, Scientific, and Cultural Organisation, France

Rufino Bomasang, PNOC Exploration Corporation, Philippines

Hernán Bravo, Instituto Costarricense de Electricidad, Costa Rica

Timothy Brennand, University of East Anglia, U.K.

Anthony Derrick, IT Power Ltd., U.K.

Bernard Devin, ADEME, UN-CERND, France

Daniel Doukoure, Ministère de l'Energie, Côte d'Ivoire

Danilo Feretic, Faculty of Electrical Engineering and Computing, Croatia

H.E. Irene Freudenschuss-Reichl, Austrian Mission to the United Nations, Austria

Zdravko Genchev, Center for Energy Efficiency EnEffect, Bulgaria

Gustav R. Grob, CMDC-WSEC (World Sustainable Energy Coalition), Switzerland

Filino Harahap, Institute of Technology of Bandung, Indonesia

Anhar Hegazi, Economic and Social Commission for Western Asia, Lebanon

Sawad Hemkamon, Ministry of Science Technology and Environment, Thailand

Nesbert Kanyowa, Zimbabwe Mission, Switzerland

Christian Katsande, Ministry of Transport and Energy, Zimbabwe

Jean-Étienne Klimpt, Hydro-Québec, Canada

Ron Knapp, World Coal Institute, U.K.

Mansika Knut, Ministry of Petroleum and Energy, Norway

Catherine P. Koshland, University of California at Berkeley, U.S.

George Kowalski, Economic Commission for Europe, Switzerland

Raymond Lafitte, International Hydropower Association, Switzerland

Hans Larsen, RISØ National Laboratory, Denmark

Kevin Leydon, European Commission, Belgium

Paul Llanso, World Meteorological Organization, Switzerland

Alphonse MacDonald, United Nations Population Fund, Switzerland

Andrei Marcu, United Nations Development Programme, U.S.

Manuel F. Martínez, Universidad Nacional Autonoma de Mexico, Mexico

William R. Moomaw, IVM Free University of Amsterdam, Netherlands

Mark J. Mwandosya, University of Dar-Es-Salaam, Tanzania

Raymond Myles, INFORSE, Integrated Sustainable Energy and Ecological Development Association, India

Gary Nakarado, United Nations Foundation, U.S.

Merle S. Opelz, International Atomic Energy Agency, Switzerland

Janos Pasztor, United Nations Framework Convention on Climate Change, Germany

Neculai Pavlovschi, Romanian Gas Corporation (Romgaz-S.A.), Romania

H.E. Per Kristian Pedersen, Royal Ministry of Foreign Affairs, Norway

Atiq Rahman, Bangladesh Centre for Advanced Studies, Bangladesh

Morris Rosen, International Atomic Energy Agency, Austria

Pranesh Chandra Saha, Economic and Social Commission for Asia and the Pacific, Thailand

T. Lakshman Sankar, Administrative Staff College of India, India

E.V.R. Sastry, Ministry of Non-conventional Sources of Energy, India

Hari Sharan, DESI Power, India

Slav Slavov, Economic Commission for Europe, Geneva

Youba Sokona, Environment Development Action in the Third World (ENDA-TM), Senegal

Lee Solsbery, Foundation for Business and Sustainable Development, U.K.

Istvan Tokes, United Nations Development Programme, Hungary

Eric Usher, United Nations Environment Programme, France

Dmitri Volfberg, Ministry of Science and Technologies, Russia

Yasmin Von Schirnding, World Health Organization, Switzerland

Peer Reviewers

Mark Reed Aberdeen

Dean E. Abrahamson, University of Minnesota, U.S.

Jiwan Sharma Acharya, University of Flensburg, Germany

Jim Adam, Executive Assembly, World Energy Council, U.S.

Adam Edow Adawa

Anthony O. Adegbulugbe, Obafemi Awolowo University, Nigeria

Bernard Aebisher, ETH Zentrum, Switzerland

Carlos Alberto Aguilar Molina, Ministerio de Medio Ambiente y Recursos Naturales, El Salvador

Husamuddin Ahmadzai, Swedish Environmental Protection Agency (SIDA), Sweden

Rafeeuddin Ahmed, United Nations Development Programme, U.S.

Francois Ailleret, World Energy Council, France

Ali Ainan Farah, Ministère de l'Industrie de l'Énergie et des Mines, Djibouti

Arif Alauddin, Ministry of Water & Power, Pakistan

M. Albert, Union for the Coordination of Production and Transmission of Electricity, Portugal

Issam Al-Chalabi, Consultant, Jordan

Abdlatif Y. Al-Hamad, Arab Fund for Economic and Social Development (AFSED), Kuwait

Suleiman Abu Alim, Ministry of Energy and Mineral Resources, Jordan

Hugo Altomonte

Popescu Anca, Institute of Power Studies and Design, Romania

Per Dannemand Andersen, Denmark

Dean Anderson, Center for Economic Analysis r.e. (ECON), Norway

Dean Anderson, Royal Institute of International Affairs, U.K.

Michael J. Antal, Jr., University of Hawaii at Manoa, U.S.

H.E. Bagher Asadi, Permanent Mission of the Islamic Republic of Iran to the United Nations, U.S.

Mie Asaoka, Yanaginobanba-dori, Japan

Harry Audus, International Energy Agency, France

Mohamaed M. Awad, Egyptian Electricity Authority, Egypt

Kazi Obaidul Awal, Bangladesh Atomic Energy Commission, Bangladesh

A. Awori, Kenya Energy and Environment Organisations (KENGO), Kenya

Emine Aybar, Ministry of Energy and Natural Resources, Turkey

Murfat Badawi, Arab Fund for Economic & Social Development, Kuwait

Sheila Bailey, NASA Glen Research Center, U.S.

Venkatrama Bakthavatsalam, Indian Renewable Energy Development Agency, Ltd., India

Juraj Balajka, Profing, s.r.o., Slovak Republic

Guillermo R. Balce, Asean Centre for Energy, Indonesia

Alexander Barnes, World Energy Council, France

Fritz Barthel, World Energy Council, Germany

A. Bartle, International Hydropower Association, U.K.

Reid Basher, International Research Institute for Climate Prediction (IRI), U.S.

Sujay Basu, Jadavpur University, India

Bauer, Mexican Autonomous National University (UNAM), Mexico

Pierre Beaudouin, Federation Rhone-Alpes de Protection de la Nature (FRAPNA), France

Carol Bellamy, United Nations Children's Fund, U.S.

Abdelali Bencheqroun, Ministry of Energy and Mines, Morocco

Natan Bernot, World Energy Council, Slovenia

Gustavo Best, Food and Agriculture Organization, Italy

Jos Beurskens, Netherlands Energy Research Foundation (ECN), Netherlands

Somnath Bhattacharjee, Tata Energy Research Institute, India

Zbigniew Bicki, Zbigniew Bicki Consulting, Poland

Jakob Bjornsson, Iceland

Edgar Blaustein, Energy21, France

Arie Bleijenberg, Centrum voor Engergiebesparing en Scvhone Technologie, Netherlands

Kornelis Blok, Ecofys Cooperatief Advies- en Onderzoeksbureau, Netherlands

David Bloom, Harvard Institute for International Development, U.S.

Brenda Boardman, St. Hilda's College, University of Oxford, U.K.

Teun Bokhoven, Netherlands

Bert Bolin, Stockholm Environment Institute, Sweden

James Bond, World Bank, U.S.

Pal Borjesson, Sweden

Daniel Bouille, Hydro-Québec, Canada

Messaoud Boumaour, Silicon Technology Development Unit, Algeria

Jean-Marie Bourdaire, International Energy Agency and Organisation for Economic Co-operation and Development, France

Christophe Bourillon, European Wind Energy Association, U.K.

Gunnar Boye Olesen, International Network for Sustainable Energy (INFORSE), Denmark

Duncan Brack, Royal Institute of International Affairs, U.K.

Adrian John Bradbrook, University of Adelaide, Australia

Rob Bradley, Climate Network Europe, Belgium

Roberto Brandt, World Energy Council, U.K.

Klaus Brendow, World Energy Council, Switzerland

Henri Bretaudeau, World Bank, U.S.

Lucien Y. Bronicki, ORMAT Industries Ltd., Israel

Jenny Bryant, United Nations Development Programme, Fiji

Tommy Buch, INVAP, Argentina

Marites Cabrera, Asian Institute of Technology, Thailand

Andre Caille, Hydro-Québec, Canada

Martin Cames, Institute for Applied Ecology, Germany

Allen Chen, Lawrence Berkeley National Laboratory, U.S.

Viravat Chlayon, Electricity Generating Authority of Thailand, Thailand

Joy Clancy, University of Twente, Netherlands

Gerald Clark, Uranium Institute, U.K.

Andrew Clarke, World Association of Nuclear Operators, U.K.

Denis Clarke, World Bank, U.S.

Suani Teixeira Coelho, National Reference Center on Biomass (CENBIO), Brazil

Gerry Collins, Canadian International Development Agency, Canada

Helene Connor, Helio Global Sustainable Energy Observatory, France

Stefano Consonni

Michael Corrigall, World Energy Council, South Africa

Jos Cosijnsen, The Environmental Defense Fund, Netherlands

Teodorescu Cristinel-Dan, Romanian Gas Corporation (Romgaz S.A.), Romania

James Currie, European Commission, DG XI, Belgium

Zhou Da Di, Energy Research Institute, State Planning Commission, China

Anibal de Almeida, University of Coimbra, Portugal

Piet de Klerk, International Atomic Energy Agency, Austria

Dmitry Derogan, Ukraine

Jean Pierre Des Rosiers, International Energy Agency, France

V. V. Desai, ICICI, India

Eric Donni, European Commission, DG VIII, Belgium

Seth Dunn, Worldwatch Institute, U.S.

Knut Dyrstad, Statkraft, Norway

Anton Eberhard, University of Cape Town, South Africa

Simon Eddy, Ministry of Energy, Cote d'Ivoire

Dominique Egré, Hydro-Québec, Canada

Mohamed T. El-Ashry, Global Environment Facility, U.S.

Mohamed El-Baradei, International Atomic Energy Agency, Austria

Baldur Eliasson, ABB Corporate Research, Switzerland

R. Bryan Erb, Sunsat Energy Council, U.S.

Andre Faaij, Utrecht University, Netherlands

Malin Falkenmark, Stockholm International Water Institute, Sweden

Ugo Farinelli, Conferenza Nazionale Energia E Ambiente, Italy

Lilian Fernandez, Asia Pacific Energy Research Centre, Japan

Susan Fisher, University of California at Berkeley, U.S.

Pamela Franklin, University of California at Berkeley, U.S.

Jean-Romain Frisch, Environmental Defense Fund, France

Yasumasa Fujii, University of Tokyo, Japan

Howard Geller, American Council for an Energy-Efficient Economy, U.S.

Shokri M. Ghanem, Organization of the Petroleum Exporting Countries, Austria

Marc Georges Giroux, International Atomic Energy Agency, France

S. Goethe Vattenfall, Sweden

Donna Green, Australia

Reg Green, International Federation of Chemical, Energy & General Workers' Unions, Belgium

Inna Gritsevich, Center for Energy Efficiency, Russia

Violetta Groseva, European Commission Energy Centre Sofia, Bulgaria

Gaétan Guertin, Hydro-Québec, Canada

Shen Guofang, Permanent Mission of the People's Republic of China to the United Nations, U.S.

H.E. Ali Hachani, Permanent Mission of Tunisia to the United Nations, U.S.

Oystein Haland, Statoil, Norway

Richard Heede, Rocky Mountain Institute, U.S.

Peter Helby, University of Lund, Sweden

Sam Holloway, British Geological Survey, U.K.

Ian Hore-Lacy, Uranium Information Centre, Australia

Roberto Hukai, BVI Technoplan, Brazil

Hassan Ibrahim, Asia Pacific Energy Research Centre, Japan

Istrate Ioan Ilarie, Romanian Gas Corporation (Romgaz S.A.), Romania

Jon Ingimarsson, Ministries of Industry and Commerce Arnarhvoli, Iceland

H.E. Samuel Rudy Insanally, Permanent Mission of Indonesia to the United Nations, U.S.

Karin Ireton, Industrial Environmental Forum of Southern Africa, South Africa

A. Jagadeesh, Nayudamma Centre for Development Alternatives, India

Antero Jahkola, Finnish Academies of Technology, Finland

Rodney Janssen, Helio International, France

Gilberto Januzzi, Lawrence Berkeley National Laboratory, U.S.

Tamas Jaszay, Technical University of Budapest, Hungary

Karl Jechoutek, World Bank, U.S.

Sathia Jothi, New Clean Energy Development Society (NERD), India

Tian Jun, China

Yonghun Jung, Asia Pacific Energy Research Centre, Japan

Olav Kaarstad, Statoil R&D Centre, Norway

Vladimir Kagramanian, International Atomic Energy Agency, Austria

Daniel M. Kammen, University of California at Berkeley, U.S.

Owen MacDonald Kankhulungo, Ministry of Water Development, Malawi

René Karottki, International Network for Sustainable Energy, Zimbabwe

Arun Kashyap, The Rockefeller Foundation, U.S.

Badr Kasme, Syrian Mission to the United Nations, Switzerland

Martti Kätkä, World Energy Council, Finland

Yoichi Kaya, World Energy Council, Japan

William Kennedy, United Nations Fund for International Partnerships, U.S.

Andrzej Kerner, Energy Information Centre, Poland

Nancy Kete, World Resources Institute, U.S.

Hyo-Sun Kim, Korea Gas Corporation, Korea

Evans N. Kituyi, Kenya National Academy of Sciences, Kenya

Tord Kjellstorm, Health and Environment International Consultants, New Zealand

Israel Klabin, Fundacao Brasileira Para O Desenvolvimento Sustentavel, Brazil

Hans Jurgen Koch, International Energy Agency, France

Serguei Kononov, International Atomic Energy Agency, Austria

Keith Kozloff, World Resources Institute, U.S.

Tom Kram, Netherlands Energy Research Foundation (ECN), Netherlands

Florentin Krause, International Project for Sustainable Energy Paths (ISEP), U.S.

Emilio La Rovere, Federal School of Rio de Janeiro, Brazil

Oddvar Lægreld, Royal Ministry of Foreign Affairs, Norway

Ari Lampinen, University of Jyvaskyla, Finland

Jonathan Lash, World Resources Institute, U.S.

Tõnu Lausmaa, Renewable Energy Center TAASEN, Estonia

Gerald Leach, Stockholm Environment Institute, U.K.

Barrie Leay, New Zealand

Thierry Lefevre, Centre for Energy-Environment Research & Development; Asian Institute of Technology, Thailand

Jostein Leiro, Permanent Mission of Norway to the United Nations, U.S.

Stella Lenny, Hydro-Québec, Canada

Jip Lenstra, Ministry of the Environment, Netherlands

Andre Liebaert, European Commission, DG VIII/E/5, Belgium

Krister Lönngren, Ministry for Foreign Affairs, Finland

Laurraine Lotter, Chemical and Allied Industries' Association, South Africa

Philip Lowe, European Commission, DG VIII, Belgium

Haile Lul Tebicke, TERRA plc, Ethiopia

Joachim Luther, Germany

Erik Lysen, University of Utrecht, Netherlands

Robert Mabro, Oxford Energy Policy Club, England

Tim Mackey, Department of Industry, Science and Resources, Australia

Birger Madson, Denmark

Preben Maegaard, Folkecenter for Renewable Energy, Denmark

Maswabi M. Maimbolwa, The World Conservation Union (IUCN), Zambia

Alexj Makarov, Energy Research Institute, Russia

Markku J. Makela, Geological Survey of Finland, Finland

Jose Malhaes da Silva, Developing Countries Committee, Brazil

Julio Torres Martinez, Ministerio de Ciencia Technologia y Medio Ambiente, Cuba

John Michael Matuszak, U.S.

Charles McCombie, Pangea Resources International, Switzerland

Gene McGlynn, Organisation for Economic Co-operation and Development, France

J. F. Meeder, International Gas Union, Netherlands

Anita Kaniz Mehdi Zaidi, Pakistan Public Health Foundation, Pakistan

Wafik M. Meshref, Committee on Energy and Natural Resources for Development (UN-CENRD), Egypt

Tim Meyer, Fraunhofer Institute for Solar Energy Systems ISE, Germany

Axel Michaelowa, France

Joseph Milewski, Hydro-Québec, Canada

David Mills, University of Sydney, Australia

Sandor Molnar, Systemexpert Consulting Ltd., Hungary

Barros Monteiro, Ministry of Economy, Portugal

Claus Montenem, Technology for Life, Finland

Robert B. Moore, U.S.

José Roberto Moreira, Biomass Users Network, Brazil

John O. Mugabe, African Centre for Technology Studies, Kenya

Surya Mulandar, Climate Action Network South East Asia, Indonesia

Pablo Mulás del Pozo, World Energy Council, Mexico

J. M. Muller, International Organization of Motor Vehicle Manufacturers (OICA), France

Michel Muylle, World Bank, U.S.

Emi Nagata, Japan

Weidou Ni, Tsinghua University, China

Lars J. Nilson, Lund University, Sweden

Ainun Nishat, Bangladesh University of Engineering and Technology, Bangladesh

M. Nizamuddin, United Nations Population Fund, U.S.

Richard Noetstaller, Registered Consulting Office, Austria

Kieran O'Brien, EirGrid, Ireland

Jose Ocampo, Economic Commission for Latin America and the Caribbean, Chile

Peter Odell, Erasmus University Rotterdam, Netherlands

Andy Oliver, International Petroleum Industry, U.K.

Derek Osborn, U.K.

Richard Ottinger, Pace University, U.S.

Nataa Oyun-Erdene, Mongolia

Rajenda K. Pachauri, Tata Energy Research Institute, India

Jyoti P. Painuly, RISØ National Laboratory, Denmark

Claudia Sheinbaum Pardo

Alain Parfitt, Energy Charter Secretariat, Belgium

Jyoti Parikh, Indira Gandhi Institute of Development Research, India

Jean-Michel Parrouffe, ENERZONIA, Canada

Maksimiljan Peènik, Slovenian Nuclear Safety Administration, Slovenia

Stanislaw M. Pietruszko, Warsaw University of Technology – Solar Energy – Photovoltaics, Polish Society for Solar Energy (ISES), Poland

Asif Qayyum Qureshi, Sustainable Development Policy Institute, Pakistan

Pierre Radane, Institut d'Evaluation des Strategies sur l'Energie et l'Energie et l'Environnement, France

Jamuna Ramakrishna, Hivos, India

Robert L. Randall, The RainForest ReGeneration Institute, U.S.

Chris Rapley, British Antarctic Survey, U.K.

Jean-Pierre Reveret, Université du Quebec à Montreal, Canada

John B. Robinson, University of British Columbia, Canada

Zoilo Rodas, Environmental Assessment, Paraguay

Humberto Rodriguez, National University, Colombia

Carlos Rolz, Guatemalan Academy of Sciences, Guatemala

Felix A. Ryan, Ryan Foundation, India

Jacques Saint-Just, Gaz de France, France

Hiroshi Sakurai, The Engineering Academy of Japan, Japan

Liam Salter, Climate Network Europe, Belgium

Angelo Saullo, ICC Energy Commission, Italy

Fulai Sheng, World Wildlife Fund, U.S.

Ralph E.H. Sims, Massey University, U.S.

Rajendra Singh, Pricing Energy in Developing Countries Committee

Wim C. Sinke, Netherlands Energy Research Foundation (ECN), Netherlands

Doug Smith

Eddy Kofi Smith, Committee on Energy and Natural Resources for Development (UN-CENRD), Ghana

Bent Sørensen, Roskilde University, Denmark

Manuel Soriano, PT Hagler Bailly, Indonesia

S. Kamaraj Soundarapandian, Non-conventional Energy and Rural Development Society, India

Randall Spalding-Fecher, University of Cape Town, South Africa

Helga V.E. Steeg, Ruhr-Universität Bochum, Germany

Achim Steiner, World Commission on Dams, South Africa

Jeffrey Stewart, U.S.

Andy Stirling, University of Sussex, U.K.

Peter Stokoe, Natural Resources Canada, Canada

Carlos Enrique Suárez, Fundación Bariloche, Argentina

Budi Sudarsono, National Nuclear Energy Agency, Indonesia

R. Taylor, International Hydropower Association, U.K.

Teng Teng, Chinese Academy of Social Sciences; Tsinghua University, China

Jefferson Tester, Massachusetts Institute of Technology, U.S.

Jacques Theys, Ministère de l'Equipement, du Logement, des Transports et du Tourisme, France

Steve Thorne, Energy Transformations cc, South Africa

Yohji Uchiyama, Central Research Institute of Electric Power Industry, Japan

Matthew Vadakemuriyil, Malanadu Development Society, India

Giap van Dang, Asian Institute of Technology, Thailand

Maarten J. van der Burgt, Energy Consultancy B.V., Netherlands

Nico van der Linden, Netherlands Energy Research Foundation (ECN), Netherlands

Frank van der Vleuten, Free Energy Europe, Netherlands

Jean-Marc van Nypelseer, Association for the Promotion of Renewable Energies (APERE), Belgium

Rangswamy Vedavalli, U.S.

Toni Vidan, Green Action, Zelena Akcija Zagreb, Croatia

Antonio Vignolo, Regional Electrical Integration Commission (CIER), Uruguay

Delia Villagrasa, Climate Network Europe, Belgium

Arturo Villevicencio

Michael S. Von Der, United Nations Development Programme, Iran

Shem O. Wandiga, Kenya National Academy of Sciences, Kenya

Xiaodong Wang, Global Environment Facility, U.S.

Werner Weiss, Arbeitsgemeinschaft Erneuerbare Energie – AEE, Austria

John Weyant, Stanford University, U.S.

H.E. Makarim Wibisono, Permanent Mission of Indonesia to the United Nations, U.S.

Quentin Wodon, World Bank, U.S.

Nobert Wohlgemuth, RISØ National Laboratory, Denmark

Beth Woroniuk, Goss Gilroy Inc, Canada

Ernst Worrell, Lawrence Berkeley National Laboratory, U.S.

Raymond M. Wright, Petroleum Corporation of Jamaica PCJ Resource Center, Jamaica

Anatoli Yakushau, Institute Power Engineering Problem, National Academy of Sciences, Belarus

Remko Ybema, Netherlands Energy Research Foundation (ECN), Netherlands

Keiichi Yokobori, Asia Pacific Research Centre, Japan

S. Zarrilli, United Nations Commission on Trade and Development, Switzerland

Guocheng Zhang, Ministry of Science and Technology, China

ZhongXiang Zhang, University of Groningen, Netherlands

Fengqi Zhou, State Development Planning Commission, China

index

Note: Page numbers followed by letters *b, f, n,* and *t* indicate material presented in boxes, figures, notes, and tables, respectively.

A

prices of, 35
    projections for, 123, 123*t*
    as source of insecurity, 122–124
resource base of, adequacy of, 116
security with, 119–124
importance of, 114
stocks of, 121
trade of, 34–35
transportation of, 122
versatility of, 114
Crystalline silicon films (f-Si), photovoltaic cell, 238*t*
CSD. *See* Commission on Sustainable Development
Current energy, tidal and marine, 259–260
    current status of, 260*t*
Cyprus, solar collectors in, 248*t*
Czech Republic
    gasification-based projects in, 298*t*
    IGCC project in, 283*t*, 284
    intensity trends in, 179, 180*t*
    sulphur dioxide emissions in, 402*f*
    urban PM$_{10}$ concentrations in, 75*f*

D

Dams, hydroelectric
    construction of, advanced technologies for, 252
    energy densities of, 156
    impact of, 77–80
        on ecosystems, 79, 79*t*
        future of, 102
        on greenhouse gas emissions, 79–80
        on humans, 78–79, 156
    prevalence of, 77–78
Debt, national
    vs. natural debt, 94*b*
    oil prices and, 23, 41
Decentralisation
    regulatory options for, 425–427
    of rural energy planning, 375–379, 381, 421–422
Deforestation
    greenhouse gas emissions from, 91
    vs. dam systems, 79–80
    household fuel demand and, 66
Demand, energy
    climate change and, 91
    in developing countries, rise in, 394
    economic development and, shifts in, 118*f*
    factors affecting, 399–400
    focus on, *vs.* supply, 41–42
    and GDP (*See* Intensity)
    by households, for woodfuel, 66
    per capita use and, 51
    population growth and, 51, 409
    projections for, 127–128, 395, 399
        efficiency and, 199–200
        spatial distribution of, 352, 352*f*
    recent trends in, 178*b*

Demand-side management, and energy efficiency, 428
Dematerialization, and demand, 178*b*
Demographic transitions, 7, 9*t*, 50–51, 340*b*
Demonstrated resources, 138
Demonstration projects, 437
    in developing countries, need for, 439
Denmark
    biomass energy conversion in, 224, 227*t*, 228
    efficiency in, policies on, 209*t*
    energy R&D in, funding for, 448
    intensity trends in, 179*f*
    renewables obligation in, 427
    solar district heating in, 249
    urban PM$_{10}$ concentrations in, 75*f*
    wind energy programme in, 231*t*, 266
        costs of, 234*f*
Desertification
    causes of, 66
    fuel demand and, 66
Desiccant cooling, 249
Developing countries. *See also specific countries*
    air quality goals in, challenge of addressing, 319*n*
    carbon dioxide emissions in
        changes in, 444*t*
        scenarios of, 405–406, 407*f*
    carbon emissions in, 92, 92*f*, 93–94
    comparative advantage in using renewable energy, 405
    consumption in, 33–34, 33*t*
        projections for, 395
        rates of, 4–5
        by wealthy, 51
    definition of, 26*n*
    demand in
        projections for, 23
        rise in, 394
    demographic transition in, 51
    demonstration projects in, need for, 439
    efficiency in, 399
        intensity trends and, 180–181, 180*t*
        measures to increase, 428
        obstacles to, 202–205
        policies on, 207
    technology transfer and, 181–183
    environmental problems in, 23, 51
    and global warming, 402
    health concerns in, for women, 49
    improved cooking stoves in, dissemination of, 370*b*, 371
    intensities in, 127, 180–181, 180*t*
    investment needs of, 430
    living standards in, 44
    oil trade and, 34–35, 35*f*
    policies for, 25
    pollution in
        from biomass consumption, 397
        options for reducing, 401–404
        in urban areas, 76–77
    population growth in, 51

poverty in, 43–46
private investment in power sectors of, 409*t*, 431
    conditions for attracting, 430*b*, 431
privatisation of electric sector in, 254
and research and development, 435, 449
rural areas of, 21–22
    energy needs of, 368–388
    lack of adequate energy services in, 369
security in
    economic growth and, 127
    problems with, 114–115
    of supply, 118
technological innovation in, encouraging, 438–441
technology transfer in, private-sector led, 440
transportation in, 55
under-pricing of electricity in, 425
urban areas of, air pollution in, 76–77
Development
    economic (*See* Economic development)
    of energy systems, 6–7, 36–37
    human, 3, 44, 340–341
Development assistance
    conditionality in, 432
    decline in, 440
    inadequacy of, 420–421
    official, 6, 37
Diesel-engine generators, electrification with, 375, 376*b*
Diesel fuel
    esters suited to replace, 225
    prices of, 74
Diesel vehicles
    air pollutant emissions, costs of, 278*t*
    exhaust from, in coal mining, 72
    particulate emissions from, 85
Diffusion, technological
    projections for, implications of, 353–355, 356–357
    supporting, 439–440
Digestion, anaerobic, of biomass, 224*t*, 224–225
Dimethyl ether (DME), 294, 295
    advantages of, 379
    applications of, 276
    crop residues converted into, 387, 388
    production of, liquid-phase reactor technology for, 298
Direct current, renewed interest in, 261
Direct investments, foreign, 6, 37, 37*f*, 430*b*, 431
Disease(s)
    burden of
        definition of, 104*n*
        global, 70*f*
        from household solid fuel use, 69, 69*b*
    climate change and, 90, 91
    hydroelectric dams and, 79
Dish/engine power plants, 246
Distributed utility (DU), concept of, 261–262

District heating, solar energy and, 249
DME. *See* Dimethyl ether
Dominican Republic, photovoltaic system in, 377
Droughts, climate change and, 89
DU. *See* Distributed utility
Dung
    harvesting of, environmental impact of, 66
    household use of, greenhouse gas emissions from, 71*f*

EAR-I resources, 151
EAR-II resources, 151
Earth Summit, 419, 443
    goals developed in, 3, 42–43
Eastern Europe. *See also specific countries*
    carbon dioxide emissions in, 92*f*
        changes in, 444*t*
    coal resources in, 148*t*, 149*t*
    efficiency in
        economic potential of, 190–192, 190*t*
        obstacles to, 202, 205
        policies on, 207
    GDP in, per capita, 343*t*
    geothermal potential in, 165*t*
    household fuel choice in, 65–66, 65*f*
    hydroelectric potentials in, 154*t*, 155*f*, 253*t*
    intensity trends in, 177–179, 180*t*
        projections for, 343, 344*f*
    natural gas resources in, 145*t*, 146*t*
    oil reserves in, 139*t*, 140*t*–141*t*
    regional emissions in, 80*t*
    solar energy potential in, 163*t*
    sulphur dioxide emissions in, 81–82, 82*f*
    thorium resources in, 152
    uranium resources in, 150*t*, 151*t*
    water resources in, 159*t*
    wind energy resources in, 164*t*
Economic costs. *See* Cost(s)
Economic development
    assistance for, inadequacy of, 420–421
    consumption and, 34, 34*f*
    and demand, shifts in, 118*f*
    distribution of, 341, 342*f*
    and electrification, 375
    energy access and, 421
    and environmental risk transitions, 95–96
    projections for, 340–342, 342*f*
Economic efficiency, and energy regulation, 410
Economic potentials, definition of, 138
Economic prosperity
    energy and, 23–24, 393–402
    environmental policies and, 394
Economic and Social Council (ECOSOC), 138
Economy, energy intensity of, 399
ECOSOC. *See* Economic and Social Council
Ecuador, urban PM$_{10}$ concentrations in, 75*f*

Edison, Thomas, 261
Education
  liberal market policies and, 408b
  of women, 50, 53
Efficiency, energy
  and consumption, 58
  definition of, 26n
  and demand, 400
  in developing countries, 399
  economic
    and energy regulation, 410
    increasing, 423–429
  end-use (See End-use efficiency)
  funding for, 435
  improvements in, poverty
    reduction with, 46
  and intensity, 128
  market barriers for, 427
  raising, 427–429
  security and, 128
  transition to modern fuels and
    gains in, 398
Egypt
  consumption in, 396t
  economic efficiency potential
    in, 198
  solar thermal electricity
    developments in, 244b
  urban PM$_{10}$ concentrations
    in, 75f
El Niño/Southern Oscillation, global
  warming and, 90
El Salvador
  geothermal development in, 256
  geothermal electricity generation
    capacity in, 256t
Electric vehicles, 78b
Electricity
  access to, global population
    and, 374t
  biomass conversion routes, 223f,
    224, 224t
    cost of, 227
  from coal and natural gas, cost
    of, 292t, 292–293
  for cooking, 374
  coproduction with synthetic
    liquefied petroleum
    gas, 387–388
  costs of, with alternative
    engine-generators, 386t
  diesel-engine generators
    for, 375, 376b
  fuel-cycle analysis of, 103b
  generation of, efficiency of, 36–37
  grids for, regional, 130
  hydrogen compared with, 280b
  hydropower generation
    of, 251–255
    small-scale, 375–376
  lack of, health impacts of, 7
  nuclear, costs of, 307–308
  photovoltaics for, 376–377
  price of, 36
  in rural areas, 374t, 374–379
    costs of, 369
    technological options for, 380t
  security with, 113, 114–115
    cost of, 115, 115b
  solar thermal, 243–247
  storage of, 262–263
    costs for, 263, 263t

supplies of, unreliable,
    dysfunctional markets
    and, 423b
Electricity system
  design, rethinking of, 262
  institutional innovations and, 261
  pillars of, 261
  technical innovations and, 261
Electrification programmes, 374–379
  centralised approach, 374–375
  decentralised approach, 375–
    379, 381, 421–422
Electropaulo, 421, 425
Emissions. See also Air pollution;
    specific types
  contaminant content of fuels
    and, 66
  health damages from, cost
    of, 319n
  from households, 66–70, 66b, 67f
  physical form of fuels and, 66
  trading of, greenhouse gases, 424
Encephalitis, hydropower and,
    252–253
Encyclopaedia of Occupational
    Safety and Health (Stellman), 70
End-use efficiency, 13–14, 173–211
  intensities and, 13, 175–181
  obstacles to, 13, 200–205, 206f
  policies on, 14, 24–25,
    205–211, 206f
  potentials for, 13–14, 175,
    176f, 184b
    long-term, 199–200
    by region and sector, 184–198
    systemic approach to,
      198–199
    types of, 183–184, 183f
  technology transfers for, benefits
    of, 181–183
Energy Charter Conference, 125
Energy Charter Protocol on Energy
    Efficiency and Related Environ-
    mental Aspects, 211
Energy Charter Treaty, 12, 26n, 114,
    122, 124–125, 442
Energy Efficiency and Related
    Environmental Aspects
    protocol, 122
Energy Research Corporation, 287
Energy after Rio: Prospects and
    Challenges (UNDP), 43
Energy sector
  components of, 32
  liberalisation of, 24, 32
  occupational hazards in, 70–73
  restructuring of, 24, 425–427
    regulations for, 25
  trends in, 261–262
Energy technology innovation
    pipeline, 265
Energy for Tomorrow's World
    (World Energy Council), 83
Energy Work Group, 122
Environmental costs
  with biomass use, 46
  of fossil fuels, 277t, 277–278, 278t
  internalising, 264, 423–424
  of nuclear power production, 306
  reductions in
    policies for, 422–423
    transition to modern fuels
      and, 398

of technological innovation, 438
Environmental policies
  and economic prosperity, 394
  market liberalisation and, 409
  trade and, 420
Environmental protection
  energy efficiency and, 400
  increased energy consumption
    and, 400–408
Environmental quality, 61–104
  awareness of problems with, 41
  impacts on, 9–11, 10t, 63, 64t
    community-level, 73–80
    cross-scale, 95–101
    future of, 101–104
    global, 86–95
    household-level, 65–70
    projections for, 358–360
    regional, 80–86
  population growth and, 51
  and security, 128
  urbanisation and, 54, 55
  win-win strategies for, 96–98
  and women, 49
Environmental risk transitions,
    95–96, 95f
EPR. See European pressurised
    water reactor
Equity issues
  economic development
    and, 340–342, 342f
  photovoltaic technology
    and, 377b
Erosion
  biomass energy systems
    and, 225
  on biomass plantations, 161–162
Eskom, photovoltaic programme
    of, 376–377, 421
Ester, biomass production of, 225
Estonia
  intensity trends in, 179
  oil shale resources in, 141
Ethanol
  as alternative automotive
    fuel, 293–294
  biomass production of, 225
  emissions from, 293–294
Ethiopia
  economic efficiency potential
    in, 198
  improved cooking stoves
    disseminated in, 371t
Eucalyptus plantations, 162, 169n
  cost of, 227
  energy production from, 224
  water-use efficiency of, 225–226
Europe. See also specific countries
  acid deposition in, 83–84
  biomass potential in, 159
  coal prices in, 276
  consumption in, 395t
  geothermal energy use in, 255t
  health impacts in, costs of, 99, 99t
  hydroelectric dams in, 78
  ozone concentrations in, 85
  solar collectors in, 248t
  solar domestic hot water systems
    in, 248t
  solar energy market in, 248
  water balance in, 153t
  wind energy programme in, 231t

European Business Council for
    Sustainable Energy Future, 444
European Energy Charter, 122
European pressurised water reactor
    (EPR), 314
European Union
  carbon dioxide emissions
    in, changes in, 444t
  geothermal energy use in, 255t
  photovoltaic solar energy
    programme in, 242b
Evaporation
  climate change and, 89
  in global water balance, 153t
Experience curves, 435, 436f
  with renewable technologies,
    14, 16f
Exportation, security and, 118
  projections for, 357–358
Externalities
  biomass energy and, 230
  including in energy prices, 423–424

F

f-Si. See Crystalline silicon films
F-T process. See Fischer-
    Tropsch process
Fast breeder reactors (FBRs), 315–316
Federal Institute for Geosciences
    and Natural Resources, 139
Feedbacks
  in climate change, 86, 89, 105n
  definition of, 104n
Fertilisers, biomass energy
  systems and, 226
Fertility
  benefits and costs of, 7, 52–53
  commercial energy use and, 42f
  definition of, 59n
  transitions in
    and population size, 50–51
    preconditions for
      decline, 7, 52–53
Final energy
  conversion of, efficiency of, 32
  requirements of, projections
    for, 348–351, 350f
Financing
  of hydroelectric power
    projects, 254
  of pollution control, 403
  private sector
    attracting, 431–432
  in developing countries, 409t
  for R&D, 435, 447–448
  public sector, for R&D, 433–434,
    437, 448–449
  of renewable energy technolo-
    gies, 264, 431, 435
  of research and development, 435
  trends in, 447–449
  of rural energy projects, 382–383,
    383b, 422
  of sustainable energy
    systems, 430–433
Finland
  biomass in energy system
    of, 227t
  research and development in,
    funding for, 448

Quadgeneration, 296t, 297
Quality of service, and energy
    regulation, 410
Quota systems, as incentive for
    renewable energy use, 235